# THE MṚICHCHHAKAṬIKA OF ŚŪDRAKA

# The Mṛichchhakaṭika of Śūdraka

*Edited with the Commentary of Pṛithvidhara (enlarged where necessary), Various Readings, A Literal English Translation, Notes, and an exhaustive Introduction*

M. R. Kale

MOTILAL BANARSIDASS PUBLISHERS
PRIVATE LIMITED • DELHI

*11th Reprint : Delhi, 2017*
*First Edition : Poona, 1924*



ISBN: 978-81-208-0081-6 (Cloth)
ISBN: 978-81-208-0082-3 (Paper)

MOTILAL BANARSIDASS
41 U.A. Bungalow Road, Jawahar Nagar, Delhi 110 007
8 Mahalaxmi Chamber, 22 Bhulabhai Desai Road, Mumbai 400 026
203 Royapettah High Road, Mylapore, Chennai 600 004
236, 9th Main III Block, Jayanagar, Bengaluru 560 011
8 Camac Street, Kolkata 700 017
Ashok Rajpath, Patna 800 004
Chowk, Varanasi 221 001

*MLBD Cataloging-in-Publication Data*
The Mṛichchakaṭika of Śūdraka
*by* M.R. Kale
Includes, Introduction, Sanskrit Text,
English Translation and Explanatory Notes
ISBN: 978-81-208-0081-6 (Cloth)
ISBN: 978-81-208-0082-3 (Paper)
I. Mṛichchakaṭika, II. Śūdraka,
III. Sankrit Literature, IV. M.R. Kale

*Printed in India*
by RP Jain at NAB Printing Unit,
A-44, Naraina Industrial Area, Phase I, New Delhi–110028
and published by JP Jain for Motilal Banarsidass Publishers (P) Ltd,
41 U.A. Bungalow Road, Jawahar Nagar, Delhi-110007

# PREFACE

No apology is needed for this new edition of the Mrichchhakatika, as there is at present no suitable edition available which satisfies the needs of the University students, who have often to study this play for their examination. I have tried to make this book as comprehensive and useful as possible, inspite of the short time at my disposal, as the edition was undertaken at the urgent request of the publishers somewhat late in the beginning of this year. To the commentary of Prithvidhara, which is somewhat abrupt and meagre in places, I have made considerable additions where I felt them to be necessary for the elucidation of the text. The relation of this play to Bhasa's *Charudatta* has been fully discussed in the Introduction, along with other usual matters. The Prakrit passages, which prove a hindrance to the student in the class, have been printed below the text, as in my other editions of Sanskrit plays, along with the text, only the Sanskrit rendering being given above; the utility of this contrivance has been established in actual use. I have fully availed myself of the labours of my predecessors in this field; but I must make special mention of the editions of Jivanand Vidyasagar and N. B. Godbole, and the scholarly translation of Dr Ryder, as also his supplementary *Notes* issued in the Journal of the American Oriental Society. To all these my best acknowledgements are due. But I have specially to thank a friend of mine who materially assisted me in the preparation of this edition and but for whose able help in every way the edition could not have been brought out in the short space of six months. Any suggestions or corrections, &c., that might help to make this edition still more useful, will be most thankfully received.

*June 1924.* M. R. KALE.

*February 1962.*

## IMPORTANT ABBREVIATIONS.

*A. G.*—Apte's Guide to Sanskrit Composition.
*A. K.*—Amarakosa.
*Bg*—Bhagavadgita.
*Bh.*—Bhartrihari's Satakas.*
*Bhatt.*—Bhattikavya.*
*Brih.-Up.*—Brihadaranyakopanishad.
*Br.-Su.*—Brahmasutras.
*Char.*—Charudatta of Bhasa.
*Chhan.-Up.*—Chhandogyopanishad.
*Com.*—Commentary; commentator.
*D.-K.*—Dasakumaracharita.*
*D.-R.*—Dasarupaka.
*Git.*—Gitagovinda.
*Hitop.*—Hitopadesa.*
*J. V.*—Jivanand Vidyasagara.
*Kad.*—Kadambari.*
*Kav.-D.*—Kavyadarsa.
*Kav.-S.*—Kavyalamkara Sutras of Vamana.
*Kir.*—Kiratarjuniya.*
*K.-P.*—Kavya Prakasa.
*Kum.*—Kumarasambhava.*
*L.-D.*—Lalla-Dikshita.
*Mah.-Bh.*—Mahabharata.
*Malav.*—Malavikagnimitra.*
*Malli.*—Mallinatha.
*Mal.-Madh.*—Malati-Madhava.*
*Megh.*—Meghaduta.
*Mrich.*—Mrichchhakatika.*
*M.-S.*—Manusmriti.
*Mud.*—Mudrarakshasa.*
*Nag.*—Nagananda.*
*Pan.*—Panini's Ashtadhyayi.
*Pri.*—Prithvidhara.
*Pt.*—Panchatantra.*
*Ragh.*—Raghuvamsa.*
*Rama.*—Ramayana.
*Ratn.*—Ratnavali.*
*Rig.-V.*—Rig Veda.
*Ritu.*—Ritusamhara.*
*Sak.*—Sakuntala.*
*S.-D.*—Sahitya-Darpana.
*Sid.-K.*—Siddhanta-Kaumudi.
*Sis.*—Sisupalavadha.
*Up.*—Upanishad.
*Uttar.*—Uttararamacharita.*
*Vart.*—Varttika.
*Veni.*—Venisamhara.*
*Vik.*—Vikramorvasiya.*
*V.-P.*—Vishnu Purana.

---

* Annotated by the Editor.

# CONTENTS

# INTRODUCTION

## I. THE SANSKRIT DRAMA[1].

We shall begin with a brief outline of the general structure and arrangement of the Sanskrit Drama, without a knowledge of which the tecnical remarks on the construction of the present play here, as well as those made in the Notes, will not be intelligible to the general reader[2]. Poetry in Sanskrit, from its inherent nature as apart from its intrinsic merit, is divided into two kinds—दृश्य 'what is capable of being seen or exhibited' and श्रव्य 'what can only be heard or chanted.' The drama falls under the first division. 'Rupaka' is the general term in Sanskrit for all dramatic compositions, which also comprises a subordinate class called *Uparupaka.* The 'Rupaka',[3] which has Rasa or Sentiment for its substratum, is divided into ten classes, *viz.*, नाटकं सप्रकरणं भाणः प्रहसनं डिमः । व्यायोगसमवकारौ वीथ्यङ्केहामृगा इति ॥. Of the Uparupakas or Minor Dramas there are eighteen species, the most important of which are *Natikas*, such as the Ratnavali, Viddhasalabhanjika &c., *Trotakas* such as the Vikramorvasiya, and *Sattakas* such as the Karpuramanjari,—all differing very little from the general features of a *Nataka.*

Having thus disposed of the divisions into which the whole of the scenic art is capable of falling, we turn to the principle of

---

1 The first Section is almost the same as that prefixed to our Sakuntala.

2 The information given here has been mainly culled from the Dasarupaka. The minor particulars not noticed here will be found in my Sahityasararasamgraha (Nir. Ed.).

३ अवस्थानुकृतिर्नाट्यं रूपं दृश्यतयोच्यते । रूपकं तत्समावेशाद्दशधैव रसाश्रयम् ॥ D-R.; रूप्यतेऽभिनयैर्यत्र वस्तु तद्रूपकं विदुः । नाटकाद्यैर्दशविधम् । *Natya* is another and perhaps a wider term for the drama or the dramatic art, and is so called because it represents the different situations in (the scenes presented by) life. The sage Bharata is the founder of the science of music and dramaturgy and his work is styled the *Natya-Sastra. Natya* is also *Rupa,* inasmuch as it has *drisyata* or the capability of being seen, and *Rupaka* inasmuch as its subject-matter is represented by actors assuming particular characters division among the *Rupakas* themselves, which is threefold[1] :—(1) वस्तु or the Plot of the play; (2) नेता or the Hero; (3) and रस or the Sentiment. These three are the essential constituents, nay the very life-blood, of every dramatic piece. Each of these we shall succinctly deal with in its order.

## (A) VASTU OR THE PLOT.

*Vastu* is primarily of two kinds : आधिकारिक or 'Principal' and प्रासङ्गिक or 'Accessary.' The Principal is that which relates to the chief characters or the persons concerned with the essential interest of the piece, and pervades the whole arrangement. The Accessary is that which appears in furtherance of the main topic, and is concerned with characters other than the Hero or the Heroine. This latter is of two kinds; *viz. Pataka* and *Prakari*. The 'Pataka' or 'Banner' is an episode by which the progress of the plot is illustrated, furthered or hindered (so as to give additional interest to it). It is of considerable length, and sometimes extends to the very end of a play. The 'Prakari' is also an episodical incident-of limited duration and minor importance-one in which the principal characters take no part. Besides these two, there are three other elements requisite for the development of the plot. These are बीज or the seed, बिन्दु or the drop, and कार्य or the final issue. *Bija* is the circumstance leading to the ultimate end briefly stated, which, as the plot develops, bears multifarious results[2], and which is as it were the seed of the plot. *Bindu*[3] is what cements a break in the plot caused by the introduction of some other incident. *Karya* is the final object of the plot, which being attained the whole is finished. These five are technically called Arthaprakritis (अर्थप्रकृतयः)

The *Vastu*, which is thus divided into five classes, may again be divided into three classes according to the source of its derivation. It may be borrowed from history or tradition, or it may be fictitious, or mixed, *i. e.* partly drawn from history and partly the creation of the poet's fancy. A *Nataka* belongs to the first class, a *Prakarana* to the second.

---

१ वस्तु नेता रसस्तेषां भेदकः ।

२ स्वल्पोद्दिष्टस्तु तद्धेतुर्बीजं विस्तार्यनेकधा ।

३ अवान्तरार्थविच्छेदे बिन्दुरच्छेदकारणम् ।

As regards its development a dramatic plot has five stages or conditions called *Avasthas*. They are–(1) आरम्भ beginning or setting on foot of the enterprise, (2) यत्न efforts, (3) प्राप्त्याशा prospect of success, (4) नियताप्ति certain attainment through the removal of obstacles, and (5) फलागम obtainment of the desired object. While these five stages are in progress there must be some links to connect them with the principal and subordinate parts of the main action ( the episodes and incidents ). These are called the *Samdhis*. They are five in number, answering to the five *Arthaprakritis*, each of which they join with its corresponding stage, *viz.* मुख, प्रतिमुख, गर्भ, अवमर्श and निर्वहण (also called उपसंहृति or उपसंहार). Thus *Mukha samdhi* is the combination of the Bija and Arambha, *i. e.* wherein the seed is sown, so to speak, with all its *Rasas*. In the *Pratimukha* there is the means ( *yatna* ) to the chief end, as originally implied by the Bija in the Mukha which herein sprouts up. In the *Garbha* there is attainment and non-attainment of the desired end implying a further sprouting up of the original Bija. There are impediments, but the main plot gains ground under resistance. The *Avamarsa samdhi* is that in which the seed attains a more luxuriant growth than in the *Garbha*, being accompanied by *Niyatapti* of the end, but whose final result is postponed further off by fresh impediments of various sorts ( as in the Sakuntala the King's forgetting Sakuntala after marriage owing to Durvasas' curse ). The *Nirvahana* or consummation is the harmonious combination of all the aforesaid parts in the final catastrophe.

The subject matter, whether historical, fictitious or mixed, is, from its inherent nature, capable of a twofold division. It is divided into—( 1 ) सूच्य deserving to be suggested or implied only as being of a dry or otherwise unfit character; and ( 2 ) दृश्यश्रव्य fit to be represented and heard as being highly sentimental and pleasing. The suggestions or implications are made in five ways, विष्कम्भचूलिकाङ्कास्याङ्कावतारप्रवेशकैः ॥ ( 1 ) For *Vishkambha* see Notes Act II. ( 2 ) *Chulika* is the suggestion of some incident from behind the scene (नेपथ्ये) (3) An अङ्कास्य[1] is one wherein is suggested by the actors at the time of their departure the connexion between the Act finished and the one to be commenced, which otherwise

१ अङ्कान्तपात्रैरङ्कास्यं छिन्नाङ्कस्यार्थसूचनात् ।

would look disconnected, as the speech of Kamandaki and others at the end of the 3rd Act of the Mal.-Madh. ( 4 ) अङ्कावतार[1] consists in casting the seed of the subject matter of an Act in the previous Act before it has drawn to its close, so that the Act following is a continuation of the one preceding; *e.g.* the sixth Act of the Sak., the germ of which is implanted at the end of the fifth Act; *cf.* also Malav. II. and Mal-Madh. II. ( 5 ) A प्रवेश or 'Introducer' is one which being interposed between any two Acts suggests like the Vishkambhaka some past or future event to show the connexion between the parts of the story through the conversation of *low* characters. It can never introduce the first Act. According to Jagaddhara, the language in a प्रवेशक is generally Sauraseni or any similar dialect as opposed to the Sanskrit found in a Suddha-vishkambhaka.

The subject-matter is further divided into three kinds–सर्वश्राव्यं or प्रकाशं, अश्राव्यं or स्वगतं, and नियतश्राव्यम्. The terms are explanatory of themselves. The last is of two kinds, जनान्तिकं and अपवारितकं (which are explained in the Notes). Independent of these divisions, there is one called आकाशभाषितं (आकाशे) or 'Speech from the void.'

*

## ( B ) NETA OR THE HERO.

The Hero is required to be modest, decorous, comely, munificent, civil, of sweet address, eloquent, sprung from a noble family, &c.[2] Heroes are mentioned to be of four kinds; *viz.* धीरोदात्त, धीरललित, धीरशान्त and धीरोद्धत. '*Dhirodatta*' or the Hero of sublime qualities, is one who is magnanimous, patient, not given to boasting, self-possessed, of firm resolve, whose high spirit is concealed and who is true to his engagements. We are not concerned with

१ अङ्कावतारस्त्वकान्ते पातोऽङ्कस्याविभागतः । The distinction, however, between an Ankasya and an Ankavatara is considered by some to be merely imaginary. Visvanatha actually supplants the latter by Ankamukha which he defines as that where, in one Act, the substance of all the other Acts is suggested.

२ नेता विनीतो मधुरस्त्यागी दक्षः प्रियंवदः । रक्तलोकः शुचिर्वाग्मी रूढवंश स्थिरो युवा ।। बुद्ध्युत्साहस्मृतिप्रज्ञाकलामानसमन्वितः । शूरो दृढश्च तेजस्वी शास्त्रचक्षुश्च धार्मिकः ।। भेदैश्चतुर्धा ललितशान्तोदात्तोद्धतैरयम् ।।

the other three classes of Heroes here. Each of these Heroes may be of one or other of four sorts. He may be दक्षिण or 'gallant,' *i. e.* equally devoted to many women though principally attached to one; or शठ 'sly', *i. e.* one, who being attached to one lady, covertly acts in a way unpleasant to her; or he may be धृष्ट 'bold' openly making his professions to another, and not ashamed even when reproached; or lastly, he may be अनुकूल 'favourable,' devoted to one Heroine only. The धीरोदात्त hero has eight manly qualities शोभा, विलास, माधुर्य, गांभीर्य, धैर्य, तेजस्, लालित्य and औदार्य.

Among the assistants of the Hero, the principal is पीठमर्द the hero of the Pataka or episode, clever in discourse, devoted to his master, and a little inferior to him in qualities. Next comes the Vidushaka, his constant companion whose business consists in the repartees of wit, in helping his friend in his love-intrigues and thus assisting in the general *denouement* of the play. The third, and of equal rank with the Vidushaka, is Vita, who knows one art only and is thereby useful to the Hero. The Hero thus equipped may still take into his service ministers of state and ministers of religion, ascetics, allies, &c. as well as eunuchs, mutes, barbarians (Yavanas) &c. Sometimes there may be a Rival-Hero called प्रतिनायक, who is avaricious, bold, impetuous, criminal and of evil conduct.

The Nayika or the Heroine, who must be possessed of qualities similar to those of the Hero, is of three kinds[1]. She may be the wife of the hero (स्वीया), as Sita in the Uttar., or one belonging to another (अन्या परकीया), or a common woman (सामान्या or साधारणस्त्री), as Vasantasena in the Mrich. The परकीया (so called because she is in the power of her guardian) may be a maiden or the wife of another. But the latter must not be introduced as the Heroine in a play[2]. The maiden's love, however, better helps the *rasa* and is, therefore, the most favourite theme with many Sanskrit poets. Further divisions and subdivisons of the *Nayika* are not introduced here, as they have very little to do with the construction of the drama. For her assistants the Heroine may have a सखी, दासी, धात्रेयी, प्रतिवेशिका and others, possessing qualities corresponding to those of the friends of the Hero.

---

१ स्वान्या साधारणस्त्रीति तद्गुणा नायिका त्रिधा।

२ अन्यस्त्री कन्यकोढा च नान्योढाङ्गिरसे क्वचित्।

## (C) RASA OR SENTIMENT.

*Rasa* is that lasting impression or feeling produced to his overwhelming delight in a man of poetic sensibility by the proper action of the *Vibhavas*, and *Anubhavas*, as well as the *Sattvikabhavas* and the *Vyabhicharibhavas*[1]. Bhava or feeling is the complete pervasion of the heart by any emotion, whether of pleasure or of pain, arising from the object under sight. Vibhava or an Exitant is that which being perceived nourishes the main sentiment. It is divided into *Alambana*, that which is, as it were, the support or subsratum of the *Rasa*, the person or thing with reference to which a sentiment arises—such as the Hero or the Heroine, and *Uddipana*, or what exites or enhances ( adds to the development of ) the sentiment, such as the moon, the beauties of the vernal season &c. beauty, decorations &c. of the principal character, in the case of शृङ्गार *Anubhava* or an Ensuant is the outward manifestation of internal feeling through the eyes, face &c. The Sattvika or natural *bhavas* are a subdivison of *Anubhava*, and are mentioned as eight in number–स्तम्भप्रलयरोमाञ्चाः स्वेदो वैवर्ण्यवेपथू। अश्रुवैस्वर्यमित्यष्टौ।. The *Vyabhicharis* or the Accessaries are those Bhavas which are not strictly confined to any *Rasa*, but appearing and disappearing, like waves in the ocean, they serve as feeders to the prevailing sentiment and strengthen it in different ways. *Sthahibhava* (स्थायिभाव) or the Permanent Sentiment of a composition is one—the ocean melting all salt into water—which not being interrupted by any sentiment contrary or akin to its nature occurring at intervals, converts all of them into its own nature[2]. Now a *Rasa* would prove contrary to another if the आश्रय or substratum of both were the same. But as अङ्गी ( principal ) and अङ्ग ( subordinate ) a रस may be mixed with one or more of others.

There are eight Sthayibhavas, रति, हास, शोक, क्रोध, उत्साह, भय, जुगुप्सा and विस्मय on which are based respectively the eight senti.

---

१ विभावैरनुभावैश्च सात्त्विकैर्व्यभिचारिभिः। आनीयमानः स्वाद्यत्वं स्थायीभावो रसः स्मृतः॥ सुखदुःखादिकैर्भावैर्भावस्तद्भावभावनम्। ज्ञायमानतया तत्र विभावो भावपोषकृत्॥ आलम्बनोद्दीपनत्वप्रभेदेन स च द्विधा। अनुभावो विकारस्तु भावसंसूचनात्मकः॥

२ विरुद्धैरविरुद्धैर्वा भावैर्विच्छिद्यते न यः। आत्मभावं नयत्यन्यान्स स्थायी लवणाकरः॥

ments–शृङ्गार the Erotic, हास्य the Comic, करुण the Pathetic, रौद्र the Furious, वीर the Heroic, भयानक the Terrible, बीभत्स the Loathsome, and अद्भुत the Marvellous. There is a ninth sentiment, that of शान्त the Quietistic, having शम or tranquillity for its Sthayibhava. But it is not suited to dramatic purposes and rarely occurs as a main sentiment in a drama. Of these eight sentiments शृङ्गार and हास्य, वीर and अद्भुत, बीभत्स and भयानक, and रौद्र and करुण are akin to each other, as they proceed from the same condition of the mind. As we are concerned with Erotic alone, that being the prevailing sentiment in Kalida's plays, we shall say something about it here. शृङ्गार is mainly divided into विप्रलम्भ or Love in separation, and संभोग or Love in union. The former, the Dasarupaka subdivides into two kinds, अयोग the Non consummation of marriage, and विप्रयोग the separation of the lovers deep in love after marriage. The former, which arises from the dependent position of one or the other of the parties, or through distance, or through the intervention of adverse fate, has ten stages, अभिलाषा, चिन्ता &c. mentioned in the com; चिन्ता 'anxiety' occurs through मान, प्रवास or some such cause. मान 'jealous anger', arises from a breach in the duties of love (प्रणयभङ्ग) and may be on both sides (rarely, however, the Nayak is mani). This मान has several varieties, such as ईर्ष्यमान, आनुमानिकमान, &c. It is capable of being dispelled in six ways–साम्ना भेदेन दानेन नत्युपेक्षारसान्तरै and is called गुरु, लघु or मध्यम according to the greatness or the smallness of the effort required to make the Nayika give it up. संभोग is when the two lovers are in the enjoyment of each other's company, engaged in looking at each other, kissing each other, &c.

## (D) THE GENERAL CONDUCT OF THE NATAKA

Every dramatic piece opens with a prelude or prologue (प्रस्तावना) which is itself introduced by what is called the *Nandi.* This Nandi, according to some, must suggest the gist of the whole plot. The Sutradhara may sometimes retire after the recital of the Nandi, in which case another actor called स्थापक (for he *establishes* as it were the topic of the play) takes his place. In the Prelude, which may begin with a brief allusion to the poet's literary attainments, his genealogy, &c., the Sutradhara or the Sthapaka suggests the subject in the form of the Bija, or by a simple beginning, or by naming the character about to enter (as in the Sakuntala). He must please the audience with sweet songs descriptive of some season and couched in the Bharati vritti. The प्रस्तावना is of two kinds—(1) प्ररोचना as in the Ratn., and (2) आमुख in which the Sutradhara holds conversation with the actress or his assistants, bearing on the subject to be introduced. This latter is of three kinds, of which one is प्रयोगातिशय. When the entry of a character is directly indicated by Sutradhara saying 'Here he enters,' that is Prayogatisaya.

The Prelude being over the piece is commenced, being hereafter arranged and exhibited in the manner indicated in the three foregoing Sections. The whole matter should be well determined and divided into Acts and Scenes. A Nataka may consist of from five to ten Acts. The Hero should be Dhirodatta. The prevailing sentiment should be शृङ्गार or वीर (or sometimes करुण), others being introduced as conducive to its development. Nothing should be introduced in the play which either misbeseems the Hero or is discordant with the main sentiment. An Act must not be tiresomely long, should be full of *Rasa*, and introduced by *Vishkambhaka*, &c. according to necessity. Its close is marked by the exit of all characters. Such incidents as journeys, massacres, wars, &c., should not be represented in a play; they may only be indicated. The death of the Hero must never be exhibited. This accounts for the somewhat monotonous character of Sanskrit plays and the absence of tragedies in Sanskrit.[1] The play should end, as it began, with a benediction or prayer, called the Bharata-

1. Wilson observes—"They (the Hindu plays) never offer a calamitous conclusion, which, as Johnson remarks, was enough to constitute a Tragedy in Shakespeare's days; and although they propose to excite all the emotions of the human breast, terror and pity included, they never effect this object by leaving a painful impression upon the mind of the spectator. The Hindus in fact have no Tragedy........The absence of tragic catastrophe in the Hindu dramas is not merely an unconscious omission; such a catastrophe is prohibited by a positive rule. The conduct of what may be termed the classical drama of the Hindus is exemplary and dignified. Nor is its moral purport neglected; and one of their writers declares, in an illustration familiar to ancient and modern poetry, that the chief end of the Theatre is to disguise by the insidious sweet the unpalatable but salutary bitter, of the cup."

vakya, as it is repeated by the principal personage in his character of an actor, and contains an expression of wishes for general prosperity and happiness. The Unity of interest or action must be maintained throughout. As regards the language to be used in a piece, the Hero and the higher characters speak in classical Sanskrit, while females and other minor characters speak in the different Prakrit dialects.

The student will have seen from the foregoing sketch, that the characteristic peculiarities of the Indian drama are mainly three :—(1) its peculiar structure; (2) the absence of the distinction between Comedy and Tragedy; and (3) the diversity of languages to be spoken by the characters. The above-mentioned general characteristics of a Nataka belong with certain modifications to the other divisions of the Rupaka as well. Of these we may notice the Prakarana and the Trotaka. The plot of a प्रकरण should be fictitous and drawn from real life in a respectable class of society. The Hero, who must be धीरप्रशान्त, may be of ministerial rank, or a Brahmana, or a merchant (Vaisya). The Heroine may be a maiden of a noble family, or a courtesan. The most appropriate sentiment is the Erotic. Gamblers and other low characters should be introduced. There should be ten Acts. The Mal.-Madh. and the Mrich. belong to this species. A Trotaka may consist of 5, 7, 8 or 9 Acts. The characters to be represented should be celestial as well as human (as in the Vik.). The Vidushaka should take a prominent part in it and be present in every Act. The prevailing sentiment should be शृङ्गार. In other particulars it does not differ from the Nataka.

## II. THE POET.

It is a regrettable fact that, barring a few well-established landmarks (*e g* the date of Bana), the chronology of Sanskrit literature is still in an unsettled condition. The dates of very few writers are given by themselves or by their contemporaries; and consequently in the majority of cases they have to be inferred or evolved, from a mass of literary material which may or may not be sufficient to yield satisfactory conclusions. Very often the result consists in the summing up of the different coflicting theories, and approximating towards what *appears* to be the probable solution. Examining the same arguments, or re-stating them in varying forms, or re-arranging them round a different point, might help to make the position more clear; but nothing except discoveries of important new facts will carry the inquiry any further. This has been well illustrated in the case of the *Mrichchhakatika*, concerning whose age and authorship not much was definitely known, when recently the unexpected discovery of the plays of Bhasa provided us with new data and brought to light the drama *Charudatta*[1], whose enlarged and completed version the *Mrichchhakatika* seems to be. Since then valuble contributions have been made to the discussion by several scholars, which have added to our knowledge of the sources of the play and finally laid to rest several doubts and hypotheses. But though the inquiry has been carried to a second and a more promising stage, we are not yet in a position to fix the date of the play with the degree of accuracy desired by the earnest inquirer; we can only make a near approach to it; and perhaps future discoveries of important texts, which have hitherto remained unknown or have been taken for lost, might throw fresh light on the problem. That this is not improbable might be gathered from the success with which South Indian scholars have recently unearthed Sanskrit works believed to have been no longer extant.

The querist who would seek to know something about our poet is confronted at the threshold by the fact that the very name of the author of the *Mrichchhakatika* is more or less shrouded in mystery. Indian tradition has attributed the drama to one Sudraka, some curious and scrappy details about whose life are given in the *Prastavana* of the play itself ( *vide* slokas 3-7 ). We are here told that Sudraka was a Kshatriya king, though of what country is not mentioned; he was brave and handsome in appearance; he knew Rigveda and Samaveda, mathematics, the arts regarding courtesans, and the science of training elephants; he was a devotee of Siva and had performed the Asvamedha sacrifice; he died[2] at the ripe age of a hundred

1 First published in 1914 by Pandit T. Ganapati Shastri in the Trivandrium Sanskrit Series.

2. There is some doubt about the exact meaning of the expressions चक्षुषी उपलभ्य and अग्नि प्रविष्ट:, for which see our Notes. According to some they signify that the king was blind and later on recovered his eye-sight through the favour of Siva, and that he voluntarily immolated himself on the funeral pyre. The word द्विज ( in sl. 3 ) has been understood by some to mean 'a Brahamana,' and not 'a Kshatriya.' We shall refer to this later on.

years and ten days, and composed ("चकार") this story of the loves of Charudatta and Vasantasena. This *Prastavana*, however, is on the face of it a later interpolation in the play, though of not far distant date, and it is doubtful how far its statements are historically true. But it seems pretty safe to assume that either Sudraka wrote the play or some one wrote it for him, and that this Sudraka was a king

It would clear the ground if we state in the beginning that we see no reason to reject these two assumptions, which are handed down by tradition. Nowhere in Sanskrit literature will be found any alternative authorship affirmed. And whoever wrote the Prologue could have had no interest in deliberately fabricating the name of Sudraka or in wantonly connecting him with the present play. Whether Sudraka personally composed the drama or whether some Pandit at his court wrote it for him cannot be exactly ascertained, for neither is improbable. In India there have been kings who were literary artists themselves, and a king might compose a work for pleasure just like any other lesser individual; while the practice of proteges writing in the name of their patrons was also quite common (*cf.* the words of Mammata श्रीहर्षादेर्धावकादीनामिव धनम् । K.-P. I.). The point may well be left undecided; for after all it does not affect the question of the poet's date. There is a suitable possibility, pointed out by some critics, that while it may be true that some person named Sudraka wrote the play, he might not be identical with Sudraka the king; in a later age the comparitavely unknown poet might easily have come to be identified with his better-known namesake Sudraka, the king. In effect this means that we must carefully look for all the Sudrakas whose existence is recorded, before we fix the authorship of the Mrich. on any one of them, king or no king. This will be done below, but it may be pointed out that there are no specific grounds for accepting only the name शूद्रक: from the Prastavana and discarding his chief qualification नृप:; they seem to go together, and must be so understood in the absence of something definite to the contrary.

There have been some scholars, however, who, because of the Prologue being an interpolation, or probably because of the difficulty of identifying Sudraka with any particular monarch, were led to seek for a solution in other hypotheses. Once the name of Sudraka is brushed aside, there arise all sorts of possibilities giving ample scope for fanciful conjectures. If Sudraka did not write the *Mrichchhakatika,* who wrote it ? To this question three different answers have been suggested. (i) It is said to have been written anonymously by some one who was neither Sudraka nor his protege. But if this were so we fail to understand how or why later on it came to be attribuled to king Sudraka, for there is no getting behind the Prastavana which is found in all the MSS. of the play and which, though put in afterwards, seems hardly to be written for recording *invented* facts. A work, originally written anonymously, can be attributed afterwards to almost any writer; but, if it is to carry any conviction, there must exist sound independent evidence to connect the author with the work; without such evidence the work will continue to remain anonymous. But the connexion of Sudraka's name with the Mrich. appears to be of such a long standing, and has so completely remained unchallenged by Indian tradition, that we cannot believe in the existence of an anonymons author, especially as there is nothing to support such a conjecture. This view is, however, supported by no less an authority than Prof. Keith[1], who writes—" That Sudraka, the alleged author, was a real person, who wrote the drama, seems most implausible..........The obvious conclusion is that the rewriter and reviver of the *Charudatta* preferred to remain nameless, and to ascribe his work to the legendary Sudraka " But why should an unknown author select in particular the name of the famous king Sudraka to father his own work on ? Prof. Levi's suggestion was that " he chose Sudraka for this purpose because he lived after Vikramaditya, patron of Kalidasa, and wished to give his work the appearance of antiquity by associating it with a prince who preceded Vikramaditya. " This suggestion is rejected by Prof. Keith, and rightly, as being " far-fetched; " but the learned scholar has offered no explanation of his own, though one was expected. And until satisfactory reasons are forthcoming, it is difficult for us to accept his assumption of anonymity. (ii) The late Dr Pischel boldly formulated

---

1 See his *Sanskrit Drama* (1924), p. 130. The quotation in the text is from his later article in the *Bu letin of the School of Oriental Studies,* Vol. III. pt. II (1924), in which he has re-affirmed his opinion.

the theory that the poet Dandin, the author of the *Dasakumara-charita*, was also the author of the *Mrichchhakatika*. There is a verse of Rajasekhara (Sarng.—P. 174) which states त्रयो दण्डि-प्रबन्धाश्च त्रिषु लोकेषु विश्रुताः. As only two works of Dandin were known, *viz.*, the *Dasakumaracharita* and the *Kavyadarsa*, the learned doctor picked out the *Mrichchhakatika* for occupying the third place, but on such slender and fantastic grounds that very few scholars[1] were prepared to endorse his view. His main reasons were two:—(*a*) that the verse लिम्पतीव तमोऽङ्गानि &c., which occurs in the Kavyad. (II. 226), also occurs in the Mrichchhakatika (I. 34), pointing to the probability of both the works being by the same author; and (*b*) that the state of society described in the Dasakum. closely resembles that depicted in the Mrich. It was unfortunate that neither of these reasons was sound or cogent. Apart from the questionable nature of the argument which attributes the same authorship to two works simply because they happen to have *one verse* in common, we now know that the stanza in question belonged orginally neither to the Kavyad. nor to the Mrich., as it is found twice in the works of Bhasa.[2] Dr. Pischel's second argument, if pursued to its logical conclusion, would entail the preposterous supposition that all works describing the same kind of social conditions were written by one and the same author! We need hardly dwell longer on Dr. Pischel's theory, as, happily, it never received any serious support and is now suitably consigned to oblivion. (iii) Greater interest attaches to a suggestion recently put forward that Bhasa himself, and none else, is the author of the Mrich., शूद्रक कवि being a sobriquet bestowed upon him on account of his being a *Sudra* by caste, and that the Mrich. is simply an amplification by Bhasa of his own work *Charudatta*. As we shall deal fully with the relations between Bhasa's *Charudatta* and our play in a

1 With the notable exception, strange to say, of Prof. Macdonell, who in his *History of Sanskrit Literature* (1900) haltingly accepted Dandin as the author of the *Mrichchhakatika*. His words are: "It is probably the work of........perhaps Dandin, as prof. Pischel thinks" (p. 361). As early as 1891 Dr. Peterson had refuted Dr. Pischel's theory in his Introduction to the Dasak.-Ch. (Bombay Sanskrit Series).

2 *I. e.*, in the *Balacharita* and the *Charudatta*. It is also ascribed by different writers to various different poets, from which it would appear to have become a kind of floating *Subhashita*; Dandin must have quoted it as such.

2

subsequent Section, we shall not enlarge on this topic at this stage, beyond remarking that if Bhasa wrote the *Mrichchhakatika*, then there is no reason why that alone, and not his other works, should bear his appellation of Sudraka; moreover, the Sudraka of the Mrich. was a king, which Bhasa most certainly was not. This hypothesis appears to us nothing but a wild attempt at originality and spectacular theorizing.

We are then left with the task of finding out who this Sudraka was to whom this play is ascribed, and what may be the age in which he should be held to have flourished. One of the familiar difficulties that beset the path of the Sanskrit student wishing to settle chronological problems is the plurality of writers bearing the same name. As is well known, many different poets bore the name Kalidasa; lesser poets than the famous author of the *Sakuntala* could hardly escape being confused with their namesakes, both anterior and posterior in time. Sudraka has met with the same fate, and one comes across a bewilderingly ample array of literary records that mention Sudraka by name. Some of them supply new and additional details concerning his life career and personality, and it would be interesting to take note of the more prominent of these and to try to see which one of these Sudrakas was probably the author of the Mrich.

(1) A passage from the Kumarikakhanda of the Skandapurana[1] mentions that a great king named Sudraka would reign in the year 3290 of the *Kali* era, *i. e.* in 190 A D. Col. Wilfred was the first to identify this Sudraka of the Skandapurana with the founder of the Andhrabhritya dynasty whose name is given as *Simuka*. The grounds given for this identification are (*a*) that the *Bhagvata-purana*[2] describes the first Andhra king as a *Vrishala* or *Sudra*, and thus it is likely that he was commonly known as *Sudraka*; and (*b*) that the name *Simuka* is variously

1. त्रिषु वर्षसहस्रेषु कलेर्यातेषु पार्थिव । त्रिशतेषु दशन्यूनेष्वस्यां भुवि भविष्यति ॥१॥ शूद्रको नाम वीराणामधिपः सिद्धिमत्र सः । चर्चितायां समाराध्य लप्स्यते भूभयापहः ॥ २ ॥

2. Sec Dr. Bhandarkar's *Early History of the Dekkan*, 1884, p. 25; the verse from the Bhag., not given there, is :—हत्वा कण्वं सुशर्माणं तद्भृत्यो वृषलो बली । गां भोक्ष्यत्यन्ध्रजातीयः कंचित्कालमसत्तमः ॥ Sk. XII. Adh. I. Sl. 20.

given as *Sindhuka*, *Sisuka*, and *Sipraka*, in various authorities, showing that its exact form was not quite settled, and might as well have been *Sudraka* originally. This is quite probable, and here we have a proof of the existence of a great Sudra—or Sudraka—king whose exploits afterwards came to figure in later literature when he had acquired a legendary or mythical character. The date[1] of the founder of the Andhrabhrityas is given as about 200 B C. Though this does not agree with the date of the Skanda-purana, we can easily explain the discrepancy if we remember that the chronology of the Sk.-P. might not have been so very accurate, since its compiler was quoting a traditional date from memory, without reference to historical exactitude in our sense of the term. As will be seen below, the date of this Sudraka does not conflict with the date to which the internal evidence of the play seems to point, nor does it conflict with the date to be assigned to his predecessor Bhasa. It is thus highly probable, and may be accepted as a working hypothesis, that Sudraka the founder of the Andhrabhritva dynasty, who ruled about 200 B C, was the author of the *Mrichchhakatika*. The play could thus be placed about 150 years before the productions of Kalidasa[2].

There are two collateral considerations which further support the conclusion arrived at above. (i) The Andhrabhrityas were a southern race. A Commentary on Vamana's Kavya-S-V. describes king Sudraka as "राजा कोमतिः"; now *Komati* is the name of a great trading caste in the Madras Presidency from which it would appear that Sudraka was a native of South India. The fact that our play is very rarely quoted by northern rhetoricians would also tend to show that it was produced in the south. In the play itself we find that the poet makes the Chandalas describe the goddess Durga as सह्यवासिनी[3] (p 382), and not as विन्ध्यवासिनी, which in our opinion is a strong indication of the author being a resident of South India. Further, the play contains a number of peculiar words and expressions which are used only in the

1. See V. A. Smith's *Early History of India* (ed. 1914), p. 216.

2. See V. A Smith's *Early History of India*, p. 307. He is inclined to place Sudraka earlier than Kalidasa.

3 Like our author, Bhavabhuti, too, who was a southerner, describes Durga as सह्यवासिनी in his Malatimadhava ; northern writers commonly use the form विन्ध्यवासिनी.

south ( *e. g.* खुण्टमोडक कर्णाटकलह &c.), and the author has mentioned the दाक्षिणात्यs along with a number of Mlechchha tribes ( Act VI, p. 236 ) which are mostly to be found in South India. And again, the Prakrit dialects are used extensively in our play, the significance of which will be noticed if we bear in mind how partial the Andhrabhrityas were to the Prakrits, as is evinced from their copper-plate grants. ( ii ) In the plot there runs the thread of a political revolution wrought, wherein one Palaka, king of Ujjayini, is deposed and Aryaka succeeds him on the throne. As this revolution has nothing directly to do with the action of the play, it could very well have been dispensed with. But the fact that it is there shows that it is deliberately included, and here is most probably a reference to some contemporary revolution which the audience remembered and could easily follow. The first of the Andhrabhrityas established himself as the result of a revolution, and very likely the author must have had that in his mind ; the actual names that he mentions were not of course those of the recent revolution, but such as were in his days past history. According to the Jaina *Harivamsa*, which is a work of the fourth century B. C., a king Palaka ruled in the sixth century B. C.; the persons Palaka and Aryaka are not imaginary, but are shown to be historical, and the political upheaval in which they were embroiled is described as having taken place shortly after the death of Gautama Buddha.[1] Though to us it seems obscure, the incident of the deposition of Palaka must have been current in Sudraka's time; its inclusion in the play, for no obvious purpose, could only be justified on the supposition that Sudraka is referring to his own exploits at the beginning of his career.

( 2 ) In the *Avantisundarikathasara*, a work of Dandin recently discovered in Madras, a life-sketch of king Sudraka is given. He is described as a Brahmana king of Ujjayini and a great poet, and is said to have defeated Svati, a prince of the Andhrabhritya dynasty. Dandin's verse in the Avanti.-K. in praise of this Sudraka runs as follows :—

शूदकेणासकृज्जित्वा स्वच्छया खड्गधारया ।
जगद्भूयोऽभ्यवष्टब्धं वाचा स्वचरितार्थया ॥

---

1 Vide Prof. Keith's *Sanskrit Drama*, p. 130.

From the words वाचा स्वचरितार्थया, it appears that in Dandin's days it was understood that Sudraka's writings consisted of autobiographical matter.[1] Thus it has been pointed out that the Mrich. embodies several incidents from Sudraka's life; Charudatta is said to represent Bandhudatta, who was Sudraka's intimate friend and frequently assisted him in times of danger, and Aryaka is said to be intended for Sudraka himself. As Svati the Andhrabhritya prince whom he defeated, ruled till about 56 B. C., an attempt has been made to identify this Sudraka with king Vikramaditya, the founder of the *Samvat* era; at present however it remains merely in the form of a suggestion. This Sudraka, whose date would thus be about 56 B. C., must obviously be different from the founder of the Andhrabhritya dynasty. Their dates, however, are not far separated from each other, and one is tempted to believe that there is probably some confusion somewhere in this account, and that the two Sudrakas might after all merge into one and the same person. For the present, how ever, we must continue to treat Dandin's Sudraka separately, and the final pronouncement on this vexed question must be suspended till we learn more of this king, either from Dandin's own woak or some similar source. Those who are not prepared to accept Col. Wilfred's identification might, as the next alternative, accept this Sudraka[2] as the author of the Mrich. The particulars given by Dandin neither agree nor conflict with those found in the Prastavana of our play, except perhaps in one particular. Dandin has described Sudraka as a Brahmana, and in the Prastavana he is described as द्विजमुख्यतमः, " the best among the Brahmanas ", if we accept the natural meaning of the compound as it appears at first sight. It is, however, a minor point, and cannot be made the basis of any serious identification between the two kings.

---

1 The above particulars are taken from a learned paper on Dandin's *Avantisundarikatha* by M. R. Kavi, M. A., read at the Second Oriental Conference of Calcutta and published in its *Proceedings* ( 1923 ) pp. 193–201. The original work of Dandin has been announced for publication.

2 For instance, Mr. Kavi unhesitatingly accepts him thus in his paper to which we have referred above.

(3) The adventures of a king Sudraka were sung by the poets Ramila and Somila,[1] who were probably his contemporaries or lived after him. Somila appears to be the same as Saumillaka, whom Kalidasa has mentioned with respect in the Malavikagnimitra;[2] thus the date of Ramila and Somila would fall before that of Kalidasa, whom we place in 56 B. C., though how long before we cannot say. This Sudraka, therefore, about whom Ramila and Somila have written, might have been the Andhrabhritya Sudraka, rather than Dandin's Sudraka, as we must allow for some time to elapse before a host of legends can gather around a king so that a कथा may be composed concerning his life. The name of Sudraka also occurs in the titles of three other works, विक्रान्तशूद्रक, a drama by an unknown author which is quoted in the Sarasvatikanthabharana, शूद्रकवध, which is a Parikatha referred to by Rayamukuta, and शूद्रकचरित, by an author named Panchasikha. As these works are not at present accessible, it is not possible to investigate whether they yield any historical information. The name of Sudraka became so famous that a host of Indian rulers, especially of the Pallava and the West-Ganges families, adopted titles, consisting of the word शूद्रक as a symbol of valour.[3]

(4) The famous name of Sudraka soon acquired a legendary halo of antiquity and was freely introduced into numerous tales; it is found mentioned in many well-known Sanskrit works. Thus, to quote Prof. Keith, "He was to Kalhana in the *Rajtaramgini* a figure to be set beside Vikramaditya; the *Vetalapanchavimsati* knows of his age as a hundred, and gives as his capital either Vardhamana or Sobhavati, which is the scene of his activities according to the *Kathasaritsagara*, which tells of the sacrifice of a Brahmin who saves him from imminent death and secures his life of a hundred years by killing himself. In the *Kadambari* he is located at Vidisa, and in the *Harshacharita* we hear of the device by which he got rid of his enemy Chandraketu, prince of Chakora; while Dandin in the *Dasakumaracharita* refers to his adventures

---

1 *Cf.* तौ शूद्रककथाकारौ रम्यौ रामिलसौमिलौ । काव्यं ययोर्द्वयोरासीद-र्धनारीनरोपमम् ॥ Rajasekhara. Prof. Bhide assumes that Ramila and Somila were the court-poets of Sudraka. *Vide* his Introd. to Svapna. p. 35.

2 प्रथितयशसां भासकविपुत्रसौमिल्लकादीनां प्रबन्धानातिक्रम्य &c., p. 2.

3 Introduction to *Chaturbhani* (Madras 1922), p. IV.

in several lives." These statements go to show that Sudraka was more or less a mythical personage to these later authors, and there is little historical truth to be gleaned from these accounts; they do not help us at all in ascertaining to which of the two Sudrakas the Mrich. should rightly be ascribed.

(5) Vamana, in his Kavyal-S.-V., mentions Sudraka by name as famed for writings exhibiting the श्लेषगुण. He does not state whether Sudraka was a king, and, as the Mrich. is not a work that particularly excels in श्लेषगुण, it is even doubtful if he knew Sudraka as the author of the Mrich. Probably he had before him some other works of our author. So, although we know when Vamana flourished, which is about 800 A. D., we gather next to nothing from his work concerning our author or our play, nor do we get any new data for Sudraka's age. Unfortunately we do not find that the Mrich. is quoted by any other writer on rhetorics whose date can be placed before Vamana's. The *Dasarupaka* quotes from the Mrich., though it does not mention Sudraka; as however it was written at the end of the tenth century A. D., its testimony serves no purpose in our inquiry.

(6) Prof. Konow, in his work on the Sanskrit drama, has started the theory that Sudraka is to be identified with an Abhira prince called Sivadatta who ruled in the third century A. D. This, however, seems to be extremely doubtful. The sole argument that is put forward to establish this result is the fact that in our play Palaka is represented as having been overthrown by Aryaka, who was the son of 'a herdsman' (गोपाल), and the word आभीर means 'a herdsman'. This is obviously too slender a reed to rely upon, and Prof. Konow's theory has consequently not found acceptance among scholars.

(7) Similar efforts have been made, on the strength of solitary words and expressions occurring in the play, to place Sudraka in the second century A. D.; *e. g.*, the expression रुद्रो राजा (VIII. 34, p. 286) is held to refer to king Rudradamana of the Kshatrapa dynasty, whose date is given as 130 A. D., so that the Mrich. would be posterior to that; the word नाणक occurring in I. 23 is believed to have come into use by the time of king Kanishka who lived in the first century A. D., so that the Mrich. would have to be placed after that. These attempts fall in the

category of Prof. Konow's inference from the word गोपाल, and cannot be considered as convincing.

We are thus left to make a choice between the Sudrakas described under ( 1 ) and ( 2 ); the materials for this choice are lacking, though it is clear that the Mrich. must have come from the pen of one of these two. It will thus have to be placed either in the third or the first century B. C.,[1] which makes it one of the earliest of Sanskrit plays now extant. We shall proceed to examine how far this claim to antiquity is supported by internal evidence; we shall find that it is all in favour of an early date. But here, too, critics have twisted various points to suit their own pet theories; as an instance we might mention that the law-suit described in the ninth Act is stated to be "in accordance with the rules of the law-books of the 6th or 7th century ," the implication being that the Mrich. cannot be older than that; but what grounds are there for supposing that similar rules *did not hold good* in the first century B. C. too ? Until that is definitely disproved the argument is of no value at all. The following are among the principal features of the internal evidence afforded by the play:—(*a*) The drama refers to a period when Buddhism was in a flourishing condition. The *Bhikshu* is introduced as an ascetic to whom respect is paid by the people, and his practices are described with great detail and accuracy of observation ; he finally becomes the head of all the monasteries ( *cf.* तत्पृथिव्यां सर्वविहारेषु कुलपतिरयं क्रियताम् । p. 404 ). Buddhism began to decline about the beginning of the Christian era, before which period, therefore, the play can safely be held to have been composed ; indeed, as is pointed out by Sir Dr. Bhandarkar,[2] under the Andrabhrityas the religion of Buddha was in a flourishing condition. (b) Many minute rules

---

1 This would of course make Sudraka a predecessor of Kalidasa Some scholars, who would like to see Sudraka put later than Kalidasa, put forward the plea that since Kalidasa does not mention Sudraka, while he refers to Bhasa, Kaviputra, and Saumillaka with respect, Sudraka must not have been known to him and therefore did not exist before him. Such "argument by silence" is always ineffective, and can never be said to prove what it seeks to prove ; for Kalidasa was not expected to enumerate *all* the famous poets with whose works he was acquainted. We have referred to it here. as reasoning on similar lines is not infrequently met with in antiquarian discussions.

2 *Early History of the Dekkan*, p. 31.

given by later writers on dramaturgy, such as those relating to the predominence of a particular *rasa*, and the assignment of a particular Prakrit dialect to a particular character, seem to be not observed by or unknown to Sudraka. ( *c* ) The reference to वैशिकी कला ( I. 4 ) and the introduction of a courtesan as the heroine seem to be synchronous with the period when Vatsyayana wrote the वैशिक chapter of his Kama-Sutra, and Vatsyayana cannot be placed later than about 100 B. C. ( *d* ) The play contains many references to astrological science. In sl. 33 of Act IX the planet मङ्गल is described as the enemy of बृहस्पति, which is contrary to the opinion of modern astrologers led by Varahamihira, but is in strict agreement with the view of ancient writers to whom Varahamihira refers ( see Brihajjataka II. 16, 15 ). As Varahamihira flourished at about 500 A. D., the Mrich. must be placed many centuries before that. ( *e* ) The general style of the play represents, in its simple grace and picturesque expression, the earlier style of Sanskrit dramatists, such as Bhasa ; it is not so polished as that of Kalidasa, and not at all as elaborate and artificial as that of Bhavabhuti and Bhattanarayana. While none of these considerations would by themselves assign any specific date to our play, still, taken together and in conjunction with the other previously known facts, they substantially strengthen the probability of the Mrich. being a production of the 2nd century B. C.

We have thus tried to show that the tradition which ascribes the Mrich. to king Sudraka may be relied upon, a being universally current, and that this Sudraka was either identical with the founder of the Andhrabhritya dynasty ( 200 B. C., and this is more probable ); or may be a king of Ujjayini described by Dandin ( 56 B. C. ). As regards the details of his life, those in the Prologue have not been denied by any authority, and might therefore be taken as fairly accurate ; if we accept Dandin's description of Sudraka, we get several additional facts which conflict with none in the Prologue. Beyond them little else is known about our author.

As regards Sudraka's works, nothing was known to be written by him except the *Mrichchhakatika* ; only recently a Bhana called *Padmaprabhritaka* has been published in South India,[1] and its

1 In the booklet titled *Chaturbhāni*, which is referred to before.

editors claim that it is by the well-known author of the Mrich. This Bhana is an inferior production covering twenty-eight pages in print, whose style of composition bears little or no affinity to that of the Mrich., but is on a par with the conventional mode affected by later writers. We have, therefore, very great hesitation in accepting the piece as a genuine production of our author. A third work *Vatsarajacharita* (also called *Vinavasavadatta*) is ascribed to him by Vallabhadeva; an edition of it has been announced for publication by the same editors, but the work is not yet accessible to us and hence its authenticity cannot be discussed at present; it may be assumed, however, on the authority of Vallabhadeva. The editors further state, in their introduction to the Padmaprabhritaka, that Sudraka, probably wrote a fourth drama, a Prakarana styled *Kamadutta*. On this point, too, the information available is tantalizingly meagre. Possibly we may be on the eve of important discoveries, which would be eagerly welcomed by all interested in the life and writings of the great artist who wrote the *Mrichchhakatika*.

*

## III. THE PLAY.

### (1) THE PLOT.

The *Mrichchhkatika* is a drama in ten Acts based on the story of the love of Charudatta, a prominent but poor inhabitant of Ujjayini, and Vasantasena, an exquisitely beautiful but pure-minded courtesan of the same city. The following is a summary of the plot as it is developed in the course of the various Acts:—

**Act I.** In the Prelude (*Prastavana*), after the Benedictory stanza (*Nandi*), the Sutradhara gives some interesting particulars about the author of the play which he is about to stage. A conversation between him and his wife (Nati), which follows, is intended chiefly to lead up to the entrance of the Vidushaka (Maitreya), at which point the action of the play properly begins. Maitreya is a poor Brahmana and an honest and sincere friend of Charudatta, a wealthy citizen of Ujjayini who, however, no longer possesses his former wealth, having spent it all in noble and charitable deeds. One Churnavriddha, who is Charudatta's friend, sends a cloak by Maitreya with instructions to give the same to his master. Charudatta enters, and the cloak is duly handed over to him. Their conversation for a while turns upon Charudatta's poverty; then Vasantasena comes upon the scene. She is being pursued by Sakara (Samsthanaka), the brother-in-law of king Palaka of Ujjayini, and the villain of the piece. He is a debauchee, a coward and a fool, with an exaggerated idea of his own importance and power; he is accompanied by two of his followers, Vita and Cheta. They entreat, cajole and threaten Vasantasena by turns, but all the same with great indignation she rejects Sakara's suit. She takes refuge in Charudatta's mansion; and in the darkness of the night her pursuers light on Radanikà, a maid in Charudatta's employ, mistaking her for the object of their search. Maitreya intervenes and turns them all out. Vasantasena is next introduced to Charudatta; she had already heard of his virtues and fallen in love with him, contrary though it was to the profession of a courtesan to become attached to a penniless man. Wishing to keep up the acquaintance, she employs an ingenious device; she leaves her ornaments with Charudatta, ostensibly for safe custody, but really with the object that they should serve as an excuse for further communication with him. She then leaves, escorted by Charudatta who on returning makes over the ornaments to Maitreya for safe keeping.

**Act II.** Vasantasena, talking in confidence with her maid Madanika, reveals the warmth of her feeling for Charudatta, and also the real reason of depositing those ornaments with him. Then follows a scene introducing a number of gamblers; one of them, Samvahaka, is running away without paying his debt, and is being pursued by his creditor and the master of the gaming-house. Assisted by another gambler, Samvahaka escapes and takes shelter in the house of Vasantasena, who in her kindness pays his debt for him and rids him of his pursuers. Samvahaka is tired of gambling, and leaves after declaring his resolve of donning the robes of a Buddhist mendicant (Bhikshu). One of Vasantasena's servants then enters and relates how he had just rescued a Bhikshu (—*i. e.*, presumably, Samvahaka—) and how his brave act was rewarded by Charudatta by the gift of his own cloak. This affords her another proof of the noble generosity of the worthy Charudatta; she takes the cloak and wears it herself, for she loves everything belonging to her beloved and worshipped hero.

**Act III.** There was a Brahmana in Ujjayini named Sarvilaka, who having fallen in love with Madanika, the slave-maid of Vasantasena, wanted to pay her ransom and marry her. Being himself poor, he had turned a burglar to obtain the necessary amount of gold. He breaks into Charudatta's house by night when all are wrapped in the arms of slumber, and happens to steal those very ornaments of Vasantasena which Maitreya had to keep with himself. The theft is soon discovered. Charudatta is distressed by the loss, not because the money meant anything to him, but because the ornaments were kept with him *as a deposit*, which he was bound in honour to return on demand. His wife Dhuta, however, whose nobility is on a par with her husband's, hands over her own necklace to help him out of the difficulty. Charudatta thereupon asks the Vid. to go to Vasa with that necklace, which he was to offer to her in exchange for her own ornaments, which, he was to state, were lost by his master at gambling, under the belief that they belonged to himself.

**Act IV.** Sarvilaka calls upon Madanika with a view to buy her freedom with those stolen ornaments. On being questioned as to the source of his sudden accession to wealth, he half-confesses that they belonged to Charudatta. Madanika, however, had recognized them as the property of her mistress; she recommends that Sarvilaka had better return them to where he had taken them from Sarvilaka, however, could not face Charudatta as a declared thief; as an alternative, therefore, she urges him to see Vasantasena and offer them to her, professing that Charudatta had sent them back by him, as his house was thought unsafe. Sarvilaka does so; but Vasantasena, who has listened to the preceding conversation, is not taken in by the pseudo-messenger. Nevertheless in her goodness of heart she bestows Madanika on her adventurous suitor. Sarvilaka has to leave suddenly in a hurry to go to the assistance of his friend Aryaka, whom king Palaka had imprisoned for fear he might become the king, as a seer had predicted he would. Vasa. is next visited by Maitreya, who, it may be remembered, is deputed by Charudatta to offer her his wife's necklace in exchange for those lost ornaments. Vasantasena is deeply touched by this fresh proof of Charudatta's nobility, and she sends word with the Vid. that she would be calling upon Charudatta that evening.

**Act V.** Vasantasena pays her promised visit, inspite of a terrible thunderstorm raging in the streets. [ This gives the poet an opportunity to introduce several fine stanzas descriptive of rain, thunder and lightning ]. On reaching Charudatta's house, she returns those ornaments to him under the plea that she had lost *his* necklace, just as he had formerly lost *her* ornaments, thereby intimating that she had seen through the ruse, well-meant though it was. The lovers have now come together, and there is nothing left that can mar their happy union, with which consummation the central theme of the play reaches its climax.

**Act VI** Vasantasena passes the night in Charudatta's house, in his company. In the morning Charudatta leaves home early, with instructions to his servant to bring Vasa. to the *Pushpaka-randaka* garden, in a carriage. Before that is done, we have a touching scene, where Rohasena, Charudatta's son, is described as crying because he was given *an earthen toy-cart* (*Mrichchhakatika*) to play with, instead of a golden one desired by him. Vasa. gives him her ornaments out of which the boy is to get a toy-cart made, and thus sends him away happy. [This is the incident that gives our play its title ]. Then the servant Vardhamanaka comes in and announces that the carriage is ready; Vasantasena asks him to wait, while she finishes her toilet. He, however, suddenly remembers that he has forgotten the carriage cushions, and goes back to bring them. In the meanwhile there comes in Sakara's servant, Sthavaraka, who, too, is driving his master's carriage in the same direction. Vasantasena gets into his carriage, by mistake, without his being aware of it, and is thus taken to the garden (where she would reach a little later than she was expected to do). Just at this time Aryaka, whom Palaka had imprisoned, has escaped from his cell; he hapnens to meet the carriage of Vardhamanaka as the latter was coming back. While the back of the driver was turned, Ayraka gets into his carriage, Vardhamanaka believing that it was Vasa. who had entered. Thus they drive on, but are shortly stopped by two of the city's guards who insist upon inspecting the carriage. One of them, Chandanaka, looks in first; he recognizes the prisoner, but promises to help him to escape; he therefore deliberately picks a quarrel with the other guard, Viraka, whom he beats and drives off. The road now being clear, Aryaka escapes in safety, Vardhamanaka never discovering all the while whom he was really driving.

**Act VII.** Vardhamanaka brings the carriage to the *Pushpakarandaka* garden, where Charudatta is awaiting Vasantasena ; as it is, however, it is Aryaka, and not Vasa., who steps out of the carriage. True to the innate generosity of his heart, Charudatta promises him safety and advises him to proceed further in the same carriage, as that would allay suspicion ; they two part the best of friends, Aryaka in gratitude and Char. in the consciousness of a good deed performed. Char. leaves without further waiting there for Vasantasena, for he did not like to be seen there after he had assisted in the escape of Aryaka, which was virtually treason towards she king.

**Act VIII.** The Bhikshu ( Samvahaka ) visits the *Pushpakarandaka* garden to wash his robe, where he is variously harassed by Sakara and finally driven away. Sakara is waiting for his carriage, which at length arrives ; he is surprised to find Vasantasena inside, though of course it is a very welcome surprise, as it affords him an opportunity to renew his attentions to her. She spurns him ; whereupon Sakara, like the fool that he is, conceives the idea of killing her by way of punishment He asks his followers, Vita and Cheta, to do the killing, which they promptly and emphatically refuse. Sakara then decides to kill her himself; he gets rid of Vita and Cheta under one pretext and another, and then strangles the helpless girl. She falls down senseless, though not dead ; he however, believes that he has killed her On the return of Vita and Cheta on the scene, Sakara boasts of his exploit ; Vita is disgusted with his master and his ways, and leaves him to join the newly formed party of Aryaka. Sakara orders the Cheta to go to his palace, where he intends to hold him a prisoner, lest he might give out the secret concerning the real author of the crime Finally, he hits upon the idea of proclaiming Charudatta as the murderer of Vasantasena ; this would be sweet and complete revenge ; for Charudatta was his rival in her affections, and it was for *his* sake that she spurned him, as he believed. On the departure of Sakara, the Bhikshu comes back to the spot to dry his robe, and discovers Vasantasena. He restores her by rendering her first-aid, and takes her to a convent (*Vihara*) hard by.

**Act IX**. The scene is now shifted to the court of justice, where in the presence of a presiding Judge and two assessors,

Sakara formally charges Charudatta with having enticed Vasa. to his garden and there murdered her for the sake of her ornaments. The Judge opens the case by calling for Vasantasena's mother, who gives evidence about the existence of a love affair between her daughter and the citizen Charudatta; she also states that so far as she knew Vasa. was then supposed to be in Charudatta's house Next Charudatta himself is sent for, who denies any exact knowledge of Vasantasena's movements. In the meantime Viraka arrives to lay information against his fellow-guard Chandanaka who had mauled and assaulted him while be was trying to inspect a carriage which belonged to Charudatta and in which Vasantasena was supposed to be travelling in the direction of *Pushpakarandaka* garden. The Judge sends him to find out if a woman's dead body was lying in the garden. As ill luck would have it, a dead body of a woman *was* lying there, who had been accidentally killed by the fall of a tree. Viraka comes back and reports what he has seen. This is sufficient evidence to charge Charudatta with Vasantasena's murder; he, however, makes no very serious effort to establish his innocence, so much weighed down he is with the thought that now that Vasantasena was no more, life would be without interest to him, and further that he, being penniless, would not be believed in what he would say to the contrary and that the Judge would not give him a fair hearing. As a matter of fact, the Judge is quite favourable, but he has to investigate the truth; the guilt of Char. is already apparent by his half silence; and further damning evidence is unwittingly given by Maitreya who brings with him Vasantasena's ornaments, the same that she had given to Rohasena; the ornaments are pointed out by Sakara as the motive of the crime, and they belonged to Vasa. and came from Charudatta's house. The chain of evidence is now practically complete. Charudatta does not give any satisfactory explanation, and t e Judge has to declare him guilty. King Palaka, thereupon, pronounces the death-sentence upon the murderer, as Charudatta is now adjudged to be. He is to be taken to the cemetery and there impaled as a warning to all similar wrong-doers.

**Act X** Charudatta is being taken to the cemetery by two Chandalas, who are to act as his executioners, though they don t much relish their job. Charu.'s guilt is proclaimed at each proclamation-station on the way. Maitreya brings in Rohasena so that his father might have a last look at his son's face; Maitreya entreats the Chandalas to release Charu., which of course they cannot. Then Sakara's servant Cheta, whom his master had put in irons, hears the proclamation; anxious to declare the truth, he resolutely jumps into the street, chains and all, from the room wherein he was confined. He denounces Sakara as the guilty party, but the latter arrives there at this juncture and somehow manages to prove, to the satisfaction of the simple-minded Chandalas, that the Cheta was a thief and a liar and that therefore his statement was not to be relied on. Then they reach the place of execution, where Charu. is now about to be impaled. But the Bhikshu accompanied by Vasantasena arrives there in the nick of time; the charge of murder falls through and the innocence of Char. is at once fully established, as also Sakara's guilt. Sarvilaka then enters and announces that Aryaka had killed the wicked king Palaka and installed himself on his throne as his successor. For the valuable aid rendered by him in times of need, Char. is rewarded by Aryaka with the gift of the kingdom of Kusavati. The title of 'wife' is conferred upon the virtuous Vasantasena, to whom the stigma of being called a courtesan would now no longer attach. Similar suitable honours are also conferred upon Samvahaka, Sthavaraka, the Chandalas, Chandanaka, and even the villainous Sakara, for Char. was not the person to revenge himself on a fallen enemy. After this happy conclusion, the play terminates with the usual stanza (*Bharatavakya*) containing an expression of goodwill towards all and unhappiness for none.

The student will see, from the foregoing sketch of the story, that the principal points in the development of the plot are:—(1) The handing over by Vasa. of her ornaments into Char.'s keeping as a deposit; (2) Samvahaka's being introduced to Vasantasena, who lays him under an obligation by paying his debt; (3) Sarvilaka's theft of Vasa.'s ornaments, and their subsequent return by him to Vasa. herself; (4) Charudatta's sending the necklace in exchange for the ornaments; (5) Vasantasena's visit to Char. and their union; (6) the interchange of the carriages, owing to which Aryaka and Charudatta become friends and which gives Sakara an opportunity to lay violent hands on Vasa.; (7) Vasantasena's rescue by Samvahaka; (8) the charge of murder against Charudatta, which is apparently proved by (*a*) the discovery of the female corpse, and (*b*) the finding of Vasa.'s ornaments on the person of Maitreya; (9) the death-sentence passed on Char.; and (10) the arrival of the Bhikshu and Vasantasena on the scene of the execution, which brings about the denouement.

## (2) The Sources of the Plot.

### Bhasa's Charudatta as the Basis of the Mrich.

The foregoing ananlysis of the plot would show that it has been constructed with no inconsiderable skill, the author having successfully welded together a variety of exciting incidents so as to maintain the spectators' interest right up to the end. The Mrich. stands at the head of all Sanskrit plays in providing us with a plot that is neither poor nor colourless; it is a love-story full of adventures that stand apart by themselves outside the conventional class of super-human agency or insipid intrigues. The credit for inventing this distinctly fresh and vigorous plot had long been given to Sudraka, as a writer of original creative power, when the discovery of Bhasa's *Charudatta* threw a flood of light on the construction of our play. It was immediately seen that the *Charudatta*, which too is based on the loves of Char. and Vasant., bore an extraordinary resemblance to the *Mrichchhakatika*; the two plays accorded with each other with such completeness of detail that it was patent, even on a most cursory examination, that one of them must have been an adaptation of the other. The following is a brief analysis of the plot of Bhasa's play:—

**Act I**. Without any Benedictory stanza or description of the author, the play opens with the entrance of the Sutradhara who carries on a conversation with his wife ( Nati ) which leads to the introduction of the Vidushaka in the same manner as in the Mrich. The Vid. then enters and is represented as paying a visit to Charudatta. A short conversation between the two, on the evils of poverty, is followed by the entrance of Vasantasena, who is pursued by Sakara and Vita. Vasa. takes refuge in the house of

Charudatta, while her pursuers, coming on in the darkness, mistake Char.'s maid Radanika for the fugitive, and seize her. The Vidushaka's entrance with a lamp makes them realize their error and they depart in peace. Vasa. is then introduced to Char.; she hands over her ornaments to him for safe keeping and then returns home, escorted by Vidushaka.

**Act II.** Vasantasena has a confidential talk with her maid-servant [as in the Mrich.], wherein she describes the warmth of her attachment to and the merits of her worshipped hero. Then enters Samvahaka who is pursued by a creditor of his to whom he owed money at gambling. The creditor is not introduced on the stage, but Vasantasena's maid goes out at the instructions of her mistress and pays him off. The Samvahaka leaves, after declaring that being disgusted with his present mode of life he had resolved to turn an ascetic. Next enters a servant of Vasa. and he describes how he had just rescued an ascetic from the teeth of an enraged elephant and how he was rewarded for his brave deed by Charudatta, who had witnessed it.

**Act III.** Charu. and Vid. have returned from a concert, and they go to sleep in their house. Sajjalaka, a burglar [*Sarvilaka* in the Mrich.] breaks into the house and steals the ornaments of Vasantasena from Vidu.s keeping, The alarm is raised; Charu. is greatly distressed at the loss of the deposit, when his wife dutifully hands over her own jewel-necklace to be given to the courtesan in exchange for her ornaments. Charu instructs Vid. to call upon her for that purpose, and the latter agrees, though under a protest.

**ACT IV.** Vasa. is in her mansion, love-sick and pining for a union with her lover; she even declines to perform her usual toilet for any other suitor than the beloved Charudatta. Sajjalaka enters; he loves Madanika, the maid-servant of Vasa.; he shows to her the ornaments which he had stolen from Char.'s house and with which he proposes to ransom her off from bondage. She, however, recognizes the ornaments; and after some persuasion her gallant lover agrees to restore the stolen property to its rightful owner, Vasantasena. In the meantime the Vidu. calls upon the courtesan to offer her the jewel-necklace in exchange. He departs after accomplishing his mission, and thereupon Sajjalaka comes in, accompanied by the maid (Madanika). He professes to be a messenger from Charu. and returns to her the ornaments as coming from him. Vasa. sees through the device, but she graciously releases Madanika from slavery and sends her off happy in the company of her lover. She then remarks to her attendant that the affairs were happening just as though in a dream ( ' जाग्रत्या मया स्वप्नो दृष्टः " ),and the maid responds by characterzing the incidents as an " अमृताङ्कनाटक ", *i. e.* 'a one-Act play sweet as nectar," referring to the happy conclusion which she forces, Then Vasa. proposes to start on a visit to Charudatta, and the play ends, somewhat abruptly, with her departure.

The student will have observed that the above is substantially the same as the story of the Mrich. (Acts I–IV.), and, on a perusal of the *Charudatta*, every page, nay almost every line and every word of it, will be found to have been reproduced, with or without embellishments, in the *Mrichchhakatika*. Here is a strange spectacle of a whole play being simply re-written and transformed into another with a different title, except that the story of the *Charudatta*, which is in 4 Acts, is carried on in the Mrich by the addition of six more Acts The identical words, expressions, sentences, stanzas, ideas and similes are to be found in both the plays, generally in an amplified and expanded form in the Mrich. and in a simple and brief one in the Charu. The number of these is too large to be specified here; the more important of them we have quoted in the Notes and it is unnecessary to set them out here in detail; for that would be practically copying out the whole of the *Charudatta*, side by side with the Mrich; moreover, the complete similarity between the two is so obvious that nobody would even attempt to deny it. What, then, is the explanation of this unique phenomenon ?

The obvious answer, and one on which most scholars are agreed, is that the Mrich is ***an enlarged version*** of the Charudatta. We have seen above how the extant portion of the *Charudatta* ends suddenly without any denouement. This completely spoils its chances as a stage-piece; for the spectators want, before everything else, a complete and well-developed story. Sudraka must have conceived the idea of continuing and finishing the play; had he merely added the remaining Acts, the result viewed as a whole would have been an incongruous piece of workmanship; hence he re-wrote and worked over the original four Acts also, making several changes and additions, and followed these up with the next six. The *Charudatta* seems to have been left incomplete by Bhasa, though we do not know why; there are indications in the play itself that he had intended to complete it. Thus, among other things, we read towards the end गणिका—एहि। इमं अलंकारं गृहीत्वा आर्यचारुदत्तमभिसरिष्यावः। चेटी—अज्जुके तथा। एतत्पुनः अभिसारिकासहायभूतं दुर्दिनमुन्नमितम्। (p. 86); where is the necessity of mentioning the दुर्दिन, unless it were to lead up to Act V. which would show Vasantasena going to her lover in rain and thunder? Some have believed that Bhasa might have composed the whole play, but a portion of it came to be lost afterwards, so that only a fragment is available to us. But this is most unlikely; for had the whole play been accessible to Sudraka, surely there could have been no motive for him simply to re-write the same and copy everything from start to finish. In Sudraka's days too the play must have been known as a fragment, and hence there was an opportunity for a skilled hand to revise it and complete it for presentation; and if Sudraka knew the play as a fragment, the probability is that Bhasa never completed it, not that the latter part was lost in the short interval separating the two poets.

In giving a more polished and a completer form to the work of his illustrious predecessor, Sudraka has preserved the original almost intact, especially its fine passages and special witticisms; thus the play on the words वसन्तसेना (f.) and वसन्तसेन (m.) (Char. p. 60) is preserved in the Mrich., though in a different context (p. 246), and so too is the following dialogue (Char. pp. 59-60):—

चेटी—वृक्षवाटिकापक्षद्वारे संधिं छित्त्वा चोरः प्रविष्टः।
विदू०—चोरं छित्त्वा संधिः प्रविष्टः।
चेटी—हताश, संधिं छित्त्वा चोरः प्रविष्टः।

In innumerable places, however, a finished and amplified turn of expression is substituted in the Mrich. in the place of the crudeness and simple abruptness which are a characteristic of Bhasa's style; thus, to compare only a few out of many passages:—

| ( चारुदत्त ) | ( मृच्छकटिक ) |
|---|---|
| भाव, नष्टा नष्टा। (p. 16) | भाव भाव, बलीयस्यन्धकारे माषराशिप्रविष्टेव मसीगुटिका दृश्यमानैव प्रनष्टा वसन्तसेना। (p. 38) |
| शृणोमि गन्धं श्रवणाभ्याम्। अन्धकारपूरिताभ्यां नासापुटाभ्यां सुष्टु न पश्यामि। (p. 20) | शृणोमि माल्यगन्धम्। अन्धकारपूरितया पुनर्नासिकया न सुव्यक्तं पश्यामि भूषणशब्दम्। (p. 40) |
| स्वरान्तरेण दक्षा हि व्याहर्तुं तन्न मुच्यताम्। (p. 22) | वञ्चनापण्डितत्वेन स्वरनैपुण्यमाश्रिता। (p. 46) |
| तव च मम च दारुणः क्षोभो भवति। (p. 25) | मरणान्तिकं वैरं भविष्यति। (p. 54) |
| वासपादपविनाशेन (p. 44) | वासपादपविसंष्ठुलतया। (p. 92) |
| ततः सर्वो जनो भणति अहो चेटस्य कर्मेति। (p 46) | तत आर्ये साधु रे कर्णपूरक साधु इत्येतावन्मात्रं भणन्ती विषमभराक्रान्तेव नौः एकतः पर्यस्ता सकलोज्जयिन्यासीत्। (p. 98) |
| उत्कण्ठितस्य हृदयानुगता सखीव। (p. 49) | उत्कण्ठितस्य हृदयागुणा वयस्या। (p. 104) |
| यावदारभे कर्म। (p. 55) | तत्कस्मिन्नुद्देशे संधिमुत्पादयामि। (p. 112) |
| नमः खरपटाय। नमो रात्रिगोचरेभ्यो देवेभ्यः। (p. 57) | नमो वरदाय कुमारकार्तिकेयाय नमः कनकशक्तये ब्रह्मण्यदेवाय देवव्रताय नमो भास्करनन्दिने नमो योगाचार्याय। (p. 114) |
| शतसहस्रमूल्या (p. 67) | चतुःसमुद्रसारभूता (p. 130) |
| कोऽप्युपचारोऽपि नैतया भणितः। (p. 82) | अहो गणिकाया लोभोऽदक्षिणता च यतो न कथाऽपि कृताऽन्या। अनेकधा स्नेहानुसारं भणित्वा किमप्येवमेव गृहीता रत्नावली। एतावत्या ऋद्ध्या न तयाऽहं भणितः—आर्य मैत्रेय विश्रम्यताम्। मल्लकेन पानीयमपि पीत्वा गम्यतामिति। (p. 180) |

It is needless to multiply instances to show how skilfully Sudraka has improved the somewhat meagre and uncouth style of Bhasa. In addition to refining the literary expression[1], our author has made the following principal alterations and additions :—( 1 ) The Sutradhara in the Char. speaks in Prakrit only; in the Mrich. he begins in Sanskrit and changes afterwards into Prakrit. ( 2 ) In the Char., no reason is assigned to the visit of Vid. to the hero; in the Mrich. he is described as carrying a cloak to be given to Char. from a friend of his. ( 3 ) In the Char., Vasa. is pursued by two persons only, Vita and Sakara; in the Mrich. Cheta is added to their company, presumably to give more variety to their dialogue. ( 4 ) In the Char., Vasa. is escorted home by the Vidushaka; in the Mrich. it is Charudatta himself who sees her home. In his anxiety to show off Charudatta as a gallant lover, attentive to his mistress, our poet has exhibited on the stage a rather improbable journey between the residences of the two lovers; this cannot be said to be a happy improvement. ( 5 ) The gamblers' Scene in Act II., introducing Mathura, Dardura, &c., is an addition which constitutes a distinct gain to the histrionic interest of the piece. It shows that Sudraka was not a slavish imitator but a constructive artist of high ability. ( 6 ) In the Char. Sajjalaka appears before Vasa. *after* the departure of Vid.; in the Mrich. he appears *before* his arrival; this is a most judicious change; for there is great poetic charm in showing that the proof of her lover's magnanimity so touches and stirs Vasa. that she immediately decides upon going to see him. The Madanika-Sajjalaka episode, if it came after the Vid.'s visit, would have thrown this effect into the back-ground. (7) The Aryaka-Palaka story is nowhere hinted at in the Char.; its earliest hint in the Mrich. is found in Act II. ( p. 84, कथितं च मम प्रियवयस्येन शर्विलकेन यथा किल आर्यकनामा गोपालदारकः &c ) and it is developed further on. This is a deliberate addition whose significance we have already pointed out in our remarks on the Poet. (8) The description of Vasa.'s mansion occupies only 4 lines in the Charu. (अहो गणिकावाटस्य सश्रीकता &c., p. 79, quoted in our Notes, p. 85 ); in the Mrich. it is given at great length and comprises more than a third of the whole Act.

All these changes, both in the manner of their relation and in the subject-matter of the piece, serve to heighten the charm of

1 Sudraka was a master of lively dialogue; the one on p. 54 is not in the Char., but it is entirely an invention of our author.

the original. In nearly all cases they are effected with true poetic judgement and scenic propriety, revealing that our author was no mediocre plagiarist, but possessed the true inspiration of a poet and the balanced discretion of a critic. It is true that he cannot be credited with originality in the invention of his plot; but it should be remembered that what he chose to do was to raise the superstructure of his new play on the *Charudatta* serving as the basis. He was therefore bound to take over the story of the original, and his skill and originality were to be seen in proportion to the success with which he would compose a complement to that fragment, which would form a fitting sequel to the incidents already narrated. In that he has achieved a rare triumph; for the last six Acts have proved to be even more exciting and more interesting than the preceding four, surpassing them in the vividness and variety of their incidents. In the construction of these last Acts lies the proof of the originality of Sudraka; they give ample evidence that our author is in no way inferior as a dramatist to his renowned model, and that, had he so chosen, he could independently have written an equally powerful play. Doubtless his glorious achievement suffers to some extent from the fact that he borrowed his initial material from his predecessor; but it cannot be denied that he has surpassed him in many respects, so that the value of the *Charudatta*, as observed by Dr. Keith[1], seems less to us by the side of the completed and elaborated *Mrichchhakatika*.[2]

There have been some critics, however, who, though unable to deny the too-obvious resemblance between the two plays, are not inclined to admit that the Char. served as the prototype of the Mrich.; their main reason for seeking an alternative explanation lies in the obscurity that surrounds the plays of Bhasa as now known to us. Ever since Pandit T. Ganapati Sastri first brought to light the works of Bhasa, there have been a number of

---

1 *Sanskrit Drama*, p. 107.

2 It may be noticed here that the current recension of the Mrich. shows tracts of *four different hands* concerned in giving it its present shape :—There is first the original *Charudatta* of Bhasa in four Acts; next comes the re-written version by Sudraka, supplemented by six new Acts; thirdly, some unknown writer has supplied the introductory account of the author in the Prastavana (p. 8); and finally, one Nilakantha has added one Scene in the tenth Act (pp. 396 to 402), which was not in Sudraka's work. We shall revert to a consideration of this last addition in a subsequent section.

scholars who have remained sceptical about their authenticity. In their opinion these plays do not belong to the famous dramatist eulogized by Kalidasa, but are probably[1] "compilations and adaptations made for the stage of Kerala not earlier than the 8th Century A. D., derived to some extent from the works of Bhasa, which, however, are lost." If this view were to be accepted, the present discussion would assume an entirely different aspect, as the *Charudatta* would cease to be anterior to our play. To investigate the authenticity or otherwise of Bhasa's dramas lies strictly outside the scope of our inquiry; we may state, however, that the majority of leading Sanskrit scholars, both in India and outside, have accepted the published plays as genuine, though there are some who decline to subscribe to such a conclusion. Dr. V. S. Sukthankar, who, among others, has made a very exhaustive study of the problem, has summarized in a lucid paper[2] the pros and cons of this question; in his opinion the balance between them is so evenly held that it is hardly possible to say on which side the truth lies, so that "the Bhasa question is now as far away from being settled as ever before". No useful purpose can be served therefore by our entering into that discussion here; under the circumstances we must be content to assume that the extant *Charudatta* is a genuine Bhasa play, and to accept Bhasa's authorship of the Trivandrum dramas, tentatively, as a working hypothesis (which is also the position taken by Dr. Sukthankar). Even if, however, it were to be proved that Bhasa had nothing to do with the extant fragment, it seems to us undeniable that the *Charudatta* whoever its author might have been, is quite distinctly an *earlier* version than the Mrich. An examination of the passages we have set out above in parallel columns, and of many more which the student can easily collect, would show that if one of these plays is based on the other—and of that there is no doubt—it must be the Mrich.; for in each case the expression of the Char. appears to be the original upon which the author of the Mrich. improved afterwards; the *Charudatta* does not read at all anywhere as an abridgement; for an abridgement generally retains the good points of the original, while we find that they are absent

1 As concisely put by Dr. Keith in a recent article in the Bulletin of the School of Oriental Studies, London.

2 In No. 75 (1923) of the *Journal* of the Bombay Branch of the R. A. Society, pp. 230 ff.

in the Char. The Mrich. invariably offers better readings and finer conceits, the worse and commonplace ones being found in the Char.; it is almost inconceivable how this could happen if the Char. were based on our play ; it is quite possible that a later writer might try to abridge a lengthy play like the Mrich., by compiling an abridged edition of it suited to acting, but it would scarcely be so inferior to the original from the literary standpoint; it is contrary to all experience; and we are compelled to admit therefore that the Mrich. is an adaptation and an amplified edition of the *Charudatta*. The Prakrit of the Mrich. has been declared by competent authorities to be later than the Prakrit of the Char., a fact which must not be lost sight of in this discussion, and which further strengthens our conclusion. Those who deny that the Char. served as the model of the Mrich. have to explain away their similarity by postulating one of these hypotheses :—(1) The Char. may be an abridged version of the Mrich. We have just shown how a cursory perusal of the two plays renders this view quite untenable. Moreover, since the Mrich. is available complete, it is but reasonable to expect that its abridgement too should have been complete ; but the fragmentary condition of the Char. militates against this view. (2) There is a theory propounded by some, to which we have already referred, that Bhasa himself wrote both these plays. Why Bhasa should have chosen to write two different plays on the same theme, and in almost identical language, is a mystery of which no solution is offered by these critics ; and why he should have left the Char. incomplete is another mystery which is equally insoluble ; for it is too far-fetched to assume that a portion of one play became lost and the other remained intact; further, there is no reason why one of them was known to be the work of Bhasa and the other came to be attributed to king Sudraka. (3) It is no doubt within the bounds of possibility that both the Mrich. and the Char. are derived from a common original now lost; in that case we should have *three* poets working on the same theme and producing such extraodinarily similar works; this appears to us so unlikely, however, that we need not give it any serious consideration, especially as there is no evidence to support such a conjecture. As matters now stand, we think that it is abundantly clear that the Char. is the earlier version and forms the basis of the Mrich., quite apart from its genuineness or otherwise as a work from the pen of the great Bhasa; and scholars who have made a minute study of the two plays have also arrived at the same conclusion. Bhasa has been generally placed in the 6th century B. C., and Sudraka, representing a stage of literary style which in finish and general polish is intermediate between Bhasa and Kalidasa, may be taken to have flourished at about 200 B. C., which is the date we have assigned to him before.

*

## (3) Time-Analysis of the Play.

The action of the Mrich. begins on a day which is not actually mentioned in the play, though we can determine approximately what it must have been. It is known from Sakara's statement (कामदेवायतनोद्यानात्प्रभृति &c. p. 54), as well as from that of Vasantasena (त्वं मया सह कामदेवायतनोद्यानं गताऽऽसी: p. 68), that it was at some festival held in Cupid's shrine that she first fell in love with Charudatta. This must have been the festival commonly known as वसन्तोत्सव or मदनमहोत्सव, which is celebrated to herald the advent of spring and which is referred to in the Malavik., the Ratanavali, and other Sanskrit plays. Its beginning was conventionally placed on the fifth day of the bright half of the month of Magha, popularly known as *Vasanta-panchami.* (Also the Vidushaka, when he goes to Vasantasena's house, mentions certain trees and plants, Ashoka and others, which he finds in blossom and which blossom when spring sets in; see p. 170). The first Act shows Vasa. in love with Charu., and we might assume a period of a fortnight to have elapsed between the day she saw him first and the one on which the action of the play commences. We may thus sefely infer that the first Act begins on the sixth day of the dark half of Magha, for at the end of the Act the moon is just rising (उदयति हि शशाङ्कः &c. p. 64), and the night is so far advanced that there are few persons abroad (राजमार्गः शून्यः p. 64); this would be at about 11 o'clock on the sixth night of a *dark half* of a month; the reading षष्ठीव्रतकृतदेवकार्यस्य instead of सिद्धीकृतदेवकार्यस्य (p. 20), which seems to be the poet's original

1 Among these may be mentioned Dr. Morgenstierne, who has written an exhaustive monograph on the subject. Dr. Keith in his *Sanskrit Drama* (p. 131) endorses the same view, with which Dr. Sukthankar also concurs.

reading (see our Notes), enables us to fix the *sixth* as the exact date, rather than the fifth or the seventh. Only when we place the action at the commencement of the *Vasanta* season we see the propriety of Churnavriddha's present to Charu. of a cloak scented with *jati* flowers; for the *jati* does not blossom in the spring (न स्याज्जाती वसन्ते S.-D, VII. 25), and it would, therefore, be a valuable gift in that season, a fact which does not escape the notice of Vasantasena who exclaims (p. 58)—आश्चर्यम् । जातीकुसुमवासितः प्रावारकः ।. Having thus determined माघ कृष्ण षष्ठी—a so because the cold season has not entirely passed yet; for Rohasena is spoken of as शीतार्तं (see p 58)—as probably the first day of the action, the further analysis of its time presents no difficulties, except on two points. (i) Dr Ryder, Mr. Paranjpe and others, do not allow a long interval between Acts II. and III., which they place on the same day, while we consider that an interval of a fortnight between them to be quite essential. (ii) Dr. Ryder assigns two successive days to Acts IX. and X., while in our opinion they refer to one and the same day. We shall analyse each Act in detail and proceed to state our reasons below.

Act I—begins, as shown above, presumably on माघ कृष्ण षष्ठी, in the evening at about 9 o'clock, when it was pitchy dark (*cf.* एतस्यां प्रदोषवेलायां p 26; and the verse लिम्पतीव तमोऽङ्गानि &c. p. 40). It lasts for about two hours, when Vasa. returns home. By that time the moon has risen, as it would do at that time that night.

Act II.—begins in the morning, when Vasa. has yet to take her bath (*cf* स्नाता भूत्वा &c., p. 66); it is mentioned further on (p 98) that Charu. has given away that same *jati*-scented cloak to Karnapuraka, which shows that it must be the morning of the day following Act I. The action lasts for about three hours, as we must allow an hour or so for the dispute between the gamblers and at least two hours more for Samvahaka to get shaved and furnish himself with the paraphernalia of a Bhikshu, and for Karnapuraka to preserve him from the elephant.

Act III.—Charudatta has gone to attend a musical concert and it is mid-night before he returns (अतिक्रामत्यर्धरजनी p. 104); at that time the moon—the crescent-moon—is described as setting (अस्तं व्रजत्युन्नतकोटिरिन्दुः p. 106). This must be the moon, say, of the 8th day of the *bright half*, obviously of Phalguna ( the month following Magha ). Thus there must be an interval of over a fortnight between the last Act and this, and it is erroneous to place the two Acts on the same day. There are several other considerations, too, which require us to understand some such interval; thus, when the Cheta hands over Vasa.'s ornaments to Maitreya ( p. 108 ), the latter exclaims अद्याप्येतत्तिष्ठति, and abuses them as निद्राचौर, which he could not be well understood to do unless they had worried him continually for a few days at least and robbed him nightly of his sleep. Moreover, if the ornaments had remained with Char. for *one day* only, it is most unlikely that he would be giving it as his excuse that he lost them under the impression that they were his own; for a previous day's deposit is such a fresh incident in one's memory on the following day that such an excuse would be too lame, and, in fact, would not be offered. So we must allow some days to pass during which the ornaments lie in Char.'s house; this interval could as well be a fortnight. Note also how in Act V. sl. 37, Char. speaks of having passed some nights sleeplessly after his meeting with Vasantasena. The action of Act III. begins at about mid-night and lasts for over four hours, during which time Char. and Vid. are lying asleep (p. 108) and Sarvilaka enters and commits the theft. It was dawn when the alarm was raised, and here the Act ends (*cf.* अहमपि कृतशौचः संध्यामुपासे p. 130.)

ACT IV.—The very next day after the burglary, Sarvilaka goes to ransom off his Madanika ( *cf.* अद्य रात्रौ मया भीरु त्वदर्थे साहसं कृतम् p. 138) ; this must have been at about 8 o'clock in the morning, for he says further on, अयि प्रभाते मया श्रुतं &c (p 140). Vasa. promises to pay a visit to Char, the same night (अहमपि प्रदोषे आर्यं प्रेक्षितुमागच्छामि p. 174). The action of this Act lasts for about two hours.

ACT V.—This begins the same night of the day of the last Act, and Vasa. herein pays the proposed visit. An untimely storm is raging (अकालदुर्दिन p. 176 ), and a storm in the month of Phalguna would no doubt be an " untimely " one. The action lasts for well over two hours, until upto midnight.

ACT VI.—begins early in the morning of the very next day ( *cf.* सुष्ठु न निध्यतिो रात्रौ। तदद्य प्रत्यक्ष प्रेक्षिष्ये p. 214 ). The action lasts for over three hours, to allow for the interchange of the carriages, the quarrel between the guards, and the escape of Aryaka.

Act VII.—synchronizes with the last and begins the same morning, when Char. is shown as awaiting the arrival of Vasantasena whom he was expecting in the Pushpakarandaka garden. The events of this Act follow immediately after those of the last, and would not occupy more than an hour.

Act VIII.—In the last Act Charudatta left the garden just when the Bhikshu was entering it ( pp. 250, 252 ); so this Act, following immediately after that, is concerned with the events of the same day. The time is somewhere near mid-day ( *cf.* नभोमध्यगत: सूर: &c. p. 260; माध्याह्निक: सूर्य: p. 264 ). The action ends with the restoring of Vasa. to consciousness; its stirring incidents, occurring in rapid succession, would occupy a period of three to four hours at the most, in the afternoon. Thus these three Acts (VI. VII. and VIII.) cover one day only.

Act IX.—is to be placed early in the morning of the next day, since Viraka expressly mentions that he has passed one night since his fellow-guard insulted him ( *cf.* रात्रि: प्रभाता मे p. 332 ). The trial would occupy about two hours, at the end of which Char. is given in custody and the Chandalas are instructed to get ready for their job ( p. 350 ). This would be at about 10 A. M.

Act X.—must be placed a few hours after the last, and on the same day, as Char. is now shown as being led to the execution-ground by the Chandalas. That could not be the next day, as Dr. Ryder and others have assumed; for if that were so, the news of the trial of Char. and the death-sentence passed on such a prominent citizen of Ujjayini would have spread like wild-fire through the city, so that the Bhikshu and Vasr. would have heard of it the same day and run to his rescue; but it is herein described that they learn it on the road, through the proclamation, which shows that this Act practically follows on the heels of the last Act. Again, had one day passed between Acts IX and X., the meeting between Char. and his son, which Maitreya is asked to arrange, would obviously have taken place not on the public road but rather at Charudatta's place of confinement. The action of this Act would occupy about three hours.

Thus it is clear that the action of the play is spread over the various Acts as follows:—(Presumably) माघ कृष्ण षष्ठी, early night, Act I.; the second day, Act II; then an interval of over a fortnight. Next (presumably) फाल्गुन शुक्ल अष्टमी, midnight, Act III.; the second day, Acts IV. and V.; the third day, Acts VI., VII., and VIII.; and the fourth day, Acts IX and X. The action, therefore, comprises the events of a period of about twenty days, and not five or six days as some critics would have it.

## (4) TECHNICAL REMARKS.

The *Mrichchhākaṭika* belongs to the division of dramatic compositions technically known as प्रकरण, which is thus[1] defined:—

अथ प्रकरणे वृत्तमुत्पाद्यं लोकसंश्रयम् ।
अमात्यविप्रवणिजामेकं कुर्याच्च नायकम् ॥
धीरप्रशान्तं सापायं धर्मकामार्थतत्परम् ।
शेषं नाटकवत्सन्धिप्रवेशकरसादिकम् ॥
नायिका तु द्विधा नेतुः कुलस्त्री गणिका तथा ।
क्वचिदेकैव कुलजा वेश्या वाऽपि द्वयं क्वचित् ॥
कुलजाऽभ्यन्तरा बाह्या वेश्या नातिक्रमोऽनयोः ।
आभिः प्रकरणं त्रेधा संकीर्णं धूर्तसंकुलम् ॥

The plot should be neither legendary nor historical, but one of the poet's own invention. The hero should be a minister, Brahmana, or a merchant, of the type known as धीरशान्त[2] (calm and self-controlled), undergoing misfortune, and with Virtue, Pleasure and Wealth as his chief objects. The heroine should be either a high-born lady, or a courtesan; it is also permissible to introduce both these types of heroines in the same play, but in that case *they should never be shown as meeting on the stage.* A प्रकरण is called शुद्ध if it has the first kind of heroine विकृत if

1. We have quoted from the *Dasa-Rupaka*, Pari. III., as it gives a concise definition; other definitions, more or less detailed, will be found in Bharata's Natya-Sastra, Adh. 18, and in Sah.-D., Pari. VI.

2. सामान्यगुणयुक्तस्तु धीरशान्तो द्विजादिकः । D.-R. II. 4. A धीरशान्त hero is a Brahmana or a similar highly respectable person, possessed of the generic merits of hero (given in the verses नेता विनीतो मधुरः &c.)

the second (*i. e.* a courtesan), and संकीर्ण if both; the संकीर्ण variety abounds in rogues. In other respects ( *e. g.* Samdhis, Interludes, Rasas, &c. ) it does not differ materially from a नाटक.

It may be remarked here that dramas like those of Bhasa, Sudraka and Kalidasa, being the earlier productions, composed at a period when the hard-and-fast rules of Sanskrit dramaturgy were yet to be evolved, will not be found to conform precisely to all the numerous minutiae as elaborated in rhetorical treatises. Thus, for example, Sudraka does not appear to have followed the rule of the Sah.-D which lays down that a प्रकरण should be named after the hero and the heroine ( *e. g.* Malati-Madhava ); his play has been named after a certain incident in Act VI. ( pp. 216–220 ) where Charudatta's son Rohasena is crying because he was given a clay-cart (मृच्छकटिका) to play with when he wanted one of gold, and where Vasa gives him her ornaments out of which he is asked to get such a one made for himself. Since those very ornaments have afterwards served as the final and damning proof of Charudatta's supposed crime, it may be perceived that the poet's choice of the word मृच्छकटिका for the title of the play is not only appropriate but it also serves to pique the curiosity of the audience as regards the subject-matter of the piece Again we may note that the Dasa-R [2] prescribes that the hero should appear in *every* Act, while Charudatta does not appear in four Acts out of the ten of the Mrich , as the student can verify for himself. But rules such as these were made later on, from an observation of a majority of specimens, for the general guidance of students of literary forms; they must not be treated as being rigidly binding on the early writers in every detail. The student will have seen how closely the Mrich , *in its broad outlines*, conforms to the definition cited above; the plot is fictitious; the hero is a Brahmana, dignified and calm, in adverse circumstances and engaged in the pursuit of Dharma, Artha and Kama in due proportion; there are two heroines, Dhuta being a कुलस्त्री and Vasantasena a गणिका There appears to be a glaring discrepancy when these two not only meet on the stage but also exchange greetings ( Act X , p. 402 ); for this is expressly prohibited in the

1 नायिकानायकाख्याना संज्ञा प्रकरणादिषु । VI. 143.

2 प्रत्यक्षनेतृचरितः (अङ्कः) । III 33.

definition[1] The fault lies not with Sudraka, however, as that Scene is known to be a later addition by one Nilakantha, who, in his anxiety to bring Dhuta on the stage, has forgotten the canon and committed a serious breach of dramatic propriety. The Mrich., being thus a Prakarna of the संकीर्ण variety, abounds in rogues (धूर्तs), among whom may be classed the three gamblers in Act II., and even Sarvilaka, in his character as a burglar.

The वस्तु of the play is two-fold, (1) Principal (मुख्य), which is the love of Char. and Vasa., and (2) Secondary ( प्रासङ्गिक ), which is the dethronement of king Palaka of Ujjayini and Aryaka's accession to the throne. The predominant रस is शृङ्गार (Love), assisted by the occasional introduction of करुण ( *e. g.* in Act X. ), हास्य ( in the witticisms of the Vid. and the dialogues of Sakara ) बीभत्स ( in Act VIII, when Vasa. is strangled on the stage ) &c. The play begins with a नान्दी followed by a प्रस्तावना, in which the Sutradhara introduces the author and the play to the audience; then the ten Acts of the drama[2] follow in succession, without any intervening विष्कम्भकs or प्रवेशकs, whose absence is a noteworthy feature of this play; at the close there is the usual भरतवाक्य or the valedictory stanza ( X. 61 ).

It is neither necessary nor possible to point out here the various *angas* or minor sub-divisions of the development of the plot, but we might notice the broad demarcations of the five *Samdhis.* (1) The मुखसंधि is a combination of the बीज and आरम्भ and it extends to the end of the 1st Act; the बीज or seed is contained in the meeting between Char. and Vasa. in Cupid's shrine, which is twice or thrice referred to in the play (pp. 54, 68); and the आरम्भ is indicated when Vasa. take refuge in the house of Char., when pursued by Sakara. (2) The प्रतिमुखसंधि indicates the further sprouting up of the बीज by some new

1 In the words नार्तिक्रमोऽनयोः. Bharata, too, in his Natya-Sastra has forbidden the bringing together of the two heroines. The reason for such a prohibition is obvious; for no कुलस्त्री would like to be confronted with a गणिका as her rival in her husband's affections, though as a dutiful wife she would be ready to meekly submit to his choice.

2 The attention of the student is drawn to the manner in which, on p. 62, a future incident is foreshadowed in the dialogue; such an episode-indication is technically termed a पताकास्थानक and is a common device in Sanskrit plays. ( *Vide* our notes on the passage ).

incidents which maintain the continuity of the action; such are, here, the receipt by Vasa. of Char.'s cloak through Karnapuraka (p. 98), and later of his jewel-necklace through the Vidushaka (p. 172). It thus extends to the end of Act IV. (3) The गर्भसंधि consists of the fifth Act, while (4) the अवमर्शसंधि covers the next four, and (5) the निर्वहणसंधि, where all events converge to the desired goal, forms the subject-matter of Act X. It should be borne in mind that the union of the hero and the heroine, which takes place towards the end of Act V., is not a real union, being temporary and of short duration; the permanent union, which is the consummation, is brought about in the final Act only.

*

## (5) General and Critical Remarks

Among the known dramatic compositions of the Hindus, the *Mrichchhakatika* of Sudraka occupies a very high and distinguished position. It is a creation of outstanding brilliance, not unworthy of being classed with the productions of acknowledged masters of the dramatic art, such as Bhasa and Kalidasa. By virtue of its high dramatic charm and its great literary excellence it has endeared itself to generations of spectators and readers; the play has been adapted in many Indian vernaculars, and in that modern form still continues to draw admiring crowds to witness its performance, when the fortunes of Charudatta and Vasantasena are followed with the same breathless interest as when, over two thousand years ago, the play was staged for the first time, probably in Ujjayini. The Mrich. possesses several unique features which have enabled it to achieve such unqualified success and assure to itself an ever-widening circle of readers. Preeminent among those is its cleverly conceived and successfully constructed plot; it is a picture of contemporary society, not a dull narration of the doings of divine or semi-divine personages; and its interest is heightened by a variety of stirring episodes that arouse alternating emotions of joy, curiosity, wonder, pity, and even fear, among the spectators. It is owing to a lack of such variety of action that the majority of later Sanskrit plays lack the dramatic flavour and read more like dramatic poems than dramas, which should be word-pictures of real life. No other Sanskrit play exhibits such a large array of enlivening incidents or thrilling dramatic situations as go to make up the ingeniously-wrought story of the Mrich. Thus we see in the first Act Vasa. being pursued in the dark of the night by a group of hooligans, one of them a royal brother-in-law. Vasa. flying in terror before them "like a doe pursued by huntsmen," and finally taking shelter in Charu.'s house. In the second Act, there is a similar Scene where the gambler Samvahaka is pursued by his creditors; there is a hand-to-hand fight[1] on the stage (p. 84), which is an incident that always appeals to a certain section of the audience; the playwright who aims at being successful must seek to please a mixed house, the intellectuals as well as the unlettered simple-minded folk; moreover the fight is not a forced one, but quite a natural seqnence of a quarrel among low characters, especially a quarrel over monetary transactions. In the third Act we have the burglary scene, where Sarvilaka is seen stepping in stealthily in the stillness of the night and proceeding scientifically to demonstrate the art of house-breaking. The fifth Act is staged amidst thunder, rain and lightning. The sixth contains the exciting episodes of the interchange of the carriages and the flight and pursuit of Aryaka; in the eighth there is the strangling of Vasa, which only a realistic writer of the calibre of Sudraka would have dared to introduce, and which for the moment strikes the audience dumb with the appalling brutality of the crime. The ninth Act describes Charudatta's trial, and the tenth his being taken to the place of execution, which, however, is averted at the last moment by the opportune arrival of Vasantasena. The interest thus never flags from Act to Act, and the humour and variety of the events of the earlier Acts and the pathos of the later Acts, which form a virtual tragedy, make the play throb with life and action and constitute its chief charm. "From force to tragedy, from satire to pathos, runs the story, with a breadth truly Shakespearian." (Dr. Ryder).

The story is further interspersed with many memorable stanzas of great beauty conveying homely morals or embodying worldly wisdom (*e g* Char.'s remarks on the evils of poverty and Sarvilaka's comments on the fickleness of women), which form not the least of its attractive features. The long description of the

1. Sudraka seems to be rather fond of describing such scuffles; one will be found in Act VI. (p. 238) and another in Act IX. (p. 340).

rainy season in Act V. may be slightly out of place, but its vivid imagery and rhythmically flowing verse have made it an idyllic piece of rare operatic charm. Sudraka's expression is forcible, graphic and pithy, both the prose and poetry being remarkably free from unwieldy compounds or involved constructions; with a few exceptions the meaning is clear and direct and readily comprehended. The play compares favourably in this respect with the works of Bhavabhuti, whose dramas would hardly be understood at first hearing without previous study, except by the learned few, and whose austere grandeur comes in the way of his being more popular. It must be admitted that Sudraka lacks the eloquence or the beauty of expression of Bhavabhuti, who is also superior to him in the delineation of passion, in all its variations of emotion and minuteness of feeling. Nor does he possess the supremely elegant grace of Kalidasa's muse, with its dazzling polish and incomparable command over sense and sound. In these respects he does not dispute the palm with the masters, but he still retains his superiority over all other lesser dramatists such as Visakhadatta[1] and Bhatta-Narayana; while of Bhasa he may be considered to be the equal, if not his superior; for though ostensibly his imitator, he has not only put new ideas in the *Charudatta* as adapted by him, but also made it pulsate with new life. Sudraka's dialogues are pointed and witty, and as examples we may note those on pp. 54, 76-78, 82, 186-188, which show him as a master of ready invention. Above all, he excels in humour, which is an element almost entirely neglected in Sanskrit plays. Sudraka's humour depends for its effect not merely on puns on words (*e. g.* that on *sena* and *vasanta* at p 188), but on the situations as well (*e. g.* when the eyes of Mathura are blinded with dust thrown into them and he is asked कथं द्रक्ष्यसि and her eplies hurl- एवं प्रेक्षिष्ये;—or when the two guards in Act VI are opprobriously hurling choice epithets at each other's caste). It is never coarse or vulgar, and is far removed in thisr espect from the so-called humour or *hasya rasa* of Bhanas and similar pieces, in which licentious jokes run riot and are the pivots on which their interest depends.

1 Dr. Keith has pointed out how the last Act of the *Mudrarakshasa* wherein Chandanadasa is led to be executed, seems to be based on, and inspired by the last Act of our play; there are the two Chandalas, and the wife and the son of condemned man, who appear on the stage during that scene only; even the language in that portion reads like an echo of the Mrich.

Sudraka's humor, as observed by Dr. Ryder, has an American flavour, both in its puns and in its situations. It " runs the whole gamut, from grim to farcical, from satirical to quaint. Its variety and keenness are such that king Sudraka need not fear a comparison with the greatest of Occidental writers of comedies. "

Next to the variety of incidents and a style pervaded by simplicity and humour, must be ranked the third great element contributing to our play's popularity, *viz.* its characterization, which is more powerful and varied than in any other Sanskrit drama and over which rich encomiums are deservedly bestowed by Indian as well as western scholars. Sudraka has painted a large number of characters, almost a cosmopolitan crowd; it comprises a learned Brahmana, a rich courtesan, robbers, gamblers, and headsmen, portly judges and royal rakes; with a few deft touches he brings out the salient characteristics of each, but his greatest triumph lies undoubtedly in the creation of the villain, the king's brother-in-law. His original name was Samsthanaka, but the poet endowed him with a drawl and a lisp and the expressive sobriquet of Sakara ( the 'Sh'–man ), which is the title under which he is familiar to the multitude of play-goers. He is represented as an empty-headed fool; but the emptiness seems more put on than real, for where necessary he shows the devil's own depth of cunning and knows much better than a common fool how to look after number one.[1] Charudatta is another character, set in quite a different mould, the beau-ideal of a gentleman, with a high sense of honour and famous for his charitable deeds, to whom by common consent was applied the title of *Arya*, the 'noble one.' Then there is Vasantasena, a courtesan by profession but almost a कुलस्त्री in her principles, who, once her heart is attached to Char., loves him the more for his poverty and disdains to look at any other suitor, not even one of royal connexion. In Maitreya Sudraka has created a somewhat different type of Vidushaka, distinct from the common glutton and fool who plays antics on the stage; he is honest, simple-minded, and straightforward, his blunders are the result of his simplicity, and do not originate in a spirit of buffoonery; he is a faithful retainer of his patron Char. to whom he

1. A more detailed analysis of the various characters will be found in a subsequent Section.

clings through riches and poverty, sunshine and clouds, sharing his joys and sorrows, ready to follow him even in death. Even the servants Sthavaraka and Vardhamanaka, and Radanika and Madanika, have distinct characteristics of their own, which make them live before us; in fact one almost fancies that the author has devoted as much care to portraying the slave Sthavaraka as to delineating his master Sakara; he would obey his employer upto a certain point, beyond which he ceases to be a pliant tool and becomes a human being with a moral sense of right and wrong, which he does not hesitate to assert, being willing even to lose his life in an attempt to save the innocent Charudatta from being unjustly killed. The gamblers, the Chandalas, the assessors, in fact all the different characters, have been shown in their proper relief. Other authors[1] appear to bestow all their care on their principal dramatis personæ, and neglect the rest; Sudraka gives the same meticulous attention to each. As Prof. Levi has observed, "Each of the twenty-seven personages who take part in the action *bears a particular mark*, a special trait which strongly characterizes him." Sudraka has been compared in this respect to Shakespeare and Moliere, names which enjoy an honoured place in the dramatic literature of the world, and that he should be mentioned in such glorious company is sufficient proof of the esteem in which he is held by those most competent to judge; higher praise than that there cannot be.

In spite of the skill and attention of the author, several slight flaws of construction have crept into the play, though they are not so serious as to interfere with its manifold attractions. We need not attach any undue importance to trifling lapses, for these are almost inevitable in a play of such great length and embracing such complex and varied situations. We have already referred to the inadvertence which has led the author to represent Char. as escorting Vasa. to her house (p. 64), and to stage such a long journey without even a word of description, so that Char. is heard describing the moonlight when he starts, and is immediately and abruptly shown as arriving at his destination; it almost reads as

1. For instance, Kalidasa in his *Sakuntala* introduces a fisherman, two policemen, and a royal brother-in-law, but some how they fail to excite as much interest as similar types in the Mrich. They are characters without characteristics, being of no interest to the poet except so far as they serve to disclose the discovery of the ring.

if some portion is missing from the text towards the end of Act I. In the second Act we see Samvahaka leaving the stage after declaring his resolve to turn a Bhikshu, and almost immediately we are told that he, dressed as a monk, was rescued by Karnapuraka from the teeth of an enraged elephant. This is rather putting a stretch on the imagination; for no sufficient time appears to have elapsed to enable Samvahaka to change his dress, get his head shaved, and don the paraphernalia of a Buddhist monk In the next Act, where Sarvilaka is shown as a burglar, it looks very strange, indeed, that he should not have known whose house it was that he was breaking into. He appears to have been a resident of Ujjayini, since he was intimate with Vasa.'s maid and counted Rebhila (p. 152) and Chandanaka (p 242) among his friends. He knew Charu. by name (p. 140), and even if he had never seen him, it is inconceivable that he should not have known where the first citizen of Ujjayini lived,[1] so that he failed to recognize his mansion even when he had inspected it carefully from the outside ( p. 110 ) before effecting his entrance. In the fourth Act, when the Vid. describes the splendours of Vasa.'s mansion, much seems to have been left to the imagination of the audience, since the things described are so varied and numerous ( including even Vasa.'s mother and brother ) that it is improbable that even a small portion of them could have been shown on the stage; this scene partakes more of the nature of a *sravya* than a *drisya* composition. Similarly, in the thunderstorm scene in Act V., many of the descriptions are purely conventional and completely discordant with the time and place. It was a dark night, with the moonlight obscured by screening clouds ( p. 190 ); still we listen immediately afterwards to the sun being similarly obscured ( sl. 20 ) and rain-bows ( p. 212 ) gleaming across—rainbows at midnight ! In the sixth Act, it does not appear why Char. should have left so very early in the morning, arranging that Vasa. should follow him, since he could as well have proceeded to the garden in her company in the same carriage; the carriage was a covered one, and nobody could even have seen them. If the poet saw the necessity of making Vasa. travel

1. The remark of the Vidushaka on p. 122 is quite appropriate ; the thief could only have been either a complete stranger or a student of the science of house-breaking. But we know that Sarvilaka was neither ; how, then, would the author reconcile this?

alone, we expect that he should have invented some sound reason for Char.'s early and abrupt departure. Finally, when in Act IX. Char. is being tried for murder, his silence appears to us to be quite puzzling and out of place. The poet somehow wanted to have him adjudged guilty on the circumstantial evidence; but he has thereby overlooked the resulting weakness imparted to the character of Charudatta. Further, even if we assume that Char. was far too much weighed down by the thoughts of his own condition to offer a proper defence, we expect that the Vidushaka at least ought to have explained the source of the ornaments, as it was a matter of life and death to his friend; but it is astonishing to see that he utters not a word, beyond asking Charu. why the truth should not be told ( p. 342 ). The silence of Maitreya appears to be much more inexplicable than that of his friend, and it remains a flaw in the construction.

Barring these faults mentioned above, the play, viewed as a whole, presents a well-proportioned and harmonious story, where one Act naturally arises out of the other and each incident possesses some bearing on the development of the plot. Dr. Ryder, however, perceives a lack of proportion in the play; he calls it "too long," and he considers that the main action halts through Acts II.–V., remarking that the contents of these Acts are not quite pertinent to the rest of the play and they might have been easily dispensed with, so to say, so far as the central theme of the love of Char. and Vasa. is concerned. Now, it may be admitted that the play is a long one; but it is not too long for presentation, as has been demonstrated by actual performances, nor can its length be characterized as boring or tiresome; for, as we have seen, the rapid succession of its incidents keeps the audience interested and on the tiptoe of expectation throughout. Further, the learned doctor appears to have missed the point altogether when he charges Acts II.–V. as being unnecessary. As a matter of fact, they comprise technically the sprouting of the seed of the action, and are quite indispensable for its proper development. The second Act serves two very important purposes; in the first place, the Samvahaka's debt has been paid off by Vasa., and his deep sense of gratitude for this disinterested act of kindness makes him render invaluable assistance to her later on; and secondly, the rescue of Samvahaka, effected by

Karnapuraka, is narrated by the poet solely to introduce the topic of Char.'s munificence as shown by his gift of the cloak; this touches Vasa. and serves to heighten her love for the hero. It is surprising therefore to find Dr. Ryder remarking that the second Act "*has little real connexion with the main plot.*" Neither is the third Act unnecessary; for without that robbery there could not have been the exchange of the pearl-necklace for the lost ornaments, which is a subsidiary incident serving solely the purpose of again illustrating the boundless generosity of Char. and deepening Vasa.'s passion. The fourth Act is a necessary sequence of the third, and the fifth of the fourth, showing Vasa. proceeding to her lover's house in the garb of an *abhisarika*; the only really unessential portions here would be the passages descriptive of Vasa.'s mansion and of the rainy season; but they do not cover more than a sixth of the ground traversed by these four Acts, and hardly justify the criticism passed on them by the learned scholar.

There is one important aspect of the play as a stage-piece, which is likely to puzzle the reader. We refer to the seeming impracticability of staging different incidents in the same scene without any shifting of curtains or por.ions of stage-property. Thus, for example, on p 26 Char. and Vid. are present on the stage, which they do not leave; when Vasa. enters and there is the commotion of her pursuit, we see Charu. and Vid. conversing, in the same scene, but without being aware of the presence of Vasa. and her pursuers. This kind of mixing up in one scene, of incidents which in a modern play would be shown in several separate scenes, is to be found throughout the play; different incidents are represented as taking place simultaneously on the same stage, as though they are in different places. This arrangement seems possible only when we understand, as Wilson has pointed out, that the stage must have been divided into several compartments by suspending curtains *traversely;* so that while these were open equally to the audience they screened one group of actors from the other as if these were in different parts of the same house and street. All the diffculties of understanding the staging of the drama would disappear if we bear in mind that some such arrangement must have been made on the stage without which the effect would be highly ludicrous indeed.

A detailed consideration of the various Prakrit dialects used in the play, interesting though it would be, lies outside the scope of this edition, which is intended to help the University student and not to overburden his memory with matter which is both dry and unnecessary ; but we may notice here their distribution, in which the play closely follows the lines laid down by Bharata in the Natya-sastra. According to the com. Prithvidhara, *Sauraseni* is spoken by the Sutradhara (when he changes from Sanskrit into Prakrit), the Nati, Vasantasena, Dhuta, Vasa.'s mother Karnapuraka, the assessors, Sodhanaka, Madanika and Radanika; *Avantika* is spoken by Viraka and Chandanaka; *Prachya* by the Vidushaka; *Magadhi* by Samvahaka (Bhikshu), Sthavaraka, Kumbhilaka, Vardhamanaka, and Rohasena; *Sakari* by Sakara; *Chandali* by the two Chandalas; and *Dhakki* by the gamblers[1]. The ancient grammarian Vararuchi whose date (1st Cent. B. C.) is nearest to our author's gives only four principal Prakrit dialects, Sauraseni, Magadhi, Maharashtri and Paisachi [ the two latter being not instanced in our play ]; the further sub divisions known as Avantika, Prachya &c. were made by later grammarians. Dr. Keith has shown how all the seven different varieties mentioned by Prith. are reducible to only two principal dialects, *Sauraseni* and *Magadhi*; for Avantika and Prachya are really to be classed under the former, and Sakari and Chandali under the latter, Dhakki being kept apart as very little is definitely known concerning that obscure form of Prakrit.

The literary style of Sudraka is, as we have already remarked, characterized by a simplicity of diction and naturalness of expression, and in this respect he stands nearer to Bhasa than to any other Sanskrit writer. Coming between Bhasa and Kalidasa, he lacks the polished grace of the language of the latter, in whose works Classical Sanskrit is to be seen in its best and most pleasing form. Sudraka's vocabulary is large and most varied. Unlike his predecessor he rarely uses, in his Sanskrit, unfamiliar words or expressions that have become obsolete, though his Prakrit is full of them (*e.g.*, चरण्डलम्बुक p. 14, मल्लक p. 20, वरटा p. 24, दधिशर p. 46, तलित p. 56, लुप्तदण्डक p. 78, गण्ड p. 78, सैरिभ p. 158, कूर p. 158, रूपिन् p. 162, महल्लक p. 166, कार्द-

1 See Prithvidhara's introductory remarks for the several linguistic characteristics that distinguish these dialects from one another.

कडाकिनी p. 168, कोष्टक p. 254, वोडी p. 294, and many more which the student can easily collect), He rarely uses long compounds, except in the description of Vasa.'s mansion in Act IV.; but herein he seems to have been influenced by a desire of exhibiting his mastery over grandiose descriptions in prose; for prose, according to Dandin, should be pervaded by the quality of *Ojas*, which signifies an abundance of compounds ( ओजः समासभूयस्त्वमेतद् गद्यस्य जीवितम् । Kavyad. I. 80). In the rare cases where he uses compounds in verse ( *e.g.* in निष्पन्दीकृत &c. V. 24), they are generally easily intelligible. His constructions are ordinarily simple and straightforward; the ambiguity that is sometimes met with is frequently due to defective Prakrit readings as they are found in MSS. His verse is commonly smooth and easy-flowing, though occasionally containing awkward compounds. He lacks the economy of expression which enables a master-stylist like Kalidasa to say a thing in the fewest possible words. Sudraka has frequently found it difficult to avoid using superfluous words in his verses; notice, for instance, the way in which he fills the space by the inclusion of particles like च, हि, तु and वै in stanzas such as II. 10, VII. 3, VIII. 15, VIII. 43, IX 42, X. 47 &c. His descriptions also are rarely touched by the glow of imagination and are seldom lifted into the sphere of the sublime, like those of Kalidasa. On the whole his writing is vigorous, pointed and forcible; he avoids uugrammatical forms, involved constructions, elaborate *alamkaras*, as also difficult puns. And to crown all, he has a facile power of dexterously clothing homely proverbs and simple morals in sentences of great beauty and stanzas of haunting melody; many of these have obtained currency in the common language of the people, by whom they are treasured up as *subhashitas*.[1]

*

## (6) The State of Society Depicted in the Play.

The student must have observed that the principal characters of the Mrich. are drawn from the upper middle-class, while its subsidiary episodes introduce such low class people as gamblers, hangmen, &c, This was inevitable in a play whose plot was

1 Most of these will be found collected in the list given at the end of our Text, pp. 408–411.

to be लौकिक or " drawn from real life " ( *vide supra,* the Def. of a Prakarana), and it is but natural that we see therein an exact reflex of the conditions and manners of contemporary society,[1] including its government and its laws in particular.

The king is not actually introduced in the play. It seems that he ruled as an absolute monarch. and, if he happened to be a tyrant (as Palaka was), discontent would be rife among the subjects, being a direct incentive to armed rebellion as soon as opportunity would offer. The king was assisted by cousellors (IX, 14), and was also the head of the army ( X, 48 ); there were the usual departments of state such as revenue ( VII, 1 ), justice (IX), police (VI.) &c. The ninth Act gives us special insight into the judicial administration. The judge was assisted by two assessors, and justice appears to have been both impartial and speedy; the presiding judge had to follow well-formulated rules of evidence and procedure in recording facts and in examining witnesses; but he could give his decision only in the form of a recommendation, the passing of the final orders lying with the sovereign If the facts were not clearly established by the evidence, recourse was to be had to four kinds of ordeals (IX 43), a trial by ordeal being fairly common in ancient society for serious offences The person under trial had to confess his crime when proved by facts ( p. 346 ). A criminal punished capitally could be set free if an adequate ransom was paid or some great event happened ( p. 378 ). The executioners had some discretionary powers; they could release a prisoner if found innocent and even punish the real offender ( p. 376). A creditor had absolute power over the person of his debtor; he could inflict bodily punishment on him with impunity, or even sell him for the recovery of his money ( p. 78 ). The officers of the king

1 That the Mrich. draws a realistic picture of society as it presented itself to its author is patent on the face of it; it is strange to find, therefore, that Prof. Levi holds the view that "*the Indian society has certainly never resembled a picture which the Mrich. traces in it.*" The learned scholar finds it difficult to believe, for instance that an insurgent rebel should be able to perform such a lightning *coup* as Aryaka is represented to have done, forgetting that history has time and again proved that revolutions, when people are ready for them, have been successfully accomplished in a very short time even in modern civilized nations, and much more so, therefore, in those remote times. Prof. Levi is sceptical about a courtesan like Vasa. owning such

seem to have been zealous in the performance of their duties; Viraka and Chandanaka pursue the escaped prisoner with as much vigour and promptitude as though it was an affair in which they were personally concerned; and although in the end Chandanaka proves a traitor to his employer, it was not due to bribery or cowardice, but to an appeal to his innate sense of compassion for one wrongfully oppressed.

The caste-system seems to have been fully recognized in those days The Brahmanas were held in great reverence and enjoyed certain privileges, immunity from capital punishment being among these (IX. 39); notice, too, how Sarvilaka declines to rob a Brahmana of his gold (IV. 6), presumably accumulated for sacrificial purposes. Brahmanas often took to commerce since the ancestors of Charudatta, who was a Brahmana, got rich through trade and were known as सार्थवाहs ( p. 320 ). Among other castes, the Kayasthas seem to have been held low in popular estimation ( *cf.* कायस्थसर्पस्पिदं p 324 ). The vituperations hurled against each other's caste by Viraka and Chandanaka ( p. 238 ) show how strong a hold the system had on people; in spite of its rigidity, however, the view that caste is no criterion of a man's worth was of general acceptance, since even the Chandalas discourse on it ( p 362 ). Buddhism, though on its decline, was yet in a flourishing state, being patronized by kings and princes, and the Bhikshus seem to have been generally respected, though a certain prejudice prevailed against them among the upper classes, who considered their sight inauspicious ( p. 250 ) Commerce was carried on on an extensive scale, Indian ships (यानपात्राणि p 168 ) sailing to the furthest ends of the earth; this must have contributed largely to the prosperity of the land. The wealth of the trading classes appears to have been almost fabulous, if we are to judge by the donations and public charities of Charudatta ( पुरस्थापनविहारारामदेवालयतडागकूपयूप &c 340 ); a large portion of

---

a vast palace, and considers it improbable that a robber like Sarvilaka should be priding himself on his skill in the burglar's art. We, however, see no improbability in either of these, and do not think that the types and manners of play are "borrowed from the imaginary world of tales and romances," as categorically declared by the Professor. Happily, he seems to be alone in holding such a curiously extreme view, most scholars agreeing to treat the Mrich. as a picture of contemporary society, which it undoubtedly is.

this wealth eventually passed into the hands of the courtesan class, so that Vasa came to own a palace which rivalled that of Kubera ( p. 170 ) in splendour. Such wealth meant luxury on a grand scale, and its necessary consequences, such as the vices of drinking ( p. 168 ), gambling (II.) and prostitution; if merchants could give golden toy-carts to their sons ( p. 218 ), courtesans could go a step further and keep Scent-elephants (p. 94). That a courtesan should be made the heroine of a play may seem a little strange to modern readers It appears, however, that low as the profession of a गणिका was, so that Charudatta is ashamed to confess his connexion with one ( p. 328 ), it had a certain recognized status, for even the sage Vatsyayana, in his treatise on Erotics, devotes a special chapter to the description of that class. A courtesan of course could never usurp the place of a legally wedded wife ( p. 214 ), but the fact that Vasa. is afterwards invested with the title of a वधू ( p. 402 ) is significant, and probably points to mixed marriages being in vogue in those days.

Slavery was common, and a slave could be bought (p. 78), sold, and ransomed by the payment of money (p. 138). Gambling was a legalized vice; there was an association which formulated the rules of play, and keepers of gaming saloons saw to it that these were strictly enforced ( p 76 ). The social, religious and superstitious observances seem to have been not materially different from those that obtain in modern Hindu society : there are refernces to बलीs (p. 20), उपवासs ( p. 128 ), and उत्सवs (p. 68), and the sciences of astrology and augury were universally believed in ( *cf.* pp. 228, 322, 84, 250, 290 &c ). The play contains references to music parties (p. 104) and drawing and painting (p 132), showing therefore, that the fine arts seem to have been cultivated on a large scale, as would be expected in a wealthy society. The general economic condition of the people appears to have been prosperous on the whole, free from petty worries and minor troubles.

## ( 7 ) The Principal Characters.

### CHARUDATTA.

The poet has chosen for his hero Charudatta, a Brahmana youth of Ujjayini, whose ancestors had amassed a large fortune in trade, which subsequently disappeared and left him penniless. This poverty, however, was brought on him by the extreme generosity of his nature—even his name is significant, meaning 'he who gives nobly' ( चारु दत्तं दानं यस्य ); the play shows that he had spent large sums in deeds of private charity ( p. 88 ) and public utility ( p. 340 ). Munificence was a habit which had become a second nature with him, so that, when he has nothing of value to give away, he parts with the very cloak he happens to be wearing ( p. 98 ); his high sense of honour makes him replace the stolen ornaments by a costly necklace ( p 172 ), and do such deeds of nobleness as could win him the love of a courtesan, young, rich and beautiful ( *cf.* अत एव काम्यसे । p. 206 ). He is to be seen in the very first Act as lamenting at great length over his poverty ( p 22 ), which is considered by some critics as unworthy of a great man whom mere want of money should not have rendered so despondent; it may be urged in his justification, however, that Char. mourns his condition, not because he wants money for enjoyment, but because he is thereby deprived of the opportunities of doing good to others ( *cf.* I. 12; p. 208 ). His silence in the law-court, when charged with murder, cannot be so easily explained; for it is expected that he should defend himself suitably, not merely to save his life, but also to clear his personal reputation. Except on this one occasion, the poet has portrayed his character with consistency, as the beau ideal of a noble person, whom everybody knows and loves ( p. 232), the Judge ( p. 324 ) as well as the hangmen ( p. 358 ). He is considered to be an ornament to the city ( p. 48 ); he is so large-hearted that he could even admire a burglar for his skill ( p 122 ), and so kind that he would even incur treason in helping Aryaka to escape in safety ( p. 250 ); his magnanimity would not allow him to revenge himself on a fallen enemy ( X. 55 ); he had the highest regard for truth ( p 126 ), and he valued honour above life itself ( X. 27 ). In brief, he is an embodiment of all the virtues, as expressively summarized by the Vita in the gorgeous and impressive stanza दीनानां कल्पवृक्षः स्वगुणफलनतः सज्जनानां कुटुम्बी &c. (I. 48).

## SAKARA.

In the Sakara ( Samsthauaka ), the poet has created a character unique in Sanskrit dramatic literature, combining the fool and the villain, of the worst type, in one. The Vidushaka as the conventional fool is put in the background, and it is the tall talk and vapid nonsense of Samsthanaka that consitutes the chief element of humour in the play. His very mannerisms of speech are sufficient to cause laughter; prominent among these are:—his substitution of 'Sh' for S (*e g.* वशन्तशेणा for वसन्तसेणा), his habit of using redundant words ( IX. 1 ), his absurd mythology (I. 25), his inversion of the order of words ( *e. g.* न च्छिन्नो वृषभो । न मृता रज्जवः । p 266), and his quaint similes (VIII 19). He happens to be the King's brother-In-law, and as such is surrounded by servants and parasites; these, however, are not mere flatterers; they know his worth (VIII. 6) and do not hesitate to delare it where necessary ( pp. 52, 282 ). But apart from his mannerisms there is nothing entertaining about the Sakara's behaviour; he is a pervert debauchee and a cruel and remorseless villain, and, as may be expected, a rank coward. He hurriedly withdraws from the scene in Act I. (p. 56), when he finds that his friend has left; and later, when the same friend shows fight, he is so much frightened that he falls down senseless on the ground (p 282) ; he is of course boastful enough to declare himself brave against the weaker sex (p. 34). It is true that he has not much sense; for otherwise he would not have pursued Vasa. when she loved him not, nor would he have so foolishly attempted to murder her in that way. Within the limits of his understanding, however, he possesses a deep cunning and is in no way a common fool; the manner in which he tries to shift the guilt on Char. and thus to save himself and at the same time have his enemy sent out of the world, clearly establishes that. Moreover, the trick that he plays on the Vita in Act VIII ( p. 284) lulling him into a false sense that all was well, and the device that he employs to secure the silence of the Cheta by putting him in chains (p, 298), the qu ckness with which he seizes the opportunity to point out the ornaments as a link in the chain of evidence (p. 342), and, in particular, the cleverness with which, by the episode of the bangle (p. 372), he hoodwinks the Chandalas, abundantly prove that he had more sense than he is generally credited with. That he finally begs and cringes and throws himself on the protection of those very persons whom he had most injured (p 394), merely serves to bring out his abject cowardice in full relief. Certainly, one almost wishes, with Sarvilaka, that Char. had not taken pity on such a scamp and saved him from a fate (X. 54) which he richly deserved.

## VASANTASENA

Vasantasena, the heroine, is a professional courtesan born and bred as such; but she is as pure-minded as any lady of noble station. She falls in love with Charudatta the very first time she sees him at a festival in Cupid's shrine (p. 68), and from that time onward she cannot tolerate the very idea of entertaining any other suitor; it is needless to remark that upon such as Sakara she looks with loathing and contempt. She is generous-hearted, as is shown by her readily paying off the debt of Samvahaka (p. 92), and releasing Madanika from her bondage (p. 150) with equal alacrity. Her passion for Charudatta grows so intense in the end that she goes to visit him as an *abhisarika* (p. 190), inspite of a raging thunderstorm; when in his house she gives a further proof of her generous nature by handing over her own ornaments to her lover's son for making a golden toy-cart. When, finally, in Act VIII., Sakara persecutes her with his attentions, she is ready even to accept death at his hands rather than prove faithless to one that was enshrined in her heart; and, to all appearances, she dies with his name on her lips (p 288). She thus gives the greatest possible proof that lay in her power of the depth of her affection and the loyalty of her love, for which she receives recognition later at the hands of king Aryaka, who bestows upon her the title of a वधू (p. 402). The development of Vasa.'s passion has been delineated by the poet with touches of such tenderness as raise her character to a very high degree in our eyes; compare, for instance, her behaviour (p. 218) when Rohasena, the innocent-minded son of Char., declines to consider her as his mother because she happened to be wearing ornaments. In fact, the more one sees of

Vasantasena the more one thinks of her as a कुलस्त्री and the less as a गणिका, so far removed she is from the ways that one naturally associates with the latter. And if we find the nature of Vasa. not rising to the high or sublime level of Sita or Sakuntala that is because the situation and environment are different.

## MAITREYA

The Vidushaka in this play differs from the Vidushakas one meets with in the works of later poets; in these he is generally depicted as a glutton and a buffoon; not that he entirely lacks these qualities (see pp 20, 48, 108, 162, 180 &c.), but he possesses them in such a small degree that they sink into insignificance before his other and nobler qualities. In the Mrich. he appears in the role of the hero's faithful friend and retainer, ready to defend him at all times (p. 48) and even prepared to lay down his life for him if need be (p. 364). The sorrows and joys of his friend arouse corresponding emotions in his breast (p. 54). He is a simpleminded, guileless and lovable companion, and it is his blunders (pp. 18, 188), rather than his jokes, which raise a laugh among the spectators. He does not think very highly of the reckless liberality of his friend (p. 130), nor does he approve of his attachment to a courtesan (p. 182); he protests against both, feeling it his duty to do so, but never carries his protests to the point of offence (p. 115). His behaviour in the last Act, including his offer of self-immolation in precedence (p 400) to Dhuta, is a further proof of his dogged and faithful affection for his friend and patron.

## OTHER MINOR CHARACTERS.

As we have already observed, Sudraka has skilfully invested each one of even his minor characters with some special trait that distinguishes him or her from others. Thus, Dhuta is shown to be a devoted wife, who gives her most valuable ornament to her lord in his hour of need (p. 128); in fact she is represented as a type of the old *Pativrata*, who regards her husband's good as her all-in-all and is ready to minister to his comfort even at the sacrifice of her own comfort and weal; thus she receives without a word of complaint a courtesan as a rival (p. 216), and later even greets her as an equal (p. 402). Rohasena is a boy, a child in his simple innocence, who cries for a golden toy-cart, but has the feelings of maturer persons, being ready to offer his own life to save that of his father (p. 374). The Vita is an outspoken companion of Sakara, frank and straightforward, ready even to give a thrashing to his friend (p. 282) if too much annoyed. The judge as an officer is fair-minded, loyal and honest, as are the captains of the city's guard, Viraka and Chandanaka. The slave Sthavaraka is a God-fearing soul, who would serve his master willingly, but within limits; while the Chandalas exhibit the sense and judiciousness of persons in far superior walks of life. Many other minor particulars the student can asily notice and collect for himself.

---

# DRAMATIS PERSONÆ

## MALES

सूत्रधार—The Manager of the Play.

मैत्रेय (विदूषक)—A Brahmana, a friend and companion of Charudatta.

चारुदत्त—The hero, a citizen of Ujjayini.

शकार (संस्थानक)—The brother-in-law of the king of Ujjayini and the villain of the Play.

विट—A friend of Sakara.

चेट (स्थावरक)—A servant of Sakara.

संवाहक (later भिक्षु)—A professional shampooer, who takes to gambling and afterwards turns a Buddhist monk.

माथुर (सभिक)—A keeper of a gambling den.

दर्दुर—A gambler.

द्यूतकर—Another gambler.

कर्णपूरक—A servant of Vasantasena.

चेट (वर्धमानक)—A servant of Charudatta.

शर्विलक—A Brahamana-adventurer who commits a robbery for obtaining money to ransom off the servant-girl Madanika whom he loves.

चेट (कुम्भीलक)—An attendant of Vasantasena.

बन्धुल—A bastard, parasite of Vasantasena.

विट—An attendant of Vasantasena.

रोहसेन—The son of Charudatta.

आर्यक—A cowherd and insurgent, later the king of Ujjayini

वीरक, चन्दनक—Two officers of the city's police.

शोधनक—A beadle of the law-court.

श्रेष्ठिन्, कायस्थ—Two assessors.

अधिकरणिक—A Judge.

चाण्डालौ (आहीन्त and गोह)—Two executioners.

## FEMALES.

नटी—The wife the Sutradhara.

वसन्तसेना—The heroine of the play, a courtesan who loves Charudatta.

रदनिका (चेटी)—Charudatta's maid-servant.

मदनिका (चेटी)—Vasantasena's maid-servant.

धूता—The wife of Charudatta.

छत्रधारिणी—An attendant of Vasantasena.

वृद्धा—The old mother of Vasantasena.

## OTHER PERSONS MENTIOND.

चूर्णवृद्ध—A friend of Charudatta.

पालक—The king of Ujjayini, afterwards dethroned and killed by Aryaka.

रेभिल—A merchant of Ujjayini, and a friend of Charudatta.

The brother of Vasantasena.

## SCENE.

The city of Ujjayini and its environs ( including the *Pushpakarandaka* garden ).

# भूमिका।

शूद्रकेणासकृज्जित्वा स्वच्छया खड्गधारया।
जगद्भूयोऽभ्यवष्टब्धं वाचा स्वचरितार्थया ॥

—आचार्यश्रीदण्डिनः।

इह खलु सकलविद्याकलाकलापादिपीठेऽस्मिन्भारते वर्षे निजयशःपरिमलसुरभीकृतदिगन्ताः प्रतिभाशालिनः परःशताः कवीश्वरा भासकालिदासादयो निजकृताभरणैर्वाग्वधूं सुरुचिरं मण्डयन्ति स्म। तेषां च केचन प्रबन्धप्रमोदितरसिककदम्बाः शब्दसर्जनावर्जितोर्जितयशस्का विदग्धपुंगवाः प्रतापसंतापितारातिचक्राश्चक्रवर्तिनो राजानोऽभूवन्नित्यहो निर्माणचातुरी विधेः। एतेषु श्रीमद्धर्षयशोवर्मभीमटभोजादिष्वग्रेसरीभूतः श्रीशूद्रकाभिधो नृपतिरितो वर्षशतैकविंशतेः प्रागुज्जयिनीं प्रशशास यमुद्दिश्य प्रसस्रुर्नानाकवीनां प्रशंसामधुरा वाक्प्रवाहाः। यश्चैतद्रसभावनिरन्तरं रूपकमूर्धन्यपदप्रतिष्ठितं **मृच्छकटिकाख्यं** चारुतरं प्रकरणं निबबन्ध। यद्यपि कविनृपतेरस्य भूपतेर्विषये किमपीतिवृत्तादि जिज्ञासुभिः स्फुटं निश्चिततया नोपलभ्यते तथाऽपि शताधिकद्विसहस्रमितवर्षेभ्यः प्रागन्ध्रभृत्यराजवंशं बद्धमूलं कृतवतान्ध्रभृत्यानामादिमनृपेण सिमुकाभिधेनास्याविभिन्नत्वमुपस्थापयन्ति भूयांसः संख्यावन्तः प्राचीनवार्ताभिज्ञाः। तेषां च मतमिदं केचन प्रत्यवतिष्ठन्ते। तदभिप्रायेण कविरयमाचार्यश्रीदण्डिविरचितावन्तिसुन्दरीकथासारे समुपवर्गिताच्छूद्रकान्नान्यः संभवतीत्यस्तीह महती विप्रतिपत्तिः। श्रीशूद्रकस्य किमपि चरितमत्रैव प्रकरणे प्रस्तावनायां त्रिभिः श्लोकैरुपनिबद्धं दृश्यते। अथ तु तस्यापि याथातथ्यविषये भूयांसो विकल्पाः पाश्चात्यविद्वद्भिः प्रदर्शिताः कष्टयन्ति चेतः शिष्टानाम्। वयं तु मन्यामहे यदिदं श्लोकत्रयोपवर्णितं वृत्तं न कथमप्यनृतत्वपदवीमारोहेदिति। अथ चात्र प्रस्ताविता ये नानाविधाः कल्पनोपजल्पा न तेषामिह परीक्षणमावश्यकमित्यलं पल्लवितेन। मृच्छकटिकं विहाय नान्यः कोऽपि शूद्रकविरचितो ग्रन्थो दृष्टिपथमारूढः। यत्किल **पद्मप्राभृतक**—**वत्सराजचरित**—**कामदत्ता**दिरूपकाण्यपि शूद्रकेण व्यरच्यन्तेति कैश्चिद्दाक्षिणात्यविपश्चिद्भिरुपन्यस्तं न तत्प्रायोऽद्ययावद्विश्वसनीयत्वकक्षामवगाढम्।

श्रीमाञ्शूद्रको नाटककृच्चक्रवर्तिनः श्रीभासस्य कृतिष्वेकतमं **चारुदत्ताख्यं** खण्डितरूपकं समुपजीव्यैवात्मनः प्रबन्धं प्रणिनायेति सर्वैरभ्युपगतप्रायोऽयमर्थः। दृश्यते च चारुदत्तमृच्छकटिकयोः प्रतिपदं च प्रतिवाक्यं च प्रतिश्लोकं च बंहिष्ठं साम्यम्। तत्रभवाञ्शूद्रको भासीयचारुदत्तादेव चतुर्ष्वङ्केषु ग्रथितं वस्तु तथैवाविकृतं

संगृह्य तस्य परतोऽसमाप्ततया स्वयमेवोर्वरितं वस्तु सम्यक्प्रकल्प्य शेषाञ्षडङ्कान्विरचयांबभूवेति लेशतोऽपि नास्ति संदेहावकाशः। रूपकेऽस्मिन्कविप्रवरः श्रीशूद्रको वैदर्भीं रीतिमेव परिगृहीतवानिति सुविशदमेवावलोकयताम्। यां च रीतिं श्रीबिल्हण इत्थमुपवर्णयति—"अनभ्रवृष्टिः श्रवणामृतस्य सरस्वतीविभ्रमजन्मभूमिः। वैदर्भरीतिः कृतिनामुदेति सौभाग्यलाभप्रतिभूः पदानाम्॥" इति। श्लेषप्रसादमाधुर्यादि काव्यगुणैः प्रगुणीकृतसरसत्वं सरलत्वमस्य कृतौ समुल्लसतितराम्। पद्ये ह्यसमस्तपदप्राचुर्याद्गद्ये च सुस्पष्टायाः सरलाया वाचो निबन्धनात्कविरयं भासकालिदासादिकविवरश्रेण्यामेव प्रधानमास्पदमलंकरोतीति न केषांचन न संमतम्। अस्मिन्प्रकरणे दशभिरङ्कैरुज्जयिनीवास्तव्यस्यौदार्यगुणनिधेर्दैवादवाप्तदारिद्र्यस्य कुलपुत्रशेखरस्य श्रीमतश्चारुदत्तस्य तत्रत्याया रूपयौवनविभवादिशालिन्या वसन्तसेनाभिधाया गुणानुरागित्वाच्चारुदत्तबद्धभावायाः प्रधानगणिकायाश्च प्रेमप्रधानं चारित्र्यं प्रपञ्चितम्। तदिदं कथावस्तु पिपठिषूणां सुखावबोधार्थं सारांशतोऽङ्कानुक्रमेण विभक्तमत्र प्रदर्श्यते—

**प्रथमाङ्के** तावदादौ नान्दीपठनम्। ततः प्रस्तावनायामादौ नाटकस्य कर्तृत्वाभिधानाद्युपनिबद्धम्। पश्चात्सूत्रधारनटीप्रवेशेन कथारम्भत्वेन विदूषकमैत्रेयस्य प्रवेशः संसूचितः। तदनन्तरं मैत्रेयः प्रविश्य बलिकर्मव्यापृताय स्वप्रियवयस्याय चारुदत्ताय तत्सुहृदा चूर्णवृद्धेनानुप्रेषितं प्रावारकमार्पयत्। चारुदत्तश्च प्रस्तावत आत्मनो दारिद्र्यजनितां मानसीमाधिमुपवर्णितवान्। ततो विटचेटाभ्यां सहितेन राजश्यालकसंस्थानकेन शकारेण प्रार्थ्यमानाया वसन्तसेनाया गणिकायाः प्रवेशः। तदभ्यर्थनामनङ्गीकृत्य चारुदत्तगृहं प्रविष्टायां वसन्तसेनायां शकारादयोऽपसृताः। अथ सा तत्र बलीयसाऽनुरागेण परवशीकृता किमपि मनीषितमुद्दिश्य चारुदत्तहस्त आत्मनोऽलंकारं न्यासत्वेन निक्षेप्तुमुद्युक्ताऽऽसीत्। 'नेदं वित्तहीनस्य गृहं न्यासस्य योग्यम्' इति च प्रत्यादेशपरं तं 'आर्य अलीकम्। पुरुषेषु न्यासा निक्षिप्यन्ते न पुनर्गेहेषु' इति निजस्नेहानुकूलं प्रतिभाष्यालंकारं तत्रैव न्यस्य पश्चात्स्वगृहं प्रतिनिवृत्ता।

**द्वितीयाङ्के**--आदौ वसन्तसेनायास्तच्चेट्या मदनिकायाश्च प्रवेशे वसन्तसेनाऽऽत्मनो हृदि निगूढं चारुदत्तनिबन्धनं भावमुपवर्ण्य 'सहसाऽभिसार्यमाणः प्रत्युपकारदुर्बलतया माऽसौ प्रियजनो दुर्लभदर्शनः पुनर्भविष्यति' इत्येवंरूपं चात्मनोऽलंकारस्य न्यासकरणं प्रख्यापितवती। ततो द्यूतं शीलयित्वा दशसुवर्णकस्य कृते रुद्धस्य प्रपलायितस्य प्रधानसभिकेन माथुरेणान्विष्यमाणस्य द्यूतकरसंवाहकस्य प्रवेशः। अन्यतमद्यूतकरसाहाय्येन संवाहको माथुरगृहीतोऽपि तद्धस्तादपक्रम्य वसन्तसेनागृहं प्रविवेश। तस्मै चाभयं प्रदायोदारशीलाऽसौ गणिका तेन धारितं सुवर्णं माथुराय प्रतिपाद्य तमुपकृतवती। आत्मनो द्यूतकरभावेन निर्विण्णः संवाहकः शाक्यश्रमणको बुभूषुर्निष्क्रान्तः। समनन्तरमेव वसन्तसेनायाः किंकरः कर्णपूरकः प्रविश्य संवाहकस्य मत्तहस्तिदंष्ट्रान्तरादात्मकृतं मोचनं तद्विलोक्य च चारुदत्तेन स्वप्रावार-

कस्य तस्मै पारितोषिकतया प्रदानं हृष्टः संकथयामास। अनेन चित्तचमत्कारिवृत्तान्तश्रवणेन च वसन्तसेना चारुदत्ते दृढतरमनुरागिणी बभूव।

तृतीयाङ्के—तत्रभवांश्चारुदत्तो गान्धर्वं श्रोतुं सार्थवाहरेभिलस्य गृहं मैत्रेयेण समं गतवानासीत्। अतिक्रान्तायामर्धरजन्यां ततः प्रतिनिवृत्य स्वगृहमागत्योभावपि सुखेन निद्रामारेभतुः। अथ शर्विलकाख्यः कश्चिद्दरिद्रो ब्राह्मणयुवा वसन्तसेनाचेट्यां मदनिकायां बद्धभावस्तामभुजिष्यां कर्तुमिच्छन्नपि स्वस्य वित्तविहीनतामवलोक्य तत्संपादनार्थं चौरमार्गमङ्गीकृत्य गृहीततत्तत्साधनश्चारुदत्तस्य गृहं प्राप्तः। तत्र च स संधिं कृत्वा प्रविश्य यः पूर्वं वसन्तसेनया न्यासीकृतस्तमेवालंकारं विदूषकेण रात्रौ रक्ष्यमाणं तस्य हस्तादपाच्छिद्य निश्चक्राम। अथ जागरितेषु सर्वेषु तमलंकारं चौरेणापहृतं श्रुत्वा 'कथममुं न्यासं प्रतिनिर्यातयिष्ये' इति चारुदत्तस्य भूयसी चिन्ता समजनि। किं तु ज्ञातैतद्वृत्तान्तया तदीयब्राह्मण्याऽऽर्याधूतया निजकण्ठादेका बहुमूल्या रत्नमालाऽवतारिता विदूषकस्य च हस्ते समर्पिता यां मैत्रेयः 'इदं ते सदृशदारसंग्रहस्य फलम्' इत्युपन्यस्य चारुदत्तायार्पयामास। तदनु वीतचिन्तश्चारुदत्तः 'गच्छ रत्नावलीमिमामादाय वसन्तसेनायाः सकाशम्। वक्तव्या च सा यत्खल्वस्माभिः सोऽलंकार आत्मीय इति कृत्वा विस्रम्भाद् द्यूते हारितः। तस्य कृते गृह्यतामियमिति।' इति संदिश्य विदूषकं गणिकासमीपं प्रेषयांचकार।

चतुर्थाङ्के—अथ प्रभाते शर्विलकश्चोरितालंकारं गृहीत्वा वसन्तसेनाभवनं प्रतियातः। तत्र च मदनिकया संगत्य यावदसौ तत्सुवर्णभाण्डं तस्यै दर्शयति तावत्तया दृष्टपूर्वं तत्स्वस्वामिन्याः संबन्धीत्यभिज्ञातम्। तदनु निर्बन्धपृष्टः शर्विलकः स्वस्तेयं प्राख्यापयत्। प्रिययाऽनुनीतश्च तद्वचनानुसारेण तद्वसन्तसेनायै प्रत्यर्पयितुकामः स चारुदत्तसंबन्धीत्यात्मानं संदर्श्य 'सार्थवाहस्त्वां विज्ञापयति—जर्जरत्वाद्गृहस्य दूरक्ष्यमिदं भाण्डम्। तद्गृह्यताम्' इति वसन्तसेनायै तमलंकारं प्रतिप्रदाय गन्तुमुद्युक्तः। अथ तु मदनिकाशर्विलकयोः संलापमादित एवामूलं श्रुतवती वसन्तसेना तमलीकदूतं विज्ञायाप्युदारशीलतया मदनिकां दास्यान्मोचयित्वा तस्मै दत्तवती। अथ परितुष्टे गते तस्मिन्विदूषको रत्नावलीमादायाष्टप्रकोष्ठं बहुविधसंपन्निचितं वसन्तसेनाभवनं प्राप्य यथादेशं ससंदेशं तां रत्नमालां तस्या हस्ते स्थापितवान्। अथ गणिकाऽपि तामादाय 'कथं चौरेणापहृतमपि शौण्डीरतया द्यूते हारितमिति भणति। अत एव काम्यते' इति स्वगतमाभाष्य 'आर्य विज्ञापयार्यचारुदत्तम्—अहमपि प्रदोष आर्यं प्रेक्षितुमागच्छामि' इति प्रतिसंदिश्य विदूषकं विसर्जयांचकार।

पञ्चमाङ्के—अथोन्नमति दुर्दिने प्रसृते भीषणान्धकारे गर्जत्सु मेघेषु विद्योतमानासु तडित्सु वसन्तसेना यथाप्रतिज्ञमभिसारिकावेषेण चारुदत्तभवनं गत्वा तेन सह संगता भूत्वा परं मोदमवाप। चारुदत्तोऽपि प्रियया संगत्य हृष्टमना विस्मृतदारिद्र्यव्यथो धन्यमात्मानं मेने। अनन्तरमुभावप्यभ्यन्तरं प्रविश्य सुखेन निशामनयताम्।

**षष्ठाङ्के**—अथान्येद्युः प्रभाते चारुदत्तः पूर्वं प्रस्थायोज्जयिनीबहिर्भूतं पुष्पकरण्डकं नाम जीर्णोद्यानं गतः। अथ प्रबुद्धायां वसन्तसेनायां चारुदत्तदारको रोहसेनः सौवर्णशकटिकां क्रीडार्थमिच्छंस्तामलभमानस्तत्स्थाने मृन्निर्मितां शकटिकां प्रदत्तामस्वीकुर्वन्रुदन्नेव तस्याः समीपं प्राविशत्। तत उदारचरिता वसन्तसेना स्वदेहादात्मनोऽलंकारानवतार्य 'गृहाणैतान्। कारय सौवर्णशकटिकाम्' इति सास्रं च सस्नेहं च भणित्वा तं हृष्टं विसर्जयामास। [ तदेवेदं वृत्तमधिकृत्य मृच्छकटिकमिति यथार्थं स्वप्रबन्धाभिधानं कृतवान्कविः।] तदनु वसन्तसेनामुद्यानं नेतुं प्रवहणं योजयित्वा वर्धमानकश्चेट उपस्थित आत्मानं तस्यै निवेदयामास। किं तु यानास्तरणानि विस्मृतानीत्युपलभ्य तान्यानेतुमकथयित्वैव तां पुनः सप्रवहणो निर्यातः। एतदन्तरे शकारस्यापि प्रवहणवाहकश्चेटः स्थावरकस्तेनैव पथा प्रवहणं वाहयंश्चारुदत्तस्य पक्षद्वारकनिकटे क्षणं तत्स्थापयित्वा कुत्रचिद्यातः। तदेव प्रवहणं चारुदत्तीयमिति मत्वा वसन्तसेना तस्मिन्नारूढा स्थावरकोऽपि प्रत्यागत्य अविज्ञाततया निजं प्रवहणं शून्यमेव मन्वानस्तद्वाहयन्नपक्रान्तः। अत्रान्तरे कोऽप्यार्यकनामा गोपालो राजा भविष्यतीति सिद्धादेशपरित्रस्तेन पालकेन राज्ञा गूढकारागारे बद्ध आसीत्। स गुप्तिं भङ्क्त्वा सनिगडमपक्रामन्यातप्रतिनिवृत्तस्य वर्धमानकस्यैव प्रवहणं पृष्ठतोऽधिरूढः। चेटोऽपि पश्चादनवलोक्यार्यकमेव गणिकां मन्वानस्तथैव प्रवहणमवाहयत्। तच्च प्रवहणं नगररक्षिणामेकतमेन चन्दनकेन प्रलोकितमार्यकश्चाभिज्ञातः। किं तु जातकारुण्यः स तस्मा अभयं दत्त्वा न तद्रहस्यं प्राकाशयद्येन वर्धमानकोऽपि तदजानन्नेव प्रवहणं वाहयन्नपचक्राम।

**सप्तमाङ्के**—पुष्पकरण्डकोद्याने प्रियां प्रतिपालयंश्चारुदत्तस्तस्याः स्थान आर्यकमुपस्थितं विलोक्य भृशं विस्मितस्तस्मा अभयं प्रदाय तेन सह सौहृदं संपाद्य 'एवमेवानेन प्रवहणेन शीघ्रमपक्रामतु भवान्' इति तं सुरक्षितं प्रास्थापयत्। नृपतेः कृतव्यलीकतया तत्र परतोऽवस्थानमयुक्तं मत्वा स्वयं चापससार।

**अष्टमाङ्के**—अथ पुष्पकरण्डकोद्याने स्वप्रवहणेनागतां वसन्तसेनामालोक्य परं मोदमापन्नः शकारस्तामनुनेतुं बहुप्रकारं येते। किं तु चारुदत्त एव दृढबद्धभावां तां परिज्ञाय जातरोषोऽसौ तां गले निपीड्य मारयितुं प्रावर्तत। अथ तां निश्चेष्टां भूमौ पतितां निरूप्य मृतेत्येव तामवगच्छंस्तन्महापापं चारुदत्ते पातयितुं निश्चित्य शकारो द्रुतमपचक्राम। अत्रान्तरे संवाहकेन शाक्यभिक्षुभूतेन यदृच्छया तत्रागतेन वसन्तसेना प्रत्युज्जीविता समाश्वासनार्थं समीपवर्तिविहारं प्रापिता च।

**नवमाङ्के**—शकारोऽधिकरणमण्डपं गत्वा व्यवहारमलेखयद्यथा किल चारुदत्तेनाकार्यकारिणा वसन्तसेनाऽर्थस्य कारणात्पुष्पकरण्डकोद्यानं प्रवेश्य बाहुपाशेन मारितेति। अधिकरणिकैराकारितश्चारुदत्त आर्यकवृत्तान्तं गोपायितुमिच्छन्न किंचित्सम्यगुत्तरं ददौ। ततस्तत्स्त्रीवधपातकं तस्मिन्नेव सुलग्नतया निर्णीतं बभूव येन

पालकेन राज्ञा 'डिण्डिमं ताडयित्वा दक्षिणश्मशानं नीत्वा कृतमहापापमेनं शूले भङ्क्त' इति तस्य शारीरो दण्डः प्रतिपन्नः ।

**दशमाङ्के**—अथ चाण्डालाभ्यामनुगम्यमानो धृतवध्यचिह्नश्चारुदत्तः शूलमारोपयितुं श्मशानमनीयत । मार्गे च स्थाने स्थाने तस्य पापं चाण्डालैर्डिण्डिमघोषणापूर्वकमुद्घोष्यत । तच्छ्रुत्वा शकारस्य चेटः स्थावरकः स्वस्वामिना रहस्यभेदशङ्कया निगडैर्बद्धोऽपि प्रासादादवप्लुत्य रथ्यायामागत्य शकारमेव स्त्रीवधपातकिनमुद्घोषयामास । किं तु न कोऽपि तस्मिन्विशश्वास । एतदन्तरे वसन्तसेना भिक्षुणा समं तत्रैव प्राप्ता यामवलोक्य चारुदत्तस्यानपराधित्वं सुव्यक्तमेवासीत् सर्वेषाम् । अत्रान्तरे शर्विलकोऽपि पालकं हत्वाऽऽर्यकस्य राज्यारोहणं प्रख्यापयंस्तत्रोपस्थितः । आर्यकश्च चारुदत्ताय कुशावत्या राज्यमतिसृष्टवान्वसन्तसेनामपि वधूशब्देनालंचकार । एवं चारुदत्तेनापि कारुणिकेन शकारोऽभयं दत्त्वा मृत्युभयाद्रक्षितः। एवं सर्वं स्वन्तमुपन्यस्य कविरन्ते भरतवाक्येन स्वकृतिं समाप्तिं नीतवान् ।

अथ

# मृच्छकटिकम् ।

## प्रथमोऽङ्कः ।

पर्यङ्कग्रन्थिबन्धद्विगुणितभुजगाश्लेषसंवीतजानो-
रन्तः प्राणावरोधव्युपरतसकलज्ञानरुद्धेन्द्रियस्य ।
आत्मन्यात्मानमेव व्यपगतकरणं पश्यतस्तत्त्वदृष्टया
शंभोर्वः पातु शून्येक्षणघटितलयब्रह्मलग्नः समाधिः ॥ १ ॥

अपि च ।

पातु वो नीलकण्ठस्य कण्ठः श्यामाम्बुदोपमः ।
गौरीभुजलता यत्र विद्युल्लेखेव राजते ॥ २ ॥

[ नान्द्यन्ते । ]

**सूत्रधारः**—अलमनेन परिषत्कुतूहलविमर्दकारिणा परिश्रमेण[1] । एवमहमार्यमिश्रान्प्रणिपत्य विज्ञापयामि—यदिदं वयं मृच्छकटिकं नाम प्रकरणं प्रयोक्तुं व्यवसिताः । एतत्कविः किल

---

शेमुषीप्रौढजीवातुर्विवृतिर्मृच्छकटिके ।
पृथ्वीधरैश्चिकीर्षद्भिर्गणेशो गण्यते गुरुः ॥

तथा—

बालानां सुखबोधाय गुरूणां वचनं शुभम् ।
लिख्यते गहनेऽप्यत्र हेरम्बावनतिस्थिरः ॥

प्रकरणं चेदम् । तस्य च लक्षणम्—'यत्र कविरात्मबुद्ध्या वस्तु शरीरं च नायकं चैव । विरचयति समुत्पाद्य तज्ज्ञेयं प्रकरणं नाम ॥ चतस्रो वृत्तयः पञ्च संधयोऽष्ट रसादयः । प्रकरणेनो नाटकं विहाय नृपनायकम् ॥' (इत्यादि) । आदिशब्दात्षड्भमादिग्रहणम् । नाटकादौ बहुप्रकारप्राकृतप्रपञ्चेषु चतस्र एव भाषाः प्रयुज्यन्ते-शौरसेन्यवन्तिकाप्राच्यामागध्यः । अपभ्रंशप्रपञ्चेषु चतस्र एवः भाषाः प्रयुज्यन्ते-शकारी-चाण्डालीशाबरीढक्कदेशीयाः । मृच्छकटिके तु शबरपात्राभावच्छावरी नास्ति । प्राकृते 'मागध्यवन्तिजा प्राच्या शौरसेन्यर्धमागधी । बाह्लीका दाक्षिणात्या च सप्तभाषाः प्रकीर्तिताः ॥' महाराष्ट्र्यादयः काव्य एव प्रयुज्यन्ते । अपभ्रंशे—'शकाराभीर-

---

१ परिभ्रमेण.

# MRICHCHHAKATIKA

## ACT I.

May the abstract meditation (*Samadhi*) of Siva, concentrated on Brahma owing to the ( intense ) absorption produced by the absence of any perception, protect you !—(of Siva), whose knees are wrapped round with the doubly-tightened fold of the snake, while he sits having formed a knot (with his legs) in the *Paryanka* posture ( by bending them cross-wise ) : ( the operation of ) whose sense is so suspended as to cause the cessation of all perception, by reason of the vital airs being confined within ; and who, with the eye of truth, is visualizing within himself his own self ( as the Universal Soul )—with a total identification of the two ( *lit.* with the function of the senses having totally ceased ) ( or, which is destitute of all kinds of organs ). (1)

Moreover—

May the neck of ( the black-throated deity, *viz.* ) Siva, resembling a dark cloud, protect you !—( the neck ) whereon the creeper-like arm of Parvati shines like a streak of lightning. (2)

[ *At the end of the Benediction* ]

SUTRADHARA—Enough of an exertion that causes distraction of the curiosity of the audience.—Having saluted ( these ) honourable gentlemen, I will thus respectfully address them : That ( here ) we have undertaken to stage this *Prakarana* ( play ) called ***Mrichchhakatika.*** It is stated that the poet, its author—

---

चाण्डालशबरद्राविडोड्रजाः। हीना वनेचराणां च विभाषाः सप्त कीर्तिताः॥ 'विविधा भाषा विभाषाः। हीनपात्रप्रयोज्यत्वाद्धीनाः। वनेचराणां चेति ढक्कभाषासंग्रहः। तत्रास्मिन्प्रकरणे प्राकृतपाठकेषु सूत्रधारो नटी रदनिका मदनिका वसन्तसेना तन्माता चेटी कर्णपूरकश्चारुदत्तब्राह्मणी शोधनकः श्रेष्ठी एते एकादश शौरसेनीभाषापाठकाः। सूत्रधारोऽप्यत्र प्राकृती 'कार्यवशात्' इति वक्ष्यते। अवन्तिभाषापाठकौ वीरकचन्दनकौ। प्राच्यभाषापाठको विदूषकः। संवाहकः शकारवसन्तसेनाचारुदत्तानां चेटकत्रितयं भिक्षुश्चारुदत्तदारकः एते षण्मागधीपाठकाः। अपभ्रंशपाठकेषु शकारीभाषापाठको राष्ट्रियः। चाण्डालीभाषापाठकौ चाण्डालौ। ढक्कभाषापाठकौ माथुरद्यूतकरौ। तथा—शौरसेन्यवन्तिजा प्राच्या एतासु दन्त्यसकारता। तत्रावन्तिजा

द्विरदेन्द्रगतिश्चकोरनेत्रः परिपूर्णेन्दुमुखः सुविग्रहश्च ।
द्विजमुख्यतमः कविर्बभूव प्रथितः शूद्रक इत्यगाधसत्त्वः ॥ ३ ॥

अपि च ।

ऋग्वेदं सामवेदं गणितमथ कलां वैशिकीं[१] हस्तिशिक्षां
ज्ञात्वा शर्वप्रसादाद्व्यपगततिमिरे चक्षुषी चोपलभ्य ।
राजानं वीक्ष्य पुत्रं परमसमुदयेनाश्वमेधेन चेष्ट्वा
लब्ध्वा चायुः शताब्दं दशदिनसहितं शूद्रकोऽग्निं प्रविष्टः ॥ ४ ॥

अपि च ।

समरव्यसनी प्रमादशून्यः ककुदं वेदविदां तपोधनश्च ।
परवारणबाहुयुद्धलुब्धः क्षितिपालः किल शूद्रको बभूव ॥ ५ ॥

अस्यां च तत्कृतौ ।

अवन्तिपुर्यां द्विजसार्थवाहो युवा दरिद्रः किल चारुदत्तः ।
गुणानुरक्ता गणिका च यस्य वसन्तशोभेव वसन्तसेना ॥ ६ ॥

तयोरिदं सत्सुरतोत्सवाश्रयं नयप्रचारं व्यवहारदुष्टताम् ।
खलस्वभावं भवितव्यतां तथा चकार सर्वं किल शूद्रको नृपः ॥ ७ ॥

( परिक्रम्यावलोक्य च । ) अये शून्येयमस्मत्संगीतशाला[२] । क्व नु गताः कुशीलवा भविष्यन्ति । ( विचिन्त्य । ) आं ज्ञातम् ।

---

रेफवती लोकोक्तिबहुला । प्राच्या स्वार्थिककाकरप्राया । मागधी तालव्यशकारवती । शकारीचाण्डाल्योस्तालव्यशकारता । रेफस्य च लकारता । वकारप्राया ढक्कविभाषा । संस्कृतप्रायत्वे दन्त्यतालव्यसशकारद्वययुक्ता च । 'अपार्थमक्रमं व्यर्थं पुनरुक्तं हतोपमम् । लोकन्यायविरुद्धं च शकारवचनं विदुः ॥' अपार्थं निरर्थकम् । व्यर्थं विरुद्धार्थम् । यद्वा । निश्चितानन्वयं पदजातं वाक्यजातं चापार्थकम् । व्यर्थं निरर्थकमेव । हतोपमम् व्याहतोपमम् । 'शकारप्रायभाषित्वाच्छकारो राष्ट्रियः स्मृतः । एकविद्यो विटश्चान्यो हास्यकृच्च विदूषकः ॥' स्वार्थिकः ककारः सर्वत्र । द्विवचनं चतुर्थीविभक्तिश्च नास्त्येव । द्वित्वे तु बहुवचनम् । चतुर्थ्यर्थे षष्ठी । परस्मैपदात्मनेपदविपर्ययः । पूर्वनिपातानियमश्च । बहुलं छन्दसो निदर्शनमप्रसिद्धच्छन्दोज्ञानार्थम् । पाठविप्लवनिरासार्थं च । [ चिकीर्षितस्य प्रकरणस्य निर्विघ्नपरिसमाप्त्यर्थं 'तथाऽप्यवश्यं कर्तव्या नान्दी विघ्नोपशान्तये ।' इति वचनानुसारेण 'आशीर्वचनसंयुक्ता स्तुतिर्यस्मात्प्रयुज्यते । देवद्विजनृपादीनां तस्मान्नान्दीति संज्ञिता ॥' इत्युक्तलक्षणां नान्दीं तावदवतारयति--] **पर्यङ्केत्यादि** । पर्यङ्कः पर्यस्तिका तस्य (ग्रन्थिः रचनं तस्य) बन्धेन द्विगुणितो यो भुजगस्तस्य (आश्लेषेण) संबन्धन (संवीते)

---

१ वैशिखीं. २ संगीतक०.

Was a famous scholar, Sudraka by name, who was the very best of the twice-born (Kshatriyas), and of unfathomable mental calibre. His gait was like that of an excellent elephant; his eyes resembled those of a *chakora* bird; his face vied with the full moon (in beauty); and he possessed a handsome body. (3)

Again—

He knew the Rigveda, the Samaveda, mathematics, the (fine) arts (practised by courtesans), and the science of (the training and management of) elephants; and he obtained, through Siva's favour, eyes from which the darkness (of ignorance) (or, blindness) had departed. Having seen his son installed (on the throne) as king, having performed the exalting *Asvamedha* sacrifice, and having enjoyed a life of one hundred years together with ten (more) days, Sudraka entered the (sacred) fire (*i. e.*, died). (4)

Moreover—

Passionately fond of war; free from negligence; chief of those who knew the Vedas; rich in penance; and eager to fight with his two arms the elephants of his enemies—such indeed was King Sudraka. (5)

And in this work of his—

(It is related that) there lived, as was said, in the city of Ujjayini, (one) Charudatta, a leader of the Brahmanas, who was young and poor; and a courtesan called Vasantasena, (lovely) like the beauty of *Vasanta* (Spring), who loved him for his virtues. (6)

King Sudraka has delineated in that (excellent) way these, in connexion with those two, *viz.*, the course of virtuous life based on the pleasures of true love, corruptness of legal procedure, the nature of villains, and (the workings of) Destiny. (7)

(*Walking about and observing*). How now! This music-hall of ours is quite empty! Where could the actors have gone? (*Reflecting*). Ah! I have it!

---

स्थगिते जानुनी यस्य । [अन्तः अन्तःशरीरे यः प्राणानां प्राणापानादिवायूनामवरोधः नियमनं तेन व्युपरतं निवृत्तं सकलं बाह्यविषयज्ञानं येषां तानि तथा रुद्धानि संयतानि इन्द्रियाणि यस्य । तदुक्तं योगसागरे–'करणान्यबहिष्कृत्य स्थाणुवन्निश्चलात्मकः । आत्मानं हृदये ध्यायेन्नासाग्रन्यस्तलोचनः ॥' इति ।] आत्मनि शरीर एव (व्यपगतं स्वव्यापाराद्) उपरतं करणमिन्द्रियं यथा स्यादेवं तत्त्वदृष्टयाऽनारोपितज्ञानेन [ब्रह्मै-

शून्यमपुत्रस्य गृहं चिरशून्यं नास्ति यस्य सन्मित्रम् ।
मूर्खस्य दिशः शून्याः सर्वं शून्यं दरिद्रस्य ॥ ८ ॥

कृतं च सगीतकं मया । अनेन चिरसंगीतोपासनेन[१] ग्रीष्मसमये प्रचण्डदिनकर-किरणोच्छुष्कपुष्करबीजमिव प्रचलिततारके क्षुधा ममाक्षिणी खटखटायेते । तद्यावद्-गृहिणीमाहूय[२] पृच्छामि, अस्ति किमपि[३] प्रातराशो न वेति । एषोऽस्मि भोः कार्य-वशात्प्रयोगवशाच्च प्राकृतभाषी संवृत्तः ।—अविद अविद भोः । चिरसंगीतोपासनेन शुष्कपुष्करनालानीव मे बुभुक्षया म्लानान्यङ्गानि । तद्यावद्गृहं गत्वा जानामि, अस्ति किमपि कुटुम्बिन्योपपादितं न वेति । (परिक्रम्यावलोक्य च ।) इदं तदस्माकं गृहम् । तत्प्रविशामि । ( प्रविश्यावलोक्य च । ) आश्चर्यम् । किं नु खल्वस्माकं गृहेऽन्यदिव संविधानकं वर्तते । आयामितण्डुलोदकप्रवाहा रथ्या लोहकटाहपरिवर्तन-कृष्णसारा कृतविशेषकेव युवत्यधिकतरं शोभते भूमिः । स्निग्धगन्धेनोद्दीप्यमाने-वाधिकं बाधते मां बुभुक्षा । तत्किं पूर्वार्जितं निधानमुत्पन्नं भवेत् । अथ वाऽहमेव बुभुक्षातोऽन्नमयं जीवलोकं पश्यामि । नास्ति किल प्रातराशोऽस्माकं गृहे । प्राणा-त्ययं बाधते मां बुभुक्षा । इह सर्वं नवमिव संविधानकं वर्तते । एका वर्णकं पिनष्टि अपरा सुमनसो गुम्फति । (विचिन्त्य ।) किं न्विदम् । भवतु । कुटुम्बिनीं शब्दाय्य परमार्थं ज्ञास्यामि । (नेपथ्याभिमुखमवलोक्य ।) आर्ये इतस्तावत् । (अविद[४] अविद भोः । चिरसंगीदोवासणेण[५] सुक्खपोक्खरणालाइं विअ मे बुभुक्खाए मिलाणाइं अङ्गाइं ता जाव गेहं गदुअ आणामि, अत्थि किं पि कुटुम्बिणीए उववादिदं ण वेत्ति । एद तं अम्हाणं गेहम् । ता पविसामि । हीमाणहे । किं णु क्खु अम्हाणं गेहे अण्णं विअ संविहाणअं वट्टदि । आआमितण्डुलोदअप्पवाहा रच्छा लोहकडाहपरि-वत्तणकसणसारा[६] किदविसेसआ विअ जुअदी अहिअदरं सोहदि भूमी । सिणिद्ध-गन्धेण उद्दीविअन्ती[७] विअ अहिअं बाधेदि मं बुभुक्खा । ता किं पुव्वज्जिदं णिहाणं उव्वणं[८] भवे । आदु अहं ज्जेव बुभुक्खादो अण्णमअं जीअलोअं पेक्खामि । णत्थि किल पादरासो[९] अम्हाणं गेहे । पाणच्चअं[१०] बाधेदि मं बुभुक्खा । इध सव्वं णवं विअ संविहाणअं[११] वट्टदि । एक्का वण्णअं पीसेदि अवरा सुमणाओ गुम्फेदि । किं ण्णेदम् । भोदु । कुडुम्बिणिं सद्दाविअ परमत्थं जाणिस्सम् । अज्जे इदो दाव ।

---

वाहमिति निर्विकल्पज्ञानेनेत्यर्थः । आत्मानं पश्यता साक्षात्कुर्वतः । एतादृशः शंभोः ईशस्य] शून्येक्षणे निराकारालोचने घटितोऽत्यन्तसंबद्धो यो लयस्तत्प्रवणताविशेषस्तेन ब्रह्मणि परमे रूप आसक्तः समाधिध्यानं [ शून्यं बाह्यप्रपञ्चासंयुक्तं यदीक्षणं तेन

---

१ संगीतको०. २ गृहं गत्वा गृहिणी०. ३ किंचित्. ४ अविद भोः, अविहा भो भोः. ५ संगीदकोवास०. ६ कटाह; परिअत्तण, परिअन्तण ( परियन्त्रण ). ७ उद्दीवन्ती. ८ उपवण्णं ( उपान्नम् ). ९ पादरासोवि. १० पाणाधिअं (टी०) ११ संविहाणं.

The home of a sonless person is empty ; he who has not a real friend finds all time empty ; the quarters are empty to a fool; and everything is empty to a poor man. (8)

Well, I have finished the musical concert. By having thus practised music for a long time, my eyes, whose pupils are rolling, are crackling ( with pain ) owing to hunger, like lotus-seeds scorched by the rays of the fierce sun in summer-time. I shall therefore now call my wife and ask (her) if there is any breakfast ( available ) or not. Here have I, sirs, turned a Prakrit-speaking person, as required by my business and the exigence of the performance, too.—Alack-a-day ! By having practised music for a long time my limbs are drooping in hunger, like the parched stalks of lotuses. I shall therefore now go home and ascertain if my wife has arranged for anything ( to eat ) or not. ( *Walking about and observing* ) Here is that house of ours. Well, I shall go in. ( *Entering and observing* ). Heigh-ho ! How is it that there is quite a new development in our house ! The passage is full of a long stream of rice-water ; and the floor, which is dark-grey by reason of the iron saucepans having been moved over it, is now looking more charming, like a woman with a variegated *tilaka* mark painted ( on her forehead ). And my hunger is paining me the more, as if it wese greatly excited by ( this ) inviting smell. Could it be, then, that some ( buried ) treasure, belonging to our ancestors, has been discovered ? Or rather, it is I myself who in my hunger am looking upon the world as consisting of nothing but eatables ! Indeed, there could not be any breakfast in our house. Hunger is paining me so as to take away my very life. Here all things are wearing a new aspect to-day. One womon is pounding unguents, while another is wreathing flowers. ( *Pondering* ). What could this be ? Never mind ; I shall call for my wife and ascertain what it all really is. ( *Looking towards the curtain* ). Lady, come here, please.

---

घटितः संपादितः यो लयः एकतानताप्रवाहः तेन ब्रह्मणि लग्नः समाधिः चित्तैकाग्रतया चिन्तनं ] वो युष्मान्रक्षतु । [ स्रग्धरावृत्तम् । तल्लक्षणं—'म्रभ्नैर्यानां त्रयेण त्रिमुनियतियुता स्रग्धरा कीर्तितेयम् ।' इति ] ॥ १ ॥ पात्विति । [ नीलकण्ठस्य श्यामश्चासौ अम्बुदश्च श्यामाम्बुदः तेन उपमा यस्य सः कण्ठः वः पातु । यत्र यस्मिन् गौर्याः भुजः लता इव । कण्ठाश्लेषे वेष्टनसाम्यात् । विद्युल्लेखा इव विराजते ॥ २ ॥ सूत्रधारः—'वर्तनीयतया सूत्रं प्रथमं येन सूच्यते । रङ्गभूमिं

**नटी**—(प्रविश्य।) आर्य इयमस्मि। (अज्ज[१] इअं म्हि।)

**सूत्रधारः**—आर्ये स्वागतं ते। (अज्जे सादअं दे।)

**नटी**—आज्ञापयत्वार्यः को नियोगोऽनुष्ठीयतामिति। (आणवेदु अज्जो[२] को णिओओ अणुचिट्ठीअदु त्ति।)

**सूत्रधारः**—आर्ये। ('चिरसंगीदोवासणेण' इत्यादि पठित्वा[३]।) अस्ति किमप्यस्माकं गेहेऽशितव्यं न वेति। (अज्जे अत्थि किं पि अम्हाणं गेहे असिदव्वं ण वेत्ति।)

**नटी**—आर्य सर्वमस्ति। (अज्ज[४] सव्वं अत्थि।)

**सूत्रधारः**—किं किमस्ति। (किं किं अत्थि।)

**नटीः**—तद्यथा गुडौदनं घृतं दधि तण्डुला आर्येणात्तव्यं रसायनं सर्वमस्तीति। एवं तव देवा आशासन्ताम्। (तं जधा गुडोदणं घिअं[५] दहीं तण्डुलाइं अज्जेण[६] अत्तव्यं रसाअणं सव्वं अत्थि त्ति। एव्वं दे देवा आसासेन्तु[७]।)

**सूत्रधारः**—आर्ये किमस्माकं गेहे सर्वमस्ति। अथवा परिहससि। (अज्जे किं अम्हाणं गेहे सव्वं अत्थि। आदु परिहससि।)

---

समाक्रम्य सूत्रधारः स उच्यते ॥' इति संगीतसर्वस्वे उक्तलक्षणः। विमर्दकारिणा हानिकरेण। परिश्रमेण अधिकतरनान्दीपठनायासेन।] आर्यान्मान्यान् मिश्रानभ्यस्तबहुशास्त्रान्। चारुदत्तपुत्ररोहसेनक्रीडनार्थं षष्ठेऽङ्क उक्तं मृच्छकटमत्रास्ति। 'अत इनिठनौ' इति ठन्। मृदः शकटिकाऽस्मिन्निति वा बहुव्रीहिः। **द्विरदेन्द्रेति**। द्विजमुख्यतमः क्षत्रजातिश्रेष्ठः। 'त्रयो वर्णा द्विजातयः' इति स्मृतेः क्षत्रियेऽपि द्विजप्रयोगः। [द्वौ रदौ एषां ते द्विरदाः तेषु इन्द्र इव द्विरदेन्द्रः तस्य इव गतिर्यस्य। चकोरस्य इव नेत्रे यस्य। शोभनः विग्रहः शरीरं यस्य। अगाधं सत्त्वं बलं यस्य सः। उपमालंकारः। औपच्छन्दसिकं वृत्तम्] ॥३॥ **ऋग्वेदमिति**। वेशोऽत्र कार्त्स्न्येन वेश्यापरः। तत्र भवा विद्यमाना। अध्यात्मादित्वाठ्ठक्। यद्वा वेशोऽग्निनिवेशाख्यो राजा तेन कृताम्। कलां चतुःषष्टिकलाप्रतिपादकं प्रबन्धम्। [यद्वा वेशः नेपथ्यग्रहणं तत्संबन्धिनीं कलां नाटयशास्त्रमित्यर्थः।] शर्वो महादेवः। [तस्य प्रसादात् व्यपगतं तिमिरं अज्ञानं यस्मात्तथाविधं ज्ञानस्वरूपं चक्षुः प्राप्य। पुत्रं राजानं वीक्ष्य राज्ये स्थापयित्वेत्यर्थः। परमः श्रेष्ठः समुदयः उत्कर्षः यस्मात् तेन। अश्वस्य मेधः पशुत्वेनोपालम्भनं यत्र सोऽश्वमेधस्तेन इष्ट्वा।] लब्ध्वा चायुः शताब्दमग्निं प्रविष्ट इति जातकादिगणितद्वारा ज्ञात्वा। आगामिसूत्रधारवचनापेक्षया 'अग्निं प्रविष्टः' इत्यादिभूतकालप्रत्ययो न विरुद्ध इति मर्मज्ञाः। अग्निप्रवेशोऽपि सर्वस्वारनामके यज्ञविशेषे यथा शरभङ्गेण कृतस्तथा बोद्धव्यम्। [स्रग्धरा छन्दः। लक्षणं

---

१ अज्जउत्त. २ अज्जउत्तो. ३ पठति. पूर्वोक्तं पठित्वा. ४ अज्जउत्त. ५ पिअं (प्रिय). ६ अज्जउत्तेण. ७ आसासेन्दु.

NATI—( *Entering* ). Sir, here I am.

SUTRA.—Lady, my greetings to you!

NATI—May your honour command what duty is to be executed ( by me ).

SUTRA.—Lady, ( *Saying—' By having practised music for a long time' &c.* ) is there anything to eat in our house, or not?

NATI.—Sir, there is everything.

SUTRA—What things are there?

NATI.—They are as follows; rice seasoned with *guda*, ghee, curds, (simple) rice, and all elixir-like ( *i. e.* delicious ) things fit to be eaten by you. May the gods thus (ever) favour you!

SUTRA.—What, are all these things (really) in our house? Or are you joking?

---

तूक्तम् ] ॥ ४ ॥ **समरेति** । [ समरेषु व्यसनं यस्य । महावीर इत्यर्थः । प्रमादेन अनवधानतया शून्यः । स्वकार्यदक्ष इत्यर्थः । वेदविदां ककुदं श्रेष्ठः । तप एव धनं यस्य स तपोधनः तपोनिष्ठः । परा उत्कृष्टा वारणा गजास्तैः सह बाहुयुद्धे लुब्धः । यद्वा परेषां वारणाः । यद्वा परेषां शत्रूणां वारणौ निवारकौ यौ बाहू ताभ्यां युद्धे लुब्धः । ] ककुदं चिह्नभूतं प्राधान्ये वा । तथा चामरः—' प्राधान्ये राजलिङ्गे च वृषाङ्गे ककुदोऽस्त्रियाम् ' इति । वारणो हस्ती । [ औपच्छन्दसिकं वृत्तम् ] ॥ ५ ॥ **अवन्तीति** । अवन्तिपुर्युज्जयिनी । ' अस्यां च तत्कृतौ अवन्ति-' इत्यादावस्तिद्वयानुषङ्गः । [ अवन्तिपुर्यां द्विजश्चासौ वणिक्कर्मकारित्वात्सार्थवाहश्च द्विजसार्थवाहः । यद्वा सार्थं समूहं वाहयतीति सार्थवाहः । द्विजश्रेष्ठ इत्यर्थः । चारुदत्त आसीत् किल । यस्य च गुणैः दयादाक्षिण्यादिभिः अनुरक्ता वसन्तशोभा मधुलक्ष्मीरिव वसन्तसेना नाम गणिका च आसीत् । उपेन्द्रवज्रा वृत्तम् । ' उपेन्द्रवज्रा जतजास्ततो गौ ' इति तल्लक्षणम् ] ॥६॥ **तयोरिति** । [ तयोः तत्संबद्धमित्यर्थः । सत् श्लाघ्यं सुरतमेवोत्सवः स आश्रयः यस्य तम् । ] नयः नीतिस्तस्य प्रचारो व्यवहारस्तं नयप्रचारम् । [ व्यवहारस्य दुष्टतां चारुदत्तस्य वसन्तसेनाघातकत्वेन निर्णयदानात् दुष्टतां सदोषतां खलानां शकारादीनां स्वभावं तथा भवितव्यतां च इदं सर्वं अस्यां तत्कृतौ शूद्रको नृपः चकार । वंशस्थविलं वृत्तम् ] स्वहितं व्यवहारः ॥ ७ ॥ [ **शून्यमिति** । ] चिरशून्यमिति कर्मधारयः । चिरं दीर्घः कालो निरवधि समयः । शून्यमभिमतकार्यरहितम् । सन्मित्रस्य हि ससहायत्वेन कार्यनिष्पत्तेः सदा पूर्ण इव समयोऽत्रभासते । [ आर्या छन्दः ] ॥ ८ ॥ [ प्रचण्डः यो दिनकरः तस्य किरणैः उच्छुष्कं यत्पुष्करबीजं कमलबीजं तद्वत् । खटखट इत्यव्यक्तशब्द इव आचरतः खटखटायते । ] खडित्यव्यक्तानुकरणम् । संगीतकेन चक्षुषी खटखटायेते इत्यसंबद्धप्रलापेन भाविनः शकारासंबद्धभाषणस्य सूचनम् । प्रातराशः कल्यभोजनम् । कार्य-

**नटी**--( स्वगतम् । ) परिहसिष्यामि तावत् । (प्रकाशम् ।) आर्य अस्त्यापणे। (परिहसिस्सं दाव । अज्ज[१] अत्थि आवणे।)

**सूत्रधारः**--( सक्रोधम् । ) आः अनार्ये एवं तवाशा छेत्स्यते । अभावं च गमिष्यसि । यदिदानीमहं वरण्डलम्बुक इव दूरमुत्क्षिप्य पातितः। (आः अणज्जे एव्वं दे आसा छिज्जिस्सदि। अभावं अ गमिस्ससि। अं दाणि अहं वरण्डलम्बुओ[२] विअ दूरं उक्खिविअ पाडिदो।)

**नटी**--मर्षतु मर्षत्वार्यः। परिहासः खलु मया कृतः। (मरिसेदु मरिसेदु अज्जो[३]। परिहासो क्खु[४] मए कदो।)

**सूत्रधारः**--तत्किं पुनरिदं नवमिव संविधानकं वर्तते । एका वर्णकं पिनष्टि अपरा सुमनसो गुम्फति इयं च पञ्चवर्णकुसुमोपहारशोभिता भूमिः । (ता किं उण इदं णवं विअ संविहाणअं वट्टदि । एक्का वण्णअ पीसेदि अवरा[५] सुमणाओ गुम्फेदि इयं अ पञ्चवण्णकुसुमोवहारसोहिदा भूमी ।

**नटी**--अद्योपवासो गृहीतः। (अज्ज उपवासो गहिदो।)

**सूत्रधारः**--किंनामधेयोऽयमुपवासः। (किंणामधेओ अअं उववासो।)

**नटी**--अभिरूपपतिर्नाम। (अहिरूअवदी णाम।)

**सूत्रधारः**--आर्ये इहलौकिकोऽथ वा पारलौकिकः । ( अज्जे इहलोइओ आदु पारलोइओ। )

**नटी**--आर्य पारलौकिकः। ( अज्ज[६] पारलोइओ। )

---

वशात्प्रयोगवशाच्चेति । कार्यं बोध्यायाः स्त्रियो झटिति ज्ञानम् । यदुच्यते-'स्त्रीषु ना प्राकृतं वदेत्' इति। सुकुमारत्वेन सुप्रयोगत्वं प्राकृतस्य। यदुक्तम्—'पुरिसा सक्कअजप्पा पाउअगुम्फो वि होइ सुउमारो' ( पुरुषाः संस्कृतजल्पाः प्राकृतगुम्फोऽपि भवति सुकुमारः।) तथा षष्ठेऽङ्के प्रवहणविपर्यासे वीरकचन्दनकयोः कलहे संभ्रमागतवचनसंवरणार्थं भाषाव्यत्यासाच्चन्दनकस्य पाठः संस्कृतेन। तथा पञ्चमाङ्के दुर्दिने कार्यवशाद्वसन्तसेनायाः श्लोकपाठः संस्कृतेन। चारुदत्तस्य दारिद्र्यवर्णनासूचनयोग्यप्राकृतपरिग्रहः। यदाहुः—'कार्यतश्चोत्तमादीना कार्यो भाषाव्यतिक्रमः।' इति। एतत्सर्वमनेन सूचितमिति । अविद अविदेति निर्वेदे। कष्टं कष्टमित्यर्थः। 'अदृष्टाश्रुतसप्राप्तावविदाविदभोःपदम्' इति च प्राञ्चः। हीमाणहे विस्मये। [ संविधीयते सम्यग् निष्पाद्यते इति संविधानं भोज्यवस्तुनिर्माणसंरम्भः।] आयामो दीर्घस्तण्डुलप्रक्षालनजलप्रवाहो यत्र तादृशी रथ्या। लोहस्य कटाहो भाजनविशेषस्तत्परिवर्तनेन [इतस्ततश्चालनात् घर्षणेन] मार्जनेन कृष्णसारा [ कृतः विशेषको यया सा कृतविशेषका] कृततिलका युवतिवद्भूमिरधिकं शोभते। कृष्णसारा भूमिरित्यनेन

---

१ अज्जउत्त. २ वरण्डु. ३ अज्जउत्तो. ४ क्ख एसो. ५ अण्णा कुसुमाइं. ६ अज्जउत्त.

NATI—(*To herself*). Well, I'll joke (with him). (*Aloud*). Hnsband, they are—in the market.

SUTRA.—(*With anger*). Ah! You hussy, your hopes will be similarly frustrated, and you too would be made away with, since just now (by you) I have been raised aloft and thrown down, like the stone at the end of the Varanda.*

NATI—Pardon, sir, pardon! I indeed played a joke.

SUTRA.—Well, then, what are these preparations that seem to be (quite) new here? One lady is pounding unguents; another is wreathing flowers; and this floor here is decked with the offerings of flowers of five colours.

NATI—I have to-day undertaken a fast.

SUTRA.—What is the name of this fast?

NATI—It is called *Abhirupa-Pati* ('The giver of a handsome husband').

SUTRA.—Lady, in this world or in the next?

NATI—Sir, in the next.

---

चतुर्थाङ्के भवनकोष्ठकस्य विशेषसूचनम् । तत्किं पूर्वार्जितं निधानं बहुसंख्यं धनमुत्पन्नं भवेत् । आदु अथ वेत्यर्थः । पाठान्तरे ओदनमयम् । [ प्राणात्ययं प्राणानामत्ययो नाशो यथा स्यात्तथा । क्रियाविशेषणम् । ] प्राणाधिकं प्राणेष्वधिकं यथा स्यादेवम् । एका वर्णकं कस्तूर्यादिकं समालम्भनं पिनष्टि । अपरा सुमनसः पुष्णाणि ग्रथ्नाति । इत्यनेनापि कोष्ठकस्यैव सूचनम् । असिदव्वं अन्नरूपं द्रव्यम् । अत्तव्वं रसाअणमिति प्रायेणात्तव्यं रसायनमस्तीति । [ रसानामयनमाश्रयभूतं सरसमन्नजातमित्यर्थः । ] एवं तव देवा आशासन्तामिति संदिग्धवाक्योपन्यासः । आर्य अस्त्यापणे वणिग्वीथ्याम् । एवं तवाशा । छेत्स्यति अभावं च गमिष्यसीत्यनेन वसन्तसेनायाः प्रवहणविपर्यासमोटनयोः सूचनम् । वरण्डो दीर्घकाष्ठं तस्य लम्बुकस्तत्प्रान्तनिबद्धो मृत्तिकास्थूणः । स हि द्रोण्यां पानीयोद्धारे दूरमुत्थाप्याधः पात्यते । केचिदाहुः— वरण्ड इष्टकागृह उन्नतीभूतो दीर्घो भित्तिप्रदेशस्तत्र लम्बुकोऽत्रयवभूत इष्टकासंघः । सोऽपि हि संयोजनार्थं दूरमुत्थाप्यते । अनन्तरं निपतत्यपीति । उपवासः । उपवासरूपं व्रतमित्यर्थः । अधिकरणघञन्तोऽयम् । पारलौकिक इत्यनेन पालकव्युदासेन नायकान्तरलाभसूचनम् । ममकेरकेण मदीयेन । भत्तपरिव्वएण भक्तपरिव्ययेन । ओदनव्ययेनेत्यर्थः । यद्वा । भर्तृपरित्यागेन । पारलौकिको भर्ताऽन्विष्यते । त्वमेव जन्मातरे भविष्यसीति । आः आक्षेपे । छयं आदुत्या आकारान्तादेशे कृते चूर्णवृद्धा इति । एवं च 'दूआ तीआ' इत्यादौ च बोद्धव्यम् । कप्पिन्तं छेद्यमानम् । वधूपक्षे कल्प्यमानं संसज्यमानम् । नव-

---

* A long beam or bamboo forming part of a sort of machine for drawing water.

**सूत्रधारः**—( सरोषम् । ) प्रेक्षन्तां प्रेक्षन्तामार्यमिश्राः । मदीयेन भक्तपरिव्ययेन पारलौकिको भर्ताऽन्विष्यते । ( पेक्खन्तु अज्जमिस्सा । ममकेरकेण[१] भत्तपरिव्वएण[२] पारलोइओ भत्ता अण्णेसीअदि । )

**नटी**—आर्य प्रसीद प्रसीद । त्वमेव जन्मान्तरे भविष्यसीति । ( अज्ज[३] पसीद पसीद । तुमं ज्जेव जम्मन्तरे भविस्ससि त्ति । )

**सूत्रधारः**—अयमुपवासः केन तवोपदिष्टः । ( अअं उववासो केण दे उवदिट्ठो । )

**नटी**—आर्यस्यैव प्रियवयस्येन चूर्णवृद्धेन । ( अज्जस्स[४] ज्जेव पिअवअस्सेन चुण्णवुड्ढेण[५] । )

**सूत्रधारः**—( सकोपम् । ) आः दास्याःपुत्र चूर्णवृद्ध कदा नु खलु त्वां कुपितेन राज्ञा पालकेन नववधूकेशकलापमिव सुगन्धं छेद्यमानं प्रेक्षिष्ये । ( आः दासीएपुत्ता[६] चुण्णवुड्ढा कदा णु क्खु[७] तुमं कुविदेण रण्णा पालएण[८] णववहूकेसकलावं[९] विअ सुअन्धं कप्पिज्जन्तं पेक्खिस्सम् । )

**नटी**—प्रसीदत्वार्यः । नन्वार्यस्यैव पारलौकिकोऽयमुपवासोऽनुष्ठीयते । ( इति पादयोः पतति । ) ( पसीददु[१०] अज्जो[११] । णं अज्जस्स ज्जेव पारलोइओ अअं उपवासो अणुचिठ्ठीअदि ।

**सूत्रधारः**—आर्ये उत्तिष्ठ उत्तिष्ठ । कथय कथयात्रोपवासें केन कार्यम् । ( अज्जे उठ्ठेहि उठ्ठेहि । कधेहि कधेहि एत्थ उववासे[१२] केण[१३] कज्जम् । )

---

वधूकेशहस्तमिव बासितं सुगन्धम् । 'वज्जन्तम' इति पाठे वध्यमानम् । अनेन संहाराङ्के चारुदत्तनिग्रहसूचनम् । अम्हारिसजणजोग्गेण अस्मत्सदृशेन ब्राह्मणेन । अहमप्युपनिमन्त्रयामि । ईदृश्यामुज्जयिन्यां समृद्धायाम् । कोऽर्थः । यदा दुस्थिता भवन्ति ब्राह्मणास्तदा चारणादीनामपि गृहे कुर्वन्ति भोजनम् । भवतु इममुपनिमन्त्रयिष्ये । अद्य मैत्रेय अस्माकं गृहे भोक्तुम् । अग्रणीः। प्रष्ठोऽग्रगामीति यावत् । 'अदिधी भोदु' इत्यपि पाठः । तत्रातिथिः भवत्वित्यर्थः । वावडो व्यापृतः । अहमिदानीं कार्यान्तरव्यासक्तः । दाणिं इदानीम् । संपन्नं मृष्टम् । णीसवतं च । पितॄणां समुत्सृष्टं घृतादिसहिततण्डुलपूर्णपात्रम् । 'निःस्राव' इति यस्य प्रसिद्धिः । 'णीसवत्तं निःसपत्नम् । विपक्षस्यापरस्याभावात्' इति केचित् । अपि च दक्षिणाऽपि ते भविष्यति । एकोऽपिः संभावनायाम्, अपरः समुच्चये । मं माम् । पदे पदे अणुबन्धेदुं अनुरोद्धुम् । प्रस्तावनेत्यामुखसंधिपर्यायः । यदुक्तम् –'सूत्रधारेण सहिताः संलापं यत्र कुर्वते । नटी विदूषको वाऽपि पारिपार्श्वक एव वा ।। आमुखं नाम तस्यैव सैव प्रस्तावना मता ।। '

---

१ मइएण, ममकेरेण. २ परिअएण. ३ अज्जउत्त. ४ अज्जउत्तस्स. ५ जूण० इति सर्वत्र. ६ उत्ता. ७ हु. ८ ०एण बन्धिज्जन्तं (बध्यमानं) सुअन्धं पेक्खि०. ९ हत्थं. १० पसीददु पसी०. ११ अज्जउत्तो. १२ उपवासए, १३ केण केण.

SUTRA—( *Angrily* ). Look, worthy gentlemen, look! At the expense of *my* food, a (good) husband is sought for in the next world!

NATI—Be pleased, sir, be pleased! I have observed the fast that you yourself should be my husband in the next birth.

SUTRA.—By whom was this fast recommended to you?

NATI—By Churnavriddha, your own dear friend.

SUTRA.—(*Angrily*). Ah! You son-of-slave, Churnavriddha! When, indeed, shall I see you being cut up by (the orders of) the enraged king Palaka, just like the scented, braided hair of a new bride!

NATI—May your honour be appeased! This fast, which is to bear fruit in the next world, is with reference to no one but your honour! ( *She falls at his feet* ).

SUTRA.—Lady, get up, pray get up; tell me what is required for this fast.

---

प्रावार: उत्तरीयं यस्ते यस्य । आमन्तणआइं आमन्त्रणकानि । पच्छिदव्वाइं समीहितव्यानि । [ उद्गारेषु सुरभिः गन्धो येषां तैः ] मोदकैरेवाशितस्तृप्तः । मल्लकशतपरिवृतः । मल्लकः पात्रविशेषः पत्रपुटो वा । 'दोना' इति प्रसिद्धो विदूषकपक्षे । चित्रकरपक्षे वर्णिकापात्रं मल्लकः । अभ्यन्तरचतुःशालकद्वारे उपविष्टः । चित्रकर इव छिविअ छिविअ स्पृष्ट्वा स्पृष्ट्वाऽङ्गुल्यग्रैरपनयामि न भक्षयामि । अत्यन्तं तृप्तत्वादित्यर्थः । चित्र-करोऽप्यङ्गुलीसंस्थितलेखनिकया वर्णिकाभाण्डं स्पष्ट्वा स्पृष्ट्वाऽपनयति विक्षिपति।अन्यथा वर्णिका।बिन्दुपातः स्यादिति । नवबद्धवृषभ इव रोमन्थायमानस्तिष्ठामि । 'आपणे नगरचत्वरवृषभ इव' इति पाठान्तरेऽपि व्याख्या । यत्र कुत्रापि चरित्वा गृहपारावत इवावासनिमित्तं शयनार्थमत्रागच्छामि । सिद्धीकिददेवकज्जरस्स निष्पादितदेवकार्यस्य [ देवकार्यं देवतार्चनम् ] । पाठान्तरे तु—षष्ठीव्रतकृतदेवकार्यस्येत्यर्थः । बलिं पूजाम् । यासामिति । [ यासां मम गृहं मद्गृहं तस्य देहल्यः तासां उदुम्बर 'उमरठा' इति ख्यातानाम् । तत्र दत्त इत्यर्थः । बलिः हंसैश्च सारससमूहैश्च । पूर्वं विलुप्तः विलुप्तपूर्वः । तासु एव संप्रति दारिद्र्यात्किंकराभावान्मृजाविरहात् विरूढतृणाङ्कुरासु ] विरूढा उपचितास्तृणाङ्कुरा यासु । कीटमुखास्वादितो बीजाञ्जलिः पतति । [वसन्ततिलका वृत्तम् । 'उक्ता वसन्ततिलका तभजा जगौ गः' इति तल्लक्षणम् ] ।। ९ ।। सुखमित्यादि । दुःखान्यनुभूय सुखं शोभते । न तु सुखमनुभूय दुःखमिति तात्पर्यम् । [ घनान्धकारेषु निबिडतमसि । सुखात्सौख्यमनुभूय । 'ल्यब्लोपे कर्मण्यधिकरणे च' इति पञ्चमी । ] स मृत एव जीवति । शरीरेण धृतः शरीरेण वेष्टितः । चर्मभस्त्रावदित्यर्थः । [ उपमालंकारः । वंशस्थविलं वृत्तम् ] ।।१०।। दारिद्र्यादिति । अल्पसमयदुःखदत्वान्मरण-

**नटी**--अस्मादृशजनयोग्येन ब्राह्मणेनोपनिमन्त्रितेन। (अम्हारिसजणजोग्गेण बम्हणेण उवणिमन्तिदेण।)

**सूत्रधारः**--तेन हि गच्छत्वार्या। अहमप्यस्मादृशजनयोग्यं ब्राह्मणमुपनिमन्त्रयामि। (तेणहि[१] गच्छदु अज्जा। अहं पि अम्हारिसजणजोग्गं बम्हणं उवणिमन्तेमि।)

**नटी**--यदार्य आज्ञापयति। (इति निष्क्रान्ता) (जं [२]अज्जो आणवेदि।)

**सूत्रधारः**--(परिक्रम्य।) आश्चर्यम्। तस्मात्कथं मयैवं सुसमृद्धायामुज्जयिन्यामस्मादृशजनयोग्यो ब्राह्मणोऽन्वेष्टव्यः। (विलोक्य।) एष चारुदत्तस्य मित्रं मैत्रेय इत एवागच्छति। भवतु। प्रक्ष्यामि तावत्। आर्य [अद्य] मैत्रेय अस्माकं गृहेऽशितुमग्रणीर्भवत्वार्यः। (हीमाणहे। ता कधं मए एव्वं[३] सुसमिद्धाए उज्जइणीए अम्हारिसजणजोग्गो बम्हणो अण्णेसिदव्वो। एसो चारुदत्तस्स मित्तं मित्तेओ इदो जेव्व आअच्छदि। भोदु। पुच्छिस्सं[४] दाव। अज्ज मित्तेअ अम्हाणं गेहे असिदुं अग्गणी[५] भोदु अज्जो[६]।)

(नेपथ्ये।)

भो अन्यं ब्राह्मणमुपनिमन्त्रयतु भवान्। व्यापृत इदानीमहम्। (भो अण्ण बम्हणं उवणिमन्तेदु भवं। वावुडो दाणिं अहं।)

**सूत्रधारः**--आर्य संपन्नं भोजनं निःसपत्नं च। अपि च दक्षिणा काऽपि ते भविष्यति। (अज्ज संपण्णं भोअणं[७] णीसवत्तं[८] अ। अवि अ दक्खिणा का वि दे भविस्सदि।)

(पुनर्नेपथ्ये।)

भो यदिदानीं प्रथममेव प्रत्यादिष्टोऽसि तत्क इदानीं ते निर्बन्धः पदे पदे मामनुबन्द्धुम्। (भो जं[९] दाणिं पढमं ज्जेव पच्चादिठ्ठोसि ता को दाणिं दे णिब्बन्धो पदे पदे मं अनुबन्धेदुम्।[१०])

**सूत्रधारः**--प्रत्यादिष्टोऽस्म्येतेन। भवतु। अन्यं ब्राह्मणमुपनिमन्त्रयामि। (पच्चादिठ्ठोम्हि एदिणा। भोदु। अण्णं[९] बम्हणं उवणिमन्तेमि।) (इति निष्क्रान्तः।)

---

मल्पक्लेशम्। बहुसमयव्यापित्वादाकाङ्क्षितापगमाद्दारिद्र्यमनन्तकं दुःखम्॥ ११॥ अलं संतप्तेन। यद्यसद्व्ययेनार्थाः स्वदोषेण नाश्यन्ते तदा संतापः क्रियते। तव तु न तथेति भावः। प्रणयी जनः स्निग्धबान्धवोऽर्थी च। **प्रणयिजने** संक्रामितः अर्थः। येन तस्य तव। **एतदिति**। क्षीणार्थमिति कृत्वाऽस्मद्गृहमतिथयः संत्यजन्ति इति यद् एतन्मां दहति। कालात्यये मदसमयापगमे धनलाभसमयापगमे च [ संशुष्का शोषं प्राप्ता सान्द्रा मदलेखा यस्य तं करिणः कपोलं भ्रमन्तः मधुकरा इव। उपमालंकारः।

---

१ अदो (अतः), ता. २ अज्जउत्तो. ३ ईरिसाए (ईदृश्यां). ४ एणं दाव उवणिभन्तिस्सं (इमं तावदुपनिमन्त्रयिष्ये). ५ अदिधी (अतिथिः). ६ भवं. ७ ओअणं. ८ णीसवणं (निःश्रावकं). ९ जधा. १० अणुसंघिदुं (अनुसंधातुं).

NATI—We must invite a Brahmana befitting (the station of) people like ourselves.

SUTRA.—If that is so, you can go; I too shall (proceed to) invite a Brahmana suitable for people like us.

NATI—As your honour commands. (*Exit*).

SUTRA.—(*Walking about*), Well, well! Now, how am I to find, in this very prosperous city of Ujjayini, a Brahmana befitting persons like us? (*Seeing*). Here is this Maitreya, Charudatta's friend, coming in this very direction. Well, I will ask him first.—Sir Maitreya, kindly be the first to dine in our house to-day

( *Behind the Scenes* )

Sir, you should invite ( some ) other Brahmana. I am engaged at present.

SUTRA.—Sir, the food is rich, and there is to be no rival. Moreover, there will be some *Dakshina* ( money gift ) too, for you.

( *Again behind the Scenes* ),

Sir, I have already refused ( your invitation ); why this persistence on your part now to importune me again and again?

SUTRA.—I am given a refusal by him. Well, I shall invite ( some ) other Brahmana. ( *Exit* ).

---

वसन्ततिलका वृत्तम् ] ॥ १२ ॥ दासीपुत्रा अर्थरूपप्रातराशाः । वरटा 'वीरणी' इति ख्याता । ततस्त्रस्ताः । अरण्ये गोपालपुत्रका इव यत्र यत्र न खाद्यन्त उपभुज्यन्ते तत्र तत्र यान्ति । सत्यमिति । विभवनाशकृता मम चिन्ता नास्ति । कथमित्यत आह— भाग्यक्रमेण लब्धव्यक्रमेण धनानि भवन्ति । तर्हि चिन्ता कुत इत्यत आह–एतत्तु मां दहति यन्नष्टधनाश्रयस्य मम सौहृदादपि मैत्रीतोऽपि जनः शिथिलीभवन्ति । अर्थशून्येन समं प्रयोजनाभावान्मैत्रीमपि न केऽपि कुर्वते । [ काव्यलिङ्गमलंकारः । वसन्ततिलका वृत्तम् ] ॥१३॥ दारिद्र्यादिति । [ नरः दारिद्र्यात् ] लज्जां गच्छति । आकाङ्क्षितासामर्थ्यात् । यदा लज्जां गतः [ लज्जापहृत इत्यर्थः ] तदा तेजसः प्रभ्रष्टो भवति यावत्तावत्कारणात् । तेजःशून्यः परिभूयते भयाभावात् । परिभवान्निर्वेदं गच्छति मानम्लानेः । ततः शुचमेति वृथा जीवनमिति । ततस्त्यज्यते बुद्ध्या । निर्बुद्धिः क्षयं गच्छति । तदुक्तम्––'बुद्धिनाशात्प्रणश्यति' इति । अत एव सर्वासामापदां स्थानमित्युपसंहरति । [ कारणमालालंकारः । 'यथोत्तरं चेत्पूर्वस्य पूर्वस्यार्थस्य हेतुता । तदा कारणमाला स्यात्' इति तल्लक्षणम् । शार्दूलविक्रीडितं वृत्तम् ] ॥१४॥ कल्लवर्त्तः प्रातराशः । एतद्रूपत्वे चार्थस्य तावद्रूपद्रव्यत्वाज्जनान्तरानवगाहितत्वाच्च तद्विस्मृत्य धर्मचित्ताः साधवो भवन्तीत्याशयः । निवास इति । चिन्ताया निवासः कथं मम निर्वाहः स्यादित्येवंरूपायाः । परस्य परिभव इति षष्ठीसमासः । कर्मधारयो

इत्यामुखम् ।

(प्रविश्य प्रावारहस्तः । )

**मैत्रेयः**—('अण्णं बम्हणं' इति पूर्वोक्तं पठित्वा । ) अथ वा मयाऽपि मैत्रेयेण परस्यामन्त्रणकानि प्रेक्षितव्यानि । हा अवस्थे तुलयसि । यो नामाहं तत्रभवतश्चारुदत्तस्य ऋद्धयाऽहोरात्रं प्रयत्नसिद्धैरुद्गारसुरभिगन्धिभिर्मोदकैरेवाशितोऽभ्यन्तरचतुःशालकद्वार उपविष्टो मल्लकशतपरिवृतश्चित्रकर इवाङ्गुलीभिः स्पृष्ट्वा स्पृष्ट्वाऽपनयामि नगरचत्वरवृषभ इव रोमन्थायमानस्तिष्ठामि स इदानीमहं तस्य दरिद्रतया यत्र तत्र चरित्वा गृहपारावत इवावासनिमित्तमत्रागच्छामि । एष चार्यचारुदत्तस्य प्रियवयस्येन चूर्णवृद्धेन जातीकुसुमवासितः प्रावारकोऽनुप्रेषितः सिद्धीकृतदेवकार्यस्यार्यचारुदत्तस्योपनेतव्य इति । तद्यावदार्यचारुदत्तं पश्यामि । (परिक्रम्यावलोक्य च । ) एष आर्य चारुदत्तः सिद्धीकृतदेवकार्यो गृहदेवतानां बलिं हरन्नित एवागच्छति । (अध वा मए वि मित्तेएण परस्स आमन्तणआइं पच्छिदव्वाइं[१] । हा अवत्थे तुलीअसि । जो णाम[२] अहं तत्तभवदो चारुदत्तस्य रिद्धीए अहोरत्तं पअतणसिद्धेहिं उग्गारसुरहिगन्धेहिं मोदकेहिं ज्जेव असिदो अब्भन्तरचदुस्सालअदुआए[३] उवविट्टो मल्लकसदपरिवुदो[४] चित्तअरो विअ अङ्गुलीहिं[५] छिविअ छिविअ अवणेमि णअरचत्तरवुसहो विअ रोमन्थाअमाणो चिट्ठामि सो दाणिं अहं तस्स दलिद्ददाए जहिं[६] तहिं चरिअ गेहपारावदो विअ आवासणिमित्तं इध आअच्छामि । एसो अ अज्जचारुदत्तस्स पिअवअस्सेण चुण्णवुड्ढेण जादीकुसुमवासिदो [७]पावारओ अनुप्पेसिदो सिद्धीकिददेवकज्जस्स अज्जचारुदत्तस्स उवणेदव्वो त्ति । ता जाव अज्जचारुदत्तं पेक्खामि । एसो अज्जचारुदत्तो सिद्धीकिददेवकज्जो गिहदेवदाणं बलिं हरेन्तो[९] इदो ज्जेव आअच्छदि ।)

(ततः प्रविशति यथानिर्दिष्टश्चारुदत्तो रदनिका च । )

**चारुदत्तः**—(ऊर्ध्वमवलोक्य सनिर्वेदं निःश्वस्य । )

**यासां बलिः सपदि मद्गृहदेहलीनां**
**हंसैश्च सारसगणैश्च विलुप्तपूर्वः ।**
**तास्वेव संप्रति विरूढतृणाङ्कुरासु**
**बीजाञ्जलिः पतति कीटमुखावलीढः ॥ ९ ॥**

(इति मन्दं मन्दं परिक्रम्योपविशति । )

---

१. भक्खिदव्वाई (भक्षितव्यानि). २. दाणिं. ३. चतुःसाल. ४. गल्लक; उणो उणो चेडजणदिण्णं सव्वोवक्करजुत्तं णिज्जिदसुवण्णवण्णाणेअपत्तघडिदं तम्बोलं चव्विज्जन्तो (पुनः पुनश्चेटजनदत्तं सर्वोपस्करयुक्तं निर्जितसुवर्णवर्णानेकपत्रघटितं ताम्बूलं चर्वयन्). ५. अग्गङ्गुलीहिं. ६. तहिं तहिं. ७. जूण्ण०. ८. पावरओ. ९ करेन्तो (कुर्वन्.)

END OF THE PROLOGUE.

( *Entering with a cloak in his hand* ).

MAITREYA—( *Having repeated—'Sir, you should invite' &c., uttered before* ). Or I, too, Maitreya, have to look for invitations from others! Ah! Fortune, you do indeed make light of a person! I, who, indeed, when my friend Charudatta was prosperous, used to feed, day and night, upon the sweetmeats, emitting savoury smells at the effusion of breath, and prepared with great care, and who, sitting at the entrance of his interior quadrangle, surrounded by hundreds of dishes, used repeatedly to touch them with my fingers and put them aside ( when satiated ), just like a painter surrounded by hundreds of colour pots ( touching each with his fingers and removing it after use ), and who used to remain, ruminating like a bull in a ( public ) square of the city;—I, the very same man, now take my food anywhere at random, owing to his being reduced to poverty; and come here like a domestic pigeon merely to rest ( at night ). Churnavriddha, who is a dear friend of our noble Charudatta, has sent by me this cloak scented with jasmine-flowers, asking that it should be presented to the noble Charudatta after he has finished his ( daily ) worship of the gods. Well, then, I will first see Charudatta. ( *Walking about and observing* ). Here comes Charudatta in this very direction, carrying the *Bali* ( offering ) to the household deities after having finished his worship of the gods.

( *Then enter* Charudatta *as described, and* Radanika ).

CHARUDATTA—( *Looking upwards and sighing dejectedly* ).

On the grounds near the thresholds of my house, the ( ample ) offering ( of food ) made whereon was formerly eagerly eaten by swans and flocks of doves,—on those same grounds now overgrown with shoots of grass, ( an offering consisting of ) a handful of corn falls to be devoured by insects' mouths. (9)

( *With these words he walks about slowly and slowly, and sits down* ).

---

वा । एतच्चाविश्वसनीयतया निर्धनानां ज्ञेयम् । जुगुप्सा मित्राणामिति । प्रत्युपकारासमर्थत्वात् । स्वजनानां बन्धूनाम् । जनानामन्येषामुदासीनानाम् । विद्वेषस्य करणं कृतिः [ साधनं वा ] । कर्तरि करणे वा ल्युट् । भवति चेति चकारो हेतौ । वनगमने कलत्रपरिभवो हेतुः । [ मालारूपकम् । शिखरिणी वृत्तम् । 'रसै रुद्रैश्छिन्ना यमनसभला गः शिखरिणी' इति लक्षणम् ] ॥ १५ ॥ न [ प्रसीदन्ति ] फलं दर्शयन्ति । नित्योऽयं

**विदूषकः**--एष आर्यचारुदत्तः। तद्यावत्सांप्रतमुपसर्पामि। (उपसृत्य।) स्वति भवते। वर्धतां भवान्। (एसो अज्जचारुदत्तो। ता जाव संपदं उवसप्पामि[1]। सोत्थि भवदे। वड्ढदु भवं।

**चारुदत्तः**--अये सर्वकालमित्रं[2] मैत्रेयः प्राप्त। सखे स्वागतम्। आस्यताम्।

**विदूषकः**--यद्भवानाज्ञापयति। (उपविश्य।) भो वयस्य एष ते प्रियवयस्येन चूर्णवृद्धेन जातीकुसुमवासितः प्रावारकोऽनुप्रेषितः सिद्धीकृतदेवकार्यस्यार्यचारुदत्तस्य त्वयोपनेतव्य इति। (जं भवं आणवेदि। भो वअस्स एसो दे पिअवअस्सेण चुण्णवुड्ढेण जादीकुसुमवासिदो पावारओ अणुप्पेसिदो सिद्धीकिददेवकज्जस्स अज्जचारुदत्तस्स[3] तुए उवणेदव्वो त्ति।) (समर्पयति।)

**चारुदत्तः**--(गृहीत्वा सचिन्तः स्थितः।)

**विदूषकः**--भोः किमिदं चिन्त्यते। (भो किं इदं चिन्तीअदि।)

**चारुदत्तः**--वयस्य।

**सुखं हि दुःखान्यनुभूय शोभते घनान्धकारेष्विव दीपदर्शनम्।**
**सुखात्तु यो याति नरो दरिद्रतां धृतः[4] शरीरेण मृतः स जीवति॥ १०॥**

**विदूषकः**--भो वयस्य मरणाद्दारिद्र्याद्वा कतरत्ते रोचते। (भो वअस्स मरणादो दालिद्दादो वा कदरं दे रोअदि।)

**चारुदत्तः**--वयस्य।

**दारिद्र्यान्मरणाद्वा मरणं मम रोचते न दारिद्र्यम्।**
**अल्पक्लेशं मरणं दारिद्र्यमनन्तकं दुःखम्॥ ११॥**

**विदूषकः**--भो वयस्य अलं संतप्तेन। प्रणयिजनसंक्रामितविभवस्य सुरजनपीतशेषस्य प्रतिपच्चन्द्रस्येव परिक्षयोऽपि तेऽधिकतरं रमणीयः। (भो वअस्स अलं संतप्पिदेण[5]। पणइजणसंकामिदविहवस्स सुरजणपीदसेसस्स पडिवच्चन्दस्स विअ परिक्खओ वि दे अहिअदरं रमणीओ।)

**चारुदत्तः**--वयस्य। न ममार्थान्प्रति दैन्यम्। पश्य।

**एतत्तु मां दहति यद्गृहमस्मदीयं**
**क्षीणार्थमित्यतिथयः परिवर्जयन्ति।**
**संशुष्कसान्द्रमदलेखमिव भ्रमन्तः**
**कालात्यये मधुकराः करिणः कपोलम्॥ १२॥**

---

विधिः। अकरणे प्रत्यवायात्। तपसेति। [तपसा व्रताद्याचरणेन। बलिकर्मभिश्च पूजिताः देवताः शमिनां शमवतां फलाप्राप्तौ अकुप्यतामित्यर्थः। नित्यं तुष्यन्ति।

---

१ पविसामि. २ सार्वकाल. ३ अज्जस्स. ४ मृतः शरीरेण धृतः. ५ संदाविदेण.

VIDUSHAKA—Here is Charudatta. Well, then, I shal now approach him. ( *Going up to him* ). My greetings to you May you ( ever ) prosper !

CHAR.—Ah ! Here comes Maitreya, our friend at all times ( good or bad ). Friend, you are welcome ; please be seated.

VID.—As you command. ( *Sitting* ). Friend, your dear friend Churnavriddaa has sent by me this cloak, scented with the blossoms of jasmine, asking me to present it to you when you had finished your worship of the deities. ( *He hands it over* ).

CHAR.—( *Takes it and remains absorbed in thought* ).

VID.—Friend, what is this that you are thinking about ?

CHAR.—Friend,

Verily happiness appears splendid ( tastes pleasanter ) after a person has experienced troubles, like the sight of a lamp when there has been pitchy darkness. But, when a man is reduced to penury after he has enjoyed luxury, he lives a dead man, existing only by keeping up his body. (10)

VID.—O friend, out of death or poverty, which do you prefer ?

CHAR.—Friend,

Out of ( these two, *viz.* ) poverty and death, I like death, but not poverty. ( For ) death causes short-lived pain, while poverty is ( *i. e.* entails ) unending misery. (11)

VID.—Friend, you need not worry yourself. Even the reduced condition of you, who have bestowed your wealth on the needy, looks more charming, like that of the moon of the first day ( of the lunar month ), that remains after it has been drunk up by the gods.

CHAR.—Friend, my misery is not due to (my loss of) money. Observe :—

This alone burns ( pains ) me that guests avoid ( coming to ) my house because it has lost its riches, just as the bees, flying off ( to another place ), desert, when the season ( of ichor-flow ) has passed away, the elephant's cheek, the thick line of rut whereon has totally dried up. (12)

---

विचारितैः वितर्कैः किम् । न कोऽपि लाभ इत्यर्थः । ] तुष्यन्ति परलोकमुत्कृष्टं प्रयच्छन्ति । यतः श्राद्धकृदतिथिप्रियो गृहस्थोऽपि मुच्यत इति भावः ॥ १६ ॥

**विदूषकः**—भो वयस्य एते खलु दास्याः पुत्रा अर्थकल्यवर्ता वरटाभीता इव गोपालदारका अरण्ये यत्र यत्र न खाद्यन्ते तत्र तत्र गच्छन्ति। ( भो वअस्स एदे क्खु दासीएपुत्ता अत्थकल्लवत्ता वरडाभीदा विअ गोवालदारआ अरण्णे जहिं जहिं ण खज्जन्ति तहिं तहिं गच्छन्ति ।)

**चारुदत्तः**—वयस्य ।

**सत्यं न मे विभवनाशकृताऽस्ति चिन्ता**
**भाग्यक्रमेण हि धनानि भवन्ति यान्ति ।**
**एतत्तु मां दहति नष्टधनाश्रयस्य**
**यत्सौहृदादपि जनाः शिथिलीभवन्ति ॥ १३ ॥**

अपि च

**दारिद्र्याद्ध्रियमेति ह्रीपरिगतः[1] प्रभ्रश्यते तेजसो**
**निस्तेजाः परिभूयते परिभवान्निर्वेदमापद्यते ।**
**निर्विण्णः शुचमेति शोकविहतो[2] बुद्ध्या परित्यज्यते[3]**
**निर्बुद्धिः क्षयमेत्यहो निधनता सर्वापदामास्पदम् ॥ १४ ॥**

**विदूषकः**—भो वयस्य तमेवार्थकल्यवर्तं स्मृत्वाऽलं संतापितेन। ( भो वअस्स तं ज्जेव अत्थकल्लवत्तअं सुमरिअ[4] अलं संतप्पिदेण ।)

**चारुदत्तः**—वयस्य दारिद्र्यं हि पुरुषस्य

**निवासश्चिन्तायाः परपरिभवो वैरमपरं**
**जुगुप्सा मित्राणां स्वजनजनविद्वेषकरणम् ।**
**वनं गन्तुं बुद्धिर्भवति च कलत्रात्परिभवो**
**हृदिस्थः शोकाग्निर्न च दहति संतापयति च ॥ १५ ॥**

तद्वयस्य कृतो मया गृहदेवताभ्यो बलिः। गच्छ त्वमपि चतुष्पथे मातृभ्यो बलिमुपहर।

**विदूषकः**—न गमिष्यामि। ( ण गमिस्सं। )

**चारुदत्तः**—किमर्थम् ।

**विदूषकः**—यत एवं पूज्यमाना अपि देवता न ते प्रसीदन्ति तत्को गुणो देवेष्वर्चितेषु। ( जदो एव्वं पूइज्जन्ता वि देवदा ण दे पसीदन्ति[5] ता को गुणो देवेसु अच्चिदेसु। )

**चारुदत्तः**—वयस्य मा मैवम् । गृहस्थस्य नित्योऽयं विधिः।

**तपसा मनसा वाग्भिः[6] पूजिता बलिकर्मभिः ।**
**तुष्यन्ति शमिनां नित्यं देवताः किं विचारितैः ॥ १६ ॥**

---

१ तत्परि०. २ पिहितः. ३ परिभ्रश्यते. ४ सुमरिअ सुमरिअ. ५ पसादं देन्ति. ६ वाऽपि.

VID.—Friend, these rascally ( *lit.* slave-born ) riches, as insignificant as a morning meal, visit those places ( only ) where they are not consumed, just like the cow-boys in a forest who, afraid of wasps, go wherever they would not be bitten by them.

CHAR.—Friend,

I am not really feeling any anxiety on account of the loss of my fortune; for riches come and go, following the course of one's luck. But this burns me ( as it were ), that people become remiss even in their affection towards a person who has lost his support of wealth. (13)

Moreover—

From penury a person passes to ( feels ) shame; being overcome by shame, he loses his spirit; devoid of spirit he is slighted; being slighted, he feels dejected; full of dejection, he comes to be sorry; being smitten with sorrow, he is left by his reason; and destitute of reason, he perishes. Ah! Pennilessness is the abode of all sorts of misfortunes! (14)

VID.—Friend, enough of feeling uneasy by remembering that same wealth which is of as little consequence as a morning meal.

CHAR.—Friend, poverty in the case of a man—

Is the abode of anxiety; it is ( the source of ) the highest insult; it is a different phase of enmity; it breeds disgust in his friends; and it is the exciter of the hatred of his kinsmen and of the general public. He feels an inclination to retire to the forest; he suffers insults even from his own wife. It is the fire of grief that dwells in his heart; it does not ( actually ) burn him, but it heats ( *i. e.*, pains ) him ( continually ). (15)

Well, friend, I have made the offering to the household deities. You, too, go and offer a *Bali* ( oblation ) to the Holy Mothers at the public square.

VID.—I shan't go.

CHAR.—Why not?

VID.—For, even when thus worshipped, the deities do not show their favour to you. Where is then the use of worshipping them?

CHAR.—Nay, friend, say not so. This is the bounden ( *lit.* obligatory ) duty of a house-holder.

Being worshipped by means of ( physical ) penance, a devoted mind, praises, and the offerings of oblations, the deities are always pleased with their tranquil-minded ( devotees ). What is the use of questionings about it? (16)

तद्गच्छ । मातृभ्यो बलिमुपहर ।

**विदूषकः**—भोः न गमिष्यामि । अन्यः कोऽपि प्रयुज्यताम् । मम पुनर्ब्राह्मणस्य सर्वमेव विपरीतं परिणमति । आदर्शगतेव छाया वामतो दक्षिणा दक्षिणतो वामा । अन्यच्चैतस्यां प्रदोषवेलायामिह राजमार्गे गणिका विटाश्चेटा राजवल्लभाश्च पुरुषाः संचरन्ति । तस्मान्मण्डूकलुब्धस्य कालसर्पस्य मूषिक इवाभिमुखापतितो वध्य इदानीं भविष्यामि । त्वमिहोपविष्टः किं करिष्यसि । ( भो ण गमिस्सं । अण्णो को वि पउज्जीअदु । मम उंण बम्हणस्स सव्वं ज्जेव विपरीदं परिणमदि । आदंसगदा विअ छाआ वामादो दक्खिणा दक्खिणादो वामा । अण्णं अ एदाए पदोसवेलाए इध राअमग्गे गणिआ विडा चेडा राअवल्लहा अ पुरिसा संचरन्ति । ता मण्डूअलुद्धस्स कालसप्पस्स मूसिओ विअ अहिमुहावदिदो[1] वज्झो दाणिं भविस्सं । तुमं इध उवविट्ठो किं करिस्ससि । )

**चारुदत्तः**—भवतु । तिष्ठ तावत् । अहं समाधिं निर्वर्तयामि ।

( नेपथ्ये । )

तिष्ठ वसन्तसेने तिष्ठ ।

( ततः प्रविशति विटशकारचेटैरनुगम्यमाना वसन्तसेना । )

**विटः**—वसन्तसेने तिष्ठ तिष्ठ ।

**किं त्वं भयेन परिवर्तितसौकुमार्या**
**नृत्यप्रयोगविशदौ चरणौ क्षिपन्ती ।**
**उद्विग्नचञ्चलकटाक्षविसृष्टदृष्टि-**
**र्व्याधानुसारचकिता हरिणीव यासि ॥ १७ ॥**

---

विपरीतमुपनमति [ अनिष्टं पर्यवस्यतीत्यर्थ । आदर्शगता छायेव । आदर्शस्थ-प्रतिबिम्बे वामो भागो दक्षिणे दृश्यते दक्षिणश्च वाम इति वस्तुगतिः । संचरन्ति । एतेन विटादीनां प्रवेशं सूचयति । 'नासूचितस्य प्रवेशः' इति । **किं त्वमिति** । [ परिवर्तितं त्वरितगमनार्थमन्यथाकृतं परित्यक्तमिति यावत् सौकुमार्यं यया । नृत्यप्रयोगेण] विशदौ संचरणलाघवगुणान्वितौ । पटू इति यावत् । उद्विग्नचञ्चलकटाक्षरूपेण [ यद्वा उद्विग्ना व्याकुला चञ्चलाश्च कटाक्षा अपाङ्ग-दर्शनानि यस्मिन्कर्मणि तथा ] विसृष्टा दृष्टिर्यया सा तथा । अनुसारोऽनुगमनम् । व्याधेन यदनुगमनं तेन त्रस्ता मृगीव । [ किं किमर्थं यासि । उपमा । वसन्ततिलका वृत्तम् ] ॥ १७ ॥ शकारभाषायां चवर्गशिरस्थितोऽन्तस्थो यकारो लेख्यः । 'पूस्पृष्टा तालव्य' इति वचनात् । स च संयोगः प्रयत्नलाघवात्पूर्वस्य गुरुत्वं न करोति । य्चिष्ठ तिष्ठ । **किं यासीत्यादि** । वसन्ततिलकच्छन्दसा श्लोकः । प्रस्खलन्ती । प्रस्खलनं निम्नोन्नतादौ गतिविघटनम् । 'बाला स्याद्वासूः' इत्यमरः । न म्रियसे ।

---

१ मुहावत्थिदो. २ वर्जित.

Go, then, and offer the oblation to the Holy Mothers.

VID.—Sir, I won't go. You may order somebody else. For, in the case of me, a ( poor ) Brahmana, everything turns out in a contrary manner : just like the reflection in a mirror, the left appearing to the right and the right to the left. Moreover, at this time of the night there are walking about, on this royal road, courtesans, their parasites and attendants, and men who are royal favourites. I shall, therefore, just fall a prey ( to them ), if I come face to face with them, like a mouse with a black snake greedy of frogs. And what will you do sitting here ?

CHAR.—All right ; wait awhile. I will go through my holy meditation.

( *Behind the Scenes* ).

Stay, Vasantasena, stay !

( ***Then enter*** Vasantasena, *being followed by* Vita, Sakara *and* Cheta ).

VITA.—Stay, Vasantasena, stay !

Why are you, setting aside (*lit.* having changed) your tenderness ( of limbs ) owing to fear, and plying your feet which are trained by the practice of dancing, running away like a female deer, frightened when being pursued by a hunter, with eyes casting affrighted and tremulous side-glances ? (17)

---

तिष्ठ तावत् । हडक्के हृदयम् । तपस्वि वराकम् । अङ्गारराशिपतितं मांसखण्डमिव कामेन दह्यते ॥ १८ ॥ अज्जुके गणिके । उत्त्रासितेत्यादि । उपजातिच्छन्दसा श्लोकः । उत्त्रासिता गच्छस्यन्तिकान्मम । यद्वा । अत्तिका ज्येष्ठा मे भगिनी । 'अत्तिका भगिनी ज्येष्ठा ' इत्यमरः । संपूर्णपक्षेत्र ग्रीष्ममयूरी । ओवग्गदी अववल्गति । ससंभ्रममागच्छतीत्यर्थः । शामिअभट्टके स्वामिभट्टारकः । वने गतः कुक्कुटशावक इव । गडे इति प्रथमान्तस्यैकारान्तत्वम् । 'गतभृतकृतानां डः' इति डः ॥ १९ ॥ किं यासीति । [ पवनेन लोला दशा यस्य तादृशं रक्तांशुकं वहन्ती । रक्तोत्पलानां प्रकरः । तद्घटितमाल्यमिति यावत् । तद्गतं कुड्मलं ससंभ्रमगमनाद् उत्सृजन्ती पातयन्ती । पक्षे रक्तोत्पलप्रकरवत् कुड्मलान् कुड्मलसदृशप्रस्तरखण्डान् उत्क्षिपन्ती । ] ' टङ्कः पाषाणदारणः ' इत्यमरः । विदारणक्षणे हि निर्मला दीप्तिः प्रसरतीति । कुड्मलं कलिका । मनःशिलगुहेति । महाभारते मनःशिलशब्दोऽपि दृश्यत इति तथा प्रयुक्तः । ' मनःशिला तु कुनटी ' इत्यमरः ।

शकारः--तिष्ठ वसन्तसेनिके तिष्ठ। ( चिश्ट वसन्तशेणिए चिश्ट। )

(किं याशि धावशि पलाअशि पक्खलन्ती
वाशू पशीद ण मलीहिशि[1] चिश्ट दाव।
कामेण दज्जदि हु मे हडके तवश्शी
अङ्गाललाशिपडिदे विअ मंशखण्डे॥)

किं यासि धावसि पलायसे प्रस्खलन्ती
वासु प्रसीद न मरिष्यसि तिष्ठ तावत्।
कामेन दह्यते खलु मे हृदयं तपस्वि
अङ्गारराशिपतितमिव मांसखण्डम्॥ १८॥

चेटः--आर्यके तिष्ठ तिष्ठ। ( अज्जुए[2] चिट्ठ चिट्ठ। )

(उत्ताशिता गच्छशि अन्तिका[3] मे शंपुण्णपुच्छा विअ गिम्हमोरी।
ओवग्गदी शामिअभश्टके मे वणे गडे कुक्कडशावके[4] व्व॥)

उत्त्रासिता गच्छस्यन्तिकान्मम संपूर्णपक्षेव ग्रीष्ममयूरी।
अववल्गति स्वामिभट्टारको मम वने गतः कुक्कुटशावक इव॥ १९॥

विटः—वसन्तसेने तिष्ठ तिष्ठ।

किं यासि बालकदलीव विकम्पमाना
रक्तांशुकं पवनलोलदशं वहन्ती
रक्तोत्पलप्रकरकुड्मलमुत्सृजन्ती[5]
टङ्कैर्मनःशिलगुहेव विदार्यमाणा॥ २०॥

---

[ वसन्ततिलका वृत्तम् ]॥ २०॥ मम मदनमित्यादि। मालिनीछन्दसा श्लोकः। मम मदनमनङ्गं मन्मथं वर्धयन्ती निशि च शयनके मम निद्रामाक्षिपन्ती। प्रसरसि प्रगच्छसि। 'प्रस्वरसि दात्यूहवद्विरौषि' इति केचित्। भयभीतेति। भयशब्दोऽयमपार्थकः। मदनमनङ्गमित्यादि पुनरुक्तम्। रावणस्येव कुन्तीति हतोपमम्। तथा चोक्तम्–'आगमलिङ्गविहीनं देशकलान्यायविपरीतम्। व्यर्थैकार्थमपार्थं भवति हि वचनं शकारस्य॥' इति॥ २१॥ किं त्वमिति। विशेषयन्ती अतिशयाना। [ पतगेन्द्रः गरुडस्तस्माद्भयं तेन पीडिता त्रस्ता ] व्याली सर्पी [ इव यासि। अनेन तस्याः शीघ्रगतित्वं वक्रगमनं च सूचितम्। ]प्रविसृतः प्रचलितः [ वातं निरुन्ध्यां गृह्णीयाम्। न रुन्ध्यामिति पाठे ] वातं न रुणध्मि अपि तु रुणध्म्येव। नकारः काकौ। हे वरगात्रि त्वन्निग्रहे मम प्रयत्नः न। अनायासेनैव त्वां निगृह्णीयामित्यर्थः। यद्वा एवं सत्यपि त्वन्निग्रहे बलात्कारेण ग्रहणे मम प्रयत्नः न। अपि तु अनुनये एव।

---

१ मलीहशि, मलिश्शसि. २ अज्जए, अज्जुके. ३ अत्तिका. ४ कुक्कुर. ५कुण्डलं.

SAKARA.—Stay, Vasantasena stay!

Why do you go, run and scamper and stumble? Be pleassed, O girl! you won't die. Stay awhile. Indeed, my poor heart is being burnt by passion, just like a piece of flesh fallen on a heap of burning charcoal. (18)

CHETA.—Stay, lady, stay!

You are running away from me in terror, like a pea-hen in the hot season with her tail fully grown ( and outstreched ). Here is my lord and master bounding ( after you ) like a young cock in the forest. (19)

VITA.—Stay, Vasantasena, stay!

Why do you run away, quaking like a young plantain tree, trailing ( after you ) your red silken garment with its ends fluttering in the breeze, and dropping off the numerous buds of red lotuses ( in your hair ), like a cave of red arsenic, being excavated ( shattered ) with a chisel? (20)

---

उपमालंकारः। वसन्ततिलका वृत्तम् ] ॥ २२ ॥ 'भावो विद्वान्' इत्यमरः। **एषा नाणकेत्यादि** । शार्दूलविक्रीडितच्छन्दसा श्लोकः । एषा । नाणं शिवाङ्कटङ्कादिवित्तं तस्य मोषणशीलः कामो यस्य तस्य कशिका चर्मकाष्ठिका । चौराणां किंचित्तया चोपकरणं भवति । तदत्र कशोक्ता । कशा चाश्वताडनी । चर्मसडि कोच्यते। मच्छाशिका मत्स्यभक्षिका। 'मच्छं शुष्कमांसम्' इत्येके। लाशिका नर्तकी। णिण्णाशा निम्ननासा। कुलणाशिका कुलं वंशस्तन्नाशयति पातित्यजननात्। णीशाशा। [निःस्वाशा] इति पाठे निःस्वानामाशा। कुलनाशिकेत्यर्थः। न वशिका [अवशिका] अनायत्ता दानेनापि कस्याप्यायत्ता न भवति। कामस्य मञ्जूषिका पात्रविशेषः। कन्दर्पभाजनमिव। वर्तुलीभूतः काम इवेत्यर्थः। एषा वेशवधूः। 'वेशो वेश्याजनाश्रयः' इत्यमरः। सुवेशनिलया शोभनानां वेशानामलंकाराणां निलय आश्रयो यस्यां सा। वेशाङ्गना। वेशिका। वेशोऽस्यास्तीति वेशिका। एतान्यस्या दश नामकानि मया कृतानि अद्यापि मां नेच्छति। यदि देवताया अष्टौ दश द्वादश नामानि पठ्यन्ते तदा सा प्रसन्ना भवति। इयं त्वेतावताऽपि न प्रसन्नेति भावः। अत्र पूर्वार्धोत्तरार्धयोः एषैषेति पुनरुक्तं न्यूनमधिकं वा कृतम्। दशेति व्यर्थम् ॥ २३ ॥ **प्रसरसीत्यादि**। प्रचलिताभ्यां कुण्डलाभ्यां घृष्टं गण्डयोः पार्श्वं यस्याः सा। अत एव विटनखपरिमृष्टवीणातुल्या। मनोहरत्वाच्छब्दवत्त्वाद्वा वीणातुल्यत्वम्। विटसदृशी कुण्डली। [ जलधरस्य गर्जितं तेन भीता सारसी इव। मालोपमालंकारः। पुष्पिताग्रा वृत्तम् ] ॥ २४ ॥ **झणज्झणायेति**। वसन्ततिलकं छन्दः। झाणज्झणन्तेत्यव्यक्तानुकरणम्। अव्यक्तशब्दविशेषयुक्तबहुभूषणशब्देन मिश्रं यथा स्यादेवम्। किं द्रौपदीव

शकारः—तिष्ठ वसन्तसेने तिष्ठ। ( चिश्ट वशन्तशेणिए चिश्ट। )

(मम मअणमणङ्गं मम्मथं[1] वड्ढअन्ती
णिशि अ शअणके[2] मे णिद्दअं पक्खिवन्ती[3]।
पशलशि भअभीदा पक्खलन्ती खलन्ती
मम वशमणुजादा लावणश्शेव कुन्ती॥ )

मम मदनमनङ्गं मन्मथं वर्धयन्ती
निशि च शयनके मम निद्रां प्रक्षिपन्ती।
प्रसरसि भयभीता प्रस्खलन्ती स्खलन्ती
मम वशमनुयाता रावणस्येव कुन्ती॥ २१॥

विटः—वसन्तसेने

किं त्वं पदैर्मम पदानि विशेषयन्ती
व्यालीव यासि पतगेन्द्रभयाभिभूता।
वेगादहं प्रविसृतः पवनं निरुन्ध्यां[4]
त्वन्निग्रहे तु वरगात्रि न मे प्रयत्नः॥ २२॥

शकारः—भाव भाव

एषा नाणकमोषिकामकशिका मत्स्याशिका लासिका
निर्नासा कुलनाशिका अवशिका कामस्य मञ्जूषिका।
एषा वेशवधूः सुवेशनिलया वेशाङ्गना वेशिका
एतान्यस्या दश नामकानि मया कृतान्यद्यापि मां नेच्छति॥ २३॥

( भावे भावे
एशा णाणकमूशिकामकशिका मच्छाशिका लाशिका
णिण्णाशा कुलणाशिका अवशिका कामस्स[5] मञ्जूशिका।
एशा वेशबहू शुवेशणिलआ वेशङ्गणा वेशिआ
एशे शे दश णामके मइ कले अज्जावि मं णेच्छदि॥)

विटः—

प्रसरसि भयविक्लवा किमर्थं प्रचलितकुण्डलघृष्टगण्डपार्श्वा।
विटजननखघट्टितेव[6] वीणा जलधरगर्जितभीतसारसीव॥ २४॥

---

पलायसे रामभीता। एष हरामि झटिति यथा हनुमान्विश्वावसोर्भगिनीमिव तां सुभद्राम्। विश्वावसोः सिद्धराजविशेषस्य न भगिनी सुभद्रा किं तर्हि कृष्णस्य। यथा इवेति पुनरुक्तम्॥ २५॥ रमयेत्यादि। प्रतिपादं चतुर्दशमात्रत्वान्मात्रासमकं छन्दः।

---

१ बम्महं. २ शअणए. ३ आक्खि०. ४ न रुन्ध्यां (टी०). ५ कामाह. ६ परिघाटितेव, नखखण्डितेव.

SAKARA—Stay, Vasantasena, stay!

You inflame my love, my passion, my lust, and forcibly deprive me of my sleep when lying on my bed at night; and you are running away stumbling and falling, being agitated by fear, now that you have come into my power, like Kunti into that of Ravana. (21)

VITA—O Vasantasena,

Why do you, surpassing my steps (*i.e.*, speed) with your own, run away like a female snake overcome with the terror of the lord of birds (the eagle)? Starting off with speed, I can overtake wind itself; but to overtake you, O fair-limbed one, I need make no (special) effort (or, my effort is not for seizing you by force). (22)

SAKARA—Friend, friend!

She is an inciter of (*lit.* a whip to) the passion (even) of stealers of coins (*i. e*, thieves); she is a fish-eater; a figurante; a flat-nosed maiden; a destroyer of families (of her lovers); an untameable (shrew); a casket of love; a courtesan; an inhabitant of the fine harlot's quarter (or, a repository of fine ornaments); a prostitute; and a concubine.—I have given her (praised her by) these ten names; and still she desires (loves) me not. (23)

VITA—

Why do you run away, overcome with fear, while the sides of your cheeks are rubbed against by your ear-rings tossing to and fro, (appearing) like a lute hard-struck with their nails by *vitas*, or like a female crane frightened by the rumbling of clouds? (24)

---

लामेहि अ रमय च । चकारो भिन्नक्रमः । राजवल्लभं चेत्यर्थः । तो खाहिशि ततः खादिष्यसि मत्स्यमांसकम् । 'तो इत्योकारो लघुश्छन्दोनुरोधात्' इत्याहुः । 'एओकारौ हलन्तस्थौ शुद्धौ वाऽप्यपदान्वितौ । दीर्घात्परौ लघू स्यातां छन्दोविचितिभाषया ॥' इत्युक्तम् । एदेहिं मच्छमंशकेहिं एताभ्यां मत्स्यमांसाभ्यां हेतुभ्याम् । 'मश्कलेहिं' इति पाठे मत्स्यशुष्कमांसाभ्यामित्यर्थः । ककारः स्वार्थे । शुणआ श्वानः । मृतकं न सेवन्ते । नकारः शिरश्चालने । न सेवन्ते इति न अपि तु सेवन्त एवेत्यर्थः ॥२६॥ किं [त्वमिति । ताराभिः मुक्ताभिः विचित्रश्चासौ रुचिरश्च तम् ।] वक्त्रेण लक्षिता नगरदेवतावत्प्रयासि । कीदृशेन वक्त्रेण । [निर्मथितः अत एव चूर्णः मनःशिलस्तेन लक्षणया] निर्मथितचूर्णमनःशिलातुल्येन [यद्वा निर्मथिता पराभूता चूर्णमनःशिला येन तेन । नगरदैवतेन तुल्यं नगरदैवतवत् । द्रुतं प्रयासि । तद्धितोपमा । वसन्त-

---

* Or, of the God of Love that robs (men of their) coins (money).

शकारः--

झणज्झणायमानबहुभूषणशब्दमिश्रं
किं द्रौपदीव पलायसे रामभीता।
एष हरामि सहसेति यथा हनूमा-
न्विश्वावसोर्भगिनीमिव तां सुभद्राम् ॥ २५॥

(झाणज्झणन्तबहुभूशणशद्दमिश्शं[1] किं दोव्वदी[2] विअ पलाअशि लामभीदा।
एशे हूलामि शहशत्ति जधा हणूमे विश्शावशुश्श बहिणिं[3] विअ तं शुभद्दं ॥)

चेट :—

रमय च राजवल्लभं ततः खादिष्यसि मत्स्यमांसकम्।
एताभ्यां मत्स्यमांसाभ्यां श्वानो मृतकं न सेवन्ते ॥ २६॥

(लामेहि अ लाअवल्लहं तो[4] खाहिशि मच्छमंशकम्[5]।
एदेहिं मच्छमंशकेहिं[6] शुणआ मडअं[7] ण शेवन्ति ॥)

विटः--भवति वसन्तसेने

किं त्वं कटीतटनिवेशितमुद्वहन्ती
ताराविचित्ररुचिरं रशनाकलापम्।
वक्त्रेण निर्मथितचूर्णमनःशिलेन
त्रस्ता[8] द्रुतं नगरदैवतवत्प्रयासि ॥ २७॥

शकारः--

अस्माभिश्चण्डमभिसार्यमाणा वने शृगालीव कुक्कुरैः।
पलायसे शीघ्रं त्वरितं सवेगं सवृन्तं मम हृदयं हरन्ती ॥२८॥

(अम्हेहि चण्डं अहिशालिअन्ती वणे शिआली विअ कुक्कुलेहिं।
पलाशि शिग्घं तुलिदं शवेग्गं शवेण्टणं[9] मे हलअं हलन्ती ॥

वसन्तसेना—पल्लवक पल्लवक परभृतिके परभृतिके। (पल्लवआ पल्लवआ परहुदिए परहुदिए।)

शकारः—(सभयम्।) भाव भाव मनुष्या मनुष्याः। (भावे भावे मणुश्शे मणुश्शे।)

विटः---न भेतव्यं न भेतव्यम्।

वसन्तसेना---माधविके माधविके। (माहविए माहविए।)

विटः--(सहासम्।) मूर्ख परिजनोऽन्विष्यते।

---

१ झणज्झ०. २ दोवदी. ३ वहिणिं. ४ ता. ५ मंशमच्छकम्. ६ मंशमच्छकेहिं. ७ मलअं. ८ त्रस्तादभुतं. ९ शवेठणं.

SAKARA—

Mixing up the sounds made by your numerous jingling ornaments, why do you fly away like Draupadi afraid of Rama? Here I (shall) carry you off suddenly, as Hanumat did that (well-known) Subhadra, the sister of Visvavasu. (25)

CHETA—

Admit to your caresses this royal favourite (Sakara,) and then you will get fish and flesh to eat. By getting these two, *viz*, fish and flesh, (even) dogs feed not on dead bodies. (26)

VITA—Madam, Vasantasena,

Why do you, wearing the girdle-zone fastened round your sloping hips and shining with divers lustre like (that of) stars and with a face excelling (in ruddiness of complexion) powdered red arsenic, run away quickly in fright, looking like the guardian deity of the city? (27)

SAKARA—

Being hard pursued by us, like a female jackal by dogs in the forest, you are running away quickly, and with speed, hastily taking away (with you) my heart together with its stem (*i. e.* support). (28)

VASANTASENA—Pallavaka, Pallavaka! Parabhritika, Parabhritika!

SAKARA—(*With fear*). Friend, friend! Men, men!

VITA—Fear not, fear not.

VAS.—Madhavika, Madhavika!

VITA—(*With a laugh*). You fool! She is looking for her servants!

---

तिलका वृत्तम्] ॥ २७ ॥ **अस्माभिरिति** । उपेन्द्रवज्रा छन्दः । **अस्माभिश्चण्डं** शीघ्रमभिसार्यमाणा वने शृगालीव कुक्कुरैः । पलायसे शीघ्रं त्वरितं सवेगं शवेण्टणं सवृन्तं समूलबन्धम् । मे हलअं मम हृदयम् । हरन्ती । 'शवेठणं सवेष्टन-मित्यर्थः' इत्येके ॥ २८ ॥ पल्लवकः परभृतिका च वसन्तसेनायाः परिचारकः परि-चारिका च । माधविका अपरा परिचारिका । भावे भावे इति संबोधनम् । **मणुश्शे** मनुष्यः । स्त्रीनामश्रवणेन सगर्वमाह–स्त्रीणां शतं मारयामि । हद्धी हद्धो हा धिक् । हा धिक् । विलप । किमेकदेशविलापेन सकलं वसन्तमासं वा । अत्र पक्षे एको वाशब्दः शकारवचनतया व्यर्थ एव प्रयुक्तः । अनेकार्थत्वान्निपातानामवधारणे वा । सर्वमेव वसन्तमासमित्यर्थः । कः तुमं त्वां परित्रायते । **किं भीमसेन इत्यादि** । इन्द्रवज्राश्लोकः । किं भीमसेनो जमदग्निपुत्रः कुन्तीसुतो वा दशकन्धरो वा । एते चत्वारः । एषोऽहं

**शकारः**—भाव भाव स्त्रियमन्विष्यति। (भावे भावे इत्थिआं अण्णेशदि।)

**विटः**—अथ किम्।

**शकारः**—स्त्रीणां शतं मारयामि। शूरोऽहम्। (इत्थिआणं शदं मालेमि। शूले हग्गे।)

**वसन्तसेना**—(शून्यमवलोक्य।) हा धिक् हा धिक्। कथं परिभ्रष्टः परिजनः। अत्र मयाऽऽत्मा स्वयमेव रक्षितव्यः। (हद्धी हद्धी। कधं परिब्भट्टो[1] परिअणो। एत्थ मए अप्पा सअं ज्जेव रक्खिदव्वो।)

**विटः**—अन्विष्यतामन्विष्यताम्।

**शकारः**—वसन्तसेनिके विलप विलप परभृतिकां वा पल्लवकं वा सर्वं वा वसन्तमासम्। मयाऽभिसार्यमाणां त्वां कः परित्रास्यते। (वसन्तशेणिए विलव विलव परहुदिअं वा पल्लवअं वा शव्वं वा[२] वशन्तमाशं। मए अहिशालिअन्तीं तुमं के पलित्ताइश्शदि।)

**किं भीमसेनो जमदग्निपुत्रः कुन्तीसुतो वा दशकन्धरो वा।**
**एषोऽहं गृहीत्वा केशहस्ते दुःशासनस्यानुकृतिं करोमि॥ २९॥**
(किं भीमशेणे जमदग्गिपुत्ते कुन्तीशुदे वा दशकन्धले[3] वा।
एशे हगे गेह्णिय केशहश्ते[4] दुश्शाशणश्शाणुकिदिं कलेमि॥)

ननु प्रेक्षस्व ननु प्रेक्षस्व। (णं पेक्ख णं पेक्ख।)

**असिः सुतीक्ष्णो वलितं च मस्तकं कल्पये शीर्षमुत मारयामि वा।**
**अलं तवैतेन पलायितेन मुमूर्षुर्यो भवति न स खलु जीवति॥ ३०॥**
(असी शुतिक्खे वलिदे अ मश्तके कप्पेमर्[5] शीशं उद मालएम[6] वा।
अलं तवेदेण पलाइदेण मुमुक्खु जे होदि ण शे क्खु जीअदि॥)

**वसन्तसेना**—आर्य अबला खल्वहम्। (अज्ज अबला क्खु अहम्।)

**विटः**—अत एव ध्रियसे।

**शकारः**—अत एव न मार्यसे। (अदो ज्जेव ण मालीअशि[7]।)

**वसन्तसेना**—(स्वगतम्।) कथमनुनयोऽप्यस्य भयमुत्पादयति। भवतु। एवं तावत् (प्रकाशम्।) आर्य अस्मात्किमप्यलंकरणं तर्क्यते। (कथं अणुणओ वि शे भअं उप्पादेदि। भोदु। एव्वं दाव। अज्ज इमादो किंपि अलंकरणं तक्कीयदि।)

**विटः**—शान्तं[8] पापम्। भवति वसन्तसेने न पुष्पमोषमर्हत्युद्यानलता। तत्कृतमलंकरणैः।

**वसन्तसेना**—तत्किं खल्विदानीम्। (ता किं क्खु दाणिम्।)

---

गृहीत्वा केशहस्ते दुःशासनस्यानुकृतिं करोमि॥ २९॥ णं ननु। पेक्ख प्रेक्षस्व। **असिरिति।** वंशस्थेन्द्रवज्रादिभिर्द्वादशैकादशवर्णैर्विजात्युपजातिः। असि सुतीक्ष्णो वलितो लालितः। मस्तकम्। कल्पये छिनद्मि। तव शीघ्रं मारयामि वा॥ ३०॥

---

१ परिअणो वि मे परि०. २ एवत्र. ३ कन्धलो. ४ हत्थे. ५ कप्पेध. ६ मालएध. ७ मालीहशि. ८ शान्तम्; शान्तं पापं शान्तं पापम्.

SAKARA—Friend, friend! Is she calling some woman?

VITA—Surely.

SAKARA—I can kill a hundred of women! I am (very) brave!

VAS.—(*Seeing no one about*). Oh! ill-luck! How now! Even the servants have disappeared! Now I have got to protect myself by my own self.

VITA—Seek them out, seek them out!

SAKARA—Vasantasena, cry out, cry out for (your) Parabhritika, or (your) Pallavaka, or the whole of the month of Vasanta (Spring). When I am pursuing you, who can save you?

Can Bhimasena, the son of Jamadagni, or can the ten-necked Ravana, the Son of Kunti (save you)? Here by seizing you by your massive hair, I am going to play (*lit.* imitate) Duhshasana. (29)

Look here, I say, look here!

My sword is very keen, and your head is turned (towards me); I will dissect your head, or kill you. So away with this running away of yours: he who is destined to die can never live. (30)

VAS.—Sir, I am only a woman!

VITA—Hence you are (still) alive!

SAKARA—Hence it is that you are not killed!

VAS.—(*To herself*). How! Even his courtesy strikes terror! Well, I will (proceed) thus. (*Aloud*), Sir, do you expect to get some ornament from (*i. e.* by seizing) this person?

VITA—Heaven forbid! O Vasantasena, a garden-creeper deserves not to be robbed of its blossoms. So we have nothing to do with ornaments.

VAS.—Then what, indeed, can it be now?

---

[न बलं यस्याः सा] अबला [दीनेत्यर्थः] खल्वहम् । अत एव ध्रियसे जीवसि । बलवान्धारयितुं न शक्यत एवेति तात्पर्यम् । अत एव न मार्यसे । तक्कीअदि अन्विष्यते । कृतं निष्फलमलंकरणैः । यत उद्यानलता पुष्पमोषं नार्हति । अहं वरपुरुषमनुष्यो वासुदेवः कामयितव्य इति तर्क्यत इत्याशयः । सन्तं शान्तम् । अनार्यमनर्हम् । सतालिकम् । विटस्य हस्ते तालदानं कृत्वेत्यर्थः । मं अन्तरेण । 'मयीत्यर्थः' इत्येके । अन्तरेण चित्तेन अन्योन्यं सुस्निग्धैषा गणिकादारिका ननु । हगे अहं न ग्रामान्तरगतो न नगरान्तरागतः । ग्रामान्तरागतो नगरान्तरगतश्च श्रान्तः क्लान्तश्च भवति । न त्वहमीदृश इत्याशयः । अज्जुके भट्टालिके । भावस्य विटस्य । शीर्षेणात्मीयाभ्यां पादाभ्यां शपे । यदग्रे वक्ष्यमाणं तत्सत्यमित्यर्थः । तवैव

**शकारः**--अहं देवपुरुषो मनुष्यो वासुदेवः कामयितव्यः । (हग्गे देवपुलिशे[१] मणुश्शे वाशुदेवके कामइदव्वे ।)

**वसन्तसेना**--( सक्रोधम् । ) शान्तं शान्तम् । अपेहि । अनार्यं मन्त्रयसि । (शन्तं शन्तम्[२] । अवेहि । अणज्जं मन्तेसि ।

**शकारः**--(सहस्ततालं[३] विहस्य ।) भाव भाव प्रेक्षस्व तावत् । अन्तरेण सुस्निग्धैषा गणिकादारिका ननु । येन मां भणति--'एहि । श्रान्तोऽसि । क्लान्तोऽसि ' इति । अहं न ग्रामान्तरं न नगरान्तरं वा गतः । आर्यके [भट्टालिके] शपे भावस्य शीर्षमात्मीयाभ्यां पादाभ्याम् । तवैव पृष्ठानुपृष्ठिकयाऽऽहिण्डमानः श्रान्तः क्लान्तोऽस्मि संवृत्तः । (भावे भावे पेक्ख दाव[४] । अन्तलेण[५] शुशिणिद्धा एशा गणिआदालिआ[६] णं । जेण मं भणादि--'एहि । शन्तेषि । किलिन्तेशि' त्ति । हगे ण ग्गामन्तलं[७] ण णगलन्तलं वा गडे । अज्जुके शवामि भावश्श शीशं अत्तणकेहिं[८] पादेहिं । तव ज्जेव पश्चाणुपश्चिआए आहिण्डन्ते शन्ते किलिन्ते म्हि शंवुत्ते ।)

**विटः**--:( स्वगतम् । ) अये कथं शान्तमित्यभिहिते श्रान्त इत्यवगच्छति मूर्खः । ( प्रकाशम् । ) वसन्तसेने वेशवासविरुद्धमभिहितं भवत्या । पश्य ।

**तरुणजनसहायश्चिन्त्यतां वेशवासो**
**विगणय गणिका त्वं मार्गजाता लतेव ।**
**वहसि हि धनहार्यं पण्यभूतं शरीरं**
**सममुपचर भद्रे सुप्रियं चाप्रियं[९] च ॥ ३१ ॥**

अपि च ।

**वाप्यां स्नाति विचक्षणो द्विजवरो मूर्खोऽपि वर्णाधमः**
**फुल्लां नाम्यति वायसोऽपि हि लतां या नामिता बर्हिणा ।**
**ब्रह्मक्षत्रविशस्तरन्ति च यया[१०] नावा तयैवेतरे**
**त्वं वापीव लतेव नौरव जनं वेश्याऽसि सर्वं भज ॥ ३२ ॥**

---

पृष्ठानुपृष्ठिकया । आहिण्डन्ते उद्भ्राम्यन् । श्रान्तः क्लान्तोऽस्मि संवृत्तः । **तरुणे-त्यादि** । वेशो वेश्याजनवासस्थानं [तरुणजनः सहायो यस्य तथा । तरुणजनापेक्षी-त्यर्थः । इति चिन्त्यतामवधार्यताम् । विगणय विजानीहि । धनेन हार्यं धनहार्यम् । केनापि तरुणजनेनेति शेषः । सुप्रियं च अप्रियं च नरं सममविशेषेण उपचर । उपमा काव्यलिङ्गं च अलंकारौ । मालिनी वृत्तम् ] ॥ ३१ ॥ **वाप्यामित्यादि** । [ वर्णे-नाधमः वर्णाधमः शूद्रादिः । ] नाम्यति नमयति । नाम्यतीति कण्ड्वादिपाठात् 'नामं

---

१ वरपुलिशमनुश्शे. २ पावं ( पापम् ). ३ सतालकम्. ४ दाव मं. ५ मं अन्त०. ६ गणिकादारिकेत्यादि नास्ति पुस्तकान्तरे. ७ अण्णग्गाम०; न्तलं गडे. ८ अत्ताणकेलकेहिं, ०केरेहिं. ९ वाऽप्रियं वा. १० यथा...तथै०.

SAKARA—That I, a heavenly personage, a man, and Vasudeva (Krishna), should be loved (by you).

VAS.—(*Angrily*). Enough, no more of this! Get away! You talk wickedly (*lit.*, what is unworthy of an Arya).

SAKARA—(*Clapping his hands and laughing*) Friend, friend! Just see. This courtesan girl is indeed very much attached (to me) at heart; and hence she says to me, 'come, you are fatigued, you are exhausted'; while I have not gone to another village, nor to another city. Lady, I swear by my friend's head and by my feet, I am fatigued and wearied while tramping close at your back here and there.

VITA—(*To himself*). Oh! The fool understands shranta (fatigued) when she said *shanta* (enough). (*Aloud*). O Vasantasena, you have spoken in a manner contrary to your stay (*i. e.* life) in the courtesans' quarter. See—

Remember that the courtesans' quarter is (mainly) dependent on young men for help; and consider (also) that you, a courtesan are just like a creeper growing by the wayside. You possess a body that can be bought for money and hence is like an article for sale. (Therefore), O good maiden, serve equally one much coveted by you and one disliked by you. (31)

Moreover—

An erudite eminent Brahmana, and also an idiot of the lowest caste—both bathe in the same well. Even a crow bends (*i. e.* sits upon) the same creeper in bloom, that had been bent by a peacock (sitting upon it). And by the same boat do other fellows (*i. e.* Chandalas, etc.) cross (a river), by which Brahmanas, Kshatriyas and Vaisyas cross it. You are a harlot, and (therefore) are like a well, or a creeper, or a boat. Wait upon all (equally). (32)

---

करोति' इत्यर्थे यक्यकारलोपे च रूपम् । यथा मगधशब्दे मागध्यतीति भवति । 'नामं करोतीत्यर्थे णिवि संज्ञापूर्वको विधिरनित्य इति गुणमकृत्वा यणादेशे नाम्यतीति रूपम् इत्येके । 'ण्यन्तात्संपदादिपाठमभ्युपेत्य क्विपिक्यचि रूपम्' इत्यपरे ॥ ३२ ॥ गर्भदासी जन्मप्रभृतिचेटी । [कामदेवायतनोद्यानात् कामदेवायतनोद्यानगतात् चारुदत्तदर्शनादारभ्येत्यर्थः ।] वामतः पार्श्वे तस्य चारुदत्तस्य गृहम् । परिहर्तव्यम् । चारुदत्तवासोऽतिनिकट इति वसन्तसेनायाः कथयितुं नार्हतीति तदेव च तेनोक्तम् । तद्वचनं परिहारविषयः । काणेलीमातः । 'काणेली कन्यकामाताः' इति देशीप्रकाशः । 'असती काणेली' इत्येके । भाव बलीयानन्धकारः ।

**वसन्तसेना**——गुणः खल्वनुरागस्य कारणं न पुनर्बलात्कारः (गुणो[1] क्खु अणुराअस्स कारणं ण उण बलक्कारो।

**शकारः**——भाव भाव एषा गर्भदासी कामदेवायतनोद्यानात्प्रभृति तस्य दरिद्रचारुदत्तस्यानुरक्ता न मां कामयते। वामतस्तस्य गृहम्। यथा तव मम च हस्तान्नेषा परिभ्रश्यति तथा करोतु भावः। (भावे भावे एशा गब्भदाशी कामदेवाअदणुज्जाणादो पहुदि ताह[2] दलिद्दचालुदत्ताह अणुलत्ता ण मं कामेदि। वामदो तश्श घलम्। जधा तव मम अ हत्तादो ण एशा पलिभंशदि तधा कलेदु भात्रे।)

**विटः**——(स्वगतम्।) यदेव परिहर्तव्यं तदेवोदाहरति मूर्खः। कथं वसन्तसेनाऽऽर्यचारुदत्तमनुरक्ता। सुष्ठु खल्विदमुच्यते रत्नं रत्नेन संगच्छत इति। तद्गच्छतु। किमनेन मूर्खेण। (प्रकाशम्।) काणेलीमातः वामतस्तस्य सार्थवाहस्य गृहम्।

**शकारः**——अथ किम्। वामतस्तस्य गृहम्। (अध इं। वामदो तश्य घलम्।

**वसन्तसेना**——(स्वगतम्।) आश्चर्यम्। वामतस्तस्य गृहमिति यत्सत्यमपराध्यताऽपि दुर्जनेनोपकृतं येन प्रियसंगमं प्रापिता। (अम्महे। वामदो तश्श गेहं त्ति जं सच्चं अवरज्झन्तेण वि दुज्जणेण[3] उवकिदं जेण पिअसंगमं पाविदा[4]।)

**शकारः**——भाव भाव बलीयसि खल्वन्धकारे माषराशिप्रविष्टेव मसीगुटिका दृश्यमानैव प्रनष्टा वसन्तसेना। (भावे भावे बलिए क्खु अन्धआले माशलाशिपविश्टा विअ मशीगुडिआ दीशन्दी[5] ज्जेव पणश्टा वशन्तशेणिआ।

**विटः**——अहो बलवानन्धकारः। तथा हि।

> **आलोकविशाला मे सहसा तिमिरप्रवेशविच्छिन्ना।**
> **उन्मीलिताऽपि दृष्टिर्निमीलितेवान्धकारेण॥ ३३॥**

---

माषराशिप्रविष्टेव मसीगुटिका दृश्यमानैव प्रनष्टा वसन्तसेना। आलोकेति। आलोके दर्शने। विशाला महती। [तिमिरे प्रवेशस्तेन विछिन्ना विलुप्ता। निमीलिता इवेति उत्प्रेक्षा]॥ ३३॥ **लिम्पतीत्यादि**। [असत्पुरुषसेवेवेत्यनेन शकारसेवाया निष्फलत्वं ध्वनितम्। विगतं फलं यस्याः सा विफला तस्या भावः विफलता ताम्। उपमोत्प्रेक्षयोः संसृष्टिः]॥ ३४॥ चिह्नं भूषणशब्दादि। उपलक्षणं माल्यगन्धादि। 'अस्ति किंचिच्चिह्नमुपलक्षयसि' इति पाठान्तरार्थो व्यक्त एव। किं विअ। कीदृशमिवेत्यर्थः। शृणामि मल्लगन्धम्' इत्यादिना लोकविरुद्धोक्तिः। **काममित्यादि**। [प्रदोषतिमिरेण निशामुखान्धकारेण। जलदोदरसंधौ लीना। वसन्ततिलका वृत्तम्।]॥ ३५॥ श्रुतमवधारितम्। गृहीतमस्य

---

१ गुणाः. २ तस्स...दत्तस्स. ३ णेण पिअशंगमं (प्रियसंगमः). ४ पाविदं. ५ दीशन्दी दीशन्दी.

VAS.—But it is merit indeed that is the cause of love, and not force

SAKARA—Friend, friend ! This accursed wench ( *lit.* slave-from-her-birth ) does not love me, having fallen in love with that penniless Charudatta ever since (she visited) the garden of Cupid's shrine. Here is his house to the left. So you will please so manage that she shall not slip from your hands or from mine.

VITA—( *To himself* ). The fool utters the very thing that should have been avoided ! What, Vasantsena has fallen in love with the noble Charudatta ! It is indeed well said that 'a jewel unites with a jewel.' Well, then, let her eseape ; what do I care for this fool ? ( *Aloud* ) Son of an unmarried woman, is that Sarthavaha's house to the left ?.

SAKARA—Surely ; his house *is* to the left.

VAS.—( *To herself* ). Wonderful ! To tell the truth, ( by saying ) his house is to the left, a favour has been conferred upon me by this villain even when doing evil to me, since I am enabled to meet my beloved,

SAKARA—Friend, friend ! in this pitchy darkness Vasantsena has disappeared while being just in sight, like a pellet of lampblack fallen in a heap of black beans.

VITA—Ah ! The darkness is indeed very dense. For—

Long-ranged in light, but suddenly deprived of their power by their entrance into the darkness, my eyes, although wide open have been closed as it were owing to the darkness. (33)

---

तात्पर्यमप्याकलितम् । अये मातः भित्तिपरामर्षसूचितं पक्षद्वारं खल्वेतत् । जानामि संयोगेन स्पर्शनेन्द्रियानुभवेन गृहस्य संवृतं पक्षद्वारकम् । **दारिद्र्यादित्यादि** । बान्धवजनो वाक्ये न संतिष्ठते । वचनं न करोतीत्यर्थः । प्रतापाभावात् । स्फारीभवन्त्येकीभवन्ति । [ ततो विस्तारं यान्तीत्यर्थः । ] तत्तस्य संभाव्यते चौर्यादिकमिदमस्य नासीदिदानीं कथमित्यादि ॥ ३६ ॥ **सङ्गमित्यादि** । [ सङ्गं सङ्गतिम् । अवज्ञया सहितं यथा तथा सावज्ञं सतिरस्कारम् । ] अल्पच्छदो वस्त्रविहीनः । [ षष्ठं-पञ्चमहापातकानि मनुनोक्तानि यथा-'ब्रह्महत्या सुरापानं स्तेयं गुर्वङ्गनागमः । महान्ति पातकान्याहुः संसर्गश्चापि तैः सह ॥' इति । उत्प्रेक्षालंकारः । उभयोः शार्दूलविक्रीडितं वृत्तम् ] ॥ ३७ ॥ **दारिद्र्येति** । भवन्तमेवं [ भवन्तमेव इ. पा. ] शोचामि । [ विपन्नः देहः यस्य तस्मिन् विपन्नदेहे ] विनष्टदेहे मयि क्व यास्यसि । अस्मत्सदृक्सार्वदिकः सुहृत्कोऽपि नास्तीत्यर्थः । अर्थ-

अपि च ।

लिम्पतीव तमोऽङ्गानि वर्षतीवाञ्जनं नभः ।
असत्पुरुषसेवेव दृष्टिर्विफलतां[१] गता ।। ३४ ।।

**शकारः**--भाव भाव अन्विष्यामि वसन्तसेनिकाम् । ( भावे भावे अण्णेशामि वशन्तशेणिअं । )

**विटः**--काणेलीमातः अस्ति किंचिच्चिह्नं[२] यदुपलक्षयसि ।

**शकारः**--भाव भाव किमिव । ( भावे भावे किं विअ । )

**विटः**--भूषणशब्दं सौरभ्यानुविद्धं माल्यगन्धं वा ।

**शकारः**--श्रृणोमि माल्यगन्धम् । अन्धकारपूरितया पुनर्नासिकया न सुव्यक्तं पश्यामि भूषणशब्दम् । ( शुणामि मल्लगन्धं । अन्धआलपूलिदाए उण णाशिआए ण शुव्वत्तं पेक्खामि भूशणशद्दं । )

**विटः**--( जनान्तिकम् ) वसन्तसेने ।

कामं प्रदोषतिमिरेण न दृश्यसे[३] त्वं
सौदामनीव जलदोदरसंधिलीना[४]
त्वां सूचयिष्यति तु माल्यसमुद्भवोऽयं
गन्धश्च भीरु मुखराणि च नूपराणि ।। ३५ ।।

श्रुतं वसन्तसेने ।

**वसन्तसेना**--( स्वगतम् । ) श्रुतं गृहीतं च । ( नाटयेन नूपुराण्युत्सार्य माल्यानि चापनीय किंचित्परिक्रम्य हस्तेन परामृश्य । ) अहो भित्तिपरामर्शसूचितं पक्षद्वारकं खल्वेतत् । जानामि च संयोगेन गेहस्य संवृतं पक्षद्वारकम् । ( सुदं गहिदं अ । अम्मो भित्तिपरामरिससूइदं पक्खदुआरअं क्खु एदं । जाणामि अ संजोएण गेहस्य संवुदं पक्खदुआरअं । )

**चारुदत्तः**--वयस्य समाप्तजपोऽस्मि । तत्सांप्रतं गच्छ । मातृभ्यो बलिमुपहर ।

**विदूषकः**--भोः न गमिष्यामि । ( भो ण गमिस्समम् । )

**चारुदत्तः**--धिक्कष्टम् ।

---

परत्वात्पुंलिङ्गत्वम् । यद्वा 'तमेवं भवमुत्पत्ति स्मरामि' इति कुव्याख्या । सुहृन्मित्रम् । अतो हेतोः मयि विनष्टदेहे क्व यास्यसि त्वमिति मे चारुदत्तस्य चिन्ता । उपजातिच्छन्दः ] ।। ३८ ।। सहायिनी द्वितीया । अभ्युपपत्तिरनुग्रहः । स्थगितद्वारेणापसरणाभावात्पिण्डीभूतेनैकीभूतेन प्रतिबन्धकत्वादपावृते पक्षद्वारे सति निर्वापितो दीपः । गृहीता प्राप्ता । तत इत एकप्रदेशे भूत्वैकान्ते हे भाव

---

१ निष्क०. २ किं चिह्नं ३ दृश्यतें. ४ संविलीना.

Moreover—

The darkness is, as if, besmearing the limbs; the sky is, as it were, showering down (black) collyrium; and eye-sight has been of no avail, like service rendered unto a wicked man. (34)

SAKARA—Friend, friend! I shall search for Vasantasena.

VITA—Bastard, is there any sign (of her) that you mark?

SAKARA—Friend, friend, of what kind?

VITA—(For example) the sound of her ornaments or the scent of her chaplets, with its fragrance closely following (its track)?

SAKARA—I hear the scent of her chaplets: but, my nose being choked up with darkness, I do not very clearly see the sound of her ornaments.

VITA—(*Aside*). O Vasantasena,

True that owing to this nocturnal darkness you cannot be seen, like lightning lying concealed in the gap of the interior of a cloud. But, O timid one, this scent proceeding from your chaplets, as well as (these your) jingling anklets, will betray you. (35)

Did you hear me, Vasantasena?

VAS.—(*To herself*). I have heard, and comprehended too. (*She shows that she takes off her anklets, and removes her chaplets; then walking about a little, and feeling with her hand*). Ah! Here, surely, is a side-door which I have discovered by feeling over the wall. And I know, by its being closed, that this side-entrance of the house is fastened (from within).

CHAR.—Friend, I have finished my prayers. So you may now go and offer the oblation to the Holy Mothers.

VID.—Sir, I won't go.

CHAR.—Ah! Fie!

---

तिष्ठ । इदो भाव इत्यादि भ्रमव्युदासाय सुनिश्चयं करोति । युवां द्वावपि तावदेकान्ते तिष्ठतम् । संपदं सांप्रतम् । अन्धकार इत्यादि । अनुष्टुप् । [ मालाएव माल्यम् । चतुर्वर्णादिष्यञ् । तस्य गन्धेन ] माल्यगन्धेन सूचिता । केशहस्ते केशवृन्दे परामृष्टा [ स्पष्टा ] ॥ ३९ ॥ एषेति । कुलपुत्रानुसारिणी चारुदत्तानुरक्ता । ] कुसुमाढ्येषु पुष्पैः समृद्धेषु । भूषितेष्वित्यर्थः । सेवितव्येष्वलंकार्येषु ॥ ४० ॥ एषाऽसीति । इन्द्रवज्रायाः श्लोकः । एषाऽसि बाला । [ वासु बाले ] अधिचण्डम-

दारिद्र्यात्पुरुषस्य बान्धवजनो वाक्ये न संतिष्ठते
सुस्निग्धा विमुखीभवन्ति सुहृदः[1] स्फारीभवन्त्यापदः ।
सत्त्वं ह्रासमुपैति शीलशशिनः कान्तिः परिम्लायते[2]
पापं कर्म च यत्परैरपि कृतं तत्तस्य संभाव्यते ।। ३६ ।।

अपि च

सङ्गं नैव हि कश्चिदस्य कुरुते संभाषते[3] नादरा-
त्संप्राप्तो गृहमुत्सवेषु धनिनां सावज्ञमालोक्यते ।
दूरादेव महाजनस्य विहरत्यल्पच्छदो लज्जया
मन्ये निर्धनता प्रकाममपरं षष्ठं महापातकम् ।। ३७ ।।

अपि च

दारिद्र्य शोचामि [4]भवन्तमेवमस्मच्छरीरे सुहृदित्युषित्वा ।
विपन्नदेहे मयि मन्दभाग्ये ममेति चिन्ता क्व गमिष्यसि त्वम् ।। ३८ ।।

विदूषकः—( सवैलक्ष्यम् । ) भो वयस्य यदि मया गन्तव्यं तदेषाऽपि मम सहायिनी रदनिका भवतु । ( भो वअस्स जइ मए गन्तव्वं ता एसा वि मे सहाइणी रदणिआ भोदु । )

चारुदत्तः—रदनिके मैत्रेयमनुगच्छ ।

चेटी:[5]—यदार्य आज्ञापयति । (जं अज्जो आणवेदि ।)

विदूषकः—भवति रदनिके गृहाण बलिं प्रदीपं च । अहमपावृतं पक्षद्वारकं करोमि । ( तथा करोति । ) (भोदि रदणिए गेण्ह बलिं पदीवं अ । अहं अपावुदं पक्खदुआरअं करेमि । )

वसन्तसेना—ममाभ्युपपत्तिनिमित्तमिवापावृतं पक्षद्वारकम् । ( दृष्ट्वा । ) तद्यावत्प्रविशामि । हा धिक् हा धिक् । कथं प्रदीपः । ( पटान्तेन निर्वाप्य प्रविष्टा । ) ( मम अब्भुववत्तिणिमित्तं विअ अवावुदं पक्खदुआरअम् । ता जाव पविसामि । हद्धी हद्धी । कधं पदीवो । )

चारुदत्तः—मैत्रेय किमेतत् ।

---

त्युच्चैः । हिशब्द एव वा । चण्डं महादेवं च ।। ४१ ।। आर्यमिश्रैर्मान्यैः । [ आर्याश्च ते मिश्राश्चेति समासः । व्यवसितं कर्तुमारब्धम् । अन्यः वसन्तसेनाया भिन्नः । ] भात्र यथा दधिभक्तलुब्धायां मार्जारिकायां स्वरपरिवृत्तिर्भवति तथैतया स्वरपरिवृत्तिः [ ध्वनेरन्यथाकरणं ] कृता । 'दहिशर' इति पाठे 'छलिल' इति पाठेऽपि शरो दध्न उपरिभागः । इयमिति । [ रङ्गः नृत्यशाला तत्र प्रवेशेन । तत्र भिन्नभिन्नस्वरानुकरणशिक्षयेत्यर्थः । वञ्चना प्रतारणा तस्यां पण्डितत्वेन पाटवेन । स्वरनैपुण्यं स्वर-

---

१. सहसा. २. परं. ३. संभाष्यते. ४. मेव ह्य०. ५. रदनिका.

Owing to poverty a man's relatives do not abide by his order; his bosom friends turn away from him; his difficulties multiply; his spirit languishes; the brilliance of the moon of his character grows entirely dim; and whatever evil deed may have been done even by other persons, the same is attributed to him. (36)

Moreover—

Nobody keeps company with him, or talks respectfully to him; if he goes to the mansions of the rich on festive occasions, he is looked at with contempt. Scantily clad, in shame he keeps himself at a distance from the great. I consider poverty to be, forsooth, another great sin, the sixth ( of the class of the usual five ). (37)

Moreover

O Poverty, I am sorry just for you : I feel concerned as to where you can go, when I, the unlucky one, shall have departed this body, you having thus ( so long ) resided in my frame like a friend. (38)

VID.—( *With shame* ). Well, friend, if I have to go, then let this Radanika, too, be my companion.

CHAR.—Radanika, follow Maitreya.

THE MAID—As Your Honour commands.

VID.—Girl Radanika, take you the oblation as well as the lamp. I shall unfasten the side-door. ( *He does so* ).

VAS.—The side-door has opened, as though to favour me. Well, then, I shall get in. ( *Seeing* ). Oh ! Pity ! How now ! Here is a lamp !

*She extinguishes it with the hem of her garment and then enters* ).

CHAR.—Maitreya, what is that ?

---

विकृतिचातुर्यम् । समुच्चयालंकारः ] ॥ ४२ ॥ ही ही भो इति परितोषे । पशुबन्धोपनीतस्येव छागलस्य हृदयं फुरफुरायति अत्यर्थं प्रकम्पते प्रदीपः । युक्तं नेदम् । नः काकौ । किं एसो । किं प्रश्ने । स्वकीयगृहसमीपे कुक्कुरोऽपि बलीयान्भवति । एतेनास्मादृशजनभागधेयवक्रेण दण्डकाष्ठेन । दुष्टस्येव । कृतद्वेषस्य वैरिणो महादुष्टस्यानिग्रहेऽपि ममापराधो भवत्येवेत्यर्थः । यद्वा । दुष्टश्चानपराधोऽपि निग्रहं प्राप्नोत्येवेत्यर्थः । पाठान्तरे चोडे कर्णनासिकाशून्यः । शुष्कवंशप्रहारेण । शुष्कोऽतिदीर्घत्वप्रतिपादनाय । एवंभूतस्य शिरः कुट्यते । तथा तत्र शिरः कुट्टिष्यामि । राजश्यालकेत्यादि । संस्थानक

**विदूषकः**—अपावृतपक्षद्वारकेण पिण्डीभूतेन वातेन निर्वापितः प्रदीपः । भवति रदनिके निष्क्राम त्वं पक्षद्वारकेण । अहमप्यभ्यन्तरचतुःशालातः प्रदीपं प्रज्वाल्यागच्छामि । ( इति निष्क्रांतः । ) ( अवावुदपक्खदुआरएण पिण्डीभूदेन[१] वादेण णिव्वाविदो पदीवो । भोदि रदणिए णिक्कम तुमं पक्खदुआरएण । अहं पि[२] अब्भन्तरचदुस्सालादो पदीवं पज्जालिअ आअच्छामि ।)

**शकारः**—भाव भाव अन्वेषयामि वसन्तसेनिकाम् । ( भावे भावे अण्णेशामि वशन्तशेणिअम् ।)

**विटः**—अन्विष्यतामन्विष्यताम् ।

**शकारः**—( तथा कृत्वा । ) भाव भाव गृहीता गृहीता । ( भावे भावे गहिदा गहिदा ।)

**विटः**—मूर्ख नन्वहम् ।

**शकारः**—इतस्तावद्भूत्वैकान्ते भावस्तिष्ठतु । ( पुनरन्विष्य चेटं गृहीत्वा ।) भाव भाव गृहीता गृहीता । ( इदो दाव भविअ एअन्ते भावे चिश्टदु । भावे भावे गहिदा गहिदा ।

**चेटः**—भट्टारक चेटोऽहम् । (भट्टके चेडे हगे ।)

**शकारः**—इतो भाव इतश्चेटः । भावश्चेटश्चेटो भावः । युवां तावदेकान्ते तिष्ठतम् । (पुनरन्विष्य रदनिकां केशेषु गृहीत्वा ।) भाव भाव सांप्रतं गृहीता गृहीता वसन्तसेनिका ।

> **अन्धकारे पलायमाना माल्यगन्धेन सूचिता ।**
> **केशहस्ते परामृष्टा चाणक्येनेव द्रौपदी ।। ३९ ।।**

(इदो भावे इदो चेडे । भावे चेडे चेडे भावे । तुम्हे दाव एअन्ते चिट्ट । भावे भावे शंपदं गहिदा गहिदा वशन्तशेणिआ ।

> अन्धआले पलाअन्ती मल्लगन्धेण शूइदा ।
> केशहश्ते[३] पलामिट्टा चाणक्केणेव्व दोव्वदी ।।)

**विटः**—

> **एषाऽसि वयसो दर्पात्कुलपुत्रानुसारिणी ।**
> **केशेषु कुसुमाढ्येषु सेवितव्येषु कर्षिता ।। ४० ।।**

**शकारः**—**एषाऽसि वासु शिरसि गृहीता केशेषु बालेषु शिरोरुहेषु ।**
> **आक्रोश विक्रोश लपाधिचण्डं शंभुं शिवं शंकरमीश्वरं वा ।। ४१ ।।**

> एशाशि वाशू शिलशि ग्गहीदा[४] केशेशु बालेशु शिलोलुहेशु ।
> अक्कोश विक्कोश लवाहिचण्डं शंभुं शिवं शंकलमीशलं वा ।।

---

१ किदेण (कृतेन). २ वि. ३ विन्दे (वृन्दे). ४ ग्गिहीदा.

VID.—The lamp has been blown out by the breeze coming in with a burst ( *lit.* that was collected together ), the side-door being opened. Girl, Radanika, you may go out through the side-door. I too shall follow you after having lighted the lamp from the interior quadrangle. ( *Exit* ).

SAKARA—Friend, friend ! I shall look for Vasantasena.

VITA—Do look; please, do.

SAKARA—( *Does accordingly*). Friend, friend ! I have caught her !

VITA--Blockhead, it is I !

SAKARA—You should come this side and stand in a corner. ( *Again searching, and catching* Cheta ). Friend, friend ! I have caught her !

CHETA--Master, I am Cheta.

SAKARA—Here is friend ( Vita ), here is Cheta. Vita and Cheta; Cheta and Vita ! As for you, you both stand in a corner. ( *Again searching, and catching* Radanika *by the hair* ). Friend, friend, I have this time ( really ) caught her; I have caught Vasantasena !

Like Chanakya seizing Draupadi, I have caught her by her massive hair, as she was indicated by the scent of her chaplets while running away in the dark. ( 39 )

VITA—

Here, you, who in your pride of youth were going to seek a noble-born person ( *i. e.* Charudatta ),—you have now been seized by the hair, which is richly decorated with flowers and which deserves to be ( so ) honoured. (40)

SAKARA—

Here you are caught by your head, O maiden,—caught by your hair, by your tresses, by your locks ! Now cry or scream or shout very loudly for Sambhu, Siva, Samkara, or Isvara ! (41)

---

इति तस्य नाम। उपमर्दो निग्रहः। मा दुर्गत इति। गाथा। कृतान्तस्य दैवस्य दुर्गतो नाम। नाम संभावनायाम्। चारित्रेण विहीन आढ्योऽपि दुर्गतो दरिद्रो भवति ॥ ४३ ॥ महाब्राह्मणश्चाण्डालः। सकामेति। सकामा स्वाधीनयौवनेति-पदाभ्यामस्या धारणं नापराधाय। सा वेश्या तिष्ठति न त्वियमित्याशयः। शील-वञ्चना दुश्चरितसंभावना [ शीलस्य सद्वृत्तस्य वञ्चना प्रतारणा। परस्त्रीपरामर्श-रूपवृत्तलोप इत्यर्थः। ]॥ ४४ ॥ जानन्ननुनयामि। आदरविषयताऽनुनयः। समयः क्रियाबन्धः। समयमेवाह—यदीममिति। एष इति। [ प्रणयः मत्प्रार्थना-

रदनिका—( सभयम्। ) किमार्यमिश्रैर्व्यवसितम् । ( किं अज्जमिस्सेहिं ववसिदम् ।)

विटः—काणेलीमातः अन्य एवैष स्वरसंयोगः ।

शकारः—भाव भाव यथा दधिशरपरिलुब्धाया मार्जारिकायाः स्वरपरिवृत्तिर्भवति तथा दास्याःपुत्र्या स्वरपरिवृत्तिः कृता । (भावे भावे जधा [1]दहिशरपलिलुद्धाए मज्जालीए शलपलिवत्ते होदि तधा दाशीएधीए शलपलिवत्ते कडे । )

विटः—कथं स्वरपरिवर्तः कृतः । अहो चित्रम् । अथ वा किमत्र चित्रम् ।

इयं रङ्गप्रवेशेन कलानां चोपशिक्षया ।
वञ्चनापण्डितत्वेन स्वरनैपुण्यमाश्रिता ।। ४२ ।।

(प्रविश्य ।)

विदूषकः—आश्चर्यं भोः प्रदोषमन्दमारुतेन पशुबन्धोपनीतस्येव छागलस्य हृदयं फुरफुरायते प्रदीपः । (उपसृत्य रदनिकां तथा दृष्ट्वा ।) भो रदनिके। (ही ही भोः पदोसमन्दमारुदेण पसुबन्धोवणीदस्य विअ छागलस्स हिअअं फुरफुराअदि पदीवो । भो रदणिए ।)

शकारः—भाव भाव मनुष्यो मनुष्यः । (भावे भावे मणुश्शे मणुश्शे ।)

विदूषकः—युक्तं न्विदं सदृशं न्विदं यदार्यचारुदत्तस्य दरिद्रतया सांप्रतं परपुरुषा गेहं प्रवेश्यन्ते। (जुत्तं ण्णेदं सरिसं ण्णेदं जं अज्जचारुदत्तस्य दलिद्ददाए संपदं परपुरिसा गेहं पवेसीअन्ति[2] ।)

रदनिका—आर्य मैत्रेय प्रेक्षस्व मे परिभवम् । (अज्ज मित्तेअ पेक्ख मे परिहवम् ।)

विदूषकः—किं तव परिभवः । अथ वाऽस्माकम् । (किं तव परिहवो । आदु अम्हाणम् ।)

रदनिका—ननु युष्माकमेव । (णं तुम्हाणं ज़्जेव ।)

विदूषकः—किमेष बलात्कारः । ( किं एसो बलक्कारो । )

रदनिका—अथ किम् । ( अध इं । )

विदूषकः—सत्यम् । ( सच्चं । )

रदनिका—सत्यम् । ( सच्चम् । )

---

नुमतिरूपः । ] गुणशस्त्रैः गुणा एव शस्त्राणि तैः।। ४५ ।। किविणं कृपणम् । अशितव्यं भोक्तव्यमपि नास्ति । यद्वा अन्हिअदव्वं पि आह्निकद्रव्यमद्य भोक्तव्यमपीत्यर्थः । स इति । [अस्माकमिव विधा प्रकारो येषां तेऽस्मद्विधाः । अर्थिनः । तेषां] प्रणयः प्रार्थनाभि [प्रार्थनानुरूपार्थदानैः।] 'स्नेहप्रकारैः समयोचितदानैरित्यर्थः' इत्येके । [विभवैः

---

१ दहिछलिल. २ पविशन्ति.

RADANIKA—( *With alarm* ). What are the noble ones ( bent upon ) doing ?

VITA—Bastard, this consonance of the voice seems to be quite different !

SAKARA—Friend, friend ! That whore's-daughter has changed her voice, just as a she-cat changes hers when coveting the cream of curds.

VITA—How ! She has changed her voice ! Oh ! Strange ! Or rather, what is there strange about it ?

She has attained skill in ( the use of ) her voice, by her acting on the ( dancing ) stage, by the training she has received in the arts, and her cleverness in ( the art of ) deception. ( 42 )

(*Entering*).

VID.—Ah ! Wonderful ! Owing to the gentle night-breeze, the lamp is fluttering like the heart of a goat brought in for being tied to the sacrificial post ( as a victim ), ( *Approaching and seeing* Radanika *in that state* ) O Radanika !

SAK.—Friend, friend ! A man, a man !

VID.—Is it indeed proper, is it at all becoming, that the poverty of our noble Charudatta should now make even strangers invade his house ( with impunity ) ?

RAD.—Sir Maitreya, see how I am being insulted !

VID.—What ! Is that an insult to you or to us ?

RAD.—Well, to you, surely !

VID.—Is this violence ?

RAD.—What else ?

VID.—Really ?

RAD.—Really.

---

संपद्गर्वादित्यर्थः। वंशस्थं वृत्तम् ]॥४६॥ **शूर इति।** श्लोको वैश्वदेव्या वृत्तेन। आहो उपायास्तेन रामेण जातः इदं व्यर्थं विरुद्धार्थम्। श्वेतकेतुरौद्दालकिर्दुर्वासो मातुलः ऋषिविशेषः। इन्द्रदत्तो बृहत्कथाप्रलम्बके स्त्र्यंशे संस्थितः ॥ ४७ ॥ **दीनानामिति।** [ स्वस्य गुणाः स्वगुणाः। स्वगुणा एव फलानि तैः नतः नम्रः कल्पवृक्षः। ] सज्जनानां कुटुम्ब्युपजीव्यः। [ आदर्शः मुकुर इव निदर्शनभूतः। सुचरितस्य निकर्षः कषपट्टिकेव स्थितः। शीलमेव वेला तस्याः समुद्रः। समुद्रवेलामिव न कदापि शीलमतिक्रामतीत्यर्थः। दीनानां नावमन्तेत्यर्थः। पुरुषगुणानां दयादाक्षिण्यादीनां निधिः। दक्षिणं सरलमुदारं महत् च सत्त्वं यस्य स तथा। अधिका इतरातिशायिनो गुणा यस्य स तस्य भावस्तया। अन्ये केवलमुच्छ्वसन्ति चर्मभस्त्रेवेति शेषः। मालारूपकम्। स्रग्धरा वृत्तम्]

**विदूषकः**--( सक्रोधं दण्डकाष्ठमुद्यम्य। ) मा तावत्। भोः स्वके गेहे कुक्कुरोऽपि तावच्चण्डो भवति किं पुनरहं ब्राह्मणः। तदेतेनास्मादृशजनभागधेय-कुटिलेन दण्डकाष्ठेन दुष्टस्येव शुष्कवेणुकस्य मस्तकं ते प्रहारैः कुट्टयिष्यामि। ( मा दाव। भो सके गेहे कुक्कुरो वि दाव चण्डो भोदि किं उण अहं बम्हणो। ता एदिणा अह्मारिसजणभाअवेअकुडिलेण दण्डकठ्ठेण दुठ्ठस्स विअ सुक्खाण-वेणुअस्स[१] मत्थअं दे पहारेहिं कुट्टइस्सम्[२]। )

**विटः**--महाब्राह्मण मर्षय मर्षय।

**विदूषकः**--( विटं दृष्ट्वा। ) नात्रैषोऽपराध्यति। ( शकारं दृष्ट्वा। ) एष खल्वत्रापराध्यति। अरे रे राजश्यालक संस्थानक दुर्जन दुर्मनुष्य युक्तं न्विदम्। यद्यपि नाम तत्रभवानार्यचारुदत्तो दरिद्रः संवृत्तः तत्किं तस्य गुणैर्नालंकृतोज्जयिनी येन तस्य गृहं प्रविश्य परिजनस्येदृश उपमर्दः क्रियते। (ण एत्थ एसो अवरज्झदि। एसो क्खु एत्थ अवरज्झदि। अरे रे राअसालअ संठ्ठाणअ दुज्जण दुम्मणुस्स जुत्तं ण्णेदम्। जइ वि णाम तत्तभवं अज्जचारुदत्तो दलिद्दो संवुत्तो ता किं तस्स गुणेहिं ण अलंकिदा उज्जइणी जेण तस्स गेहं पविसिअ परिअणस्स ईरिसो उवमद्दो करीअदि।)

**मा दुर्गत इति परिभवो नास्ति कृतान्तस्य दुर्गतो नाम।**
**चारित्रेण विहीन आढ्योऽपि च दुर्गतो भवति॥ ४३॥**

( मा दुग्गदोत्ति परिहवो णत्थि कअन्तस्य दुग्गदो णाम।
चारित्तेण विहीणो अड्ढो वि अ दुग्गदो होइ॥)

**विटः**—( सवैलक्ष्यम् ) महाब्राह्मण मर्षय मर्षय। अन्यजनशङ्कया खल्विद-मनुष्ठितं न दर्पात्। पश्य।

**सकामाऽन्विष्यतेऽस्माभिः**

**विदूषकः**--किमियम्। (किं इअम्। )

---

॥४८॥ नष्टा अदर्शनं गता। **अन्धस्येति**। [आतुरस्य रुग्णस्य। सिद्धिः कार्यसफलता। स्वल्पा मन्दा स्मृतिर्यस्य तस्य। तथा च व्यसनिनः आपद्गतस्य मृगयादिव्यसनपरस्य वा। परमा उत्कृष्टा विद्या वेदान्तविद्या वा। रतिरनुरागः। वसन्ततिलका वृत्तम्]॥४९॥ **आलान इति**। [ आलाने बन्धनस्तम्भे गृह्यते निरुध्यते। वल्गासु खलीनाकर्षणेन। हृदये तस्या अनुरागपूर्णं हृदयं चेदित्यर्थः। ] यदि चेदर्थे। चेन्नास्ति। यदिदं इति पाठे यद् यस्मादिदं अनुरक्तं हृदयं] नास्ति ततः तदा गम्यताम्॥ ५०॥

---

१ सुक्खवेणु. २ पाडइस्सं.

VID.—( *Angrily raising his wooden stick* ) This cannot be allowed! Look here, even a dog becomes formidable when in his own kennel; what then of a Brahamana like me? So, by means of this wooden stick which is crooked like the luck of people like us, I will batter with blows your head, like the top of a spoiled dry bamboo!

VITA.—Pardon, worthy Brahmana, pardon!

VID.—( *Looking at* Vita ). He is not the guilty party in this matter. ( *Looking at* Sakara ). *This* fellow, obviously, is the offender in this affair. O you, king's brother-in-law, Samsthanaka, bad man, villain! Is this indeed becoming? Even though it is true that the noble Charudatta has been reduced to poverty, still, are not his merits an ornament to this Ujjayini, that you should enter his house and thus insult his servants?

Insult no man because he is poor: for indeed fate treats none as poor; moreover, even a rich person is poor if he be destitute of good character. ( 43 )

VITA—( *Feeling ashamed* ). Pardon, worthy Brahmana, pardon! This was done, not in insolence, but owing to our having msitaken her for another person (whom we were following). See—

An amorous woman is sought by us—

VID.—What, *this* one?

---

अभावमदर्शनम् । काकपदशीशमश्तका इति । द्यूताद्यकार्यप्रवृत्तौ काकपदाकारा ये धूर्तास्तेषां शीर्षप्राया ग्रामण्यस्तेषां मस्तकभूत धूर्तचक्रवर्तिनामपि प्रधानभूत। एतेनाचारकुलयोराक्षेपः कृतः । केचित्तु—'काकपदशीर्षं काकपदवत्पञ्चधा शीर्षं मस्तकं यस्य । पञ्चेत्युपलक्षणम् । अष्टकपालः [ तेनालक्षणयुक्तमस्तक इत्यर्थः ] ' इत्याहुः । अत्र च मते शीशमश्तका इति शकारवाणीत्वेन पुनरुक्तत्वं न दोषः। दुष्टबटो । ततोऽधिकरणे व्यवहारं विना इत्यनेन व्यवहारनाम्नो नवमाङ्कस्य सूचनम्। [ अधिकरणे न्यायसभायायाम् । व्यवहारं निर्णयकरणम् ] लघु शीघ्रम् । णिज्जाद-माणाह निर्यातयतः । तव मयाऽनुबद्धा प्रीतिर्भविष्यति । कूष्माण्डीत्यादि । उपजातिच्छन्दसा । कूष्माण्डी गोमयलिप्तवृंता शाकं च शुष्कं पलिरं प्रचुरप्रलेहं मांसम् । [ तलितं घृतपक्वम् । तदुक्तं भावप्रकाशे—'शुद्धमांसविधानेन मांसं सम्यक्प्रसाधितम् । पुनस्तदाज्ये संभृष्टं तलितं प्रोच्यते बुधैः ॥ ' इति । ] 'तलिदं स्नेहपक्वे देशी' इत्येके । 'भडिदे' इति पाठे भटित्रमित्यर्थः । 'शूलाकृतं भटित्रं च' इत्यमरः । भक्तं च हैमन्तिकरात्रिसिद्धं लीणे अ [वेले लीनायां च वेलायाम् । गते

**विट**:—शान्तं[1] पापम् ।

**काचित्स्वाधीनयौवना ।**

**सा नष्टा[2] शङ्कया तस्याः प्राप्तेयं शीलवञ्चना ॥ ४४ ॥**

सर्वथेदमनुनयसर्वस्वं गृह्यताम् । (इति खड्गमुत्सृज्य कृताञ्जलिः पादयोः पतति ।)

**विदूषकः**—सत्पुरुष उत्तिष्ठोत्तिष्ठ । अजानता मया त्वमुपालब्धः । सांप्रतं पुनर्जानन्ननुनयामि । (सप्पुरिस उठ्ठेहि उठ्ठेहि । अआणन्तेण मए तुमं उवालद्धे । संपदं उण जाणन्तो अणुणेमि । )

**विटः**—ननु भवानेवात्रानुनेयः । तदुत्तिष्ठामि समयतः ।

**विदूषकः**—भणतु भवान् । ( भणादु भवम् । )

**विटः**—यदीमं वृत्तान्तमार्यचारुदत्तस्य[3] नाख्यास्यसि[4] ।

**विदूषकः**—न कथयिष्यामि । ( ण कधइस्सम् । )

**विटः**—

**एष ते प्रणयो विप्र शिरसा धार्यते मया ।**

**गुणशस्त्रैर्वयं येन शस्त्रवन्तोऽपि निर्जिताः ॥ ४५ ॥**

**शकारः**—( सासूयम् । ) किंनिमित्तं पुनर्भाव एतस्य दुष्टबटुकस्य कृपणाञ्जलिं कृत्वा पादयोर्निपतितः । (किंणिमित्तं उण भावे एदश्श दुट्ठबडुअश्श किविणअञ्जलिं[5] कदुअ पाएशु णिवडिदे ।)

**विटः**—भीतोऽस्मि ।

**शकारः**—कस्मात्त्वं भीतः । ( कश्श तुमं भीदे ।)

**विटः**—तस्य चारुदत्तस्य गुणेभ्यः ।

**शकारः**—के तस्य गुणा यस्य गृहं प्रविश्याशितव्यमपि नास्ति । ( के तश्श गुणा जश्श गेहं पविशिअ अशिदव्वं पि णत्थि ।)

**विटः**—मा मैवम् ।

**सोऽस्मद्विधानां प्रणयैः कृशीकृतो**
**न तेन कश्चिद्विभवैर्विमानितः ।**
**निदाघकालेष्विव सोदको ह्रदो**
**नृणां स तृष्णामपनीय शुष्कवान् ॥ ४६ ॥**

**शकारः**—( सामर्षम् । ) कः स गर्भदास्याः पुत्रः ।

**शूरो विक्रान्तः पाण्डवः श्वेतकेतुः**
**पुत्रो राधाया रावण इन्द्रदत्तः ।**
**आहो कुन्त्यां तेन रामेण जातः**
**अश्वत्थामा धर्मपुत्रो जटायुः ॥ ४७ ॥**

---

१ शान्तं पापं शान्तं पापम्. २ भ्रष्टा. ३ आर्येति नास्ति क्वचित्. ४ नाख्यापयसि. ५ किं विणअं.

VITA—Heaven forbid !

—Who is a courtesan ( *lit.* the mistress of her youth ). She disappeared, and, mistaking this lady for her, we came to commit this breach of decorum ( *lit.* good character ). ( 44 )

Please accept this all-in-all of conciliation ( unconditional apology ). *He throws away his sword, and folding his hands prostrates himself at his feeet* ).

VID.—Good man, get up, get up. I blamed you as I did not know ( your real nature ). Now that I know it, I will apologize to you.

VITA—It is indeed you to whom we owe an apology in this affair. So, I will get up, ( but ) on condition.

VID.—Speak ( what it is ).

VITA—( I will get up ) if you will not tell Charudatta of this incident.

VID.—I will not tell.

VITA--

This favour of you, O Brahmana, I bear on my head ( i. e. accept with great respect ), ( of you ) by whom, we, even though armed with real weapons, have been conquered with the weapons of virtues. ( 45 )

SAK.—( *With jealous anger.* ). Well, for what reason did you fall at this rascally fellow's feet, folding your hands cringingly ?

VITA—Because I am afraid.

SAK.—Of what are you afraid ?

VITA—Of the virtues of that Charudatta.

SAK.—What sort of virtues does he possess, when on entering his house one does not find even eatables there ?

VITA—Nay, say not so.

He has become impoverished by ( granting ) the prayers of persons like us ; never did he insult anyone in his ( pride of ) wealth. He has dried up ( i. e. become poor ) by having satisfied the thirst ( i. e. needs ) of men, like a reservoir, full of water, in the hot season. ( 46 )

SAK.—( *Indignantly*). Who is he, that son-of-a-born-slave ?

Is he Svetaketu, the brave and valiant son of Pandu ? Or is he Ravana, the Indra-given son of Radha ? Or is he Asvatthama, born of Kunti from that ( well-known ) Rama ? Or is he Jatayu, the son of Dharma ? (47)

( के शे गब्भदासीएपुत्ते ।

शूले विक्कन्ते पण्डवे शेदकेदू पुत्ते लाधाए लावणे इन्ददत्ते ।

आहो कुन्तीए तेण लामेण जादे अश्शत्थामे धम्मपुत्ते जडाऊ ॥ )

**विटः**—मूर्ख आर्यचारुदत्तः खल्वसौ ।

**दीनानां कल्पवृक्षः स्वगुणफलनतः सज्जनानां कुटुम्बी**
**आदर्शः[1] शिक्षितानां सुचरितनिकषः शीलवेलासमुद्रः ।**
**सत्कर्ता नावमन्ता पुरुषगुणनिधिर्दक्षिणोदारसत्त्वो**
**ह्येकः श्लाघ्यः स जीवत्यधिकगुणतया चोच्छ्वसन्तीव चान्ये ॥ ४८ ॥**

तदितो गच्छामः ।

**शकारः**—अगृहीत्वा वसन्तसेनाम् । ( अगेण्हिअ वशन्तशेणिअम् । )

**विटः**—नष्टा वसन्तसेना ।

**शकारः**—कथमिव । ( कधं विअ ।)

**विटः**—

**अन्धस्य दृष्टिरिव, पुष्टिरिवातुरस्य ।**
**मूर्खस्य बुद्धिरिव, सिद्धिरिवालसस्य ।**
**स्वल्पस्मृतेर्व्यसनिनः परमेव विद्या**
**त्वां प्राप्य सा रतिरिवारिजन प्रनष्टा ॥ ४९ ॥**

**शकारः**—अगृहीत्वा वसन्तसेनां न गमिष्यामि । (अगेण्हिअ वशन्तशेणिअं ण गमिश्शम् ।)

**विटः**—एतदपि न श्रुतं त्वया ।

**आलाने गृह्यते हस्ती वाजी वल्गासु गृह्यते ।**
**हृदये गृह्यते नारी यदीदं[2] नास्ति गम्यताम् ॥ ५० ॥**

**शकारः**—यदि गच्छसि गच्छ त्वम् । अहं न गमिष्यामि । (यदि गच्छशि गच्छ तुमम् । हगे ण गमिश्शम् ।)

**विटः**—एवम् । गच्छामि । (इति निष्क्रान्तः ।)

---

समये इत्यर्थः । लीणे वेळे इति पुंलिङ्गं शकारवचनत्वेन न दोषः । अतः पूर्वमेवोक्तं—'आगमलिङ्गविहीनम्' इत्यादीति ध्येयं सुधीभिः । न खलु भवति पूतिर्दुर्गन्धताऽपि तु भवत्येव इति काकुः—इति लल्लादीक्षितः । ] ऋणं च वैरं च न भवति । पूदी पूति । चिरंतनत्वेन प्रशिथिलं स्वकार्यम् ॥ ५१ ॥ शोश्तकं शोभनम् । लश्तकं सकपटम् । भणिष्यसि । तथा भणिश्यसि । भणेशीति भविष्यद्वर्तमानयोस्तुल्यं रूपम् । यथाऽहमात्मकीयायां प्रासादस्य बालाग्रलक्षितायां कपोतपालिकायां विटङ्के । 'बालाग्रं मत्तवारणम् । कपोतपालिका उपरिगृहश्रेणीति दक्षिणापथे लोकोक्तिरियम्' इति प्राचीनटीका । तस्यामुपविष्टः शृणोमि । अन्यथा यदि भणसि तदा कपाट-

---

१ चादर्शः. २ यदिदं.

VITA—You fool! He is, as is well-known, the worthy Charudatta :

To the distressed, he is the wish-yielding tree, bent down with (the load of) the fruit of his virtues. To the virtuous he is a family-head. To the learned he is a mirror ( reflecting learning ). He is the touch-stone of moral conduct, and the ocean having righteousness for its coast-line ( *i. e.* never transgressing it ). He is (ever) hospitable, and never shows disrespect. He is a treasure of all manly virtues, and is courteous and magnanimous by nature. By reason of his manifold virtues, he alone, deserving of praise, really lives; while others are (merely) breathing as it were. (48)

So we shall go away from this place.

SAK.—Without taking Vasantasena (with us) ?

VITA—Lost is your Vasantasena !

SAK.—How, indeed ?

VITA,—

Meeting with you, she has vanished, like the sight of a blind man, or the robustness of a sick person, or the common sense of a fool, or the achievement of an idle fellow, or the highest kind of ( *i. e.* Vedic ) learning in the case of one of weak memory and addicted to vices, or like the feeling of love towards an enemy. (49)

SAK —I will not go without taking Vasantasena (with me).

VITA—Have you not heard even this ?—

" An elephant can be held by means of a tying-rope, a horse by means of reins, and a woman by the heart : if you haven't this, then go away." (50)

SAK.—If you want to go, you may. I won't go.

VITA--All right. I am off. (*Exit*).

---

प्रविष्टं कपित्थगुलिकमिव मस्तकं तव शब्दविशेषयुक्तं [ मडमड इति शब्दयुक्तं ] तथा भक्षयिष्यामि लोकोक्त्या मडमडायिश्शमिति व्याख्यायते । कपित्थं फलविशेषः । 'लस्तकं शोस्तकं द्वयमपि शोभनार्थम्' इति प्राचीनटीका । [ अपवार्येति । तल्लक्षणं--'तद्भवेदपवारितम् । रहस्यं तु यदन्यस्य परावृत्य प्रकाशते ।।' इति । ] गतो भावो विटः सत्यम् । एषोऽसिः । भट्टारकः स्वामिकः । **निर्वल्कलमित्यादि** । उपजातिच्छन्दसा । निर्वल्कलं [ निर्गतं वल्कलं लक्षणया कोशः यस्य तं विकोशमित्यर्थः । ] मूलकपेशिवर्णम् । पेशी त्वक् । मूलकत्वग्वर्णम् । आलोहितमित्यर्थः । [ एतादृशमसि ] स्कन्धेन गृहीत्वा च कोशीसुप्तम् । अल्पार्थे स्त्रीत्वम् । कोशावस्थितमित्यर्थः । **कोशावस्थितं** कृत्वेति यावत् । ] कुक्कुरैः कुक्कुरीभिश्च शब्दायमानो

**शकारः**—गतः खलु भावोऽभावम् । (विदूषकमुद्दिश्य ।) अरे काकपदशीर्षमस्तक दुष्टबटुक उपविशोपविश । ( गडे क्खु भावे अभावम् । अले काकपदशीशमश्तक[1] दुश्टबडुका उवविश उवविश । )

**विदूषकः**—उपवेशिता एव वयम् । ( उववेसिदा ज्जेव अम्हे । )

**शकारः**—केन । ( केण । )

**विदूषकः**—कृतान्तेन । ( कअन्तेण ।)

**शकारः**—उत्तिष्ठोत्तिष्ठ । (उठ्ठेहि उठ्ठेहि । )

**विदूषकः**—उत्थास्यामः । ( उट्ठिस्सामो । )

**शकारः**—कदा । ( कदा । )

**विदूषकः**—यदा पुनरपि दैवमनुकूलं भविष्यति । ( जदा पुणो वि देव्वं अणुऊलं भविस्सदि । )

**शकारः**—अरे रुदिहि रुदिहि । ( अले लोद लोद । )

**विदूषकः**—रोदिता एव वयम् । ( रोदाविदा ज्जेव अम्हे ।)

**शकारः**—केन । ( केण । )

**विदूषकः**—दुर्गत्या । (दुग्गदीए ।)

**शकारः**—अरे हस हस । ( अले हश हश ।)

**विदूषकः**—हसिष्यामः । ( हसिस्सामो । )

**शकारः**—कदा । ( कदा । )

**विदूषकः**—पुनरपि ऋद्ध्याऽऽर्यचारुदत्तस्य । ( पुणो वि ऋद्धीए[2] अज्जचारुदत्तस्स[3] । )

**शकारः**—अरे रे दुष्टबटुक भणिष्यसि मम वचनेन तं दरिद्रचारुदत्तकम्—'एषा ससुवर्णा सहिरण्या नवनाटकदर्शनोत्थिता सूत्रधारीव वसन्तसेना नाम गणिकादारिका कामदेवायतनोद्यानात्प्रभृति त्वामनुरक्ताऽस्माभिर्बलात्कारानुनीयमाना तव गेहं प्रविष्टा । तद्यदि मम हस्ते स्वयमेव प्रस्थाप्यैनां समर्पयसि ततोऽधिकरणे व्यवहारं विना लघु निर्यातयतस्तव मयाऽनुबद्धा प्रीतिर्भविष्यति । अथ वाऽनिर्यातयतो मरणान्तिकं वैरं भविष्यति । अपि च प्रेक्षस्व प्रेक्षस्व । ( अलेले[4] दुश्टबडुका भणेशि मम वअणेण तं दलिद्दचालुदत्तकम्— 'एशा शशुवण्णा शहिलण्णा णवणाडअदंशणुट्ठिदा शुत्तधालिव्व वशन्तशेणा णाम गणिआदालिआ कामदेवाअदणुज्जाणादो पहुदि तुमं अणुलत्ता अम्हेहिं बलक्कालाणुणीअमाणा तुह गेहं पविश्टा । ता जइ मम हश्ते[5] शअं ज्जेव पट्ठाविअ एणं शमप्पेशि तदो अधिअलणे ववहालं विणा लहुं णिज्जादमाणाह तव मए अणुबद्धा पीदी हुविश्शदि । आदु अणिज्जादमाणाह मलणन्तिके वेले हुविश्शदि । अवि अ पेक्ख पेक्ख ।)

---

१ पदमश्तशीशक. २ सिद्धीए. ३ अज्ज इति नास्ति क्वचित्. ४ अले. ५ हत्थे.

SAK.—Well, he has taken himself off! (*To the* Vid.). You villainous fellow, with your pate and head of the shape of a crow's foot! Sit down, sit down!

VID.—We have been already made to sit down.

SAK.—By whom?

VID.—By fate.

SAK.—Well, get up, get up.

VID.—We shall get up.

SAK.—When?

VID.—When fate will again become favourable

SAK.—Eh, weep, weep!

VID.—We have been already made to weep.

SAK.—By whom?

VID.—By poverty.

SAK.—Eh, laugh, laugh i

VID.—We shall laugh.

SAK.—When?

VID.—When the noble Charudatta attains prosperity again.

SAK.—You villainous fellow! Say to that beggar Charudatta at my bidding (as follows):—" This courtesan, named Vasantasena decked with gold and covered with gold, (and charming) like the chief actress rising up for (or, at) the exhibition of a new play, who has fallen in love with you since (her visit to) the garden of Cupid's temple, has entered your house while we were trying to win her over by force; so, if you, of your own accord, send her away and place her in my hands, then there will subsist permanent friendliness between you and me, by your quickly restoring her without (any recourse on my part to) judicial proceedings in a court af law. And if you don't restore her, there will be (between us) a feud lasting till death. Moreover, observe carefully—

---

यथा शृगालस्तथा स्वगृहं प्रयामि । विदूषकरदनिके कुक्कुरकुक्कुरीस्थाने ॥ ५२ ॥ [संयतमुखी नियन्त्रितवदना । नाहं कथंचिन्निवेदयामीत्यर्थः । ] एव ण्णेदमिति एवार्थे । रोहसेनश्चारुदत्तसुतः । अम्हहे विस्मये । अनुदासीनं साभिलाषम् । तदनुरूपचेष्टा-योगात् । अभ्यन्तरगमनस्याभागिनी । वेश्यात्वात् । यदेति । भाग्यं शोभनं कर्म [यदा नरः भाग्यक्षयेण विभवनाशेन पीडितां संकटां कृतान्तेन दैवेन उपहितां प्रापितां दशां प्रतिपद्यते तदा । विरज्यते विरक्तो भवति । वंशस्थं वृत्तम् ] ॥५३॥ अविज्ञातेति । [ अविज्ञाता यथार्थतोऽज्ञाता । अत एव अवसक्तेनाङ्गलग्नेन मम वाससा दूषिता । यद्वा अविज्ञातायामवसक्तेन लग्नेन इति एकं पदम् । अविज्ञातं यथा

**कूष्माण्डी गोमयलिप्तवृन्ता शाकं च शुष्कं तलितं खलु मांसम् ।**
**भक्तं च हैमन्तिकरात्रिसिद्धं लीनायां च वेलायां न खलु भवति पूति ॥५१॥**

(कश्चालुका[1] गोच्छडलित्तवेण्टा शाके अ शुक्खे तलिदे[2] हु मंशे ।
भत्ते अ हेमन्तिअलत्तिशिद्धे लीणे अ वेले ण हु होदि पूदी ॥ ')

शोभनं भणिष्यसि । सकपटं भणिष्यसि । तथा भणिष्यसि यथाऽहमात्मकीयायां प्रासादबालाग्रकपोतपालिकायामुपविष्टः शृणोमि । अन्यथा यदि भणसि तदा कपाटप्रविष्टकपित्थगुलिकमिव मस्तकं ते मडमडायिष्यामि । (शोश्तकं[3] भणेशि । लश्तकं[4] भणेशि । तधा भणेशि जधा हगे अत्तणकेलिकाए पाशादबालग्गकवोदवालिआए उववि‍श्टे शुणामि । अण्णधा[5] जदि भणेशि ता कवालपविठ्ठकविस्थगुडिअं[6] विअ मस्तअं दे मडमडाइश्शम् ।)

**विदूषकः**––भणिष्यामि । (भणिस्सम् ।)

**शकारः**––( अपवार्य । ) चेट गतः सत्यमेव भावः । (चेडे गडे शच्चकं ज्जेव भावे ।)

**चेटः**––अथ किम् । (अध इं ।)

**शकारः**––तच्छीघ्रमपक्रमावः । (ता शिग्घं अवक्कमम्ह ।)

**चेटः**––तद्गृह्णातु भट्टारकोऽसिम् । (ता गेण्हदु[7] भट्टके अशिम् ।)

**शकारः**––तवैव हस्ते तिष्ठतु । (तव ज्जेव हत्थे चिश्ठदु । )

**चेटः**––एष भट्टारकस्य । गृह्णात्वेनं भट्टारकोऽसिम् । (एशे भट्टालकस्य । गेण्हदु णं भट्टके अशिम् ।)

**शकारः**––(विपरीतं गृहीत्वा ।)

**निर्वल्कलं मूलकपेशिवर्णं स्कन्धेन गृहीत्वा च कोशसुप्तम् ।**
**कुक्कुरैः कुक्कुरीभिश्च बुक्कयमानो यथा शृगालः शरणं प्रयामि ॥५२।**

(णिव्वक्कलं मूलकपेशिवण्णं खन्धेण घेत्तूण अ कोशशुत्तम्[8] ।
कुक्केहिं कुक्कीहिं अ [9]बुक्कअन्ते जधा शिआले शलणं पलामि ॥ )

( परिक्रम्य निष्क्रान्तौ । )

**विदूषकः**––भवति रदनिके न खलु तेऽयमपमानस्तत्रभवतश्चारुदत्तस्य निवेदयितव्यः । दौर्गत्यपीडितस्य मन्ये द्विगुणतरा पीडा भविष्यति । (भोदि रदणिए ण क्खु दे अअं अवमाणो तत्तभवदो चारुदत्तस्य णिवेदइदव्वो । दोग्गच्चपीडिअस्स मण्णे दिउणदरा पीडा हुविस्सदि ।

**रदनिका**––आर्य मैत्रेय रदनिका खल्वहं संयतमुखी । ( अज्ज मित्तेअ रदणिआ क्खु अहं संजदमुही ।)

---

१ कक्कालुका ( कर्कालुका ). २ पलिर. ३ शोट्टकं (स्वस्तिकं). ४ लहुअं (लघुकं). ५ तधा जदि ण. ६ कवालतल. ७ गेण्ह मं. ८ कोशि० ९ भुक्क.

A pumpkin whose stalk is besmeared with cow's dung, a vegetable that has been dried, meat which is fried, and boiled rice that has been cooked at night in the cold season—these do not get spoiled (*lit.* putrefy) even by lapse of time. ( And so will be my enmity ever-lasting )." (51)

Speak well, and speak craftily ; speak in such a ( loud ) voice that I may hear you when seated in the elephant-corniced upper terrace of my palace. If you speak in any other manner, I will crunch your head like a round *Kapittha* fruit crushed by being inserted between the panels of a door.

VID.—I will speak ( as you desire .

SAK.—( *Aside* ). Cheta, has Vita really gone ?

CHETA—He has.

SAK.—Then let us be off quickly.

CHETA—Then let the master take the sword.

SAK.—Let it be in your own hand.

CHETA—It belongs to the master. Let the master keep it with him.

SAK.—( *Seizing it by the wrong end* ).

Like a jackal pursued with yells by dogs and bitches ( going to his lair ), I go to my house, bearing on my shoulder this unsheathed sword resembling in colour the radish-skin, after making it rest in its scabbard. (52)

( *They walk about and depart* ).

VID.—Girl, Radanika, you should not inform Charudatta about this insult offered to you ; for I think he would be doubly pained ( to hear it ), afflicted as he already is by poverty.

RAD.—Sir Maitreya, I am, indeed, Radanika ; my lips are sealed.

---

तथा अवसक्तेनेति वा । ननु भूषिता इत्यनेन औदार्याख्यो नायिकालंकार: प्रदर्शित: । 'औदार्यं विनय: सदा ' इति लक्षणात् । ] दूषिता परपुरुषत्वात् ॥ ५४ ॥ ययेति । [ क्षीणे नष्टे विभवविस्तरे संपन्निधौ सति यया जनित: मम काम: साफल्याभावात् । कुत्सित: पुरुष: कुपुरुष: निस्तेजस्क: पुमांस्तस्य क्रोध इव स्वगात्रेष्वेव ] सीदति कर्तव्यासामर्थ्यात्प्रव्यक्तो न भवति । [ तत्रैव विलीयते इत्यर्थ: । ] अत्र 'अलं परकलत्रशङ्कया ' इत्यारभ्य ' अये इयं वसन्तसेना ' इत्यन्तेन नायकोपकारिकाया अर्थसंपत्तेरवगमात्प्रथमं पताकास्थानमिदम् । तदुक्तं– ' सहसैवार्थसंपत्तिर्नायकस्योपकारिका । पताकास्थानकं संधौ प्रथमे तन्मतम् '

**विदूषकः**--एवं न्विदम् । (एवं ण्णेदम् । )

**चारुदत्तः**--( वसन्तसेनामुद्दिश्य । ) रदनिके मारुताभिलाषी प्रदोषसमयशीतार्तो[1] रोहसेनः । ततः प्रवेश्यतामभ्यन्तरमयम् । अनेन प्रावारकेण छादयैनम् । (इति प्रावारकं प्रयच्छति ।)

**वसन्तसेना**--(स्वगतम् ।) कथं परिजन इति मामवगच्छति । ( प्रावारकं गृहीत्वा समाघ्राय च स्वगतं सस्पृहम् ।) आश्चर्यम् । जातीकुसुमवासितः प्रावारकः । अनुदासीनमस्य यौवनं प्रतिभासते । (अपवारितकेन प्रावृणोति ।) (कधं परिअणोत्ति मं अवगच्छदि । अम्हहे । जादीकुसुमवासिदो पावारओ । अणुदासीणं से ज्जोव्वणं पडिभासेदि । )

**चारुदत्तः**--ननु रदनिके रोहसेनं गृहीत्वाऽभ्यन्तरं प्रविश ।

**वसन्तसेना**--( स्वगतम् । ) मन्दभागिनी खल्वहं तवाभ्यन्तरस्य । ( मन्दभाईणी क्खु अहं तुम्हे अब्भन्तरस्स ।)

**चारुदत्तः**--ननु रदनिके प्रतिवचनमपि नास्ति । कष्टम् !

**यदा तु भाग्यक्षयपीडितां दशां नरः कृतान्तोपहितां प्रपद्यते ।**
**तदाऽस्य मित्राण्यपि यान्त्यमित्रतां चिरानुरक्तोऽपि विरज्यते जनः ॥५३॥**

(उपसृत्य[2] रदनिका विदूषकश्च ।)

**विदूषकः**—भो इयं सा रदनिका । (भो इअं सा रदणिआ ।)

**चारुदत्तः**—इयं सा रदनिका । इयमपरा का ।

**अविज्ञातावसक्तेन दूषिता मम वाससा ।**

**वसन्तसेना**—(स्वगतम् ।) ननु भूषिता । (णं भूसिदा ।)

**चारुदत्तः**—

**छादिता शरदभ्रेण चन्द्रलेखेव दृश्यते ॥ ५४ ॥**

अथ वा न युक्तं परकलत्रदर्शनम् ।

**विदूषकः**—भोः अलं परकलत्रदर्शनशङ्कया । एषा वसन्तसेना कामदेवायतनोद्यानात्प्रभृति भवन्तमनुरक्ता । (भो अलं परकलत्रदंसणसङ्काए । एसा वसन्तसेणा कामदेवाअदणुज्जाणादो पहुदि भवन्तमणुरत्ता । )

**चारुदत्तः**—अये[3] इयं वसन्तसेना । (स्वगतम् ।)

**यया मे जनितः कामः क्षीणे विभवविस्तरे ।**
**क्रोधः कुपुरुषस्येव स्वगात्रेष्वेव सीदति ॥ ५५ ॥**

**विदूषकः**—भो वयस्य एष खलु राजश्यालो भणति । (भो वअस्स एसो क्खु राअसालो भणादि ।)

---

१ समयः । शीता०. २ विदूषकः रदनिकामुपसृत्य. ३ अये इति नास्ति क्वचित्.

VID.—Well, so be it.

CHAR.—( *To Vasantasena* ). Radanika ( the boy ) Rohasena covetous of ( enjoying ) the breeze, is now suffering from the chilliness of the night-time. So let him be carried inside. And cover him with this cloak. ( *He gives her the cloak* ).

VAS.—(*To herself*). How now ! He takes me for his servant ! ( *Taking up the cloak she smells it : then longingly to herself* ). Ah ! This cloak bears the scent of jasmine flowers ! His youth seems to be not indifferent ( to the pleasures of life ), after all. ( *She turns aside and covers herself with it* ).

CHAR.—I say, Radanika, take Rohasena and go inside.

VAS.—( *To herself* ). Alas ! I have not the good fortune to ( enter ) your inside.

CHAR.—I say, Radanika, you don't even make a reply ! Alas !

When a man attains a state brought on by fate and painful on account of the loss of prosperity, even his friends turn into his enemies, and even persons who have long been attached to him grow cold. (53)

( Radanika *and* Vidushaka *approach* )

VID.—Sir, *here* is that Radanika.

CHAR.—This is our Radanika ! Then who is this another lady,

Who is desecrated by my garment which I threw at her in ignorance—

Vas.—( *To herself* ). Say rather *consecrated.*

CHAR.—

—And who appears like the lunar digit obscured by an autumnal cloud ? (54)

Or rather, it is improper to look at another's wife.

VID.—Sir, you need not have any fear about looking at another's wife. This is Vasantasena, who has fallen in love with you since ( her visit to ) the garden of Cupid's shrine.

CHAR.—Ah, this is Vasantasena ! ( *To himself* ).

—The passion inspired in me by whom subsides in my limbs like the anger of a cowardly person, now that my ample ( large ) fortune has declined. (55)

VID.—My friend, this is what the king's brother-in-law says—

**चारुदत्तः**—किम् ।

**विदूषकः**—एषा ससुवर्णा सहिरण्या नवनाटकदर्शनोत्थिता सूत्रधारीव वसन्तसेना नाम गणिकादारिका कामदेवायतनोद्यानात्प्रभृति त्वामनुरक्ताऽस्माभिर्बलात्कारानुनीयमाना तव गेहं प्रविष्टा । (एसा ससुवण्णा सहिलण्णा णवणाडअदंसणुट्ठिदा सुत्तधालिव्व वसन्तसेणा णाम गणिआदालिआ कामदेवाअदणुज्जाणादो पहुदि तुमं अणुलत्ता अम्हेहिं बलक्कालाणुणीअमाणा तुह गेहं पविट्ठा ।)

**वसन्तसेना**—(स्वगतम् ।) बलात्कारानुनीयमानेति यत्सत्यमलंकृताऽस्म्येतैरक्षरैः । (बलक्कालाणुणीअमाणेत्ति जं सच्चं अलंकिदम्हि एदेहिं अक्खरेहिं ।)

**विदूषकः**—तद्यदि मम हस्ते स्वयमेव प्रस्थाप्यैनां समर्पयसि ततोऽधिकरणे व्यवहारं विना लघु निर्यातयतस्तव मयाऽनुबद्धा प्रीतिर्भविष्यति । अन्यथा मरणान्तिकं वैरं भविष्यति । (ता जइ मम हत्थे सअं ज्जेव्व पट्ठाविअ एणं समप्पेसि तदो अधिअलणे ववहालं विणा लहुं णिज्जादमाणाह तव मए अणुबद्धा पीदी हुविस्सदि । अण्णधा मलणन्तिके वेले हुविस्सदि ।)

**चारुदत्तः**—(सावज्ञम् ।) अज्ञोऽसौ । (स्वगतम् ।) अये कथं देवतोपस्थानयोग्या युवतिरियम् । तेन खलु तस्यां वेलायां

> **प्रविश गृहमिति प्रतोद्यमाना**
> **न चलति भाग्यकृतां दशामवेक्ष्य ।**
> **पुरुषपरिचयेन च प्रगल्भं**
> **न वदति यद्यपि भाषते बहूनि ॥ ५६ ॥**

(प्रकाशम् ।) भवति वसन्तसेने अनेनाविज्ञानादपरिज्ञातपरिजनोपचारेणापराद्धोऽस्मि । शिरसा भवतीमनुनयामि ।

**वसन्तसेना**—एतेनानुचितभूमिकारोहणेनापराद्धाऽऽर्यं शीर्षेण प्रणम्य प्रसादयामि (एदिणा अणुचिदभूमिआरोहणेण अवरज्झा अज्जं सीसेण पणमिअ पसादेमि ।)

---

इति ॥ ५५ ॥ एषेत्यादि पूर्वोक्तमेव भणति । अलंकृताऽस्मीति । ममान्यत्राभिलाषो नास्तीत्यर्थः ] । देवतेवोपस्थानं [ स्तुत्योपचरणम् । यद्वा देवतया उपस्थानं समागमः । तस्य योग्या । तस्यां वेलायां रोहसेनस्य गृहप्रवेशाज्ञादानकाले । ] [ अनेन विलोभनं नामाङ्गमुपक्षिप्तम् । 'गुणाख्यानं विलोभनम्' इति तल्लक्षणम् । ] **प्रविश गृहमिति** । [ प्रतोद्यमाना सपरुषाक्षरमनुरुध्यमानाऽपि । भाग्यकृतां मद्दैवकृतामवस्थामवेक्ष्य दाक्षिण्यात् न चलति अन्यत्र न गता । यद्यपि गणिकात्वेन लब्धपाटवत्वाद्बहूनि भाषते तथाऽपि अधुना पुरुषपरिचयेन मादृशस्य पुरुषस्य संगत्या प्रगल्भं धृष्टं न भाषते । सविनयमेव वक्तीत्यर्थः । ] पुष्पिताग्रा वृत्तम् ॥ ५६ ॥ [ अज्ञानात् अपरिज्ञातायां त्वयि यः परिजनवदुपचारः आज्ञाकरणादिरूपः तेन । ]

CHAR.—What is it ?

VID.—" This courtesan, named Vasantasena, decked with gold and covered with gold, ( and charming ) like the chief actress rising up for ( or, at ) the exhibition of a new play, who has fallen in love with you since ( her visit to ) the garden of Cupid's temple, has entered your house while we were trying to win her over by force.

VAS.—( *To herself* ). To tell the truth, I have been obliged ( *lit.* decked ) by these words ( of his ), *viz.* " trying to win her over by force."

VID.—" So, if you, of your own accord, send her away and place her in my hands, then there will subsist permanent friendliness between you and me, by your quickly restoring her without (any recourse on my part to) judicial proceedings in a court of law. Otherwise there will be ( between us ) a feud lasting till death."

CHAR.—( *Contemptuously* ). He is a fool ! ( *To himself* ). Ah ! How now ! She is indeed a lady fit to be waited upon ( worshipped ) like a goddess ! Hence it was that at that time,

She, although ordered to enter the house. did not move away, observing my ( penurious ) condition brought upon by fate. And although she can talk boldly in a variety of ways owing to her familiarity with men, she does not speak boldly. (56)

( *Aloud* ). Madam Vasantasena, I have offended you by thus treating you like a servant, not recognizing you through my ignorance. So here I ask your pordon with my ( bent ) head,

VAS.—*I* have to conciliate your honour by bowing down to you with my head, since I have offended you by this intrusion into a place of which I am unworthy.

---

अनुचितं भूमिसमारोहणं पक्षद्वारेणावासप्रवेशादिकम् । [ कलमः शालिविशेषः केदारः क्षेत्रं च ताविव । ] करभ उष्ट्रशिशुः तस्य जानु तत्सदृशेन । अवर्तुलेन निम्नोन्नतेन चेति भावः । तिष्ठतु प्रणयः आस्तामियं प्रणयोक्तिः । अयं प्रणयः स्नेहः तिष्ठतु स्थिरो भवत्विति गूढाभिसंधिः । ] प्रणय इत्यनेन संभोगप्रार्थना कटाक्षिता । ईदृशेन गहीतसंभोगोपकरणादिना । पापा अकार्यकारिणः । भग्नत्वाद्रक्षकाभावाच्चायोग्यता । अत्यन्तप्रश्रयवत्त्वादनुग्रहः । चोरेहिं हरिज्जउ इति संधिच्छेदनाम्नस्तृतीयाङ्कस्य सूचनम् । [ तेन चेह तृतीयं पताकास्थानकमुक्तम् । 'अर्थोपक्षेपकमनुलीनं सविनयं भवेत् । श्लिष्टप्रत्युत्तरोपेतं तृतीयमिदमुच्यते ॥ ' इति । ] चतुष्पथोपनीत इवोपहारो

**विदूषकः**--भो द्वावपि युवां सुखं प्रणम्य कलमकेदारावन्योन्यशीर्षेण शीर्षं समागतौ। अहमप्यमुना करभजानुसदृशेन शीर्षेण द्वावपि युवां प्रसादयामि। ( इत्युत्तिष्ठति। ) (भो दुवेवि तुम्हे सुखं[1] पणमिअ कलमकेदारा अण्णोण्णं सीसेण सीसं समाअदा। अहं पि इमिणा करहजाणुसरिसेण सीसेण दुवेवि तुम्हे पसादेमि।[2]

**चारुदत्तः**--भवतु। तिष्ठतु प्रणयः।

**वसन्तसेना**--( स्वगतम्।) चतुरो मधुरश्चायमुपन्यासः। न युक्तमद्येदृशेनेहागतया मया प्रतिवस्तुम्। भवतु। एवं तावद्भणिष्यामि। (प्रकाशम्।) आर्य यद्येवमहमार्यस्यानुग्राह्या तदिच्छाम्यहमिममलंकारकमार्यस्य गेहे निक्षेप्तुम्। अलंकारस्य निमित्तमेते पापा अनुसरन्ति। ( चदुरो मधुरो अ अअं उवण्णासो। ण जुत्तं अज्ज एरिसेण इध आअदाए मए पडिवसिदुम्। भोदु। एव्वं दाव भणिस्सम्। अज्ज जइ एव्वं अहं अज्जस्स अणुगेज्झा ता इच्छे अहं इमं अलंकारअं अज्जस्स[3] गेहे णिक्खिविदुम्। अलंकारस्स णिमित्तं एदे पावा अणुसरन्ति।)

**चारुदत्तः**--अयोग्यमिदं न्यासस्य गृहम्।

**वसन्तसेना**--आर्य अलीकम्। पुरुषेषु न्यासा निक्षिप्यन्ते न पुनर्गेहेषु। (अज्ज अलीअम्। पुरुसेसु णासा णिक्खिविअन्ति ण उण गेहेसु। )

**चारुदत्तः**--मैत्रेय गृह्यतामयमलंकारः।

**वसन्तसेना**--अनुगृहीताऽस्मि। ( इत्यलंकारमर्पयति। ) (अणुग्गहिदम्हि। )

**विदूषकः**--(गृहीत्वा। ) स्वस्ति भवत्यै। ( सोत्थि भोदीए।)

**चारुदत्तः**--धिङ मूर्ख न्यासः खल्वयम्।

**विदूषकः**--(अपवार्य।) यद्येवं तदा चौरैर्ह्रियताम्--( जइ एव्वं ता चोरेहिं हरिज्जउ--)

**चारुदत्तः**--अचिरेणैव कालेन--

**विदूषकः**--एषोऽस्या अस्माकं विन्यासः। (एसो से अम्हाणं विण्णासो।)

**चारुदत्तः**--निर्यातयिष्ये।

**वसन्तसेना**--आर्य इच्छाम्यहमनेनार्येणानुगम्यमाना स्वकं गेहं गन्तुम्। (अज्ज इच्छे अहं इमिणा अज्जेण अणुगच्छिज्जन्ती सकं गेहं गन्तुम्।)

**चारुदत्तः**--मैत्रेय अनुगच्छ तत्रभवतीम्।

**विदूषकः**--त्वमेवैतां कलहंसगामिनीमनुगच्छन्राजहंस इव शोभसे। अहं पुनर्ब्राह्मणो यत्र तत्र जनैश्चतुष्पथोपनीत इवोपहारः कुक्कुरैरिव खाद्यमानो विपत्स्ये। ( तुमं ज्जेव एदं कलहंसगामिणीं अणुगच्छन्तो[5] राअहंसो विअ सोहसि। अहं उण बम्हणो जहिं तहिं जणेहिं चउप्पहोवणीदो विअ उवहारो कुक्कुरेहिं विअ खज्जमाणो विवज्जिस्सम्।

---

१ सुसंपण्णा–सुसंपुण्णा–विअ. २ पसादेमि उठ्ठेब त्ति. ३ अज्जगेहे. ५ अणु गच्छ०.

VID.—Well, both of you happily saluting each other, have mutually approached ( each other ) with your heads, like two paddy-fields. I too will ask pardon of you both, with this head of mine resembling a camel-colt's knee. ( *He gets up* ).

CHAR.—Let it go ; no ceremony is needed !

VAS.—( *To herself* ). The beginning of the talk has been clever as well as sweet. But it will not be proper for me to stay with him, having thus come here, he being in such ( poor ) condition. Well, I will speak to him thus. (*Aloud*). Sir, if your Honour would like thus to favour me, then I wish to keep this ornament in your house as a deposit ; it is for the sake of ornaments that these wicked fellows pursue one.

CHAR.—This house is not a fit place for (keeping) a deposit.

VAS.—Sir, that is not true ; (for) deposits are entrusted to *persons*, and not to *houses*.

CHAR.—Maitreya, take that ornament.

VAS.—I am indeed obliged. ( *Hands over the ornament* ).

VID.—( *Receiving it* ). May you be happy !

CHAR.—You fool, it is a deposit ( and not a gift ) !

VID.—( *Aside* ). If so, then may thieves steal—

CHAR.—In a very short time—

VID.—this deposit entrusted to us by her—

CHAR.—I will return it ( to her ).

VAS.—Sir, I wish to repair to my house in the company of this gentleman.

CHAR.—Maitreya, accompany her ladyship.

VID.—You yourself will look charming, like a royal swan, tripping after this lady with her swan-like gait. But I, a ( poor) Brahmana, will come to grief ( or, perish ) being harassed at every step by people, just as an offering made in a public square is gobbled up by dogs.

---

देवताबलिरूप;। ही आश्चर्ये। यत एव निर्धनोऽत एवापमानितः [ कामुकः याभिः।] निःस्नेहा निरनुरागा निस्तैलाश्च। स्नेहोऽनुरागस्तैलं च। भवत्वित्युपसंहारोक्तिः । उदयतीति । [ कामिन्या गण्ड इव पाण्डुः स्निग्धोज्ज्वलः। ग्रहगणः परिवारः अस्य। राजमार्गस्य प्रदीप इवेति रूपकम्। न तु दीपिकावदल्पप्रदेशवर्तिप्रकाश;। उदयति।] यस्य हिमांशोस्तमोवृन्दमध्ये शुभ्रा रश्मयः पतन्ति। यथा प्रभूतजले कर्दमे दुग्धधाराः। [ मालिनी वृत्तम् ] ॥ ५७ ॥ [ राजमार्गं इति। ]

**चारुदत्तः**—एवं भवतु। स्वयमेवानुगच्छामि तत्रभवतीम्। तद्राजमार्गविश्वासयोग्याः प्रज्वाल्यन्तां प्रदीपिकाः।

**विदूषकः**—वर्धमानक प्रज्वालय प्रदीपिकाः। (वड्ढमाणअ पज्जालेहि पदीविआओ।)

**चेटी**—(जनान्तिकम्।) अरे तैलेन विना प्रदीपिकाः प्रज्वाल्यन्ते। (अले तेल्लेण विणा पदीविआओ पज्जालीअन्ति।)

**विदूषकः**—(जनान्तिकम्।) आश्चर्यम्। ताः खल्वस्माकं प्रदीपिका अपमानितनिर्धनकामुका इव गणिका निःस्नेहा इदानीं संवृत्ताः। (ही। ताओ क्खु अम्हाणं पदीविआओ अवमाणिदनिद्धणकामुआ विअ गणिआ णिस्सिणेहाओ दाणिं संवुत्ता।

**चारुदत्तः**—मैत्रेय भवतु। कृतं प्रदीपिकाभिः[1]। पश्य।

**उदयति हि शशाङ्कः कामिनीगण्डपाण्डु**
**ग्रहगणपरिवारो राजमार्गप्रदीपः।**
**तिमिरनिकरमध्ये रश्मयो यस्य गौराः**
**स्रुतजल इव पङ्के क्षीरधाराः पतन्ति ॥ ५७ ॥**

(सानुरागम्[2]।)भवति वसन्तसेने इदं भवत्या गृहम्। प्रविशतु भवती।

**वसन्तसेना**—(सानुरागमवलोकयन्ती[3] निष्क्रान्ता।)

**चारुदत्तः**—वयस्य गता वसन्तसेना। तदेहि। गृहमेव गच्छावः।

**राजमार्गो हि शून्योऽयं रक्षिणः संचरन्ति च।**
**वञ्चना परिहर्तव्या बहुदोषा हि शर्वरी ॥ ५८ ॥**

(परिक्रम्य।) इदं च सुवर्णभाण्डं रक्षितव्यं त्वया रात्रौ वर्धमानकेनापि दिवा।

**विदूषकः**—यथा भवानाज्ञापयति। (जधा भवं आणवेदि)

(इति निष्क्रान्तौ)

**इति मृच्छकटिकेऽलंकारन्यासो[4] नाम प्रथमोऽङ्कः।**

---

शून्यः जनसंचाररहितः। केवलं रक्षिणः संचरन्ति। तथाऽपि वञ्चना प्रतारणा। वसन्तसेनालंकारापहाररूपेति यावत्। हि यतः शर्वरी रात्रिः बहवः दोषाः स्तेयादिरूपा यस्यां सा तथोक्ता ॥ ५८ ॥

इति महोपाध्यायश्रीपृथ्वीधरकृतौ मृच्छकटिकविवृतौ
न्यासार्पणो नाम प्रथमोऽङ्कः ॥

---

१ दीपिकाभिः. २ उत्थाय सानु०. ३ पश्यन्ती. ४ मृच्छकटिकायाम्.

CHAR.—All right. I myself will accompany her ladyship. So light ( some ) torches, such as can be relied upon ( to light up ) the king's high-road.

VID.—Vardhamanaka, light ( some ) torches.

THE SERVANT—( *Aside to* Vid ). Here, how are torches to be lighted without oil ?

VID.—( *Aside to* Char. ). Ah ! Those torches of ours have now become void of *sneha* ( oil ), like courtesans who, slighting penniless lovers, lose their *sneha* ( affection ) for them.

CHAR.—Maitreya, let it be ; there is no need ( now ) of the torches. See—

Here indeed, rises the moon, palish-white like the cheek of an amorous lady, having the starry clusters as his retinue, and serving as the lamp on the king's road,—( the moon ) whose white beams fall in the midst of the dense darkness like streams of milk over (dried) mud from which all the water has oozed out. (57)

( *With love* ). Lady Vasantasena, here is your house ; you may now get in.

VAS —( *Looking at him lovingly*; *exit.* )

CHAR.—Friend, Vásantasena has gone in. Come then ; we too shall go home.

Deserted is this royal road, and guards are patrolling it. We must avoid being duped, for night is full of ( *i. e.* affords scope for ) many crimes. ( 58 )

( *Walking about* ). And this golden casket should be guarded by you at night and by Vardhamanaka by day.

VID. —As Your Honour commands.

( *Exeunt both* ).

*End of Act I. of the* Mrichchhakatika, *styled*
'The Depositing *of the* Ornament.'

# द्वितीयोऽङ्कः ।

( प्रविश्य । )

**चेटी**--मात्राऽऽर्यासकाशं संदेशेन प्रेषिताऽस्मि । तद्यावत्प्रविश्यार्यासकाशं गच्छामि । ( परिक्रम्यावलोक्य च । ) एषाऽऽर्या हृदयेन किमप्यालिखन्ती तिष्ठति। तद्यावदुपसर्पामि । ( अत्ताए अज्जआसआसं संदेसेण पेसिदम्हि । ता जाव पविसिअ अज्जआसआसं गच्छामि । एसा अज्जआ हिअएण किं पि आलिहन्ती चिठ्ठदि । ता जाव उपसप्पामि । )

( ततः प्रविशत्यासनस्था सोत्कण्ठा वसन्तसेना मदनिका च । )

**वसन्तसेना**—चेटि ततस्ततः । ( हञ्जे तदो तदो । )

**मदनिका**[1]—आर्ये न किमपि मन्त्रयसे । किं ततस्ततः । ( अज्जए ण किं पि मन्तेसि । किं तदो तदो । )

**वसन्तसेना**—किं मया भणितम् । ( किं मए भणिदम् । )

**चेटी**—ततस्तत इति । ( तदो तदो त्ति । )

**वसन्तसेना**--( सभ्रूक्षेपम् । ) आ एवम् । ( आ एव्वम् । )

(उपसृत्य)

**प्रथमा चेटी**--आर्ये माताऽऽदिशति स्नाता भूत्वा देवतानां पूजां निर्वर्तयेति (अज्जए अत्ता आदिसदि ण्हादा भविअ देवदाणं पूअं णिव्वत्तेहि त्ति । )

**वसन्तसेना**--चेटि विज्ञापय मातरम् । अद्य न स्नास्यामि तद्ब्राह्मण एव पूजां निर्वर्तयत्विति । ( हञ्जे विण्णवेहि अत्तम् । अज्ज ण ण्हाइस्सं ता बम्हणो ज्जेव्व पूअं णिव्वत्तेदु त्ति । )

**चेटी**—यदार्याऽऽज्ञापयति (इति निष्क्रान्ता ।) (जं अज्जआ आणवेदि ।)

**मदनिका**--आर्ये स्नेहः पृच्छति न पुरोभागिता । तत्किं न्विदम् । (अज्जए सिणेहो पुच्छदि ण पुरोभाइदा । ता किं णेदम् । )

**वसन्तसेना**--मदनिके कीदृशीं मां प्रेक्षसे । ( मदणिए केरिसिं मं पेक्खसि । )

**मदनिका**—आर्यायाः शून्यहृदयत्वेन जानामि हृदयगतं कमप्यार्याऽभिलषतीति । ( अज्जआए सुण्णहिअअत्तणेण जाणामि हिअअगदं कं पि अज्जआ अहिलसदि त्ति । )

---

[ इत आरभ्य चतुर्थाङ्कसमाप्तिं यावत्प्रतिमुखसंधिः । तल्लक्षणं-'फलप्रधानोपायस्य मुखसंधिनिवेशिनः । लक्ष्यालक्ष्य इवोद्भेदो यत्र प्रतिमुखं च

---

1 चेटी.

# ACT II

( *Entering* ).

A MAID—The mother has sent me with a message to my mistress; so I will just enter and approach her. ( *Walking about and observing* ). Here is seated my lady, brooding over something in her heart. Well, then, I will approach her.

( *Then enter love-sick* Vasantasena *seated, and also* Madanika ).

VAS.—Friend, what next ?

MAD.—Lady, you have not spoken about anything. How then ( do you ask ) 'what next' ?

VAS.—What did I say ?

MAD.—You asked, 'what next' ?

VAS.—( *Knitting her eye-brows* ). Ah ! Yes !

( *Approaching* )

THE FIRST MAID—Lady, the mother asks that you should take your bath and go through the worship of the deities.

VAS.—Friend, tell mother that I am not going to bathe to-day ; let therefore the Brahmana himself perform the worship.

THE MAID—As your ladyship commands. ( *Exit* )

MAD.—Madam, it is my love that prompts me to inquire, and not the disposition to find faults : so tell me, please, what all this means.

VAS.—Madanika, what do you see me to be like ?

MAD.—I can see from your ladyship's absent-mindedness that you have fallen in love with somebody whom you have treasured up in your heart.

---

तत् ॥ ' इति । तदत्र मदनिकामैत्रेयाभ्यां ज्ञाततया वसन्तसेनामात्रादिभिरज्ञाततया च अनुरागरूपबीजस्य लक्ष्यालक्ष्यतयोद्भेदः । ] अत्ताए वसन्तसेनामात्रा । [ अत्ता इति मातुः श्वश्र्वाश्च प्राकृते संज्ञा । ] अज्जआस्रआसं वसन्तसेनासकाशम् । संदेशेन प्रयोजनार्थम् । [ संदेशं दत्त्वेत्यर्थः । ] [ हञ्जे इति चेटीसंबोधनम् । 'हण्डे हञ्जे हलाऽऽह्वाने नीचां चेटीं सखीं प्रति ' इत्यमरः । 'हञ्जे तदो तदो' इत्युन्माददशारीत्युपन्यासः । अत्र विप्रलम्भशृङ्गाराङ्गभूतः प्रलाप उपक्षिप्तः । तल्लक्षणम्- 'अलक्ष्यवाक् प्रलापः स्याच्चेतसो भ्रमणाद्भृशम् ' इति ।

**वसन्तसेना**--सुष्ठु त्वया ज्ञातम् । परहृदयग्रहणपण्डिता मदनिका खलु त्वम् । (सुठठु[1] तुए जाणिदम् । परहिअअग्गहणपण्डिआ मदणिआ क्खु तुमम् ।)

**मदनिका**--प्रियं मे प्रियम् । कामः खलु नामैष भगवाननुगृहीतो महोत्सवस्तरुणजनस्य । तत्कथयत्वार्या किं राजा राजवल्लभो वा सेव्यते । ( पिअं मे पिअम् । कामो क्खु णाम असो भअवं अणुगहिदो[2] महूसवो तरुणजनस्य । ता कधेदु अज्जआ किं राआ राअवल्लहो वा सेवीअदि ।)

**वसन्तसेना**--चेटि रन्तुमिच्छामि न सेवितुम् । ( हञ्जे रमिदुमिच्छामि नसेविदुम् ।)

**मदनिका**--विद्याविशेषालंकृतः किं कोऽपि ब्राह्मणयुवा काम्यते । ( विज्जाविसेसालंकिदो किं को वि वम्हणजुआ[3] कामीअदि ।)

**वसन्तसेना**--पूजनीयो मे ब्राह्मणजनः । (पूअणीओ[4] मे बह्मणजणो ।)

**मदनिका**--किमनेकनगराभिगमनजनितविभवविस्तारो वाणिजयुवा वा काम्यते ।(किं अणेअणअराहिगमणजणिवुविहववित्थारो वाणिअजुआ वा कामीअदि ।)

**वसन्तसेना**--हञ्जे उपारूढस्नेहमपि प्रणयिजनं परित्यज्य देशान्तरगमनेन वाणिजजनो महद्वियोगजं दुःखमुत्पादयति । ( हञ्जे उवारूढसिणेहं पि पणइजणं परिच्चइअ देसन्तरगमणेण वाणिअजणो महन्तं विओअजं[5] दुक्खं उप्पादेदि ।)

**मदनिका**--आर्ये न राजा न राजवल्लभो न ब्राह्मणो न वणिजजनः । तत्क इदानीं स भर्तृदारिकया काम्यते । (अज्जए ण राआ ण राअवल्लहो ण बह्मणो ण वाणिअजणो । ता को दाणिं सो भट्ठिदारिआए कामीअदि । )

**वसन्तसेना**--हञ्जे त्वं मया सह कामदेवायतनोद्यानं गताऽऽसीः । (हञ्ज तुमं मए सह कामदेवाअदणुज्जाणं गदा आसि ।)

**मदनिका**--आर्ये गताऽऽस्मि । (अज्जए गदह्मि ।)

**वसन्तसेना**--तथाऽपि मामुदासीनेव पृच्छसि । (तह वि मं उदासीणा विअ पुच्छसि ।)

---

अज्जआ वसन्तसेनैव । [ स्नेहः पृच्छति स्नेहात्पृच्छामीत्यर्थः । ] पुरोभाइदा पुरोभागिता दोषदर्शिता । 'दोषैकदृक्पुरोभागी' इत्यमरः । दोषशून्यत्वेनेति भावः । [ भगवान् कामः खलु य एवं विकारयति इत्यर्थः । यद्वा भगवान् काम एवाद्यानुग्रहीतः इति वाक्यम् । ] 'भअवदा' इत्यपि पाठः । भगवता हरेण । स्वीकृतोऽनुगृहीतो वा । ण सेविदुम् । कामोपभोगरसिकाऽस्मि न द्रव्यार्थिनीत्यर्थः । पूजनीयाश्च ये भवन्ति तेषां विलासवैमुख्यं सदेति भावः । उवारूढसिणेहं विवृद्धस्नेहम् । भट्ठिदारिआए ईश्वरसुतया । [ उदासीना मध्यस्था वृत्तान्तमजानतीत्यर्थः । शरणागता गृहं प्रविष्टा । ] सुहिदा सुखयुक्ता । अभ्युपपन्ना स्वीकृता । सुगृहीतनामधेयो दातृत्वेन ।

---

१ सुठ्ठु क्खु. २ अणवगहीदो. ३ बह्मणो. ४ हञ्जे पूअ०. ५ विओदुक्खं.

VAS.—Rightly have you guessed! You are indeed Madanika, clever in fathoming the hearts of others!

MAD.—Well, I am glad, I am glad indeed! Herein you are indeed obliging the mighty Cupid, who is ( *i. e.* occasions ) a glorious festive joy to all young persons. So your ladyship will please tell whether he is a king, or a king's favourite, who is ( thus desired ) to be served!

VAS.—Girl, I want to *enjoy*, not to *serve*.

MAD.—Do you love some Brahmana youth, distinguished for his deep erudition?

VAS.—I have a veneration for all Brahmanas.

MAD.—Do you then love some young merchant, who has amassed a great fortune by visiting many cities?

VAS.—Friend, a merchant causes great pain of separation, by going to other countries, leaving behind his beloved person even though her love for him be very deep.

MAD.—Madam, he is not a king, nor a king's favourite, nor a Brahmana, nor a merchant. Who may he be then, that my mistress desires?

VAS.—Girl, you visited with me the garden of Cupid's shrine?

MAD.—I did, Madam.

VAS.—And still you ask me (about it), as if you are a stranger ( in the matter )?

---

दरिद्रपुरुषदत्तमना अवचनीया भवति अर्थानभिलाषित्वात् । [ अवचनीयाऽर्थानभिलाषेण गुणमात्रानुरागेण च वागगोचरमाहात्म्यानुशालिनीत्यर्थः–इति लल्लादीक्षिताः । ] अतिस्वश्चारुदत्तो ब्राह्मणः अनध्यापकत्वेनं विलासी । अन्यश्च श्रोत्रियः तर्कतन्त्रप्रवीणः पूजनीयः न काम्यो विलासवैमुख्यादित्याशयः । महुअरीओ इति । मधु कुर्वन्ति सेवन्ते । मत्ता इत्यर्थः । [ मधु कुर्वन्त्येव केवलं न स्वयं सेवन्ते । तथा गणिका धनार्थमेव केवलं स्वदेहं परोपकरणीकृत्य अलब्धरतयो वृथाजन्मभाजो भवन्तीत्यर्थः । सहसा विस्रम्भोत्पादनात्प्रागभिसार्यमाणः प्रत्युपकारे दुर्बलतया अक्षमतया पुनरात्मानं न दर्शयिष्यति एवं दुर्लभदर्शनः स्यादिति सहसा न गम्यते । ] भट्टेति द्यूतकरस्य संबोधनम् । दशसुवर्णकृते लुद्धु रुद्धः । दश सुवर्णा लभ्या यस्य पार्श्वे स द्यूतकरः प्रपलायितः । अतो गृहाण धारय । 'लब्धः' इति पाठे दशसुवर्णानां द्यूतकरो लब्धः प्रपलायित इत्यर्थः । [ 'नामूचितस्य पात्रस्य प्रवेशो निर्गमोऽपि च' इत्युक्तेः अत्र संवाहकस्य तिरस्करिणीमाक्षिप्य प्रवेशः सूचनाभावात् । ] सभ्यानुद्दिश्य ब्रूते । हीमाणहे इति विस्मये । कष्ट एव द्यूतकरभावः । नवबन्धनेत्यादि । चित्रजातिः । गद्दहीए गर्धभीनामधेय्या । हा कष्टम् । ताडितोऽस्मि । गद्दहीति वराटिका-

**मदनिका**––ज्ञातम् । किं स एव येनार्या शरणागताऽभ्युपपन्ना । (जाणिदम् । किं[1] सो ज्जेव्व जेण अज्जआ सरणाअदा अब्भुववण्णा । )

**वसन्तसेना**––किंनामधेयः खलु सः । ( किंणामहेओ क्खु सो ।)

**मदनिका**––स खलु श्रेष्ठिचत्वरे प्रतिवसति । ( सो क्खु सेट्ठिचत्तरे पडिवसदि ।)

**वसन्तसेना**––अयि नामास्य पृष्टासि । (अइ णाम से[2] पुच्छिदासि ।)

**मदनिका**––स खल्वार्ये सुगृहीतनामधेय आर्यचारुदत्तो नाम । (सो क्खु अज्जए सुगहिदणामहेओ अज्जचारुदत्तो णाम ।)

**वसन्तसेना**––(सहर्षम् ।) साधु मदनिके साधु । सुष्ठु त्वया ज्ञातम् । (साहु मदणिए साहु । सुट्ठु तुए जाणिदम् ।)

**मदनिका**––(स्वगतम् ।) एवं तावत् । (प्रकाशम् ।) आर्ये दरिद्रः खलु स श्रूयते । (एव्वं दाव । अज्जए दलिद्दो क्खु सो सुणीअदि ।)

**वसन्तसेना**––अत एव काम्यते । दरिद्रपुरुषसंक्रान्तमनाः खलु गणिका लोकेऽवचनीया भवति । (अदो ज्जेव्व कामीअदि । दलिद्दपुरिससंकन्तमणा क्खु गणिआ लोए अवअणीआ भोदि ।)

**मदनिका**––आर्ये किं हीनकुसुमं सहकारपादपं मधुकर्यः पुनः सेवन्ते । (अज्जए किं हीणकुसुमं सहआरपादवं महुअरीओ उण सेवन्ति ।)

**वसन्तसेना**––अत एव ता मधुकर्य उच्यन्ते । (अदो ज्जेव्व ताओ महुअरीओ वुच्चन्ति ।)

**मदनिका**—आर्ये यदि स मनीषितस्तत्किमर्थमिदानीं सहसा नाभिसार्यते । (अज्जए जइ सो मणीसिदो ता कीस दाणिं सहसा ण अहिसारीअदि ।)

**वसन्तसेना**—चेटि सहसाऽभिसार्यमाणः प्रत्युपकारदुर्बलतया मा तावज्जनो दुर्लभदर्शनः पुनर्भविष्यति । (हञ्जे सहसा अहिसारिअन्तो पच्चुअआरदुब्बलदाए मा दाव जणो दुल्लहदंसणो पुणो भविस्सदि ।)

**मदनिका**—किमत एव सोऽलंकारस्तस्य हस्ते निक्षिप्तः । (किं अदो ज्जेव्व सो अलंकारओ तस्य हत्थे णिक्खित्तो ।)

**वसन्तसेना**—हञ्जे सुष्ठु त्वया ज्ञातम् । (हञ्जे सुठ्ठु दे जाणिदम् ।)

---

नाम । गर्दभीशक्तिके आर्यौ इति प्रसिद्धद्यूतके कपर्दकनामधेये । नवबन्धनान्मुक्तयेव गर्दभ्या पशुविशेषेण ताडितोऽस्मि गर्दभ्या [वराटिकया] । ताडनस्वभावा सा यतः । अङ्गराजेन कर्णेन मुक्तयेव शक्त्या अस्त्रविशेषेण घटोत्कचो भीमसेनसुत इव ताडितोऽस्मि शक्त्या ॥१॥ **लेखकेत्यादि** । गाथा । [लेख एव लेखकः । स्वार्थे कन् । यद्वा लिखतीति लेखकः । तत्र व्यापृतहृदयमासक्तचित्तं] लेखकव्यापृतहृदयं सभिकं दृष्ट्वा

---

१ अज्जुए किं. २ संपुच्छि.

MAD.—I have it! Is he that same gentleman who favourably received my mistress when she sought his help?

VAS.—Well, what is his name?

MAD.—Why, he resides in the merchants' quarter.

VAS.—Girl, I asked you his *name*!

MAD.—My lady, he, of auspicious name, is called the noble Charudatta.

VAS.—(*Joyfully*). Excellent, Madanika, excellent! You know it rightly.

MAD.—(*To herself*). I will thus (speak to her) now. (*Aloud*) My lady, it is heard that he is a poor man.

VAS.—Hence it is that I love him. For a courtesan who fixes her affections on a poor lover would not incur censure from the world.

MAD.—But, madam, do the female honey-bees frequent a mango-tree which has lost its blossoms?

VAS.—[No, they do not;] and hence they are known as 'honey-makers.'

MAD.—Lady, if you desire him, then why is it that you do not now approach him of your own accord, at once?

VAS.—Girl, if I were to go to him myself at once, then, being unable to make an adequate return (for my self-offer), he may probably make it impossible for me to visit him again, and I wish to prevent that.

MAD.—Is it for this very reason that you deposited that ornament in his hands?

VAS.—Girl, you have guessed it correctly!

---

[तस्य दर्शनपथं विहायेत्यर्थः ।] झटिति प्रभ्रष्टः । मार्गनिपतितः तन्मार्गगतः] । कं नु खल्विति विमर्शे ॥ २ ॥ विप्रतीपाभ्यां विपरीताभ्याम् । देवोभविष्यामि । [देवतावत्प्रतिमास्थाने स्थास्यामि ।] देवीति व्यन्तम् । यदि व्रजसीत्यादि । आर्या । [तरति समर्थो भवेदित्यर्थः] ॥३॥ कुत्र कुत्रेत्यादि । रुचिरा वृत्तम् । [विप्रलम्भक प्रतारक ।] रे भयपरिवेपमानाङ्गक । पदे पदे समविषमं यथा स्यादेवं स्खलन्कुलं यशश्चातिकृष्णं कुर्वन् ॥ ४ ॥ [पदं संवाहकचरणचिह्नम् । विप्रतीपेति । ढक्कभाषायामस्यामुकारान्तानि प्रथमान्तादीनीत्यवधेयम्—इति ल. दी.] । अरे विप्रतीपपादशून्यं देवकुलम् । प्रयोजनाभावेन नात्र मानुष इति भावः । 'धूर्तो द्यूतकरो विप्रतीपाभ्यां पादाभ्यां देवकुलं प्रविष्टः' इत्येके । [संज्ञाप्येति—अयं संवाहक एव

(नेपथ्ये !)

अरे भट्टारक दशसुवर्णस्य रुद्धो द्यूतकरः प्रपलायितः प्रपलायितः। तद्गृहाण गृहाण। तिष्ठ तिष्ठ। दूरात्प्रदृष्टोऽसि। (अले भट्टा दशसुवण्णाह लुद्धु जूदकरु पपलीणु पपलीणु। ता गेण्ह[1] गेण्ह। चिट्ठ चिठ्ठ। दूलात्पदिट्टो सि।)

(प्रविश्यापटीक्षेपेण संभ्रान्तः।)

**संवाहकः**—आश्चर्यम्। कष्ट एष द्यूतकरभावः। (हीमाणहे। कट्ठे एशे जूदिअलभावे।)

**नवबन्धनमुक्तयेव गर्दभ्या हा ताडितोऽस्मि गर्दभ्या।**
**अङ्गराजमुक्तयेव शक्त्या घटोत्कच इव घातितोऽस्मि शक्त्या॥१॥**
**लेखकव्यापृतहृदयं सभिकं दृष्ट्वा झटिति प्रभ्रष्टः।**
**इदानीं मार्गनिपतितः कं नु खलु शरण प्रपद्ये॥२॥**

(णवबन्धणमुक्काए[2] विअ गद्दहीए हा ताडिदो म्हि गद्दहीए।
अङ्गलाअमुक्काए विअ शत्तीए घडुक्को विअ घादिदो म्हि शत्तीए॥
लेखअवावडहिअअं शहिअं दट्ठूण[3] झत्ति पब्भट्टे।
एण्हि मग्गणिवडिदे कं णु क्खु शलणं पपज्जे॥)

तद्यावदेतौ सभिकद्यूतकरावन्यतो मामन्विष्यतः तावदहं विपरीताभ्यां पादाभ्यामेतच्छून्यदेवकुलं प्रविश्य देवीभविष्यामि। (बहुविधं नाटयं कृत्वा तथा स्थितः।) (ता जाव एदे शहिअजूदिअला अण्णदो मं अण्णेशन्ति ताव हक्के[4] विप्पडीवेहिं पादेहिं एदं शुण्णदेउलं पविशिअ देवीभविश्शम्।)

(ततः प्रविशति माथुरो द्यूतकरश्च)

**माथुरः**—अरे भट्टारक दशसुवर्णस्य रुद्धो द्यूतकरः प्रपलायितः प्रपलायितः। तद्गृहाण गृहाण। तिष्ठ तिष्ठ। दूरात्प्रदृष्टोऽसि। (अले भट्टा दशसुअण्णाह लुद्धु जूदकरु पपलीणु पपलीणु। ता गेण्ह गेण्ह। चिट्ठ चिट्ठ। दूलात्पदिट्टो सि।)

**द्यूतकरः**—

**यदि व्रजसि पातालमिन्द्रं शरणं च सांप्रतं यासि।**
**सभिकं वर्जयित्वैकं रुद्रोऽपि न रक्षितुं तरति॥३॥**

(जइ वज्जसि पाआलं इन्दं शलणं च संपदं जासि।
सहिअं वज्जिअ एकं रुद्दो वि ण रक्खिदुं तरइ॥)

---

प्रतिमारूपेणात्मानं निह्नुवान इह तिष्ठतीति संज्ञापनं कृत्वेत्यर्थः।] संज्ञापनं प्रतिमायाम्। [शिलाया इयं शैली सा चासौ प्रतिमा च शैलप्रतिमा। संवरणं गोपनं स्वस्य प्रतिमारूपेण स्थितत्वात्—इति ल. दी.]। **कत्तेति। द्यूतकरणं यया सा कत्ता। काड**

---

१ गेण्णघ गेण्हघ. २ मुक्कापुए. ३ दश्टूण..पब्भश्टे. ४ इदो.

( *Behind the Scenes* ).

O Gamester ! This gambler, bound ( to us ) for ten gold-pieces, is making off—making off ! Catch him ! Oh ! Catch him ! Stop, stop ! I see you from a distance !

( *Entering wish a toss of the curtain, and in a flurry* ).

SAMVAHAKA.—Oh ! Painful is this state of a gambler !

Oh ! I am kicked ( *i. e.* defeated ) by the *gardabhi* die, as if by a *gardabhi* ( she-ass ) just let loose from her first halter. Ah ! I am struck ( *i e.*, defeated ) by the *Sakti* die, like Ghatotkacha struck by the *Sakti* ( weapon ) discharged by Karna, the king of the Angas ! (1)

Seeing the keeper mentally occupied with the score, I suddenly escaped, and have now reached the public road ; whom shall I now approach for refuge ? (2)

Well, then while these two, the master and the gamester, are looking for me elsewhere, I shall enter this deserted temple walking backwards ( *lit.* with feet turned in the opposite direction ) and take my stand there as the goddess ( idol ). ( *He makes numerous gestures and then remains in that posture* ).

( *Then enter* Mathura, *and the* Gamester ).

MATHURA—O Bhattaraka ! This gambler here, bound to us for ten gold-pieces, is making off—making off ! Catch him ! Oh ! Catch him ! (O you) Stop, stop ! I see you from a distance !

GAMESTER—

Even if you now go to the nether regions, or seek the protection of Indra himself, nobody, not even Siva, would be able to save you, excepting the keeper alone. (3)

---

(उ) इति प्रसिद्धः । नान्दीपूरा इति प्रसिद्धे द्यूत इत्यन्ये । [ नान्दी नक्की इति भाषायाम् । पूर्वः पूरा इति भाषया प्रसिद्धः । निर्गतं नाणकमपि यस्य यस्माद्वा स तथा तस्य निर्नाणकस्य । इति ल. दी. ] । कत्ताशब्दो निर्नाणकस्य निर्धनस्य ।।५ ।। जानामीति । सुमेरुशिखरपतनसंनिभं द्यूतम् । [ सुमेरोः शृङ्गात्पतनवत् ] सुखविनाशकमित्यर्थः । कोकिलमधुरः [कोकिलशब्दवन्मधुरः] ॥ ६ ॥ मम पाठ इत्यार्थी द्यूतकरोक्तिविशेषः । गोहे पुरुषः मनुष्यः । पेदण्डा लुप्तदण्डक । उभे अपि देशी । शिरः पतति । भ्रमतीत्यर्थः । इति भूमौ निपत्य स्थितः । ही कष्टम् । अस्माभिः सर्वः समय उल्लङ्घ्यते । एषोऽस्माकं द्यूतकराणामलङ्घ्यः समयः ।

माथुरः--

कुत्र कुत्र सुसभिकविप्रलम्भक पलायसे रे भयपरिवेपिताङ्गक।
पदे पदे समविषमं स्खलन्कुलं यशोऽतिकृष्णं कुर्वन् ॥ ४ ॥
(कहिं कहिं सुसहिअविप्पलम्बआ पलासि ले भअपलिवेविदङ्गआ।
पदे पदे समविसमं[1] खलन्तआ कुलं जसं अदिकसणं कलेन्तआ ॥)

द्यूतकरः--(पदं वीक्ष्य।) एष व्रजति। इयं प्रनष्टा पदवी। (एसो वज्जदि। इअं पणट्ठा पदवी।)

माथुरः--(आलोक्य सवितर्कम्।) अरे विप्रतीपौ पादौ। प्रतिमाशून्यं देवकुलम्। (विचिन्त्य।) धूर्तो द्यूतकरो विप्रतीपाभ्यां पादाभ्यां देवकुलं प्रविष्टः। (अले विप्पदीवु पादू। पाडिमाशुण्णु देउलु। धुत्तु जूदकरु विप्पदीवेहिं पादेहिं देउलं पविट्ठो।)

द्यूतकरः--ततोऽनुसरावः। (ता अणुसरेह्म।)

माथुरः--एवं भवतु। (एव्वं भोदु।)

(उभौ देवकुलप्रवेशं निरूपयतः[2]। दृष्ट्वान्योऽन्यं संज्ञाप्य।)

द्यूतकरः--कथं काष्ठमयी प्रतिमा। (कधं कट्ठमयी पडिमा।)

माथुरः--अरे न खलु न खलु। शैलप्रतिमा। (इति बहुविधं चालयति[3]। संज्ञाप्य च।) एवं भवतु। एहि। द्यूतेन क्रीडावः। (इति बहुविधं द्यूतं क्रीडतः[4]।) (अले ण हु ण हु। शैलपडिमा। एव्वं भोदु। एहि। जूदं किलेह्म।)

संवाहकः--(द्यूतेच्छाविकारसंवरणं बहुविधं कृत्वा। स्वगतम्।) अरे।

कत्ताशब्दो निर्नाणकस्य हरति हृदयं मनुष्यस्य।
ढक्काशब्द इव नराधिपस्य प्रभ्रष्टराज्यस्य ॥ ५ ॥
जानामि न क्रीडिष्यामि सुमेरुशिखरपतनसंनिभं द्यूतम्।
तथाऽपि खलु कोकिलमधुरः कत्ताशब्दो मनो हरति ॥ ६ ॥

(अले।

कत्ताशद्दे णिण्णाणअश्श हलइ हडकं मनुश्शश्श।
ढक्काशद्दे व्व णडाधिवश्श पब्भट्ठलज्जश्श ॥
जाणामि ण कीलिश्शं शुमेलुशिहलपडणशण्णिहं जूअम्।
तह वि हु कोइलमहुले कत्ताशद्दे मणं हलदि ॥

द्यूतकरः--मम पाठे मम पाठे। (मम पाठे मम पाठे।)

माथुरः--न खलु। मम पाठे मम पाठे। (ण हु। मम पाठे मम पाठे।

---

१ शमविशमम्. २ नाटयतः. ३ चालयतः. ४ क्रीडति.

MATH.—

O you-who cheated a good keeper ! Where, Oh, where can you run away, with your limbs quaking with fear, stumbling at every step over even as well as uneven ground, and seriously darkening ( *i. e.* disgracing ) both your family and your good name ? (4)

GAM.—( *Examining the foot-prints* ). Here he goes ( *i. e.* has gone on ) ! Here the track is lost !

MATH.—( *Observing and reflecting* ). Ah ! The foot-prints are in the contrary direction, while this temple ( we know ) has no image. ( *Pondering* ). That rogue of a gambler has entered the temple, walking backward !

GAM.—Then let us follow him.

MA.—Let us do so.

( *Both show that they enter the temple: seeing, and making signs to each other* ).

GAM.—How now ! We have a wooden idol here !

MA.—No, not at all; it is a stone image. ( *He rocks it in various ways; then making a sign* ). Never mind; come, we shall have a game at gambling. ( *They play many sorts of games at dice*).

SAMVA.—( *Variously restraining the manifestations of his longing to have a game himself; to himself*). Ah !

The rattling sound of dice stirs the heart of a penniless person, just as the sound of drums does that of a king who has lost his kingdom ! (5)

I know that I shall never again play ( *i. e.* gamble); gambling is like taking a leap from the summit of the Meru mountain ! But still the rattle of dice, sweet as ( the song of ) the Cuckoo, captivates the heart ! (6)

GAM.—The throw is mine, the throw is mine !

MA.—No, no ! It is mine, it is mine !

---

'गण्डं गण्डो लग्नकः' इति पूर्वटीका। [उपस्पृश्य करे धृत्वा। ] अर्धं सभिकेन मुक्तं। अर्धं द्यूतकरेण । उभाभ्यां राशिरेव मुक्तः । इति मुक्तदेयत्वाद्यामीति ब्रूते । भट्टारका इति मध्यस्थान्संबोधयति । अद्धे अर्धेन । गण्डे कण्डे । एकस्य सभिकस्यार्धं गण्डः कृतः। अपराह अद्धेण मुक्के इत्यपरस्य द्यूतकरस्यार्धेन मुक्तोऽस्मि । तच्च सभिकेनैवोपेक्षितम् । अत्र माथुरोऽहं निपुणः । एत्थ तुए अत्र त्वया । धुत्तिज्जामि धूर्त्ये प्रतार्ये ।

**संवाहकः**—(अन्यतः सहसोपसृत्य।) ननु मम पाठे। ( णं मम पाठ।)

**द्यूतकरः**—लब्धः पुरुषः। ( लद्धे गोहे।)

**माथुरः**—( गृहीत्वा ]) अरे लुप्तदण्डक गृहीतोऽसि। प्रयच्छ तद्दशसुवर्णम्। ( अले पेदण्डा गहीदो सिं। पअच्छ तं दशसुवण्णम्।)

**संवाहकः**—अद्य दास्यामि। (अज्ज दइश्शम्।)

**माथुरः**—अधुना प्रयच्छ। ( अहुणा पअच्छ।)

**संवाहकः** – दास्यामि। प्रसादं कुरु। (दइश्शं। पशादं कलेहि।)

**माथुरः**—अरे ननु सांप्रतं प्रयच्छ। (अले णं संपद पअच्छ।)

**संवाहकः**—शिरः पतति। ( इति भूमौ पतति।) ( शिलु पडदि।)

(उभौ बहुविधं ताडयतः।)

**माथुरः**—एष त्वं खलु द्यूतकरमण्डल्या बद्धोऽसि। ( एसु[1] तुमं हु जूदिअर-मण्डलीए बद्धो सि।)

**संवाहकः**—( उत्थाय सविषादम्।) कथं द्यूतकरमण्डल्या बद्धोऽस्मि। कष्टम्। एषोऽस्माकं द्यूतकराणामलङ्घनीयः समयः। तस्मात्कुतो दास्यामि। (कधं जूदिअलमण्डलीए बद्धो म्हि। ही। एशे अम्हाणं जूदिअलाणं अलङ्घणीए शमए। ता कुदो दइश्शम्।)

**माथुरः**—अरे गण्डः क्रियतां क्रियताम्। ( अले गण्डे कुलु कुलु।)

**संवाहकः**—एवं करोमि। ( द्यूतकरमुपस्पृश्य।) अर्धं तुभ्यं ददामि अर्धं मे मुञ्चतु। ( एव्वं कलेमि। अद्धं ते देमि अद्धं मे मुञ्चदु।)

**द्यूतकरः**—एवं भवतु। ( एव्वं भोदु।)

**संवाहकः**—( सभिकमुपगम्य।) अर्धस्य गण्डं करोमि। अर्धमपि म आर्यो मुञ्चतु ( अद्धश्श[3] गण्डे कलेमि। अद्धं पि मे अज्जो मुञ्चदु।)

**माथुरः**— को दोषः। एवं भवतु। ( को दोसु। एव्वं भोदु।)

**संवाहकः**—( प्रकाशम्।) आर्य अर्धं त्वया मुक्तम्। (अज्ज अद्धे[4] तुए मुक्के।)

**माथुरः**—मुक्तम्। ( मुक्के।)

**संवाहकः**—( द्यूतकरं प्रति।) अर्धं त्वयाऽपि मुक्तम् (अद्धे तुए वि मुक्के)

**द्यूतकरः**— मुक्तम्। ( मुक्के।)

**संवाहकः**—सांप्रतं गमिष्यामि। ( संपदं गमिश्शम्।)

**माथुरः**—प्रयच्छ तद्दशसुवर्णम्। कुत्र गच्छसि। ( पअच्छ तं दशसुवण्णम्। कहिं गच्छसि।)

---

१ एसु तुहं जूदिमण्डलीए बद्धेसि। इति द्यूतमण्डलीं कृत्वा तथा करोति. २ गन्थु. ३ गन्थु. ४ अद्धं.

SAMVA.—( *Coming up suddenly from one side* ). No, no ! It is *my* throw !

GAM.—We have got our man !

MA.—( *Seizing him* ). O you, defrauder of the money staked ( *i. e.* avoider of the penalty ) ! You are caught ! Deliver up those ten gold-pieces !

SAMVA.—I will give to-day.

MA.—Give them just now.

SAMVA.—I will give ; please have a little patience ( *lit.* show me favour ).

MA.—You fellow, give them *now*, I say !

SAMVA.—My head is feeling dizzy ! ( *He falls down on the ground* ).

( Both *belabour him in various ways* ).

MA.—Here, now ! I arrest you in the name of the Players' Association !

SAMVA.—( *Gets up* ; *sorrowfully* ). How now ! I have been arrested in the name of the Players' Association ! Ah ! This is a rule which we gamblers cannot break. But from what source am I to pay it ?

MA.—Let a pledge be given ; oh, let one.

SAMVA.—So I will. ( *Approaching the* Gamester ). I will pay half ; you should forgive me the other half !

GAM.—So be it.

SAMVA.—( *Approaching the* Keeper ). I will give surety for half ; your honour will please excuse me the other half !

MA.—Where is the harm ? Let it be as you say.

SAMVA.—( *Aloud* ). Sir, half excused by you ?

MA.—Excused.

SAMVA.—( *To the* Gamester ). Half also excused by you ?

GAM.—Excused.

SAMVA.—Then I am off now !

MA.—Give those ten gold pieces ! Where are you off to ?

---

पेदण्डा लुप्तदण्डक । कुत इति लाभोपायप्रश्ने । [ आकाशे–'असंबोध्याऽदृष्टवक्त्री वाक्यादाकाशभाषितम्' इत्युक्तम् । प्रकृते त्वसंबोध्या ( न विद्यते संबंध्यो यस्यां ) वागियमिति बोध्यम् इति ल. दी ] । सहिअस्स इत्यादो सभिकस्य पार्श्वादित्यर्थः । हा आर्यचारुदत्तस्य विभवे विघटिते तस्मिन्निर्धने एष एतादृशावस्थो वर्ते । नेति ।

**संवाहकः**—प्रेक्षध्वं प्रेक्षध्वं भट्टारकाः। हा सांप्रतमेव एकस्यार्धे गण्डः कृतः अपरस्यार्धं मुक्तम्। तथाऽपि मामबलं सांप्रतमेव याचते। (पेक्खध पेक्खध भट्टालआ। हा शम्पदं ज्जेव्व एक्काह अद्धे गण्डे कडे अवलाह अद्धे मुक्के। तह वि मं अबलं शम्पदं ज्जेव्व मग्गदि।)

**माथुरः**—(गृहीत्वा।) धूर्त माथुरोऽहं निपुणः। अत्र नाहं धूर्तयामि। तत्प्रयच्छ तल्लुप्तदण्डक सर्वं सुवर्णं सांप्रतम्। (धुत्तु माथुरु अहं णिउणु। एत्थ[1] ण अहं धुत्तिज्जामि। ता पअच्छ तं पेदण्डआ सव्वं सुवण्णं संपदम्।)

**संवाहकः**—कुतो दास्यामि। (कुदो दइश्शम्।)

**माथुरः**—पितरं विक्रीय प्रयच्छ। (पिदरु विक्किणिअ पअच्छ।

**संवाहकः**—कुतो मे पिता (कुदो मे पिदा।)

**माथुरः**—मातरं विक्रीय प्रयच्छ। (मादरु विक्किणिअ पअच्छ।)

**संवाहकः**—कुतो मे माता। (कुदो मे मादा।)

**माथुरः**—आत्मानं विक्रीय प्रयच्छ। (अप्पाणं विक्किणिअ पअच्छ।)

**संवाहकः**—कुरुत प्रसादम्। नयत मां राजमार्गम्। (कलेध पशादम्। णेध मं लाजमग्गम्।)

**माथुरः**—प्रसर। (पसरु।)

**संवाहकः**—एवं भवतु। (परिक्रामति।) आर्याः क्रीणीध्वं मामस्य सभिकस्य हस्ताद्दशभिः सुवर्णकैः। (दृष्ट्वा। आकाशे।) किं भणथ—'किं करिष्यसि' इति। गेहे ते कर्मकरो भविष्यामि। कथमदत्त्वा प्रतिवचनं गतः। भवत्वेवम्। इममन्यं भणिष्यामि। (पुनस्तदेव पठति।) कथमेषोऽपि मामवधीर्य गतः। हा आर्यचारुदत्तस्य विभवे विघटिते एष वर्ते मन्दभाग्यः। (एव्वं भोदु। अज्जा विक्किणिध मं इमश्श शहिअश्श हत्थादो दशेहिं शुवण्णकेहिं। किं भणाध—'किं कलइश्शशि' त्ति। गेहे दे कम्मकले हुविश्शम्। कधं अदइअ पडिवअणं गदे। भोदु एव्वम्। इमं अण्णं भणइस्सम्। कधं एशे वि मं अवधीलिअ गदे। हा अज्जचालुदत्तस्स विहवे विहडिदे एशे वड्ढामि मन्दभाए।)

**माथुरः**—ननु देहि। (णं देहि।)

**संवाहकः**—कुतो दास्यामि। (इति पतति।) (कुदो दइश्शम्।)

(माथुरः कर्षति।)

**संवाहकः**—आर्याः परित्रायध्वं परित्रायध्वम्। (अज्जा पलित्ताअध पलित्ताअध।)

(ततः प्रविशति दर्दुरकः।)

**दर्दुरकः**—भोः द्यूतं हि नाम पुरुषस्यासिंहासनं राज्यम्।

---

१ एहिं.

SAMVA.—Look here, Sirs, look here! Oh! Just now I offered security for one half, and the other half was excused. Still he demands it just now from me, who am unable ( to pay ) !

MA.—( *Seizing him* ). You rouge, I am Mathura, and am clever enough ( as you know ). I won't allow myself to be cheated in this matter. So, you, Cheater-of-the-money-staked, pay up all those gold-pieces *now* !

SAMVA.—How can I pay them ?

MA.—Sell your father and pay.

SAMVA.—Whence have I a father ?

MA.—Sell your mother and pay.

SAMVA.—Whence have I a mother ?

MA —Sell your own self and pay.

SAMVA.—Then do this much favour : take me to the king's highway.

MA.—Come along !

SAMVA.—So be it ! ( *Walks about* ). Sirs, buy me off the hands of this Keeper here by paying ten gold-pieces ! ( *Looking up in the empty space* ). What say you ?—'What can yon do ?' I can be a menial servant in your household.—How ! He has passed by without making any answer ! Never mind ; I will speak to this another gentleman. ( *He repeats that same sentence again* ). How ! He too has despised me and gone away ! Alas ! This is how I, the unlucky one, have fared since the noble Charudatta lost his fortune !

MA.—Give it, I say !

SAMVA.—How can I pay ? ( *He falls down* ).

( Mathura *pulls him up* ).

SAMVA.—Save me, sirs, save me !

( *Then enter* Darduraka ).

DAR.—Oh, gambling is, indeed, to a man, a kingdom without a throne !

---

[ कुतश्चित्कस्माच्चिदपि पराभवं न गणयति चिन्तयति । नृपः स्वसामर्थ्यात् । द्यूतमपि द्यूतप्रसक्तस्य मानावमानविगणनादित्यर्थः । नृपः व्यवहारानुरोधेन द्यूतं च जयापजयोरनियमात् नित्यमर्थंगतिं हरति ददाति च । निकाममत्यन्तमायं लाभं पश्यतीति आयदर्शी नृपः ] अतिशयमायस्य दर्शको राजेवेश्वरेणापि पुरुषेण सेव्यते । उपमा ।

न गणयति पराभवं कुतश्चिद्धरति ददाति च नित्यमर्थजातम् ।
नृपतिरिव निकाममायदर्शी विभववता समुपास्यते जनेन ।। ७ ।।

अपि च ।

द्रव्यं लब्धं[1] द्यूतेनैव दारा मित्रं द्यूतेनैव ।
दत्तं भुक्तं द्यूतेनैव सर्वं नष्टं द्यूतेनैव ।। ८ ।।

अपि च ।

त्रेताहृतसर्वस्वः पावरपतनाच्च[2] शोषितशरीरः ।
नर्दितदर्शितमार्गः कटेन विनिपातितो यामि ।। ९ ।।

( अग्रतोऽवलोक्य । ) अयमस्माकं पूर्वसभिको माथुर इत एवाभिवर्तते । भवतु । अपक्रमितुं न शक्यते । तदवगुण्ठयाम्यात्मानम् । (बहुविधं नाट्यं कृत्वा स्थितः । उत्तरीयं निरीक्ष्य ।)

अयं पटः सूत्रदरिद्रतां गतो ह्ययं पटश्छिद्रशतैरलंकृतः
अयं पटः प्रावरितुं न शक्यते ह्ययं पटः संवृत एव शोभते ।। १० ।।

अथ वा किमयं तपस्वी करिष्यति । यो हि

पादेनैकेन गगने द्वितीयेन च भूतले ।
तिष्ठाम्युल्लम्बितस्तावद्यावत्तिष्ठति भास्करः ।। ११ ।।

**माथुरः**—दापय पापय । (द्रापय दापय । )

**संवाहकः**—कुतो दास्यामि । ( कुदो दइश्शम् । )

**माथुरः**—( कर्षति । )

**दर्दुरकः**—अये किमेतदग्रतः । (आकाशे ।) किं भवानाह—अयं द्यूतकरः सभिकेन खलीक्रियते न कश्चिन्मोचयतीति । नन्वयं दर्दुरो मोचयति[3] । (उपसृत्य ।) अन्तरमन्तरम् । (दृष्ट्वा ।) अये कथं माथुरो धूर्तः । अयमपि तपस्वी संवाहकः ।

---

पुष्पिताग्रा छन्दः ] ।।७।। **द्रव्यं लब्धमित्यादि** । [ कारकदीपकमलंकारः । ] विद्युन्माला वृत्तम् ।। ८ ।। **त्रेतेति** । त्रेता 'तीया' इति प्रसिद्धः । पावरो 'दूआ' इति ख्यातः । नर्दितो 'नान्दी' इति प्रसिद्धः । [ नर्दितपतनेन दर्शितो मार्गो यस्य स तादृशः । गृहं गच्छेति मार्गः—ल. दी.] कटेन 'पूरा' इति प्रसिद्धेन । 'पावरः पूरा कटो दूआ' इति केचित् ।।९।। **अयमिति** । [ अयं पटः सूत्राणां दरिद्रता जीर्णता तत्रतत्र लुप्तता तां गतः । सूत्राणां नाशात् । प्रावरितुं परिधातुम् । वंशस्थं वृत्तम् ] ।। १० ।। तपस्वी वराकः । **पादेनेति** । [एकेन पादेन उन्नमितेनेत्यर्थः । यावत्तिष्ठति भास्करः आसायंकालमित्यर्थः । अनेनैवं क्लेशसहस्य मम माथुरकात्कुतो भयमिति ध्वनितम् ] ।।११।। खलीक्रियते भर्त्स्यते । [ कर्षणाद्युपमर्दपात्रं क्रियते इत्यर्थः इति ल० दी० ] अन्तर-

---

१ जग्धं. २ द्वापर. ३ मोचयत्येनम्.

Like a king, a gambler cares not for defeat from any one; he always receives and gives away amounts of money; ( and ), being the recipient of an immence income ( revenue ), he is ever waited upon by wealthy persons. ( 7 )

Moreover—

Money is obtained by gambling alone; wife and friends are acquired through gambling alone; gifts are given and things enjoyed by means of gambling alone; and one's all is lost ( also ) by gambling alone. ( 8 )

Moreover—

Having lost all my wealth through the *Treta* ( Tray ), then having my body parched up by the ( wrong ) fall of the *Pavara* ( the Deuce ), and next having the road shown to me by the *Nardita* ( the Ace ), I (now) go, being (finally) felled to the ground (i. e. completely ruined ) by the *Kata* ( the Four ). ( 9 )

( *Looking before him* ). Here is our former keeper Mathura, coming in this very direction. Well, I can't escape him ( avoid his path ), so I will veil myself. ( *He gesticulates variously and then stands inspecting his cloak*).

This garment has lost most of its threads; this garment has become ornamented with hundreds of holes! This garment it is not possible to wear at all; this garment looks all right only when rolled up! ( 10 )

Or rather, what can this poor fellow ( Mathura ) do ( to me ), who verily,

Can remain stretched up, so long as the sun stands ( in the sky ), with one leg in the sky and the other on the ground! (11)

MA.—Pay, pay!

SAMVA.—How shall I pay?

MA.—( *Pulls him* ).

DAR.—Ah! What is this ( that is going on ) before me? (*In the space* ). What do you say?—'This gambler is being maltreated by the Keeper and none is setting him free'? Why, this Dardura will set him free! ( *Approaching* ). Make way, make way! ( *Seeing* ). Oh! How now! Here is the cunning Mathura, and this too is poor Samvahaka!

---

मन्तरमिति जनसंमर्दे प्रवेशायावकाशप्रार्थना । [ संवाहकस्य द्यूतक्रीडाकरणाक्षमत्वं द्योतयति-] य इति । [ यः । अहमिवेति पूरणीयम् । समुल्लम्बितः सन् दिवसान्तं

य: स्तब्धं दिवसान्तमानतशिरा नास्ते समुल्लम्बितो
यस्योद्घर्षणलोष्टकैरपि सदा पृष्ठे न जातः किणः ।
यस्यैतच्च न कुक्कुरैरहरहर्जङ्घान्तर चर्व्यते
तस्यात्यायतकोमलस्य सततं द्यूतप्रसङ्गेन किम् ॥ १२ ॥

भवतु । माथुरं तावत्सान्त्वयामि । (उपगम्य ।) माथुर अभिवादये ।)

**माथुरः**—(प्रत्यभिवादयते ।)

**दर्दुरकः**—किमेतम् ।

**माथुरः**—अयं दशसुवर्णं धारयति । (अअं दशसुवण्णं धालेदि ।)

**दर्दुरकः**—ननु कल्यवर्तमेतत् ।

**माथुरः**—(दर्दुरस्य[1] कक्षातललुण्ठीकृतं पटमाकृष्य ।) भर्तारः पश्यत पश्यत । जर्जरपटप्रावृतोऽयं पुरुषो दशसुवर्णं कल्यवर्तं भणति । (भट्टा पश्शत पश्शत । जज्जरपडप्पावुदो अअं पुलिसो दशसुवण्णं कल्लवत्तं भणादि ।)

**दर्दुरकः**—अरे मूर्ख नन्वहं दशसुवर्णान्कटकरणेन प्रयच्छामि । तत्किं यस्यास्ति धनं स किं क्रोडे कृत्वा दर्शयति । अरे

दुर्वर्णोऽसि[2] विनष्टोऽसि दशस्वर्णस्य कारणात् ।
पञ्चेन्द्रियसमायुक्तो नरो व्यापाद्यते त्वया ॥ १३ ॥

**माथुरः**—भर्तः तव दशसुवर्णं कल्यवर्तः । ममैष विभवः । (भट्टा[3] तुए दशसुवण्णु कल्लवत्तु । मए एसु विहवु ।)

**दर्दुरकः**—यद्येवं श्रूयतां तर्हि । अन्यांस्तावद्दश सुवर्णानस्यैव प्रयच्छ । अयमपि द्यूतं शीलयतु ।

**माथुरः**—तत्किं भवतु । (तत्किं भोदु ।)

**दर्दुरकः**—यदि जेष्यति तदा दास्यति ।

**माथुरः**—अथ न जयति । (अह ण जिणादि ।)

**दर्दुरकः**—तदा न दास्यति ।

---

आनतं शिरो यस्य तथा नास्ते । यस्य मम पृष्ठे इव उद्धर्षणं लोष्ठकैः पणीकृतार्थादाने सभिकादिभिः कृतं पृष्ठघर्षणं तदर्थं लोष्ठकैः कृतः किणः न जातः । यस्य च मम इव जङ्घान्तरदेशः कुक्कुरैः सदा न चर्व्यते । तस्य अस्य संवाहकस्य अत्यायतकोमलस्य अत्यन्तकोमलस्य । यद्वा अत्यायतः विपुलशरीरश्चासौ कोमलश्च तस्य द्यूतप्रसङ्गेन कोऽर्थः । न कोपीऽत्यर्थः । अप्रस्तुतप्रशंसालंकारः । शार्दूलविक्रीडितं वृत्तम् ।] उद्धर्षणः संघर्षणः । किणः 'घाटिः' इति प्रसिद्धः । 'कुक्कुरैश्चर्व्यते' इति पाठो व्यक्त एव । अत्यायतो विपुलशरीरः । तथा कोमलस्य । 'व्यायतोऽकृतश्रमः' इति

---

१ दर्दुरकक्षा०, ०कक्षलुण्डीकृतं. २ उच्छिन्नोऽसि. ३ भट्टारु एदश्श.

Why should this very tall and delicate fellow be always engaged in gambling ?—( he ) who does not remain suspended motionless till the close of the day, with his head hanging down ; whose back does not bear scars produced by rasping clods of earth; and this interior of whose thighs is not daily nibbled by the dogs ( set after him ). ( 12 )

Well, I will first appease Mathura. ( *Approaching* ). I salute you, Mathura !

MA.—( *Returns his salute.* )

DAR.—What is this ?

MA.—This fellow owes ten gold-pieces.

DAR.—Why, that's a mere trifle !

MA.—( *Pulling out the cloak lying folded up in* Dardura's *arm-pit* ). Look, sirs, look ! This man, clad in ( such ) a tattered garment, calls ten gold-pieces 'a mere trifle' !

DAR.—You fool ! I can pay off ten gold-pieces by a mere *Kata* throw. What then ! he who has money—does he take it on his bosom and display it ( publicly )? You fellow !

You are a low-caste man ! you are doomed (to perish); (since) you are killing a human being possessed of the five bodily organs, merely for the sake of ten gold-pieces. (13)

MA.—Sir, ten gold-pieces may be a trifle to you ; to me they are a fortune !

DAR.—If so, then hear me. Give ten additional gold-pieces to this very man, and let him gamble with them.

MA.—Then what would happen ?

DAR.—If he wins, he will pay you.

MA.—And if he doesn't win ?

DAR.—Then he will not pay !

---

पूर्वटीका ।। १२ ।। [लुण्डीकृतं गोलीकृतम् । भट्टा इति संबुद्धिर्जनान्प्रति । ल० दी०] कल्यवर्तं प्रातर्भोजनम् । तत्साधनमेतत् द्रव्यमिदमित्यर्थः । जीर्णपटसंवृतः । [कटकरणेन पूरापतनेन । त्वमधुना देहीति यदि वदेन्माथुरस्तत्राह—तत्किमित्यादि । क्रोडे उत्सङ्गे । इति ल० दा० । [**दुर्वर्ण इति** । [दुष्टः वर्णः यस्य स दुर्वर्णः हीनजातिः । नीच इत्यर्थः । यद्वा क्रोधावेशात् दूषितमुखरागः । विनष्टोऽसि क्रूराचरणाद्धतोऽसि । पञ्चेन्द्रियाणि चक्षुरादीनि ज्ञानेन्द्रियाणि । नरः न तु पशुः ] ।। १३ ।। भट्टा इति संबोधनोक्तिः । तदेवं सति किम् । अथायं न दृढं भद्रं जयतु । पाठान्तरे तु—**अह अथ** भद्रकं जन्यम् । [खण्डितवृत्तः प्रतारक इत्यर्थः इति

**माथुरः**—अथ न युक्तं जल्पितुम् । एवमाचक्षाणस्त्वं प्रयच्छ धूर्तक । अहमपि नाम माथुरो धूर्तो द्यूतं मिथ्याऽऽदर्शयामि । अन्यस्मादप्यहं न विभेमि । धूर्त खण्डितवृत्तोऽसि त्वम् । (अह ण जुत्तं जप्पिदुम्[१] । एव्वं अक्खन्तो[२] तुमं पयच्छ धुत्तआ । अहं पि णाम माथुरु[३] धुत्तु जूदं मिच्छा आदंसआमि । अण्णस्स वि अहं ण बिभेमि । धुत्ता खण्डिअवुत्ता सि तुमम् ।)

**दर्दुरकः**—अरे कः खण्डितवृत्तः ।

**माथुरः**—त्वं खलु खण्डितवृत्तः । (तुमं हु खण्डिअवुत्तो ।)

**दर्दुरकः**—पिता ते खण्डितवृत्तः । (संवाहकस्यापक्रमितुं संज्ञां ददाति ।)

**माथुरः**—वेश्यापुत्र नन्वेषमेव द्यूतं त्वया सेवितम् । (गोसाविआपुत्ता णं एव्वं ज्जेव जूदं तुए सेविदम् ।)

**दर्दुरकः**—मयैवं द्यूतमासेवितम् ।

**माथुरः**—अरे संवाहक प्रयच्छ तद्दशसुवर्णम् । (अले संवाहआ पअच्छ तं दशसुवण्णम् ।)

**संवाहकः**—अद्य दास्यामि । तावद्दास्यामि । (अज्ज दइश्शम् । दाव दइश्शं ।)

( माथुरः कर्षति । )

**दर्दुरकः**—मूर्ख परोक्षे खलीकर्तुं शक्यते न ममाग्रतः खलीकर्तुम् ।

(माथुरः संवाहकमाकृष्य घोणायां मुष्टिप्रहारं ददाति । संवाहकः सशोणितं मूर्च्छां नाटयन्भूमौ पतति । दर्दुरक[४] उपसृत्यान्तरयति । माथुरो दर्दुरं ताडयति । दर्दुरो विप्रतीपं ताडयति ।)

**माथुरः**—अरे अरे दुष्ट पुंश्चलीपुत्रक फलमपि प्राप्स्यसि । ( अले[५] अले दुट्ट छिणालिआपुत्तअ फलं पि पाविहसि । )

**दर्दुरकः**—अरे मूर्ख अहं त्वया मार्गगत[६] एव ताडितः । श्वो यदि राजकुले ताडयिष्यसि तदा द्रक्ष्यसि ।

**माथुरः**—एष प्रेक्षिष्ये । ( एसु पेक्खिस्सम् । )

**दर्दुरकः**—कथं द्रक्ष्यसि ।

**माथुरः**—(प्रसार्य चक्षुषी । ) एवं प्रेक्षिष्ये । ( एव्वं पेक्खिस्सम् )

(दर्दुरो माथुरस्य पांशुना चक्षुषी पूरयित्वा संवाहकस्यापक्रमितुं संज्ञां ददाति । माथुरोऽक्षिणी निगृह्य भूमौ पतति । संवाहकोऽपक्रामति । )

**दर्दुरकः**—( स्वगतम् । ) प्रधानसभिको माथुरो मया विरोधितः । तन्नात्र युज्यते स्थातुम् । कथितं च मम प्रियवयस्येन शर्विलकेन यथा किल आर्यकनामा गोपालदारकः सिद्धादेशेन समादिष्टो राजा भविष्यतीति । सर्वश्चास्मद्विधो जनस्तमनुसरति । तदहमपि तत्समीपमेव गच्छामि । ( इति निष्क्रान्तः । )

---

१ जम्पिदुं. २ आचक्खन्तो. ३ माथुरो. ४ दर्दुरः. ५ अले दुट्ठ. ६ मार्गा०.

MA.—Now it is no use talking any more ( with you in this matter ). Rogue, you who are talking in this fashion—*you* pay them! Shall I, too, the well-known gambler, Mathura gamble for nothing? I am not afraid of anyone. You rogue, you are a blackguard ( *lit.* a man false to your character as a gambler )!

DAR.—Ha! Who is a blackguard?

MA.—You, *you* are a blackguard!

DAR.—Your father is a blackguard! ( *Makes signs to* Samvahaka *to escape* ).

MA.—You son-of-a-whore! Is it (always) thus that you have played at dice?

DAR.—Yes, I have thus played at dice.

MA.—You Samvahaka! Pay up those ten gold-pieces!

SAMVA.—I'll pay to-day; I'll pay presently.

( Mathura *pulls him* ).

DAR—You fool! You can harass him in my absence, but not in my presence! ( Mathura *drags* Samvahaka *and gives a blow on his nose*; Samva. *shows that he bleeds and faints, and falls on the ground*; Dar. *goes forth and screens him*: Ma. *strikes* Dar.; Dar. *strikes in return* ).

MA.—Ah! Ah! You villain! Son-of-a-whore! You'll get the fruit of this!

DAR.—You fool, you have struck me while I was on the road; if you were to beat me to-morrow in the palace, then you'll see!

MA.—Here I am ready to see!

DAR.—How will you see?

MA.—(*Opening his eyes wide*). Thus I will see.

( Dar. *throws dust into* Ma's *eyes and makes a sign to* Samva. *to escape*; Ma. *shuts his eyes and falls to the ground*; Samva. *makes good his escape* ).

DAR.—( *To himself* ). I have made an enemy of Mathura, the principal gambling-master. So it is not advisable ( for me ) to stay (longer) in this place. My dear friend Sarvilaka has told me that, as the report goes, a cowherd's son, named Aryaka, shall be the king as has been prophesied by a *Siddha* (a Seer). And all persons, of my sort, are flocking to him. So I too will go into his presence. ( *Exit* ).

**संवाहकः**—(सत्रासं परिक्रम्य। दृष्ट्वा।) एतत्कस्याप्यपावृतपक्षद्वारकं गेहम्। तदत्र प्रविशामि। (प्रवेशं रूपयित्वा। वसन्तसेनामालोक्य।) आर्ये शरणागतोऽस्मि। (एशे कश्श वि अपावुदपक्खदुआलके[1] गेहे। ता एत्थ पविशिश्शम्। अज्जे शलणागदे म्हि।

**वसन्तसेना**:—अभयं शरणागतस्य। चेटि पिधेहि पक्षद्वारकम्। (अभअं सरणागदस्स। हञ्जे ढक्केहि पक्खदुआरअम्।)

(चेटी तथा करोति।)

**वसन्तसेना**—कुतस्ते भयम्। (कुदो दे भअम्।)

**संवाहकः**—आर्ये धनिकात्। (अज्जे धणिकादो।)

**वसन्तसेना**—चेटि सांप्रतमपावृणु पक्षद्वारकम्। (हञ्जे संपदं अवावुणु पक्खदुआरअम्।)

**संवाहकः**—(आत्मगतम्।) कथं धनिकात्तुलितमस्या भयकारणम्। सुष्ठु खल्वेत्रमुच्यते।

**य आत्मबलं ज्ञात्वा भारं तुलितं वहति मनुष्यः।**
**तस्य स्खलनं न जायते न च कान्तारगतो विपद्यते॥ १४॥**

अत्र लक्षितोऽस्मि।

(कवं धणिकादो तुलिदं शे भअकालणम्। शुठ्ठु क्खु एव्वं वुच्चदि।
जे अत्तबलं जाणिअ भालं[2] तुलिदं वहेइ माणुस्से।
ताह खलणं ण जाअदि ण अ कन्तालगदो विवज्जदि॥
एत्थ लक्खिदो म्हि।)

**माथुरः**—(अक्षिणी प्रमृज्य। द्यूतकरं प्रति।) अरे देहि देहि। (अले देहि देहि।)

**द्यूतकरः**—भर्तः यावदेव वयं दर्दुरेण कलहायितास्तावदेव स पुरुषोऽपक्रान्तः। (भट्ठा जावदेव अम्हे दद्दुरेण कलहाविदा तावदेव सो गोहो अवक्कन्तो।)

**माथुरः**—तस्य द्यूतकरस्य मुष्टिप्रहारेण नासिका भग्नाऽऽसीत्। तदेहि। रुधिरपथमनुसरावः। (तस्स जूदकलस्स मुट्ठिप्पहालेण णासिका भग्गा आसि। ता एहि। रुहिरपहं अणुसरेम्ह।)

(अनुसृत्य।)

**द्यूतकरः**—भर्तः वसन्तसेनागृहं प्रविष्टः सः। (भट्ठा वसन्तसेणागेहं पविट्ठो सो।)

**माथुरः**—भूतानि सुवर्णानि। (भूदाइं सुवण्णाइं।)

**द्यूतकरः**—राजकुलं गत्वा निवेदयावः। (लाअउलं गदुअ णिवेदेम्ह।)

---

१ अपलाबुद (अपरावृत); अणपा०. २ लाभं.

SAMVA.—( *Walks about in fear* ; *observing* ). Here is somebody's house with its side-door open. So I'll get in here. ( *Shows that he enters* ; *seeing* Vasantasena ). Lady, I beseech your protection !

VAS.—Have no fear, you who seek my protection ! Girl, close the side-door.

( *The maid does as ordered* ).

VAS.—Whom are you afraid of ?

SAMVA.—Of a creditor, madam.

VAS.—Girl, you may now open the side-door.

SAMVA.—( *To himself* ). How now ! She makes light of any fear arising from a creditor ! Rightly it has been said that—

A person, who, knowing his own strength, takes up a load which is proportionate (to it), will never stumble ( come to grief ) ; nor will he perish even if he (comes to) be in a wilderness. (14)

Of (the truth of) this I myself am an illustration !

MA.—( *Rubbing his eyes* ; *to the* Gambler ). Eh ! Give, give !

THE GAMESTER—Master, that fellow escaped just as we came into scrape with Dardura !

MA.—That gambler had his nose broken by the blow of my fist. So come along ; we shall follow the track of its blood.

( *Following the track* ).

GAMESTER—Master, he has gone into Vasantasena's house !

MA.—Then our gold-pieces are secure.

THE PLAYER—Let us go and inform the police ( *lit.* the court ).

---

ल० दी० ]। एवमहं पत्तुआ धुत्तिज्जामि प्रतार्ये । अहमपि नाम मथुराभर्त्रा द्यूतकरो द्यूतं मिथ्या दर्शयामि । अन्यस्माच्च नाहं बिभेमि । अहमेवान्यं निर्भयः प्रतारयामि । न तु मामन्य इत्यर्थः । तेन त्वमपि धूर्तोऽसीति भावः । गोसाविआ वेश्या । ढक्केहि पिधेहि । तुलिदमाकलितम् । **य आत्मेत्यादि** । वैतालीयं छन्दः । [ यः नरः तुलितं वोढुं शक्य इति निश्चितं भारं वहति सः कान्तारगतः कृच्छ्रगतोऽपि न विपद्यते ] ॥ १४ ॥ तुलितं कलितमिति 'वा पदान्त-' इति त्रिन्दोर्लघुत्वम् । वसन्तसेनाया अशक्यविषये व्यापार उक्तः । गोहो मनुष्यः । तस्य दुरात्मनो मया मुष्टिप्रहारेण नासा भग्ना । तदागच्छतु । चिरमेतदनुसरावः । एहि तावत् । अदो अतः ।

**माथुरः**—एष धूर्तोऽतो निष्क्रम्यान्यत्र गमिष्यति। तदुपरोधेनैव गृह्णीवः। (एसो धुत्तो अदो णिक्कमिअ अण्णत्त गमिस्सदि। ता उअरोधेणेव्व गण्हेम्ह।)

**वसन्तसेना**—(मदनिकायाः संज्ञां ददाति।)

**मदनिका**—कुत आर्यः। को वाऽऽर्यः। कस्य वाऽऽर्यः। कां वा वृत्तिमार्य उपजीवति। कुतो वा भयम्। (कुदो अज्जो। को वा अज्जो। कस्स वा अज्जो। कं वा वित्तिं अज्जो उवजीअदि। कुदो वा भअम्।)

**संवाहकः**—शृणोत्वार्या। आर्ये पाटलिपुत्रं मे जन्मभूमिः। गृहपतिदारकोऽहम्। संवाहकस्य वृत्तिमुपजीवामि। (शुणादु अज्जआ। अज्जए पाडलिउत्तं मे जम्मभूमी। गहवइदालके हग्गे। संवाहअश्श वित्तिं उवजीआमि।

**वसन्तसेना**—सुकुमारा खलु कला शिक्षिताऽऽर्येण। (सुउमारा क्खु कला सिक्खिदा अज्जेण।)

**संवाहकः**—आर्ये कलेति शिक्षिता। आजीविकेदानीं संवृत्ता। (अज्जए कलेत्ति शिक्खिदा। आजीविआ दाणिं संवुत्ता।)

**चेटी**[१]—अतिनिर्विण्णमार्येण प्रतिवचनं दत्तम्। ततस्ततः। (अदिणिव्विण्णं अज्जेण पडिवअणं दिण्णम्। तदो तदो।)

**संवाहकः**—तत आर्ये एष निजगेह आहिण्डकानां मुखाच्छ्रुत्वाऽपूर्वदेशदर्शन-कुतूहलेनेहागतः। इहापि मया प्रविश्योज्जयिनीमेक आर्यः शुश्रूषितः। यस्तादृशः प्रियदर्शनः प्रियवादी दत्त्वा न कीर्तयत्यपकृतं विस्मरति। किं बहुना प्रलपितेन। दक्षिणतया परकीयमिवात्मानमवगच्छति शरणागतवत्सलश्च। (तदो अज्जए एशे णिजगेहे आहिण्डकाणं मुहादो शुणिअ अपुव्वदेशदंशणकुदूहलेण इह आगदे। इह वि मए पविशिअ उज्जइणिं एक्के अज्जे शुश्शूशिदे। जे तालिशे पिअदंशणे पिअवादी दइअ ण कित्तेदि अवकिदं विशुमलेदि। किं बहुणा पलन्तेण। दक्खिणदाए पलकेलकं विअ अत्ताणअं अवगच्छदि शलणागअवच्छले अ।)

**चेटी**—क इदानीमार्याया मनोरथान्तरस्य गुणांश्चोरयित्वोज्जयिनीमलंक-रोति। (को दाणिं अज्जआए मणोरहन्तरस्स गुणाइं चोरिअ उज्जइणिं अलंकरेदि।)

**वसन्तसेना**—साधु चेटि साधु। मयाप्येवमेव हृदयेन मन्त्रितम्। (साहु हञ्जे साहु। मए वि एव्वं ज्जेव्व हिअएण मन्तिदम्।)

**चेटी**—आर्य ततस्ततः। (अज्ज तदो तदो।)

**संवाहकः**—आर्ये स इदानीमनुक्रोशकृतैः प्रदानैः—(अज्जए शे दाणिं अणु-क्कोशकिदेहिं पदाणेहिं—)

**वसन्तसेना**—किमुपरतविभवः संवृत्तः। (किं उवरदविहवो संवुत्तो।)

**संवाहकः**—अनाख्यातमेव कथमार्यया विज्ञातम्। (अणाचक्खिदे ज्जेव्व कधं अज्जआए विण्णादम्।)

MA.—That rascal might leave this place and go elsewhere. So we had better capture him by means of a blockade.

VAS.—( *Makes a sign to* Madanika ).

MAD.—Whence do you come ? Who may you be ? To whom do you belong ? What profession do you follow for a living ? And whence is your fear ?

SAM.—May the lady hear !—Madam, my birth-place is Pataliputra, and I am the son of a village headman. I earn my living by the profession of a shampooer.

VAS.—It is a very dainty art that you have learnt.

SAM.—Lady, I learnt it as an art, but it has now become my means of earning a livelihood !

THE MAID.—You have given a reply indicative of extreme dejection ! Well, what next ?

SAM.—Then, lady, having at home heard ( about this city ) from the lips of travellers, I came down to this place out of a curiosity to visit a country never seen before. And, having entered this Ujjayini, I took service with a certain gentleman. He is so very handsome in appearance and of a sweet address ! He makes gifts, but makes no mention of them ; and forgets any ill ( done unto him by others ). Why waste words ?—On account of his courtesy he considers himself as belonging to ( *i. e.* at the service of ) others ; and he is kind to those who approach him for refuge.

THE MAID.—Who may he be that now graces Ujjayini, having appropriated to himself ( *lit.* stolen ) the virtues of the object ( *i. e.* Charudatta ) of my lady's desires ?

VAS.—Well spoken, wench, well spoken ! I too thought just the same in my mind.

THE MAID—Sir, what next ?

SAM.—Lady, owing to the large gifts he bestowed in compassion, he now—

VAS.—Has lost all his fortune ?

SAM.—How did your ladyship know it, even before it was told to you ?

---

[ उपराधेन निर्गममार्गविरोधेन । संज्ञां ददाति नामादि सर्वं पृच्छेति कटाक्षेण सूचयतीत्यर्थः इति ल. दी. ]। गृहपतिर्ग्रामाध्यक्षः । संवाहकस्य शरीरयन्त्रमर्दकस्य व्यापारमुपजीवामि । स्वगृहपर्यटकानां भिक्षुकादीनां वचनं श्रुत्वा । मणोरहन्तरस्स

**वसन्तसेना**—किमत्र ज्ञायते । दुर्लभा गुणा विभवाश्च । अपेयेषु तडागेषु बहुतरमुदकं भवति । (किं एत्थ जाणीअदि । दुल्लहा गुणा[१] विहवा अ । अपेएसु तडाएसु बहुदरं उदअं भोदि ।)

**चेटी**—आर्य किंनामधेयः खलु सः । (अज्ज किंणामधेओ क्खु सो ।)

**संवाहकः**—आर्ये क इदानीं तस्य भूतलमृगाङ्कस्य नाम न जानाति । स खलु श्रेष्ठिचत्वरे प्रतिवसति । श्लाघनीयनामधेय आर्यचारुदत्तो नाम । (अज्जे के दाणिं तश्श भूदलमिअङ्कस्स णामं ण जाणादि । शो क्खु शेट्ठिचत्तले[२] पडिवशदि । शलाहणिज्जणामधेए अज्जचालुदत्ते णाम ।)

**वसन्तसेना**—(सहर्षमासनादवतीर्य ।) आर्यस्यात्मीयमेतद्गेहम् । चेटि देह्यस्यासनम् । तालवृन्तकं गृहाण । परिश्रम आर्यस्य बाधते । (अज्जस्स अत्तणकेरकं एदं गेहम् । हञ्जे देहि से आसणम् । तालवेण्ठअं गेण्ह । परिस्समो अज्जस्स बाधेदि ।)

(चेटी तथा करोति ।)

**संवाहकः**—(स्वगतम् ।) कथमार्यचारुदत्तस्य नामसंकीर्तनेनेदृशो म आदरः । साधु आर्यचारुदत्त साधु । पृथिव्यां त्वमेको जीवसि । शेषः पुनर्जनः श्वसिति । (इति पादयोर्निपत्य ।) भवत्वार्ये भवतु । आसने निषीदत्वार्या । (कधं अज्जचालुदत्तस्स णामशंकीत्तणेण ईदिशे मे आदले । शाहु अज्जचालुदत्त शाहु । पुहवीए तुमं एक्के जीवशि । शेशे उण जने शशदि । भोदु अज्जए भोदु । आशणे णिशीददु अज्जआ ।

**वसन्तसेना**—(आसने समुपविश्य ।) आर्य कुतः स धनिकः । (अज्ज कुदो सो धणिओ ।)

**संवाहकः**—

**सत्कारधनः खलु सज्जनः कस्य न भवति चलाचलं धनम् ।**
**यः पूजयितुमपि जानाति स पूजाविशेषमपि जानाति ॥ १५ ॥**

(शक्कालधणे क्खु शज्जणे काह ण होइ चलाचले धणे ।
जे पूइदुं पि आणादि[३] शे पूआविशेशं पि आणादि ॥)

**वसन्तसेना**—ततस्ततः । (तदो तदो ।)

**संवाहकः**—ततस्तेनार्येण सवृत्तिः परिचारकः कृतोऽस्मि । चारित्र्यावशेषे च तस्मिन्द्यूतोपजीव्यस्मि संवृत्तः । ततो भागधेयविषमतया दशसुवर्णं द्यूते हारितम् । (तदो तेण अज्जेण शवित्ती पलिचालके किदो ह्मि । चालित्तावशेशे अ तश्शि जूदोवजीवि ह्मि शंउत्ते । तदो भाअधेअविशमदाए दशशुवण्णअं जूदे हालिदम् ।)

---

१ गुणविहवा. २ चउत्तले. ३ ण जाणा०.

VAS.—What is there to be known ? Virtues and riches are seldom found ( to exist ) together. Water is most plentiful in those pools which are unfit to be drunk from.

THE MAID—Sir, what may his name be ?

SAM.—Lady, who is there that does not know the name of that Moon on this Earth ? He resides in the merchants' quarter; he, of auspicious name, is called the noble Charudatta.

VAS.—( *Joyfully getting down from her seat* ). This house is your honour's own ! Girl, give him a seat. And take up a fa his honour is weary with fatigue.

( *The* Maid *does as ordered* )

SAM.—( *To himself* ). How ! By the mere mention of the noble Charudatta's name they are showing me so much respect ! Excellent, noble Charudatta, excellent ! You alone ( really ) *live* in this world, while all other persons merely *breathe* ! ( *Falling at* Vas.'s *feet* ). No, no, madam ! You may sit on the seat !

VAS.—( *Sitting down on it* ). Sir, whence is that ( how can he, *i.e.* Charudatta, be ) a rich man ?

SAM.—

A good man's wealth really consists in his hospitable nature ; (otherwise) who does not possess riches which are transitory ? He who knows how to respect (others) knows also ( *i. e.* can appreciate ) the significance of the respect (paid by others to him). (15)

VAS.—Well, go on.

SAM.—Then that gentleman took me into his personal service on wages; when he had only his good name left to him, I took to gambling as a means of sustenance. Then, my luck going against me, I lost ten gold-pieces at play.

---

मनोरथाभिमुखस्य । अनुक्रोशः करुणा । आजीविका वृत्तिः । [अपेयेषु नीरसत्वात्पानानर्हजलेषु । श्लाघनीयं प्रशंसार्हं नामधेयं यस्य । चारु दत्तं दानं यस्येत्यर्थाव्यभिचारित्वादिति भावः । तालवृन्तकं गृहाण गृहीत्वा वीजयेत्यर्थः ।] सत्कारेति । मात्रासमकम् । प्रतिपादं चलाचले धणे शे इत्येकारत्रयं लघु । छन्दोनुरोधात् । सत्कारधनः [सत्कारः अन्येषामादरदर्शनं धनं यस्य सः । चलाचलमस्थिरम् । कस्य न भवति सर्वस्यापि भवतीत्यर्थः । सज्जनत्वं न धननिबन्धनमित्यर्थः ] यः पूजितुमपि न जानाति स पूजाविशेषं जानाति । अपि तु न जानात्येव ॥ १५ ॥ सवृत्तिः कृतवर्तनः । चारित्रमात्रावशेषे धनशून्ये तस्मिन् । [वासपादपस्य निवासवृक्षस्य

**माथुरः**—उत्सादितोऽस्मि । मुषितोऽस्मि । (उच्छादिदो ह्मि । मुसिदो ह्मि ।)

**संवाहकः**—एतौ तौ सभिकद्यूतकरौ मामनुसंधत्तः । सांप्रतं श्रुत्वाऽऽर्या प्रमाणम् । (एदे दे शहिअजूदिअला मं अणुशंधअन्ति । शंपदं शुणिअ अज्जआ पमाणम् ।)

**वसन्तसेना**—मदनिके वासपादपविसंष्ठुलतया पक्षिण इतस्ततोऽप्याहिण्डन्ते । चेटि तद्गच्छ । एतयोः सभिकद्यूतकरयोरयमार्य एव प्रतिपादयतीति इदं हस्ताभरणकं त्वं देहि । (इति हस्तात्कटकमाकृष्य चेटयाः प्रयच्छति ।)( मदणिए वासपादवविसंठुलदाए पक्खिणो इदो तदो वि आहिण्डन्ति । हञ्जे ता गच्छ । एदाणं सहिअजूदिअराणं अअं अज्जो ज्जेव पडिवादेदि त्ति इमं हत्थाभरणअं तुमं देहि ।)

**चेटी**—(गृहीत्वा ।)यदार्याऽऽज्ञापयति । ( इति निष्क्रान्ता । ) (जं अज्जआ आणवेदि ।)

**माथुरः**—उत्सादितोऽस्मि मुषितोऽस्मि । (उच्छादिदो म्हि । मुसिदो म्हि ।)

**चेटी**—यथैतावूर्ध्वं प्रेक्षेते दीर्घं निश्वसितो विचारयतश्चाभिलपतश्च द्वारनिहितलोचनौ तथा तर्कयाम्येतौ तौ सभिकद्यूतकरौ भविष्यतः । (उपगम्य ।) आर्य वन्दे । (जधा एदे उद्धं पेक्खन्ति दीहं णीससन्ति विसूरअन्ति अ अहिलहन्ति अ दुआरणिहिदलोअणा तधा तक्केमि एदे दे सहिअजूदिअरा हुविस्सन्ति । अज्ज वन्दामि ।

**माथुरः**—सुखं तव भवतु । (सुहं तुए होदु ।)

**चेटी**—आर्य कतरो युवयोः सभिकः । (अज्ज कदमो तुम्हाणं सहिओ ।)

**माथुरः**—

> **कस्य त्वं तनुमध्ये अधरेण रतदष्टदुर्विनीतेन ।**
> **जल्पसि मनोहरवचनमालोकयन्ती कटाक्षेण ॥ १६ ॥**

नास्ति मम विभवः । अन्यत्र व्रज ।

> (कस्स तुहं[१] तणुमज्झे अहरेण रददठ्ठदुव्विणीदेण
> जम्पसि मणहलवअणं आलोअन्ती कडक्खेण ॥

णत्थि मम विहवो । अण्णत्त व्वज ।)

**चेटी**—यदीदृशानि ननु मन्त्रयसे तदा न भवसि द्यूतकरः । अस्ति कोऽपि युष्माकं धारकः । (जइ ईदिसाइं णं मन्तेसि ता ण होसि जूदिअरो । अत्थि को वि तुम्हाणं धारओ ।

**माथुरः**—अस्ति । दशसुवर्णं धारयति । किं तस्य । ( अत्थि । दशसुअण्णं धालेदि । किं तस्स ।)

**चेटी**—तस्य कारणादार्येदं हस्ताभरणं प्रतिपादयति । न हि न हि । स एव प्रतिपादयति । ( तस्स कारणादो अज्जआ इमं हत्थाभरणं पडिवादेदि । ण हि ण हि । सो ज्जेव पडिवादेदि ।)

---

१ तुमं.

MA.—I am totally undone ! I am robbed !

SAM.—Here are they, the keeper and the gamester, both on my track. So now, having heard (my story), your ladyship may decide (what to do).

VAS.—Madanika, the birds wander anywhere at random, when the tree whereon they dwell is tottering. Go, then, girl, and give this bracelet (*lit.* hand-ornament) to those two, the keeper and the player, saying that it is given by this gentleman himself. ( *She removes the bracelet from her hand and gives it to the* Maid ).

THE MAID—( *Taking it* ). As your ladyship commands. ( *Exit* ).

MA.—I am totally undone ! I am robbed !

THE MAID—As these two are looking upwards, sighing deeply, pondering, and talking with their eyes fixed on our door, I guess that these must be those very persons, the keeper and the gamester. ( *Approaching* ). Sir, I bow to you !

MA.—May you fare well !

THE MAID—Sir, which of you two is the keeper ?

MA—

O you slender-waisted damsel ! With your lower lip bitten in love sport and looking ungainly, to whom are you addressing alluring words, casting side-glances ? (16)

I am not a rich man. So go elsewhere.

THE MAID—If you can talk thus, then surely you can't be the gambler.—Is there any person who owes you money ?

MA.—There is. He owes ten gold-pieces. What of him ?

THE MAID—On his account my lady has given this bracelet—Ah ! no !—he himself has given it.

---

विसंष्ठुलतया अस्थिरतया ] पक्षिणो भ्राम्यन्ति । दिनान्ते भूतप्राय इत्यर्थः (?) । आर्यः संवाहकः । [ प्रतिपादयति ददाति । ] अहिणेन्ति अभिनीयन्ते । दुवारमुले द्वारमूल सुहवा सुभगा । कस्येति । गाथा । दुर्विनीतेन रते दष्टेनाधरेण जल्पसि । [ मनोहरवचनमिति क्रियाविशेषणम् ] ॥ १६ ॥ धारयति । यस्य पार्श्वलभ्यमीदृशं तं संवाहकं कुलपुत्रम् । भूतो गण्डः । सुविधानमित्यर्थः । 'खण्ड' इति मरहट्टप्रसिद्धः । तत्पुनरपि द्यूतं रमामहे । इयं कला संवाहनरूपा । शाक्यश्रमणकः शाक्यबौद्धभिक्षुः । एतान्यक्षराणि द्यूतेनेति । गाथा । द्यूतेन तत्कृतं मम सर्वस्माज्जनाद्विभ्यते यत् । 'यद्विभ्यतः ।

**माथुरः**—(सहर्षं गृहीत्वा।) अरे भणसि तं कुलपुत्रम्—भूतस्तव गण्डः। आगच्छ। पुनर्द्यूतं रमस्व। (अले भणेशि तं कुलवुत्तम्—भूदं तुए गण्डे[1]। आअच्छ। पुणो जूदं रमह।)

(इति निष्क्रान्तौ।)

**चेटी**—(वसन्तसेनामुपसृत्य।) आर्ये परिपुष्टौ गतौ सभिकद्यूतकरौ। (अज्जए पडितुट्टा गदा सहिअजूदिअरा।)

**वसन्तसेना**—तद्गच्छत्वार्यो बन्धुजनं समाश्वासयितुम्। (ता गच्छदु अज्जो[2] बन्धुअणं समस्सासिदुं।)

**संवाहकः**—आर्ये यद्येवं तदियं कला परिजनहस्तगता क्रियताम्। (अज्जए जइ एव्वं ता इअं कला पलिअणहत्थगदा कलीअदु।)

**वसन्तसेना**—आर्य यस्य कारणादियं कला शिक्ष्यते स एवार्येण शुश्रूषितपूर्वः शुश्रूषितव्यः। (अज्ज जस्स कारणादो इअं कला सिक्खीअदि सो ज्जेव अज्जेण सुस्सूसिदपुरुव्वो सुस्सूसिदव्वो।)

**संवाहकः**—(स्वगतम्।) आर्यया निपुणं प्रत्यादिष्टोऽस्मि। कथं प्रत्युपकरिष्ये। (प्रकाशम्।) आर्ये अहमेतेन द्यूतकरापमानेन शाक्यश्रमणको भविष्यामि। तत्संवाहको द्यूतकरः शाक्यश्रमणकः संवृत्त इति स्मर्तव्यान्यार्ययैतान्यक्षराणि। (अज्जआए णिउणं पच्चादिट्टो म्हि। कधं पच्चुवकलिश्शम्। अज्जए अहं एदिणा जूदिअलावमाणेण शक्कशमणके हुविश्शम्। ता संवाहके जूदिअले शक्कशमणके शंवुत्तेत्ति शुमलिदव्वा अज्जआए एदे अक्खलु।)

**वसन्तसेना**—आर्य अलं साहसेन। (अज्ज अलं साहसेण।)

**संवाहकः**—आर्ये कृतो निश्चयः। (इति परिक्रम्य।)

**द्यूतेन तत्कृतं मम यद्विहस्तं जनस्य सर्वस्य।**
**इदानीं प्रकटशीर्षो नरेन्द्रमार्गेण विहरिष्यामि॥ १७॥**

(अज्जए कले णिच्चए।)

जूदेण तं कदं मे जं वीहत्थं जणश्श शव्वश्श।
एण्हि पाअडशीशे णलिन्दमग्गेण विहलिश्शम्॥)

(नेपथ्ये कलकलः)

**संवाहकः**—(आकर्ण्य।) अरे किं न्विदम्। (आकाशे।) किं भणथ—एष खलु वसन्तसेनायाः खुण्टमोडको नाम दुष्टहस्ती विचरतीति। अहो आर्याया गन्धगजं प्रेक्षिष्ये गत्वा। अथ वा किं ममैतेन। यथाव्यवसितमनुष्ठास्यामि। (इति निष्क्रान्तः।) (अले किं ण्णेदम्। किं भणाध—एशे क्खु वशन्तशेणआए खुण्टमोडके णाम दुट्टहत्थी विअलेदि त्ति। अहो अज्जआए गन्धगअं पेक्खिश्शं गदुअ। अह वा किं मम एदिणा। जधाववशिदं अणुचिट्ठिश्शम्।)

---

१ गन्थु. २ अज्ज बन्धुअणो समस्ससदु (अद्य बन्धुजनः समाश्वसितु).

MA.—( *Joyfully taking it* ). Aye, you say to that good chap that we have got the security; so he might come and again have a throw at dice.

( *Exeunt both* ).

THE MAID—( *Approaching* Vas. ) Mistress, the keeper and the gamester have both gone away satisfied.

VAS.—Then you may depart, sir, and comfort your (anxious) relatives.

SAM.—Madam, if so, then kindly allow this art ( of mine ) to be imparted to your made-servants.

VAS,—Sir, you should (go and) serve that same person whom you served before, for whose sake this art is to be learnt ( by us ).

SAM.—( *To himself* ). Her ladyship has skilfully declined my offer! How then shall I repay her kindness? ( *Aloud* ). Madam, being thus disgraced as a gambler I will now become a Buddhist monk. So madam should carefully remember these words. *viz.* that Samvahaka the gambler has turned a Buddhist monk.

VAS.—Sir, don't be rash.

SAM.—Madam, my resolve is taken ( *Walking about* ).

Gambling has done to me that which places me beyond the power of all people. Now I will roam about on the king's highway freely holding up my head. (17)

( *An uproar behind the Scenes* )

SAM.—( *Listening* ) Ah! What may this be? ( *In the void* ) What say you?—'Here has broken loose Vasantasena's rogue elephant named Khuntamodaka? Oh! I shall then go and have a look at her ladyship's Scent-elephant. Or rather, what have I to do with this? I shall do as I have resolved. (*Exit.*)

---

सर्वस्य जनस्य' इनि प्राचीनटीका । [ सर्वजनस्य यद्विहस्तं हस्तशब्देन हस्तशस्त्रं विगतहस्तशस्त्रं भवति निर्भयमित्यर्थः। तन्मम द्यूतेन कृतमिति वाक्यार्थः । ल. दी. ] इदानीं द्यूतदेयदशसुवर्णदेयकाले । प्रकटशीर्षो नरेन्द्रमार्गेण विहरिष्यामि । भयविरहादित्याशयः ॥ १७ ॥ [ खुण्टमोडकः स्तम्भभञ्जकः । ] विअलेदि विचरति । [ गन्धप्रधानो गजः गन्धगजः । तदुक्तं पालकाप्ये—' यस्य गन्धं समाघ्राय न तिष्ठन्ति प्रतिद्विपाः । तं गन्धहस्तिनं प्राहुर्नृपतेर्विजयावहम् ' इति । ] 'विकलयति' इत्येके । गलुअदां गुरुत्वम् । महावैभवशालित्वात् । यथाव्यवसितं परिव्रज्यानुष्ठान-

(ततः[1] प्रविशत्यपटीक्षेपेण प्रहृष्टो विकटोज्जलवेषः कर्णपूरकः ।)

**कर्णपूरकः**—कुत्र कुत्रार्या । (कहिं कहिं अज्जआ ।)

**चेटी**—दुर्मनुष्य किं त उद्वेगकारणं यदग्रतोऽवस्थितामार्यां न प्रेक्षसे । (दुम्मणुस्स किं ते उव्वेअकालणं जं अग्गदो वट्ठिदं अज्जअं ण पेक्खसि ।)

**कर्णपूरकः**—( दृष्ट्वा । ) आर्ये वन्दे । ( अज्जए वन्दामि । )

**वसन्तसेना**—कर्णपूरक परितुष्टमुखो लक्ष्यसे । तत्किं न्विदम् । (कण्णऊरअ परितुट्ठमुहो लक्खीअसि । ता किं ण्णेदम् ।)

**कर्णपूरकः**—(सविस्मयम् ।) आर्ये वञ्चिताऽसि यथाऽद्य कर्णपूरकस्य पराक्रमो न दृष्टः । (अज्जए वञ्चिदासि जाए अज्ज कण्णऊरअस्स परक्कमो ण दिट्ठो ।)

**वसन्तसेना**—कर्णपूरक किं किम् । (कण्णऊरअ किं किम् ।)

**कर्णपूरकः**—शृणोत्वार्या । यः स आर्यायाः खुण्टमोडको नाम दुष्टहस्ती स आलानस्तम्भं भङ्क्त्वा महामात्रं व्यापाद्य महन्तं संक्षोभं कुर्वन्राजमार्गमवतीर्णः । ततोऽत्रान्तरे उद्घुष्टं जनेन—

**'अपनयत बालकजनं त्वरितमारोहत वृक्षप्रासादम् ।**
**किं न खलु प्रेक्षध्वं पुरतो दुष्टो हस्तीत एति' ॥ १८ ॥**

अपि च ।

**विचलति नूपुरयुगलं छिद्यन्ते च मेखला मणिखचिताः ।**
**वलयाश्च सुन्दरतरा रत्नाङ्कुरजालप्रतिबद्धाः' ॥ १९ ॥**

ततस्तेन दुष्टहस्तिना करचरणरदनैः फुल्लनलिनीमिव नगरीमुज्जयिनीमवगाहमानेन समासादितः परिव्राजकः । तं च परिभ्रष्टदण्डकुण्डिकाभाजनं शीकरैः सिक्त्वा दन्तान्तरे क्षिप्तं प्रेक्ष्य पुनरप्युद्घुष्टं जनेन—हा परिव्राजको व्यापाद्यत इति । (सुणादु अज्जआ । जो सो अज्जआए खुण्टमोडओ णाम दुट्टहत्थी सो आलाणत्थम्भं[2] भञ्जिअ महमेत्थं वावादिअ महन्तं संखोहं करन्तो राअमग्गं ओदिण्णो । तदो एत्थन्तरे उग्घुट्टं जणेण—

'अवणेध बालअजणं तुरिदं आरुहध वुक्खपासादम्[3] ।
किं ण[4] हु पेक्खध पुरदो दुट्टो हत्थी इदो एदि ' ॥

अवि अ ।

'विचलइ णेउरजुअलं छिज्जन्ति अ मेहला मणिक्खइआ ।
वलआ अ सुन्दरदरा रअणङ्कुरजालपडिबद्धा ' ॥

तदो तेण दुट्टहत्थिणा कलचलणरदणेहिं फुल्लणलिणिं विअ णअरिं उज्जइणिं अवगाहमाणेण समासादिदो परिव्वाजओ । तं च परिब्भट्टदण्डकुण्डिआभाअणं सीअरेहिं सिञ्चिअ दन्तन्तरे क्खित्तं पेक्खिअ पुणो वि उग्घुट्टं जणेण—हा परिव्वाजओ वावादीअदि त्ति ।)

---

१ प्रविश्य कर्णपूरो हृष्टोऽपटी०; प्रविशत्यपटा०. २ खम्भं. ३ रुक्ख. ४ उण.

*( Then enter with a toss of the curtain* Karnapuraka *highly jubilant and in a formidable and gaudy dress )*

KAR.—Where, where is her ladyship ?

THE MAID—You rude fellow, what is the cause of your excitement that you do not see her ladyship seated just in your front ?

KAR.—(*Seeiny*). Madam, I bow to you!

VAS.—Karnapuraka, you seem to be mightily pleased, from your face! So what can this be ?

KAR.—( *With great pride* ). My lady, you've missed a treat (*lit.* you have been cheated ) inasmuch as you saw not Karnapuraka's exploit, to-day!

VAS.—Karnapuraka, what is it, what is it ?

KAR —May your ladyship listen —That rogue elephant of yours, called Khuntamodaka,—he broke the post to which he was tied, killed his keeper, and got down to the king's highway, causing tremendous excitement. Then in the meantime people began to shout out—

'Remove the children—Quickly mount trees or house-tops.—Don't you see that the furious elephant is just coming towards you this way ?" (18)

And again—

"Pairs of anklets have dropped off! Broken are girdle-zones set with jewels! And so, too, are very lovely bracelets inlaid with a network of the shooting rays of gems !" (19)

Then that rogue elephant came upon a monk, as he was dashing through the city of Ujjayini, as though it were a lake full of blooming lotuses through which he was wading with his trunk, legs and tusks. Seeing that he discharged a shower of spray at the monk who had (already, in fear) dropped his staff, his gourd, and his alms-pot, and took him up between his tusks, the people again shouted out—"Oh! The monk is being killed!"

---

रूपम् । [ दुर्मनुष्य तस्य संभ्रमपारवश्यादेवमुक्तम् ।] अज्जअं वसन्तसेनाम् । आलानस्तम्भं बन्धनस्तम्भम् । महामात्रं हस्त्यारोहम् । अपनयतेत्यादि । गाथाद्वयम् ॥ १८ ॥ विचलतीति । नूपुरं वलयाश्च विघटन्ते [ भयसंभ्रमाद् दूरमप-

**वसन्तसेना**—(ससंभ्रमम् ।) अहो प्रमादः । अहो प्रमादः । (अहो पमादो । अहो पमादो ।)

**कर्णपूरकः**—अलं संभ्रमेण । शृणोतु तावदार्या । ततो विच्छिन्नविसंष्ठुलशृङ्खलाकलापमुद्वहन्तं दन्तान्तरपरिगृहीतं परिव्राजकमुद्वहन्तं तं प्रेक्ष्य कर्णपूरकेण मया—न हि न हि । आर्याया अन्नपिण्डपुष्टेन दासेन—वामचरणेन द्यूतलेखकं उद्घुष्योद्घुष्य त्वरितमापणाल्लोहदण्डं गृहीत्वाऽऽकारितः स दुष्टहस्ती । (अलं संभमेण । सुणादु दाव अज्जआ । तदो विच्छिण्णविसंठुलसिङ्खलाकलावअं उव्वहन्तं दन्तन्तरपरिग्गहिदं परिव्वाजअं उव्वहन्तं तं पेक्खिअ कण्णऊरएण मए—ण हि ण हि । अज्जआए अण्णपिण्डउठ्ठेण दासेण—वामचलणेण जूदलेक्खअं उग्घुसिअ उग्घुसिअ तुरिदं आवणादो लोहदण्डं गेण्हिअ आआरिदो सो दुट्ठहत्थी ।)

**वसन्तसेना**—ततस्ततः । (तदो तदो ।)

**कर्णपूरकः**—

**आहत्य सरोषं तं हस्तिनं विन्ध्यशैलशिखराभम् ।**
**मोचितो मया स दन्तान्तरसंस्थितः परिव्राजकः ॥ २० ॥**

(आहणिऊण सरोसं तं हत्थिं विञ्झसैलसिहराभम् ।
मोआविओ मए सो दन्तन्तरसंठिओ[1] परिव्वाजवो ।)

**वसन्तसेना**—सुष्ठु त्वया कृतम् । ततस्ततः । (सुट्ठु दे किदम् । तदो तदो ।)

**कर्णपूरकः**—तत आर्ये साधु रे कर्णपूरक साधु इत्येतावन्मात्रं भणन्ती विषमभराक्रान्ता इव नौरेकतः पर्यस्ता सकलोज्जयिन्यासीत् । तत आर्ये एकेन शून्यान्याभरणस्थानानि परामृश्योर्ध्वं प्रेक्ष्य दीर्घं निःश्वस्यायं प्रावारको ममोपरि क्षिप्तः । (तदो अज्जए साहु रे कण्णऊरअ साहु त्ति एत्तिअमेत्तं भणन्ती विसमभरक्कन्ता विअ णावा एक्कदो पल्हत्था सअला उज्जइणी आसि । तदो अज्जए एक्केण सुण्णाइं आहरणट्ठाणाइं परामसिअ उद्धं पेक्खिअ दीहं णीससिअ अअं पावारओ मम उवरि क्खित्तो[2] ।)

**वसन्तसेना**—कर्णपूरक जानीहि तावत्किमेष जातीकुसुमवासितः प्रावारको न वेति । ( कण्णऊरअ जाणीहि दाव किं एसो जादीकुसुमवासिदो पावारओ ण वेत्ति।

**कर्णपूरकः**—आर्ये मदगन्धेन सुष्ठु तं गन्धं न जानामि । (अज्जए मदगन्धेण सुट्ठु तं गन्धं ण जाणामि ।)

**वसन्तसेना**—नामापि तावत्प्रेक्षस्व । ( णामं पि दाव पेक्ख ।

**कर्णपूरक**—इदं नाम । आर्यैव वाचयतु । (इति प्रावारकमुपनयति ।) (इमं णामं । अज्जआ एव्व वाएदु ।)

---

1 परिट्ठिदो 2 णिक्खित्तो.

VAS.—(*In agitaion*). Oh! the carelessness! Oh! the mishap!

KAR.—-Away with agitation! May your ladyship just listen.-Then seeing the elephant who carried along a mass of broken chains that were dangling about and bore that monk held between his tusks, I, Karnapuraka—-no, no! This slave nourished upon the rice-balls got from your ladyship—-running in a zigzag way, calling out (assuring words all the while) to that writer of gambling-scores (*i. e.* the monk), quickly seized an iron bar from a shop and challenged that mad elephant (to halt).

VAS.—What happened then?

KAR.—

I struck at that infuriated elephant who looked like a peak of the Vindhya mountain, and released that recluse held between his tusks. (20)

VAS.—It was bravely done by you! What followed?

KAR.—Then, lady, like a boat unevenly loaded with freight, all Ujjayini crowded over on one side, simply calling out 'Bravo! Karnapuraka, Bravo!' Then, lady, one person (from amongst them), touching those parts of his body where he should have had ornaments, and finding that they weren't there, looked up, heaved a deep sigh, and threw this cloak over me.

VAS.—Karnapuraka, just see whether that cloak is scented with jasmine flowers or not.

KAR.—Lady, owing to the smell of ichor I cannot well distinguish its scent.

VAS.—-Just see if it has any name.

KAR.—-Here's a name. May madam read it herself. (*Takes the cloak to her*).

---

सरन्तीनां स्त्रीणामिति शेषः। रत्नाङ्कुराणां प्रसृमररत्नकिरणानां जालैः प्रतिबद्धाः स्यूताः] ॥ १९ ॥ समासादितः प्राप्तः। परिव्राजकः संवाहक एव भिक्षुकरूपः। फुल्लनलिनीं पुष्पितकमलिनीमिव। कुण्डिका कमण्डलुः। [हस्तिना करशीकरैः सिक्त्वा।] [विच्छिन्ना त्रुटिता अत एव विसंष्ठुला स्खलन्ती शृङ्खला तस्याः कलापः गुणमेलकः तम्।] विसंष्ठुलशृङ्खलाकलापमिति क्रियाविशेषणम्। [वामचलनेन वक्रगत्या] द्यूतलेखकमुत्प्राथ्य। आपणात्क्रयविक्रयस्थानात्। [आकारितः स्पर्धयाऽऽहूतः।] आहत्येति। गाथा। [आहत्य लोहदण्डेन प्रहृत्य।] स परिव्राजकः ॥ २० ॥ पल्हत्था पर्यस्ता। परामुसिअ परामृश्य। आं सोहदीति। मया

**वसन्तसेना**--आर्यचारुदत्तस्य। (इति वाचयित्वा सस्पृहं गृहीत्वा प्रावृणोति।) (अज्जचारुदत्तस्य।)

**चेटी**—कर्णपूरक शोभत आर्याया: प्रावारक:। (कण्णऊरअ सोहदि अज्जआए पावारओ।)

**कर्णपूरकर**:--आं शोभत आर्याया: प्रावारक:। (आं सोहदि अज्जआए पावारओ।)

**वसन्तसेना**---कर्णपूरक इदं ते पारितोषिकम्। (इत्याभरणं प्रयच्छति।) (कण्णऊरअ इदं दे पारितोसिअम्।)

**कर्णपूरकर**:--(शिरसा गृहीत्वा प्रणम्य च।) सांप्रतं सुष्ठु शोभत आर्याया प्रावारक:। (संपदं सुट्ठु सोहदि अज्जआए पावारओ।)

**वसन्तसेना**—कर्णपूरक एतस्यां वेलायां कुत्रार्यचारुदत्त:। (कण्णऊरअ एदाए वेलाए कहिं अज्जचारुदत्तो।)

**कर्णपूरक**:—एतेनैव मार्गेण प्रवृत्तो गन्तुं गेहम्। (एदेण ज्जेव मग्गेन पवुत्तो गन्तुं गेहम्।)

**वसन्तसेना**—चेटि उपरितनमलिन्दकमारुह्यार्यचारुदत्तं पश्याम:। (हञ्जे उवरिदणं [1]अलिण्दअं आरुहिअ अज्जचारुदत्तं पेक्खेम्ह।)

(इति निष्क्रान्ता: सर्वे।)

(**इति[2] द्यूतकरसंवाहको नाम द्वितीयोऽङ्क:।**)

---

साहसार्जितेन न युक्तमेतदिति भाव:। प्रवृत्तश्चलित:॥

इति द्यूतकरसंवाहको नाम द्वितीयोऽङ्क:।

---

१ आलि०. २ इति मृच्छकटिकायां.

VAS.--"This (cloak) belongs to the noble Charudatta." (*Reading it she takes it lovingly and wraps herself with it.*)

THE MAID--Karnapurka, the cloak becomes our lady well.

KAR.—Surely; it becomes her well!

VAS.—Karnapuraka, here's a reward for you. (*Gives him an ornament*).

KAR.—(*Receiving it with bowed head, and saluting her*). Now that cloak does, indeed, become her ladyship beautifully!

VAS.--Karnapuraka, where may the noble Charudatta be at this time?

KAR.--He started to go home by this very road.

VAS.—Wench, we shall ascend the upper terrace and have a look at the noble Charudatta.

(*Exeunt all*)

*Thus ends Act II., styled.*

'Samvahaka, the Gambler.'

---

## तृतीयोऽङ्कः

( ततः[1] प्रविशति चेटः । )

**चेटः** —

**सुजनः खलु भृत्यानुकम्पकः स्वामी निर्धनकोऽपि शोभते ।**
**पिशुनः पुनर्द्रव्यगर्वितो दुष्करः खलु परिणामदारुणः ।। १ ।।**

अपि च ।

**सस्यलम्पटबलीवर्दो न शक्यो वारयितु-**
**मन्यकलत्रप्रसक्तो न शक्यो वारयितुम् ।**
**द्यूतप्रसक्तमनुष्यो न शक्यो वारयितुं**
**योऽपि स्वाभाविकदोषो न शक्यो वारयितुम् ।। २ ।।**

(सुअणे[2] क्खु भिच्चाणुकम्पके शामिए णिद्धणके वि शोहदि ।
पिशुणे उण दव्वगव्विदे दुक्कले क्खु पलिणामदालुणे[3] ।।

अवि अ ।

शश्शपलक्कबलद्दे ण शक्कि वालिदुं अण्णकलत्तपशत्ते ण शक्कि वालिदुम् ।
जूदपशत्तमणुश्शे ण शक्कि वालिदुं जे वि शहाविअदोशे ण शक्कि वालिदुम् ।।)

---

१ प्रविश्य चेटः. २ एतत्समानार्थकं पाठान्तरं छन्दोभिन्नं च—

सुअणे हु कुभिच्चपालए धणहीणे अपहू वि शोहदि ।
पिशुणे उण दव्वगव्विदे ण अ लच्छीविहवावलंविदे ।।

**(सुजनः खलु कुभृत्यपालको धनहीनोऽप्रभुरपि शोभते ।**
**पिशुनः पुनर्द्रव्यगर्वितो न च लक्ष्मीविभवावलम्बितः ।। )**

[अस्य ल० दी० कृतं व्याख्यानं—कुभृत्यस्यापि मादृशस्य कार्यकरणासमर्थस्य वर्धमानकादेरपि पालकः । किं पुनर्वाच्यं सुभृत्यपालक इति । ईदृशः सुजनः इ० । पिशुनः पुनः प्रभुः लक्ष्मीविभवावलम्बितो यतोऽतो द्रव्यगर्वितः इत्येवं पौनरुक्तयं परिहरणीयम्।

३ अस्मात्परमिदं पद्यद्वयं क्वचित्–तिउसाहु विंट तित्तउ तित्तउ बम्हणे निलक्खले । अलसबहुआ वि त्तित्तिआ ण जणाहदलिद्द तित्तए ।। ( **त्रपुषस्य वृन्तं तिक्तं तिक्तो ब्राह्मणो निरक्षरः । अलसा वधूरपि तिक्ता न जन्मदरिद्रस्तिक्तः ।।** ) **अपि च ।** कुणाडअं ण रोएइ पढुमकालअ असई । सइत्तणे सा गव्वइ अंचलं लंबं पढुम एच्छइ ।। **(कुनाटकं न रोचते प्रथमकालमसती । सतीत्वे सा गर्वति अञ्चलं दीर्घं प्रथममाच्छादयति ।। ).** ४ अण्णपशत्तकलत्ते ( अन्यप्रसक्तकलत्रम् ).

# ACT III

( *Then enter Cheta* )

CHETA--

A master, who is kind and compassionate to his servants, is pleasing ( *lit.* shines ) even though he may be poor But again, one who is mean and purse-proud is forsooth difficult to serve, and proves formidable in the end.* (1)

Moreover--

It is not possible to turn away a bull who is greedy of corn, nor a man who is deeply attached to another's wife, nor one who is addicted to gambling; nor is it possible to cure what is one's natural defect. (2)

---

[ चेटोऽयं वर्धमानकनामा चारुदत्तस्येति बोध्यम् । ] **सुजन इति**। वैतालीयम् । 'सुअणे' इत्येकारो लघु: छन्दोनुरोधात् । [ स्वामी सुजन: तथा भृत्येषु दयावान् निर्धनकोऽपि शोभते खलु। स पिशुन: दुर्जन: चेत् दुष्कर: दु:सेव्य इत्यर्थ:। परिणामे सुसेवितोऽपि अवसाने फलदानसमये दारुण: च। अनेन शकार: कटाक्षित:। अत्र पूर्वार्धेन चारुदत्तस्योत्तरार्धेन च शकारस्य तादृशप्रस्तुतस्य वर्णनेनावगमादप्रस्तुतप्रशंसालंकार:। ] खलु यस्मादर्थे। दुष्करो यत: अत: परिणामदारुण: ॥ १ ॥ **सस्येत्यादि**। शक्वरी जाति:। पलक्को लम्पट:। 'पडकला' इति महाराष्ट्रभाषायाम् । योऽपि स्वाभाविको दोष: सोऽपीत्यर्थान्न शक्यो वारयितुम् । अतिरिक्तदातृत्वं दोष एवेति। तं च मम स्वामी न त्यजतीति भाव: ॥ २ ॥ गन्धव्वं गन्धर्वम्। गीतमित्यर्थ:। **उत्कण्ठितस्येति**। [ 'सर्वेन्द्रियसुखास्वादो यत्रास्तीत्यभिमन्यते। तत्प्राप्तीच्छां ससंकल्पामुत्कण्ठां कवयो विदु:॥' इत्युक्तलक्षणा उत्कण्ठा

---

* Instead of this some MSS. read—"A good man ( master ) who keeps in his service servants even though they be worthless, and who is himself poor and without power, is pleasing ( *lit.* shines ); but not so a purse-proud, mean master, laden though he may be with immense wealth."

After this some MSS. also read the following two verses:—"The stalk of a cucumber is bitter ( in taste ); an illiterate Brahmana is bitter ( *i. e.* unwelcome ); so, too, is a lazy wife; and a man who is poor from his very birth."

"First an unchaste woman does not like to behave virtuously, which to her is unpleasant acting; but she feels proud when she behaves like a chaste woman; and in the beginning she covers her ( upper ) body with a long hem ( as becomes a chaste lady )."

काऽपि वेलाऽऽर्यचारुदत्तस्य गान्धर्वं श्रोतुं गतस्य। अतिक्रामत्यर्धरजनी। अद्यापि नागच्छति। तद्यावद्बहिर्द्वारशालायां गत्वा स्वप्स्यामि। (इति तथा करोति।) (का वि वेला अज्जचारुदत्तश्श गन्धव्वं शुणिदुं गदश्श। अदिक्कमदि अद्धलअणी। अज्ज वि ण आअच्छदि। ता जाव बाहिलदुआलशालाए गदुअ शुविश्शम्।)

(ततः प्रविशति चारुदत्तो विदूषकश्च।)

**चारुदत्तः**—अहो[1] साधु साधु रेभिलेन[2] गीतम्। वीणा हि नामासमुद्रोत्थित रत्नम्। कुतः[3]।

**उत्कण्ठितस्य हृदयानुगुणा वयस्या**
**संकेतके चिरयति प्रवरो विनोदः।**
**संस्थापना प्रियतमा विरहातुराणां**
**रक्तस्य रागपरिवृद्धिकरः[4] प्रमोदः॥ ३॥**

**विदूषकः**—भो एहि। गृहं गच्छावः। (भो एहि। गेहं गच्छेम्ह।)

**चारुदत्तः**—अहो सुष्ठु भावरेभिलेन गीतम्।

**विदूषकः**—मम तावद्द्वाभ्यामेव हास्यं जायते। स्त्रिया संस्कृतं पठन्त्या मनुष्येण च काकलीं गायता। स्त्री तावत्संस्कृतं पठन्ती दत्तनवनस्येव गृष्टिरधिकं सूसूशब्दं क ोति। मनुष्योऽपि काकलीं गायञ्शुष्कसुमनोदामवेष्टितो वृद्धपुरोहित इव मन्त्रं जपन्दृढं मे न रोचते। (मम दाव दुवेहिं ज्जेव्व हस्सं जाअदि। इत्थिआए सक्कअं पठन्तीए मणुस्सेण अ काअलीं गाअन्तेण। इत्थिआ दाव सक्कअं पठन्ती दिण्णणवणस्सा विअ गिट्ठी अहिअं सुसुआअदि। मणुस्सो वि काअलीं गाअन्तो सुक्खसुमणोदामवेट्ठिदो बुड्ढपुरोहिदो विअ मन्तं जवन्तो दिढं मे ण रोअदि।)

**चारुदत्तः**—वयस्य सुष्ठु खल्वद्य गीतं भावरेभिलेन। न च भवान्परितुष्टः।

**रक्तं च नाम मधुरं च समं[5] स्फुटं च**
**भावान्वितं च ललितं च मनोहरं च।**
**किं वा प्रशस्तवचनैर्बहुभिर्मदुक्तै-**
**रन्तर्हिता[6] यदि भवेद्वनितेति मन्ये॥ ४॥**

---

संजाता अस्य असौ उत्कण्ठितः। विरहोत्सुको वा हृदयानुगुणा मनोनुरूपा वयस्या सखी। संकेतके कृतसंकेते जने चिरयति विलम्बं कुर्वति। प्रवरः उत्कृष्टः विनोदः। विरहातुराणां प्रियतमा अत्यन्तेष्टा संस्थापना शरीरस्वास्थ्यकरणं मनस आश्वासो वा। रक्तस्यानुरक्तस्य रागपरिवृद्धिकरः प्रमोदः। वीणावादनमिति शेषः। प्रथमचरणे रूपकालंकारः। इतरत्र कारणे कार्योपचारादतिशयोक्तिः। वसन्ततिलका वृत्तम्] ॥ ३॥ [काकलीं सूक्ष्ममधुरध्वनियक्तां गीतिम्। दत्ता नस्या नासारज्जुर्यस्याः

---

१ अहो अहो. २ रेभिलकेन. ३ यतः. ४ करप्रमोदः. ५ समस्फुटं. ६ अन्तर्हितः.

A long time has passed since the noble Charudatta went to attend the musical concert. It is past midnight, and still he hasn't come. So then I'll go to the room near the outer entrance, and go to sleep (there). (*He does acccrdingly*).

( *Then enter* Charudatta *and* Vidushaka ).

CHAR.—Oh! Splendid! Rebhila sang just beautifully! The lute is indeed a jewel, (only that it was) not produced from the ocean. For—

To a love-sick person, it is a companion agreeable to (the state of) his heart; if the lover who has made an appointment is long in coming, it serves as an excellent means to pass time; to those suffering from (the pangs of) separation, it is the most welcome means of consolation; and to a person actually in love, it yields delight that intensifies his passion. (3)

VIDUSHAKA—Sir, come along; let us go home.

CHAR.--Master Rebhila did, indeed, sing charmingly!

Vid.—As for me, a smile is produced in me by two things: by a woman reading Sanskrit, and by a man singing in in a low, sweet tone. For when a woman reads Sanskrit, she noisily snuffles ( *lit.* makes a 'Soo, Soo' sound ), like a young cow that has had a new rope put through the septum of her nose. A man, too, when he is singing in a low, sweet tone, is emphatically not to my liking, like an old priest repeating *Mantras* and having a garland of dried-up flowers ( round his neck ).

CHAR.--Friend, Master Rebhila did indeed, sing wonderfully to-day! And ( how is it that ) you were not pleased?

Really his song was impassioned, sweet, smooth, clear, and full of emotion, and graceful, and charming. Or where is the use of many words of praise uttered by me?--Methinks it was as if some woman concealed who sang ( and not he ). (4)

---

सा। नासायै हिता नस्या। गृष्टिः सकृत्प्रसूता गौः।] णस्सा नासिकाविवररज्जुः। सुसुआअदीत्यव्यक्तशब्दानुकरणम्। शुष्कसुमनोदामवेष्टितत्वेन चिरकालजपप्रवणत्वमुक्तम्। रक्तमिति। [रक्तं रागयुक्तम्। मधुरं कर्णस्वादु। समं रागोत्थापकस्वराणां वैपरीत्यरहितम्।] भावान्वितं रत्यास्पदम्। ललितं लालित्याख्यधर्मविशेषशालि। [किं वा बहुभिः मदुक्तैः प्रशस्तं प्रशस्तिः तस्य वचनैः किम्। अन्तर्हिता पुरुषरूपच्छन्ना वनिता यदि भवेदपि नाम स्यादिति मन्ये।] पिहिता योषिदेव गायति न पुरुष इति

अपि च ।

तं तस्य स्वरसंक्रमं मृदुगिरः[1] श्लिष्टं च तन्त्रीस्वनं[2]
वर्णानामपि मूर्छनान्तरगतं तारं विरामे मृदुम् ।
हेलासंयमितं पुनश्च ललितं रागद्विरुच्चारितं[3]
यत्सत्यं विरतेऽपि गीतसमये गच्छामि शृण्वन्निव ॥ ५ ॥

**विदूषकः**—भो वयस्य आपणान्तररथ्याविभागेषु सुखं कुक्कुरा अपि सुप्ताः। तद्गृहं गच्छावः। (अग्रतोऽवलोक्य।) वयस्य पश्य पश्य। एषोऽप्यन्धकारस्येवावकाशं ददद्न्तरिक्षप्रासादादवतरति भगवांश्चन्द्रः। (भो वअस्स आवणन्तररच्छाविहाएसु सुहं कुक्कुरा वि सुत्ता[4]। ता गेहं गच्छेम्ह। वअस्स पेक्ख पेक्ख। एसो वि अन्धआरस्स विअ अवआसं देन्तो अन्तरिक्खपासादादो ओदरदि भअवं चन्दो।)

**चारुदत्तः**—सम्यगाह भवान्।

असौ हि दत्त्वा तिमिरावकाशमस्तं व्रजत्युन्नतकोटिरिन्दुः।
जलावगाढस्य वनद्विपस्य तीक्ष्णं विषाणाग्रमिवावशिष्टम् ॥ ६ ॥

**विदूषकः**—भो इदमस्माकं गेहम्। वर्धमानक वर्धमानक उद्घाटय द्वारम्। ( भो एदं अम्हाणं गेहम्। वड्ढमाणअ वड्ढमाणअ उग्घाटेहि दुआरअम्। )

**चेटः**—आर्यमैत्रेयस्य स्वरसंयोगः श्रूयते। आगत आर्यचारुदत्तः। तद्यावद्द्वारमस्योद्घाटयामि। ( तथा कृत्वा। ) आर्य वन्दे। मैत्रेय त्वामपि वन्दे। अत्र विस्तीर्ण आसने निषीदतमार्यौ। ( अज्जमित्तेआह शलशंजोए शुणीअदि। आगदे अज्जचालुदत्ते। ता जाव दुआलअं शे उग्घाटेमि[5]। अज्ज वन्दामि। मित्तेअ तुमं पि वन्दामि। एत्थ वित्थण्णे आशणे णिशीदन्तु अज्जा। )

(उभौ नाट्येन प्रविश्योपविशतः।)

**विदूषकः**—वर्धमानक रदनिकामाकारय पादौ धावितुम्। ( वड्ढमाणअ रअणिअं सद्दावेहि पादाइं धोइदुम्। )

**चारुदत्तः**--(सानुकम्पम्।) अलं सुप्तजनं प्रबोधयितुम्।

**चेटः**—आर्य मैत्रेय अहं पानीयं गृह्णामि। त्वं पादौ धाव। ( अज्ज मित्तेअ अहं पाणिअं गेण्हे। तुमं पादाइं धोवेहि। )

**विदूषकः**—(सक्रोधम्।) भो वयस्य एष इदानीं दास्याःपुत्रो भूत्वा पानीयं गृह्णाति। मां पुनर्ब्राह्मणं पादौ धावयति। ( भो वअस्स एसो दाणिं दासीएपुत्तो भविअ पाणिअं गेण्हेदि। मं उण बम्हणं पादाइं धोवावेदि। )

**चारुदत्तः**—वयस्य मैत्रेय त्वमुदकं गृहाण। वर्धमानकः पादौ प्रक्षालयतु।

---

१ मृदुगिरा श्लिष्टं. २ स्वरं. ३ रागाद्द्वि०. ४ पसुत्ता. ५ देमि ( ददामि ).

Moreover--

To tell the truth, I feel that, although the time of the musical concert is over, I am as it were still listening, as I walk, to the cadence of the notes of his sweet voice; and to those well-blended notes of the lute, high-pitched when following up with the harmonious swell and fall of the sounds of the syllables ( of the song ), but low towards the close;--and to the song, sung with due regard to the pitch of sounds, graceful and repeated twice where the *raga* ( passion ) required it. (5)

VID.--Friend, even the dogs are fast asleep in the various lanes that stretch across the market-place. So let us go home. ( *Looking before him* ). Friend, see, see ! Here is the divine Moon descending from his skyey mansion, as though to make room for darkuess !

CHAR.--Your remark is quite proper.

There sets the moon, giving room to darkness, and with one end raised upwards, looking as if it were the sharp tip remaining ( visible ) outside, of the tusk of a wild elephant submerged in water. (6)

VID --Well, here's our house Vardhamanaka, Vardhamanaka ! Open the door !

CHETA--I hear the revered Maitreya's voice; the noble Charudatta has arrived. Well, then, let me open the door for him. ( *He does so* ). Sir, my bow to you ! Maitreya, to you too ! May you both sit on this commodious seat !

( *Both show that they enter and sit down* ).

VID.--Vardhamanaka, call Radanika to wash our feet.

CHAR.--( *With compassion* ). You need not awaken a person who is asleeping.

CHETA--Sir Maitreya, I'll hold the water, and you may wash (Charudatta's) feet.

VID.--( *Angrily* ). Frind, here is this fellow, the son-of-a-slave, going to hold the water, while he wants to make *me*, who am a Brahmana, wash your feet !

CHAR.—Friend Mitreya, you may hold the water and. Vardhamanaka will wash my feet.

**चेटः**—आर्य मैत्रेय देह्युदकम्। (अज्ज मित्तेअ देहि उदअम्।)

(विदूषकस्तथा करोति। चेटश्चारुदत्तस्य पादौ प्रक्षाल्यापसरति।)

**चारुदत्तः**—दीयतां ब्राह्मणस्य पादोदकम्।

**विदूषकः**—किं मम पादोदकैः। भूम्यामेव मया ताडितगर्दभेनेव पुनरपि लोठितव्यम्। (किं मम पादोदएहिं। भूमीए ज्जेव मए ताडिदगद्दहेण विअ पुणो वि लोठ्ठिदव्वम्।)

**चेटः**—आर्य मैत्रेय ब्राह्मणः खल त्वम्। (अज्ज मित्तेअ बम्हणे क्खु तुमम्।)

**विदूषकः**—यथा सर्वनागानां मध्ये डुण्डुभस्तथा सर्वब्राह्मणानां मध्येऽहं ब्राह्मणः। (जधा सव्वणागाणं मज्झे डुण्डुहो तधा सव्वबम्हणाणं मज्झे अहं बम्हणो।)

**चेटः**—आर्य मैत्रेय तथाऽपि धाविष्यामि। (तथा कृत्वा।) आर्य मैत्रेय एतत्तत्सुवर्णभाण्डं मम दिवा तव रात्रौ च। तद्गृहाण। (इति दत्त्वा निष्क्रान्तः।) (अज्ज मित्तेअ तधा वि धोइश्शम्। अज्ज मित्तेअ एदं तं शुवण्णभण्डअं मम दिवा तुह लत्तिं च। ता गेण्ह।)

**विदूषकः**—(गृहीत्वा।) अद्याप्येतत्तिष्ठति। किमत्रोज्जयिन्यां चौरोऽपि नास्ति य एतं दास्याःपुत्रं निद्राचौरं नापहरति। भो वयस्य अभ्यन्तरचतुःशालकं प्रवेशयाम्येनम्। (अज्ज वि एदं चिठ्ठदि। किं एत्थ उज्जइणीए चोरो वि णत्थि जो एदं दासीएपुत्तं णिद्दाचोरं ण अवहरदि। भो वअस्स अब्भन्तरचतुस्सालअं पवेसआमि णम्।)

**चारुदत्तः**—

**अलं चतुःशालमिमं प्रवेश्य प्रकाशनारीधृत एष यस्मात्।**<br>
**तस्मात्स्वयं धारय विप्र तावद्यावन्न तस्याः खलु भोः समर्प्यते ॥ ७ ॥**

(निद्रां नाटयन्[१] 'तं तस्य स्वरसंक्रमं–' (३।५) इत्यादि पुनः पठति।)

**विदूषकः**—अपि निद्राति भवान्। (अवि णिद्दाअदि भवम्।)

**चारुदत्तः**—अथ किम्।

**इयं हि निद्रा नयनावलम्बिनी ललाटदेशादुपसर्पतीव माम्।**<br>
**अदृश्यरूपा चपला जरेव या मनुष्यसत्त्वं परिभूय वर्धते ॥ ८ ॥**

---

भासते। [वसन्ततिलका वृत्तम्]॥४॥ **तमिति।** [यद्गीतसमये विरतेऽपि गतेऽपि सर्वमिदं शृण्वन्निवाहं गच्छामि तत्सत्यमित्यन्वयः। इदं किम्। मृदुगिरः कोमलकण्ठस्वरस्य तस्य रेभिलस्य तमिदानीं श्रुतं स्वरसंक्रमं स्वराणां निषादर्षभगान्धारषड्जमध्यमधैवतपञ्चमानां सप्तानां प्रसिद्धानां समीचीनं क्रममारोहावरोहरूपम्। शृण्वन्नित्यत्रान्वयः सर्वद्वितीयान्तानाम्। श्लिष्टं गीताक्षरैरभिन्नतया श्रूयमाणम्। तन्त्री वीणा तस्याः

---

१ नाटयति चारु०

CHETA—Sir Maitreya, pour the water.

(VID. *does accordingly*; Cheta *washes* Char's *feet and moves away*).

CHAR.—You should also pour water over (i. e. wash) the Brahmana's (Maitreya's) feet.

VID.—What good will water for my feet do? I shall again (soon) have to roll on the ground, like a beaten ass?

CHETA—Sir Maitreya, you are indeed, a Brahmana!

VID.—Yes I am a Brahmana among all the Brahmanas, like the (harmless and despised) *dundubha* among all the serpents!

CHETA—Sir Maitreya, still I shall wash your feet. (*Does so*) Sir Maitreya, here's that golden casket which I have to guard by day and you by night. So please take it. (*Gives it*). (*Exit*).

VID.—(*Taking it*). This still remains with us! What, is there not even a thief in this Ujjayiṇi who would rid me of this vile thing, this robber of my sleep? Friend, I am going to keep it inside, in the interior quadrangle.

CHAR.—

Do not take it inside the quadrangle; for it has been worn by a courtesan; therefore, O Brahmana, you should keep it with you till it is returned to her. (7).

(*Showing that he is about to sleep, he again recites the former verse, "To tell the truth" &c.*)

VID.—Are you going to sleep?

CHAR—Yes.

Here is this sleep approaching me as it were from my forehead, seizing my eys; of invisible form and elusive, it gains strength, like old age, overcoming the (opposing) vitality of a person. (8)

---

स्वनं च शृण्वन्नित्यर्थः। वर्णानां गानाक्षराणां मूर्छना। 'यथा कुटुम्बिनः सर्वे एकीभूता भवन्ति हि। तथा स्वराणां संदोहो मूर्छनेत्यभिधीयते' इति। तस्या अन्तरगतं मध्यगतम्। तारमुच्चम्। विरामे समाप्तौ मृदुम्। इदं विशेषणत्रयं तन्त्रीस्वनस्येति बोध्यम्। हेला रागस्यारोहावरोहयोरनौचित्यम्। तत्र संयमितं नियमितम्। अनौचित्यान्निवृत्तमिति भावः। पुनश्च ललितं रागेषु द्विरुच्चारितं द्विस्त्रिरुक्तं गीतं शृण्वन्नित्यर्थः। इति ल०दी०। शार्दूलविक्रीडितं छन्दः] ॥ ५ ॥ आपणमध्यरथ्याविभागेषु कुक्कुरा अपि सुप्ताः। ओदरदि अवतरति। अस्ताभिमुखं यातीत्यर्थः। असाविति। [हि असौ उन्नते कोटी अग्रे यस्य स उन्नतकोटिः इन्दुः। अनेनार्धचन्द्रो गम्यते। तिमिरस्य अवकाशं

विदूषकः—तत्स्वपिव: । (नाटयेन स्वपिति[१] ।) (ता सुवेम्ह ।)

(ततः प्रविशति शर्विलकः ।)

शर्विलकः—

कृत्वा शरीरपरिणाहसुखप्रवेशं
शिक्षाबलेन च बलेन च कर्ममार्गम् ।
गच्छामि भूमिपरिसर्पणघृष्टपार्श्वो
निर्मुच्यमान इव जीर्णतनुर्भुजङ्गः[२] ॥ ९ ॥

(नभोऽवलोक्य । सहर्षम् ।) अये कथमस्तमुपगच्छति[३] स भवान्मृगाङ्कः। तथा हि ।

नृपतिपुरुषशङ्कितप्रचारं परगृहदूषणनिश्चितैकवीरम् ।
घनतिमिरनिरुद्धसर्वभावा[४] रजनिरियं जननीव संवृणोति ॥ १० ॥

वृक्षवाटिकापरिसरे संधिं कृत्वा प्रविष्टोऽस्मि मध्यमकम् । तद्यावदिदानीं चतुःशालकमपि दूषयामि । भोः ।

---

प्रसरणावसरं दत्वा अस्तं व्रजति। जलावगाढस्य जलनिमग्नस्य वनद्विपस्य अवशिष्टं तीक्ष्णं विषाणाग्रमिव दृश्यमान इत्यर्थः। वनपदेन साग्रदन्तवत्त्वं व्यज्यते। तेन च तीक्ष्णं विषाणाग्रं दन्ताग्रमिवेत्युपमाऽपि संगच्छते। वृत्तमुपजातिः] ॥ ६ ॥ संयोगः समवधानम् । द्वारं देमि ददामि । कवाटमुद्घाट्य अवकाशं बिभर्मीत्यर्थः । अलमिति । प्रकाशनारी वेश्या [तया धृतः परिहितः । अतः कुटुम्बिन्यलंकारनिवेशनस्थाने स्थापयितुमयोग्य इत्यर्थः । उपजातिः छन्दः] ॥ ७ ॥ इयमिति । मनुष्यसत्त्वं । नृसत्ताम् । [मनुष्यसत्त्वं मनुष्यबलं परिभूय तिरस्कृत्य । उत्प्रेक्षानुप्राणितोपमालंकारः । वंशस्थं वृत्तम्] ॥८॥ कृत्वेति । [शिक्षाबलेन विद्यासामर्थ्येन बलेन शक्त्या च शरीरस्य परिणाहो विशालता तस्य सुखः अक्लिष्टः सुखेन वा प्रवेशो यत्र तादृशं कर्ममार्गं भित्तौ संधिं कृत्वा भूमिपरिसर्पणेन घृष्टौ पार्श्वौ यस्य तथा गच्छामि । जीर्णतनुः कञ्चुकेन निर्मुच्यमानः भुजङ्गः इव गच्छामि । उपमा । वसन्ततिलका वृत्तम् ।] यथा जीर्णतनुः सर्पः मुच्यमानकञ्चुको गच्छति ॥ ९ ॥ नृपतीति । [घनं निबिडं च तत्तिमिरं च तेन निरुद्धा छन्नाः सर्वे भावाः पदार्था यस्यां सा इयं रजनिः । नृपतिपुरुषेभ्यः नगररक्षकेभ्य इत्यर्थः । शङ्कितः शङ्कापूर्वं कृत इत्यर्थः । प्रचारो यस्य तम् । परगृहस्य यद् दूषणं चौर्येण धनहरणं तत्र निश्चितश्चासौ एकवीरश्च तम् । मादृशमिति शेषः । संवृणोति गोपायति । घनं यत्तिमिरं प्रेमान्ध्यं तेन निरुद्धः सर्वभावो यस्याः तादृशी । जननी केवलं वात्सल्यप्रेरितेत्यर्थः । यथा कुटिलगामिनमतिदुर्वृत्तमपि स्वपुत्रं संवृणोति दूषणाद्रक्षति तथा । 'घनपटलतमोनिरुद्धतारा ' इति पाठे घनं पटलं समूहो यस्य तथाभूतं तमः तेन निरुद्धाः ताराः नक्षत्राणि यस्यां सा । पक्षे घनं यत्पटलं नेत्ररोगविशेषस्तस्य तमसा निरुद्धा

---

१ स्वपितः. २ जीर्णतनुः. ३ अस्तं ग०. ४ घनपटलतमोनिरुद्धतारा.

VID.--Well, we shall both sleep. (*Shows that he falls asleep*).

(*Then enter Sarvilaka*),

SAR.--

Having made a passage (for my business), by the power of my training and physical strength, (a passage) large enough to easily admit a man of my build, I move about, my sides being scratched by my creeping along the ground, like a snake with his old (worn-out) body casting off his slough. (9)

(*Looking at the sky : joyfully*). Ah! How now! The divine Moon is about to set! For now--

This night, in which all the objects are hidden (from sight) by the pitchy darkness, is concealing me as fondly) as a mother (conceals her son,--a mother) in whom all other sentiments are overpowered by the intense blindness (of love);--(me) who walk about in fear of the king s watchmen, and who, supremely brave, am bent upon burgling the houses of others. (10)

Having made a hole in the surrounding wall of the park, I have (now) reached the central building. So now I shall force an entry into the (inner) quadrangle also. Oh!

---

व्याप्ता तारा अक्ष्णः कनीनिका यस्याः तथाभूता जननी पुत्रं संवृणोति आलिङ्गनेनाच्छादयति तथा । उपमालंकारः । पुष्पिताग्रा वृत्तम् ] ॥ १० ॥ काममिति । [ यत् चौर्यं स्वप्ने निद्रावस्थायां न तु जाग्रदवस्थायामिति भावः । वर्धते प्रसरति तद् इदं नीचं कर्म इति तथा च यद् विश्वस्तेषु शङ्कारहितेषु वञ्चना प्रतारणा तद्रूपः पराभवः । इति यद् तद् हि न शौर्यमिति पुरुषः कामं वदन्तु । काममित्यर्धाङ्गीकारे । न मम तत्सर्वथा संमतम् । स्वाधीना स्वायत्ता वचनीयता निन्दाऽपि वरं मनाक् प्रिया । अत्र वचनीयताशब्देन तत्कारणं चौर्यादि लक्ष्यते । बद्धः सेवाञ्जलिर्न वरम् । श्ववृत्तिः सेवा । तदपेक्षया स्वातन्त्र्योपेतं चौर्यादिकमपि वरमिति भावः । एतदेव पुरावृत्तोपन्यासेनोत्तम्भयति । हि यतः एष मार्गः विश्वस्तवञ्चनारूपः पूर्वं द्रौणिना प्रशस्तवीरेणेत्यर्थः । नरेन्द्राणां सौप्तिकवधे सुप्तं निद्रा तत्र भवः सौप्तिकः वधस्तत्र कृतः अवलम्बितः । ] अश्वत्थाम्ना पाण्डवपक्षपातिनो राजानो रात्रौ संधिं कृत्वा मारिताः । सौप्तिकमिति भावक्तान्तादध्यात्मादित्वाट्ठञ् । शार्दूलविक्रीडितं छन्दः ] ॥ ११ ॥ देश इति । [ को नु भित्तीनां देशः भागः जलावसेकेन शिथिलः यस्मिन्खननजन्यः शब्दः न भवेत् । यत्र च संधिः बिलं करालः तुङ्गः भीषणो वा अत एव दर्शनान्तरगतः न भवेत् । क्षारेण क्षीणतया दुर्बलतया हर्म्यं लोष्टकैः कृश

कामं नीचमिदं वदन्तु[1] पुरुषाः स्वप्ने च यद्वर्धते
विश्वस्तेषु च वञ्चनापरिभवश्चौर्यं न शौर्यं हि तत् ।
स्वाधीना वचनीयताऽपि हि वरं बद्धो न सेवाञ्जलि-
र्मार्गो ह्येष नरेन्द्रसौप्तिकवधे पूर्वं कृतो द्रौणिना ॥ ११ ॥

तत्कस्मिन्नुद्देशे[2] संधिमुत्पादयामि ।

देशः को नु जलावसेकशिथिलो यस्मिन्न शब्दो भवे-
द्भित्तीनां च न दर्शनान्तरगतः संधिः करालो भवेत् ।
क्षारक्षीणतया च लोष्टककृशं जीर्णं[3] क्व हर्म्यं भवे-
त्कस्मिन्स्त्रीजनदर्शनं च न भवेत्स्यादर्थसिद्धिश्च मे ॥ १२ ॥

( भित्तिं परामृश्य । ) नित्यादित्यदर्शनोदकसेचनेन[4] दूषितेयं भूमिः क्षारक्षीणा । मूषिकोत्करश्चेह । हन्त सिद्धोऽयमर्थः । प्रथममेतत्स्कन्दपुत्राणां सिद्धिलक्षणम् । अत्र कर्मप्रारम्भे कीदृशमिदानीं संधिमुत्पादयामि । इह खलु भगवता कनकशक्तिना चतुर्विधः संध्युपायो दर्शितः । तद्यथा—'पक्वेष्टकानामाकर्षणमामेष्टकानां छेदनं पिण्डमयानां सेचनं काष्ठमयानां पाटनमिति । तदत्र पक्वेष्टक इष्टकाकर्षणम् । तत्र

---

शीर्णलोष्टमिति यावत् । अत एव जीर्णमयत्नपाति क्व भवेत् । तथा च कस्मिन्स्थाने स्त्रीजनदर्शनं न भवेत् । स्त्रीणां स्तेयशास्त्रे निषिद्धत्वादिति भावः । मे अर्थसिद्धिश्च भवेत् । ] संधिः किंभूतः । दर्शनान्तरगतो दर्शनान्तरं कनकशक्त्यादिमतविशेषस्तदनुगतस्तद्बोधितः । करालो विपरीतः । स्त्रीजनदर्शनं हि तदनिष्टाचरणं वीरजनगर्हितं संभाव्येत । [ शार्दूलविक्रीडितं छन्दः ] ॥ १२ ॥ [ मूषिकोत्करः मूषकोद्धृतमृत्पुञ्जः । स्कन्दपुत्राणां स्कन्दोपजीविचौराचार्याणाम् । कनकशक्तिना कनकस्य शक्तिः आयुधविशेषो यस्य तेन स्कन्देन । पद्मव्याकोशमित्यादि । वैश्वदेवीछन्दः । [ पद्मव्याकोशादयः संधिसंज्ञाः ।] वापी विस्तीर्णमिति द्वे नामनी । यदुक्तवान्—'इष्टकाभित्तौ च संस्कारवशेन पद्मव्याकोशादयः सप्त संज्ञाः' इति । भास्करो मण्डलाकारः । अन्येऽपि नामसदृशाः सप्त संधयः । [ आत्मशिल्पं संधिनिर्माणकौशलम् । ] ॥ १३ ॥ अन्यास्विति । [ क्षारेण क्षतासु जीर्णासु विषमासु कठिनासु च कल्पनासु रचनासु मया पाटितासु । प्रतिवेशिवर्गः आसन्नवर्तिजनसमूहः । ] कौशलं चेति चकारोऽप्यर्थे ॥ १४ ॥ कार्त्तिकेयः परमगुरुः । 'ब्रह्मण्यदेवादयोऽपरगुरवः' इत्याहुः सर्वे । 'कार्तिकेयविशेषणम्' इत्येके । 'ब्रह्मण्याय देवाय' इति क्वचित्पाठः । [ योगः मायाप्रयोगः तेन साधिता रोचना गोरोचना । ] अनयेति । [ समालब्धं लिप्तगात्रम् । ] ॥ १५ ॥ एतेनेति । कर्मसु संधिरचनासु कर्ममार्गं प्रवेशानुकूलसंधिपरिमाणमिति यावत् । भूषणसंप्रयोगानिति कटकादेर्घर्मावकीलकसुश्लिष्टसंयोजनाभेदान् ।

---

१ वदन्ति. २ कस्मिन्नु देशे; कस्मिन्देशे. ३ क्षीणं. ४ नित्यादित्यादर्शनोदकसेवनेन. ५ पक्वेष्टिका.

Let people call, as they will, this a vile trade, which thrives well when people are asleep; and that getting the better of people by cheating them when they are unsuspicious, is mere thieving, and by no means a brave deed. Still, even a condemnable position of independence is preferable to serving others with folded hands. And this is the path that was followed of yore by Drona's son ( Asvatthaman) when he assassinated the Kashatriya prince in sleep. (11)

So now, in what spot shall I effect a breach ?

What is that spot, which is loose (soft) by being sprinkled over with water, so that it would produce no sound (when being bored through) ? Where could be made a hole in the wall, wide but not in sight (of the passers-by) ? What portion of this building is dilapidated, having its masonry worn out by the corroding action of saline exudations ? And where shall I not come upon (*lit.* see) women-folk, and still accomplish my purpose ? (12)

( *Touching the wall* ). Here's a spot, worn out by saline action, and weakened by being sprinkled every day with water at the sight of the sun. And here's a pile of rubbish excavated by rats ! My purpose in hand here is (as good as) accomplished ! (For ) this is the best (*lit.* first) omen of success for us thieves, the followers ( *lit.* sons ) of Karttikeya (our patron-saint). Now I have to begin my job ; what sort of hole shall I make here ? In connexion with this the divine Kanakasakti has laid down four modes of making a breach they are as follows :—to pull out the bricks when they are baked, to chip them off if unbaked, to wet them with water if they are of common clay, and to cut them through if they are of wood. Now this is a wall of baked bricks ; so I shall have to pull them out. Here (seven kinds of holes are possible, *viz.*)

---

[ वसन्ततिलकं वृत्तम् ] ॥ १६ ॥ **शिखेति** । [ प्रदीपस्य सुवर्णवत् पिञ्जरा पिङ्गलवर्णा महीतले संधिद्वारेण निर्गता पर्यन्ते यत्तमसेन समावृता वेष्टिता कषे निकषपाषाणे निवेशिता सुवर्णरेखेव विभाति । उपमा । वंशस्थं वृत्तम् ] ॥ १७ ॥ प्रतिपुरुषं कृत्रिम-पुरुषाकृतिम् । ] 'प्रतीक्ष्य' इत्यत्र 'प्रतीच्छ्य' इति पाठो दृश्यते । तच्च प्रतीच्छा-ग्रहणं कृत्वेत्यत्रार्थे णिचि समासे क्त्वाप्रत्यये ल्यपि रूपम् । लक्ष्यसुप्तं व्याजसुप्तम् । **निःश्वास इति** । [ अस्य पुरुषद्वयस्य निःश्वासः शङ्कितः संजातशङ्कः न । शङ्कितस्य पुरुषस्य इव नेत्यर्थः । यतः सुविशदः स्फीतः ] । तुल्यमविषममन्तरमन्तरालो यथा

[1]पद्मव्याकोशं भास्करं बालचन्द्रं
वापीं विस्तीर्णं स्वस्तिकं पूर्णकुम्भम् ।
तत्कस्मिन्देशे दर्शयाम्यात्मशिल्पं
दृष्ट्वा श्वो यं यद्विस्मयं यान्ति पौराः ॥ १३ ॥

तदत्र पक्वेष्टके पूर्णकुम्भ एव शोभते । तमुत्पादयामि ।

अन्यासु भित्तिषु मया निशि पाटितासु
क्षारक्षतासु विषमासु च कल्पनासु ।
दृष्ट्वा प्रभातसमये प्रतिवेशिवर्गो
दोषांश्च मे वदति कर्मणि कौशलं च ॥ १४ ॥

नमो वरदाय कुमारकर्त्तिकेयाय नमः कनकशक्तये ब्रह्मण्यदेवाय देवव्रताय नमो भास्करनन्दिने नमो योगाचार्याय यस्याहं प्रथमः[2] शिष्यः । तेन च परितुष्टेन योगरोचना[3] मे दत्ता ।

अनया हि समालब्धं न मां द्रक्ष्यन्ति रक्षिणः ।
शस्त्रं च पतितं गात्रे रुजं नोत्पादयिष्यति ॥ १५ ॥

(तथा करोति ।) धिक्कष्टम् । प्रमाणसूत्रं मे विस्मृतम् । (विचिन्त्य ।) आं इदं यज्ञोपवीतं[4] प्रमाणसूत्रं भविष्यति । यज्ञोपवीतं हि नाम ब्राह्मणस्य महदुपकरणद्रव्यं[5] विशेषतोऽस्मद्विधस्य[6] । कुतः ।

एतेन मापयति भित्तिषु कर्ममार्ग-
मेतेन मोचयति भूषणसंप्रयोगान् ।
उद्घाटको भवति यन्त्रदृढे कपाटे
दष्टस्य कीटभुजगैः परिवेष्टनं च ॥ १६ ॥

---

स्यादेवं वर्तते । कपटसुप्तस्य विषमान्तरालवत्त्वात् । [दृष्टिः गाढं दृढं यथा तथा निमीलिता न विकला विश्लिष्टा अभ्यन्तरे व्याजसुप्तस्य इव न चञ्चला । गात्रं स्रस्ताश्च ते शरीरसंधयश्च तैः शिथिलं विश्लथम् । शय्यायाः प्रमाणं तस्मादधिकं हस्तपादस्य स्वैरप्रसरणात् । व्याजसुप्तो हि न तथा कुर्यात् । तथा च यदि लक्ष्यसुप्तं स्यादभिमुखं दीपं न मर्षयेत्सहेत । तत्प्रकाशमित्यर्थः । अतः परमार्थसुप्तमिदमिति निश्चयः । अत्रोक्तार्थस्य समर्थनाय कारणसमुदायस्योपादानात्समुच्चयालंकारः । शार्दूलविक्रीडितं छन्दः ] ॥ १८ ॥ [ दर्दुरपणवौ वाद्यभेदौ । ] स्फारीभवति । अभिमन्त्रितो बीजविशेषो धनसहितभूतले क्षिप्तो बहुलीभवतीति प्रसिद्धिः । लघुत्वाच्चपलत्वात् । [ लघुः नीचः खलु उत्स्वप्नायते न तु महाशय इति भावः । गोकाम्या गवेच्छा ब्राह्मणकाम्या ब्राह्मणेच्छा । ताभ्यां शापितः शपथं प्रापितः । सति संभवे गोब्राह्मण-

---

१ पद्मं. २ आद्यः. ३ रचना. ४ मे यज्ञो०. ५ उपकरणम्. ६ ह्यस्म०.

Padmavyakosa, Bhaskara, Balachandra, Vapi, Vistirna, Svastika and Purnakumbha,* So in what spot shall I exhibit my skill, seeing which to-morrow the citizens would be filled with astonishment? (13)

Well, in this (particular case of a) baked-brick wall, the *Purnakumbha* breach alone would look well. I will make that.

When at night other walls were breached by me, as also hard structures, weakened by the action of saltpetre, the neighbours, seeing them in the morning, have condemned my crime, and praised my skill of handiwork as well. (14)

My bow to Kumara Karttikeya, the bestower of boons! Reverence to Kanakasakti, the deserving of praise, whose law is divine! Salutation to Bhaskaranandin! And reverence to Yogacharya, whose first pupil I am. Highly pleased with me, he gave me magic ointment.

When I am besmeared with it, the watchmen will be unable to see me; nor will any weapon striking my body, produce pain. (I5)

(*He does accordingly*). Ah! Alas! I have forgotten my measuring tape! (*Reflecting*). Well, this sacred thread will serve as the measuring tape! Indeed, the sacred thread is a very important serviceable article to a Brahmana, particularly to one of my profession! For—

With this, one measures the passage to be made in the wall: with this one breaks off the fastenings (*e. g.* hooks &c.) of ornaments; this serves as a key when a door is securely locked; and it also serves as a ligature when one is bitten by insects or snakes. (16)

---

योरिच्छा पूरणीयैवास्तिकैरिति धर्मदर्शनराद्धान्तः । गोब्राह्मणयोरिच्छायाः प्रतिघाते महत्पातकमिति निर्णयसिन्धुप्रमुखग्रन्थेषु स्पष्टम् । इति ल. दी.] गोकाम्येति । कामयतेर्लिङ्सामान्ये अचो यति पश्चात्स्त्रीत्वं विवक्षणीयम् । गोब्राह्मणसहिताया भङ्गं त्वं करोषि यदीदं न गृह्णासीति शपथार्थः । प्रणयोऽभ्यर्थना । **धिगिति** । [ निर्वेदः अस्य संजात इति निर्वेदितं न निर्वेदितमनिर्वेदितं प्रकृतार्थेऽकृतनिश्चयमित्यर्थः । तथाभूतं पौरुषं यस्मिन् । ] प्रकरणनिश्चयो निर्वेदः तदभावोऽनिर्वेदः ॥ १९ ॥ पदशब्द इत्यनेन रदनिकाप्रवेशसूचनम् ।

---

* These names are significant: see Notes for full explanations.

मापयित्वा कर्म समारभे । (तथा कृत्वाऽवलोक्य च ।) एकलोष्टावशेषोऽयं संधिः । धिक्कष्टम्[1] । अहिना दष्टोऽस्मि । यज्ञोपवीतेनाङ्गुलीं बद्ध्वा विषवेगं नाटयति । चिकित्सां कृत्वा । ) स्वस्थोऽस्मि । (पुनः कर्म कृत्वा दृष्ट्वा च ।) अये ज्वलति प्रदीपः । तथा हि ।

शिखा प्रदीपस्य सुवर्णपिञ्जरा महीतले संधिमुखेन निर्गता ।
विभाति पर्यन्ततमःसमावृता सुवर्णरेखेव कषे निवेशिता ।। १७ ।।

( पुनः कर्म कृत्वा । ) समाप्तोऽयं संधिः । भवतु । प्रविशामि । अथ वा न तावत्प्रविशामि । प्रतिपुरुषं निवेशयामि[2] । ( तथा कृत्वा । ) अये न कश्चित् । नमः कार्त्तिकेयाय । (प्रविश्य[3] दृष्ट्वा च ।) अये पुरुषद्वयं सुप्तम् । भवतु । आत्मरक्षार्थं द्वारमुद्घाटयामि । कथं जीर्णत्वाद्गृहस्य विरौति कपाटम्[4] । तद्यावत्सलिलमन्वेषयामि । क्व न खलु सलिलं भविष्यति । ( इतस्ततो दृष्ट्वा सलिलं गृहीत्वा क्षिपन्सशङ्कम् । ) मा तावद्भूमौ पतच्छब्दमुत्पादयेत् । भवतु । एवं तावत् । (पृष्ठेन प्रतीक्ष्य कपाटमुद्घाट्य । ) भवतु । एवं तावत् । इदानीं परीक्षे किं लक्ष्यसुप्तमुत[5] परमार्थसुप्तमिदं द्वयम् । ( त्रासयित्वा परीक्ष्य च । ) अये परमार्थसुप्तेनानेन भवितव्यम् । तथा हि ।

निःश्वासोऽस्य न शङ्कितः सुविशदस्तुल्यान्तरं[6] वर्तते
दृष्टिर्गाढनिमीलिता न विकला नाभ्यन्तरे[7] चञ्चला ।
गात्रं स्रस्तशरीरसंधिशिथिलं शय्याप्रमाणाधिकं
दीपं चापि न मर्षयेदभिमुखं स्याल्लक्ष्यसुप्तं यदि ।। १८ ।।

(समन्तादवलोक्य ।) अये कथं मृदङ्गः । अयं दर्दुरः । अयं पणवः । इयमपि वीणा । एते वंशाः । अमी पुस्तकाः । कथं नाट्याचार्यस्य[8] गृहमिदम् । अथ वा भवनप्रत्ययात् प्रविष्टोऽस्मि ।

---

मार्जार इति । [क्रमणे लङ्घने मार्जारः प्रसरणे शीघ्रगमने मृगः । ग्रहेण आक्रमणेन लुञ्चनं लक्ष्यस्य छेदने श्येनः । सुप्तस्यासुप्तस्य च मनुष्यस्य वीर्यस्य शक्तेस्तुलने श्वा । सर्पणे भूमितलवक्रगमने पन्नगः । रूपमाकारः शरीरं पश्वाद्याकृतिवेशः च एतेषां रचने माया । अतिपटुरित्यर्थः । देशभाषान्तरे तत्तद्देशभाषायाः परिज्ञाने भाषणे च वाक् सरस्वती । रात्रिषु दीपः । दीप इव सर्वं निरपेक्षः पश्यामीति भावः । संकटेषु दुर्गमप्रदेशेषु डुडुभः सर्पविशेषः । स्थले वाजी अश्व इव शीघ्रगामी । जले नौरिव प्लवनशीलः । शार्दूलविक्रीडितं वृत्तम् ।] ग्रहणयुक्तमालुञ्चनं ग्रहालुञ्चनम् । श्वा कुक्कुरः । माया शाम्बरी विद्या । रूपमाकारः । वेशोऽलंकारादियोजना ।।२०।।
भुजग इति । [परिसर्पणे सवेगं परिभ्रमणे पतगपतेः गरुडस्य तुल्यः । भुवनस्य

---

१ हा धिक्क० . २ प्रवेश० . ३ इति प्र० . ४ कपाटः. ५ लक्ष० . ६ स्वप्नान्तरं. ७ नाभ्यन्तरं. ८ चार्यगृ० .

So, I'll take measurements and start on my work. ( *Does so; then inspecting* ). Only one brick remains (to be taken out) from this breach. Ah! Pity! I am bitten by a cobra! ( *He binds up his finger with his sacred thread, and shows that he is affected by the poison; then applying the cure* ). I am all right now! ( *Again works at the breach; observing* ). Ah! A lamp is burning! For—

This flame of the lamp, yellowish like gold, emerging through the hole and lying across the ground, being surrounded by darkness on all sides, looks like a streak of gold scratched on a touchstone. (17)

( *Again working at the breach* ). Here's the hole finished! Well, let me get in. Or rather, I won't go in at once; I will first shove in a dummy man. ( *Does so* ). Ah! There's nobody about! Bow to Karttikeya! ( *Enters; observing* ). Ah! Here are a couple of men asleep! Well, I'll open the door to provide a means of escape for myself. How! The house being old, the door creaks! Well, now, I'll first look for water. Where indeed might water be? ( *Searches here and there; finding water, he sprinkles it about; then with apprehension* ). I hope it won't make a noise when being sprinkled on the ground. Well, now, I will do this. ( *Looking behind, he opens the door* ). Well, this is all right. Now I'll see if these two are feigning sleep or are really asleep. ( *Frightening them, and observing* ). Ah! They must be really asleep. For—

Their breathing is free ( *lit.* unsuspicious), is quite distinct, and occurs at regular intervals. Their eyes are firmly closed; they neither *blink* nor are they unsteady behind the lids. Their limbs lie loose, owing to the bodily joints being relaxed, and they stretch beyond the limits of the bed. Moreover, if they were shamming sleep, they could not have borne the ( gleam of the ) lamp held before their face. (18)

(*Looking about him* ). Ah! How now! Here is a tabour; here a flute, and here a *panava!* Here too is a lute; here are reedpipes and here these puppets! How! This turns out to be the house of a professor of music! Or why, I have entered by trusting to the ( external grandeur of the ) mansion.—

तत्किं परमार्थदरिद्रोऽयमुत राजभयाच्चौरभयाद्वा भूमिष्ठं द्रव्यं धारयति। तन्ममापि नाम शर्विलकस्य भूमिष्ठं द्रव्यम्। भवतु। बीजं प्रक्षिपामि। (तथा कृत्वा।) निक्षिप्तं बीजं न क्वचित्स्फारीभवति। अये परमार्थदरिद्रोऽयम्। भवतु। गच्छामि।

**विदूषकः**—(उत्स्वप्नायते।) भो वयस्य संधिरिव दृश्यते। चौरमिव पश्यामि। तद्गृह्णातु भवानेतत्सुवर्णभाण्डम्। (भो वअस्स संधी[1] विअ दिज्जदि। चोरं विअ पेक्खामि। ता गेण्हदु भवं एदं सुवण्णभण्डअम्।)

**शर्विलकः**—किं न खल्वयमिह मां प्रविष्टं ज्ञात्वा दरिद्रोऽस्मीत्युपहसति। तत्किं व्यापादयामि उत लघुत्वादुत्स्वप्नायते। (दृष्ट्वा।) अये जर्जरस्नानशाटीनिबद्धं दीपप्रभयोद्दीपितं सत्यमेवैतदलंकरणभाण्डम्। भवतु। गृह्णामि। अथ वा न युक्तं तुल्यावस्थं[2] कुलपुत्रजनं पीडयितुम्। तद्गच्छामि।

**विदूषकः**—भो वयस्य शापितोऽसि गोब्राह्मणकाम्यया यद्येतत्सुवर्णभाण्डं न गृह्णासि। (भो वअस्स साविदोसि गोब्ह्मणकामाए जइ एदं सुवण्णभण्डअं ण गेह्णसि।)

**शर्विलक**—अनतिक्रमणीया[3] भगवती गोकाम्या ब्राह्मणकाम्या च। तद्गृह्णामि। अथ वा ज्वलति प्रदीपः। अस्ति च मया प्रदीपनिर्वापणार्थमाग्नेयः कीटो धार्यते। तं तावत्प्रवेशयामि। तस्यायं[4] देशकालः। एष मुक्तो मया कीटो यात्वेवास्य[5] दीपस्योपरि मण्डलैर्विचित्रैर्विचरति। एष पक्षद्वयानिलेन निर्वापितो भद्रपीठेन[6]। धिक्। कृतमन्धकारम्। अथ वा मयाऽप्यस्मद्ब्राह्मणकुले धिक् कृतमन्धकारम्। अहं हि चतुर्वेदविदोऽप्रतिग्राहकस्य पुत्रः शर्विलको नाम ब्राह्मणो गणिकामदनिकार्थमकार्यमनुतिष्ठामि। इदानीं करोमि ब्राह्मणस्य प्रणयम्। (इति जिघृक्षति।)

**विदूषकः**—भो वयस्य शीतलस्तेऽग्रहस्तः। (भो वअस्स सीदलो दे अग्गहत्थो।)

---

निलयस्थानस्यावलोकने शश इव। भिन्नसाधारणधर्मा मालोपमाऽलंकारः। पुष्पिताग्रा छन्दः।] वृक इति हुण्डार इति प्रसिद्धः ॥२१॥ कप्पिअ क्लृप्त्वा। निर्मायेत्यर्थः। **उपरीति**। उपरिभागे तलभागे च [उपरितलादूर्ध्वप्रदेशात्] निपातिता आकृष्टा इष्टका यत्र। 'उपरितन—' इति पाठे उपरितनी उपरिभवा। शेषं तुल्यम्। [शिरसि उपरिभागे तनुः अल्पविस्तारः मध्यदेशे मध्यभागे विपुलः विस्तृतः। कुम्भाकार इति भावः। असदृशजनस्य चौरादेः संप्रयोगः आत्मनि व्यापारः तस्माद्भीरोः महागृहस्य स्फुटितं हृदयमिव स्थितः। उत्प्रेक्षालंकारः। पुष्पिताग्रा वृत्तम्]॥ २२॥ **वैदेश्येनेति**। [विदेशे भवः वैदेश्यः तेन। व्यापारं संधिकरणमभ्यस्यता मम गृहे संधिः कृतो भवेत्। अतः असौ नरः धनैर्विरहितमतः विस्रब्धं

---

१ संधी विअ दि० संधी विअ दि०. २ तुल्यावस्थकु० ३ ०क्रमणी मम. ४ तथा कृत्वा। अये निर्वापितः प्रदीपः. ५ यात्येवास्य, यात्वेवास्य...रितुम्. ६ कीटेन.

Now, is he really a poor man, or does he keep his money underground, from fear of the king or of thieves ? Ah, can there be a treasure buried to Sarvilaka ? Well, I'll scatter the (magical) seeds. ( *Does so* ). The seeds, when scattered, nowhere multiply (or expand ). Oh ! He must really be a poor man ! Well, I'll depart.

VID.—(*Talking in his sleep*). Friend, I see something like a hole ! I see someone like a thief ! So take hold of this casket containing gold ornaments.

SAR.—What ! Can it be that he, knowing that I entered here, is mocking me that he is poor ! Shall I then kill him ?—Or is he talking in sleep owing to lightheadedness ? ( *Seeing* ). Ha ! This thing, wrapped up in a worn-out bathing-garment, is really a casket of gold ornaments, as it gleams in the light of the lamp. All right; I'll take it — Or rather, it is not proper to injure (*i. e.* rob ) a person of high birth similarly situated with myself ( *i. e.* poor ). So I'll go away.

VID.—Frind, I adjure you by the wishes of cows and Brahmanas; do take this gold casket.

SAR.—The (adjuration by the) saintly wishes of cows and Brahmanas must not be transgressed. So I'll take it. But no ! Here's a lamp burning ! I carry with me a fire-insect ( *i. e.* a moth) for extinguishing lamps. So I'll let it loose; this is the (proper) place and time for it. Here this insect, set free by me, flies straightway and whirls over the lamp, describing wonderful circles. Here is the lamp extinguished by Bhadrapitha with the flutter ( *lit.* breeze) of its wings ! Oh ! It has caused darkness ! Or rather, fie on me, who too have caused darkness in ( *i. e.* brought ignominy upon) our Brahmana family ! For here am I, a Brahmana, Sarvilaka by name, the son of one who knew (by heart) all the four Vedas and who never accepted any gifts, doing this foul deed for the sake of the courtesan Madanika ! Now I will grant the Brahmana's request. ( *Proceeds to take the casket* ).

VID.—Friend, your fingers are cold !

---

यथा तथा सुप्त जनं न वेदितवान् । असौ अस्माकं महतीं निवासरचनां दृष्ट्वा प्राग् आशान्वितः सुचिरं संधिच्छेदनखिन्नः पश्चाद् द्रव्यालाभे निराश एव गतः। [ शार्दूलविक्रीडितं वृत्तम् ] ॥ २३ ॥ निष्क्रामयिष्यामि बहिः करिष्यामीति दिष्टया हर्षे।

शर्विलकः—धिक्प्रमादः । सलिलसंपर्काच्छीतलो मेऽग्रहस्तः । भवतु । कक्षयोर्हस्तं[1] प्रक्षिपामि । (नाटयेन[2] सव्यहस्तमुष्णीकृत्य[3] गृह्णाति ।)

विदूषकः—गृहीतम् । (गहिदम् ।)

शर्विलकः—अनतिक्रमणीयोऽयं ब्राह्मणप्रणयः । तद्गृहीतम् ।

विदूषकः—इदानीं विक्रीतपण्य इव वणिगहं सुखं स्वप्स्यामि । (दाणि विक्किणिदपण्णो विअ वाणिओ अहं सुहं सुविस्सम् ।)

शर्विलकः—महाब्राह्मण स्वपिहि वर्षशतम् । कष्टमेवं मदनिकागणिकार्थे ब्राह्मणकुलं[4] तमसि पातितम् । अथ वाऽऽत्मा[5] पातितः ।

धिगस्तु खलु दारिद्र्यमनिर्वेदितपौरुषम्[6] ।
यदेतद्गर्हितं कर्म निन्दामि च करोमि च ॥ १९ ॥

तद्यावन्मदनिकाया निष्क्रयणार्थं वसन्तसेनागृहं गच्छामि । (परिक्रम्यावलोक्य च ।) अये पदशब्द इव । मा नाम रक्षिणः । भवतु । स्तम्भीभूत्वा तिष्ठामि । अथ वा ममापि नाम शर्विलकस्य रक्षिणः । योऽहं

मार्जारः क्रमणे मृगः प्रसरणे श्येनो ग्रहालुञ्चने[7]
सुप्तासुप्तमनुष्यवीर्यतुलने श्वा सर्पणे पन्नगः ।
माया रूपशरीरवेशरचने वाग्देशभाषान्तरे
दीपो रात्रिषु संकटेषु डुडुभो वाजी स्थले नौर्जले ॥ २० ॥

अपि च ।

भुजग इव गतौ गिरिः स्थिरत्वे पतगपतेः परिसर्पणे च तुल्यः ।
शश इव भुवनावलोकनेऽहं वृक इव च ग्रहणे बले च सिंहः ॥ २१ ॥

(प्रविश्य)

रदनिका—हा धिक् हा धिक् बहिर्द्वारशालायां प्रसुप्तो वर्धमानकः सोऽप्यत्र न दृश्यते । भवतु । आर्यमैत्रेयमाह्वयामि । (इति परिक्रामति ।) (हद्धी हद्धी बाहिरदुआरसालाए पसुत्तो वड्ढमाणओ सोवि एत्थ ण दीसइ । भोदु । अज्जमित्तेअं सद्दावेमि ।)

---

क इति । [ भूतार्थं यथावृत्तमर्थं चौरेणापहृतं रत्नभाण्डमिति । तुलयिष्यति लघूकरिष्यति । ] निष्प्रतापा निष्पौरुषा । [ अर्थान्तरन्यासोऽलंकारः ] ॥ २४ ॥ यदीति । [ कृतान्तेन दैवेन ] । प्रणयोऽर्थित्वम् । [ दूषितं मलिनीकृतम् । लोकैः । ममैवापहारकत्वेनावस्थापनात् इति भावः ] ॥ २५ ॥ भैक्षेणेति । [ न्यासस्य प्रतिक्रियां तन्निष्क्रयद्रव्यमित्यर्थः । भैक्षेण भिक्षालब्धद्रव्यसंघातेन अर्जयिष्यामि ] ॥ २६ ॥ अव-

---

१ कक्षायां. २ इति नाटयेन. ३ स्वहस्तं. ४ ब्रह्मकुलं. ५ आत्माऽपि. ६ निर्वेदित. ७ गृहा०.

SAR.—Oh ! What carelessness (on my part) ! My fingers are cold owing to their (recent) contact with water. Well, I'll hold my hand (for a while) inside my arm-pit. (*He acts warming his right hand, and then takes the casket*).

VID.--Have you got it ?

SAR.--Of course, I couldn't say 'no' to this request of a Brahmana; so I've accepted it.

VID.--Now I can sleep soundly, like a merchant that has sold off his goods.

SAR.--Worthy Brahmana, you may sleep for a hundred years ! Alas ! For the sake of the courtesan Madanika, I havs thus brought degradation upon (*lit.* cast into darkness) my Brahmana family ; or why, I have degraded my own soul ?

Fie upon poverty, on account of which one's manly nature ceases to feel disgust (for unworthy acts) ! For instance, here I am censuring this ignoble deed, but am doing it all the same ! (19)

Well now let me repair to Vasantsena's mansion to buy Madanika's freedom. (*Walking about and observing*). Ah ! It sounds like somebody's footsteps ! I hope they are not policemen ! Never mind--I'll become (rigid like) a pillar and stand (here). Or rather--Are the police of any accout to me Sarvilaka ?--I, who.

Am a (veritable) cat in leaping, a deer in bounding off, a hawk in seizing prey and tearing it to pieces, a dog in judging of the strength of a man according as he is asleep or awake, a snake in crawling, magic (personified) in assuming different characters, postures and dresses the goddess of speech in (talking in) the various dialects of different countries, a lamp during nights, a dudubha in (slipping away from) intricate places, a horse on land, and a boat on water ! (20)

Moreover--

In movement I am (quick) like a snake; in steadiness, like a mountain; in flying, I resemble the lord of birds (the eagle). In surveying the whole country, I am like a hare; in effecting a capture, like a wolf; and in strength, a lion. (21)

(*Entering*).

RADANIKA--Oh ! Alas ! How now ! Vardhamanaka was sleeping in the room adjoining the outer gate; he, too, is not to be seen here ! Well, I'll call out to the worthy Maitreya. (***Walks about***).

**शर्विलकः**—(रदनिकां हन्तुमिच्छति। निरूप्य।) कथं स्त्री। भवतु। गच्छामि। (इति निष्क्रान्तः।)

**रदनिका**—(गत्वा सत्रासम्।) हा धिक् हा धिक् अस्माकं गृहे संधिं कर्तयित्वा[1] चौरो निष्क्रामति। भवतु। मैत्रेयं गत्वा प्रबोधयामि। (विदूषकमुपगम्य।) आर्य मैत्रेय उत्तिष्ठोत्तिष्ठ। अस्माकं गेहे संधिं कर्तयित्वा चौरो निष्क्रान्तः। (हद्धी हद्धी अम्हाणं गेहे संधिं कप्पिअ चोरो णिक्कमति। भोदु। मित्तेअं गदुअ पबोधेमि। अज्ज मित्तेअ उठ्ठेहि उठ्ठेहि। अम्हाणं गेहे संधिं कप्पिअ चोरो णिक्कन्तो।)

**विदूषकः**—(उत्थाय।) आः दास्याःपुत्रिके किं भणसि। चौरं कर्तयित्वा संधिर्निष्क्रान्तः। (आः दासीएधीए किं भणासि। चोरं[2] कप्पिअ संधी णिक्कन्तो।)

**रदनिका**—हताश अलं परिहासेन। किं न प्रेक्षस एतद्। (हदास अलं परिहासेण। किं ण पेक्खसि एणम्।)

**विदूषकः**—आः दास्याःपुत्रिके किं भणसि द्वितीयमिव द्वारमुद्घाटितमिति। भो वयस्य चारुदत्त उत्तिष्ठोत्तिष्ठ। अस्माकं गेहे संधिं दत्त्वा चौरो निष्क्रान्तः। (आः दासीएधीए किं भणासि दुदिअं विअ दुआरअं उग्घाडिदं त्ति। भो वअस्स चारुदत्त उठ्ठेहि उठ्ठेहि। अम्हाणं गेहे संधिं दइअ चोरो णिक्कन्तो।)

**चारुदत्तः**—भवतु। भोः अलं परिहासेन।

**विदूषकः**—भोः न परिहासः। प्रेक्षतां भवान्। (भो ण परिहासो। पेक्खदु भवम्।)

**चारुदत्तः**—कस्मिन्नुद्देशे।

**विदूषकः**—भोः एषः। (भो एसो।)

**चारुदत्तः**—(विलोक्य।) अहो दर्शनीयोऽयं संधिः।

> [3]**उपरितलनिपातितेष्टकोऽयं शिरसि तनुर्विपुलश्च मध्यदेशे।**
> **असदृशजनसंप्रयोगभीरोर्हृदयमिव स्फुटितं महागृहस्य॥ २२॥**

कथमस्मिन्नपि कर्मणि कुशलता।

**विदूषकः**—भो वयस्य अयं संधिर्द्वाभ्यामेव दत्तो भवेत्। अथ वाऽऽगन्तुकेन शिक्षितुकामेन वा। अन्यथाऽत्रोज्जयिन्यां कोऽस्माकं गृहविभवं न जानाति। (भो वअस्स अअं संधी दुवेहिं ज्जेव्व दिण्णो भवे। आदु आगन्तुएण सिक्खिदुकामेण वा। अण्णधा इध उज्जइणीए को अम्हाणं घरविहवं ण जाणादि।)

**चारुदत्तः**—

> **वैदेश्येन कृतो भवेन्मम गृहे व्यापारमभ्यस्यता**
> **नासौ वेदितवान्धनैर्विरहितं विस्रब्धसुप्तं[4] जनम्।**
> **दृष्ट्वा प्राङ्महतीं निवासरचनामस्माकमाशान्वितः**
> **संधिच्छेदनखिन्न एव सुचिरं पश्चान्निराशो गतः॥ २३॥**

ततः सुहृद्भ्यः किमसौ कथयिष्यति तपस्वी। सार्थवाहसुतस्य गृहं प्रविश्य न किंचिन्मया[5] समासादितमिति।

---

**१ कल्पयित्वा. २ चोरो कप्पिदो. ३ उपरितन. ४ विश्रब्ध. ५ मयाऽसादितम्.**

SAR.—(*Prepares to strike down Radanika; but observing*). Ah! She is a woman! Never mind, then, I am going. (*Exit*).

RAD.—(*Moving on; with fear*). Ha! What's that! A thief has burgled our house and is escaping! Well, I'll go and rouse Maitreya. (*Approaching* Vid.). Sir Maitreya, get up, get up; in our house a thief has cut a hole and escaped!

VID—(*Getting up*) Ah! What do you say, you slave-born wench? A hole has cut a thief and escaped?

RAD.—You silly fellow, don't you be joking; can't you see this hole?

VID.—Ah! What do you say, you slave-born wench? That he has cut open a second door as it were? Here, friend Charudatta, get up, get up; a chief has cut a hole in our house and escaped!

CHAR.—Enough; don't you be joking.

VID.—My dear friend, this is no joke; you should see for yourself.

CHAR—In what place (is it);

VID.—Here it is.

CHAR.—(*Observing*). Ah! It is a fine looking hole!

This breach, formed with the bricks pulled out from the upper part (downwards), which is narrow at the top and wide in the central part, looks as if it were the heart of our stately mansion, burst in fear at coming in contact with an unworthy person (*i. e.* the thief). (22)

How! There is a certain skill even in such kind of work!

VID.—Friend, this hole could have been made only by two sorts of persons; either by a stranger, or by one who wished to try his hand; for otherwise, who is there in this Ujjayini that does nct know the wealth of our house!

CHAR.—

This (hole) in our house must have been made by a foreigner who wanted to practise his art; he did not know that people here were sleeping soundly because they were moneyless! At first, on seeing the magnificent structure of our house, he was filled with hopes (and entered); but he must have afterwards gone disappointed, being just fatigued, having long toiled at boring that hole. (23)

So what will that poor fellow say to his friends?—that he entered the house of a leading merchant's son (Char.) but got nothing?

**विदूषकः**—भोः कथं तमेव चौरहतकमनुशोचसि। तेन चिन्तितं महदेतद्गृहम्। इतो रत्नभाण्डं सुवर्णभाण्डं वा निष्क्रामयिष्यामि। (स्मृत्वा। सविषादमात्मगतम्।) कुत्र तत्सुवर्णभाण्डम्। (पुनरनुस्मृत्य। प्रकाशम्।) भो वयस्य त्वं सर्वकालं भणसि। मूर्खो मैत्रेयोऽपण्डितो मैत्रेय इति। सुष्ठु मया कृतं तत्सुवर्णभाण्डं भवतो हस्ते समर्पयता। अन्यथा दास्याःपुत्रेणापहृतं भवेत्। (भो कधं तं ज्जेव्व चोरहदअं अणुसोचसि। तेण चिन्तिदं महन्तं एदं गेहम्। इदो रअणभण्डअं सुवण्णभण्डअं वा णिक्कामइस्सामि। कहिं तं सुवण्णभण्डअम्। भो वअस्स तुमं सव्वकालं[1] भणासि। मुक्खो मित्तेअओ अपण्डिदो मित्तेअओ त्ति। सुट्ठु[2] मए किदं तं सुवण्णभण्डअं भवदो हत्थे समप्पअन्तेण। अण्णधा दासीएपुत्तेण अवहृदं भवे।)

**चारुदत्तः**—अलं परिहासेन।

**विदूषकः**—भोः यथा नामाहं मूर्खस्तत्किं परिहासस्यापि देशकालं न जानामि। (भो जह णाम अहं मुक्खो ता किं परिहासस्स वि देशआलं ण जाणामि।

**चारुदत्तः**—कस्यां वेलायाम्।

**विदूषकः**—भोः यदा त्वं मया भणितोऽसि शीतलस्तेऽग्रहस्तः। (भो जदा तुमं मए भणिदो सि शीदलो दे अग्गहत्थो।)

**चारुदत्तः**—कदाचिदेवमपि स्यात्। (सर्वतो निरूप्य। सहर्षम्।) वयस्य दिष्टया ते प्रियं निवेदयामि।

**विदूषकः**—किं नापहृतम्। (किं ण अवहृदम्।)

**चारुदत्तः**—हृतम्।

**विदूषकः**—तथाऽपि किं प्रियम्। (तधा वि किं पिअम्।)

**चारुदत्तः**—यदसौ कृतार्थो गतः।

**विदूषकः**—न्यासः खलु सः। (णासो क्खु सो।)

**चारुदत्तः**—कथं न्यासः। (मोहमुपगतः[3]।)

**विदूषकः**—समाश्वसितु भवान्। यदि न्यासश्चौरेणापहृतस्त्वं किं मोहमुपगतः। (समस्ससदु भवम्। जइ णासो चोरेण अवहृदो तुमं किं मोहं उवगदो।)

**चारुदत्तः**—(समाश्वस्य।) वयस्य।

> **कः श्रद्धास्यति भूतार्थं सर्वो मां तुलयिष्यति।**
> **शङ्कनीया हि लोकेऽस्मिन्निष्प्रतापा दरिद्रता॥ २४॥**

भोः कष्टम्।

> **यदि तावत्कृतान्तेन प्रणयोऽर्थेषु मे कृतः।**
> **किमिदानीं नृशंसेन चारित्रमपि[4] दूषितम्॥ २५॥**

---

१ सव्वं. २ सुट्ठु क्खु. ३ उपागतः. ४ चरि०.

VID.—Sir, how is it that you feel sorry for that rascally thief? He must have thought: Here is a big mansion; from here I shall carry off a casket of jewels or of gold.—(*Remembering: sorrowfully, to himself*). Ah! Where's that golden casket?—(*Again remembering; aloud*). Friend, you are always saying that Maitreya is a fool, that Maitreya is a blockhead. But I acted wisely in that I delivered over that golden casket into your hands! Otherwise that son-of-a-slave (thief) would have taken it away.

CHAR.—Enough of joking.

VID.—Sir, though I may be a fool, still do I not know even the time and place for joking?

CHAR.—At what time (did you give it to me)?

VID.—Sir, just when I said to you that your fingers were cold.

CHAR.—Perhaps it might have been even as you say.—(*Looking everywhere; joyfully*). Friend, good luck! I'll tell you something pleasant!

VID.—What, it is not stolen?

CHAR.—It is.

VID.—Then what is it that is pleasant?

CHAR.—That he went away satisfied.

VID.—But it was a deposit!

CHAR.—Ah! A deposit? (*Faints*).

VID.—Come to yourself, Sir. If a thief has stolen the deposit, why should you faint (for that)?

CHAR.—(*Recovering*). Friend,

Who will believe the real fact? Everyone will think lightly of me. For, in this world, inglorious poverty is always prone to be suspected. (24)

Ah! Bad luck!

If, indeed, Fate did desire my riches,—why did now the cruel one spoil my character also? (25)

---

रक्खणजणस्य अपगतं रक्षणं यस्यासौ अपरक्षणो जनः । [पुष्करपत्रं कमलपत्रं तत्पतिता जलबिन्दवस्तद्वच्चञ्चलैः । अतिशौण्डीरतया अत्युन्नतचित्ततया । पुरस्तान्मुखः प्राचीमुखः । प्रतिग्रहे तस्यावश्यकत्वात् ।] पौरत्थिआहिमुहो पौरस्त्याभिमुखः । पूर्वदिगवलम्बितमुख इत्यर्थः । रअणसट्ठि रत्नषष्ठिकाभिधं व्रतम् । 'अरण्य-

**विदूषकः**—अहं खल्वपलपिष्यामि केन दत्तं केन गृहीतं को वा साक्षीति। ( अहं क्खु अवलविस्सं केण दिण्णं केण गहिदं को वा सक्खि त्ति। )

**चारुदत्तः**—अहमिदानीमनृतमभिधास्ये।

**भैक्षेणाप्यर्जयिष्यामि[1] पुनर्न्यासप्रतिक्रियाम्।**
**अनृतं नाभिधास्यामि चारित्रभ्रंशकारणम्॥ २६॥**

**रदनिका**:—तद्यावदार्याधूतायै गत्वा निवेदयामि। ( इति निष्क्रान्ता। ) ( ता जाव अज्जाधूदाए[2] गदुअ णिवेदेमि। )

( ततः[3] प्रविशति चेटया सह चारुदत्तवधूः। )

**वधूः**—( ससंभ्रमम्। ) अयि सत्यमपरिक्षतशरीर आर्यपुत्र आर्यमैत्रेयेण सह। ( अइ सच्चं अवरिक्खदसरीरो अज्जउत्तो अज्जमित्तेएण सह। )

**चेटी**—भर्त्रि सत्यम्। किं तु यः स वेश्याजनस्यालंकारः सोऽपहृतः। (भट्टिणि सच्चम्। किं तु जो सो वेस्साजणकेरको अलंकारओ सो अवहदो।)

**वधूः**—( मोहं नाटयति। )

**चेटी**—समाश्वसित्वार्या धूता। ( समस्ससदु[4] अज्जा धूदा। )

**वधू**—( समाश्वस्य। ) चेटि किं भणसि अपरिक्षतशरीर आर्यपुत्र इति। वरमिदानीं स शरीरेण परिक्षतः न पुनश्चारित्रेण। सांप्रतमुज्जयिन्यां जन एवं मन्त्रयिष्यति दरिद्रतयाऽऽर्यपुत्रेणैवेदृशमकार्यमनुष्ठितमिति। ( ऊर्ध्वमवलोक्य निःश्वस्य च। ) भगवन्कृतान्त पुष्करपत्रपतितजलबिन्दुचञ्चलैः क्रीडसि दरिद्रपुरुषभागधेयैः। इयं च म एका मातृगृहलब्धा रत्नावली तिष्ठति। एतामप्यतिशौण्डीरतयाऽऽर्यपुत्रो न ग्रहीष्यति। चेटि आर्यमैत्रेयं तावच्छब्दापय। ( हञ्जे किं भणासि अवरिक्खदसरीरो अज्जउत्तो त्ति। वरं दाणिं सो सरीरेण परिक्खदो ण उण चारित्तेण। संपदं उज्जइणीए जणो एव्वं मन्तइस्सदि दलिद्ददाए अज्जउत्तेण ज्जेव्व ईदिसं अकज्जं अणुचिट्ठिदं त्ति। भअवं कअन्त पोक्खरवत्तपडिदजलबिन्दुचञ्चलेहिं कीलसि दलिद्दपुरिसभाअधेएहिं। इअं च मे एक्का मादुघरलद्धा रअणावली चिट्ठदि। एदं पि अदिसोण्डीरदाए अज्जउत्तो[5] ण गेण्हिस्सदि। हञ्जे अज्जमित्तेअं दाव सद्दावेहि। )

**चेटी**—यदार्या धूताऽऽज्ञापयति। ( विदूषकमुपगम्य। ) आर्य मैत्रेय धूता त्वामाह्वयति। ( जं अज्जा धूदा आणवेदि। अज्ज मित्तेअ धूदा दे सद्दावेदि। )

**विदूषकः**—कुत्र सा। ( कहिं सा। )

**चेटी**—एषा तिष्ठति। उपसर्प। ( एसा चिट्ठदि। उवसप्प। )

**विदूषकः**—( उपसृत्य। ) स्वस्ति भवत्यै। (सोत्थि भोदीए।)

---

१ भैक्ष्येण. २ अज्जाए. ३ प्रविश्य चेटया. ४ समस्स० समस्स०. ५ एसो अज्ज०.

VID.—I would, indeed deny it ( and say )—Who made the deposit ? Who accepted it ? Who was the witness ?

CHAR.—Am I now to tell a lie ? ( No ).

I'll again acquire the means of returning the deposit, even by begging ( if necessary ); but I'll never utter a falsehood, which would lead to loss of character. ( 26 )

RAD.—Well, then, let me go and tell ( all this ) to the worthy Dhuta. ( *Exit* ).

( *Then enter* Charudatta's wife, *accompanied by the* Maid ).

Wife—( *Excitedly* ). Well, is my lord ( i. e. husband ) really safe ( *lit.* uninjured ) in body, along with the worthy Maitreya ?

THE MAID—Mistress, he is really safe. But that ornament belonging to the courtesan,—that is stolen.

Wife—( *Acts swooning* ).

THE MAID—Worthy Dhuta, is compose yourself !

WIFE—( *Recovering* ). Girl, What did you say ?—that my lord was safe in body ? It were now far better that he was injured in body, than in charactor. ( For ) now in Ujjayini people will ( everywhere ) say that my husband himself, being poor, committed such a vile deed. ( *Looking upwards and sighing* ). O mighty Fate ! You do, indeed, play with the fortunes of poor people, unstable as the drops of water fallen on lotus-leaves !—Now, I have only a jewel-necklace left, come from my mother's family. But even this, my husband would refuse to accept, on account of his extreme pride ! Girl, just call the worthy Maitreya here.

THE MAID—As the noble Dhuta orders. ( *Approaching the* Vid. ) Sir Maitreya, Dhuta is calling you.

VID.—Where is she ?

THE MAID—Here is she ; go to her.

VID.—( *Approaching* ). My blessings to your ladyship.

---

षष्ठिका नाम ग्रीष्मव्रतम् ' इत्येके । [ प्रतिग्राहयितव्यः यतो दक्षिणया व्रतं सुसिद्धं भवति । ] [ वैक्लव्यात् चित्तस्य दौःस्थित्यात् । अकार्यमात्मघातादि । आत्मेति । आत्मभाग्येन स्वस्य दुर्दैवेन क्षत द्रव्यं यस्य सः । अर्थतः धनाद्धेतोः । द्रव्याभावादित्यर्थः । [ अर्थतः अर्थसंबन्धेन ] ॥ २७ ॥ विभवेति । [ विभवमनुगतो विभवानुरूपं

**वधूः**—आर्य वन्दे। आर्य पुरस्तान्मुखो भव। (अज्ज वन्दामि। अज्ज पुरत्थिआमुहो[1] होहि।)

**विदूषकः**—एष भवति पुरस्तान्मुखः संवृत्तोऽस्मि। (एसो भोदि पुरत्थिआमुहो संवुत्तो म्हि।)

**वधूः**—आर्य प्रतीच्छेमाम्। (अज्ज पडिच्छ इमम्।)

**विदूषकः**—किं न्विदम्। (किं ण्णेदम्।)

**वधूः**—अहं खलु रत्नषष्ठीमुपोषिताऽऽसम्। तत्र यथाविभवानुसारेण ब्राह्मणः प्रतिग्राहयितव्यः। स च न प्रतिग्राहितः। तत्तस्य कृते प्रतीच्छेमां रत्नमालिकाम्। (अहं[2] क्खु रअणसट्ठिं उववसिदा आसि। तहिं जधाविहवाणुसारेण बम्हणो पडिग्गाहिदव्वो[3]। सो अ ण पडिग्गाहिदो। ता तस्स किदे पडिच्छ इमं रअणमालिअं।)

**विदूषकः**—(गृहीत्वा।) स्वस्ति। गमिष्यामि। प्रियवयस्याय निवेदयामि। (सोत्थि। गमिस्सम्। पिअवअस्सस्स णिवेदेमि।)

**वधूः**—आर्य मैत्रेय मा खलु मां लज्जितां कुरु। (इति निष्क्रान्ता।) (अज्ज मित्तेअ मा क्खु मं लज्जावेहि।)

**विदूषकः**—(सविस्मयम्।) अहो अस्या महानुभावता। (अहो से महाणुभावदा।)

**चारुदत्तः**—अये चिरयति मैत्रेयः। मा नाम वैक्लव्यादकार्यं कुर्यात्। मैत्रेय मैत्रेय।

**विदूषकः**—(उपसृत्य।) एषोऽस्मि। गृहाणैताम्। (रत्नावलीं दर्शयति।) (एसो म्हि। गेण्ह एदम्।)

**चारुदत्तः**—किमेतत्।

**विदूषक**—भोः यत्ते सदृशदारसंग्रहस्य फलम्। (भो जं दे सरिसदारसंगहस्स फलम्।)

**चारुदत्त**—कथं ब्राह्मणी मामनुकम्पते। कष्टम्। इदानीमस्मि दरिद्रः।

**आत्मभाग्यक्षतद्रव्यः स्त्रीद्रव्येणानुकम्पितः।**
**अर्थतः पुरुषो नारी या नारी साऽर्थतः पुमान्॥ २७॥**

अथ वा। नाहं दरिद्रः। यस्य मम

**विभवानुगता भार्या सुखदुःखसुहृद्भवान्।**
**सत्यं च न परिभ्रष्टं यद्दरिद्रेषु दुर्लभम्॥ २८॥**

मैत्रेय गच्छ रत्नावलीमादाय वसन्तसेनायाः[4] सकाशम्। वक्तव्या च सा मद्वचनात्। यत्खल्वस्माभिः सुवर्णभाण्डमात्मीयमिति[5] कृत्वा विस्रम्भाद्द्यूते हारितम्। तस्य कृते गृह्यतामियं रत्नावलीति।

---

१ पौरत्थिआहि० (पौरस्त्याभि०). २ अज्ज अहं. ३ गहि०. ४ सेनागृहम्. ५ अस्मदीयं.

WIFE--Sir, my bow to you! Sir, just turn your face towards the east.

VID.--Lady, here I have turned my face towards the east.

WIFE--Sir, take this.

VID.--What may this be?

WIFE--I had observed a fast on Ratnashashthi day. For that I had to bestow a gift on a Brahmana, in accordance with my position ( *lit.* riches ). But no Brahmana was yet given a gift; so you should accept this jewel-necklace ( from me ) on his account.

VID.--( *Receiving* ). God bless you! (Now) I will go and tell (this) to my dear friend ( Charudatta ).

WIFE--Sir Maitreya, but ( take care ) you do not put me to shame thereby! ( *Exit* ).

VID.--(*With wonder*). Oh! What a nobility of mind she shows!

CHAR.--How now! Maitreya yet tarries. I hope he won't do anything rash in his (present) distracted condition. Maitreya! Maitreya!

VID--( *Approaching* ). Here I am. Take this. (*Shows the jewel-necklace* ).

CHAR.--What's this?

VID.--Sir, this is (what I would describe as) the fruit of your having married a worthy wife!

CHAR.--Alas! Even my wife takes pity on me! Ah! Now I am truly a poor man!

I, having lost my money through my own (bad) luck, am now shown pity by my wife's ( *i.e.* my wife has given me ) money! Through (the absence of) money, a man becomes a woman; and she who is a woman becomes a man, also through (the possession of) money! (27)

Or rather, I am not a poor man, I whose

Wife follows me through (the turns of) my fortune; who have a friend in you, (unchanged) in happiness as well as in sorrow, and who have not swerved from truth (*i.e.* honesty), which is rarely to be found in the poor. (28)

Maitreya, go with that jewel-necklace to Vasantasena and say to her at my instance--"Kindly accept this jewel-necklace in exchange for that golden casket of yours, which we thought to be our own and in that belief lost at gambling."

**विदूषकः**—मा तावदखादितस्याभुक्तस्याल्पमूल्यस्य चौरैरपहृतस्य कारणाच्चतुःसमुद्रसारभूता रत्नावली दीयते। (मा दाव अक्खाइदस्स अभुत्तस्स अप्पमल्लस्स चोरेहिं अवहृदस्स कारणादो चदुस्समुद्दसारभूदा रअणावली दीअदि।)

**चारुदत्तः**—वयस्य मा मैवम्।

**यं समालम्ब्य विश्वासं न्यासोऽस्मासु तया कृतः।**
**तस्यैतन्महतो मूल्यं प्रत्ययस्यैव दीयते ॥ २९ ॥**

तद्वयस्य अस्मच्छरीरस्पृष्टिकया शापितोऽसि नैनामग्राहयित्वाऽत्रागन्तव्यम्। वर्धमानक[1]।

**एताभिरिष्टकाभिः संधिः क्रियतां सुसंहतः शीघ्रम्।**
**परिवादबहल[2]दोषान्न यस्य[3] रक्षां परिहरामि ॥ ३० ॥**

वयस्य मैत्रेय भवताऽप्यकृपणशौण्डीर्यमभिधातव्यम्।

**विदूषकः**—भो दरिद्रः किमकृपणं मन्त्रयते। (भो दलिद्दो किं अकिवणं मन्तेदि।)

**चारुदत्तः**—अदरिद्रोऽस्मि सखे यस्य मम ('विभवानुगता भार्या' (३।२८) इत्यादि पुनः पठति।) तद्गच्छतु भवान्। अहमपि कृतशौचः संध्यामुपासे।

(इति निष्क्रान्ताः सर्वे।)

**इति संधिच्छेदो[4] नाम तृतीयोऽङ्कः।**

---

वर्तमाना। यद् एतत्त्रितयम्।] ॥ २८ ॥ चतुःसमुद्रेति। चतुःसमुद्राणां रत्नाकराणां सारभूता। **यमिति**। [यं विश्वासं समालम्ब्य तयाऽस्मासु न्यासः कृतः तस्य महतः प्रत्ययस्य विश्वासस्यैवैतन्मूल्यं दीयते] ॥ २९ ॥ [स्पृष्टिकया स्पर्शेन।] **एताभिरिति**। [संधिः शीघ्रं सुसंहतः सुपूर्णः क्रियताम्। यतः परिवादस्य लोकनिन्दायाः यः बहलः दोषः तस्माद्यस्य रक्षां न परिहरामि उपेक्षे] ॥ ३० ॥ [अकृपणममन्दं शौण्डीर्यमौदार्यं यत्र तद्यथा तथा।]

इति संधिच्छेदो नाम तृतीयोऽङ्कः।

---

१ वर्ध० वर्ध०. २ बहुल. ३ नयस्य, नृपस्य. ४ मृच्छकटिकायां सं०.

VID.—Don't you give away this jewel-necklace, which is (as it were) the best produce of the four oceans, for the sake of that thing of (comparatively) little value, which was neither swallowed nor enjoyed but was stolen by thieves !

CHAR.--Nay, friend, say not so.

This price is being paid, (not for that ornament, but) for that high trust, by relying on which she kept that deposit with us. (29)

So friend, I adjure you by the touch of my body --you must not return here without inducing her to accept it. Vardhamanaka !

Quickly fill up the opening wall with these bricks; I do not wish it to remain; for scandal has many evils. (30)

Friend Maitreya, you should also address her with (due) dignity and nobility of mind.

VID.--Friend, can one talk ignobly, even though one may be poor ?

CHAR.--Friend, I am not indeed poor, I whose (—*Repeats again the verse, "Wife follows me" &c.*). So you may go now. I too will purify myself and attend to morning prayers.
(Exeunt all.)

*Thus ends Act III-, styled*
'The Making of a Breach.'

# चतुर्थोऽङ्कः ।

( ततः प्रविशति चेटी । )

**चेटी**—आज्ञप्ताऽस्मि मात्राऽऽर्यायाः सकाशं गन्तुम् । एषाऽऽर्या चित्रफलकनिषण्णदृष्टिर्मदनिकया सह किमपि मन्त्रयमाणा तिष्ठति । तद्यावदुपसर्पामि । ( इति परिक्रामति । ) ( आणत्तम्हि अत्ताए अज्जआए[1] सआसं गन्तुम् । एसा अज्जआ चित्तफलअणिसण्णदिट्‌ठी मदणिआए सह किंपि मन्तअन्ती चिठ्ठदि । ता जाव उवसप्पामि । )

( ततः प्रविशति यथानिर्दिष्टा वसन्तसेना मदनिका च । )

**वसन्तसेना**—हञ्जे मदनिके अपि सुसदृशीयं चित्राकृतिरार्यचारुदत्तस्य । ( हञ्जे मदणिए अवि सुसदिसी इअं चित्ताकिदी अज्जचारुदत्तस्स । )

**मदनिका**—सुसदृशी । ( सुसदिसी । )

**वसन्तसेना**—कथं त्वं जानासि । ( कधं तुमं जाणासि । )

**मदनिका**—येनार्यायाः सुस्निग्धा दृष्टिरनुलग्ना । ( जेण अज्जआए सुसिणिद्धा दिट्‌ठी अनुलग्गा । )

**वसन्तसेना**—हञ्जे किं वेशवासदाक्षिण्येन मदनिके एवं भणसि । ( हञ्जे किं वेसवासदाक्खिण्णेण मदणिए एव्वं भणासि । )

**मदनिका**—आर्ये किं य एव जनो वेशं प्रतिवसति स एवालीकदक्षिणो भवति । ( अज्जए किं जो ज्जेव जणो वेसे पडिवसदि सो ज्जेव अलीअदक्खिणो भोदि । )

**वसन्तसेना**—हञ्जे नानापुरुषसङ्गेन वेश्याजनोऽलीकदक्षिणो भवति । ( हञ्जे णाणापुरिससङ्गेण वेस्साजणो अलीअदक्खिणो भोदि । )

**मदनिका**—यतस्तावदार्याया दृष्टिरिहाभिरमते हृदयं च तस्य कारणं किं पृच्छ्यते । ( जदो दाव अज्जआए दिट्‌ठी इध अभिरमदि हिअअं च तस्स कारणं किं पुच्छीअदि । )

---

अथोत्कण्ठितायाः प्रियस्य चित्रदर्शनेन विरहं विनोदयन्त्या वसन्तसेनायाः प्रवेशसूचनार्थमादौ चेटीप्रवेशः । वसन्तसेनामात्रा माधवसेनया । चित्रफलके निषण्णा संसक्ता दृष्टिर्यस्याः । प्रियप्रतिकृतिदर्शनं हि उत्कण्ठितानां विरहविनोदनोपायः । तदुक्तम्—'वियोगावस्थासु प्रियजनसदृक्षानुभवनं ततश्चित्रं कर्म स्वपनसमये दर्शनमपि ।

---

१ अज्जुआस०.

# ACT IV

( *Then enter a* Maid ).

THE MAID—The mother has asked me to be in attendance upon her ladyship (Vasantasena). Here she is, talking about something with Madanika, her eyes fixed on a painting-board. Well, then, I'll approach her. ( *Walks about* ).

( *Then enter* Vas., *as described, and* Mad. )

VAS.—Girl, Madanika, is this portrait a most faithful representation of the worthy Charudatta ?

MAD —It is a most faithful one.

VAS.—How do you know ?

MAD — Because your eyes are gazing upon it with great fondness.

VAS.—Girl, Madanika, do you speak thus because of the courtesy bred in you by your residence in the courteans' quarter ?

MAD.—My lady, is it (a fact) that every person who lives in the courtesans' quarter is falsely courteous ?

VAS.—Girl, courtesans *are* false in their courtesy on account of their coming in contact with various sorts of men.

MAD.—Since in the first place your ladyship's eyes as well as heart take delight in this (picture), where is the need to ask the reason ?

---

तदङ्गस्पृष्टानामुपगतवतां स्पर्शनमपि प्रतीकारः कामव्यथितमनसां कोऽपि कथितः ॥' इति । चित्रे निवेशिता आकृतिः चित्राकृतिः । वेशो वेश्यावसतिः तत्र यो वासः तेन यद्दाक्षिण्यं परच्छन्दानुवृत्तिचातुर्यं तेन । 'वेशवासदाक्षिण्येन' इति पाठे वेशानां वेश्याश्रितानां यो वासस्तस्य दाक्षिण्यमिति ल. दी. । स सर्व एवालीकदक्षिणो मिथ्याप्रियवादी भवति । किमिति शेषः । ] यत्र चक्षुर्हृदये लग्ने तत्र कारणं किं पर्यालोच्यते । अतिप्रियनामासावलं विलम्बेनेत्याशयः । [ गृहीतावगुण्ठनमाच्छादन-महापटाच्छादितम् । 'कर्णीरथः प्रवहणम्' इति कोशः । स्त्रीणां स्थितियोग्योऽभितः समाछन्नो रथः प्रवहणम् । इति ल० दी० । सुवर्णं दशमासिकं तेषां दश-सहस्रं तेन लभ्यः सुवर्णदशसाहस्रिकः । ] संदेशेनेति । मया संदेशः कथितो नात्र

**वसन्तसेना**—हञ्जे[1] सखीजनादुपहसनीयतां रक्षामि। ( हञ्जे सहीजणादो उवहसणीअदां रक्खामि। )

**मदनिका**—आर्ये एवं नेदम्। सखीजनचित्तानुवर्त्यबलाजनो भवति। ( अज्जए एव्वं णेदम्। सहीजणचित्ताणुवत्ती अबलाजणो भोदि। )

**प्रथमा चेटी**—( उपसृत्य। ) आर्ये माताऽऽज्ञापयति—'गृहीतावगुण्ठनं पक्षद्वारे सज्जं प्रवहणम्। तद्गच्छ' इति। (अज्जए अत्ता आणवेदि—'गहिदावगुण्ठणं पक्खदुआरए सज्जं पवहणम्। ता गच्छ' त्ति। )

**वसन्तसेना**—हञ्जे[1] किमार्यचारुदत्तो मां नेष्यति। ( हञ्जे किं अज्जचारुदत्तो मं णइस्सदि। )

**चेटी**—आर्ये येन प्रवहणेन सह सुवर्णदशसाहस्रिकोऽलंकारोऽनुप्रेषितः। (अज्जए जेण पवहणेण सह सुवण्णदससाहस्सिओ अलंकारओ अणुप्पेसिदो। )

**वसन्तसेना**—कः पुनः सः। ( को उण सो। )

**चेटी**—एष एव राजश्यालः संस्थानकः। (एसो ज्जेव राअसालो संठाणओ।)

**वसन्तसेना**—(सक्रोधम्।) अपेहि। मा पुनरेवं भणिष्यसि। (अवेहि। मा पुणो एव्वं भणिस्ससि।)

**चेटी**—प्रसीदतु प्रसीदत्वार्या। संदेशेनास्मि प्रेषिता। (पसीददु पसीददु अज्जआ। संदेसेण म्हि पेसिदा।)

**वसन्तसेना**—अहं संदेशायैव कुप्यामि। (अहं संदेसस्स ज्जेव कुप्पामि।)

**चेटी**—तत्किमिति मातरं विज्ञापयिष्यामि। ( ता किंति[2] अत्तं विण्णविस्सम्। )

**वसन्तसेना**—एवं विज्ञापयितव्या—यदि मां जीवन्तीमिच्छसि तदेवं न पुनरहं मात्राऽऽज्ञापयितव्या। ( एव्वं विण्णाविदव्वा[3]–जइ मं जीअन्तीं इच्छसि ता एव्वं ण पुणो अहं अत्ताए आणविदव्वा। )

**चेटी**—यथा ते रोचते। ( इति निष्क्रान्ता। ) ( जधा दे रोअदि। )

( प्रविश्य। )

**शर्विलकः**—

**दत्त्वा निशाया[4] वचनीयदोषं निद्रां च जित्वा नृपतेश्च रक्षान्[5]।**
**स एष सूर्योदयमन्दरश्मिः क्षपाक्षयाच्चन्द्र इवास्मि जातः ॥ १ ॥**

---

मम दोष इति भावः। **दत्त्वेति**। [ निशायाः वचनीयदोषं चौर्यादिकं स्याच्चेन्निशाया एव दोष इत्येवंरूपं दत्त्वा निद्रां जित्वा अवधय नृपतेः रक्षान् रक्षापुरुषांश्च जित्वा तद्दृष्टिं परिहृत्येत्यर्थः। स एवाहं क्षपाक्षयान्निशावसानात् सूर्योदयेन मन्दा रश्मयः तेजः पराक्रमश्च यस्य सः सूर्योदयविगतप्रभः चन्द्र इव जातोऽस्मि।

---

१ चेटि. २ किं अत्तअं. ३ विण्णवि०. ४ निशायां. ५ रक्षान्.

VAS.--Girl, I wish to avoid incurring the ridicule of my friends.

MAD.--It couldn't be so, my lady; for we women always act in accordance with the wishes of our friends' hearts.

THE FIRST MAID--( *Approaching* ). Mistress, the mother says--" A veiled (*i.e.* closed) carriage is ready (waiting) at the side-door; so you should go "

VAS --Wench, has the noble Charudatta sent for me ?

THE MAID--Mistress, (it is one) who has sent, along with the carriage, an ornament worth ten thousand gold-pieces.

VAS.—But *who* is he ?

THE MAID—He is the self same King's brother-in-law, Samsthanaka.

VAS.—( *Angrily* ). Get away! Don't you talk like that again !

THE MAID—Pardon, mistress, pardon! I was sent with (such) a message.

VAS.—It is the message itself that I am angry with !

THE MAID—Then what shall I say to the mother ?

VAS.—Say this—" If you wish that I should live, I should never again be asked to do such a thing by mother. "

THE MAID—As you wish. ( *Exit* ).

( *Entering.* ).

SARVILAKA—

Having cast on the night the slur of censure, having conquered sleep, and having got the better of the King's watchmen, here have I become devoid of lustre ( *i.* e. power ) at sunrise, like the moon at the close of the night (1)

---

उपजातिश्छन्दः ] ॥ १ ॥ **य इति** । [ यः कश्चित् त्वरितगतिं त्वरया गच्छन्तं मां निरीक्षते । तथा च संभ्रान्तं चकितं यथा तथा स्थितं द्रुतमुपसर्पति । तं सर्वं अन्तरात्मा दूषितः संजातशङ्कः तुलयति मद्दोषशङ्कितमिव संभावयतीत्यर्थः । मनुष्यो हि स्वदोषैः शङ्कितो भवति । अर्थान्तरन्यासोऽलङ्कारः । प्रहर्षिणी वृत्तम् ] ॥ २ ॥ **परिजनेति** । [ परिजनकथायामासक्तः कश्चिन्नरः उमुपेक्षितः । तस्य गृहं न प्रविष्टमित्यर्थः । नारी नाथः यस्य नार्याधिष्ठितं पुरुषाभावात् । तद्विवर्जित त्यक्तम् । नरपतिबले नगररक्षिबले समीपमागते । गृहदारुवन्निश्चलं स्थितम् । एवंप्रायैः व्यवसितशतैः निशा दिवसीकृता जाग्रता एव नीता । हरिणी वृत्तम् ]॥ ३ ॥ **मदनमिति** ।

अपि च ।

यः कश्चिच्चरितगति[१] निरीक्षते मां
संभ्रान्तं द्रुतमुपसर्पति स्थितं वा ।
तं सर्वं तुलयति दूषितोऽन्तरात्मा[२]
स्वैर्दोषैर्भवति हि शङ्कितो मनुष्यः ॥ २ ॥

मया खलु मदनिकायाः कृते साहसमनुष्ठितम् ।

परिजनकथासक्तः कश्चिन्नरः समुपेक्षितः
क्वचिदपि गृहं नारीनाथं निरीक्ष्य विवर्जितम् ।
नरपतिबले पार्श्वायाते स्थितं गृहदारुव-
द्व्यवसितशतैरेवंप्रायैर्निशा दिवसीकृता ॥ ३ ॥

( इति परिक्रामति )

**वसन्तसेनाः**—चेटि इमं तावच्चित्रफलकं मम शयनीये स्थापयित्वा तालवृन्तं गृहीत्वा लघ्वागच्छ । (हञ्जे इमं दाव चित्तफलअं मम सअणीए ठाविअ तालवेण्टअं गेण्हिअ लहु[२] आअच्छ ।)

**मदनिका**—यदार्याऽऽज्ञापयति । (इति फलकं गृहीत्वा निष्क्रान्ता ।) (जं अज्जआ आणवेदि ।)

**शर्विलकः**—इदं वसन्तसेनाया गृहम् । तद्यावत्प्रविशामि । ( प्रविश्य ) क्व नु मया मदनिका द्रष्टव्या ।

( ततः प्रविशति तालवृन्तहस्ता मदनिका । )

**शर्विलकः**—(दृष्ट्वा ।) अये इयं मदनिका ।

मदनमपि गुणैर्विशेषयन्ती रतिरिव मूर्तिमती विभाति येयम् ।
मम हृदयमनङ्गवह्नितप्तं भृशमिव चन्दनशीतलं करोति ॥ ४ ॥

मदनिके ।[३]

**मदनिका**—( दृष्ट्वा । ) आश्चर्यम् । कथं शर्विलकः । शर्विलक स्वागतं ते । कुत्र त्वम् । ( अम्मो । कधं सव्विलओ । सव्विलअ साअदं दे । कहिं तुमम् । )

**शर्विलकः**—कथयिष्यामि ।

( इति सानुरागमन्योन्यं पश्यतः । )

---

[ गुणैः सौन्दर्यादिभिर्मदनमपि विशेषयन्ती सातिशयं कुर्वती । येयमनङ्गवह्नितप्तं कामानलसंतप्तं मे हृदयं भृशं चन्दनशीतलमिव करोति । पुष्पिताग्रा छन्दः ] ॥ ४ ॥
[ अभुजिष्यामन्येन केनाप्यभोग्याम् । कलत्रवत्स्वगृहस्थां स्वाधीनामित्यर्थः । यद्वा

---

१ गतिः. २ तान्तरात्मा. २ मदनिके मद०.

Moreover—

Whoever stares closely at me as I walk rapidly, or approaches me quickly as I stand in a state of distraction,—my suspicious mind internally treats all such persons equally; for it is one's own faults that fill a man with apprehension. (2)

It was, indeed, for Madanika's sake that I undertook a risky adventure.

In some place I had to let go a man who was busy talking to his servants; in another I passed by a house seeing that it was inhabited by women (only); and (sometimes) I had to stand like a wooden pillar of a house when a posse of the King's watchmen came near me. By hundreds of acts, mostly like these, I turned the night into day. (3)

(*Walks about*).

VAS.—Girl, just take this painting-board and place it on my bed; then come back here quickly with a fan.

MAD.—As the mistress commands. (*Exit with the board*).

SAR.—Here's Vasantasena's house. Well, then, let me go in (*Entering*). Where, possibly, can I find Madanika)?

(*Then enter* MAD. *with a fan in her hand*).

SAR.—(*Seeing*). Ah! Here's Madanika!—

—This is she, who, excelling even Madana by the excellence (of her charms), looks as if she were Rati herself in bodily form. She renders my heart, heated by the fire of Love, exceedingly cooled as it were with sandal-paste. (4)

O Madanika!

MAD.—(*Seeing*). Ah! What! Here's Sarvilaka! You are welcome, Sarvilaka! What brings you here?

SAR.—I'll just tell you.

(*They lovingly cast glances at each other*).

---

अकिंकरीम् । स्वतन्त्रामित्यर्थः । ] स्वाधीनामिति यावत् । मम छन्दो ममाभिलाषः । **दारिद्रयेणेति।** दारिद्रयोपहतेन तथाऽपि त्वयि स्नेहस्त्वत्स्नेहस्तेनानुगतेन । अनुरागवतेत्यर्थः । साहसं चौर्यरूपम् ॥ ५ ॥ साहसे जीवितानपेक्षकर्मणि । न खल्वाचरितम् । अपि त्वाचरितमेव । **नो मुष्णामीति** । [ धनार्थी अहं विप्रस्वं **ब्राह्मणस्य स्वस्वामिकं द्रव्यम् । अथो अथ** वा यज्ञार्थमभ्युद्धृतं पृथङ्निहितं काञ्चनं

**वसन्तसेना**—चिरयति मदनिका। तत्कुत्र नु खलु सा। (गवाक्षकेन दृष्ट्वा।) कथमेषा केनापि पुरुषकेण सह मन्त्रयमाणा तिष्ठति। यथाऽतिस्निग्धया निश्चलदृष्ट्याऽऽपिबन्तीवैतं निध्यायति तथा तर्कयामि एष स जन एतामिच्छत्यभुजिष्यां कर्तुम्। तद्रमतां रमताम्। मा कस्यापि प्रीतिच्छेदो भवतु। न खल्वाकारयिष्यामि। (चिरअदि मदणिआ। ता कहिं णु क्खु सा। कधं एसा केनावि पुरिसकेण सह मन्तअन्ती चिट्ठदि। जधा अदिसिणिद्धाए णिच्चलदिट्ठीए आपिवन्ती विअ एदं णिज्झाअदि तधा तक्केमि एसो सो जणो एदं इच्छदि अभुजिस्सं कादुम्। ता रमदु रमदु। मा कस्सावि पीदिच्छेदो भोदु। ण क्खु सद्दाविस्सम।)

**मदनिका**—शर्विलक कथय। (सव्विलअ कधेहि।)

**शर्विलकः**—(साशङ्कं[1] दिशोऽवलोकयति।)

**मदनिका**—शर्विलक किं निवन्दम्। सशङ्क इव लक्ष्यसे। (सव्विअल किं णेदम्। ससङ्को विअ लक्खीअसि।)

**शर्विलकः**—वक्ष्ये त्वां किंचिद्रहस्यम्। तद्विविक्तमिदम्।

**मदनिका**—अथ किम्। (अध इ।)

**वसन्तसेना**—कथं परमरहस्यम्। तन्न श्रोष्यामि। (कधं परमरहस्सम्। ता ण सुणिस्सम्।)

**शर्विलकः**—मदनिके किं वसन्तसेना मोक्ष्यति त्वां निष्क्रयेण।

**वसन्तसेना**—कथं मम सम्बन्धिनी कथा। तच्छ्रोष्याम्यनेन गवाक्षेणापवारितशरीरा। (कधं मम सम्बन्धिणी कधा। ता सुणिस्सं इमिणा गवक्खेण ओवारिदसरीरा।)

**मदनिका**—शर्विलक भणिता मयाऽऽर्या। तदा भणति—यदि मम च्छन्दस्तदा विनाऽर्थं सर्वं परिजनमभुजिष्यं करिष्यामि। अथ शर्विलक कुतस्त एतावान्विभवः येन मामार्यसकाशान्मोचयिष्यसि। (सव्विलअ भणिदा मए अज्जआ। तदो भणादि—जइ मम छन्दो तदा विणा अत्थं सव्वं परिजणं अभुजिस्सं करइस्सम्। अध सव्विलअ कुदो दे एत्तिओ विहवो जेण मं अज्जआसआसादो मोआइस्ससि।)

**शर्विलकः**—

> **दारिद्र्येणाभिभूतेन त्वत्स्नेहानुगतेन च।**
> **अद्य रात्रौ मया भीरु त्वदर्थे साहसं कृतम्॥ ५॥**

**वसन्तसेना**—प्रसन्नाऽस्याकृतिः। साहसकर्मतया पुनरुद्वेजनीया। (पसण्णा से आकिदी। साहसकम्मदाए उण उव्वेअणीआ।)

---

१ सशङ्कम्.

VAS.—Madanika has taken a long time (to come); where, then, I wonder, could she have gone? (*Looks through the window*). Ha! Here is she, engaged in talking with some man. Since she is gazing at him fixedly as if drinking him up with her steady and very loving glances, I guess that this must be that person who is desirous of freeing her from her bondage. Let them enjoy—let them! Let nobody suffer from interruption in love-making. I will not at all call her.

MAD.—Sarvilaka, tell it now).

SAR.—(*Looks about him in all directions in fear*).

MAD.—Sarvilaka, what can this be? You seem to be afraid as it were (of something)!

SAR.—I am going to tell you some secret So, is this spot quite secluded?

MAD.—Yes (*lit*.. what else?).

VAS.—What, some deep secret! I shall not listen to it, then.

SAR.—Madanika, will Vasantasena set you at liberty by accepting a ransom?

VAS.—How! They are talking about me! Then I will listen to it through this window, keeping myself (*lit.* my body) hidden (from them).

MAD.—Sarvilaka, I did ask her ladyship, when she said—"If I had my will, I would set free all my servants from their bondage, (even) without any money whatever." So, Sarvilaka, how could you ever possess so much money, so that you could liberate me from her ladyship's service?

SAR.—

Over-powered by poverty and led on by my love for you, O timid one, I committed a crime last night, (all) for your sake. (5)

VAS.—His appearance is plassing (to sight), but it inspires fear on account of his adventurous deed.

---

न मुष्णामि। कार्याकार्यविचारिणी युक्तायुक्तविवेकिनी।] शूद्रस्वर्णहरणे न तथा पातकमिति विप्रेत्यादिनोक्तम्। शार्दूलविक्रीडितं वृत्तम्॥ ६॥ अयमिति। तव वसन्तसेनायाः। अनुचितः प्रकाशो यस्य सोऽप्रकाशः। अनेनास्माकं दण्ड इत्यनेन न प्रकाशयितव्य इत्यर्थः॥ ७॥ अयं जनो वसन्तसेनास्वरूपः [यस्याप्रकाश-

**मदनिका**—शर्विलक स्त्रीकल्यवर्तस्य कारणनोभयमपि संशये विनिक्षिप्तम्। (सव्विलअ इत्थीकल्लवत्तस्स कारणेण उहअं पि संसए विणिक्खित्तम्।)

**शर्विलक**—किं किम्।

**मदनिका**—शरीरं चारित्रं च। (सरीरं चारित्तं च।)

**शर्विलकः**—अपण्डिते, साहसे श्रीः प्रतिवसति।

**मदनिका**—शर्विलक अखण्डितचारित्रोऽसि। तन्न खलु त्वया मम कारणात्साहसं कुर्वताऽत्यन्तविरुद्धमाचरितम्। (सव्विलअ अखण्डिदचारित्तो सि। ता ण खु ते मम कारणादो साहसं करन्तेण अच्चन्तविरुद्धं आचरिदम्।)

**शर्विलकः**—

**नो मुष्णाम्यबलां विभूषणवतीं फुल्लामिवाहं लतां**
**विप्रस्वं न हरामि काञ्चनमथो यज्ञार्थमभ्युद्धृतम्।**
**धात्र्युत्सङ्गगतं हरामि न तथा बालं धनार्थी क्वचि-**
**त्कार्याकार्यविचारिणी मम मतिश्चौर्येऽपि नित्यं स्थिता॥ ६॥**

तद्विज्ञाप्यतां वसन्तसेना—

**अयं तव शरीरस्य प्रमाणादिव निर्मितः।**
**अप्रकाशो[१] ह्यलंकारो मत्स्नेहाद्धार्यतामिति॥ ७॥**

**मदनिका**—शर्विलक अप्रकाशोऽलंकारः। अयं च जन इति द्वयमपि न युज्यते। तदुपनय तावत्। पश्याम्येनमलंकारम्। (सव्विलअ अप्पकाशो अलंकारओ[२]। अअं च जणो त्ति दुवेवि ण जुज्जदि। ता उवणेहि दाव। पेक्खामि एदं अलंकारअम्।

**शर्विलकः**—इदमलंकरणम्। (इति साशङ्कं समर्पयति।)

**मदनिका**—(निरूप्य।) दृष्टपूर्व इवायमलंकारः। तद्भण कुतस्त एषः। (दिट्ठपुरुव्वो विअ अअं अलंकारओ। ता भणेहि कुदो दे एसो।

**शर्विलकः**—मदनिके किं तवानेन। गृह्यताम्।

**मदनिका**—(सरोषम्।) यदि मे प्रत्ययं न गच्छसि तत्किंनिमित्तं मां निष्क्रीणासि। (जइ मे पच्चअं ण गच्छसि ता किंणिमित्तं मं णिक्किणासि।)

**शर्विलकः**—अयि प्रभाते मया श्रुतं श्रेष्ठिचत्वरे यथा सार्थवाहस्य चारुदत्तस्येति।

(वसन्तसेना मदनिका च मूर्छां नाटयतः।)

---

मलंकारधारणमसंभाव्यमिति भावः। 'सप्रमाणव्यवहारकारिजनशिरोमणिः' इति ल दी]। अपिरनुनये। 'अयं जनः शर्विलकः' इति प्राचीनटीका। तन्न बुद्ध्यते। वेश्यात्वे वसन्तसेनाया निभृतं संगतमित्यभिप्रायः। **विषादेति**। [विषादेन खेदेन स्रस्तं

---

१ अप्रकाश्यं २ कारओ च त्ति दुवे.

MAD.—Sarvilaka, for the sake of the trifling thing (called) woman, you have (now) placed both these in jeopardy--

SAR.--What two things ?

MAD.—Your body ( *i.e.* life), and your character.

SAR.--You ignorant girl, fortune abides in adventure (favours the brave).

MAD --Sarvilaka, you have hitherto been of blameless (*i.e.* uninjured) character. So (may I hope that) when for my sake you committed that crime, you did nothing which was very objectionable ?

SAR.--

I do not rob a woman with ornaments on, looking like a creeper in blossom; I do not steal a Brahmana's wealth, nor gold collected for the purpose of a sacrifice; so, too, I never, during my search after money, rob a child lying on a nurse's lap. (Thus) my mind has always been given to the discrimination of what is right and wrong, even in the act of committing a theft. (6)

So please request Vasantasena (in these words):—

" Please wear in secret, out of love for me, this ornament which looks as if it had been ( specially ) manufactured to the (exact) measure of your body." (7)

MAD.—Sarvilaka, an ornament (to be worn) in secret, and this person (i. e. the courtesan Vasantasena to wear it)—both these are inconsistent. So bring it to me, please; I shall have a look at the ornament.

SAR.—Here's the ornament. (*Gives it to her, hesitatingly*),

MAD.—( *Inspecting it* ). This ornament looks like one seen before. Se tell me where you got it from ?

SAR.—Madanika, what have you to do with it ? Take it.

MAD.—( *Angrily* ). If you don't trust me, then why do you want to ransom me ?

SAR.--Well, I heard it in the morning in the merchants' square that it belonged to the merchant Charudatta.

( *Both* Vas. *and* Mad. *act swooning* ).

शर्विलकः—मदनिके समाश्वसिहि[1]। किमिदानीं त्वं

विषादस्त्रस्तसर्वाङ्गी संभ्रमभ्रान्तलोचना ।
नीयमानाऽभुजिष्यात्वं[2] कम्पसे नानुकम्पसे ॥ ८ ॥

मदनिका—(समाश्वस्य ।) साहसिक न खलु त्वया मम कारणादिदमकार्यं कुर्वता तस्मिन्गेहे कोऽपि व्यापादितः परिक्षतो वा । (साहसिअ ण क्खु तुए मम कारणादो इमं अकज्जं करन्तेण तस्सिं गेहे कोवि वावादिदो परिक्खदो वा । )

शर्विलकः—मदनिके भीते सुप्ते न शर्विलकः प्रहरति । तन्मया न कश्चिद् व्यापादितो नापि परिक्षतः ।

मदनिका—सत्यम् । (सच्चम् ।)

शर्विलकः—सत्यम् ।

वसन्तसेना—(संज्ञां लब्ध्वा ।) आश्चर्यम् । प्रत्युपजीविताऽस्मि । (अम्महे । पच्चुवजीविदम्हि ।)

मदनिका—प्रियम् । (पिअम् ।)

शर्विलकः—(सेर्ष्यम् ।) मदनिके किं नाम प्रियमिति ।

त्वत्स्नेहबद्धहृदयो हि करोम्यकार्यं
सद्वृत्तपूर्वपुरुषेऽपि कुले प्रसूतः ।
रक्षामि[3] मन्मथविपन्नगुणोऽपि[4] मानं
मित्रं च मां व्यपदिशस्यपरं च यासि ॥ ९ ॥

(साकूतम् ।)

इह सर्वस्वफलिनः कुलपुत्रमहाद्रुमाः ।
निष्फलत्वमलं यान्ति वेश्याविहगभक्षिताः ॥ १० ॥

अयं च सुरतज्वालः कामाग्निः प्रणयेन्धनः ।
नराणां यत्र हूयन्ते यौवनानि धनानि च ॥ ११ ॥

वसन्तसेना—( सस्मितम् । ) अहो अस्यास्थान आवेगः । (अहो से अत्थाणे आवेओ । )

शर्विलकः—सर्वथा—

अपण्डितास्ते पुरुषा मता मे ये स्त्रीषु च श्रीषु च विश्वसन्ति ।
श्रियो हि कुर्वन्ति तथैव नार्यो भुजङ्गकन्यापरिसर्पणानि ॥ १२ ॥

---

गलितं सर्वमङ्गं यस्यः सा । संभ्रमेण भयेन चित्तवृत्त्यनवस्थानेन वा भ्रान्ते लोचने यस्याः सा । अभुजिष्यात्वमदासीत्वम् । नीयमाना भुजिष्यात्वमिति वा पदच्छेदः । ]

---

१ समा० समा०. २ माना भुजि०, भुजिष्या त्वं. ३ वक्ष्यामि. ४ अद्य.

SAR.—Madanika, compose yourself! Why do you now,

Quake and do not show compassion to me, when you are being freed from bondage, (you), with all your limbs drooping in despair, and your eyes rolling in agitation!

MAD.—(*Recovering*). You rash fellow, I hope you didn't kill or wound anybody in that house, when you committed this foul deed for my sake?

SAR.—O Madanika, Sarvilaka strikes not a person who is afraid, nor one who is asleep. So (you may rest assured that) I neither killed nor wounded anybody.

MAD.—Really

SAR.—Really.

VAS.—(*Regaining consciousness*). Wonderful! I am (now) restored to life again!

MAD.—It is pleasant news to me!

SAR.—(*Jealously*). Madanika, what do you mean by saying it is pleasant news?

Although born in a family with its ancestors all men of righteous conduct, still I committed a sinful deed, my heart being dominated by love for you. But, although my virtues have perished through my passion, still I do preserve my (sense of) honour. You call me a friend, and yet at the same time you run after another (lover)! (9)

(*Significantly*)

In this world, the fine trees in the form of nobly-born youths having their whole wealth for their fruit, are completely divested of their fruit when devoured by the birds in the form of courtesans. (10)

And this fire of Love has amorous sports for its flames and affection for its fuel, wherein are offered as oblations men's youths and riches. (11)

VAS.—(*smilingly*). Oh! His excitement is quite out of place (ungrounded).

SAR.—In every way,

Senseless are those men, I esteem, who trust in women or in riches; for riches as well as women move about as tortuously a female snakes. (12)

स्त्रीषु न रागः कार्यो रक्तं पुरुषं स्त्रियः परिभवन्ति ।
रक्तैव हि रन्तव्या विरक्तभावा तु[1] हातव्या ॥ १३ ॥

सुष्ठु खल्विदमुच्यते—

एता हसन्ति च रुदन्ति च वित्तहेतो-
विश्वासयन्ति पुरुषं न तु[2] विश्वसन्ति ।
तस्मान्नरेण कुलशीलसमन्वितेन ।
वेश्याः श्मशानसुमना[3] इव वर्जनीयाः ॥ १४ ॥

अपि च ।

समुद्रवीचीव चलस्वभावाः संध्याभ्रलेखेव मुहूर्तरागाः ।
स्त्रियो हृतार्थाः[4] पुरुषं निरर्थं [5]निष्पीडितालक्तकवत्त्यजन्ति ॥ १५ ॥

स्त्रियो नाम चपलाः—

अन्यं मनुष्यं हृदयेन कृत्वा [6]अन्यं ततो दृष्टिभिराह्वयन्ति[7] ।
अन्यत्र मुञ्चन्ति मदप्रसेकमन्यं शरीरेण च कामयन्ते ॥ १६ ॥

सूक्तं खलु कस्यापि—

न पर्वताग्रे नलिनी प्ररोहति न गर्दभा वाजिधुरं वहन्ति ।
यवाः प्रकीर्णा न भवन्ति शालयो न वेशजाताः[8] शुचयस्तथाऽङ्गनाः ॥ १७ ॥

आः दुरात्मन् चारुदत्तहतक अयं न भवसि । (इति कतिचित्पदानि गच्छति[9] । )

**मदनिका**—( अञ्चले गृहीत्वा । ) अयि असंबद्धभाषक असंभावनीये कुप्यसि । (अइ असंबद्धभासअ असंभावणीए कुप्पसि । )

**शर्विलकः**—कथमसंभावनीयं नाम ।

**मदनिका**—एष खल्वलंकार आर्यासंबन्धी । ( एसो क्खु अलंकारओ अज्ज-आकेरओ । )

**शर्विलकः**—ततः किम् ।

**मदनिका**—स च तस्यार्यस्य हस्ते विनिक्षिप्तः । ( स च तस्स अज्जस्स हत्थे विणिक्खित्तो[10] । )

**शर्विलकः**— किमर्थम् ।

**मदनिका**—( कर्णे । ) एवमिव । ( एव्वं विअ । )

---

॥ ८ ॥ त्वदिति । [ सद्वृत्तं येषां ते सद्वृत्ताः । सद्वृत्ताः पूर्वपुरुषा यस्मिंस्तस्मिन्कुले प्रसूतोऽप्यहं त्वत्स्नेहबद्धहृदयोऽकार्यं करोमि । कामातुरोऽन्यस्य मानं न रक्षति । अहं तु कामातुरोऽपि रक्षामीत्याह । व्यपदिशसि बाह्यतो दर्शयसि । ] मन्मथेन विपन्नो गुणो

---

१ नु. २. च. ३ स्मशान. ४ हितार्थाः. ५ निपी०. ६ त्वन्यं. ७ आह्वयन्त्यः. ८ याताः. ९ ददाति. १० णिक्खित्तो.

( Undue ) love should not be shown to women; women disrespect a man who is (over-) attached to them. Only that woman should be loved who is herself in love; but one whose heart is cold should be let alone. (13)

It is indeed truly observed :

" These women ( harlots ) laugh, and weep too, for money; they make a man confide in them, but themselves never trust him. Therefore, a man of high birth and good character should avoid courtesans, like, flowers (*Or*, jasmines ) in cremation-grounds." (14)

" Of an unstable nature like the waves of the ocean, and exhibiting *raga* ( passion—redness ) for a short time like the ridges of clouds in the evening, women, having taken a man's money, abandon him, when he is penniless, like ( a ball of ) *alaktaka* ( red lac, ) with all its colour squeezed out. " ( 15 )

Indeed women, who are fickle,

Having fixed upon one man in their heart, invite another by their glances; they pour an effusion of joy ( *or*, intoxicating caresses ) on a third one, while they carnally desire quite another still. ( 16 )

Indeed, it has been truly said by some one that—

" The lotus-plant grows not on mountain-top; asses bear not the yoke of horses; nor do grains of barley, when sown, yield a crop of rice; ( and ) similarly, women born in the courtesans' quarter can never be pure. " (17)

O you villain, accursed Charudatta ! Here you cease to exist ! —( *Walks a few steps* ).

MAD.—( *Catching him by the hem of his cloak* ). You utterer of nonsense, you have got angry at what is inconceivable.

SAR.—How inconceivable, pray ?

MAD.—This ornament, indeed, belongs to her ladyship.

SAR.—What of that ?

MAD.—And it was kept as a deposit with that gentleman.

SAR.—For what purpose ?

MAD.—( *In his ear* ). It was like this.

---

यस्य । ईदृशोऽपि देहं रक्षामि । मदनिकार्थचौर्याहरणेन हीनगुणत्वं व्यक्तम् ।
[ " मन्मथेत्यादिना देहमिति पाठे ध्वनिः । देहं स्त्रीयं रक्षामि कामपीडितांऽप्यहमिति

**शर्विलकः**—( सवैलक्ष्यम् । ) भोः कष्टम् ।

**छायार्थं[1] ग्रीष्मसंतप्तो यामेवाहं समाश्रितः ।**
**अजानता मया सैव पत्रैः शाखा वियोजिता ॥ १८ ॥**

**वसन्तसेना**—कथमेषोऽपि संतप्यत एव । तदजानतैतेनैवमनुष्ठितम् । (कधं एसो वि संतप्पदि ज्जेव । ता अजाणन्तेण एदिणा एव्वं अणुचिट्ठिदम् ।)

**शर्विलकः**—मदनिके किमिदानीं युक्तम् ।

**मदनिका**—अत्र त्वमेव पण्डितः । (इत्थ तुमं ज्जेव पण्डिओ ।)

**शर्विलकः**—नैवम् । पश्य ।

**स्त्रियो हि नाम खल्वेता निसर्गादेव पण्डिताः ।**
**पुरुषाणां तु पाण्डित्यं [2]शास्त्रैरेवोपदिश्यते ॥ १९ ॥**

**मदनिका**—शर्विलक यदि मम वचनं श्रूयते तदा तस्यैव महानुभावस्य प्रतिनिर्यातय । (सव्विलअ जइ मम वअणं सुणीअदि ता तस्स ज्जेव महाणुभावस्स पडिणिज्जादेहि ।)

**शर्विलकः**—मदनिके यद्यसौ राजकुले मां कथयति[3] ।

**मदनिका**—न चन्द्रादातपो भवति । (ण चन्दादो आदवो होदि ।)

**वसन्तसेना**—साधु मदनिके साधु । (साहु मदणिए साहु ।)

**शर्विलकः**—मदनिके ।

**न खलु मम विषादः साहसेऽस्मिन्भयं वा**
**कथयसि हि किमर्थं तस्य साधोर्गुणांस्त्वम् ।**
**जनयति मम वेदं[4] कुत्सितं कर्म लज्जां**
**नृपतिरिह शठानां मादृशां किं नु[5] कुर्यात् ॥ २० ॥**

तथाऽपि नीतिविरुद्धमेतत् । अन्य उपायश्चिन्त्यताम् ।

---

वाच्यार्थः । परकीयमपि देहं रक्षामि नो चेत्प्रहरेयमिति व्यङ्ग्यम्" इति. ल. दी.] ॥ ९ ॥ [परपुरुषानुरक्ता मदनिकेति शङ्कमानः शर्विलकः वेश्याजनं निन्दति- **इहेति** । इह अस्मिञ्जगति सर्वाणि स्वानि धनान्येव फलानि सन्त्येषां ते **सर्वस्व-फलिनः** । 'अत इनिठनौ' इति मत्वर्थे इनिः । कुलपुत्रा एव महाद्रुमास्ते वेश्या एव विहगास्तैर्भक्षिताः अलं निष्फलत्वं यान्ति । हृतसर्वस्वा भवन्तीति भावः । समस्तवस्तु-विषयं सावयवं रूपकमलंकारः] ॥ १० ॥ **अयमिति** । [अयं कामरूपाग्निः सुरतमेव ज्वाला यस्य तथा । प्रणयोऽनुराग एव इन्धनं यस्य तादृशः अस्ति । यत्र यस्मिन्नराणां यौवनानि धनानि च हूयन्ते । 'अत्र विशेषणयोः समस्तं व्यस्तं विशेषे सावयवरूप-मलंकारः' इति ल० दी०] ॥ ११ ॥ [अस्थाने अयुक्ते अकारणे इति यावत् ।

---

१ छायार्थी. २ शास्त्रेणैव. ३ कथयिष्यति. ४ चेदं. ५ न.

SAR.—( *With shame* ). Ah ! Alas !

That branch ( of a tree ), to which I had resorted for shade when suffering from summer's heat,—that very branch has been despoiled of its foliage by me, in my ignorance. ( 18 )

VAS.—How now ! Even he is pained ! So he must have done it in ignorance.

SAR.—O Madanika, what is now proper ( to be done ) ?

MAD.—As to that matter you yourself are clever enough ( to know ).

SAR.—Nay, say not so. See :

These women, as is well-known, are forsooth clever by their very nature; while cleverness has to be taught to men by means of the Sastras. ( 19 )

MAD.—Sarvilaka, if you will listen to ( *i.e.* follow ) my advice, then restore this to that same high personage.

SAR.—Madanika, what if he were to inform against me at the royal palace ?

MAD.— Heat comes not from the Moon.

VAS.—Well said, Madanika, well said !

SAR.—O Madanika,

For this my adventure I do not indeed feel sorrow nor fear.—Why do you then narrate to me that good man's virtues ?—Does this ignoble deed produce any shame in me ?— And what can the king do to rogues like me ? ( 20 )

Still, this is against policy. ( So ) think of ( some ) other way.

---

कामप्रतिघाते क्रोधः शक्तस्याशक्तस्य तु विषाद इति शास्त्रात्क्रुद्धः शर्विलको वेश्याजनं निर्भर्त्स्य स्त्रीमात्रमिदानीं निर्भर्त्सयति । इति ल० दी० । ] अपण्डिता इति । [ भुजङ्गकन्या भुजङ्गयस्तासामिव परिसर्पणानि वक्राणि त्वरितानि च चलनानि । उपजातिः छन्दः ॥ १२ ॥ स्त्रीष्विति । रागः प्रीतिः । परिभवन्ति विगणयन्ति । विरक्तभावा स्नेहशून्यान्तःकरणवृत्तिः । हातव्या त्याज्या । आर्या छन्दः ॥ १३ ॥ स्त्रीजनं निन्दन्नेव विशेषेण वेश्या निन्दति ] एता इति । [—श्मशाने सुमनाः पुष्पाणि । जात्यैकवचनम् । ] सुमनसः पुष्पवृत्तेरेकवचनान्ततापि । यथा–' अप्रत्याख्येये दधिसुमनसी ' इति [ प्राचीनप्रयोगात् । अथ वा ] ' सुमना मालती लता ' ' सुमना मालतीजातिः ' इत्यमरोक्तेः । तां यथा श्मशानवर्तिनीं न कोऽपि स्पृशति तद्वत् । वर्जनीयाः । क्रियादीपकोपमयोः संसृष्टिः । ] वचनभेदेऽपि सतामनुद्वेजकत्वाददुष्टत्वमुपमायाः ।

**मदनिका**—सोऽयमपर उपायः। (सो अअं अवरो उवाओ।)

**वसन्तसेना**—कः खल्वपर उपायो भविष्यति। (को क्खु अवरो उवाओ हुविस्सदि।)

**मदनिका**—तस्यैवार्यस्य संबन्धी भूत्वैतमलंकारमार्यया उपनय। (तस्स ज्जेव अज्जस्स केरओ भविअ एदं अलंकारअं अज्जआए उवणेहि।)

**शर्विलकः**—एवं कृते किं भवति।

**मदनिका**—त्वं तावदचौरः सोऽप्यार्योऽनृणः। आर्यया स्वकोऽलंकार उपगतो भवति। (तुमं दाव अचोरो सो वि अज्जो अरिणो। अज्जआए सकं अलंकारअं उवगदं भोदि।)

**शर्विलकः**—नन्वतिसाहसमेतत्।

**मदनिका**—अयि उपनय। अन्यथाऽतिसाहसम्। (अइ उवणेहि। अण्णधा अदिसाहसम्।)

**वसन्तसेना**—साधु मदनिके साधु। अभुजिष्ययेव मन्त्रितम्। (साहु मदणिए साहु। अभुजिस्साए विअ मन्तिदम्।)

**शर्विलकः**—

**मयाऽऽप्ता महती बुद्धिर्भवतीमनुगच्छता।**
**निशायां नष्टचन्द्रायां दुर्लभो मार्गदर्शकः॥ २१॥**

**मदनिका**—तेन हि त्वमस्मिन्कामदेवगेहे मुहूर्तकं तिष्ठ यावदार्यायै तवागमनं निवेदयामि। (तेण[1] हि तुमं इमस्सिं कामदेवगेहे मुहुत्तअं चिट्ठ जाव अज्जआए तुह आगमणं णिवेदेमि।)

**शर्विलकः**—एवं भवतु।

**मदनिका**—(उपसृत्य।) आर्ये एष खलु चारुदत्तस्य सकाशाद्ब्राह्मण आगतः। (अज्जए एसो क्खु चारुदत्तस्स सआसादो बम्हणो आअदो।)

**वसन्तसेना**—हञ्जे तस्य संबन्धीति कथं त्वं जानासि। (हञ्जे तस्स केरअं त्ति कधं तुमं जाणासि।)

**मदनिका**—आर्ये आत्मसंबन्धिनमपि न जानामि। (अज्जए अत्तणकेरअं वि ण जाणामि।)

**वसन्तसेना**—(स्वगतं सशिरःकम्पं विहस्य।) युज्यते। (प्रकाशम्।) प्रविशतु। (जुज्जदि। पविसदु।)

**मदनिका**—यदार्याऽऽज्ञापयति। (उपगम्य।) प्रविशतु शर्विलकः। (जं अज्जआ आणवेदि। पविसदु सव्विलओ।)

---

१ तेण तुमं.

MAD.—Then here's another way—

VAS.—What may that other way possibly be ?

MAD.—Be a person connected with that same gentleman, and take this ornament to her ladyship.

SAR.—If I do so, what would come of it ?

MAD.—In the first place, you will be no thief; while that gentleman, too, will be out of debt; and her ladyship would get back her own ornament.

SAR.—Why, this is very risky !

MAD.—My dear fellow, take it to her; if you don't, *that* would be very risky !

VAS.—Noble, Madanika, noble ! You have spoken like a gentlewoman ( *lit.* one who is not a slave ) !

SAR.—

By following you, I have obtained excellent wisdom. When at night the moon is not visible, it is hard to find a guide ( who would point out the way ). ( 21 )

MAD.—Then please wait for a short while in this Cupid's temple, while I shall announce your arrival to her ladyship.

SAR.—So be it !

MAD.—( *Approaching* ). Lady, here has come a Brahmana from Charudatta.

VAS.—Girl, how do you know that he belongs to Charudatta ?

MAD.—Lady, do I not know my own connexions ?

VAS.—( *To herself, shaking her head and smiling* ). Properly said ! ( *Aloud* ). Let him come in.

MAD.—As your ladyship commands. ( *Approaching* ) Sarvilaka, you may come in.

---

वसन्ततिलकं वृत्तम् ॥ १४ ॥ [ **समुद्रवीचींवेति** । वीची तरङ्गः । मुहूर्तं रागः अनुरागः रक्तिमा च यासां यस्याः च । निरर्थं निर्द्रव्यम् । उपजातिर्वृत्तम् ॥ १५ ॥ चपलाः चञ्चलाः । चपला विद्युत एवेति रूपकध्वनिः । **अन्यमिति** । हृदयेन कृत्वा अभिसंधाय । तस्मिन्मनो निवेशयेति यावत् । मदप्रसेकं आनन्दसंदोहं वीर्यसिञ्चनं च । क्रियादीपकम् । इन्द्रवज्रा वृत्तम् ॥ १६ ॥ **न पर्वतेति** । नलिनी गभीरनीरोद्भवा कमलिनी । वाजिनः धुरं वाजिधुरमश्ववाह्यां धुरमित्यर्थः । अत्र ल० दी०–पद्यं प्राचीनम् । अत एवोक्तं सूक्तं कस्यापीति । विलक्षणमिदं छन्दः । प्रथमपादे द्वादशा-

**शर्विलकः**—(उपसृत्य । सवैलक्ष्यम् ।) स्वस्ति भवत्यै ।

**वसन्तसेना**—आर्य वन्दे । उपविशत्वार्यः । (अज्ज वन्दामि । उवविसदु अज्जो ।)

**शर्विलकः**—सार्थवाहस्त्वां विज्ञापयति—जर्जरत्वाद्गृहस्य दूरक्ष्यमिदं भाण्डम् । तद्गृह्यताम् । (इति मदनिकायाः समर्प्य प्रस्थितः ।)

**वसन्तसेना**—आर्य ममापि तावत्प्रतिसंदेशं तत्रार्यो नयतु । (अज्ज ममावि दाव पडिसंदेसं तहिं अज्जो णेदु ।)

**शर्विलकः**—(स्वगतम् ।) कस्तत्र यास्यति । (प्रकाशम् ।) कः प्रतिसंदेशः ।

**वसन्तसेना**—प्रतीच्छत्वार्यो मदनिकाम् । (पडिच्छदु अज्जो मदणिअम् ।)

**शर्विलकः**—भवति न खल्ववगच्छामि ।

**वसन्तसेना**—अहमवगच्छामि । (अहं अवगच्छामि ।)

**शर्विलकः**—कथमिव ।

**वसन्तसेना**—अहमार्यचारुदत्तेन भणिता—य इममलंकारकं समर्पयिष्यति तस्य त्वया मदनिका दातव्या । तत्स एवैतां ते ददातीत्येवमार्येणावगन्तव्यम् । (अहं अज्जचारुदत्तेण भणिदा—जो इमं अलंकारअं समप्पइस्सदि तस्स तुए मदणिआ दादव्वा । ता सो ज्जेव एदं दे देदित्ति एव्वं अज्जेण अवगच्छिदव्वम् ।)

**शर्विलकः**—(स्वगतम् ।) अये विज्ञातोऽहमनया । (प्रकाशम् ।) साधु आर्यचारुदत्त साधु ।

**गुणेष्वेव हि कर्तव्यः प्रयत्नः पुरुषैः सदा ।**
**[1]गुणैर्युक्तो दरिद्रोऽपि नेश्वरैरगुणैः समः ॥ २२ ॥**

अपि च ।

**गुणेषु यत्नः पुरुषेण कार्यो न किंचिदप्राप्यतमं गुणानाम् ।**
**गुणप्रकर्षादुडुपेन [2]शंभोरलङ्घ्यमुल्लङ्घितमुत्तमाङ्गम् ॥ २३ ॥**

**वसन्तसेना**—कोऽत्र प्रवहणिकः । (को एत्थ पवहणिओ ।)

(प्रविश्य सप्रवहणः ।)

**चेटः**—आर्ये सज्जं प्रवहणम् । (अज्जए सज्जं पवहणम् ।)

**वसन्तसेना**—हञ्जे मदनिके सुदृष्टां मां कुरु । दत्ताऽसि । आरोह प्रवहणम् । स्मरसि माम् । (हञ्जे मअणिए सुदिट्ठं मं करेहि । दिण्णासि । आरुह पवहणम् । सुमरेसि मम् ।)

**मदनिका**—(रुदती ।) परित्यक्ताऽस्म्यार्यया । (इति पादयोः पतति ।) (परिच्चत्तम्हि[3] अज्जआए ।)

---

**१ गुणयुक्तः. २ रलङ्घितं. ३ परिच्चअम्हि (परिच्युताऽस्मि).**

SAR.—( *Approaches; with embarrassment* ). Hail to your ladyshipl !

VAS.—Sir, I salute you. Please be seated.

SAR.—The merchant ( Charudatta ) sends this message:— " On account of the dilapidated state of my house, it is difficult to guard this casket. So please take it back. " ( *He gives it to* Madanika, *and starts to go* ).

VAS.—Sir, you should carry back to him a counter-message from me, too.

SAR.—( *To himself* ). Who is going there ? ( *Aloud* ). What is the counter-message ?

VAS.—Your honour should take Madanika ( with you ).

SAR.—Lady, I do not understand ( this ).

VAS.—But I do.

SAS.—What do you mean ?

VAS.—I was told by noble Charudatta that I was to give Madanika to him who would hand over to me that ornament. So you may understand that he himself is bestowing her on you.

SAR.—( *To himself* ). Ah ! I have been found out by her ! ( *Aloud* ). Excellent, noble Charudatta, excellent !

Men should always make an effort to acquire virtues. A virtuous person, poor though he may be, cannot be the equal of ( *i. e.* is superior to ) persons who are rich, but not virtuous. (22)

Moreover—

An effort should be made by man to acquire virtues; for there is nothing that is exceedingly unattainable by means of them. ( Thus ) the Moon, on account of the excellence of his merits, came to occupy Siva's head which is ( otherwise ) inaccessible. (23)

VAS.—Is there any driver here ?

( *Entering with a carriage* ).

A SERVAT—Your ladyship, the carriage is ready !

VAS.—Girl Madanika, look at me very well. You are given away. Mount the carriage; and remember me.

MAD.—( *Weeping* ) Your ladyship has abandoned me ! ( ***She falls at her feet*** ).

**वसन्तसेना**—सांप्रतं त्वमेव वन्दनीया संवृत्ता । तद्गच्छ । आरोह प्रवहणम् । स्मरसि माम् । (संपदं तुमं ज्जेव वन्दणीआ संवुत्ता । ता गच्छ । आरुह पवहणम् । सुमरेसि मम् ।)

**शर्विलकः**—स्वस्ति भवत्यै । मदनिके ।

**सुदृष्टः क्रियतामेष शिरसा वन्द्यतां जनः ।**
**यत्र ते दुर्लभं प्राप्तं वधूशब्दावगुण्ठनम् ॥ २४ ॥**

( इति मदनिकया सह प्रवहणमारुह्य गन्तुं प्रवृत्तः । )

(नेपथ्ये ।)

कः कोऽत्र भोः । राष्ट्रियः समाज्ञापयति—एष खल्वार्यको गोपालदारको राजा भविष्यतीति सिद्धादेशप्रत्ययपरित्रस्तेन पालकेन राज्ञा घोषादानीय[1] घोरे बन्धनागारे बद्धः । ततः स्वेषु स्वेषु स्थानेष्वप्रमत्तैर्भवितव्यम् ।

**शर्विलकः**—( आकर्ण्य । ) कथं राज्ञा पालकेन प्रियसुहृदार्यको मे बद्धः । कलत्रवांश्चास्मि संवृत्तः । आः कष्टम् । अथ वा ।

**द्वयमिदमतीव लोके प्रियं नराणां सुहृच्च वनिता च ।**
**संप्रति तु सुन्दरीणां शतादपि सुहृद्विशिष्टतमः ॥ २५ ॥**

भवतु अवतरामि । (इत्यवतरति ।)

**मदनिका**— (सास्रमञ्जलिं बद्ध्वा ।) एवं न्विदम् । तत्परं नयतु मामार्यपुत्रः समीपं गुरुजनानान् । (एव्वं ण्णेदम् । ता परं णेदु मं अज्जउत्तो समीवं गुरुअआणम् ।)

**शर्विलकः**—साधु प्रिये साधु अस्मच्चित्तसदृशमभिहितम्[2] । (चेटमुद्दिश्य )। भद्र[3] जानीषे रेभिलस्य सार्थवाहस्योदवसितम् ।

**चेटः**—अथ किम् । (अध इं ।)

**शर्विलकः**—तत्र प्रापय प्रियाम्[4] ।

**चेटः**—यदार्य आज्ञापयति । (जं अज्जो आणवेदि ।)

**मदनिका**—यथाऽऽर्यपुत्रो भणति । अप्रमत्तेन तावदार्यपुत्रेण भवितव्यम् । ( इति निष्क्रान्ता । ) (जधा अज्जउत्तो भणादि । अप्पमत्तेण दाव अज्जउत्तेण होदव्वम् ।)

**शर्विलकः**—अहमिदानीं ।

**ज्ञातीन्विटान्स्वभुजविक्रमलब्धवर्णा-**[5]
**न्राजापमानकुपितांश्च नरेन्द्रभृत्यान् ।**
**उत्तेजयामि सुहृदः परिमोक्षणाय**
**यौगंधरायण इवोदयनस्य राज्ञः ॥ २६ ॥**

---

१ आनीय चोर इव. २ समभिहितम्. ३ अयि. ४ प्रियतमाम्. ५ शब्दान्.

VAS.—Now you yourself have become worthy of salutation ( by others ). So go and ascend the car. And remember me.

SAR.—Good bye, madam ! O Madanika,

Take a good view of her ladyship and bow to her with (bent) head, from whom you have obtained the addition ( *lit.* the veil ) of the title of 'a bride' which is hard to obtain. (24)

( *Mounts the caarriage along with* Madanika, *and starts to go* ).

( *Behind the scenes* )

Who is there ? ( Listen ). The chief of the police orders : "King Palaka, alarmed on account of his belief in the prophecy of a seer ( Siddha ) that Aryaka, a cowherd's son, would be the king, has now brought him from his hamlet and confined him in a dreadful dungeon. So you should all watch carefully at your respective stations."

SAR.—( *Listening* ). What ! King Palaka has arrested my dear friend Aryaka; and here I have just got a wife ! Oh ! Bad. luck ! Or rather—

In this world, these two things are exceedingly dear to men, *viz.* a friend and a wife; but now ( the circumstances are such that ) the friend has become more important than even a hundred fair wives. (25)

All right. I'll get down. ( *Gets down* ).

MAD.—( *Tearfully; folding her hands* ). It is just so. Well, then let my lord send me now to my elders.

SAR.—Good, my dear, well said ! You have spoken just what is in accord with my mind ! ( *To the servant* ). My good fellow, do you know the house of Rebhila, the merchant ?

THE SERVANT—Yes.

SAR.—Take my wife there.

THE SERVANT—As your honour orders.

MAD.—As my lord says. But my lord should be careful ( *Exit.* ).

SAR.—Now I will—

Incite ( to rebellion ) kinsmen ( mine and Aryaka's ), the city rakes, men that have won fame through the valour of their own arms ( *i. e.* free-lances ), and such servants of the King as ave been alienated through being insulted by him,—( all ) for the release of my friend ( Aryaka ), just as Yaugandharayana did ( incite people ) for the release of king Udayana. (26)

अपि च ।

प्रियसुहृदमकारणे गृहीतं
रिपुभिरसाधुभिराहितात्मशङ्कैः ।
सरभसमभिपत्य मोचयामि
स्थितमिव राहुमुखे शशाङ्कबिम्बम् ॥ २७ ॥

(इति निष्क्रान्तः ।)

(प्रविश्य ।)

**चेटः**—आर्ये दिष्टया वर्धसे । आर्यचारुदत्तस्य सकाशाद्ब्राह्मण आगतः । (अज्जए दिट्ठिआ वड्ढसि । अज्जचारुदत्तस्स सआसादो बम्हणो आअदो ।)

**वसन्तसेना**—अहो रमणीयताऽद्य दिवसस्य । तद्धञ्जे सादरं बन्धुलेन समं प्रवेशयैनम् । (अहो रमणीअदा अज्ज दिवसस्स । ता हञ्जे सादरं बन्धुलेण समं पवेसेहि णम् ।)

**चेटी**—यदार्याऽऽज्ञापयति । (इति निष्क्रान्ता ।) (जं अज्जआ आणवेदि ।)

(विदूषको बन्धुलेन सह प्रविशति[1] ।)

**विदूषकः**—आश्चर्यं भोः । तपश्चरणक्लेशविनिर्जितेन राक्षसराजो रावणः पुष्पकेण विमानेन गच्छति । अहं पुनर्ब्राह्मणोऽकृतनतपश्चरणक्लेशोऽपि नरनारीजनेन गच्छामि । (ही हो भोः तवच्चरणकिलेसविणिज्जिदेण रक्खसराओ रावणो पुप्फकेण विमाणेण गच्छदि । अहं उण बह्मणो अकिदतवच्चरणकिलेसो वि णरणारीजणेण[2] गच्छामि ।)

**चेटी**--प्रेक्षतामार्योऽस्मदीयं गेहद्वारम् । ( पेक्खदु अज्जो अम्हकेरकं गेहदुआरम् ।)

---

क्षराणि द्वितीये एकादशाक्षराणि च सन्ति । प्रथमपादे **जतजभ** एते गणा लभ्यन्ते द्वितीये तु जतजगल इति । उत्तरार्धं तु वंशस्थं छन्दः । ] ॥ १७ ॥ [ एवमिव चारुदत्तस्याकिंचनतया भोगस्य भूरिधनसाध्यत्वादयमलंकारो न्यासनिषेण तस्य हस्ते विनिक्षिप्त इति सकेतार्थः । अप्रस्तुतवृत्तान्तेन प्रस्तुतवृत्तान्तमुपपादयन्नाह—इति ल०दी०] **छायार्थमिति** । [ग्रीष्मसन्तप्तोऽहं यामेव शाखां छायार्थं समाश्रितः सैव । **पत्रैः** छायाहेतुभिः । अप्रस्तुतप्रशंसालंकारः] ॥ १८ ॥ **स्त्रियो हीति** । निसर्गादशिक्षयैव । शास्त्रैरेवोपदिश्यते शास्त्राध्ययनादेव जायते ॥ १९ ॥ **नेति** । [ अस्मिन्साहसे चौर्यरूपे । तस्य साधोर्गुणान्किमर्थं कथयसि येनाहं प्रतिनिवृत्यालंकारं तस्मै प्रत्यर्पयिष्यामि । इदं कुत्सित कर्म मम लज्जां जनयति वा । मादृशानां शठानां सर्वा युक्तीर्जानतामित्यर्थः । किं नु कुर्यात् । न किमपि । मालिनी वृत्तम् ] ॥ २० ॥ **अथ** निजपतित्वेनैवमाह—**तुमं दावेति** । इदानीं ब्राह्मणभार्यात्वेनेति **भावः** ।

---

१ प्रविष्टः; प्रविश्य. २ णअर.

Moreover—

My dear friend, who has been arrested causelessly by the wicked enemies, feelling alarmed in their minds, I will release by a sndden onset, as if he were the lunar orb lying in the jaws of Rahu. (27) (*Exit*).

(*Entering*).

A SERVANT—Lady, fortune smiles on you! A Brahmana has come from the noble Charudatta.

VAS.—Oh! How charming is this day! So, girl, bring him in with (due) respect, attended by one of the bastard-pages.

THE MAID—As your ladyship commands. (*Exit*).

(*Enter* Vidushaka, *attended by a bastard-page*)

VID.—Oh! Wonder! Ravana, the king of the Rakshasas, used to travel by the aerial car, Pushpaka, which he had conquered by means of (the merit born of) the pain he suffered in practising penance. But here I, a Brahmana, am moving about, attended by a number of men and women, although I have suffered no pain due to the practice of penance.

THE MAID—Sir, please look at this entrance to our abode.

---

[ अभुजिष्ययेव यथा कलत्रं मन्त्रयति तथा मन्त्रितमित्यर्थः । ल० दी० ] **मयेति** । भवतीमनुगच्छताऽनुवर्तमानेन । नष्टचन्द्रायां तिमिराच्छादितायामित्यर्थः । **कार्या-कार्यपर्याकुलत्वे** सतीति यावत् ॥ २१ ॥ अत्तणकेरअं वोति चारुदत्तस्यानुचरत्वं स्वीकृत्य ब्रूते । दूरक्ष्यं रक्षितुं दुःशकम् । **गुणेष्वेवेति** । गुणेषु गुणोपार्जने । **गुणयुक्तो** नरः दरिद्रोऽपि अगुणैः ईश्वरैः धनिकैः न समः । ततोऽप्यधिक इति भावः ॥ २२ ॥ **गुणेष्विति** । गुणानामप्राप्यतममत्यन्तमलभ्यम् । गुणवद्भिः सर्वमेव सुखेन लभ्यते इत्यर्थः । [ गुणप्रकर्षाद्गुणाधिक्यात् । उडूनि पातीति उडुपः चन्द्रः तेन अलङ्घ्यं केनापि लङ्घयितुमशक्यं शंभोः उत्तमाङ्गं शिरः लङ्घितमाक्रान्तम् । अत्र गुणप्रकर्षादुडुपकृत-शिवशिरोलङ्घनरूपेण विशेषेण सामान्यस्य समर्थनादर्थान्तरन्यासोऽलंकारः । उपेन्द्र-वज्रा वृत्तम् ] ॥ २३ ॥ [ **त्वमेव वन्दनीयेति—तवेदानीमभुजिष्यात्वेन वधूत्वं प्राप्तम्। अस्माकं तु कोटिपतित्वेऽपि एकपतित्वेऽपि वेश्यापदवाच्यतैवेति भावः।** इति ल० दी०। ] **सुदृष्ट इति**। [ एष जनः वसन्तसेना । **यत्र यस्याः सकाशात्** । वधूशब्दावगुण्ठनं वधू-शब्दरूपमवगुण्ठनमावरणम् । **केनाप्यनवलोकनस्वरूपमित्यर्थः** । ] यत्र ते इति । हेता-वाधारविवक्षया '**यत्र**' इति सप्तमी । **कर्तुः शेषत्वविवक्षया** 'ते' इति षष्ठी ॥२४॥ [ राष्ट्रे अधिकृतो राष्ट्रियः। '**राष्ट्रावारपाराद्धखौ**' इति घः । सिद्धः त्रकालिक-यथार्थज्ञानवान् । तस्यादेशो **प्रत्ययो विश्वासस्तेन** परित्रस्तः तेन । घोषाद्व्रजात् । ]

**विदूषकः**—( अवलोक्य[१] । सविस्मयम् । ) अहो सलिलसिक्तमार्जितकृतहरितोपलेपनस्य विविधसुगन्धिकुसुमोपहारचित्रलिखितभूमिभागस्य गगनतलावलोकनकौतूहलदूरोन्नामितशीर्षस्य दोलायमानावलम्बितैरावणहस्तभ्रमायितमल्लिकादामगुणालंकृतस्य समुच्छ्रितदन्तिदन्ततोरणावभासितस्य महारत्नोपरागोपशोभिना पवनबलान्दोलनाललच्चञ्चलाग्रहस्तेन 'इत एहि' इति व्याहरतेव मां सौभाग्यपताकानिवहेनोपशोभितस्य तोरणधरणस्तम्भवेदिकानिक्षिप्तसमुल्लसद्धरितचूतपल्लवललामस्फटिकमङ्गलकलशाभिरामोभयपार्श्वस्य महासुरवक्षःस्थलदुर्भेद्यवज्रनिरन्तरप्रतिबद्धकनककपाटस्य दुर्गतजनमनोरथायासकरस्य वसन्तसेनाभवनद्वारस्य सश्रीकता । यत्सत्यं मध्यस्थस्यापि जनस्य बलाद्दृष्टिमाकारयति । (अहो सलिलसित्तमज्जिदकिदहरिदोवलेवणस्स विविहसुअन्धिकुसुमोवहारचित्तलिहिदभूमिभाअस्स[२][३] गअणतलाअलोअणकोदूहलदूरुण्णामिदसीसस्स[४][५] दोलाअमाणावलम्बिदैरावणहत्थब्भमाइदमल्लिआदामगुणालकिदस्स समुच्छिददन्तिदन्ततोरणावभासिदस्स[६] महारअणोवराओवसोहिणा पवणबलन्दोलणाललन्तचञ्चलग्गहत्थेण 'इदो एहि' त्ति वाहरन्तेण विअ मं सोहग्गपडाआणिवहेणोवसोहिदस्स तोरणधरणत्थम्भवेदिआणिक्खित्तसमुल्लसन्तहरिदचूदपल्लवललामफटिहमङ्गलकलसाभिरामोहअपास्सस्स महासुरवक्खत्थल[७]दुब्भेज्जवज्जणिरन्तरपडिबद्धकणअकवाडस्स दुग्गदजणमणोरहाआसकरस्स वसन्तसेणाभवणदुआरस्स सस्सिरीअदा । जं सच्चं मज्झत्थस्स वि जणस्स बलाद्दिट्ठिं आआरेदि ।)

---

**द्वयमिति** । [ संप्रति सुहृदां विपत्तेः कार्यकाले समुपस्थिते । विशिष्टतमस्यैव रक्षणस्यात्यावश्यकत्वादिति भावः । आर्या छन्दः ]॥ २५॥ उदवसितं गृहम् । **ज्ञातीनिति** । [ **यौगंधरायणः** तन्नामकः प्रधानसचिवः **उदयनस्य** राज्ञः वत्सराजस्य इव सुहृदः आर्यकस्य परिमोक्षणाय बन्धनागारान्मुक्त्यर्थं ज्ञातीन् बन्धून् विटान् स्वभुजविक्रमेण लब्धो वर्णः यशः यैस्तादृशान्वीरपुरुषान् । तथा राज्ञा पालकेन कृतापमानेन कुपितान् । विरक्तानिति यावत् । नरेन्द्रभृत्यानुत्तेजयामि राज्ञः पालकस्योच्छेदार्थं प्रोत्साहयिष्यामि । पुरा किल कौशाम्बीनृपो वत्सराजः उज्जयिनीपतिना चण्डसेनेन केनापि मिषेण गृहीत्वा कारागारे निक्षिप्तस्तत्सचिवेन यौगंधरायेण प्रकृतिकोपमुत्पाद्य बन्धनान्मोचित इति कथासरित्सागरकथाऽत्रानुसंधेया । उपमापरिकरावलंकारौ । वसन्ततिलकं वृत्तम् ]॥ २६ ॥ **प्रियेति** । [ अकारणं कारणाभावेऽपि असाधुभिः आहिता आत्मनि शङ्का आर्यको राजा भविष्यतीति यैस्तैः । **स्वयमेव भीतैः गृहीतं** प्रियसुहृदं आर्यकं सरभसं सवेगं समभिपत्य शत्रूनभियात्य मोचयामि राहुमुखे स्थितं

---

१ विलोक्य. २ सुअन्ध...कुसुमचित्त. ३ चित्तलिदभूमिआ० (चित्रितभूमिका०.) ४ तलालोअण (तलालोकन). ५ ण्णामिद. ६ समुद्धद. ७ णिब्भेज्ज.

VID.—( *Looks, admiringly* ). Oh ! How beautiful is this gate of Vasantasena's mansion ! It is besprinkled with waters swept, and then besmeared with greenish cow-dung. Its floor space is attractively (*lit.* diversely) decorated with the offerings of various kinds of sweet-smelling flowers. It has raised its top to a great height, as if out of curiosity to have a sight of the celestial regions. It is adorned with a string of a (huge) garland of jasmine flowers which is tossing about and hanging down from it, making one mistake it for the trunk of ( Indra s elephant ) Airavata. It is splendidly decked with a lofty arch of ivory. It is decorated with a number of auspicious banners, which look lovely with the lustre of costly jewels, whose finger-like tips are tremulously shaking as they are tossed about by the force of the wind, and which thus seem to be as it were beckoning me to get in. Both its sides are rendered attractive by auspicious crystal-jars which are kept on the pedestals of the pillars supporting the archway, and which are charming on account of the green mango-leaves placed gracefully therein. Its golden panels are thickly set with diamonds, and are as hard to break open as the chest of a big demon. It tortures the desires of indigent persons. To tell the truth, it forcibly arrests the eye even of an indifferent looker-on ( like me).

---

शशिबिम्बमिव । पुष्पिताग्रा छन्दः ] ॥ २७ ॥ बन्धुलेन । [ बन्धुलस्त्वसतीसुतः' इत्यमरः] अत्रैवाङ्के पञ्चमप्रकोष्ठके [पञ्चमप्रकोष्ठकवर्णने] 'परगृहललिताः' (४।२८) इत्यादि बन्धुललक्षणं करिष्यते। ही ही भो इति विस्मये। तपश्चरणक्लेशविनिर्जितेन स्वाधीनेन । पुष्पकेण विमानविशेषेण । अकृततपश्चरणक्लेशः । नरयुक्ता नारी नरनारी सोद्वाहिका यस्य । पुष्पकमपि सा नरनारी सीतारूपा उद्वहनीया यस्येदृशम् । शब्दच्छलेन साम्यम् । अहो वसन्तसेनाभवनद्वारस्य सश्रीकता । किंभूतस्य । [ आदौ सलिलेन सिक्तं पश्चान्मार्जितं च कृतं हरितोपलेपनं यस्य तस्य । [ कृतहरितोपलेपनस्य । कृतगोमयोपलेपनस्येत्यर्थात् । [ विविधानि च तानि सुगन्धीनि कुसुमानि च तेषामुपहारैः चित्रं यथा तथा लिखितः भूमिभागो यस्य । ०लोकने कौतूहलं तेन दूरोन्नामितं शीर्षं येन तस्य ।] उच्छ्रायप्रकर्षपरमेतत् । [ दोलायमानः यः अवलम्बितः ऐरावणः ऐरावतस्तस्य हस्तः शुण्डा तस्य भ्रमायितः भ्रममागतः मल्लिकादामगुणः मल्लिकाकुसुममाला तेनालंकृतस्य । महारजनोपरागेति पाठे महारजनं कुसुम्भं तस्योपरागः रञ्जनं तैरुपशोभते इति तेन । पवनबलेन या आन्दोलना तया ललत् चलदत एव चञ्चलं अग्रं एव हस्तो यस्य तेन । सौभाग्याय सौभाग्यलक्षणा वा याः पताकास्तासां निवहेन । तोरणस्य धरणं धारणं तदर्थं

**चेटी**—एत्वेतु। इमं प्रथमं प्रकाष्ठं पविशत्वार्यः (एदु एदु। इमं पढमं पओट्ठं पविसदु अज्जो।)

**विदूषकः**—(प्रविश्यावलोक्य[1] च।) आश्चर्यं भोः। इहापि प्रथमे पकोष्ठे शशिशङ्खमृणालसच्छाया विनिहितचूर्णमुष्टिपाण्डुरा विविधरत्नप्रतिबद्धकाञ्चनसोपानशोभिताः प्रासादपङ्क्तयोऽवलम्बितमुक्तादामभिः स्फटिकवातायनमुखचन्द्रैर्निर्ध्यायन्तीवोज्जयिनीम्। श्रोत्रिय इव सुखोपविष्टो निद्राति दौवारिकः। सदध्ना कलमौदनेन प्रलोभिता न भक्षयन्ति वायसा बलिं सुधासवर्णतया। आदिशतु भवती। (ही ही भोः। इध वि पढमे पओट्ठे ससिसङ्खमुणालसच्छाहाओ विणिहिदचुण्णमुट्ठिपाण्डुराओ विविहरअणपडिबद्धकञ्चणसोवाणसोहिदाओ पासादपन्तिओ[2] ओलम्बिदमुत्तादामेहिं फटिहवादाअणमुहचन्देहिं णिज्झाअन्ती विअ उज्जइणिम्। सोत्तिओ विअ सुहोवविट्ठो णिद्दाअदि दोवारिओ। सदहिणा कलमोदणेण पलोहिदा ण भक्खन्ति वायसा बलिं सुधासवण्णादाए। आदिसदु भोदी।)

**चेटी**—एत्वेत्वार्यः। इमं द्वितीयं प्रकोष्ठं प्रविशत्वार्यः (एदु एदु अज्जो। इमं दुदिअं पओट्ठं पविसदु अज्जो।)

**विदूषकः**—(प्रविश्यावलोक्य च।) आश्चर्यं भोः। इहापि द्वितीये प्रकोष्ठे पर्यन्तोपनीतयवसबुसकवलसुपुष्टास्तैलाभ्यक्तविषाणा बद्धाः प्रवहणबलीवर्दाः। अयमन्यतरोऽवमानित इव कुलीनो दीर्घं निश्वसिति सैरिभः। इतश्चापनीतयुद्धस्य मल्लस्येव मर्द्यते ग्रीवा मेषस्य। इत इतोऽपरेषामश्वानां केशकल्पना क्रियते। अयमपरः पाटच्चर इव दृढबद्धो मन्दुरायां शाखामृगः। (अन्यतोऽवलोक्य।) इतश्च कूरच्युततैलमिश्रं पिण्डं हस्ती प्रतिग्राह्यते मात्रपुरुषैः। आदिशतु भवती। (ही ही भोः। इध वि दुदिए पओट्ठे पज्जन्तोवणीदजवसबुसकवलसुपुट्ठा तेल्लब्भङ्गिदविसाणा[3] बद्धा पवहणबइल्ला। अअं अण्णदरो अवमाणिदो विअ कुलीणो दीहं णीससदि सेरिहो। इदो अ अवणीदजुज्झस्स मल्लस्स विअ मद्दीअदि गीवा मेसस्स। इदो इदो अवराणं अस्साणं केसकप्पणा करीअदि। अअं अवरो पाडच्चरो विअ दढबद्धो मन्दुराए साहामिओ। इदो अ कूरच्चुअतेल्लमिस्सं पिण्डं हत्थी पडिच्छावीअदि मेत्थपुरिसेहिं। आदिसदु[4] भोदी।)

---

स्तम्भौ तयोः वेदिका तस्यां निक्षिप्तौ निहितौ च तौ। समुल्लसन्तः च ते हरिताश्च चूतपल्लवा आम्रपल्लवास्तैः ललामौ स्फटिकनिर्मितौ मङ्गलकलशौ ताभ्यामभिरामौ उभयपार्श्वौ यस्य। महासुरवक्षःस्थलवद् दुर्भेद्यं वज्रैः हीरकैः निरन्तरं प्रतिबद्धं प्रत्युप्तं कनककपाटं यस्य तस्य। दुर्गतः दरिद्रः जनः। आयासकरस्य द्रव्याभावादलभ्यत्वात्। आकारयत्याकर्षति।] प्रथमप्रकोष्ठवर्णनम्—[शशिशङ्खमृणालसच्छायाः शशिशङ्खमृणालैः समाना छाया कान्तिर्येषां ते। विविधैः रत्नैः प्रतिबद्धानि

---

१ दृष्ट्वा च. २ वन्तिओ. ३ विसाणबद्ध. ४ आदेसेदु.

THE MAID—Come, come (this way): please enter this first quadrangle.

VID.—(*Entering and looking about*). Oh! Wonderful! Here, too, in this first quadrangle, are rows of balconies resembling in colour the moon, or conches, or lotus-stalks, which are whitened with handfuls of chunam-powder laid over them (as paint), which are adorned with golden stairs inlaid with various kinds of gems, and which seem to be, as it were, gazing down fixedly on Ujjayini with their moon-like faces in the form of the crystal-windows from which pearlstrings ore dangling. Here the door-keeper is comfortably sleeping, lying at ease like a learned Brahmana! The crows, though enticed by means of *Kalama* rice mixed with curds, do not eat the oblations, they being of the same colour as chunam-paint (and therefore indistinguishable from it)—Please direct me (further), madam.

THE MAID—Come, sir, come (this way); please enter this second quadrangle.

VID—(*Entering and looking about*). Oh! Wonderful; Here, too, in this second quadrangle, there are tied the carriage-oxen, fattened on the mouthfuls of grass and corn-husks that are placed before them, and having their horns anointed with oil. Here's one buffalo, snorting (*lit.* emitting deep sighs) like a high-born man when slighted. Here they are rubbing the neck of a ram as if he were a wrestler, after the fight is over. And here in this direction they are dressing the hair of some horses. Here's a monkey, fastened in its stable securely like a thief. (*Looking in another direction*). And here an elephant is being fed by the keepers with balls of boiled rice mixed with ghee.—Please direct me (further), madam.

---

खचितानि काञ्चनस्य सोपानानि तैः शोभिताः । अवलम्बितानि मुक्तादामानि येषु तैः स्फटिकवातायनान्येव मुखचन्द्रास्तैः । निध्यायिन्तीव पश्यन्तीव । कलमोदनेन शाल्योदनेन । ] [ पर्यन्तेषु उपनीतानि यवसानि तृणानि बुसानि धान्यत्वचश्च तेषां कवलैः सुपुष्टाः । ] इह सैरिभो महिषः । [ केशकल्पना केशसज्जना । केशानां संस्कार इत्यर्थः । "कूरेति भक्तेत्यर्थः । तल्लेति घृतेत्यर्थः । मात्रेति महामात्रेत्यर्थः ।" इति ल० दी० । ] पाटच्चर इव चौर इव । इतोऽपि भक्ततैलघृतमिश्रपिण्डं ग्राह्यते हस्ती हस्तिपकपुरुषैः । [ कुलपुत्राः गर्भेश्वराः । पाशकपीठे मञ्चे इति ल० दी० । यद्वा शारीपटे । ] पुस्तकं कामशास्त्रस्येत्यर्थात् । स्वाधीनम् । 'सारितम्' इति पाठे प्रसारित-

**चेटी**—एत्वेत्वार्यः। इमं तृतीयं प्रकोष्ठं प्रविशत्वार्यः। एदु एदु अज्जो। इमं तइअं पओट्ठं पविसदु अज्जो।)

**विदूषकः**—( प्रविश्य दृष्ट्वा च। ) आश्चर्यं भोः। इहापि तृतीये प्रकोष्ठे इमानि तावत्कुलपुत्रजनोपवेशननिमित्तं विरचितान्यासनानि। अर्धवाचितं पाशकपीठे तिष्ठति पुस्तकम्। एतच्च मणिमयसारिकासहितं पाशकपीठम्। इमे चापरे मदनसंधिविग्रहचतुरा विविधवर्णिकाविलिप्तचित्रफलकाग्रहस्ता इतस्ततः परिभ्रमन्ति गणिका वृद्धविटाश्च। आदिशतु भवती। (ही ही भोः। इध वि तइए पओट्ठे इमाइं दाव कुलउत्तजणोववेसणणिमित्तं विरचिदाइं आसणाइं। अद्धवाचिदो [1]पासअपीठे चिठ्ठइ पोत्थओ। एसो अ [2]मणिमअसारिआसहिदो पासअपीठो। इमे अ अवरे मअणसंधिविग्गहचदुरा विविहवण्णिआविलित्तचित्तफलहअग्गहत्था इदो तदो परिब्भमन्ति गणिआ वुड्ढविडा अ। आदिसदु भोदी।)

**चेटी**—एत्वेत्वार्यः। इमं चतुर्थं प्रकोष्ठं प्रविशत्वार्यः (एदु एदु अज्जो। इमं चउठ्ठं पओठ्ठं पविसदु अज्जो।)

**विदूषकः**—( प्रविश्यावलोक्य च। ) आश्चर्यं भोः। इहापि चतुर्थे प्रकोष्ठे युवतिकरताडिता जलधरा इव गम्भीरं नन्दन्ति मृदङ्गाः। क्षीणपुण्या इव गगनात्तारका निपतन्ति कांस्यतालाः। मधुकरविरुतमिव मधुरं वाद्यते वंशः। इयमपरेर्ष्याप्रणयकुपितकामिनीवाङ्कारोपिता कररुहपरामर्शेन सार्यते वीणा। इमा अपराः कुसुमरसमत्ता इव मधुकर्योऽतिमधुरं प्रगीता गणिकादारिका नर्त्यन्ते नाट्यं पाठ्यन्ते सशृङ्गारम्। अपवलिगना गवाक्षेषु वातं गृह्णन्ति सलिलगर्गर्यः। आदिशतु भवती। (ही ही भोः। इध वि चउट्ठे पओट्ठे जुवदिकरताडिदा जलधरा विअ गम्भीरं णदन्ति मुदङ्गा[3] हीणपुण्णाओ[4] विअ गअणादो तारआओ णिवडन्ति कंसतालआ महुअरविरुअं[5] विअ महुरं वज्जदि वंसो। इअं अवरा ईसाप्पणअकुविदकामिणी विअ अङ्कारोविदा कररुहपरामरिसेण सारिज्जदि वीणा। इमाओ अवराओ कुसुमरसमत्ताओ विअ महुअरिओ अदिमहुरं पगीदाओ गणिआदारिआओ णच्चीअन्ति णट्ठअं पठीअन्ति ससिङ्गारओ। ओवग्गिदा गवक्खेसु वादं गेण्हन्ति सलिलगग्गरीओ। आदिसदु भोदी।)

---

मित्यर्थः। 'स्वाधीनमकृत्रिमम्' इति प्राचीनटीका। [मदनसंबन्धी यः संधिः परस्परानुनयनं विग्रहः प्रणयकलहश्च तत्र चतुराः। विविधा वर्णिका नीलपीतादयो वर्णास्तैः विलिप्ताः कृतालेख्याः चित्रफलका अग्रहस्ते येषां ते।] विविधवर्णिकावलिप्तं

---

१ वासपीठे ( व्यासपीठे ). २ साहीणमणि० ( स्वाधीनमणि० ). ३ मुरआ (मुरजाः). ४ झीण. ५ विरुअमहुरं (विरुतमधुरं).

THE MAID—Come, sir, come ( this way ); please enter this third quadrangle.

VID.—( *Entering and looking about* ). Oh ! Wonderful ! Here, too, in this third quadrangle, are these seats, duly arranged, for the use of well-born youths. There is a half-read volume lying on a gaming-table. Here's this gaming-table with chessmen made of precious stones. And here are these courtesans and aged gallants, wandering in all directions, who are skilled in managing love-unions and love-quarrels, carrying in their hands ( *lit.* fingers ) picture-boards covered with paintings in various colours.—Please direct me ( further ), madam.

THE MAID—Come, sir, come ( this way ); please enter this fourth quadrangle.

VID.—( *Entering and looking about* ). Oh ! wonderful ! Here, too, in this fourth quadrangle, the tabors struck by the hands of ladies are sounding deeply like clouds; cymbals of bell-metal beating time are falling ( with a flash ), like the stars from heaven when their merit is exhausted; and bamboo-pipes are being sweetly played upon, ( sounding ) like the hum of bees. Here's a lute which, after being placed on the lap like a maiden angered in jealous love, is being played upon ( stroked ) with the touch of the nails ( fingers ). Here are some courtesan-girls singing very sweetly, like female bees intoxicated with the honey of flowers‹ who are being taught to dance and made to learn a drama full ot erotic sentiment. And water-jars, turned upside down, are kepf suspended in the windows to receive the ( cooling ) breeze.—Please direct me ( further ), madam.

---

चित्रफलकं वहमानाः । गम्भीरं धीरम् । निपतन्ति वैदग्ध्यवादनादेव निपातः । मधुकराभिरुतमिव । [ अपरस्याः ईर्ष्यया अनुरागासहिष्णुतया प्रणयकुपिता कामिनीव । कररुहपरामर्शेन नखाग्राघातेन । कामिनीपक्षे स्पर्शनेन ] । 'गणिकादारिका वेश्याविशेषा' इतिगुणपताकायामुक्तम् । [ नर्त्यन्ते नृत्यं शिक्ष्यन्ते । ] नाटयन्ते नाटचम् । पाठयन्ते सशृङ्गारं । अपवल्गिता अवलम्बिताः । सलिलगर्गर्यः [ पात्रविशेषाः ] । एतच्च जनानां पानार्थम् । हिङ्गुतैलगन्ध आ समन्ताद्धरति । [ महानसं पाकस्थानम् । ] अधिकं रोमाञ्चयति [ उत्सुकयतीति वाऽर्थः । भुज्यते अनेनेति भोजनम् । करणे ल्युट् । व्यञ्जनमिति व्युत्पत्तेः । अतो न पौनरुक्त्यमिति ध्येयम् । इति ल० दी० भोजनं करणे ल्युटि व्यञ्जनादिवचनः । पटच्चरमिव जीर्णवस्त्रमिव [ पेशीं मांसपिण्डीम् । ] छेद्यपट्टमनेकाधारशोणिताभ्यामुपहतत्वात् । रूपिदारओ । रूपशब्दः

**चेटी**—एत्वेत्वार्यः । इमं पञ्चमं प्रकोष्ठं प्रविशत्वार्यः । (एदु एदु अज्जो । इमं पञ्चमं पओट्ठं पविसदु अज्जो ।)

**विदूषकः**—( प्रविश्य दृष्ट्वा च । ) आश्चर्यं भोः । इहापि पञ्चमे प्रकोष्ठेऽयं दरिद्रजनलोभोत्पादनकर आहरत्युपचितो हिङ्गुतैलगन्धः । विविधसुरभिधूमोद्गारैर्नित्यं संताप्यमानं निःश्वसितीव महानसं द्वारमुखैः । अधिकमुत्सुकायते मां साध्यमानबहुविधभक्ष्यभोजनगन्धः । अयमपरः पटच्चरमिव हतपशूदरपेशिं धावति रूपिदारकः । बहुविधाहारविकारमुपसाधयति सूपकारः । बध्यन्ते मोदकाः पच्यन्तेऽपूपकाः । (आत्मगतम् ।) अपीदानीमिह वर्धितं भुङ्क्ष्वेति पादोदकं लप्स्ये । (अन्यतोऽवलोक्य । ) इतो गन्धर्वाप्सरोगणैरिव विविधालंकारशोभितैर्गणिकाजनैर्बन्धुलैश्च यत्सत्यं स्वर्गायत एतद्गेहम् । भो के यूयं बन्धुला नाम । (ही ही भोः । इध वि पञ्चमे पओट्ठे अअं दलिद्दजणलोहुप्पादणअरो आहरइ उवचिदो हिङ्गुतेल्लगन्धो । विविहसुरहिधूमुग्गारेहिं णिच्चं संताविज्जमाणं णीससदि विअ महाणसं दुवारमुहेहिं । अधिअं उसुसावेदि[1] मं साहिज्जमाणबहुविहभक्खभोअणगन्धो । अअं अवरो पडच्चरं विअ पोट्टिं धोअदि रूपिदारओ । बहुविहाहारविआरं उवमाहेदि सूवआरो । बज्झन्ति मोदआ पच्चन्ति अपूवआ । अवि दाणिं इह वड्ढिअं भुञ्जमु त्ति पादोदअं लहिस्सम् । इदो[2] गन्धव्वच्छरगणेहिं[3] विअ विविहालंकारसोहिदेहिं गणिआजणेहिं बन्धुलेहिं अ जं सच्चं सग्गीअदि[4] एदं गेहम् । भो के तुम्हे बन्धुला णाम ।)

**बन्धुलाः**—वयं खलु

**परगृहललिताः परान्नपुष्टाः परपुरुषैर्जनिताः पराङ्गनासु ।**
**परधननिरता गुणेष्ववाच्या गजकलभा इव बन्धुला ललामः**[5] ॥ २८ ॥

**विदूषकः**—आदिशतु भवती । (आदिसदु भोदी ।)

**चेटी**—एत्वेत्वार्यः । इमं षष्ठं प्रकोष्ठं प्रविशत्वार्यः । ( एदु एदु अज्जो । इमं[6] छठ्ठं पओट्ठ पविसदु अज्जो ।)

---

पशुवचनस्तद्योगाद्रूपी खट्टिकस्तस्य दारकः पुत्रः । यद्वा रूपी रूपसंघस्तस्य दारकश्छेदकः । खट्टिक एव । यत्र मांसं छिद्यते तं पदं धावति प्रक्षालयति । अपीदानीमहं भोक्तुं पादोदकं लप्स्ये । 'वर्धितम्' इति पाठे 'व्यञ्जनादिसामग्र्योपचितं वर्धितकम्' इति पूर्वटीका । **परगृहेति** । [ परगृहे ललिताः पालिताः । ] गुणेष्ववाच्याः । अनभिधानीयगुणा इत्यर्थः । 'ऋणेषु' इति पाठे ऋणेष्ववाच्या ऋणमेवावसीय सर्वैरभिमुह्यामह इत्यर्थः । ललामो विलसामः । 'लल विलासे' भौवादिकः । अनुप्रासानुरोधेनानयोरैक्यम् । 'ललामाः' इति पाठे श्रेष्ठा इत्यर्थः ॥ २८ ॥ [ कर्मणा कार्येण चित्रघटनयेत्यर्थः । निर्मितानि तोरणानि । ] वस्तुविशेषे निक्षिप्तानि प्रसा-

---

१ ओआसावेदि. २ इदो अ. ३ सुर. ४ सग्गाअदि. ५ ललामाः. ६ एदं.

THE MAID—Come. sir, come ( this way ); please enter this fifth quadrangle.

VID.—( *Entering and looking about*). Oh ! Wonderful ! Here, too, in this fifth quadrangle, there pervades an over-powering odour of asafœtida and oil, exciting the appetite of a poor person. The kitchen, being always heated ( pained ), is sighing, as it were, through its mouths in the shape of its doors, sending forth effusions of fragrant smoke of different kinds. The smell of the many varieties of edibles and condiments that are being prepared is exciting me (*i.e.*) my appetite ) very much. Here is this butcher's boy washing the entrails of a killed animal, looking like ( a piece ) of an old garment. The cook is preparing various kinds of different eatables : *modakas* are being made and *apoopas* fried. (*To himself*). Oh, how I long I should be offered here water for my feet, with a request to eat to my heart's content ! ( *Looking in another direction* ). To tell the truth, this mansion in this spot, with its bastards and courtesan-folk adorned with different kinds of ornaments, looks as if it were heaven itself, with its crowds of Gandharvas and Apsarasas.—Sirs, who are you that go by the name of '*Bandhulas*' ?

THE BASTARDS—We are, indeed,

*Bandhulas* ( bastards ), that sport about like the cubs of elephants, being reared in other people's houses, fed on others' food, begotten by other men upon stranger-women, enjoying others' riches, and possessing no ( particular ) merits to speak of. (28)

VID.—Please direct me ( further ), madam,

THE MAID—Come, sir, come ( this way ); please enter this sixth quadrangle.

---

रितानीन्द्रायुधस्थानकमिव दर्शयन्ति । नीलरत्नेष्वारोपितानीन्द्रायुधमिव दृश्यन्त इत्याशयः । प्रवालककर्केतरौ मणिविशेषौ । जातरूपैः सुवर्णैः । लोहितसूत्रैर्ग्रथ्यन्ते मौक्तिकाभरणानि । शाणे घृष्यन्ते प्रवालानि । शोष्यन्ते ओल्लविदमवतारिता आर्दिता वा कुङ्कुमप्रस्तराः । 'प्रस्तरः कुङ्कुमाधारश्चर्मपुटः' इत्याहुः । सालीअदि आर्द्रीक्रियते । सेलज्जअं कस्तूरिका । शल्यवद्वेधकत्वात् । आज्यमिव मृगमदन्वात् । इमेऽन्येऽवज्ञातपुत्रदारवित्ता मनुष्याः [ आसवकरकैश्चषकैः आपीता मदिरा यैः ] आसवकरकेणापीतमदिरा गणिकाजनैर्ये मुक्तास्ते वाटं पिबन्ति । अयमर्थः— मद्यपानभाण्डेनापीतमद्या अनादृतनिजपरिवारास्त्यक्तान्यकर्तव्या अत एव तत्रै-

**विदूषकः**—(प्रविश्यावलोक्य च ।) आश्चर्यं भोः । इहापि षष्ठे प्रकोष्ठेऽमूनि तावत्सुवर्णरत्नानां कर्मतोरणानि नीलरत्नविनिक्षिप्तानीन्द्रायुधस्थानमिव दर्शयन्ति । वैदूर्यमौक्तिकप्रवालकपुष्परागेन्द्रनीलकर्केतरकपद्मरागमरकतप्रभृतीन्रत्नविशेषानन्योन्यं विचारयन्ति शिल्पिनः । बध्यन्ते जातरूपैर्माणिक्यानि । घटघन्ते सुवर्णालंकाराः । रक्तसूत्रेण ग्रथ्यन्ते मौक्तिकाभरणानि । घृष्यन्ते धीरं वैदूर्याणि । छिद्यन्ते शङ्खाः । शाणैर्घृष्यन्ते प्रवालकाः । शोष्यन्त आर्द्रकुङ्कुमप्रस्तराः । सार्यंते[1] कस्तूरिका । विशेषेण घृष्यते चन्दनरसः । सयोज्यन्ते गन्धयुक्तयः । दीयते गणिकाकामुकानां[2] सकर्पूरं ताम्बूलम् । अवलोक्यते सकटाक्षम् । प्रवर्तते हासः । पीयते चानवरतं ससीत्कारं मदिरा । इमे चेटा इमाश्चेटिका इमेऽपरेऽवधीरितपुत्रदारवित्ता मनुष्या आसवकरकापीतमदिरैर्गणिकाजनैर्ये मुक्तास्तें पिबन्ति । आदिशतु भवति । (ही ही भोः । इध वि छट्ठे पओट्ठे अमुं दाव सुवण्णरअणाणं कम्मतोरणाइं णीरलअणविणिक्खिताइं इन्दाउहट्ठाणं विअ दरिसअन्ति । वेदुरिअमोत्तिअपवालअपुप्फराअइन्दणीलकक्केतरअपउमराअमरगअपहुदिआइं रअणविसेसाइं अण्णोण्णं विचारेन्ति सिप्पिणो । बज्झन्ति जादरूवेहिं मणिक्कांइं । घडिज्जन्ति सुवण्णालंकारा । रत्तसुत्तेण गत्थीअन्ति मोत्तिआभरणाइं । घसीअन्ति धीरं वेदुरिआइं । छेदीअन्ति सङ्खआ । साणिज्जन्ति पवालआ । सुक्खविअन्ति ओल्लविदकुङ्कुमपत्थरा । सालीअदि सेलज्जअम् । विस्साणीअदि चन्दणरसो । संजोईअन्ति गंधजुत्तीओ । दीअदि गणिआकामुकाणं सकप्पूरं तम्बोलम् । अवलोईअदि सकडक्खअम् । पअट्टदि हासो । पिबीअदि अ अणवरअं ससिक्कारं मइरा । इमे चेडा इमा चेडिआओ इमे अवरे अवधीरिदपुत्तदारवित्ता मणुस्सा आसवकरआपीदमदिरेहिं गणिआजणेहिं जे मुक्का ते पिअन्ति । आदिसदु भोदी ।

**चेटी**—एत्वेत्वार्यः । इमं सप्तमं प्रकोष्ठं प्रविशत्वार्यः । (एदु एदु अज्जो । इमं सत्तमं पओट्ठं पविसदु अज्जो ।)

**विदूषकः**—( प्रविश्यावलोक्य च । ) आश्चर्यं भोः । इहापि सप्तमे प्रकोष्ठे सुश्लिष्टविहंगवाटीसुखनिषण्णान्यन्योन्यचुम्बनपराणि सुखमनुभवन्ति पारावतमिथुनानि । दधिभक्तपूरितोदरो ब्राह्मण इव सूक्तं पठति पञ्जरशुकः । इयमपरा

---

वात्यन्तमवस्थाना गणिकाभिर्ये मुक्ता निःसारिता इत्युक्तं ते पुरुषा वारंवारं पुनः पुनर्मद्यमेव पिबन्ति । मदिराया अवारितसत्रत्वमुक्तम् । इह सप्तमे प्रकोष्ठे सुश्लिष्टायां विहङ्गपाल्यां ( –वाट्यां ) कपोतपालिकायाम् । सूक्तमृक्समुदायम् । शोभनोक्तं च यथा स्यादेवम् । [ कुम्भदासीव कुट्टिनीव । ] परपुष्टा कोकिला । आलम्बिता नागदन्तेषु गृहभित्तिस्थदारुविशेषेषु । नागदन्तका इति प्रकृष्टौ कः ।

---

१ क्षाल्यते. २ कामुकयोः.

VID.—( *Entering and looking about* ). Oh ! Wonderful ! Here, too, in this sixth quadrangle, these architectural arches, made of jewels set in gold, and embossed on ( a background of ) blue gems ( sapphires ), exhibit as it were a spot full of rain-bows. Goldsmiths are consulting one another as regards various kinds of jewels, such as lapis lazuli, pearls, corals, topazes, sapphires, cat's-eyes, rubies, emeralds, etc. Rubies are being set in gold ; golden ornaments are being manufactured ; pearl-ornaments are being strung on threads of red silk ; lapis lazuli are being gently polished ; conches are being cut ; and corals are being ground on whetting stones. Layers of wet saffron-paint are exposed for drying ; musk is being moistened ; sandal-juice is being made up. Betel-rolls with camphor are being offered to the lovers of the courtesans ; side-glances are being cast; laughter is going on ; and wine is being incessantly drunk with sounds of merriment. Here are drinking these men-servants, these maid-servants, and also these men who have forsaken their children, wives and property, and are left ( to themselves ) by the courteans who have ( gone away, having ) drunk wine from liquor-cups.—Please direct me (further) madam.

THE MAID--Come, sir, come ( this way ); please enter this seventh quadrangle.

VID.—( *Entering and looking about* ). Oh ! Wonderful ! Here, too, in this seventh quadrangle, pairs of pigeons are enjoying happiness, perched comfortably in snug dove-cots and busy in kissing each other. The parrot in its cage, fed on curds and rice, is reciting a Vedic hymn, like a Brahmana whose belly is filled with rice and curds.

---

कपिञ्जला गौरास्तित्तिरयः । प्रेष्यन्ते पञ्जरकपोताः । योद्धुमित्यर्थात् । इतस्ततो विविधमणिविचित्रित इवायं सहचरीसहितः सहर्षं नृत्यन्नविकिरणसंतप्तं पक्षोत्क्षेपैर्वीजयतीव प्रासादं गृहमयूरः । चन्द्रपादाश्चन्द्रकिरणाः । [ वृद्धमहल्लका वृद्धश्रेष्ठा इत्यर्थः । इति ल. दी. ] प्रसारणकं दत्तं गणिकाभिर्नानापक्षिसमूहे । [ एत्वार्यः । अत्र एत्वेत्विति न वीप्सा । प्रकोष्ठमर्यादासमाप्तेरभ्यन्तरगृहस्यागतत्वेन गन्तव्यस्य प्रकोष्ठान्तरस्य विरहाच्चेति ध्येयम् । इति ल० दी० ] पट्टप्रच्छदप्रावृतोऽधिकतरमत्यद्भुतपुनरुक्तालंकारालंकृतः । **मा तावदिति** । आर्या । त्रितातायामिव अमेध्य इवेति पाठान्तरे इत्यर्थः । अनभिगम्योऽनभिगमनीयः ॥ २९ ॥ पुष्पप्रावारकप्रावृता [ सूक्ष्मसूत्रपुष्पाणि कृत्रिमाणि यत्र भवन्ति स पुष्पपट इति प्रसिद्धः । इति ल० दी० ]

संमाननालब्धप्रसरेव गृहदासी अधिकं कुरकुरायते मदनसारिका । अनेकफलरसास्वादप्रहृष्टकण्ठा कुम्भदासीव कूजति परपुष्टा । आलम्बिता नागदन्तेषु पञ्जरपरंपराः । योध्यन्ते लावकाः । आलाप्यन्ते कपिञ्जलाः । प्रेष्यन्ते पञ्जरकपोताः । इतस्ततो विविधमणिचित्रित इवायं सहर्षं नृत्यन्रविकिरणसंतप्तं पक्षोत्क्षेपैर्विधुवतीव प्रासादं गृहमयूरः । (अन्यतोऽवलोक्य ।) इतः पिण्डीकृता इव चन्द्रपादाः पदगतिं शिक्षमाणानीव कामिनीनां पश्चात्परिभ्रमन्ति राजहंसमिथुनानि । एतेऽपरे वृद्धमहल्लका इवेतस्ततः संचरन्ति गृहसारसाः । आश्चर्यं भोः । प्रसारणं कृतं गणिकाया नानापक्षिसमूहैः । यत्सत्यं खलु नन्दनवनमिव मे गणिकागृहं प्रतिभासते । आदिशतु भवती । (ही ही भोः । इध वि सत्तमे पओट्ठे सुसिलिट्ठविहङ्गवाडीसुहणिसण्णाइं अण्णोणचुम्बणपराइं सुहं अणुभवन्ति पारावदमिहुणाइं । दहिभत्तपूरिदोदरो बम्हणो विअ सुत्तं पढदि पञ्जरसुओ । इअं अवरा संमाणणालद्धप्पसरा विअ घरदासी[1] अधिअं कुरकुरायदि मदणसारिआ । अणेअफलरसास्सादपन्हुट्ठकण्ठा कुम्भदासी विअ कूअदि परपुट्ठा[3] । आलम्बिदा णागदन्तेसु पञ्जरपरम्पराओ । जोधीअन्ति लावआ । आलवीअन्ति कविञ्जला । पेसीअन्ति पञ्जरकवोदा । इदो तदो विविहमणिचित्तलिदो विअ अअं सहरिसं णच्चन्तो रविकिरणसंतत्तं पक्खुक्खेवेहिं विधुवेदि विअ पासादं घरमोरो । इदो पिण्डीकिदा विअ चन्दपादा पदगदिं सिक्खन्ता[4] विअ कामिणीणं पच्छादो परिब्भमन्ति राअहंसमिहुणा । एदे अवरे बुड्ढमहल्लका विअ इदो तदो संचरन्ति घरसारसा[5] । ही ही भोः । पसारणअं किदं गणिआए णाणापक्खिसमूहेहिं । जं सच्चं क्खु[6] णन्दणवणं विअ मे गणिआघरं पडिभासदि । आदिसदु[7] भोदी ।)

**चेटी**—एत्वार्यः । इममष्टमं प्रकोष्ठं प्रविशत्वार्यः । (एदु[8] अज्जो । इमं अट्ठमं पओट्ठं पविसदु अज्जो ।)

**विदूषकः**—(प्रविश्यावलोक्य च ।) भवति क एष पट्टप्रावारकप्रावृतोऽधिकतरमत्यद्भुतपुनरुक्तालंकारालंकृतोऽङ्गभङ्गैः परिस्खलन्नितस्ततः परिभ्रमति । (भोदि को एसो पट्टपावारअपाउदो अधिअदरं अच्चब्भुदपुणरुत्तालंकारालंकिदो अङ्गभङ्गेहिं परिक्खलन्तो इदो तदो परिब्भमदि ।)

**चेटी**—आर्य एष आर्याया भ्राता भवति । (अज्ज एसो अज्जआए[9] भादा भोदी ।)

**विदूषकः**—कियत्तपश्चरणं कृत्वा वसन्तसेनाया भ्राता भवति । अथ वा ।

**मा तावद्यद्यप्येष उज्ज्वलः स्निग्धश्च सुगन्धश्च ।**
**तथाऽपि श्मशानवीथ्यां जात इव चम्पकवृक्षोऽनभिगमनीयो लोकस्य ॥ २९ ॥**

---

१ गृहदासी. २ पदुट्ट (प्रतुष्ट). ३ परउ-बु-द्ठा. ४ सिक्खन्ति. ५ सारसाओ. ६ क्खु एदं. ७ आदेसेदु. ८ एदु एदु. ९ आए अअं.

And this talking thrush is chattering lustily like a house-maid that has gained ascendancy on account of the consideration shown to her. The cuckoo is cooing like a procuress, with her throat delighted by having tasted the juice of numerous fruits. Rows of cages are suspended from pegs. Quails are incited to fight ; partridges are being made to talk ; caged pigeons are being set upon (each other) while this domestic peacock, looking as if decked with various kinds of gems, is, as it were, fanning the ( whole ) mansion heated with the sun's rays, with the flutter of his tail, as he dances about joyfully hither and thither. ( *Looking in another direction*). Here these pairs of royal swans, looking as if they were the moon's rays rolled up ( into that shape ), are walking behind lovely damsels, as though learning their gait ( *lit.* movement of feet ). And here these tame cranes are moving here and there, like aged eunuchs. Oh ! Wonderful ! An extensive scene is presented by the courtesan's collection of various kinds of birds ! To tell the truth, this mansion of the courtesan appears to me like the Nandana garden ( of Indra ) !—Please direct me ( further ), madam.

THE MAID—Come, sir; please enter this eighth quadrangle.

VID.—( *Entering and looking about* ). Girl, who is this person clad in a silken cloak and gorgeously decked with a superfluity of very wonderful ornaments, moving about haltingly and with distortions of the body ?

THE MAID—Sir, this is her ladyship's brother.

VID.—How much penance has a person to practise to become Vasantasena's brother ? Or rather,—

I must not ( think highly of him ). For, although he is gaily dressed, gentle, and well-perfumed, still he is to be shunned by the people, just like a *Champaka* tree growing in the enclosure of a cremation-ground, although it may be bright ( with blossoms ), attractive, and sweet-smelling. (29)

---

पादाभ्यां लक्षिता। 'करट्ट' इति पाठे अशौचाभ्यवहरणप्रयुक्तकरट्टब्राह्मणवत्। तत्किमितीमां प्रवेशयेत्यादि। अन्यथा अनेन द्वारेणास्या गृहे न प्रवेशः स्यादित्याशयः। एषा खल्वस्माकं माता चातुर्थिकेन ज्वरविशेषेण पीड्यते। तेनेदृशी दशेत्युक्तम्। [ चतुर्थे अहनि भवः चातुर्थिकः। 'कालाट्ठञ्' इत्यनेन ठञ्। 'ठस्येकः' इतीकादेशः। ]

(केत्तिअं तवच्चरणं कदुअ वसन्तसेणाए भादा भोदि । अध वा ।

मा दाव जइ वि एसो उज्जलो सिद्धिणो अ सुअन्धो अ ।
तह वि मसाणवीधीए जादो विअ चम्पअरुक्खो अणहिगमणिओ लोअस्स ॥)

(अन्यतोऽवलोक्य ।) भवति एषा पुनः का पुष्पप्रावारकप्रावृतोपानद्युगलनिक्षिप्त-तैलचिक्कणाभ्यां पादाभ्यामुच्चासन उपविष्टा तिष्ठति ।

(भोदि एसा उण का फुल्लपावारअपाउदा उवाणहजुअलणिक्खित्ततेल्लचिक्कणेहिं पादेहिं उच्चासणे उवविट्टा चिट्ठदि ।)

**चेटी**—आर्य एषा खल्वस्माकमार्याया माता । (अज्ज एसा क्खु अम्हाणं अज्जआए अत्तिआ ।)

**विदूषकः**—अहो अस्याः कपर्दकडाकिन्या उदरविस्तारः । तत्किमेतां प्रवेश्य महादेवमिव द्वारशोभेह गृहे निर्मिता । (अहो से कवट्ठडाइणीए[१] पोट्टवित्थारो । ता किं एदं पवेसिअ महादेवं विअ दुआरसोहा इह घरे णिम्मिदा ।)

**चेटी**—हताश मैवमुपहसास्माकं मातरम् । एषा खलु चातुर्थिकेन पीडयते । (हदास मा एव्वं उवहस अम्हाणं अत्तिअम् । एसा क्खु चाउत्थिएण पीडिअदि ।)

**विदूषकः**—(सपरिहासम् ।) भगवंश्चातुर्थिक एतेनोपकारेण मामपि ब्राह्मणमालोकय । (भअवं चाउत्थिअ एदिणा उवआरेण मं पि बम्हणं आलोएहि ।)

**चेटी**—हताश मरिष्यसि । (हदास मरिस्ससि ।)

**विदूषकः**—(सपरिहासम् ।) दास्याःपुत्रि वरमीदृशः शूनपीनजठरो मृत एव ।

**सीधुसुरासवमत्ता एतावदवस्थां गता हि माता ।**
**यदि म्रियतेऽत्र माता भवति श्रृगालसहस्रपर्याप्ता ॥** ३० ॥

भवति किं युष्माकं यानपात्राणि वहन्ति । (दासीएधीए[२] वरं ईदिसो शूणपीणजठरो मुदो ज्जेव ।

[३]सीहुसुरासवमत्तिआ एआवत्थं गदा हि अत्तिआ ।
जइ मरइ एत्थ अत्तिआ भोदि सिआलसहस्सपज्जत्तिआ ॥[४]

भोदि किं तुम्हाणं जाणवत्ता वहन्ति ।)

**चेटी**—आर्य न हि न हि । (अज्ज ण हि ण हि ।)

---

सपरिहासम् । शूणपीणजठरो शूनमुच्छूनं पीनं महाभोगं जठरं यस्य सः । **सीधुसुरासवेत्यादि** । उपजातिविशेषः । सीधुसुरासवा मदिराविशेषाः । [ 'सीधुरिक्षुरसैः पक्वैरपक्वैरासवं भवेत्' इति माधवः । ] एतावदवस्थामापन्नपीनत्वरूपां गता यदि म्रियतेऽत्र मृता भवति श्रृगालानां पर्याप्तिका सौहित्यम् ॥ ३० ॥ [ युष्माकं यान-

---

१ करट्ट (अपवित्र). २ आ दासी०. ३ सोधु. ४ ज्जत्तिआ (यात्रा).

(*Looking in another direction*). Girl, and who is this woman occupying a lofty seat, clad in a garment embroidered with flowers with her oil-greasy feet thrust into a pair of shoes ?

THE MAID—Sir, she is the mother of our mistress.

VID.—Oh ! How great is the expanse of the belly of this ugly she-ghoul ! What, then, was the beautiful entrance of this house constructed after she was set up here, as is done with a (huge) idol of Siva ?

THE MAID—You knave, you mustn't jeer at our mother in this fashion. She is suffering from a quartan fever.

VID—(*With a burst of laughter*). Holy quartan fever, look thou also upon me, a Brahmana, with such a favour !

THE MAID—You wretch, you will die then !

VID.—(*Jestingly*). Thou slave-born wench, better is a fat and bloated belly like this dead !

The mother has been reduced to such a condition, having intoxicated hereself with spirits, liquors and wines. If the mother were now to die, she would provide sufficient food for a thousand jackals ! (30)

Girl, have you any sailing vessels going abroad (for trade) ?

THE MAID—Sir, no, not at all.

---

पात्राणि पोतादीनि वाणिज्यार्थे वहन्ति किम् । अन्यथा कथमीदृशी संपदिति भावः ।] उद्वाहकेनार्जितविभवस्यैव परमियान्विस्तारो भवतीति प्रष्टुरभिप्रायः । [ परिच्छेदः एकदेशः । 'परिच्छदो विस्तारः' इति ल० दी० ] [ अच्छरीतयः सम्यक्प्रकाराः कुसुमप्रस्ताराः पुष्पोद्गमा येषां ते । निर्गतमन्तरं येषां ते निरन्तराः पादपाः युवतिजनजघनानुरूपप्रमाणा इत्यर्थः । पट्टनिर्मिता दोला पट्टदोला । सुवर्णानि चम्पकानि हरिचन्दनकुसुमानि वा । यूथिकादयः पुष्पविशेषाः । ] सर्वकुसुमप्रस्तारा पट्टदोला । लघूकरोतीव नन्दनवनस्य सश्रीकत्वम् । [ संध्यायते संध्यावदाचरति । ] **एष इत्यादि ।** गाथा । [ घना लोहितपङ्कस्य रुधिरकर्दमस्य ] चर्चा यस्य सः ॥ ३१ ॥ **गुणेति ।** [ गुणाः संगीतज्ञानं कलापाटवमित्यादयः कृत्रिमाः ते एव प्रवालाः पल्लवा यस्य तम् । विनय एव प्रशाखा मुख्यशाखा यस्य तम् । विश्रम्भः सर्वलोकानां विश्वास एव मूलं यस्य तम् । महनीयं पूज्यत्वं यश इत्यर्थः एव पुष्पं यस्य तम् । स्वगुणैः सहजैः गुणैः दयादाक्षिण्यकुलशीलादिभिः फलैः आढ्यं संपन्नम् । एवंविधं साधुः चारुदत्तः एव वृक्षस्तं सुहृद एव विहङ्गाः पक्षिणस्ते सुखमाश्रयन्ति अपि । भवादृशास्तं यथापूर्वं सेवन्ते किमित्यर्थः । रूपकमलंकारः । उपजातिश्छन्दः ] ।

**विदूषकः**—किं वाऽत्र पृच्छयते। युष्माकं खलु प्रेमनिर्मलजले मदनसमुद्रे स्तननितम्बजघनान्येव यानपात्राणि मनोहराणि। एवं वसन्तसेनाया बहुवृत्तान्तमष्ट-प्रकोष्ठं भवनं प्रेक्ष्य यत्सत्यं जानाम्येकस्थमिव त्रिविष्टपं दृष्टम्। प्रशंसितुं नास्ति मे वाग्विभवः। किं तावद्गणिकागृहमथ वा [१]कुबेरभवनपरिच्छेद इति। कुत्र युष्माकमार्या। (किं वा एत्थ पुच्छिअदि। तुम्हाणं क्खु पेम्मणिम्मलजले मअण-समुद्दे त्थणणिअम्बजहणा ज्जेव जाणवत्ता मणहरणा। एव्वं वसन्तसेणाए बहुवुत्तन्तं अट्टपओट्ठं भवणं पेक्खिअ जं सच्चं जाणामि एकत्थं विअ तिविट्ठअं दिट्ठम्। पसंसिदुं णत्थि मे वाआविहवो। किं दाव गणिआघरो अह वा कुबेरभवणपरिच्छेदो[१] त्ति। कहिं तुम्हाणं अज्जआ।)

**चेटी**—आर्य एषा वृक्षवाटिकायां तिष्ठति। यत्प्रविशत्वार्यः। (अज्ज एसा रुक्खवाडिआए चिट्ठदि। ता पविसदु अज्जो।)

**विदूषकः**—(प्रविश्य दृष्ट्वा च।) आश्चर्यं भोः। अहो वृक्षवाटिकायाः सश्रीकता। अच्छरीतिकुसुमप्रस्तारा रोपिता अनेकपादपाः निरन्तरपादपतलनिर्मिता युवतिजनजघनप्रमाणा पट्टदोला सुवर्णयूथिकाशेफालिकामालतीमल्लिकानवमालिका-कुरबकातिमुक्तकप्रभृतिकुसुमैः स्वयं निपतितैर्यत्सत्यं लघूकरोतीव नन्दनवनस्य सश्रीकताम्। (अन्यतोऽवलोक्य।) इतश्च उदयत्सूर्यसमप्रभैः कमलरक्तोत्पलैः संध्यायत इव दीर्घिका। अपि च।

> **एषोऽशोकवृक्षो नवनिर्गतकुसुमपल्लवो भाति।**
> **सुभट इव समरमध्ये घनलोहितपङ्कचर्चिकः॥ ३१॥**

भवतु। तत्कुत्र युष्माकमार्या। (ही ही भोः। अहो रुक्खवाडिआए सस्सिरीअदा। अच्छरीदिकुसुमपत्थारा[२] रोविदा अणेअपादवा [३]णिरन्तरपादवतलणिम्मिदा जुवदि-जणजहणप्पमाणा[४] पट्टदोला सुवण्णजूधिआसेहालिआमालईमल्लिआणोमालिआ-कुरबआअदिमोत्तअप्पहुदिकुसुमेहिं[५] सअं णिवडिदेहिं जं सच्चं लहुकरेदि विअ णन्दणवणस्स सस्सिरीअदम। इदो अ उदअन्तसूरसमप्पहेहिं कमलरत्तोप्पलेहिं संझाअदि विअ दीहिआ। अवि अ।

> एसो असोअवुच्छो [६]णवणिग्गअकुसुमपल्लवो भादि।
> सुभडो व्व समरमज्झे घणलोहिदपङ्कचच्चिक्को॥

भोदु। ता कहिं तुम्हाणं अज्जआ।)

**चेटी**—आर्य अवनमय दृष्टिम्। पश्यार्याम्। (अज्ज ओणामेहि दिट्ठिम्। पेक्ख अज्जअम्।)

**विदूषकः**—(दृष्ट्वा उपसृत्य।) स्वस्ति भवत्यै। (सोत्थि भोदीए।)

---

१ परिच्छदो. २ अच्छरीअकुसुमा जत्थ रोविदा (आश्चर्यकुसुमा यत्र रोपिताः) ३ णिरन्तरम्. ४ जव०. ५ कुरवआ. ६ णिग्गम (निर्गम).

VID.—Or rather, why ask a question in this matter? (For) surely, in this ocean of your passion, having affection for its pure waters, your beasts, hips and buttocks are themselves the charming sailing vessels! To tell the truth, having thus seen this mansion of Vasantasena with its eight quadrangles and its numerous appurtenances, I feel I have, as it were, seen the three worlds brought together in one spot. I have not the power of speech to praise it (as it deserves), whether (it should be called) a courtesan's house, or a portion of Kubera's palace. Where is your mistress?

THE MAID—Sir, here she is, in this garden; may your honour enter.

VID.—(*Entering and looking about*). Oh! Wonderful! How beautiful is this garden! Numerous trees have been planted here, that have put forth ample blossoms in a very charming manner. There is a silken swing, hung, beneath thickly-growing trees, and big enough to accommodate ladies' hips. To tell the truth, the garden throws into the back-ground as it were the beauty of (Indra's) Nandana garden, by means of the flowers that have spontaneously dropped down, of the *Champaka*, the *Yuthika*, the *Sephalika*, the *Malati*, the *Mallika*, the *Navamalika*, the *Kurabaka*, the *Atimukta* and other plants. (*Looking in another direction.*) And here this oblong well looks like (red) twilight as it were, owing to the lilies and the red lotuses (blooming therein), whose lustre resembles that of the rising sun. Moreover—

Here this Asoka tree, having recently put forth blossoms and foliage, looks like a brave warrior in the thick of the battle, amply splashed all over with clotted blood. (31)

Well, where is your mistress?

THE MAID—Sir, bring down your eyes, and you'll see her ladyship.

VID.—(*Seeing her and approaching*). My greetings, madam!

---

॥ ३२ ॥ अथ किम् अनुमतौ । राअवत्थहारी वार्त्तिकः शौण्डीर्येणाशयमहत्त्वेन । [हीनकुसुमादिति दारिद्र्यं गताच्चारुदत्ताद्रत्नावलीरूपस्यालंकारस्य प्राप्तिरित्यर्थः । अकाले दुर्दिनं मेघध्वान्तं सूर्यकिरणरोधकारि मेघमण्डलमित्यर्थः उन्नमति आविर्भवति ।] उदयन्त्विवति । [वर्षं वृष्टिः । अविरतमविश्रान्तम् । दयिताभिमुखेन प्रियगमनोत्सुकेन ॥ ३३ ॥ अत्र चारुदत्तानुरागः परमार्थः । अत्र चेटीवचनेन वसन्तसेनावाक्येन च अव्यवहितमेव पञ्चमाङ्कादौ वर्षर्तुवर्णनावतारः सूच्यते इति ल०दी० ।]

इति मदनिकाप्रदानो नाम चतुर्थोऽङ्कः ॥

**वसन्तसेना**—( संस्कृतमाश्रित्य । ) अये मैत्रेयः । ( उत्थाय । ) स्वागतम् । इदमासनम् । अत्रोपविश्यताम् ।

**विदूषकः**—उपविशतु भवति । (उपविसदु भोदी ।)

( उभावुपविशतः । )

**वसन्तसेना**—अपि कुशलं सार्थवाहपुत्रस्य ।

**विदूषकः**—भवति कुशलम् । (भोदी कुशलम् ।)

**वसन्तसेना**—आर्य मैत्रेय अपीदानीं

**गुणप्रवालं विनयप्रशाखं विश्रम्भमूलं महनीयपुष्पम् ।**
**तं साधुवृक्षं स्वगुणैः फलाढ्यं सुहृद्विहङ्गा सुखमाश्रयन्ति ॥ ३२ ॥**

**विदूषकः**—(स्वगतम् ।) सुष्ठूपलक्षितं दुष्टविलासिन्या । (प्रकाशम् ।) अथ किम् । (सुट्ठु उवलक्खिदं दुट्ठविलासिणीए । अध इं ।)

**वसन्तसेना**—अये किमागमनप्रयोजनम् ।

**विदूषकः**—श्रृणोतु भवती । तत्रभवांश्चारुदत्तः शीर्षेऽञ्जलिं कृत्वा भवतीं विज्ञापयति । ( सुणादु भोदी । तत्तभवं चारुदत्तो सीसे अञ्जलिं कदुअ भोदिं विण्णवेदि ।)

**वसन्तसेना**—(अञ्जलिं बद्ध्वा ।) किमाज्ञापयति ।

**विदूषकः**—मया तत्सुवर्णभाण्डं विश्रम्भादात्मीयमिति कृत्वा द्यूते हारितम् । स च सभिको राजवार्ताहारी न ज्ञायते कुत्र गत इति । ( मए तं सुवण्णभण्डअं विस्सम्भादो अत्तणकेरकेत्ति कदुअ जूदे हारिदम् । सो अ सहिओ राअवत्थहारी[१] ण जाणिअदि कहिं गदो त्ति ।)

**चेटी**—आर्ये दिष्टया वर्धसे । आर्यो द्यूतकरः संवृत्तः ( अज्जए दिट्ठआ वड्ढसि । अज्जो जूदिअरो संवुत्तो ।)

**वसन्तसेना**—(स्वगतम ।) कथं चौरेणापहृतमपि शौण्डीरतया द्यूते हारितमिति भणति । अतएव काम्यते । ( कधं चोरेण अवहिदं पि सोण्डीरदाए जूदे हारिदं त्ति भणादि । अदो ज्जेव कामीअदि ।)

**विदूषकः**—तत्तस्य कारणाद्गृह्णातु भवतीमां रत्नावलीम् । (ता तस्स कारणादो गेण्हदु भोदी एदं[२] रअणावलिम् ।)

**वसन्तसेना**—( आत्मगतम् । ) किं दर्शयामि तमलंकारम् । ( विचिन्त्य । ) अथ वा न तावत । (किं दंसेमि तं अलंकारअम् । अध वा ण दाव ।)

---

१ राआवत्थआरी (राजापथ्यकारी). २ इमं (इमां).

VAS.—(*Speaking in Sanskrit*). Oh ! Here's Maitreya ! (*Getting up* ). Welcome sir ! Here's a seat; pray be seated here.

VID.—You ( too ) may sit down.

( *Both sit down* )

VAS.—Is the merchant's son ( Charudatta ) all well ?

VID.—Madam, he is well.

VAS —Sir, Maitrey, do now

The birds in the form of friends happily resort to that tree in the form of a good man ?—the tree which has accomplishments for its foliage, modesty for its principal branches, (popular) trust for its root, and fame for its flowers, and which is richly endowed with fruits in the form of merits ? (32)

VID. (*To himself*). The roguish blonde has observed acutely ! ( *Aloud* ). Yes, ( so they do ).

VAS.—Now, what may be the object of your visit ?

VID.—May madam listen ! His honour Charudatta, placing his folded hands on his head, begs to say—

VAS.—( *Folding her hands* ).—What does he command ?

VID.—" I lost that golden casket at gambling, in the confident belief that it belonged to me. And I do not know where that gambling-master, the King's emissary, is gone (at present )."

THE MAID—I congratulate you, madam ! His honour has turned a gambler !

VAS.—( *To herself* ). How ! Although it was stolen by a thief, still he says, out of his magnanimity, that it was lost at play ! Hence it is that I love him !

VID.—"—So in exchange for that, your ladyship may kindly accept this jewel-necklace. "

VAS.—( *To herself* ). Shall I show him that ornament ? ( *Considering* ). Or rather, not so soon.

**विदूषकः**—किं तावन्न गृह्णाति भवत्येतां रत्नावलीम् । (किं दाव ण गेण्हदि भोदी एदं रअणावलीम् ।)

**वसन्तसेना**—( विहस्य[1] सखीमुखं पश्यन्ती । ) मैत्रेय कथं न ग्रहीष्यामि रत्नावलीम् । (इति गृहीत्वा पार्श्वे स्थापयति । स्वगतम् ।) कथं हीनकुसुमादपि सहकारपादपान्मकरन्दबिन्दवो निपतन्ति । (प्रकाशम् ।) आर्य विज्ञापय तं द्यूतकरं मम वचनेनार्यचारुदत्तम्—अहमपि प्रदोष आर्यं प्रेक्षितुमागच्छामीति । (मित्तेअ कधं ण गेण्हिस्सं रअणावलिम् । कधं झीणकुसुमादो वि सहआरपादवादो मअरन्दबिन्दओ णिवडन्ति । अज्ज विण्णवेहि तं जूदिअरं मम वअणेण अज्जचारुदत्तम्—अहं पि पदोसे अज्जं पेक्खिदुं आअच्छामि[2] त्ति ।)

**विदूषकः**—( स्वगतम् । ) किमन्यत्तत्र गत्वा ग्रहीष्यति । ( प्रकाशम् । ) भवति भणामि । ( स्वगतम् । )—निवर्ततामस्माद्गणिकाप्रसङ्गादिति । ( इति निष्क्रान्तः ।) (किं अण्णं तहिं गदुअ गेण्हिस्सदि । भोदि भणामि ।—णिअत्तीअदु इमादो गणिआपसङ्गादो त्ति ।)

**वसन्तसेना**—चेटि गृहाणैतमलंकारम् । चारुदत्तमभिरन्तुं गच्छावः । (हञ्जे गेण्ह एदं अलंकारअम् । चारुदत्तं अहिरमिदुं गच्छम्ह । )

**चेटी**—आर्ये पश्य पश्य । उन्नमत्यकालदुर्दिनम् । (अज्जए पेक्ख पेक्ख । उण्णमदि अकालदुद्दिणम् ।)

[3]**वसन्तसेना**—

**उदयन्तु नाम मेघा भवतु निशा वर्षमविरतं पततु ।**
**गणयामि नैव सर्वं दयिताभिमुखेन हृदयेन ॥ ३३ ॥**

चेटि हारं गृहीत्वा लघ्वागच्छ । (हञ्जे हारं गेण्हिअ लहुं[4] आअच्छ ।)

(इति निष्क्रान्ताः सर्वे ।)

[5]**मदनिकाशर्विलको नाम चतुर्थोऽङ्कः ।**

---

१ इदं नास्ति क्वचित्. २ आगमिस्समिति. ३ अस्मात्परं—' संस्कृतमाश्रित्य इत्यधिकं क्वचित्. ४ लहु लहु. ५ मृच्छकटिके. ०टिकप्रकरणे चतु०.

VID.—What then ? Is not your ladyship disposed to accept this jewel-necklace ?

VAS.—( *Laughs; looking at the face of her* Maid ) O Maitreya, how shall I not accept the jewel-necklace ( *Taking it keeps it by her side; and to herself* ). How ! Even from the mango-tree denuded of all blossoms there still do fall drops of honey ! ( *Aloud* ). Sir, please tell the worthy Charudatta, the gambler, in my name, that I too shall be visiting him this evening.

VID.—(*To himself*). What other thing will she get by going there ? ( *Aloud* ). Lady, I will tell him. ( *To himself* ).—That he should refrain from having anything to do with this courtesan. (*Exit*).

VAS.—-Girl, keep this ornament. We shall ( now ) go to sport in the company of Charudatta.

THE MAID—Lady, look, look here; an untimely storm is gathering ( in the sky ).

VAS.—

Let clouds gather as they will; let it turn night; ( or ) let rain fall incessantly. With my heart yearning for my beloved, I care not for all of them. (33)

Girl, take a garland and come quickly.

( *Exeunt Omnes* )

*End of the Act IV, Styled*

'Madanika and Sarvilaka'

# पञ्चमोऽङ्कः ।

(ततः प्रविशत्यासनस्थः सोत्कण्ठश्चारुदत्तः ।)

**चारुदत्तः**—( ऊर्ध्वमवलोक्य । ) उन्नमत्यकालदुर्दिनम् । यदेतत्

**आलोकितं गृहशिखण्डिभिरुत्कलापै-**
**र्हंसैर्यियासुभिरपाकृतमुन्मनस्कैः**[1] **।**
**आकालिकं सपदि दुर्दिनमन्तरिक्ष-**
**मुत्कण्ठितस्य हृदयं च समं रुणद्धि ॥ १ ॥**

अपि च ।

**मेघो जलार्द्रमहिषोदरभृङ्गनीलो**
**विद्युत्प्रभारचितपीतपटोत्तरीयः ।**
**आभाति संहतबलाकगृहीतशङ्खः**
**खं केशवोऽपर इवाक्रमितुं प्रवृत्तः ॥ २ ॥**

---

पूर्वाङ्केऽङ्कावतारेणैव सूचितस्य प्रकरणनायकस्य प्रवेशः । * [ अत्राङ्के तावदासमाप्ति वर्षर्तुवर्णनं चारुदत्तेन वसन्तसेनाया च विटेन च यथायथं क्रियते । तदिदं वसन्तसेनाचारुदत्तयोरन्योनानुरागोद्दीपनविभावत्वेनावतरतीति ध्येयम् इति ल० दी० ।] [ अधुना पूर्वाङ्कान्ते सूचितं वसन्तसेनाया अभिसारिकावेषेण चारुदत्ताभिसरणमुपक्षेप्तुं पूर्वाङ्कान्तसूचितस्य नायकस्य प्रवेशं निर्दिशति-ततः प्रविशतीत्यादिना । सोत्कण्ठः वसन्तसेनाविषयकोत्कण्ठासहित इत्यर्थः । इत आरम्याङ्कसमाप्ति यावद्गर्भसंधिः ।] **आलोकितमिति** । [ उद्गतः कलापो येषां तैः उत्कलापैः उन्नमितबर्हैः गृहशिखण्डिभिः आलोकितम् । उन्मनस्कैः उत्कण्ठितैः यियासुभिः मानसं सरो

---

*अस्मात्परं—तथा चोक्तम्—'प्रवेशश्चूलिका चैव तथा विष्कम्भकोऽपरः । अङ्कावतारोऽङ्कमुखमर्थोपक्षेपपञ्चकम् ॥' इति । प्रवेशयतीति प्रवेशः । पचाद्यच् । प्रवेशको ण्वुलन्त उच्यते । अधमपात्रप्रयोज्यः प्रवेशकः । तदुक्तम्—'भृत्यवर्गकथावच्च कर्तव्यस्तु प्रवेशकः । अन्तर्जवनिकासंस्थैस्तथा मागधबन्दिभिः ॥ अर्थोपक्षेपणं यत्र क्रियते सा हि चूलिका ॥ विष्कम्भस्तु द्विधा सोऽयं शुद्धः संकीर्ण एव च । शुद्धो मध्यमपात्रेण संकीर्णो मध्यमाधमैः ॥' इति ॥—इत्यधिको ग्रन्थष्टीकायामुपलभ्यमानोऽप्यनुपयोगित्वान्नात्र निवेशितः ।

---

१ उपाकृत.

## Act. V

( *Then enter seated love-sick* Charudatta ).

CHAR.—( *Looking upward* ). An untimely storm is gathering. For here this,

Untimely storm, which is ( joyfully ) gazed upon by the tame peacocks with their uplifted tails, and is disliked by the distressed swans who are about to depart ( to the Manasa lake ). quickly pervades the sky, and also ( pervades, i. e. afflicts ) at the same time the heart of a lover. (1)

Moreover—

The cloud, looking dark like a bee or like the belly of a buffalo wet with water, wearing an upper garment of yellow silk constituted by the flash of lightning, and bearing conches in the form of serried flocks of cranes, is about to traverse the sky, as though it were a second Vishnu ( who is dark like &c., wears an upper garment of yellow silk like the flash of lighting, and has in his hand a conch white and looking like a flock of cranes ). (2)

---

गन्तुमिच्छुभिः हंसैः ] अपाकृतं निरस्तम् । अनभिनन्दितमिति यावत् । [ अकाले भवम् आकालिकम् । 'कालाट्ठञ्' इति ठञ् । दुर्दिनं मेघावरणं सपदि अन्तरिक्ष उत्कण्ठितस्य विरहिजनस्य हृदयं च समं रुणद्धि व्याप्नोति । सहोक्तिरलंकारः । वसन्ततिलकं वृत्तम् ] ॥ १ ॥ मेघ इति । [ जलेनार्द्रं जलार्द्रं च तन्महिषोदरं च जलार्द्रमहिषोदरं भृङ्गश्च तद्वन्नीलः । महिषस्य स्वतः श्यामत्वेऽपि जलार्द्रस्यातिश्यामलता ततोऽप्युदरदेशे नैलाधिक्यमिति तथा ग्रहणम् । विद्युत्प्रभया रचितं पीतपटवदुत्तरीयं यस्य । पक्षे विद्युत्प्रभा इव रचितं पीतपटः पीताम्बरमेव उत्तरीयं येन । संहताः बलाका बका एव गृहीतः शङ्खः येन । अत्र बलाकशब्दः पुंलिङ्गः । 'बलाकश्च बको मतः' इति विश्वशाश्वतौ । पक्षे संहतबलाकवद् गृहीतः शङ्खः पाञ्चजन्यो येन । एतादृशो मेघः अपरः केशव इव खमाकाशमाक्रमितुं प्रवृत्तः । उत्प्रेक्षालंकारः । यद्वा अपरः केशवः वामनावतारः विष्णुरिव खमाक्रमितुं प्रवृत्तः । एतत्पक्षे उपमालंकारः । वृत्तं पूर्वोक्तम् ॥ २ ॥ उक्तार्थमेव भङ्ग्यन्तरेणाह—**केशवेत्यादि** । केशवगात्रश्यामः । कुटिला चासौ बलाकावली च तया रचितः शङ्खो येन । विद्युद्गुण एव कौशेयं यस्य सः । मेघः चक्रधरो विष्णुरिवोन्नतः । उपमालंकारः । आर्या

अपि च ।

केशवगात्रश्यामः कुटिलबलाकावलीरचितशङ्खः ।
[१]विद्युद्गुणकौशेयश्चक्रधर इवोन्नतो मेघः ॥ ३ ॥

एता निषिक्तरजतद्रवसंनिकाशा
धारा जवेन पतिता जलदोदरेभ्यः ।
विद्युत्प्रदीपशिखया क्षणदृष्टनष्टा-[२]
श्छिन्ना इवाम्बरपटस्य दशाः पतन्ति ॥ ४ ॥

संसक्तैरिव चक्रवाकमिथुनैर्हंसैः प्रडीनैरिव
व्याविद्धैरिव मीनचक्रमकरैर्हर्म्यैरिव प्रोच्छ्रितैः ।
तैस्तैराकृतिविस्तरैरनुगतैर्मेघैः समभ्युन्नतैः
पत्रच्छेद्यमिवेह भाति गगनं [३]विश्लेषितैर्वायुना ॥ ५ ॥

एतत्तद्धृतराष्ट्रचक्रसदृशं[४] मेघान्धकारं नभो
हृष्टो गर्जति चातिदर्पितबलो दुर्योधनो वा शिखी ।
अक्षद्यूतजितो युधिष्ठिर इवाध्वानं[५] गतः कोकिलो
हंसाः संप्रति पाण्डवा इव वनादज्ञातचर्यां[६] गताः ॥ ६ ॥

(विचिन्त्य ।) चिरः खलु कालो मैत्रेयस्य वसन्तसेनायाः सकाशं गतस्य । नाद्या-प्यागच्छति ।

---

छन्दः ॥ ३ ॥ एता इति । निषिक्तः स्रावितः यः रजतद्रवः तस्य सदृश्यः ०द्रव-संनिकाशाः । जलदोदरेभ्यः जवेन वेगेन पतिताः । विद्युदेव प्रदीपशिखा तया क्षणं दृष्टाः पश्चान्नष्टाः । एता धारा वर्षोदकस्येति शेषः । छिन्ना अम्बरमेव पटः तस्य दशा अग्राणीव पतन्ति । वसन्ततिलकं वृत्तम् ॥ ४ ॥ संसक्तैरिति । संसक्तैः अन्योन्यं मिलितैः चक्रवाकमिथुनैः इव । प्रडीनैः उत्पतितैः हंसैः इव । व्याविद्धैः समुद्रक्षोभादितस्ततः उत्क्षिप्तैः मीनचक्रैः मकरैश्च । प्रोच्छ्रितैः ऊर्ध्वं गतैः हर्म्यैः इव । एतादृशैः तैस्तैः बहुविधैः आकृतिविस्तरैः अनुगतैः प्राप्तानेकाकृतिविस्तरैरिति यावत् । समभ्युन्नतैः वायुना विश्लेषितैश्च मेघैः इह एतद्भूतलोर्ध्वभागे गगनं पत्रच्छेद्यमिव पत्रच्छेदैर्घटितं चित्रमालेख्यमिव भाति । उपमालंकारः । शार्दूलविक्रीडितं छन्दः । ] प्रडीनैरिति कर्मणि क्तः । व्याविद्धैर्भ्रान्तैः चक्रं समूहः । पत्रस्य छेदः खण्डनं विचल यत्र चित्रे तत्पत्रछेद्यं चित्रम् । तदिव गगनं शोभते ॥ ५ ॥ एतदिति । [ मेघैरन्धकारो यस्मिन् तद् एतन्नभः । तत्प्रसिद्धं धृतराष्ट्रचक्रं कौरवकटकं तेन सदृशम् । 'सादृश्यं चानयोराभूवियन्मण्डलमन्धकारकारित्वेन विनष्टचन्द्रार्कतया च बोध्यम्' इति ल० दी० । ०वक्त्र० इति पाठे धृतराष्ट्रवक्त्रे दृष्टिशून्यत्वादन्ध-

---

१ विद्युद्गण. २ नष्टदृष्टाः—दष्टाः. ३ विश्लेषितं. ४ वक्त्र. ५ वारण्यं. ६ चर्यं.

Moreover—

There rises forth a cloud, dark like the body of Vishnu, forming an appearance of conches by means of the crooked lines of cranes, and having the ( yellow ) siken mantle in the form of the streaks of lightning,—as though it were Vishnu ( *lit.* the discus-bearer ) himself, ( who is called Kesava and is dark-bodied, who wields a conch white and shaped like a curved line of cranes, and who wears a silken garment made of threads bright like streaks of lightning ). ( 3 )

Here these streams of water, resembling ( downpours of ) molten silver, dropped rapidly from the interiors of clouds, fall, like the rent hems of the garment of the sky, seen for a moment in ( the light of ) the flame of the lamp of lightning, and then lost ( to view ). ( 4 )

This sky looks as if it had been adorned with decorative paintings ( of leafy lines ), owing to the high-soaring clouds, scattered by the wind, and assuming various expansive shapes (some) resembling thronging couples of *Chakravaka* birds, ( some ) flying swans, ( some ) alligators and fish-swarms thrown about pell-mell, and ( some ) lofty mansions. ( 5 )

Here is this sky, darkened with clouds, that resembles the army of the Kauravas ( producing a darkness like that of the clouds ). This peacock, greatly flushed with the pride of his vigour, is shouting in glee, like Duryodhana whose army was mightily proud. The cuckoo has ceased cooing, like Yudhishthira taking to the path ( of the forest ) when conquered at dice-play. And, on account of the ( muddy ) water, the swans have now gone off to dwell in an unknown place, like the Pandavas living incognito after leaving the forest. (6)

(*Reflecting*). It is a long time since Maitreya went to Vasantasena. How is it that he does not come even now ?

---

कारः । नभसि सूर्यचन्द्रमसोरिति सादृश्यम् । अतिदर्पितं बलं सारः यस्य स शिखी मयूरः । अतिदर्पितं बलं सैन्यं यस्य स दुर्योधनः वा इव । वा शब्द इवार्थे । गर्जति । अक्षद्यूते जितः युधिष्ठिरः अध्वानं वनमार्गमिव कोकिलः अध्वानं ध्वनिराहित्यं गतः । संप्रति हंसा वनात् जलाद्धेतोः पाण्डवा वनादरण्यवासादिव अज्ञातचर्यां गताः । मानसं सरो गता अदृश्या अभवन्नित्यर्थः । ] धृतराष्ट्रवक्त्रसदृशं नष्टचन्द्रार्कत्वात् । वा इवार्थे । शिखी मयूरः । वनादिति ल्यब्लोपे कर्मणि पञ्चमी ।

(प्रविश्य)

**विदूषकः**—अहो गणिकाया लोभोऽदक्षिणता च यतो न कथाऽपि कृताऽन्या। अनेकधा स्नेहानुसारं भणित्वा किमप्येवमेव गृहीता रत्नावली। एतावत्या ऋद्धया न तयाऽहं भणितः—आर्य मैत्रेय विश्रम्यताम्। मल्लकेन पानीयमपि पीत्वा गम्यतामिति। तन्मा तावद्दास्याःपुत्र्या गणिकाया मुखमपि द्रक्ष्यामि। (सनिर्वेदम्।) सुष्ठु खलूच्यते—अकन्दसमुत्थिता पद्मिनी अवञ्चको वणिक् अचौरः सुवर्णकारः अकलहो ग्रामसमागमः अलुब्धा गणिकेति दुष्करमेते संभाव्यन्ते। तत्प्रियवयस्यं गत्वाऽस्माद्गणिकाप्रसङ्गान्निवर्तयामि। (परिक्रम्य दृष्ट्वा।) कथं प्रियवयस्यो वृक्षवाटिकायामुपविष्टस्तिष्ठति। तद्यावदुपसर्पामि। (उपसृत्य।) स्वस्ति भवते। वर्धतां भवान्। (अहो गणिआए लोभो अदक्खिणदा अ जदो ण कधा वि किदा अण्णा। अणेकहा[1] सिणेहाणुसारं भणिअ किं पि एअमेअ गहिदा रअणावली। एत्तिआए ऋद्धीए ण तए अहं[2] भणिदो—अज्ज मित्तेअ वीसमीअदु। मल्लकेण[3] पाणीअं पि पिबिअ गच्छीअदुत्ति। ता मा दाव दासीएधीआए गणिआए मुहं पि पेक्खिस्सम्। सुष्ठु क्खु वुच्चदि—अकन्दसमुत्थिता पउमिणी अवञ्चओ वाणिओ अचोरो सुवण्णआरो अकलहो गामसमागमो अलुद्धा गणिआ त्ति दुक्करं एदे संभावीअन्ति। ता पिअवअस्सं गदुअ इमादो गणिआपसङ्गादो णिवत्तावेमि। कधं पिअवअस्सो रुक्खवाडिआए उवविट्ठो चिट्ठदि। ता जाव उवसप्पामि। सोत्थि भवदे[4]। वड्ढदु भवम्।)

**चारुदत्तः**—(विलोक्य।) अये सुहृन्मे[5] मैत्रेयः प्राप्तः। वयस्य स्वागतम्। आस्यताम्।

**विदूषकः**—उपविष्टोऽस्मि। (उवविट्ठो[6] म्हि।)

**चारुदत्तः**—वयस्य कथय तत्कार्यम्।

**विदूषकः**—तत्खलु कार्यं विनष्टम्। (तं क्खु कज्जं विणट्टम्।)

**चारुदत्तः**—किं[7] तया न गृहीता रत्नावली।

**विदूषकः**—कुतोऽस्माकमेतावद्भागधेयम्। नवनलिनकोमलमञ्जलिं मस्तके कृत्वा प्रतीष्टा। (कुदो अम्हाणं एत्तिअं[8] भाअधेअम्[9]। णवणलिणकोमलं अञ्जलिं मत्थए कदुअ पडिच्छिआ।)

**चारुदत्तः**—तत्किं ब्रवीषि विनष्टमिति।

**विदूषकः**—भो कथं न विनष्टं यदभुक्तपीतस्य चौरैरपहृतस्याल्पमूल्यस्य सुवर्णभाण्डस्य कारणाच्चतुःसमुद्रसारभूता रत्नमाला हारिता। (भो कधं ण विणट्टं जं अभुत्तपीदस्स चोरेहिं अवहिदस्स अप्पमुल्लस्स सुअण्णभण्डअस्स कारणादो चदुस्समुद्दसारभूदा रअणमाला हारिदा।)

---

१ अणाअरेण ज्जेव अभणिअ किं पि एअमेअ इ. (अनादरेणैवाभणित्वा किमप्येवमेव इ.). २ एवं पि. ३ मल्ल०. ४ भो ते. ५ कथं सु०. ६ ०विठ्ठोम्हि. ७ किं न. ८ एत्तिआ. ९ भागधेआ.

( *Entering*) .

VID.—Oh, the greed and the want of courtesy of that courtesan, that she did not even talk about anything else ! She spoke variously about something in a manner befitting her affection and thus accepted the jewel-necklace. With all that wealth she did not say to me—" Sir Maitreya, rest yourself ( here ); you may depart after you have drunk water at least, in a cup. " Never then shall I so much as even look at the face of that slave-born harlot ! ( *Sorrowfully* ). Truly do they say: " A lotus-plant that grows without a root; a tradesman that does not cheat; a goldsmith that doesn't steal; a village-meeting that is without a quarrel; and a courtesan that is not avaricious;—these are hard to be found ( or conceived )." So I'll go to my friend and dissuade him from this his attachment to that courtesan. ( *Walking about and observing* ). How ! Here's my dear friend sitting in the garden. Well, I'll approach him. ( *Approaching* ). My greetings to you ! May you prosper !

CHAR.—( *Seeing* ). Ah ! My friend Maitreya has come ! Welcome, friend ! Pray be seated.

VID.—I have taken my seat.

CHAR.—Friend, tell me about that business.

VID.—Well, that business has failed !

CHAR.—What, did she not accept that jewel-necklace ?

VID.—Whence could we have so much luck ! She took it, placing on her head her folded hands delicate like fresh water-lilies.

CHAR.—Then how do you say that the business failed ?

VID.—Friend, how has it not failed, since you have given away the jewel-necklace, the very essence ( as it were ) of the four oceans, in exchange for a golden casket of ( comparatively ) little value, that we neither ate nor drank, and that was stolen by thieves ?

---

वनं प्राप्येत्यर्थः ॥ ६ ॥ पाठान्तरे–नैव कथा कथं हारितमलंकारभाण्डमित्यादिका नैव कथानुसारः कुतोऽस्या रत्नावल्या भाव इत्यादिकः । मल्लको भाजनविशेषः । तन्मा तावत् । यद्भोजनाद्यर्थमपि न तथा भणितोऽहम् । चोरैरेवापहृतस्य । **यमिति** । [तु. २९ श्लो. द्रष्टव्यः] ॥७॥ बहुप्रत्यवायात् बहवः प्रत्यवाया दोषा यत्र तस्मात् ।

**चारुदत्तः**—वयस्य मा मैवम्[१]।

> यं समालम्ब्य विश्वासं न्यासोऽस्मासु तया कृतः।
> तस्यैतन्महतो मूल्यं[२] प्रत्ययस्यैव दीयते ॥ ७ ॥

**विदूषकः**—भो वयस्य एतदपि मे द्वितीयं संतापकारणं यत्सखीजनदत्तसंज्ञया पटान्तापवारितं मुखं कृत्वाहऽमुपहसितः तदहं ब्राह्मणो भूत्वेदानीं भवन्तं शीर्षेण पतित्वा विज्ञापयामि—निवर्त्यतामात्माऽस्माद्बहुप्रत्यवायाद्गणिकाप्रसङ्गात्। गणिका नाम पादुकान्तरप्रविष्टेव लेष्टुका दुःखेन पुनर्निराक्रियते। अपि च भो वयस्य गणिका हस्ती कायस्थो भिक्षुश्चाटो रासभश्च यत्रैते निवसन्ति तत्र दुष्टा अपि न जायन्ते। (भो वअस्स एदं पि मे दुदिअं[३] संतावकारणं जं सहीअणदिण्णसण्णाए पडन्तोवारिदं[४] मुहं कदुअ अहं उवहसिदो[५]। ता अहं बम्हणो भविअ दाणिं भवन्तं सीसेण पडिअ विण्णवेमि—णिवत्तीअदु अप्पा इमादो बहुपच्चवाआदो गणिआपसङ्गादो। गणिआ णाम पादुअन्तरप्पविट्टा विअ लेठ्ठुआ दुक्खेण उण णिराकरीअदि। अवि अ भो वअस्स गणिआ हत्थी काअत्थओ भिक्खु चाटो रासहो अ जहिं एदे णिवसन्ति तहिं दुट्टा वि ण जाअन्ति।)

**चारुदत्तः**—वयस्य अलमिदानीं सर्वं[६] परिवादमुक्त्वा। अवस्थयैवास्मि निवारितः। पश्य।

> वेगं करोति तुरगस्त्वरितं प्रयातुं
> प्राणव्ययान्न चरणास्तु तथा वहन्ति।
> सर्वत्र यान्ति पुरुषस्य चलाः स्वभावाः
> खिन्नास्ततो[७] हृदयमेव पुनर्विशन्ति ॥ ८ ॥

अपि च वयस्य।

> यस्यार्थास्तस्य सा कान्ता धनहार्यो ह्यसौ जनः।

(स्वगतम्।) न गुणहार्यो ह्यसौ जनः (प्रकाशम्।)

> वयमर्थैः परित्यक्ता ननु त्यक्तैव सा मया ॥ ९ ॥

**विदूषकः**—(अधोऽवलोक्य। स्वगतम्।) यथैष ऊर्ध्वं प्रेक्ष्य दीर्घं निःश्वसिति तथा तर्कयामि मया विनिवार्यमाणस्याधिकतरं वृद्धाऽस्योत्कण्ठा। तत्सुष्ठु खल्वेवमुच्यते—कामो वाम इति। (प्रकाशम्।) भो वयस्य भणितं च तया—भण चारुदत्तमद्य प्रदोषे मयाऽत्रागन्तव्यमिति। तत्तर्कयामि रत्नावल्याऽपरितुष्टाऽपरं याचितुमागमिष्यतीति। (जधा एसो उद्धं पेक्खिअ दीहं णिस्ससदि तधा तक्केमि मए विणिवारिअन्तस्य अधिअदरं वड्ढिदा से उक्कण्ठा। ता सुठ्ठु क्खु एव्वं वुच्चदि—कामो वामो त्ति। भो वअस्स भणिदं अ ताए—भणेहि चारुदत्तं अज्ज पओसे मए एत्थ आअन्तव्वं त्ति। ता तक्केमि रअणावलीए अपरितुट्ठा अवरं मग्गिदुं आअमिस्सदि त्ति।)

---

१ मैवम् पश्य. २ मौल्यं. ३ दुदिअस०. ४ पडन्ताबवारिदं. ५ ०सिदोम्हि. ६ सर्वंपरि०. ७ तदा.

CHAR.—Nay, friend, say not so!

This price is being paid, ( not for that ornament, but ) for that high trust, by relying on which she kept that deposit with us. (7)

VID.—O friend, I have this another reason, too, for being angry, inasmuch as she made a sign to her maid, and, veiling her face with the end of her garment, she laughed derisively at me. So I, being a Brahmana, now bow to you with my bent head and request you that you should turn yourself away from this affair with that courtesan, which is full of many pitfalls. A courtesan is just like a pebble got inside a shoe, that is got rid of afterwards with great difficulty. Moreover, O friend, a courtesan, an elephant, a Kayastha ( a scribe ), a mendicant, a spy and a donkey,—where these dwell, there not even villains can flourish.

CHAR.—Friend, now you need no longer give vent to all these strictures; I am warded off ( from that pursuit ) by my condition itself. See :

A ( wearied ) horse puts on speed to go quickly, but his legs do not move to that extent for want of vigour. ( Similarly ), the volatile desires of a man wander everywhere ( *i. e.* aspire to everything ), but, weary ( at failure ), they afterwards enter once more ( *i. e.* lie dormant ) in his bosom. (8)

Moreover, friend,—

Whoever has riches, will have that lady; for she is to be bought with money.

( *To himself* ). No; she is surely to be bought with merits! ( *Aloud* ).—

But riches have left me; she therefore is, of course, left by me. (9)

VID.—( *Looking down; to himself* ). Since he is looking upward and sighing deeply, I conclude that his passion must have become still more inflamed as I tried to dissuade him. So it has been truly said that " Love is perverse. " ( *Aloud* ). O friend, she also said : " Tell Charudatta that I shall visit him there this evening. " So I guess that not being satisfied with that jewel-necklace, she is coming to demand something in addition.

---

चाटो क्षुद्रविषयभोक्ता । न जायन्ते वृद्धिं गच्छन्ति । **वेगमिति** । [ तुरगस्त्वरितं प्रयातुं वेगं करोति किं तु प्राणव्ययात् शक्तिक्षयात् तस्य चरणाः तथा वेगानुरूपं न

**चारुदत्तः**—वयस्य आगच्छतु । परितुष्टा यास्यति ।

**चेटः**—(प्रविश्य ।) अवेत मानवाः ।

**यथा यथा वर्षत्यभ्रखण्डं तथा तथा तिम्यति पृष्ठचर्म ।**
**यथा यथा लगति शीतवातस्तथा तथा वेपते मे हृदयम् ॥ १० ॥**

( प्रहस्य । )

**वंशं वादयामि सप्तच्छिद्रं सुशब्दं वीणां वादयामि सप्ततन्त्रीं नदन्तीम् ।**
**गीतं गायामि गर्दभस्यानुरूपं को मे गाने तुम्बुरुर्नारदो वा ॥ ११ ॥**

आज्ञप्तोऽस्म्यार्यया वसन्तसेनया—कुम्भीलक गच्छ त्वं ममागमनमार्यचारुदत्तस्य निवेदयेति । तद्यावदार्यचारुदत्तस्य गेहं गच्छामि । (परिक्रम्य प्रविष्टकेन दृष्ट्वा ।) एष चारुदत्तो वृक्षवाटिकायां तिष्ठति । एषोऽपि स दुष्टबटुकः । तद्यावदुपसर्पामि । कथमाच्छादितं द्वारं वृक्षवाटिकायाः । भवतु । एतस्य दुष्टबटुकस्य संज्ञां ददामि । ( इति लोष्टगुटिकाः[1] क्षिपति ।) (अवेध माणहे ।

जधा जधा वश्शदि अब्भखण्डे तधा तधा तिम्मदि पुट्ठिचम्मे ।
जधा जधा लग्गदि शीदवादे तधा तधा वेवदि मे हलक्के[2] ॥
वंशं वाए शत्तछिद्दं शुशद्दं वीणं वाए शत्ततन्ति णदन्ति ।
गीअं गाए गद्दहश्शाणुलूअं के मे गाणे तुम्बुलू णालदे वा ॥

आणतम्हि अज्जआए वशन्तशेणाए—कुम्भीलआ गच्छ तुमं मम आगमणं अज्जचारुदत्तश्श णिवेदेहि त्ति । ता जाव अज्जचारुदत्तश्श गेहं गच्छामि । एशे चालुदत्ते रुक्खवाडिआए चिट्ठदि । एशे वि शे दुट्ठबडुके । ता जाव उपशप्पेमि । कधं ढक्किदे दुवाले रुक्खवाडिआए । भोदु । एदश्श दुट्ठबडुकश्श शण्णं देमि ।)

**विदूषकः**—अये क इदानीमेष प्राकारवेष्टितमिव कपित्थं मां लोष्टकैस्ताडयति । (अए को दाणिं एसो पाआरवेट्ठिदं विअ कइत्थं मं लोट्टकेहिं ताडेदि[3] ।

**चारुदत्तः**—आरामप्रासादवेदिकायां क्रीडद्भिः पारावतैः पातितं भवेत् ।

**विदूषकः**—दास्याःपुत्र दुष्टपारावत तिष्ठ तिष्ठ यावदेतेन दण्डकाष्ठेन सुपक्वमिव चूतफलमस्मात्प्रासादाद्भूमौ पातयिष्यामि । (इति दण्डकाष्ठमुद्यम्य धावति ।) (दासीएपुत्त[4] दुट्ठपारावअ चिट्ठ चिट्ठ जाव एदिणा दण्डकट्ठेण सुपक्कं विअ चूअफलं इमादो पासादादो भूमीए पाडइस्सम् ।)

---

वहन्ति । पुरुषस्य चलाः स्वभावा मनोवृत्तयः सर्वत्र सर्वेषु विषयेषु यान्ति । ततः खिन्नाः अलब्धकामत्वात्खेदं प्राप्ताः पुनः उत्पत्तिस्थानं हृदयमेव प्रविशन्ति । तत्रैव विलीयन्ते इत्यर्थः । वसन्ततिलकं वृत्तम् ]॥ ८ ॥ **यस्येति** । असौ जनः गणिका वसन्तसेना ॥ ९ ॥ [ कामो वाम इति । तदुक्तं रामायणे—‘ वामः कामो मनुष्याणां

---

१ गुटिकां. २ हडक्के. ३ सीसे ताडेदि.

CHAR.—Friend, let her come. She will go satisfied.

CHETA—( *Entering* ) Listen, (all) people !

The more the bank of clouds rains, the more wet does the skin of my back become; and the more the cold wind beats, the more does my heart quake. (10)

( *Laughing loudly* ).

I can play upon the loud-sounding flute with seven holes and ( also ) upon the resounding lute with seven strings. I can sing songs just like an ass. What is Tumburu or Narada as compared to me, in singing ? (11)

I am ordered by her ladyship Vasantasena :—" Kumbhilaka, go and inform the worthy Charudatta of my arrival " So I'll go to the house of the noble Charudatta. ( *Walks about ; entering and seeing* ). Here is Charudatta, seated in his garden. Here, too, is that rascally fellow. Well, then, I'll approach them. How ! The gate of the garden is closed ! Never mind ; I'll make a sign to this rascally chap. ( *Throws lumps of mud.* )

VID.—Ah ! Who is this here that is now pelting me with clods, as if I were a *Kapittha* tree enclosed within a fence ?

CHAR.—Perhaps ( a clod ) might have been let fall by the pigeons playing on the terrace of the garden-house.

VID—You slave-born wretch of a pigeon, you just wait till with this wooden staff I fell you on the ground from off this house, as if you were a ripe mango-fruit ! ( *Lifts his wooden staff and runs* ).

---

यस्मिन्किल निबध्यते । जने तस्मिन्ननुक्रोशः स्नेहश्च किल जायते ॥' इति ।] अवेत अवगच्छत मानवाः । यथा यथेति । उपेन्द्रवज्रया श्लोकः । अभ्रखण्डं [ मेघशकलं मेघसमहो वा ।] तिम्यति आर्द्रीभवति पृष्ठचर्म ॥ १० ॥ वंशमिति । उपजातिविशेषः । पादत्रयं जगतीजात्या । चतुर्थः पादः शालिन्या । सप्तच्छिद्रं सप्तरन्ध्रम् । को मे तुल्यस्तुम्बुरुनारदो वा ॥ ११ ॥ [ तत्पातनार्थम् । आरामप्राकारेति । आरामः उपवनं तद्गतप्राकारवेष्टितं प्राचीरपरिवृतं ] कपित्थं कपित्थवृक्षफलार्थमिव । [ प्रासादस्य वेदिकायाम् । तपस्वी वराकः । वृद्धरङ्कः वृद्धभिक्षुः ।] इन्द्रमहकामुकः काकः । ' इन्द्रमहकाकपोदओ [ ०काकपोतकः ] विअ ' इति पाठो व्यक्तार्थ एव । [ कान्तमभिसरतीत्यभिसारिका । उज्ज्वलवेषत्वं वेश्यात्वात् । तदुक्तं—' विचित्रोज्ज्वलवेषा तु चलन्नूपुरनिःस्वना । प्रमोदस्मेरवदना स्याद्वेश्याऽ-

**चारुदत्तः**—(यज्ञोपवीत[1] आकृष्य।) वयस्य उपविश। किमनेन। तिष्ठतु दयितासहितस्तपस्वी पारावतः।

**चेटः**—कथं पारावतं पश्यति। मां न पश्यति। भवतु। अपरया लोष्ट-गुटिकया पुनरपि ताडयिष्यामि। (तथा करोति।) (कधं पारावदं पेक्खदि। मं ण पेक्खदि। भोदु। अवराए लोट्टगुडिकाए पुणो वि ताडइस्सम्।)

**विदूषकः**—(दिशोऽवलोक्य[2]।) कथं कुम्भीलकः। तद्यावदुपसर्पामि। (उप-सृत्य। द्वारमुद्घाटय।) अरे कुम्भीलक प्रविश। स्वागतं ते। (कधं कुम्भीलओ। ता जाव उवसप्पामि। अरे कुम्भीलअ पविश। साअदं दे।)

**चेटः**—(प्रविश्य।) आर्य वन्दे। (अज्ज वन्दामि।)

**विदूषकः**—अरे कुत्र त्वमीदृशे दुर्दिनेऽन्धकार आगतः (अरे कहिं तुमं ईदिसे दुद्दिणे अन्धआरे आअदो।)

**चेटः**—अरे एषा सा। (अले एशा शा।)

**विदूषकः**—कैषा का। (का एसा का।)

**चेटः**—एषा सा। (एशा शा।)

**विदूषकः**—किमिदानीं दास्याःपुत्र दुर्भिक्षकाले वृद्धरंकः इवोर्ध्वकं श्वासा-यसे—एषा सा सेति। (किं दाणिं दासीएपुत्ता[3] दुब्भिक्खकाले वुड्ढरङ्को विअ उद्धकं सासाअसि—एसा सा सेत्ति।)

**चेटः**—अरे त्वमपीदानीमिन्द्रमहकामुक इव सुष्ठु किं काकायसे—का केति। (अले तुमं पि दाणिं इन्दमहकामुको विअ सुट्ठु किं काकाअसि—का केत्ति।)

**विदूषकः**—तत्कथय। (ता कहेहि।)

**चेटः**—(स्वगतम्।) भवतु। एवं भणिष्यामि। (प्रकाशम्।) अरे प्रश्नं ते दास्यामि। (भोदु। एव्वं भणिश्शम्। अले पण्हं दे दइश्शम्।)

**विदूषकः**—अहं ते मस्तके पादं दास्यामि। (अहं दे मुण्डे गोडं दइस्सम्।)

**चेटः**—अरे जानीहि तावत्तेन हि कस्मिन्काले चूता मुकुलिता भवन्ति। (अले जाणाहि दाव[4] तेण हि कश्शि काले चूआ मौलेन्ति।)

**विदूषकः**—अरे दास्याःपुत्र ग्रीष्मे। (अरे दासीएपुत्ता गिम्हे।)

**चेटः**—(सहासम्।) अरे न हि नहि। (अले ण हि ण हि।)

**विदूषकः**—(स्वगतम्।) किमिदानीमत्र कथयिष्यामि। (विचिन्त्य।) भवतु। चारुदत्तं गत्वा प्रक्ष्यामि। (प्रकाशम्।) अरे मुहूर्तकं तिष्ठ। (चारुदत्त-मुपसृत्य।) भो वयस्य प्रक्ष्यामि तावत्कस्मिन्काले चूता मुकुलिता भवन्ति। (किं दाणिं एत्थ कहिस्सम्। भोदु। चारुदत्तं गदुअ पुच्छिस्सम्। अरे मुहुत्तअं चिट्ठ। भो वअस्स पुच्छिस्सं दाव कस्सिं काले चूआ मौलेन्ति।)

---

१ ०वीतेन. २ विलोक्य. ३ आ दासीए०. ४ दाव इति नास्ति क्वचित्.

CHAR.—( *Holding him by his sacred thread* ) Sit down, friend; why do you bother yourself with him ? Leave that poor pigeon alone, who is in the company of his mate.

CHETA—How ! He is looking at the pigeon, and not at me ! Well, I'll again strike him with another lump of mud. ( *Does so* ).

VID.—( *Looking in all directions* ), Ah ! It is Kumbhilaka ! Well then, I'll go to him. ( *Approaching and opening the door* ) Well, Kumbhilaka, come in; you are welcome.

CHETA—( *Entering* ). Sir, I salute you !

VID.—Where have you come, man, on such a rainy day, and in darkness ?

CHETA—You see, she is here.

VID.—What 'she' ( you mean ) ? What 'she' ?

CHETA—*She*. See ? *She* !

VID.—You son-of-a-slave, what makes you now hiss forth 'she-see-she,' like an old beggar in famine-time ?

CHETA--Eh, why do you too now shout out--'what, what' ( ka, ka ), regularly like a greedy crow ( crowing ) during Indra's festival ?

VID.—All right. Tell me.

CHETA—( *To himself* ). Well, I'll speak thus. ( *Aloud* ) Eh, I'll set a puzzle to you !

VID.—And I'll set my foot on your head !

CHETA—Oh, all right ! Then just find out in what season the mango-trees blossom.

VID.--You son-of-a-slave, in the *Grishma* ( summer ) season !

CHETA—( *Laughing* ). Ah, no ! no !

VID.--( *To himself* ). What answer then should I make here ? ( *Pondering* ). Well, I'll go to Charudatta and ask him. ( *Aloud* ) Eh, you wait awhile. ( *Approaching* Charudatta ) O friend, let me just ask you in what season the mango trees blossom.

---

भिसरेद्यदि ॥' इति ] अपद्मेति । [ रतिसमये लज्जा तस्यां प्रणयिनी प्रीति-मती रतिक्षेत्रे क्रीडाभूमौ एव रङ्गे प्रियैः पथिकसार्थैरनुगता सलीलं गच्छन्ती ] एषा वसन्तसेनेति संनिकर्षेण । अपद्मा पद्मरहिता श्रीर्लक्ष्मीः अनङ्गस्य कामस्य

**चारुदत्तः**—मूर्ख वसन्ते ।

**विदूषकः**—(चेटमुपगम्य ।) मूर्ख वसन्ते । (मुक्ख वसन्ते ।)

**चेटः**—द्वितीयं ते प्रश्नं दास्यामि । सुसमृद्धानां ग्रामाणां का रक्षां करोति । (दुदिअं दे पण्णं दइश्शम् । शुशमिद्धाणं गामाणं का लक्खअं कलेदि ।)

**विदूषकः**—अरे रथ्या । (अरे रच्छा ।)

**चेटः**—(सहासम् ।) अरे न हि न हि । (अले ण हि ण हि ।)

**विदूषकः**—भवतु । संशये पतितोऽस्मि । (विचिन्त्य ।) भवतु । चारुदत्तं पुनरपि प्रक्ष्यामि । (पुनर्निवृत्य चारुदत्तं तथैवोदाहरति ।) (भोदु । संसए पडिदोम्हि । भोदु । चारुदत्तं पुणो वि पुच्छिस्सम् ।)

**चारुदत्तः**—वयस्य सेना ।

**विदूषकः**—(चेटमुपगम्य ।) अरे दास्याःपुत्र सेना । (अरे दासीएपुत्ता सेणा ।)

**चेटः**—अरे द्वे अप्येकस्मिन्कृत्वा शीघ्रं भण । (अले दुवे वि एक्कश्शि कदुअ शिग्घं भणाहि ।)

**विदूषकः**—सेनावसन्ते । (सेणावसन्ते ।)

**चेटः**—ननु परिवृत्य भण । (णं पलिवत्तिअ भणाहि ।)

**विदूषकः**—(कायेन परिवृत्य ।) सेनावसन्ते । (सेणावसन्ते ।)

**चेटः**—अरे मूर्ख वटुक पदे परिवर्तय । (अले मुक्ख बडुका[1] पदाइं पलिवत्तावेहि ।)

**विदूषकः**—(पादौ परिवर्त्य ।) सेनावसन्ते । (सेणावसन्ते ।)

**चेटः**—अरे मूर्ख अक्षरपदे परिवर्तय । (अले मुक्ख अक्खलपदाइं पलिवत्तावेहि ।)

**विदूषकः**—(विचिन्त्य ।) वसन्तसेना । (वसन्तसेणा ।)

**चेटः**—एषा साऽऽगता । (एशा शा आअदा ।)

**विदूषकः**—तद्यावच्चारुदत्तस्य निवेदयामि । (उपसृत्य ।) भो चारुदत्त धनिकस्त आगतः । (ता जाव चारुदत्तस्स णिवेदेमि । भो चारुदत्त धणिओ दे आअदो ।)

**चारुदत्तः**—कुतोऽस्मत्कुले धनिकः ।

**विदूषकः**—यदि कुले नास्ति तद्द्वारेऽस्ति । एषा वसन्तसेनाऽऽगता । (जइ कुले णत्थि ता दुवारे अत्थि । एसा वसन्तसेना आअदा ।)

**चारुदत्तः**—वयस्य किं मां प्रतारयसि

**विदूषकः**—यदि मे वचने न प्रत्येषि तदेतं कुम्भीलकं पृच्छ । अरे दास्याःपुत्र कुम्भीलक उपसर्प । (जइ मे वअणे ण पत्तिआअसि ता एदं कुम्भीलअं पुच्छ । अरे दासीएपुत्ता कुम्भीलअ उवसप्प ।)

---

१ बटुवका (बटुवक).

CHAR.—In *Vasanta* ( Spring ), you fool !

VID.—( *Going to Cheta* ). In *Vasanta* ( Spring ), you fool !

CHETA—I'll set you another puzzle.—Who affords protection to prosperous villages ?

VID.—Eh, *Rathya* ( military cars ).

CHETA—( *Laughs* ). Ah, no ! no !

VID.—Oh ! well, I have fallen into doubt. ( *Pondering* ). Never mind; I'll again ask Charudatta. ( *Again goes back and asks* Charudatta *as before* ).

CHAR.—Friend, *Sena* ( the army ).

VID.—( *Approaching Cheta* ). You son-of-a-slave, *Sena* ( the army ).

CHETA—Now put the two together and repeat it quickly.

VID.—Sena-vasante !

CHETA—No, say it turned around.

VID.—( *Bodily turning around* ). Sena-vasante !

CHETA—You foolish fellow, turn the *padas* ( words )

VID.—( *Turning his* padas, *i. e. feet* ). Sena-vasante !

CHETA—You idiot, turn the *padas* ( words ) formed by those letters !

VID —( *Pondering* ). Vasanta-sena !

CHETA—Here she has arrived !

VID.—Well, I'll just go and tell Charudatta. ( *Approaching* ). Sir Charudatta, a *Dhanika* ( rich person—creditor ) has come to see you !

CHAR.—Why should a *Dhanika* ( creditor ) visit my house ?

VID.—If not in your house, the *Dhanika* ( rich person ) is at your door. Here's Vasantasena come ( to see you ) !

CHAR.—Why do you deceive me friend ?

VID —If you don't believe what I say, then ask this Kumbhilaka.—You son-of-a-slave, Kumbhilaka, come here !

---

ललितं सुकुमारं प्रहरणम् । कुलस्त्रीणां शोकः तासां पतीनां चित्ताकर्षकत्वेन विश्लेषणादिति भावः । मदन एव वरवृक्षस्तस्य कुसुमम् । अस्तीति शेषः । मालापकमलंकारः । शिखरिणी वृत्तम् ॥ १२ ॥ गर्जन्तीति । वियुक्ताश्च ता वनिताश्च तासां हृदयानुकाराः धूसरा इत्यर्थः । शैलशिखरेषु विलम्बिबिम्बा मेघा गर्जन्ति ।

**चेटः**—(उपसृत्य ।) आर्य वन्दे । (अज्ज वन्दामि ।)

**चारुदत्तः**—भद्र स्वागतम् । कथय सत्यं प्राप्ता वसन्तसेना ।

**चेटः**—एषा साऽऽगता वसन्तसेना । (एशा शा आअदा वसन्तशेणा ।)

**चारुदत्तः**—(सहर्षम् ।) भद्र न कदाचित्प्रियवचनं[1] निष्फलीकृतं मया । तद्गृह्यतां पारितोषिकम् । (इत्युत्तरीयं प्रयच्छति ।)

**चेटः**—(गृहीत्वा प्रणम्य सपरितोषम् ।) यावदार्याया निवेदयामि । (इति निष्क्रातः ।) (जाव अज्जआए णिवेदेमि ।)

**विदूषकः**—भो अपि जानासि किंनिमित्तमीदृशे दुर्दिन आगतेति । (भो अवि जाणासि किंणिमित्तं ईदिसे दुद्दिणे आअदेत्ति ।)

**चारुदत्तः**—वयस्य न सम्यगवधारयामि ।

**विदूषकः**—मया ज्ञातम् । अल्पमूल्या रत्नावली बहुमूल्यं सुवर्णभाण्डमिति न परितुष्टाऽपरं याचितुमागता । (मए जाणिदम् । अप्पमुल्ला रअणावली बहुमुल्लं सुअण्णभण्डअं त्ति ण परितुट्ठा अवरं मग्गिदुं आअदा ।)

**चारुदत्तः**—(स्वगतम् ।) परितुष्टा यास्यति ।

(ततः प्रविशत्युज्ज्वलाभिसारिकावेषेण वसन्तसेना सोत्कण्ठा छत्रधारिणी विटश्च ।)

**विटः**—(वसन्तसेनामुद्दिश्य ।)

**अपद्मा श्रीरेषा प्रहरणमनङ्गस्य ललितं**
**कुलस्त्रीणां शोको मदनवरवृक्षस्य कुसुमम् ।**
**सलीलं गच्छन्ती रतिसमयलज्जाप्रणयिनी**
**रतिक्षेत्रे रङ्गे प्रियपथिकसार्थैरनुगता ॥ १२ ॥**

वसन्तसेने पश्य पश्य ।

**गर्जन्ति शैलशिखरेषु विलम्बिबिम्बा**
**मेघा वियुक्तवनिताहृदयानुकाराः ।**
**एषां रवेण सहसोत्पतितैर्मयूरैः**
**खं वीज्यते मणिमयैरिव तालवृन्तैः ॥ १३ ॥**

अपि च ।

**पङ्कक्लिन्नमुखाः पिबन्ति सलिलं धाराहता दर्दुराः**
**कण्ठं मुञ्चति बर्हिणः समदनो नीपः प्रदीपायते ।**
**संन्यासः कुलदूषणैरिव जनैर्मेघैर्वृतश्चन्द्रमा**
**विद्युन्नीचकुलोद्गतेव युवतिर्नैकत्र संतिष्ठते[2] ॥ १४ ॥**

---

१ कदाचिदपि. २ विश्राम्यति

CHETA.—( *Approaching* ). Sir, I salute you!

CHAR.—Welcome, my good man, tell me, has Vasantasena *really* come?

CHETA—Here she has come, our Vasantasena.

CHA'R.—( *Joyfully* ). My good fellow, I have never let a welcome announcement go by without bestowing a reward. So take this reward. ( *Gives his upper garment* ).

CHETA--( *Takes it and bows; with delight* ). Well, I'll tell her ladyship. ( *Exit* )

VID.—Sir, do you know for what purpose she has come on such a rainy day?

CHAR—Friend, I can't quite understand it.

VID.—But I do. Not being satisfied, as the necklace is of small value and her golden casket more valuable she has come to demand something in addition!

CHAR.--( *To himself* ) She shall go away fully satisfied.

( *Then enter love-sick* Vasantasena *brilliantly attired as an* Abhisarika, *accompanied by her* Umbrella-bearer *and by* Vita )

VITA—( *With reference to Vasantasena* )

She is the goddess Lakshmi, without the lotus ( in her hand ); she is the lovely weapon or the bodiless one ( Cupid ); She is the ( cause of ) grief to high-born ( chaste ) ladies; and she is the flower of the excellent tree in the form of Love. Exhibiting bashfulness at the time of amorous sports, she is followed by hosts of gallants wandering after her, as she walks gracefully over the stage in the form of Love's field. ( 12 )

See, Vasantasena, see!

With their forms hanging low on the peaks of mountains, and resembling ( in colour ) the ( darkened ) hearts of ladies in separation, the clouds are thundering, whose roar makes the peacocks start up suddenly, so that the sky is fanned ( by their opened tails ) as though by jewelled fans. (13)

And also--

The frogs, pelted by rain-showers, and with their mouths besmirched with mud, are drinking water; the impassioned peacock lets loose his voice, *i. e.* shrieks loudly; the *nipa* tree ( with its red blossoms ) glows like a bright lamp; the clouds have taken off ( *i. e.* obscured ) the moon, like rakes ( *lit.* disgracers of family ) taking to the life of a *Samnyasin*; while the lightning stays not in one ( fixed ) spot, like a woman born of a low family. ( 14 )

वसन्तसेना—भाव सुष्ठु ते भणितम् । एषा[1] हि । (भाव सुठ्ठु दे भणिदम् ।)

मूढे निरन्तरपयोधरया मयैव
कान्तः सहाभिरमते यदि किं तवात्र ।
मां गर्जितैरिति[2] मुहुर्विनिवारयन्ती
मार्गं रुणद्धि कुपितेव निशासपत्नी ॥ १५ ॥

विटः—भवतु । एवं तावत् । उपालभ्यतां तावदियम् ।

वसन्तसेना—भाव किमनया स्त्रीस्वभावदुर्विदग्धयोपालब्धया[3] । पश्यतु भावः ।

मेघा वर्षन्तु गर्जन्तु मुञ्चन्त्वशनिमेव वा[4] ।
गणयन्ति न शीतोष्णं [5]रमणाभिमुखाः स्त्रियः ॥ १६ ॥

विटः—वसन्तसेने पश्य पश्य । अयमपरः

पवनचपलवेगः स्थूलधाराशरौघः
स्तनितपटहनादः[6] स्पष्टविद्युत्पताकः ।
हरति करसमूहं खे शशाङ्कस्य मेघो
नृप इव पुरमध्ये मन्दवीर्यस्य शत्रोः ॥ १७ ॥

वसन्तसेना—एवं न्विदम् । तत्कथमेषोऽपरः । (एव्वं ण्णेदम् । ता कधं एसो अवरो[7] ।)

एतैरेव यदा गजेन्द्रमलिनैराध्मातलम्बोदरै-
र्गर्जद्भिः [8]सतडिद्वलाकशबलैर्मेघैः सशल्यं मनः ।
तत्किं प्रोषितभर्तृवध्यपटहो[9] हा हा हताशो बकः
प्रावृट् प्रावृडिति ब्रवीति शठधीः क्षारं क्षते प्रक्षिपन् ॥ १८ ॥

---

येषां रवेण रवं श्रुत्वा सहसा उत्पतितैः मयूरैः मणिमयैस्तालवृन्तैरिव खमाकाशं वीज्यते इत्युत्प्रेक्षा । वसन्ततिलकं वृत्तम् ॥ १३ ॥ पङ्केति । पङ्केन कर्दमेन क्लिन्नं मुखं एषां ते पङ्कक्लिन्नमुखा धाराहताः दर्दुरा भेका सलिलं पिबन्ति । समदनः बर्हिणः मयूरः कण्ठं मुञ्चति मुक्तकंठं रौति । नीपः कदम्बवृक्षः प्रदीपायते आरक्त-कुड्मलभरेण प्रदीप इवाचरति । कुलदूषणैः जनैः संन्यास इव मेघैः चन्द्रमा वृतः । नीचकुलोत्पन्ना युवतिरिव विद्युदेकत्र न संतिष्ठते । शार्दूलविक्रीडितं छन्दः ॥ १४ ॥ 'कार्यतश्चोत्तमादीनां कार्यो भाषाव्यतिक्रमः' इति भरतोक्त्यनुसारेण वसन्त-सेनायाः संस्कृतोक्तिः । ] मूढे इति । मूढे इति वसन्तसेनायाः साक्षेपसंबोधनम् । [ यदि निरन्तराः पयोधरा यस्यां सा तया सान्द्रमेघया । निरन्तरौ सुश्लिष्टौ पयो-धरौ स्तनौ यस्यास्तया च । मयैव सह कान्तः अभिरमते तर्हि अत्र तव किम् ।

---

१ (संस्कृतमाश्रित्य ।) एषा. २ रपि. ३ दग्धोपा० ४ च. ५ दयिताभि०. ६ स्वनित. ७ अवरो (संस्कृतमाश्रित्य). ८ तडित्पताक. ९ बद्ध.

VAS.—Sir, you have described correctly. See, here this—

Co-wife in the form of the night is blocking my path in anger, forbidding me now and again with its thundering, as though saying—"You foolish woman, what business have you here when your lover sports with me alone, possessing plump *payodharas* (breasts—clouds ) ? " (15)

VITA—Yes; it is as you say. You may therefore scold her,

VAS.—Sir, what is the use of scolding her who is obstinate as is women's nature ? And sir, observe—

Let the clouds pour in torrents, thunder or shoot forth lightning; women who go to ( meet ) their lovers do not mind cold or heat. (16)

VITA—See, Vasantasena, see ! This other—

Cloud, having its speed augmented by the breeze, discharging a stream of arrows in the form of big torrents, with its rumbling serving as the beat of drums, and displaying banners in the form of lightning, seizes ( *i.* e. obscures ) the cluster of the moon's rays, in the sky, like a king receiving from an enemy, weak in valour, large tributes in the latter's capital,—( a king ) having movements rapid like those of the wind, discharging streams of arrows like big torrents, with sounds of drums like the rumbling of clouds, and displaying banners like lightning. (17)

VAS.—So it is. But then how is it that here this another—

Wicked crane, with villainous intentions, and serving as the drum that sounds the doom of ladies whose husbands have gone on a journey, is also crying '*Pravrit, Pravrit*', ( Rain, Rain ), sprinkling salt on their wounds ( as it were ), when their minds are already tortured by these thundering clouds dark like big elephants, with their interiors swollen and hanging low, and variegated with cranes and with lightning-flashes ? (18)

---

इति कुपिता इव गर्जितैः मुहुः मां निवारयन्ती निशासपत्नी मार्गं रुणद्धि । वसन्ततिलकं वृत्तम् ।] पयोधरो मेघः स्तनौ च ॥ १५ ॥ मेघा इति । [रमणाभिमुखाः प्रियाभिगामिन्यः ] ॥ १६ ॥ अयमपर इति शत्रोः पुनर्मध्य इत्यर्थात् । पवनेति । [पवनेन चपलः वेगो यस्य सः । पक्षे पवनवत् चपलो वेगो यस्य । स्थूला धारा एव शरौघा यस्य । पक्षे स्थूलधारा इव शरौघा यस्य । स्तनितं गर्जितमेव पटहनादः यस्य । पक्षे स्तनितवत्पटहनादो यस्य । स्पष्टा विद्युदेव विद्युदिव च पताका यस्य । स मेघः खे शशाङ्कस्य करसमूहं किरणजालं हरति । मन्दवीर्यस्य शत्रोः पुरमध्ये करसमूहं राजदेयद्रव्यमिव । रूपकानुप्राणिता उपमालंकारः । श्लेषश्च । मालिनी-

विटः—वसन्तसेने एवमेतत् । इदमपरं पश्य ।

बलाकापाण्डुरोष्णीषं विद्युदुत्क्षिप्तचामरम् ।
मत्तवारणसारूप्यं कर्तुकाममिवाम्बरम् ॥ १९ ॥

वसन्तसेना—भाव पश्य पश्य । (भाव पेक्ख पेक्ख[1] ।)

एतैरार्द्रतमालपत्रमलिनैरापीतसूर्यं नभो
वल्मीकाः शरताडिता इव गजाः सीदन्ति धाराहताः ।
विद्युत्काञ्चनदीपिकेव रचिता प्रासादसंचारिणी
ज्योत्स्ना दुर्बलभर्तृकेव वनिता प्रोत्सार्य मेघैर्हृता[2] ॥ २० ॥

विटः—वसन्तसेने पश्य पश्य ।

एते हि विद्युद्गुणबद्धकक्षा गजा इवान्योन्यमभिद्रवन्तः[3] ।
शक्राज्ञया वारिधराः सधारा[4] गां रूप्यरज्ज्वेव[5] समुद्धरन्ति ॥ २१ ॥

अपि च पश्य ।

[6]महावाताध्मातैर्महिषकुलनीलैर्जलधरै-
श्चलैर्विद्युत्पक्षैर्जलधिभिरिवान्तःप्रचलितैः ।
इयं गन्धोद्दामा नवहरितशष्पाङ्कुरवती[7]
धरा धारापातैर्मणिमयशरैर्भिद्यत इव ॥ २२ ॥

वसन्तसेना—भाव एषोऽपरः । (भाव एसो अवरो ।)

---

छन्दः] ॥ १७ ॥ एतैरिति । [यदा गजेन्द्रवन्मलिनैः । श्यामैः । आध्मातानि अत एव लम्बानि उदराणि येषां तैः । आध्माताः शब्दायमानाश्च ते लम्बोदराः स्वरूपविस्तारवन्तश्चेति कर्मधारयः—इति ल० दी० । गर्जद्भिः सतडिद्बलाकैः शबलैः मेघैः मनः सशल्यं सवेदनमित्यर्थः । तत्तदा प्रोषितभर्तृणां विरहिणीनामित्यर्थः । वध्यपटहः विपत्तिसूचकः पटहः । ] प्रोषितभर्तृशब्दात् 'न नित्यः समासान्तः' इति न 'नद्यृतश्च' इति कप् । [हताशः शठधीः वञ्चकः बकः क्षते क्षारं सिञ्चन् इव हा हा प्रावृट् प्रावृट् इति ब्रवीति । शार्दूल० छन्दः ॥ १८ ॥ बलाकेति । बलाका बकपङ्क्तिरेव पाण्डुरोष्णीषो यस्य । पक्षे बलाकावत्पाण्डुर उ० । विद्युदेव पक्षे विद्युदिव उत्क्षिप्तं चामरं यस्य । तादृगम्बरं मत्तवारणसारूप्यं कर्तुकाममिव भातीति शेषः । रूपकानुप्राणितोत्प्रेक्षालंकारः ॥ १९ ॥ एतैरिति । एतैः आर्द्राणि यानि तमालपत्राणि तद्वन्मलिनैः नीलैः मेघैः नभः आपीतः निगीर्णः पिहितः इत्यर्थः । सूर्यः यस्मिन् तथा भूतम् । मेघैः धाराहताः वल्मीकाः शरताडिता गजा इव सीदन्ति । विद्युत् प्रासादसंचारिणीं काञ्चनदीपिकेव रचिता । दुर्बलभर्तृका वनिता इव ज्योत्स्ना प्रोत्सार्य हृता । शार्दूल०

---

१ पेक्ख (संस्कृतमाश्रित्य ।). २ हता. ३ अतिद्र०. ४ सरागा. ५ रूप. ६ वातोद्ध्मा. ७ शस्या.

VITA—So it is, O Vasantasena ! But see this another thing :-

The sky, having a white head-dress in the form of the cranes, and waving *chowries* in the form of lightning-flashes, is, as it were, desirous of imitating the appearance of an infuriated elephant ( whose head-dress is white like cranes and who has waving *chowries* on his head that resemble lightning-flashes ). ( 19 )

VAS.—See, sir, see !

By these clouds, dark like the wet leaves of the *tamala* tree, the sun has been completely hidden (*lit.* drunk up) in the sky; the ant-hills, beaten with the torrential rains, crumble down, like elephants cowering down when struck by arrows; lightning is made to move through the mansions like a golden lamp; and the moon-light, like the wife of an imbecile husband, has been taken away ( obscured ) after being forcibly seized. ( 20 )

VITA—See, Vasantsena, see !

These clouds pouring torrents of rain with their sides girt by streaks of lightning, and rushing against each other, like elephants round whose arm-pits are fastened lightning—like chains (made of gold ), are, as it were, lifting up the earth with silver chains, at the command of Indra (their lord ). ( 21 )

And see also—

By the clouds, thundering in the strong gale, dark like a herd of buffaloes, and moving about like oceans in the sky on their wings in the form of lightning, this earth, emitting a strong odour, and covered with the blades of new green grass, is pierced with the sharp falling showers, as if with arrows made of jewels. ( 22 )

VAS.—Sir, here this another—

---

वृत्तम् ॥ २० ॥ **एत इति** । एते विद्युद्गुणेन विद्युल्लतया पक्षे विद्युदिव गुणः रज्जुस्तेन बद्धा कक्षा मध्यभागः मध्यबन्धनं वा येषां ते विद्युद्गुणबद्धकक्षाः । अन्योन्यमभिद्रवन्तः गजा इव सधारा वारिधरा शक्राज्ञया गां महीं रूपरज्ज्वा समुद्धरन्ति इव । उपमोत्प्रेक्षयोः संसृष्टिः । उपजातिच्छन्दः ॥ २१ ॥ **महावातेति** । महावातैः आध्माताः शब्दिताः । 'आध्मातः शब्दिते दग्धे' इति मेदिनी । तैः महिषकुलवन्नीलैः चलैः । विद्युत एव पक्षा येषां तैः । अन्तः गगनमध्ये प्रचलितैः जलधिभिः इव स्थितैः जलधरैः कर्तृभिः । गन्धेन नववर्षजलसेकजनितमृद्गन्धेन उद्दामा गन्धेन मदेनोद्दामा च नवाना हरितानां शष्पाणामङ्कुरास्तद्वती इयं धरा धारापातैः मणिमयशरैः भिद्यते इव इत्युत्प्रेक्षा । शिखरिणीछन्दः । ] शष्पाङ्कुरा संलग्न-

एह्येहीति शिखण्डिनां पटुतरं केकाभिराक्रन्दितः
प्रोड्डीयेव[1] बलाकया सरभसं [2]सोत्कण्ठमालिङ्गितः ।
हंसैरुज्झितपङ्कजैरतितरां सोद्वेगमुद्वीक्षितः
कुर्वन्नञ्जनमेचका इव दिशो मेघः समुत्तिष्ठति[3] ॥ २३ ॥

विटः—एवमेतत् । तथा हि पश्य[4] ।

निष्पन्दीकृतपद्मषण्डनयनं[5] नष्टक्षपावासरं
विद्युद्भिः क्षणनष्टदृष्टतिमिरं[6] प्रच्छादिताशामुखम् ।
निश्चेष्टं स्वपितीव संप्रति पयोधारागृहान्तर्गतं
स्फीताम्भोधरधामनैकजलदच्छत्रापिधानं जगत् ॥ २४ ॥

वसन्तसेना—भाव एवं न्विन्दम् । तत्पश्य पश्य । (भाव एव्वं ण्णेदम् । ता पेक्ख पेक्ख[7] ।)

गता नाशं तारा उपकृतमसाधाविव जने
वियुक्ताः कान्तेन स्त्रिय इव न राजन्ति ककुभः ।
प्रकामान्तस्तप्तं त्रिदशपतिशस्त्रस्य शिखिना
द्रवीभूतं मन्ये पतति जलरूपेण गगनम् ॥ २५ ॥

अपि च पश्य ।

उन्नमति नमति वर्षति गर्जति मेघः करोति तिमिरौघम् ।
प्रथमश्रीरिव पुरुषः करोति रूपाण्यनेकानि ॥ २६ ॥

विटः—एवमेतत् ।

विद्युद्भिर्ज्वलतीव संविहसतीवोच्चैर्बलाकाशतैः
माहेन्द्रेण विवल्गतीव धनुषा [8]धाराशरोद्गारिणा ।
विस्पष्टाशनिनिःस्वनेन रसतीवाघूर्णतीवानिलै-
र्नीलैः सान्द्रमिवाहिभिर्जलधरैर्धूपायतीवाम्बरम्[9] ॥ २७ ॥

वसन्तसेना—

जलधर निर्लज्जस्त्वं यन्मां दयितस्य वेश्म गच्छन्तीम् ।
स्तनितेन भीषयित्वा धाराहस्तैः परामृशसि ॥ २८ ॥

---

शरतुल्याः ॥ २२ ॥ एह्येहीति । [ शिखण्डिनां केकाभिः पटुतरं यथा तथा एहि एहि इति आक्रन्दित आहूतः । बलाकया बलाकमालया सरभसं प्रोड्डीय सोत्कण्ठमालिङ्गित इव स्थितः । हंसैः उज्झितपङ्कजैः त्यक्तकमलैः अतितरां सोद्वेगमुद्वीक्षितः । एष अपरः मेघः दिशः अञ्जनवन्मेचकाः श्यामाः कुर्वन् समुत्तिष्ठति ।

---

१ प्रोत्थायेव. २ सोद्गाढं. ३ ०त्तिष्ठते, समुज्जृम्भते. ४ पश्य पश्य. ५ खण्ड. ६ दृष्टनष्ट. ७ पेक्ख (संस्कृतमाश्रित्य ।). ८ धातो०. ९ धूमाय०.

Cloud is rising forth, darkening the quarters as if with ( black ) collyrium, very loudly welcomed by the cries of peacocks shouting 'come, come'; ardently and lovingly embraced, as it were, by the cranes flying up; and looked at with very great distress by the swans that have left the lotus-beds. ( 23 )

VITA—So it is. And also mark:—

The ( whole ) world is now sleeping motionless, as it were, lying in the inside of the mansion formed by the torrents of water; its eyes in the from of lotus-clusters are rendered motionless; it has lost ( all consciousness of ) night and day; owing to the lightning-flashes, the darkness therein momentarily disappears and becomes visible again; its face in the form of the quarters is veiled; and it has a covering ( *lit.* umbrella-like ) canopy of numerous clouds in the spacious sky, the abode of clouds. (24)

VAS.—Sir, it is as you say; and again also observe :—

The stars have vanished ( become invisible ), like the good done to a bad person; and the ( moonless ) quarters do not look charming, like women separated from their husbands. I think the sky itself, being intensely heated within by the fire of the weapon ( the thunderbolt ) of Indra, the lord of gods, is liquefied, and so is falling down in the form of water. (25)

And also mark--

The cloud now rises, now descends, now pours ( its showers ), now thunders, and now produces a mass of darkness;—thus it puts on manifold appearances, like a man getting wealth for the first time ( *i. e.* an upstart ). (26)

VITA--So it is.

The sky is ablaze, as it were, on account of the lightning-flashes; it laughs aloud, as it were, owing to hundreds of cranes; it is dancing, as it were, on account of Indra's ( rain— ) bow, discharging arrows of water-torrents; it is shrieking, as it were, owing to the loud clap of thunder; it is reeling, as it were, because of the gales; and it is emitting ( curling ) smoke, as it were, on account of the throng of dark and snake-like clouds. (27)

VAS.—

You are shameless, O cloud, since you frighten me, who am going to the house of my beloved, with your thunder, and touch me with your hands in the form of streams. (28)

भोः शक्र।

किं ते ह्यहं पूर्वरतिप्रसक्ता यस्त्वं नदस्यम्बुदसिंहनादैः।
न युक्तमेतत्प्रियकाङ्क्षितायाः मार्गं निरोद्धुं मम वर्षपातैः ॥ २९ ॥

अपि च।

यद्वदहल्याहेतोर्मृषा वदसि शक्र गौतमोऽस्मीति।
तद्वन्ममापि दुःखं निरपेक्ष[1] निवार्यतां जलदः ॥ ३० ॥

अपि च।

गर्ज वा वर्ष वा शक्र मुञ्च वा शतशोऽशनिम्।
न शक्या हि स्त्रियो रोद्धुं प्रस्थिता दयितं प्रति ॥ ३१ ॥
यदि गर्जति वारिधरो गर्जतु तन्नाम निष्ठुराः पुरुषाः।
अयि[2] विद्युत्प्रमदानां त्वमपि च दुःखं न जानासि ॥ ३२ ॥

विटः—भवति अलमलमुपालम्भेन। उपकारिणी तवेयम्।

ऐरावतोरसि चलेव सुवर्णरज्जुः
शैलस्य मूर्ध्नि निहितेव सिता पताका।
आखण्डलस्य [3]भवनोदरदीपिकेय-
माख्याति ते प्रियतमस्य हि संनिवेशम् ॥ ३३ ॥

वसन्तसेना—भाव एवम्। तदेवैतद्गेहम्। (भाव एव्वं। तं ज्जेव एदं गेहम्।)

विटः—सकलकलाभिज्ञाया न किंचिदिह [4]तवोपदेष्टव्यमस्ति। तथाऽपि स्नेहः प्रलापयति। अत्र प्रविश्य कोपोऽत्यन्तं न कर्तव्यः।

यदि कुप्यसि नास्ति रतिः कोपेन विनाऽथ वा कुतः कामः।
कुप्य च कोपय च त्वं प्रसीद च त्वं प्रसादय च कान्तम् ॥ ३४ ॥

भवतु। एवं तावत्। भो भोः निवेद्यतामार्यचारुदत्ताय।

एषा फुल्लकदम्बनीपसुरभौ काले घनोद्भासिते
कान्तस्यालयमागता समदना हृष्टा जलार्द्रालका।
विद्युद्वारिदगर्जितैः सचकिता त्वद्दर्शनाकाङ्क्षिणी
पादौ नूपुरलग्नकर्दमधरौ[5] प्रक्षालयन्ती स्थिता ॥ ३५ ॥

---

समुत्तिष्ठते इति पा॰ 'उदोऽनूर्ध्वकर्मणि' इत्यात्मनेपदं चिन्त्यम्। उत्प्रेक्षालंकारः। शार्दूल॰ वृत्तम् ॥ २३ ॥ **निष्पन्दीति**। संप्रति निष्पन्दीकृतानि पद्मषण्डान्येव नयनानि यस्य तत्। नष्टा क्षपा वासरश्च यस्मिंस्तत्। विद्युद्भिः क्षणं नष्टं पश्चाद्दृष्टं तिमिरं यस्मिंस्तत्। प्रच्छादितानि पिहितानि आशा दिश एव मुखानि यस्य तत्। पयोधारा एव गृहं तस्यान्तर्गतं स्फीते अम्भोधराणां धामनि निवासे गगने नैके

---

१ निरवेक्ष्य. २ अपि. ३ भुवनो. ४ तवादे. ५ भरौ.

O Indra !

Was I ever before attached to you amorously, that you are thundering ( at me ) with the lion-like roars of clouds ? It is not proper that you should block my path with downpours of rain, when I am yearning for ( the company of ) my beloved. ( 29 )

Moreover—

Just as, O Indra, you ( being love-smitten ) falsely said that you were Gautama, for the sake of Ahalya, so I too am suffering the pangs ( of love ) ; therefore, O you who are indifferent ( to my pain ), please draw off ( your obstructing ) clouds. ( 30 )

Moreover--

You may thunder. O Indra, or pour down showers, or send down hundreds of thunderbolts: you cannot stop women who have started to meet their lovers. ( 31 )

If the cloud thunders, well, let him do so; for men are ( known to be ) cruel. But, O Lightning, how is it that even you, ( who are a woman ), cannot understand the sufferings of ( young ) women ? ( 32 )

VITA--Madam, enough, enough of upbraiding her; she has laid you under an obligation :

For, like a slippery gold-chain on the chest of the ( dark ) Airavata, or like a white flag planted on the top of a mountain, this lightning, which is ( as it were ) the lamp illuminating the interior of Indra's abode ( *i. e.* the sky ), points out to you the residence of your lover. ( 33 )

VAS.--Sir, it is as you say, here is that same house.

VITA--Since you have mastered all the arts, there is nothing on which you need advice in this matter. Still, my affection prompts me to speak. When you go in here, you must not show too much anger.

If you get angry, there is no ( scope for ) love; but again, whence could there be ( charming ) love without anger ? ( So ) you may get angry and anger him too; ( but at the same time ) you should be pacified and also pacify your lover. ( 34 )

Well, so much for that--Who is there ? Please inform the worthy Charudatta :--

" Here she, full of love and joy, and with her hair dripping with water, has come to the house of you, her lover, desirous of seeing you, at a time rendered charming by the clouds and fragrant with the *Kadamba* and the *Nipa* trees in bloom, terrified though she was by lightning and the clap of thunder; she is (now) busy washing her feet which are covered with mud that has stuck to her anklets." (35)

**चारुदत्तः**—( आकर्ण्य ) वयस्य ज्ञायतां किमेतदिति ।

**विदूषकः**—यद्भवानाज्ञापयति । ( वसन्तसेनामुपगम्य सादरम् । ) स्वस्ति भवत्यै । ( जं भवं आणवेदि । सोत्थि भोदीए । )

**वसन्तसेना**—आर्य वन्दे । स्वागतमार्यस्य । (विटं प्रति । ) भाव एषा छत्र-धारिका भावस्यैव भवतु । (अज्ज वन्दामि । साअदं अज्जस्स । भाव एसा छत्त-धारिआ भावस्स ज्जेव भोदु । )

**विटः**—(स्वगतम् । ) अनेनोपायेन निपुणं प्रेषितोऽस्मि । (प्रकाशम् । ) एवं भवतु । भवति वसन्तसेने ।

**साटोपकूटकपटानृतजन्मभूमेः**
**शाठ्यात्मकस्य रतिकेलिकृतालयस्य**
**वेश्यापणस्य[1] सुरतोत्सवसंग्रहस्य**
**[2]दाक्षिण्यपण्यसुखनिष्क्रयसिद्धिरस्तु** ॥ ३६ ॥

(इति निष्क्रान्तो विटः । )

**वसन्तसेना**—आर्य मैत्रेय कुत्र युष्माकं द्यूतकरः । ( अज्ज मित्तेअ कहिं तुम्हाणं जूदिअरो । )

**विदूषकः**—(स्वगतम् ।) आश्चर्यं भोः द्यूतकर इति भणन्त्याऽलंकृतः प्रिय-वयस्यः । (प्रकाशम् । ) भवति एष खलु शुष्कवृक्षवाटिकायाम् । (ही ही भो जूदि-अरो त्ति भणन्तीए अलंकिदो पिअवअस्सो । भोदि एसो क्खु सुक्खरुक्खवाडिआए ।

**वसन्तसेना**—आर्य का युष्माकं शुष्कवृक्षवाटिकोच्यते । ( अज्ज का तुम्हाणं सुक्खरुक्खवाटिआ वुच्चदि । )

**विदूषकः**—भवति यत्र न खाद्यते न पीयते । ( भोदि जहिं ण खाईअदि ण पीईअदि । )

---

अनेके जलधरा एव छत्रं तदेव अपिधानं यस्य तत् । जगत् निश्चेष्टं स्वपिति इव । उत्प्रेक्षालंकारः । शार्दूल० छन्दः ॥ २४ ॥ **गता इति** । असाधौ जने उपकृतमिव तारा अदर्शनं गताः । कान्तेन वियुक्ताः स्त्रिय इव दिशः चन्द्रेण वियुक्ता न राजन्ति । त्रिदशपतिरिन्द्रस्तस्य शस्त्रस्य वज्रस्य शिखिना अग्निना प्रकाममन्त-स्तप्तमत एव द्रवीभूतं गगनं जलरूपेण पतति इति मन्ये इत्युत्प्रेक्षा । पूर्वार्धे उपमालंकारः । शिखरिणी वृत्तम् ॥ २५ ॥ **उन्नमतीति** ॥ प्रथमा प्रथमं प्राप्ता श्रीः येन स पुरुष इव मेघः अनेकानि रूपाणि करोति आकारान्प्रकटयति । तदेव प्रतिपादयति उन्नमतीत्यादिना । कारकदीपकोपमयोः संसृष्टिः । आर्या छन्दः ॥ २६ ॥

---

१ जनस्य. २ पुण्य, पण्यमुख.

CHAB—( *Listening* ). Friend, find out what this is.

VID.—As your honour commands. (*Approaching* Vasantasena; *respectfully* ). I greet you, madam !

VAS.—Sir, I salute you ! You are well seen ! ( *To* Vita ). Sir, let this umbrella-bearer be for you only ( *i. e.* take her away with you ).

VITA—( *To himself* ). She has cleverly dismissed me by means of this plan ! ( *Aloud* ). All right. Lady Vasantasena.

May you achieve success in easily disposing of your courtesy ( to your lover ), which is the commodity offered for sale in the market of a courtesan's profession, which is the birth-place of hypocrisy, deceit, treachery and falsehood, which consists of perfidy, wherein love-sports have made their home, and where the stock in-trade consists of the festival of union. (36)

( *Exit* ).

VIS.—Sir Maitreya, where is that gambler of yours ?

VID —( *To himself* ). Oh ! Wonderful ! By calling him a gambler, she has complimented my dear friend. ( *Aloud* ). Lady, here he is, in the garden of dried-up trees.

VAS. —Sir, what is that which you describe as your 'garden of dried up-trees' ?

VID.—Lady, it is a place wherein one can neither eat nor drink !

---

**विद्युद्भिरिति ।** अम्बरं विद्युद्भिर्ज्वलति इव । हासस्य कविसमयसिद्धश्वेतत्वादाह— बलाकाशतैः उच्चैः विहसति इव । धारा एव शरास्तानुद्गिरति इति धाराशरोद्गारि तेन माहेन्द्रेण धनुषा विवल्गति प्रस्फुरति इव । विस्पष्टः स्फुटं प्रतीयमानः यः अशनिनिःस्वनः तेन रसति उच्चैर्विक्रोशति इव । अनिलैः आघूर्णति भ्रमति इव । जलधरैः हेतुभिः नीलैः अहिभिः कृष्णसर्पैः सान्द्रं धूपायति धूपवदाचरति धूमितं भवति इति । धूमायति इति पाठे धूमवद्भवतीत्यर्थः । मालोत्प्रेक्षा । शार्दूल० छन्दः ॥ २७ ॥ **जलधरेति ।** हे जलधर त्वं निर्लज्जः । यत् यतः दयितस्य वेश्म गच्छन्तीं मां स्तनितेन गर्जितेन भीषयित्वा धारा एव हस्तास्तैः परामृशसि स्पृशसि ॥ २८ ॥ **किमिति ।** किमहं ते पूर्वं रत्या संभोगेन प्रसक्ता संबद्धा आसमिति शेषः । यद् यस्मात्त्वं अम्बुदानां सिंहनादैः नदसि । प्रियेण चारुदत्तेन काङ्क्षितायाः प्रियकाङ्क्षितायाः ; यद्वा काङ्क्षितः प्रियो यया सा प्रियकाङ्क्षिता । परनिपातः । तस्यः मम एतद् मार्गं निरोद्धुं निरोधनं न युक्तम् ॥ २९ ॥] **यद्वदिति ।**

( वसन्तसेना स्मितं करोति । )

**विदूषक**--तस्मात्प्रविशतु भवती । (ता पविसदु भादी ।)

**वसन्तसेना**:--(जनान्तिकम् । ) अत्र प्रविश्य किं मया भणितव्यम् । ( एत्थ पविसिअ किं मए भणिदव्वम् । )

**चेटी**--द्यूतकर अपि सुखस्ते प्रदोष इति । (जूदिअर अवि सुहो दे पदोसो त्ति ।)

**वसन्तसेना**--अपि पारयिष्यामि । (अवि पारइस्सम् । )

**चेटी**--अवसर एव पारयिष्यति । ( अवसरो ज्जेव पारइस्सदि । )

**विदूषकः**--प्रविशतु भवती । ( पविसदु भोदी । )

**वसन्तसेना**--( प्रविश्योपसृत्य च । पुष्पैस्ताडयन्ती । ) अयि द्यूतकर अपि सुखस्ते प्रदोषः । ( अइ जूदिअर अवि सुहो दे पदोसो ।

**चारुदत्तः**--( अवलोक्य । ) अये वसन्तसेना प्राप्ता । ( सहर्षमुत्थाय । ) अयि प्रिये ।

**सदा प्रदोषो मम याति जाग्रतः**
**सदा च मे निःश्वसतो गता निशा ।**
**त्वया समेतस्य विशाललोचने**
**ममाद्य शोकान्तकरः प्रदोषकः ।। ३७ ।।**

तत्स्वागतं भवत्यै । इदमासनम् । अत्रोपविश्यताम् ।

**विदूषकः**--इदमासनम् । उपविशतु भवती । ( इदं आसणम् । उवविसदु भोदी । )

( वसन्तसेनाऽऽसीना[1] । ततः सर्व[2] उपविशन्ति । )

**चारुदत्त** :--वयस्य पश्य पश्य ।

**वर्षोदकमुद्गिरता श्रवणान्तविलम्बिना कदम्बेन ।**
**एकः स्तनोऽभिषिक्तो नृपसुत इव यौवराज्यस्थः ।। ३८ ।।**

तद्वयस्य क्लिन्ने वाससी वसन्तसेनायाः । अन्ये प्रधानवाससी [3]समुपनीयेतामिति ।

---

हे शक्र [ यद्वद् अहल्याहेतोः अहल्याप्राप्त्यर्थं ] यथा अहल्याया अप्राप्तिदुःखेन गौतमोऽस्मीत्यसत्यं ब्रूषे । हे निरपेक्ष परपीडानभिज्ञ तद्वन्ममापि दुःखं जानीहीत्यर्थात् । ततः किं कर्तुमुचितमित्याह—[ जलदः ] निवार्यतां [ निषिध्यताम् ] । प्रियभवनगमनं प्रति विरोधकत्वादित्याशयः ।। ३० ।। गर्जेति । [ हे शक्र गर्ज वा ६० । दयितं प्रति प्रस्थिताः । स्त्रियो रोद्धुं न शक्या हि ।। ३१ ।। यदीति । यदि वारिधरो मेघः गर्जति तत् गर्जतु नाम । यतः पुरुषा निष्ठुराः । अयि विद्युत् त्वमपि प्रमदा सत्यपीत्यर्थः ।

---

१ नाट्येनासीना. २ सर्वे उप०. ३ समुपा०

( Vasantasena *smiles.* )

VID.—So, you may enter it.

VAS.—( *Aside, to her* Maid ). What am I to say on entering it ?

THE MAID—" O gambler, do you find the evening delightful ?

VAS.—Shall I be able to say it ?

THE MAID—The occasion itself will lend you strength.

VID.—Please enter, madam.

VAS.—( *Entering and approaching; striking him with flowers* ). O gambler, do you find the evening delightful ?

CHAR—( *Seeing* ) Ah ! Vasantasena has come ! ( *Joyfully getting up* ). My darling

My evenings always pass in wakefulness, and my nights too have always been passed in sighing. But to-day, O lady with elongated eyes, the evening has put an end to my grief, since I am now united with you! (37)

So I welcome you; here's a seat; pray be seated here.

VID.—Here's a seat; your ladyship should sit down.

( Vasantasena *takes a seat; then all seat themselves* ).

CHAR.—Friend, see, see !

By the *Kadamba* flower which is hanging from the tip of her ear and is dripping rain-water, one of her breasts is besprinkled ( with water ), as though it were a royal prince being crowned as heir-apparent. (38)

Well, friend, Vasantasena's garments are wet; let another pair of excellent garments be brought ( for her ).

---

प्रमदानां दुःखं न जानासि येन दृष्टिग्रहणमोक्षाभ्यां गमनविघ्नं करोषि ॥ ३२ ॥ **ऐरावतोरसीति** । हि यस्मात् ऐरावतोरसि चला सुवर्णरज्जुः इव । शैलस्य मूर्ध्नि निहिता सिता धवला पताका इव । आखण्डलस्य इन्द्रस्य भवनोदरदीपिका इव । इयं विद्युत् ते प्रियतमस्य उपस्थितं संनिवेशं आख्याति प्रकाशेन दर्शयति । वसन्ततिलकं वृत्तम् ॥ ३३ ॥ **यदीति** । यदि कुप्यसि कुपितैव तिष्ठसीत्यर्थः । तर्हि रतिः रतिसुखमित्यर्थः । नास्ति । अथ वा कोपेन विना कामः कुतः । ईर्ष्याकृतकोपेन विना शृङ्गाररसोत्थं सुखं नास्तीत्यर्थः । अतः त्वं कुप्य कान्तं च कोपयेत्या० । आर्या ॥ ३४ ॥ **एषेति** । फुल्लैः कदम्बैः नीपैः च सुरभौ सुगन्धौ मनोज्ञे वा घनैः उद्भासिते शोभिते काले समदना सकामा हृष्टा । जलेन आर्द्रा अलकाः केशा यस्याः

**विदूषकः**—यद्भवानाज्ञापयति । ( जं भवं आणवेदि ।)

**चेटी**—आर्य मैत्रेय तिष्ठ त्वम् । अहमेवार्यां शुश्रूषयिष्यामि । (तथा करोति।) ( अज्ज मित्तेअ चिट्ठ तुमम् । अहं ज्जेव अज्जअं सुस्सूसइस्सम् ।)

**विदूषकः**—( अपवारितकेन । ) भो वयस्य पृच्छामि तावत्तत्रभवतीं किमपि। ( भो वअस्स पुच्छामि दाव तत्थभोदिं किं पि ।)

**चारुदत्त** :—एवं क्रियताम् ।

**विदूषक** :—(प्रकाशम् । ) अथ किंनिमित्तं पुनरीदृशे प्रनष्टचन्द्रालोके दुर्दिनान्धकार आगता भवती। (अध किंणिमित्तं उण ईदिसे पणट्ठचन्दालोए [1]दुद्दिण-अन्धआरे आअदा भोदी। )

**चेटी**—आर्ये ऋजुको ब्राह्मणः । (अज्जए उजुओ[2] बम्हणो ।)

**वसन्तसेना**—ननु निपुण इति भण । (णं णिउणोत्ति भणाहि ।)

**चेटी**—एषा खल्वर्यैवं प्रष्टुमागता–कियत्तस्या रत्नावल्या मूल्यमिति । (एसा क्खु अज्जआ एव्वं पुच्छिदुं आअदा—केत्तिअं ताए रअणावलीए मुल्लं त्ति ।)

**विदूषकः**—( जनान्तिकम् ।) भोः भणितं मया यथाऽल्पमूल्या रत्नावली बहुमूल्यं सुवणभाण्डम् । न परितुष्टाऽपरं याचितुमागता । (भो भणिदं मए जधा अप्पमुल्ला रअणावली बहुमुल्लं सुवण्णभण्डअम्। ण परितुट्टा अवरं मग्गिदुं आअदा।)

**चेटी**—सा खल्वार्ययाऽऽत्मीयेति भणित्वा द्यूते हारिता। स च सभिको राज-वार्ताहारी न ज्ञायते कुत्र गत इति। (सा क्खु अज्जआए अत्तणकेरकेत्ति भणिअ जूदे हारिदा। सो अ सहिओ राअवत्थहारी[3] ण जाणीअदि कहिं गदो त्ति । )

**विदूषकः**—भवति मन्त्रितमेव मन्त्र्यते । ( भोदि मन्तिदं ज्जेव मन्तीअदि ।)

**चेटी**—यावत्सोऽन्विष्यते तावदिदमेव गृहाण सुवर्णभाण्डम्। (इति दर्शयति।) (जाव सो अण्णेसीअदि ताव एदं ज्जेव गेण्ह सुवण्णभण्डअम् ।)

( विदूषको विचारयति। )

**चेटी**—अतिमात्रमार्यो निध्यायति । तत्किं दृष्टपूर्वं ते । ( अदिमेत्तं अज्जो णिज्झाअदि। ता किं दिट्ठपुरुव्वं दे। )

**विदूषकः**—भवति शिल्पकुशलतयाऽवबध्नाति दृष्टिम् । (भोदि सिप्पकुसलदाए ओबन्धेदि दिट्ठिम् ।)

**चेटी**—आर्य वञ्चितोऽसि दृष्टया । तदेवेदं सुवर्णभाण्डम् । ( अज्ज वञ्चिदोसि दिट्ठीए। तं ज्जेव एदं सुवण्णभण्डअम् ।)

---

१ दुद्दिणे. २ उज्जओ (उज्ज्वलः); उज्जुओ (ऋजुकः). ३ राआवत्थआरी (राजापथ्यकारी) राआवच्छहारी (राजावश्यकारी).

VID.—As your honour commands.

THE MAID—Sir, Maitreya, you need not go. I shall wait upon her ladyship myself. ( *Does accordingly* ).

VID.—( *Aside; to* Charudatta ). Friend, I want to ask her ladyship about something.

CHAR—Do so.

VID.—( *Aloud* ). Well, now, for what purpose has your ladyship come here in such darkness of a rainy day when the moonlight has vanished ?

THE MAID—Lady, how simple is this Brahmana !

VAS.—Say, rather, 'clever' !

THE MAID—This our lady has come to ask this : 'What is the price of that jewel-necklace ?'

VID.—( *Aside*; *to* Charudatta ). Sir, it was already said by me that the jewel-necklace was of little value, and the golden casket of greater value; she was not satisfied with that and has come to ask for something else.

THE MAID—For, it was lost by our mistress at gambling, believing ( *lit.* saying ) that it was her own. And it cannot be discovered where that gaming-master, the King's emissary, has gone.

VID.—Madam, you are simply repeating what I myself said to you !

THE MAID—So, while we are looking for him, you may receive this golden casket ( in exchange ). ( *She shows it* ).

( *The* Vid. *remains in deep thought* )

THE MAID—Your honour is gazing at it very fixedly. What then; was it ever seen by you before ?

VID.—Madam, it captivates my eyes by its skilled craftsmanship.

THE MAID—Sir, your eyes are deceiving you ! It is that very same golden casket !

---

सा। विद्युद्भिः वारिदगर्जितैः च सचकिता भीता त्वद्दर्शनाकाङ्क्षिणी। कान्तस्य आलयमागता वसन्तसेना नूपुरलग्नकर्दमधरौ पादौ प्रक्षालयन्ती स्थिता इति निवेद्यतामिति संबन्धः। शार्दूल० छन्दः ] ॥ ३५ ॥ **साटोपेति**। आटोपो दम्भः [ तेन सहितं साटोपं ] कूटं माया कपटं छद्म अनृतं मृषाभाषणम्। निह्नवप्राकट्य-

**विदूषकः**—( सहर्षम्[१] । ) भो वयस्य तदेवेदं सुवर्णभाण्डं यदस्माकं गृहे चौरैरपहृतम् । ( भो वअस्स तं ज्जेव एदं सुवण्णभण्डअं जं अम्हाणं गेहे चोरेहिं अवहृदम् । )

**चारुदत्तः**—वयस्य ।

योऽस्माभिश्चिन्तितो व्याजः कर्तुं न्यासप्रतिक्रियाम् ।
स एव प्रस्तुतोऽस्माकं किं तु सत्यं[२] विडम्बना ॥ ३९ ॥

**विदूषकः**—भो वयस्य सत्यं शपे ब्राह्मण्येन । ( भो वअस्स सच्चं सवामि बह्मण्णेण । )

**चारुदत्तः**—प्रियं नः प्रियम्[३] ।

**विदूषकः**—( जनान्तिकम् । ) भोः पृच्छामि ननु कुत इदं समासादितमिति । ( भो पुच्छामि णं कुदो एदं समासादिदं त्ति । )

**चारुदत्तः**—को दोषः ।

**विदूषकः**—( चेटयाः कर्णे । ) एवमिव । ( एव्वं विअ । )

**चेटी**—( विदूषकस्य कर्णे । ) एवमिव । ( एव्वं विअ । )

**चारुदत्तः**—किमिदं कथ्यते । किं वयं बाह्याः ।

**विदूषकः**—( चारुदत्तस्य कर्णे । ) एवमिव । ( एव्वं विअ । )

**चारुदत्तः**—भद्रे सत्यं तदेवेदं सुवर्णभाण्डम् ।

**चेटीः**—आर्य अथ किम् । ( अज्ज अध इं । )

**चारुदत्तः**— भद्रे न [४]कदाचित्प्रियनिवेदनं निष्फलीकृतं मया । तद्गृह्यतां पारितोषिकमिदमङ्गुलीयकम् । (इत्यनङ्गुलीयकं हस्तमवलोक्य लज्जां नाटयति । )

**वसन्तसेना**—( आत्मगतम् । ) अत एव काम्यसे । ( अदो ज्जेव कामीअसि । )

**चारुदत्तः**—( जनान्तिकम् । ) भोः कष्टम् ।

---

भेदात्कूटकपटयोर्भेदः । एतेषां जन्मभूमेः । [ शाठ्यं धौर्त्यं आत्मा यस्य तस्य । रतिकेलिभिः शृङ्गारक्रीडाभिः कृतालयस्य कृताश्रयस्य । सुरतमेव उत्सवस्तस्य संग्रहः यत्र तस्य ] वेश्यापणो वेश्याव्यवहारः [ तस्य ] । व्यञ्जकस्येत्यर्थः । [ दाक्षिण्येन यत्पण्यसुखं तस्य निष्क्रयसिद्धिः अस्तु । वसन्त०वृत्तम् । ] दाक्षिण्यपण्यप्रधानं निष्क्रयो मूल्यम् ॥ ३६ ॥ **सदेति** । [ सदा मम जाग्रतः प्रदोषः निशामुखं याति । निःश्वसतः त्वद्विरहवेदनातुरत्वादिति भावः । निशा गता । जातावेकवचनम् । प्रदोषा निशाश्च व्यतीताः । हे विशाललोचने अद्य त्वया समेतस्य मम प्रदोषकः शोकान्तकरः शोकस्य नाशकरः । अद्य रात्रिः सुखेन यास्यतीति भावः । वंशस्थं वृत्तम् ॥ ३७ ॥ **वर्षोदकमिति** । [ वर्षोदकमुद्गिरता क्षरता श्रवणान्ते कर्णान्ते विलम्बते असौ तेन कदम्बेन कदम्बपुष्पेण यौवराज्यस्थः नृपसुत इव एकः स्तनः अभिषिक्तः । उपमा ।

---

१ सहर्षं जनान्तिकम्. २ सत्त्वं. ३ प्रियं नः. ४ कदाऽपि.

VID.—( *Joyfully* ). O friend, this is that very same golden casket that was stolen by the thieves from our house!

CHAR.—Friend,

The very device that was thought of ( employed ) by us for returning that deposit is now being used against us. But is it really true, or only a mockery ? ( 39 )

VID.—O friend, it is true,—I swear by my Brahmanahood!

CHAR.—It is gratifying, highly gratifying to me!

VID.—( *Aside; to Cha'r.* ). Sir, I'll ask her as to whence they obtained it.

CHAR.—( There is ) no harm ( in that ).

VID.—( *Whispering in the* Maid's *ear* ). Was it like that ?

THE MAID—( *Whispering in the* Vid's *ear* ). It was like that.

CHA'R.—What is this that is being communicated ? Am I an outsider ( *i. e.* to be excluded from the communication ) ?

VID.—( *Whispering in* Char's *ear* ). It was like this.

CHA'R.—My good girl, is it really that very same golden casket ?

THE MAID—Noble one, just so.

CHA'R.—Girl, I have never allowed a welcome announcement to go unrewarded. So, then, please accept this ring as a reward. ( *Seeing his hand ringless, he exhibits shame* ).

VAS.—( *To herself* ). Hence it is that you are loved ( by me )!

CHA'R.—( *Aside; to the* Vid ). Alas, Oh!

---

आर्या वृत्तम् ॥ ३८ ॥ प्रधानवाससी उत्कृष्टवस्त्रे । प्रनष्टः चन्द्रलोको यस्मिन् । ऋजुकः सरलः अनागरिक इत्यर्थः । [ अन्विष्यते सभिकः । ] निध्यायति निरूपयति । य इति । [ न्यासस्य न्यासीकृतभाण्डस्य प्रतिक्रियां प्रत्यर्पणं कर्तुं अस्माभिः यो व्याजः अपदेशः चिन्तितः स एव व्याजः अस्माकं प्रस्तुतः । किं तु सत्यं अथ वा विडम्बना ] स एव व्याजो विडम्बनाऽस्माकं प्रस्तुत आरब्धः ॥ ३९ ॥ अथ वा सत्यमेवेदम् । अथ वेति प्रकरणात्प्रतीयते । [धनैरिति । धनैः वियुक्तस्य नरस्य लोके जीवितेन किम् । आदित एव तावत् यस्य प्रतीकारे निरर्थकत्वात् कोपप्रसादा विफलीभवन्ति कोपे प्रतिकर्तुं प्रसादे चोपकर्तुमसमर्थतया तयोर्वैयर्थ्यमित्यर्थः । इति ल० दी० ] ॥ ४० ॥ पक्षेति । [ पक्षाभ्यां विकलः पक्षविकलः गतपक्षः पक्षी । उद्धृता दंष्ट्रा यस्य स उद्धृतदंष्ट्रः सर्पश्च एतत्सर्वं लोके तुल्यम् ॥ ४१ ॥ ] शून्यैरिति । [ दरिद्राः पुरुषाः शून्यैः गृहैः तोयरहितैः कूपैः शीर्णैः तरुभिश्च समाः खलु । ] यद् यतो यस्माद्दृष्टपूर्वस्य जनस्य संगमेनोत्तरलतया वर्तमानस्वदैन्यविस्मृतानां विस्मरणवतां पुंसां

धनैर्वियुक्तस्य नरस्य लोके किं जीवितेनादित[1] एव तावत्।
यस्य प्रतीकारनिरर्थकत्वात्कोपप्रसादा विफलीभवन्ति[2] ॥४०॥

अपि च।

पक्षविकलश्च पक्षी शुष्कश्च तरुः सरश्च जलहीनम्।
सर्पश्चोद्धृतदंष्ट्रस्तुल्यं[3] लोके दरिद्रश्च ॥४१॥

अपि च[4]।

शून्यैर्गृहैः खलु समाः पुरुषा दरिद्राः
कूपैश्च तोयरहितैस्तरुभिश्च शीर्णैः।
यद्दृष्टपूर्वजनसंगमविस्मृताना[5]-
मेवं भवन्ति विफलाः परितोषकालाः ॥ ४२ ॥

विदूषकः—भोः अलमतिमात्रं संतापितेन। ( प्रकाशं सपरिहासम्।) भवति समर्प्यतां मम स्नानशाटिका। ( भो अलं अदिमेत्तं संतप्पिदेण[6]। भोदि समप्पीअदु ममकेरिआ ण्हाणसाडिआ। )

वसन्तसेना—आर्य चारुदत्त युक्तं न्विदमनया रत्नावल्येमं जनं तुलयितुम्। ( अज्ज चारुदत्त जुत्तं ण्णेदं इमाए रअणावलीए इमं तुलइदुम्।)

चारुदत्तः—( सविलक्षस्मितम्। ) वसन्तसेने पश्य पश्य।

कः श्रद्धास्यति भूतार्थं सर्वो मां [7]तुलयिष्यति।
शङ्कनीया हि लोकेऽस्मिन्निष्प्रतापा दरिद्रता ॥ ४३ ॥

विदूषकः—चेटि किं भवत्येहैव स्वप्तव्यम्। ( हञ्जे किं भोदिए इध ज्जेव सुविदव्वम्।)

चेटी —( विहस्य।) आर्य मैत्रेय अतिमात्रमिदानीमृजुमात्मानं दर्शयसि। ( अज्ज मित्तेअ अदिमेत्तं दाणिं उजुअं अत्ताणअं दंसेसि।)

विदूषकः—भो वयस्य एष खल्वपसारयन्निव सुखोपविष्टं जनं पुनरपि विस्तारिवारिधाराभिः प्रवृष्टः पर्जन्यः। ( भो वअस्स एसो क्खु ओसारअन्तो विअ सुहोवविठ्ठं जणं पुणोवि वित्थारिवारिधाराहिं पविट्ठो पज्जण्णो।)

चारुदत्तः—सम्यगाह भवान्।

अमूर्हि भित्त्वा[8] जलदान्तराणि पङ्कान्तराणीव मृणालसूच्यः।
पतन्ति चन्द्रव्यसनाद्विमुक्ता[9] दिवोऽश्रुधारा इव वारिधाराः ॥ ४४ ॥

---

[ परितोषकालाः एवं विफला भवन्ति। वसन्त० वृत्तम् ]॥४२॥ मत्संबन्धिनी स्नानशाटिका।तुलयितुं लब्धालब्धजिज्ञासया बहुमूल्यया रत्नावल्या अल्पमूल्यसुवर्णभाण्डस्य

---

१ जीवितैरा०. २ विफला भ०, ३ तुल्यः. ४ च वयस्य. ५ विस्मितानां. ६ संकथिदेण, ७ तूल०. ८ भिन्ना. ९ वियुक्ता.

In this world, to a man who has lost his money, of what use is his very life in the first place ?--Since he is unable ( suitably ) to counter-act, both his anger and his favour remain ineffectual. (40)

Again—

A bird maimed of its wings; a dried-up tree; a lake without water; a cobra with its fangs pulled off; and a pauper: all these are on the same level, in this world. ( 41 )

And also—

Poor men are, indeed, like houses that are tenantless, wells devoid of water, and trees that are shrivelled, since, as they forget ( their penniless condition ) in the company of their ( beloved ) acquaintances ( *lit.* persons seen before ), the moments of their gratification thus prove fruitless. ( 42 )

VID.—Sir, do not grieve too much. ( *Aloud* ; *laughingly* ). Madam, please return my bathing-garment.

VAS.—Sir, Charudatta, was it indeed fair of you to test ( the worth of ) this person ( myself ) by that jewel-necklace ?

CHA'R.—( *With an embarrassed smile* ). Mark, Vasantasena, mark !

Who would have believed the real fact ? Every one would have lightly thought of me. For, in this world, inglorious poverty is always prone to be suspected. ( 43 )

VID.—Girl, are you going to sleep in this very place ?

THE MAID—( *Laughing* ). Sir Maitreya, you are now showing yourself exceedingly simple, indeed !

VID.—O friend, here now the rain has begun to fall again, in torrential showers of water, as if wishing to drive away people comfortably seated.

CHA'R.—You have observed truly.

For, here are falling these showers of water, breaking through the cloud-spaces, like the spires of lotus-stalks ( piercing ) through the intervening mud, as though they were the showers of tears shed by the sky owing to the calamity that has befallen the Moon. ( 44 )

---

कृते[ प्रत्यर्पणेन परीक्षितुं इदं युक्तं न । नाहमर्थलुब्धेति भाव: ।] क इति । व्याख्यातपूर्वोऽयं ३अ० २४श्लो० ] ॥४३॥ अमूरिति । [ हि अमू: वारिधारा मृणालसूच्य: बिसाग्राणि पङ्कान्तराणि इव जलदान्तराणि भित्त्वा चन्द्रस्य प्रियस्य व्यसनाद् आवरणरूपसंकटात्

अपि च।

धाराभिरार्यजनचित्तसुनिर्मलाभि-
श्चण्डाभिरर्जुनशरप्रतिकर्कशाभिः ।
मेघाः स्रवन्ति बलदेवपटप्रकाशाः
शक्रस्य मौक्तिकनिधानमिवोद्गिरन्तः ॥ ४५ ॥

प्रिये पश्य पश्य ।

एतैः पिष्टतमालवर्णकनिभैरालिप्तमम्भोधरैः
संसक्तैरुपजीवितं सुरभिभिः शीतैः प्रदोषानिलैः ।
एषाऽम्भोदसमागमप्रणयिनी स्वच्छन्दमभ्यागता
रक्ता कान्तमिवाम्बरं प्रियतमा विद्युत्समालिङ्गति ॥ ४६ ॥

( वसन्तसेना श्रृङ्गारभावं नाटयन्ती चारुदत्तमालिङ्गति । )

चारुदत्तः—(स्पर्शं नाटयन्प्रत्यालिङ्ग्य ।)

भो मेघ गम्भीरतरं नद त्वं तव प्रसादात्स्मरपीडितं मे ।
संस्पर्शरोमाञ्चितजातरागं कदम्बपुष्पत्वमुपैति गात्रम् ॥ ४७ ॥

विदूषकः—दास्याःपुत्र दुर्दिन अनार्य इदानीमसि त्वं यदत्रभवतीं विद्युता भीषयसि। ( दासीएपुत्त दुद्दिण अणज्जो दाणिं सि तुमं जं अत्तभोदिं[1] विज्जुआए भाआवेसि। )

चारुदत्तः—वयस्य नार्हस्युपालब्धुम् ।

वर्षशतमस्तु दुर्दिनमविरतधारं शतह्रदा स्फुरतु ।
अस्मद्विधदुर्लभया यदहं प्रियया परिष्वक्तः ॥ ४८ ॥

अपि च वयस्य ।

धन्यानि तेषां खलु जीवितानि ये कामिनीनां गृहमागतानाम् ।
आर्द्राणि मेघोदकशीतलानि गात्राणि गात्रेषु परिष्वजन्ते ॥ ४९ ॥

---

विमुक्ता 'दवो नायिकाया अश्रुधारा इव पतन्तीति उत्प्रेक्षा। उपजातिर्वृत्तम्] ॥४४॥ [धाराभिरिति। बलदेवपटप्रकाशा बलरामवस्त्रसदृशा नीला इत्यर्थः। मेघाः आर्यजनचित्तसुनिर्मलाभिः चण्डाभिः तीव्राभिः अर्जुनशरप्रतिकर्कशाभिः धाराभिः शक्रस्य मौक्तिकनिधिं मुक्तासमहं उद्गिरन्त इव स्रवन्ति। उपमोत्प्रेक्षयोः संसृष्टिः। वसन्ततिलकं वृत्तम् ॥ ४५ ॥ एतैरिति। पिष्टतमालवर्णकनिभैः पिष्टतमालपत्राणां यद्वर्णकं विलेपनं तत्सदृशैः नीलैः अम्भोधरैः आलिप्तम्। संसक्तैः सुरभिभिः शीतैः प्रदोषानिलैः उपवीजितं अम्बरं अम्भोदसमागमे प्रणयिनी स्वच्छन्दं स्वेच्छयैव

---

१ एव्वं भोदिं.

And again—

The clouds, looking ( dark ) like the garments of Balarama, are pouring down in showers which are very pure like the mind of a noble ( Arya ) person, and which, being fierce, are hard ( *i. e.* terrible ) like Arjuna's shafts, as if they are pouring forth Indra's collection of pearls. ( 45 )

See, beloved, see—

Here this red lightning, desiring to be united with the clouds, has appeared of its own will and is embracing the sky, like a beloved mistress ( who, being in love, desires union with her lover at the advent of clouds and goes to him of her own will ) embracing her lover;—the sky which ( like a lover ) is covered ( *lit.* anointed ) with these clouds resembling the paint of ( the juice of ) crushed *tamala* leaves and which is fanned by the continual, fragrant and cool breezes of the evening. (46)

( Vasantsena, *displaying the emotion of love, embraces* Charudatta. )

CHA'R.—( *Displaying the pleasure of her touch, and embracing her in return* ).

Roar still louder, O cloud ! ( For ) by your favour this body of mine, suffering the anguish of love, has become as though it were ( full of ) *Kadamba* flowers, with its hair risen on end and its passion inflamed by ( Vasantasena's ) touch. (47)

VID.—You rainy day, son-of-a-slave, you are, indeed, an ungentlemanly fellow, since now you are frightening her ladyship with the lightning !

CHA'R.—Friend, you should not rebuke it.

Let the storm, pouring showers continually, last for a hundred years ( if it pleases ), and ( so ) let the lightning flash ( too ); for ( owing to them ) I have been embraced by this beloved lady, ( otherwise ) inaccessible to persons like me. (48)

And moreover, O friend,

Blessed, indeed, are the lives of those who closely press, against their own bodies, the bodies, wet and cooled by rain-water, of their mistresses come to their house ( of their own accord ). (49)

---

अभ्यागता रक्ता एषा विद्युत् अम्बरं प्रियतमा कान्तमिव समालिङ्गति। शार्दूल० वृत्तम् ॥ ४६ ॥ भो मेघेति। भो मेघ त्वं गम्भीरतरं नद। स्मरपीडितं मे गात्रं

प्रिये वसन्तसेने ।

स्तम्भेषु प्रचलितवेदिसंचयान्तं
शीर्णत्वात्कथमपि धार्यते वितानम् ।
एषा च स्फुटितसुधाद्रवानुलेपा-
त्संक्लिन्ना सलिलभरेण चित्रभित्तिः ।। ५० ।।

(ऊर्ध्वमवलोक्य ।) अये इन्द्रधनुः । प्रिये पश्य पश्य ।

विद्युज्जिह्वेनेदं महेन्द्रचापोच्छ्रितायतभुजेन
जलधरविवृद्धहनुना विजृम्भितमिवान्तरीक्षेण[१] ।। ५१ ।।

तदेहि : अभ्यन्तरमेव प्रविशावः । ( इत्युत्थाय परिक्रामति[२] ।)

तालीषु तारं विटपेषु मन्द्रं[३] शिलासु [४]रूक्षं सलिलेषु चण्डम् ।
संगीतवीणा इव ताड्यमानास्तालानुसारेण पतन्ति धाराः ।। ५२ ।।

( इति निष्क्रान्ताः सर्वे । )

[५]दुर्दिनो नाम पञ्चमोऽङ्कः ।

---

तव प्रसादात् वसन्तसेनाप्रापणरूपात् संस्पर्शेन रोमाञ्चितं जातरोम उत्पन्नसंभोगाभिलाषं च कदम्बपुष्पत्वमुपैति । काव्यलिङ्गनिदर्शनालंकारौ । उपजातिश्छन्दः ] ।।४७।। **वर्षेति** । [ अविरता अविच्छिन्ना धारा यस्मिंस्तद् अविरतधारं दुर्दिनं वर्षशतमस्तु । शतह्रदा स्फुरतु । ] यदहमस्मद्विधदुर्लभया दरिद्रस्य वेश्यावाप्त्यसंभवात् । [ प्रियया परिष्वक्त आलिङ्गितः ।। ४८ ।। **धन्यानीति** । ये पुमांसः गृहमागतानां कामिनीनां मेघोदकशीतलानि आर्द्राणि गात्राणि आत्मनः गात्रेषु परिष्वजन्ते तेषां जीवितानि धन्यानि खलु । इन्द्रवज्रा वृत्तम् ।।४९।। **स्तम्भेष्विति** । स्तम्भेषु प्रचलितः शिथिलित इत्यर्थः । यः वेदिसंचयः तस्य अन्तं यावत् शीर्णत्वाद्वितानं कथमपि धार्यते उपरि ध्रियते । एषा च चित्रभित्तिः स्फुटितसुधाद्रवानुलेपात् सलिलभरेण वर्षोदकाधिक्येन संक्लिन्ना अत्यार्द्रा । प्रहर्षिणी वृत्तम् । ] प्रकृतिच्छन्दसा । वितानं चन्द्रातपः ।।५०।। **विद्युदिति** । [ विद्युदेव जिह्वा यस्य तेन । महेन्द्रचापमेव उच्छ्रितौ आयतौ च भुजौ यस्य तेन । जलधर एव विवृद्धा हनुर्यस्य तेन । अन्तरीक्षेण विजृम्भितं जृम्भाप्रदानं

---

१ अन्तरि; २ क्रामतः; अस्मात्परं-प्रिये पश्य, पश्य पश्य. ३ मन्दं. ४ रुक्षं.
५ इति मृच्छकटिकायां, मृ०प्रकरणे दु०.

Dear Vasantasena,

The canopy, as it is torn, is with great difficulty supported on the pillars, as the ends of their close-bricked pedestals have been loosened. And this painted wall, owing to its chunam paint being cracked, is thoroughly drenched by the torrent of water. (50)

( *Looking upwards* ). Ah ! Here's a rain-bow ! See, my dear, see !

The sky has here given a yawn as it were, with ( *i. e.* exhibiting ) its tongue in the form of the lightning, its uplifted long arms in the shape of ( Indra's ) rain-bow, and an expansive chin in the form of the clouds. (51)

Come, then; let us enter the inside ( *Gets up and walks about* ).

Shrilly on the *tala* leaves, rumbling on the branches, harshly on stones and fiercely on the waters,—thus do the showers fall, resembling lutes played upon in musical concerts to the keeping of time. (52)

( *Exeunt Omnes* ).

*Thus ends Act V Styled*

' A STORMY DAY. '

---

कृतमिवेत्युत्प्रेक्षा ।] आर्या। अनया च वेतालादिभयानकरूपवर्णनम् ॥ ५१ ॥ **तालीष्विति** । [ तालीषु तालीपत्रेषु तारं विटपेषु शाखासु मन्द्रं शिलासु रूक्षं सलिलेषु चण्डं तुमुलस्वनम् । एवं ताड्यमाना संगीतवीणा इव धाराः तालानुसारेण पतन्ति । उपमा । उपजातिच्छन्दः ॥ ५२ ॥ ]

इति दुर्दिनो नाम पञ्चमोऽङ्कः ॥

# षष्ठोऽङ्कः ।

(ततः प्रविशति चेटी ।)

**चेटी**—कथमद्याप्यार्या न विबुध्यते । भवतु । प्रविश्य प्रतिबोधयिष्यामि । (इति नाटयेन परिक्रामति ।) (कधं अज्ज वि अज्जआ ण विबुज्झदि । भोदु । पविसिअ पडिबोधइस्सम् ।)

(ततः प्रविशत्याच्छादितशरीरा प्रसुप्ता वसन्तसेना ।)

**चेटी**—(निरूप्य ।) उत्तिष्ठतूत्तिष्ठत्वार्या । प्रभातं संवृत्तम् । (उत्थेदु उत्थेदु अज्जआ । पभादं संवुत्तम् ।)

**वसन्तसेना**—(प्रतिबुध्य[1] ।) कथं रात्रिरेव प्रभातं संवृत्तम् । (कधं रत्ति ज्जेव पभादं संवुत्तम् ।)

**चेटी**—अस्माकमेतत्प्रभातम् । आर्यायाः पुना रात्रिरेव । (अम्हाणं एसो पभादो । अज्जआए उण रत्ति ज्जेव ।)

**वसन्तसेना**—चेटि कुतः पुनर्युष्माकं द्यूतकरः । (हञ्जे कहिं उण तुम्हाणं जूदिअरो ।)

**चेटी**—आर्ये वर्धमानकं समादिश्य पुष्पकरंडकं जीर्णोद्यानं गत आर्यचारुदत्तः । (अज्जए वड्ढमाणअं समादिसिअ पुप्फकरण्डअं जिण्णुज्जाणं गदो अज्जचारुदत्तो ।)

**वसन्तसेना**—किं समादिश्य । (किं समादिसिअ[2] ।)

**चेटी**—योजय रात्रौ प्रवहणं वसन्तसेना गच्छत्विति । (जोएहि रादीए पवहणं वसन्तसेना गच्छदु त्ति ।)

**वसन्तसेना**—चेटि कुत्र मया गन्तव्यम् । (हञ्जे कहिं मए गन्तव्वम् ।)

**चेटी**—आर्ये यत्र चारुदत्तः । (अज्जए जहिं चारुदत्तो ।)

**वसन्तसेना**—(चेटीं परिष्वज्य ।) चेटि सुष्ठु न निर्ध्यातो रात्रौ । तदद्य प्रत्यक्षं प्रेक्षिष्ये । चेटि किं प्रविष्टाऽहमिहाभ्यन्तरचतुःशालकम् । (हञ्जे सुट्ठु ण णिज्झाइदो रादीए । ता अज्ज[3] पच्चक्खं पेक्खिस्सम् । हञ्जे किं पविट्ठा अहं इह अब्भन्तरचदुस्सालअम् ।)

**चेटी**—न केवलमभ्यन्तरचतुःशालकम् । सर्वजनस्यापि हृदयं प्रविष्टा । (ण केवलं अब्भन्तरचदुस्सालअम् । सव्वजणस्स वि हिअअं पविट्ठा ।)

**वसन्तसेना**—अपि संतप्यते चारुदत्तस्य परिजनः । (अवि संतप्पदि चारुदत्तस्स परिअणो ।)

---

१ प्रबुध्य. २ संदिसिअ (संदिश्य); समासादिअ. ३ अपय्यत्तं (अपर्याप्तं) (टी०)

## ACT VI

( *Then enter a* Maid )

THE MAID--How is it that her ladyship does not wake up yet ? Well, I shall go in and rouse her. ( *Gesticulates walking about* ).

( *Then enter* Vasantasena, *asleep, with her body covered up* ).

THE MAID--( *Observing* ). Get up, madam, get up ! It is day-break !

VASANTASENA '--( *Awakening* ). Ha ! How can it be morning when it is still night !

THE MAID--This is morning *to us*; but to your ladyship it is still night.

VAS.--Girl, and where is that gamester of yours ?

THE MAID--Madam, the noble Charudatta has gone to the old garden, *Pushpakarandaka*, after giving orders to Vardhamanaka.

VAS.--What orders did he give ?

THE MAID--" Get the chariot ready at night, so that Vasantasena might depart. "

VAS.--Girl, where am I to go ?

THE MAID--Madam, where Charudatta has gone.

VAS.--( *Embracing the* Maid ). Girl, I could not take a good view of him at night. So to-day I'll observe him with my own eyes. Girl, have I here entered the inner quadrangle ?

THE MAID--Not only the inner quadrangle, but you have entered ( *i. e.* captured ) the hearts of all persons ( here ), too.

VAS —Do the servants of Charudatta feel distressed ?

---

अपय्यत्तं अपर्याप्तं । [ निध्यातः सम्यग्दृष्टः । संतप्यते ममात्रागमनेनात्मनः सपत्नीभावादित्यर्थः । संतप्स्यति तव विश्लेषादिति भावः । मया प्रथमं संतप्तव्यं— गृहीतरत्नावलीकायां गतायां मयि निजमित्रचारुदत्तपरिजनपरितापे पश्चान्मम बहुपश्चात्तापः स्यादिति प्रथममेव मया संतप्तव्यम् । यथा मित्रपरिजनानुतापो न भवेदिति भावः । इति ल० दी० ] [ 'भर्ता हि परमं नार्या भूषणं भूषणैर्विना' इति मन्यमानाऽऽह—आर्यपुत्र एवेत्यादि । [ कृतान्त विधे । पुष्करपत्रं कमलपत्रं तस्मिन्पतिता जलबिन्दवस्तत्सदृशैः चञ्चलैरित्यर्थः । ] अलीकम-

**चेटी**—संतप्स्यति । (संतप्पिस्सदि ।)

**वसन्तसेना**—कदा । (कदा ।)

**चेटी**—यदाऽऽर्या गमिष्यति । (जदो अज्जआ गमिस्सदि ।)

**वसन्तसेना**—तदा मया प्रथमं संतप्तव्यम् । (सानुनयम्[1] ।) चेटि गृहाणेमां रत्नावलीम् । मम भगिन्या आर्याधूतायै गत्वा समर्पय । वक्तव्यं च—अहं श्रीचारुदत्तस्य गुणनिर्जिता दासी तदा युष्माकमपि। तदेषा तवैव कण्ठाभरणं भवतु रत्नावली । (तदो मए पढमं संतप्पिदव्वम् । हञ्जे गेण्ह एदं रअणावलिम् । मम बहिणिआए अज्जाधूदाए गदुअ समप्पेहि । भणिदव्वं च—अहं सिरिचारुदत्तस्स गुण-णिज्जिदा दासी तदा तुम्हाणं पि । ता एसा तुह ज्जेव कण्ठाहरणं होदु रअणावली ।)

**चेटी**—आर्ये कोपिष्यति चारुदत्त आर्यायै तावत् । (अज्जए कुपिस्सदि चारुदत्तो अज्जाए दाव ।)

**वसन्तसेना**—गच्छ । न कोपिष्यति । (गच्छ । ण कुपिस्सदि ।)

**चेटी**—(गृहीत्वा ।) यदार्याज्ञापयति । ( इति निष्क्रम्य पुनः प्रविशति ।) आर्ये भणत्यार्या धूता—आर्यपुत्रेण युष्माकं प्रसादीकृता । न युक्तं ममैतां ग्रहीतुम् । आर्यपुत्र एव ममाभरणविशेष इति जानातु भवती । (जं अज्जआ आणवेदि । अज्जए भणादि अज्जा धूदा—अज्जउत्तेण तुम्हाणं पसादीकिदा । ण जुत्तं मम एदं गेण्हिदुम् । अज्जउत्तो ज्जेव मम आहरणविसेसो त्ति जाणादु भोदी ।)

(ततः प्रविशति दारकं गृहीत्वा रदनिका ।)

**रदनिका**—एहि वत्स शकटिकया क्रीडावः । (एहि वच्छ सअडिआए कीलम्ह ।)

**दारकः**—(सकरुणम् ।) रदनिके किं मम एतया मृत्तिकाशकटिकया । तामेव सौवर्णशकटिकां देहि । (रदणिए किं मम एदाए मट्टिआसअडिआए । तं ज्जेव सोवण्णसअडिअं देहि ।)

**रदनिका**—( सनिर्वेदं निःश्वस्य । ) जात कुतोऽस्माकं सुवर्णव्यवहारः । तातस्य पुनरपि ऋद्ध्या सुवर्णशकटिकया क्रीडिष्यसि । तद्यावद्विनोदयाम्येनम् । आर्याया वसन्तसेनायाः समीपमुपसर्प्स्यामि । (उपसृत्य ।) आर्ये प्रणमामि । (जाद कुदो अम्हाणं सुवण्णववहारो । तादस्य पुणो वि रिद्धीए सुवण्णसअडिआए कीलिस्ससि । ता जाव विणोदेमि णम् । अज्जआए वसन्तसेणाए समीवं उव-सप्पिस्सम्[2] । अज्जए पणमामि ।)

**वसन्तसेना**—रदनिके स्वागतं ते । कस्य पुनरयं दारकः । अनलंकृतशरीरोऽपि चन्द्रमुख आनन्दयति मम हृदयम् । (रदणिए साअदं दे । कस्स उण अअं दारओ । अणलंकिदसरीरो वि चन्दमुहो आणन्देदि मम हिअअम् ।)

---

१ सानुकम्पम्. २ उपसप्पामि.

THE MAID—They will feel distressed.

VAS.—When ?

THE MAID—When your ladyship will depart.

VAS.—Then I shall be the first to be distressed ! ( *Persuasively* ). Girl, take this jewel-necklace and go and give it to my sister, the worthy Dhuta. And sap to her ( in my name ):—"I am a slave, of his honour Charudatta, bought by his merits; and so I am of you also. Let, therefore, this pearl-necklace be ( worn as ) an ornament round the neck by you."

THE MAID—Madam, but Charudatta would get angry with her ladyship !

VAS.—Go; he won't be angry.

THE MAID—( *Takes it* ) As your ladyship orders ( *Goes out and again enters* ). Madam, her ladyship Dhuta says :— " This is given to you by my husband as ( a mark of ) his favour. So it would not be right for me to take it. And please be it known to you that my husband himself is my best ornament. "

( *Then enter* Radanika, *with* Charudatta's Son ).

RAD.—Come, dear, we shall play with this little cart.

THE SON—( *Crying* ). O Radanika, what do I care for this small clay-cart ? Give me that same golden cart.

RAD.—( *Sighing dejectedly* ). Child, whence can we handle gold now ? When prosperity will come to your papa again, then you will play with a golden cart.— Let me in the meanwhile ( try to ) amuse him ( *i. e.* divert his attention ). I'll go into the presence of her ladyship Vasantasena. ( *Approaching* ). Madam, I salute you !

VAS.—Welcome to you, O Radanika ! Well, whose son is this ? The moon-faced one gladdens my heart, even though his body is unadorned with ornaments.

---

सत्यम् । बालहस्ताभ्यां सुवर्णपूर्णां शकटिकां दारकं च स्वयं गृहीत्वा निष्क्रान्ता । उद्घाटितपक्षद्वारकम् । ही ही इत्यकस्मात्स्मरणविषये । जाणत्थलके यानास्तरणकम् । णस्साकदुआ नासिकारज्ज्वा दुःसहाः । अतोऽतिक्रमः संभाव्यते 'णस्साकडुआ' इत्यपि पाठः । तत्र नस्यकटुका इत्यर्थः । बइल्ला बलीवर्दाः । द्यूतपलायित इव द्यूतकरः सभिकमिव मां दृष्ट्वा प्रच्छादितशरीरः । एतेनार्यकस्य पलायनमुपक्षिप्तम् । एआई तवस्सी एकाकी वराकः । एशे आअदे इति चक्रपरिवर्त्तिदानार्थम् ।

**रदनिका**—एष खल्वार्यचारुदत्तस्य पुत्रो रोहसेनो नाम। (एसो क्खु अज्जचारुदत्तस्स पुत्तो रोहसेणो णाम।)

**वसन्तसेना**—(बाहू प्रसार्य।) एहि मे पुत्रक आलिङ्ग। (इत्यङ्क उपवेश्य।) अनुकृतमनेन पितू रूपम्। (एहि मे पुत्तअ आलिङ्ग। अणुकिदं अणेण पिदुणो रूवम्।)

**रदनिका**—न केवलं रूपं शीलमपि तर्कयामि। एतेनार्यचारुदत्त आत्मानं विनोदयति। (ण केवलं रूपं सीलं पि तक्केमि। एदिणा अज्जचारुदत्तो अत्ताअणं विणोदेदि।)

**वसन्तसेना**—अथ किंनिमित्तमेष रोदिति। (अध किंणिमित्तं एसो रोअदि।)

**रदनिका**—एतेन प्रतिवेशिगृहपतिदारकस्य सुवर्णशकटिकया क्रीडितम्। तेन च सा नीता। ततः पुनस्तां याचतो मयेयं मृत्तिकाशकटिका कृत्वा दत्ता। ततो भणति—रदनिके किं ममैतया मृत्तिकाशकटिकया। तामेव सौवर्णशकटिकां देहीति। (एदिणा पडिवेसिगहवइदारअकेरिआए सुवण्णसअडिआए कीलिदम्। तेण अ सा णीदा। तदो उण तं मग्गन्तस्स मए इअं मट्टिआसअडिआ कदुअ दिण्णा। तदो भणादि—रदणिए किं मम एदाए मट्टिआसअडिआए। तं ज्जेव सोवण्णसअडिअं देहि त्ति।)

**वसन्तसेना**—हा धिक् हा धिक्। अयमपि नाम परसंपत्त्या संतप्यते। भगवन्कृतान्त पुष्करपत्रपतितजलबिन्दुसदृशैः क्रीडसि त्वं पुरुषभागधेयैः। (इति सास्रा[1]।) जात मा रुदिहि। सौवर्णशकटिकया क्रीडिष्यसि। (हद्धी हद्धी। अअं पि णाम परसंपत्तीए सतप्पदि। भअवं कअन्त पोक्खरवत्तपडिदजलबिन्दुसरिसेहिं कीलसि तुमं पुरिसभाअधेएहिं। जाद मा[2] रोद। सोवण्णसअडिआए कीलिस्ससि।)

**दारकः**—रदनिके कैषा। (रदणिए का एसा।)

**वसन्तसेना**—पितुस्ते गुणनिर्जिता दासी। (पिदुणो दे गुणणिज्जिदा दासी।)

**रदनिका**—जात आर्या ते जननी भवति। (जाद अज्जआ दे जणणी भोदि।)

**दारकः**—रदनिके अलीकं त्वं भणसि। यद्यस्माकमार्या जननी तत्किमर्थमलंकृता। (रदणिए अलिअं तुमं भणासि। जइ अम्हाणं अज्जआ जणणी ता कीस अलंकिदा।)

**वसन्तसेना**—जात मुग्धेन मुखेनातिकरुणं मन्त्रयसे। (नाट्येनाभरणान्यवतार्य रुदती।) एषेदानीं ते जननी संवृत्ता। तद्गृहाणैतमलंकारम्। सौवर्णशकटिकां कारय। (जाद मुद्धेण मुहेण अदिकरुणं मन्तेसि। एसा दाणीं दे जणणी संवुत्ता। ता गेण्ह एदं अलंकारअम्। सोवण्णसअडिअं घडावेहि।)

---

१ सास्रम्. २ मा रोद मा रोद.

RAD.—He is the son of the worthy Charudatta, Rohasena by name.

VAS.—( *Stretching forth her arms* ). Come, my child, embrace me ! ( *Seating him on her lap* ). He resembles his father in his beauty.

RAD.—Not only in beauty, but I think in character, too. The noble Charudatta finds recreation in his company.

VAS.—And for what reason is he crying ?

RAD.—He was playing with a small golden cart belonging to the son of a gentleman ( *lit.* head of a house ) who lives next door. And that was taken away by him. Then, as he asked for it again, I made this clay-cart and gave it to him. Thereupon he says—" O Radanika, what do I care for this small clay-cart ! Give me that same golden one. "

VAS.—Oh, alas ! Oh, alas ! He, too, should be distressed at ( the sight of ) other people's wealth ! O divine Fate, you do indeed sport with the fortunes of men, resembling ( *i. e.* as evanescent as ) the drops of water fallen on lotus-leaves ! ( *Tearfully* ). Child, do not cry; you will play with a cart of gold.

THE SON—O Radanika. who is this lady ?

VAS.—A slave of your father, bought by his merits.

RAD.—Child, her ladyship is your mother.

THE SON—Radanika, you are telling a lie; ( for ) if her ladyship is my mother, then why has she put on ornaments ?

VAS.—Child, with your innocent lips you are saying something most touching. ( *Gesticulates taking off the ornaments; weeping.* ). Now here I have become your mother ! So please take these ornaments, and get a golden cart made ( out of them ).

---

अतोऽपि च शकारलाघवमुक्तमित्यवधेयम् । भारवत् सभारमित्यर्थः । मत्वर्थीयः । गोणा गावः । परिभ्भट्टो बन्धनभेदादपगतः । हित्वेति । [ महान्तं नरपतिना बन्धनं कारागृहेऽवरोधः नरपतिबन्धनमपदेशो यस्याः सा नरपतिबन्धनापदेशा या व्यापत्तिः तत्संबन्धि यद् व्यसनं दुःखं संकट वा तदेव महार्णवस्तं हित्वा । पादाग्रस्थितः निगडस्य एकपाशस्तं कर्षतीति तथा सन् अहं बन्धनात्प्रभ्रष्टः गज इव भ्रमामि । प्रहर्षिणी वृत्तम् ॥ १ ॥ विशसने वधस्थानभूते । मारणाय इति वा । 'निमित्तात्कर्मयोगे' इति सप्तमी । गूढागारे कारागृहे । भाग्यानीति । यदि मे भाग्यानि । राज्यप्राप्तिरूपं भाग्यमित्यर्थः । तदा मम कः अपराधः यद्यस्मात् तेन राज्ञा वन्य-

**दारकः**—अपेहि । न ग्रहीष्यामि । रोदिषि त्वम् । (**अवेहि । ण गेण्हिस्सम् ।** रोदसि तुमम् ।)

**वसन्तसेना**—(अश्रूणि प्रमृज्य ।) जात न रोदिष्यामि । गच्छ । क्रीड । (अलंकारैर्मृच्छकटिकं पूरयित्वा ।) जात कारय सौवर्णशकटिकाम् । (जाद ण रोदिस्सम् । गच्छ । कील । जाद कारेहि सोवण्णसअडिअं ।)

(इति दारकमादाय निष्क्रान्ता रदनिका ।)

(प्रविश्य प्रवहणाधिरूढः ।)

**चेटः**—रदनिके रदनिके निवेदयार्यायै वसन्तसेनायै—अपवारितं[1] पक्षद्वारके सज्जं प्रवहणं तिष्ठति । (लदणिए लदणिए णिवेदेहि अज्जआए वशन्तशेणाए—ओहालिअं पक्खदुआरए शज्जं पवहणं चिश्टदि ।)

(प्रविश्य ।)

**रदनिका**—आर्ये एष वर्धमानको विज्ञापयति—पक्षद्वारे सज्जं प्रवहणमिति । (अज्ज ए एसो वड्ढमाणओ विण्णवेदि—पक्खदुआरए सज्जं पवहणं त्ति ।)

**वसन्तसेना**—चेटि तिष्ठतु मुहूर्तकम् । यावदहमात्मानं प्रसाधयामि । (हञ्जे चिट्ठदु मुहुत्तअम् । जाव अहं अत्ताणअं पसाधेमि ।)

**रदनिका**—(निष्क्रम्य ।) वर्धमानक तिष्ठ मुहूर्तकम् । यावदार्याऽऽत्मानं प्रसाधयति । (वड्ढमाणआ चिट्ठ मुहुत्तअम् । जाव अज्जआ अत्ताणअं पसाधेदि ।)

**चेटः**—ही ही भोः । मयाऽपि यानास्तरणं विस्मृतम् । तद्यावद्गृहीत्वाऽऽगच्छामि । एतौ नासिकारज्जुकटुकौ बलीवर्दौ । भवतु प्रवहणेनैव गतागतिं करिष्यामि । (इति निष्क्रान्तश्चेटः ।) (ही ही भो । मए वि जाणत्थलके विशुमलिदे । ता जाव गेण्हिअ आअच्छामि । एदे णश्शालज्जुकडुआ बइल्ला । भोदु । पवहणेण ज्जेव गदागदिं कलिश्शम् ।)

**वसन्तसेना**—चेटि उपनय मे प्रसाधनम् । आत्मानं प्रसाधयिष्यामि । (इति प्रसाधयन्ती स्थिता ।) (हञ्जे उवणेहि मे पसाहणम् । अत्ताणअं पसाधइस्सम् ।)

(प्रविश्य प्रवहणाधिरूढः ।)

---

नाग इव संयमितोऽस्मि बद्धोऽस्मि । दैवी देवसंबन्धिनी सिद्धिः लङ्घयितुं न शक्या च । बन्धनं न भाव्यार्थप्रतीकार इति भावाः । तथापि गम्यो नृपः सर्वेषां सेव्यो हि राजा । बलवता सह कः विरोधो वैरम् । वसन्ततिलका वृत्तम् ]॥ २ ॥ **इदमिति** । [ इदं गृहं भिन्नं विश्लिष्टसंधिबन्धनमित्यर्थः । **महाकपाटः अदत्तः दण्डः** अर्गला यस्य तथा विशीर्णः संधिः फलकसंयोगो यस्य तथाभूतश्च । **ध्रुवं** नूनमयं

---

१ अवघाटितं (अपवृतं) इति च्छायापा०.

THE SON—Get away! I won't take them! You are weeping!

VAS—( *Wiping her tears* ). Child, I will not cry. Go and play. ( *Fills the clay-cart with her ornaments* ). Child, get a golden cart made ( out of these ).

( *Exit* Radanika, *with the* Son. )

( *Entering, mounted on a chariot* ).

CHETA—Radanika, O Radanika! Please tell her ladyship Vasantsena, that the covered car is ready at the side-door.

( *Entering* ).

RAD.—Madam, here this Vardhamanaka announces that the carriage is ready at the side-door.

VAS.—Girl, let it wait for some time; in the meanwhile I shall get through my toilet.

RAD.—( *Going out* ). Vardhamanaka, wait awhile, until her ladyship has finished her toilet.

CHETA—Ah, yes! I too have forgotten the carriage cushions. So in the meanwhile, I'll just ( go and ) come back with them But these bullocks are restive because of their ( new ) nose-rope. Well, I'll go and come back in the car itself.

( *Exit* Cheta ).

VAS.—Bring me my toilet things, girl. I'll get through my toilet. ( *Remains engaged in dressing* ).

( *Entering, mounted on a car* )

---

कुटुम्बी गृहस्वामी व्यसनाभिभूतां दारिद्र्योपहतां दशां प्रपन्नः सन् मम तुल्यभाग्यः मत्सदृशभागधेयो वर्तते। उपेन्द्रवज्रा वृत्तम् ॥ ३ ॥ **भवेदिति**। इदं विषमशीलैः विसदृशस्वभावैः न च अधिगतम्। गोष्ठी समाजस्तस्य यानं भवेत्। अथ वा वधूसंयानं स्त्रीवाहनं तस्या अभिगमनायोपस्थितं भवेत्। वा अथ वा प्रवरजनयोग्यं सद्विधिवशाद्दैवबलाद्वहिर्नेतव्यं भवेत्। विविक्तत्वात्परिजनादिराहित्यात् शून्यं मम खलु दैवविहितं दैवप्रापितं भवेत्। सदेहालंकारः। शिखरिणी वृत्तम्] ॥ ४ ॥ **किमित्यादि**। गाथा। [किं विश्रद्धा असंरब्धाः गच्छथ। यः स गोपालदारको बद्धः स नरपतिहृदयं च बन्धनं चापि समं युगपदेव भित्त्वा व्रजति] ॥ ५ ॥ पुरत्थिमे पूर्वस्मिन्। [प्रतोलीद्वारे रथ्यामुखे। पूर्वनगरद्वारे इत्यर्थः।] **आगच्छतेति**। गाथापञ्चकम्। [विश्वस्ताः सुविश्रब्धा आगच्छत। लघु द्रुतं कुरुत कार्यं। निर्वहत] ॥६॥ **उद्यानेष्विति** ॥ ७ ॥ **रे रे इति** ॥ ८ ॥ **कस्याष्टम इति**। **भणेति**। [युग्मम्। अष्टमः जन्मराशितोऽष्टमराशिस्थः। एवमुत्तरत्रापि। भार्गवग्रहः शुक्रः। भूमिसुतो

**स्थावरकः चेटः**—आज्ञप्तोऽस्मि राजश्यालकसंस्थानेन—स्थावरक प्रवहणं गृहीत्वा पुष्पकरण्डकं जीर्णोद्यानं त्वरितमागच्छेति । भवतु । तत्रैव गच्छामि ।—वहतं बलीवर्दौ वहतम् । (परिक्रम्यावलोक्य च ।) कथं ग्रामशकटै रुद्धो मार्गः । किमिदानीमत्र करिष्यामि । (साटोपम् ।) अरे रे अपसरत अपसरत । (आकर्ण्य ।) किं भणथ—एतत्कस्य प्रवहणमिति । एतद्राजश्यालकसंस्थानस्य प्रवहणम् । तच्छीघ्रमपसरत । (अवलोक्य ।) कथमेषोऽपरः सभिकमिव मां प्रेक्ष्य सहसैव द्यूतपलायित इव द्यूतकरोऽपवार्यात्मानमन्यतोऽपक्रान्तः । तत्कः पुनरेषः । अथ वा किं ममैतेन । त्वरितं गमिष्यामि । अरे रे ग्राम्याः अपसरत अपसरत । किं भणथ—मुहूर्तकं तिष्ठ । चक्रपरिवृत्तिं देहीति । अरे रे राजश्यालकसंस्थानस्याहं शूरश्चक्रपरिवृत्तिं दास्यामि । अथ वैष एकाकी तपस्वी । तदेवं करोमि । एतत्प्रवहणमार्यचारुदत्तस्य वृक्षवाटिकायाः पक्षद्वारके स्थापयामि । (इति प्रवहणं संस्थाप्य ।) एषोस्म्यागतः । (इति निष्क्रान्तः ।) (आण्णत्तम्हि लाअशालअशंठाणेण—थावलआ पवहणं गेण्हिअ पुप्फकलण्डअं जिण्णुज्जाणं तुलिदं आअच्छेहि त्ति । भोदु । तहिं ज्जेव गच्छामि ।—वहध बइल्ला वहध । कधं गामशअलेहिं लुद्धे मग्गे । किं दाणिं एत्थ कलइश्शम् । अले ले ओशलध ओशलध । किं भणाध—एशे कश्शकेलके पवहणे त्ति । एशे लाअशालअशंठाणकेलके पवहणम् । ता शिग्घं ओशलध । कधं एशे अवले शहिअं विअ मं पेक्खिअ शहश ज्जेव जूदपलाइदे विअ जूदिअले ओहालिअ अत्ताणअं अण्णदो अवक्कन्ते । ता को उण एशे । अध वा किं मम एदिणा । तुलिदं गमिश्शम् । अले ले गामेलुआ ओशलध ओशलध । किं भणाध—मुहुत्तअं चिट्ठ । चक्कपलिवट्टिं देहित्ति । अले ले लाअशालअशंठाणकेलके हगे शूले चक्कपलिवट्टिं दइश्शम् । अध वा एशे एआई तवश्शी । ता एव्वं कलेमि । एदं पवहणं अज्जचालुदत्तश्श रुक्खवाडिआए पक्खदुआलए थावेमि । एशे म्हि आअदे ।)

**चेटी**—आर्ये नेमिशब्द इव श्रूयते । तदागतं प्रवहणम् । (अज्जए णेमिसद्दो विअ सुणीअदि । ता आअदो पवहणो ।)

**वसन्तसेना**—चेटि गच्छ । त्वरते मे हृदयम् । तदादिश पक्षद्वारम् । (हञ्जे गच्छ । तुवरदि मे हिअअम् । ता आदेसेहि पक्खदुआलम् ।)

**चेटी**—एत्वेत्वार्या । (एदु एदु अज्जआ ।)

**वसन्तसेना**—(परिक्रम्य ।) चेटि विश्राम्य त्वम् । (हञ्जे वीसम तुमम् ।)

**चेटी**—यदार्याऽऽज्ञापयति । (इति निष्क्रान्ता ।) (जं अज्जआ आणवेदि ।)

**वसन्तसेना**—(दक्षिणाक्षिस्पदं सूचयित्वा प्रवहणमधिरुह्य च ।) किं न्विदं स्फुरति दक्षिणं लोचनम् । अथ वा चारुदत्तस्यैव दर्शनमनिमित्तं प्रमार्जयिष्यति । (किं ण्णेदं फुरदि दाहिणं लोअणम् । अध वा चारुदत्तस्स ज्जेव दंसणं अणिमित्तं पमज्जइस्सदि ।)

STHA'VARAKA CHETA—Samsthanaka, the King's brother-in-law, has ordered me—"Sthavaraka, take the car and come quickly to the old garden, *Pushpakarandaka.*" Well, then, I'll just go there.—Speed on, bullocks, speed on! (*Driving on and observing*). How! The village carts have blocked the road! Now, what shall I do here? (*Haughtily*). You there get out, get out (of the way)! (*Listening*). What do you ask—"Whose car is that"? This is the car of Samsthanaka, the King's brother-in-law! So get out (of the way) quickly! (*Seeing*). How! Here's a person who, on seeing me, suddenly concealed himself and made off in another direction, like a gambler, (who is) running away from the game, (making off) at the sight of the gambling-master! So who may he be? Or, what have I to do with him? I'll go on quickly. You there, yokels, get out, get out (of my way)! What do you say—"Stop awhile, and give a turn to this wheel"? Eh, you! Am I, the brave (servant) of Samsthanaka, the King's brother-in-law, to help you to a twist of the wheel? Or rather, he is alone, poor chap. So I'll manage thus: I'll stop this car near the side-door of the garden of the noble Charudatta. (*Stopping the car accordingly*). Here I am coming! (*Exit*).

THE MAID—Madam, a sound like that of the rims (of wheels) is heard. So the carriage must have come.

VAS.—Maid, go; my mind is in a hurry; so tell me (the way to) the side-door.

THE MAID—Come (this way), madam, come!

VAS—(*Walking about*). Girl, you may (now) retire.

THE MAID—As your ladyship orders. (*Exit*).

VAS—(*Showing that her right eye throbs, and mounting the car*). Why, I wonder, does this right eye of mine throb? Or, rather the sight of Charudatta himself will dispel (all) evil omens!

---

मङ्गलः । जीवो गुरुः । सूरः सूर्यस्तत्सुतः शनिः । एते ग्रहा उक्तस्थानस्थिता अत्यन्तानिष्टा जीवितापहाः । गोपालदारकमपहरतः कस्य मृत्युरुपस्थित इत्यर्थः । अष्टमसूर्यफलं मरणम् । चतुर्थचन्द्रफलं कुक्षिरोगः । षष्ठशुक्रफल बुद्धिहानिः । पञ्चममङ्गलफलं क्षतिः । षष्ठगुरुफलं शोकः शत्रुपीडा च । नवमशनैश्चरफलमर्थनाशः । अत्र बादरायणः—'हुतवहभयमारश्चन्द्रजः सौख्यमुग्रं धनहरणमथार्किर्भार्गवश्चार्थलाभम् । मरणमथ पतङ्गः स्थाननाशं सुरेज्यः सृजति निधनसंस्थो नेत्ररोगं च चन्द्रः ।

( प्रविश्य । )

**स्थावरक: चेट:**—अपसारिता मया शकटा: । तद्यावद्गच्छामि । (इति नाटचेनाधिरुह्य चालयित्वा । स्वगतम् ।) भारवत्प्रवहणम् । अथ वा चक्रपरिवर्तनेन परिश्रान्तस्य भारवत्प्रवहणं प्रतिभासते । भवतु । गमिष्यामि ।—यातं गावौ यातम् । ( ओशालिदा मए शअडा । ता जाव गच्छामि । भालिके पवहणे । अध वा चक्कपलिवट्टिआए पलिश्शन्तश्श भालिके पवहणे पडिभाशेदि । भोदु । गमिश्शम् । —जाध गोणा जाध ।)

( नेपथ्ये । )

अरे रे दौवारिका: अप्रमत्ता: स्वेषु स्वेषु गुल्मस्थानेषु भवत । एषोऽद्य गोपालदारको गुप्तिं भङ्क्त्वा गुप्तिपालकं व्यापाद्य बन्धनं भित्त्वा परिभ्रष्टोऽपक्रामति । तद्गृह्णीत गृह्णीत । (अरे रे दोवारिआ अप्पमत्ता सएसु सएसु गुम्मठ्ठाणेसु होध । एसो अज्ज गोवालदारओ गुत्तिअं भञ्जिअ गुत्तिवालअं वावादिअ बन्धणं भेदिअ परिब्भट्टो अवक्कमदि । ता गेण्हध गेण्हध ।)

( प्रविश्यापटीक्षेपेण संभ्रान्त एकचरणलग्ननिगडोऽवगुण्ठित आर्यक: परिक्रामति । )

**चेट:**—( स्वगतम् । ) महान्नगर्यां संभ्रम उत्पन्न: । तत्त्वरितं त्वरितं गमिष्यामि । (इति निष्क्रान्त: ।) (महन्ते णअलीए शंभमे उप्पण्णे । ता तुलिदं तुलिदं गमिश्शम् ।)

**आर्यक:**—

**हित्वाऽहं नरपतिबन्धनापदेश-**
**व्यापत्तिव्यसनमहार्णवं[1] महान्तम् ।**
**पादाग्रस्थितनिगडैकपाशकर्षी[2]**
**प्रभ्रष्टो गज इव बन्धनाद्भ्रमामि ॥ १ ॥**

भो: अहं खलु सिद्धादेशजनितपरित्रासेन राज्ञा पालकेन घोषादानीय विशसने गूढागारे बन्धनेन बद्ध: । तस्माच्च प्रियसुहृच्छर्विलकप्रसादेन बन्धनात्परिभ्रष्टोऽस्मि । ( अश्रूणि विसृज्य । )

**भाग्यानि मे यदि तदा मम कोऽपराधो**
**यद्बन्यनाग इव संयमितोऽस्मि तेन ।**
**दैवी च सिद्धिरपि लङ्घयितुं न शक्या**
**गम्यो नृपो बलवता सह को विरोध: ॥ २ ॥**

तत्कुत्र गच्छामि मन्दभाग्य: । ( विलोक्य । ) इदं कस्यापि साधोरनावृतपक्षद्वारं गेहम् ।

---

१ महार्हणं. २ पाशकर्षम्.

( *Entering* )

STHAVARAKA CHETA—I have cleared off these ( blocking ) carts. So then I'll proceed. ( *Shows that he mounts and drives; to himself* ). The vehicle is heavy ! Or rather, it appears heavy to me as I have been fatigued with turning that wheel. All right I'll proceed.—Push on, bullocks, push on !

( *Behind the curtains* )

O you ( all ) gate-keepers ! Keep a vigilant watch at your respective guard-posts ! For now this cowhere's son ( Aryaka ) has broken through the prison by killing his jailor ; he has cut his chains, and has given us the slip ; he is escaping ! So capture him, do capture him !

( *Then enter with a toss of the curtain in great hurry, A'ryaka, veiled, and with a chain still clinging to one foot ; he walks about* ).

CHETA.—( *To himself* ). There has sprung up a great commotion in the city. So I'll go very quickly. ( *Exit* ).

ARYAKA—

Like an elephant that has broken loose from his tying-post, I am ( now ) wandering about, dragging the one remaining fetter of the chain clinging to the forepart of my foot, having escaped from the terrible great ocean of the calamity of death (commonly) called 'the king's prison'. ( 1 )

Oh ! I was forsooth brought from the cowherd's hamlet by king Palaka, frightened by the prophecy of a seer, and was then kept bound with a chain in a secret death-dealing dungeon. And I have ( now ) escaped from that imprisonment by the favour of my dear friend, Sarvilaka. ( *Shedding tears* ).

If I do possess ( future ) good luck, then what fault is it of mine, that he should have imprisoned me, as one does a wild elephant ? And moreover, one cannot oppose the workings of Destiny. ( But still ), the king is one to whom all pay homage ; what hostility can there be against ( such ) a powerful person ? (2)

So then, where shall I, the unlucky one, go ? ( *Seeing* ). Here is the house of some good man, with its side-door open !

---

सूक्ष्मां शास्त्रविबोधिकामपि धियं मूढां करोत्यङ्गिरा घोरां दुःखपरंपरां दिनकरः कुक्ष्यामयं चन्द्रमाः । सौम्यो रोगविनाशमिच्छति नृणां रोगभयं भार्गवो भौमः शत्रुभयं चतुर्थभवने सौरिश्च वित्तक्षयम् ॥ स्थिताः षष्ठे राशौ दिनकरमहीजार्कतनया

इदं गृहं भिन्नमदत्तदण्डो[1] विशीर्णसंधिश्च महाकपाटः ।
ध्रुवं कुटुम्बी व्यसनाभिभूतां दशां प्रपन्नो मम तुल्यभाग्यः ॥ ३ ॥

तदत्र तावत्प्रविश्य तिष्ठामि ।

( नेपथ्ये । )

यातं गावौ यातम् । (जाध गोणा जाध ।)

आर्यकः—(आकर्ण्य ।) अये प्रवहणमित एवाभिवर्तते ।

भवेद्गोष्ठीयानं न च विषमशीलैरधिगत
वधूसंयानं वा तदभिगमनोपस्थितमिदम् ।
बहिर्नेतव्यं वा प्रवरजनयोग्यं विधिवशा-
द्विविक्तत्वाच्छून्यं मम खलु भवेद्दैवविहितम् ॥ ४ ॥

( ततः प्रवहणेन सह प्रविश्य । )

वर्धमानकः चेटः—आश्चर्यम । आनीतं मया यानास्तरणम् । रदनिके निवेदयार्यायै वसन्तसेनायै—अवस्थित सज्जं प्रवहणमधिरुह्य पुष्पकरण्डकं जीर्णोद्यानं गच्छत्वार्या । (हीमाणहे । आणीदे मए जाणत्थलके । लदणिए णिवेदेहि अज्जआए वशन्तशेणाए—अवत्थिदे शज्जे पवहणे अहिलुहिअ पुप्फकलण्डअं जिण्णुज्जाणं गच्छदु अज्जआ । )

आर्यकः—( आकर्ण्य ) गणिकाप्रवहणमिदम् । बहिर्यानं च । भवतु । अधिरोहामि । ( इति स्वैरमुपसर्पति । )

चेटः—( श्रुत्वा । ) कथं नूपुरशब्दः । तदागता खल्वार्या । आर्ये इमौ नासिकारज्जुकटुकौ बलीवर्दौ । तत्पृष्ठत एवारोहत्वार्या । (कधं णेउलशद्दे । ता आअदा क्खु अज्जआ । अज्जए इमे णश्शालज्जुकडुआ बइल्ला । ता पिट्ठदो[2] ज्जेव आलुहदु अज्जआ । )

( आर्यकस्तथा करोति । )

चेटः—पादोत्फालचालितानां नूपुराणां विश्रान्तः शब्दः । भाराक्रान्तं च प्रवहणम् । तथा तर्कयामि सांप्रतमार्ययाऽऽरूढया भवितव्यम् । तद्गच्छामि ।—यात गावौ यातम् । ( इति परिक्रामति । ) ( पादुप्फालचालिदाणं णेउलाण वीशन्तो शद्दो । भलक्कन्ते अ पवहणे । तथा तक्केमि शपदं अज्जआए आलूढाए होदव्वम् । ता गच्छामि ।—जाध गोणा जाध । )

( प्रविश्य । )

वीरकः—अरे रे अरे जय जयमान-चन्दनक-मङ्गल-पुष्पभद्र-प्रमुखाः ।

किं गच्छथ विश्रब्धाः यः स गोपालदारको बद्धः ।
भित्वा समं व्रजति नरपतिहृदयं च बन्धनं चापि ॥ ५ ॥

---

१ मनायतार्गलम्. २ पिश्टदो.

This house is in ruins ; and this big panel of its gate has no belt fixed to it, and is cracked at its joints. Surely this householder, whose fortunes resemble mine, must have been ( recently ) reduced to a wretched ( i. e. penniless ) condition ! ( 3 )

( *Behind the curtains* )

Push on, bullocks, push on !

ARYAKA—( *Listening* ). Ah ! A carriage is coming in this very direction !

Can it be the carriage of a picnic-party, not occupied by ill-natured people ? Or perhaps it is a bride's carriage, arriving to take her away. Or by good luck, it is to be taken outside ( the city ), intended for some high personage. As it is unattended I fervently hope that it may be empty, sent unto me by my good luck ! ( 4 )

( *Then entering with the chariot* )

VARDHAMA'NAKA CHETA—Fine ! I have brought those carriage-cushions. O Radanika, tell her ladyship Vasantasena, that she may get into the carriage which stands ( here ) ready, and proceed to the old garden *Pushpakarandaka.*

ARYAKA----( *Listening* ). This carriage belongs to a courtesan; and it is to go outside ( the city ). All right; I'll mount it. ( *Approaches gently* )

CHETA—( *Hearing* ). How ! These are anklets jingling ! So her ladyship must have come.--Madam, these bullocks are restive on account of their ( new ) nose-rope. So you should mount it from the back.

( Aryaka *does accordingly* ).

CHETA--The jingling of the anklets shaken by the movement of the feet has ( now ) ceased; and the carriage has become heavy. So I take it that her ladyship must have now mounted. So then I'll proceed.--Speed on, bullocks, speed on ! ( *Drives on* ).

( *Entering* )

VIRAKA--Ho, there ! You, Jaya, Jayamana Chandanaka, Mangala, Pushpabhadra, and the rest !

How is it that you are walking about at ease ? That cowherd's son who was put in jail,—he is escaping, having simultaneously broken the heart of the king and his chains ! ( 5 )

अरे पुरस्तात्प्रतोलीद्वारे तिष्ठ त्वम् । त्वमपि पश्चिमे त्वमपि दक्षिणे त्वमप्युत्तरे । योऽप्येष प्राकारखण्ड एनमधिरुह्य चन्दनेन समं गत्वाऽवलोकयामि । एहि चन्दनक एहि । इतस्तावत् ।

(अरे रे अरे जअ-जअमाण-चन्दणअ-मङ्गल-फुल्लभद्द-प्पमुहा ।
किं [1]अच्छध वीसद्धा जो सो गोवालदारओ बद्धो ।
भेत्तूण समं वच्चइ णरवइहिअअं अ बन्धणं चावि ॥

अले पुरत्थिमे पदोलीदुआरे चिट्ठ तुमम् । तुमं पि पच्छिमे तुमं पि दक्खिणे तुमं पि उत्तरे । जो वि एसो पाआरखण्डो एद अहिरुहिअ चन्दणेण समं गदुअ अवलोएमि । एहि चन्दणअ एहि । इदो दाव ।)

( प्रविश्य संभ्रान्तः । )

**चन्दनकः**—अरे रे वीरक-विशल्य-भीमाङ्गद-दण्डकालक-दण्डशूर-प्रमुखाः ।

आगच्छत विश्वस्तास्त्वरितं यतध्वं लघु कुरुत ।
लक्ष्मीर्येन न राज्ञः प्रभवति गोत्रान्तरं गन्तुम् ॥ ६ ॥

(अरे रे वीरअ-विसल्ल-भीमङ्गअ-दण्डकालअ-दण्डसूरप्पमुहा ।
आअच्छध वीसत्था तुरिअं जत्तेह लहुं करेज्जाह ।
लच्छी जेण ण रण्णो पहवइ गोत्तन्तरं गन्तुम् ॥ )

अपि च ।

उद्यानेषु सभासु च मार्गे नगर्यामापणे घोषे ।
तं तमन्वेषयत त्वरितं शङ्का वा जायते यत्र ॥ ७ ॥
रे रे वीरक किं किं दर्शयसि भणसि तावद्विश्रब्धम् ।
भित्त्वा च बन्धनकं कः स गोपालदारकं हरति ॥ ८ ॥
कस्याष्टमो दिनकरः कस्य चतुर्थश्च वर्तते चन्द्रः ।
षष्ठश्च भार्गवग्रहो भूमिसुतः पञ्चमः कस्य ॥ ९ ॥
भण कस्य जन्मषष्ठो जीवो नवमस्तथैव सूरसुतः ।
जीवति चन्दनके कः स गोपालदारकं हरति ॥ १० ॥

(अवि अ ।

उज्जाणेसु सहासु अ मग्गे णअरीअ आवणे घोसे ।
तं तं जोहह तुरिअं सङ्का वा जाअए जत्थ ॥
रे रे वीरअ किं किं दरिसेसि भणाहि दाव वीसद्धम् ।
भेत्तूण अ बन्धणअं को सो गोवालदारअं हरइ ॥

---

१ 'स्थ,' 'तिष्ठथ,' इति च्छायाया०.

Eh, you, stand at the eastern gate of the main street! And you, too, at the western;--and you at the southern;—and you at the northern! And this part of the rampart here,--to the same I'll go and mount, and observe ( the place around ) in the company of Chandanaka. Come, Chandanaka, come! This way, here!

( *Entering, in excitement* )

CHANDANAKA—Ho, there! Viraka, Visalya, Bhimangada, Dandakalaka, Dandasura, and the rest of you!

Come confidently; strive quickly and make haste, so that Royalty will be unable to move to another family! ( 6 )

And moreover--

In gardens, in gambling saloons, on roads, in the city, in markets, and in stables,--quickly search every person about whom you may have a suspicion! (7)

Oh, O Viraka! What--what do you want me to see? You may speak without hesitation. Who is he that is rescuing that cowherd's son, having cut asunder his fetters? (8)

Who has the Sun in the eighth mansion ( in his horoscope )? —or the Moon in the fourth, or the planet Venus in the sixth, or Mars, the son of the Earth, in the fifth? (9)

Say, who has Jupiter in the sixth mansion of his birth-horoscope, or Saturn, the son of the Sun, in the ninth? Who is he that is rescuing that cowherd's son, while Chandanaka is alive? (10)

---

बुधश्चन्द्रश्चैवं प्रचुरधनधान्यानि ददति । समृद्धिं शत्रूणां मनसिजविषादं सुरगुरु-भृंगुर्नाशं कुर्याद्युवतिकृतवैरं च परमम् ॥ दौर्भाग्यं शशलाञ्छनः क्षितिसुतश्चोद्विग्नतां चेतसः' इत्यादि । 'धर्मस्थाने दिनकरसुतो नाशमर्थस्य कुर्यात्' इत्यादि । अत्र पृथ्वीधरोक्तश्लोकांशाः सम्यक्तया नोपलभ्यन्ते इति न निवेशिताः । ते बृहत्संहितायां द्रष्टव्याः ॥ ९ ॥ १० ॥ अपहरतीत्यादि । गाथा । खुटितः छिन्नबन्ध इत्यर्थः प्राकृतम् ॥ ११ ॥ अपवारितमित्यादि । गाथा । उद्घाटितं प्रवहणम् । एवं तावद्विचारय कस्य कुत्र वा प्रवसितं प्रवहणमिति ॥ १२ ॥ कस्तमिति । द्वावेवेति । गाथाद्वयम् । [गुणानामरविन्दं कमलं मधुन इव निवासस्थानम् । यद्वा गुणा अरविन्दं इव यस्य । शीलस्य मृगाङ्कं चन्द्रमिव स्थितम् । आपन्नानां विपद्ग्रस्तानां शरणमागतानां वा मोक्षं दुःखमुक्तिस्थानम् । यद्वा ] आपन्नदुःखस्य मोक्षो यतस्तं चतुःसागरसारकं रत्नम् । [तिलक-

कस्सट्ठमो दिणअरो कस्स चउत्थो अ वट्टए चन्दो ।
छट्ठो अ भग्गवगहो भूमिसुओ पञ्चमो कस्स ॥
भण कस्स जम्मछट्ठो जीवो णवमो तहेअ सूरसुओ ।
जीअन्ते चन्दणए को सो गोवालदारअं हरइ ॥ )

वीरकः—भट चन्दनक ।

अपहरति[1] कोऽपि त्वरितं चन्दनक शपे तव हृदयेन ।
यथाऽर्धोदितदिनकरे गोपालदारकः खुटितः[2] ॥ ११ ॥

(भड चन्दणआ ।

अवहरइ कोवि तुरिअं चन्दणअ सवामि तुज्ज हिअएण ।
जह अद्धुइददिणअरे गोवालअदारओ खुडिदो ॥ )

चेटः—यातं गावौ यातम् । (जाध गोणा जाध ।)

चन्दनकः—(दृष्ट्वा ।) अरे रे पश्य पश्य ।

अपवारितं प्रवहणं व्रजति मध्येन राजमार्गस्य ।
एतत्तावद्विचारय कस्य कुत्र प्रोषितं प्रवहणमिति ॥ १२ ॥

(अरे रे पेक्ख पेक्ख ।

ओहारिओ पवहणो वच्चइ मज्झेण राअमग्गस्स ।
एदं दाव विआरह कस्स कहिं पवसिओ पवहणोत्ति ॥ )

वीरकः—(अवलोक्य ।) अरे प्रवहणवाहक मा तावदेतत्प्रवहणं वाहय । कस्यैतत्प्रवहणम् । को वेहारूढः । कुत्र वा व्रजति । (अरे पवहणवाहआ मा दाव एवं पवहणं वाहेहि । कस्सकेरकं एदं पवहणम् । को वा इध आरूढो । कहिं वा वज्जइ ।)

चेटः—एतत्खलु प्रवहणमार्यचारुदत्तस्य । इहार्या वसन्तसेनाऽऽरूढा । पुष्पकरण्डकं जीर्णोद्यानं क्रीडितुं चारुदत्तस्य नीयते । (एशे क्खु पवहणे अज्जचालुदत्ताह-केलके । इध अज्जआ वशन्तशेणा आलूढा । पुप्फकरण्डअं जिण्णुज्जाणं कीलिदुं चालुदत्तश्श णीअदि ।)

वीरकः—(चन्दनकमुपसृत्य ।) एष प्रवहणवाहको भणति—आर्यचारुदत्तस्य प्रवहणम् । वसन्तसेनाऽऽरूढा । पुष्पकरण्डकं जीर्णोद्यानं नीयत इति । (एसो पवहणवाहओ भणादि—अज्जचालुदत्तस्स पवहणं । वशन्तशेणा आलूढा । पुप्फ-करण्डअं जिण्णुज्जाणं णीअदि त्ति ।)

चन्दनकः—तद्गच्छतु । (ता गच्छदु ।)

वीरकः—अनवलोकित एव । (अणवलोइदो ज्जेव ।)

---

१ अवह०. २ खण्डितः.

VIRAKA—Soldier Chandanaka!

I swear by your heart, O Chandanaka, that someone must be we they carrying off that cowherd's son; for he was found missing when the sun was just half risen. (11)

CHETA—Push on, bullocks, push on!

CHAND—(*Seeing*). Eh, there! Just see--see!

A closed carriage is being driven along the middle of the high road; so just inquire to whom it belongs, and where it is going. (12)

VIRAKA--(*Seeing*). You, driver of the car, just stop driving that carriage! To whom does it belong? And who is seated inside? And whither is it going?

CHETA—Well, this carriage belongs to the noble Charudatta. Her ladyship Vasantasena is seated within. And she is being taken to the old garden *Pushpakarandaka*, for sporting with Charudatta.

VIRAKA—(*Approaching* Chandanaka). This carriage-driver says that the car belongs to the noble Charudatta, that Vasantasena is inside, and that she is being taken to the old garden *Pushpakarandaka.*

CHAND.—Then allow it to go.

V'IRAKA—Without being inspected at all?

---

भूतो अलंकारभूतो। धर्मनिधिः पुण्यैकसंचयः] ॥ १३ ॥ १४ ॥ **जानामीति** । गाथा । [राजकार्ये राज्ञः प्राप्ते कार्ये कर्तव्यत्वेनोपस्थिते ।] प्राप्ते चेति चकारः पुनरर्थे ॥१५॥ **एकेति** ॥ १६ ॥ तन्त्रिलश्चिन्तापरः । **भीमस्येति** । [भीमस्य शस्त्रं विना बाहुभ्यामेव युध्यमानस्य।] व्यायच्छतः परपरिभवं कुर्वतः ॥ १७ ॥ **त्यजतीति** ॥ १८ ॥ पत्ररथः पक्षी । शाकुनिकस्य पक्षिणां हन्तुः । **भीताभयेति** । गाथा । भीतेभ्यः अभयप्रदानं ददतः परोपकारे निरतस्य ॥ १९ ॥ परिभूता रथाधिरोहणेन धर्षिता । **संभ्रमेत्यादि** । गाथा । [त्वमपि धीरोऽसि । संभ्रमेण भयव्याकुलतया घर्घरः कण्ठो यस्य।] यस्त्वं जातोऽसि ॥ २० ॥ [कर्णाटकलहः मिथ्याकलहः तस्य प्रयोगं करोमि।] **जानन्नपीति** । गाथा । [शीलविभवेन मम शीलस्य विभवेन औन्नत्येन ] ॥ २१ ॥ संज्ञां ददातीति जात्युचितक्रियाभिनयः । **शीर्णेत्यादि** । गाथा [शीर्णं शिलातलं क्षुरादितेजनशिलाखण्डः हस्ते यस्य स शीर्णशिलातलहस्तः । पुरुषाणां कूर्चग्रन्थिसंस्थापनः सम्यक्स्थापकः । अनेन पर्यायेण नापितजातिर्दर्शिता ] ॥ २२ ॥ **जातिस्तवेति** । गाथा । [करटकस्य वाद्यविशेषस्य भ्राता । अत्र चर्मावगुण्ठित-

**चन्दनकः**—अथ किम् । (अध इं ।)

**वीरकः**—कस्य प्रत्ययेन । (कस्स पच्चएण ।)

**चन्दनकः**—आर्यचारुदत्तस्य । (अज्जचारुदत्तस्स ।)

**वीरकः**—क आर्यचारुदत्तः का वा वसन्तसेना येनानवलोकितं व्रजति । (को[1] अज्जचारुदत्तो का वा वसन्तसेणा जेण अणवलोइदं वच्चदि ।)

**चन्दनकः**—अरे आर्यचारुदत्तं न जानासि न वा वसन्तसेनाम् । यद्यार्यचारुदत्तं वसन्तसेनां वा न जानासि तदा गगने ज्योत्स्नासहितं चन्द्रमपि त्वं न जानासि ।

**कस्तं गुणारविन्दं शीलमृगाङ्कं जनो न जानाति ।**
**आपन्नदुःखमोक्षं चतुःसागरसारं रत्नम् ॥ १३ ॥**
**द्वावेव पूजनीयाविह नगर्यां तिलकभूतौ च ।**
**आर्या वसन्तसेना धर्मनिधिश्चारुदत्तश्च ॥ १४ ॥**

(अरे अज्जचारुदत्तं ण जाणासि ण वा वसन्तसेणिअम् । जइ अज्जचारुदत्तं वसन्तसेणिअं वा ण जाणासि ता गअणे जोण्हासहिदं चन्दं पि तुमं ण जाणासि ।

को तं गुणारविन्दं शीलमीअङ्कं जणो ण जाणादि ।
आवण्णदुक्खमोक्खं चउसाअरसारअं रअणम् ॥
दो ज्जेव[2] पूअणीआ इह णअरीए तिलअभूदा अ ।
अज्जा वसन्तसेणा धम्मणिही चारुदत्तो अ ॥)

**वीरकः**—अरे चन्दनक ।

**जानामि चारुदत्तं वसन्तसेनां च सुष्ठु जानामि ।**
**प्राप्ते च राजकार्ये पितरमप्यहं न जानामि ॥ १५ ॥**

(अरे चन्दणआ ।

जाणामि चारुदत्तं वसन्तसेणं अ सुट्ठु जाणामि ।
पत्ते अ राअकज्जे पिदरं पि अहं ण जाणामि ॥)

**आर्यकः**—(स्वगतम् ।) अयं मे पूर्ववैरी । अयं मे पूर्वबन्धुः । यतः ।

**[3]एककार्यनियोगेऽपि नानयोस्तुल्यशीलता ।**
**विवाहे च चितायां च यथा हुतभुजोर्द्वयोः ॥ १६ ॥**

**चन्दनकः**—त्वं तन्त्रिलः सेनापती राज्ञः प्रत्ययितः । एतौ धारितौ मया बलीवर्दौ अवलोकय । (तुमं तन्तिलो सेणावई रण्णो पच्चइदो । एदे धारिदा मए बइल्ला अवलोएहि ।)

**वीरकः**—त्वमपि राज्ञः प्रत्ययितो बलपतिः । तस्मात्त्वमेवावलोकय । (तुमं पि रण्णो पच्चइदो बलवई । ता तुमं ज्जेव अवलोएहि ।)

---

१ को स. २ वेव्व. ३ एकाकार्य.

CHAND.—Yes. Why not ?

VIRAKA—Trusting whom ?

CHAND.—The noble Charudatta.

VIRAKA—Who is the noble Charudatta or Vasantasena, that it is to go uninspected ?

CHAND.—Ah ! Don't you know the noble Charudatta, nor Vasantasena ? If you don't know the noble Charudatta, nor Vasantasena, then you don't know even the moon in the sky, with its light !

What person does not know that Charudatta, whose virtues are like ( i. e., as charming as ) lotuses, whose character is like ( i. e., as attractive as ) the moon, who relieves the misery of the affected, and who is ( as it were ) a jewel, the essence of the four oceans ? ( 13 )

In this city only two persons deserve to be honoured, and are an ornament to it, *viz.*, her ladyship Vasantasena, and Charudatta, the store of righteousness. ( 14 )

VIRAKA—O Chandanaka !

I know Charudatta, and I know Vasantasena, too, quite well. But, when the king's business is to be done, I don't know even my own father ! ( 15 )

ARYAKA—( *To himself* ). This person ( Viraka ) must have been my past enemy, and this one ( Chandanaka ) my past friend, since—

Although appointed to discharge the same function, these two do not behave in the same manner, just like the two fires, the one at a wedding and the other at a funeral. ( 16 )

CHAND.—You are an investigating officer in the army, trusted by the king. I have held these bullocks ; you may ( therefore ) inspect.

VIRAKA—You, too, are an officer in the army, trusted by the king. So you may inspect yourself.

---

वाद्यानां मातापितृत्वाद्यारोपणेन भङ्ग्यन्तरेण चर्मकारजातिरुक्ता । ] ॥ २३ ॥ अये इति । [पुंसो दक्षिणबाहुस्पन्दः सौभाग्यसूचकः] ॥ २४ ॥ अत्रेति । [प्रत्ययिता राज्यलाभेन सिद्धादेशे जातविश्वासा । लुब्धः द्रव्यगृध्नुः ] सन्न भणामि ॥ २५ ॥

**चन्दनकः**—मयाऽवलोकितं त्वयाऽवलोकितं भवति। (मए अवलोइदं तुए अवलोइदं भोदि।)

**वीरकः**—यस्त्वयाऽवलोकितं तद्राज्ञा पालकेनावलोकितम्। (जं तुए अवलोइदं तं रण्णा पालएण अवलोइदम्।)

**चन्दनकः**—अरे उन्नमय धुरम्। (अरे उण्णामेहि धुरम्।)

(चेटस्तथा करोति।)

**आर्यकः**—(स्वगतम्।) अपि रक्षिणो मावलोकयन्ति। अशस्त्रश्चास्मि मन्दभाग्यः। अथ वा।

**भीमस्यानुकरिष्यामि बाहुः शस्त्रं भविष्यति।**
**वरं व्यायच्छतो मृत्युर्न गृहीतस्य बन्धने॥ १७॥**

अथ वा साहसस्य तावदनवसरः।

(चन्दनको नाट्येन प्रवहणमारुह्यावलोकयति।)

**आर्यकः**—शरणागतोऽस्मि।

**चन्दनकः**—(संस्कृतमाश्रित्य।) अभयं शरणागतस्य।

**आर्यकः**—

**त्यजति किल तं जयश्रीर्जहति च मित्राणि बन्धुवर्गश्च।**
**भवति च सदोपहास्यो यः खलु शरणागतं त्यजति॥ १८॥**

**चन्दनकः**—कथमार्यको गोपालदारकः श्येनवित्रासित इव पत्ररथः शाकुनिकस्य हस्ते निपतितः। (विचिन्त्य।) एषोनपराधः शरणागत आर्यचारुदत्तस्य प्रवहणमारूढः प्राणप्रदस्य म आर्यशर्विलकस्य मित्रम्। अन्यतो राजनियोगः। तत्किमिदानीमत्र युक्तमनुष्ठातुम्। अथ वा यद्भवतु तद्भवतु। प्रथममेवाभयं दत्तम्।

**भीताभयप्रदानं ददतः परोपकाररसिकस्य।**
**यदि भवति भवतु नाशस्तथाऽपि खलु लोके गुण एव॥ १९॥**

(सभयमवतीर्य।) दृष्ट आर्यः—(इत्यर्धोक्ते[1]।) न, आर्या वसन्तसेना। तदेषा भणति—युक्तं न्विदं सदृशं न्विदं यदहमार्यचारुदत्तमभिसर्तुं गच्छन्ती राजमार्गे परिभूता। (कधं अज्जओ गोवालदारओ सेणवित्तासिदो विअ पत्तरहो साउणिअस्स हत्थे णिवडिदो। एसो अणवराधो सरणाअदो अज्जचारुदत्तस्स पवहणं आरूढो पाणप्पदस्स मे अज्जसव्विलअस्स मित्तम्। अण्णदो राअणिओओ। ता किं दाणि एत्थ जुत्तं अणुचिट्ठिदुम्। अध वा जं भोदु तं भोदु। पढमं ज्जेव अभअं दिण्णम्।

भीदाभअप्पदाणं दत्तस्स परोवआररसिअस्स।
जइ होइ होउ णासो तहवि हु लोए गुणो ज्जेव्व॥

दिट्ठो अज्जो—ण, अज्जआ[2] वसन्तसेणा। तदो एसा भणादि—जुत्तं ण्णेदं सरिसं ण्णेदं जं अहं अज्जचारुदत्तं अहिसरिदुं गच्छन्ती राअमग्गे परिभूदा।)

---

1 र्धोक्तेन. २ अज्जुआ.

CHAND.—If I inspect, would it be as good as being inspected by you ?

VIRAKA—What is inspected by you is ( as though it were ) inspected by king Palaka himself.

CHAND. —You there, raise up the yoke !

( Cheta *does so* ).

ARYAKA—( *To himself* ). Would the guards find me out ? Unlucky that I am, I am without weapons, too ! Or rather—

I shall imitate Bhima ; my arm shall be my weapon ! It is better to die fighting, rather than in chains, as a prisoner. ( 17 )

Or rather, this is no time for rash enterprise.

(Chandanaka *gesticulates mounting the carriage, and looks in* ).

ARYAKA—I seek your protection, Sir !

CHAND —( *Speaking in Sanskrit* ). Safety to one who seeks protection !

ARYAKA—

Whoever deserts a person that seeks his protection, he is forsaken by the goddess of success, by his friends, and by all his relatives ; and he is always exposed to derision (everywhere). (18)

CHAND.—How ! The cowherd's son Aryaka has, like a bird frightened by ( *i e.* flying from ) a hawk, fallen into the hands of a fowler ! (*Reflecting*). [ On one hand ] this innocent man, seeking my protection and riding in the noble Charudatta's carriage, is the friend of the worthy Sarvilaka, who ( once ) saved my life. And on the other hand there is my official duty. So, now, what is the right thing to do under these circumstances ? Or rather, come what may ; I have already promised him freedom from fear.

If ruin befalls a man who, intent on obliging others, promises safety to a frightened person, why, let it befall ; but all the same, in the world it would be ( regarded as ) a righteous deed. ( 19 )

( *Getting down in fear* ). I have seen him—( *Leaving it half-said* )—no, her ladyship Vasantasena. And she says—" Is it proper, is it becoming, that I should be insulted on the high road while going to meet the noble Charudatta ? "

---

चन्दन इति । तथा यदीत्यादि । राज्यप्राप्तिरूपः ॥ २६ ॥ अभयमित्यादि । आर्या । । २७ ॥ विरोधिदो विरोधितः । पुत्रभ्रातृप्रभृतिभिः सहितः । तमार्यकमेव ।

इति प्रवहणविपर्यासो नाम षष्ठोऽङ्कः ।

**वीरकः**—चन्दनक अत्र मे संशयः समुत्पन्नः। (चन्दणआ एत्थ मह संसओ समुप्पण्णो।)

**चन्दनकः**—कथं ते संशयः। (कधं दे संसओ।)

**वीरकः**—

संभ्रमघर्घरकण्ठस्त्वमपि जातोऽसि यत्त्वया भणितम्।
दृष्टो मया खल्वार्यः पुनरप्यार्या वसन्तसेनेति॥ २०॥

अत्र मेऽप्रत्ययः।

(संभमघग्घरकण्ठो तुमं पि जादो सि जं तुए भणिदम्।
दिट्ठो मए क्खु अज्जो पुणो वि अज्जा वसन्तसेणेत्ति॥

एत्थ मे अप्पच्चओ।)

**चन्दनकः**—अरे कोऽप्रत्ययस्तव। वयं दाक्षिणात्या अव्यक्तभाषिणः। खश-खत्ति-खड-खडठ्ठ-विड-कर्णाट-कर्ण-प्रावरण-द्राविड-चोल-चीन–बर्बर–खेर–खान-मुख-मधुघात-प्रभृतीनां म्लेच्छजातीनामनेकदेशभाषाभिज्ञा यथेष्टं मन्त्रयामहे दृष्टो दृष्टा वा। आर्य आर्या वा (अरे को अप्पच्चओ तुह। वअं दक्खिणत्ता अव्वत्तभासिणो। खस-खत्ति खड-खडठ्ठ-विलअ-कण्णाट-कण्ण-प्पावरणअ-दविड-चोल-चीण-बर्बर-खेर-खान-गुख-मधुघाद-पहुदाणं मिलिच्छजादीणं अणेअदेसभासाभिण्णा जहेट्ठं मन्तआम दिट्ठो दिट्ठा वा अज्जो अज्जआ वा[1]।)

**वीरकः**—नन्वहमपि प्रलोकयामि। राजाज्ञैषा। अहं राज्ञः प्रत्ययितः। (णं अहं पि पलोएमि। राअअण्णा एसा। अहं रण्णो पच्चइदो।)

**चन्दनकः**—तत्किमहमप्रत्ययितः संवृत्तः। (ता किं अहं अप्पच्चइदो संवुत्तो।)

**वीरकः**—ननु स्वामिनियोगः। (णं समिणिओओ।)

**चन्दनकः**—(स्वगतम्।) आर्यगोपालदारक आर्यचारुदत्तस्य प्रवहणमधिरुह्यापक्रामतीति यदि कथ्यते तदाऽऽर्यचारुदत्तो राज्ञा शास्यते। तत्कोऽत्रोपायः। (विचिन्त्य।) कर्णाटकलहप्रयोग करोमि। (प्रकाशम्।) अरे वीरक मया चन्दनकेन प्रलोकितं पुनरपि त्वं प्रलोकयसि। कस्त्वम्। (अज्जगोवालदारओ अज्जचारुदत्तस्स पवहणं अहिरुहिअ अवक्कमदित्ति जइ कहिज्जदि तदो अज्जचारुदत्तो रण्णा सासिज्जइ। ता को एत्थ उवाओ। कण्णाटकलहप्पओअं कलेमि। अरे वीरअ मए चन्दणकेण पलोइदं पुणो वि तुमं पलोएसि। को तुमम्।)

**वीरकः**—अरे त्वमपि कः। (अरे तुमं पि को।)

**चन्दनकः**—पूज्यमानो मान्यमानस्त्वमात्मनो जातिं न स्मरसि। (पूइज्जन्तो माणिज्जन्तो तुमं अप्पणो जादिं ण सुमरेसि।)

**वीरकः**—(सक्रोधम्।) अरे का मम जातिः। (अरे का मह जादी।)

**चन्दनकः**—को भणतु। (को भणउ।)

**वीरकः**—भणतु। (भणउ।)

---

१ अस्मात्परं 'किं शब्दविचारः। स्त्रीपुंनपुंसकव्याख्यानमप्रस्तुतम्' इत्य०ए०पु०।

VIRAKA—Chandanaka, a suspicion has arisen in my mind about this.

CHAND.—How is it that you entertain a suspicion ?

VIRAKA—

Your voice sounded hoarse with nervousness when you said I have seen him, ' and immediately again, ' her ladyship Vasantsasena.' ( 20 )

So I can't believe ( you ) in this matter.

CHAND.—Ah, why should you not believe me ? We natives of the south speak indiscriminately. We are conversant with the various dialects of different countries, as spoken by the Mlechchha ( barbarian ) tribes, such as Khasa, Khatti, Khada, Khadaththa, Vida, Karnata, Karna, Pravarana, Dravida, Chola, China, Barbara, Khera, Khana, Mukha, Madhughata, and the others: and we speak as we please, saying either 'I have seen *him*', or 'I have seen *her*' ( *i. e.* without distinction of gender ).

VIRAKA—Still, let me also inspect; ( for ) such is the king's order; and I have the king's trust.

CHAND.—What, then, have I become one who is *not* trusted ( by the king ) ?

VIRAKA—Still, there's the king's order.

CHAND.—( *To himself* ). If it were to get reported that the worthy cowherd's son escaped by riding in the carriage of the noble Charudatta, then our noble Charudatta would be punished by the king. So, what is the remedy in this matter ? (*Pondering*). I shall stir up a quarrel after the manner of the people in Karnataka. ( *Aloud* ). You, Viraka, are you going to re-inspect what has been inspected by *me*, Chandanaka ? Wko are you, eh ?

VIRAKA—Ho ! And who are *you* ?

CHAND.—Honoured and respected as you are, you don't ( now ) remember your lineage.

VIRAKA—( *Angrily* ) Ho ! And what ( do you think ) is my lineage ?

CHAND.—Who can say ?

VIRAKA—Speak.

**चन्दनकः**—अथ वा न भणामि । (अह वा ण भणामि ।)

**जानन्नपि खलु जातिं तव च न भणामि शीलविभवेन ।**
**तिष्ठतु ममैव मनसि किं च कपित्थेन भग्नेन ॥ २१ ॥**

(जाणन्तो वि हु ज जादिं तुज्झ अ ण भणामि सीलविहवेण ।
चिट्ठउ मह्च्चिअ मणे किं च कइत्थेण भग्गेण ॥)

**वीरकः**—ननु भणतु भणतु । (णं भणउ भणउ ।)

(चन्दनकः संज्ञां ददाति ।)

**वीरकः**—अरे किं न्विदम् । (अरे किं ण्णेदम् ।)

**चन्दनकः**—

**शीर्णशिलातलहस्तः पुरुषाणां कूर्चग्रन्थिसंस्थापनः ।**
**कर्तरीव्यापृतहस्तस्त्वमपि सेनापतिर्जातः ॥ २२ ॥**

(सिण्णसिलाअलहत्थो पुरिसाणं कुच्चगण्ठिसंठवणो ।
कत्तरिवावुदहत्थो तुमं पि सेणावई जादो ॥ )

**वीरकः**—अरे चन्दनक त्वमपि मान्यमान आत्मनो जातिं न स्मरसि । (अरे चन्दणआ तुमं पि माणिज्जन्तो अप्पणोकेरिकं जादिं ण सुमरेसि ।)

**चन्दनकः**—अरे का मम चन्दनकस्य चन्द्रविशुद्धस्य जातिः । (अरे का मह चन्दणअस्स चन्दविसुद्धस्स जादी ।)

**वीरकः**—को भणतु । (को भणउ ।)

**चन्दनकः**—भणतु भणतु । (भणउ भणउ ।)

(वीरको नाटयेन संज्ञां ददाति ।)

**चन्दनकः**—अरे किं न्विदम् । (अरे किं ण्णेदम् ।)

**वीरकः**—अरे शृणु शृणु ।

**जातिस्तव विशुद्धा माता भेरी पिताऽपि ते पटहः ।**
**दुर्मुख करटकभ्राता त्वमपि सेनापतिर्जातः ॥ २३ ॥**

(अरे सुणाहि सुणाहि ।
जादी तुज्झ विसुद्धा मादा भेरी पिदा वि दे पडहो ।
दुम्मुह करडअभादा तुमं पि सेणावई जादो ॥)

**चन्दनकः**—( सक्रोधम् । ) अहं चन्दनकश्चर्मकारः । तत्प्रलोकय प्रवहणम् । (अहं चन्दणओ चम्मारओ । ता पलोएहि पवहणम् ।)

**वीरकः**—अरे प्रवहणवाहक परिवर्तय प्रवहणम् । प्रलोकयिष्यामि । (अरे पवहणवाहआ पडिवत्तावेहि पवहणम् । पलोइस्सम् ।)

(चेटस्तथा करोति । वीरकः [1]प्रवहणमारोढुमिच्छति । चन्दनकः सहसा केशेषु गृहीत्वा पातयति पादेन ताडयति [2]च ।)

---

१ नाटयेन प्र०. २ पादप्रहारेण दूरीकरोति वीरकम्.

CHAND.—I'd rather *not* speak of it.

Although I know what your lineage is, I do not speak it out, owing to the loftiness of my character. Let it ( therefore ) remain in my mind. What is the good of breaking open a *Kapittha* fruit ? (21)

VIRAKA—Nay, speak; out with it !

( Chandanaka *makes signs* [ *indicative of his caste* ] ).

VIRAKA—Ho ! What is that ?

CHAND.—

( Once ) you held in your hand a broken piece of ( whet- ) stone, trimming the scrubby beards of men, your fingers busy with the scissors. And ( now ) you have become an officer in the army ! (22)

VIRAKA—You, Chandanaka, you too, the honoured one, don't remember your own parentage.

CHAND.—Ho ! What is the parentage of *me*, Chandanaka, who am as pure as the moon ?

VIRAKA—Who can say ?

CHAND.—Speak; out with it !

( Viraka *gesticulates and makes signs* ).

CHAND—Ho ! What is that ?

VIRAKA—Listen, man, listen !

Your parentage is most pure ( indeed ) ! Your mother was a kettle-drum, your father was a drum, and you had a tambourine for your brother, O you ugly-faced one ! And ( now ) you have become an officer in the army ! (23)

CHAND.—( *Angrily* ). Am I, Chandanaka, a shoe-maker ? Very well, Inspect the carriage.

VIRAKA—You there, driver of the carriage, turn it back ! I am going to inspect it.

( Cheta *does accordingly*. Viraka *is about to mount the carriage*. Chandanaka *suddenly seizes him by the hair, throws him down, and kicks him* ).

**वीरकः**—(सक्रोधमुत्थाय ।) अरे अहं त्वया विश्वस्तो राजाज्ञप्तिं कुर्वन्सहसा केशेषु गृहीत्वा पादेन ताडितः । तच्छृणु रे अधिकरणमध्ये यदि ते चतुरङ्गं न कल्पयामि तदा न भवामि वीरकः । (अरे अहं तुए विसत्थो राआणत्तिं करेन्तो सहसा केसेसु गेण्हिअ पादेन ताडिदो । ता सुणु रे अहिअरणमज्झे जइ दे चउरङ्गं ण कप्पावेमि तदो ण होमि वीरओ ।)

**चन्दनकः**—अरे राजकुलमधिकरणं वा व्रज । किं त्वया शुनकसदृशेन । (अरे राअउलं अहिअरणं वा वच्च । किं तुए सुणअसरिसेण ।)

**वीरकः**—तथा । (इति निष्क्रान्तः ।) (तह ।)

**चन्दनकः**—(दिशोऽवलोक्य ।) गच्छ रे प्रवहणवाहक गच्छ । यदि कोऽपि पृच्छति तदा भण—चन्दनकवीरकाभ्यामवलोकितं प्रवहणं व्रजति । आर्ये वसन्तसेने इदं चाभिज्ञानं ते ददामि । (इति खड्गं प्रयच्छति ।) (गच्छ रे पवहणवाहआ गच्छ । जइ को वि पुच्छेदि तदो भणेसि—चन्दणअवीरएहिं अवलोइदं पवहणं वच्चइ । अज्जे वसन्तसेणे इमं च अहिण्णाणं दे देमि ।)

**आर्यकः**—(खड्गं गृहीत्वा सहर्षमात्मगतम् ।)

> अये शस्त्रं मया प्राप्तं स्पन्दते दक्षिणो भुजः ।
> अनुकूलं च सकलं हन्त संरक्षितो ह्यहम् ॥ २४ ॥

**चन्दनकः**—आर्ये ।

> अत्र मया विज्ञप्ता प्रत्ययिता चन्दनकमपि स्मरसि ।
> न भणाम्येष लुब्धः स्नेहस्य रसेन ब्रूमः ॥ २५ ॥

(अज्जए ।

> एत्थ मए विण्णविदा[1] पच्चइदा चन्दणं पि सुमरेसि ।
> ण भणामि एस लुद्धो णेहस्स रसेण[2] बोल्लामो ॥

**आर्यकः**—

> चन्दनश्चन्द्रशीलाढ्यो दैवादद्य सुहृन्मम ।
> चन्दनं भोः स्मरिष्यामि सिद्धादेशस्तथा यदि ॥ २६ ॥

**चन्दनकः**—

> अभयं तव ददातु हरो विष्णुर्ब्रह्मा रविश्च चन्द्रश्च ।
> हत्वा शत्रुपक्षं शुम्भनिशुम्भौ यथा देवी ॥ २७ ॥

> (अभअं तुह देउ हरो विण्हू बम्हा रवी अ चन्दो अ ।
> हत्तूण सत्तुवक्खं सुम्भणिसुम्भे जधा देवी ॥)

---

१ विण्णादा. २ वसेण.

VIRAKA—(*Getting up in rage*). You fellow, you have suddenly seized me by the hair and kicked me, while I, the trusted ( officer of the King ), was executing the royal command. Ho ! Just listen ( to what I say ). If I don't see you drawn and quartered in the court of law, then I shall cease to be (called) Viraka !

CHAND.—Oh go to the King's palace or to the law-Court ! What do I care for you, ( who are ) like a dog ?

VIRAKA—All right. ( *Exit* ).

CHAND.—(*Looking in all directions*). Go, go away, O carriage-driver ! And, if any one inquires, you should say that the carriage was inspected and allowed to pass by Chandanaka and Viraka. And, madam Vasantsena, I'll give you this token. (*Hands over his sword* ).

ARYAKA—( *Takes the sword; joyfully, to himself* ).
Oh ! I have obtained a weapon. My right arm throbs. Everything is ( therefore going to be ) favourable to me. Oh ! I am saved ! (24)

CHAND—Madam,
I hope you'll remember Chandanaka, now that I have spoken to you and shown that I am to be trusted. I do not say this out of greed, but out of a feeling of affection. (25)

ARYAKA—
Chandanaka, possessing a noble nature like (*i. e.* as attractive as ) the moon, has to-day become my friend, by good luck. Well, Sir, I'll remember Chandanaka, if the prophecy of the seer ever comes true. ( 26 )

CHAND.—
May Siva, Vishnu, Brahma, the Sun and the Moon, ( all ) grant you safety, after killing all the followers of your foe, just as the goddess Parvati, after killing Sumbha and Nisumbha (granted safety to the gods ). ( 27 )

(चेटः प्रवहणेन निष्क्रान्तः ।)

**चन्दनकः**—(नेपथ्याभिमुखमवलोक्य ।) अरे निष्क्रमतो मम प्रियवयस्यः शर्विलकः पृष्ठत एवानुलग्नो गतः । भवतु । प्रधानदण्डधारको वीरको राजप्रत्ययकारो विरोधितः । तद्यावदहमपि पुत्रभ्रातृपरिवृत एतमेवानुगच्छामि । (इति निष्क्रान्तः ।) (अरे णिक्कमन्तस्स मे पिअवअस्सो सव्विलओ पिट्ठदो ज्जेव अणुलग्गो गदो । भोदु । पधाणदण्डधारओ वीरओ राअपच्चअआरो विरोधिदो । ता जाव अहंपि पुत्तभादुपडिवुदो एदं ज्जेव अणुगच्छामि ।)

**इति [1]प्रवहणविपर्ययो नाम षष्ठोऽङ्कः ।**

---

१ मृच्छकटिकायां प्रवहण०; मृच्छ० प्रकरणे.

( *Exit* Cheta *with the carriage* )

CHAND.—( *Looking towards the curtain* ). Ah ! As he left, my dear friend Sarvilaka too has gone, following just close at his back. Well, I have made an enemy of Viraka, the chief of the police, who is the King's confidant. So, then, I also will follow him, together with my sons and brothers. ( *Exit* ).

*Thus ends Act VI., styled*
' The Exchange of the Carriages.'

---

## सप्तमोऽङ्कः ।

( ततः प्रविशतो चारुदत्तो विदूषकश्च । )

**विदूषकः**—भोः पश्य पश्य पुष्पकरण्डकजीर्णोद्यानस्य सश्रीकताम् । ( भो पेक्ख पेक्ख पुप्फकरण्डअजिण्णुज्जाणस्स सस्सिरीअदाम् । )

**चारुदत्तः**—वयस्य एवमेतत् । तथा हि ।

> वणिज इव भान्ति तरवः पण्यानीव स्थितानि कुसुमानि ।
> शुल्कमिव साधयन्तो मधुकरपुरुषाः प्रविचरन्ति ॥ १ ॥

**विदूषकः**—भोः इदमसंस्काररमणीयं शिलातलमुपविशतु भवान् । (भो इमं असक्काररमणीअं सिलाअलं उवविसदु भवम् । )

**चारुदत्तः**—(उपविश्य । ) वयस्य चिरयति वर्धमानकः ।

**विदूषकः**—भणितो मया वर्धमानकः—वसन्तसेनां गृहीत्वा लघु लघ्वागच्छेति । (भणिदो मए वड्ढमाणओ—वसन्तसेणिअं गेण्हिअ लहुं लहुं आअच्छ त्ति ।)

**चारुदत्तः**—तत्किं[1] चिरयति ।

> किं यात्यस्य पुरः शनैः प्रवहणं तस्यान्तरं मार्गते
> भग्नेऽक्षे परिवर्तनं प्रकुरुते छिन्नोऽस्य वा प्रग्रहः ।
> [2]वर्त्मान्तोज्झितदारुवारितगतिर्मार्गान्तरं याचते
> स्वैरं प्रेरितगोयुगः[3] किमथ वा स्वच्छन्दमागच्छति ॥ २ ॥

( प्रविश्य गुप्तार्यकप्रवहणस्थः । )

**चेटः**—यातं गावौ यातम् । (जाध गोणा जाध । )

**आर्यकः**—(स्वगतम् । )

> नरपतिपुरुषाणां दर्शनाद्भीतभीतः
> सनिगडचरणत्वात्सावशेषापसारः ।
> अविदितमधिरूढो यामि साधोस्तु[4] याने
> परभृत इव नीडे रक्षितो वायसीभिः ॥ ३ ॥

अहो नगरात्सुदूरमपक्रान्तोऽस्मि[5] । तत्किमस्मात्प्रवहणादवतीर्य वृक्षवाटिकागहनं प्रविशामि । उताहो प्रवहणस्वामिनं पश्यामि । अथ वा कृतं वृक्षवाटिकागहनेन । अभ्युपपन्नवत्सलः खलु तत्रभवानार्यचारुदत्त श्रूयते । तत्प्रत्यक्षीकृत्य गच्छामि ।

---

१ भणितस्तत्किम्. २ कर्मान्तो०. ३ प्रेषित. ४ सुयाने. ५ आगतः.

## ACT VII.

( *Then enter* Charudatta *and* Vidushaka ).

VID.—Oh, just observe the beauty of this old Pushpakarandaka garden !

CHAR.—Friend, it is as you say. For,

The trees appear like merchants ; the flowers stand out like the articles for sale ; and the bees are wandering about, as if they were the men collecting the toll. ( 1 )

VID.—Sir, you may sit down on this stone-slab which is charming without any ( artificial ) decoration.

CHAR.—( *Having seated himself* ). Friend, Vardhamanaka tarries long !

VID.—Vardhamanaka was told by me to come very quickly with Vasantasena.

CHAR.—Then why is he tardy ?

Can it be that another carriage is passing slowly in his front, and he is seeking room to pass it ? Or, the axle being broken, is he replacing it by another ? Or have the reins snapped ? Or, is he waiting to have the road cleared, his path being blocked by logs of wood lying in the middle of the road ? Or can it be that he is driving his two bullocks slowly, and is coming ( in a leisurely fashion ) as he pleases ? ( 2 )

( *Entering with carriage, with* A'ryaka *concealed therein* ).

CHETA—Push on, bullocks, push on !

ARYAKA—( *To himself* ).

Greatly frightened at the sight of the king's officers, and with my escape yet not fully effected owing to the chain still clinging to my foot, I am moving on, having mounted the good man's vehicle without the fact being known, and ( thus ) resembling a cuckoo reared by the female crows in their nest. ( 3 )

Oh ! I have come far away from the city ! So, then, shall I get down from this carriage and enter this dense grove of trees ? Or shall I (remain and) see the master of the carriage ? Or rather, let me not think of the dense grove of trees. It is reported that his honour the noble Charudatta is kind towards those who seek his help. So I'll leave after I have seen him personally.

स तावदस्माद्व्यसनार्णवोत्थितं[1] निरीक्ष्य साधुः समुपैति निर्वृतिम् ।
शरीरमेतद्गतमीदृशीं दशां धृतं मया तस्य महात्मनो गुणैः ॥ ४ ॥

**चेटः**—इदं तदुद्यानम् । यावदुपसर्पामि । (उपसृत्य ।) आर्य मैत्रेय । (इमं तं उज्जाणम् । जाव उवशप्पामि । अज्ज मित्तेअ ।)

**विदूषकः**—भोः प्रियं ते निवेदयामि । वर्धमानको मन्त्रयते । आगतया वसन्तसेनया भवितव्यम् । (भो पिअं दे णिवेदेमि । वड्ढमाणओ मन्तेदि । आगदाए वसन्तसेणाए ह्योदव्वम् ।)

**चारुदत्तः**—प्रियं नः प्रियम् ।

**विदूषकः**—दास्याःपुत्र किं चिरायितोऽसि । (दासीएपुत्ता किं चिरइदोसि ।)

**चेटः**—आर्य मैत्रेय मा कुप्य । यानास्तरणं विस्मृतमिति कृत्वा गतागतिं कुर्वंश्चिरायितोऽस्मि । (अज्ज मित्तेअ मा कुप्प । जाणत्थलके विशुमलिदे त्ति कदुअ गदागदिं कलेन्ते चिलइदेम्हि ।)

**चारुदत्तः**—वर्धमानक परिवर्तय प्रवहणम् । सखे मैत्रेय अवतारय वसन्तसेनाम् ।

**विदूषकः**—किं निगडेन बद्धावस्याः पादौ येन स्वयं नावतरति । (उत्थाय प्रवहणमुद्घाटच ।) भोः न वसन्तसेना वसन्तसेनः खल्वेषः । (किं णिअडेण बद्धा से गोडा जेण सअं ण ओदरेदि । भो ण वसन्तसेणा वसन्तसेणो क्खु एसो ।)

**चारुदत्तः**—वयस्य अलं परिहासेन । न कालमपेक्षते स्नेहः । अथ वा स्वयमेवावतारयामि । (इत्युत्तिष्ठति ।)

**आर्यकः**—(दृष्ट्वा ।) अये अयमेव प्रवहणस्वामी । न केवलं श्रुतिरमणीयो दृष्टिरमणीयोऽपि । हन्त रक्षितोऽस्मि ।

**चारुदत्तः**—(प्रवहणमधिरुह्य दृष्ट्वा च ।) अये तत्कोऽयम् ।

करिकरसमबाहुः सिंहपीनोन्नतांसः
पृथुतरसमवक्षास्ताम्रलोलायताक्षः ।
कथमिदमसमानं प्राप्त एवंविधो यो
वहति निगडमेकं[2] पादलग्नं महात्मा ॥ ५ ॥

ततः[3] को भवान् ।

**आर्यकः**—शरणागतो गोपालप्रकृतिरार्यकोऽस्मि ।

**चारुदत्तः**—किं घोषादानीय योऽसौ राज्ञा पालकेन बद्धः ।

**आर्यकः**—अथ किम् ।

---

१ नार्णवो०. २ निगडयुग्मं. ३ तत्को.

That good man will surely be gratified to see me, recently liberated from this calamity. It was owing to the virtues of that high-souled person that I saved this body of mine reduced to such a plight. ( 4 )

CHETA.--This is that garden. So I'll go near. (*Approaching*) Sir Maitreya !

VID.—Oh ! I have good news for you ! Vardhamanaka is calling. So Vasantasena must have arrived.

CHAR.--It is welcome ( news ) to me, welcome, indeed !

VID.—You son-of-a slave, why are you ( so ) late ?

CHETA—Sir, Maitreya, don't be angry ; I was delayed as I had to go back and return, because of my having forgotten the carriage-cushions.

CHAR.—Vardhamanaka, turn the carriage round. Friend Maitreya, you may help Vasantasena to get down.

VID.—Have her feet been tied by chains, that she cannot get down herself ? ( *Getting up and opening the carriage* ) Oh ! This is not Mistress Vasantasena ! Here's Mister Vasantasena !

CHAR.—Friend, away with joking ; ( for ) love brooks no delay. Or rather, I'll myself help her to alight. ( *He gets up* ).

ARYAKA— ( *Seeing* ). Oh ! Here is the owner of the carriage himself ! He is charming not only to hear about, but also to look upon ! Oh ! I am saved !

CHAR.—( *Mounting the carriage and seeing* ). Oh ! who, then, may this person be ?

Having arms ( huge ) like the trunk of an elephant, shoulders plump and lofty like those of a lion, a chest very broad and even, and eyes reddish and restless,—how did this high-souled person, of such ( noble ) appearance, come to such a state, not befitting ( his dignity ), *viz.* that he should be wearing a chain clinging to his foot ? ( 5 )

Well, then, who may you be ?

ARYAKA—I am Aryaka. a cowherd by birth, seeking your protection !

CHAR.—What, the same that was brought by king Palaka from the hamlet of cowherds and imprisoned ?

ARYAKA—None else.

**चारुदत्तः**—

**विधिनैवोपनीतस्त्वं चक्षुर्विषयमागतः ।**
**अपि प्राणानहं जह्यां न तु त्वां शरणागतम् ।। ६ ।।**

( आर्यको हर्षं नाटयति । )

**चारुदत्तः**—वर्धमानक चरणान्निगडमपनय ।

**चेटः**—यदार्य आज्ञापयति । (तथा कृत्वा[१] ।) आर्य अपनीतानि निगडानि । (जं अज्जो आणवेदि । अज्ज अवणीदाइं णिगलाइं ।)

**आर्यकः**—स्नेहमयान्यन्यानि दृढतराणि दत्तानि[२] ।

**विदूषकः**—संगच्छस्व निगडानि । एषोऽपि मुक्तः । सांप्रतं वयं व्रजिष्यामः । (संगच्छेहि णिअडाइं । एसो वि मुक्को । संपदं अम्हे वजिस्सामो ।)

**चारुदत्तः**—धिक्शान्तम्[३] ।

**आर्यकः**—सखे चारुदत्त अहमपि प्रणयेनेदं प्रवहणमारूढः तत्क्षन्तव्यम् ।

**चारुदत्तः**—अलंकृतोऽस्मि [४]स्वयंग्राहप्रणयेन भवता ।

**आर्यकः**—अभ्यनुज्ञातो भवता गन्तुमिच्छामि ।

**चारुदत्तः**—गम्यताम् ।

**आर्यक**—भवतु । अवतरामि ।

**चारुदत्तः**—सखे नावतरितव्यम् । प्रत्यग्रापनीतसंयमनस्य भवतोऽलघुसंचारा[५] गतिः । सुलभपुरुषसंचारेऽस्मिन्प्रदेशे प्रवहणं विश्वासमुत्पादयति । तत्प्रवहणेनैव गम्यताम् ।

**आर्यकः**—यथाऽऽह भवान् ।

**चारुदत्तः**—

**क्षेमेण व्रज बान्धवान्**

**आर्यकः**—

**ननु मया लब्धो भवान्बांधवः**

**चारुदत्तः**—

**स्मर्तव्योऽस्मि कथान्तरेषु भवता**

**आर्यकः**—

**स्वात्माऽपि विस्मर्यते ?**

---

**वणिज इति** । [ पण्यानि विक्रेयवस्तूनि । ] शुल्कं राजदेयम् ।। १ ।। **असत्कारमिति** । अकृत्रिमं स्वभावत एवेत्वर्थः । **किमिति** । [तस्य अन्तरं गमनायावकाशम् । अक्षे कूबराख्ये । परिवर्तनं विनिमयम् । प्रग्रहः रश्मिः । वर्त्मान्ते अध्वप्रान्ते

---

१ करोति. २ लग्नानि. ३ धिक् । धिक् । शान्तं पापम्. ४ ग्रह. ५ ०संवारा; लघुसं०.

CHAR.—

Fate itself brought you here; as you ( thus ) came within the range of my sight. I will abandon my life even, but not you who seek my protection. (6)

( *Aryaka gesticulates delight* ).

CHAR.—Vardhamanaka, remove the chain from his foot.

CHETA—As your honour orders. ( *Does accordingly* ). Sir, the fetters are removed.

ARYAKA—But other and firmer ones, made of love, have been put on !

VID.—Take up those fetters. He has been set free ; let us ( therefore ) now take our departure.

CHAR.—Fie ! Not so quick !

ARYAKA—Friend Charudatta, it was out of affection ( for you ) that I got in in this chariot of yours ; so kindly forgive it.

CHAR.—I am honoured ( *lit.* adorned ) by you by thus voluntarily showing your love.

ARYAKA—I wish to go now, with your permission.

CHAR.—Yo can go.

ARYAKA—All right ; I'll get down.

CHAR.—Friend, do not get down. As your fetters have been only just recently removed, you will not be able to walk with a quick gait. While the carriage would ( also ) create confidence in this locality, where the officers are moving about in large numbers. So you should travel in the carriage just as before.

ARYAKA—As your honour says.

CHAR.—

Go to yonr relatives in safety.

ARYAKA—

Well, I have just acquired a relative in your honour.

CHAR.—

I should be remembered by you during the course of conversation.

ARYAKA—

Can I forget my own self ? ( *Or,* then I shall forget my own self ).

---

उज्झितानि दारूनि तैः वारिता गतिर्यस्य । कर्मान्तेति पाठे ] कर्मान्तो राजादीनां नियोगविशेषः । तत्संबन्धिनि धर्मे त्यक्तकाष्ठानि तैः प्रतिरुद्धगमनः ॥ २ ॥

चारुदत्तः—

त्वां रक्षन्तु पथि प्रयान्तममराः

आर्यकः—

संरक्षितोऽहं त्वया

चारुदत्तः—

स्वैर्भाग्यैः परिरक्षितोऽसि

आर्यकः—

ननु हे तत्रापि हेतुर्भवान् ॥ ७ ॥

चारुदत्तः—यदुद्यते[1] पालके महती रक्षा न वर्तते तच्छीघ्रमपक्रामतु भवान् ।

आर्यकः—एवं पुनर्दर्शनाय । (इति निष्क्रान्तः ।)

चारुदत्तः—

कृत्वैवं मनुजपतेर्महद्व्यलीकं
स्थातुं हि क्षणमपि न प्रशस्तमस्मिन् ।
मैत्रेय[2] क्षिप निगडं पुराणकूपे
पश्येयुः क्षितिपतयोहि चारदृष्टया ॥ ८ ॥

(वामाक्षिस्पन्दनं सूचयित्वा ।) सखे मैत्रेय वसन्तसेनादर्शनोत्सुकोऽयं जनः । पश्य ।

अपश्यतोऽद्य तां कान्तां वामं स्फुरति लोचनम् ।
अकारणपरित्रस्तं हृदयं व्यथते मम ॥ ९ ॥

तदेहि । गच्छावः (परिक्रम्य ।) कथमभिमुखमनाभ्युदयिकं श्रमणकदर्शनम् । (विचार्य ।) प्रविशत्वयमनेन पथा । वयमप्यनेनैव पथा गच्छामः । (इति निष्क्रान्तः ।)

[3]इत्यार्यकापहरणं नाम सप्तमोऽङ्कः ।

---

**नरपतीति** । [ निगडेन शृङ्खलया सहितः चरणः यस्य तस्य भावस्तत्त्वं तस्मात् । ] सावशेषः किंचिदवशिष्टः अपसारो निर्गमो यस्य । कोकिलपक्षे नरपतिपुरुषाः शाकुनिकाः । सनिगड इव । सनिगडो बाल्यान्मन्दगमनः यानेऽधिरूढोऽनवस्थितः । काकस्त्रीरक्षितकोकिल उपमानम् । [ मालिनी वृत्तम् ] ॥ ३ ॥ [ अभ्युपपन्नेषु आश्रितेषु वत्सलः । ] **स इति** । [ स साधुः अस्मात् । व्यसनाद्राजनिग्रहरूपात् नवोत्थितं मां निरीक्ष्य निर्वृतिं सुखं समुपैति तावत् । ] चन्दनकेन रक्षितत्वात् । [ वंशस्थं वृत्तम् ] ॥ ४ ॥ **करीति** । [ करिणः करः शुण्डादण्डः तेन समौ बाहू यस्य । सिंहस्येव पीनौ उन्नतौ च अंसौ यस्य । पृथुतरमतिविपुलं समं च वक्षो यस्य सः । ताम्रे लोले आयते च अक्षिणी यस्य सः । यः एवंविधो महात्मा इदं असमानमननुरूपं पादलग्नमेकं निगडं कथं वहति । मालिनी वृत्तम् ] ॥ ५ ॥

---

१ यत्नोद्यते, यत्नेनो०...रक्षा वर्तते. २ ( दृष्टा । ) मैत्रेय. ३ मृच्छकटिकायामा०; ०कारुये प्रकरणे.

CHAR.—

May the gods guard you as you travel along the road !

ARYAKA—

( Rather ) it is you who have guarded me !

CHAR —

You were guarded by your own good luck.

ARYAKA—

Still, Sir, your honour was the cause even of that. ( 7 )

CHAR.—Since there can be no great protection ( safety ) ( for a culprit ) when Palaka is up and exerting himself, you should quickly make good your escape.

ARYAKA—So ( I'll go, hoping ) to meet again. ( *Exit* ).

CHAR.—

It is undesirable to linger here even for a moment ( more ), since we have thus committed a very grave offence against the king. O Maitreya, throw that chain in that old well; ( for ) kings can see ( such things ) through the eyes of their spies. ( 8 )

( *Showing that his left eye throbs* ). Friend Maitreya, this person ( *i. e.* myself ) is eager to get a sight of Vasantasena. Mark :—

As I haven't seen that beloved of mine to-day, my left eye is throbbing, and my heart feels uneasy, frightened without any ( apparent ) cause. ( 9 )

So, come : let us ge. ( *Walking about* ). How ! Just before me I see a Buddhist mendicant, a sight of evil omen ! ( *Reflecting*). Let him come in by this path ; while we shall depart by this ( other ) path. ( *Exit* ).

*Thus ends Act VII., styled*
'The Escape of Aryaka.'

---

अलघुर्मन्दः संचारो यत्र । लघुरिति पाठे अल्पः । **क्षेमेणेति** । अत्र चारुदत्तार्यकयोरुत्तरोत्तरेण अष्टखण्डः श्लोकः । [एवमुपकृतवांस्त्वं विस्मर्यसे चेन्मया स्वात्माऽपि विस्मर्यते । शार्दूलविक्रीडितं वृत्तम् ] ॥ ७ ॥ पालके राजनि रक्षक एव वा । रक्षणे महानभिनिवेश इत्यर्थः । **कृत्वेति** । [ मनुजपतेः राज्ञः एवं महत् व्यलीकमप्रियं कृत्वा अस्मिन्देशे इ० । निगडमार्यकपादादपनीतम् । चारदृष्टया यतः चारचक्षुषः राजानः । तदुक्तम्—' चारैः पश्यन्ति राजानश्चक्षुर्भ्यामितरे जनाः ' इति । प्रहर्षिणी वृत्तम ] ॥ ८ ॥ **अपश्यत इति** ॥ ९ ॥ [ अभ्युदय उत्कर्षः प्रयोजनमस्याभ्युदयिकम् । ' प्रयोजनम् ' इति ठञ् । नाभ्युदयिकमनाभ्युदयिकमनिष्टफलम् । ' काषायीगुडतक्रपङ्कविधवाकुब्जा न दृष्टाः शुभाः ' इत्युक्तेः । ] श्रमणको भिक्षुः । अशकुनपरंपरा च चारुदत्तवसन्तसेनयोरनिष्टस्याग्रे भविष्यतः सूचनाय ।

इत्यार्यकापवाहनो नाम सप्तमोऽङ्कः ।

## अष्टमोऽङ्कः ।

(ततः प्रविशत्यार्द्रचीवरहस्तो भिक्षुः ।)

**भिक्षुः**—अज्ञाः कुरुत धर्मसंचयम् ।

**संयच्छत निजोदरं नित्यं जागृत ध्यानपटहेन ।**
**विषमा इन्द्रियचौरा हरन्ति चिरसंचितं धर्मम् ॥ १ ॥**

अपि च । अनित्यतया प्रेक्ष्य केवलं तावद्धर्मिणां शरणमस्मि ।

**पञ्चजना येन मारिता स्त्रियं[1] मारयित्वा ग्रामो रक्षितः ।**
**अबलश्च चण्डालो मारितोऽवश्यं स नरः स्वर्गं गाहते ॥ २ ॥**

**शिरो मुण्डितं तुण्डं मुण्डितं चित्तं न मुण्डितं किमर्थं[2] मुण्डितम् ।**
**यस्य पुनश्च चित्तं मुण्डितं साधु सुष्ठु शिरस्तस्य मुण्डितम् ॥ ३ ॥**

गृहीतकषायोदकमेतच्चीवरं यावदेतद्राष्ट्रियश्यालकस्योद्याने प्रविश्य पुष्करिण्यां प्रक्षाल्य लघु लघ्वपक्रमिष्यामि । (परिक्रम्य तथा करोति ।)

(अज्ञा[3] कलेध धम्मशंचअम् ।

शजम्मध[4] णिअपोटं णिच्चं जग्गेध झाणपडहेण ।
विशमा इन्दिअचोला हलन्ति चिलशंचिदं धम्मम् ॥

अवि अ । अणिच्चदाए पेक्खिअ णवलं[5] दाव धम्माणं शलणम्हि ।

पञ्चजण जेण मालिदा इत्थिअ मालिअ गाम लक्खिदे ।
अबले अ[6] चण्डाल मालिदे अवस[7] शे णले शग्ग गाहदि ॥

शिल मुण्डिदे तुण्ड मुण्डिदे चित्त ण मुण्डिदे कीश मुण्डिदे ।
जाह उण अ चित्त मुंडिदे शाहु शुठ्ठु शिल ताह मुण्डिदे ॥

गिह्दिकशाओदए एशे चीवले जाव एदं लश्टिअशालकाह्केलके उज्जाणे पविशिअ पोक्खलिणीए पक्खालिअ लहुं लहुं अवक्कमिश्शम् ।)

---

[अथ पूर्वाङ्कान्तसूचितं भिक्षुं प्रवेश्य तदनु शकारस्यापि प्रवेशं प्रवहण-विपर्ययेण राष्ट्रियशकटमधिरूढाया वसन्तसेनयाः संकटं वर्णयितुं प्रस्तौति । ] **संयच्छतेति** । गाथा । [ निजोदरं संयच्छत केवलमुदरपरायणा मा भवतेत्यर्थः । ध्यानमेव पटहस्तेन जागृत । अज्ञाननिद्रामग्ना मा भवतेत्यर्थः । विषमा दुर्ग्राह्या

---

१ अविद्यां. २ कुतः, किं. ३ अज्जा (आर्याः). ४ संजयमध णिअमुदलं णिच्चं जग्गध. ५ णवल (नरः). ६ क-कक (टी०). ७ अवसं वि.

# ACT VIII

( *Then enter a Buddhist* mendicant, *with a wet garment in his hand* ).

THE MENDICANT—Ye, ignorant people, accumulate religious merit !

Keep a check over your appetites; remain ever wide awake with the help of the drum in the form of meditation. ( For ) these cunning thieves in the form of the senses steal away religious merit stored for a long time. ( 1 )

Moreover, looking ( at the world ) through ( its aspect of ) transitoriness, I fly for support to religious deeds only.

That man most surely attains heaven, who has killed five men ( *viz.* the senses ), and, after killing a woman ( *viz.* Nescience ) has guarded the town ( *viz.* the body ), and has also killed the helpless Chandala ( *viz.* egotism ). ( 2 )

The head is shaved; the face is shaved; but the heart is not shaved ( *i. e.* purified ). Then what is tbe good of shaving ? But, if a person has his heart shaved, then his shaved head becomes him very well, indeed ! ( 3 )

I'll first enter this garden of the king's brother-in-law, and there in the lotus-pond wash this garment which has been dyed with red-coloured water ; and then I'll very quickly come away. ( *Walks about and does accordingly* ).

---

इन्द्रियाणि एव चौराः चिरसंचितं चिरोपार्जितं धर्मं पुण्यं हरन्ति ]॥ १ ॥ **पञ्चजना इति । शिर इति ।** वैतालीछन्दसा द्वयम् । पञ्चेति । ज्जणसंयोगात्पञ्चेति पञ्चशब्दो गुरुः छन्दोनुरोधात् । पञ्चजणेति णकारः । अबले केति केवलः ककारः एकारश्च लघुः । अवसं वोत्यत्र सकारो न प्रविष्टः । अन्यथा अवस्सं वीति स्यात् । शे णले इत्येकारद्वयेऽन्यतरो न गाहतीत्यत्र 'गा' इत्याकारस्य गुरुत्वम् । पञ्चजनाः पञ्चेन्द्रियाणि । ग्रामः शरीरम् । लक्खिदे रक्षितः । दुष्टत्वविकृतिपातात् । चण्डालोऽहंकारः । अबलोऽसहायः । अथ वेन्द्रियादिविनाशात् । अवश्यं स नरः स्वर्गं गाहते ॥ २ ॥ चित्तं न मुण्डितं न संयत्तीकृतम् । किं मुण्डितम् । साधु शिरो मुण्डितम् । [ सत्यामेव चित्तशुद्धौ बहिःसंन्यासः शोभते इत्यर्थः ] ॥ ३ ॥ राष्ट्रियश्यालकत्वेन च पुनः संयोगः प्रकर्षख्यापनार्थः । अपूपौ द्वावितिवत् वा न पुनरुक्तम् ।

( नेपथ्ये । )

शकारः—तिष्ठ रे दुष्टश्रमणक तिष्ठ । (चिश्ट ले दुश्टशमणका चिष्ट ।)

भिक्षुः—( दृष्ट्वा सभयम् । ) आश्चर्यम् । एष स राज्यश्यालसंस्थानक आगतः । एकेन भिक्षुणाऽपराधे कृतेऽन्यमपि यत्र यत्र भिक्षुं पश्यति तत्र तत्र गामिव नासिकां विद्ध्वापवाहयति ।तत्कुत्राशरणः शरणं गमिष्यामि । अथ वा भट्टारक एव बुद्धो मे शरणम् । (ही अविद माणहे । एशे शे लाअशालशंठाणे आअदे । एक्केण भिक्खुणा अवलाहे किदे अण्णं पि जहिं जहिं भिक्खुं पेक्खदि तहिं तहिं गोणं विअ णासं विन्धिअ ओवाहेदि । ता कहिं अशलणे शलणं गमिश्शम् । अध वा भट्टालके ज्जेव बुद्धे मे शलणे ।)

(प्रविश्य सखड्गेन विटेन सह ।)

शकारः—तिष्ठ रे दुष्टश्रमणक तिष्ठ । आपानकमध्यप्रविष्टस्येव रक्तमूलकस्य शीर्षं ते भङ्क्ष्यामि । ( इति ताडयति । ) ( चिश्ट ले दुश्टशमणका चिष्ट । आवाणअमज्झपविश्टश्श विअ लत्तमूलअश्श शीशं दे मोडइश्शम् ।)

विटः—काणेलीमातः न युक्तं निर्वेदधृतकाषायं[१] भिक्षुं ताडयितुम् । तत्किमनेन । इदं तावत्सुखोपगम्यमुद्यानं[२] पश्यतु भवान् ।

**अशरणशरणप्रमोदभूतैर्वनतरुभिः क्रियमाणचारुकर्म ।**
**हृदयमिव दुरात्मनामगुप्तं नवमिव राज्यमनिर्जितोपभोग्यम् ॥ ४ ॥**

भिक्षुः—स्वागतम् । प्रसीदतूपासकः । (शाअदम् । पशीददु उवाशके ।)

शकारः—भाव पश्य पश्य । आक्रोशति माम् । ( भावे पेक्ख पेक्ख । आक्कोशदि मम् ।)

विटः—किं ब्रवीति ।

शकारः—उपासक इति मां भणति । किमहं नापितः । ( उवाशके त्ति मं भणादि । किं हग्गे णाविदे ।)

विटः—बुद्धोपासक इति भवन्तं स्तौति ।

शकारः—स्तुहि श्रमणक स्तुहि । (थुणु शमणका थुणु ।)

भिक्षुः—त्वं धन्यस्त्वं पुण्यः । ( तुमं धण्णे तुमं पुण्णे । )

शकारः—भाव धन्य पुण्य इति मां भणति । किमहं चार्वाकः कोष्टकः कुम्भकारो वा । (भावे धण्णे पुण्णे त्ति मं भणादि । किं हग्गे शलावके कोश्टके कोम्भकाले वा ।)

विटः—काणेलीमातः ननु धन्यस्त्वं पुण्यस्त्वमिति भवन्तं स्तौति ।

शकारः—भाव तत्किमर्थमेष इहागतः । (भावे ता कीश एशे इध आगदे ।)

---

१ कषायं. २ गम्यमान०.

( *Behind the curtain* ).

SAKARA—Stop, stop, you rascally mendicant !

THE MENDICANT—( *Seeing* ; *with fright* ). Alack-a-day ! Here comes that king's brother-in-law, Samsthanaka. Since a certain mendicant once happened to offend him, wherever now he sees any mendicant, the same or another, he bores a hole through his nose, as if he were a bullock, and then drives him away. So whom shall I approach for help, helpless that I am ? Or rather, Lord Buddha himself will be my refuge !

( *Entering, with* Vita, *armed with a sword* ).

SAK.—Stop, stop, you rascally mendicant ! I'll break your head, like that of a red radish brought in the midst of a drinking party. ( *He beats him* ).

VITA—Bastard, it is not right to strike a mendicant who has put on red robes owing to his being weary of the world. So, why bother about him ? Please glance at this garden, pleasant to visit.

Noble deeds are done in it by the sylvan trees, which are both the refuge and the joy of homeless persons. It lies unguarded ( *i. e.* is free of access ), like the heart of wicked persons (which is unchecked in its licence ) ; like a newly-acquired kingdom, it is one to be enjoyed without the restraint of conquest (possession).(4)

THE MENDICANT—Welcome ! Be kind, O *Upasaka* ( worshipper of Buddha ) !

SAK.—Mark, friend, mark; he is calling me names.

VITA—What does he say ?

SAK.—He calls me an *Upasaka*. Am I then a barber ?

VITA—He is praising you by describing you as a worshipper of Buddha.

SAK.—Praise, O mendicant, praise !

THE MENDICANT—You are *dhanya* ( blessed ) ; you are *punya* ( holy ).

SAK.—Friend, he calls me *dhanya* and *punya*. Am I a materialist, or a watering trough, or a potter ?

VITA—Bastard, he is forsooth praising you by saying that you are blessed and are holy.

SAK.—Well, friend, why has he come here ?

भिक्षुः—इदं चीवरं प्रक्षालयितुम् । (इदं चीवलं [1]पक्खालिदुम् ।)

शकारः—अरे दुष्टश्रमणक एतन्मम भगिनीपतिना सर्वोद्यानानां प्रवरं पुष्पकरण्डोद्यानं दत्तं यत्र तावच्छुनकाः शृगालाः पानीयं पिबन्ति । अहमपि प्रवरपुरुषो मनुष्यको न स्नामि । तत्र त्वं पुष्करिण्यां पुराणकुलित्थयूषसवर्णान्युग्रगन्धीनि चीवराणि प्रक्षालयसि । तत्त्वामेकप्रहारिकं करोमि । (अले दुश्टशमणका एशे मम बहिणीवदिणा शव्वुज्जाणाणं पवले पुप्फकलण्डुज्जाणे दिण्णे जहिं दाव शुणहका शिआला पाणिअं पिअन्ति । हग्गे वि पवलपुलिशे मणुश्शके ण ण्हाआमि । तहिं तुमं पुक्खलिणीए पुलाणकुलुत्थजूशशवण्णाइं[2] उश्शगन्धिआइं[3] चीवलाइं पक्खालेशि । ता तुमं एक्कपहालिअं कलेमि ।)

विटः—काणेलीमातः तथा तर्कयामि [4]यथाऽनेनाचिरप्रव्रजितेन भवितव्यम् ।

शकारः—कथं भावो जानाति । (कधं भावे जाणादि ।)

विटः—किमत्र ज्ञेयम् । पश्य ।

> अद्याप्यस्य[5] तथैव केशविरहाद्गौरी ललाटच्छविः
> कालस्याल्पतया च चीवरकृतः स्कन्धे न जातः किणः ।
> नाभ्यस्ता च कषायवस्त्ररचना दूरं निगूढान्तरो[6]
> वस्त्रान्तश्च पटोच्छ्रयात्प्रशिथिलः स्कन्धे न संतिष्ठते ॥ ५ ॥

भिक्षुः—उपासक एवम् । अचिरप्रव्रजितोऽहम् । ( उवाशके एव्वम् । अचिलपव्वजिदे हग्गे ।

शकारः—तत्किमर्थं त्वं जातमात्र एव न प्रव्राजतः । ( इति ताडयति । ) ( ता कीश तुमं जातमेत्तक[7] ज्जेव ण पव्वजिदे ।)

भिक्षुः—नमो बुद्धाय । (णमो बुद्धश्श ।)

विटः—किमनेन ताडितेन तपस्विना । मुच्यताम् । गच्छतु ।

शकारः—अरे तिष्ठ तावद्यावत्संप्रधारयामि । ( अले चिश्ट दाव जाव शंपधालेमि । )

विटः—केन सार्धम् ।

शकारः—आत्मनो हृदयेन । (अत्तणो हडक्केण ।)

---

[ चीवरं शाक्यभिक्षुप्रावरणम् । ] ही अविद माणहे इति विस्मयखेदे । आपानकं पानगोष्ठी । पिबन्त्यस्मिन्नित्यधिकरणे ल्युट् । रक्तमूलकस्य शीर्षमिव । मद्यपाः पत्रमयमग्रभागमपनीय मूलकमुपदंशीकुर्वन्ति । [ कषायेण लोहितद्रव्यविशेषेण रक्तं काषायम् । 'तेन रक्तं रागात्' इत्यण् । निर्वेदाद्वैराग्येण धृतं काषायं येन तम् । ]

---

१ पच्छालिदुं. २ शबलाइं. ३ उद्‌दुश्श (उग्र); उग्गविस्सगन्धि०. ४ तेनाचिर०. ५ अद्यार्यस्य. ६ ०न्तरं वस्त्रान्तं (टी०). ७ मेत्तकं.

THE M.--To wash this garment.

SAK.—Eh, you rascally mendicant, this *Pushpakarandaka* garden was given to me by my sister's husband, as being the best of all gardens. Dogs and jackals drink water here. I, too, the best of mortals, and a man, do not bathe here. And here, in this lotus-pond, you are washing those horribly stinking garments, having a colour like the broth of old *Kulittha* grain. So I'll kill you with one blow!

VITA—Bastard, I guess that he must have but recently turned an ascetic.

SAK.—Friend, how do you know?

VITA—What is there to be known? See:—

Even now, having shorn his hair, the complexion of his forehead is bright-red as before. And, as only a short time has elapsed, on his shoulder no scar is produced by his ascetic robe. Moreover, he is not yet (sufficiently) practised in wearing his brown garments; and the end of his garment, which is very loose on account of the bagginess of the cloth, and which completely hides the middle part of his body, does not sit well on his shoulder. (5)

THE M.—It is as you say, O Upasaka! I have but recently turned a monk.

SAK.—Then why did you not become a monk the moment you were born? (*Beats him*).

THE M.—My bow to Buddha!

VITA—What is the use of beating this poor fellow? Leave him; let him go.

SAK.—Eh, just wait till I hold a consultation.

VITA—With whom?

SAK.—With my heart.

---

**अशरणेति** । [ अशरणानां गृहाद्याश्रयरहितानां शरणमाश्रयस्तेन प्रमोदभूतैः आनन्दरूपैर्जातैः । वनतरुभिरुद्यानवृक्षैः क्रियमाणं चारु मनोहरं कर्म यस्मिन् तत् । दुरात्मनां त्वादृशामिति ध्वनिः । हृदयमिव अगुप्तं प्रकटमनियन्त्रितप्रवेशं च । पुनश्च ] अनिर्जितमनात्मसात्कृतम् । [ अत उपभोग्यं च सर्वैरिति शेषः । सर्वोपभोग्यत्वाद्भिक्षोः प्रवेशो न निषेध्य इत्यर्थः । मालोपमालंकारः । पुष्पिताग्रा

**विटः**— हन्त न गतः ।

**शकारः**—पुत्रक हृदय भट्टारक पुत्रक एष श्रमणकोऽपि नाम किं गच्छतु किं तिष्ठतु । ( स्वगतम् । ) नापि गच्छतु नापि तिष्ठतु । ( प्रकाशम् । ) भाव संप्रधारितं मया हृदयेन सह । एतन्मम हृदयं भणति । ( पुत्तका[1] हडक्का भश्टके पुत्तके एशे शमणके अवि णाम किं गच्छदु किं चिश्टदु । णावि गच्छदु णावि चिश्टदु । भावे शंपधालिदं मए हडक्केण शह । एशे मह हडक्के भणादि ।)

**विटः**—किं ब्रवीति ।

**शकारः**—माऽपि गच्छतु मापि तिष्ठतु । माऽप्युच्छ्वसितु माऽपि निःश्वसतु । इहैव झटिति पतित्वा म्रियताम् । (मावि गच्छदु मावि चिश्टदु । मावि ऊशशदु[2] मावि णीशशदु । इध ज्जेव झत्ति[3] पडिअ मलेदु । )

**भिक्षुः**—नमो बुद्धाय । शरणागतोऽस्मि । (णमो बुद्धश्श । शलणागदेम्हि । )

**विटः**—गच्छदु ।

**शकारः**—ननु समयेन । ( णं शमएण ।)

**विटः**—कीदृशः समयः ।

**शकारः**—तथा कर्दमं प्रक्षिपतु यथा पानीयं पंकाविलं न भवति । अथ वा पानीयं पुञ्जीकृत्य कर्दमे क्षिपतु । (तधा कद्दमं फेलदु जधा पाणिअं पङ्काइलं ण होदि । अध वा पाणिअं पुञ्जीकदुअ कद्दमे फेलदु ।)

**विटः**—अहो मूर्खता ।

**विपर्यस्तमनश्चेष्टैः शिलाशकलवर्ष्मभिः ।**
**मांसवृक्षैरियं मूर्खैर्भाराक्रान्ता वसुंधरा ॥ ६ ॥**

( भिक्षुर्नाटयेनाक्रोशति । )

**शकारः**—किं भणति । (किं भणादि ।)

**विटः**—स्तौति भवन्तम् ।

**शकारः**—स्तुहि स्तुहि । पुनरपि स्तुहि । (थुण थुण । पुणो वि थुण ।)

( तथा कृत्वा निष्क्रान्तो भिक्षुः । )

**विटः**—काणेलीमातः पश्योद्यानस्य शोभाम् ।

**अमी हि वृक्षाः फलपुष्पशोभिताः कठोरनिष्पन्दलतोपवेष्टिताः[4] ।**
**नृपाज्ञया रक्षिजनेन पालिता नराः[5] सदारा इव यान्ति निर्वृतिम् ॥ ७ ॥**

---

वृत्तम् ]॥ ४ ॥ नापितः । स ह्युपासको दृष्ट इत्याशयः । गलावकश्चार्वाकः । [स हि धनमर्हतीति धन्यः । केवलमर्थकामपरः । 'अनित्यानि शरीराणि ऋणं कृत्वा घृतं पिबेत्' इति तस्योपदेशः ।] कोष्टकमिष्टकादिरचितं [निपानं यत्र पशवः पानीयं पिबन्ति ।] एकप्रहारवन्तं करोमि । एकप्रहारेण मारणोक्तावयं प्रयोगः ।

---

१ पुश्तका. २ ओशशदु (उपविशतु). ३ झत्ति अ. ४ निष्यन्द. ५ नरः

VITA—Oh ! He hasn't (yet) gone !

SAK.—O my child, my heart, my master. my child! Should this mendicant be allowed to go, or should he be made to stay? (*To himself*). He should neither go nor stay. (*Aloud*). Friend, I have consulted my heart. This is what my heart says :—

VITA—What does it say ?

SAK.—He shall neither go nor stay! He shall neither breathe in nor breathe out! He shall immediately fall down here and die!

THE M.—My bow to Buddha! I seek your protection

VITA—Let him go.

SAK.—Yes, but on one condition.

VITA—What sort of condition ?

SAK.—He should throw mud in water in such a manner that the water does not turn muddy. Or else, he should collect the water in a heap and throw it in the mud.

VITA—What folly!

This earth is bent (*i. e.* groaning) under the weight of fools, whose thoughts and deeds are all perverse, whose bodies ar simply like (so many) pieces of stones, and who are merely growths (*lit.* trees) of flesh. (6)

(*The* Mendicant *gesticulates cursing*).

SAK.—What is he saying ?

VITA—He is praising you.

SAK.—Praise, praise; do praise me once again.

(*The* Mendicant *does accordingly and exit*).

VITA—Bastard, see the beauty of this garden :—

These trees, guarded by watchmen under the king's orders, decked with fruits and flowers, and encircled by full-grown, motionless creepers, are enjoying happiness, like men in the company of their wives. (7)

---

अद्यापोति । गौरी ललाटे शोभा [ तथैव गृहस्थाश्रमस्थितस्यैव ] भवति । किण: संघर्षजो व्रणाकार: । वस्त्रकषायीकरणं न शीलितम् । [ दूरं निगूढमन्तरं शरीरभागो येन स तथा । पटस्योच्छ्रयाद्दैर्घ्याद्विशालतया वा प्रशिथिल: असंस्थित: ] वस्त्रान्तं स्कन्धे न संतिष्ठते । नपुंसकत्वं चिन्त्यम् । निगूढमवकाशो यस्य तत् । संकोचित-प्रदेशमित्यर्थः । [ काव्यलिङ्गसमुच्चयालंकारौ । शार्दूलविक्रीडितं वृत्तम् ] ॥ ५ ॥ तपस्विना वराकेण । हडक्केन हृदयेन । न गतस्तर्हि न गमिष्यतीत्यर्थः । पङ्काविलं कलुषमिति यावत् । विपर्यस्तेति । [ विपर्यस्ता विपरीता लोकविरुद्धा मनश्चेष्टा

**शकारः**—सुष्ठु भावो भणति ।

**बहुकुसुमविचित्रिता च भूमिः कुसुमभरेण विनामिताश्च वृक्षाः ।**
**द्रुमशिखरलतावलम्बमानाः पनसफलानीव वानरा ललन्ति ॥ ८ ॥**

(शुश्टु भावे भणादि ।

बहुकुशुमविचित्तिदा अ भूमी कुशुमभलेण[1] विणामिदा अ रुक्खा ।
दुमशिहललदाअलम्बमाणा पणशफला विअ वाणला ललन्ति ॥)

**विटः**—काणेलीमातः इदं शिलातलमध्यास्यताम् ।

**शकारः**—एषोऽस्म्यासितः । (इति विटेन सहोपविशति ।) भाव अद्यापि तां वसन्तसेनां स्मरामि । दुर्जनवचनमिव हृदयान्नापसरति । (एशे म्हि आशिदे । भावे अज्ज वि तं वशन्तशेणिअं शुमलामि । दुज्जणवअणं विअ हडक्कादो ण ओशलदि ।)

**विटः**—(स्वगतम् ।) तथा निरस्तोऽपि स्मरति ताम् । अथ वा !

**स्त्रीभिर्विमानितानां कापुरुषाणां विवर्धते मदनः ।**
**सत्पुरुषस्य स एव तु[2] भवति मृदुर्नैव वा भवति ॥ ९ ॥**

**शकारः**—भाव काऽपि वेला स्थावरकचेटस्य भणितस्य प्रवहणं गृहीत्वा लघु लघ्वागच्छेति । अद्यापि नागच्छतीति चिरमस्मि बुभुक्षितः । मध्याह्ने न शक्यते पादाभ्यां गन्तुम् । तत्पश्य पश्य ।

**नभोमध्यगतः सूरो दुष्प्रेक्षः कुपितवानरसदृक्षः ।**
**भूमिर्दृढसंतप्ता हतपुत्रशतेव गान्धारी ॥ १० ॥**

(भावे का वि वेला थावलकचेडश्श भणिदश्श पवहणं गेण्हिअ लहुं लहुं आअच्छे त्ति । अज्ज वि ण आअच्छदि त्ति चिलम्हि बुभुक्खिदे । मज्झण्हे ण शक्कीअदि पादेहिं गन्तुम् । ता पेक्ख पेक्ख ।

णहमज्झगदे शूले दुप्पेक्खे कुविदवाणलशलिच्छे ।
भूमी दढशंतत्ता[3] हदपुत्तशदेव्व गन्धाली ॥)

**विटः**—एवमेतत् ।

**छायासु प्रतिमुक्तशष्पकवलं निद्रायते गोकुलं**
**तृष्णार्तैश्च निपीयते वनमृगैरुष्णं पयः सारसम् ।**
**संतापादतिशङ्कितैर्न नगरीमार्गो नरैः सेव्यते**
**तप्तां भूमिमपास्य च प्रवहणं मन्ये क्वचित्संस्थितम् ॥ ११ ॥**

---

मनोव्यापारो एषां तैः । यद्वा विपर्यस्ते मनः चेष्टा च येषां तैः । शिलाशकलानि पाषाणखण्डा इव वर्ष्माणि शरीराणि येषां तैः । मांसस्य वृक्षा इव तैः । मूर्खैः इयं

---

१ बलेण. २ नु. ३ दिढ.

SAK.—My friend has spoken truly.

The ground is picturesque owing to the numberless flowers (fallen thereon); the trees are bent down with the load of blossoms; and the monkeys, hanging from the branches at the tops of the trees, look as graceful as *panasa* fruits. (8)

VITA—Bastard, here's a stone-slab; please sit down.

SAK.—Here I seat myself. (*He sits down, and so does* Vita). Friend, even now I remember that Vasantasena. Like the words of a wicked man, she does not leave my mind.

VITA—(*To himself*). Although he was spurned in that (contemptuous) manner, he still remembers her! Or rather :—

In the case of low persons, their passion waxes stronger if they are spurned by women; but in the case of a good man, the same becomes milder, or even disappears altogether. (9)

SAK.—Friend, a long time has passed since I asked the Cheta, Sthavaraka, to come here very quickly with the carriage. He hasn't yet arrived. And I have been feeling hungry long since. It is now noon, and I cannot walk with my legs. Just mark, mark :—

The sun, occupying the middle of the sky, is difficult to gaze upon, like an enraged monkey. And the ground is extremely hot, like Gandhari (suffering great anguish) when her hundred sons were all killed. (10)

VITA—So it is.

The herd of bullocks is sleeping under shade, letting fall their mouthfuls of grass. And the wild deer, suffering from thirst, are drinking the water of the lake, hot though it is. Men are not walking on the roads of the city, being exceedingly afraid of the heat. I think (therefore) that the carriage must have halted somewhere (on its way), leaving off the heated track. (11)

---

वसुंधरा । भाराक्रान्ता भारनिपीडिता । ] ॥ ६ ॥ आक्रोशति जुगुप्सते । **अमा इति ।** [ अमी फलपुष्पशोभिताः कठोराः निष्पन्दा निश्चलाश्च ता लताश्च ताभिः ॥ कठोरं निर्दयं निष्पन्दं निश्चलं च यथा तथा इति वा । उपवेष्टिता आलिङ्गिताः वृक्षाः नृपाज्ञया रक्षिजनेन पालिताः सदारा नरा इव निर्वृतिं सुखं यान्ति । वंशस्थं वृत्तम् ॥ ७ ॥ **बहुकुसुमेत्यादि ।** [ बहुभिः नानावर्णैः कुसुमैः विचित्रिता भूमिः । वृक्षाः विनामिता विनामं प्रापिताः । द्रुमाणां शिखरलताभ्यः शिखरशाखाभ्यः अवलम्बमानाः वानराः पनसफलानीव ललन्ति शोभन्ते । ] पुष्पिताग्राच्छन्दः । रुक्खा वृक्षाः । ललन्ति विहरन्ति

**शकारः**—भाव ।

**शिरसि मम निलीनो भाव सूर्यस्य पादः**
**शकुनिखगविहङ्गा वृक्षशाखासु लीनाः ।**
**नरपुरुषमनुष्या उष्णदीर्घं श्वसन्तो**
**गृहशरणनिषण्णा आतपं निर्वहन्ति ॥ १२ ॥**

भाव अद्यापि स चेटो नागच्छति । आत्मनो विनोदननिमित्तं किमपि गास्यामि । ( इति गायति । ) भाव भाव श्रुतं त्वया यन्मया गीतम् । (भावे ।
शिलशि मम[1] णिलीणे भाव शुज्जश्श पादे शउणिखगविहङ्गा लुक्खशाहाशु लीणा ।
णलपुलिशमणुश्शा उण्हदीहं शशन्ता घलशलणणिशण्णा आदवं णिव्वहन्ति ॥
भावे अज्ज वि शे चेडे णाअच्छदि । अत्तणो विणोदणणिमित्तं किं पि गाइश्शम् । भावे भावे शुदं तुए जं मए गाइदम् ।)

**विटः**—किमुच्यते । गन्धर्वो[2] भवान् ।

**शकारः**—कथं गन्धर्वो न भविष्यामि ।

**हिङ्गूज्ज्वला जीरकभद्रमुस्ता वचाया ग्रन्थिः सगुडा च शुण्ठी ।**
**एषा मया सेविता गन्धयुक्तिः कथं नाहं मधुरस्वर इति ॥ १३ ॥**

भाव पुनरपि तावद्गास्यामि । ( तथा[3] करोति । ) भाव भाव श्रुतं त्वया यन्मया गीतम् । (कधं गन्धव्वे ण भविश्शम् ।

हिङ्गुज्जले जीलकभद्दमुश्ते वचाह गण्ठी शगुडा अ शुण्ठी ।
एशे मए शेविद गन्धजुत्ती कधं ण हग्गे मधुलश्शलेत्ति ॥

भावे पुणो वि दाव गाइश्शम् । भावे भावे शुदं तुए जं मए गाइदम् ।)

**विटः**—किमुच्यते । गन्धर्वो भवान् ।

**शकारः**—कथं गन्धर्वो न भवामि ।

**हिङ्गूज्ज्वलं दत्तमरीचचूर्णं व्याघारितं तैलघृतेन मिश्रम् ।**
**भुक्तं मया पारभृतीयमांसं कथं नाहं मधुरस्वर इति ॥ १४ ॥**

भाव अद्यापि चेटो नागच्छति । (कधं गन्धव्वे ण भवामि ।

हिङ्गुज्जले दिण्णमरीचचुण्णे वग्घालिदे तेल्लघिएण[4] मिश्शे ।
भुत्ते मए पालहुदीअमंशे कधं ण हग्गे मधुलश्शलेत्ति ॥

भावे[5] अज्जवि चेडे णाअच्छदि ।)

**विटः**—स्वस्थो भवतु भवान् । संप्रत्येवागमिष्यति ।

---

॥ ८ ॥ **स्त्रीभिरिति** । [ स्त्रीभिः विमानितानां अवज्ञया तिरस्कृतानां कापुरुषाणामधीराणां मदनः कामः वर्धते । मृदुः स्ववशः भवति विनश्यति वा ] ॥ ९ ॥ **नभोमध्येत्यादि** । गाथा । [ सूरः सूर्यः । संतप्ता भूमिरातपेन गान्धारी शोकेन । ]

---

१ मह. २ गन्धर्वोऽसि. ३ इति तथा. ४ ०घिएहि. ५ भावे भावे.

SAK.—Friend,

O friend, the rays of the sun have rested on my head; birds, feathered creatures, and sky-rangers are sheltering among the branches of the trees; and men, persons and people, heaving hot and deep sighs, are passing ( the period of ) the sun's heat by remaining in their houses and homes. ( 12 )

Friend, stilll that Cheta hasn't come. I'll sing something to amuse myself. ( *He sings* ). Friend, friend, did you hear what I sang ?

VITA—Why describe it ? You are ( verily ) a Gandarva !

SAK.—How should I not be a Gandharva ?

Cumin seed and nut-grass mixed ( *lit.* brightened ) with asafœtida, and a piece of orris-root with ginger and treacle,—this fragrant mixture I have taken; How, then, shall I not be sweet-voiced ? ( 13 )

Friend, I'll sing once again. ( *Does so* ). Friend, friend, did you hear what I sang ?

VITA—What to say of it ? You are ( verily ) a Gandharva !

SAK.—How should I not be a Gandharva ?

I have eaten cukoo's flesh, seasoned with asafœtida, with black-pepper powder added to it, fried in ghee, and besprinkled with oil and clarified butter: How, then, shall I not be sweet-voiced ? ( 14 )

Fridnd, still the Cheta hasn't arrived !

VITA—You need not be anxious; he'll come just now.

---

गान्धारी दुर्योधनादिपुत्रशतमाता ॥ १० ॥ **छायास्विति** । [ प्रतिमुक्तः मुखात्त्यक्ताः शष्पस्य कवला ग्रासा येन तत् । गोकुलं गोसमूहः । सरस इदं सारसम् । 'तस्येदम्' इति अण् । संतापात्सूर्यस्य प्रचण्डातपादतिशङ्कितैः भीतैः । अपास्य हित्वा । क्वचित्प्रच्छाये देशे । स्वभावोक्तिः । शार्दूल० छन्दः ] ॥ ११ ॥ **शिरसीति** । मालिन्या श्लोकः । [ गृहमेव शरणं रक्षितृ तत्र निषण्णा । यद्वा गृहं शरणमिति पुनरुक्तिता शकारोक्तत्वान्न दोषाय । निर्वहन्ति यापयन्ति ] ॥ १२ ॥ **हिङ्गूज्ज्वलेति** । उपजातिच्छन्दसा । [ वचा उग्रगन्धाभिधा ओषधिः । 'वेखण्ड' इति भाषायाम् । गन्धयुक्तिः गन्धद्रव्ययोजना ] ॥ १३ ॥ **हिङ्गूज्ज्वलमिति** । [ हिङ्गुना उज्ज्वलम् । दत्तं निक्षिप्तं मरीचचूर्णं यस्मिन् । व्याघारितं घृताक्तम् । तैलघृतेन मिश्रमिति विरुद्धार्थं पुनरुक्तं च । परभृत एव पारभृतः कोकिलस्तस्येदं पारभृतीयम्

(ततः प्रविशति प्रवहणाधिरूढा वसन्तसेना चेटश्च)

**चेटः**—भीतः खल्वहम् । माध्याह्निकः सूर्यः । मेदानीं कुपितो राजश्यालकसंस्थानको भविष्यति । तत्त्वरितं वहामि ।—यातं गावौ यातम् । ( भीदे क्खु हग्गे । मज्झण्हिके शुज्जे । मा[1] दाणिं कुविदे लाअशालशंठाणे हुविश्शदि । ता तुलिदं वहामि ।—जाध गोणा जाध ।)

**वसन्तसेना**—हा धिक् हा धिक् । न खलु वर्धमानकस्यायं स्वरसंयोगः । किन्विदम् । किं नु खल्वार्यचारुदत्तेन वाहनपरिश्रमं परिहरताऽन्यो मनुष्योऽन्यत्प्रवहणं प्रेषितं भविष्यति । स्फुरति दक्षिणं लोचनम् । वेपते मे हृदयम् । शून्याः दिशः । सर्वमेव विसंष्ठुलं पश्यामि । (हद्धी हद्धी । ण क्खु वड्ढमाणअस्स अअं सरसंजोओ । किं ण्णेदम् । किं णु क्खु अज्जचारुदत्तेण वाहणपरिस्समं परिहरन्तेण अण्णो मणुस्सो अण्णं पवहणं पेसिदं भविस्सदि । फुरदि दाहिणं लोअणम् । वेवदि मे हिअअम् । सुण्णाओ दिसाओ । सव्वं ज्जेव विसंठुलं पेक्खामि ।)

**शकारः**—( नेमिघोषमाकर्ण्य । ) भाव भाव आगतं प्रवहणम् । ( भावे भावे आगदे पवहणे ।)

**विटः**—कथं जानासि ।

**शकारः**—किं न पश्यति भावः । वृद्धशूकर इव घुरघुरायमाणं लक्ष्यते ।(किं ण पेक्खदि भावे । बुड्ढशूअले विअ घुलघुलाअमाणे लक्खीअदि ।)

**विटः**—(दृष्ट्वा ।) साधु लक्षितम् । अयमागतः ।

**शकारः**—पुत्रक स्थावरक चेट आगतोऽसि । ( पुश्तका[2] थावलका चेडा आगदे शि ।)

**चेटः**—अथ किम् । (अध इं ।)

**शकारः**—प्रवहणमप्यागतम् ( पवहणे वि आगदे । )

**चेटः**—अथ किम् । (अध इं ।)

**शकारः**—गावावप्यागतौ । (गोणा वि आगदे ।)

**चेटः**—अथ किम् । (अध इं ।)

**शकारः**—त्वमप्यागतः । (तुमं पि आगदे । )

**चेटः**—(सहासम् ।) भट्टारक अहमप्यागतः । (भट्टके अहं पि आगदे ।)

**शकारः**—तत्प्रवेशय प्रवहणम् । (ता पवेशेहि पवहणम् । )

**चेटः**—कतरेण मार्गेण (कदलेण मग्गेण ।)

**शकारः**—एतेनैव प्राकारखण्डेन । (एदेण ज्जेव पाआलखण्डेण[3] ।)

---

१ मा दाव. २ पुत्तका, पुश्यका. ३ पगाल.

( *Then enter* Vasantasena *riding in the carriage, and* Cheta. )

CHETA—I am rather afraid. The sun is in the middle of the sky ; I hope the royal brother-in-law, Samsthanaka, won't be getting angry now ! Let me, therefore, drive quickly—Push on, bullocks, push on !

VAS.—Oh, alas ! Oh, alas ! This is surely not the voice of Vardhamanaka ! What may it mean ? Could it be that the worthy Charudatta, not wishing to weary the bullocks, has sent another driver and a different carriage ? My right eye throbs, my heart quakes, and all the quarters look void. I see everything turned upside down !

SAK.—( *Hearing the sound of the wheels* ). Friend, friend, the carriage has arrived !

VITA—How do you know ?

SAK.—Don't you notice it, friend ? It appears to be croaking, like an old hog.

VITA—( *Seeing* ) You marked correctly. Here he comes !

SAK.—Sthavaraka, my servant, my son, have you come ?

CHETA—I have.

SAK.—And the car also has come ?

CHETA—By all means.

SAK.—And the bullocks, too, have come ?

CHETA—Certainly.

SAK.—And you, too, have arrived ?

CHETA—( *With a laugh* ). Master, I, too, have arrived !

SAK.—Then bring the carriage in.

CHETA—By what path ?

SAK.—Along this broken part of the wall.

---

वृद्धाम्बुकः ' इति छः । मांसं भुक्तम् ] ।। १४ ।। किं न प्रेक्षते भावः । घुरघुरेत्यव्यक्तशब्दानुकरणम् । अव्यक्तं शब्दं कुर्वाणो लक्ष्यते । पगारुखण्डेण प्राकारखण्डपथेनैव प्रवेशय । दैवगत्या तु न भग्नं प्रवहणमित्याह—कथं न भग्नमिति । ण छिण्णा लज्जू ण मला गोणा इति वक्तव्ये शकारोक्तत्वाद्भ्रमणम् । मम गुरुः । गुरुरित्यतिमान्यत्वपरम् । एवं त्वं प्रेक्ष्यसे । [प्रेक्ष्यसे मयेति शेषः सादरकः आदरयुक्तः । अभ्यन्तरको रहस्येऽभ्यन्तरीकृतः । पुरस्करणीयः संमाननीयः ।] मूशे खज्जे इति विपरीतोक्तिः शकारवाक्यत्वात् । अवनतेस्याबि । [ पथि मार्गे वर्षेण धारा-

**चेटः**—भट्टारक वृषभौ म्रियेते । प्रवहणमपि भज्यते । अहमपि चेटो म्रिये । (भट्टके गोणा मलेन्ति । पवहणे वि भज्जेदि । हग्गे वि चेडे मलामि ।)

**शकारः**—अरे राजश्यालकोऽहम् । वृषभौ मृतौ अपरौ क्रेष्यामि । प्रवहणं भग्नमपरं कारयिष्यामि । त्वं मृतः अन्यः प्रवहणवाहको भविष्यति । (अले लाअशालके हग्गे । गोणा मले अवले किणिश्शम् । पवहणे भग्गे अवलं घडाइश्शम् । तुमं मले अण्णे पवहणवाहके हुविश्शदि ।)

**चेटः**—सर्वमुपपन्नं भविष्यति । अहमात्मीयो न भविष्यामि । (शव्वं उववण्ण हुविश्शदि । हग्गे अत्तणकेलके ण हुविश्शम् ।)

**शकारः**—अरे सर्वमपि नश्यतु । प्राकारखण्डेन प्रवेशय प्रवहणम् । (अले शव्वं पि णश्शदु । पाआलखण्डेण पवेशेहि पवहणम् ।)

**चेटः**—विभज्यस्व रे प्रवहण समं स्वामिना विभज्यस्व । अन्यत्प्रवहणं भवतु । भट्टारकं गत्वा निवेदयामि । (प्रविश्य ।) कथं न भग्नम् । भट्टारक एतदुपस्थितं प्रवहणम् । (विभज्ज[1] ले पवहण शमं शामिणा विभज्ज । अण्णे पवहणे भोदु । भट्टके गदुअ विणेदेमि । कधं ण भग्गे । भट्टके एशे उवत्थिदे पवहणे ।)

**शकारः**—न च्छिन्नौ वृषभौ । न मृता रज्जवः । त्वमपि न मृतः । (ण छिण्णा गोणा । ण मला लज्जू । तुमं पि ण मले ।)

**चेटः**—अथ किम् । (अध इं ।)

**शकारः**—भाव आगच्छ । प्रवहणं पश्यावः । भाव त्वमपि मम गुरुः परमगुरुः । प्रेक्ष्यसे सादरकोऽभ्यन्तरक इति पुरस्करणीय इति । त्वं तावत्प्रवहणमग्रतोऽधिरोह । (भाव आअच्छ । पवहणं पेक्खामो । भावे तुमं पि गुलु पलमगुलु । पेक्खीअशि शादलके अब्भन्तलकेत्ति पुलक्कलण्णीएत्ति[2] । तुमं दाव पवहणं अग्गदो अहिलुह ।)

**विटः**—एवं भवतु । (इत्यारोहति ।)

**शकारः**—अथ वा तिष्ठ त्वम् । तव पितृसंबन्धि[3] प्रवहणं येन त्वमग्रतोऽधिरोहसि । अहं प्रवहणस्वामी । अग्रतः प्रवहणमधिरोहामि । (अध वा चिश्ट तुमम् । तुह[4] बप्पकेलके पवहणे जेण तुमं अग्गदो अहिलुहशि । हग्गे पवहणशामी । अग्गदो पवहणं अहिलुहामि ।)

**विटः**—भवानेवं[5] ब्रवीति ।

**शकारः**—यद्यप्यहमेवं भणामि तथाऽपि तवैष आचारोऽधिरोह भट्टारकेति भणितुम् । ( जइ वि हग्गे एव्वं भणामि तधा वि तुह एशे आदले अहिलुह भश्टकेत्ति भणिदुम् ।)

---

१ विभज्ज विभज्ज २ पुक्कलणीआ (पुष्कलनीयः). ३ पितुः प्रव० इति क्वचिच्छाया. ४ तुहप्पके (तव संबन्धि).५ भवानेव.

CHETA—Master, the bullocks will die; the carriage will be smashed; and I, too, your servant, shall die.

SAK.—Well, I'm the king's brother-in-law! If the bullocks die, I'll buy others; if the carriage is smashed, I'll get another built; and if you die, I'll find another carriage-driver.

CHETA—That would all be right; but then I shall cease to be my own self!

SAK.—Eh, you, let everything perish; ( but ) bring in the carriage along the broken part of the wall.

CHETA—Break, thou carriage, go to pieces along with the master! Let there be another carriage. I'll go to the master and inform him ( to that effect. ) ( *Entering* ). How; It is not broken! Master, here is come your carriage!

SAK.—Are not the bullocks snapped, and the reins dead, and you too have not perished?

CHETA—That's so.

SAK.—Friend, come; we shall inspect the carriage. Friend, you are my preceptor, my most revered preceptor. I look upon you with respect, as one to be treated with confidence and honour. So you should get into the carriage before me.

VITA—So be it. ( *He goes to mount* ).

SAK.—Or rather, you stand aside. Is it your father's carriage ( as it were ) that you get in before me? *I* am the master of the carriage, and *I* therefore shall go in first.

VITA—But your honour said so ( *i. e.* asked me to do it ).

SAK.—Even though I did say so, still it would have been proper etiquette on your part to say—" Master, please get in ( first yourself )."

---

सारेण ताडितानि अक्षीणि येषां ते वर्षताडिताक्षाः अत एव अवनतशिरसः वृषभा इव अवनतशिरसः शीघ्रं प्रयाम । सदसि सभायां गौरवमात्मनि बहुमानः प्रियः यस्य तस्य मम चक्षुः कुलजनदर्शनकातरं कुलस्त्रीविलोकनभीरु हि । सामान्यस्त्रीदर्शनं त्वदुष्टमिति ध्वनिः । पुष्पिताग्रा वृत्तम् ] ॥ १५ ॥ [ ऊषरक्षेत्रे क्षारभूमौ । ] बुड्ढचेडे निन्दितश्रोतः । 'वृद्धश्रोत्रोन्नेषांह्म इत्यावाचकः । अकारणात्' इति पूर्वटीका । अक्षिभ्यां भक्ष्यते दन्तैः प्रेक्ष्यते । शकारवाक्यत्वाद्विपरीतोक्तिः । शरदिति । [ शरच्चन्द्रप्रतीकाशं शरदिन्दुधवलं पुलिनान्तरे सैकतप्रदेशे शेते इति तं हंसम् । वसन्तसेना रूपादिगुणसंपन्नं चारुदत्तं विहाय मूर्खं

विटः—आरोहतु भवान् ।

शकारः—एष सांप्रतमधिरोहामि । पुत्रक स्थावरक चेट परिवर्तय प्रवहणम् । (एशे शंपदं अहिलुहामि । पुत्तका थावलका चेडा पलिवत्तावेहि पवहणम् ।)

चेटः—(परावर्त्य[1]) अधिरोहतु भट्टारकः । (अहिलुहदु भट्टालके ।)

शकारः—(अधिरुह्यावलोक्य च शङ्कां[2] नाटयित्वा त्वरितमवतीर्य विटं कण्ठेऽवलम्ब्य ।) भाव भाव मृतोऽसि मृतोऽसि । प्रवहणाधिरूढा राक्षसी चौरो वा प्रतिवसति । तद्यदि राक्षसी तदोभावपि मुषितौ । अथ चौरः तदोभावपि खादितौ । (भावे भावे मलेशि मलेशि । पवहणाधिरूढा लक्खशी चोले वा पडिवशदि । ता जइ लक्खशी तदो उभे वि मूशे । अध चोले तदो उभे वि खज्जे ।)

विटः—न[3] भेतव्यम् । कुतोऽत्र वृषभयाने राक्षस्याः[4] संचारः[5] । मा नाम ते मध्याह्नार्कतापच्छिन्नदृष्टेः[6] स्थावरकस्य सकञ्चुकां[7] छायां दृष्ट्वा भ्रान्तिरुत्पन्ना ।

शकारः—पुत्रक स्थावरक चेट जीवसि । (पुश्तका[8] थावलका चेडा जीवेशि ।)

चेटः—अथ किम् । (अध इं ।)

शकारः—भाव प्रवहणाधिरूढा स्त्री प्रतिवसति । तदवलोकय । (भावे पवहणाधिलूढा[9] इश्थिआ[10] पडिवशदि ता[11] अवलोएहि ।)

विटः—कथं स्त्री ।

अवनतशिरसः प्रयाम शीघ्रं पथि वृषभा इव वर्षताडिताक्षाः ।
मम हि सदसि गौरवप्रियस्य कुलजनदर्शनकातरं हि चक्षुः ॥ १५ ॥

वसन्तसेना—(सविस्मयमात्मगतम् ।) कथं मम नयनयोरायासकर एव राजश्यालः । तत्संशयिताऽस्मि मन्दभाग्या । एतदिदानीं मम मन्दभागिन्या ऊषरक्षेत्रपतित इव बीजमुष्टिर्निष्फलमिहागमनं संवृत्तम् । तत्किमत्र करिष्यामि । (कधं मम णअणाणं आआसअरो ज्जेव राअसालओ । ता संसइदम्हि मन्दभाआ । एसो दाणिं मम मन्दभाइणीए ऊसरक्खेत्तपडिदो विअ बीअमुट्ठी णिप्फलो इध आगमणो संवुत्तो । ता किं एत्थ करइस्सम् ।)

शकारः—कातरः खल्वेष वृद्धचेटः प्रवहणं नावलोकयति । भाव आलोकय प्रवहणम् । (कादले क्खु एशे वुड्ढचेडे[12] पवहणं णावलोएदि । भावे आलोएहि पवहणम् ।)

विटः—को दोषः । भवतु । एवं तावत् ।

---

१ परावृत्य. २ त्रासं. ३ न भेतव्यं न भेत०. ४ राक्षससंचारः. ५ अवसरः. ६ खिन्न. ७ सकूर्चकाम्. ८ पश्यका; पुत्तका. ९ पवहणाहिं (प्रवहणान्तः). १० इत्थिआ. ११ अतो पलोएहि. १२ वुड्ढखोडे.

VITA—( Well, then ), let your honour get in.

SAK.—Here now I'll mount it. Sthavaraka, my servant, my son, turn the car around.

CHETA—( *Having turned it around* ). May master mount it.

SAK.—( *Mounts and looks in ; shows fear, quickly dismounts, and clings to the neck of* Vita ). Friend, friend, you're dead, you're dead ! There is a demoness or a thief seated inside the car. So, if she is a demoness, then we are stolen, both of us ; and if it is a thief, then we are gobbled up, both of us !

VITA—Don't you fear. How can a demoness come to occupy this bullock-cart ? May it not be that your eyes being dazzled with the heat of the mid-day sun, there arose this hallucination on your seeing the shadow of Sthavaraka, with the cloak on ?

SAK.—Sthavaraka, my servant, my son, are you alive ?

CHETA—Yes, I am.

SAK.—Friend, there is a female seated inside the carriage. You had better see it.

VITA—What ! A woman ?

Let us pass away quickly by the road, with bent heads, like bullocks whose eyes are dazzled by the falling rain-drops ; for the eyes of me, to whom esteem in public assemblies is dear, are afraid to gaze upon high-born ladies. (15)

VAS.—( *With surprise ; to herself* ). What ! Here is the same royal brother-in-law, who is an eyesore to me ! Then indeed I am in peril, I, the unlucky one ! Now this visit of my unlucky self here has turned out fruitless, like a handful of seed sown in saline soil. So what shall I do here ?

SAK.—This old fellow, Cheta, is a coward ; he won't peep in the carriage. Friend, you look into it.

VITA—Where's the harm ? All right : so be it.

---

शकारं कथमुपस्थितेत्यर्थः । अप्रस्तुतप्रशंसालंकारः सारूप्यनिबन्धनः ॥ १६ ॥ पूर्वमिति । [ पूर्वं प्रथमाङ्के शकारानुगमने मानाद्राजश्यालमवज्ञाय संप्रति जननीवशान्मात्राज्ञानुरोधाद् द्रव्यार्थे आगतेति शेषः । अशौण्डीर्यमनौदार्यं कृपणमत्त्वमिति यावत् । तत्स्वभावः यस्य तेन वेशभावेन आगताऽसीति मन्यते ] ॥ १७ ॥ भक्खिदे भक्षितः । विपरीतोक्तिः पूर्ववत् । अथ वेत्यतलस्थोक्तिः । शृगाला उड्डीयन्त इत्यादि चतुष्टयमपक्रमम् । [ धुर्याणां प्रवहणबलीवर्दयोः । सामान्याभिप्रायं

**शकारः**—कधं शृगाला उड्डयन्ते वायसा व्रजन्ति । तद्यावद्भावोऽक्षिभ्यां भक्ष्यते दन्तैः प्रेक्ष्यते तावदहं पलायिष्ये । (कधं शिआला उड्डेन्ति वाअशा वच्चेन्ति । ता जाव भावे अक्खीहिं भक्खीअदि दन्तेहिं पेक्खीअदि ताव हग्गे पलाइश्शम् ।)

**विटः**—(वसन्तसेनां दृष्ट्वा । सविषादमात्मगतम् । ) कथमये मृगी व्याघ्रमनुसरति । भोः कष्टम् ।

**शरच्चन्द्रप्रतीकाशं पुलिनान्तरशायिनम् ।**
**हंसी हंस परित्यज्य वायसं समुपस्थिता ॥ १६ ॥**

(जनान्तिकम् ।) वसन्तसेने न युक्तमिदं नापि सदृशमिदम् ।

**पूर्वं मानादवज्ञाय द्रव्यार्थे जननीवशात् ।**

**वसन्तसेना**—न । (इति शिरश्चालयति ।) (ण ।)

**विटः**—

**[१]अशौण्डीर्यस्वभावेन वेशभावेन मन्यते ॥ १७ ॥**

ननूक्तमेव मया भवतीं प्रति—'सममुपचर भद्रे सुप्रियं चाप्रियं च ।'

**वसन्तसेना**—प्रवहणविपर्यासेनागता शरणागतास्मि । (पवहणविपज्जासेण आगदा । सरणागदम्हि ।)

**विटः**—न भेतव्यं न भेतव्यम् । भवतु । एनं वञ्चयामि । (शकारमुपगम्य ।) काणेलीमातः सत्यं राक्षस्येवात्र प्रतिवसति ।

**शकारः**—भाव भाव यदि राक्षसी प्रतिवसति तत्कथं न त्वां मुष्णाति । अथ चौरः तदा किं त्वं न भक्षितः । (भावे भावे जइ लक्खशी पडिवशदि ता कीश ण तुमं मूशेदि । अध[२] चोले ता किं तुमं ण भक्खिदे[३] ।)

**विटः**—किमनेन निरूपितेन । यदि पुनरुद्यानपरंपरया पद्भ्यामेव नगरीमुज्जयिनीं प्रविशावः तदा को दोषः स्यात् ।

**शकारः**—एवं कृते किं भवति । (एव्वं किदे किं भोदि ।)

**विटः**—एवं कृते व्यायामः सेवितो धुर्याणां च परिश्रमः[४] परिहृतो भवति ।

**शकारः**—एवं भवतु । स्थावरक चेट नय प्रवहणम् । अथ वा तिष्ठ तिष्ठ । देवतानां ब्राह्मणानां चाग्रतश्चरणेन गच्छामि । नहि नहि । प्रवहणमधिरुह्य गच्छामि । येन दूरतो मां प्रेक्ष्य भणिष्यन्ति—एष स राष्ट्रियश्यालो भट्टारको गच्छति । (एवं भोदु । थावलआ चेडा णेह पवहणम् । अध वा चिश्ट चिश्ट । देवदाणं बह्मणाणं च अग्गदो चलणेण गच्छामि । ण हि ण हि । पवहणं अहिलुहिअ गच्छामि जेण दूलदो मं पेक्खिअ भणिश्शन्ति—एशे शे लश्टिअशाले भश्टालके गच्छदि ।)

---

१ अशौटीर्य. २ अध वा. ३ खज्जे (खादितः). ४ श्रमः.

SAK.—How ! The jackals are flying about in the sky and the crows scampering along ! So I'll run away before my friend is eaten up with eyes and gazed upon with teeth !

VITA—( *Seeing* Vasantasena; *sorrowfully, to himself*). Ah ! How is it that the doe is following a tiger ! Oh, alas ;

Leaving the male swan, resplendent like the autumnal moon, and reclining on a stretch of ( white ) sand, the female swan has taken herself to a crow ! (16)

( *Aside; to* Vasantasena ) O Vasantasena, this is neither proper nor becoming.

Having first proudly spurned him, you're now come at the bidding of your mother, for the sake of money :—

VAS.—No ! ( *She nods her head* ).

VITA—

Then I think ( you came ) owing to the profession of a courtesan being characterized by absence of generosity ( *i. e.* by a desire for money ). (17)

Why, I did ( formerly ) say to you—" O good maiden, serve equally one much coveted by you and one disliked by you."

VAS —I came owing to an interchange of carriages. I beseech your protection !

VITA--Be not afraid; be not afraid.--All right; I will deceive him. ( *Approaching* Sakara ). Bastard, it is true; there's actually a demoness inside.

SAK.--Friend, friend, if there's a demoness, then how has she not stolen you ? And if a thief, then how haven't you been devoured ?

VITA—What is the good of discussing that ?—Well, now, if we enter the city of Ujjayini going on foot, through the row of orchards, then what is the harm ( in that ) ?

SAK.--If we do so, what good would it do ?

VITA—If we do so, we get exercise and avoid giving trouble to the bullocks.

SAK.—So be it. Sthavaraka, my servant, take away the carriage. Or rather, stay—stay. Am I to walk on foot before ( *i e.* in the presence of ) the deities and the Brahmanas ? No, no ! I'll mount the carriage and go, so that, seeing me from afar, they will say :—" Here goes our master, the king's brother-in-law."

**विटः**—( स्वगतम् । ) दुष्करं विषमौषधीकर्तुम्[1] । भवतु । एवं तावत् । (प्रकाशम् ।) काणेलीमातः एषा वसन्तसेना भवन्तमभिसारयितुमागता ।

**वसन्तसेना**—शान्तं पापम् । शान्तं पापम् । (सन्तं[2] पावम् । सन्तं पावम् ।)

**शकारः**—( सहर्षम् । ) भाव भाव मां प्रवरपुरुषं मनुष्यं वासुदेवकम् । (भावे भावे मं पबलपुलिशं[3] मणुश्शं वाशुदेवकम् ।)

**विटः**—अथ किम् ।

**शकारः**—तेन ह्यपूर्वा श्रीः समासादिता । तस्मिन्काले मया रोषिता । सांप्रतं पादयोः पतित्वा प्रसादयामि । (तेण हि अपुव्वा शिली शमाशादिदा । तश्शि काले मए लोशाइदा[4] । शंपदं पादेशुं पडिअ पशादेमि ।)

**विटः**—साध्वभिहितम् ।

**शकारः**—एष पादयोः पतामि । (इति वसन्तसेनामुपसृत्य ।) मातः अम्बिके शृणु मम विज्ञप्तिम् ।

**एष पतामि चरणयोर्विशालनेत्रे**
**हस्ताञ्जलिं दशनखे तव शुद्धदन्ति ।**
**यत्तव मयाऽपकृतं मदनातुरेण**
**तत्क्षामिताऽसि वरगात्रि तवास्मि दासः ॥ १८ ॥**

(एशे पादेशुं पडेमि । अत्तिके अम्बिके शुणु मम विण्णत्तिम् ।

एशे पडामि[5] चलणेशु विशालणेत्ते हश्तञ्जलिं दशणहे[6] तव शुद्धदन्ति ।
जं तं मए अवकिदं मदणातुलेण[7] तं खम्मिदाशि वलगत्ति तव म्हि दाशे ॥)

**वसन्तसेना**—(सक्रोधम् ।) अपेहि । अनार्यं मन्त्रयसे । इति पादेन ताडयति । (अवेहि । अणज्जं मन्तेसि ।)

**शकारः**—(सक्रोधम् ।)

**यच्चुम्बितमम्बिकामातृकाभिर्गतं न देवानामपि यत्प्रणामम् ।**
**तत्पातितं पादतलेन मुण्डं वने शृगालेन यथा मृताङ्गम् ॥ १९ ॥**

अरे स्थावरक चेट कुत्र त्वयैषा समासादिता ।

(जे चुम्बिदे अम्बिकमादुकेहिं गदे ण देवाण[8] वि जे पणामम् ।
शे पाडिदे पादतलेण मुण्डे वणे शिआलेण जधा मुदङ्गे[9] ॥

अले थावलआ चेडा कहिं तुए एशा शमाशादिदा ।)

---

१ ओष०. २ शन्तं. ३ पुलिशमणु० ४ लोशायिदा. ५ पडेमि. ६ दशणहं. ७ मदणाउलेन. ८ देवाणं. ९ मिदङ्गे.

VITA—( *To himself* ). It is difficult (*i. e.* impossible ) to convert poison into medicine. All right. Let it be thus. (*Aloud*). Bastard, here's Vasantasena, come to you of her own accord, as an *abhisarika*.

VAS.—Heaven forbid—heaven forbid !

SAK.—( *Joyfully* ). Friend, friend, has she come to *me*, the great man, a human being, ( another ) Krishna ?

VITA—Yes.

SAK.—Then I have attained unprecedented good fortune! On that occasion I had angered her : now I'll fall at her feet and reconcile her.

VITA—You have spoken well !

SAK.—Here I'll fall at her feet. ( *Approaching* Vasantasena). Mother, mamma, listen to my request :—

Here I prostrate myself at your feet, O you with large eyes; O pearly-toothed one, I place my folded hands on the ten nails of your feet.—O beautiful-limbed damsel, I beseech your forgiveness for whatever ill I, tormented by love, did towards you. I am your slave ! (18)

VAS.—( *Angrily* ). Get away ; you are speaking wickedly. ( *Strikes him with the foot* )

SAK.—( *Wrathfully* ).

This head of mine, which was caressed by my mother and mamma, and which did not bow even to the gods, has been struck down ( by her ) with her foot, as a jackal treats a carcass in the jungle. (19)

You, Sthavaraka, my slave, where did you come across her ?

---

बहुवचनम् । ] देवदाणं अग्गदो गच्छामि । न हि न होति न्यायविरुद्धम् । [ विषमौषधीकर्तुं दुर्जनमानुकूल्येन परिवर्तयितुमित्यर्थः । वासुदेव इव वासुदेवकः तम् । 'इवे प्रतिकृतौ' इति इवार्थे कन् । ] **एष पतामीत्यादि** । [ हे विशालनेत्रे एषोऽहं तव चरणयोः पतामि । हे शुद्धदन्ति शुद्धा दन्ता यस्याः तत्संबुद्धिः । तव दश नखे चरणयोः दशसु नखेषु हस्ताञ्जलिं करोमीति शेषः । मदनातुरेण कामपीडितेन मया यत्तव अपकृतं तत् क्षामिताऽसि तदर्थं क्षमां याचिताऽसि । हे वरगात्रि तव-

**चेट:**—भट्टक ग्रामशकटै रुद्धो राजमार्ग:। तदा चारुदत्तस्य वृक्षवाटिकायां प्रवहणं स्थापयित्वा तत्रावतीर्य यावच्चक्रपरिवृत्तिं करोमि तावदेषा प्रवहणविपर्यासेनेहारूढेति तर्कयामि। (भट्टके गामशअलेहिं लुद्धे लाअमग्गे। तदो चालुदत्तश्श लुक्खवाडिआए पवहणं थाविअ तहिं ओदलिअ जाव चक्कपलिवट्टिअं कलेमि ताव एशा पवहणविपज्जाशेण[1] इह आलूढेत्ति तक्केमि।)

**शकार:**—कथं प्रवहणविपर्यासेनागता। न मामभिसारयितुम्। तदवतरावतर मदीयात्प्रवहणात्। त्वं तं दरिद्रसार्थवाहपुत्रकमभिसारयसि। मदीयौ गावौ वाहयसि। तदवतरावतर। गर्भदास्यवतरावतर। (कधं पवहणविपज्जाशेण[2] आगदा। ण मं अहिशालिदुम्। ता ओदल ओदल ममकेलकादो पवहणादो। तुमं तं दलिद्दशत्थवाहपुत्तक[3] अहिशालेशि। ममकेलकाइं गोणाइं वाहेशि। ता ओदल ओदल। गब्भदाशि ओदल ओदल।)

**वसन्तसेना**—तमार्यचारुदत्तमभिसारयसीति यत्सत्यमलंकृताऽस्म्यमुना वचनेन। सांप्रतं यद्भवतु तद्भवतु। (तं अज्जचारुदत्तं अहिसारेसित्ति जं सच्चं अलंकिदम्हि इमिणा वअणेण। संपदं जं भोदु तं भोदु।)

**शकार:**—

**एताभ्यां ते दशनखोत्पलमण्डलाभ्यां**
**हस्ताभ्यां चाटुशतताडनलम्पटाभ्याम्।**
**कर्षामि ते वरतनुं निजयानका-**
**त्केशेषु वालिदयितामिव यथा जटायु:॥ २०॥**

(एदेहिं दे दशणहुप्पलमण्डलेहिं
हश्तेहिं[4] चाडुशदताडणलम्पडेहिं।
कट्टामि[5] दे वलतणुं णिअजाणकादो
केशेशु वालिदइअं वि जहा जडाऊ[6]॥)

---

दास: अस्मि। वसन्ततिलकम्।]॥ १८॥ **यच्चुम्बितमिति**। [यदम्बिकया मात्रा चुम्बितम्। यद्देवानामपि प्रणामं न गतं तान्न प्रणतम्। तन्मे मुण्डं शिर: वनशृगालेन मृताङ्गं शवशरीरमिव पादतलेन पातितम्। अम्बिकामातृभिरिति पुनरुक्तं सर्वत्र पुंल्लिङ्गबहुवचनत्वं च शकारवचनत्वादित्यवसेयम्।] उपजात्या। ये चुम्बिता मातृकाम्बिकाभिर्गता न देवानामपि ये प्रणामम्। ते पातिता: पादतलेन मुण्डा वने शृगालेन यथा मृदङ्गा:॥ मातृका इति स्वार्थे क:। मुण्डा इति बहुवचनमप्यनर्थकम्॥ १९॥ [गर्भदासि जन्मत एव दासि। अत: कस्ते गर्व इति भाव:।]

१ विपलट्टणेण (विपर्ययेण); २ पलिवट्टणेण (परिवर्तनेन). ३ पुत्तहकं. ४ हत्थेहिं ५ वड्ढामि, वट्टामि. ६ हणूमे (हनूमान्).

CHETA—Master, the highway was blocked by the rustic carts. I therefore stopped my car near Charudatta's garden; and while I got down there and was giving a turn to the wheels (of another's cart), she must have got in by mistaking our carriage for her own; so I infer.

SAK.—What! She came owing to an interchange of carriages, and not to meet me (as her lover)! Then get down, get down from my carriage! You are going to meet that penniless son of a merchant (*i. e.*, Charudatta), and you make my bullocks carry you! Ah, get down, get down! You born servant-maid, get down!

VAS.—To tell the truth, I feel honoured by these words (of his), *viz.* that I am going to meet that worthy Charudatta. Now whatever must happen, let it come.

SAK.—

Seizing you by the hair with these two hands of mine, which are decked with a row of lotuses in the form of their ten nails, and which were yearning to pat you to the accompaniment of hundreds of fond words, I shall (forthwith) drag down your lovely body from my carriage, just as Jatayu did the wife of Vali. (20)

---

**ताभ्यामित्यादि** । वसन्ततिलकच्छन्दसा । सबिन्दोः पाक्षिकगुरुत्वात् एदेहिं हत्थेहिं इत्यनयोर्लघुत्वम् । [ दश नखा एव उत्पलमण्डलं ययोस्ताभ्याम् । चाटुशतेन प्रियवचनशतेन यत्ताडनं तत्र लम्पटाभ्यामुत्सुकाभ्याम् । एताभ्यां हस्ताभ्यां ते वरतनुं केशेषु गृहीत्वा निजयानकात्कर्षामि । यथा इव । ] कर्षयामि दे त्वाम् । वरतनुं निजयानकात्केशेषु वालिदयितामिव यथा केशेषु जटायुराकृष्टवान् । पाठान्तरे हनूमानित्यर्थः । [ ते ते इति यथा इव इति च पुनरुक्तम् । वालिदयिताया जटायुना कर्षणाभावात् ] व्याहतोपमं चेदम् । [ शकारोक्तित्वेन चमत्कृतिमत् ] ॥ २० ॥ **अग्राह्या इति** । [ गुणसमन्विताः सौन्दर्यादिगुणोपेताः । दृष्टान्तालंकारः ] ॥ २१ ॥ **योऽसौ सोऽद्यैतस्याः इत्यादि** । ततः सांप्रतं मारयाम्येनाम् । **यदीच्छसीत्यादि** । उपजातिच्छन्दसा । प्रावारकं प्रच्छन्दं सूत्रशतैर्ग्रथितम् । [ यदि इच्छसि मत्त इति शेषः । ] मत्स्यं च खादितुम् । चुहू चुहू चुक्कु चुहू चुहूत्ति इत्यनुकरणम् ॥ २२ ॥ **बालामिति** । [ वेश्यां तथाऽपि अवेशसदृशः । कुलस्त्रीजनोचित इत्यर्थः । प्रणयोपचारः यस्याः । धनलोभविरहादिति भावः । अनागसं निरपराधामेनां यदि घातयामि । केनोडुपेन प्लवेन । तरिष्ये अत्रात्मनेपदं चिन्त्यम् । वसन्त० वृत्तम् । ]

**विटः**—

**अग्राह्या मूर्धजेष्वेताः स्त्रियो गुणसमन्विताः ।**
[१]**न लताः**[२] **पल्लवच्छेदमर्हन्त्युपवनोद्भवा**[३]**: ॥ २१ ॥**

तदुत्तिष्ठ त्वम्[४] । अहमेनामवतारयामि । वसन्तसेने अवतीर्यताम् ।

( वसन्तसेनाऽवतीर्यैकान्ते स्थिता । )

**शकारः**—( स्वगतम् । ) योऽसौ मम वचनावमानेन तदा रोषाग्निः संधुक्षितोऽद्यैतस्याः पादप्रहारेणानेन प्रज्वलितः । तत्सांप्रतं मारयाम्येनाम् । भवतु । एवं तावत् । (प्रकाशम् ।) भाव भाव ।

**यदीच्छसि लम्बदशाविशालं प्रावारकं सूत्रशतैर्युक्तम् ।**
**मांसं च खादितुं तथा तुष्टिं कर्तुं चुहू चुहू चुक्कु चुहू चुहू इति ॥ २२ ॥**

(जे शे मम वअणावमाणेण तदा लोशग्गी शंधुक्खिदे अज्ज एदाए पादप्पहालेण अणेण पज्जलिदे । तं शंपदं मालेमि णम् । भोदु । एव्वं दाव । भावे भावे ।

जदिच्छशे लम्बदशाविशालं पावालअं शुत्तशदेहिं जुत्तम् ।
मंशं च खादुं तह तुश्टिं कादुं चुहू चुहू चुक्कु चुहू [५]चुहूत्ति ॥)

**विटः**—ततः किम् ।

**शकारः**—मम प्रियं कुरु । (मम पिअं कलेहि ।)

**विटः**—बाढं करोमि वर्जयित्वा त्वकार्यम् ।

**शकारः**—भाव अकार्यस्य गन्धोऽपि नास्ति । राक्षसी काऽपि नास्ति । ( भावे[६] अकज्जाह गन्धे वि णत्थि । लक्खशी कवि णत्थि ।)

**विटः**—उच्यतां तर्हि ।

**शकारः**—मारय वसन्तसेनाम् । (मालेहि वसन्तशेणिअम् ।)

**विटः**—(कर्णौ पिधाय ।)

**बालां स्त्रियं च नगरस्य**[७] **विभूषणं च**
**वेश्यामवेशसदृशप्रणयोपचाराम् ।**
**एनामनागसमहं यदि घातयामि**
**केनोडुपेन परलोकनदीं तरिष्ये ॥ २३ ॥**

**शकारः**—अहं त उडुपं[८] दास्यामि । अन्यच्च विविक्त उद्यान इह मारयन्तं कस्त्वां प्रेक्षिष्यते । ( अहं ते भेडकं दइश्शम् । अण्णं च विवित्ते उज्जाणे इध मालन्तं को तुमं पेक्खिश्शदि ।)

---

१ नु. २ लता.....त्युपवनोद्भवा. ३ न्तूपव०. ४ त्वहमेनाम्. ५ चुहुत्ति. ६ भावे भावे. ७ नरलोकवि. ८ एडकम्.

VITA—

Ladies like these, who are accomplished, should not be seized by the hair; for, the creepers growing in orchards deserve not to have their foliage lopped off. (21)

So you may stand off; I'll help her to dismouut. O Vasantasena, please get down.

( Vasantasena *dismounts and stands in one corner* ).

SAK.—( *To himself* ). That fire of my anger, which was kindled on that occasion when she spurned my suit, has to-day been inflamed by this her insult of ) kicking. So I'll now kill her. All right; I'll ( proceed ) in this way. ( *Alond* ). Friend, friend!

If you desire ( to wear ) a large cloak, with long fringes and having hundreds of tassels, and to dine upon flesh and derive satisfaction (therefrom), (munching) with the sounds *chuhoo-chuhoo, chukku, chuhoo-chuhoo,*— (22)

VITA—Then what?

SAK.—Do what I wish.

VITA—Very well. I'll do it, but excepting an execrable [ sinful ] deed ( that cannot be done ).

SAK.—Friend, there is not even the remotest trace of the job being such as [ being difficult ] cannot be done. There is no demoness whatever in it.

VITA—Speak out, then ( what it is ).

SAK.—Kill Vasantasena!

VITA—( *Closing his ears* )

If I kill her who is young, a woman, and an ornament of our city, and who, although a courtesan, bestows her love in a manner unlike that of the courtesans' quarter, and who is ( withal ) innocent, then with what boat shall I cross the river of the next world? ( 23 )

SAK.—I will give you a boat. And moreover, in this deserted garden, who would see you killing her?

---

अवेशसदृशेति । अवेश्यापाठकोचितमकृत्रिमम् ॥ २३ ॥ [एकडमिति पाठे मेषम् । परलोकनदीतरणायेति शेषः । ] विविक्ते विजने । पश्यन्तीति । [ अयमिति गगनस्थितसूर्यस्य हस्तेन निर्देशः । अनिलः वायुः । सुकृतदुष्कृतयोः पुण्यपापकर्मणोः

विटः—

पश्यन्ति मां दश दिशो वनदेवताश्च
चन्द्रश्च दीप्तकिरणश्च दिवाकरोऽयम् ।
धर्मानिलौ च गगनं च तथाऽन्तरात्मा
भूमिस्तथा सुकृतदुष्कृतसाक्षिभूता ॥ २४ ॥

शकारः—तेन हि पटान्तापवारितां कृत्वा मारय । (तेण हि पडन्तोवालिदं[1] कदुअ मालेहि ।)

चेटः—मूर्ख अपध्वस्तोऽसि ।[2]

शकारः—अधर्मभीरुरेष वृद्धशृगालः । भवतु । स्थावरकं चेटमनुनयामि । पुत्रक स्थावरक चेट सुवर्णकटकानि दास्यामि । (अधम्मभीलू एशे बुड्ढकोले[3] । भोदु । थावलअं चेडं अणुणेमि । पुश्थका[4] थावलका चेडा शोवण्णखडुआइं[5] दइश्शम् ।)

चेटः—अहमपि परिधास्यामि । (अहं पि पहिलिश्शम् ।)

शकारः—सौवर्णं ते पीठकं कारयिष्यामि। (शोवण्णं दे [6]पीठकं कालइश्शम् ।)

चेटः—अहमप्युपवेक्ष्यामि । (अहं पि उवविशिश्शम् ।)

शकारः—सर्वं त उच्छिष्टं दास्यामि । (शव्वं दे उच्छिश्टं [7]दइश्शम् ।)

चेटः—अहमपि खादिष्यामि । (अहं पि खाइश्शम् ।)

शकारः—सर्वचेटानां महत्तरकं कारयिष्यामि । (शव्वचेडाणं[8] महत्तलकं कलइश्शम् ।)

चेटः—भट्टक भविष्यामि । (भश्टके[9] हुविश्शम् ।)

शकारः—तन्मन्यस्व मम वचनम् । (ता मण्णेहि[10] मम वअणम् ।)

चेटः—भट्टक सर्वं करोमि वर्जयित्वाऽकार्यम् । (भश्टके शव्वं कलेमि वज्जिअ अकज्जम् ।)

शकारः—अकार्यस्य गन्धोऽपि नास्ति । (अकज्जाह गन्धे वि णत्थि[11] ।)

चेटः—भणतु भट्टकः । (भणादु भश्टके ।)

शकारः—एनां वसन्तसेनां मारय । (एणं वशन्तशेणिअं मालेहि ।)

चेटः—प्रसीदतु भट्टकः । इयं मयाऽनार्येणार्या प्रवहणपरिवर्तनेनानीता । (पशीददु भश्टके । इअं मए अणज्जेण अज्जा पवहणपलिवत्तणेण आणीदा ।)

---

१ वलितं (वलितां). २ धिक्कृतः. ३ खोले (शृगालः). ४ पुत्तका. ५ खण्डाइं. ६ पीठके. ७ ०श्टअं. ८ चेडआणं. ९ भट्टके. १० माणेहि (मानय). ११ णश्ति.

VITA—

The ten quarters are seeing me, and the sylvan deities, and the moon, and this sun with his brilliant rays, and Dharma (Righteousness), and Wind, and the sky, and the internal soul, and also the Earth, the witness to all holy and unholy acts. ( 24 )

SAK.—Then put your cloak over her, and kill her.

VITA—Fool, you are damned !

SAK.—This old jackal is afraid of ( committing) sin. All right; I'll persuade my servant Sthavaraka. Sthavaraka, my slave, my son, I'll give you golden bracelets.

CHETA—And I will put them on.

SAK.—I'll get a golden seat made for you.

CHETA—And I will sit ( on it ).

SAK.—I'll give you all the leavings of my food.

CHETA—And I will eat them.

SAK.—I'll make you the head of all my servants.

CHETA—Master, I will become ( the head ).

SAK.—Then do my bidding,

CHETA—Master, I will do everything, excepting such as cannot be done.

SAK.—There is no trace of impossibility about it.

CHETA—Let my master speak out ( what it is ).

SAK.—Kill this Vasantasena ?

CHETA—Please, master [ don't ask me that ] this noble lady was brought here by my unworthy self owing to an interchange of cars.

---

साक्षिभूता प्रत्यक्षद्रष्ट्री । एतल्लिङ्गवचनविपरिणामेन सर्वत्र योज्यम् ॥ २४ ॥ खड्आइं बाहुवलयविशेषान् । पीढके पीठम् । उच्छिश्टअं भोजनावशिष्टम् । **येनेति** । [ येन कर्मणा अहं भागधेयदोषैः दुर्भाग्यदोषैः गर्भदासः आजन्मसेवकः विनिर्मितोऽस्मि तत्कर्म ईदृशकर्मणा अधिकं न क्रेष्यामि संपादयिष्यामि । तेनाकार्यं परिहरामि ] ॥ २५ ॥ **अपीति** । [ एष परिभूता निकृष्टा दशा यस्य तथा अपि दरिद्रः प्रेष्यः सेवकोऽपि परत्र परलोके फलं पुण्यकर्मण इति यावत् इच्छति । अस्य भर्ता तु न । तस्माद्ये शकारसदृशाः अद्य असदृशं कर्म पापादि असदृशमयोग्यं पुरुषं वा वर्धयन्ति सदृशं पुण्यं कर्म योग्यं पुरुषं वा त्यजन्ति ते कथमिव नाशं न यान्ति । यास्य-

**शकारः**—अरे चेट तवापि न प्रभवामि। (अले[1] चेडा तवावि ण पहवामि।)

**चेटः**—प्रभवति भट्टकः शरीरस्य न चारित्रस्य। तत्प्रसीदतु प्रसीदतु भट्टकः। बिभेमि खल्वहम्। (पहवदि भश्टके[2] शलीलाह ण चालित्ताह। ता पशीददु पशीददु भश्टके। भाआमि क्खु अहम्।)

**शकारः**—त्वं मम चेटो भूत्वा कस्माद्बिभेषि। (तुमं मम चेडे भविअ कश्श भाआशि।)

**चेटः**—भट्टक परलोकात्। (भश्टके पललोअश्श।)

**शकारः**—कः स परलोकः। (के शे पललोए।)

**चेटः**—भट्टक सुकृतदुष्कृतस्य परिणामः। (भश्टके शुकिददुक्किदश्श पलिणामे।)

**शकारः**—कीदृशः सुकृतस्य परिणामः। (केलिशे[3] शुकिदश्श पलिणामे।)

**चेटः**—यादृशो भट्टको बहुसुवर्णमण्डितः। (जादिशे भश्टके बहुशुवण्ण-मण्डिदे।)

**शकारः**—दुष्कृतस्य कीदृशः। (दुक्किदश्श केलिशे।)

**चेटः**—यादृशोऽहं परपिण्डभक्षको भूतः। तदकार्यं न करिष्यामि। (जादिशे हग्गे पलपिण्डभक्खके[4] भूदे। ता अकज्जं ण कलइश्शम्।)

**शकारः**—अरे न मारयिष्यसि। (इति बहुविधं ताडयति।) (अले ण मालिश्शशि।)

**चेटः**—ताडयतु भट्टको मारयतु भट्टकः। अकार्यं न करिष्यामि।

> **येनास्मि गर्भदासो विनिर्मितो भागधेयदोषैः।**
> **अधिकं च न क्रेष्यामि तेनाकार्यं परिहरामि॥ २५॥**

(पिश्टदु[5] भश्टके मालेदु भश्टके। अकज्जं ण कलइश्शम्।

> जेणम्हि गब्भदाशे विणिम्मिदे भाअधेअदोशेहिं।
> अहिअं च ण कीणिश्शं[6] तेण[7] अकज्जं पलिहलामि॥

**वसन्तसेना**—भाव शरणागताऽस्मि। (भाव शरणागदम्हि।)

**विटः**—काणेलीमातः मर्षय मर्षय। साधु स्थावरक साधु।

> **अप्येष[8] नाम परिभूतदशो[9] दरिद्रः**
> **प्रेष्यः परत्र फलमिच्छति नास्य भर्ता।**
> **तस्मादमी कथमिवाद्य न यान्ति नाशं**
> **ये वर्धयन्त्यसदृशं सदृशं त्यजन्ति॥ २६॥**

---

१ अले अले. २ भट्टके. ३ कीलिशे, कीशिदे. ४ पुश्टके, पुट्टके. ५ पिठ्ठदु, विठ्ठदु. ६ कीलिश्शं. ७ तेण अहं. ८ अप्येवमेव. ९ दृशः.

SAK.—You, slave, have I no mastery even over you ?

CHETA—Your honour is the master of my body, but not of my morals. So please, master, excuse me; I am verily afraid.

SAK.—Being *my* servant, of whom are you afraid ?

CHETA—Of the next world, master.

SAK.—What is that 'next world' ?

CHETA—Master, it is the consequence of one's good and bad acts.

SAK.—Of what kind is the consequence of good acts ?

CHETA—(To be) like my master, adorned with many golden ornaments.

SAK.—And of what sort (is the consequence) of bad acts ?

CHETA.—( To be ) like me, who have become an eater of others' food. So I will not do an unholy deed.

SAK.—Aye, you won't kill her ? ( *He beats him in a variety of ways* ).

CHETA—The master may beat me or kill me; but I won't do an unholy deed.

Since I am made a born slave by the faults of my luck, I shall not buy any further ( store of evil luck ), and for this reason I refrain from committing a sinful deed. ( 25 )

VAS.—Sir, I beseech your protection !

VITA—Bastard, forbear, forbear ! Good, Sthavaraka, good !

Even this penniless man, in such a miserable condition, and a menial, desires reward in the next world; but not so his master. Then why do such persons not meet with instant ruin, who multiply unworthy deeds and never do a worthy one ? ( 26 )

---

न्त्येवेत्यर्थः। वसन्ततिलकं वृत्तम् ] ॥२६॥ **रन्ध्रेति**। [कृतान्तः विधिः रन्ध्रानुसारी छिद्रानुवर्ती विषमो विपरीतकारी च यद् यस्मात्कारणाद् । अस्य चेटस्य । शषं स्पष्टम् । उपजातिच्छन्दः ]॥ २७ ॥ कस्मात् बिभेमि । अपि तु न कस्मादपीत्यर्थः। अपवारके । गृहविशेष इत्यर्थः । परिकरं काछ इति प्रसिद्धम् । **सर्वकालमित्यादि** । वैरिको वैरी । स्वार्थे कः ॥ २८ ॥ शण्णा उपदेशः । एदं विटम् । कथमहं एवं बृहतो मल्लकप्रमाणात् । समुद्रप्रमाणादिति वक्तव्ये मौर्ख्यान्मल्लकप्रमाणतया कुलमुपमिनोति । 'मल्लिका पत्रपुटिका तया कुलस्य महत्त्वं मौर्ख्यादुपमिनोति' इति प्राचीनटीका । **किं कुलेनेति** । [ कुलेन उपदिष्टेन कथितेन किं किं प्रयोजनम् ।

अपि च ।

**रन्ध्रानुसारी विषमः कृतान्तो यदस्य दास्यं तव चेश्वरत्वम् ।**
**श्रियं त्वदीयां यदयं न भुङ्क्ते यदेतदाज्ञां न भवान्करोति ॥ २७ ॥**

**शकारः**—( स्वगतम् । ) अधर्मभीरुको वृद्धशृगालः । परलोकभीरुरेष गर्भदासः । अहं राष्ट्रियश्यालः कस्माद्बिभेमि वरपुरुषमनुष्यः । (प्रकाशम् ।) अरे गर्भदास चेट गच्छ त्वम् । अपवारके प्रविश्य विश्रान्त एकान्ते तिष्ठ । (अधम्मभिलुए[1] बुड्ढखोडे । पललोअभीलू एशे गब्भदाशे । हग्गे लश्टिअशाले कश्श भाआमि वलपुलिशमणुश्शे । अले[2] गब्भदाशे चेडे गच्छ तुमम् । ओवलके पविशिअ वीशन्ते एअन्ते चिश्ट ।)

**चेटः**—यद्भट्टक आज्ञापयति । ( वसन्तसेनामुपसृत्य । ) आर्ये एतावान्मे विभवः (इति निष्क्रान्तः ।) (जं भट्टके आणवेदि । अज्जए एत्तिके मे विहवे ।)

**शकारः**—( परिकरं बध्नन् । ) तिष्ठ वसन्तसेने तिष्ठ । मारयिष्यामि । (चिश्ट वसन्तशेणिए चिश्ट । मालइश्शम् ।)

**विटः**—आः ममाग्रतो व्यापादयिष्यसि[3] । (इति गले गृह्णाति ।)

**शकारः**—(भूमौ पतति ।) भावो भट्टकं मारयति । (इति मोहं नाटयति । चेतनां लब्ध्वा ।)

**सर्वकालं मया पुष्टो मांसेन च घृतेन च ।**
**अद्य कार्ये समुत्पन्ने जातो मे वैरिकः कथम् ॥ २८ ॥**

( विचिन्त्य । ) भवतु । लब्धो मयोपायः । दत्ता वृद्धशृगालेन शिरश्चालनसंज्ञा । तदेतं प्रेष्य वसन्तसेनां मारयिष्यामि । एवं तावत् । (प्रकाशम् ।) भाव यत्त्वं मया भणितः तत्कथमहमेवं बृहत्तरैः मल्लकप्रमाणैः कुलैर्जातोऽकार्यं करोमि । एवमेतदङ्गीकारयितुं मया भणितम् । (भावे[4] भट्टकं मालेदि ।

शव्वकालं मए पुश्टे[5] मंशेण अ घिएण अ ।
अज्ज कज्जे शमुप्पण्णे जादे मे वैलिए[6] कधम् ॥

भोदु । लद्धे मए उवाए । दिण्णा बुड्ढखोडेण शिरश्चालणशण्णा । ता एदं पेशिअ वशन्तशेणिअं मालइश्शम् । एव्वं दाव । भावे जं तुमं[7] मए भणेदि तं कधं हग्गे एव्वं वड्ढकेहिं मल्लकप्पमाणेहिं[8] कुलेहिं जादे अकज्जं कलेमि । एव्वं एदं अङ्गीकलावेदुं[9] मए भणिदम् ।)

**विटः**—

**किं कुलेनोपदिष्टेन शीलमेवात्र कारणम् ।**
**भवन्ति सुतरां स्फीताः सुक्षेत्रे कण्टकिद्रुमाः[10]॥ २९ ॥**

---

१ भीलू (भीरुः). २ अले अले. ३ ष्यति. ४ भावे भविअ. ५ पुट्टे. ६ वेलिए. ७ तुमे. ८ गल्लक; ०पमाणाहिं. ९ कालीवेदुं, कालिदुं. १० कण्टक.

Moreover—

Providence, ever searching for weak points is unjust, since slavery is his ( Sthavaraka's ) lot and mastery yours : and since he does not enjoy your wealth and you are not made to do his bidding. (27)

SAK.—(*To himself*). The old jackal is afraid of unrighteousness, and this born slave is afraid of the next world. But I am the king's brother-in-law, an aristocratic gentleman ! Whom do I fear ? ( *Aloud* ). You born slave, Cheta, you go away. Getting into a secluded spot, you wait there, enjoying rest in solitude.

CHETA—As the master orders. ( *Approaching* Vasantasena ) Lady, only thus far lay my power. ( *Exit* ).

SAK.—( *Girding up his loins* ). Stay, Vasantasena, stay. I am going to kill you !

VITA—Ah, will you kill her in my presence ? ( *He seizes him by the neck* ).

SAK.—( *Falls on the ground* ). My friend is killing (me), the master. ( *Shows that he faints; regaining consciousness* ).

I have always fattened him on meat and ghee; but now that a business has arisen ( to be done ), how is it that he has turned my enemy ? (28)

( *Reflecting* ). Well : I have found the remedy. The old jackal has given me a warning by shaking my head. So I'll (first) send him away and then kill Vasantasena. I'll ( proceed ) in this way. ( *Aloud* ). Friend, as to what I said to you; how can I, born in such a very large family, of the size of a *mallaka* ( cup ), ever do such a wicked deed ? I spoke ( in that fashion ) simple to force her into compliance with my proposal.

VITA—

Why talk of one's family, since in such matters it is a man's character that makes him ( what he is ) ? Even thorny trees grow exceedingly large in a fertile field. (29)

---

न किंचिदित्यर्थः। अत्र अकार्यकरणे शीलमेव कारणम्। यतः सुक्षेत्रे कण्टकिद्रुमा स्फीताः संप्ररूढा भवन्ति। एवं महाकुलेऽपि दुष्कृतकारिणो भवन्ति ॥ २९ ॥ अस्मदिति। [ वसन्तसेना शौण्डीर्यभावात्स्वाभिमानात् अस्मत्समक्षं न युक्तमिदं नापि सदृशमिदमिति मया पूर्वोक्तत्वात् मूर्खं न भजेत सेवेत। तस्माद् विविक्तं

**शकारः**—भाव एषा तवाग्रतो लज्जते। न मामङ्गीकरोति। तद्गच्छ। स्थावरकचेटो मया ताडितो गतोऽपि। एष प्रपलाय्य गच्छति। तस्मात्त्वं गृहीत्वाऽऽगच्छतु भावः। (भावे एशा तव अग्गदो लज्जाअदि। ण मं अङ्गीकलेदि। ता गच्छ। थावलअचेडे मए पिट्टिदे गदे वि। एशे[1] पलाइअ गच्छदि। ता तं गेण्हिअ आअच्छदु[2] भावे।)

**विटः**—(स्वगतम्।)

**अस्मत्समक्षं हि वसन्तसेना शौण्डीर्यभावान्न भजेत मूर्खम्।**
**तस्मात्करोम्येष विविक्तमस्या विविक्तविश्रम्भरसो हि कामः॥ ३०॥**

(प्रकाशम्।) एवं भवतु। गच्छामि।

**वसन्तसेना**—(पटान्ते गृहीत्वा।) ननु भणामि शरणागताऽस्मि। (णं भणामि शलणागदम्हि।)

**विटः**—वसन्तसेने न भेतव्यं न भेतव्यम्। काणेलीमातः वसन्तसेना तव हस्ते न्यासः।

**शकारः**—एवम्। मम हस्त एषा न्यासेन तिष्ठतु। (एव्वम् मम हश्ते एशा णाशेण चिश्टदु[3]।)

**विटः**—सत्यम्।

**शकारः**—सत्यम्। (शच्चम्।)

**विटः**—(किंचिद्गत्वा।) अथ वा मयि गते नृशंसो हन्यादेनाम्। तदपवारितशरीरः पश्यामि तावदस्य चिकीर्षितम्। (इत्येकान्ते स्थितः।)

**शकारः**—भवतु। मारयिष्यामि। अथ वा कपटकापटिक एष ब्राह्मणो वृद्धशृगालः कदाऽप्यपवारितशरीरो गत्वा शृगालो भूत्वा कपटं करोति। तदेतस्य वञ्चनानिमित्तमेवं तावत्करिष्यामि। (कुसुमावचयं कुर्वन्नात्मनं मण्डयति।) बाले बाले वसन्तसेने एहि। (भोदु। मालइश्शम्[4]। अध वा कवडकावडिके एशे बम्हणे बुड्ढखोडे कदावि ओवालिदशलीले गडिअ शिआले भविअ हुलुभुलिं कलेदि। ता एदश्श वञ्चणाणिमितं एव्वं दाव कलइश्शम्। वाशू वाशू वशन्तशेणिए एहि।

**विटः**—अये कामी संवृत्तः। हन्त निर्वृतोऽस्मि। गच्छामि। (इति निष्क्रान्तः।)

**शकारः**—

**सुवर्णकं ददामि प्रियं वदामि पतामि शीर्षेण सवेष्टनेन।**
**तथाऽपि मां नेच्छसि शुद्धदन्ति किं सेवकं कष्टमया मनुष्याः॥ ३१॥**

(शुवण्णअं देमि पिअं वदेमि पडेमि शीशेण [5]शवेश्टणेण।
तधा वि मं णेच्छसि शुद्धदन्ति किं शेवअं कश्टमआ मणुश्शा॥)

---

१ गदे वि एशे. २ आअश्छदु ३ चिठ्ठदु. ४ माडिश्शम्. ५ शवेट्टणेण.

SAK.—Friend, she feels bashful in your presence, and (therefore) does not accept me. So you should take yourself off. The slave Sthavaraka, whom I beat, has already gone. (See),—here he goes away running. So please ( catch him and then ) come back with him.

VITA—( *To himself* ).

Vasantasena would not accept this fool in my presence, out of a sense of pride. So I'll just secure privacy for her ( by going away ) : for love becomes enjoyable ( *or*, gains flavour ) only through the confidence born of privacy. (30)

( *Aloud* ). All right. I'll go.

VAS—( *Seizing him by the hem of his cloak* ). I repeat, sir, that I beseech your protection !

VITA.—Fear not, fear not, O Vasantasena ! Bastard, let Vasantasena ramain a pledge in your hands.

SAK.—Yes. Let her remain in my hands as a pledge ( *also*, to perish ).

VITA—Honestly ?

SAK.—Honestly.

VITA—( *Going a little distance* ). Or rather, this wicked fellow might kill her when I am gone. So I'll conceal myself and just observe what he intends to do. ( *He remains in a corner* ).

SAK.—Well, (now) I'll kill her. Or rather, this cunning rascally Brahmana, this old jackal, might perhaps go and hide himself, and behaving like a fox might cheat me. So I'll just do this to deceive him. ( *He collects some flowers and decorates himself* ). Girl, girl, Vasantasena, come !

VITA—Oh ! He has turned a gallant ! Ah ! Now I feel at ease. I'll go now. ( *Exit* ).

SAK.—

I give you gold, speak caressingly, and fall down ( at your feet ) with my head having the turban on. Still, O damsel with pure teeth, why don't you desire to accept me as your servant ? Men, alas, have to suffer anguish ! (31)

---

विजनं करोमि । हि यत: विविक्ते यो विश्रम्भस्तेन रसो रागो यत्र तथाभूत: काम: भवति । अर्थान्तरन्यास: । उपजातिच्छन्द: ।। ३० ।। णाशेण न्यासेन विनाशेन च ।

**वसन्तसेना**—कोऽत्र संदेहः। (अवनतमुखी[1] 'खलचरित' इत्यादि श्लोकद्वयं पठति।)

**खलचरित निकृष्ट जातदोषः**
**कथमिह मां परिलोभसे धनेन।**
**सुचरितचरितं विशुद्धदेहं**
**न हि कमलं मधुपाः परित्यजन्ति॥ ३२॥**

**यत्नेन सेवितव्यः पुरुषः कुलशीलवान्दरिद्रोऽपि।**
**शोभा[2] हि पणस्त्रीणां सदृशजनसमाश्रयः कामः॥ ३३॥**

अपि च। सहकारपादपं सेवित्वा न पलाशपादपमङ्गीकरिष्यामि। (को एत्थ संदेहो। अवि अ। सहआरपादवं सेविअ ण पलासपादवं[3] अङ्गीकरिस्सम्।)

**शकारः**—दास्याःपुत्रि दरिद्रचारुदत्तकः सहकारपादपः कृतः। अहं पुनः पलाशो भणितः। किंशुकोऽपि न कृतः। एवं त्वं मह्यं गालीं ददत्यद्यापि तमेव चारुदत्तकं स्मरसि। (दाशीएधीए दलिद्दचालुदत्तके[4] शहआलपादवे कडे। हग्गे उण पलाशे[5] भणिदे। किंशुके वि ण कडे। एव्वं तुमं मे गालिं देन्ती अज्जवि तं ज्जेव चालुदत्तकं शुमलेशि।)

**वसन्तसेना**—हृदयगत एव किमिति न स्मर्यते। (हिअअगदो ज्जेव किंत्ति ण सुमरीअदि।)

**शकारः**—अद्यापि ते हृदयगतं त्वां च सममेव मोटयामि। तद्दरिद्रसार्थवाहकमनुष्यकामुकिनि तिष्ठ तिष्ठ। (अज्ज वि दे हिअअगदं तुमं च शमं ज्जेव मोडेमि। ता दलिद्दशत्थवाहअमणुश्शकामुकिणि[6] चिश्ट चिश्ट[7]।)

**वसन्तसेना**—भण भण पुनरपि भण श्लाघनीयान्येतान्यक्षराणि। (भण भण पुणो वि भण[8] सलाहणिआइं एदाइं अक्खराइं।)

**शकारः**—परित्रायतां दास्याःपुत्रो दरिद्रचारुदत्तकस्त्वाम्। (पलित्ताअदु[9] दाशीएपुत्ते दलिद्दचालुदत्तके तुमम्।)

**वसन्तसेना**—परित्रायते यदि मां प्रेक्षते। (परित्ताअदि जदि मं पेक्खदि।)

**शकारः**—

**किं स शक्रो वालिपुत्रो महेन्द्रो रम्भापुत्रः कालनेमिः सुबन्धुः।**
**रुद्रो राजा द्रोणपुत्रो जटायुश्चाणक्यो वा धुन्धुमारस्त्रिशङ्कुः॥ ३४॥**

अथ वैतेऽपि त्वां न रक्षन्ति।

---

१ संस्कृतमाश्रित्यावन०. २ शोभा पण्य०. ३ पलाश. ४ दत्ताके. ५ पडाशे. ६ शट्ठघाह, शत्तवाह. ७ चिठ्ठ चिठ्ठ. ८ भण। सला०. ९ पडिअत्तदु.

VAS.—What doubt is there about that ?

( *With face bent down she recites these two verses, beginning* 'You man of evil deeds' &c. ).

You man of evil deeds, you wretch ! Full of sin that you are, why do you tempt me with money, in this matter ? For the bees never abandon a lotus of graceful actions and pure ( beautiful ) form. (32)

An effort should be made to serve a man of (good) family and ( virtuous ) character, even though he may be in reduced circumstances. For, love for a worthy personage constitutes the glory of courtesans. (33)

Moreover, having resorted to the mango-tree, I shall not betake myself to the *Palasa* tree.

SAK.—You slave-born maid, you've called that penniless Charudatta a mango-tree, while me you have described as a *Palasa*, and not even as a *Kimsuka !* You, who have been thus calling me names,—still you remember that same Charudatta ?

VAS.—When he is enshrined just in my heart, why should he not be remembered ?

SAK.—Now I'll crush you, and him who is still stationed in your heart, both together ! So wait, O you who love that penniless merchant-man, wait !

VAS.—Speak, speak; speak out once more those charming syllables !

SAK.—Now let that slave-born penniless Charudatta save you ( if he can ) !

VAS.—He will save me if he will see me !

SAK.—

What ! Is he Indra, the great Indra, the son of Vali; or Kalanemi, the son of Rambha; or Subadhu; or King Rudra; or Jatayu, the son of Drona; or Chanakya, or Dhundhumara, or Trisanku ? ( 34 )

Or why ? Even these can't save you !

---

कपटेन चरतीति कापटिकः । कपटेषु कापटिकः वञ्चकाग्रणीरित्यर्थः । सुवर्णकमिति । [ सवेष्टनेन सोष्णीषेण । शुद्धदन्ति तथाऽपि मां सेवकं किं नेच्छसि । मनुष्याः कष्टमयाः खलु । केचित् किं शे वअं इति पदच्छेदं कृत्वा 'किं ते वयं

चाणक्येन यथा सीता मारिता भारते युगे ।
एवं त्वां मोटयिष्यामि जटायुरिव द्रौपदीम् ॥ ३५ ॥

( इति ताडयितुमुद्यतः । )

(किं शे शक्के वालिपुत्ते महिन्दे लम्भापुत्ते कालणेमी शुबन्धू ।
लुद्दे लाआ दोणपुत्ते जडाऊ चाणक्के वा धुन्धुमाले तिशङ्कू ॥

अध वा एदे वि दे ण लक्खन्ति ।

चाणक्केण जधा शीदा मालिदा भालदे जुए ।
एव्वं दे मोडइश्शामि जडाऊ विअ दोव्वदिम् ॥)

**वसन्तसेना**—हा मातः कुत्रासि । हा आर्यचारुदत्त एष जनोऽसंपूर्णमनोरथ एव विपद्यते । तदूर्ध्वमाक्रन्दयिष्यामि । अथ वा वसन्तसेनोर्ध्वमाक्रन्दतीति लज्जनीयं खल्वेतत् । नम आर्यचारुदत्ताय । (हा अत्ते कहिं सि । हा अज्जचारुदत्त एसो जणो असंपुण्णमणोरधो ज्जेव विवज्जदि । ता उद्धं अक्कन्दइस्सम् । अध वा वसन्तसेणा उद्धं अक्कन्दति त्ति लज्जणीअं क्खु एदम् । णमो अज्जचारुदत्तस्स ।)

**शकारः**—अद्यापि गर्भदासी तस्यैव पापस्य नाम गृह्णाति । (इति कण्ठे पीडयन् ।) स्मर गर्भदासि स्मर । (अज्जवि गब्भदाशी[1] तश्श ज्जेव पावस्स णामं गेण्णदि । शुमल गब्भदाशि शुमल ।)

**वसन्तसेना**—नम आर्यचारुदत्ताय । (णमो अज्जचारुदत्तस्स ।)

**शकारः**—म्रियस्व गर्भदासि म्रियस्व । (नाटयेन कण्ठं निपीडयन्मारयति ।) (मल गब्भदाशि मल ।)

(वसन्तसेना मूर्छिता निश्चेष्टा पतति ।)

**शकारः**—(सहर्षम् ।)

एतां दोषकरण्डिकामविनयस्यावासभूतां खलां
रक्तां तस्य किलागतस्य रमणे कालागतामागताम् ।
किमेष समुदाहरामि निजकं बाह्वोः शूरत्वं
निःश्वासाऽपि म्रियतेऽम्बा सुमृता सीता यथा भारते ॥ ३६ ॥

(एदं दोशकलण्डिअं[2] अविणअश्शावाशभूदं खलं
लत्तं तश्श किलागदश्श लमणे कालागदं आअदम् ।
किं एशे शमुदाहलामि णिअअं बाहूण शूलत्तणं[3]
णीशाशे वि मलेइ[4] अम्ब शुमला शीदा जधा भालदे ॥)

---

१ ०दाशि...गेण्हसि. २ कलण्डअं. ३ शूलक्खणं. ४ मले इअं अ सुमला (म्रियते इयं च सुमृता)

Just as in the Bharata age Sita was killed by Chanakya, so I'll kill you, like Jatayu (killing) Draupadi ! (35)

(*He is about to strike her*).

VAS.—O mother, where are you ? O noble Charudatta, this person is now dying, with her desires still unfulfilled ! Now I will cry out loudly (*i. e.* for help). Or no, it would be surely a disgrace that Vasantasena should be crying aloud—Bow to the noble Charudatta !

SAK.—Still the born slave is calling out the name of that same villain ! (*He seizes her by the throat*). Remember, thou born slave, remember !

VAS.—Bow to the noble Charudatta !

SAK.—Die, thou born slave, die ! (*Gesticulates strangling her and killing her*).

Vasantasena *faints and falls down senseless*).

SAK.—(*Gleefully*).

(I have killed) that wicked girl, who was a repository of faults and a dwelling place of immodesty, and who, full of love, came to sport with that Charudatta, who had come here, her end being near. But why am I thus describing the valour of my arms ? The poor woman dies even when deprived of her breath, so as never to rise again, as did Sita in the Bharat (age). (36)

---

काष्ठमया मनुष्याः' इति च्छायामिच्छन्ति । तें वयं काष्ठमयाः पुरुषाः न तु परमार्थतः इति व्याख्यान्ति च । उपजातिर्वृत्तम् । ] किं सेवकाः कष्टमया मनुष्याः ॥ ३१ ॥ **खलचरितेति** । [ हे खलचरित दुष्टचरित हे निकृष्ट अधम । इति संबोधनद्वयम् । जातदोषः उत्पन्नपापः इह मां कथं धनेन परिलोभसे विलोभयसि । सुचरितं चरितं आह्लादकरत्वादि यस्य तत्सुचरितचरितं विशुद्धदेहं भास्वरशरीरं कमलं मधुपाः न परित्यजन्ति हि । अत्र अप्रस्तुतप्रशंसया चारुदत्तं न परित्यजामीति सूचितम् । पुष्पिताग्रा वृत्तम् । ] ॥ ३२ ॥ **यत्नेनेति** । कुलशीलवान् पुरुषः दरिद्रोऽपि यत्नेन सेवितव्यः । सदृशजनः अनुरूपपुरुषः समाश्रयो यस्य तादृशः कामः पणप्रधानाः स्त्रियः पणस्त्रियः वेश्याः तासां शोभा हि भूषणावहः खलु । आर्या ] ॥ ३३ ॥ पलाशपदेन राक्षसोऽप्यभिधीयते । [ पलं मासमश्नातीति । ] गालि देन्ती साक्षेपं वदन्ती इति देशीति चिरंतनटीका । **किं स शक्र इति** । शक्वरीविशेषच्छन्दसा श्लोकः । [ स चारुदत्तः किं शक्रः वालिपुत्रः महेन्द्रः । अत्र शक्रः महेन्द्र इति पुनरुक्तं वालिपुत्र इति आगमविरुद्धम् । अथ वा रम्भापुत्रः कालनेमिः सुबन्धुः ।

इच्छन्तं मां नेच्छतीति गणिका रोषेण मया मारिता
शून्ये पुष्पकरण्डक इति सहसा पाशेनोत्त्रासिता ।
सेवावञ्चितो भ्राता मम पिता मातेव सा द्रौपदी
योऽसौ पश्यति नेदृशं व्यवसितं पुत्रस्य शूरत्वम् ॥ ३७ ॥

भवतु । सांप्रतं वृद्धशृगाल आगमिष्यतीति ततोऽपसृत्य तिष्ठामि । (तथा करोति ।)

(इच्छन्तं मम णेच्छति[1] त्ति गणिआ लोशेण[2] मे मालिदा
शुण्णे पुप्फकलण्डके त्ति शहशा पाशेण उत्ताशिदा ।
शेवावञ्चिद भादुके मम पिदा मादेव शा दोप्पदी
जे शे पेक्खदि णेदिशं ववशिदं पुत्ताह शूलत्तणम् ॥

भोदु शंपदं[3] बुड्ढखोडे आगमिश्शदित्ति ता ओशलिअ चिश्टामि ।)

( प्रविश्य चेटेन सह । )

**विटः**—अनुनीतो मया स्थावरकश्चेटः । तद्यावत्काणेलीमातरं पश्यामि । (परिक्रम्यावलोक्य च ।) अये मार्ग एव पादपो[4] निपतितः । अनेन च पतता स्त्री व्यापादिता । भोः पाप किमिदमकार्यमनुष्ठितं त्वया । तवापि पापिनः पतनात्स्त्रीवधदर्शनेनातीव[5] पातिता वयम् । अनिमित्तमेतत् । यत्सत्यं वसन्तसेनां प्रति शङ्कितं मे मनः । सर्वथा देवताः[6] स्वस्ति करिष्यन्ति । ( शकारमुपसृत्य । ) काणेलीमातः एवं मयाऽनुनीतः स्थावरकश्चेटः ।

**शकारः**—भाव स्वागतं ते । पुत्रक स्थावरक चेट तवापि स्वागतम् ।' (भावे शाअदं दे । पुश्तका[7] थावलका चेडा तवावि शाअदम् ।)

**चेटः**—अथ किं । (अध इं ।)

**विटः**—मदीयं न्यासमुपनय ।

**शकारः**—कीदृशो न्यासः । (कीदिशो णाशे ।)

---

एवमितरत्रापि आगमविरुद्धं यथायथमूह्यम् । कालनेमिः असुरविशेषः । सुबन्धुः कविः । धुन्धुमारः त्रिशङ्कुश्च राजविशेषौ । शालिनी वृत्तम् ]॥ ३४ ॥ चाणक्येनेत्यादि । भारते युगे भारतावच्छिन्ने समये । [मोटयिष्यामि मारयिष्यामि ] ॥ ३५ ॥ [ ऊर्ध्वमुच्चैःस्वरेण । निश्चेष्टा चङ्गनवलनादिरहिता । ] एतामिति । खलां दुर्जनस्वभावाम् । तस्य चारुदत्तस्य रमणे संभोगनिमित्तं कालागतामागताम् । कालां कृष्णाम् । [ दोषाणां करण्डिकां पेटिकां अविनयस्य आवासभूतां खलां रक्तां आगतस्य अथ वा अगतस्य गतिरहितस्य दुर्गतस्येत्यर्थः । तस्य चारुदत्तस्य रमणे रमणार्थं कालागतां कालप्राप्तां तथा आगताम् एताम् हतवा-

---

१ णेच्छसि. २ पाशेण. ३ संपदं. ४ पादयोर्नि०. ५ दर्शनादतीव. ६ देवता... करिष्यति. ७ पुश्थका, पुत्तका.

Because she wouldn't accept me who was courting her, I killed in my wrath that courtesan. Seeing that the *Pushpakarandaka* garden was lonely, I suddenly frightened her ( *i. e.* strangled her ) with the noose ( of my arms ). My brother and my father, and my mother like Draupadi, who have not witnessed this sort of valorous exploit of their son, have indeed, missed a treat ( to their sight ). ( 37 )

Very well. Now that old jackal would come back; so I'll move away hence and wait (in another spot). ( *Does accordingly* )

( *Entering, with the* Cheta )

VITA—I have persuaded the Cheta Sthavaraka (to come back). So I'll now see the bastard. ( *Walking about and observing* ). Ha! Here's a tree fallen just in our way! And while falling it has killed a woman! You sinful ( tree ), what a wicked deed you have committed! Now, we too have been completely brought down ( into ill luck ), by the sight of the woman killed by the fall of your sinful self. This is a bad omen; so, to tell the truth, my mind is full of misgivings about ( the fate of ) Vasantasena. May the gods grant safety in all ways! ( *Approaching* Sakara ). Bastard, here I have induced the Cheta Sthavaraka (to come back).

SAK.—You're welcome, friend. My son, my slave, Sthavaraka, you too are welcome!

CHETA—Thank you.

VITA—Return my pledge.

SAK.—Pledge? Of what sort?

---

मिति शेषः। एष बाह्वोः निजकं शूरत्वं किं समुदाहरामि। निःश्वासा अपि अम्बा वसन्तसेना म्रियते। भारते सीता यथेति हतोपमम्। शार्दूल० ]॥ ३६॥ इच्छन्तमिति। [इच्छतं मां गणिका नेच्छतीति मे मया रोषेण मारिता। शून्ये पुष्पकरण्डके सहसा पाशेन बाहुपाशेन इति उत्त्रासिता। योऽसौ मम भ्राता पिता च सेवावञ्चितः। सा द्रौपदी इव मे माता च सेवावञ्चिता या ईदृशं पुत्रस्य व्यवसितं शूरत्वं न पश्यति। शार्दूल० वृत्तम्।] मया रोषेण मारिता इति विपर्यस्य योजना। माता च सा द्रौपदी। या सा पश्यति॥ ३७॥ पाप इति वृक्षं संबोधयति। अनिमित्तमसंकुलम्। पिट्ठदो पृष्ठतः। दक्षिणदिग्गतत्वं मृतत्वमपि। न प्रत्येषि पराक्रमे। दाक्षिण्येति। [दाक्षिण्यमेव उदकं तस्य नदी विगलिता नष्टा। रतिः प्रीतिः स्वदेशं याता। हे अलंकृतभूषणे अलंकृतानि भूषणानि यया तत्संबुद्धिः। सुवदने। क्रीडायां रसः तेन उद्भासिनि शोभमाने। प्रहासः पुलिनं यस्याः तादृशि हा

**विटः**—वसन्तसेना ।

**शकारः**—गता । (गडा ।)

**विटः**—क्व ।

**शकारः**—भावस्यैव पृष्ठतः । (भावश्श ज्जेव पिश्टदो ।)

**विटः**—(सवितर्कम् ।) न गता खलु सा तया दिशा ।

**शकारः**—त्वं कतमया दिशा गतः । (तुमं कदमाए दिशाए गडे[1] ।)

**विटः**—पूर्वया दिशा ।

**शकारः**—साऽपि दक्षिणया गता । (शा वि दक्खिणाए गडा ।)

**विटः**—अहं दक्षिणया ।

**शकारः**—साऽप्युत्तरया । (शा वि उत्तलाए ।)

**विटः**—अत्याकुलं कथयसि । न शुध्यति[2] मेऽन्तरात्मा । तत्कथय सत्यम् ।

**शकारः**—शपे भावस्य शीर्षमात्मीयाभ्यां पादाभ्याम् । ततः संस्थापय हृदयम् । एषा मया मारिता । (शवामि भावश्श शीशं अत्तणकेलकेहिं पादेहिं । ता शंठावेहि हिअअम् । एशा मए मालिदा ।)

**विटः**—(सविषादम् ।) सत्यं त्वया व्यापादिता ।

**शकारः**—यदि मम वचने न प्रत्ययसे तत्पश्य प्रथमं राष्ट्रियश्यालसंस्थानस्य शूरत्वम् । ( इति दर्शयति । ) (जइ मम वअणे न पत्तिआअशि ता पेक्ख पढमं लश्टिअशालशंठाणाह शूलत्तणम्[3] ।)

**विटः**—हा हतोऽस्मि मन्दभाग्यः । (इति मूर्छितः पतति ।)

**शकारः**—ही ही । उपरतो भावः । (ही ही । उवलदे भावे ।)

**चेटः**—समाश्वसितु समाश्वसितु भावः । अविचारितं प्रवहणमानयतैव मया प्रथमं मारिता । ( शमश्शशदु शमश्शशदु भावे । अविचालिअं पवहणं आणन्तेण ज्जेव मए पढमं मालिदा ।)

**विटः**—(समाश्वस्य सकरुणम् ।) हा वसन्तसेने ।

> **दाक्षिण्योदकवाहिनी विगलिता याता स्वदेशं रति-**
> **र्हा हाऽलंकृतभूषणे सुवदने क्रीडारसोद्भासिनि[4] ।**
> **हा सौजन्यनदि प्रहासपुलिने हा मादृशामाश्रये[5]**
> **हा हा नश्यति मन्मथस्य विपणिः सौभाग्यपण्याकरः ।। ३८ ।।**

(सास्रम् ।) कष्टं भोः कष्टम् ।

---

१ गदे. २ बुध्यति. ३ पलक्कमं (पराक्रमम् ।). ४ सरोद्भा०. ५ आश्रमे.

VITA—Vasantasena.

SAK.—She's gone !

VITA—Where ?

SAK.—Just immediately after you ( *lit.* at your back ).

VITA—( *Surmisingly* ). Surely, she couldn't have gone in that direction !

SAK.—In what direction did you go ?

VITA—In the east.

SAK.—Well, she went towards the south !

VITA—I went to the south !

SAK.—She went to the north !

VITA—You are telling something in great agitation ( *or*, what is extremely contradictory ). My mind does not feel at ease ( entertains a doubt ). So tell ( me ) the truth.

SAK.—I swaear it by your head and by my feet. So compose your heart. I killed her !

VITA—( *Sorrowfully* ). You have really killed her ?

SAK.—If you don't believe in my words, then observe this first exploit of Samsthanaka, the king's brother-in-law ! ( *Shows* [ *her body* ] ).

VITA—Alas, I am undone, unlucky that I am ! ( *Swoons and falls down* ).

SAK.—Ho, ho ! My friend has breathed his last !

CHETA—Compose yourself, sir, compose yourself ! It was really I who first killled her by thoughtlessly bringing that carriage here.

VITA—( *Coming to himself*; *mournfully*). O Vasantasena !

The river of the water in the form of innocence is dried up. Love has departed to its original home ! Alas, alas ! O you who were an adornment of your ornaments, you with that sweet face, you that shone with your fondness for amorous sports ! You that were the river of goodness, with laughter for the sandy bank, the refuge of persons like me ! Alas, alas ! The market of passion, the treasure-house of merchandise of beauty, is now pulled down ! (38)

( *Tearfully* ). Alas, Oh, alas !

**किं नु नाम भवेत्कार्यमिदं येन त्वया कृतम् ।**
**अपापा पापकल्पेन नगरश्रीर्निपातिता ॥ ३९ ॥**

(स्वगतम् ।) अये कदाचिदयं पाप[1] इदमकार्यं मयि संक्रामयेत् । भवतु । इतो गच्छामि । (इति परिक्रामति ।)

( शकार उपगम्य धारयति । )

**विटः**—पाप मां[2] मा स्प्राक्षीः । अलं त्वया । गच्छाम्यहम् ।

**शकारः**—अरे वसन्तसेनां स्वयमेव मारयित्वा मां दूषयित्वा कुत्र पलायसे । सांप्रतमीदृशोऽहमनाथः प्राप्तः । (अले वशन्तशेणिअं शअं ज्जेव मालिअ मं दूशिअ कहिं पलाअशि । शंपदं ईदिशे हग्गे अणाधे पाविदे ।)

**विटः**—अपध्वस्तोऽसि ।

**शकारः**—

**अर्थं शतं ददामि सुवर्णकं ते कार्षापणं ददामि सवोडिकं ते ।**
**एष दोषस्थानं पराक्रमो मे सामान्यको भवतु मनुष्यकाणाम् ॥ ४० ॥**

(अत्थं शदं देमि शुवण्णअं[3] दे कहावणं देमि शवोडिअं[4] दे ।
एशे दुशट्ठाणं पलक्कमे[5] मे शामाण्णए भोदु मणुश्शआणम् ॥)

**विटः**—धिक् । तवैवास्तु ।

**चेटः**—शान्तं पापम् । (शन्तं पावम् ।)

(शकारो हसति ।)

**विटः**—

**अप्रीतिर्भवतु[6] विमुच्यतां हि हासो**
**धिक्प्रीतिं परिभवकारिकामनार्याम् ।**
**मा भूच्च त्वयि मम संगतं कदाचि-**
**दाच्छिन्नं धनुरिव निर्गुणं त्यजामि ॥ ४१ ॥**

**शकारः**—भाव प्रसीद प्रसीद । एहि । नलिन्यां प्रविश्य क्रीडावः । (भावे पशीद पशीद । एहि । णलिणीए पविशिअ कीलेम्ह ।)

---

सौजन्यस्य नदि । हा मादृशामाश्रये आश्रयभूते । हा हा सौभाग्यमेव पण्यं विक्रेय-वस्तुजातं तस्य आकरः खनिः मन्मथस्य कामस्य विपणिः पण्यवीथिका नश्यति । शार्दूल० वृत्तम् ] ॥ ३८॥ **किं न्विति ।** [ किं नु नाम तत्कार्यं भवेद्येनेदं त्वया कृतम् ।

---

१ पापमिदं. २ मा. ३ सुवण्णअं. ४ शवेडिअं. ५ फलक्कमे (फलक्रमः). ६ स्खलतु.

What indeed could be the purpose for which you committed this deed ? The sinless beauty of this city has been felled by you who are almost an embodiment of sin ( wickedness ). (39)

( *To himself* ). Ah, this wicked fellow might perhaps shift on me (the guilt of) this criminal deed. All right; I'll leave this place. ( *Walks about* ).

( Sakara *approaches and holds him* ).

VITA—You sinner, don't touch me! I have had enough of you! Let me go!

SAK.—Ah you! Having yourself killed Vasantasena, where do you escape now, putting the guilt on me? Now I have been rendered so very helpless.

VITA—Oh, go to the devil!

SAK.—

I will give you money to the extent of a hundred gold coins; I will give you a *karshapana*,* together with a *vodi*.* Let this my exploit, which is the abode of ( *i. e.* of the nature of ) crime, be common to all persons ( *i. e.* do not disclose my name ). (40)

VITA—Fie! Let it belong to you alone.

CHETA—Heaven forbid!

( *Sakara laughs* ).

VITA—

Let there be absence of joy ( on your part; *i. e.* feel sorry ); give up this laughter; fie upon your friendship which is humiliating and dishonourable! May I never come in contact with you again! I cast you off, who are without *guna* (virtue), like a broken bow ( without *guna*-string ). (41)

SAK.—Friend, please be not angry. Come; we'll descend into this lotus-pool and sport ( in its waters ).

---

पापकल्पेन पापादीषन्न्यूनेन । अपापा नगरस्य श्रीः शोभा त्वया निपातिता । ] ॥ ३९ ॥ हे पाप हे पापसंकल्प । अयं शतमिति । [ ते शतं सुवर्णमर्थं ददामि । वोडी पणचतुर्थांशः तत्सहितं सवोडिकं कार्षापणं षोडशपणात्मकं सुवर्णं ते ददामि । ] वोडी विंशतिकपर्दकः गौडे प्रसिद्धः । तच्चतुष्टयं पणः । ते षोडश कार्षापणः कहावण इत्येके । साधारणो भवतु । [ उपजातिर्वृत्तम् ] ॥ ४० ॥ अप्रीतिरिति । [ अप्रीतिः

---

* Names of different coins.

**विटः**—

अपतितमपि तावत्सेवमानं भवन्तं
पतितमिव जनोऽयं मन्यते मामनार्यम् ।
कथमहमनुयायां त्वां हतस्त्रीकमेनं
पुनरपि [1]नगरस्त्रीशङ्कितार्धाक्षिदृष्टम् ॥ ४२ ॥

(सकरुणम् ।) वसन्तसेने ।

अन्यस्यामपि जातौ मा वेश्या भूस्त्वं हि सुन्दरि ।
चारित्र्यगुणसंपन्ने[2] जायेथा विमले कुले ॥ ४३ ॥

**शकारः**—मदीये पुष्पकरण्डकजीर्णोद्याने वसन्तसेनां मारयित्वा कुत्र पलायसे । एहि । मम आवुत्तस्याग्रतो व्यवहारं देहि । ( इति धारयति[3] । ) ( ममकेलके[4] पुप्फकलण्डकजिण्णुज्जाणे वशन्तशेणिअं मालिअ कहिं पलाअशि । एहि । मम आवुत्तश्श अग्गदो ववहालं[5] देहि ।)

**विटः**—आः तिष्ठ जाल्म । (इति खड्गमाकर्षति[6] ।)

**शकारः**—( सभयमपसृत्य । ) किं रे भीतोऽसि । तद्गच्छ । ( किं ले भीदेशि । ता गच्छ[7] ।)

**विटः**—(स्वगतम् ।) न युक्तमवस्थातुम् । भवतु । यत्रार्यशर्विलकचन्दनक-[8] प्रभृतयः सन्ति तत्र गच्छामि । (इति निष्क्रान्तः ।)

**शकारः**—निधनं गच्छ । अरे स्थावरक पुत्रक कीदृशं मया कृतम् । (णिधणं गच्छ । अले थावलका पुश्तका[9] कीलिशे मए कडे ।)

**चेटः**—भट्टक महदकार्यं कृतम् । (भश्टके[10] महन्ते अकज्जे कडे ।)

**शकारः**—अरे चेट किं भणस्यकार्यं कृतमिति । भवतु । एवं तावत् । (नानाभरणान्यवतार्य ।) गृहाणेममलंकारं मया तावद्दत्तम् । यावत्यां वेलायामलंकरोमि तावतीं वेलां मम । अन्यदा तव । (अले चेडे किं भणाशि अकज्जे कडेत्ति । भोदु । एव्वं दाव । गेण्ह एदं अलंकारअं मए ताव दिण्णं । जेत्तिके वेले अलंकलेमि तेत्तिकं वेलं मम । अण्णं तव ।)

**चेटः**—भट्टक एवैते शोभन्ते । किं ममैतैः । (भश्टके[10] ज्जेव एदे शोहन्ति । किं मम एदेहिं ।)

**शकारः**—तद्गच्छ । एतौ वृषभौ गृहीत्वा मदीयायां प्रासादबालाग्रप्रतोलिकायां तिष्ठ यावदहमागच्छामि । (ता गच्छ । एदाइं गोणाइं गेण्हिअ ममकेलकाए पाशादबालग्गपदोलिकाए[11] चिश्ट जाव हग्गे आअच्छामि ।)

**चेटः**—यद्भट्टक आज्ञापयति । (इति निष्क्रान्तः ।) (जं भश्टके आणवेदि ।)

---

१ रश्री. २ चारित्र. ३ ताडयति. ४ केरके. ५ ववहाले. ६ कर्षयति. ७ गश्छ. ८ चन्दनप्रभृ०. ९ पुत्तका, पुत्थका. १० भट्टके. ११ पडोलिआए.

VITA—

The people (of this city) consider me as if degraded and wicked (*or*, sinful) while serving you even when you had not fallen (so low as now). How, then, can I still follow you, who have now killed a woman, and who will again be fearfully looked at with half-closed eyes by the women of this city? (42)

(*Sorrowfully*). Vasantasena!

O fair one, may you never become a courtesan in your next birth; O you possessed of the excellences of character, may you be born in a pure family! (43)

SAK.—Where are you now escaping, having killed Vasantasena in my old Pushpakarandaka garden? Come, you must make your deposition before my brother-in-law (the king)! (*Seizes him*).

VITA—Ah, just wait, you villain! (*Draws his sword*).

SAK.—(*Moving off in fear*). What, are you afraid? Well, you may go.

VITA—(*To himself*). It is not desirable to stay here (longer). All right; I will go to the place where there are the worthy Sarvilaka, Chandanaka, and others. (*Exit*)

SAK.—Go to perdition! Well, Sthavaraka my son, what sort of a deed have I done?

CHETA—Master, you have committed a most heinous crime!

SAK.—What, you slave, what do you say? —That I committed a crime? All right; (I will manage) thus. (*Takes off many ornaments*). Take these ornaments, which I hand over to you. They are mine during the time that I have to decorate myself; on other occasions they shall be yours.

CHETA.—These look well on my master's own body; of what use are they to me?

SAK.—Well, then, be off; take away those bullocks and stay in the aisle of the elephant-corniced upper terrace of my palace, until I come there.

CHETA—As my master orders. (*Exit*).

---

अनुतापः दुःखं वा भवतु । हासो विमुच्यतां हि । परिभवकारिकां अनार्यां प्रीतिं धिक् । त्वयि मम संगतं कदाचिदपि मा भूत् । आच्छिन्नं शत्रुणा विध्वस्तं निर्गुणं विगतज्यं धनुरिव निर्गुणं दयादिगुणरहितं त्वां त्यजामि । प्रहर्षिणी वृत्तम् ] ॥४१॥ [ नलिन्यां दीर्घिकायाम् । नलानि सन्त्यस्यामिति नलिनी ।] अपतितमपीति ।

शकारः—आत्मपरित्राणे भावो गतोऽदर्शनम् । चेटमपि प्रासादबालाग्रप्रतोलिकायां निगडपूरितं कृत्वा स्थापयिष्यामि । एवं मन्त्रो रक्षितो भवति । तद्गच्छामि । अथ वा पश्यामि तावदेनाम् । किमेषा मृताऽथ वा पुनरपि मारयिष्यामि । (अवलोक्य ।) कथं सुमृता । भवतु । एतेन प्रावरकेण प्रच्छादयाम्येनाम् । अथ वा नामाङ्कित एषः । तत्कोऽप्यार्यपुरुषः प्रत्यभिज्ञास्यति । भवतु । एतेन वातालीपुञ्जितेन शुष्कपर्णपुटेन प्रच्छादयामि । ( तथा कृत्वा विचिन्त्य । ) भवतु । एवं तावत् । सांप्रतमधिकरणं गत्वा व्यवहारं लेखयामि यथाऽर्थस्य कारणात्सार्थवाहकचारुदत्तकेन मदीयं पुष्पकरण्डकं जीर्णोद्यानं प्रवेश्य वसन्तसेना व्यापादितेति । (अत्तपलित्ताणे भावे गदे अदंशणम् । चेडं वि पाशादबालग्गपदोलिकाए णिगलपूलिदं[१] कदुअ थावइश्शम् । एव्वं मन्ते लक्खिदे भोदि । ता गच्छामि । अध वा पेक्खामि दाव एदम् । किं एशा मला आदु पुणो वि मालइश्शम् । कधं शुमला । भोदु । एदिणा पावालएण पच्छादेमि णम् । अध वा णामङ्किदे एशे । ता के वि अज्जपुलिशे पच्चहिजाणेदि । भोदु । एदिणा वादालीपुञ्जिदेण शुक्खपणपुडेण पच्छादेमि[२] । भोदु । एव्वं दाव । संपदं अधिअलणं गच्छिअ ववहालं लिहावेमि जहा[३] अत्थश्श कालणादो शत्थवाहचालुदत्ताकेण[४] ममकेलकं पुप्फकलण्डकं जिण्णुज्जाणं पवेशिअ वशन्तशेणिआ वावादिदे त्ति । )

चारुदत्तविनाशाय करोमि कपटं नवम् ।<br>
नगर्यां विशुद्धायां पशुघातमिव दारुणम् ।। ४४ ।।

(चालुदत्तविणाशाय कलेमि कवडं णवम् ।<br>
णअलीए विशुद्धाए पशुघादं व्व[५] दालुणम् ।।)

भवतु । गच्छामि । ( इति निष्क्रम्य दृष्ट्वा । सभयम् । ) अविद मादिके । येन येन गच्छामि मार्गेण तेनैवैष दुष्टश्रमणको गृहीतकषायोदकं चीवरं गृहीत्वाऽऽगच्छति । एष मया नासां छित्त्वा वाहितः कृतवैरः कदाऽपि मा प्रेक्ष्यैतेन मारितेति प्रकाशयिष्यति । तत्कथं गच्छामि । (अवलोक्य । ) भवतु । एतमर्धपतितं प्राकारखण्डमुल्लङ्घ्य गच्छामि । (भोदु । गच्छामि । अविद मादिके । जेण जेण गच्छामि मग्गेण तेण ज्जेव एशे दुट्टशमणके गहिदकशाओदकं चीवलं आअच्छदि । एशे मए णशिं[६] च्छिंदिअ वाग्दिे किदवेले कदावि मं पेक्खिअ एदेण मालिदेत्ति पआशइश्शदि । ता कधं गच्छामि । भोदु । एवं अद्धपडिदं पाआलखण्डं उल्लङ्घिअ गच्छामि ।)

[ अपतितमपि भवन्तं सेवमानं मां अयं जनः अनार्यं पतितमिव मन्यते । एवं सति हतस्त्रीकं पुनरपि नगरस्त्रीभिः शङ्कितं सभयं यथा स्यात्तथा अर्धाक्षिभिः अर्धो-

१ णिअल०. २ पश्छा. ३ जधा. ४ शठुवाहउत्तचा०. ५ च. ६ णश्शिअ ( नासारज्ज्वा ); णशि च्छिअ ( नसिच्छित्त्वा ).

SAK.—My friend has made himself scarce, to save his own skin. Now this slave also I am going to put in fetters and keep (imprisoned) in the elephant corniced terrace room of my palace. Thus my secret will be kept safe. Now let me go; or no—first let me have a look at her, whether she is dead or whether I shall have to kill her again. (*Observing*). How! She is quite dead! Well, now, I'll cover her up with this cloak. But, no,—this is marked with my name: so some gentleman might recognize it. All right; I'll cover her up with this lot of dried leaves which have been heaped together by the gusts of wind. (*Does so; reflecting*), Well I'll now proceed in this way: I shall forthwith go to the law-court and file a written charge that the merchant Charudatta enticed Vasantasena into my old garden, Pushpakarandaka, and killed her for the sake of her money.

I'll invent a new fraud, for the destruction of Charudatta, horrible like the slaughter of an animal (*i. e.* a cow) in a holy city. (44)

All right; I'll depart. (*Goes out and sees; with fear*). Alack-a-day! By whatever path I (try to) leave, by that same path I find this rascally Buddhist medicant coming in, with his garment dyed with red-coloured water. He is inimical towards me, as I had bored a hole through his nose and turned him out; seeing me, perhaps he might give out that it was I who killed her. So how shall I leave? (*Seeing*). Yes. I'll jump over this half-fallen broken wall, and take myself off.

---

न्मीलितनेत्रैः दृष्टं त्वामहं कथमनुयायाम् । मालिनी वृत्तम् ] ॥ ४२ ॥ **अन्यस्यामिति** । [ हे सुन्दरि त्वमन्यस्यां जातौ आगामिनि जन्मनि अपि वेश्या मा भूः । हे चारित्र्यमेव गुणस्तेन संपन्ने सुशीले विमले निर्दोषे कुले जायेथाः ] ॥ ४३ ॥ आवुत्तश्श भगिनीपतेः । व्यवहारं विचारम । निघनं गच्छ त्वमिति विटं प्रति । आत्मपरित्राणे आत्मरक्षार्थम् । प्रासादबालाग्रप्रतोलिकायां प्रासादोपरिगृहविशेष इति पश्चाद्व्याख्यातम् । निगलपूरितं अतिगुरुबन्धनोक्तिरियम् । प्रावारेण प्रच्छदपटेन । णामङ्किदे नामाङ्कितः वसन्तसेनाया इति शकारस्य वेति लिखिताक्षरः । तथा कृत्वा । पूर्वोक्तेन स्थगितां कृत्वेत्यर्थः । **चारुदत्तेति** । [ चारुदत्तस्य विनाशाय वधाय नवं कपटं मायां करोमि रचयिष्यामि । विशुद्धायां नगर्यां दारुणं पशुघातमिव । गोवधमिव ] ॥ ४४ ॥ अविद मादिके सभयविस्मये । नश्तिय नासारज्ज्वा बाधितः । **एषोहमित्यादि** । गाथा । [ एषोऽहं लङ्कानगर्यां गगने भूम्यां पाताले हनूमच्छिखरे महेन्द्र इव त्वरितत्वरितो गच्छन्नस्मि । ] भूमौ पाताले हनूमच्छिखरा-

एषोऽहं त्वरितत्वरितो लङ्कानगर्यां गगने गच्छन् ।
भूम्यां पाताले हनूमच्छिखर इव महेन्द्रः ॥ ४५ ॥

(एशे म्हि तुलिदतुलिदे लङ्काणअलीए गअणे गच्छन्ते ।
भूमीए पाआले हणूमशिहले विअ महेन्दे ॥)

(इति निष्क्रान्तः ।)

( प्रविश्यापटीक्षेपेण[1] संवाहकः । )

भिक्षुः—प्रक्षालितमेतन्मया चीवरखण्डम् । किं नु खलु शाखायां शुष्कं करिष्यामि । इह वानरा विलुम्पन्ति । किं नु खलु भूम्याम । धूलीदोषो भवति । तत्कुत्र प्रसार्य शुष्कं करिष्यामि । (दृष्ट्वा ।) भवतु इह वातालीपुञ्जिते शुष्कपत्र-संचये प्रसारयिष्यामि । ( तथा कृत्वा ।) नमो बुद्धाय । (इत्युपविशति ।) भवतु । धर्माक्षराण्युदाहरामि । ('पञ्चजण जेण मालिदा' (८।२) इत्यादि पूर्वोक्तं पठति । अथ वाऽलं ममैतेन स्वर्गेण । यावत्तस्या वसन्तसेनाया बुद्धोपासिकायाः प्रत्युपकारं न करोमि यया दशानां सुवर्णकानां कृते द्यूतकराभ्यां निष्क्रीतस्ततः प्रभृति तया क्रीतमिवात्मानमवगच्छामि । (दृष्ट्वा ।) किं नु खलु पर्णोदरे समुच्छ्वसिति । अथ वा । (पक्खालिदे[2] एशे मए चीवलखण्डे । किं णु क्खु शाहाए शुक्खावइश्शम् । इध वाणला विलुप्पन्ति । किं णु क्खु भूमीए । धूलीदोशे होदि । ता कहिं पशालिअ शुक्खावइश्शम् । भोदु । इध वादालीपुञ्जिदे[3] शुक्खवत्तसंचए पशालइश्शम् । णमो बुद्धश्शं । भोदु । धम्मक्खलाइं उदाहलामि । अध वा अलं मम एदेण शग्गेण । जाव ताए वसन्तशेणिआए बुद्धोवाशिआए पच्चुवकालं ण कलेमि जाए दशाणं शुवण्णकाणं किदे जूदिअलेहि णिक्कीदे तदो पहुदि ताए कीदं विअ अत्ताणअं अवगच्छामि । किं णु क्खु पण्णोदले शमुश्शदि । अध वा ।)

वातातपेन तप्तानि चीवरतोयेन स्तिमितानि पत्राणि ।
एतानि विस्तीर्णपत्राणि मन्ये पत्राणीव स्फुरन्ति ॥ ४६ ॥

(वादादवेण तत्ता चीवलतोएण तिम्मिदा पत्ता ।
एदे विश्थिण्णपत्ता मण्णे पत्ता विअ फुलन्ति[4] ॥

( वसन्तसेना संज्ञां लब्ध्वा हस्तं दर्शयति । )

भिक्षुः—हा हा शुद्धालंकारभूषितः स्त्रीहस्तो निष्क्रामति । कथम् । द्वितीयोऽपि हस्तः । (बहुविधं निर्वर्ण्य ।) प्रत्यभिजानामीवैतं हस्तम् । अथ वा किं विचारेण । सत्य स एव हस्तो येन मेऽभयं दत्तम् । भवतु । पश्यामि । ( नाटयेनोद्घाट्य दृष्ट्वा प्रत्यभिज्ञाय च । ) सैव बुद्धोपासिका । (हा हा शुद्धालंकालभूशिदे इत्थि-आहत्थे णिक्कमदि । कधम् । दुदिए वि हत्थे । पच्चभिआणामि विअ एदं हत्थम् । अध वा किं विचालेण । शच्चं शे ज्जेव हत्थे जेण मे अभअं दिण्णम् । भोदु । पेक्खिश्शम् । शा ज्जेव बुद्धोवाशिआ ।)

---

१ पटाक्षेपेण. २ पच्छाडिदे ३ पुञ्जिदेशु..संचएशु ४ फुरन्ति.

Here I go with very great speed, like (the monkey) Mahendra going to the city of Lanka, through the sky, over the earth, through the nether regions, and over the summit of (the mountain) Hanumat. (45) (*Exit*)

(*Entering, with a toss of the curtain*, Samvahaka, *now appearing as*)

A BUDDHIST MENDICANT—I have washed this piece of cloth. What, shall I dry it by hanging it on the branch (of some tree)? Here the monkeys might make off with it. Shall I then spread it over the ground? (There) it would be spoiled by the dust. So, where shall I spread it for drying? (*Seeing*). All right; I'll spread it here on this heap of dry leaves collected together by the gusts of wind. (*Does so*) Bow to Buddha! (*Sits down*). Well, now, let me recite holy words. (*He recites the verses beginning with* 'That man most surely attains heaven' &c., *which he had repeated before*). Or no—I have had enough of this (seeking after) heaven; so long as I do not requite the obligations of that Vasantasena, the devotee of Buddha, who bought me off from those two gamesters by paying ten gold-pieces. From that time I consider myself as having been purchased by her [as a slave]. (*Seeing*). Ha! What may this be, that is heaving inside these leaves? Or rather :—

I think that these leaves are throbbing as they were (first) heated by the hot breezes and (then) moistened by the water of my garment, (the leaves which) resemble wings (of birds) with their feathers extended. (46)

(Vasantasena *regains consciousness and puts forth her hand*).

THE M.—Ha! What! A woman's hand is coming out, adorned with fine ornaments! What! Another hand, too! (*Observes it variously*). I seem to recognize this hand. Or why what doubt can there be? Surely it is that same hand which granted me safety (*i. e.* freedom)! Well; I will see. (*Gesticulates uncovering it; observing and recognizing*). It is she, that same devotee of Buddha!

---

दिव महेन्द्रः । महेन्द्रशिखरादिव हनूमानिति वक्तव्ये शकारोक्तत्वाद्विपरीतम् । 'अट्टअ' इति पाठे अष्टकशिखरादित्यर्थः । व्याहतोपममिदं तावत् ॥ ४५ ॥ तथेति प्रसार्य । तदो पहुदि निष्क्रयप्रभृति । **वातातपेनेति** । गाथा । वातातपेन तप्तानि चीवरतोयेन तिम्मितत्वमार्द्रत्वं प्राप्तानि । तिम्मिदा इति भावप्रधानो निर्देशः । एतानि

(वसन्तसेना पानीयमाकाङ्क्षति ।)

भिक्षुः—कथमुदकं याचते । दूरे च दीर्घिका । किमिदानीत्र करिष्यामि । भवतु । एतच्चीवरमस्या उपरि गालयिष्यामि । ( तथा करोति । ) ( कधं उदअं मग्गेदि । दूले च दिग्घिआ । किं दाणि एत्थ कलइश्शम् । भोदु । एदं चीवलं शे उवलि गालइश्शम्[१] ।)

( वसन्तसेना संज्ञां लब्ध्वोत्तिष्ठति । भिक्षुः पटान्तेन वीजयति । )

वसन्तसेना—आर्य कस्त्वम् । (अज्ज को तुमम् ।)

भिक्षुः—किं मां न स्मरति बुद्धोपासिका दशसुवर्णनिष्क्रीतम् । किं मं ण शुमलेदि बुद्धोवाशिआ दशशुवण्णणिक्कीदम् ।)

वसन्तसेना—स्मरामि । न पुनर्यथाऽऽर्यो भणति । वरमहमुपरतैव । ( सुमरामि । ण उण जधा अज्जो भणादि । वरं अहं उवरदा ज्जेव ।)

भिक्षुः—बुद्धोपासके किं न्विदम् । (बुद्धोवाशिए किं ण्णेदम् ।)

वसन्तसेनाः—(सनिर्वेदम् ।) यत्सदृशं वेशभावस्य । (जं सरिस वेसभावस्स ।)

भिक्षुः—उत्तिष्ठतूत्तिष्ठतु बुद्धोपासिकैतां पादपसमीपजातां लतामवलम्ब्य । ( इति लतां नामयति[२] । ) (उट्ठेदु उट्ठेदु बुद्धोवाशिआ एदं पादवसमीवजादं लदं ओलम्बिअ । )

( वसन्तसेना गृहीत्वोत्तिष्ठति । )

भिक्षुः—एतस्मिन्विहारे मम धर्मभगिनी तिष्ठति । तत्र समाश्वस्तमना भूत्वोपासिका गेहं गमिष्यति । तच्छनैः शनैर्गच्छतु बुद्धोपासिका । (इति परिक्रामति । दृष्ट्वा । ) अपसरत आर्याः अपसरत । एषा तरुणी स्त्री एष भिक्षुरिति शुद्धो ममैष धर्मः ।

---

विस्तीर्णं प्राप्तं प्रसारितं यत्र तानि पत्राण्येव स्फुरन्ति विजृम्भन्ते । [ विस्तीर्णपत्राः प्रसारितपक्षाः मन्ये पत्राः पक्षिणः इव स्फुरन्ति । इति ल० दी० ] ।। ४६ ।। शुद्धं केवलं कटकादि एवालंकरणं यत्र सः । दीर्घिका वापी । गालयिष्यामि जलसेकार्थम् । वरं मनागिष्टम् । हस्तेति । [ स खलु मनुष्यः । यो हस्ते हस्तेन वा संयतः अकार्यान्निवर्तितहस्तः । मुखसंयतः असत्यवाक्यादेर्निवृत्तः । इन्द्रियसंयतः कामान्निवर्तितेन्द्रियवृत्तिः । तस्य राजकुलं किं करोति । धर्मनिष्ठस्य तस्य न काऽपि भीतिरिति भावः । तस्य हस्ते परलोको निश्चलः ध्रुवः ] ।। ४७ ।।

इति मोटनो नामाष्टमोऽङ्कः ।

---

१ चाल०. २ नमयति.

( Vasantasena *shows a desire for water* )

THE M.—How ! She asks for water ! And the well is far off ! What shall I now do about this ? All right; I will let this garment drip over her. ( *Does so* ).

( Vasantasena *regains consciousness and rises. The* Mendicant *fans her with the hem of his cloak* ).

VAS.—Sir, who may you be ?

THE M.—What, does not your ladyship, the worshipper of Buddha, remember me ( whom you ) purchased with ten gold-pieces ?

VAS.—I do remember (now). But it isn't as you say.—It were far better that I was dead !

THE M.—O worshipper of Buddha, what may this be ?

VAS.—( *With dejection* ). What befits the profession of a courtesan.

THE M.—Please stand up, O worshipper of Buddha, stand up, by supporting yourself with this creeper growing near this tree. ( *Bends down the creeper* ).

( Vasantasena *seizes it and stands up* ).

THE M.—In this *Vihara* ( convent ) hard by, there dwells ( a nun ), sister of mine by faith. You, the devotee ( of Buddha ) should recover the composure of your mind in that place, and then go home. So, please walk very slowly, O worshipper of Buddha ! ( *Walks about* ; *seeing* ). Make way, worthy sirs, make way ! Here's a young lady, and here's a mendicant ; ( still ) this is my righteous ( holy ) duty.

हस्तसंयतो मुखसंयत इन्द्रियसंयतः स खलु मनुष्यः ।
किं करोति राजकुलं तस्य परलोको हस्ते निश्चलः ।। ४७ ।।

( एदश्शि[१] विहाले मम धम्मबहिणिआ चिट्ठदि । तहिं शमश्शशिदमणा भविअ उवाशिआ गेहं गमिश्शदि । ता शेणं शेणं गच्छदु बुद्धोवाशिआ । ओशलध[२] अज्जा ओशलध । एशा तलुणी इत्थिआ एशो भिक्खु त्ति शुद्धे मम एशे धम्मे ।

हत्थशंजदो[३] मुहशंजदो इन्दियशंजदो शे क्खु माणुशे ।
किं कलेदि लाअउले तश्श पललोओ[४] हत्थे णिच्चले ।।)

इति वसन्तसेनामोटनो[५] नामाष्टमोऽङ्कः ।

---

१ एत्थ शिराविहाघले (अत्र श्रावकगृहे). २ ओशलध ओशलध. ३ शंजद-दे मुहशंजद-दे इन्दिअशंजद-दे. ४ पललोअ. ५ ०सेनामारणं नाम; इति मृच्छकटिकायां वस०.

He is ( really to be called ) a man who is restrained ( in the use of ) his hands, his mouth, and his senses. What can the king's ( law-- ) court do to him ? The next world lies firmly ( grasped ) in his hand. (47)

( *Exeunt Omnes* ).

*Thus ends Act VIII., styled*

'The Killing of Vasantasena.'

---

# नवमोऽङ्कः ।

( ततः प्रविशति शोधनकः । )

**शोधनकः**—आज्ञप्तोऽस्म्यधिकरणभोजकैः—अरे शोधनक व्यवहारमण्डपं गत्वाऽऽसनानि सज्जीकुर्विति । तद्यावदधिकरणमण्डपं सज्जितुं गच्छामि । ( परिक्रम्यावलोक्य च । ) एषोऽधिकरणमण्डपः । एष प्रविशामि (प्रविश्य संमार्ज्यासनमाधाय । ) विविक्तः कारितो मयाऽधिकरणमण्डपः । विरचितानि मयाऽऽसनानि । तद्यावदधिकरणिकानां पुनर्निवेदयामि । (परिक्रम्यावलोक्य च ।) कथमेष राष्ट्रियश्यालो दुष्टदुर्जनमनुष्य इत एवागच्छति । तद्दृष्टिपथं परिहृत्य गमिष्यामि । ( इत्येकान्ते स्थितः । ) (आणत्तम्हि अधिअरणभोइएहिं—अरे सोहणआ ववहारमण्डवं[1] गदुअ आसणाइं सज्जीकरेहि त्ति । ता जाव अधिअरणमण्डवं सज्जिदुं गच्छामि । एदं अधिअरणमण्डवम् । एस[2] पविसामि । विवित्तं कारिदं मए अधिअरणमण्डवम् । विरइदाइं मए आसणाइं । ता जाव अधिअरणिआणं उण णिवेदेमि । कधं एसो रट्ठिअस्सालो दुट्ठदुज्जणमणुस्सो इदो एव्व आअच्छदि । ता दिट्ठिपधं परिहरिअ गमिस्सम् ।)

( ततः प्रविश्यत्युज्ज्वलवेषधारी शकारः । )

**शकारः**—

**स्नातोऽहं सलिलजलैः पानीयैरुद्यान उपवनकानने निषण्णः ।**
**नारीभिः सह युवतीभिः स्त्रीभिर्गन्धर्व इव सुविहितैरङ्गकैः ॥ १ ॥**

(ण्हादेहं[3] सलिलजलेहिं पाणिएहिं उज्जाणे उववणकाणणे णिशण्णे ।
णालीहिं शह जुवदीहिं इश्तिआहिं गन्धव्वेव[4] शुविहिदेहिं अङ्गकेहिं ॥)

---

[ अधिक्रियते विवादाद्यत्रेत्यधिकरणं तस्य भोजयन्ति पालयन्तीति भोजकाः प्रभवस्तैः । व्यवहारो विवादः तस्य मण्डपः । 'परस्परं मनुष्याणां स्वार्थविप्रतिपत्तिषु । वाक्यान्न्यायाद्व्यवस्थानं व्यवहार उदाहृतः ॥' इति मिताक्षरा । ] अधिकरणे न्यायविवादविषये नियुक्तत्वात्तदेषामस्ति । 'अत इनिठनौ' इति ठन् । अपवादो दोषवाच्येति यावत् । **स्नातोऽहमिति** । प्रहर्षिणीच्छन्दसा । जलेहिं जुवदीहिं शुविहिदएहिं इत्यत्र स्वानुस्वाराणामप्यन्त्याक्षराणां लाघवम् । छन्दोनुरोधात् । स्नातोऽहं सलिलजलैः स्वच्छैः । पाठान्तरे पानीयैः । नारीभिर्युवतीभिः स्त्रीभिः सह उद्याने

---

१ मण्डपं सज्जिदुं गच्छेत्ति ता गच्छामि. २ ता प०. ३ ण्हादोहं. ४ गन्धव्वेहिं शुविहिदएहिं; गन्धवे विअ शुहिदेहिं; गन्धव्वो शुवि०.

# ACT IX

( *Then enter* Sodhanaka, *the beadle* )

SODHANAKA—The officers of the law-court have ordered me : " O Sodhanaka, go to the judicial hall and see that the seats are ready." So then I will just go to the judicial chamber to make them ready. ( *Walking about and seeing* ). Here is the court of justice. I will just enter it. (*Enters, sweeps it and arranges the seats* ). I have swept the court-hall clean and arranged the seats. So I will now go and report ( the same ) to the judges. ( *Walks about* ; *seeing* ). How now ! Here's that wicked fellow, villain and rogue, the King's brother-in-law, coming in this very direction ! So I will (first) keep out of the range of his sight and then go. ( *He stands aside in a corner* ).

( *Then enter* Sakara, *dressed in gaudy attire* ).

SAK.—

I have bathed with water, fluids and liquids, and sat in orchards, gardens and groves in the company of ladies, damsels and women, like a Gandharva having well-shaped ( *or*, well-decorated ) limbs. (1)

---

उपवनकानने निषण्ण इति विपर्यस्य योजना । गन्धर्व इव सुविहितैरङ्गकैर्लक्षितः । 'गन्धव्वेहिं' इति पाठे तृतीया प्रथमार्थे रूपकं च । पौनरुक्त्यादि शकारोक्तत्वात् ॥ १ ॥ क्षणेनेति । उपेन्द्रवज्रया । हगे इत्यत्र एकारस्य लघुत्वम् । छन्दोनुरोधात् । एतच्छत्रकमुष्टिकं पावालबन्ध इत्येके । क्षणेन ग्रन्थिः । पाठान्तरे घृष्टिका । क्षणजूलिका मे क्षणेन बालाः क्षणकुन्तला वा । जनिकाज्वलिकयोर्विशेषः (?) । 'चित्ते ण चित्तो ' इति पाठे चित्रं न चित्रं यतोऽहं राजश्याल इति व्याख्येयम् । राजश्यालत्वेन मयि सर्वं संभाव्यते इति भावः ॥ २ ॥ [विषग्रन्थ्यभ्यन्तरे प्रविष्टः कीटो यथा विषतापमसहमानः बहिर्निर्गमनार्थं रन्ध्रं मार्गयते तथा स्वनाशपरिहारायोपायं मार्गमाणेन मया लब्ध उपाय इत्यर्थः। श्रेष्ठी वणिक् । अलंकरणादिपरीक्षणधनगणनाद्यर्थं लोकरञ्जनार्थं च तस्याधिकरणे नियोगः । तदुक्तं कात्यायनेन—'कुलशीलवयोवृत्तवित्तवद्भिरमत्सरैः । वणिग्भिः स्यात्कतिपयैः कुलभूतैरधिष्ठितम् ॥' इति । कायस्थो व्यवहारलेखकः व्यवहारदर्शी । 'व्यवहारः प्रतिज्ञोत्तरसंशयहेतुपरामर्शप्रमाणनिर्णयप्रयोजनात्मकः' इति मिताक्षरा । तस्य पराधीनतया अर्थिप्रत्यर्थिसाक्ष्या-

क्षणेन ग्रन्थिः क्षणजूटको मे क्षणेन बालाः क्षणकुन्तला वा।
क्षणेन मुक्ताः क्षणमूर्ध्वचूडाश्चित्रो विचित्रोऽहं राजश्यालः ॥ २ ॥

अपि च। विषग्रन्थिगर्भप्रविष्टेनेव कीटकेनान्तरं मार्गमाणेण प्राप्तं मया महदन्तरम्। तत्कस्येदं कृपणचेष्टितं पातयिष्यामि। (स्मृत्वा।) आं स्मृतं मया। दरिद्रचारुदत्तस्येदं कृपणचेष्टितं पातयिष्यामि। अन्यच्च। दरिद्रः खलु सः। तस्य सर्वं संभाव्यते। भवतु। अधिकरणमण्डपं गत्वाऽग्रतो व्यवहारं लेखयिष्यामि यथा चारुदत्तेन वसन्तसेना मोटयित्वा मारिता। तद्यावदधिकरणमण्डपमेव गच्छामि। (परिक्रम्यावलोक्य च।) एष सोऽधिकरणमण्डपः। अत्र प्रविशामि। (प्रविश्यावलोक्य च।) कथमासनानि दत्तानि तिष्ठन्ति। यावदागच्छन्त्यधिकरणभोजकाः तावदेतस्मिन्दूर्वाचत्वरे मुहूर्तमुपविश्य प्रतिपालयिष्यामि। (तथा स्थितः।)

(खणेण गण्ठी खणजूलके[1] मे खणेण बाला[2] खणकुन्तले वा।
खणेण मुक्के खण उद्धचूडे चित्ते विचित्ते हगे लाअशाले ॥

अवि अ। विशगण्ठिगब्भपविश्टेण विअ कीडएण अन्तलं मग्गमाणेण पाविदं मए महदन्तलम्। ता कश्श एदं किविणचेश्टिअं पाडइश्शम्। आं शुमलिदं मए। दलिद्दचालुदत्तश्श एदं किविणचेश्टिअं पाडइश्शम्। अण्णं च। दलिद्दे क्खु शे। तश्श शव्वं शंभावीअदि। भोदु। अधिअलणमण्डवं गदुअ अग्गदो ववहालं लिहावइश्शं जधा चालुदत्ताकेण वशन्तशेणिआ मोडिअ मालिदा। ता जाव अधिअलणमण्डवं ज्जेव्व गच्छामि। एदं तं अधिअलणमण्डवम्। एत्थ पविशामि। कधं आशणाइं दिण्णाइं चिश्टन्ति। जाव आअश्शन्ति अधिअलणभोइआ दाव एदश्शि दुव्वचत्तले[3] मुहुत्तअं उवविशिअ पडिवालइश्शम्।)

**शोधनकः**—(अन्यतः परिक्रम्य। पुरो[4] दृष्ट्वा।) एतेऽधिकरणिका आगच्छन्ति। तद्यावदुपसर्पामि। (इत्युपसर्पति।) (एदे अधिअरणिआ आअच्छन्ति। ता जाव उपसप्पामि।)

(ततः प्रविशति श्रेष्ठिकायस्था[5]दिपरिवृतोऽधिकरणिकः[6]।)

**अधिकरणिकः**—भो भोः श्रेष्ठिकायस्थौ।

**श्रेष्ठिकायस्थौ**[7]—आज्ञापयत्वार्यः। (आणवेदु अज्जो।)

**अधिकरणिकः**—अहो व्यवहारपराधीनतया[8] दुष्करं खलु परचित्तग्रहणमधिकरणिकैः।

---

१ खण (क्षणं) जूदिका. २ मे चञ्चलकुन्तले वा. ३ उच्चच०. ४ पुरतः. ५ स्थादिभिः. ६ आधिक०; एवं सर्वत्र. ७ तौ; उभौ. ८ हाराधी०.

For one moment I have my hair knotted; in the next I wear it matted and bound up (like an ascetic). For one moment I have long, flowing tresses; in another curly hair. One moment I keep them loose; in the next I have them rolled up on my crest. (Thus) I am a picturesque and a wonderful brother-in-law of the king! (2)

Moreover, I have found a broad way out, like a worm seeking a way, having got within the interior of the knotted root of a poisonous herb. So on whom shall I shift this evil deed of mine? (*Recollecting*). Yes, I remember it! I'll lay (the blame of) this vile act on the penniless Charudatta! Moreover, he is known to be poor; everything will be (believed as) possible in his case.—All right. I'll go to the court of justice and lodge a written complaint, before (anyone else has done so), that Charudatta strangled Vasantasena and murdered her. So, then, I'll just repair to the law-court. (*Walking about and observing*). Here's that law-court! I'll enter it. (*Entering and looking on*). How! They have kept the seats ready arranged! So, until the judges arrive, I'll sit down here for a while in this grassy quadrangle, and wait. (*Stays accordingly*).

SO.—(*Walking in another direction*; *looking before him*). Here the judges are coming! So then I will approach them. (*Draws near*).

(*Then enter a* Judge, *accompanied by a* Sreshthin, *a* Kayastha, *and* others).

THE JUDGE—Sirs, Sreshthin and Kayastha!

SR. & K.—We await your honour's commands!

THE JUDGE—See, it is verily difficult for judges to find what lies in the minds of others, as a judicial trial is dependent on (a number of) other matters.

---

दीनां युक्तिनिष्ठतया व्यवहारपराधीनतया । परचित्तग्रहणं परेषामर्थिप्रत्यर्थ्यादीनां चित्तस्य भावस्य ग्रहणं यथार्थज्ञानम् ।] छन्नमिति । [पुरुषाः व्यवहर्तारः न्यायेन प्रत्यक्षादिप्रमाणादिना दूरीकृतं विवर्जितं छन्नं सत्यं कार्यमसत्येनाच्छादितमसत्यं च सत्यवत्कृत्वा कार्यमुपक्षिपन्ति निर्णयार्थमुपन्यस्यन्ति । रागाभिभूताः स्वकार्यसंपादनप्रसक्त्याऽभिभूताः अधिकरणे स्वयं स्वान् दोषान् न कथयन्ति । तैः पक्षापरपक्षाभ्यामर्थिप्रत्यर्थिवादाभ्यां वर्धितं बलं येषां तैः । उपचितैरित्यर्थः । दोषैः नृपः स्पृश्यते । यतो न्यायस्य स एव परमाधिष्ठानम् । तदुक्तं मनुना—'अदण्ड्यान्दण्डयन्राजा

छन्नं कार्यमुपक्षिपन्ति पुरुषा न्यायेन दूरीकृतं
स्वान्दोषान्कथयन्ति नाधिकरणे रागाभिभूताः स्वयम् ।
तैः पक्षापरपक्षवर्धितबलैर्दोषैर्नृपः स्पृश्यते
संक्षेपादपवाद एव सुलभो द्रष्टुर्गुणो दूरतः ॥ ३ ॥

अपि च ।

छन्नं दोषमुदाहरन्ति कुपिता न्यायेन दूरीकृताः
स्वान्दोषान्कथयन्ति नाधिकरणे सन्तोऽपि नष्टा ध्रुवम् ।
ये पक्षापरपक्षदोषसहिताः पापानि संकुर्वते
संक्षेपादपवाद एव सुलभो द्रष्टुर्गुणो दूरतः ॥ ४ ॥

यतोऽधिकरणिकः खलु—

शास्त्रज्ञः कपटानुसारकुशलो वक्ता न च क्रोधन-
स्तुल्यो[1] मित्रपरस्वकेषु चरितं[2] दृष्ट्वैव दत्तोत्तरः ।
क्लीबान्पालयिता शठान्व्यथयिता धर्म्यो न लोभान्वितो
द्वार्भावे[3] परतत्त्वबद्धहृदयो[4] राज्ञश्च कोपापहः ॥ ५ ॥

**श्रेष्ठिकायस्थौ**—आर्यस्यापि नाम गुणे दोष इत्युच्यते । यद्येवं तदा चन्द्रालोकेऽप्यन्धकार इत्युच्यते । (अज्जस्स वि णाम गुणे दोसो त्ति वुच्चदि । जइ एव्वं ता चन्दालोए वि अन्धआरो त्ति वुच्चदि ।)

**अधिकरणिकः**—भद्र शोधनक अधिकरणमण्डपस्य मार्गमादेशय ।

**शोधनकः**—एत्वेत्वधिकरणभोजक एतु । ( एदु एदु अधिअरणभोइओ एदु ।)

( इति परिक्रामन्ति[5] । )

**शोधनकः**—अयमधिकरणमण्डपः । तत्प्रविशन्त्वधिकरणभोजकाः । ( एदं अधिअरणमण्डवम् । ता पविसन्तु अधिअरणभोइआ ।)

( सर्वे च प्रविशन्ति । )

**अधिकरणिकः**—भद्र शोधनक बहिर्निष्क्रम्य ज्ञायतां कः कः कार्यार्थीति ।

**शोधनकः**—यदार्य आज्ञापयति । (इति निष्क्रम्य ।) आर्याः अधिकरणिका भणन्ति—कः क इह कार्यार्थीति । (जं अज्जो आणवेदि । अज्जा अधिअरणिआ भणन्ति—को को इह कज्जत्थी त्ति ।)

---

दण्ड्यांश्चैवाप्यदण्डयन् । अयशो महदाप्नोति नरकं चाधिगच्छति ॥ ' इति । न्यायदर्शिनस्तु को लाभ इत्याह—संक्षेपात् सारतः । किं बहुनेत्यर्थः । द्रष्टुः प्राड्विवाकस्य अपवादः निन्दा एव सुलभः । गुणः प्रशंसालाभस्तु दूरत एव । न सुखलभ्य इत्यर्थः ।

---

१ ल्योऽमित्र. २ चरिते दृष्टे च. ३ द्वाभ्यां वै. ४ तन्त्र. ५ क्रामति.

People ( *i. e.* contending parties ) bring up ( for trial ) transactions which are ( *i. e.* whose real character is ) hidden and far removed from justice. Themselves swayed by self-interest, they never tell in the court their own faults. (So) the king incurs the blame ( for the failure of justice ), whose intensity is augmented by ( the contentions of ) one party as well as the other. In short, nothing but odium is commonly to be got by a judge, appreciation but seldom ( falling to his lot ). (3)

Moreover--

People, completely ignoring law, wrathfully complain of the offences ( of others ), but they never confess in the court their own faults. Even learned persons ( counsels ) who commit sin, sharing in the crimes of the contending parties, are verily lost. In short, blame is very easy for a judge to get; applause is far removed from him ( seldom falls to his lot ). (4)

Hence, a judge—

Should be learned in law; expert in tracing ( the course of ) fraud; eloquent; never losing his temper; equally impartial towards friends, strangers and relatives; giving his decision only after ( carefully ) investigating the facts ; a protector of the weak ; a terror to the rogues : righteous ; free from greed even when the means exist for him ( to take bribes ) ; sincerely bent in his mind on ( discovering ) the real truth, and able to avert the anger of the king. (5)

SR. & K.--Can they speak of merits as faults, even in your honour's case ? If so, then they would say that there is darkness even when there is moonlight.

THE J.—Sodhanaka, my good man, point out the way to the court of justice.

SO.--Please come, come ; step ( this way ), your worship !

( *They walk about* ).

SO.—Here is the court of justice. So may the officers enter.

( *Then* all *enter* ).

THE J.—Sodhanaka, my good man, just go out and ascertain who there are that desire to present cases ( to-day ).

SO.—As your worship orders. ( *Going out* ). Gentlemen, the judges ask, who are here that desire to present cases ?

**शकारः**—( सहर्षम् । ) उपस्थिता अधिकरणिकाः। ( साटोपं परिक्रम्य । ) अहं वरपुरुषो मनुष्यो वासुदेवो राष्ट्रियश्यालो राजश्यालः कार्यार्थी । (उवत्थिए अधिअलणिए। हग्गे वलपुलिशे मणुश्शे वाशुदेवे लश्टिअशाले लाअशाले कज्जत्थी ।)

**शोधनकः**—(ससंभ्रमम् ।) हन्त प्रथममेव राष्ट्रियश्यालः कार्यार्थी । भवतु । आर्य मुहूर्तं तिष्ठ । तावदधिकरणिकानां निवेदयामि । ( उपगम्य । ) आर्याः एष खलु राष्ट्रियश्यालः कार्यार्थी व्यवहारमुपस्थितः । (हीमादिके पढमं ज्जेव रट्टिअसालो कज्जत्थी । भोदु । अज्ज मुहुत्तं चिट्ठ । दाव अधिअरणिआणं णिवेदेमि । अज्जा एसो क्खु रट्टिअसालो कज्जत्थी ववहारं उवत्थिदो ।)

**अधिकरणिकः**—कथम् । प्रथममेव राष्ट्रियश्यालः कार्यार्थी । यथा सूर्योदय उपरागो महापुरुषनिपातमेव कथयति । शोधनक व्याकुलेनाद्य व्यवहारेण भवितव्यम् । भद्र निष्क्रम्योच्यताम्—गच्छाद्य न दृश्यते तव व्यवहार इति ।

**शोधनकः**—यदार्य आज्ञापयति । ( इति निष्क्रम्य शकारमुपगम्य । ) आर्य अधिकरणिका भणन्ति—अद्य गच्छ । न दृश्यते तव व्यवहारः । (जं अज्जो आणवेदि । अज्ज अधिअरणिआ भणन्ति—अज्ज गच्छ । ण दीशदि तव ववहारो ।)

**शकारः**—(सक्रोधम् ।) आः किं न दृश्यते मम व्यवहारः । यदि न दृश्यते तदाऽऽवुत्तं राजानं पालकं भगिनीपतिं विज्ञाप्य भगिनीं मातरं च विज्ञाप्यैतमधिकरणिकं दूरीकृत्यात्रान्यमधिकरणिकं स्थापयिष्यामि । ( इति गन्तुमिच्छति । ) (आः किं ण दीशदि मम ववहाले । जइ ण दीशदि तदो आवुत्तं लाआणं पालअं बहिणीवदिं विण्णविअ बहिणिं अत्तिकं च विण्णविअ एदं अधिअलणिअं दूले फेलिअ एत्थ अण्णं अधिअलणिअं ठावइश्शम् ।)

**शोधनकः**—आर्य राष्ट्रियश्याल मुहूर्तं तिष्ठ । तावदधिकरणिकानां निवेदयामि । ( अधिकरणिकमुपगम्य[1] । ) एष राष्ट्रियश्यालः कुपितो भणति—( इति तदुक्तं भणति) । ( अज्ज रट्टिअशालअ मुहुत्तअं चिट्ठ । दाव अधिअरणिआणं णिवेदेमि । एसो रट्टिअशालो कुविदो भणादि—।)

**अधिकरणिकः**—सर्वमस्य मूर्खस्य संभाव्यते । भद्र उच्यताम्—आगच्छ । दृश्यते तव व्यवहारः ।

**शोधनकः**—(शकारमुपगम्य । ) आर्य अधिकरणिका भणन्ति—आगच्छ । दृश्यते तव व्यवहारः । तत्प्रविशत्वार्यः । (अज्ज अधिअरणिआ भणन्ति—आअच्छ । दीसदि तव ववहारो । ता पविसदु अज्जो ।)

---

समुच्चयालंकारः । शार्दूलविक्रीडितं वृत्तम् ]॥ ३ ॥ [ उक्तमेवार्थं किंचिद्विशिष्य पुनराह—छन्नमिति । न्यायेन दूरीकृताः वर्जिताः कुपिताः पुरुषाः छन्नं गूढं दोषं

---

१ ०कानुप०.

SAK.—( *Joyfully* ). The judges have arrived! ( *Walking forth arrogantly* ). Here am I, the best of men, a gentleman, ( another ) Krishna ( as it were ), the king's brother-in-law, the brother-in-law of the king, who want to present a case!

SO.—( *In flurry* ). Ah! At the very commencement here's the royal brother-in-law desiring to present a case! All right. Sir, please wait awhile, so that I will just announce ( your presence ) to the judges. ( *Going to them* ). Gentlemen, here is this king's brother-in-law come to the court, who wishes to present a case.

THE J.—How! At the very commencement there is the king's brother-in-law wanting to present a case! It is just like an eclipse at sunrise, foretelling the death of some great man! Sodhanaka, the hearing of cases to-day will prove troublesome! Go out, my good man, and say to him that he might go away, as his suit can't be heard to-day.

SO.—As Your Honour orders. ( *Going out and approaching* Sakara ). Sir, the judges say that you might go away as your suit won't be heard to-day.

SAK.—( *Wrathfully* ). What, ho! *My* suit won't be heard? If it be not heard, then I will inform my brother-in-law, the king Palaka, who is my sister's husband, and I will tell my sister and my mother, and I'll have this judge removed and another appointed in his place. ( *He is about to leave* ).

SO.—Sir, royal brother-in-law, stay awhile, so that I will just inform the judges ( of what you have said ). ( *Approaching the* Judge ). Our royal brother-in-law here says in anger—( *Repeats what was said by him* ).

THE J.—Everything is possible in the case of that fool. My good man, say to him that he might come in, and that we will look into his suit.

SO.—( *Approaching* Sakara ). Sir, the judges say that you might come in, and that they will look into your suit. Please, sir, you may therefore go in.

---

परकीयस्य अधिकरणे उदाहरन्ति । स्वान् दोषान् अधिकरणे न कथयन्ति । ये सन्तः पक्षापरपक्षदोषसहिताः पापानि संकुर्वते ते ध्रुवं नष्टाः । शेषं व्याख्यातम् ] ॥ ४ ॥ [ अथाधिकरणिकस्वरूपमाह । अधिकरणिकः खलु एवं स्यात्—शास्त्रज्ञ इत्यादि ।

**शकारः**—प्रथमं भणन्ति न दृश्यते सांप्रतं दृश्यत इति। तन्नाम भीतभीता अधिकरणभोजकाः। यद्यदहं[1] भणिष्यामि तत्तत्प्रत्याययिष्यामि। भवदु। प्रविशामि। (प्रविश्योपसृत्य।) सुसुखमस्माकं युष्माकमपि सुखं ददामि न ददामि च। (पढमं[2] भणन्ति ण दीशदि संपदं दीशदि त्ति। ता णाम भीदभीदा अधिअलणभोइआ। जेत्तिअं हग्गे भणिश्शं तेत्तिअं पत्तिआवइश्शम्। भोदु। पविशामि। शुशुहं अम्हाणं तुम्हाणं पि शुहं देमि ण देमि अ।)

**अधिकरणिकः**—(स्वगतम्।) अहो स्थिरसंस्कारता व्यवहारार्थिनः। (प्रकाशम्।) उपविश्यताम्।

**शकारः**—आँ आत्मीयैषा भूमिः। तद्यत्र मह्यं रोचते तत्रोपविशामि। (श्रेष्ठिनं प्रति।) एष उपविशामि। (शोधनकं प्रति।) नन्वत्रोपविशामि। (इत्यधिकरणिकमस्तके हस्तं दत्त्वा।) एष उपविशामि। (इति भूमावुपविशति।) (आं अत्तणकेलका शे भूमी। ता जहिं मे रोअदि तहिं उवविशामि। एश उवविशामि। णं एत्थ उवविशामि। एश उवविशामि।)

**अधिकरणिकः**—भवान्कार्यार्थी।

**शकारः**—अथ किम्। (अध इं।)

**अधिकरणिकः**—तत्कार्यं कथय।

**शकारः**—कर्णे कार्यं कथयिष्यामि। एवं बृहति मल्लकप्रमाणस्य कुलेऽहं जातः। (कण्णे कज्जं कधइश्शम्। एव्वं वड्ढके मल्लक्कप्पमाणाह कुले हग्गे जादे।)

**राजश्वशुरो मम पिता राजा तातस्य भवति जामाता।**
**राजश्यालोऽहं ममापि भगिनीपती राजा॥ ६॥**
(लाअशशुले मम पिदा लाआ तादश्श होइ जामादा।
लाअशिआले हग्गे ममावि बहिणिवदी लाआ॥)

**अधिकरणिकः**—सर्वं ज्ञायते।

**किं कुलेनोपदिष्टेन शीलमेवात्र कारणम्।**
**भवन्ति नितरां स्फीताः सुक्षेत्रे कण्टकिद्रुमाः[3]॥ ७॥**

तदुच्यतां कार्यम्।

---

शास्त्रज्ञः धर्मशास्त्रवित्। कपटस्य वादिप्रतिवादिकृतस्यानुसारे अनुगमने। यथार्थज्ञाने इत्यर्थः। कुशलः। वक्ता अवगतार्थप्रतिपादनसमर्थः। न च क्रोधनः क्रोधशीलः। मित्रपरस्वकेषु मित्रशत्रुस्वजनेषु तुल्यः समदर्शनः। पक्षपातरहित इति यावत्। चरितं व्यवहारिणामिति शेषः। दृष्ट्वा सम्यग्विचार्य एव दत्तोत्तरः उत्तरदायी।

---

१ यावदहं भणिष्यामि तावत्प्रत्येष्यन्ते. २ ही पढमं भणादि. ३ कण्टक.

SAK.—First they say that they wouldn't look into it, and now that they would. So, obviously, the judges must have got mightily frightened! Whatever I'll say, the same I'll compel them to accept as true. Very well; I'll go in. ( *Entering and approaching* ). I am doing very well! As to you, I can give or not give you happiness ( as I please )!

THE J.—( *To himself* ). Oh! Even when presenting a complaint, his usual habits do not leave him ( *lit.* are firm with him )! (*Aloud*). Pray seat yourself.

SAK.—Ah! This place belongs to me; so I'll sit where I like! ( *To the* Sreshthin ). I'll sit here! (*To* Sodhanaka). No, I'll sit here! ( *Then placing his hand on the head of the* Judge ). I'll sit here! ( *Thereupon he sits on the ground* ).

THE J.—So you wish to lodge a complaint?

SAK.—Yes.

THE J.—Then tell us what it is.

SAK.—I will whisper my business in your ear. I am born in a very big family, of the size of a *mallaka* ( cup ).

My father is the king's father-in-law; the king is the son-in-law of my father. I myself am the king's brother-in-law; while the king is the husband of my sister. (6)

THE J.—All that is known ( to us ).

Why describe one's family, since one's own character itself is the determining factor herein? Even thorny trees grow exceedingly large in a good soil. (7)

So describe your business.

---

क्लीबान्दुर्बलान् पालयिता । शठान् व्यथयिता तेषां निग्रहात्पीडाकारी । धर्मादनपेतो धर्म्यः । न लोभान्वितः । द्वार्भवे द्वारुपायः तस्य भावः सत्त्वं तस्मिन्सति । परतत्त्वे अर्थिप्रत्यर्थिनोः याथार्थ्यज्ञाने बद्धहृदयः आहितमतिः । राज्ञश्च वस्तुनो यथार्थस्वरूपकथनेन सदुपदेशेन च कोपापहः कोपमपहन्तीति तथोक्तः । शार्दूल० छन्दः ] ॥ ५ ॥ [ यदुक्तं 'संक्षेपादपवाद एव सुलभः' तदुद्दिश्याह—आर्यस्यापि नाम गुणे दोष इति । ] [ उपरागः राहुणा सूर्यस्य चन्द्रस्य वा ग्रासः । व्याकुलेन विक्षोभितेन । ] आः क्रोधे । आवुत्त भगिनीपतिम् । आवुत्तमित्यादावुक्त्वा पुनर्भगिनीपतिमिति पुनरुक्तम् । युष्माकं सुखं ददामि न ददामि । शकारोक्तेर्व्याकुलता । मल्लकः पात्रविशेषः । राजश्वशुर इत्यादि । गाथा ॥ ६ ॥ किं कुलेनेत्यादि । [ अष्टमाङ्के २९ तमं पद्यं द्रष्टव्यम् ] ॥ ७ ॥ एतेन यदुक्तं भवति तदाह—अपराद्धस्यापि न मे किमपि

**शकारः**—एवं भणामि। अपराद्धस्यापि न च मे किमपि करिष्यति। ततस्तेन भगिनीपतिना परितुष्टेन मे क्रीडितुं रक्षितुं सर्वोद्यानानां प्रवरं पुष्पकरण्डकजीर्णोद्यानं दत्तम्। तत्र च प्रेक्षितुमनुदिवसं शुष्कं कारयितुं शोधयितुं पुष्टं कारयितुं लूनं कारयितुं गच्छामि। दैवयोगेन पश्यामि न पश्यामि वा स्त्रीशरीरं निपतितम्। (एव्वं भणामि। अवलद्धाह वि ण अ मे किं पि कलइश्शदि। तदो तेण बहिणीवदिणा परितुश्टेण मे कीलिदुं लक्खिदुं शव्वुज्जाणाणं पवले पुप्फकलण्डकजिण्णुज्जाणे दिण्णे। तहिं च पेक्खिदुं अणुदिअहं शोशावेदुं शोधावेदुं पोश्टावेदुं लुणावेदुं गच्छामि। देव्वजोएण पेक्खामि ण पेक्खामि वा इत्थिआशलीलं णिवडिदम्।)

**अधिकरणिकः**—अथ ज्ञायते का स्त्री विपन्नेति।

**शकारः**—अहो अधिकरणिकभोजकाः किमिति न जानामि तां तादृशीं नगरमण्डनं काञ्चनशतभूषणाम्। केनापि कुपुत्रेणार्थकल्यवर्तस्य कारणाच्छून्यं पुष्पकरण्डकजीर्णोद्यानं प्रविश्य बाहुपाशबलात्कारेण वसन्तसेना मारिता। न मया। (इत्यर्धोक्ते मुखमावृणोति।) (हंहो अधिअलणभोइआ किंत्ति ण जाणामि तं तादिशिं णअलमण्डणं काञ्चनशदभूशणिअं। केण वि कुपुत्तेण अत्थकल्लवत्तश्श कालणादो शुण्णं पुप्फकलण्डकजिण्णुज्जाणं पविशिअ बाहुपाशबलक्कालेण वशन्तशेणिआ मालिदा। ण मए।)

**अधिकरणिकः**—अहो नगररक्षिणां प्रमादः। भोः श्रेष्ठिकायस्थौ न मयेति व्यवहारपदं प्रथममभिलिख्यताम्।

**कायस्थः**—यदार्य आज्ञापयति। (तथा कृत्वा।) आर्य लिखितम्। (जं अज्जो आणवेदि। अज्ज लिहिदम्।)

**शकारः**—(स्वगतम्।) हीमादिके। उत्त्वरायमाणेनेव पायसपिण्डारकेणाद्य मयाऽऽत्मैव निर्नाशितः। भवतु। एवं तावत्। (प्रकाशम्।) अहो अधिकरणभोजकाः ननु भणामि मयैव दृष्टा। किं कोलाहलं कुरुत। (इति पादेन लिखितं[1] प्रोञ्छति।) (हीमादिके। उत्तलाअन्तेण विअ पाअशपिण्डालकेण अज्ज मए अत्ता एव्व णिण्णाशिदो। भोदु। एव्वं दाव। अहो अधिअलणभोइआ णं भणामि मए ज्जेव्व दिट्ठा। किं कोलाहलं कलेध।)

**अधिकरणिकः**—कथं त्वया ज्ञातं यथा खल्वर्थनिमित्तं बाहुपाशेन व्यापादिता।

**शकारः**—हंहो नूनं शूनशूनया मोघस्थानया ग्रीवालिकया निःसुवर्णकैराभरणस्थानैस्तर्कयामि। (हंहो णूणं शूणशूणाए[2] मोघट्ठाणाए[3] गीवालिआए णिशुवण्णकेहिं आहलणट्ठाणेहिं तक्केमि।)

**श्रेष्ठिकायस्थौ**—युज्यत इव। (जुज्जदि विअ।)

---

१ लिखनं. २ परिशूणाए. (परिशून्यया). ३ मोटणाए (मोटनया).

SAK.—I will just tell you. (But understand that) he (*i. e.* the king) won't do anything to me even if I am guilty! Well, that brother-in-law of mine, being pleased with me, bestowed upon me the old garden *Pushpakarandaka*, the best of all gardens, for sport as well as for custody. And I daily go there, to look after it, to see that it is (properly) drained, and swept, and growing luxuriantly, and trimmed (as necessary). As fate would have it, I saw therein—or no, I didn't see—the body of a woman lying (dead) on the ground.

THE J.—And could you discover who that dead woman was?

SAK.—O you judges, how could it be that I shouldn't recognize that lady, so well-known, the adornment of our city and wearing hundreds of ornaments? Vasantasena, who was enticed into the old *Pushpakarandaka* garden, when it was deserted, was killed by some villainous fellow for the sake of filthy lucre after having forcibly strangled her with the noose of his arms; but not by me—(*Leaving it half-said, he covers his mouth*).

THE J.—What negligence on the part of the city's police! O Sreshthin and Kayastha, first write down the words '*Not by me*' as part of the plaint.

K.—As your worship orders. (*Does so*). Sir, I have written it.

SAK.—(*To himself*). Hang it all! I have to-day simply brought ruin on my own self, like the beggar gulping down the hot *payasa* (milk preparation) in a hurry. Never mind; I will (proceed) in this way. (*Aloud*). O judges, what I was saying was that it was by me that she was seen. Why do you make such a fuss about it? (*With his foot he rubs out what was written*)

THE J.—How do you know that she was killed for her money, and with the noose of arms?

SAK.—Well, surely, I could guess it from her neck, which was very much swollen, and bare in the place (where an ornament is worn), and also from her limbs (*lit.* places on her body) where ornaments are worn, but which were devoid of golden ornaments.

SR. & K.—It seems quite plausible.

---

करिष्यति। जीर्णेति विशेषणं विजनत्वख्यापनार्थम्। तत्र च प्रेक्षितुमित्यत्र तत्रेति करणाधिकरणत्वेन विवक्षितत्वात्तदित्येवार्थः [ न गच्छामीति पूर्वोक्तविरुद्धं शकार-

**शकारः**—( स्वगतम् । ) दिष्ट्या प्रत्युज्जीवितोऽस्मि । अविद मादिके । (दिश्टिआ पच्चुजीविदम्हि । अविद मादिके ।)

**श्रेष्ठिकायस्थौ**—भोः कमेष व्यवहारोऽवलम्बते । (भो कं एसो ववहारो अवलम्बदि ।)

**अधिकरणिकः**—इह हि द्विविधो व्यवहारः ।

**श्रेष्ठिकायस्थौ**—कीदृशः । (केरिसो ।)

**अधिकरणिकः**—वाक्यानुसारेण अर्थानुसारेण च । यस्तावद्वाक्यानुसारेण स खल्वर्थिप्रत्यर्थिभ्यः[१] । यश्चार्थानुसारेण स चाधिकरणिकबुद्धिनिष्पाद्यः ।

**श्रेष्ठिकायस्थौ**—तद्वसन्तसेनामातरमवलम्बते व्यवहारः । (ता वसन्तसेणामादरं अवलम्बदि ववहारो ।)

**अधिकरणिकः**—एवमिदम् । भद्र शोधनक वसन्तसेनामातरमनुद्वेजयन्नाह्वय ।

**शोधनकः**—तथा[२] । ( इति निष्क्रम्य गणिकामात्रा[३] सह प्रविश्य । ) एत्वेत्वार्या । (तधा । एदु एदु अज्जा ।)

**वृद्धा**—गता मे दारिका मित्रगृहमात्मनो यौवनमनुभवितुम् । एष पुनर्दीर्घायुर्भणति—आगच्छ । अधिकरणिक आह्वयति । तन्मोहपरवशमिवात्मानमवगच्छामि । हृदयं मे प्रकम्पते । आर्य आदिश मह्यमधिकरणमण्डपस्य मार्गम् । (गदा मे दारिआ मित्तघरअं अत्तणो जोव्वणं[४] अणुभविदुम् । एसो उण दीहाऊ भणादि-आअच्छ । अधिअरणिओ सद्दावेदि । ता मोहपरवसं विअ अत्ताअणं अवगच्छामि । हिअअं मे थरथरेदि । अज्ज आदेसेहि मे अधिअरणमण्डवस्स मग्गम् । )

**शोधनकः**—एत्वेत्वार्या । (एदु एदु अज्जा ।)

( उभौ परिक्रामतः । )

**शोधनकः**—एषोऽधिकरणमण्डपः । अत्र प्रविशत्वार्या । ( एदं अधिअरणमण्डवम् । एत्थ पविसदु अज्जा ।)

(इत्युभौ प्रविशतः ।)

**वृद्धा**—(उपसृत्य ।) सुखं युष्माकं भवतु भावमिश्राणाम् । ( सुहं तुम्हाणं भोदु भावमिस्साणम् । )

**अधिकरणिकः**—भद्रे स्वागतम् । आस्यताम् ।

**वृद्धा**—तथा । (इत्युपविष्टा ।) (तधा ।)

**शकारः**—(साक्षेपम् ।) आगताऽसि वृद्धकुट्टिनि आगताऽसि । ( आगदाशि बुड्ढकुटटणि[५] आगदाशि । )

**अधिकरणिकः**—अये त्वं किल वसन्तसेनायाः[६] माता ।

---

१ अर्थं प्रत्यर्थेभ्यः. २ तथेति नि०. ३ गणिकायाः. ४ जोव्वणसुहं. ५ कुट्टिणि, कुट्टणिआ. ६ सेनामाता.

SAK.—( *To himself* ). Most fortunate ! I feel I have obtained a new lease of life ! Heigh ho !

SR. &. K.—Sir, on whom does ( the investigation of ) this suit depend ?

THE J.—Well, in law the complaints are of two kinds.

SR. & K.—What are they ?

THE J.—One depending on arguments ( *or*, oral statements ) and the other on actual facts. The one which depends on argument is ( to be settled) by the plaintiff and the defendant (arguing against each other ). And what depends on facts is to be decided by the Judge with the help of his own wisdom.

SR. & K.—So, then, this case depends on the mother of Vasantasena ( giving evidence ).

THE J.—That's so. Sodhanaka, my good man, please call Vasantasena's mother (here), without frightening her.

SO.—Yes. ( *Goes out and comes in with the courtesan's* mother ). Come, come ( this way ), madam !

THE OLD LADY—My daughter has gone to her friend's house to enjoy her youth. But this long-lived gentleman says that I am to go ( with him ) as the Judge calls me. Therefore I feel as though a faintness is overpowering me, and my heart trembles ( with fear ). Sir, kindly show me the way to the law-court.

SO.—Come, come (this way), madam.

( *Both walk about* )

SO.—This is the law-court. May madam enter it.

( *Thereupon both go in* ).

THE OLD LADY—( *Approaching* ). May you be happy, worthy sirs !

THE J.—Welcome, good lady ! Please take a seat.

THE O. L.—Yes. ( *Sits down* ).

SAK.—( *Abusively* ). So you have come, you old bawd, have you ?

THE J.—Madam, are you the mother of Vasantasena ?

---

वचनत्वात् । बाहुपाशबलात्कारेण । व्रणशून्यत्वाद्बलवद्बाहुपीडनेन । ] न मयेति तस्य बोध्यत्वेन व्यवहारपदम् । [ हीमादिके इति खेदे भये वा । उत्त्वरायमाणेण त्वरया

वृद्धा—अथ किम् । (अध इं ।)

अधिकरणिकः—अथेदानीं वसन्तसेना क्व गता ।

वृद्धा—मित्रगृहम् । (मित्तघरअम् ।)

अधिकरणिकः—किंनामधेयं तस्या मित्रम् ।

वृद्धा—(स्वगतम् ।) हा धिक् हा धिक् । अतिलज्जनीयं खल्वेतत् । (प्रकाशम् ।) जनस्य पृच्छनीयोऽयमर्थो न पुनरधिकरणिकस्य । (हद्धी हद्धी । अदिलज्जणीयं क्खु एदम् । जणस्स पुच्छणीओ अअं अत्थो ण उण अधिअरणिअस्स ।)

अधिकरणिकः—अलं लज्जया । व्यवहारस्त्वां पृच्छति ।

श्रेष्ठिकायस्थौ—व्यवहारः पृच्छति । नास्ति दोषः । कथय । (ववहारो पुच्छदि । णत्थि[1] दोसो । कधेहि ।)

वृद्धा—कथं व्यवहारः । यद्येवं तदा श्रृण्वन्त्वार्यमिश्राः । स खलु सार्थवाहविनयदत्तस्य नप्ता सागरदत्तस्य तनयः सुगृहीतनामधेय आर्यचारुदत्तो नाम श्रेष्ठिचत्वरे प्रतिवसति । तत्र मे दारिका यौवनसुखमनुभवति । (कधं ववहारो । जइ एव्वं ता सुणन्तु अज्जमिस्सा । सो क्खु सत्थवाहविणअदत्तस्स णत्तिओ साअरदत्तस्स तणओ सुगहिदणामहेओ[2] अज्जचारुदत्तो णाम सेट्ठिचत्तरे पडिवसदि । तहिं मे दारिआ जोव्वणसुहं अणुभवदि ।)

शकारः—श्रुतमार्यैः । लिख्यन्तामेतान्यक्षराणि । चारुदत्तेन सह मम विवादः । (शुदं अज्जेहिं । लिहीअन्तु एदे अक्खला । चालुदत्तेण शह मम विवादे ।)

श्रेष्ठिकायस्थौ—चारुदत्तो मित्रमिति नास्ति दोषः । (चारुदत्तो मित्तो त्ति णत्थि दोसो ।)

अधिकरणिकः—व्यवहारोऽयं चारुदत्तमवलम्बते ।

श्रेष्ठिकायस्थौ—एवमिव । (एवं विअ ।)

अधिकरणिकः—धनदत्त वसन्तसेनाऽऽर्यचारुदत्तस्य गृहं गतेति लिख्यतां व्यवहारस्य प्रथमः पादः । कथमार्यचारुदत्तोऽप्यस्माभिराह्वाययितव्यः । अथ वा व्यवहारस्तमाह्वयति । भद्र शोधनक गच्छ । आर्यचारुदत्तं स्वैरमसंभ्रान्तमनुद्विग्नं सादरमाह्वय प्रस्तावेन—अधिकरणिकस्त्वां द्रष्टुमिच्छतीति ।

शोधनकः—यदार्य आज्ञापयति । (इति निष्क्रान्तः । चारुदत्तेन सह प्रविश्य च ।) एत्वेत्वार्यः । (जं अज्जो आणवेदि । एदु एदु अज्जो ।)

चारुदत्तः—(विचिन्त्य ।)

परिज्ञातस्य मे राज्ञा शीलेन च कुलेन च ।
यत्सत्यमिदमाह्वानमवस्थामभिशङ्कते ॥ ८ ॥

(सवितर्कं स्वगतम् ।)

---

१ ण एत्थ. २ सुगिहिद.

THE O. L.—Yes.

THE J.—And where has Vasantasena gone now ?

THE O. L.—To the house of her friend.

THE J.—What is her friend's name ?

THE O. L.—( *To herself* ). Oh, fie ! Oh, fie ! This is truly very shameful ! ( *Aloud* ) This thing may be asked by a (common) person, but not by a judge !

THE J.—Do not feel any shame ; it is a legal necessity that is asking you.

SR. & K.—It is a legal necessity that is putting the question. There is no harm ( in telling ). (So) please answer.

THE O. L.—What, a legal necessity ! If so, then may you gentlemen hear ! He is that well-known grandson of the merchant Vinayadatta, and the son of Sagaradatta, who is called the worthy Charudatta, and whose name it is auspicious to invoke ;—he who dwells in the merchants' quarter. With him my daughter is enjoying the pleasures of youth !

SAK.—You have heard, gentlemen ! Write down these words ( of hers ). My complaint is against Charudatta !

SR. & K.—There is no harm in ( the mere fact ) that Charudatta should be her friend.

THE J.—This suit ( now ) depends on Charudatta ( giving evidence ).

SR. & K.—So it does.

THE J.—Dhanadatta, write down, as the first portion of this case, that Vasantasena went to the house of the worthy Charudatta. How now ! We have to summon even the worthy Charudatta ! Or rather, it is the law that calls him ( and not we). Sodhanaka, my good man, go and respectfully summon the worthy Charudatta (here), gently, without hurry, and without alarming him, telling him—' the judge wishes to see you '.

SO.—As Your Worship orders. ( *Exit. Then entering with* Charudatta ). Come, sir, come ( this way ) !

CHAR.—( *Thoughtfully* ).

To tell the truth, this summoning of me, who am very well known to the King as regards my character and lineage, bespeaks a suspicion ( on his part ) owing to my ( present ) condition ( of poverty ). (8)

( *Reflecting. To himself* ).

ज्ञातो नु[1] किं स खलु बन्धनविप्रयुक्तो
मार्गागतः[2] प्रवहणेन मयाऽपनीतः ।
चारेक्षणस्य नृपतेः श्रुतिमागतो वा
येनाहमेवमभियुक्त इव प्रयामि ॥ ९ ॥

अथ वा किं विचारितेन । अधिकरणमण्डपमेव गच्छामि । भद्र शोधनक अधिकरणस्य[3] मार्गमादेशय ।

**शोधनकः**—एत्वेत्वार्यः । (एदु एदु अज्जो ।)

( इति परिक्रामतः । )

**चारुदत्तः**—(सशङ्कम् ।) तत्किमपरम् ।

रूक्षस्वरं वाशति[4] वायसोऽयममात्यभृत्या मुहुराह्वयन्ति ।
सव्यं च नेत्रं स्फुरति प्रसह्य ममानिमित्तानि हि खेदयन्ति ॥ १० ॥

**शोधनकः**—एत्वेत्वार्यः स्वैरमसंभ्रान्तम् । (एदु एदु अज्जो सैरं असंभन्तम् ।)

**चारुदत्तः**—(परिष्क्रम्याग्रतोऽवलोक्य च ।)

शुष्कवृक्षस्थितो ध्वाङ्क्ष आदित्याभिमुखस्तथा ।
मयि चोदयते वामं [5]चक्षुर्घोरमसंशयम् ॥ ११ ॥

(पुनरन्यतोऽवलोक्य ।) अये कथमयं सर्पः ।

मयि [6]विनिहितदृष्टिर्भिन्ननीलाञ्जनाभः
स्फुरितविततजिह्वः शुक्लदंष्ट्राचतुष्कः ।
अभिपतति सरोषो जिह्मिताध्मातकुक्षि-
र्भुजगपतिरयं मे मार्गमाक्रम्य सुप्तः ॥ १२ ॥

---

ऊर्ध्वं निष्क्रामता पायसपिण्डारकेण पायसान्नेन इव । शूनशूनया अतिशोथवत्या । मोघस्थानया ग्रैवेयाद्यलंकारहरणाद्रिक्तस्थानया । ग्रीवैव ग्रीवालिका ।] अविद मादिके इत्याश्वासे । [ वाक्यानुरोधादर्थिप्रत्यर्थिनोस्तत्साक्षिणां च वचनानुरोधात् । अर्थानुसारेण वाक्यविप्रतिपत्तौ विषयस्वरूपप्रबोधनेन निर्णयः । ] अनुद्वेजयन दुहितृमृत्युवार्ताकथनेनोद्विग्नामकुर्वन् । अर्थो न पुनरधिकरणिकानामिति वेश्यापतिरूपतया ज्ञानेन शिष्टानां लज्जाकरत्वादिति भावः । धनदत्तेति कायस्थसबोधनम् । स्वैरं स्वच्छन्दम् । असभ्रान्तं संभ्रमशून्यम् । परिज्ञातस्येति । अवस्थामीदृशीं दशाम् ॥ ८ ॥ ज्ञात इति । [ स मार्गागत आर्यकः प्रवहणेन मयाऽपनीतः अपवाहितः

---

१ हि किं नु. २ मार्गं गतः. ३ ०णमण्डपस्य. ४ वासति. ५ चक्षुश्चौर. ६ विनिहत.

Could it be that the King found out that Aryaka, whom I met in the road as he was escaping from custody, was sent off by me in my carriage, or did he, having spies for his eyes, come to hear of him ( as being helped by me ), that I am now marching thus as if I were an accused person ? (9)

Or rather, why should I think over that ? I will forthwith repair to the law-court. Sodhanaka, my good man, show the way to the court.

SO.—Come, sir, come ( this way ).

( *They walk about* )

CHAR.—( *With apprehension* ). And what is this next ?

The crow is shrieking in a harsh voice; the ministerial servants are calling out for me repeatedly; and my left eye is throbbing violently. These evil omens make me ( very ) anxious ! (10)

SO.—Come, sir, come ( this way ), gently and without hurry.

CHAR.—( *Walking about and looking before him* ). This crow (here) seated on a withered tree, and facing the sun, is casting his left eye at me. There is no doubt that a dire calamity is to befall me. (11)

( *Again looking in another direction* ). Ah ! How is it that here is a snake !

This huge snake, who was lying asleep across my path with his coiled and swollen belly, is now darting at me in rage, with his eyes fixed on me, ( his body ) looking (dark) like powdered antimony, with his quivering tongue stretched out, and possessing four white fangs. (12)

---

नृपतेः ज्ञातः किम् । अथ वा चारा ईक्षणं यस्य तस्य श्रुतिमागतो वा । येनाहमेवमभियुक्तः अपराधित्वेन दूषित इव प्रयामि । वसन्ततिलकं वृत्तम् ] ॥ ९ ॥ रूक्षाति । 'शासृ वासृ शब्दे' । भ्वादिः । आत्मनेपदानित्यत्वाच्च परस्मैपदम् । [वायसो रूक्षस्वरं वाशति शब्दं करोति । लल्लादीक्षितास्तु 'वासति' इति पठित्वा चञ्चुपुटमुद्घास्य विरौति इति व्याख्यान्ति । वायसस्य कर्कशारावः महाभयदः । तदुक्तं वराहमिहिरेण—'दारुणनादस्तरुकोटरोगपो वायसो महाभयदः' इति । अमात्यानामत्राधिकरणिकानां भृत्याः मुहुराह्वयन्ति । सव्यं वामं च नेत्रं प्रसह्य बलवत्स्फुरति । पुंसां वामनेत्रस्फुरणमनिमित्तमनिष्टसूचकम् । एतानि अनिमित्तानि मम मां खेद-

अपि चेदम् ।

स्खलति चरणं भूमौ न्यस्तं न चार्द्रतमा मही
स्फुरति नयनं वामो बाहुर्मुहुश्च विकम्पते ।
शकुनिरपरश्चायं तावद्विरौति हि नैकशः
कथयति महाघोरं[1] मृत्युं न चात्र विचारणा ॥ १३ ॥

सर्वथा देवता स्वस्ति करिष्यन्ति ।

शोधनकः—एत्वेत्वार्यः । इममधिकरणमण्डपं प्रविशत्वार्यः (एदु एदु अज्जो। इमं अधिअरणमण्डवं पविसदु अज्जो ।)

चारुदत्तः—( प्रविश्य । समन्तादवलोक्य । ) अहो अधिकरणमण्डपस्य परा श्रीः । इह हि—

चिन्तासक्तनिमग्नमन्त्रिसलिलं दूतोर्मिशङ्खाकुलं
पर्यन्तस्थितचार[2]नक्रमकरं नागाश्व[3]हिंस्राश्रयम् ।
नानावाशक[4]कङ्कपक्षिनिचितं[5] कायस्थसर्पास्पदं
नीतिक्षुण्णतटं च राजकरणं[6] हिंस्रैः समुद्रायते ॥ १४ ॥

भवतु । (प्रविशञ्शिरोघातमभिनीय सवितर्कम् । अहह इदमपरम् ।

सव्यं मे स्पन्दते चक्षुर्विरौति वायसस्तथा ।
पन्थाः सर्पेण रुद्धोऽयं स्वस्ति चास्मासु दैवतः[7] ॥ १५ ॥

तावत्प्रविशामि । (इति प्रविशति ।)

अधिकरणिकः—अयमसौ चारुदत्तः । य एषः—

घोणोन्नतं मुखमपाङ्गविशालनेत्रं
नैतद्धि[8] भाजनमकारणदूषणानाम् ।
नागेषु गोषु तुरगेषु तथा नरेषु
न ह्याकृतिः सुसदृशं विजहाति वृत्तम् ॥ १६ ॥

यन्ति । ममेति द्वितीयार्थे कर्मणः शेषत्वविवक्षया षष्ठी । उपजातिः ]॥ १० ॥ शुष्केति । [ ध्वाङ्क्षः काकः शुष्कवृक्षस्थितस्तथा आदित्याभिमुखः सन् मयि घोरं वामं चक्षुः असंशयं यथा तथा चोदयते प्रेरयति । महाभयसूचकमेतत् । तदुक्तं बृहत्संहितायां—'छिन्नाग्रेऽङ्गच्छेदः कलहः शुष्कद्रुमस्थिते ध्वाङ्क्षे । ऐन्द्रादिदिगवलोकी सूर्याभिमुखो रुवन् गृहे गृहिणः । राजभयचौरबन्धनकलहाः स्युः पशुभयं चेति ॥' इति ]॥ ११ ॥ [ अपरमपशकुनमाह—मयीति । भिन्नं सम्यग्मृदितं यन्नीलाञ्जनं तस्येव आभा यस्य सः । स्फुरिता वितता जिह्वा यस्य सः । शुक्लं दंष्ट्राचतुष्कं

१ महामृत्युं घोरं. २ चारु. ३ हिंसा. ४ वासक. ५ रचितं, रुचिरम्. ६ भवनं. ७ दैवताः ८ विभाजनं.

And moreover, there's this :—

My foot planted on the ground slips, and yet the earth is not very wet ( muddy ). My (left) eye throbs, and so does my left arm, again and again. And here again is this another bird ( crow *or* vulture ) uttering frequent cries. All this indicates most terrible death : there's no doubt about it. (13)

May the gods grant welfare in all ways !

SO.—Come, sir, come ( this way ). May your honour enter this law-court.

CHAR.—( *Entering* ; *looking on all sides* ). Oh, the supreme grandeur of the court of justice ! For here—

Owing to its cruel elements, this royal court of justice looks like an ocean ; it has water in the shape of the ministers deeply engaged in thought ; it is full of waves and conches in the form of the envoys ( *or*, advocotes ) ; it has within its environs sharks and alligators in the form of the spies; it is the abode of ferocious animals in the form of elephants and horses; it is thronged with *Kanka* birds in the form of the litigants shouting various complaints; it is the resort of serpents in the form of the Kayasthas ( writers ) ; and it has its shores cut in by [ the rivers in the form of ] politics ( rules about the conduct of cases ). (14)

Well. ( *Trying to enter* ; *gesticulates that his head strikes against the door. Reflecting* ). Alack-a-day ! Here's another ( additional ill omen ) !

My left eye throbs; and the crow is crying; and just now my way was blocked by that snake. May good betide me through fate ! (15)

Let me then get in. ( *Enters* ).

THE JUDGE—Here's that Charudatta, he who—

[ Possesses ] a face having a prominent nose and eyes with large corners. Such a face, surely, could never be the abode of having crimes wantonly attributed to it. For in the case of elephants, bullocks, horses and men, the form is never without a corresponding excellence of conduct. (16)

---

यस्य सः । मे मार्गमाक्रम्य सुप्तः अयं भुजगपतिः कृष्णसर्पः सरोषः जिह्मितः वक्रीकृतः आध्मातः वायुपूरितः कुक्षिर्यस्य तथा । मयि विनिहितदृष्टिः अभिपतति । एतदपि महाभयसूचकम् । उक्तं च बृहत्संहितायां—' फणिनोऽभिमुखागमोऽरिसङ्गं

**चारुदत्तः**—भोः अधिकृतेभ्यः स्वस्ति । हंहो नियुक्ताः अपि कुशलं भवताम् ।

**अधिकरणिकः**—( ससंभ्रमम् । ) स्वागतमार्यस्य । भद्र शोधनक आर्यस्यासनमुपनय ।

**शोधनकः**—( आसनमुपनीय । ) एतदासनम् । अत्रोपविशत्वार्यः । ( एदं आसनम् । एत्थ उवविसदु अज्जो । )

( चारुदत्त उपविशति । )

**शकारः**—( सक्रोधम् । ) आगतोऽसि रे स्त्रीघातक आगतोऽसि । अहो न्याय्यो व्यवहारः अहो धर्म्यो व्यवहारः यदेतस्मै स्त्रीघातकायासनं दीयते । (सगर्वम् ।) भवतु । ननु दीयताम् । ( आगदेशि ले इश्थिआघादआ आगदेशि । अहो णाए ववहाले अहो धम्मे ववहाले जं एदाह इश्थिआघादकाह आशणे दोअदि । भोदु । णं दीअदु ।)

**अधिकरणिकः**—आर्य चारुदत्त अस्ति भवतोऽस्या आर्याया दुहित्रा सह प्रसक्तिः प्रणयः प्रीतिर्वा ।

**चारुदत्तः**—कस्याः ।

**अधिकरणिकः**—अस्याः । (इति वसन्तसेनामातरं दर्शयति ।)

**चारुदत्तः**—(उत्थाय ।) आर्ये अभिवादये ।

**वृद्धा**—जात चिरं मे जीव । ( स्वगतम् । ) अयं स चारुदत्तः । सुनिक्षिप्तं खलु दारिकया यौवनम् । (जाद चिरं मे जीव । अअं सो चारुदत्तो । सुणिक्खितं क्खु दारिआए जोव्वणम् ।)

**अधिकरणिकः**—आर्य गणिका तव मित्रम् ।

(चारुदत्तो लज्जां नाटयति ।)

---

कथयति बन्धवधात्ययं च यातुः ' इति स्वभावोक्तिः । मालिनी वृत्तम् ]॥ १२ ॥ स्खलतीति । [ भूमौ न्यस्तं चरणं स्खलति । न च मही आर्दतमा अत्यन्तमार्द्रा । एतदपि अनिष्टसूचकम् । तदुक्तं वसन्तराजेन—'स्वपादयानस्खलनं नृपाणां भङ्गः क्वचिद्यानपलायनं च । द्वाराभिघाताध्वगशस्त्रपाताः प्रस्थानविघ्नं कथयन्ति यातुः ॥' इति । नयनं वाममित्यर्थात् । स्फुरति । वामो बाहुश्च मुहुः विकम्पते । अयमपरः पूर्वोक्तादन्यः गृध्रादिः शकुनिः तावदनेकशः वारं वारं विरौति विकटं शब्दायते । एतत्सर्वं महाघोरं मृत्युं कथयति । अत्र विचारणा न च । हरिणी वृत्तम् ]॥ १३ ॥ चिन्तासक्तेति । चिन्तामार्गे [ चिन्तायां कार्यार्थपर्यालोचने आसक्ताः ] निमग्नाश्च मन्त्रिणः एव सलिलानि यत्र । दूत आह्वायको गतागतनियुक्तो वीरश्च गूहपुरुषः । [दूता एव ऊर्मयः शङ्खाश्च । यद्वा ऊर्म्यूढाः शङ्खाः तैः आकुलम् ' चाराः प्रणिधय एव नक्रा मकराश्च यत्र । नागा गजाश्च अश्वाश्च नामाश्वा ते एव हिंस्राः तेषा-

CHAR.—My greetings to the Judges ! Well, assessors, how do you do ?

THE J.—( *Hurriedly* ). Welcome to you, noble sir ! Sodhanaka, my good man, bring a seat for the noble one.

SO.—( *Bringing a seat* ). Here's a seat. Please, sir, be seated on it.

( Charudatta *sits* )

SAK.—(*Angrily*). Oh ! You have come, have you, you woman-killer ! Oh, how very fair, how very righteous, is this legal procedure, that a seat should be offered to this woman-killer ! ( *Haughtily* ). Never mind ; let him have it.

THE J.—Sir Charudatta, have you any close acquaintance with, or affection, or love, for the daughter of this worthy lady ?

CHAR.—Of what lady ?

THE J.—Of this one, here. ( *Points out the mother of* Vasantasena ).

CHAR.—( *Rising* ). Madam, I bow to you !

THE OLD LADY—May you live long, my son ! ( *To herself* ) Here's that Charudatta ! Verily my daughter has most fittingly bestowed her youth !

THE J.—Sir, the courtesan is your friend ?

( Charudatta *betrays shame* ).

---

माश्रयमावासभूतम् । नागानां पादतलेन वध्यविनाशार्थं अश्वानां च झटिति संदेशहरणाद्यर्थं तत्र स्थापितत्वात् हिंस्रसाम्यम् । ] नाना बहुप्रकाराः [ ये वाश्यन्ते इति वाशकाः अनेकधा शब्दायमाना अर्थिप्रत्यर्थिजनाः ते एव ] शब्दं कुर्वन्तो ये कङ्कःपक्षिणस्तै रचितं [ निचितं ] व्याप्तम् । पर्यन्तेषु स्थिताः अशुभसूचकत्वेन तेषां समवधानमुक्तम् । अब्धिपक्षे तु व्यक्तमेव । 'पक्ष' इति पाठे तेषां पक्षाणां रचितम् । नानाक्रमणिकया निर्मितभेदो यत्रेत्यर्थः । कङ्को मांसादः पक्षिविशेषः । [ कायस्थाः एव सर्पाः तेषां स्वभावकौटिल्यादसूयापरत्वात् प्राणहरराजशासनलेखनाद्वा सर्पसाम्यम् । तेषामास्पदं स्थानम् । नीतिभिः नदीभिरिव क्षुण्णतटम् । एवंविधं राज्ञः करणं न्यायाधिकरणं समुद्रायते । समुद्रवद् दुष्प्रवेश्यमित्यर्थः । 'कर्तुः क्यङ्—' इत्यनेन क्यङ । रूपकोपमयोः संकरः । शार्दूलविक्रीडितं वृत्तम् ] ॥ १४ ॥ **सव्यमिति** । [ अस्मासु दैवतः भागधेयादेव स्वस्ति अस्तु ] ॥ १५ ॥ **घोणेति** । घोणा उन्नता यत्र घोणया वा उन्नतमुत्कृष्टम् । अपाङ्गो विशालो यत्र । [ तादृशे नेत्रे यस्य । यद्वा अपाङ्गयोः विशाले नेत्रे यस्य तत् । ] एतेन नेत्रविशालत्वमुक्तम् ।

**शकारः**—

> **लज्जया भीरुतया वा चारित्रमलीकं निगूहितुम् ।**
> **स्वयं मारयित्वाऽर्थकारणादिदानीं गूहति न तद्धि भट्टकः ॥ १७ ॥**
> (लज्जाए भीलुदाए वा चालित्तं अलिए णिगूहिदुम् ।
> शअं मालिअ अत्थकालणा दाणिं गुहदि ण तं हि भश्टके ॥)

**श्रेष्ठिकायस्थौ**—आर्य चारुदत्त भण । अलं लज्जया । व्यवहारः खल्वेषः । (अज्ज चारुदत्त भणाहि । अलं लज्जाए । ववहारो क्खु एसो ।)

**चारुदत्तः**—(सलज्जम् ।) भो अधिकृताः मया कथमीदृशं वक्तव्यं यथा गणिका मम मित्रमिति । अथ वा यौवनमत्रापराध्यति न चारित्र्यम्[1] ।

**अधिकरणिकः**—

> **व्यवहारः सविघ्नोऽयं त्यज्ज लज्जां हृदि स्थिताम् ।**
> **ब्रूहि सत्यमलं धैर्यं छलमत्र न गृह्यते ॥ १८ ॥**

अलं लज्जया । व्यवहारस्त्वां पृच्छति ।

**चारुदत्तः**—अधिकृत[2] केन सह मम व्यवहारः ।

**शकारः**—(साटोपम् ।) अरे मया सह व्यवहारः । (अले मए शह ववहाले ।)

**चारुदत्तः**—त्वया सह मम व्यवहारः सुदुःसहः ।

**शकारः**— अरे स्त्रीघातक तां तादृशीं रत्नशतभूषणां वसन्तसेनां मारयित्वा सांप्रतं कपटकापटिको भूत्वा निगूहसि । (अले इश्थिआघादआ तं तादिशिं लअणशदभूशणिअं वशन्तशेणिअं मालिअ शंपदं कवडकावडिके भविअ णिगूहेशि ।)

---

[एवंविधमेतन्मुखमकारणदूषणानां अकारणेन हठेन दूरणानां भाजनं न भवति हि । यतः नागेषु गोषु तुरगेषु तथा नरेषु आकृतिः रम्याकारः सुसदृशं आकारसदृशं रमणीयं वृत्तं न विजहाति त्यजति । सुरूपाकृतिर्गुणविसंवादिनी न भवतीति भावः । वसन्ततिलकं वृत्तम् ] ॥ १६ ॥ प्रसक्तिः [ संङ्गः संपर्को वा ] प्रणयो रागानुबन्धः प्रीतिः स्नेहमात्रम् । **लज्जयेत्यादि** । वैतालीयम् । एइं इति सबिन्दुविकारो लघुः छन्दोनुरोधात् । लज्जया भीरुकतया च लक्षितः । त्वमित्यर्थात् । **कुत** एवमित्याह स्वयं मारयित्वाऽर्थनिमित्तमिदानीं गृह्णाति न नष्टके । अपि तु नष्ट एव । 'नष्टके' इत्यपि पाठः । [ अर्थकारणात् स्वयं वसन्तसेनां मारयित्वा लज्जया भीरुतया वा अलीकं चरित्रं निगूहितुं यतसे इति शेषः । किं तु भट्टकः राजा पालकः अधिकरणिको वा तन्न गूहति हि । 'अलीको निगूहतु' इति पाठः साधीयान् ] ॥ १७ ॥ **व्यवहार इति** । [ अयं व्यवहारः सविघ्नः । हृदि स्थितां लज्जां त्यज । सत्यं ब्रूहि । **धैर्य-**

---

१ चारित्रम्. २ अधिकृताः.

SAK.—

Having himself killed her for her money, he is ( now ) trying to conceal his wicked deed either in shame or out of cowardice. But surely, the king won't conceal it ( will bring it to light ). (17)

SR & K.—Noble Charudatta, you may speak out; don't be ashamed. This is simply the legal procedure.

CHAR.—( *In shame* ). Ye officials, how should I utter such a thing, *viz.* that a courtesan is my friend ? Or rather, herein it is youth that is at fault, and not my character.

THE J.—

So leave off all the shame you feel in your mind. Tell the truth : enough of delaying ( *or*, have courage enough to tell the truth ). An equivocal statement would not be accepted here. (18)

Don't be ashamed. It is the law-suit that is putting you the question.

CHAR.—Your Honour, with whom does my law suit lie ?

SAN.—( *Arrogantly* ). Ah you, your suit is with *me* !

CHAR.—A law-suit with you would be extremely unbearable ( detrimental ) to me.

SAK.—Ah, you woman-killer, having killed that Vasantasena so beautiful and adorned with hundreds of jewels, you now turn a deceitful rogue and hide it ?

---

मलं विलम्बो माऽस्तु इत्यर्थः। यद्वा धैर्यं अलं सत्यकथनायेति शेषः। अस्तु। ] छलपरिहारार्थं चिरं समीक्ष्यत इत्याशङ्क्याह—छलमत्र नेति। [ यद्वा अत्र अस्मिन् व्यवहारे छलमाकारगोपनादिकं न गृह्यते स्वीक्रियते ] ॥ १८ ॥ अभ्युक्षित इति। [ चाषस्य पक्षिविशेषस्य अग्रपक्षः पक्षाग्रं तत्सदृशं यथा तथा अन्तराले आकाशे वचनमध्ये च बलाहकानां मेघानां सलिलैः न अभ्युक्षितोऽसि। एतद्भवतो वचनं मिथ्या। तथा हि। इदं भवतः आननं हेमन्तपद्ममिव निष्प्रभतामुपैति। वसन्ततिलकं वृत्तम् ] ॥ १९ ॥ तुलनमिति। चारुदत्तस्य दूषणमद्रिराजस्य तुलनमिव। अन्त्यताशक्यमित्यर्थः। एवमन्यत्र ॥ २० ॥ वेदार्थानित्यादि। अतिधृतिजातिः। [ त्वं प्राकृतः नीचः अपकृष्टवर्ण इत्यर्थः। वेदार्थान् वदसि। न च ते जिह्वा निपतिता। ] वेदार्थविरोधिनो वचने जिह्वापातो युज्यते। [ विचलिता स्थानाद्भ्रष्टा प्रतिहता वा। चारित्र्याच्चारुदत्तं चलयसि प्रच्यावयसि। भूः ते देहं न हरति च। चित्रमेतदित्यर्थः। विशेषोक्तिप्रतिवस्तूपमालंकारौ। सुमधुरा वृत्तम् ]॥ २१ ॥ कृत्वेति। [ येन समुद्रं उदकोच्छ्रय उदकस्योन्नतिराधिक्यमिति यावत्। तन्मात्रावशेषं कृत्वा।

**चारुदत्तः**—असंबद्धः खल्वसि ।

**अधिकरणिकः**—आर्य चारुदत्त अलमनेन । ब्रूहि सत्यम् । अपि गणिका तव मित्रम् ।

**चारुदत्तः**—एवमेव ।

**अधिकरणिकः**—आर्य वसन्तसेना क्व ।

**चारुदत्तः**—गृहं गता ।

**श्रेष्ठिकायस्थौ**—कथं गता कदा गता गच्छन्ती वा केनानुगता ? (कधं गदा कदा गदा गच्छन्ती वा केण अणुगदा ।)

**चारुदत्तः**—(स्वगतम् ।) किं प्रच्छन्नं गतेति ब्रवीमि ।

**श्रेष्ठिकायस्थौ**—आर्य कथय । (अज्ज कधेहि ।)

**चारुदत्तः**—गृहं गता । किमन्यद्ब्रवीमि ।

**शकारः**—मदीयं पुष्पकरण्डकजीर्णोद्यानं प्रवेश्यार्थनिमित्तं बाहुपाशबलात्कारेण मारिता । अये सांप्रतं वदसि गृहं गतेति । ( ममकेलकं पुप्फकलण्डकजिण्णुज्जाणं पवेशिअ अत्थणिमित्तं बाहुपाशबलक्कालेण मालिदा । अये शंपदं वदशि घलं गदे त्ति ।)

**चारुदत्तः**—आः असंबद्धप्रलापिन् ।

अभ्युक्षितोऽसि सलिलैर्न बलाहकानां
चाषाग्रपक्षसदृशं भृशमन्तराले ।
मिथ्यैतदाननमिदं भवतस्तथा हि
हेमन्तपद्ममिव निष्प्रभतामुपैति ॥ १९ ॥

**अधिकरणिकः**—( जनान्तिकम् । )

तुलनं चाद्रिराजस्य समुद्रस्य च तारणम् ।
ग्रहणं चानिलस्येव[1] चारुदत्तस्य दूषणम् ॥ २० ॥

( प्रकाशम् । ) आर्यचारुदत्तः खल्वसौ कथमिदमकार्यं[2] करिष्यति । ( 'घोणा— ( ९।१६ ) इत्यादि पठति ।)

**शकारः**—किं पक्षपातेन व्यवहारो दृश्यते । ( किं पक्खवादेण ववहाले दीशदि । )

---

उद्धृतरत्नत्वात् । अनपेक्षितानि दानशौण्डत्वान्मुक्तहस्तानि धनानि दत्तानि । स श्रेयसां एकनिधिः महात्मा धनार्थं अवीरजुष्टं कृपणसेवितं पापं कथं करिष्यति ? 'अवैरिजुष्टम्' इति पाठे वैरिभिरप्यसेवितमित्यर्थः । वसन्त० वृत्तम् ] ॥ २२ ॥

---

१ वाऽनिल०. २ कथमकार्यं.

CHAR.—You are surely talking nonsense!

THE J.—Noble Charudatta, never mind him. Tell us the truth. Is that courtesan your friend?

CHAR.—That's so.

THE J.—Well, where is Vasantasena ( at present )?

CHAR.—She has gone home.

SR. & K.—How did she go? When did she go? And who accompanied her when she went?

CHAR.—( *To himself* ). What! Shall I say that she went unobserved?

SR. & K.—Sir tell it ( please ).

CHAR.—She went home. What more should I tell?

SAK.—You enticed her to my old *Pushpakarandaka* garden and killed her for her money by forcibly strangling her with the noose of your arms. Ah, and now you say that she went home?

CHAR.—Ah, you, talker of nonsense!

You are not thoroughly wetted by the waters of the clouds in the sky, like the tips of the wings of a *chasha* bird, ( and still your face is darkened, without any cause ). What you asssert is false. For, this face of yours loses its lust like the lotus in winter. ( 19 )

THE J.—( *Aside; to the* assessors )

Imputing a crime to Charudatta is like weighing the Himalaya mountain, or like crossing the ocean ( by swimming ), or like capturing the wind. (20)

( *Aloud* ). He is, indeed the 'noble' Charudatta! How would he do this evil deed? ( *Repeats the verse beginning* 'A face having a prominent nose' &c. ).

SAK.—What! Are you investigating this case with ( such ) partiality?

---

पादेत्यादि । गाथा । पादप्रहारेण परिभव आक्रमः स एव विमानना तया बद्धगुरुकवैरस्य । अनुशोचमानस्येयं कथमपि रात्रिः प्रभाताऽपगता मम ॥ २३ ॥ एष इति । [ भो इति खेदे । एष निर्मला ज्योत्स्ना यस्य स निर्मलज्योत्स्नः शशी । निर्दोषश्चारुदत्त इत्यर्थः । कलुषायते आविलं भवति । अपवादेन दुष्यति इत्यर्थः । रूपकातिशयोक्तिः ] ॥ २४ ॥ यथेति । [ इदं चारुदत्तवृत्तं यथा यथा निपुणं

अधिकरणिकः—अपेहि[1] मूर्ख ।

वेदार्थान्प्राकृतस्त्वं वदसि न च ते जिह्वा निपतिता[2]
मध्याह्ने वीक्षसेऽर्कं[3] न तव सहसा दृष्टिर्विचलिता ।
दीप्ताग्नौ पाणिमन्तः क्षिपसि स[4] च ते दग्धो भवति नो
चारित्र्याच्चारुदत्तं चलयसि[5] न ते देहं हरति भूः ॥ २१ ॥

आर्यचारुदत्तः कथमकार्यं[6] करिष्यति ।

कृत्वा समुद्रमुदकोच्छ्रयमात्रशेषं
दत्तानि येन हि धनान्यनपेक्षितानि ।
स श्रेयसां कथमिवैकनिधिर्महात्मा
पापं करिष्यति धनार्थमवीरजुष्टम्[7] ॥ २२ ॥

वृद्धा[8]—हताश यस्तदानीं न्यासीकृतं सुवर्णभाण्डं रात्रौ चौरैपहृतमिति तस्य कारणाच्चतुःसमुद्रसारभूतां रत्नावलीं ददाति स इदानीमर्थकल्यवर्तस्य कारणादिदमकार्यं करोति । हा जाते एहि मे पुत्रि । ( इति रोदिति । ) ( हदास जो तदाणिं णासीकिदं सुवण्णभण्डअं रत्ति चोरेहिं अवहिदं त्ति तस्स कारणादो चदुस्समुद्दसारभूदं रअणावलिं देदि सो दाणिं अत्थकल्लवत्तस्स[9] कारणादो इमं अकज्जं करेदि । हा जादे एहि मे पुत्ति ।)

अधिकरणिकः—आर्य चारुदत्त किमसौ पद्भ्यां गता उत प्रवहणेनेति ।

चारुदत्तः—ननु मम प्रत्यक्षं न गता । तन्न जाने किं पद्भ्यां गता उत प्रवहणेनेति ।

( प्रविश्य सामर्षः । )

वीरकः—

पादप्रहारपरिभवविमाननाबद्धगुरुकवैरस्य ।
अनुशोचत इयं कथमपि रात्रिः प्रभाता मे ॥ २३ ॥

तद्यावदधिकरणमण्डपमुपसर्पामि । (प्रवेष्टकेन ।) सुखमार्यमिश्राणाम् ।

(पादप्पहारपरिभवविमाणणाबद्धगरुअवेरस्स[10] ।
अणुसोअन्तस्स इयं कधं पि रत्ती पभादा मे ॥

ता जाव अधिअरणमण्डवं उवसप्पामि । सुहं अज्जमिस्साणम् ।)

अधिकरणिकः—अये नगररक्षाधिकृतो वीरकः । वीरक किमागमनप्रयोजनम् ।

---

१ अवेहि. २ निपतति. ३ सेऽर्के. ४ न च ते तत्क्षणं दह्यतेऽसौ. ५ छलयसि. ६ कथमयम०. ७ ०मवैरि०. ८ अस्मात्प्राक्–शकारः–किं पक्खवादेण ववहालो दीशदि. ९ अत्थकारणादो. १० लद्ध (लब्ध).

THE J.—Begone, you fool!

You, a low cast fellow, are explaing the sense of the Vedas, and (yet) your tongue does not fall off! You are gazing at the sun at mid-day, and (still) your eyes are not suddenly struck blind! You are putting your hand inside the blazing fire, and (yet) that hand of yours is not burnt! You are depriving Charudatta of his good name, and (still) the Earth does not (yawn and) gulp down your body! (21)

How can the noble Charudatta do an evil deed?

He who left only the mass of waters in the ocean (which was the repository of jewels), and gave away undreamt quantities of money,—how can that high-souled person, the unique abode of all noble qualities, commit, for the sake of money, a crime that is committed only by mean persons? (22)

THE OLD L.—You wretch! He who, on that occasion, gave a jewel-necklace, the essence (as it were) of the four oceans, in return for the golden ornaments deposited with him because they were stolen at night by thieves,—would he now commit this evil deed for the sake of filthy lucre? oh, my daughter! Come (to me), my daughter! (*weeps*).

THE J.—Worthy Charudatta, did she go walking or in a carriage?

CHAR.—Well, she did not leave in my presence. So I do not know whether she went walking or in a carriage.

(*Entering enraged*)

VIRAKA—

Nursing a bitter hatred (towards Chandanaka) for humiliating me with the insult of striking me with foot, as I lay (awake) brooding over it all this night, it has somehow dawned. (23)

So, then, let me just repair to the law court. (*Entering*) Good day, gentlemen!

THE J.—Ah, (here's) Viraka, the officer appointed to keep guard over the city. Well, Viraka, what brings you here?

---

सूक्ष्मतया विचार्यते विमृश्यते तथा तथा संकटमकुशलपरिणामि एव दृश्यते। अहो व्यवहारनीतयः व्यवहारन्यायाः सुसन्नाः सुसंहताः।] सुसन्ना व्यवहारनीतय इति सामान्यविशेषभावेन विशेषणम्। [मे मतिस्तु पङ्कगता गौः इव सीदति। न तु उत्थातुं शक्नोति। निर्दोषमपि चारुदत्तं मोक्तुं न शक्नोतीत्यर्थः। वंशस्थं वृत्तम्]

वीरकः—ही ही बन्धनभेदनसंभ्रम आर्यकमन्वेषयन् अपवारितं प्रवहणं व्रजतीति विचारं कुर्वन्नन्वेषयन् अरे त्वयाऽप्यालोकितं मयाऽप्यालोकितव्यमिति भणन्नेव चन्दनमहत्तरकेण पादेन ताडितोऽस्मि । एतच्छ्रुत्वाऽऽर्यमिश्राः प्रमाणम् । (ह्वी ह्वी बन्धणभेअणसंभमे अज्जकं अण्णेसन्तो ओवाडिदं पवहण वच्चदि त्ति विआरं करन्तो अण्णेसन्तो अरे तुए वि आलोइदे मए वि आलोइदव्वो त्ति भणन्तो ज्जेव्व चन्दणमहत्तरएण पादेण ताडिदो म्हि । एदं सुणिअ अज्जमिस्सा पमाणम् ।)

अधिकरणिकः—भद्र जानीषे कस्य तत्प्रवहणमिति ।

वीरकः—अस्यार्यचारुदत्तस्य । वसन्तसेनाऽऽरूढा पुष्पकरण्डकजीर्णोद्यानं क्रीडितुं नीयत इति प्रवहणवाहकेन कथितम् । (इमस्स अज्जचारुदत्तस्स । वसन्तसेणा आरूढा पुप्फकरण्डकजिण्णुज्जाणं कीलिदुं णीअदि त्ति पवहणवाहएण कहिदम् ।)

शकारः—पुनरपि श्रुतमार्यैः । (पुणो वि शुदं अज्जेहिं[1] ।)

अधिकरणिकः—

एष भो निर्मलज्योत्स्नो राहुणा ग्रस्यते शशी ।
जलं कूलावपातेन प्रसन्नं कलुषायते ॥ २४ ॥

वीरक पश्चादिह भवतो न्यायं द्रक्ष्यामः । य एषोऽधिकरणद्वार्यश्वस्तिष्ठति तमेनमारुह्य गत्वा पुष्पकरण्डकोद्यानं दृश्यतामस्ति तत्र काचिद्विपन्ना[2] स्त्री न वेति ।

वीरकः—यदार्य आज्ञापयति । ( इति निष्क्रान्तः । प्रविश्य च । ) गतोऽस्मि तत्र । दृष्टं च मया स्त्रीकलेवरं श्वापदैर्विलुप्यमानम् । ( जं अज्जो आणवेदि । गदो म्हि तहिं । दिट्ठं च मए इत्थिआकलेवरं सावदेहिं विलुप्पन्तम् ।)

श्रेष्ठिकायस्थौ—कथं त्वया ज्ञातं स्त्रीकलेवरमिति । ( कधं तुए जाणिदं इत्थिआकलेवरं त्ति । )

वीरकः—सावशेषैः केशहस्तपाणिपादैरुपलक्षितं मया । (सावसेसेहिं केसहत्थपाणिपादेहिं उवलक्खिदं मए ।)

अधिकरणिकः—अहो विग्वैषम्यं लोकव्यवहारस्य ।

यथा यथेदं निपुणं विचार्यते तथा तथा संकटमेव दृश्यते ।
अहो सुसन्ना व्यवहारनीतयो मतिस्तु गौः पङ्कगतेव सीदति ॥ २५ ॥

चारुदत्तः—(स्वगतम् ।)

यथैव पुष्पं प्रथमे विकाशे समेत्य पातुं मधुपाः पतन्ति ।
एवं मनुष्यस्य विपत्तिकाले छिद्रेष्वनर्था बहुलीभवन्ति ॥ २६ ॥

अधिकरणिकः—आर्यचारुदत्त सत्यमभिधीयताम् ।

---

१ अज्जमिश्शेहिं. २ काचित्स्त्री विपन्ना.

VIR.—Oh! Oh! While I was hunting for Aryaka in the tumult following his escape from prison, I grew suspicious about a closed carriage that was passing along, and was going to search it; but then, just as I said—'Oh, although you have inspected (the carriage) I too wish to inspect it,' I was kicked by captain Chandanaka. Having heard this, may your honours decide (what to do).

THE J.—Well, my good man, do you know to whom that carriage belonged?

VIR.—To this gentleman, the worthy Charudatta. (And) the carriage-driver said that Vasantsena was inside, and that she was being taken to the old garden *Pushpakarandaka* for sporting (with him).

SAK.—You have (now) once more heard it (the same story), gentlemen!

THE J.—

Alas, here is the moon, shedding a pure light, being eclipsed by Rahu! The clear water is being rendered muddy by the falling in of the banks! (24)

Viraka, we'll look into this complaint of yours afterwards. (For the present) just mount this horse which is standing outside near the entrance to the court, and go to the *Pushpakarandaka* garden and see if there is any woman lying dead there, or not.

VIR.—As Your Honour orders. (*Exit. Then entering again*). I have just been there. Well, I *did* see a woman's corpse that the jackals (*lit.* beasts) were eating up.

SR. & K.—How did you know that it was a woman's corpse?

VIR.—I found it out by the remains (portions) of the hair, arms, hands and legs (that were uneaten).

THE J.—Oh, fie upon the intricacy of wordly transactions! (*Or*, how difficult is the investigation of law-suits!)

The more carefully is the (case) looked into, the darker it appears. Alas! The points of law (proof) are very clear (*lit.* well-connected); but my judgment finds it difficult to proceed (*lit.* sinks), like a cow in a quagmire. (25)

CHAR.—(*To himself*).

Just as, at its first blooming the bees come in swarm to a flower to suck its honey, so, in times of calamity, a man's troubles multiply when there are weak points. (26)

THE J.—Noble Charudatta, tell the truth.

**चारुदत्तः**—

दुष्टात्मा परगुणमत्सरी मनुष्यो
रागान्धः परमिह हन्तुकामबुद्धिः ।
किं यो यद्वदति मृषैव जातिदोषा-
त्तद्ग्राह्यं भवति न तद्विचारणीयम् ॥ २७ ॥

अपि च ।

योऽहं लतां कुसुमितामपि पुष्पहेतो-
राकृष्य नैव कुसुमावचयं करोमि ।
सोऽहं कथं भ्रमरपक्षरुचौ सुदीर्घे
केशे प्रगृह्य[1] रुदतीं प्रमदां निहन्मि ॥ २८ ॥

**शकारः**—हंहो अधिकरणभोजकाः किं यूयं पक्षपातेन व्यवहारं पश्यत येनाद्याप्येष हताशचारुदत्त आसने धार्यते । ( हंहो अधिअलणभोइआ किं तुम्हे पक्खवादेण ववहालं पेक्खध ज्जेण अज्ज वि एशे हदाशचालुदत्ते आशणे धालीअदि ।)

**अधिकरणिकः**—भद्र शोधनक एवं क्रियताम् ।

(शोधनकस्तथा करोति ।)

**चारुदत्तः**—विचार्यताम् । भो अधिकृताः[2] विचार्यताम् । (इत्यासनादवतीर्य भूमावुपविशति ।)

**शकारः**—(स्वगतम् । सहर्षं नर्तित्वा ।) ही अनेन मया कृतं पापमन्यस्य मस्तके निपतितम् । तद्यत्र चारुदत्त उपविशति तत्राहमुपविशामि । (तथा कृत्वा ।) चारुदत्त पश्य पश्य माम् । तद्भण भण मया मारितेति । (ही अणेण मए कडे पावे अण्णश्श मश्तके णिवडिदे । ता जहिं चालुदत्ताके[3] उवविशदि तहिं हग्गे उवविशामि । चालुदत्ता पेक्ख पेक्ख मम् । ता भण भण मए मालेदि त्ति ।)

**चारुदत्तः**—भो अधिकृताः । ('दुष्टात्मा–' (९।२७) इति पूर्वोक्तं पठति । सनिःश्वासम् स्वगतम् ।)

मैत्रेय भोः किमिदमद्य ममोपघातो
हा ब्राह्मणि[4] द्विजकुले विमले प्रसूता ।
हा रोहसेन न हि पश्यसि मे विपत्तिं
मिथ्यैव नन्दसि [5]परव्यसनेन नित्यम् ॥ २९ ॥

प्रेषितश्च मया तद्वार्तान्वेषणाय मैत्रेयो वसन्तसेनासकाशं शकटिकानिमित्तं च तस्य प्रदत्तान्यलंकरणानि प्रत्यर्पयितुम् । तत्कथं चिरयते ।

---

१ विगृह्य. २ अधिकृते. ३ चालुदत्ते. ४ ब्राह्मणी निजकुले. ५ परिव्यस०.

CHAR.—

Whatever a person, who is evil-souled, jealous of another's virtues, blinded by passion, and desirous of ruining another, tells falsely here ( *i. e.*, in the law-court ), through the evil bent of his very nature,—is all that to be accepted ( as true ) ? Is it not to be investigated ?* (27)

Moreover :—

I, who do not even bend down a flowering creeper for plucking its blossoms, and never gather its flowers thus,—how could that I ever kill a weeping woman, seizing her by her long tresses having the ( dark ) shine of bees' wings ? (28)

SAK.—You judges, do you conduct your proceedings with partiality, that you allow this wretch, Charudatta, to occupy a seat even now ?

THE J.—Sodhanaka, my good man, do as he says.

( Sodhanaka *does accordingly* )

CHAR.—Consider, O judges, consider ( what you are doing ! ) ( *He then leaves his seat and sits on the bare ground* ).

SAK.—( *To himself. Dancing in joy* ). Heigh-ho ! By this the sinful deed done by me has fallen on another's head ! So I'll sit where Charudatta sat. ( *Does so* ). Charudatta, look, look at me ! Say, then, say that you killed her !

CHAR.—Sirs, judges ! ( *Repeats what he had said before, viz.* ' Whatever a person who is evil-souled ', &c. *Then heaving a sigh ; to himself* ).

O Maitreya, what is this ( going on ) ? It will end to-day in my destruction ! O my wife, born in a spotless Brahmana family ! O Rohasena ! you do not certainly see my calamity ! You are ever cheerful, calamities being far aff ( from us ); but it is in vain ( that you do so ). (29)

I have sent Maitreya to get news of Rohasena, and also to Vasantasena, to return to her the ornaments given by her to him for ( making ) a golden toy-cart ( out of them ). But why is he late ?

* Or, that should not be accepted as true ; it should be considered.

(ततः प्रविशति गृहीताभरणो विदूषकः ।)

**विदूषकः**–प्रेषितोऽस्म्यार्यचारुदत्तेन वसन्तसेनासकाशं तत्रालंकरणानि गृहीत्वा यथा—आर्य मैत्रेय वसन्तसेनया वत्सो रोहसेन आत्मनोलंकारेणालंकृत्य जननी-सकाशं प्रेषितः । अस्या आभरणं दातव्यं न पुनर्ग्रहीतव्यम् । तत्समर्पयेति । तद्यावद्वसन्तसेनासकाशमेव गच्छामि । ( परिक्रम्य अवलोक्य च । आकाशे । ) कथं भावरेभिलः । भो भावरेभिल किंनिमित्तं त्वमुद्विग्न उद्विग्न इव लक्ष्यसे । (आकर्ण्य ।) किं भणसि—प्रियवयस्यश्चारुदत्तोऽधिकरणमण्डप आहूत इति । तन्न खल्वल्पेन कार्येण भवितव्यम् । (विचिन्त्य ।) तत्पश्चाद्वसन्तसेनासकाशं गमिष्यामि । अधि-करणमण्डपं तावद्गमिष्यामि । ( परिक्रम्यावलोक्य च । ) अयमधिकरणमण्डपः । तद्यावत्प्रविशामि । (प्रविश्य ।) सुखमधिकरणभोजकानाम् । कुत्र मम प्रियवयस्यः । (पेसिदोम्हि अज्जचारुदत्तेण वसन्तसेणासआसं तहिं अलंकरणाइं गेण्हिअ जधा-अज्ज मित्तेअ वसन्तसेणाए वच्छो रोहसेणो अत्तणो अलंकारेण अलंकरिअ जणणीसआसं पेसिदो । इमस्स आहरणं दादव्वं ण उण गेण्हिदव्वम् । ता समप्पेहि त्ति । ता जाव वसन्तसेणासआसं ज्जेव्व गच्छामि । कधं भावरेभिलो । भो भावरेभिल किंणिमित्तं तुमं उव्विग्गो उव्विग्गो विअ लक्खीअसि । किं भणासि—पिअवअस्सो चारुदत्तो अधि-अरणमण्डवे सद्दाइदो त्ति । ता ण हु अप्पेण कज्जेण होदव्वम् । ता पच्छा वसन्त-सेणासआसं[१] गमिस्सम् । अधिअरणमण्डवं दाव गमिस्सम् । इदं अधिअरणमण्डवम् । ता जाव पविसामि । सुहं अधिअरणभोइआणम् । कहिं मम पिअवअस्सो ।)

**अधिकरणिकः**—नन्वेष तिष्ठति ।

**विदूषकः**—वयस्य स्वस्ति ते । (वअस्स सोत्थि दे ।)

**चारुदत्तः**—भविष्यति ।

**विदूषकः**—अपि क्षेमं ते । (अवि क्खेमं दे ।)

**चारुदत्तः**—एतदपि भविष्यति ।

**विदूषकः**—भो वयस्य किंनिमित्तमुद्विग्न उद्विग्न इव लक्ष्यसे । कुतो वाऽऽहूतः । (भो वअस्स किंणिमित्तं [२]उव्विग्गो उव्विग्गो विअ लक्खीअसि । कुदो वा सद्दाइदो ।)

**चारुदत्तः**—वयस्य ।

**मया खलु नृशंसेन परलोकमजानता ।**
**स्त्री रतिर्वाऽविशेषेण[३] शेषमेषोऽभिधास्यति ॥ ३० ॥**

**विदूषकः**—किं किम् । (किं किम् ।)

**चारुदत्तः**—(कर्णे ।) एवमेवम्[४] ।

---

१ गेहं. २ उण उव्वि०ः. ३ रतिश्चावि०. ४ एवमिति.

( *Then enter* Vidushaka, *carrying the ornaments* ).

VID.—The worthy Charudatta has sent me to Vasantasena, to go to her place, with the ornaments, saying—" Worthy Maitreya, Vasantasena sent dear Rohasena to his mother, after adorning him with her own ornaments. It was all right for her to give those ornaments, but not ( for us ) to accept them. So please return them ( to her )." So, then, I'll just go to Vasantasena. ( *Walking about and observing* ; *in the Void* ). How ! Here is friend Rebhila ! Ho, sir Rebhila, why do you look as if you were exceedingly distressed ? ( *Listening* ). What do you say ?—that my dear friend Charudatta has been summoned to ( appear in ) the law-court ? Ah, then, surely, it could not have been on any ordinary business ! ( *Pondering* ). Well, I'll go to Vasantasena afterwards. Let me first proceed to the law-court. ( *Walking about and looking on* ). Here is the court of justice; let me then enter it. ( *Entering* ). Hail to you, judges ! Where is my dear friend ?

THE J.—Here he is !

VID.—Friend, happiness to you !

CHAR.—That will be.

VID.—( Why ), I hope you are all right ?

CHAR.—That, too, will be.

VID.—O friend, why are you looking as if you were extremely distressed ? And why have you been summoned here ?

CHAR.—Friend,

Verily, by me, who am cruel and ignorant of (the existence of) the next world, a woman,—or rather, Rati herself, without any distinction,......The rest this person will tell. (30)

VID.—What, what is it ?

CHAR.—( *Whispering in his ear* ). Thus; like this.

---

॥ २५ ॥ **यथैवेति** । [ यथा एव प्रथमे विकासे विकासारम्भे एव पुष्पं लक्षणया तन्मकरन्दं पातुं मधुपाः भ्रमराः समेत्य संघातं कृत्वा पतन्ति । एवं मनुष्यस्य विपत्तिकाले छिद्रेषु सत्सु अनर्था बहुलीभवन्ति विपुला भवन्ति । उपमाऽप्रस्तुतप्रशंसालंकारौ । उपजातिर्वृत्तम् ॥ २६ ॥ **दुष्टेति** । [ इहास्मिन्नधिकरणे यः नरः दुष्टात्मा परगुणेषु मत्सरोऽस्यास्तीति मत्सर्यमर्षणः रागान्धः परं हन्तुकामबुद्धिः जातिदोषात् हीनजातित्वात् मृषैव यद्वदति तत् किं ग्राह्यं भवति । नैवेत्यर्थः । तत्

**विदूषकः**—क एवं भणति। (को एव्वं भणादि।)

**चारुदत्तः**—(संज्ञया शकारं दर्शयति[१]।) नन्वेष तपस्वी हेतुभूतः कृतान्तो मां व्याहरति।

**विदूषकः**—(जनान्तिकम्।) एवं किमर्थं न भण्यते गृहं गतेति। (एव्वं कीस ण भणीअदि गेहं गदे त्ति।)

**चारुदत्तः**—उच्यमानमप्यवस्थादोषान्न गृह्यते।

**विदूषकः**—भो भो आर्या येन तावत्पुरस्थापनविहारारामदेवालयतडागकूपयूपैरलंकृता नगर्युज्जयिनी सोऽनीशोऽर्थकल्यवर्तकारणादीदृशमकार्यमनुतिष्ठतीति। (सक्रोधम्।) अरे रे कुलटापुत्र राजश्यालसंस्थानक उच्छृङ्खलक कृतजनदोषभण्ड बहुसुवर्णमण्डितमर्कटक भण भण ममाग्रतः। य इदानीं मम प्रियवयस्यः कुसुमितां माधवीलतामप्याकृष्य कुसुमावचयं न करोति कदाचिदाकृष्टतया पल्लवच्छेदो भवतीति स कथमीदृशमकार्यमुभयलोकविरुद्धं करोति। तिष्ठ रे कुट्टनीपुत्र तिष्ठ। यावदेतेन तव हृदयकुटिलेन दण्डकाष्ठेन मस्तकं ते शतखण्डं करोमि। (भो भो अज्जा जेण दाव पुरट्ठावणविहारारामदेउलतडागकूवजूवेहिं[२] अलंकिदा णअरी उज्जइणी सो अणीसो अत्थकल्लवत्तकारणादो एरिसं अकज्जं अणुचिट्ठदि त्ति। अरे रे काणेलीसुदा राअश्शालसंठाणआ [३]उस्सुङ्खलआ किदजणदोसभण्डआ बहुसुवण्णमण्डिदमक्कडआ भण भण मम अग्गदो। जो दाणिं मम पिअवअस्सो कुसुमिदं माधवीलदं पि आकिट्ठिअ[४] कुसुमावचअं ण करेदि कदा वि आकिट्ठिदाए पल्लवच्छेदो भोदि त्ति सो कधं एरिसं अकज्जं उहअलोअविरुद्धं करेदि। चिट्ठ रे कुट्टणिपुत्ता चिट्ठ। जाव एदिणा तव हिअअकुडिलेण दण्डअट्ठेण मत्थअं दे सदखण्डं करेमि।)

**शकारः**—(सक्रोधम्।) श्रृण्वन्तु श्रृण्वन्त्वार्यमिश्राः। चारुदत्तेन सह मम विवादो व्यवहारो वा। तत्किमर्थमेष काकपदशीर्षमस्तको मम शिरः शतखण्डं करोति। मा तावत्। रे दास्याःपुत्र दुष्टबटुक। (शुणन्तु शुणन्तु अज्जमिश्शा। चालुदत्ताकेण शह मम विवादे ववहाले वा। ता कीश एशे काकपदशीशमश्तका मए शिले शदखण्डे कलेदि। मा दा। ले दाशीएपुत्ता दुट्टबडुका।)

(विदूषको दण्डकाष्ठमुद्यम्य पूर्वोक्तं पठति। शकारः सक्रोधमुत्थाय ताडयति। विदूषकः प्रतीपं ताडयति। अन्योन्यं ताडयतः। विदूषकस्य कक्षादेशादाभरणानि[५] पतन्ति।)

---

किं न विचारणीयम्। अपि तु सदसद्वेति विमर्शनीयमेव। प्रहर्षिणी वृत्तम्]॥ २७॥ **योऽहमिति**। [योऽहं कुसुमान्यस्याः संजातानि असौ कुसुमिता तां लतां पुष्पहेतोः आकृष्य इ०। सोऽहं भ्रमरपक्षयोरिव रुचिः कान्तिर्यस्य तस्मिन्भ्रमरवन्नीले केशे

---

१ निर्दिशति. २ देउलेहिं. ३ दुस्संकणआ (दुःशङ्कन). ४ आअंबिअ. ५ कक्षदे०.

VID.—Who says so ?

CHAR.—( *Points out* Sakara *by a sign* ). Why, this poor fellow, who has been the instrument of the god of Death says so of me !

VID.—( *Aside; to* Charudatta ). Why don't you tell them that she went home ?

CHAR.—Although told it is not believed in, owing to my poverty ( *lit.* the fault of my condition ).

VID.—O you gentlemen! He who adorned this city of Ujjayini by founding suburbs, and by means of monasteries, gardens, temples, tanks, wells, and sacrificial posts—would he, because he is poor, commit such an evil deed for the sake of filthy lucre ? ( *Wrathfully* ). Oh, you, a whore's son, royal brother-in-law, Samsthanaka, a lost libertine, you scoundrel imputing crimes to people, you monkey decked with numerous golden ornaments, say it in *my* presence ! This dear friend of mine, who does not even bend down the *madhavi* creeper in bloom and thereby gather flowers, for fear that perchance its leaves might get torn ( off the stalk ) when it is bent,—how could he commit such an evil deed, despicable in both the worlds ? Wait, you son of a bawd, just wait ! I will just break your head into a hundred pieces with this wooden staff, which is as crooked as your heart !

SAK.—( *Angrily* ). Listen, listen, ye gentlemen ! It is with Charudatta that I have a quarrel, or a suit. Why then should this crow-foot-pated fellow break my head into a hundred pieces ? You can't do it, you slave-born, knavish Brahmana !

( Vidushaka *raises his wooden staff and repeats what he had said before.* Sakara *gets up in anger, and beats him.* Vidushaka *beats* Sakara *in return. They both beat each other. The ornaments drop down from under* Vid's *arm-pit* ).

---

प्रगृह्य बलाद् गृहीत्वा रुदतीं प्राणत्राणार्थं क्रोशन्तीं प्रमदां कथं निहन्मि । न हन्यामेव । वसन्ततिलकं वृत्तम् ] ॥ २८ ॥ अथ मित्रभार्यापुत्रान् बुद्ध्युपस्थापितानुद्दिश्याह—मैत्रेयेति । [ भो मैत्रेय किमिदम् । अद्य ममोपघातः विनाशः प्राप्तः । हा इति खेदे । ब्राह्मणि त्वं विमले द्विजकुले प्रसूताऽसि । अतः तव पत्युरीदृशो विनाशस्तेऽनुचितः इति भावः । हा रोहसेन मे प्राणविपत्तिं न पश्यसि हि नैव जानासि । परं दूरम् । अज्ञातमिति यावत् । च तद् व्यसनं च तेन नित्यं नन्दसि किं तु तन्मिथ्यव । परेण श्रेष्ठेन व्यसनेन उपस्थितपितृघातरूपेणोपलक्षितस्त्वमिति

**शकारः**—(तानि गृहीत्वा दृष्ट्वा ससाध्वसम् ।) पश्यन्तु पश्यन्त्वार्याः । एते खलु तस्यास्तपस्विन्या अलंकाराः । ( चारुदत्तमुद्दिश्य । ) अस्यार्थकल्यवर्तस्य कारणादेषा मारिता व्यापादिता च । (पेक्खन्तु पेक्खन्तु अज्जा । एदे क्खु ताए तवश्शिणीएकेलका अलंकाला । इमश्श अत्थकल्लवत्तश्श कालणादो एशा मालिदा वावादिदा अ ।)

(अधिकृताः सर्वेऽधोमुखाः स्थिताः ।)

**चारुदत्तः**—( जनान्तिकम् । )

**अयमेवंविधे काले दृष्टो भूषणविस्तरः ।**
**अस्माकं भाग्यवैषम्यात्पतितः पातयिष्यति** ॥ ३१ ॥

**विदूषकः**—भोः किमर्थं भूतार्थो न निवेद्यते । ( भो कीस भूदत्थं ण णिवेदीअदि ।)

**चारुदत्तः**—वयस्य ।

**दुर्बलं नृपतेश्चक्षुर्नैतत्तत्त्वं निरीक्षते ।**
**केवलं वदतो दैन्यमश्लाघ्यं मरणं भवेत्** ॥ ३२ ॥

**अधिकरणिकः**—कष्टं भोः कष्टम् ।

**अङ्गारकविरुध्दस्य प्रक्षीणस्य बृहस्पतेः ।**
**ग्रहोऽयमपरः पार्श्वे धूमकेतुरिवोत्थितः** ॥ ३३ ॥

**श्रेष्ठिकायस्थौ**—( विलोक्य । वसन्तसेनामातरमुद्दिश्य । ) अवहिता तावदार्येदं सुवर्णभाण्डमवलोकयतु तदेवेदं न वेति । ( अवहिदा दाव अज्जा एदं सुवण्णभण्डअं अवलोएदु सो ज्जेव एसो ण वेत्ति ।)

**वृद्धा**—( अवलोक्य । ) सदृशमेतत् । न पुनस्तत् । ( सरिसो एसो । ण उण सो ।)

**शकारः**—आं वृद्धकुट्टनि अक्षिभ्यां मन्त्रितं वाचा मूकितम् । (आं बुड्ढकुट्टणि अक्खीहिं मन्तिद वाआए मूकिदम् ।)

**वृद्धा**—हताश अपेहि । (हदास अवेहि ।)

**श्रेष्ठिकायस्थौ**—अप्रमत्तं कथय तदेवैतन्न वेति । (अप्पमत्तं कधेहि सो ज्जेव एसो ण वेत्ति ।)

---

परेण केवलेन व्यसनेन बाल्योचितक्रीडनेन इति च केचिद्व्याख्यान्ति । वसन्ततिलकं वृत्तम् ]॥ २९ ॥ **मयेति** । [ परलोकमजानता नृशंसेन घातुकेन मया खलु स्त्री सामान्या योषित् वा अथ वा अविशेषेण रतिः स्वरूपेण कामप्रिया वा मूर्तिमती प्रीतिर्वा । हतेति वक्तुमसमर्थ आह—शेषमिति । एष शकारः । ] ॥ ३० ॥ [ तपस्वी शोच्यः । कृतान्तः विधिः । मम दुर्दैवमित्यर्थः । पुरस्थापनं पुरा-

SAK.—( *Picking them up and looking at them ; showing fear* ) Look, gentlemen look! These are verily the ornaments of that poor girl! ( *Pointing to* Charudatta ). For the sake of this filthy lucre he strangled and killed her!

( *The* officers *all bend down their faces* ).

CHAR.—( *Aside* ; *to* Vid. ).

This group of ornaments, seen at such a time, and dropped ( from your person ) owing to my ill-luck, will ruin me. (31)

VID.—Well, why don't you tell them the truth ?

CHAR.—Friend,

The royal eye is weak, and it cannot perceive the truth in this matter. If I were to tell, it would be ( simply ) humiliation, and there would be inglorious death. (32)

THE J.—Alas, Oh, alas!

By the side of Jupiter, powerless and opposed by Mars, there has appeared this another planet, like a comet. (33)

SR. & K.—( *Observing, and addressing* Vasantasena's mother ) Madam, please just inspect these golden ornaments carefully, ( and find out ) if they are the same or not.

THE OLD L.—( *Seeing* ). They are similar, but they are not the same.

SAK.—Ha! You old bawd, your eyes have spoken, if your tongue has concealed it!

THE O. L.—Off with you, you wretch!

SR. & K.—Please answer, without making any mistake, whether these are the same or not.

---

वस्थितिः । पुरनिर्माणमिति यावत् । विहाराः सौगतावसथाः । आरामा उपवनानि । यूपः कृतस्य यज्ञस्य चिह्नभूतः । अनीशः दरिद्रतां गतोऽपि । उच्छृङ्खलक स्वैरवृत्तः । कृतजनदोषश्चासौ भण्डश्चेति विशेषणसमासः । कुट्टनीपुत्र असतीपुत्र । अयमिति । [ एवंविधे काले दोषारोपसमये अस्माकं भाग्यवैषम्याद्विधेः वक्रतया पतितः अयं भूषणविस्तरः आभरणसमूहः दृष्टः मां पातयिष्यति ] ॥ ३१ ॥ दुर्बलमिति । [नृपतेः चक्षुः अधिकरणादिरूपं दुर्बलमर्थस्य याथार्थ्यग्रहणासमर्थम् । एतत् चक्षुः तत्त्वं न निरीक्षते । बहिःप्रमाणान्येवाश्रयते इत्यर्थः । अतः वदतः परमार्थवादिनः दैन्यमेव केवलं निश्चितम् । अश्लाघ्यं मरणं च भवेत् ।] ॥ ३२ ॥ अङ्गारकेति । [ अङ्गारको मङ्गलग्रहः विरुद्धो यस्य तस्य । यद्वा अङ्गारकेण विरुद्धस्य । प्रक्षीणस्य क्षीणबलस्य अथ वा नीचस्थानस्थितत्वाद्दुर्बलस्य । बृहस्पतेः सौम्यग्रहस्य पार्श्वे अयमलंकारपातोऽपरो धूमकेतुरिवोत्थितः । एकदेशविवर्तिना वाक्यार्थोपमालंकारः ] ॥ ३३ ॥

**वृद्धा**—आर्य शिल्पिकुशलतयाऽवबध्नाति दृष्टिम् । न पुनस्तत् । (अज्ज सिप्पिकुसलदाए ओबन्धेदि दिट्ठिम् । ण उण सो ।)

**अधिकरणिकः**—भद्रे अपि जानास्येतान्याभरणानि ।

**वृद्धा**—ननु भणामि न खलु न खल्वनभिज्ञातः । अथ वा कदाऽपि शिल्पिना घटितो भवेत् । (णं भणामि ण हु ण हु अणभिजाणिदो[१] । अह वा कदा वि सिप्पिणा घडिदो भवे ।)

**अधिकरणिकः**—पश्य श्रेष्ठिन् ।

> **वस्त्वन्तराणि सदृशानि भवन्ति नूनं**
> **रूपस्य भूषणगुणस्य च कृत्रिमस्य ।**
> **दृष्ट्वा क्रियामनुकरोति हि शिल्पिवर्गः**
> **सादृश्यमेव कृतहस्ततया च दृष्टम् ॥ ३४ ॥**

**श्रेष्ठिकायस्थौ**—[२]आर्यचारुदत्तीयान्येतानि । (अज्जचारुदत्तस्स केरकाइं एदाइं ।)

**चारुदत्तः**—न खलु न खलु ।

**श्रेष्ठिकायस्थौ**—तदा कस्य । (ता कस्स ।)

**चारुदत्तः**—इहात्रभवत्या दुहितुः ।

**श्रेष्ठिकायस्थौ**—कथमेतानि तस्या वियोगं गतानि । (कधं एदाइं ताए विओअं गदाइं ।)

**चारुदत्तः**—एवं गतानि । आं इदम् ।

**श्रेष्ठिकायस्थौ**—आर्य चारुदत्त अत्र सत्यं वक्तव्यम् । पश्य पश्य ।

> **सत्येन सुखं खलु लभ्यते सत्यालापे न भवति पातकम् ।**
> **सत्यमिति द्वे अप्यक्षरे मा सत्यमलीकेन गूहय ॥ ३५ ॥**

> (अज्ज चारुदत्त एत्थ सच्चं वत्तव्वम् । पेक्ख पेक्ख ।
> सच्चेण सुहं क्खु लब्भइ सच्चालावे ण होइ पावम् ।
> सच्चं त्ति दुवे वि अक्खरा मा सच्चं अलिएण गूहेहि ॥)

**चारुदत्तः**—आभरणान्याभरणानीति न जाने । किं त्वस्मद्गृहादानीतानीति जाने ।

**शकारः**—उद्यानं प्रवेश्य प्रथमं मारयसि । कपटकापटिकतया सांप्रतं निगूहसि । (उज्जाणं पवेशिअ पढमं मालेशि । कवडकावडिआए । शंपदं णिगूहेशि ।)

**अधिकरणिकः**—आर्य चारुदत्त सत्यमभिधीयताम् ।

---

१ अणणदो अह कदापि (अन्यतोऽथ कदाऽपि). २ चारुदत्तस्य.

THE O. L.—Sir, owing to the workman's skill, they captivate my sight, but they are not the same.

THE J.—Madam, do you recognize these ornaments ?

THE O. L.—I say that I do not, I do not, indeed. They are not recognized by me. Or perhaps they might have been made by the same workman.

THE J.—See, Sreshthin :—

Surely different articles ( ornaments ) resemble each other in form and beauty which are imparted by human art. For all workmen copy the model which they have seen ; and perfect resemblance itself is seen on account of their skilled handiwork. (34)

SR. & K.—Then they belong to the noble Charudatta.

CHAR.—No, surely not !

SR. & K.—Then to whom do they belong ?

CHAR.—To the daughter of this worthy dame here.

SR. & K.—How did they come to be separated from her person ?

CHAR.—They did in this way. Oh, this—

SR. & K.—Sir Charudatta, you should tell the truth in this matter. For see, see—

Verily, happiness is got by ( telling ) the truth. By telling the truth one does not incur sin. *Sa* and *Tya* ( Truth ) only two syllables ( *akshara* ) are these, but they are imperishable ( *akshara* ). Do not hide the truth by telling a lie. (35)

CHAR.—I don't know this much fuss about ornaments ; I only know that they were brought ( here ) from my house.

SAK.—First you kill her by enticing her into the garden; and now you hide it by your deceitful cunning !

THE J.—Noble Charudatta, please tell the truth.

---

**वस्त्वन्तराणीति** । [ कृत्रिमस्य कार्येण निर्वृत्तस्य रूपस्य भूषणगुणस्य अलंकारसौष्ठवस्य वस्त्वन्तराणि सदृशानि नूनं भवन्ति । हि शिल्पिवर्गः कारुजनः दृष्ट्वा क्रियामनुकरोति । अतः शिल्पिवर्गस्य कृतहस्ततया हस्तकौशलेन इति हेतुना सादृश्यं शिल्पकौशलमेव दृष्टम् । काव्यलिङ्गमलंकारः । वसन्ततिलकम् वृत्तम् ] ॥ ३४ ॥ एवं आं इदं एवमिदं स्मर्यते । **सत्येनेत्यादि** । वैतालीयम् । सत्येन सत्याश्रयणेन । **सत्यालापे** । सत्यमालापयतीति क्विपि सत्यालापः । तत्र । न भवति पापकम् ।

इदानीं सुकुमारेऽस्मिन्निः शङ्कं[1] कर्कशाः कशाः ।
तव गात्रे पतिष्यन्ति [2]सहास्माकं मनोरथैः ॥ ३६ ॥

**चारुदत्तः**—

अपापानां कुले जाते मयि पापं न विद्यते ।
यदि संभाव्यते पापमपापेन च किं मया ॥ ३७ ॥

( स्वगतम् । ) न च मे वसन्तसेनाविरहितस्य जीवितेन कृत्यम् । ( प्रकाशम् । ) भोः किं बहुना ।

मया किल[3] नृशंसेन लोकद्वयमजानता[4] ।
स्त्रीरत्नं[5] च विशेषेण शेषमेषोऽभिधास्यति ॥ ३८ ॥

**शकारः**—व्यापादिता । अरे त्वमपि भण मया व्यापादितेति । (वावादिदा । अले तुमं पि भण मए वावादिदेत्ति ।)

**चारुदत्तः**—त्वयैवोक्तम् ।

**शकारः**—श्रृणुत श्रृणुत भट्टारकाः एतेन मारिता । एतेनैव संशयश्छिन्नः । एतस्य दरिद्रचारुदत्तस्य शारीरो दण्डो धार्यताम् । (शुणेध शुणेध भट्टारका एदेण मालिदा । एदेण ज्जेव शंशए छिण्णे । एदश्श दलिद्दचालुदत्तश्श शालीले दण्डे धालीअदु ।)

**अधिकरणिकः**—शोधनक यथाऽऽह राष्ट्रियः । भो राजपुरुषाः गृह्यतामयं चारुदत्तः ।

(राजपुरुषा गृह्णन्ति ।)

**वृद्धा**—प्रसीदन्तु प्रसीदन्त्वार्यमिश्राः । ('जो तदाणिं..चोरेहिं अवहिदंत्ति...' इत्यादि पूर्वोक्तं पठति ।) तद्यदि व्यापादिता मम दारिका व्यापादिता । जीवतु मे दीर्घायुः । अन्यच्च । अर्थिप्रत्यर्थिनोर्व्यवहारः । अहमर्थिनी । तन्मुञ्चतैतम् । (पसीदन्तु पसीदन्तु अज्जमिस्सा । ता जदि वावादिदा मम दारिआ वावादिदा । जीवदु मे दीहाऊ । अण्णं च । अत्थिपच्चत्थिण्णं ववहारो । अहं अत्थिणी । ता मुञ्चध एदम् ।)

**शकारः**—अपेहि गर्भदासि गच्छ । किं तवैतेन । (अवेहि गब्भदाशि गच्छ । किं तव एदिणा ।)

**वृद्धा**—हा जात हा पुत्रक । (इति रुदती निष्क्रान्ता ।) (हा जाद हा पुत्तअ ।)

**शकारः**—( स्वगतम् । ) कृतं मयैतस्यात्मनः सदृशम् । सांप्रतं गच्छामि । (इति निष्क्रान्तः ।) (कडं मए एदश्श अत्तणो शलिशम् । शंपदं गच्छामि ।)

---

१ निःशङ्काः. २ सदा. ३ खलु. ४ परलोक. ५ स्त्री रतिश्च.

(For) now, most assuredly, the heavy lashes (of punishment) will fall on this delicate body of yours, and so, too, will our wishes (to acquit you as innocent fall to the ground. (36)

CHAR.—

I who am born in a family of sinless persons have committed no sin. But if sin is thought to be committed by me, then what avails my being sinless ? (37)

'*To himself*'. And life is without purpose to me, now that I am separated (for ever) from Vasantasena. (*Aloud*) Gentlemen what more need I say ?

As is said, by me who am cruel and know neither of the two worlds, a woman, and especially a jewel (among women), ......The rest this person will say. (38)

SAK.—"Was killed." Oh ! say you too—"By me (she) was killed."

CHAR.—You yourself have said it !

SAK.—Listen, gentleman, listen ! She was killed by him ! He himself has removed your doubt ! So let capital punishment be inflicted upon this penniless Charudatta.

THE J.—Sodhanaka, (it shall be) as the King's brother-in-law says. Well, guards, arrest this Charudatta !

(*The guards arrest him*).

THE OLD L.—Be kind, gentlemen, please be merciful. (*Repeats what she had said before, viz.* "*He who on that occasion ......because it was stolen by thieves......*" *&c.*). So, if my daughter has been killed, well, she has been killed. But let my long-lived one, Charudatta, live. Moreover, a suit lies between the complainant and the defendant; and *I* am the (real) complainant (in this matter). So please release him.

SAK.—Get away, you born slave, off with you ! What have you to do with him ?

THE J.—Madam, you may go (now). Guards, please show her out.

THE O. L.—O my dear, my child ! (*Exit weeping*).

---

सत्यमिति द्वे अप्यक्षरे इति स्वरूपोक्तिः। 'न भवति पापस्य निमित्तमिति यस्मात्' इति प्राचीनटीका। अलीकं कर्तुं ! सत्यापेक्षया बह्वक्षरमपीत्यर्थः। सत्यं पूर्वोक्तस्वरूपत्वाद्द्व्यक्षरमपि कर्मभूतम्। मा निगूहय मा संवृणु इति ॥ ३५ ॥ [गूहादा-

**अधिकरणिकः**—आर्य चारुदत्त निर्णये वयं प्रमाणम्। शेष तु[1] राजा। तथाऽपि शोधनक विज्ञाप्यतां राजा पालकः—

**अयं हि पातकी विप्रो न वध्यो मनुरब्रवीत्।**
**राष्ट्रादस्मात्तु निर्वास्यो [2]विभवैरक्षतैः सह॥ ३९॥**

**शोधनकः**—यदार्य आज्ञापयति। (इति निष्क्रम्य पुनः प्रविश्य। सास्रम्।) आर्याः गतोऽस्मि तत्र। राजा पालको भणति—येनार्थकल्यवर्तस्य कारणाद्वसन्तसेना व्यापादिता तं तान्येवाभरणानि गले बद्ध्वा डिण्डिमं ताडयित्वा दक्षिणश्मशानं नीत्वा शूले भङ्क्तेति। यः कोऽप्यपर ईदृशमकार्यमनुतिष्ठति स एतेन सनिकारदण्डेन शास्यते। (जं अज्जो आणवेदि। अज्जा गदम्हि तहिं। राआ पालओ भणादि—जेण अत्थकल्लवत्तस्स कालदाणो वसन्तसेणा वावादिदा तं ताइं[3] ज्जेव आहरणाइं गले बन्धिक डिण्डिमं ताडिअ दक्खिणमसाणं णइअ सूले भज्जेधत्ति। जो को वि अवरो एरिसं अकज्जं अणुचिट्ठदि सो एदिणा सणिआरदण्डेन सासीअदि।)

**चारुदत्तः**—अहो अविमृश्यकारी[4] राजा पालकः। अथ वा।

**ईदृशे व्यवहाराग्नौ मन्त्रिभिः परिपातिताः।**
**स्थाने खलु महीपाला गच्छन्ति कृपणां [5]दशाम्॥ ४०॥**

अपि च।

**ईदृशैः श्वेतकाकीयैः राज्ञः शासनदूषकैः।**
**अपापानां सहस्राणि हन्यन्ते च हतानि च॥ ४१॥**

सखे मैत्रेय गच्छ। मद्वचनाद[6]म्बाम[7]पश्चिममभिवादयस्व। पुत्रं च मे रोहसेनं परिपालयस्व।

**विदूषकः**—मूले छिन्ने कुतः पादपस्य पालनम्। (मूले छिण्णे कुदो पादवस्स पालणम्।)

**चारुदत्तः**—मा मैवम्।

**नृणां लोकान्तरस्थानां[8] देहप्रतिकृतिः सुतः।**
**मयि यो वं तव स्नेहो रोहसेने स युज्यताम्॥ ४२**

---

नीतानि न तु पुष्पकरण्डकोद्यानादिति रहस्यम्।] अतिकापटिकतया निगूहसि। **इदानीमिति**। कशा अश्वताडिनीः। [ताः पतिष्यन्ति। सत्यख्यापनार्थमिति भावः। अस्माकं मनोरथैः तव दोषवारणरूपैः] ॥ ३६॥ **अपापानामिति**। [यदि पापं संभाव्यते युष्माभिः। अपापेन मया किम्। युष्माकं निर्णय एव प्रमाणमित्यर्थः] ॥ ३७॥ **मयेति**। स्त्री रत्नमिव। उत्कृष्टा स्त्री ॥ ३८॥ **अयमिति**। [अयं विप्रः

---

१ एतन्नास्ति क्वचित्. २ रक्षितैः. ३ तहिं (तत्र). ४ अविवेको अविमृ०. ५ श्रियम्. ६ मम. ७ अम्बां मम पश्चि०; अम्बामपि मम अभिवा०. ८ लोकोत्तर.

SAK.—( *To himself* ). I have done to him something which is worthy of myself ! Now I'll go. (*Exit* ).

THE J.—Sir Charudatta, we are authorized ( merely ) to give our decision ( in a case ); but the rest ( *i. e.* the actual punishment ) depends on the King. Still, O Sodhanaka, let king Palaka be informed ( in these words ):—

" He is a sinner. But Manu has laid down that a Brahmana is not to be killed; ( so ) he might be banished from this country together with all his property intact." (39)

SO.—As Your Honour orders. ( *Goes out and again comes back; tearfully* ). Gentlemen, I had gone there. But king Palaka says—" Tie those very ornaments round the neck of him who killed Vasantasena for the sake of a paltry sum of money; and, beating the drum, take him to the southern burning-ground and have him impaled there. Whoever else commits a similar crime will be visited with this ( same ) punishment, accompanied by great disgrace."

CHAR.—Ah ! How thoughtlessly has king Palaka acted ! Or rather—

It is but right that kings ( *lit.* the protectors of the earth ) are reduced to pitiable plight, when pushed into such a fire of legal trials by their counsellors. (40)

Also—

By such-like men ( *i. e.* judges ), who would even believe that a crow ( which is black ) is white, and who disgrace the king's ( judicial ) administration, thousands of sinless ( innocent ) persons are being, and have been, killed. (41)

Friend Maitreya, please go, and at my request give, for the last time, my salute to my dear mother. And please look after my son, Rohasena.

VID.—When the root itself is cut off, how can the tree be looked after ?

CHAR.—Nay, say not so.

The son is the physical substitute of persons who have departed to the other world. So please bestow on Rohasena that very affection which you had for me. (42)

---

पातकी स्थापितदोषः हि । तथाऽपि विप्रः न वध्य इति मनुरब्रवीत् । तस्मादक्षतैः यथास्थितैः विभवैः सहास्माद्राष्ट्रान्निर्वास्यः विवासयितव्यः । अत्र मनुः—'न जातु ब्राह्मणं हन्यात्सर्वपापेष्वपि स्थितम् । राष्ट्रादेनं बहिः कुर्यात्समग्रधनमक्षतम् ॥

**विदूषकः**—भो वयस्य अहं ते प्रियवयस्यो भूत्वा त्वया विरहितान्प्राणान्धारयामि। (भो वअस्स अहं ते पिअवअस्सो भविअ तुए विरहिदाइं पाणाइं धारेमि।)

**चारुदत्तः**—रोहसेनमपि[1] तावद्दर्शय।

**विदूषकः**—एवम् युज्यते। (एव्वम् जुज्जदि।)

**अधिकरणिकः**—भद्र शोधनक अपसार्यतामयं बटुः[2]।

(शोधनकस्तथा करोति।)

**अधिकरणिकः**—कः कोऽत्र भोः। चाण्डालानां[3] दीयतामादेशः।

(इति चारुदत्तं विसृज्य[4] निष्क्रान्ताः सर्वे राजपुरुषाः।)

**शोधनकः**—इत आगच्छत्वार्यः। (इदो आअच्छदु अज्जो।)

**चारुदत्तः**—( सकरुणम् 'मैत्रेय भोः किमिदमद्य' (९।२९) इत्यादि पठति। आकाशे। )

**विषसलिलतुलाग्निप्रार्थिते मे विचारे**
**क्रकचमिह शरीरे वीक्ष्य दातव्यमद्य।**
**अथ रिपुवचनाद्वा ब्राह्मणं मां निहंसि**
**पतसि नरकमध्ये पुत्रपौत्रैः समेतः॥** ४३॥

**अयमागतोऽस्मि।**

( इति निष्क्रान्ताः सर्वे। )

[5]**इति व्यवहारो नाम नवमोऽङ्कः**[6]।

---

**मौण्ड्यं** प्राणान्तिको दण्डो ब्राह्मणस्य विधीयते।' इति॥ ३९॥ **निकारः** विप्रकारः। अधिक्षेप इति यावत्। तेन सहितः दण्डः तेन।] **ईदृश इति**। [ईदृशे व्यवहार एव अग्निः तस्मिन्। कुदृष्टव्यवहाररूपाग्नौ इत्यर्थः। मन्त्रिभिः परिपातिताः महीपालाः कृपणां दीनां दशां गच्छन्ति इति स्थाने युक्तं खलु]॥ ४०॥ **ईदृशैरिति**। [ईदृशैः श्वेतकाकीयैः श्वेतः काक इति विततार्थं वाक्यं श्वेतकाकीयम्। 'इवे प्रतिकृतौ' इत्यधिकारस्थितेन 'समासाच्च तद्विषयात्' इत्यनेन छप्रत्ययः। तद्वादिनः श्वेतकाकीयाः विततार्थदर्शिनस्तैः। शासनदूषकैः। अधिकरणिकैः। एतन्मनसि कृत्वैवोक्तं प्रथमाङ्के 'व्यवहारदुष्टतां' इति। अपापानामनपराधिनां सहस्राणि हन्यन्ते हतानि च। 'श्वा च एतः हरिणश्च काकश्च तत्सदृशैः। सादृश्यं च स्वामिसेवापरत्वभयचकितत्वेङ्गितज्ञत्वैर्बोध्यम्' इति केचित्। उत्पातकल्पैरिति पृथ्वीधरः]॥ ४१॥ **नृणामिति**। [लोकान्तरस्थानां मृतानाम्। सुतः देहप्रतिकृतिः स्वप्रतिनिधिः तथा च श्रुतिः—'सा जाया जाया भवति यदस्यां जायते पुनः' इति।

---

1 मपि च. 2 बहिः. 3 चण्डा०. 4 विसर्ज्य. 5 इति मृच्छकटिके प्र०; ०कटिकप्र०. 6 अङ्कः समाप्तः.

VID.—O friend, shall I ( be able to ) support life separated from you, having been your dear friend ( so long ) ?

CHAR.—At any rate, please let me have a sight of Rohasena.

VID.—Quite so; that is all right.

THE J.—Well, Sodhanaka, let this fellow be removed ( from here ).

( Sodhanaka *does so* ).

THE J.—Ho ! Who is there ? Let orders be issued to the Chandalas.

( *Then exeunt all the* officers *leaving alone* Charudatta ).

SO.—Sir, please come this way.

CHAR.—( *Sorrowfully recites the verse beginning 'O Maitreya, what is this to-day' etc. Then in the void* )—

After my case had been investigated ( decided ), by means of ( the ordeals of ) poison, water, balance, and fire, then with justice you might have to-day ordered a saw to be used on this body of mine. But as you are killing me, a Brahmana, relying simply on the words of my enemy, you will ( surely ) fall into hell, along with your sons and grandsons ! (43)

Here I am coming !

( *Exeunt all* )

*Thus ends Act IX., styled*

'The Trial.'

---

'अङ्गादङ्गात्संभवसि हृदयादधिजायसे । आत्मा वै पुत्रनामासि स जीव शरदः शतम् ॥' इति च ] ॥ ४२ ॥ विषसलिलेति । अथ विचारनिरपेक्षं नृपतिं हृदि स्वीकृत्य वदति । [ विषं विषपानं सलिलं सलिलमज्जनं तुला तुलारोहणं अग्निः अग्निधारणमित्येतैः दिव्यैः प्राथिते निर्णयार्हे इत्यर्थः । मे मम विचारे व्यवहारविमर्शे । इह मम शरीरे क्रकचं वीक्ष्य दातव्यम् । अथ वा रिपुवचनात् शकारवचनात् मां ब्राह्मणं निहंसि अतः पुत्रपौत्रैः समेतः नरकमध्ये पतसि पतिष्यसि । अनेन भावि मरणं सूच्यते । मालिनी छन्दः ] विषादिपरीक्षाप्रार्थितेऽन्विष्टे । विचारे । क्रकचं दातव्यम् । अर्हे तव्यः ॥ ४३ ॥

इति व्यवहारो नाम नवमोऽङ्कः ।

# दशमोऽङ्कः ।

(ततः प्रविशति [1]चाण्डालद्वयेनानुगम्यमानश्चारुदत्तः ।)

**उभौ**—

**तत्किं न कलय कारणं नववधबन्धनयने निपुणौ ।**
**अचिरेण शीर्षच्छेदनशूलारोपेषु कुशलौ स्वः ॥ १ ॥**

**अपसरतार्याः अपसरत । एष आर्यचारुदत्तः—**

**दत्तकरवीरदामा गृहीत आवाभ्यां वध्यपुरुषाभ्याम् ।**
**दीप इव मन्दस्नेहः स्तोकं स्तोकं क्षयं याति ॥ २ ॥**

(तक्किं ण कलअ कालण णववहबन्धणअणे णिउणा ।
अचिलेण[2] शीशछेअणशूलालोवेशु कुशलम्इ ॥
ओशलध अज्जा ओशलध । एशे अज्जचालुदत्ते—
दिण्णकलवीलदामे गहिदे अम्हेहिं वज्झपुलिसेहिं[3] ।
दीवे व्व मन्दणेहे थोअं थोअं खअं जादि ॥)

**चारुदत्तः**—(सविषादम् ।)

**नयनसलिलसिक्तं पांशुरूक्षीकृताङ्गं[4]**
**पितृवनसुमनोभिर्वेष्टितं मे शरीरम् ।**
**विरसमिह रटन्तो[5] रक्तगन्धानुलिप्तं**
**बलिमिव परिभोक्तुं वायसास्तर्कयन्ति ॥ ३ ॥**

---

[इतः समाप्ति यावत्कार्यफलयोगरूपः निर्वहणसंधिः । वसन्तसेनासंज्ञालाभेन चारुदत्तस्य मोक्षः आर्यकस्य राज्यप्राप्तिः शर्विलकस्य संगमेन चारुदत्तस्य सर्वार्थसिद्धिश्चाङ्कस्य प्रतिपाद्यविषयः । तत्र तावद्वध्यभूमिं नीयमानस्य चारुदत्तस्य प्रवेशः प्रस्तूयते—ततः प्रविशतीत्यादिना । तत्र चाण्डालावन्योन्यं वदतः । **तत्किमिति** । तत् किमिति कारणं वधनिमित्तं न कलय विचारय । नवः वधः बन्धश्च तयोः । यद्वा नवः वधाय बन्धस्तस्य नयने प्रापणे निपुणौ स्वः । स्पष्टमन्यत् ॥ १ ॥ **दत्तेति** दत्तं करवीराणां दाम वध्यस्रक् यस्य सः । आवाभ्यां वधे नियुक्तः वध्यः । वध्यौ पुरुषौ वध्यपुरुषौ । यद्वा वध्यग्राहकौ पुरुषौ इति मध्यमपदलोपी समासः । ताभ्यां गृहीतः । मन्दस्नेहोऽल्पतैलो दीप इव स्तोकं स्तोकं क्षयं नाशं याति ॥ २ ॥

---

१ चण्डा०. २ अइलेण. ३ वज्ज. ४ रुक्षी०. ५ लगन्तः.

# ACT X.

( *Then enter* Charudatta, *accompanied by two Chandalas* ).

BOTH—

What then! Seek not the reason. ( It is this, that ) we are experts in chaining and leading a recently condemned criminal to the gallows, and are skilled in cutting off his head or impaling him without loss of time. ( 1 )

Make way, gentlemen, make way! Here's the worthy Charudatta—

On whom are put garlands of *karavira* flowers and who is in the custody of us two, his executioners; he is now slowly losing lustre, like a lamp with its oil exhausted. (2)

CHAR.—( *Mournfully* )

These crows, cawing harshly near by, are expecting to feed on my body as though it were an oblation,—my body which is drenched with tears, has its limbs soiled with dust, is covered with ( garlands of ) funeral flowers, and is besmeared with red sandal-paste. (3)

---

**नयनेति** । इह विरसं कर्कशं यथा तथा रटन्तः शब्दायमाना वायसा नयनसलिलै- रश्रुभिः सिक्तं पांशुना रथ्याधूल्या रूक्षीकृतानि अङ्गानि यस्य तत्तथा । पितृवनं श्मशानं तत्संबन्धिसुमनोभिः पुष्पमालाभिः वेष्टितं मे शरीरं बलिमिव परिभोक्तुं तर्कयन्ति उत्प्रेक्षन्ते । मालिनी वृत्तम् ] ।। ३ ।। **किमिति** । [ कालः कृतान्तः स एव परशुः तस्य धाराभिः छिद्यमानं सत्पुरुषम् । अपि च सुजना एव शकुनाः पक्षिण- स्तेषामधिवासम् । पुरुष एव द्रुमः पुरुषद्रुमः । सज्जनानां छायाकरत्वात्पुरुषद्रुमः । तमेतं किं पश्यत ।। ४ ।। **सवति** । सर्वगात्रेषु विन्यस्तैर्दत्तैः रक्तचन्दनहस्तकैः पञ्चाङ्गुलिचिह्नैः । हस्ता एव हस्तकाः । इवार्थे कन् । पिष्टचूर्णैः । पिष्टरजोभिः **अवकीर्णः** । 'पिष्टचूर्णाभ्यामवकीर्णः व्याप्तः । पिष्टं तण्डुलानां चूर्णं तिलानाम्' इति लल्लादीक्षिताः । पिष्टचूर्णं श्यामतण्डुलचूर्णमिति पृथ्वीधरः । अहं पुरुषः सन् पशूकृतः । अपशुः पशुर्यथा संपद्यते तथा कृतः । ] पशुदेवतार्थं छागादिः ।। ५ ।। **अमी इति** । [ अमी हि पौराः मदुपेतं मया प्राप्तमेतद्व्यसनं दृष्ट्वा मर्त्यं मनुष्य- धर्माणं धिगस्तु इति उक्त्वा उपजातबाष्पा मां व्यसनाद्रक्षितुमशक्नुवन्तः स्वर्गं लभस्वेति वदन्ति । ] मदिति पञ्चम्येकवचनान्तकम् । मदुपगतमीदृशमवस्थान्तरं

**चाण्डालौ**—अपसरतार्याः अपसरत ।

किं पश्यथ छिद्यमानं सत्पुरुषं कालपरशुधाराभिः ।
सुजनशकुनाधिवासं सज्जनपुरुषद्रुममेतम् ॥ ४ ॥

आगच्छ रे चारुदत्त आगच्छ । (ओशलध अज्जा ओशलध ।)

(किं पेक्खध छिज्जन्तं शप्पुलिशं कालपलशुधालाहिं ।
शुअणशउणाधिवाशं शज्जणपुलिशद्दुमं एदम् ॥

आअच्छ ले चारुदत्ता आअच्छ ।)

**चारुदत्तः**—पुरुषभाग्यानाम[1]चिन्त्याः[2] खलु व्यापारा यदहमीदृशीं दशामनुप्राप्तः ।

सर्वगात्रेषु विन्यस्तै रक्तचन्दनहस्तकैः ।
पिष्टचूर्णावकीर्णश्च पुरुषोऽहं पशूकृतः ॥ ५ ॥

(अग्रतो निरूप्य ।) अहो तारतम्यं नराणाम् । (सकरुणम् ।)

अमी हि दृष्ट्वा [3]मदुपेतमेतन्मर्त्यं धिगस्त्वित्युपजातबाष्पाः[4] ।
अशक्नुवन्तः परिरक्षितुं मां स्वर्गं लभस्वेति वदन्ति पौराः ॥ ६ ॥

**चाण्डालौ**—अपसरतार्याः अपसरत । किं पश्यथ ।

इन्द्रः प्रवाह्यमाणो गोप्रसवः संक्रमश्च ताराणाम् ।
सुपुरुषप्राणविपत्तिश्चत्वार इमे न द्रष्टव्याः ॥ ७ ॥

(ओशलध अज्जा ओशलध । किं पेक्खध ।
इन्दे प्पवाहिअन्ते गोप्पसवे शंकमं[5] च तालाणम् ।
शुपुलिशपाणविपत्ती चत्तालि इमे ण दट्ठव्वा ॥)

**एकः**—अरे आहीन्त पश्य पश्य ।

नगरीप्रधानभूते वध्यमाने कृतान्ताज्ञया ।
किं रोदित्यन्तरिक्षमथ [6]वाऽनभ्रं पतति वज्रम् ॥ ८ ॥

(हण्ड[7] आहिन्ता पेक्ख पेक्ख ।
णअलीपधाणभूदे वज्झीअन्ते कदन्तअण्णाए ।
किं लुअदि अन्तलिक्खे अणब्भे पडदि वज्जे ॥)

**द्वितीयः**—अरे गोह ।

---

दृष्ट्वेति वाऽर्थः ॥ ६ ॥ इन्द्र इत्यादि । गाथा । इन्द्रः [ इन्द्रध्वजः ] प्रवास्यमानो यद्वा प्रवाह्यमाणः न द्रष्टव्यः । [ 'उत्थापयेत्तूर्यरवैः सर्वलोकस्य वै पुरः । रह्रो विसर्जयेत्केनु विशेषोऽयं प्रपूजने ॥ ' इति । ] गोप्रसवो [ गोप्रसूतिः ] निरतनं च

---

१ भावानां. २ अविचिन्त्याः. ३ मम देहमेतं. ४ खेदाः. ५ संकमं. ६ अनभ्रे. ७ हण्डे.

CH.—Make way, gentlemen, make way!

Why should you look at this good man being hewn asunder by the edge of Death's axe, this tree in the shape of a righteous man, being the residence of birds in the form of virtuous persons? (4)

Come, O Charudatta, come away!

CHAR.—The workings of a person's destiny are verily inscrutable, since I have been reduced to such a condition :

By the prints of ( the extended ) hand dipped in red-sandal paste, impressed over all my limbs and covered over with rice-flour and sesamum-powder, I, a man, am turned into an animal ( about to be slaughtered ). (5)

( *Looking before him* ). Oh, the commonsense of the people! (*mournfully* ).

Here these citizens, seeing the state to which I have now fallen, are saying 'Fie upon this moral lot,' with tears welling up ( in their eyes ), and being unable to save me, are blessing me with words 'May you go to heaven!' (6)

THE TWO CH.—Make way, sirs, make way! What are you seeing?

The Indra-pole being carried away, the delivery of a cow, the falling of a star, and the execution of a virtuous man,—these four ought not to be looked at! (7)

ONE CH.—Eh, Ahinta see, see!

When the chief man of the city is about to be slain by the fiat of the Fate, is the sky weeping, or is the thunderbolt falling ( even ) though there are no clouds? (8)

THE SECOND CH.—O Goha.

---

ताराणाम् । सत्पुरुषस्य प्राणविपत्तिर्नाशः । चत्वार इमे न द्रष्टव्याः ॥ ७ ॥ हण्डे इति नीचसंबोधने । **नगरीत्यादि** । गाथा । नगरीप्रधानभूते [ चारुदत्ते ] कृतान्ताज्ञया [ विधिनियोगेन । यद्वा कृतान्तसदृशपालकाज्ञया । किं अन्तरिक्षं रोदिति अथ वा अनभ्र मेघरहितं तथा यथा वज्र पतति । ] वध्यमाने नगरीप्रधानवधो वज्र इवेत्युत्प्रेक्षा ॥ ८ ॥ **न चेति** । गाथा । स्त्रीसमूहमेघान्निपतति । नयनाम्बु कर्तृ । धाराभिः ॥ ९ ॥ **वध्ये नीयमान इति** । आर्या । वध्ये वध्यभूमिं नीयमाने । रेणुः रथ्यातो नोन्नमति नोद्गच्छति ॥ १० ॥ **एता इति** । [ एता हर्म्यगताः स्त्रियः पुनः वातायनार्धेन वातायनैकदेशेन विनिःसृतानि आस्यानि यासां ताः निर्गतवदनाः हा

न च रोदित्यन्तरिक्षं नैवानभ्रं पतति वज्रम् ।
महिलासमूहमेघान्निपतति नयनाम्बु धाराभिः ॥ ९ ॥

अपि च ।

वध्ये नीयमाने जनस्य सर्वस्य रुदतः ।
नयनसलिलैः सिक्तो रथ्यातो नोन्नमति रेणुः ॥ १० ॥

(अले[1] गोहा ।

ण अ लुअदि अन्तलिक्खे णेअ अणब्भे पडदि वज्जे ।
महिलाशमूहमेहे निवडदि णअणम्बु धाराहिं ॥

अवि अ ।

वज्झम्मि णीअमाणे जणश्श शव्वश्श लोदमाणश्श ।
णअणशलिलेहिं शित्ते लच्छादो ण उण्णमइ लेणू ॥)

**चारुदत्तः**—(निरूप्य सकरुणम् ।)

एताः पुनर्हर्म्यगताः स्त्रियो मां वातायनार्धेन विनिःसृतास्याः[2] ।
हा चारुदत्तेत्यभिभाषमाणा बाष्पं प्रणालीभिरिवोत्सृजन्ति ॥ ११ ॥

**चाण्डालौ**—आगच्छ रे चारुदत्त आगच्छ । इदं घोषणस्थानम् । आहत डिण्डिमम् । घोषयत घोषणाम् । (आअच्छ ले चालुदत्ता आअच्छ । इमं घोषणट्ठाणम् । आहणेध डिण्डिमम् । घोशेध घोषणम् ।)

**उभौ**—शृणुतार्याः शृणुत । एष सार्थवाहविनयदत्तस्य नप्ता सागरदत्तस्य पुत्रक आर्यचारुदत्तो नाम । एतेन किलाकार्यकारिणा गणिका वसन्तसेनाऽर्थकल्यवर्तस्य कारणाच्छून्यं पुष्पकरण्डकजीर्णोद्यानं प्रवेश्य बाहुपाशबलात्कारेण मारितेत्येष सलोप्त्रो गृहीतः स्वयं च प्रतिपन्नः । ततो राज्ञा पालकेन वयमाज्ञप्ता एतं मारयितुम् । यद्यपर ईदृशमुभयलोकविरुद्धमकार्यं करोति तमपि राजा पालक एवमेव शास्ति । (शुणाध[3] अज्जा शुणाध । एशे शत्थवाहविणअदत्तश्श णत्थिके शाअलदत्तश्श पुत्तके[4] अज्जचालुदत्ते णाम । एदिणा किल अकज्जकालिणा गणिआ वशन्तशेणा अत्थकल्लवत्तश्श कालणादो शुण्णं पुप्फकलण्डअजिण्णुज्जाणं पवेशिअ बाहुपाशबलक्कालेण मालिदे त्ति एशे शलोत्ते गहिदे शअं अ पडिवण्णे । तदो लण्णा पालएण अम्हे आणत्ता एदं मालेदुम् । जदि अवले ईदिशं उभअलोअविलुद्धं अकज्जं कलेदि तं पि लाआ पालए एव्वं ज्जेव शाशदि ।)

**चारुदत्तः**—(सनिर्वेदं स्वगतम् ।)

---

चारुदत्तेति अभिभाषमाणाः प्रणालीभिरिव स्थूलधाराभिरित्यर्थः । बाष्पमुद्गिरन्ति उत्सृजन्ति । इन्द्रवज्रा वृत्तम् ] ॥ ११ ॥ [ मखेति । मखानां यज्ञानां शतैः परिपूतं

---

१ अले ले. २ विनिःशृताक्ष्यः. ३ शुणध. ४ पुश्तके.

The sky is not weeping, nor is the thunderbolt falling in the absence of clouds. ( But ) these are the tears, flowing in torrents, from the clouds in the form of the assembled ladies. (9)

Moreover :—

As the condemned man is being led on, the dust does not rise up from the streets, being sprinkled over with the tears of all people who are weeping. ( 10 )

CHAR.—( *Observing; mournfully* )

And these ladies in their mansions, putting forth their faces through the ( lower ) halves of the windows, are saying, with reference to me, 'Alas, O Charudatta !' and are shedding tears by conduits as it were ( *i. e.* in profusion ). ( 11 )

THE TWO CH.—Come, O Charudatta, come along ! Here's a proclamation-station. Beat the drum, and repeat aloud the proclamation !

BOTH—Listen gentlemen, listen ! This is the grandson of the merchant Vinayadatta, and the son of Sagaradatta, who is called the worthy Charudatta. By him, who has done an evil deed, the courtesan Vasantasena was enticed into the old deserted *Pushpakarandaka* garden for the sake of a trifle, *viz.* her money, and was there killed by being forcibly strangled with the noose of his arms; then he was caught with the booty, and himself also confessed ( his crime ). Thereupon King Palaka ordered us to slay him. If anyone else commits a similar crime, which is good neither for this world nor for the next, him too King Palaka will condemn similarly ( to death ).

CHAR.—( *With dejection; to himself* ).

---

पवित्रं मे गोत्रं पुरस्तात्पूर्वस्मिन्काले सदसि यज्ञमण्डपे निबिडानि घनानि चैत्यानि आयतनानि तत्र ब्रह्मणां वेदानां घोषैः । चित्यस्य चयनीयस्याग्नेः संबन्धिभिश्चैत्यैः इति केचित् । उद्भासितम् । मरणदशायां वर्तमानस्य मम तद्गोत्रं पापैः असदृशमनुष्यैः नीचैश्चाण्डालै घोषणायामपराधप्रख्यापनस्थाने घुष्यते । मालिनी वृत्तम् ] ॥ १२ ॥ उद्वीज्य उद्वेगं कृत्वा । शशीति । [ शशिनः चन्द्रस्य विमलमयूखा धवलकिरणा इव शुभ्रा दन्ता यस्यास्तत्संबुद्धिः । सुरुचिरो यः विद्रुमः प्रवालः तत्सदृशः अधरोष्ठो यस्यास्तादृशि । तव वदनोत्पन्नममृतं निपीय अवशः परवशोऽहं अयशोरूपं विषं कथं पिबामि । विषमालंकारः । पुष्पिताग्रा वृत्तम् ] ॥ १३ ॥ एष इति । [ एष चारुदत्तः गुणा एव रत्नानि तेषां निधिः । सज्जनदुःखानामुत्तरण-

मखशतपरिपूतं गोत्रमुद्भासितं मे
सदसि निबिडचैत्यब्रह्मघोषैः पुरस्तात् ।
मम मरणदशायां वर्तमानस्य पापै-
स्तदसदृशमनुष्यैर्घुष्यते घोषणायाम् ॥ १२ ॥

(उद्वीज्य[1] कर्णौ पिधाय ।) हा प्रिये वसन्तसेने ।

शशिविमलमयूखशुभ्रदन्ति[2] सुरुचिरविद्रुमसंनिभाधरौष्ठि[3] ।
तव वदनभवामृतं निपीय कथमवशो ह्ययशोविषं पिबामि ॥ १३ ॥

उभौ—अपसरतार्याः अपसरत ।

एष गुणरत्ननिधिः सज्जनदुःखानामुत्तरणसेतुः ।
असुवर्णं मण्डनकमपनीयतेऽद्य नगरीतः ॥ १४ ॥

अन्यच्च ।

सर्वः खलु भवति लोके लोकः सुखसंस्थितानां चिन्तायुक्तः ।
विनिपतितानां नराणां प्रियकारी दुर्लभो भवति ॥ १५ ॥

(ओशलध अज्जा ओशलध

एशे गुणलअणणिही शज्जणदुक्खाण उत्तलणशेदू ।
अशुवण्णं मण्डणअं अवणीअदि अज्ज णअलीदो ॥

अण्णं च ।

शव्वे क्खु होइ लोए लोए शुहशंठिदाण तत्तिल्लः[4] ।
विणिवडिदाण[5] णलाणं पिअकाली दुल्लहो होदि ॥)

चारुदत्तः—(सर्वतोऽवलोक्य ।)

अमी हि वस्त्रान्तनिरुद्धवक्त्राः[6] प्रयान्ति मे दूरतरं वयस्याः ।
परोऽपि बन्धुः समसंस्थितस्य मित्रं न कश्चिद्विषमस्थितस्य ॥ १६ ॥

चाण्डालौ—अपसारणं कृतम् । विविक्तो राजमार्गः । तदानयतैतं दत्तवध्यचिह्नम् । (ओशालणं किदम् । विवित्तं लाअमग्गम् । ता आणेध एदं दिण्णवज्झचिण्हम् ।)

(चारुदत्तो निःश्वस्य 'मैत्रेय भोः किमिदमद्य' (९।२९) इत्यादि पठति ।)

(नेपथ्ये ।)

हा तात हा प्रियवयस्य । (हा ताद हा पिअवअस्स ।)

चारुदत्तः—(आकर्ण्य सकरुणम् ।) भोः स्वजातिमहत्तर इच्छाम्यहं भवतः सकाशात्प्रतिग्रहं कर्तुम् ।)

१ उद्वीक्ष्य. २ दन्तं. ३ धरोष्ठं; धरोष्ठि. ४ तत्तिल्ला. ५ वडिदाणं. ६ न्तरुद्ध०.

My family, which was formerly sanctified by ( the performance of ) hundreds of sacrifices, and made illustrious by the chanting of Vedic hymns in crowded halls in sacrificial assemblies, is now being loudly named in the proclamation and polluted by ( such ) persons, unholy and quite different from them ( my ancestors ), as I am now a man condemned to death. ( 12 )

( *Shuddering and covering up his ears* ). Oh, dear Vasantasena !

O you, with teeth white like the pure rays of the moon and with the lower lip resembling the beautiful coral, having drunk the nectar from your mouth, how can I, who am ( so ) helpless, ( now ) swallow the poison ( in the form ) of ignominy ? ( 13 )

BOTH—Make way, sirs, make way !

This store of the jewels ( *or* ocean ) of virtues, ( this ) bridge for the good to cross ( the ocean of ) their miseries, ( this ) ornament, though not one of gold,—this person is to-day being taken away from the city. ( 14 )

Moreover:—

Verily, in this world, all interest themselves in other persons when these ( latter ) are in easy circumstances. But it is difficult to find one who will show kindness to men who have fallen. (15)

CHAR.—( *Looking on all sides* )

These friends of mine, covering up their faces with the ends of their garments, are going further away from me. Even a stranger is ( *i. e.* behaves like ) a relative towards a person in normal circumstances; but no one befriends a man whose circumstances are reversed. ( 16 )

THE TWO CH.—We have turned away ( the crowd ). The high road is now clear. So bring him up, with the signs of the condemned put on.

( Charudatta *sighs and recites the verse beginning ' O Maitreya, what is this to-day ' &c.* )

( *Behind the curtain* )

Alas, father ! Alas, dear friend !

CHAR.—( *Listening; mournfully* ). O you, the chief of your caste, I wish to ask a favour at your hands.

**चाण्डालौ**—किमस्माकं हस्तात्प्रतिग्रहं करोषि। (किं अम्हाणं हत्थादो पडिग्गहं कलेशि।)

**चारुदत्तः**—शान्तं पापम्। नापरीक्ष्यकारी[1] दुराचारः पालक इव चाण्डालः। तत्परलोकार्थं[2] पुत्रमुखं द्रष्टुमभ्यर्थये।

**चाण्डालौ**—एवं क्रियताम्। (एव्वं कलीअदु।)

(नेपथ्ये।)

हा तात हा पितः। (हा ताद हा आवुक।)

(चारुदत्तः श्रुत्वा सकरुणं 'भोः स्वजातिमहत्तर' इत्यादि पठति।)

**चाण्डालौ**—अरे पौराः क्षणमन्तरं दत्त। एष आर्यचारुदत्तः पुत्रमुखं पश्यतु। (नेपथ्याभिमुखम्।) आर्य इत इतः। आगच्छ रे दारक आगच्छ। (अले पउला[3] खणं अन्तलं देध। एशे अज्जचालुदत्ते पुत्तमुहं पेक्खदु। अज्ज इदो इदो। आअच्छ ले दालआ आअच्छ।)

(ततः प्रविशति दारकमादाय विदूषकः।)

**विदूषकः**—त्वरतां त्वरतां भद्रमुखः। पिता ते मारयितुं नीयते। (तुवरदु तुवरदु भद्दमुहो। पिदा दे मारिदुं णीअदि।)

**दारकः**—हा तात हा पितः। (हा ताद हा आवुक।)

**विदूषकः**—हा प्रियवयस्य कुत्र मया त्वं द्रष्टव्यः। (हा पिअवअस्स कहिं मए तुमं पेक्खिदव्वो।)

**चारुदत्तः**—(पुत्रं मित्रं च वीक्ष्य।) हा पुत्र हा मैत्रेय। (सकरुणम्।) भोः कष्टम्।

**चिरं खलु भविष्यामि परलोके पिपासितः।**
**अत्यल्पमिदमस्माकं निवापोदकभोजनम्[4] ॥ १७ ॥**

किं पुत्राय प्रयच्छामि। (आत्मानमवलोक्य[5]। यज्ञोपवीतं दृष्ट्वा।) आं इदं तावदस्ति मम च।

**अमौक्तिकमसौवर्णं ब्राह्मणानां विभूषणम्।**
**देवतानां पितॄणां च भागो येन प्रदीयते ॥ १८ ॥**

(इति यज्ञोपवीतं ददाति।)

---

सेतुः उत्तरणसाधनम्। असुवर्णं मण्डनमद्य नगरीतोऽपनीयते ॥१४॥ **सर्व इति।** लोके सर्वः खलु सुखसंस्थितानां सुखिनां चिन्तायुक्तः क्षेमचिन्तनपरः भवति। चिन्तापर उपयुक्त इत्यर्थ इति पृथ्वीधरः। विनिपतितानामापन्नानां नराणां प्रियकारी दुर्लभः

---

१ नापरीक्षितकारी. २ ०कार्थे. ३ पउला जणा. ४ भाजनम्. ५ वीक्ष्य.

THE TWO CH.—What! You would take a favour from *our* hands?

CHAR.—Heaven forbid! (Still), a Chandala is not like the ill-behaved king Palaka, who acts without due investigation. So, I request you for getting a (last) sight of my son's face, so that I might (easily) obtain heaven,

THE TWO CH.--You may do so.

(*Behind the curtain*).

Alas, Alas, father!

(Charudatta, *hearing it, mournfully repeats*—'*O you the chief of your caste*' *&c.*).

THE TWO CH.—Ye citizens, make room for a moment. Let this worthy Charudatta have a look at his son's face (*Facing the curtain*). Sir, (come) this way, in this direction! Come, boy, come up here!

(*Then enter* Vidushaka *with the* boy).

VID.—Make haste, my sweet-faced one, make haste; your father is being taken for being killed!

THE SON—Oh, papa! Oh, father!

VID.—Oh, dear friend! Where shall I see you (again)?

CHAR.—(*Seeing his* son *and his* friend). Ah, my son! Ah, Maitreya! (*Mournfully*). Oh! Alas!

Verily I shall have to remain thirsty for a long time in the next world; (for) very small, indeed, would be this libation of water offered to me after death (as the boy's hands are so small). (17)

What shall I bequeath to my son? (*Looking over his own body and seeing his sacred thread*). Ah, yes! Here's a thing which I do possess—

Which is an ornament to the Brahmanas, though not made of pearls or of gold, and through which oblations are offered to the gods and the manes. (18)

(*He hands over his sacred thread*)

---

भवति ।] ॥ १५ ॥ [अमी हीति । अमी हि मे वयस्याः वस्त्रान्तेन निरुद्धं संवृतं वक्त्रं यैस्तथा सन्तः दूरतरं प्रयान्ति । समसंस्थितस्य सुखावस्थात्रस्थितस्य परोऽपि बन्धुर्भवति । उपजातिः ]॥१६॥ हा आवुक पितः। चिरमिति । [पिपासितः तृषितः।

**चाण्डालः**—आगच्छ रे चारुदत्त आगच्छ। (आअच्छ ले चालुदत्ता आअच्छ।)

**द्वितीयः**—अरे आर्यचारुदत्तं निरुपपदेन नाम्नाऽऽलपसि। अरे पश्य।

**अभ्युदयेऽवसाने तथैव रात्रिदिवमहतमार्गा।**
**उद्दामेव किशोरी नियतिः खलु प्रत्येषितुं याति ॥ १९ ॥**

अन्यच्च।

**शुष्का व्यपदेशा अस्य किं विनमितमस्तकं न कर्तव्यम्।**
**राहुगृहीतोऽपि चन्द्रो न वन्दनीयो जनपदस्य ॥ २० ॥**

(अले अज्जचालुदत्तं णिलुववदेण णामेण आलवेशि। अले पेक्ख[1]।

अब्भुदए अवशाणे तहेअ[2] लत्तिदिवं अहदमग्गा।
उद्दामे व्व किशोली णिअदी क्खु पडिच्छिदुं[3] जादि ॥

अण्णं च।

शुक्खा ववदेशा[4] शे किं विणमिअमत्थए[5] ण काअव्वम्।
लाहुगहिदे वि चन्दे ण वन्दणीए जणपदश्श ॥)

**दारकः**—अरे रे चाण्डालौ कुत्र मम पितरं नयथः। (अरे[6] रे चाण्डाला, कहिं मे आवुकं णेध।)

**चारुदत्तः**—वत्स।

**अंसेन बिभ्रत्करवीरमालां स्कन्धेन शूलं हृदयेन शोकम्।**
**आघातमद्याहमनुप्रयामि शामित्रमालब्धुमिवाध्वरेऽजः[7] ॥ २१ ॥**

**चाण्डालः**—दारक।

**न खल्वावां चाण्डालौ चाण्डालकुले जातपूर्वावपि।**
**येऽभिभवन्ति साधुं ते पापास्ते च चाण्डालाः ॥ २२ ॥**

(दालआ

ण हु अम्हे [8]चाण्डाला चाण्डालकुलम्मि जादपुव्वा वि।
जे अहिभवन्ति शाहुं ते पावा ते अ चाण्डाला ॥)

**दारकः**—तत्किमर्थं मारयथः पितरम्। (ता कीस मारेध आवुकम्।)

**चाण्डालः**—दीर्घायुः अत्र राजनियोगः खल्वपराध्यति न खल्वावाम्। (दीहाओ अत्त लाअणिओओ क्खु अवलज्झदि ण क्खु अम्हे।)

---

१ पेक्ख पेक्ख. २ तह अ (तथा च). ३ पडिक्खिदुं (परीक्षितुं). ४ वि वदेशा (अपि प्रदेशाः). ५ मत्थएण (मस्तकेन); पणमिअ मत्थके (प्रणम्य मस्तके). ६ अले ले. ७ आलब्धं. ८ चण्डाला.

CH.—Come, O Charudatta, come along !

THE SEC. CH.—Ah, you are calling the worthy Charudatta without his title ( of *Arya*, 'the worthy' ) ? See, you !—

Unchecked in its course, like a female colt broken loose from the reins, Fate verily comes ( thundering along ) in pursuit of a man, by day and by night, in prosperity as well as in adversity. (19)

Moreover—

Have his titles ( noble appellations ) become empty ? Should we not bow down our heads to him ? ( We should ). Does not the moon, though eclipsed by Rahu, deserve to be saluted by the people in general ? ( 20 )

THE SON—Oh, you Chandalas, where are you taking my father ?

CHAR.—Child !

Bearing the garland of *karavira* flowers round my neck, the iron spike on my shoulder and grief in my heart, I am to-day going to the place of execution, like the goat ( at a sacrifice being led ) to the place of immolation for being killed. ( 21 )

CH.—Boy !

Verily we are not ( to be called ) Chandalas, though we have been born in a Chandala family. Those who presecute a virtuous man,—*they* are the sinners, and *they* the Chandalas. ( 22 )

SON—Then why are you killing my father ?

CH.—My long-lived boy, it is the king's command that commits the wrong ( is to blame ), and not we two.

---

इदं पुत्रदत्तं निवापोदकमेव भोजनमस्माकमत्यल्पमपर्याप्तं भविष्यति ] ॥ १७ ॥ **अमौक्तिकमिति** । [असौवर्णमसुवर्णघटितम् । येन उपवीतेन प्राचीनोपवीतरूपेण] ॥१८॥ निरुपपदेन आर्य इत्यादिविशेषणशून्येन । **अभ्युदय इत्यादि** । गाथा । [अवसाने संपदुपरमे आपदि इत्यर्थः । तथैव रात्रिदिवमहतमार्गा । अव्याहतप्रसिक्ता इत्यर्थः । उद्दामा उच्छिन्नबन्धना किशोरी बालाश्वा इव नियतिर्दैवं खलु प्रत्येषितुं पुरुषमाक्रमितुं याति । प्रतीष्टं (इष्टं पुरुषं) इति केचिच्छायामिच्छन्ति ] ॥ १९ ॥ **शुष्का इत्यादि** । गाथा । [अस्य चारुदत्तस्य व्यपदेशाः शोभननामादयः किं शुष्काः अनेनापवादेन क्षीणाः । अस्य विनमितमस्तकं किं न कर्तव्यम् । कर्तव्यमेव । राहुगृहीतश्चन्द्रो जनपदस्य न वन्दनीयः इति काकुः । वन्दनीय एवेत्यर्थः । ] शुष्का अपि प्रदेशा अङ्गानि ।

**दारकः**—व्यापादयतं माम्। मुञ्चतं पितरम्। ( वावादेध मम्। मुञ्चध आवुकम्। )

**चाण्डालः**—दीर्घायुः एवं भणंश्चिरं मे जीव। (दीहाओ एवं भणन्ते चिलं मे जीव।)

**चारुदत्तः**—(सास्रं पुत्रं कण्ठे गृहीत्वा।)

**इदं तत्स्नेहसर्वस्वं सममाढ्यदरिद्रयोः।**
**[1]अचान्दनमनौशीरं हृदयस्यानुलेपनम् ॥ २३ ॥**

( 'अंसेन बिभ्रत्--' ( १०।२१ ) इत्यादि पुनः पठति। अवलोक्य स्वगतम्। 'अमी हि वस्त्रान्तनिरुद्धवक्त्राः' ( १०।१६ ) इत्यादि पुनः पठति। )

**विदूषकः**—भो भद्रमुखौ मुञ्चतं प्रियवयस्यं चारुदत्तम्। मां व्यापादयतम्। (भो भद्दमुहा मुञ्चध पिअवअस्सं चालुदत्तम्। मं वावादेध।)

**चारुदत्तः**—शान्तं पापम्[2]। (दृष्ट्वा स्वगतम्।) अद्यावगच्छामि। ('परोऽपि ...समसंस्थितस्य' ( १०।१६ ) इत्यादि पठति। प्रकाशम्। 'एताः पुनर्हर्म्यगताः स्त्रियो माम्' ( १०।११ ) इत्यादि पुनः पठति।)

**चाण्डालः**—अपसरतार्याः अपसरत।

**किं पश्यथ सत्पुरुषमयशोवशेन प्रनष्टजीवाशम्।**
**कूपे खण्डितपाशं काञ्चनकलशमिव मज्जन्तम् ॥ २४ ॥**

(ओशलध अज्जा ओशलध।

किं पेक्खध शप्पुलिशं अजशवशेण प्पणट्टजीवाशम्।
कूवे[3] खण्डिदपाशं कञ्चणकलशं व्वि डुब्बन्तम् ॥)

(चारुदत्तः सकरुणम् 'शशिविमलमयूख–' ( १०।१३ ) इत्यादि पठति।)

**अपरः**—अरे पुनरपि घोषय। (अले पुणोवि घोशेहि।)

(चाण्डालस्तथा करोति।)

---

किं विनमितमस्तकेन अवनतशिरसा किं कर्तव्यम्। अस्य स्त्रीहृणस्य लज्जया नतशिरसोऽपि न कुत्सेत्यर्थः। कुत एवमित्यत आह—राहुगृहीत इव चन्द्रो वन्दनीयो जनपदस्य। किंशब्द आवर्त्योभयोरर्धयोर्योज्य इत्याहुः ॥ २० ॥ **अंसेनेति**। आघातं अधिकरणवधस्थानम्। 'शमिता यज्ञे' इति पाणिनेः सूत्रम्। शमितुरिदं शामित्रम्। यज्ञे पशुघातस्थानम्। आलब्धोऽभिमन्त्रितः। मारित इत्येके। अज इवाहं प्रयामि। इन्द्रवज्रा वृत्तम् ] ॥ २१ ॥ **न खल्विति**। जातपूर्वौ अपि। जन्मना चाण्डालौ न कर्मणेत्यर्थः। ते पापाः इत्यनेन पालकः शकारश्च लक्षितौ ] ॥ २२ ॥ **इदमिति**।

---

१ अचन्दनं. २ पापं शान्तं पापम्. ३ कूवम्मि खुडिदपाशं.

SON—Kill me, and let my papa go !

CH.—My long-lived child, may you that speak thus ( *i. e.* so nobly ) live long !

CHAR.—( *Embracing his weeping* son *around the neck* ).

This is the all-in-all of love, equally accessible to both, the rich and the poor ! It is a soothing ointment ( balm ) to the heart, though containing neither sandal nor *usira* paste. ( 23 )

( *He again recites the verse beginning ' Bearing round my neck ' &c.; then he observes, and again repeats to himself the verse beginning ' And these with their faces covered up with the ends of their garments ' &c.* )

VID.—You gentle ones, let go my dear friend Charudatta, and kill me ( in his stead ) !

CHAR —Heaven forbid ! ( *Observing; to himself* ), Now I learnt it ! ( *He recites again ' Of one in happy circumstances ' &c.; then aloud—he recites again the verse beginning 'And these ladies in their mansions '* &c. ).

CH.—Make way, sirs, make way !

Why should you throng to look at a virtuous man who has lost all hope of life owing to ( *i. e.* in consequence of ) ignominy ( an infamous deed ), like a golden jar sinking in a well when its rope is snapped ? ( 24 )

Charudatta *mournfully recites the verse beginning ' O you with teeth pure like the rays of the moon ' &c.* ).

THE OTHER CH.—Eh, proclaim it once more !

( *The* Chandala *does so* ).

---

[ इदं तत्पुत्रालिङ्गनजन्यं सुखं आढ्यः श्रीमान् दरिद्रश्च तयोः समं स्नेहसर्वस्वम् । अचान्दनं अनौशीरं उशीरजादन्यत् हृदयस्यानुलेपनम् ] ॥ २३ ॥ किमिति । गाथा । अयशोवशेन वसन्तसेनाघातजन्यापवादात् । प्रनष्टा जीवाशा यस्य तं पुरुषम् । खण्डितः विच्छिन्नः पाशः रज्जुः यस्य तादृशं कूपे मज्जन्तम् ] ॥ २४ ॥ प्राप्त इति । [ अहं व्यसनेन कृतामापज्जनितामनार्यां गर्ह्यां दशां प्राप्तः । यत्रेदं जीवितावसानं मरणरूपं फलमपि । घोषणा मदपराधख्यापना । प्रहर्षिणी वृत्तम् ] ॥ २५ ॥ आक्रन्दामि विरौमि । बालाग्रप्रतोलीतः प्रासादभागादित्यर्थः । कोऽयमिति । [ कालपाशस्थिते मृत्युगोचरे । द्रोणमेघः शस्यवृद्धिकरः पुष्करावर्तकाद्यन्यतमः मेघविशेषः । तदुक्तं ज्योतिस्तत्त्वे—' त्रियुते शाकवर्षे तु चतुर्भिः शेषितः क्रमात् । आवर्तं विद्धि

**चारुदत्तः**—

**प्राप्तोऽहं व्यसनकृतां[1] दशामनार्यां**
**यत्रेदं फलमपि जीवितावसानम्[2] ।**
**एषा च व्यथयति घोषणा मनो मे**
**श्रोतव्यं यदिदमसौ मया[3] हतेति ॥ २५ ॥**

(ततः प्रविशति प्रासादस्थो बद्धः स्थावरकः)

**स्थावरकः**—([4]घोषणामाकर्ण्य सवैक्लव्यम् ।) कथमपापश्चारुदत्तो व्यापाद्यते । अहं निगडेन स्वामिना बद्धः । भवतु । आक्रन्दामि । शृणुतार्याः शृणुत । अस्तीदानीं मया पापेन प्रवहणपरिवर्तेन पुष्पकरण्डकजीर्णोद्यानं वसन्तसेना नीता । ततो मम स्वामिना मां न कामयस इति कृत्वा बाहुपाशबलात्कारेण मारिता न पुनरेतेनार्येण । कथम् । विदूरतया न कोऽपि शृणोति । तत्किं करोमि । आत्मानं पातयामि । ( विचिन्त्य । ) यद्येवं करोमि तदाऽऽर्यचारुदत्तो न व्यापाद्यते । भवतु । अस्याः प्रासादबालाग्रप्रतोलिकात एतेन जीर्णगवाक्षेणात्मानं निक्षिपामि । वरमहमुपरतः न पुनरेष कुलपुत्रविहगानां वासपादप आर्यचारुदत्तः । एवं यदि विपद्ये लब्धो मया परलोकः । (इत्यात्मानं पातयित्वा ।) आश्चर्यम् । नोपरतोऽस्मि । भग्नो मे दण्ड-निगडः । तच्चाण्डालघोषं समन्विष्यामि । (दृष्टोपसृत्य ।) हं हो चाण्डालौ अन्तर-मन्तरम् । (कधं अपावे चालुदत्ते वावादीअदि । हग्गे णिअलेण शामिणा बन्धिदे । भोदु । आक्कन्दामि । शुणाध अज्जा शुणाध । अत्थि दाणिं मए पावेण पवहण-पडिवत्तेण पुप्फकलण्डअजिण्णुज्जाणं वसन्तशेणा णीदा । तदो मम शामिणा मं ण कामेशित्ति कदुअ बाहुपाशबलक्कालेण मालिदा ण उण एदिणा अज्जेण । कधम् । विदूलदाए ण को वि शुणादि । ता किं कलेमि । अत्ताणअं पाडेमि । जइ एव्वं कलेमि तदा अज्जचालुदत्ते ण वावादीअदि । भोदु । इमादो पाशादबालग्गपदोलिकादो एदिणा जिण्णगवक्खेण अत्ताणअं णिक्खिवामि । वलं हग्गे उवलदे ण उण एशे कुलपुत्तविहगाणं[5] वाशपादवे अज्जचालुदत्ते । एव्वं जइ विवज्जामि लद्धे मए पललोए । ही ही । ण उवलदम्हि । भग्गे मे दण्डणिअले । ता चाण्डालघोशं शमण्णेशामि । हंहो चाण्डाला अन्तलं अन्तलम् ।)

**चाण्डालौ**—अरे कोऽन्तरं याचते । (अले के अन्तलं मग्गेदि ।)

(चेटः 'शुणाध' इति पूर्वोक्तं पठति ।)

**चारुदत्तः**—अये ।

**कोऽयमेवंविधे काले कालपाशस्थिते मयि ।**
**अनावृष्टिहते सस्ये द्रोणमेघ इवोदितः[6] ॥ २६ ॥**

---

१ कृशां. २ पमानम्. ३ त्वया. ४ घोषणं. ५ विहंगाणं. ६ वोत्थितः.

CHAR.—

I have already been reduced to a despicable state, brought on by adversity, having for its climax the loss of my life in this fashion. And ( to add to that ) this proclamation cuts me to the quick, that I should have now to hear that that beloved of mine was killed by me ! (25)

( *Then enter* Sthavaraka *in fetters and imprisoned in the palace* ).

STH.—( *Listening to the proclamation; distressfully* ). How now ! They are killing the innocent Charudatta ! And my master has secured me with chains ! Never mind, I will shout out.—Listen, sirs, listen ! It so happened that I, the sinful wretch, took Vasantasena to the old *Pushpakarandaka* garden, owing to an interchange of carriages. Then my master killed her by violently strangling her with the noose of his arms, because she did not love him; this noble person ( Charudatta ) didn't do it. How ! Owing to the great distance nobody hears me ! Then what shall I do ? Shall I throw myself down ? ( *Reflecting* ). If I do so, the worthy Charudatta would not be killed. All right. I will throw myself down through this old window, from this elephant-corniced terrace of the palace. Better that I should be dead, rather than the noble Charudatta, the tree affording shelter to the birds in he form of ( all ) well-born youths. If I die thus, I shall have obtained heaven ! ( *Thereupon he throws himself down*). Wonderful ! I have not been killed, and ( these ) my fettering chains have snapped asunder ! Now I shall find out where that proclamation of the Chandalas comes from. ( *Observes and approaches* ). Oh, you Chandalas, make room, make room !

THE TWO CH.—Eh, who is that wants room ?

( *The* Cheta *repeats what he had said before, viz.* ' *Listen* ' *etc.*).

CHAR.—Ah !

Who is this that has sprung up at such a time, when I am held fast in the noose of Death, like the *Drona* cloud when the corn is suffering from drought ? ( 26 )

---

संवर्तं पुष्करं द्रोणमम्बुदम् । आवर्तो निर्जलो मेघः संवर्तश्च बहूदकः । पुष्करो दुष्करजलो द्रोणः शस्यप्रपूरकः ॥ ' इति ] ॥ २६ ॥ न भीत इति ॥ २७ ॥ तेनेति । [ मया अकृत वैरं यस्य तेन । क्षुद्रेण नीचेन अतिमन्दबुद्धिना स्वयं दूषितेन तेन शकारेण

भो श्रुतं भवद्भिः ।

न भीतो मरणादस्मि केवलं दूषितं यशः ।
विशुद्धस्य हि मे मृत्युः पुत्रजन्मसमो भवेत् ॥ २७ ॥

अन्यच्च ।

तेनास्म्यकृतवैरेण क्षुद्रेणात्यल्पबुद्धिना ।
शरेणेव[1] विषाक्तेन दूषितेनापि दूषितः ॥ २८ ॥

**चाण्डालौ**—स्थावरक अपि सत्यं भणसि । (थावलक अवि शच्चं[2] भणाशि ।)

**चेटः**—सत्यम् । अहमपि मा कस्यापि कथयिष्यसीति प्रासादबालाग्रप्रतोलिकायां दण्डनिगडेन बद्ध्वा निक्षिप्तः । (शच्चम् । हग्गे वि मा कश्श वि कधइश्शशित्ति पाशादबालग्गपदोलिकाए दण्डणिअलेण बन्धिअ णिक्खित्ते ।)

(प्रविश्य ।)

**शकारः**—(सहर्षम् ।)

मांसेन तिक्ताम्लेन भक्तं शाकेन सूपेन समत्स्यकेन ।
भुक्तं मयाऽऽत्मनो गेहे शालीयकूरेण गुडौदनेन ॥ २९ ॥

( कर्णं दत्त्वा । ) भिन्नकांस्यखङ्खणायाश्चाण्डालवाचायाः स्वरसंयोगः । यथा चैष उद्गीतो वध्यडिण्डिमशब्दः पटहानां च श्रूयते तथा तर्कयामि दरिद्रचारुदत्तको वध्यस्थानं नीयत इति । तत्प्रेक्षिष्ये । शत्रुविनाशो नाम मम महान्हृदयस्य परितोषो भवति । श्रुतं च मया योऽपि किल शत्रुं व्यापाद्यमानं पश्यति तस्यान्यस्मिञ्जन्मान्तरेऽक्षिरोगो न भवति । मया खलु विषग्रन्थिगर्भप्रविष्टेनेव कीटकेन किमप्यन्तरं मृगयमाणेनोत्पादितस्तस्य दरिद्रचारुदत्तस्य विनाशः । सांप्रतमात्मीयायां प्रासादबालाग्रप्रतोलिकायामधिरुह्यात्मनः पराक्रमं पश्यामि ।

---

विषाक्तेन शरेण इव दूषितोऽस्मि ] ॥ २८ ॥ **मांसेनेति** । उपजातिच्छन्दः । [ मया आत्मनो गेहे तिक्ताम्लेन तिक्ताम्लरसोपेतेन मांसेन समत्स्यकेन शाकेन शालीयकूरेण शाल्युत्पन्नेनान्नेन गुडौदनेन सह भक्तं भुक्तम । ] तप्तशाकेन शालेर्भक्तेन गुडौदनेन ॥२९॥ भिन्नकांस्यवत्खङ्खणायाः कटुस्वरायाः विकृतध्वन्याश्चाण्डालवाचः स्वरसंयोगः । यथा चैव उत्खालित उद्गतः पटहानां च शब्दस्तथा तर्कये । यः शत्रुं व्यापाद्यमानं प्रेक्षते तस्याक्षिणी शीतलायेते । विषकण्डिकामध्यप्रविष्टेन इव कीटकेन । ही विस्मये । कथमित्यर्थः । एवड्ढे एतावान्महान् । नवबलीवर्द इव नववृषभ इव मण्डितः । वृषभशब्दः संभवन्नपि शकारभाषात्वात्त्यक्तः । **अपसरतेति** । [तूष्णीका मौनिनः । अविनय एव तीक्ष्णो निशितः विषाणः शृङ्गं यस्य सः । दुष्टः बलीवर्दः

---

१ शरेणैव २ सच्चं.

Well, Sirs, have you heard ( all that ) ?

I am not afraid of death; only my fair name is tarnished [and this is what pains me]. Death to me if ( proved ) pure ( free from guilt ) will be like ( i. e. as welcome as ) the birth of a son. ( 27 )

Moreover :—

By that mean fellow ( Sakara ), whose enemy I never was and who is extremely narrow-minded, I was charged with crime —though he himself was the criminal—as with a poison-besmeared arrow. ( 28 )

THE TWO CH.—Sthavaraka, are you telling the truth ?

CHETA—( Yes ), the truth. And he also put me in chains linked together, and kept me, imprisoned in the elephant-corniced terrace of his palace, saying ' ( now ) you will not tell any one.'

( *Entering* )

SAK.—( *Gleefully* ).

In my palace I have dined on rice, and meat seasoned with pungent and sour sauces, and vegetables, soup and fish, and rice-cakes and treacled rice. ( 29 )

( *Listening* ). It seems to be the voice of a Chandala speaking, as it has the ring of cracked bell-metal. And, since this loud noise of drums and kettle-drums beaten at the time of execution is heard, I guess that the penniless Charudatta is ( now ) being taken to the place of execution. So I shall ( go and ) have a good look at it. The destruction of an enemy, in sooth, affords my heart very great pleasure. And I have heard that whoever witnesses the killing of an enemy will not suffer from any eye-disease in his next birth. I have indeed managed to bring about the ruin of that pauper Charudatta, after having sought a ( broad ) way out, like a warm stationed in the inside of the root of a poisonous herb. Now I'll ascend to the elephant-corniced upper terrace of my palace and ( from there ) witness my own exploit.

---

शकारः ] ॥ ३० ॥ [ लल्लादीक्षितास्तु सत्यकमपि इति पठित्वा 'प्रशस्तं सत्यं सत्यकम् । प्रशंसायां कन्' इति व्याख्यान्ति । विभवः सामर्थ्यम् ] । उत्तिष्ठेति । [ भोः पतितः आपद्ग्रस्तः यः साधुजनस्तस्य अनुकम्पिन् निष्कारणोपगतबान्धव धर्मशील धार्मिक उत्तिष्ठ । त्वया मम मोक्षणाय सुमहान् यत्नः कृतोऽपि यद्यपि कृतः तथाऽपि दैवं न संवदति अनुकूलत्वेनानुवर्तते । त्वयाऽद्य किं न कृतम् । सर्वं

( तथा कृत्वा दृष्ट्वा च । ) ही ही एतस्य दरिद्रचारुदत्तस्य वध्यं नीयमानस्यैतावाञ्जनसंमर्दः । यस्यां वेलायामस्मादृशः प्रवरो वरमानुषो वध्यं नीयते तस्यां वेलायां कीदृशो भवेत् । ( निरीक्ष्य । ) कथम् । एष स नवबलीवर्द इव मण्डितो दक्षिणां दिशं नीयते । अथ किंनिमित्तं मदीयायाः प्रासादबालाग्रप्रतोलिकायाः समीपे घोषणा निपतिता निवारिता च । ( विलोक्य । ) कथं स्थावरकश्चेटोऽपि नास्तीह । मा नाम तेनेतो गत्वा मन्त्रभेदः कृतो भविष्यति । तद्यावदेनमन्विष्यामि । ( इत्यवतीर्योपसर्पति । )

( मंशेण तिक्खामिलकेण भत्ते शाकेण शूपेण शमच्छकेण ।
भुत्तं मए अत्तणअश्श गेहे शालिश्शकूलेण गुलोदणेण ।।

भिण्णकंशखङ्खणाए चाण्डालवाआए शलशंजोए । जधा अ एशे उक्खालिदे[1] वज्झडिण्डिमशद्दे पडहाणं अ शुणीअदि तधा तक्केमि दलिद्दचालुदत्ताके वज्झट्ठाणं णीअदि त्ति । ता पेक्खिश्शम् । शत्तुविणाशे णाम मम महन्ते हलवकश्श पलिदोशे होदि । शुदं अ मए जे वि किल शत्तुं वावादअन्तं पेक्खदि तश्श अण्णंशि जम्मन्तले अक्खिलोगे ण होदि । मए क्खु विशगण्ठिगब्भपविट्ठेण विअ कीडएण किं पि अन्तलं मग्गमाणेण उप्पाडिदे ताह दलिद्दचारुदत्ताह विणाशे । शंपदं अत्तणकेलिकाए पाशादबालग्गपदोलिकाए अहिलुहिअ अत्तणो पलक्कमं पेक्खामि । ही ही एदाह दलिद्दचालुदत्ताह वज्झं णीअमाणाह एवड्ढे[2] जणशंमद्दे । जं वेलं अम्हालिशे पबले वलमणुश्शे वज्झं णीअदि तं वेलं कीदिशे[3] भवे । कधम् । एशे शे णवबलद्दके विअ मण्डिदे दक्खिणं दिशं णीअदि । अध किंणिमित्तं ममकेलिकाए पाशादबालग्गपदोलिकाए शमीवे घोशणा णिवडिदा णिवालिदा अ । कधं थावलके चेडे वि णत्थि इध । मा णाम तेण इदो गदुअ मन्तभेदे कडे भविश्शदि । ता जाव णं अण्णेशामि । )

**चेटः**—( दृष्ट्वा । ) भट्टारकाः एष स आगतः । ( भट्टालका एशे शे आगदे । )

**चाण्डालौ**—

**अपसरत दत्त मार्गं द्वारं पिधत्त भवत तूष्णीकाः ।**
**अविनयतीक्ष्णविषाणो दुष्टबलीवर्द इत एति ।। ३० ।।**
( ओशलध देध मग्गं दालं ढक्केध होध तुण्हीआ ।
अविणअतिक्खविशाणे दुट्टबइल्ले इदो एदि ।। )

**शकारः**—अरे अरे अन्तरमन्तरं दत्त । ( उपसृत्य । ) पुत्रक स्थावरक चेट एहि गच्छावः । ( अले अले अन्तलं अन्तलं देध । पुश्तका थावलका चेडा एहि । गच्छम्ह । )

**चेटः**—ही ही अनार्य वसन्तसेनां मारयित्वा न परितुष्टोऽसि । सांप्रतं प्रणयिजनकल्पपादपमार्यचारुदत्तं मारयितुं व्यवसितोऽसि । ( ही ही अणज्ज वशन्तशेणिअं मालिअ ण पलितुट्टे शि । शंपदं पणइजणकप्पपादवं अज्जचालुदत्तं मालइदुं ववशिदेशि । )

**शकारः**—न हि रत्नकुम्भसदृशोऽहं स्त्रियं व्यापादयामि । ( ण हि लअणकुम्भशलिशे हग्गे इत्थिअं वावादेमि । )

---

१ उस्कालिदे. २ ऐशे वडढे ( एष वृद्धः ). ३ कीदिशं.

( *Does so; seeing* ). Ha, ha ! There is so large a crowd of people when this beggar Charudatta is being taken to the execution-ground; how large then would it be when a mighty high personage like myself would be taken to be executed ? (*Peering*). How ! Here he is, decked like a newly-trained bullock, being taken in the southern direction ! But why is it that the proclamation was made in the neighbourhood of the elephant-corniced terrace of my palace, and stopped ( suddenly ) ? ( *Observing* ). How ! The slave Sthavaraka, too, is not to be seen here ! Could he have gone from this place and divulged the facts ? Let me then first seek him out.

( *Descends and approaches* ).

CHETA—(*Seeing him*). Gentlemen, here he comes !

CH.—

Move off and make way ! Shut the doors and remain silent ! For here comes this mad bull having sharp horns ( in the form ) of his arrogant deeds ! ( 30 )

SAK.—Ho, there ! Make way, make way ! ( *Approaching* ) My son, Sthavaraka, my slave, come, let us be off !

CHETA.—Oh, you villain ! You were not satisfied by the murder of Vasantasena, and ( in addition ) now you want to murder the noble Charudatta also, the wish-granting tree of all supplicants !

SAK.—Never shall I, who am like a pot filled with jewels ( *i. e.* very rich ), murder a woman ( for the sake of her money ) !

---

कृतमित्यर्थः । वसन्ततिलकं वृत्तम् ] ॥ ३१ ॥ **आश्रममिति** । [ वत्स मातरं गृहीत्वा अद्यैव आश्रमं कस्यापि मुनेः तपोवनं वा गन्तव्यम् । पुत्र पितृदोषेण त्वमपि एवमहमिव मृत्युं मा गमिष्यसि ] ॥ ३२ ॥ **किं ओहसशीत्यादि** । गाथा । किमवहससि हे ज्ञक पुरुषं दृष्ट्वा दैवपर्यस्तम् । विदितं न त्वमत्पीवत हे दुर्जन कृतान्तदंष्ट्रामापुरोऽहपि (?) ॥ पराणेमि परानयामि व्यावर्तयामि । एताए एतावता । एवमेवेत्यर्थः । इदानीमित्येके । सङ्खलेन वध्यपटहवादनदण्डेन **प्राप्येति** । [ एतद्व्यसनमेव महार्णवस्तत्र प्रपातं प्राप्य । त्रासो भीतिः । जनापवादः वसन्तसेनावधायशोरूपः स एव वह्निः ] ॥ ३३ ॥ **वज्झपालिआ** वधपर्यायः । वीरक इति चाण्डालनाम । बन्धं खण्डेदि बन्धमाच्छिद्य प्रसरति । **प्रभवतीति** । प्रबलपुरुषः नयनिर्णेतारः । तेषां वाक्यैर्भाग्यदोषाद्दूषितस्य यदि मे **धर्मः** [पुण्यसंचयः] प्रभवति तदा सुरपतिभवनस्था कदाचिज्जीवन्ती यत्र तत्र स्थिता वा सैव वसन्तसेनैव

**सर्वे**—अहो त्वया मारिता। नार्यचारुदत्तेन। (अहो तुए मारिदा। ण अज्जचारुदत्तेण।)

**शकारः**—क एवं भणति। (के एव्वं भणादि।)

**सर्वे**—(चेटमुद्दिश्य।) नन्वेषः साधुः (णं एसो साहू।)

**शकारः**—(अपवार्य सभयम्।) हन्त कथं स्थावरकश्चेटः सुष्ठु न मया संयतः। एष खलु ममाकार्यस्य साक्षी। (विचिन्त्य।) एवं तावत्करिष्यामि। (प्रकाशम्।) अलीकं भट्टारकाः। अहो एष चेटः सुवर्णचोरिकया मया गृहीतस्ताडितो मारितो बद्धश्च। तत्कृतवैर एष यद्भणति किं सत्यम्। (अपवारितकेन चेटस्य कटकं प्रयच्छति। स्वैरकम्।) पुत्रक स्थावरक चेट एतद्गृहीत्वाऽन्यथा भण। (अविदमादिके अविवमादिके कधं थावलके चेडे शुश्ठु ण मए शंजदे। एशे क्खु मम अकज्जश्श शक्खी। एव्वं दाव कलइश्शम्। अलीअं भश्टालका। हंहो एशे चेडे शुवण्णचोलिआए मए गहिदे पिश्टिदे मालिदे बद्धे अ। ता किदवेले एशे जं भणादि किं शच्चम्। पुश्तका[1] थावलका चेडा एदं गेण्हिअ अण्णधा भणाहि।)

**चेटः**—(गृहीत्वा।) पश्यत पश्यत भट्टारकाः अहो सुवर्णेन मां प्रलोभयति। (पेक्खध पेक्खध भट्टालका। हंहो शुवण्णेण मं पलोभेदि।)

**शकारः**—(कटकमाच्छिद्य।) एतत्तत्सुवर्णकं यस्य कारणान्मया बद्धः। (सक्रोधम्।) हंहो चाण्डालौ मया खल्वेष सुवर्णभाण्डारे नियुक्तः सुवर्णं चोरयन्मारितस्ताडितः। तद्यदि न प्रत्ययेथे तदा पृष्ठं तावत्पश्यतम्। (एशे शे शुवण्णके जश्श कालणादो मए बद्धे[2]। हंहो चाण्डाला[3] मए क्खु एशे शुवण्णभण्डाले णिउत्ते शुवण्णं[4] चोलअन्ते मालिदे पिश्टिदे। ता जदि ण पत्तिआअध ता पिश्टिं दाव पेक्खध।)

**चाण्डालौ**—(दृष्ट्वा।) शोभनं भणति। वितप्तश्चेटः किं न प्रलपति। (शोहणं भणादि। वितत्ते[5] चेडे किं ण प्पलवदि[6]।)

**चेटः**—हन्त ईदृशो दासभावो यत्सत्यं कमपि न प्रत्याययति। (सकरुणम्।) आर्य चारुदत्त एतावान्मे विभवः। (इति पादयोः पतति।) (हीमादिके ईदिशे दाशभावे जं शच्चं[7] कंपि ण पत्तिआअदि। अज्जचालुदत्त एत्तिके मे विहवे।)

**चारुदत्तः**—(सकरुणम्।)

> **उत्तिष्ठ भोः पतितसाधुजनानुकम्पि-**
> **न्निष्कारणोपगतबान्धव धर्मशील।**
> **यत्नः कृतोऽपि सुमहान्मम मोक्षणाय**
> **दैवं न संवदति किं न कृतं त्वयाऽद्य॥ ३१॥**

**चाण्डालौ**—भट्टक ताडयित्वैतं चेटं निष्कासय। (भट्टके[8] पिट्ठिअ एदं चेडं णिक्खालेहि।)

---

१ पुश्थका. २ वड्ढे. ३ चाण्डालआ. ४ शुवण्णअं. ५ विडत्ते. ६ प्पडवदि. ७ सच्चकं पि. (सत्यकमपि न प्रत्याय्यते). ८ भश्टके.

ALL—Oh, but she was murdered by *you*, and not by the worthy Charudatta!

SAK.—Who says so?

ALL.—( *Pointing to* Cheta ). Why, this good man!

SAK.—( *Alarmed; to himself* ). Hang it! How is it that I failed to properly secure the slave Sthavaraka? For he is the ( sole ) witness of my crime. ( *Pondering* ). Well, I'll manage it thus. ( *Aloud* ). It is a lie, gentlemen! For see, this slave was caught by me as he was stealing my gold, and beaten and cudgelled and imprisoned. So, having become my enemy, whatever he tells you—could it be the truth? ( *Aside. Gives a golden bangle to* Cheta. *Whispering* ). Sthavaraka, my son, my slave, take this and contradict what you have said ( *lit.* speak otherwise ).

CHETA.—( *Taking it* ). Look, masters, look! Oh, ( here ) he is tempting me with gold!

SAK.—( *Snatching away the bangle* ). Here's that golden ornament for which he was put in chains! ( *Angrily* ). Oh you Chandalas, I really did beat and cudgel him as he was stealing my gold when appointed to guard my treasury. And, if you don't believe me, you may just inspect his back.

CH.—( *Seeing* ) What he says is right. What will a slave when exasperated ( *lit.* scorched ) not prattle?

CHETA.—Alas! Slavery is such a ( cursed ) thing that nobody believes the truth ( told by a slave ). ( *Mournfully* ). Sir Charudatta, ( only ) thus far lay my power! ( *He prostrates himself at his feet* ).

CHAR.—( *Mournfully* ).

Rise, O you who took pity on a fallen innocent man, who came to me as a disinterested friend, and who are righteous by nature. Although you made a very great effort to set me free, Fate does not agree to it. What is it that you have not done ( for me ) to-day? (31)

CH.—Sir, thrash this slave and turn him out.

---

स्वस्वभावेनात्मरूपतया मम कलङ्कं व्यपनयतु । [ मालिनी छन्दः ] ॥ ३४ ॥
गन्तव्यम् । तत्रैव मया मर्तव्यमित्यर्थः । अर्धामति । [ दीर्घा उन्नतशरीरा गोमायवः

**शकारः**— निष्क्राम रे। (इति निष्क्रामयति[1]।) अरे चाण्डालौ किं विलम्बेथे मारयतमेतम्। ([2]णिक्कम ले। अलेचाण्डाल किं विलम्बेध। मालेध एदम्।)

**चाण्डालौ**—यदि त्वरयसे तदा स्वयमेव मारय। (जदि तुवलशि ता शअं ज्जेव मालेहि।)

**रोहसेनः**—अरे चाण्डालौ मां मारयतम्। मुञ्चतं पितरम्। (अले चाण्डाला मं मारेध। मुञ्चध आवुकम्।)

**शकारः**—सपुत्रमेवैतं मारयतम्। (शपुत्तं ज्जेव एदं मालेध।)

**चारुदत्तः**—सर्वमस्य मूर्खस्य संभाव्यते। तद्गच्छ पुत्र मातुः समीपम्।

**रोहसेनः**—किं मया गतेन कर्तव्यम्। (किं मए गदेण कादव्वम्।)

**चारुदत्तः**—

> **आश्रमं[3] वत्स गन्तव्यं गृहीत्वाऽद्यैव मातरम्।**
> **मा पुत्र पितृदोषेण त्वमप्येवं[4] गमिष्यसि॥ ३२॥**

तद्वयस्य गृहीत्वैनं व्रज।

**विदूषकः**—भो वयस्य एवं त्वया ज्ञातं त्वया विनाऽहं प्राणान्धारयामीति। (भो वअस्स एव्वं तुए जाणिदं तुए विणा अहं पाणाइं धारेमि त्ति।)

**चारुदत्तः**—वयस्य स्वाधीनजीवितस्य न युज्यते तव प्राणपरित्यागः।

**विदूषकः**—(स्वगतम्।) युक्तं न्विदम्। तथाऽपि न शक्नोमि प्रियवयस्यविरहितः प्राणान्धर्तुमिति। तद्ब्राह्मण्यै दारकं समर्प्य प्राणपरित्यागेनात्मनः प्रियवयस्यमनुगमिष्यामि। (प्रकाशम्।) भो वयस्य परानयाम्येतं लघु। (इति सकण्ठग्रहं[5] पादयोः पतति।) (जुत्तं णेदम्। तधा वि ण सक्कुणोमि पिअवअस्सविरहिदो पाणाइं धारेदुं त्ति। ता बम्हणीए दारअं समप्पिअ पाणपरिच्चाएण अत्तणो पिअवअस्सं[6] अणुगमिस्सम्। भो वअस्स पराणेमि एदं लहुम्।)

(दारकोऽपि रुदन्पतति।)

**शकारः**—अरे ननु भणामि सपुत्रकं चारुदत्तं व्यापादयतमिति। (अले णं भणामि शपुत्ताकं चालुदत्ताकं वावादेध त्ति।)

(चारुदत्तो भयं नाटयति)

**चाण्डालौ**—न ह्यस्माकमीदृशी राजाज्ञप्तिः यथा सपुत्रं चारुदत्तं व्यापादयतमिति। तन्निष्क्राम रे दारक निष्क्राम। (इति निष्क्रामयतः।) इदं तृतीयं घोषणास्थानम्। ताडयत डिण्डिमम्। (पुनर्घोषयतः।) (ण हि अम्हाणं ईदिशी लाआणत्ती जधा शपुत्तं चालुदत्तं वावादेध त्ति। ता णिक्कम ले दालआ णिक्कम। इमं तइमं घोषणट्ठाणम्। ताडेध डिण्डिमम्।)

---

१ निर्वासयति. २ णिश्शल (निस्सर). ३ आश्रमो वत्स गन्तव्यः. ४ त्वमप्यत्रगमिष्यसि. ५ ग्रहणं. ६ वअस्समग्गं.

SAK.—Here, off with you! (*He drives him out*). Well, Chandalas, why do you delay? Kill him!

CH.—If you are in such a hurry, then you may kill him yourself!

ROH.—O Chandalas, kill me; release my father!

SAK.—Kill him together with his son!

CHA'R.—Everything is possible in the case of this fool; so, my son, go to your mother.

ROH.—What am I to do by going away?

CHAR.—

Dear child, this very day you should go to (reside in) a hermitage (in a forest), along with your mother, lest you too, my son, fare similarly, through the crime of your father. (32)

So, friend Maitreya, take him and go.

VID.—O friend, have you so known it (as to think) that I could remain alive without you?

CHAR.—Friend, your life is in your own power, and it is not right for you to give it up.

VID.—(*To himself*). That is surely true; but still, I am unable to remain alive after being separated from my dear friend. So, I will give this boy into his wife's care and myself follow my dear friend by giving up my life. (*Aloud*) O friend, I shall immediately take him back. (*He embraces him around the neck and falls at his feet*).

(*The* boy, *too, weeps and prostrates himself*).

SAK.—Eh, do I not say that you should kill Charudatta along with his son?

(Charudatta *exhibits alarm*).

CH.—The king's order (to us) is not such (to the effect) that we should kill Charudatta along with his son. Here, go away, boy, off with you! (*They show him out*). Here's the third proclamation-station. Beat the drum! (*They proclaim once more*).

**शकारः**—( स्वगतम् । ) कथमेते न प्रत्ययन्ते पौराः । ( प्रकाशम् । ) अरे चारुदत्त बटुक न प्रत्ययत एष पौरजनः । तदात्मीयया जिह्वया भण मया वसन्तसेना मारितेति । (कध एशे ण पत्तिआअन्ति पौला । हंहो चालुदत्ता बडुका[1] ण पत्तिआअदि एशे पौलजणे । ता अत्तणकेलिकाए जीहाए भणाहि मए वशन्तशेणा मालिदेत्ति ।)

(चारुदत्तस्तूष्णीमास्ते ।)

**शकारः**—अरे चाण्डाल मनुष्य न भणति चारुदत्तबटुकः । तद्भणयतमनेन जर्जरवंशखण्डेन शङ्खलेन ताडयित्वा ताडयित्वा । (अले चाण्डाल गोहे ण भणादि चालुदत्तबडुके[2] । ता भणावेध इमिणा जज्जलवंशखण्डेन शङ्खलेण तालिअ तालिअ ।)

**चाण्डालः**—(प्रहारमुद्यम्य ।) भोश्चारुदत्त भण । (भो चालुदत्त भणाहि ।)

**चारुदत्तः**—( सकरुणम् । )

प्राप्यैतद्व्यसनमहार्णवप्रपातं[3]
न त्रासो न च मनसोऽस्ति मे विषादः ।
एको मां दहति जनापवादवह्नि-
र्वक्तव्यं यदिह मया हता प्रियेति ।। ३३ ।।

( शकारः पुनस्तथैव । )

**चारुदत्तः**—भो भोः पौराः । ('मया खलु नृशंसेन' (९।३०, ३८) इत्यादि पुनः पठति ।)

**शकारः**—व्यापादिता । (वावादिता ।)

**चारुदत्तः**—एवमस्तु ।

**प्रथमचाण्डालः**—अरे तवात्र वध्यपालिका । (अले तव अत्त [4]वज्झपालिआ ।)

**द्वितीयचाण्डालः**—अरे तव । (अले तव ।)

**प्रथमः**—अरे लेखं कुर्वः । (इति बहुविधं लेखकं कृत्वा ।) अरे यदि मदीयां वध्यपालिका तदा तिष्ठतु तावन्मुहूर्तकम् । (अले लेक्खअं कलेम्ह । अले जदि ममकेलिका वज्झपालिआ ता चिट्ठदु दाव मुहुत्तअम् । )

**द्वितीयः**—किंनिमित्तम् । (किंणिमित्तम् ।)

**प्रथमः**—अरे भणितोऽस्मि पित्रा स्वर्गं गच्छता यथा—पुत्र वीरक यदि तव वध्यपालिका भवति मा सहसा व्यापादयसि वध्यम् । (अले भणिदो म्हि पिदुणा शग्गं गच्छन्तेण जधा—पुत्त वीरअ जइ तुह वज्झपालिआ होदि मा शहशा[5] वावादअशि वज्झम् ।)

---

१ बडुव्वका (बटुवक।). २ बडुव्वके; बुड्ढबडुके. ३ महार्णवं; ...प्रयातं. ४ वज्झवाली. ५ शहशत्ति ( सहसेति )

SAK.—( *To himself* ). How ! These citizens do not believe it ! ( *Aloud* ). Oh, Chrudatta, you fellow ! This multitude of citizens does not believe it. So speak it with your own tongue—"I killed Vasantasena."

( Charudatta *remains silent* )

SAK.—Ho ! Chandala, man, this fellow, Charudatta, doesn't speak. So make him speak by repeatedly striking him with that broken piece of old bamboo, your drum-stick.

CH.—( *Raising his hand for a blow* ). Speak, O Charudatta !

CHAR.—( *Mournfully* ).

Having fallen in this fathomless big ocean of calamity, I feel neither terror nor sorrow in my mind. But only one thing, *viz.* the fire of popular ignominy, burns me, when now I am asked to say—"I killed my beloved." (33)

( Sakara *again says as before* ).

CHAR.—Oh, ye citizens ! ( *He recites again the verse beginning 'By my cruel self' &c.* ).

SAK.—"Was killed."

CHAR.—So be it !

THE FIRST CH.—Oh, it is your turn to-day to kill.

THE SECOND CH.—Oh, it is yours !

THE FIRST—Let us reckon by making a writing. ( *They write or draw lines in many ways* ). Ah, if it is my turn, then let it stand over for a short while.

THE SECOND—What for ?

THE FIRST—I was told by my father when about to depart to heaven, thus—"Viraka, my son, whenever it will be your turn to kill, you should never kill the condemned man at once."

---

शृगालाः प्रतिवृत्तं शूलादधोलम्बमानं कलेवरं कर्षन्ति । अर्धमपि शूललग्नमट्टहासस्य वेशो कालाट्टहासस्य रूपमिव तद्वद्भीषणमित्यर्थः । शूललग्नं स्थितम् ] ॥ ३५ ॥ उत्तिष्ठदिति ॥ ३६ ॥ आकृष्ट इति । उद्गीतिः । [ सरोषमाकृष्टः मुष्टौ त्सरौ मुष्टिना गृहीतोऽपि दारुणकः भीषणः अशनिसन्निभः निर्घातसदृशः खड्गः किमर्थं

**द्वितीयः**—अरे किंनिमित्तम् । (अले किंणिमित्तम् ।)

**प्रथमः**—कदाऽपि कोऽपि साधुरर्थं दत्त्वा वध्यं मोचयति । कदाऽपि राज्ञः पुत्रो भवति तेन वृद्धिमहोत्सवेन सर्ववध्यानां मोक्षो भवति । कदाऽपि हस्ती बन्धं खण्डयति तेन संभ्रमेण वध्यो मुक्तो भवति । कदाऽपि राजपरिवर्तो भवति तेन सर्ववध्यानां मोक्षो भवति । (कदावि कोवि साहू अत्थं दइअ वज्झं मोआवेदि । कदावि लण्णो पुत्ते भोदि तेण वद्धावेण[1] शव्ववज्झाणं मोक्खे होदि । कदावि हत्थी बन्धं खण्डेदि[2] तेण शंभमेण वज्झे मुक्के होदि । कदावि लाअपलिवत्ते होदि तेण शव्ववज्झाणं मोक्खे होदि ।)

**शकारः**—किं किं राजपरिवर्तो भवति । (किं किं लाअपलिपत्ते होदि ।)

**चाण्डालः**—अरे वध्यपालिकाया लेखं कुर्वः ।( अले वज्झपालिआए लेक्खअं कलम्हे ।)

**शकारः**—अरे शीघ्रं मारयतं चारुदत्तम् । ( इत्युक्त्वा चेटं गृहीत्वैकान्ते स्थितः । ) ( अले शिग्घं मालेध चालुदत्ताकम् । )

**चाण्डालः**—आर्य चारुदत्त राजनियोगः खल्वपराध्यति न खल्वावां चाण्डालौ । तत्स्मर यत्स्मर्तव्यम् । (अज्ज चालुदत्त लाअणिओओ क्खु अवलज्झदि ण क्खु अम्हे चाण्डाला । ता शुमलेहि जं शुमलिदव्वम् । )

**चारुदत्तः**—

> **प्रभवति यदि धर्मो दूषितस्यापि मेऽद्य**
> **प्रबलपुरुषवाक्यैर्भाग्यदोषात्कथंचित् ।**
> **सुरपतिभवनस्था[3] यत्र तत्र स्थिता[4] वा**
> **व्यपनयतु कलङ्कं स्वस्वभावेन[5] सैव[6] ॥ ३४ ॥**

भोः क्व तावन्मया गन्तव्यम् ।

**चाण्डालः**—(अग्रतो दर्शयित्वा ।) अरे एतद्दृश्यते दक्षिणश्मशानं यत्प्रेक्ष्य वध्या झटिति प्राणान्मुञ्चन्ति । पश्य पश्य ।

> **अर्धं कलेवरं प्रतिवृत्तं कर्षन्ति दीर्घगोमायवः ।**
> **अर्धमपि शूललग्नं वेश इवाट्टहासस्य ॥ ३५ ॥**

( अले एदं दीशदि दक्खिणमशाणं जं पेक्खिअ वज्झा झत्ति पाणाइं मुञ्चन्ति । पेक्ख पेक्ख ।

> अद्धं कलेवलं पडिवुत्तं कट्टन्ति दीहगोमाआ ।
> अद्धं पि शूललग्गं वेशं विअ अट्टहाशश्श ॥)

**चारुदत्तः**—हा हतोऽस्मि मन्दभाग्यः । ( इति सावेगमुपविशति ।)

---

१ वद्धावएण. २ खुट्टति (छिनत्ति). ३ भुवनस्था. ४ आस्थिता. ५ स्वस्ति०. ६ सैषा.

THE SECOND—For what reason ?

THE FIRST—Perchance some kind gentleman might set the condemned man at liberty by paying a ransom. Perhaps a son might be born to the king, and on account of that great joyous festival, all the condemned men may be released. Perchance an elephant might break loose from his chains, and in that commotion the condemned criminal might escape. Or sometimes there might be a change of kings, and then all the condemned men may be set at large.

SAK.—What, what's that ? A change of kings ?

CH.—Eh, let us reckon by writing out our turns of killing.

SAK.—You there, kill Charudatta quickly ! ( *Having said so he, with the* Cheta, *moves away and remains in a corner* ).

CH —Noble Charudatta, it is verily the king's command that is guilty towards you, and not we, Chandalas. So please think of whatever you have to think of.

CHAR.—

Although through ill luck I am somehow condemned ( declared guilty ) by the words of persons in high authority, still, if my righteousness possesses power, then let that very same ( beloved of mine ), residing in Indra's heaven,—or wherever she may be,—remove this stigma on me, by virtue of ( with ) her own ( sweet ) good nature. (34)

Well, where am I to go now ?

CH.—( *Pointing before him* ). Well, here you observe this southern cemetery at whose very sight the condemned men at once ( take fright and ) die. See, see—

Jackals with elongated bodies are pulling at the ( lower ) half of a corpse which is dangling there, while the other half still remains on the stake, like the (grinning) mask of loud laughter.(35)

CHAR.—Alas ! I am undone, unlucky that I am! ( *Sits down in agony*).

---

धरण्यां पतितः ] ॥ ३७ ॥ सह्यवासिनीति । सह्यः पर्वतविशेषः । तत्रस्थां दुर्गां स्वकुलदेवतां संबोधयति । का पुनरिति । गाथा । का पुनस्त्वरितमंसे पतता चिकुरभारेण [ कुन्तलकलापेनोपलक्षिता एषा ] व्याहरन्त्युत्थितहस्ता [ ऊर्ध्वपाणिः ]

[1]शकारः—न तावद्गमिष्यामि। चारुदत्तकं व्यापाद्यमानं तावत्पश्यामि। (परिक्रम्य दृष्ट्वा।) कथमुपविष्टः। (ण दाव गमिश्शम्। चालुदत्ताकं वावादअन्तं दाव पेक्खामि। कधं उवविश्टे।)

**चाण्डालः**—चारुदत्त किं भीतोऽसि। (चालुदत्ता किं भीदेशि।)

**चारुदत्तः**—(सहसोत्थाय।) मूर्ख। ('न भीतो मरणादस्मि केवलं दूषितं यशः' (१०।२७) इत्यादि पुनः पठति।)

**चाण्डालः**—आर्य चारुदत्त गगनतले प्रतिवसन्तौ चन्द्रसूर्यावपि विपत्ति लभेते। किं पुनर्जना मरणभीरुका मानवा वा। लोके कोऽप्युत्थितः पतति कोऽपि पतितोऽप्युत्तिष्ठते।

**उत्तिष्ठत्पततो वसनपातिका शवस्य पुनरस्ति।**
**एतानि हृदये कृत्वा संधारयात्मानम्॥ ३६॥**

(द्वितीयचाण्डालं प्रति।) एतच्चतुर्थं घोषणास्थानम्। तदुद्घोषयावः। (पुनस्तथैवोद्घोषयतः।) (अज्ज चालुदत्त गअणदले पडिवशन्ता चन्दशुज्जा वि विपत्ति लहन्ति। किं उण जणा मलणभीलुआ माणवा वा। लोए कोवि उट्ठिदो पडदि कोवि पडिदोवि उट्ठेदि।

उट्ठन्तपडन्ताह वशणपाडिआ शवश्श उण अत्थि।
एदाइं हिअए कदुअ संधालेहि अत्ताणअं॥

एदं चउट्ठं घोशणट्ठाणम्। ता उग्घोशम्ह।)

**चारुदत्तः**—हा प्रिये वसन्तसेने। ('शशिविमलमयूख'—(१०।१३) इत्यादि पुनः पठति।)

(ततः प्रविशति ससंभ्रमा वसन्तसेना भिक्षुश्च।)

**भिक्षुः**—आश्चर्यम्। अस्थानपरिश्रान्तां समाश्वास्य वसन्तसेनिकां नयन्ननुगृहीतोऽस्मि प्रव्रज्यया। उपासिके कुत्र त्वां नेष्यामि। (हीमाणहे। अट्ठाणपलिश्शन्तं शमश्शाशिअ वशन्तशेणिअं णअन्ते अणुग्गहिदम्हि पव्वज्जाए। उवाशिके कहिं तुमं णइश्शम्।)

**वसन्तसेना**—आर्यचारुदत्तस्यैव गेहम्। तस्य दर्शनेन मृगलाञ्छनस्येव कुमुदिनीमानन्दय माम्। (अज्जचारुदत्तस्स ज्जेव गेहम्। तस्स दंसणेण मिअलाञ्छणस्स विअ कुमुदिणिं आणन्देहि मम।)

**भिक्षुः**—(स्वगतम्।) कतरेण मार्गेण प्रविशामि। (विचिन्त्य।) राजमार्गेणैव प्रविशामि। उपासिके एहि। अयं राजमार्गः। (आकर्ण्य।) किं नु खल्वेष राजमार्गे महान्कलकलः श्रूयते। (कलदेण मग्गेण पविशामि। लाअमग्गेण ज्जेव पविशामि। उवाशिके एहि। इमं लाअमग्गम्। किं णु क्खु एशे लाअमग्गे महन्ते कलअले शुणीअदि।)

---

१ नेपथ्ये श०.

SAK.—I won't go just yet. Let me first see Charudatta being killed. ( *Walking about and seeing* ). How ! He has sat down !

CH.—Charudatta, are you afraid ?

CHAR.—( *Getting up at once* ). You fool ! ( *He recites again the verse beginning 'I am not afraid of death; only my good name is soiled'* &c. ).

CH.—Noble Charudatta, even the sun and the moon, who are denizens of heaven, are overtaken by calamity, what then of ( common ) people, men who are afraid of death ? In this world, any one who rises does fall, and one who falls does rise ( again ).

The dead body, rising and again falling, exhibits the manner of the casting off of a garment. So, keeping these things in your mind, you should steel yourself ( against death ). (36)

( *To the* second Chandala ). Here's the fourth proclamation-station ! Let us, therefore, proclaim it aloud. ( *They again proclaim as before* ).

CHAR.—Oh, my beloved Vasantasena ! ( *He again recites the verse beginning 'O you with teeth pure like the rays of the moon' &c.* ).

( *Then enter in a hurry Vasantasena and the Bhikshu* ).

BHIKSHU—Wonderful ! I am indeed blessed by my ascetic state, since I am leading ( *i. e.* showing the way to ) Vasantsena after having revived her who had swooned in an undesirable locality.—O, worshipper of Buddha, where shall I take you ?

VAS.—To the house of the worthy Charudatta, of course ! Kindly gladden me with his sight, like a night-lotus with that of the moon !

BH.—( *To himself* ). By what route shall I proceed ? ( *pondering* ). I will go by the high road. Come, O worshipper of Buddha ! Here is the high-road. ( *Listening* ). What, I wonder, might be the cause of this mighty uproar that I hear on the highway ?

---

इत एति । 'उच्छिअहत्था' इति पाठे उच्छ्रितहस्तेत्यर्थः ॥ ३८ ॥ [ यज्ञवाट-गतस्य यज्ञस्थानस्थितस्य । ] **केयमिति** । अभ्युद्यते उद्गते । द्रोणवृष्टिः द्रोणस्य मेघस्य वृष्टिः ॥ ३९ ॥ **वसन्तसेनेति** । [ द्वितीया मृताया अन्या । उपजाति-वृत्तम् ] ॥ ४० ॥ **किं न्विति** । [ जीवातुकाम्यया जीवनौषधेच्छया । जीवयितु-

**वसन्तसेना**—(अग्रतो निरूप्य ।) कथं पुरतो महाजनसमूहः । आर्य जानीहि तावत्किं न्विदमिति । विषमभरक्रान्तेव वसुंधरा एकवासोन्नतोज्जयिनी वर्तते । (कधं पुरदो महाजणसमूहो । अज्ज जाणाहि दाव किं णेदं त्ति । विसमभरक्कन्ता विअ वसुंधरा एअवासोण्णदा उज्जइणी वट्टदि ।)

**चाण्डालः**—इदं च पश्चिमं घोषणास्थानम् । तत्ताडयतं डिण्डिमम् । उद्घोषयतं घोषणाम् । (तथा कृत्वा ।) भोश्चारुदत्त प्रतिपालय । मा भैः । शीघ्रमेव मार्यसे । (इमं अ पच्छिमं घोषणट्ठाणम् । ता तालेध डिण्डिमम् । उग्गोशेध घोशणम् । भो चालुदत्त पडिवालेहि । मा भाआहि । लहुं ज्जेव मालीअशि ।)

**चारुदत्तः**—भगवत्यो देवताः ।

**भिक्षुः**—(श्रुत्वा ससंभ्रमम् ।) उपासिके त्वं किल चारुदत्तेन मारिताऽसीति चारुदत्तो मारयितुं नीयते । (उवाशिके तुमं किल चालुदत्तेण मालिदाशि त्ति चालुदत्तो मालिदुं णीअदि ।)

**वसन्तसेना**—(ससंभ्रमम् ।) हा धिक् हा धिक् । कथं मम मन्दभागिन्याः कृत आर्यचारुदत्तो व्यापाद्यते । भोः त्वरितं त्वरितमादेशय मार्गम् । (हद्धी हद्धी । कधं मम मन्दभाइणीए किदे अज्जचालुदत्तो वावादीअदि । भो तुरिदं तुरिदं आदेसेहि मग्गम् ।)

**भिक्षुः**—त्वरतां त्वरतां बुद्धोपासिकाऽऽर्यचारुदत्तं जीवन्तं समाश्वासयितुम् । आर्याः अन्तरमन्तरं दत्त । (तुवलदु तुवलदु बुद्धोवाशिका अज्जचालुदत्तं जीअन्त शमश्शाशिदुम् । अज्जा अन्तलं अन्तलं देध ।)

**वसन्तसेना**—अन्तरमन्तरम् । (अन्तरं अन्तरम् ।)

**चाण्डालः**—आर्य चारुदत्त स्वामिनियोगोऽपराध्यति । तत्स्मर यत्स्मर्तव्यम् । (अज्ज चालुदत्त शामिणिओओ अवलज्झदि । ता शुमलेहि जं शुमलिदव्वम् ।)

**चारुदत्तः**—किं बहुना । ('प्रभवति—'(१०।३४) इत्यादि श्लोकं पठति ।)

**चाण्डालः**—(खड्गमाकृष्य ।) आर्य चारुदत्त उत्तानो भूत्वा समं तिष्ठ एकप्रहारेण मारयित्वा त्वां स्वर्गं नयावः । (अज्ज चालुदत्त उत्ताणे भविअ समं चिट्ठ । एक्कप्पहालेण मालिअ तुमं शग्गं णेम्ह ।)

(चारुदत्तस्तथा तिष्ठति ।)

**चाण्डालः**—(प्रहर्तुमीहते । खड्गपतनं हस्तादभिनयन् ।) ही कथम् ।

**आकृष्टः सरोषं मुष्टौ मुष्टिना गृहीतोऽपि ।**
**धरण्यां किमर्थं पतितो दारुणकोऽशनिसंनिभः खड्गः ॥ ३७ ॥**

यथैतत्संवृत्तं तथा तर्कयामि न विपद्यत आर्यचारुदत्त इति । भगवति सह्यवासिनि प्रसीद प्रसीद । अपि नाम चारुदत्तस्य मोक्षो भवेत्तदाऽनुगृहीतं त्वया चाण्डालकुलं भवेत् । (ही कधम् ।

VAS.—( *Peering before her* ). How! There's a big crowd of people in our front! Sir, please just find out what it may be. Ujjayini seems to have raised itself in one spot, as though the earth had become burdened with an uneven load!

CH.—And here is the last proclamation-station. So, strike the drum and repeat aloud the proclamation! ( *Doing accordingly* ) O Charudatta, get ready! Do not fear; you will be quickly dispatched!

CHAR.—Ye gods in heaven!

BH.—( *Hearing it; excitedly* ). O worshipper of Buddha! Charudatta is being taken for being killed on a charge of having murdered you.

VAS.—(*In agitation* ). Oh, alas! Oh, alas! How is it that the worthy Charudatta is being killed on account of me, the unlucky one! Sir, please show me the way very quickly.

BH.—Make haste, O worshipper of Buddha, make haste and comfort the worthy Charudatta while he still lives! Make way, sirs, make way!

VAS.—Make room, make room!

CH.—Noble Charudatta, it is our master's command that is guilty here. So remember whatever you have to remember.

CHAR.—What more need I say? ( *Recites the verse beginning "Although I am deemed a sinner" &c.*)

CH.—( *Drawing his sword* ). Noble Charudatta, lie flat and keep straight. We will despatch you with one stroke and send you to heaven.

( Charudatta *lies as asked* ).

CH.—( *Is about to strike; gesticulating that the sword drops from his hand*). Ha! How's that?

Although I fiercely drew it by its hilt and grasped it in my fist, why has the sword, terrible like the thunderbolt, fallen on the ground? (37)

Since this has occurred, I infer that the worthy Charudatta won't be killed ( after all ). O divine Durga, thou that dwellest on the Sahya? Have mercy! If Charudatta happens to be saved, then forsooth the ( whole ) race of the Chandalas will have been blessed by you!

आअट्ठिदे[2] शलोशं मुट्ठीए मुट्ठिणा गहीदे वि ।
घलणीए कीश पडिदे दालुणके अशणिशंणिहे खग्गे ॥

जधा एदं संवुत्तं तधा तक्केमि ण विवज्जदि अज्जचालुदत्ते त्ति । भअवदि सज्झवाशिणि पशीद पशीद । अवि णाम चालुदत्तश्श मोक्खे भवे तदो अणुगहीदं तुए चाण्डालउलं भवे ।)

अपरः—यथाज्ञप्तमनुतिष्ठावः । (जधाण्णत्तं अणुचिट्ठम्ह ।)

प्रथमः—भवतु । एवं कुर्वः । (भोदु[1] । एवं कलेम्ह ।)

(इत्युभौ चारुदत्तं शूले समारोपयितुमिच्छतः ।)

('चारुदत्तः 'प्रभवति—' (१०।३४) इत्यादि पुनः पठति ।)

भिक्षुर्वसन्तसेना च—(दृष्ट्वा ।) आर्याः मा तावन्मा तावत् । आर्याः एषाहं मन्दभागिनी यस्याः कारणादेष व्यापाद्यते । ( अज्जा मा दाव मा दाव । अज्जा एसा अहं मन्दभाइणी जाए कारणादो एसो वावादीअदि ।)

चाण्डालः—(दृष्ट्वा ।)

का पुनस्त्वरितमेषांऽसपतता चिकुरभारेण ।
मा मेति व्याहरन्त्युत्थितहस्तेत एति ॥ ३८ ॥

(का उण तुलिदं एशा अंशपडन्तेण चिउलभालेण ।
मा मेत्ति वाहलन्ती उट्ठिदहत्था[2] इदो एदि ॥)

वसन्तसेना—आर्य चारुदत्त किं न्विदम् । ( इति पादयोः पतति । ) ( अज्ज चारुदत्त किं ण्णेदम् ।)

भिक्षुः—आर्य चारुदत्त किं न्विदम् । ( इति पादयोः पतति । ) ( अज्ज चालुदत्त किं ण्णेदम् ।)

चाण्डालः—(सभयमपसृत्य[3] ।) कथं वसन्तसेना । ननु खल्वावाभ्यां साधुर्न व्यापादितः । ( कधं वशन्तशेणा । णं क्खु अम्हेहिं शाहू ण वावादिदे ।)

भिक्षुः—(उत्थाय ।) अरे जीवति चारुदत्तः । (अले जीवदि चालुदत्ते ।)

चाण्डालः—जीवति वर्षशतम् । (जीवदि वश्शशदम् ।[4])

वसन्तसेना—(सहर्षं ।) प्रत्युज्जीविताऽस्मि । (पच्चुज्जीविदम्हि ।)

चाण्डालः—तद्यावदेतद्वृत्तं राज्ञो यज्ञवाटगतस्य निवेदयावः । (ता जाव एदं वुत्तं राइणो जण्णवाडगदश्श णिवेदेम्ह । )

(इति निष्क्रामतः ।)

---

१ भोदु भोदु. २ उत्थिद. ३ उपसृत्य. ४ वस्सर (वत्सर), वरिस०.

SECOND CH.—Let us do as we were ordered.

FIRST CH.—Certainly. Let us do so.

( *Thereupon both prepare to fix* Charudatta *on the stake* ).

( Charudatta *again recites the verse beginning* ' Although I am deemed a sinner ' &c. ).

BH. & VAS.—( *Observing* ). Forbear, sirs, forbear!—Gentlemen here I am, that same unlucky woman for whose sake he is being killed!

CH—( *Seeing* ).

And who may this lady be, with her ample tresses fallen over her shoulders, that is quickly coming in this direction, with her hand raised, and saying ' Forbear, forbear ' ? (38)

VAS.—Noble Charudatta, what does this mean? ( *She falls on his breast* ).

BH.—Noble Charudatta, what may this be? ( *He falls at his feet.* )

CH.—( *Moving off in alarm* ). How! ( She is ) Vasantasena! How very lucky that we did not kill an innocent person!

BH.—( *Rising* ). Man, does Charudatta live?

CH.—He lives a hundred years!

VAS.—( *Joyfully* ). I am restored to life again!

CH.—So, then, let us first report this turn of events to the king who is in the sacrificial enclosure. ( *They start to go* ).

---

मित्यर्थः। रूपानुरूपेण सदृशरूपेण ] ॥ ४१ ॥ कुत इति। [ बाष्पाम्बुधाराभिः पयोधरौ स्नपयन्ती। विद्याऽमृतसंजीवनी विद्या। ] विद्या इतरविविक्तात्मज्ञानम् ॥ ४२ ॥ त्वदर्थमिति। [देहं देहः। ' कायो देहः क्लीबपुंसोः ' इत्यमरः। उपजातिर्वृत्तम्। ॥ ४३ ॥ रक्तमिति। [ वरस्य जामातुः वस्त्रम्। यद्वा पट्टवस्त्रम्। ] वरस्य यथा जामातुरिव। [ पर्यायालंकारः। वसन्ततिलकं वृत्तम् ] ॥ ४४ ॥ पूर्वेति। [ प्रभविष्णुना सामर्थ्यवता। मनागीषत् ] ॥ ४५ ॥ तेनापि। न एतद्व्यतिरिक्तेनान्येनेत्यर्थः। न प्रत्यभिजानाति। निर्वेदः शान्तिः वैषयिकेच्छानिवृत्तिः। किमेतत्किमेतदिति शत्रूणां क्रूरः कलकलः। जयतीति। जयति सर्वोत्कर्षेण वर्तते। [ वृषभकेतुः शिवः। षण्मुखः कार्तिकेयः क्रौञ्चशत्रुः क्रौञ्चाख्यस्य दैत्यस्य हन्ता। तदुक्तं— ' क्रौञ्चे क्रौञ्चो हतो दैत्यः क्रौञ्चाद्रौ हेमकन्दरे। स्कन्देन युद्ध्वा सुचिरं चित्रमायी सुमायिना ' इति। ] तदनु जयति आत्मसात्करोति। [ शुभ्रः कैलासः केतुरिव यस्याः

शकारः—( वसन्तसेनां दृष्ट्वा । सत्रासम् । ) आश्चर्यम् । केन गर्भदासी जीवनं प्रापिता । उत्क्रान्ता मे प्राणाः । भवतु । पलायिष्ये । ( इति पलायते । ) ( ह्रीमादिके । केण गब्भदाशी जीवाविदा । उक्कन्ताइं मे पाणाइं । भोदु । पलाइश्शम् । )

चाण्डालः—( उपसृत्य । ) अरे नन्वावयोरीदृशी राजाज्ञप्तिः—येन सा व्यापादिता तं मारयतमिति । तद्राष्ट्रियश्यालमेवान्विष्यावः । ( अले णं अम्हाणं ईदिशी लाआणत्ती–जेण शा वावादिदा तं मालेध त्ति । ता लट्ठिअशालअं ज्जेव्व अण्णेशम्ह । )

(इति निष्क्रान्तौ ।)

चारुदत्तः—(सविस्मयम् ।)

केयमभ्युद्यते[1] शस्त्रे मृत्युवक्त्रगते मयि ।
अनावृष्टिहते सस्ये[2] द्रोणवृष्टिरिवागता[3] ॥ ३९ ॥

(अवलोक्य च ।)

वसन्तसेना किमियं द्वितीया समागता सैव दिवः किमित्थम् ।
भ्रान्तं मनः पश्यति वा ममैनां वसन्तसेना न मृताऽथ सैव ॥ ४० ॥

अथ वा ।

किं नु स्वर्गात्पुनः प्राप्ता मम जीवातुकाम्यया[4] ।
तस्या रूपानुरूपेण किमुतान्येयमागता ॥ ४१ ॥

वसन्तसेना—( सास्रमुत्थाय पादयोर्निपत्य । ) आर्य चारुदत्त सैवाहं पापा यस्याः कारणादियं त्वयाऽसदृश्यवस्था प्राप्ता । (अज्ज चालुदत्त सा ज्जेव्व अहं पावा जाए कारणादो इअं तुए असरिसी अवत्था पाविदा ।)

( नेपथ्ये । )

आश्चर्यमाश्चर्यम् । जीवति वसन्तसेना । (इति सर्वे पठन्ति ।) (अच्चरिअं अच्चरिअम् । जीवदि वसन्तशेणा ।)

चारुदत्तः—आकर्ण्य सहसोत्थाय [5]स्पर्शसुखमभिनीय निमीलिताक्ष एव हर्षगद्गदाक्षरम् ।) प्रिये वसन्तसेना त्वम् ।

वसन्तसेना—सैवाहं मन्दभाग्या । (सा ज्जेव्वाहं मन्दभाआ ।)

चारुदत्तः—(निरूप्य सहर्षम् ।) कथं वसन्तसेनैव । (सानन्दम् ।)

कुतो बाष्पाम्बुधाराभिः [6]स्नपयन्ती पयोधरौ ।
मयि मृत्युवशं प्राप्ते विद्येव समुपागता ॥ ४२ ॥

---

१ केय समु०. २ शस्ये. ३ सम्यग्वृष्टि. ४ जीवानु. ५ स-स-स्पर्शसुखनिमी. ६स्नाप०.

SAK.—( *Seeing* Vasantasena; *in alarm* ). Heavens! By whom was this born slave-girl brought back to life? Now my life has ( as good as ) ended! Well, let me take to my heels. ( *He runs away* ).

CH.—( *Approaching* ) Oh, the king's order to us was to this effect—" Kill him by whom she was murdered. " So let us go in pursuit of the royal brother-in-law himself.

( *Exeunt* ).

CHAR.—( *Full of wonder* ).

While the weapon was raised and I was in the jaws of death, who is this lady that has come up, like a shower from the Drona cloud, ( coming ) on the crop withering owing to drought? (39)

( *Then, having observed* ).

Is this a second Vasantasena? Or has that same ( Vasantasena ) thus come here from heaven? Or is my wandering mind seeing her ( in illusion )? Or can it be that Vasantasena never died at all, and that this is the same? (40)

Or again:

Has she come back again from heaven with a desire to restore me to life? Or is she some different lady, resembling her in appearance, that has come here? ( 41 )

VAS.—( *Tearfully rising, and falling at his feet* ). Noble Charudatta, it is my own sinful self, for whose sake you were reduced to this unmerited plight!

( *Behind the Scenes* ).

Wonder, oh, wonder! Vasantasena is alive! ( *All repeat these words* ).

CHAR.—( *Hears, immediately rises, and exhibits pleasure at* Vasantasena's *touch. Still keeping his eyes closed, and in a voice faltering in ecstasy* ). Beloved mine, are you really Vasantasena?

VAS.—The very same, my own unlucky self!

CHAR.—( *Observing; joyfully* ). How! She is Vasantasena and none else! ( *Delightedly* ).

Bathing your breasts with the streams of the water of tears, whence did you come, like the divine ( re-vivifying ) lore, when I was in the grasp of Death? ( 42 )

प्रिये वसन्तसेने ।

> त्वदर्थमेतद्विनिपात्यमानं देहं त्वयैव प्रतिमोचितं मे ।
> अहो प्रभावः प्रियसंगमस्य मृतोऽपि को नाम पुनर्ध्रियेत ॥ ४३ ॥

अपि च । प्रिये पश्य[1] ।

> रक्तं तदेव वरवस्त्रमियं च माला
> कान्तागमेन हि वरस्य यथा विभाति ।
> एते च वध्यपटहध्वनयस्तथैव
> जाता विवाहपटहध्वनिभिः समानाः ॥ ४४ ॥

**वसन्तसेना**—अतिदक्षिणतया किं न्विदं व्यवसितमार्येण । (अदिदक्खिणदाए किं ण्णेदं ववसिदं अज्जेण ।)

**चारुदत्तः**—प्रिये त्वं किल मया हतेति—

> पूर्वानुबद्धवैरेण शत्रुणा प्रभविष्णुना ।
> नरके पतता[2] तेन मनागस्मि निपातितः ॥ ४५ ॥

**वसन्तसेना**—( कर्णौ पिधाय । ) शान्तं पापम् । तेनास्मि राजश्यालेन व्यापादिता । (सन्तं पावम् । तेण म्हि राअसालेण वावादिता ।)

**चारुदत्तः**—(भिक्षुं दृष्ट्वा ।) अयमपि कः ।

**वसन्तसेना**—तेनानार्येण व्यापादिता । एतेनार्येण जीवं प्रापिताऽस्मि । (तेण अणज्जेण वावादिदा । एदिणा अज्जेण जीवाविदम्हि ।)

**चारुदत्तः**—कस्त्वमकारणबन्धुः ।

**भिक्षुः**—न प्रत्यभिजानाति मामार्यः । अहं स आर्यस्य चरणसंवाहचिन्तकः संवाहको नाम द्यूतकरैर्गृहीत एतयोपासिकयाऽऽर्यस्यात्मीय इत्यलंकारपणनिष्क्रीतोऽस्मि । तेन च द्यूतनिर्वेदेन शाक्यश्रमणकः संवृत्तोऽस्मि । एषाऽप्यार्या प्रवहणविपर्यासेन पुष्पकरण्डकजीर्णोद्यानं गता । तेन चानार्येण न मां बहु मन्यस इति बाहुपाशबलात्कारेण मारिता मया दृष्टा । (ण पच्चभिजाणादि[3] मं अज्जो । अहं शे अज्जश्श चलणशंवाहचिन्तए शंवाहके णाम । जूदिअलेहिं गहिदे एदाए उवाशिकाए अज्जश्श केलके त्ति अलंकालपणणिक्कीदे म्हि । तेण अ जूदणिव्वेदेण शक्कशमणके शंवुत्ते म्हि । एशावि अज्जा पवहणविपज्जाशेण पुप्फकलण्डकजिण्णुज्जाणं गदा । तेण अ अणज्जेण ण मं बहु मण्णेशि त्ति बाहुपाशबलक्कालेण मालिदा मए दिट्ठा ।)

---

सा ताम् । मालिनी वृत्तम् ]॥ ४६ ॥ हत्वेति । शेषभूतां पुष्पदामायमानाम् । गुणभूतामिति केचित् । [ व्यसनगतमापद्ग्रस्तम् । पुष्पिताग्रा वृत्तम् ]॥ ४७ ॥

---

१ पश्य पश्य. २ ताऽनेन. ३ ०आणादि.

Beloved Vasantasena!

This body of mine, which was about to be destroyed on your account, was saved by yourself (from that fate). Oh, the power of union with one's beloved person! (Else) who, being dead, could ever be brought back to life again? (43)

And, O my dear, see, moreover :—

By the arrival of you, my beloved, that same red garment has become (like) a bridegroom's attire, and this garland decks me as though I were a bridegroom. And similarly, these sounds of the drum of execution now resemble those of nuptial drums. (44)

VAS.—What is this that your noble self, in your extreme generosity, has brought on yourself?

CHAR.—Beloved, under a charge that you were killed by me,

I was very nearly put to death by that powerful enemy of mine, who had from the very beginning conceived a hatred (against me) and who is to fall in hell. (45)

VAS.—(*Closing her ears*). Heaven forbid! It was that royal brother-in-law who killed me.

CHAR.—(*Seeing the* Bhikshu). And who is this, too?

VAS.—I was killed by that wicked man; but this gentleman restored me to life.

CHAR.—Who are you, that (thus) befriended her disinterestedly?

BH.—Your worthy self does not recognize me. I am that same person, named Samvahaka, employed as the Shampooer-of-the-feet of your noble self. I was seized by gamblers, but this worshipper of Buddha bought me off giving an ornament as my ransom, simply because I belonged to your honour. And through the disgust (which I then felt) for gambling, I turned a Buddhist mendicant. This worthy lady had gone to the old *Pushpakarandaka* garden owing to an interchange of carriages; and she was forcibly strangled by that wicked fellow with the noose of his arms, because she didn't think highly of (*i. e.* love) him. (Afterwards) I found her.

---

**हत्वेति।** [ बलेन सुसैन्येन मन्त्रेण सुनयोपदेशेन च विहीनं रिपुं हत्वा। प्रकर्षात्प्रभावातिशयात्। समग्रवसुधाया अधिराज्यं यस्मिन् तादृक् शत्रुराज्यं बलारेः इन्द्रस्य राज्यमिव प्राप्तम्। इन्द्रवज्रा वृत्तम् ] ॥ ४८ ॥ **विष्टचेति।** [ भो

( नेपथ्ये कलकलः । )

जयति वृषभकेतुर्दक्षयज्ञस्य हन्ता
तदनु जयति भेत्ता षण्मुखः क्रौञ्चशत्रुः[1] ।
तदनु जयति कृत्स्नां शुभ्रकैलासकेतुं
विनिहतवरवैरी[2] चार्यको गां विशालाम् ॥ ४६ ॥

( प्रविश्य सहसा । )

शर्विलकः—

हत्वा तं कुनृपमहं हि पालकं भो-
स्तद्राज्ये द्रुतमभिषिच्य चार्यकं तम् ।
तस्याज्ञां शिरसि निधाय शेषभूतां
मोक्ष्येऽहं व्यसनगतं च चारुदत्तम् ॥ ४७ ॥

हत्वा रिपुं तं बलमन्त्रहीनं[3] पौरान्समाऽश्वास्य पुनः प्रकर्षात् ।
प्राप्तं समग्रं वसुधाधिराज्यं राज्यं[4] बलारेरिव[5] शत्रुराज्यम् ॥ ४८ ॥

(अग्रतो निरूप्य ।) भवतु । अत्र तेन भवितव्यं यत्रायं जनपदसमवायः । अपि नामायमारम्भः[6] क्षितिपतेरार्यकस्यार्यचारुदत्तस्य जीवितेन सफलः स्यात् । (त्वरित-तरमुपसृत्य ।) अपयात जाल्माः । (दृष्ट्वा सहर्षम् ।) अपि ध्रियते चारुदत्तः सह वसन्तसेनया । [7]संपूर्णाः [8]खल्वस्मत्स्वामिनो मनोरथाः ।

दिष्टचा भो व्यसनमहार्णवादपारा-
दुत्तीर्णं गुणधृतया सुशीलवत्या ।
नावेव प्रियतमया चिरान्निरीक्षे
ज्योत्स्नाढ्यं [9]शशिनमिवोपरागमुक्तम् ॥ ४९ ॥

तत्कृतमहापातकः कथमिवैनमुपसर्पामि । अथ वा सर्वत्रार्जवं शोभते । ( प्रकाश-मुपसृत्य बद्धाञ्जलिः ।) आर्य चारुदत्त ।

चारुदत्तः—ननु को भवान् ।

---

दिष्टचा सुदैवेन अपारात् व्यसनं महार्णव इव तस्मात् । गुणः रज्जुः तेन पक्षे गुणैः धृतया सुशीलवत्या नावा इव प्रियतमया वसन्तसेनया उत्तीर्णमुद्धृतं उपरागो राहुग्रासस्तस्मान्मुक्तं ज्योत्स्नाढ्यं शशिनमिव आर्यचारुदत्तं चिरात् निरीक्षे । उपमारूपकयोः संसृष्टिः । पुष्पिताग्रा वृत्तम् ॥ ४९ ॥ येनेति । [सोऽहं कृतं महापापं येन सः । त्वामेवापकृतमेव ] ॥ ५० ॥ आर्यकेणेति । [आर्यवृत्तेन

---

१ शत्रोः. २ ०वैरां. ३ मन्त्रि, मित्र. ४ आढ्यं. ५ सुरारेः. ६ नामारम्भः. ७ संपूर्णः...मनोरथः. ८ सत्वरम०. ९ इनाप०.

( *An uproar behind the Scenes* ).

Victory to the bull-bannered deity ( Siva ), the destroyer of Daksha's sacrifice ! After that, victory to the six-faced (Karttikeya), the cleaver and the enemy of the Krauncha mountain ! And after that, victory to Aryaka, who has killed his mighty foe ( and conquered ) the whole vast ( expanse of the ) earth, having the white Kailasa mountain for its ( white ) banner ! ( 46 )

(*Entering suddenly* ).

SARVILAKA—

Ye ( citizens ) ! Having killed that wicked king Palaka, and having immediately installed that Aryaka as sovereign of his kingdom, I have ( reverently ) received with ( bent ) head his command as if it was the cast-off garland of worship, and will ( forthwith ) release Charudatta who is in danger. ( 47 )

Having killed that enemy who lacked both strength and wise counsel, and having afterwards inspired confidence among the citizens through our ( superior ) prowess, we have acquired the whole enemy's kingdom, with sovereignty over the world, as if it were Indra's own kingdom ! ( 48 )

( *Looking before him* ). Yes. He must be just there where this crowd of citizens is (to be seen). I hope that this enterprise of king Aryaka will be crowned with success by ( the saving of ) the life of the worthy Charudatta ! ( *Walking very swiftly towards them*). Away, you rash people ! ( *Observing joyfully* ). Surely Charudatta is alive, and so is Vasantasena ! The heart's desire of my master is now fulfilled, indeed !

Aye ! By great good luck I am beholding after a long time, like the moon freed from eclipse and splendidly united with moonlight, ( Charudatta ) who has crossed the boundless and vast ocean of misery by the aid of his best beloved, possessing virtues and high moral character, as by means of a boat held fast by ropes and well-steered. (49)

But then, how possibly shall I approach him, as I have committed the great sin ( of theft, in his house ) ? Or why, straightforwardness is becoming on all occasions. ( *Coming forward before them; folding his hands* ) Sir Charudatta !

CHAR.—Ah, who are you ?

शर्विलकः—

येन ते भवनं भित्त्वा न्यासापहरणं कृतम् ।
सोऽहं कृतमहापापस्त्वामेव शरणं गतः ॥ ५० ॥

चारुदत्तः—सखे मैवम् । त्वयाऽसौ[1] प्रणयः कृतः । (इति कण्ठे गृह्णाति ।)

शर्विलकः—अन्यच्च ।

आर्यकेणार्यवृत्तेन कुलं[2] मानं च रक्षता ।
पशुवद्यज्ञवाटस्थो दुरात्मा पालको हतः ॥ ५१ ॥

चारुदत्तः—किम् ।

शर्विलकः—

त्वद्यानं यः समारुह्य गतस्त्वां शरणं पुरा ।
पशुवद्वितते यज्ञे हतस्तेनाद्य पालकः ॥ ५२ ॥

चारुदत्तः—शर्विलक योऽसौ पालकेन घोषादानीय निष्कारणं कूटागारे[3] बद्ध आर्यकनामा त्वया मोचितः ।

शर्विलकः—यथाऽऽह तत्रभवान् ।

चारुदत्तः—प्रियं नः प्रियम्[4] ।

शर्विलकः—प्रतिष्ठितमात्रेण तव सुहृदाऽऽर्यकेणोज्जयिन्यां [5]वेणातटे कुशावत्य राज्यमतिसृष्टम् । तत्प्रतिमान्यतां प्रथमः सुहृत्प्रणयः । (परिवृत्य ।) अरे रे आनीयतामयं पापो राष्ट्रियशठः ।

(नेपथ्ये ।)

यथाऽऽज्ञापयति शर्विलकः ।

शर्विलकः—आर्य नन्वयमार्यको राजा विज्ञापयति—इदं मया युष्मद्गुणोपार्जितं राज्यम् । तदुपयुज्यताम् ।

चारुदत्तः—अस्मद्गुणोपार्जितं राज्यम् ।

(नेपथ्ये ।)

अरे रे राष्ट्रियश्यालक एह्येहि । स्वस्याविनयस्य फलमनुभव ।

(ततः प्रविशति पुरुषैरधिष्ठितः पश्चाद्बाहुबद्धः शकारः ।)

---

उदात्तशीलेन । [ यज्ञवाटो यज्ञस्थानम् । एतच्चापरिच्छिन्नजनसंमर्दन प्रमादस्थानम् । तेन सर्वोत्कटवध इति सूचयितुम् । [ तत्र तिष्ठतीति यज्ञवाटस्थः । पशुवच्छागतुल्यं हतः ] ॥ ५१ ॥ त्वद्यानमिति । वितस्ते प्रसृते यज्ञे पशुवत् ।

---

१ त्वया स. २ कुलमानं. ३ गूढागारे, बन्धनेन बद्धः. ४ प्रियं नः. ५ वेणी.

SAR.—

I am that same man who broke into your house and stole that deposit; having committed that great sin, I now throw myself on your mercy ! ( 50 )

CHAR.—Friend, say not so ! It was a *kindness* which you did to me ! ( *He embraces him by the neck* ).

SAR.—Moreover :—

The wicked-souled Palaka, who was staying in the sacrificial enclosure, was slaughtered like a ( sacrificial ) animal by Aryaka, of noble deeds, thus maintaining ( the greatness of ) his family and his honour. ( 51 )

CHAR.—What !

SAR.—

He who formerly drove in your chariot and threw himself on your mercy, has to-day slain Palaka like a ( sacrificial ) animal, in the course of a sacrifice that was being performed. ( 52 )

CHAR.—Sarvilaka, ( do you mean ) that same person, named Aryaka, whom you helped to escape and who was brought by Palaka from his hamlet and imprisoned in a secret dungeon without any cause ?

SAR.—( It is ) as your honour says.

CHAR.—Then it is gratifying (news) to me, gratifying indeed !

SAR.—Immediately on his being enthroned in Ujjayini, your friend Aryaka has bestowed on you the kingdom of Kusavati on the banks of the Vena ( river ). So please honour ( by your acceptance ) this first request of your friend. ( *Turning round* ). You there ! Bring here that sinful scoundrel, the royal brother-in law !

( *Behind the Scenes* ).

As Sarvilaka orders !

SAR.—Sir, king Aryaka has indeed requested you in these words—"This kingdom was acquired by me through your goodness. It is thereefore at your disposal."

CHAR.—( What !) The kingdom was acquired through ***my*** goodness ?

( *Behind the Scenes* ).

Come, you brother-in-law of the king, come along ! Taste the fruit of your own evil deeds !

( *Then enter* Sakara, *led in by the* guard ***with his hands tied behind him*** )

शकारः—आश्चर्यम् ।

एवं दूरमतिक्रान्त उद्दाम इव गर्दभः ।
आनीतः खल्वहं बद्धः कुक्कुरोऽन्य इव दुष्करः ॥ ५३ ॥

( दिशोऽवलोक्य । ) समन्तत उपस्थित एष राष्ट्रियबन्धः । तत्कमिदानीमशरणः शरणं व्रजामि । ( विचिन्त्य । ) भवतु । तमेवाभ्युपपन्नशरणवत्सलं गच्छामि । ( इत्युपसृत्य । ) आय चारुदत्त परित्रायस्व परित्रायस्व । (इति पादयोः पतति ।) (हीमादिके

एव्वं दूलमदिक्कन्ते उद्दामे विअ गद्दहे ।
आणीदे क्खु हगे बद्धे हुडे अण्णे व्व दुक्कले ॥

शमन्तदो उवठ्ठिदे एशे लश्टिअबन्धे । ता कं दाणिं अशलणे शलणं वजामि । भोदु । तं ज्जेव्व अब्भुववण्णशलणवच्छलं[1] गच्छामि । अज्ज चालुदत्त पलित्ताआहि पलित्ताआहि ।)

(नेपथ्ये ।)

आर्य चारुदत्त मुञ्च मुञ्च । व्यापादयावैतम् । ( अज्ज चालुदत्त मुञ्च मुञ्च । वावादेम्ह एदम् ।)

शकारः—(चारुदत्तं प्रति ।) भो अशरणशरण परित्रायस्व । (भो अशलण-शलणे पलित्ताआहि ।)

चारुदत्तः—( सानुकम्पम् । ) अहह अभयमभयं शरणागतस्य ।

शर्विलकः—(सावेगम् ।) आः अपनीयतामयं[1] चारुदत्तपार्श्वात् । (चारुदत्तं प्रति ।) ननूच्यतां किमस्य पापस्यानुष्ठीयतामिति ।

आकर्षन्तु[2] सुबद्ध्वैनं श्वभिः संखाद्यतामथ ।
शूले वा [3]तिष्ठतामेष पाटयतां क्रकचेन वा ॥ ५४ ॥

चारुदत्तः—किमहं यद्ब्रवीमि तत्क्रियते ।

शर्विलकः—कोऽत्र संदेहः ।

शकारः—भट्टारक चारुदत्त शरणागतोऽस्मि । तत्परित्रायस्व तत्परित्रायस्व । यत्तव सदृशं तत्कुरु । पुनर्नेदृशं करिष्यामि । (भश्टालआ चालुदत्त शलणागदे म्हि । ता पलित्ताआहि पलित्ताआहि । जं [4]तुए शलिशं तं कलेहि । पुणो ण ईदिशं कलिश्शम् ।)

---

अद्य पालकः हतः ॥५२॥ एवमिति । [ उद्दामः छिन्नबन्धः दूरमतिक्रान्तः पलायितः अहं दुष्करः । दुर्ग्रह इत्यर्थः । कुक्कुर इव आनीतः ] ॥ ५३ ॥ [ राष्ट्रियस्य

---

१ लक्खणं (रक्षणं). १ असौ. २ आकर्षंतु. ३ भिद्यतां. ४ तुज्झ.

SAK.—Wonderful !

Although I had escaped to such a long distance, like a donkey broken loose from his reins, I have indeed been brought back a captive, as if I were an untamed ( wild ) dog. (53)

( *Looking in all directions* ) The king's brother-in-law is now surrounded on all sides by these guards. So then, being helpless, whose protection shall I now seek ? ( *Pondering* ). Yes. I will approach that very same person, who is kind to those that seek his protection. ( *So thinking, he goes fourth* ). Noble Charudatta, save me ! save me ! ( *He throws himself at his feet* ).

( *Behind the Scenes* ).

Let him off, Sir Charudatta, let him off ! We will kill him.

SAK.—( *To* Charudatta ). Save me, sir, you who are the refuge of the helpless !

CHAR.—( *Mercifully* ). Oh, pity ! ( I promise ) safety to you who seek my protection ! You are safe !

SAR.—( *Impatiently* ). Oh ! Drag him off from Charudatta's side ! ( To Charudatta ). Well, sir, tell us what should be done with this sinful wretch.

Let them ( Chandalas ) bind him tight and drag him away. And then, should he be devoured by dogs, or lie on the stake, or be cut up with a saw ? (54)

CHAR.—Well, will you do what I tell ?

SAR.—What doubt is there about that ?

SAK.—Master, Charudatta, I beseech your protection ! So save me, Oh, save me ! Do what behoves you ! I will never again behave similarly !

---

बन्धः निरोद्धा पुरुषवर्गः ] । आकर्षन्त्विति । [ एनं शकारं सुबद्ध्वा चाण्डाला आकर्षन्तु । अयं श्वभिः खाद्यतां वा । क्रकचेन करपत्रेण ] ॥ ५४ ॥ शत्रुरिति । [ उपकारेण अनुग्रहेण हतः कर्तव्यः । कृतापराधस्य शरणमागतस्य शत्रोः प्राणरक्षणमेव महान्दण्ड इत्यर्थः ] ॥ ५५ ॥ पुरुषैः सह निष्क्रान्तः । अत्र ल० दीक्षिताः— इतः परं नीलकण्ठेनापूरि । 'नेपथ्ये कलकलः । पुनर्नेपथ्ये—' इत्यारभ्याग्रे (पृ. ४०२) 'शर्वि०—दिष्टया जीवितसुहृद्वर्ग आर्यः । चारु०—युष्मत्प्रसादेन—' इत्यन्तं समाप्य 'यत्सूर्योदयभयतः कविनोचितगात्रमेलनं न कृतम् । सुन्दरयुक्तिभिररचयदाचन्दनकोक्ति नीलकण्ठस्तत् ॥' इति निजनिर्मितिसूचिकामार्यां विरच्य समापितोऽयमधिको ग्रन्थः इति ।] [ महाराजप्रासादमार्यकप्रासादम् ] । न महीति । [ हे चारुचरिते

( नेपथ्ये पौराः । )

व्यापादयतम् । किंनिमित्तं पातकी जीव्यते । (वावादेध । किंणिमित्तं पादकी जीवावीअदि ।)

(वसन्तसेना वध्यमालां चारुदत्तस्य कण्ठादपनीय शकारस्योपरि क्षिपति । )

शकारः—गर्भदासीपुत्रि प्रसीद प्रसीद । न पुनर्मारयिष्यामि । तत्परित्रायस्व (गब्भदाशीधीए पशीद पशीद । ण उण मालइश्शम् । ता पलित्ताआहि)

**शर्विलकः**—अरे रे अपनयत । आर्य चारुदत्त आज्ञाप्यताम्—किमस्य पापस्यानुष्ठीयताम् ।

**चारुदत्तः**—किमहं यद्ब्रवीमि तत्क्रियते ।

**शर्विलकः**—कोऽत्र संदेहः ।

**चारुदत्तः**—सत्यम् ।

**शर्विलकः**—सत्यम् ।

**चारुदत्तः**—यद्येवं शीघ्रमयम् ।

**शर्विलकः**—किं हन्यताम् ।

**चारुदत्तः**—न हि नहि । मुच्यताम् ।

**शर्विलकः**—किमर्थम् ।

**चारुदत्तः**—

**शत्रुः कृतापराधः शरणमुपेत्य पादयोः पतितः ।**
**शस्त्रेण न हन्तव्यः—**

**शर्विलकः**—एवम् । तर्हि श्वभिः खाद्यताम् ।

**चारुदत्तः**—न हि ।

**उपकारहतस्तु कर्तव्यः ॥ ५५ ॥**

**शर्विलकः**—अहो आश्चर्यम् । किं करोमि । वदत्वार्यः[१] ।

**चारुदत्तः**—तन्मुच्यताम् ।

**शर्विलकः**—मुक्तो भवतु ।

**शकारः**—(आश्चर्यम् ।) प्रत्युज्जीवितोऽस्मि । (इति पुरुषैः सह निष्क्रान्तः[२] ।) (हीमादिके । पच्चुज्जीविदे म्हि ।)

(नेपथ्ये कलकलः ।)

( पुनर्नेपथ्ये । )

एषाऽऽर्यचारुदत्तस्य वधूरार्या धूता पदे वसनाञ्चले विलगन्तं दारकमाक्षिपन्ती बाष्पभरितनयनैर्जनैर्निवार्यमाणा प्रज्वलिते पावके प्रविशति । (एसा अज्जचालुदत्तस्स वहुआ अज्जा धूदा पदे वसणञ्चले विलग्गन्तं दारअं आक्खिवन्ती बाप्फभरिदणअणेहिं जणेहिं णिवारिज्जमाणा पज्जलिदे पावए पविसदि ।

१ वदत्यार्यः. २ अतः परं ४०२ पृष्ठं यावन्मृच्छकटिकस्थोऽधिको ग्रन्थः.

( *Behind the Scenes; the citizens speaking* )

Kill him ! Why is the sinner allowed to live ?

( Vasantasena *removes the garland, the badge of execution, from* Charudatta's *neck and throws it on* Sakara ).

SAK.—Daughter of a born slave-maid, have mercy ! I won't kill you again ! So please save me !

SAR.—You there ! Take him away ! Noble Charudatta, please order what we should do with this sinful miscreant.

CHAB.—Well, will you do as I tell ?

SAR.—What doubt is there about that ?

CHAR.—Really ?

SAR.—Really,

CHAR.—If so, then let him be quickly—

SAR.—What, slain ?

CHAR.—No, no,—*released* !

SAR.—For what reason ?

CHAR.—

If an enemy, having done evil, beseeches protection and throws himself at the feet, he should never be killed with weapons,—

SAR.—Quite so; then he should be devoured by dogs ?

CHAR.—No !

But he should be killed ( so to say ), by being smothered with kindness ! ( 55 )

SAR.—Oh ! Wonderful ! What shall I do ? Let your honour speak ( further ).

CHAR.—So let him go !

SAR.—( Well ), let him be set free !

SAK.—Bless me, I am restored to life again ! ( *Exit with the* guards ).

( *An uproar behind the Scenes* )

( *Again, behind the Scenes* ).

Here this worthy dame Dhuta, wife of the noble Charudatta, s about to enter the blazing fire, ( even ) casting off her son who is clinging to her legs and to the hem of her garment, and even though she is being dissuaded by the people whose eyes are brimming with tears !

**शर्विलकः**—(आकर्ण्य नेपथ्याभिमुखमवलोक्य ।) कथं चन्दनकः । चन्दनक किमेतत् ।

**चन्दनकः**—( प्रविश्य । ) किं न पश्यत्यार्यः । महाराजप्रासादं दक्षिणेन महाञ्जनसंमर्दो वर्तते । ( 'एसा...... इत्यादि पुनः पठति । ) कथितं च मया तस्यै यथा—आर्ये मा साहसं कुरुष्व । जीवत्यार्यचारुदत्त इति । परं तु दुःखव्यापृततया कः शृणोति कः प्रत्ययते । (किं ण पेक्खदि अज्जो । महाराअप्पासादं दक्खिणेण महन्तो जणसंमद्दो वट्टदि । कधिदं अ मए तीए जधा—अज्जे मा साहसं करेहि । जीवदि अज्जचारुदत्तो त्ति । परं तु दुक्खवावुडदाए को सुणेदि को पत्तिआएदि ।)

**चारुदत्तः**—( सोद्वेगम् । ) हा प्रिये जीवत्यपि मयि किमेतद्व्यवसितम् । (ऊर्ध्वमवलोक्य दीर्घं निःश्वस्य च ।)

न महीतलस्थितिसहानि भवच्चरितानि चारुचरिते यदपि ।
उचितं तथाऽपि परलोकसुखं न पतिव्रते तव विहाय पतिम् ॥ ५६ ॥

( इति मोहमुपगतः[१] । )

**शर्विलकः**—अहो प्रमादः ।

त्वरया[२] सर्पणं तत्र मोहमार्योऽत्र चागतः ।
हा धिक्प्रयत्नवैफल्यं दृश्यते सर्वतोमुखम् ॥ ५७ ॥

**वसन्तसेना**—समाश्वसित्वार्यः । तत्र गत्वा जीवयत्वार्याम् । अन्यथाऽधीरत्वेनानर्थः संभाव्यते । (समस्ससिदु अज्जो । तत्त गदुअ जीवावेदु अज्जाम् । अण्णधा अधीरत्तणेण अणत्थो संभावीअदि ।)

**चारुदत्तः**—(समाश्वस्य सहसोत्थाय ।) हा प्रिये क्वासि । देहि मे प्रतिवचनम् ।

**चन्दनकः**—इत इत आर्यः । (इदो इदो अज्जो ।)

(इति सर्वे परिक्रामन्ति ।)

( ततः प्रविशति यथानिर्दिष्टा धूता चेलाञ्चलमाकर्षन्विदूषकेणानुगम्यमानो रोहसेनो रदनिका च ।)

**धूता**—(सास्रम् ।) जात मुञ्च माम् । मा विघ्नं कुरुष्व । बिभेम्यार्यपुत्रस्यामङ्गलाकर्णनात् । ( इत्युत्थायाञ्चलमाकृष्य पावकाभिमुखं परिक्रामति । ) ( जाद मुञ्चेहि मम् । मा विग्घं करेहि । भीआमि अज्जउत्तस्स अमङ्गलाकण्णणादो ।)

**रोहसेनः**—मातरार्ये प्रतिपालय माम् । त्वया विना न शक्नोमि जीवितं धर्तुम् । (इति त्वरितमुपसृत्य पुनरञ्चलं गृह्णाति ।) (माद अज्जए पडिवालेहि मम् । तुए विणा ण सक्कुणोमि[३] जीविदं धारेदुम् ।)

१ उपागतः. २ त्वरायाः. ३ सक्कणोमि.

SAR.—*Listening; looking towards the curtain*). How ! Here's Chandanaka ! Well, Chandanaka, what's this ?

CHAND.—(*Entering*). What ! Has not your honour noticed ? There's a big crowd of people to the south of the royal palace. (*He again repeats "Here this worthy dame Dhuta" &c.*). And I said to her—"Madam, please do not act (thus) rashly, for the worthy Charudatta is alive." But when one is affected by grief, who will listen and who will believe ?

CHAR.—(*In distress*). Oh, my dear, what is it that you have resolved upon, while I am still alive ? (*Looking upwards and heaving a deep sigh*).

O, you of noble character ! Although your deeds are such that the earth is not a fitting residence for them, still, O faithful wife, it is not proper on your part to enjoy the happiness of the next world, leaving your husband behind. (56)

(*He falls in a swoon*)

SAR.—Oh what a mishap !

We ought to be proceeding thither (*i. e.* to Dhuta) quickly; but here his honour has swooned ! Alas ! Our efforts seem to come to naught in all directions ! (57)

VAS.—Your honour should calm yourself ! You should go there and induce the worthy lady to live. Otherwise, by (such) weakness, a disaster will probably befall !

CHAR.—(*Coming to himself; getting up at once*). O, my dear, where are you ? Give me a reply !

CHAND.—Come, sir, come (this way) !

(*Thereupon all walk about*)

(*Then enter* Dhuta *as described, and* Rohasena *clinging to the skirts of her garment, and accompanied by the* Vidushaka, *and* Radanika).

DHU.—(*Tearfully*). Leave me child ! Do not hinder me ! I am afraid (to live longer) lest I hear the evil tidings concerning my husband. (*She gets up; frees her skirt, and walks towards the fire*).

ROH.—O Mother, O Mamma ! Please wait for me; (for) I shall not be able to remain alive without you ! (*He swiftly approaches her and again seizes her skirts*).

**विदूषकः**—भवत्यास्तावद्ब्राह्मण्या भिन्नत्वेन चिताधिरोहणं पापमुदाहरन्ति ऋषयः। (भोदीए दाव बम्हणीए भिण्णत्तणेण चिदाधिरोहणं पावं उदाहरन्ति रिसीओ।)

**धूता**—वरं पापाचरणम्। न पुनरार्यपुत्रस्यामङ्गलाकर्णनम्। (वरं पावाचरणे[1]। ण उण अज्जउत्तस्स अमङ्गलाकण्णणम्।)

**शर्विलकः**—(पुरोऽवलोक्य।) आसन्नहुतवहाऽऽर्या। तत्त्वर्यतां त्वर्यताम्।

(चारुदत्तस्त्वरितं परिक्रामति।)

**धूता**—रदनिके अवलम्बस्व दारकम्। यावदहं समीहितं करोमि। (रअणिए अवलम्ब दारअं। जाव अहं समीहिदं करेमि।)

**चेटी**—(सकरुणम्।) अहमपि यथोपदेशिन्यस्मि भट्टिन्याः। (अहं पि जधोवदेसिणिम्हि भट्टिणीए।)

**धूता**—(विदूषकमवलोक्य।) आर्यस्तावदवलम्बताम्। (अज्जो दाव अवलम्बेदु।)

**विदूषकः**—(सावेगम्।) समीहितसिद्ध्यै प्रवृत्तेन ब्राह्मणोऽग्रे कर्तव्यः। अतो भवत्या अहमग्रणीर्भवामि। (समीहिदसिद्धिए पउत्तेण बम्हणो अग्गदो कादव्वो। अदो भोदीए अहं अग्गणी होमि।)

**धूता**—कथं प्रत्यादिष्टाऽस्मि द्वाभ्याम्। (बालकमालिङ्ग्य।) जात त्वमेव पर्यवस्थापयात्मानमस्माकं तिलोदकदानाय। अतिक्रान्ते किं मनोरथैः। (सनिःश्वासम्।) न खल्वार्यपुत्रस्त्वां पर्यवस्थापयिष्यति। (कधं पच्चादिट्ठम्हि दुवेहिं। जाद तुमं ज्जेव्व पज्जवट्ठावेहि अत्ताणं अम्हाणं तिलोदअदाणाअ। अदिक्कन्ते किं मणोरहेहिं।। ण क्खु अज्जउत्तो तुमं पज्जवट्ठाविस्सदि।)

**चारुदत्तः**—(आकर्ण्य सहसोपसृत्य।) अहमेव पर्यवस्थापयामि बालिशम्[2]। (इति बालकं बाहुभ्यामुत्थाप्य वक्षसाऽऽलिङ्गति।)

**धूता**—(विलोक्य।) आश्चर्यम्। आर्यपुत्रस्येव स्वरसंयोगः। (पुनर्निपुणं निरूप्य सहर्षम्।) दिष्ट्याऽऽर्यपुत्र एवैषः। प्रियं मे प्रियम्। (अम्महे। अज्जउत्तस्स ज्जेव्व सरसंजोओ। दिट्ठिआ अज्जउत्तो ज्जेव्व एसो। पिअं मे पिअम्।)

**बालकः**—(विलोक्य सहर्षम्।) आश्चर्यम्। तातो मां परिष्वजते। (धूतां प्रति।) आर्ये वर्धसे। तात एव मां पर्यवस्थापयति (इति प्रत्यालिङ्गति। (अम्मो। आवुको मं परिस्सजदि। अज्जए वड्ढवीअसि। आवुको ज्जेव्व मं पज्जवट्ठावेदि।)

---

रमणीयवृत्ते यद्यपि भवत्याः चरितानि सत्कृत्यानि महीतलस्थितिसहानि न। स्वर्गोचितान्येवेत्यर्थः। तथाऽपि हे पतिव्रते पतिं विहाय तव परलोकसुखं न उचितम्।

---

१ वत्सं. २ चरणं. ३ पधोव० (पथोप०).

VID.—As for you, a Brahman lady, the sages have declared it a sin to mount the funeral pyre separately from ( the corpse of ) the husband.

DHU.—It is better to commit that sin, rather than hear the evil tidings about my husband !

SAR.—( *Looking before him* ). The good lady is just near the fire; so make haste, make haste !

( Charudatta *hastily walks up* ).

DHU.—O Radanika, please take care of the boy, so that I may do what I wish.

THE MAID.—( *mournfully* ). I, too, am going to do what I have learnt from my mistress !

DHU.—( *Looking at the* Vidushaka ). You, sir, please look after the child.

VID.—( *With a pang* ), Anybody setting about to accomplish his desire has to follow the lead of a Brahmana. So I will precede your ladyship ( in this matter ).

DHU.—How ! they both have refused my request ! ( *Embracing the boy* ). Child, you yourself should compose ( take care of ) yourself that you may offer to both of us the ( obsequial ) sesamum-mixed water. Of what avail are one's desires, when a thing is past( *i. e.* the person concerned is out of reach ) ? ( *Sighing* ). For your father will not indeed take care of you !

CHAR.—( *Hearing it and coming up suddenly* ). I myself will take care of my boy ! ( *He lifts up the boy with his arms and clasps him to his breast* ).

DHU.—( *Seeing*). Wonderful ! It seems like the voice of my husband ! ( *Again peering closely; joyfully* ). Oh, good luck ! It is my lord himself ! It is gratifying to me, gratifying indeed !

THE BOY—( *Seeing; with delight* ). Wonderful ! It is father who is embracing me ! ( *To* Dhuta ). Mamma, you are now happy ! It is father himself who is taking care of me ! ( *He embraces him in return* ).

---

प्रमिताक्षरा वृत्तम् ] ।। ५६ ।। त्वरयेति । [ तत्र त्वरया सर्पणं गमनं उचितम् । अत्र च आर्यो मोहमागतः । हा धिक् सर्वतोमुखं प्रयत्नवैफल्यं दृश्यते ] ।। ५७ ।। अहमेवेति । पर्यवस्थापनमाचार इति कृत्वा स्वयमेव क्षमोऽहमिति भावः

**चारुदत्तः**—(धूतां प्रति।)

**हा प्रेयसि प्रेयसि विद्यमाने कोऽयं कठोरो व्यवसाय आसीत्।**
**अम्भोजिनी लोचनमुद्रणं किं भानावनस्तगमिते करोति ॥ ५८ ॥**

**धूता**—आर्यपुत्र अत एव साऽचेतनेत्युच्यते (अज्जउत्त अदो ज्जेव सा अचेतणेत्ति उच्चीअदि[1]।)

**विदूषकः**—(दृष्ट्वा सहर्षम्।) आश्चर्यं भोः एताभ्यामेवाक्षिभ्यां प्रियवयस्यः प्रेक्ष्यते। अहो सत्याः प्रभावः यतो ज्वलनप्रवेशव्यवसायेनैव प्रियसमागमं प्रापिता। (चारुदत्तं प्रति।) जयतु जयतु प्रियवयस्यः। (ही ही भो एदेहिं ज्जेव अच्छीहिं पिअवअस्सो पेक्खीअदि। अहो सदीए पहावो जदो जलणप्पवेशव्ववसाएण ज्जेव पिअसमागमं पाविदा। जेदु जेदु पिअवअस्सो।)

**चारुदत्तः**—एहि मैत्रेय। (इत्यालिङ्गति।)

**चेटी**—अहो संविधानकम्। आर्य वन्दे। (इति चारुदत्तस्य पादयोः पतति।) (अहो संविधाणअम्। अज्ज वन्दामि।)

**चारुदत्तः**—(पृष्ठे करं दत्वा।) रदनिके उत्तिष्ठ। (इत्युत्थापयति।)

**धूता**—(वसन्तसेनां दृष्ट्वा।) दिष्टचा कुशलिनी भगिनी। (दिठ्ठिआ कुसलिणी बहिणिणा।)

**वसन्तसेना**—अधुना कुशलिनी संवृत्ताऽस्मि। (अहुणा कुसलिणी संवुत्तम्हि।)

(इत्यन्योन्यमालिङ्गतः।)

**शर्विलकः**—दिष्टचा जीवितसुहृद्वर्ग आर्यः।

**चारुदत्तः**—युष्मत्प्रसादेन।

**शर्विलकः**—आर्ये वसन्तसेने परितुष्टो राजा भवतीं वधूशब्देनानुगृह्णाति।

**वसतन्सेनाः**—आर्य कृतार्थाऽस्मि। (अज्ज कदत्थम्हि।)

**शर्विलकः**—(वसन्तसेनामवगुण्ठच चारुदत्तं प्रति।) आर्य किमस्य भिक्षोः क्रियताम्।

---

**हा प्रेयसीति।**[हा कष्टं हे प्रेयसि दयते प्रेयसि प्रियतरे मयि विद्यमाने कोऽयं कठोरः निष्ठुरः व्यवसायः अग्निप्रवेशरूपः आसीत्। भानौ अनस्तंगमिते कालेनास्तमप्रापिते अम्भोजिनी लोचनमुद्रणं पद्मसंकोचं करोति किम्। न करोत्येव। इन्द्रवज्रा वृत्तम् ॥ ५८ ॥ **लब्धेति।**[चारित्रस्य शुद्धिः निष्कलङ्कता लब्धा। वसन्तसेना-मारणापवादपरिहारादिति भावः। एष शत्रुः शकारः। प्रोत्खातमुन्मूलितमराति-कुलं येन स तथा। प्रियसुहृदार्यकः राजा सन् अचलां पृथ्वीं शास्ति। इयं प्रिया

---

१ चुम्बीअदि (चुम्ब्यते).

CHAR.—( *To* Dhuta ).

O my love! What means this terrible attempt on your part while your dearest one ( husband ) still lived? Does the sun-lotus-plant close its eyes ( *i. e.* its flowers ), while the sun has not set? (58)

DHU.—My lord, it is for that that it is described as inanimate,

( *Seeing; joyfully* ). Oh! Wonder! With these self-same eyes I am beholding my dear friend! Oh, the might of a chaste wife! By merely resolving upon immolating herself in the fire she has been united with her beloved husband! ( *To* Charudatta ). Victory to my dear friend!

CHAR.—Come, Maitreya! ( *Embraces him* ).

THE MAID.—Oh, the wonderful turn of events! Sir, I salute you! ( She *falls at* Charudatta's *feet* ).

CHAR.—( *Laying his hand on her back* ). Rise, O Radanika! ( *He helps her to rise* ).

DHU.—( Seeing Vasantasena ). Good luck! My sister is safe!

VAS.—Now I am safe, indeed!

( *They both embrace each other* ).

SAR.—By good luck all your honour's friends are now safe!

CHAR.—It is ( rather ) by your favour ( that it is so ).

SAR.—Madam Vasantasena, the king is highly pleased ( with you ) and has graciously bestowed on you the title of a wedded wife!

VAS.—Sir, my wishes are fulfilled!

SAR.—( *Putting the veil on* Vasantasena; *to* Charudatta ). Sir, what should be done for this Bhikshu?

---

भूयः पुनः प्राप्ता । प्रियसुहृदि संगतः भवान्मम बयस्यः जातः । किं चातिरिक्तं उक्तेभ्योऽन्यत् लभ्यं यदपरमधुनाऽहं भवन्तं प्रार्थये । स्रग्धरा वृत्तम् ] ॥ ५९ ॥

**कांश्चिदिति** । [ विधिः कांश्चित् तुच्छयति । तुच्छान् रिक्तानित्यर्थः । करोति । कांश्चित्प्रपूरयति कांश्चिदुन्नतिं नयति । कांश्चित्पातविधौ करोति । कांश्चित्पुनः आकुलान् स्रस्तबन्धतयाऽर्धभरितानेवावलम्बमानान् नयति । करोतीत्यर्थः । इमां लोकस्थितिं अन्योन्यं प्रतिपक्षाणामुन्नत्यवनत्यादिना संहतिर्यस्यां तादृशीं बोधयन् । एष कूपयन्त्रं वार्युद्धरणयन्त्रं तस्य या घटिकास्तासां न्यायः एकस्या अधोमज्जनमेकस्या रिक्तीभावः एकस्या जलपूरणमितिरूपः तत्र प्रसक्तः विधिः क्रीडति । अत्र

**चारुदत्तः**—भिक्षो किं तव बहुमतम् ।

**भिक्षुः**—इदमीदृशमनित्यत्वं प्रेक्ष्य द्विगुणतरो मम प्रव्रज्यायां बहुमानः संवृत्तः। ( इमं ईदिशं अणिच्चत्तणं पेक्खिअ दिउणतलं मे पव्वज्जाए बहुमाणे संवुत्ते ।)

**चारुदत्तः**—सखे दृढोऽस्य निश्चयः । तत्पृथिव्याः सर्वविहारेषु कुलपतिरयं क्रियताम् ।

**शर्विलकः**—यथाऽऽहार्यः ।

**भिक्षुः**—प्रियं नः प्रियम् । (पिअं णो पिअम् ।)

**वसन्तसेना**—सांप्रतं जीवापिताऽस्मि । (संपदं जीवाविदम्हि ।)

**शर्विलकः**—स्थावरकस्य किं क्रियताम् ।

**चारुदत्तः**—[1]सुवृत्तोऽदासो भवतु । ते चाण्डालाः सर्वचाण्डालानामधिपतयो भवन्तु । चन्दनकः[2] पृथिवीदण्डपालको भवतु । तस्य राष्ट्रियशालस्य यथैव[3] क्रिया पूर्वमासीद्वर्तमाने तथैवास्तु ।

**शर्विलकः**—एवं यथाऽऽहार्यः । परमेनं मुञ्च मुञ्च । व्यापादयामि ।

**चारुदत्तः**—अभयं शरणागतस्य । ( 'शत्रुः कृतापराधः--' (१०।५५ ) इत्यादि पठति । )

**शर्विलकः**—तदुच्यतां किं ते भूयः प्रियं करोमि[4] ।

**चारुदत्तः**--अतः परमपि[5] प्रियमस्ति ।

**लब्धा [6]चारित्रशुद्धिश्चरणनिपतितः शत्रुरप्येष मुक्तः**
**प्रोत्खातारातिमूलः प्रियसुहृदचलामार्यकः शास्ति राजा ।**
**प्राप्ता भूयः प्रियेयं प्रियसुहृदि भवान्संगतो मे वयस्यो**
**लभ्यं किं चातिरिक्तं यदपरमधुना प्रार्थयेऽहं भवन्तम् ॥ ५९ ॥**

---

समानार्थं पद्यं शाकुन्तले—'यात्येकतोऽस्तशिखरं पतिरोषधीनामाविष्कृतोऽरुणपुरःसर एकतोऽर्कः । तेजोद्वयस्य युगपद्व्यसनोदयाभ्यां लोको नियम्यत इवात्मदशान्तरेषु ॥' इति । निदर्शनालंकारः । शार्दूल० वृत्तम् ] ॥ ६० ॥ [ भरतवाक्यं नटवाक्यम् । नाटकाभिनयसमाप्तौ गृहीतां भूमिकां विहाय भरततां प्रतिपन्नेन नटेन या आशीर्दीयते सा भरतवाक्यमित्युच्यते । यदाह भरतः-'अन्ते काव्यस्य नित्यत्वात्कुर्यादाशिषमुत्तमाम्' इति ] । **क्षीरिण्य इति** । [ गावः क्षीरिण्यः प्रचुरदुग्धवत्यः सन्तु । भूमार्थे इनिः । वसुमती पृथ्वी सर्वं संपन्नं सस्यं यस्यां तथा अस्तु । पर्जन्यः

---

१ सुवृत्त अ०; त्तोऽयमदा०. २ चन्दनकस्य पृथ्वीदण्डपालकता. ३ यथैव क्रिया पूर्वं वर्तमाना तथैवास्तु,..वर्तमाने तथैवास्तु. ४ उपकरोमि. ५ परं प्रियं; परमस्ति प्रियं. ६ चारित्र्य. ७ बुद्धिः. ८ दवनीं.

CHAR.—O Bhikshu, what do you like best ?

BH.—Having witneseed this impermanence ( of things here below ), of such kind, the great liking that I had for an ascetic's life has been intensified !

CHAR.—Friend, his resolution is firm; so let him be made the head of all the Buddhistic monasteries in the country !

SAR.—As your honour directs.

BH.—It is gratifying to me, gratifying, indeed !

VAS.—Now I feel I have been ( really ) restored to life !

SAR.—How is Sthavaraka to be rewarded ?

CHAR.—Let that well-behaved servant be freed from his bondage. As for those Chandalas, let them be made the chiefs of all the Chandalas. Let Chandanaka be appointed the head of the police ( *or*, chief magistrate ) in the country. And, as regards that king's brother-in-law, whatever status he enjoyed formerly, let him continue to enjoy the same even now.

SAR.—It shall be as your honour directs. But still, please deliver him over, leave him ( to me ); I will put him to death !

CHAR.—He that seeks protection shall have it ! ( *He recites the verse beginning* " *An enemy who has wrought evil* " &c.)

SAR.—Then please say what further pleasure of yours shall be done by me.

CHAR.—Is there any further pleasure beyond this ?—

The purity of my character is restored; this enemy of mine, too, who had fallen at my feet ( for protection ), has been allowed to go free. My dear friend Aryaka, who has destroyed his foe from his very roots, is now the king and the ruler of the earth. I have gained this beloved ( Vasantasena ) of mine. And you, that are in union with your dear friend ( Aryaka ), have become my friend. What more, then, remains there to be obtained, that I should now ask of you ? ( 59 )

---

काले वर्षतीति कालवर्षी भवतु । सकलजनमनोनन्दिनः वाता वान्तु । जन्मभाजः प्राणिनः सततं मोदन्ताम् । सुखिनः सन्तु इत्यर्थः । ब्राह्मणाः अभिमताः सन्तु । सन्तः श्रीमन्तः सन्तु । प्रशमिता नाशं नीता रिपवो यैस्ते प्रशमितरिपवः धर्मनिष्ठाश्च भूपाः पृथ्वीं पान्तु । स्रग्धरा वृत्तम् । अनेन प्रशस्तिर्नाम निर्वहणसंध्यङ्गमुपक्षिप्तम् । तदुक्तमादिभरते—' देवद्विजनृपादीनां प्रशस्तिः स्यात्प्रशंसनम् ' इति ] ॥ ६१ ॥

काश्चित्तुच्छयति[१] प्रपूरयति वा कांश्चिन्नयत्युन्नतिं
कांश्चित्पातविधौ[२] करोति च पुनः कांश्चिन्नयत्याकुलान् ।
अन्योन्यं प्रतिपक्षसंहतिमिमां लोकस्थितिं बोधय-
न्नेष क्रीडति कूपयन्त्रघटिकान्यायप्रसक्तो विधिः ।। ६० ।।

तथापीदमस्तु ।

(भरतवाक्यम् ।)

क्षीरिण्यः सन्तु गावो भवतु वसुमती सर्वसंपन्नसस्या[३]
पर्जन्यः कालवर्षी सकलजनमनोनन्दिनो वान्तु वाताः ।
मोदन्तां जन्मभाजः सततमभिमता ब्राह्मणाः सन्तु सन्तः
श्रीमन्तः पान्तु[४] पृथ्वीं प्रशमितरिपवो धर्मनिष्ठाश्च[५] भूपाः ।। ६१ ।।

(इति निष्क्रान्ताः सर्वे ।)

संहारो[६] नाम दशमोऽङ्कः ।

समाप्तं[७] मृच्छकटिकम् ।

---

मृच्छकटिकविवृतिरियं गणपतिचित्तान्तपारपर्यन्ता ।
पृथ्वीधरकृतिरुपनयतु संतोषं कृतिसमुद्रे ।।

इति दशमोऽङ्कः ।।

---

१ दूषयति. २ पान. ३ शस्या. ४ पान्तु पृथ्व्यां; पान्तु सर्वाप्रतिहत. ५ ब्रह्म. ६ इति मृच्छकटिकायां संहा०; इति मृच्छकटिकप्रकरणे संहारो. ७ समाप्ता चेयं मृच्छकटिका.

It empties some and fills others; some it raises up and others it causes to go down; while some it keeps in (anxious) suspense; thus bringing home to the people this course of the world which consists of opposites mutually meeting together, does Destiny play with all creatures, being bent upon following the maxim of "the water-wheel and the buckets." (60)

Still, let there be this :—

(*The Benediction*).

May cows yield (plenty of) milk, the earth produce all kinds of grains in abundance, the clouds shower rain in due season, and the winds blow so as to gladden the hearts of all people! May all creatures always rejoice, the Brahmanas be ever respected, and the virtuous become rich. And may righteous kings subdue their foes and govern the earth (justly)! (61)

(*Exeunt Omnes*).

*Here ends Act X., styled*

"THE CONCLUSION"

---

**FINIS**

# मृच्छकटिकस्थसुभाषितसंग्रहः ।

I. Sentences. [ Page

# श्लोकसूची

# Index of Important Words

*( The figures refer to the pages of this Edition )*

# NOTES

## ACT I.

P. 7. Sanskrit writers generally introduce their works with a benediction ( आशीः ), or a salutation to their favourite deity (नमस्क्रिया). In dramas this purpose is served by the Nandi, which is enjoined by Bharata ( see com. ) as necessary for the removal of obstacles and thereby for the safe completion of the work undertaken. We find play-writers from Sudraka downwards, conforming to this rule of Bharata. Bhasa, Sudraka's predecessor, however, often dispenses with the Nandi, probably treating it as the last part of the theatrical preliminaries (पूर्वरङ्ग) which are gone through behind the curtains. Thus the *Charudatta* opens at once with the stage direction 'नान्द्यन्ते ततः प्रविशति सूत्रधारः. Sudraka was a worshipper of Siva ( see sl. 4 ), and hence he has addressed both the stanzas of the Nandi to that deity. In the first sl., Siva is referred to as completely lost in abstract meditation, and so his *Samadhi* is invoked for granting protection. Sanskrit poets often address their prayer for protection to some act of, or some thing connected with, the deity, instead of to the deity directly. *Cf.* the Nandi of Mudr. (शाठ्यमव्याद्विभोर्वः), Mal.-Madh. (वैनायक्यः वदनविधुतयः &c.), Ratna., Veni. &c.

**पर्यङ्क** &c.—The principal sentence is शंभोः शून्येक्षण० समाधिः वः पातु; the genitives go with शंभोः. **पर्यङ्क**—more generally known as वीरासन, is one of the five principal postures (for these see our notes on Ragh. XIII. 52) assumed in the practice of Yoga. It consists in sitting down with the upper part of the body raised straight up perpendicularly, with one foot placed on the other thigh passing it through the knee-joint of that leg, and then placing the other foot on the other thigh. It is thus defined by Vasishtha—एकपादमथैकस्मिन्विन्यस्योरुणि संस्थितम् । इतरस्मिंस्तथा चान्यं वीरासनमुदाहृतम् ॥ (as quoted by Malli. on Ragh. XIII. 52).

**ग्रन्थि**—the placing of the feet thus crosswise being firmly held together; तस्य बन्धाय for keeping it fast यः द्विगुणितस्य भुजंगस्य आश्लेषः तेन &c. ; see com. आश्लेष—embrace, coiling round

Siva sat in the Virasana posture; and the serpent lay doubly coiled fast, round the squatting position of the body (the base of the hips and the knees). Mr. Raddisastri contends that this is not the meaning of पर्यङ्क here; he thinks it means योगपट्टक which means 'sitting up with the knees raised up by firmly fastening an upper garment round the back and the knees.' But this meaning does not suit here at all. If the serpent was fastened like a garment round the back and the knees, then we do not get the द्विगुणितभुजगाश्लेष, and the knees, also do not become संवीत (encircled) as the garment passes *round* and not *over* the knees. Again, this posture is not suited to Samadhi at all. Patanjali defines an *asana* as स्थिरसुख, which Virasana is. For Samadhi the body must be in a state of equipoise, such as is described by Kalidasa in his Kum.; see Kum. III. 45, and Bg. VI. 11-13.

अन्तःप्राणावरोध—The restraining within of the vital airs in the body so as to arrest their functions; suppression of breath. व्युपरत—ended, suspended. इन्द्रिय is derived as इन्द्रस्य आत्मनः लिङ्गं करणेन कर्तुरनुमानात्; the sign (for inference) of the soul; fr. इन्द्र and aff. (घच्); see also Pan. V. 2 93 There are eleven *Indriyas*, the five organs of action, and the six organs of sense; मनः कर्णौ तथा नेत्रे रसना च त्वचा सह। नासिका चेति षट् तानि धीन्द्रियाणि प्रचक्षते ॥. Here the latter six are meant. रुद्ध—restrained or checked from outer perception. These six senses naturally look out; they must be turned inside. *Cf.* पराञ्चि खानि व्यतृणत्स्वयंभूस्तस्मात्पराक्पश्यति नान्तरात्मन्। &c. Kathop. II. 1. 1; see also the quotation from योगसागर given in the com. Samkara so restrained the organs of sense that there was no perception of anything external. For the compound, see com.

आत्मन्यात्मान०—व्यपगतकरणं is an adv. modifying पश्यतः. For the comp. see com.; करण is the same as इन्द्रिय. Here करण is to be understood in the secondary sense of 'its function' (व्यापार). All the 11 इन्द्रियs are meant here. The Samkhyas add two more to these, *viz*. बुद्धि and अहंकार. *Cf*. यदा पञ्चावतिष्ठन्ते ज्ञानानि मनसा सह। बुद्धिश्च न विचेष्टति तामाहुः परमां गतिम् ॥ तां योगमिति मन्यन्ते स्थिरामिन्द्रियधारणाम्। Kathop. II. 3. 10, 11. See also Bg. VI. 20, 25. व्यपगतकरणं cannot be fitly taken as an adj. to आत्मानं as some suggest; for आत्मानं refers to the Supreme Soul or Brahma, whose vision Siva was enjoying inwardly in his Samadhi; and this Brahma, pure spirit, unassociated with the gunas and undefined, has no *Karanas*; *Cf.* the Sruti **न तस्य कार्यं करणं च विद्यते न तत्समश्चाभ्यधिकश्च दृश्यते।** &c. Svet. Up. VI. 8 and अपाणिपादो जवनो ग्रहीता पश्यत्यचक्षुः स शृणोत्यकर्णः। स वेत्ति वेद्यं न च तस्यास्ति वेत्ता तमाहुरग्र्यं पुरुषं महान्तम् ॥ Svet. Up. III. 19. **तत्त्वदृष्टया**--with the eye of true knowledge, *viz.* अहमेव ब्रह्मास्मि &c. **आत्मानमेव**--The force of एव is that Siva himself being the Supreme Being could see his own self only *Cf.* Kali. स्वयं विधाता तपसः फलानां केनापि कामेन तपश्चार। Kum. I 57; and यस्मात्परं नापरमस्ति किंचित्। Svet. Up. III. 9. **पश्यतः**—*Cf* तदा द्रष्टुः स्वरूपेऽवस्थानम्। Pat Yo. Su. I. 3.

**शून्येक्षण** &c.—शून्येक्षण is the non-perception of anything external; तेन घटितः brought about यः लयः the continued resting of the mind (*cf* आत्मसंस्थ मनः कृत्वा न किंचिदपि चिन्तयेत्। Bg. VI. 25) तेन ब्रह्मणि लग्नः concentrated on **समाधिः**--Remaining lost in meditation ( a sort of psychic trance ). The following from Kum. III. will serve as a com. on the description of Siva's *samadhi* here--पर्यङ्कबन्धस्थिरपूर्वकायमृज्वायतं संनमितोभयांसम। उत्तानपाणिद्वयसंनिवेशात्प्रफुल्लराजीवमिवाङ्कमध्ये ॥ + + + नेत्रैरविस्पन्दितपक्ष्ममालैर्लक्ष्यीकृतघ्राणमधोमयूखैः ॥ अवृष्टिसंरम्भमिवाम्बुवाहमपामिवाधारमनुत्तरङ्गम्। अन्तश्चराणां मरुतां निरोधान्निवातनिष्कम्पमिव प्रदीपम् ॥ मनो नवद्वारनिषिद्धवृत्ति हृदि व्यवस्थाप्य समाधिवश्यम्। यमक्षरं क्षेत्रविदो विदुस्तमात्मानमात्मन्यवलोकयन्तम् ॥ 45–50.

**समाधिः पातु वः**—The virtual meaning is समाधिनिष्ठः शिवः वः पातु Siva is often described as given to meditation, probably because, as Wilson thinks, in some of the Puranas, especially those of a Saiva character, the origin of Yoga is ascribed to Siva who taught it in the person of Sveta on the Himalaya mountains in the beginning of the Kali age.

" This benediction alludes to the practices and notions of योग, in which, by abstract meditation (समाधि), the fusion (लय) of individual with universal spirit ब्रह्मन्) is to be effected even in the body. Spirit is said to be detached from the *Karanas*, the thirteen products of matter, or महत् intellect; अहंकार, consciousness; and the eleven organs of sense and action. The mode of effecting this union is by sitting in particular *asanas* or postures, one of which is sitting on the hams with a cloth fastened round the knees and back (पर्यङ्क-बन्धः-ग्रन्थिः), also by suppression of breath (प्राणावरोधः), by keeping the vision directed either on vacuity or inwardly (शून्येक्षण), and by preventing as vigilantly as possible the wanderings of the senses." W.

P. 7. नीलकण्ठः—Siva so called after the colour of his throat was changed to a dark-blue in consequence of his having drunk the deadly poison produced at the churning of the ocean for the the obtaining of Amrita. श्यामाम्बुदोपमः—The throat is compared to a dark cloud because both relieve the संताप (torment—heat) of the people. The fig. is लुप्तधर्मोपमा as the common quality is not mentioned. गौरीभुजलता—The word गौरी is used in preference to शिवा or so, to give prominence to her गौरत्व which bears out the comparison to विद्युल्लता. The second sl. is written by the poet very probably in order to suggest partly the subject-matter of the plot as required by a cannon of dramaturgy ('अर्थतः शब्दतो वाऽपि मनाक्काव्यार्थसूचनम्'). Thus the casting of the arm of Gauri round Siva's neck suggests the love between Charudatta and Vasantasena, while the reference to नीलाम्बुद is meant to indicate the visit of Vasantasena to Charudatta amidst rain and flashes of lightning. The contrast between white and blue also further suggests the dark ways of the world, as exemplified by the conduct of Samsthanaka, and the joys of pure love as in the case of Vasantasena. The Nandi here consists of eight *padas* (*pada* referring to the line of a sloka). It is of the Pattravali kind, since the casting of the seed of the plot is indirectly suggested in it. *Cf.* यस्यां बीजस्य विन्यासो ह्यभिधेयस्य वस्तुनः । श्लेषेण वा समासोक्त्या नान्दी पत्रावलीति सा ॥ Sah.-Dar.

नान्द्यन्ते—नन्दन्ति देवता अस्यामिति नान्दी that in which the gods take delight. It contains the praise of some deity, or Brahmanas or a king &c., combined with a benediction. See definition given in the com.; or नन्दयति इति नन्दः, नन्द् cau. and अ (अच्); नन्द एव नान्दः by adding अण् (अ) स्वार्थे; and by adding ई (fem.) we get नान्दी.

नान्द्यन्ते सूत्र०—It is the Sutradhara who recites the Nandi here. Bharata says that the Sutra. should repeat the Nandi employing a middle tone. But the word सूत्रधार is not placed before the introductory sloka, because it contains a benediction and forms no part of the drama itself, being the last part of the पूर्वरङ्ग. The Sutra. was generally a Brahmana and recited the Nandi in his own person and not in his character as the chief manager, which he did not assume till he had recited the Nandi. Another explanation is—It is the practice of Sanskrit writers to introduce their works with auspicious words, and so the word Sutradhara is not placed before the benedictory sl. *Cf.* Panini who also writes his first सूत्र as वृद्धिरादैच्, though the proper order is आदैच् वृद्धिः, which he follows when he says अदेङ् गुणः. The Sutra. was already present on the stage; hence the stage-direction प्रविश्य is not used.

Bhasa's play ( *Charudatta* ) however begins with नान्द्यन्ते ततः प्रविशति सूत्रधारः । This shows that the old practice was to recite the Nandi behind the curtain. Then the Sutra. entered and began the play. When the chief manager happened not to be a Brahmana, it seems he had no right to the title Sutra., nor did he repeat the Nandi. He was called Sthapaka, one who established the action of the play, and had qualities similar to those of the Sutra.; cf. Bharata--रङ्गपूजां विधायादौ सूत्रधारे विनिर्गते । स्थापकः प्रविशेत्पश्चात्सूत्रधारगुणाकृतिः ॥. All the plays from those of Kali. downwards make the Sutra first recite the Nandi and then carry on the Prologue.

**सूत्रधारः**—The chief manager, *lit.* he who holds the thread of the plot, *i. e.* looks after the general management, the casting of parts, &c. ( सूत्रं प्रयोगानुष्ठानं धारयतीति ). For the origin of the term and of the drama, see our note on सूत्रधार in the Sak. The following are the qualifications of the Sutra. according to मातृगुप्ताचार्य--" चतुरातोद्यनिष्णातोऽनेकभूषासमावृतः नानाभाषणतत्त्वज्ञो नीतिशास्त्रार्थतत्त्वविद् ॥ नानागतिप्रचारज्ञो रसभावविशारदः । नाट्यप्रयोगनिपुणो नानाशिल्पकलान्वितः ॥ छन्दोविधानतत्त्वज्ञः सर्वशास्त्रविचक्षणः । तत्तद्गीतानुगलयकलातालावधारणः ॥ अवधानप्रयोक्ता च योक्तॄणामुपदेशकः । एवं गुणगणोपेतः सूत्रधारोऽभिधीयते ॥ " **अलं**—" enough of "—has a prohibitive sense (वारण): ' no object is to be gained by परिश्रम ' (परिश्रमेण किंचित्साध्यं नास्ति ). **विमर्दकारिणा**—crushing, destroying. **परिश्रमेण**—( This ) exertion ( at the recitation of the Nandi ). **आर्यमिश्रान्**—The noble and learned men composing the audience. ' कुलं शीलं दया दानं धर्मः सत्यं कृतज्ञता । अद्रोह इति येष्वेतत्तानार्यान्संप्रचक्षते ॥ ' Bharata, as quoted by Jagaddhara on the Mal.-Madh. मिश्र is an honorific title added to the names of learned men; as वाचस्पतिमिश्रः, शाङ्गरव

मिश्राः Sak., &c. विज्ञापयामि—simply means—'I respectfully inform or bring to the notice of;' for here no request is addressed to the 'audience as in the Vikr. to behold the play with attention.

मृच्छकटिकं—मृदः मृन्निर्मिता वा शकटिका a small play-cart मृच्छकटिका। सा एवाभेदोपचारान्मृच्छकटिकं प्रकरणम् Or, मृच्छकटिका लक्षणया प्राधान्येन तन्निर्देशः अस्त्यस्मिन् प्रकरणे इति. The play is named after the play-cart made of earth for Rohasena, Charudatta's son, mentioned in the sixth Act, as it forms the turning point in the development of the plot. See Introd. प्रकरणं—see Intro. व्यवसिताः—'we are prepared or resolved to.' We find from the plays of Kalidasa and others that follow, that it was usual in ancient India to exhibit dramatic performances at the time of some fair or some festive occasion. But here no mention is made of the place at which the play was exhibited. This perhaps proves the antiquity of the play.

P. 8. द्विरदेन्द्र—See com. चकोरनेत्रः—The eyes of a *Chakora* ( the Greek partridge ) are reddish and beautiful. The natural redness indicates heroism on the part of Sudraka. *Cf.* the description of the eyes of Lava and Kusa—नेत्रे पुनर्यद्यपि रक्तनीले। Uttar. VI. 27. The eyes of women are generally compared to those of a *Chakora* see Ragh. VI. 59, VII. 25. सुविग्रहः—शोभनः well-built and handsome विग्रहः body यस्य. For this see Ragh. I. 13.

द्विजमुख्यतमः—The most eminent of Kshatriyas. Originally the word द्विज signified the first three classes, *viz.* the Brahmanas, Kshatriyas and Vaisyas. It was only in later times that it came specially to refer to the Brahmana class. Here it refers to a Kshatriya from the context. कविः—must be taken in the sense of 'a scholar, a Pandit,' to avoid tautology with एतत्कविः on p. 7. संज्ञावान्पण्डितः कविः। Amara. अगाधसत्त्वः—अगाध not fathomable, unflinching; सत्त्व—mental calibre, that firmness of the mind which remains unshaken under trying circumstances and enables a man to maintain his character.

वैशिकीं—Belonging to the Vesa. According to the Com. वेश refers to the residence of the courtesans. So वैशिकीं कलां ( sing. for the plural ) means the arts to be found among or cultivated by the courtesans, the elegant arts; and we know from the Dasakum. that the knowledge of the following arts among others was deemed necessary for the harlot class, *viz.* नृत्य, गीत, वाद्य, नाट्य, चित्रलेखन,

आस्वाद्य, गन्धकला, पुष्पकला and द्यूत. The words seem rather to mean 'the dramatic art or Natya-sastra' (which relates to वेश or the assumption of different dresses *i.e.* characters). हस्तिशिक्षां—The knowledge of elephants and the art of training them. The name of the treatise on हस्तिशिक्षा generally quoted is हस्त्यायुर्वेद by Palakapya.

Wilson has—"The proficiency of the Indians in this art early attracted the attention of Alexander's successors, and natives of India were so long exclusively employed in this service, that the term Indian was applied to every elephant-driver, to whatever country he might belong.—*Schlegel Indische Bibliothek.*"

व्यपगततिमिरे &c.—तिमिर is a kind of eye disease causing blindness, opacity of the cornia. But that does not seem to be intended here. Here the meaning is 'eyes free from the blindness of ignorance', eyes of knowledge; i e insight into the Brahmavidya. Siva is the deity to be propitiated for the obtainment of knowledge; *cf.* आरोग्यं भास्करादिच्छेद्धनमिच्छेद्धुताशनात् । विज्ञानं शंकरादिच्छेन्मोक्षमिच्छेज्जनार्दनात् ।। Valmiki is similarly mentioned as having got divine vision by the favour of Brahma; *cf.* अव्याहतज्योतिरार्षं ते प्रतिभातु चक्षु: । Uttar II.

परमसमुदयेन—Leading to great exaltation; Indicating supreme power. *Cf.* अये अश्वमेध इति नाम विश्वविजयिनां क्षत्रियाणामूर्जस्वल: सर्वक्षत्रपरिभावी महानुत्कर्षनिकष: । Uttar. IV. अश्वमेधेन—For the sacrifice, see our note on that word at Ragh. VI. 61. In ancient India it was the highest ambition of a king enjoying supreme power to perform one horse-sacrifice at least. One such was performed, and perhaps the last of the kind, by Pushpamitra, the father of Agnimitra, the hero of the Malav.; see Malav. p. 104.

अग्नि प्रविष्ट:—These words are not to be taken in their literal sense. They simply mean, like पुरंदरपुरातिथिरभवत् or अमरेष्वगण्यत, 'he died'. The writer has used the expression अग्नि प्रविष्ट: only to show that Sudraka was an *agnihotrin* (like Rama) till his death, as we speak of a devotee of Siva as going to the mountain Kailasa, or of Vishnu to Vaikuntha. The com. understands these words literally (and he is followed in this by Wilson and others) and cites the instance of Sarabhanga who made a voluntary cremation of himself after seeing Rama. (For his story see our notes on

Ragh. XIII. 45 ).* But the case of Sarabhanga ( or of the Sramanacharya who made a similar immolation ) is different. These sages knew how to dematerialize the body and to reduce it to a fiery state by meditation on the fiery element, and then offered up their bodies to fire. Sudraka was not an ascetic of that sort. Nor was there anything in his life to make it burdensome to him, so that he could have resorted to self-immolation. Again, if we take the words in their real sense that Sudraka terminated his life by entering fire, then the words लब्ध्वा चायुः शताब्दं &c. become meaningless; for they indicate that he died a natural death. To suit the other meaning we should expect नीत्वा instead of लब्ध्वा.

The com. explains the mention of his own death by the author by supposing that he knew by astrological computation when his death would occur exactly, and wrote about it as a past event in anticipation of the Sutradhara's alluding to it subsequently. But it seems to us that this part of the Prologue, *viz.* the whole passage from अलमनेन परिषत्कुतूहल० (p. 7) to the end of sl 7, which relates to the personal history of the author, is the work of another hand. Sudraka, like Bhasa, must have written नान्द्यन्ते । सूत्रधारः—( परिक्रम्यावलोक्य च । अये &c. p. 8

**समरव्यसनी**--Not that he liked bloodshed, but whenever there was an opportunity for fighting, like a true Kshatriys he was anxious to take advantage of it., **प्रमादशून्यः**—never committing mistakes while fighting or managing the State; vigilantly watchful of his interests. **ककुद**--*m. n.* is the hump of a bull; and as it is his chief mark of distinction, it also means 'the chief or foremost of'; *cf.* ककुदं नृपाणां Ragh. VI. 71. **तपोधनः**--who lived like an ascetic although a king. By तपस् is meant here the three kinds of penance mentioned at Bg. XVII. 14-16. **परवारण** &c—'Who fought with his arms with the elephants of his enemes, or with the most powerful elephants.' Anoth er possible imeaning is, 'who longed to fight with his arms ( and not with weapons ) the repulsers of his enemies.' The epithet is

---

* "Zarmancohagas ( Sramanacharya ) burnt himelf at Athens after the custom of his country, and Calanus ( Kalyana ) mounted the funeral pile at Pasargadae in the presence of the astonished Greeks, who were at a loss to consider the act as that of a sage or a madman, and were never of a mood to imitate such a model." ( From Wilson's note on अग्निं प्रविष्टः )

put in to show that he had enormous physical strength. किल—Verily, certainly.

P. 8. **अवन्तिपुर्यां**—अवन्तीनां जनपदानां पुरी अवन्तिपुरीं, *i. e.* उज्जयिनी (see p 18) situated on the Sipra, and the capital of the country called अवन्ति (see Megh. I. 30) which formed the eastern part of Malwa. It was also known by the names of अवन्ती and विशाला; for its description see Kathas. XI. 31-32. "Few cities," remarks Wilson, "perhaps, can boast of a more continuous repu-tation, as it has been a place of great note from the earliest periods of Hindu tradition down to the present day" It is one of the seven sacred cities (अयोध्या मथुरा माया etc.) in India visited by numerous pilgrims. The modern Ujjain is about a mile south of the ancient city. We may also take the comp. as अवन्ती चासौ पुरी च, the final ई being shortened as in कालिदास; see Pan. VI. 3. 63.

**द्विजसार्थ**०—is generally interpreted as—'A Brahmana who was a merchant by profession.' See com. But this does not seem to be so good. For there is no mention made in the play of Charudatta's having himself followed that profession. On the contrary, when the ornaments deposited with him by Vasanta-sena, are found to be stolen away and his friend Maitreya advises him to deny all knowledge of their having been deposited with him, Charudatta plainly refuses to do so and says that he would beg (which is proper for a Brahmana to do) and make good the loss (see 'भैक्षेण' &c. III. 26). He does not say 'वाणिज्येन', which he would have done had he been a merchant. So we have pre-ferred the second interpretation (see com.), and taken द्विजसा० to mean 'a leader of the Brahmana community.' For this sense of सार्थवाह *cf.* कुरु मामम्ब कृतार्थसार्थवाहम्। (Malli's Introd. verse 3 to his com. on Ragh.). Char. is called सार्थवाह later on (*e.g.* on p. 38); but it does not mean that he himself was a merchant. His grandfather had been a merchant (see सार्थवाहविनयदत्तस्य नप्ता Act IX.), and the epithet सार्थवाह seems to have been retained as a family title; it may be understood in that sense here too.

**वसन्तशोभेव**—Mark the alliterations in this line. Vasanta or Spring is especially the season of flowers; *cf.* मासो नु पुष्पाकरः Vik. I. 8; so the comparison indicates the freshness and love-liness of youth (*cf.* कुसुममिव लोभनीयं यौवनमङ्गेषु संनद्धम्। Sak. I. 9), the power to please, in fact all that makes Vasantasena a charming woman. वसन्तसेना--*Cf.* दत्तासेनान्तनामानि वेश्यानां कल्पयेत्सुधीः ।.

तयोरिदं &c.--तयोः means 'with reference to them.' इदं--is in apposition with सर्वं. Some take इदं to refer to प्रकरणं; but that is wrong The two slokas are connected with अस्यां तत्कृतौ; so it is absurd to say अस्यां च तत्कृतौ इदं प्रकरणं चकार. The construction is तयोः नयप्रचारं, तयोः व्यवहारदुष्टतां &c. सत्सुरतोत्सवाश्रयं--must be taken as an adj. to नयप्रचारं. नय०--नयेन प्रचारः नयप्रचारः a just course of conduct or life, based on the festivity *i. e.* joy of conjugal pleasures. व्यवहारदुष्टतां--the vitiation or miscarriage of justice, as instanced in the trial of Charudatta. खलस्वभावं--as exemplified in the character of Sakara. तथा भवितव्यतां--And what was fated to happen in that way. Or तथा may be taken with चकार--he depicted all this in that way, *i.e.* exactly as it happpened.

संगीतशाला--संगीतार्थं शाला a hall or chamber for the practice or exhibition of music, singing and dancing. कुशीलवाः--actors; or singers, bards आं ज्ञातं--He accounts for the desertion of his music-hall by attributing it to his poverty.

P. 10. शून्यं--Vacant, void of interest. अपुत्रस्य--*Cf.* अंतःकरणतत्त्वस्य दम्पत्योः स्नेहसंश्रयात् । आनन्दग्रन्थिरेकोऽयमपत्यमिति बध्यते ॥ Uttar. III. 17. चिरशून्यं--a perpetual blank; or, all time is blank.

संगीतम्--Samgita is a musical concert, consisting of instrumental and vocal music and dancing. नृत्यं गीतं तथा वाद्यं त्रयं संगीतमुच्यते । इति संगीतरत्नाकरे. The Sutra. had done it along with the band of choisters who had taken part in the पूर्वरङ्ग ( which is a cumbrous and a long procedure ) and hences his exhaustion. पुष्करबीज--lotus-seeds which are easily parched up by heat. The comparison shows that the Sutra.'s eyes were burning on account of wakefulness, as he had to sing till the last quarter of the night. खटखटायेते--'crackle'; a verb formed from the onomatopoetic word खटखट by adding य ( क्यष् ). A final आ (डाच्) is added to the half of a word indicating sound, when such half consists of at least two syllables, and when joined with कृ &c.; see Pan. V. 4. 57. So we get खट्खटा; and words ending in आ take the denom. aff. य by लोहितादिडाज्भ्यः क्यष् । Pan. III.

l. 13. **This is not a happy word to be used with reference to the movements of the pupils. At least it is no improvement on** Bhasa's पुष्करपत्रपतितजलबिन्दू इव चञ्चलायेते इव मेऽक्षिणी ।

**कार्यवशात्**--Here कार्यं does not refer to the business of the play but to the Sutra.'s business with his wife; *cf.* एषोऽहं कार्यवशादायोध्यक: &c. Uttar. I. **प्रयोग**.--The part he had to play. The Com. takes it in the sense of 'use, employment.' **प्राकृतभाषी**--In Bhasa's Charu the Sutra. speaks in Prakrit from the beginning. He uses Prakrit because his wife could understand it more readily. A person may change the language proper for him or her as may suit the circumstances. See Com. Here the Sutra. has to play the part of a poor person and hence has to speak in Prakrit like a low character; *cf.* भावप्रकाश--ऐश्वर्येण प्रमत्तस्य दारिद्रयोपहतस्य च । उत्तमस्यापि पठत: प्राकृतं संप्रयोजयेत् ।।

**अविद अविद**--woe, woe, O pity ! This is a combination of indeclinables expressing sorrow. According to the quotation in the com. it indicates the happening of something unseen or unheard of before; *i. e.* something untoward or unwelcome. It appears sometimes as अविहा अविहा; see Vik. p112; it may have been a corrupt form of अव इह, अव इह protect here, protect me ( from some evil).

**अपरमिव संविधानकं**—An arrangement quite of different sort, an unexpected bustle of preparation. Bhasa uses the simple word संविधा preparation of food. **परिवर्तन**--the moving about of; as the pan was turned about on the ground, it left black marks on it. **विशेषक**—an ornamental mark made with dots of different colours on the face of a woman; *cf.* प्रत्याख्यातविशेषकं कुरबकं &c, Malav. III. 5 ; अभिनवा इव पत्रविशेषका: । Ragh. IX. 29; see also Sis. X. 84. **प्राणात्ययं**--See com.; Prith. reads प्राणाधिकं 'so as to oppress life,' in a manner more than life can bear. **वर्णकं**-- a paste of coloured and scented things, such as saffron, turmeric mixed with musk, &c. The Com. thinks that by this the description of Vasantasena's hall is suggested; see Com.; see however our note on this passage below; For a parallel *cf.* अये तत्किमिदमस्मद्गृहे महोत्सव इव दृश्यते । स्वस्वकर्मण्यधिकतरमभियुक्त: परिजन: । तथा हि-वहति जलमियं पिनष्टि गन्धानियमियमुद्ग्रथते स्रजो विचित्रा: ।...भवतु । कुटुम्बिनीमाहूय पृच्छामि । Mud. I. **शब्दाख्य**-a grammatical irregularity.

आर्य–The Sutra. is thus to address his wife; *cf.* वाच्यौ नटीसूत्रधारावार्यनाम्ना परस्परम्।

P. 12. गुडौदनं—गुडेनौदनं गुडोदनं Inst Tat.; ओदन is both *m.* and *n.* in gender. तण्डुलाः–simple rice. रसायनं–savoury, delicious food. See com. एवं..आशास्ताम्—In Bhasa's Charu. the Sutra. expresses this hope and with greater propriety. आर्ये किं &c.—The Sutra. knew what he had in his house and was not sure that his wife was telling him the truth, and so he asks this question.

P. 14. वरण्डलम्बुक इव—There is some uncertainty about the meaning of this expression, and commentators are at a loss to assign a particular meaning to it. Thus Prithvidhara says that this refers to a sort of mechanism used for drawing water from wells or rivers in villages ( called ळाट in Marathi ). It consists of a long stick or bamboo resting on a fulcrum with a weight in the form of a mass of ( hardened ) clay or a big stone fastened at one end with a rope and a bucket at the other. This weight, when raised up, and the hold at the other end let go, falls down at once. Mr. Apte in his Dic. says—It seems to mean 'an overhanging or projecting wall which if raised high is sure to topple down'. According to others Varanda means the lofty part of the wall of a building, and Lambaka means another part of it made of brick or stone, to be attached to it, which when carried up to it falls down by accident. All these explanations are shown to be fanciful by the words उत्क्षिप्य and पातितः. उत्क्षिप्य does not support Prithvidhara's meaning, for the *lambaka* in that case is not उत्क्षिप्त but उद्धृत or उन्नमित. Sudraka has borrowed the expression from Bhas's अहं चण्डप्रवातलण्डित इव वरण्डः पर्वताद् दूरमारोप्य पातितः; which throws light on its meaning; there वरण्ड must refer to something that can be thrown up, a cluster or heap of grass ( तृणसंचयः; and वरण्ड is a word still used in Konkn in that sense). So here वरण्डलंबुकः means–a hanging cluster or bundle of grass which may be blown up by a strong wind and then cast down.

तत्किं पुनरिदं नवमिव संविधानकं &c.—Here by repeating the word संविधानक for the third time in the Prologue, the poet no doubt refers to the novel plot of his own play; nay, even the following sentence explaining this, is meant to covertly refer to the main incidents of the *denouement*. The words used therein are deliberately chosen Thus वर्णकं पिनष्टि refers to Sakara's attempt to crush

Charudatta ( who belonged to the chief of the Varnas ), सुमनसो गुम्फति refers to the victim's garland thrown round Char.'s neck when being conducted to the gallows, and thereby to the case got up against him; while इयं च पञ्चवर्ण० भूमिः refers to the final happy issue, wherein five desirable events are achieved, which the poet himself has summed up in X. 58. These are—(1) the re-establishment of Charudatta's purity of conduct and his consequent deliverance; (2) the granting of life to his humbled foe, the Sakara —a great humiliation to him while it redounds to the supreme generosity of Charudatta; (3) the elevation of Aryaka to the throne, which meant the removal of the oppressive king Palaka; (4) the happy union of Charudatta and Vasantasena, raised by the king to the title of a *Vadhu*; (5) the securing of the friendship of the able schemer Sarvilaka, but for whose help Aryaka could not have got the throne.

अभिरूप०—अभिलक्ष्यं रूपमस्य अभिरूपः learned and handsome; *cf.* अभिरूपो बुधे रम्ये Medini; अभिरूपः पतिर्यस्मात्. Mark the meaning of अभिरूप; she does not say अनुरूप. इहलौकिकः—Read ऐहलौकिकः which is grammatically more correct. इहलोके भवः ऐहलौकिकः by adding ठञ् (इक) in the sense of तत्र भवः. The words of the अनुशतिकादि class take वृद्धि in both the members of the comp.; so we get ऐहलौकिक; similarly पारलौकिक, सार्वलौकिक &c. The form इहलौ० may also be defended on the general principle that 'such changes are not always binding' (अनित्यत्व)

P, 16. चूर्णवृद्धेन—In the Charu. we read चूर्णगोष्ठेन. सकोपं—He is angry because Churn. advised his wife to observe such an expensive vow. सुगन्धं—goes with both त्वां and ०कलापं; in the former case the fragrance comes by means of the flowers forming the वध्यस्रक्. छेद्यमानं—The Prakrit for this is कप्पिज्जन्तं which the Com. renders in one case by छेद्यमानं and in the other ( *i. e.* with hair) by कल्प्यमानं, 'being dressed and bound up.' If the word is used with a double application then कल्प्यमानं will do in both the cases. क्लृप् cau. is found used in the sense of 'cutting up' in the Sak. also; *cf.* रोहितमत्स्यो मया कल्पितः Act. VI. The other reading वज्जन्तं may also be rendered doubly as वध्यमानं and बध्यमानं. But as the Sutra. has now here used a word with a double application in the Prologue, we have adopted the rendering छेद्यमानं in the text as applying to both, as in the second case, the ordering of the cutting of the hair of a young woman by the king would make his act revolting in the eyes of the people and thereby lead to disaffection, which it is the object of the poet to suggest.

P. 18. **ब्राह्मणेनोप०**--A Brahmana must be fed at the time of breaking a fast; otherwise the observance would bear no fruit. **सुसमृद्धायामु०**--This is put in to show that eminent Brahmanas had sufficient invitations from the rich where they could get good *Dakshina*, and were not to be easily secured by poor men; or that the Brahmanas there were rich and would not be easily induced to dine at the house of an actor. For, dining at the houses of actors, musicians and men of that sort, was supposed to be derogatory to the dignity of a pious Brahmana and it also involved loss of social status; *cf.* Mah.-Bha–'गायकः सर्वविक्रयी। ईदृशा ब्राह्मणा ज्ञेया अपाङ्क्तेया युधिष्ठिर॥.'

**अशितुमग्रणीः** &c.--is a courteous way of inviting to a dinner. **व्यापृतः**-engaged; I have my own business to attend to. **संपन्नं**--Rich, delicious. **निःसपत्नं**--The Com. seems to translate the Prakrit णीसवत्तं by नीसपात्रं, better known as निःस्राव, and assigns a technical meaning to it, *viz.* a present of rice, ghee, &c. placed in a pot and given to a Brahmana for the gratification of the *pitris*; see com. But this sense of निःस्राव is not found in the dictionaries So the trans. निःसपत्नं is preferable. The Sutra. means—There will be no other Brahmana to share the food with you; and nobody will know that you dined at our house.

**भो यदिदानीं**--Here we have sarcasm mixed with humour, which is one of the characteristics of Vidushaka's speeches.

P. 20 **आमुखं**--same as **प्रस्तावना**, for which see com. and Introd. The **प्रस्तावना** here is of the kind named **प्रयोगातिशय**, as the Vidu. is introduced here as being already engaged in conversation with the Sutra. at the time of his leaving the stage.

Wilson observes—"The scene is supposed to represent a street on one side, and on the other the first court of Charudatta's house; the outside of the house is also seen in the part next the street."

**मयाऽपि**--Vid. mourns his lot that he should be forced to look for invitations from others to dine. **प्रेक्षितव्यानि**--should be expected or waited for. Some translate पच्छिदव्वाइं by **प्रार्थयित-**

व्याणि–should be sought. Some read पडिच्छिदव्वाइं and give the *chhaya* as समीहितव्यानि; but the correct rendering is प्रत्येष्टव्यानि 'should be accepted or expected' तुलयसि—Here तुल is not a root of the tenth class (for then the form will be तोलयसि), but a nominal verb derived from तुला, meaning in the first instance 'to subject a man to a trial, to put one to test'; hence, to reduce one to a wretched state. The meaning depends upon the context; see *infra* III. 24; IV. 2; &c.; *cf.* also Megh. I. 20. उद्गार—The coming up of the air from the stomach; the agreeable smell of the Modakas was so strong that it came out with the breath when strongly exhaled; *cf.* ०मकरोद्गारसुरभिणा पयसा। Nag. IV. 4. उग्घार (उद्घार) *V. l.* is taken to mean घृतसेक putting ghee on; but it is difficult to see how the sprinkling over of ghee would add to the pleasantness of the smell, even if we take सुरभि in the sense of 'charming, delightful.' Again, the usual word is अभिघार and not उद्घार. अशित:—'I who had my meal of;' this is to be explained as अशितमस्यास्तीति by adding अ (अच्, which is added to words of the अर्शआदि class; see Pan. V. 2. 127) on the analogy of भुक्ता ब्राह्मणा:, पीता गाव: &c. See Malli. on Kir. I. 1, आसिदो (आशित:) *V. l.*-P. p. p. of अश् to eat, cau.; 'who was fed on' चतु:शालकं—चतस्र: शाला: समाहृता अत्र इति चतु:शालं-ल: and by adding क स्वार्थे we get ०शालकं—a quadrangle enclosed by four halls. Most of the large houses had such in ancient times. मल्लक—a cup or a small dish (filled with sweetmeats of different kinds (in one case) and with colours (in the other). Also read as गल्लक or गल्वर्क. चत्वर—a courtyard; or a place where four roads meet; fr. चत् 1 P. A. to go (चत्यते इति) and वर (Unadi ष्वरच्). Some read आपणे (आवणे) 'in the market', before this. This refers to bulls let loose at ceremonials who thenceforward ramble about at will without hindrance. And as it is thought to be a merit to feed such animals, such a bull is well fed and becomes stout. And the Vidu., who is a lover of sweetmeats and burly in appearance, is often compared to such a bull; *cf.* एष...विपणिगत इव बलीवर्द आर्यगौतम आसीन एव निद्रायते। Malav. IV. p.148 The reading नवबद्धवृषभ इव is bad, as such a bull must be restless and the Vidu. sitting leisurely can be ill compared with him. रोमन्थायमान:—Pres. p. of the verb from रोमन्थ, रोगं मथ्नातीति रोमन्थ:, from रोग + मन्थ and aff. अ (अण्), the ग of रोग being dropped; the comp., therefore, is of the पृषोदरादि class. It means 'rumination,' or chewing the cud, which is necessary for digestion in the case of animals like bulls. Then by adding य (क्यङ्), which forms A'tm. verbs, to रोमन्थ in the sense of 'to practise it,' we get (रोमन्थं वर्तयति) रोमन्थायते; by कर्मणो रोमन्थतपोभ्यां वर्तिचरोः Pan. III. 1. 15; so तपश्चरति तपस्यति (which is Para. by special rule). Additional reading (see foot-note)- सर्वोपस्करयुक्तं—made up with all the ingredients (which are 13 in number) such as cardamums, cloves, catechu, nutmeg &c. निर्जित०--the betel-leaves when ripe have a perfect yellow colour.

P. 20. देवकार्यं--Such as offering worship to the household deities, performance of Brahmayajna, offering libations of water to the manes, &c. For सिद्धीकृत some read सट्ठिवद्किद (षष्ठीव्रतकृत) which is found in the Charu. also. Then the meaning will be 'when he will have finished the worship to be offered in connexion with the vow to be observed on the sixth day.' This seems to be the original reading. सिद्धीकृत does not fit in well with देवकार्य; in this case we should expect समापित. Charudatta's wife further on speaks of having observed a fast on the sixth day (which she calls रत्नषष्ठी); And it appears that Charudatta also had observed a fast on that day, which was to be broken in the early night, as is done on the 4th day of a month by those who observe a fast on that day. And hence the offerings referred to here are made in the evening. And the sixth day of some month appears to be the opening day of the play. गृहदेवतानां--The deities meant here are those outside the house (generally of the spiritkind) keeping guard over the house; offerings of food, and sometimes of grains of rice. are made to these in the open air to keep them in good humour. This shows that Charudatta was a rigid performer of religious duties.

०देहलानां—देहली is properly the threshold; here the ground near the threshold. It is usual with Brahmanas to offer a quantity of rice (according to means) at the threshold to the birds (usually the crows) after the performance of the Vaisvadeva but before taking food. The pl. shows that Char. in his days of prosperity made such offerings at all the four doors of his mansion. विरूढ०—Because there were no servants to look after the grounds. *Cf.* हर्म्याग्रसंरूढतृणाङ्कुरेषु Ragh. VI. 47; see also XVI. 18. कीटमुखा०—Because it was a scanty offering of grains which did not attract birds. This sl. occurs in the Charu. with the readings भवति for

सपदि, विभक्तपुष्पः for विलुप्तपूर्वः and पूर्वबलिरूढयवाङ्कुरेषु for संप्रति विरूढतृणाङ्कुरासु.

P. 22 सर्वकाल०—*i. e.* in prosperity as well as in adversity सुखं हि दुःखान्य०—occurs in the Charu. with the readings यथाऽन्धकारादिव...दशां दरिद्रतां स्थितः शरी०. *cf.* यदेवोपनतं दुःखात्सुखं तद्रसवत्तरम्। Vik. III. 21. दारिद्र्यान्मर *cf. Hitop.* दारिद्र्यान्मरणाद्वाऽपि दारिद्र्यमवरं स्मृतम्। अल्पक्लेशेन मरणं दारिद्र्यमतिदुःसहम्. प्रणयिजन—friends and loving relatives as well as supplicants सुरजनपीत—जन a multitude. *Of* पर्यायपीतस्य सुरैर्हिमांशोः कलाक्षयः श्लाघ्यतरो हि वृद्धेः। Ragh. V. 16; मणिः शाणोल्लीढः समरविजयी हेतिनिहतो मदक्षीणो नागः शरदि सरिदाश्यानपुलिना। कलाहीनश्चन्द्रः सुरतमृदिता बालवनिता तनिम्ना शोभन्ते गलितविभवाश्चार्थिषु जनाः॥ Bh. Ni. 44. The moon is supposed to be the reservoir of Amrita or ambrosia which the gods and the manes drink during the dark half of the month. It is replenished again from the sun during the bright half. *Cf.* Devipurana—कलाः षोडश सोमस्य शुक्ले वर्धयते रविः। अमृतेनामृतं कृष्णे पीयते देवतैः क्रमात्॥ &c. See notes on Ragh. quoted above,

अर्थान् प्रति—प्रति is a कर्मप्रवचनीय and has the sense of लक्षण or indication. एतत्तु मां दहति—For संभावितस्य चाकीर्तिर्मरणादतिरिच्यते। Bg II. 34.

P. 24. अर्थकल्यवर्ताः—अर्था एव कल्यवर्ताः। कल्यं the morning; कल्ये वर्त्यते अनेन (that by which one subsists) इति कल्यवर्तः the morning meal (the same as प्रातराशः); and as this is a light one, कल्यवर्तं signifies anything trivial or unimportant. *Cf. infra,* ननु कल्यवर्तमेतत् and स्त्रीकल्यवर्तस्य कारणेन. दास्याःपुत्रा अर्थ०—*Cf.* this 'vile trash' of money, these 'rascal (base-born) counters.' Julius Caesar IV. 3 वरटा— a kind of wasp. खाद्यन्ते—is used to suit the comparison; (1) are not eaten, *i. e.* enjoyed; (2) bitten.

भाग्यक्रमेण—*cf.* नीचैर्गच्छत्युपरि च दशा चक्रनेमिक्रमेण Megh. II. 48. नष्टधना०—नष्टः धनमेवाश्रयो धनाश्रयः यस्य. सौहृदात्—शोभनं हृदयमस्य इति सुहृत् a friend; हृदय is changed to हृद् after सु and दुस् in the sense of 'a friend,' and 'an enemy' respectively. सुहृदो भावः सौहृदं; the proper form is सौहार्दं as Vriddhi of the first vowel of both the members is necessary before अण् by हृद्भगसिन्ध्वन्ते पूर्वपदस्य च। Pan. VII. 3. 19. But the form सौहृद is often used by eminent poets like Kalidasa, Bhavabhuti and others. *Cf.* सखीजनस्ते किमुतार्द्रसौहृदः

Vik I. 9.; सौहृदादपृथगाश्रयामिमां Uttar. I. 45 &c. The form, however, may be defended by having recourse to the maxim सञ्ज्ञापूर्वको विधिरनित्यः'; Vamana derives it by adding अण् to सुहृदय first and then changing हृदय to हृद्; the आदिवृद्धि is got by तद्धितेषु अचामादेः। Pan VII. 2 117 (=when a Taddhita aff having an indicatory ण् or ञ् is added, the first vowel of a stem takes its Vriddhi substitute). See Kavya Sut V. 2. 83. See Jagaddhara on the word at Mal-Madh. p 8. This sl occurs in the Charu. with the variations–धनविनाशगता विचिन्ता, धनानि पुनर्भवन्ति, and नष्टधनश्रियो मे यत्सौहृदानि सुजने.

ह्रियमेति ह्रीपरि०--Here although ह्री follows, ति is not made long and the metre is not violated as the stress of voice does not fall on it. We have a similar instance in Sis—प्रहरकमपनीय स्वं निनिद्रासतोच्चैः प्रतिपदमुपहूतः केनचिज्जागृहीति । मुहुरविशदवर्णां निद्रया शून्यशून्यां ददददपि प्रतिवाचं (*v. l.*) बुध्यते ना मनुष्यः ॥ XI 4, where the प्र in प्रतिवाचं has no phonetic action on the पि of अपि. प्रभ्रश्यते &c–सत्त्वात्परिभ्रश्यते *v. l* is not so good ह्री has direct action on तेजस् (brightness of face, the outward sign of spiritedness); सत्त्व refers to the strength of mind. निर्वेदः—despondency, lowness of spirits. This makes one feel life a burden (निर्विण्णः) बुद्ध्या—बुद्धि means power of judgment or discrimination of good from bad; *cf.* बुद्धिनाशात्प्रणश्यति Bg. II 63 निधनता—used for निर्धनता for the sake of the metre; निवृत्त धनं यस्मात्स निधनः तस्य भ वः। Here नि has the sense of निर् (*i. e* absence of); *cf* Tattvabodhini on निमूलसमूलयोः कषः Pan III. 4. 34.

परपरिभवः—परश्चासौ परिभवश्च a great humiliation, *i.e.* the source of it; a Karm. comp The Com takes it as a Geni. Tat. (परस्य कर्तुः *i. e.* coming from परिभवः); the cause of insults offered by others अपरं–another kind of; or 'supreme' (नास्ति परं यस्मात्). जुगुप्सा—sensure; abhorrence मित्राणां–Again कर्तरि षष्ठी; मित्रकर्तृका; the Com says प्रत्युपकारासमर्थत्वात–on account of the inability of a poor man to return favours. विद्वेष--great dislike or hatred. चतुष्पथे--चतुर्णां पथां समाहारः चतुष्पथं; or चत्वारः पन्थानः समाहृता यत्र तत्; the place where four roads meet. Any offering made there or a rite performed there is supposed to be efficacious; *cf.* Kad चतुष्पथे स्नपनमङ्गलानि भेजे p. 128 मातृभ्यः—The *matris* are divine Mothers said to attend on Siva, but generally on Skanda, मान्ति शिवस्य परिवारत्वेनेति मातरः or मान्यन्ते पूज्यन्ते इति मातरः. They are usually said to be eight in number—ब्राह्मी माहेश्वरी चैन्द्री वाराही वैष्णवी तथा । कौमारीत्यपि चामुण्डा चर्चिकेत्यष्ट मातरः ॥. According to some they are seven, *viz*. ब्राह्मी माहेश्वरी चैव कौमारी वैष्णवी तथा । माहेन्द्री चैव वाराही चामुण्डा सप्त मातरः ॥. While others say that they are sixteen. It is clear from the names of these that they are the personified energies of the several deities.

Wilson remarks—"Tantrika ceremonies addressed to the sixteen Matris are not uncommon, but the rite in the text appears to be a matter of course, and seems to take the place of that enjoined by Manu to the Pitris, the manes or progenitors." Sss Manu. III. 91.

**नित्योऽयं विधिः**—विधिs or sacred rites are of three kinds :— *Nitya* or obligatory, which must be performed, as the five daily Yajnas. Their performance brings no fruit; but their non-performance gives rise to sin (अकरणे प्रत्यवायहेतुः). *Kamya*, those performed with a view to attain some object, as the पुत्रेष्टि performed by Dasharatha. And Naimittika, those which are performed on certain specified occasions, such as the birth of a child the Upanayana ceremony, etc. There is a fourth class also, called नित्यनैमित्तक, *i. e.*, which are performed on occasions regularly recurring, such as पर्वश्राद्ध.

**तपसा**—By the observance of vows. **शमिनां**—शम एषां विद्यते इति शमिनः those who have subdued their passions, *i. e.* who would not allow their mind to be ruffled if a certain object is not attained.

P. 26. **प्रदोषवेलायां**—Here प्रदोष is used in the sense of 'the first watch of the night.' **विटाः**—Vita, in dramas, is the companion of a prince, a dissipated young man, or a courtesan. वेश्यानागरिकयोः संदेशं परस्परं विटति इति विटः। संभोगहीनसंपद्विटस्तु धूर्तः कलैकदेशज्ञः। वेशोपचारकुशलो वाग्मी मधुरोऽथ बहुमतो गोष्ठ्याम् ॥ Sah.-Dar. III. 41. 'He is one lacking the means of enjoyment, is subtle, versed in some arts, ingenious in dress and address, eloquent, pleasing and much esteemed in company.' **चेटः**—A servant who assists his master in love-affairs. **संचरन्ति**—This speech of the Vid. is intended to indicate the entrance of Vasantasena and her pursuers, agreeably to the rule that no character is to enter without previous intimation. तस्मान्मण्डूकलुब्धस्य &c.—Wilson remarks—"If we are to consider the antiquity of this play as established, this passage bears testimony to the early currency of apologues in India."

**विट, चेट**—are the pleasure-companions of Sakara. *Cf.* शृङ्गारेऽस्य सहाया विटचेटविदूषकाद्याः स्युः । भक्ता नर्मसु निपुणाः कुपितवधूमानभञ्जनानिपुणाः ॥ S.-Dar. III 40. शकारः—named संस्थानक, is the brother-in-law of the king, being the brother of his concubine. Sakara ought to be represented as a mixture of pride, folly, and vanity, of low origin, and raised to power only on account of his relation to the king. He is called Sakara because he speaks the Sakari dialect, which abounds in the श्-sounds; मदमूर्खताभिमानी दुष्कुलतैश्वर्यसंयुक्तः । सोऽयमनूढाभ्राता श्यालः शकार इत्युक्तः ॥ S.-D. III 80. The Sakara of this play is all this and even something more, and the mannerisms of his speech are more striking here than in the *Charudatta*. See Introduction. Perhaps the definition of a Sakara given by the Sah-D. is based on the character of Sakara as painted by Bhasa and Sudraka, as there is no reference to it in Bharata's Natyasastra.

**परिवर्तित०**—Entirely changed; given up. **विशदो**—विशद properly means 'clear,' or white, bright; and then, bright by skill. **उद्विग्न** &c—A clumsy comp.; many such awkward compounds and uncouth expressions occur in Bhasa and Sudraka, indicative of their crude and unpolished style. The comp. may best be taken as उद्विग्ना bewilderad चासौ चञ्चला च कटाक्षविसृष्टा च दृष्टिः glances यस्याः सा. It may also be taken as उद्विग्नं चञ्चलं च यथा स्यात्तथा (in a frightful and tremulous manner) कटाक्षेन विसृष्टा दृष्टिः यया सा तथा. See also com.; some dissolve it as उद्विग्नेन चञ्चलेन कटाक्षेण विसृष्टा दृष्टिर्यया निसृष्ट for विसृष्ट would have been better. **अनुसार**—Pursuit, going after. This sl. occurs in the Charu. with slight variations, as—वृत्तोपदेशवि०, निविष्टदृष्टिः, and व्याघ्रानुसार.

P. 28. **किं यासि धावसि** &c.—It will be seen that the speeches of Sakara are full of repetitions, absurd comparisons, irrelevancies, etc. for which see com. p. 8 (अपार्थमक्रमं &c.) and Introd. **वासू**—a word of rare occurrence, though used in the Das-K.-Ch. In the Charu. we have प्रधावसि प्रस्ख०; साधु प्रसीद न मार्यसे, कामेन संप्रति हि दह्यते मे शरीरं, and मध्य for राशि and चर्म for मांस in the fourth line.

**उत्त्रासिता** &c.—The Cheta's speech, too, although not full of absurdities and irrelevancies like that of his master, is full of quaint expressions and strange similes. The poetry put in the mouth of Vita is, however, of a higher order and his speeches more sensible. अन्तिकात्--*v. l.* अत्तिका 'my elder sister' (अत्तिका भगिनी ज्येष्ठा। Ak.) संपूर्ण० मयुरी--He means-Just as a pea hen, frightened at the sight of a forest-conflagration, runs away from anything red in appearance, so you are running away from us in vain fear, though we are friendly to you and love you. अववल्गति—goes by leaping or tripping (so eager he is to meet you). Some translate ओव० by अपवल्गति 'bounds aside' स्वामि०—स्वामीं चासौ भट्टारकश्च. भट्टारक is the title for a king in dramas; so here it signifies excellence; 'my noble master'. कुक्कुट०—The Cheta being a low character naturally thinks of a young cock, being the object of everyday sight. हीनानां हीनोपमेव नैसर्गिकी). कुक्कुडशा०--is also translated as कुक्कुरशावकाः, which is better, as it better refers to the surly and cruel nature of Sakara.

बालकदलीव--Vasantasena was clad in a red garment and was quaking and is fitly compared to a Kadali plant which is covered with red flowers and is easily shaken by the wind. रक्तोत्पल &c —प्रकर a collection; hence, a garland (in the first case). Vasant had worn a garland of red lotuses; and as she walked hastily with heavy steps, the lotuses fell on the ground one by one. In the second case this means—'throwing off (as worked upon by the chisel) bud-like pieces.' मनःशिल—red arsenic; the word is usually *fem.* in gender, but is here used in the *mas.*; see com.

P. 30. मदनमनङ्ग &c.--This is an instance of पुनरुक्तं (or repetition) in Sak's speech. भयभीता—Here भय is redundant. रावणस्येव कुन्ती —An instance of Sak.'s speech being हतोपमं (see com. p 8). There is no connexion whatsoever between these two who lived at different times. Such confusion of persons and events, which will often occur, is characteristic of the speech of Sakara who thus evinces his ignorance as well as pretension.

विशेषयन्ती--Causing to exceed or surpass in speed. प्रविसृतः—Here प्र has no force, as वेगात् already occurs; it is used for the metre. निरुन्ध्यां--will obstruct, stop the course of, *i. e.* by going before it. ण रुन्ध्यां– *v. l.* must be read with a *Kaku* (by changing the voice in such a way as to imply the contrary meaning); 'shall I not obstruct? Surely I shall' (न रुन्ध्यामपि तु

रुन्ध्यामेव). त्वग्निग्रहे &c.—'I shall have to make no effort to catch you, *i. e.* I shall easily overtake you.' Another meaning also is intended—'O fair-bodied one, my effort is not for seizing you,' indicating thereby that he might connive at her escape. **भाव**—Sakara thus addresses his companion, which shows that he has respect for him (and it will be also seen that he even fears him to some extent). *Cf.* सेनापतिरमात्यश्च स्यालो भावेति भाष्यते। Bhavaprakasha.

**नाणकमोषि०**—**नाणक** is a coin bearing some impression (as the figure of Siva, according to Prithvidhara). The com. here is not very clear. नाणकानि मुष्णन्तीति नाणकमोषिण: thieves; तेषां कामस्य कशिका the whip of; *i.e.* 'the inciter of the inflamer of the lust of'. Some translate this as 'the gratifier or the satisfier of'; but that is not accurate; a whip urges one (as a horse) to action. *Cf.* तस्करा: पण्डका मूर्खा: सुखप्राप्तधनास्तथा। लिङ्गिनश्छन्नकामाद्या आसां प्रायेण वल्लभा:॥ S.-D. III. 70. Or this may mean—the inflamer of passion (काम) that robs (deprives) one of one's money. Wilson translates this as—'the taper lash of that filcher of broad pieces-Kama.' **लासिका**—a dancer. **निर्नासा**—having a depressed nose; pug-nosed. Here the negation (निर्) has the sense of तदल्पत्व. Some render णिण्णासा as निम्नाशा, निम्ना आशा यस्या: सा who has a mean desire (as she simply cares for money); or निम्नेषु (for low-born persons) आशा यस्या: सा. Prithvi notices the reading णीशाशा (नि:स्वाशा); नि:स्वानां निर्धनानामाशा a mere matter of, hope for the penniless (अलभ्यत्वादाशामात्रमेव केवलम्।). **कुलनाशिका**—तदासक्तपुरुषाणामिति शेष:. Because connexion with a harlot occasions loss of social status (पातित्यजननात्); or an over-attachment to a courtesan on the part of a lewd sensualist weans his affection from his wife and leads to the loss of legal issue (वेश्यासक्तस्य स्वपत्न्यां प्रेमराहित्यादजातपुत्रत्वेन स्वकुलनाश:). **अवशिका**—One not in the power of another. **सुवेशनिलया**—is taken to mean 'an abode of good dress or ornaments;' *i. e.* one always finely dressed. But it is better to take it as 'one dwelling in the habitation of harlots,' for the sake of symmetry, as all the four epithets will then have the same meaning. **वेशिका**—वेश: अस्ति आश्रयत्वेनास्या:. वेश means courtesans collectively and all that belongs to them; or hire-money. **दश नामकानि**—They are really eleven; while he calls them ten. Such blundering in computation is also a characteristic of Sakara's speech. **मया कृतानि**—By addressing Vasant. by these appellations, Sakara wishes to win her favour, and in this he shares the general belief that addressing a god by several names is the best means to secure his good graces. *Cf.* in this respect the 12 names of Ganapati uttered at the commencement of every religious rite. Most of these epithets are far from being pleasing or complimentary to Vasant ; and yet Sakara says अद्यापि &c. Probably he does so to stir laughter. See remark on Sl. 25 below. This Sl. is full of alliterations wherein क is introduced in combination with श for the recurrence of harsh sounds, which makes the speech more striking. प्रसरसि—move hastily or with quick steps (प्रकर्षेण सरसि) कुण्डलघृष्ट०—As Vasant. moved hastily the pendants in her ears, being tossed about, rubbed harshly against her cheeks. She is therefore compared to a lute. The simile is bad, as no poetic purpose is served by it. The only point of similarity between the two is, as observed by the com. (विटसदृशौ कुण्डलौ), that Vasantasena's cheeks were struck against by the Kundalas with their points, and the Vina is struck with their nails by the Vitas (playing upon a lute).

P 32 झणज्झणायमान—Pres. p. of झणज्झणाय् a verb formed like खटखटाय्, see p. 13; ०मानानि बहूनि भूषणानि तेषां शब्देन मिश्रं यथा तथा Adv comp. द्रौपदीव पलायसे—Here again we have funny references to several names that have no connexion whatsoever with each other. Visvavasu is a Gandharva king mentioned in the Mahabharata, and has no connexion with Subhadra. This confusion may be partly due to Sakara's ignorance and carelessness and partly feigned, owing to theatrical needs. For the character of Sakara, like that of the Vidushaka, is meant to provide fun for the audience and to stir laughter. And we know that Sakara is not altogether such a great blockhead as he appears to be; for there is a great deal of shrewdness and sagacity in him, as will appear now and then, from the 9th Act.

मत्स्यमांसक—मत्स्याश्च मासं च मत्स्यमांसं तदेव मत्स्यमांसकम् Sam.-Dvan श्वान:—He means the dogs of Samsthanaka. His dogs are so plentifully fed on fish and flesh that they care not to eat dead bodies. Mark how again the speech of Cheta is adapted to his own low station. A good supply of fish and meat, although a luxury to him, has no attraction for Vasantasena. Mark the metre; see com. Prithvi. says-तो इत्योकारो &c.; this must refer to some other reading; for as we have it the second line contains fourteen Matras. It is, however, in the third line that we must take either दे or हिं in एदेहिं as short.

भवति--Vita is polite to Vasantsena; and his tone is conciliatory. कटीतट--the region of the waist. ताराबि०--तारा may mean sparkling pearls, or a starlike setting of diamonds. निर्मथित०--This is best taken as a Bah. 'which far surpasses powdered red arsenic in colour;' Vasant.'s face had grown ruddy on account of fear. Or it may mean 'having a paint of' &c.; निर्मथिता (crushed and made into a paste) चूर्णमनःशिला यत्र. Some take it to mean 'resembling red arsenic in colour;' see com.

चण्डं--Fiercely; *i.e.* with great impetuosity; hotly. पल्लव' परभृतिका--It is in the fitness of things that the servants of Vasa. are called by these names, which, meaning 'tender foliage' and 'a cuckoo', are also concerned with Vasanta, the Spring. माधविके-Madhavika also is a creeper that blooms in Spring (वासन्ती माधवी लता Ak.).

P. 34. विलप विलप--Mark the wit of Sakara, how he puns on the words पल्लवक and परभृतिका.

जमदग्निपुत्रः--Parasurama was the son of Jamadagni and not Bhimasena. केशहस्त--The mass of hair; the words पाश, पक्ष and हस्त, when coming after a word signifying 'hair,' mean 'a mass of'; पाशः पक्षश्च हस्तश्च कलापार्थाः कचात्परे । Ak दुःशासनस्य-This reference is right. He means—'I shall drag and pull you by seizing you by the hair as Duhsasana did Draupadi.'

वलितं--Turned towards (me). कल्पये--cut, dissect. मुमूर्षु--Noun from the desid. base of मृ; 'about to die.' He means—'you need not run; for we are not going to kill you. Had that been our intention, we could have done it easily; you could not have lived for another moment.' अनुनयः--For he said 'न मार्यसे'; and even this was much from the inconsiderate Sakara. तर्क्यते—तर्क् 'to have in view';—'is expected, wished for;' *cf.* for this sense त्वं चेदच्छस्फटिकविशदं तर्कयेस्तिर्यगम्भः । Megh. I. 53. शान्तं पापं--This expression is used to express one's disapproval of what is said by another, or to express a wish that an expected evil be warded off (in which case it is generally repeated).

P. 36. कामयितव्यः--इति तर्क्यते; it is a reply to Vasa.'s तत्किं खल्विदानीं (तर्क्यते). शान्तं--is used as a particle of repugnance or disapproval. 'Hush, say not so.' मन्त्रयसि--Although the root मन्त्र् is Atm. according to Pan., still it is used in the Par. by many writers and with the sanction of Patanjali. Or read मन्त्रयसे.

**अन्तरेण**— inwardly, in her heart. The Com. reads **मं अन्त०** —मामन्तरेण 'with regard to me;' but the omission of मं improves the sense. He means--'although outwardly she shows her dislike to me, internally she loves me' **सहस्ततालं**--may also mean 'striking his hand on the palm of Vita,' as the Com. takes it. **श्रान्तोऽसि**--The impatient Sakara understands शन्त in the sense of श्रान्त, the same being the Prakrit form of both. He translates the other शन्त by क्लान्त. **अज्जुके**—The com. translates this by भट्टालि (रि) के. A courtesan is thus to be addressed by her attendants; *cf.* Bharata--अज्जुकेति भवेद्वाच्या वेश्या परिजनेन तु । या त्वत्र वृद्धा सा त्वम्बा भाष्या परिजनेन तु ॥. Here Sakara wishes to flatter Vasant. by thus addressing her (परिजनवदामन्त्रणमनुरञ्जनार्थम् । ) **शीर्षं**—should properly be शीर्षेण, but the use of the wrong case is allowable in Sak.'s speech. *Cf.* Com. आगमलिङ्गविहीनं &c. p. 28. **आत्मीयाभ्यां पादाभ्यां**—The order also is reversed; the proper order would be शपे भावस्य पादाभ्यामात्मीयेन शीर्षेण च. This is अक्रमं (see p 8, com). Some supply स्पृष्टा after पादाभ्यां and construe भावस्य शीर्षं पादाभ्यां स्पृष्ट्वा; but this is not natural. Sakara respects *Vita* who is an elderly person having a hold on him, and is not likely to use such insulting words with regard to him. **पृष्ठानुपृष्ठिकया**--पृष्ठानुपृष्ठमित्यस्त्यस्यां क्रियायामिति पृष्ठानुपृष्ठिका by adding ठन् (इक); by following close at the back, *i. e.* close pursuit.

**वेशवास**—For a vivid description of courtesans' residence see Damodaragupta's Kuttanimata **विरुद्धं**—against the practices and ways of; *i. e.* a harlot ought to welcome any young man. He explains this in the following Sloka. **विगणय**—विशेषेण गणय particularly think that; remember the fact that **लतेव**—*i e* which is not the property of a particular man, any one passing by it can admire its beauty and enjoy the sweet smell of its flowers.

**पण्यभूतं**—पण्यं भूतं पण्यभूतं, सुप्सुपेति समास: like a saleable commodity; anybody can buy it. **फुल्लां**—फुल्ल p. p. p. फुल् 1 P to burst open. **नाम्यति**—used for नामयति inadvertently The form is defended, however, by commentators. One way is to take नाम (bending) as one of the words of the कण्ड्वादि group, which are nouns and verbs; when verbs they take य (यक्); adding

य and dropping the अ of नाम we get नाम्यति. Another way is to take it as a denom. verb formed from नाम by adding य; see com.

Sl. 31. The last line is repeated after VIII. 17. This sl. occurs in the Charu.

P. 38. गुणः खलु &c.--brings out the nobility of Vasantasena's mind; she is no slave of money. In the Char. she says--कुलपुत्रजनस्य शीलपरितोषोपजीविनी गणिका खल्वहम् । *Cf.* गुणशुल्काऽहं न धनशुल्का Das. p. 85; *cf.* the love of Rupanika in the Kathas.; and of Ragamanjari in Das. **गर्भदासी**—गर्भप्रभृति दासी a born slave--used as a term of reproach and abuse. **कामदेवायतनो**०--is short for ०देवायतनोद्याने चारुदत्तदर्शनात्प्रभृति.* **चारुदत्तस्यानुरक्ता**--The Loc. (or Acc.) is the proper case with अनुरक्त; but Sakara can ignore it. This statement shows that Sakara was not quite an idiot; he had his eye on Vasantasena and must have got the information from one of his agents engaged to watch her actions. **यदेव परिहर्तव्यं** &c —For, Vasant. would take advantage of the information. **चारुदत्तमनु**०--Vita uses the proper case. **रत्नं रत्नेन** &c.--जातौ जातौ यदुत्कृष्टं तद्रत्नमिति कथ्यते । *Cf.* रत्नं समागच्छतु काञ्चनेन Ragh. VI. 79. **काणेलीमातः**:--काणेली माता यस्य; the final क (to be added to Bah. compounds ending in ऋ) is not added here, as it is not absolutely necessary to do so. This way of addressing a person by referring to his mother is common in Bhasa; *Cf.* गान्धारीमातः, Pancharatra. **काणेली** is said to mean 'an unmarried woman, having children,' *i. e.*, one who lives with a man like a wife although not married to him, and who is looked upon almost as a Kulangana. Sakara's mother was a woman of this sort, her daughter living with the king like a wife. She was the head of the house, as appears from Sakara's speech in the 9th Act तदा आवुत्तं राजानं पालकं भगिनीपतिं विज्ञाप्य भगिनीं मातरं च etc., where he gives prominence to his mother instead of to his father. Hence although Vita addresses him as **काणेलीमातः** he does not resent it. Compare in this respect Chanakya who always addressed Chandragupta as

---

* Wilson remarks—"The temple of Kamadeva makes a great figure in all the dramas and tales of the Hindus of any antiquity. There was always a garden or grove attached to it, to which no sanctity, however, seems to have been ascribed, as was to those of Albunea or Dodona: it was rather the Daphne of the Hindu religion, the resort of the young of either sex at public festivals, and the scene of many love-adventures."

Vrishala. Some read काणेलीभ्रातः brother of an unmarried woman living with a man (here the king).

आलोकविशाला—Very keen in seeing things (आलोके दर्शने *com.*); or आलोके when in light विशाला of long ken, as contrasted with ०विच्छिन्ना. विछिन्ना—cut short, *i. e.* deprived of its power. This is from the Charu. with the reading संच्छन्ना for विछिन्ना.

P. 40. लिम्पतीव &c.—occurs in the Char. This Sl. is cited in the Kav. Pra. first as an instance of उत्प्रेक्षा and then of संसृष्टि. अर्थालंकारसंसृष्टिस्तु लिम्पतीव० पूर्वत्र परस्परनिरपेक्षौ यमकानुप्रासौ संसृष्टिं प्रयोजयतः उत्तरत्र तु तथाविधे उपमोत्प्रेक्षे। Also quoted and discussed by Dandin; see Kav-D. II 226. सौरभ्यान्०—closely followed by, leaving its trace behind. We should expect ०शब्दं and ०गन्धं to be in the Nom.; as they are, we must explain the Acc. by supplying उपलक्षयसि. शृणोमि &c.—see com.; he says this for fun. *Cf.* Midsummer Night's Dream quoted by Wilson—

Bottom as Pyramus:

"I see a voice: now will I to the chink,

"To spy an' I can hear my Thisby's face."

And in the same—

"Eye of man hath not heard, nor ear seen," &c.

जनान्तिकं—This stage-direction is used when a character whispers or says something to another, excluding others with the palm of the hand with its three fingers raised (त्रिपताककरेणान्यानपवार्यान्तरा कथाम्। अन्योन्यामन्त्रणं यत्स्याज्जनान्ते तज्जनान्तिकम्॥) Vita now begins actually to help Vas. in getting out of the reach of Sakara कामं—A particle indicating consent not whole-hearted; in this sense it is generally followed by तु. *Cf.* कामं न तिष्ठति मदाननसंमुखीयं भूयिष्ठमन्यविषया न तु दृष्टिरस्याः। Sak. I 28; see also Ragh. IV 13, VI. 22; Mal.-M. IX. 34 सौदामनी—सुदाम्नः (of a cloud) अपत्यं स्त्री. संधिलीना—संविलीना is a better reading and should have been adopted in the text; 'totally lost in the cloud.' सूचयिष्यति—This is a hint to her to remove the ornaments and chaplets This sl is from the Char. with the variations जलदोदरसंनिरुद्धा, हि वायुवशोपनीतो गन्धश्च शब्दमुख०

संयोगेन—see com.; it rather means 'the joining of the panes of the door.'

P. 42. स्फारीभवन्ति--A Chvi formation from स्फार great, wide. सत्त्वं--mental firmness, the stuff of which a person is made. This sl. occurs in the Charu. with the readings निर्वैरा विमुखी० स्फीता भवन्त्या० सत्त्वं हास्यमुपैति. विहरति--has his movements, moves. अल्पच्छद:--अल्प: छद: clothing यस्य. षष्ठं &c.—For the five great sins, see com. भवन्तं—The use of the *mas.* should be explained by supposing सुहृदं to be understood after it, or सुहृद् after दारिद्र्य.

सवैलक्ष्यं—विगतं लक्षमस्यासौ विलक्ष: one embarassed or abashed; विलक्षस्य भाव: वैलक्ष्यं; वैलक्ष्येण सहितं यथा स्यात्तथा । Vid. felt ashamed because his refusal caused deep sorrow to Charudatta as expressed in his above reflections on poverty.

अभ्युपपत्ति०—As if to favour me by granting me protection.

P. 44. पिण्डीभूतेन—The wind was being collected there, not finding passage in; and so it rushed in a lump. ०शालात:—Read शालत:.

भाव अन्वेषयामि—This speech follows close upon Sakara's speech शृणोमि माल्यगन्धं &c. on p. 40. The student should remember that while Sakara with Vita and Cheta was pursuing Vasantasena, Charudatta was holding discourse with Vidushaka inside the house. Now it so happens that as soon as Vasantasena reaches the door, it is opened by Vidu.; Vasanta. gets in and Radanika comes out at a time when Sakara moves forth to catch Vasantasena. The words of Sakara and Vita (अन्विष्यतां अ०) were uttered just before Radanika came out. The two scenes occur simultaneously.

चाणक्यनेव द्रौपदी—Another instance of a reckless simile (हतोपमा). Chanakya the famous statesman and writer on politics was the prime minister of Chandragupta. He lived in the 4th century B. C. and was in no way connected with Draupadi.

वयसो दर्पात्—Vita. thinking that Vasanta. was really caught, and angry that she should not have acted on his hint, says this, apparently to please Sakara—'You in your pride of youth wished to follow a nobly-born youth; but you are caught (as a punishment)' &c. Some construe दर्पात् with कर्षिता; but that is not a good way. It involves दुरान्वय; again Vita is not likely to say this in the hearing of Sakara. कुसुमाढ्येषु-कुसुमै: आढ्या: तेषु

rich in, *i. e.* profusely decorated with flowers. सेवितव्येषु—To be gently handled in love-sport. *Cf.* the Subhashita ( ते कबरीभार: ) भवति ( शिववदाचरति ) च कलापवत्त्वान्निर्जर—(a god, a young man ) सेव्य: कथं नोचेत् ।. This sl. occurs in the Charu. with the readings एषा हि......पुत्रावमानिनी । केशेषु कुसुमन्यासै...र्षिता ॥.

एषाऽसि &c.—The repetitions in this sl. can be easily marked. This sl. occurs in the Char. with the readings एषा हि वासू:....। कूज क्रन्द लप वाऽऽतं महेश्वरं शं०. व्यवसितं—set on foot, endeavoured to be done; सो with वि and अव implies determinate effort; *cf.* यमुद्वर्तुं पूषा व्यवसित इवालम्बितकर: Vik. IV. 34. स्वरसंयोग:—the union or agreement of sounds; *i. e.* voice; used with reference to a voice already heard; *cf.* आर्यकौशिकया इव स्वरसयोग: Malav. p. 180

P. 46. दधिशर—The cream of curds. दधिभक्त *v. l.*—rice mixed with curds. ०छल्लि *v. l.*—the upper surface of curds. दास्या:पुत्र्या—An *aluk* comp. (censure being implied).

रङ्गप्रवेश—Appearance on the stage, where it is necessary to change the voice to suit the particular part one has to play. This shows that acting was a part of the accomplishments of a courtesan in those days. Or रङ्ग may mean 'a music hall,' where dancing, along with music, was taught. Singing also required a knowledge of the change of tones to suit a particular *Rasa*. कलानां—such as the imitation of the sounds of birds, &c. स्वरनैपुण्यं—skill in the modulation of the voice. In the Charu. the reading of the second half is स्वरान्तरेण दक्षा हि व्याहर्तुं तन्न मुच्यताम् ।

पशुबन्धो०—पशु: बध्यते अत्र इति पशुबन्ध:; अधिकरणार्थे घञ् (अ); the place where the animal to be slaughtered at a sacrifice is tied फुरफुरायते—see note खटाखटायेते p. 13. प्रवेश्यन्ते—The reading प्रविशन्ति is better, in which case दरिद्रतया becomes करणे तृतीया.

P. 48. भागधेय—भाग एव भागधेयं fate. कुष्टस्य—spoiled by being worm-eaten. महाब्राह्मण—Generally the word महत्, when prefixed to words like ब्राह्मण, implies slight or censure; *cf.* शङ्खे तैले तथा मांसे वैद्ये ज्योतिषिके द्विजे । यात्रायां पथि निद्रायां महच्छब्दो न दीयते ॥. But here though used in good humour, it is used in a good sense as will appear from the subsequent action of Vita; *cf.* for such a use पुण्यो महाब्रह्मसमूहजुष्ट: Bhatti. I. 4.

मा परिभव:—Construe परिभव: मा (let there not be). Notice the use of मा, which is often used in this play without a verb in the Imperative. Here अस्तु may be supplied. The metre of this line is faulty; so वो in परिहवो should be read as a short syll. **नास्ति कृतान्तस्य** &c --supplies the reason for the statement in the first line. **कृतान्तस्य**--कृतान्त is used frequently in this play in the sense of 'fate' or providence. See note on sl. 53 *infra*. **नाम**--may be प्राकाश्ये ( as is well known ) or संभावनायां as the Com takes it. He means--'One who is in affluent circumstances to day may be reduced to straitened circumstances to-morrow, so one should not insult a man because he is poor.' **चारित्र्येण** &c --is another reason for the same. The loss of character is more deplorable than the loss of wealth.

**सकामा**—In the Char. we read अकामा ह्रियते and सा भ्रष्टा.

P. 50. **स्वाधीनयौवना**—स्वस्मिन्नधि स्वाधीनं, स्वाधीनं यौवनं यस्याः *i.e.* one who can dispose of her youthful person in any way she likes, hence a courtesan. The epithet सकामा is added to show that they were justified in going after her **शीलवञ्चना**—(this being led to) the loss of character. वञ्च् is used when a result follows which one does not expect. *Cf.* स्वर्गाभिसंधिसुकृतं वञ्चनामिव मेनिरे Kum. VI. 47. For a different sense *cf. infra* I. 58.

**अनुनयसर्वस्व**--The all-in-all of, *i. e.* the most convincing indication of. For, falling at the feet with the weapon cast off implies complete surrender. **समयतः**—समयः a condition, an agreement. **प्रणयः**--an act of kindness, a favour. *Cf* अलंकृतोऽस्मि स्वयंग्राहप्रणयेन भवता । *infra*, Act VII.; for a different sense see sl. 46 below

**सासूय**--With jealousy, disdainfully. असूया is intolerance of another's praise ( गुणेषु दोषाविष्करणमसूया Sid. Kau. ) **कृपणाञ्जलि**-- *lit.* folding of hands indicative of one's weakness of spirit or helplessness; hence, a humiliating bow. **अशितव्यं**--Any thing fit to be eaten; pot. p. p. used as a noun; *cf.* भवितव्यं. आह्निकद्रव्यं *v. l.*— ( see com. ) daily provisions; a day's food.

**प्रणयैः**—प्रणय a request; solicitation; hence, the gratification of supplications **कृशीकृतः**—reduced to thinness, *i. e.* to poverty. This brings out his generosity, kindliness and absence of love of money. **विभवैः**—By reason of his wealth, *i. e.* through the pride of wealth. कश्चित्--Some take this in the sense of 'an insignificant man.' **न विमानितः**—brings out his humility (**अनुद्धतत्व**); *cf.* अनुद्धताः सत्पुरुषाः समृद्धिभिः Bh. Nit. 70. **ह्रदः**—A pool with unfathomable water; तत्रागाधजलो ह्रद: Amara. तृष्णा--(1) desire for money; (2) thirst. शुष्कवान्—(1) became poor; (2) was dried. This sl. occurs in the Charu. with the readings स मद्विधानां, न तस्य कश्चिद्विभवैरमण्डित: । निदाघसंशुष्क इव ह्रदो महान् नृणां तु तृष्णामपनीय शुष्यति ।।.

पाण्डव: श्वेतकेतु—Again a reckless confusion of names and events. Svetaketu was neither a Pandava nor a warror. He is a sage figuring in the Upanishads, being the son of Uddalaka and the maternal uncle of Durvasas. *Cf.* श्वेतकेतुर्हारुणेय आस &c., and उद्दालको हारुणि: श्वेतकेतुं पुत्रमुवाच &c.; Chhand. Up. VI. 1, 1; 8. 1. According to the Mahabharata, he put a stop to the practice of married women consorting with other men, especially with Brahmanas. If we take श्वेतकेतु in the sense of Arjuna (the monkey-bannered one, श्वेत: मारुति: केतुर्यस्य) then Sakara comes to be unconsciously right. पुत्रो राधाया:—This was Karna. He was cast off in a river by Kunti, out of fear of the elders, because he was born of her when a virgin from the sun; but be was found by Adhiratha, the charioteer of Dhritarashtra, who handed over the child to his wife Radha, to bring him up. Hence he is called राधेय and सूतपुत्र. Ravana, the son of Visravas and the grandson of the sage Pulastya, is well known. इन्द्रदत्त is a character in the Brihatkatha of Gunadhya. These three names may be taken separately; but to make the inconsistency more striking they should be taken together, इन्द्रदत्त being taken as an adj. The son of Radha was not Ravana, nor was he इन्द्रदत्त, but दुर्वासोदत्त or सूर्यदत्त. आहो कुन्त्यां &c.—To associate with Kunti the name of Rama who was known for his एकपत्नीव्रत is the height of absurdity कुन्ती was the mother of the Pandavas and was not a contemporary of Rama. Again, Asvatthama was the son of कृपी. Asvatthama was powerful (अश्वस्येव स्थाम बलं यस्य, the स being dropped). *Cf.* अश्वस्येवास्य यत्स्थाम नदत: प्रदिशो गतम् । अश्वत्थामैव बालोऽयं तस्मान्नाम्ना भविष्यति ।।. धर्मपुत्रो जटायु:—Jatayu was not the son of Dharma ( that was युधिष्ठिर ) but of Aruna, ( according to some, of Garuda ). He was the younger brother of संपाति. His story is well known.

All the persons named here were distinguished for their valour. This shows that Sakara knew history but confounded these names to maintain his conventional character.

P. 52. कल्पवृक्ष:—कल्प: the desired object; तस्य वृक्ष: (जन्यजनक-

भावसंबन्धे षष्ठी ) the wish-granting tree; a Gen. Tatp.; कल्पफलक: कल्पपूरणो वा वृक्ष:; शाकपार्थिवादि:. It is one of the five trees of heaven which are in the Nandanavana of Indra (पञ्चैते देवतरवो मन्दार: पारिजातक:। संतान: कल्पवृक्षश्च पुंसि वा हरिचन्दनम् ॥ ) **दीनानां कल्प०**— Who granted every wish of the poor. **कुटुम्बी**—कुटुम्बमस्यास्तीति; the head of a family; he considered all good men as the members of his family, *i.e.* protected them. *Cf.* Hitop. उदारचरितानां तु वसुधैव कुटुम्बकम्।. **आदर्श** :—a mirror of. आदृश्यते रूपमत्र; दृश् with आ and अ ( घञ् ). That in which one's form is seen in its true nature; hence a perfect model or type of. *Cf.* आदर्श: सर्वशास्त्राणां Kad. p. 10; and 'the glass of fashion' Hamlet III. **०निकष**:—the touchstone for testing **सुचरित**; *i.e.* the standard of. **शीलवेला०**—वेला is the boundary line of the land covered by the water of the sea at high tide. Read in the com. समुद्रो वेलामिव.

**पुरुषगुण०**—virtues which characterize a perfect man, such as compassion, courtesy, truthfulness, honesty &c **दक्षिणोदार०**—may also be taken as दाक्षिणश्चासौ उदारसत्त्व: ( magnanimous ) **च. एक:........जीवति**—*Cf.* स जीवति गुणा यस्य धर्मो यस्य स जीवति। गुणधर्मविहीनो यो निष्फलं तस्य जीवितम् ॥.

**अन्धस्य दृष्टिरिव पुष्टिरिव** &c.—आतुर: a sick man. The implication is—she has vanished depriving you of the pleasure of her sight and your body of the pleasure of an embrace. **मूर्खस्य बुद्धिरिव**—As in your case when you foolishly said that Charu.'s house was near at hand. **सिद्धिरिवा०**—As a man who does not take time by the fore-lock fails to get success in his undertaking, so you were not on the alert to catch her in time and therefore she is lost to you. **व्यसनिन:** व्यसनमस्य विद्यते. One in difficulty or distress. In this case परमा विद्या will simply mean a difficult Sastra requiring great effort for mastering it. Or **व्यसनानि अस्य विद्यन्ते** a man addicted to vices, a dissipated man. The *Vyasanas* originating from काम and क्रोध are given by Manu as—मृगयाऽक्षा दिवास्वाप: परिवाद: स्त्रियो मद:। तौर्यत्रिकं वृथाट्या च कामजो दशको गण: ॥ पैशुन्यं साहसं द्रोह ईर्ष्याऽसूयाऽर्थदूषणम्। वाग्दण्डजं च पारुष्यं क्रोधजोऽपि गणोऽष्टक: ॥ VII. 47. In this case परमा विद्या means ब्रह्मविद्या or Vedanta-Vidya. *Cf.* द्वे विद्ये वेदितव्ये इति ह स्म यद् ब्रह्मविदो वदन्ति परा चैवापरा च।* * अथ परा यया तदक्षरमधिगम्यते। Mundakop. I. 1. 4 5. Implication–'You, of confounded memory and dissipated, filled her with disgust and she left you.' **अरिजने रतिरिव**—As one can have no love for one's enemy so she can never love you, as you have offended her by your indiscriminate advances. आलाने &c.—He now plainly states what was implied in the previous Sl. आलानं—a post to which an elephant is tied; it sometimes means the chain by which an elephant is tied. वल्गा—reins. हृदये गृह्यते &c.—He means :—You can capture a woman only if you have secured her real affection; force will never do.

P. 54. भाव: अभावं--A pun on the word भाव which means (1) a respectable person, here Vita; and (2) presence, existence. *Bhava* has gone to *abhava, i. e* disappeared, has left. काकपदशीर्षमस्तक—Here शीर्ष and मस्तक mean the same thing, and so one of them is redundant. Crow-foot-pated one; *lit.* one having a head bulged out on the sides and elongated and appearing in the front like the foot of a crow, *i. e.* deformed. Or शीर्ष may mean the tuft of hair on the head One having a tuft of hair like a caret on the head. काकपद is the mark caret (^) used to indicate an omission supplied afterwards. Bharata in his Natyasastra says that Vidu. should dress his hair so as to give it the form of a काकपद. But the first sense is natural. Sakara here uses his usual device of repetition and also refers to Vidu.'s deformity of head. The other sense given by the Com. द्यूताद्यकार्यप्रवृत्तो &c. (Chief of the princes of sharpers-Ryder) does not seem to be intended. Sakara is not likely to use an expression with such a far-fetched meaning.

नवनाटक &c.—नव is put in to indicate that the actress wears special decoration. सूत्रधारीव—The fem. form of Sutra. humorously used for the usual Nati, by Sakara. For, a female stage-manager is unknown to the Sanskrit drama. "A word like ताण्डवसूत्रधारी in Chaurapanchasika 7 is obviously withont bearing on the history of the drama in India. The expression in our passage cannot be used as direct evidence, since it may be nothing more than another absurdity of Samsthanaka's." Dr. Ryder.

अधिकरणं--A Court of justice; a tribunal. Hence अधिकरणिक a judge. व्यवहार--The filing of a law-suit, judicial procedure. लघु--quickly. निर्यातयत्--Handing over back, restoring. Here Sakara speaks as if Vasant. belonged to him. *Cf.* for this sense Vik. V. तदेतस्य ते भर्तु: समक्षं निर्यातितो हस्तनिक्षेप: p. 236; or अद्य......

नियर्तितो मे दीर्घायु: p. 128. अनुबद्धा--Continuons, close, ever-abiding. अथ वा &c.--Here the subject-matter of the ninth Act is hinted.

P. 34. कष्माण्डी--A pumpkin ( कोहळा in Marathi ). Some read कक्कालुका for कश्चालुका and translate it by कर्करुक: (०वृन्त:). We should have also read कूष्माण्ड: Here the use of the fem. for the *mas.* and of लीने for लीनायां is Sakarian See Com. हैमन्तिक--हेमन्तस्य इयं हैमन्तिका; है० रात्रि: हैमन्तिकरात्रि: तस्यां सिद्धं ; prepared on a wintry night (which is colder than day). लीनायां वेलायां--After the lapse of some time. पूति--putrid; when taken with कूष्माण्ड or वडा it becomes पूति: by लिङ्गविपरिणाम. These things under the conditions mentioned do not putrefy or rot even after the lapse of some time. By this Sakara means that his enmity, too, caused by Charudatta's refusal to deliver over Vasant., will not rot, *i. e* will ever remain fresh. तवानिर्यातनजन्यं वैरं न भविष्यति पूति. So the fig. of speech here is [ अत्राप्रस्तुतानां यथोक्तानां कूष्माण्डादीनां वेलातिपातेऽपि पूतिगन्धत्वाभाव-प्रतिपादनेनाप्रस्तुतस्य वसन्तसेनाऽनिर्यातनजन्यवैरस्य प्रत्ययाद् ] अप्रस्तुतप्रशंसा. Some render लीणे अ वेले as ऋणं च वैरं in Sans, adding these to the list. In this case there is no अप्रस्तुतप्र०, as वैर is actually mentioned, but कारकदीपक. L. D takes a different view. He reads the words न भवति पूति: with a Kaku. Then it would mean—Do they not get spoiled when time passes ( although care be taken to preserve them ) ? Yes, they do. So if you restore Vasantasena to me after a lapse of time, ( thinking over the matter ), it will spoil the business (चिरंतनत्वेन प्रशिथिलं स्वकार्यम्) ; the matter will lose its charm.

शोभनं—Well, in a pleasing way. स्वस्तिकं *v.l.*—favourably ( to me ); so as to lead to a happy end. सकपटं--cunningly, cleverly ( so that I should gain my object ). These two clauses show that Sakara climbs down from his former haughty position (मरणान्तिक वैर भविष्यति) लघुकं *v. l.* - means briefly, in a few words. प्रासादबालाग्र०—It is difficult to see what this exactly means. The natural meaning seems to be बाल नूतन (newly-built) अग्रं a turret or top यस्या: सा कपोतपालिका dove-cot, *i.e* upper terrace. Sakara humorously calls the upper terrace a dove-cot; the Com. assigns a technical meaning to बालाग्र, *viz.* a wild elephant; *i. e* a terrace marked with the figure or cornice of a wild elephant. अन्यथा—Otherwise, *i. e.* against my direction; in a way not favourable to me.

कपित्थगुलिकं— The round fruit of the Kapittha or wood-apple tree ( कपयस्तिष्ठन्त्यत्र इति कपित्थ:; पृषोदरादि: ). मडमडा-

**यिष्यामि**—Verb formed from the onomatopoetic word **मडमड**; I will make it produce the sound 'mad mad,' *i. e.* crush it. *Cf.* येन कपिला कल्याणी मडमडायिता । Uttar. IV. p. 101; मा दास्या-पुत्र......................कपाटसंपुटप्रविष्टमिव पक्वकपित्थं शीर्षं ते चूर्णचूर्णं मडमडायिष्ये । Charu **असि**—The same sword that was dropped by Vita, near Vidushaka. In the Charu. no mention is made of a sword. **विपरीतं**—In the reverse way, i. e seizing it by the point with the hilt raised up. **निर्वल्कलं**—Without its bark, *i. e.* covering; this is generally taken to mean 'unsheathed.' **मूलकपेशि**—The rind of a radish. **कोशसुप्तं**—To avoid the contradiction with निर्व०, we are to suppose that Saka put the sword into its sheath before taking it on his shoulder. The Sl is translated accordingly. It is better, however, to take निर्वल्कलं in the sense of 'without the outer covering of cloth.' The sheathed swords of rich men are carried by their servants on their shoulders, being placed in coverings of fine woollen or some such cloth. निर्वल्कल cannot be taken with मूलक० as proposed by some; for in that case निर्वल्कलं must be taken as compounded with मूल०; but this violates the metre. **कुक्कुरैःकु० श्च**—some think that this is meant to refer to Vid. and Radanika. **बुक्कयमानः** being barked at बुक्क् 1, 10 P. to bark. There are two other similar roots हिक्क्, and फक्क्, given in the following sl. describing the chase of Dasaratha—भल्लूक एको बहुधा जिहिक्वे रुन्धद्भिरेनं शुनकैर्बुबुक्के वने श्वकोलाहलदीर्णदिक्के वल्मीकलीनैः फणिभिः पफक्के ॥ Udaraghava I. 53.

**रदनिका खल्वहं**—Mark the pun on the word रदनिका which is her name, and also means 'one having teeth'; fr. रदन and इक (ठन्) showing possession. 'I have got 'teeth' that are always clenched fast and so my mouth is locked up'. She means that she would not tell under any circumstances. *Cf.* for a similar use विमर्दसुरभिर्बकुलावलिका खल्वहम् । Malav. III. p 96, and परहृदयग्रहणपण्डिता मदनिका खलु त्वम् further on, p.96

P. 58. **मारुताभिलाषी**—Desirous of, *i.e.* fond of, the breeze; who delights to be in open air. Sastri Raddi reads प्रदोषसमयः । शीतार्तः रोह०. This is a bad reading मारुताभिलाषी प्रदोष० is a strange expression; we can readily understand मारुता० अग्निः, but not प्रदोष०; it means 'which desires, is expectant of'; hence full of; windy. Again शीतार्त remains unexplained. If we take मारु० with **रोह०** we know why he is sitting exposed to the wind and is शीतार्त; otherwise he would have come in. In the Charu. we have मारुताभिलाषी प्रदोषः । तद्गृह्यतां प्रावारकम् । and there it is all right. Charu, offers the mantle to the supposed Rad. saying 'the evening bids fair to be windy; so take &c.' **प्रयच्छति**--We are to understand that he throws it to her from the place where he was sitting. **अनुदासीनं**--not indifferent to (carnal plesaures); from the fact that he wore a scented Pravaraka she concludes that he yet loved gaieties In the Charu. we actually have अनुदासीनं यौवनमस्य पटवासगन्धः सूचयति **अपवारितकेन**--the manner of the अपवारितक speech; *i.e.* turning aside, so as to hide the act from Charudatta.' **प्रावृणोति**—We must supply आत्मानं--covers herself with the mantle. So sincere and ardent was her love for Char. that anything from him filled her with extreme delight, and so she at once wore it. Raddi Sastri supplies रोहसेनं, apparently for the reason that in the second Act Charu. gives the same cloak to Karnapuraka, as a mark of his approbation of his heroic deed ( see p. 98 ) and it is not stated when Vasant. returned it to its owner. But this contention will not do. The word अपवारितकेन and sl. 54 leave no doubt that the cloak was worn by Vasantasena. The inconsistency is to be removed by supposing that Vasantasena restored it to Charu. when she deposited her ornament with him, and that the poet forgot to mention it.

**तवाभ्यन्तरस्य**--There is a play on the word **अभ्यन्तर** which means inside of the house as well as the inner apartment (अन्तर्गृह). Not sure that Charu. loved her with equal ardour, she says--I am not lucky enough to enter your inner apartment ( as a wife ). The Com. says वेश्यात्वात्, *i. e.* she could not enter the inside of the house, being a harlot; but this is not correct. Charudatta himself says to Vas. at the end of the fifth Act 'एहि । अभ्यन्तरमेव प्रविशावः ।' This shows that वेश्यात्व was no bar to her entrance into the house. This one sentence brings out the salient trait of Vasantasena's character, *viz.* her extreme modesty and humility. Although supremely blessed with beauty and fortune, she does not feel sure of winning Charu.'s love.

**भाग्यक्षय०**—भाग्यक्षयः decline of fortune; तस्मात्पीडा सा संजाता अस्याः ताम् । तारकादित्वादितच् The com. takes **भाग्य** in the sense of 'the stock of religious merit'; but that idea is expressed by कृतान्तोपहितां. **कृतान्तोप०**--brought on by fate or providence कृतः अन्तः निश्चयः येन स कृतान्तः ( he who fixes or pre-ordains things )

Charudatta deplores his lot that even his servants should not obey him.

**अविज्ञातावसक्तेन**--may be separated as अविज्ञाता ( not known as to her reality ) अवसक्तेन ( clinging, attaching to her body ) मम वाससा दूषिता ( defiled, desecrated ) च. Mr. Raddi says अवसक्तेन स्वगात्रसंबद्धेन । उपभुक्तेनेति यावत्. This is inaccurate. That idea is expressed by मम; अवसक्त must be taken with वसन्त०; she cannot be दूषिता unless there is **contact** of the garment. Or the whole may be taken as one word-- **अविज्ञातं यथा तथा** &c. By its coming in contact with or getting clung to her body through ignorance ( *lit.* without the matter being known ). **दूषिता**-- Wilson remarks--" This instances the great reserve that separated the virtuous part of the sexes among the Hindus. To have touched the wife of another with the **hem of the garment** was a violation of her person."

**ननु भूषिता**--Vasant. understands **दूषिता** in the sense of disfigured, made to suffer in beauty,' and so ejaculates **ननु** भूषिता decorated; she does not say **पवित्रीकृता.**

**छादिता शरद**०--Charud. could see Vasant. now, as a light was brought in by Vidu. She was clad in the thin white cloak; she is therefore compared to the bright crescent moon hidden by an autumnal cloud which is **also white** and thin. The simile shows that she was completely **veiled.** The sl. occurs in the Charu. with the variations--०तप्रयुक्तेन धर्षिता (insulted)...संवृता ...शोभते.

**अथ वा न युक्तं** &c --As a nobly-born gentleman he suddenly restrains himself from looking at her any more ( and describing her further ). *Cf.* अनिर्वर्णनीयं परकलत्रं Sak. V. p. **172.**

**यया मे** &c --It is clear from this that Charu. also was stirred by a similar passion for Vasantasena at her sight. **विभव**०— Extensive, *i.e.* large fortune; विस्तर is appropriate after क्षीण ( the expanse narrowed ). Its **क्षीणत्व** is the हेतु of सीदति ( disappears, comes to naught ). He could not profess his love to her as he was poor. **कुपुरुषस्य**—कुत्सित: निन्दित: पुरुष: कुपुरुष:; here the कुत्सितत्व lies in his being spiritless. This sl occurs in the Charu. as यत्र मे पतित.....। रोष...स्वाङ्गेष्वेवावसीदति ॥

P. 60. **यत्सत्यमलंकृतास्मि**—It was an honour to Vasant. because the words would clearly show to Charu. that Vasant.

sincerely loved him and spurned the love of Sakara. **अज्ञोऽसौ**— He is a fool to say like that **देवतोपस्थान०**—may be taken as (1) देवतावत् उपस्थानस्य योग्या fit to be waited upon like a deity; (2) देवतया उपस्थानं तस्य योग्या fit to be the companion of a deity. आदरेणैव सेव्या न तु बलात्कारेणेति भावः. **तस्यां वेलायां**—At that time, *i. e.* when I told her to take in Rohasena.

**प्रतोद्यमाना**—Being told in harsh words ( such as प्रत्युत्तरमपि नास्ति &c.); repeatedly urged. For प्रतो० some read प्रचोद्यमाना. **भाग्यकृतां** &c—Looking to the plight to which I am reduced by fate. He means—She did not come in knowing that I was poor and would not be able to receive her as she deserves. Some take **भाग्य०** as referring to Vasantasena's own state, *viz.* her being born a courtesan. But that goes against देवतोपस्थानयोग्या. Also had that been her idea, she would not have loved Charudatta at all ' The phrase probably refers to Charudatta's poverty, not to Vasantasena's profession, as Bohtlingk takes it." Ryder **पुरुषपरिचयेन** etc.—The last two lines are rather obscure. The meaning seems to be—she does not speak boldly on being acquainted with men, although he (पुरुषः) speaks much. For, she did not return a bold reply to me which she should have done on account of her familiarity with men as a courtesan. Some take पुरुषपरिचयेन with बहु भाषते—Although she talks much ( many things ) on account of her acquaintance with men, she does not speak boldly. Here we have first दूरान्वय. Secondly, Char., not being previously acquainted with Vasa., could not have known how she talked at home Thirdly, it is no compliment to her to call her बहुभाषिणी. So the first way is better. Dr Ryder also says—" But Vasantsena has not spoken a word aloud since her entry into the house; so that perhaps we have to understand ' a man ' as subject of भाषते." **अविज्ञानात्** &c— अविज्ञानात् is to be taken with अपराद्धोऽस्मि. " Through ignorance I committed an offence by thus addressing ( or treating ) as a servant you whom I did not know as such (अपरिज्ञात)." If अविज्ञानात् be taken with ०नोपचारेण the meaning will be—by this my treatment, through ignorance, of you as a servant, which was never known to you अपरिज्ञातः त्वया अननुभूतः यः परिजनवदुपचारस्तेन ). **अपराद्धोऽस्मि**—Mark the Active use; *cf.* अपराद्धोऽस्मि तत्रभवतः कण्वस्य । Sak. VII. p. 288

**अनुचितभूमिका०** —By ascending to—intruding on— a place ( a Brahmana's house ) which is not the proper place for me, *i. e.* where I, as a harlot, should not have come.

P. 62 **सुखं**—may be taken with **प्रणम्य** or **समागतौ** (have happily come together). **कलमकेदारौ**—As the stalks of paddy of two adjoining fields meet by their tops inclining to each other. Vid. says this humorously. **कलम**—is a kind of fine paddy; its stalks wave beautifully in the wind. *Cf.* तुतोष पश्यन्कलमस्य सोऽधिकं सवारिजे वारिणि रामणीयकम् । Kir. IV. 4. **करभजानु॰**—*i. e.* ugly, being depressed in some parts and protruding in others. **इति उत्तिष्ठति**—He rises to go wishing to leave them alone; instead of this some read उत्तिष्ठतमिति, as part of Vidu.'s speech. In this case the meaning is 'you should rise and go inside the house.' **तिष्ठतु प्रणयः**—'Let courtesy be set aside, let formalities cease;' implying thereby that they were on sufficiently familiar terms now to have done away with excuses. **चतुरः** &c—उपन्यास is what is set forth for consideration; hence, the beginning of a topic, introduction. *Cf.* अहो उपन्यासशुद्धिः Mal. M III p. 69; नियतिः शनकैरलीकवचनोपन्यासमालीजनः । Amarusa. 23. चतुरः—because, although addressed to the Vid., it was also intended for her and had a side-meaning—Let this love be abiding (तिष्ठतु प्रणयः). **मधुरः**—because it contained a response to her love. **ईदृशेन**—supply सह, 'with him who is poor;' *i. e.* without the means of enjoyment or of repaying obligation. See p. 70. In the Charu. she says—अदक्षिणं खलु प्रथमदर्शने यदृच्छागतया इह वस्तुम्. **पुरुषेषु न्यासाः** &c.—She means—a deposit is made, not looking to the wealth in the house, but through confidence in the worth of a man. **स्वस्ति**—स्वस्ति implies a blessing, which means that the Vid. took it as a free gift made to him. Hence Charu says धिङ्मूर्ख &c.

**चोरैः ह्रियताम्**—Let it be stolen by thieves; what do I care for it? Of course Vid. says this humorously. This speech of Vid. is not complete; the full speech is ह्रियतामेषोऽस्या **अस्माकं** विन्यासः. Similarly the full text of Charu.'s speech is.... **न्यासः खलु** अयम् । अचिरेणैव कालेन निर्यातयिष्ये । But the poet skilfully breaks them up in such a way that the parts also syntactically fit in with each other. Thus, as soon as Vid. says ह्रियतां, Charu. is made to say अचिरणैव कालेन, which, taken with Vidu.'s speech, means 'stolen in a short time,' and thus suggests the events of the third Act. The two parts अचिरेणैव कालेन and एषोऽस्या विन्यासः need not be taken together; but if so taken they will mean—'In a short time we shall lose this deposit and be free from the care of guarding it' [ विगतो न्यास; विन्यास: न्यास: विन्यास: भवेत् ], and not 'will be our property,' as Mr. Paranjpe suggests, because Charu. would never allow that. This way of suggesting parts of the story is called a Patakasthana, of the 3rd kind; see Sah.-Dar. VI. 48. *Cf.* Mud. IV राक्षस:--अपि नाम चाणक्यबटु:--दौवारिक:-(प्रविश्य।) जयतु । रा०--अतिसंधातुं शक्य: स्यात् । दौ०--अमात्य:. Or Veni. II. दुर्यो०--ममोरुयुग्मम् । ( प्रविश्य ) कञ्चुकी--देव भग्नं भग्नम् । &c. p. 47. चतुष्पथ--see p. 24.

P. 64. राजमार्गविश्वास०--That can be depended upon &c. *i. e.* shedding a powerful light, and not easily blown out on the broad road where the wind is strong. जनान्तिकं--see p. 40. नि:स्नेहा:--(1) devoid of oil; (2) destitute of affection. Perhaps the sentence contains a hint to Charudatta that he should not fall too much in the hands of Vasantasena lest he, too, may be treated like a निर्धनकामुक.

शशाङ्क:--The moon ( having the mark of a hare ). कामिनीगण्ड०--कामोऽस्या अस्तीति कामिनी a beautiful young woman; तस्या गण्ड: स इव पाण्डु: yellowish-white. Here the usual relation of उपमेय and उपमान is reversed to indicate the superiority of the cheek to the moon ( the usual standard of comparison ). This is also meant as an indirect compliment to Vasantasena. तिमिरनिकर--The heap, *i. e.* compact mass of darkness. स्रुतजले इव पङ्के--स्रुतं जलं यस्मात् Mud, from which water has trickled down; *i. e.* the surface of which is moist and unbroken. This is not a happy simile. The rays of the moon gradually removing the darkness are compared to streams of milk falling on darkish mud gradually hiding its surface and turning it white. For the comparison of rays of the moon to streams of milk, *cf.* क्षीरेण क्षालितेवोर्वी शर्वरीशे विराजति. This Sl. occurs in the Charu. with the readings -- क्लिन्नखर्जूरपाण्डुर्युवतिजनसहायो......। तिमिरनिचय०...हृतजल इव..।। भवति वस०--Here we are to imagine that they then start and reach the house of Vasantasena. राजमार्गो हि शून्योऽयं--Charudatta must be supposed to say this on reaching his house, which was also situated on the high way. The road was solitary as it was midnight. For when the moon rose it was about 11. P. M. वञ्चना--Deception, a trick ( being played upon us ). बहुदोषा--fraught with harms, abounding in evils or dangers ( coming from robbers &c. ). त्वया रात्रौ--Because Vidu. would be in the house during the night. The concluding portion of this Act is marked by extreme brevity.

# ACT II

The second Act opens with a conversation between Vasant. and her maid Madanika, in which the former makes a confession of her love for Charudatta. While they are conversing a cry is heard in the streets which finally serves to introduce Samvahaka, a shampooer, who was once in the service of Charu., but had turned a gambler afterwards, to Vasantasena. Vasanta. pays off the debt Samva. owes to the gambling-master, whereupon he resolves to become a Buddhistic mendicant. This is necessary for the proper understanding of the events that terminate in the final catastrophe. Another incident mentioned in the Act is Samvahaka's rescue from the grasp of Vasantasena's elephant by Karnapura, who gets the प्रावारक from Charu. as a reward for his heroic deed. The mention of this fact, and praise bestowed on Charu. by Samvahaka serve to further develop the love Vasant. had conceived for Charudatta. See Introd. for other particulars. The second Act consists of seven parts forming two scenes which the student can easily mark.

P. 66. **मात्रा**—*i.e.* Vasantasena's mother. **आर्यासकाशं**—Vasant. is addressed as Arya. **संदेशेन**—having charged me with a message; mark the use of the Instr. **हृदयेनालिखन्ती**—Drawing (some) picture by the heart; brooding over something. *Cf.* मनो निष्ठाशून्यं भ्रमति च किमप्यालिखति च । Mal. Madh. I. 31. L. D. reads कमप्यालिखन्ती and says अभिलषन्तीत्यर्थः **सोत्कण्ठा**—उत्कण्ठया सहिता. **उत्कण्ठा**—a love-longing; it is 'सस्पृहं आध्यानं,' thinking about a person with a desire for his or her company. It is thus defined—रागे त्वलब्धविषये वेदना महती तु या । संशोषणी तु गात्राणां तामुत्कण्ठां विदुर्बुधाः ॥. **न किमपि मन्त्रयसे**—This is the reading generally found; it means—you have not said anything and I have not replied to you. It is decidedly better to read मन्त्रये 'I have not said anything.' The mistake is due to मन्तेसि (the Prakrit for मन्त्रयसे) being misread for मन्तेमि, मि and सि being easily confounded. **आ**—or **आम्** is used when one remembers the right thing.

**स्नेहः पृच्छति**—So in the Vik. **मदनः खलु त्वामाज्ञापयति** &c. p. 73. **पुरोभागिता**—forwardness; पुरोभागः अस्यास्तीति पुरोभागी *lit.* one who takes a share foremost; hence, officious; *cf.* पुरोभागे किं स्वातन्त्र्यमवलम्बसे । Sak. V. p. 192; Vik. III. मा खलु मां पुरोभागिनीं समर्थयस्व । p 84. पुरोभागिनः भावः पुरोभागिता a fault-finding disposition *Cf.* प्रायः समानविद्याः परस्परयशःपुरोभागाः । Malav. I. 20.

P. 68. **कामः खलु नाम** &c.—The whole may be read as one sentence "It is, indeed, the divine Kama, (the god of love) who is favoured. by you; Kama, who is the great festivity (joy) of youths." *Cf.* "Love is a mighty god, who holds his holidays in youthful breasts." Wilson. Or, we may split up the sentence into two— कामः खलु एष भगवान् (य एवं विकारयति)—This is, indeed, the God of love (that has thus led you to love a man): *cf.* भ्रमति भुवने कंदर्पाज्ञा विकारि च यौवनम् and सोऽयं प्रसिद्धविभवः खलु चित्तजन्मा Mal. Madh. I. 17, 20. **अनुगृहीतो महोत्सव** &c.—The great festival of young men (*viz.* the gaining of your love) is favoured by Cupid. What is meant is—That you have set your heart on some young man is a triumph for Cupid and a source of great joy to that young man Jib. reads कः खलु नामाद्य अत्रभवत्या अनुगृहीतो महोत्सवे (at the great festival) (मधूत्सवे) तरुणजनः—which is simpler. **राजा राज॰**—Mad thinks that her mistress, so richly endowed with beauty, must have fixed her affection on some such person (*cf.* सागरं वर्जयित्वा कुत्र वा महानद्यवतरति). **सेव्यते**—equal to सेवितुमिष्यते desired to be served (*i.e.* won over by your attendance on him). **रन्तुमिच्छामि** &c— I wish to enjoy pleasures of true love and not to minister to the pleasures of the great for their money (like an ordinary courtesan, that sells her body for money). See com. Jib. considers the passage from here to the third speech of Madanika as spurious on the ground that a young woman would not express herself in such clear terms. But we must remember that Vasant. is speaking in private and can freely open her heart to her confidante. **काम्यते**—is sought as an object of love; mark the difference in the wording. The first question (सेव्यते) was asked as to a courtesan whose profession requires her to humour great persons (such as a king or his minister) for money. **पूजनीयः** &c.— She means that she would not be able freely to enjoy the company of one she would have to honour.

**हञ्जे**—A vocative particle used in addressing a maidservant; see com. **उपारूढः**—For he values money more than the company of his beloved. **भर्तृदारिकया**—Properly a term of address for a princess (भर्तुः दारिका) in dramas; and then for any mistress **उदासीनेव**—*i.e.* one who remains indifferent to what happened there. She means—Don't you know the man who attracted my attention and captivated my heart there?

* इतः परं मदनिकायास्तृतीयोक्तिपर्यन्तं प्रक्षिप्तमिति मन्यामहे। यतः 'हञ्जे रमिदुं इच्छामि' इत्येवं स्पष्टतः स्वाभिलाषव्यञ्जकं रमण्यः कदाऽपि न कथयन्ति। इत्यादि।

P. 70. शरणागता--शरणमागता; refers to Vasantasena's having taken shelter in Charu.'s house when pursued by Sakara. Vas. must have spoken about the incident on her return to her house tc Mada and others. श्रेष्ठिच०--श्रेष्ठिनां चत्वरं the quarter or residence of the chief or leading merchants. श्रेष्ठं धनादि अस्यास्तीति श्रेष्ठी--the head or president of a mercantile or other guild अयि नामा०--Mark how eager Vasant. is to hear her lover's name; it will give her unbounded pleasure.

एवं तावत्--I shall say this--to test her love. दरिद्रपुरुष०--For it is the lot of courtesans to be denounced as lovers of money only and not of persons (see *infra* V. 14).

आर्ये किं हीन०--She means--Even bees do not resort a a mango-tree that has lost its blossoms. Much less then should a discriminating woman like you love a man totally destitute of wealth. अत एव ता: &c.--Vasant. meets her argument by saying that the bees are after all called the *makers* of honey and not the *enjoyers* of honey. So a woman who, having decorated and improved the beauty of her person, only makes it an instrument of the pleasures of others, cannot enjoy life. She for herself would not be a courtesan of such type. 'A pun on the word *Madhukaras*, honey-makers or beggars.' Wilson. मनीषित:--desired, coveted by the mind Mark the Samdhi-मनस: ईषित: मनीषित: । (पररूपसंधि:) किं नाभिसा० Why don't you approach him as a lover, all at once? It will not be difficult for you to win his love; for श्रिया दुराप: कथमीप्सितो भवेत् । Sak. III. 12 प्रत्युपकारदु०--Const. मा तावत् प्रत्यु० दुर्लभदर्शनो भविष्यति । Unable to make a suitable return for my love by gifts of money or ornaments &c., he as a gentleman will feel chagrined and will not like to meet me again. So I must create confidence in him that I trust him, love him inspite of his poverty &c.; see com अत एव--*i.e.* for creating confidence in him and also to have an occasion to go to him.

P 72. नेपथ्ये--Now opens a scene which tells us what sort of people the gamblers were and acquaints us with the manner of their playing the game and the rules with which they were bound. This scene is unknown to the Char. of Bhasa. The persons introduced are Mathura, the keeper of a gambling house, two gamblers, one of them named Samvahaka who owed ten Suvarnas to the other, and Darduraka, an Ujjain rake, brought in to indicate the revolution planned in favour of Aryaka. For the dialects spoken by these see Introduction.

**भट्टारक**--(for भट्टा) refers to the winning gambler (द्यूतकर), and not to the people in the street, as some have it. **सुवर्ण**--a coin of glod, 80 *gunjas* or 10 *mashas* in weight ( a little more than 175 grains Troy ), something like the 'Mohar' of later times. "A weight of gold which, according to different data, varies from 105 grains to 227." Wilson. **सुवर्णस्य**--सुवर्णार्थं; the Gen. for the Dat. (तादर्थ्ये); or संबन्धसामान्येन हेत्वर्थे षष्ठी Raddi. **रुद्ध**:--Bound or indebted to us. **लब्ध**: *v.l.*--who was found or detained. **प्रपलायितः**--has fast (प्र) run away. Mathura shouts thus on seeing Samvahaka escape. **तिष्ठ तिष्ठ**--This he says on seeing him, after coming out of the gambling house.

**अपटीक्षेपेण**—Tossing aside the curtain ( implying hurry and fright.) पटी is properly the stage-curtain, and पटीक्षेप is the lifting up or pushing aside of a curtain ; and a dictum of Bharata says पटीक्षेपो न कर्तव्य आर्तराजप्रवेशने (The curtain should not open upon an agitated man and a king ). But as **पटीक्षेपेण** does not occur as a stage-direction in plays, commentators explain अपटीक्षेपेण as 'with a toss of the अपटी' अपटी, meaning a screen (अ being अल्पार्थे). **संभ्रान्तः**—bewildered, or in a hurry. **संवांहकः**—*Lit.* the shampooer and kneader of the limbs. **हीमाणहे** ( *Prakrit* )—may be **खेदे** or **विस्मये.**

**नवबन्धन०**--indicates that the blow is very hard. The second गर्दभी and शक्ति are the technical names of *cowries* used as dice in playing **ताडितोऽस्मि**—shows that he lost his money in part. **घातितोऽस्मि**--shows that his fate was decided by the cowrie शक्ति. He lost the whole amount. **अङ्गराज०**—अङ्गानां राजा अङ्गराजः, Karna, who was made king of the Anga country by Duryodhana. Once Indra, whose care it was to ensure the protection of his son Arjuna, came to Karna in the disguise of a Brahmana and asked for his divine cuirass and ear-rings, which Karna gave him. Indra gave him in return great strength and a Sakti ( a kind of weapon ), certain to bring about the death of whomsoever it was hurled against. When Ghatotkacha, son of Bhima by the demoness Hidimba, proved very destructive to the Kaurava host, Duryodhana pressed Karna to discharge the Sakti, which the latter had reserved for Arjuna, against him. Karna yielded, and slew Ghatotkacha with it. See Mah-Bh. Drona-P. Chs. 179-190. *Cf.* Mud. II. 15.

**लेखक**---A document; or a scribe. **सभिकं**—सभा द्यूतमाश्रयत्वेनास्यास्तीति सभिकः the keeper or master of a gambling house;

fr. सभा + इक (ठन्), which is added to the words of the व्रीह्यादि class. Samvahaka bolted away, seeing that the attention of Sabhika was taken up by some writing or his scribe. But Sabhika was on his guard; he at once noticed his escape.

The *Sabhika* is said, in the Mitakshara, to be a person who presides a the house where assemblies are held for the purposes of gambling, and who provides the dice and all other materials. The अग्निपुराण gives the following description of the Sabhika's duties and the laws of the gambling table:—"The Sabhika is entitled to five per cent. on money won at play, whenever the sum exceeds one hundred; if it fall short of that amount he is to receive ten per cent. In return for the protection of the king, he shall pay to the royal treasury a fixed proportion of his profits. It is his business to collect from the unsuccessful party whatever sums they may have lost, and transfer them to the winners, and it becomes him to do this civilly, and to adjust the payment on liberal and lenient terms. In all licensed gaming-houses, where the royal dues are regularly paid, the king should enforce the payment of all sums lost, but he should not interfere with gaming-house of a different class. In all disputes, those who have been lookers-on are to be witnesses; and if any foul play or false dice be proved against a gambler, he shall be branded and banished the kingdom. The king shall appoint proper officers to attend at gambling houses, and secure all dishonest characters; the same rules are applicable to cock-pits and other similar places, where animals are set to fight for wagers." The legal sanction thus given to gambling is very different from the sturdy and moral notions expressed by मनु who directs kings to prohibit such practices in the dominions, and even to punish with death those who engage in them themselves or induce others to do so (Manu-Samhita, IX. 221, 224), but regulations of either tendency are manifest indications of considerable progress in the vices of civilized society. (Wilson). See also याज्ञवल्क्य II. 199–202.

**विपरीताभ्यां पा०**—*i. e.* with feet turned in the opposite direction of the temple, *i. e.* walking back to it so as to give the footsteps the appearance of a man walking away from the temple. Here he imagines that the Mathura and his companion would not go into the temple finding from the foot-prints no man going in. The device was a clever one, but poor Sam. did not know that his pursuers also were grown grey in the art of deceiving and would at once find out the truth from the sudden change in the direction of the foot-prints.

**देवीभवि०**—As one word–न देवः अदेवः अदेवः देवः संपद्यमानो भविष्यामि I will turn god, *i. e.* stand there as the image of the god; as two words–देवी भविष्यामि stand there as the image of its goddess. This was his second trick. He thought that he would pass for the image of the deity of the temple in case his pursuers were to enter it in search of him. **बहुविधं**—Because he had to try several postures before he fixed himself into one.

**एकं सभिकं वर्ज०**—This shows the power which the Sabhika had over the gamblers who had to obey his word as law. **रुद्रोऽपि**—श्रीनिवासाचार्य quotes the following sl. as a parallel to this—ब्रह्मा स्वयंभूश्चतुराननो वा रुद्रस्त्रिनेत्रस्त्रिपुरान्तको वा । इन्द्रो महेन्द्रः सुरनायको वा त्रातुं न शक्ता युधि रामवध्यम् ॥

P. 74 **सुसभिक०**-- A good or just Sabhika. **समविषमं**-- irregularly, unevenly. **कुलं यशो**-Because the gamblers were bound in good faith to pay their dues; so Samva. attempting to defraud the winners, would be bringing disgrace on his family and casting a stain on his own fair name as a gambler

**एष व्रजति**--Here-so far--he has run on. **पदवी**--the line of foot prints. *Cf*. कच्चिदासादिता तस्य दुरात्मनः कौरवाधमस्य पदवी । Veni. VI p. 132. **धूर्तः**--means a gambler ( धूर्तोऽक्षदेवी कितवः Ak.) ; but as द्यूतकरः follows, this must be taken to mean a rogue, a villain; or roguish, deceitful **अन्योन्यं संज्ञाप्य**—Having made signs to each other that he was there. They knew that the temple was without an image; on seeing the image they at once conclud- ed that it was Samva standing there transfixed like an idol. But they did not say it openly as they wanted to use a trick to catch him.

**शैलप्रतिमा**—He says this purposely as he wanted a plea to go and shake the idol. **क्रीडतः**—The reading क्रीडति is bad. They began to gamble because they were confident that Samva., who they knew was there, would feel, as a gambler, an uncontrollable desire to play on seeing them engaged in play, and would at once come forward and thus reveal himself And this their expectation was fulfilled. **०विकारसंवरणं**—suppression or restraining of the manifestation of. **कत्ताशब्दः**—According to some कत्ता is a technical term for the gambling implements, such as dice or cowries; according to others it means a kind of gambling called Nandipura. **हृदयं**—attracts, the mind of, *i.e.* excites his desire for playing. **ढक्का**--ढक् इति कायति (makes a sound like) इति ढक्का; or कै to sound and अ aff. (क), A war drum, the sound of which on being heard fires the spirit of a vanquished king. *Cf*. न ते हुडुक्केन न सोऽपि ढक्कया न मर्दलैः साऽपि न तेऽपि ढक्कया (आच्छादिताः) Nai. XV. 17. Or ढक्का may mean a drum beaten on the festive occasion of the proclamation of victory of a victorious king. स्याद्यशःपटहो ढक्का Ak. जानामि--I know that, I have made up my mind that. सुमेरु--the same as मेरु, a fabulous mountain round which the heavenly bodies are said to revolve and which forms the centre of the several *dvipas* ( sometimes identified with the Himalayas). मेरुर्मध्ये भुवनानां च भर्ता । Kalikapurana. For further information see our note on Ragh I. 14. ०सन्निभं--*i.e.* causing certain ruin and great pain. कोकिलमधुरः—कोकिल must be taken to mean कोकिलरव (the note of the cuckoo) by Lakshana. पाठे--A cry (दान in Marathi) which means in the cant of the gamblers 'a desired throw or turn of the dice (or cowries).' मम--in my favour.

P. 76 लुप्तदण्डक--Defrauder of the money staked. लुप्तं दण्डकं येन. (शिरः) पतति--whirls or becomes dizzy ताडयतः--Because they thought that his falling down was a mere pretext. द्यूतकरमण्डली--The gamblers' association over which Sabhika presided. बद्धोऽसि--You are held bound to it by the association, *i. e.* you are under its arrest and responsible to it for payment. Sabhika gives this decision as the president of the gaming assembly. By the laws of the gaming table the association had the right of enforcing payment even by the detention of the debtor's person. समयः--condition. All gamblers were bound by common consent to abide by the decision of the assembly. So there was no escaping from the payment. गण्डः-- a pledge, surety (लग्नकः); see com ; give a pledge that you would pay at a certain future date if you have no money now. (यदि इदानीं द्रविणं नास्ति तर्हि कालात्यये दातुं लग्नको विधीयतामित्यर्थः । Srinivasacharya ).

अर्धस्य गण्डं करोमि--I will give security for one half. He means to impose upon him by his duplicity. So he gives *Mathura* to understand that at least half the money was safe; but he really meant the half that belonged to the gamester, which has been forgiven him already. अर्धं मुक्त—He asks the two questions in turn, always meaning the different half, while he makes them believe that it was the same half that he referred to They knew his trick, and wishing to befool him say 'मुक्तम्.' सांप्रत गमिष्यामि—I shall go now; my debt is paid off, Mathura having foregone one half and the gamester the other half. प्रयच्छ तद्दश० Here तद् may also be taken to mean तस्मात्—since you do not mean to pay us at all.

P. 78. **भट्टारका:**—Ye honourable men (addressing the people at large ). भट्टं स्वामित्वम् ऋच्छति इति भट्टारक: a master, an honourable man. एकस्य द्यूतकरस्य अर्धे गण्ड: कृत: अपरस्य माथुरस्य अर्धं तेनैव मुक्तम् । यस्य गण्ड: कृतस्तदर्धं द्यूतकरेण मुक्तम् । एवं राशिरेव मुक्त: ( the whole amount is paid off ). **निपुण**--clever or shrewd enough to know what you mean. **धूर्तयामि**--Read धूर्त्ये Pass. 1st sing. of धूर्तय् a denom. from धूर्त as given in the com.; I shall ( not ) allow myself to be treated deceitfully *i. e.* taken in.

**आत्मानं विक्रीय**—A creditor was authorized by the ancient Hindu law to enforce payment of an acknowledged debt by forcing the debtor to work in his service or by dealing with his person in any way he liked. **आकाशे**—'In the air.' This stage-direction is used when a character on the stage addresses a person not present on the stage, hears an imaginary reply from him and gives a reply to that, which is generally introduced by किं ब्रवीषि, कथयसि &c. किं ब्रवीषीति यन्नाट्ये विना पात्रं प्रयुज्यते । श्रुत्वेवानुक्तमप्यर्थं तत्स्यादाकाशभाषितम् ॥ Sah.-Dar. VI. 140. **एष वर्ते**—I am in this plight, I fare thus वर्धे *v. l.* —live, get on. **असिंहासनं—न** विद्यते सिंहासनमस्मिन् he means—a gambler is like a king, except only in that he has no throne.

P. 80. **न गणयति**--does not care for or expect. **अर्थजातं**—(1) the sums staked; (2) amounts ( as revenue and expenditure). **निकाममायदर्शी**—goes with नृपति:. Seeing, *i. e.* making great gains, having a large income. If we read ०दर्शि it may be taken with द्यूतं also. In this case it may also mean—निकामं माया येषां ते निकाममायिन: well-skilled in deceit, great cheats, swindlers; **तान् दर्शयतीति विभववता**-by rich men (न तु निर्धनेन); a king also is waited upon by rich vassals or rich men.

**द्रव्यं लब्धं**—He means-If desired wealth, wife &c. are to be obtained, they can be obtained by means of gambling alone; so complete ruin also follows from gambling.

**त्रेताहृत** &c.--In this sl. the speaker tells us how he lost everything by gambling, thereby illustrating his statement सर्वं नष्टं द्यूतेनैव. त्रेता, पावर, नर्दित and **कट** are technical names for particular throws of cowries which the com. says are respectively called (in northern India) तीया, दूआ, नान्दी (नक्की) and पूरा (Three, Two, Ace and Four), names equally unintelligible to the modern student. Wilson translates these by Tray, Deuce, Ace and doublets (four). "If correct," says Wilson, "the game alluded to is a kind of Hazard: it is played upon a table or cloth with four compartments, called severally Nakki, Dua, Tiya and Chouk or Pura, and by any number of players. Each stakes upon one or other of the compartments whatever sum the caster will set him in. The caster has sixteen cowries which he shakes in his hands and throws on the grouud; those which fall with the value uppermost are counted; and according as they corre pond to either of the divisions, that division sweeps the table. The mode of counting them refers to the favourable mode of telling off articles in India by four; and the number of one, two, &c. are not only those numbers simply, but the same in excess above four and its multiples: thus *Nakki* or Ace is counted by one, five, nine or thirteen cowries; *Dua* or Deuce by two, six, ten or fourteen; *Tiya* or Tray by three, seven, eleven and fifteen; and *Pura* by four, eight, twelve, and sixteen" Wilson further observes--"There is reason to doubt, however, whether the commentator is correct, and the word *Nardita* presents some trace of the word *Nerd*, the game presented to the Indians by the Persians in exchange for Chess, invented according to *Firdusi* by *Buzerjemehr* but improved by him according to other traditions, noticed by the author of the *Burhankati*........ And if they (the Indians) invented Chess, they might very naturally have elaborated out of this game their *Chaupur* or Chaturanga; and it may be doubted whether any other game of tables than *Chaupur* is traceable in Sanskrit books. There is a striking resemblnce between Pasas of the Hindus and Pessos of the Greeks; the latter of which Eyde identifies with dice used in *Nerdiludium.*"

Pandit Harinanda Sastri remarks on this-"We cannot concur with these views. Dice-throw is not referred to here. There is only one throw in this game which is regarded as inauspicious and is represented by त्रिश्र काणे (*lit.* three blinds.) The speaker only alludes to the fourfold cowrie throw which alone ruins the player. The plays referred to are called Soli and Nakkipura. Wilson is wrong to find some trace of Nerd in Nardita. These of course are apparently similar.:...Were the words त्रेता &c. indicative of dice-throws, the speaker could never have said हृतसर्वस्व: &c, as these do not individually ruin the gamester"

त्रेताहृत०—The game went against him four times, instead of improving his fortune. He lost his all by the adverse त्रेता throw. The पावर caused anxiety to him. The नर्दित throw going against him showed him the way out, *i. e.* made it impossible for him to stay there; while the कट ruined him completely—brought about the loss of wealth house, prestige, &c. पूर्वसभिक:-shows that Darduraka lost his money at some other gambling house and that he was Mathura's debtor also and hence his wish to avoid him. सूत्रदरिद्रतां गत:—has become threadbare, its threads being worn out by long use. J V. thinks that the repetition of अय in every line constitutes the fault अनवीकृतत्व mentioned in the Sah.-Dar. ('सदा वहति खे भानु: सदा वहति मारुत:' इत्यादिदर्पणकृदुदाहरणवत् अनवीकृतत्वदोष: स्पष्ट एवाभाति) and proposes to read the last three lines as समन्वितच्छिद्रशतैश्च सर्वश: । न वा तथा प्रावरितुं च ह्वियते ततस्त्वयं संवृत एव शोभते ।। But this spoils the charm which simplicity gives it.

अय तपस्वी—This poor fellow; refers to Mathura. तपस्वी properly means one practising penance; and as such a person has not the means of protecting himself, तपस्वी means one needing help or protection; hence one deserving to be pitied; helpless. Supply मम after कच्छति; Sudraka often leaves such words to be understood. Some take तपस्वी as referring to Darduraka, the speaker himself But it is not a good way. In the first place, the sentence is introduced by अथ वा which is used पक्षान्तरे; 'or why should I veil myself, why should I fear him.' Secondly, in the next sl. he refers to his power of endurance; so how can he call himself helpless (तपस्वी)? Again, had he feared Mathura, he would not have rushed on to rescue संवाहक saying अय दर्दुरो मोचयति (below). Dr. Ryder also thinks that अयं refers to the speaker himself saying "on the one hand it (तपस्वी) means 'poor, unfortunate (varaka),' and on the other hand 'saint'. The second meaning is made almost certain by the fact that each of these speeches is followed by a verse describing ascetic practices" But this does not seem to be the case. There is no reference to ascetic practices. यो हि—अहमिति शेष:.

पादेनैकेन—It appears from this and the next sloka that the art of hardening the body and making it proof against injury or fatigue was cultivated by gamblers like Dar., thieves like Sarvilaka, and such others, as a necessary qualification for their profession. Darduraka means—My power of endurance is so great that I can stand any torture he might put me to, and he will get nothing from me; or—I am physically so strong that Mathura dare not lay violent hands on me.

**खलीक्रियते**—is treated like a villain; *i.e.* is undeservedly maltreated. **धूर्तः**—' a gamester.'

P. 82. **यः स्तब्धं** &c.—The first three lines mention the tortures to which a defaulting debtor was put; he was suspended with his head downwards, or his back was scratched hard by means of rough stones, and dogs were made to bite off his flesh. The sl. means—A man whose body is not inured to such hardships has no business to take to a life of gambling. **आनतशिरः** *v. l.* आनतं शिरः यस्मिन्कर्मणि तद्यथा तथा; adv. comp. **अत्यायत॰**--अत्यायतः very tall चासौ कोमलश्च or अत्यायतं कोमलः extremely delicate. **अव्यायत॰**--*v.l.* noticed by the Com. is better; अव्यायतः (अकृतश्रमः) अत एव कोमलः delicate because of his body not being hardened by physical exercise. **द्यूतप्रसङ्गः**--प्रसङ्ग (प्रसक्ति) great attachment to. L. D. explains this sl as वृक्षादौ समुल्लम्बितो न आस्ते किम् । अपि तु आस्ते एव । अस्य उद्घर्षणेन लोष्टका लोष्टसदृशसूक्ष्मव्रणचिह्नानि तैः सदा यस्य पृष्ठे किणः घट्टा इति प्रसिद्धः न जातः । अपि तु जात एव ।..यस्यैतज्जङ्घान्तरं जङ्घयोर्मध्यं कुक्कुरैः श्वभिर्न चर्व्यंते। चर्व्यंत एवेत्यर्थः । तस्य संवाहकस्येदृशतीव्रवेदनाऽसहिष्णोः अत्यायतस्य अतिदीर्घस्य विपुलशरीरस्येत्यर्थः । तथा कोमलस्य विपरीतलक्षणया कठोरस्येत्यर्थः । सततं द्यूतप्रसङ्गेन किम् । किं दुःखं न किमपीत्यर्थः । It will be seen that this meaning is against the context. Samva. was not a stereotyped gambler like Dardura, who considered gambling 'a kingdom without a throne', but had taken to gambling only recently, and after a few reverses at the table he had found gambling a bed of thorns (कष्ट एष द्यूतकरभावः p. 72). Had he the bitter experiences mentioned in the sl., he would not have turned a Bhikshu.

**कल्यवर्तं**—see p. 24. **लुण्ठीकृतं**—rolled up, folded. **ननु**--surely **कटकरणेन**—By securing the throw of cowries called कट; see sl 9. above. **क्रोडे कृत्वा**—refers to the practice of carrying money tied up in the end of a cloth which is fastened round the loins or thrown across the shoulder. This speech is a retort to Mathura's **पश्यत जर्जरपटप्रावृतः** &c. He means-Does a man who has money make a show of it by carrying lt on his person ?

Certainly not. How do you not know this ? Again, for ten pieces of gold I need not go home and bring them. I can earn them here by gambling successfully.

**दुर्वर्ण**:—A man of low caste, a mean fellow. **विनष्टोऽसि**—implies a curse; 'the deuce take you.' **दशस्व०**—For the sake of a trifle like ten pieces of gold you are depriving a man of his five senses which are irrecoverable. The five *indriyas* referred to here are the five jnanendriyas. **शीलयतु**—शील् 10 conj. to practise repeatedly; *cf.* शीलयन्ति यतयः सुशीलता Kir. XIII. 43; hence, to begin again.

P. 84. **अथं न युक्तं** &c.—is generally taken to mean-Now it is not proper for you to chatter like this. It rather means—After this (*i. e.* when you are simply trifling with me saying दास्यति, न दास्यति &c.) it is not proper to talk with you in this way. 'You who propose thus, pay it off.' **अहमपि नाम** &c.—This sentence is mistranslated by Wilson and some others. **मिथ्याऽऽदर्शयामि** must be read with a *Kaku*; shall I, Mathura, the well known gambler, exhibit gambling as going for nothing ?—*i. e.*, shall I allow the rules and regulations of the institution to be treated as a dead letter, which I shall be doing if I allow Samvahaka or you to cheat me ? No. It is not so much the payment of the sum that is the matter; what is desired is the rigorous observance of the rules of the gambling-house, and in this I fear no one. *Cf.* श्रीनिवासाचार्य—अहमपि नाम माथुरो धूर्तो द्यूतं मिथ्याऽऽदर्शयामीति काकुः। पणमप्रतियाचितं त्यजन् हि द्यूतमेव वितथयति। नाहमेवं द्यूतस्य व्यपदेशं दूषयामीत्यर्थः। नेदं धनस्पृहया पीडनं किं तर्हि द्यूतधर्मरक्षार्थमिति भावः। **खण्डितवृत्तोऽसि**—You have been false to your character as a gambler, since you have become Sam's accomplice in cheating the Association. **एवमेव द्यूतं** etc.—*i. e.*, by allowing your debtor to escape, by allowing the rules of gambling to be set at naught.

**मयैवं द्यूतमा०**—Thus, *i.e.* by helping a sufferer, without torturing a poor debtor. **अन्तरयति**—screens him; hides him from him. **विप्रतीप**—in return; *lit.* in the opposite direction; प्रतीप-(प्रतिगता आपाऽत्र प्रतीपं) against the current of water; fr. प्रति + अप् water, the अ of अप् being changed to ई by द्व्यन्तरुपसर्गेभ्योऽप ईत्। Pan. VI. 3. 97.

**पुंश्चली**—पुंसः स्वपुरुषाच्चलति पुरुषान्तरं गच्छति इति. छिणालिआ is a Prakrit word for पुंश्चली, like गोसाविआ for वेश्या (above). **ताड-**

यिष्यसि—Perhaps the original reading is यदा...ताडयिष्यसे &c.; *i.e.* when I shall lodge a complaint against you for assaulting me and you will be flogged in the royal palace then &c. विरोधित:—made hostile to, or an enemy of, myself. शर्विलकेन—the Brahmana thief mentioned in the 3rd Act. सिद्धादेशेन--सिद्ध: आदेश: यस्य whose telling always comes true, a sooth-sayer. अस्मद्विधो जनस्तमनुसरति—Here we have the first indication of the revolution that was being secretly planned in the city and which forms the underplot of the play.

P. 86. पिधेहि पक्ष०—Shut the door, so that no one else should enter. She gave the order because she did not know exactly by whom the man was pursued.

धनिक:--A creditor; धनमादेयत्वेनास्यास्तीति; धन + इक (ठन्). सांप्रतमपावृणु—When Vasant learnt that it was a creditor whom the man was afraid of she asked the door to be opened; for she knew that if it came to that she could pay the creditor and set free the man But had he been pursued by a king's officer, or a mob, closing the door was the only course she could adopt.

कथं धनिकात् &c—The constr. is धनिकाद्भयकारणं अस्या: तुलितं; held or considered light. तुलितं--what is weighed or balanced; hence, considered to be quite in one's power; and hence, not of great consequence. He is surprised to see that Vasant treated the matter with little concern. भारं तुलितं वहति—तुलितं weighed and compared with one's strength; hence, proportionate to one's strength. लक्षितोऽस्मि—I am observed as to my true character, *i.e.* known to be a debtor. Or, I have become an instance in this case (अस्मिन् श्लोकोक्तविषये वैधर्म्येण दृष्टान्तीभूतोऽस्मि); I gambled and staked money without looking to my means—I undertook responsibilities that were out of proportion to my paying capacity. Mr Raddi also takes the same view when he says स्वस्थितिमनालोच्य द्यूते प्रवृत्तोऽहमित्यर्थस्य मयि समन्वयाल्लक्ष्यतां प्राप्तोऽस्मि. अक्षिणी प्रमृज्य—Now the scene shifts to where we left the gamblers scuffling. कलहायिता:—P. p p. of the Denom. from कलह (कलहाय्) to engage in a quarrel. भूतानि सुवर्णानि—The coins have come to be; *i. e.* are safe; we are sure to get them. He means—Vasantasena is kind-hearted and generous, and is sure to pay off the debt of the man who has sought her protection. *cf.* भूतस्तत्र गण्ड: p 94. Some take भूतानि in the sense of गतानि, but incorrectly. There is no reason why Mathura should have considered the money as lost merely because Samva. entered Vasantasena's house. He had the court of law open to him, and Vasantasena's house was not a house of blackguards. Again, had Mathura given up all hope of the money he could not have said further on एष धूर्तः अतो निष्क्रम्य &c राजकुलं गत्वा &c.—He says–If so, *i. e.* if we are sure to get our money now, let us go, etc.

P. 88 एष धूर्तो &c.--Mathura says–The rogue might take the money from Vasant. and go away. So let us take our money by blocking him up. संज्ञां ददाति--just after Vasant. asked her maid to open the door, she made a sign to her to ask the stranger who he was. गृहपति—The headman of a village. वृत्ति--means of livelihood, profession. कलेति--As an art; for I was the son of a rich man. आहिण्डक—a traveller; from हिण्ड् with आ to wander about. The word has also a technical meaning. It means a man of mixed origin, the son of a Nishada by a Vaidehi woman; आहिण्डिको निषादेन वेदेह्यामेव जायते Manus. X. 37. But it cannot be intended here. दक्षिणतया &c.—On account of his politeness and generous disposition he considers his own self as meant for the use of others.

मनोरथान्तरस्य—मनोरथस्यान्तरस्तस्य the object of desire (of my lady), the darling of. She means—Who is this that has exactly the virtues of Charudatta ?—*i. e.* he must be none else than Charudatta. अनुक्रोशः—compassion; *lit.*. crying after one; *cf.* Eng. 'sympathy,' which etymologically means the same thing. उपरत—ceased to exist; ended.

P. 90. गुणा विभवाश्च–She means–Where there are merits like generosity, compassion, &c., wealth cannot long remain. You can have either the one or the other. अपेयेषु etc.—*i. e.* those whose wealth is not spent in charity or in relieving the distress of the poor, are those who have considerable wealth. तालवृन्तकं गृहाण—This shows her extreme regard for Charudatta, and indicates the further development of her love for him.

कुतः स धनिकः—The phrase, as observed by Dr. Ryder, is intended to be ambiguous. It means–(1) Where is that creditor (of yours, *i.e.* Mathura)? (2) How can he be rich when he has spent much in charity? "The shampooer is shrewd enough to see that it is the hidden meaning which really interests Vasantasena, and answers accordingly." Ryder. सत्कारधनः—Hospitality to others, *i.e.* public esteem arising from it, is the wealth of a good man; and that wealth is everlasting. *Cf* for the idea युक्तः प्रजानामनुरञ्जने स्यास्तस्माद्यशो यत्परमं धनं वः। Uttar. I 11. स पूजाविशेषमपि जानाति—He also knows what distinguished honour is, *i. e.* comes to be highly esteemed; receives special honour; अतो भवती अपि सत्कार्या मम इति भावः। यः पूजयितुमपि न जानाति *v. l.* (does not know how to honour others )-In this case the last quarter must be read as a rhetorical question—स पूजाविशेषमपि जानाति। न जानात्वेव; does he know what special honour is ? He does not. The com. gives the metre of this as मात्रासमक; but it is वैतालीय in which the first and third quarters have 14 syllabic instants, and the second and the fourth 16. The last two lines are irregular. In the last line शे must be read as a short syll. In the third line ण जाणादि makes the metre iregular, or दि must be read as a long syllable. See Appendix on Metres. सवृत्तिः— With means of maintenance, *i e.* wish settled wages or salary. चारित्र्यावशेषः—*i.e.* when reduced to perfect penury.

P. 92. मुषितोऽस्मि-While Vasant. and Samva. are thus conversing, Mathura with the gamester comes to Vasantasena's door and purposely cries loudly to attract attention.

विसंष्ठुलतया—the unsettled state or the shaky condition of; where safety is uncertain. विसंष्ठुलः not stable or firmly fixed तस्य भावः तया. The meaning is—It is natural that servants should wander about in search of support when they find their master's position uncertain or find him unable to support them; so I must help this man. J. V.'s alternative explanation of this, *viz.* "यदा तिर्यञ्चः पक्षिणोऽपि स्वाश्रयस्य नाशे अदर्शने वा तमन्वेष्टुं यतन्ते तदा मानवयोरनयोः (सभिकद्यूतकरयोः) स्वजीविताश्रयीभूतस्य एतस्य नष्टस्याधमर्णस्य अन्वेषणं युक्तमेव," is far-fetched and quite out of place कस्य—goes with जल्पसि. ०दुर्विनीतेन–रते दष्टः अत एव दुर्विनीतः immodest or ill-mannered (as it betrays your lovesports); or it may mean 'obstinate,' and so, bitten in lovesports. Some take it in the sense of दुर्दर्शन, 'unseemly in appearance.' कटाक्षः—a side-glance ; कटं गण्डं अक्षति इति कटाक्षः। कर्मण्यण्. Mathura's addressing the maid in this way indicates the loose character of these gamblers.

ईदृशानि—*i. e.* नास्ति मम विभव इति that you have no money. She means—Gamblers ought to be courtesans' men, since they earn money by easy means.

P. 94. भूतः—fulfilled, redeemed. परिजनहस्तगता—Passed

into the hands of, *i. e.* learnt by; as a return for her favour he offers to teach the art to her servants, as it would be most useful to courtesans. "The phrase is one of exaggerated courtesy. Mistress, if it may be, then let this art remain in the hands of a servant (of yours); that is to say take me into your service." Dr Ryder, who quotes J. V. in support:—परिजनहस्तगता परिजनस्य पोष्यजनस्य ममेति भाव: । सेवकत्वेन मामनुमन्यस्वेति भाव:. But this is not the sense of the passage. And in J V.'s new edition we find परिजनस्य भवत्परिचारिकाया इति यावत् हस्तगता आयत्तीभूता शिक्षिता । त्वया अनुमन्यते चेदहं भवद्गृहे कियत्कालं स्थित्वा भवत्या: सेविकाजनानिमामङ्गमर्दनविद्यां शिक्षयित्वा स्वस्थानं गमिष्यामीति भाव: । **यस्य कृते**—She means Charudatta. 'If it is desired to be learnt, it is for his sake'. This also betrays her extreme love for him. **शाक्यश्र०**—A Buddha-mendicant श्रमणक, though originally meaning any ascetic, came generally to mean a 'Jain mendicant;' and so शाक्य is prefixed to fix its meaning. शाक्य or शाक्यमुनि is a name of Buddha or the last living Buddha. **स्मर्तव्यानि एतानि अक्षराणि**—He means—If by some chance I come to be of any service to you in my character as a शाक्य०, remember that he is no other than Samvahaka, the gambler, thus saved by you. **अलं साहसेन**—The life of Bud. and Jain mendicants was looked upon with a sort of odium in those days; *cf.* Das.-Ch. मम तु मन्दभाग्यस्य निन्द्यवेषं अभन्ददु:खायतनं &c. p 75.

**विहस्तं**—Commentators vary in their interpretation of this word, and it is difficult to know what this exactly means. The best way seems to be द्यूतेन मम तत् दशान्तरं कृतं (referring to his resolve to be a Bud. mendicant) यत्सर्वस्य जनस्य विहस्तं (विगत: हस्त: यस्मिन्), in which no man can lay his hands on me no man will get me into his clutches; for gambling has led me to renounce the world. *Cf.* Wilson—' In bidding adieu to gambling the hands of men are no longer armed against me.' Another way is यत्सर्वस्य जनस्य विहस्तं व्याकुलत्वं सर्वस्माज्जनाद्व्याकुलत्वं (the state of being harassed or persecuted by all) तत् द्यूतेन कृतम् । विहस्तव्याकुलौ समौ ' इति कोशात् । भावप्रधाने निर्देशे विहस्तत्वमिति लभ्यते. विहस्त: *lit.* one without (the use of hands; hence, one not knowing what to do, perplexed; *cf.* रामापरित्राणविहस्तयोधं Ragh. V. 49; and lastly, by metonymy, it means विहस्तत्वं But here we arrive at the meaning in a roundabout way. J. V. says विहस्तं व्याकुलं व्याकुलीकरणमित्यर्थ: । अवमाननमिति यावत्. L. D's explanation also is not satisfactory. बिम्यते in P.'s com. should be भीयते-यत्सर्वस्माज्जनाद्भीयते भयं प्राप्यते तत् &c.—'to a state in which one is to fear all;' this is easier, but we do not know what P's reading was. Dr. Ryder prefers Stenzler's reading बीहच्छं (बीभत्सं), a condition that fills all with disgust or dismay.

प्रकटशीर्षं :—With face openly displayed; *i.e.* having nothing to fear. खुण्टमोडक:—Prakrit for ०मोटक:; खुण्टं स्तम्भं मोटयति breaks इति दुष्ट--naughty, unmanageable, roguish विचरति—*v. l* विकलयति throws into agitation, frightens. गन्धगज—a species of elephant having a strong scent that repels ordinary elephants; see com.

P. 96. विकट—formidable (as it was disordered in his scuffle with the elephant). दुर्मनुष्य—an ill-mannered fellow; she calls him thus because he entered rudely. वञ्चिताऽसि--वञ्चित in such cases means—deprived of something fortunate or precious; hence, unfortunate. Here वञ्चिताऽसि means—You are deprived of what you would have been very glad to see; hence, you lost a sight. This shows that Karna (as his name 'the ear ornament' implies) was a favourite of Vasantasena.

आलान—see I. 50 महामात्रं—महती मात्रा worth यस्य असौ महामात्र: the chief elephant-driver (being the keeper of the गन्धगज); 'महामात्र: समृद्धे चामात्ये हस्तिपकाधिपे इति मेदिनी. The use of this word shows that Vasant. had more than one elephant. विचलति &c—explains the panic and the consequent confusion of the women folk छिद्यन्ते—their girdles snapped as they dashed against one another. रत्नाङ्कुर—The spars or shooting rays of jewels. फुल्लन०—A tank with full-blown lotuses in it; फुल्लानि नलिनानि यस्यां सा ताम्. The elephant got loose at a time when the people were out and Ujja. war bristling with the faces of men and women. परिभ्रष्टे०—परिभ्रष्टे दण्ड: कुण्डिकाभाजनं च यस्य तम्. शीकरै:—with the spray of water from his trunk.

P. 98. शृङ्खलाकलापं—a number of chains (tied to the legs and neck). उद्वहन्त—This should have been dropped as we have it again in the same line and the repetition does not look good, ०कलापं being in this case taken as a Bah. वामचरणेन &c.—This phrase is another knotty point in this Act and has caused great difficulty to the commentators. The first difficulty is about the meaning of द्यूतलेखक Srinivasacharya gives a far-fetched explanation; he supposes that the gambling-house was near at hand;

and that Karna. called out to the scribe attached to the house to give him an iron bar, and takes वामपादेन with गृहीत्वा; द्यूतलेखकं द्यूते लेखनाधिकृतं पुरुषमुद्घुष्योद्घुष्य लोहदण्डग्रहणार्थमाहूयाहूय तस्मिन्ननागते इति शेष: । He also takes द्यूतलेखक to refer to Samvahaka, like other commentators, and says यद्वा द्यूतलेखकं तमेव द्यूतकरं परिव्राजकीभूतमित्यर्थ: उद्घुष्योद्घुष्य मा भैषीरिति पुन: पुनराश्वास्येत्यर्थ:. This meaning will do; but here the difficulty is, how could Karna. recognize Samvahaka in the apparent monk, in the hurry and confusion of the hour and when the shampooer was clean shaven and had his features altered ? Again, Karna. was not near Vasant. in the course of the conversation that took place between him and her. Thirdly, Samva. was not द्यूतलेखक but द्यूतकर. But unless we make such a supposition, no meaning can be given to the line. Perhaps Karna. had often seen Samva. at the gambling-house and knew him so well as to recognize him at once. He only calls him द्यूतलेखक instead of द्यूतकर; or this difficulty can be got over by read ing द्यूतखेलकं for द्यूतलेखकं This conceded, the constr. is—त्वरितमापणात् लोहदण्डं गृहीत्वा वामचरणेन वक्रगत्या द्यूतलेखकं उद्घुष्योद्घुष्य आकारित: &c I, having quickly snatched an fron bar from an adjoining shop and moving is a zigzag way before the elephant to avoid being struck by him, and calling out to the gambler to take courage, &c. ( He had to move in that way before the elephant in order to be able to hit a blow so as to avoid the mendicant from being struck). No other meaning can be reasonably assigned to वामचरणेन. Srinivasacharya says वामचरणेन सव्यपादेन त्वरितमापणाल्लोहदण्डमायसीं यष्टिं गृहीत्वा । हस्तेन ग्रहणे हि नमन्तं हस्ती गृह्णीयाद्विलम्बश्च स्यादिति पादेन ग्रहणं &c. This is anything but satisfactory Karna. could have easily gone from behind the elephant to get an iron bar and taken it more quickly with the right hand. Dr. Ryder says—"The word लेखक is used in II. 2, where it plainly has the meaning 'a ( gambling ) score, Stenzler's *Chhaya* is right, I think, in taking उग्घुसिअ as the representative of उद्घृष्य, rather than of उद्घुष्य. The phrase then becomes simple enough: "stumbling with my left foot over a gambler's score." The suddenly metamorphosized shampooer has forgotten to rid himself of his gambling paraphernalia, which he drops when attacked by the elephant." But this is supposing too much. If the shampooer had time to change his dress and take the paraphernalia of a Bud. ascetic, he had time also to put aside his gambling implements. Again, the repetition of उद्घृष्य implies a repeated effort to push aside the thing; and even supposing the monk had his score with him, it could not have been so heavy as to require such an effort to push it aside. So this view is not acceptable.

**विषमभरा०**—Pressed down with unevenly placed load.

**मदगन्धेन**—For his nose was still stuffed up with the strong odour of the elephant's ichor. **इदं नाम**--The custom of marking garments with the owner s name is again referred to in the eighth Act in Sakara's speech (अथ वा नामाङ्कित एषः).

P. 100 **इतिवाचयित्वा** &c.—She had done the same before 'दत्तं किमपि कान्तेन धृत्वाऽङ्के मुहुरीक्षते' इत्यादिवचनात् अत्र कान्तत्यक्तवस्त्रग्रहणमनुरक्ताया अनुरागप्रकटनार्थम्। J. V. **सांप्रतं**—now that he got a reward far costlier than the mantle. **अलिन्दकं**--अल्यते भूष्यते इति अलिन्दकः; fr. अल् and aff. इन्द (किन्दच्); अलिन्द एव अलिन्दकः a dais near a door. Also written as आलिन्दः-दकः.

## ACT III

As the play is a Prakarana, this Act is not introduced either by a Pravesaka or a Vishkambhaka. It is meant for the introduction of the thief Sarvilaka, who takes a prominent part in the revolution which forms the underplot of the play. It is introduced by the direct entrance of Vardhamanaka, Charudatta's servant, who indirectly refers in the first sl. to Aryaka, the hero of the underplot and prophesied to be the king of Ujjayini, and to Palaka its present king. The theft committed is also necessary for the further development of the plot, and serves the purpose of introducing Dhuta, Charudatta's wife, as one entirely devoted to her husband, ready to sacrifice anything to uphold his fair name.

P. 102. **सुजनः खलु** &c.—Here he refers to his master Charudatta. who though poor was lovėd by his servants. **द्रव्यगर्वितः**—गर्वः अस्य संजातः असौ गर्वितः । द्रव्येण गर्वितः द्रव्यगर्वितः **दुष्करः**—hard to please or serve. This is a reference to Sakara; see X. 52.

**योऽपि स्वाभा०**—Here he refers to some of the innate virtues of Charudatta, which being carried to excess turn into faults, such as kindliness of heart, liberality of mind, courtesy, &c.

[ Readings in the foot-note :— ] **कुभृत्यपालक**—Here कु has a diminutive force, the protector of even ordinary servants, *i. e.* who does not deprive poor men in his service of food, although they happen to be men of no ability. **अप्रभुरपि**—Although not a man of power. **लक्ष्मीविभवा०**—Propped up by the power of wealth, having great wealth and hence द्रव्य० or **लक्ष्मीविभवैरव०**—resorted to, served by rich men. **त्रपुषस्य**—of cucumber. **तिक्तं**—bitter; तिक्त in other cases means unwelcome, unpleasant, or uncovetable, and an object of disrespect, respectively. Omit the न after तिक्ता. प्रथमकालं—at first; असती—immodest; सा सतीत्वे (when acting like a woman of family) गर्वति feels proud; प्रथमं दीर्घमञ्चलं आच्छादयति (which modest women do).

P. 104. **गान्धर्व**—Music (गन्धर्वस्य इदं); the Gandharvas being the heavenly musicians, the science of music is named after them.

(गान्धर्वं वेद). **रेभिलेन**--Rebhila, it seems, was a friend of Char., being a सार्थवाह like himself and an expert singer; see p. 152 where he is spoken of as a friend of Sarvilaka also, since the latter sends his wife to his house.

**वीणा**—A lute*; said to be invented by Narada; it had seven strings ( see *infra* V. 11. ), and it is therefore different from the modern *Tambura*. **असमुद्रोत्थितं रत्नं**—He raises Vina to to the high level of the fourteen jewels churned out of the ocean, given in the following well-known sl.—लक्ष्मीः कौस्तुभपारिजातकसुरा धन्वन्तरिश्चन्द्रमा गावः कामदुघाः सुरेश्वरगजो रम्भादिदेवाङ्गनाः । अश्वः सप्तमुखो विषं हरिधनुः शङ्खोऽमृतं चाम्बुधे रत्नानीह चतुर्दश प्रतिदिनं कुर्युः सदा मङ्गलम् ॥ The poet is fond of such an expression; *cf.* द्यूतं हि नाम पुरुषस्यासिंहासनं राज्यम् p. 78.

**उत्कण्ठितस्य**--one longing for the company of his beloved. **संकेतकः**--A lover who makes an appointment for meeting at a particular time. **सं थापना**--The means of composing or steadying the mind. *Cf.* Megh. II. 26, 27. **रक्त**--A person deep in attachment.

**भाव०**—भावो विद्वान् Ak.; used as a title of honour. **काकली**--a low soft tune. **नस्या**--a rope or rein passed through the nose of drift cattle. **वृद्धपुरोहितः**--who also repeats the *mantras* in a low tone.

सुष्ठु &c.--The encomium bestowed a second time on Rebhila's singing shows that Charudatta was exceedingly pleased by it.

**रक्तं**--Full of passion. **समं**--smooth; with the musical tunes well-balanced. These terms may also have their technical sense as given in the Naradasiksha (which enumerates ten special merits of गान)--तत्र रक्तं नाम वेणुवीणास्वराणामेकीभावे रक्तमित्युच्यते; *i. e.* in perfect harmony with instrumental music. मधुरं नाम स्वरभावोपनीतललितपदाक्षरगुणसमृद्धम् । व्यक्तं ( स्फुटं ) नाम पदपदार्थविकारागमलोपकृत्तद्धित...विभक्त्यर्थवचनानां सम्यगुपपादनं; *i. e.* having grammatical purity. **भावान्वितं**--emotional; *lit.* accompanied by the manifestation of internal feeling **ललितं**—graceful; मृदुपदवर्णस्वरादियोगात्सुकुमारम्. **अन्तर्हिता** &c.--He means--The voice of the singer was

---

* "A description of it may be found in the first volume of the *Researches*; it is an instrument of much sweetness and compass, but has little power," Wilson.

so soft, melodious and attractive that one would think it was some female disguised as Rebhila that was singing.

P. 106 **स्वरसंक्रमं**—The proper succession of notes, cadence. **मृदुगिरः**–qualifies तस्य. Some suggest that it may be taken as an obj. to शृण्वन्; but it has no propriety; it also breaks symmetry. **श्लिष्टं**–harmoniously blended. मूर्छनान्तरगतं, तारं and मृदु qualify both स्वरसंक्रम and तन्त्रीस्वन. L–D. is inaccurate in saying इदं विशेषणत्रयं तन्त्रीस्वनस्येति बोध्यम्. **मूर्छना**—The gradual or duly regulated rising and falling of sounds (conducting the air and the harmony through the keys in a pleasing manner, or passing from one key to another). The Sl quoted by L–D (see com.) gives the definition of ग्राम; for Malli on Sis. I. 10 quotes the Sl., though he gives the last half as तथा स्वराणां संदोहो ग्राम इत्यभिधीयते ॥ Malli. quotes the Def. of मूर्छना as क्रमात्स्वराणां सप्तानामारोहश्चावरोहणम् । सा मूर्छेत्युच्यते ग्रामस्था एताः सप्त सप्त च ॥ For further information see Malli 's com. on the above Sl **०न्तरगतं**—the voice passing from one *murchhana* to another. **तारं**—high-pitched. **हेलासं०**—हेला has a technical meaning (see com.); 'restrained from straying into a wrong note.' **राग०**—repeated through enthusiastic fondness or passion for music *Cf.* with this व्यक्तिर्व्यञ्जनधातुना दशविधेनाप्यत्र लब्धामुना &c. Nag. I. 14, and अङ्गैरन्तर्निहितवचनैः सूचितः सम्यगर्थः Malav. II. 8. **रथ्याविभागाः**—the branches of the streets.

**अस्तं व्रजति**—This must be the half moon of the eighth day, as it was a little after midnight that Char. came home. This mention of the setting of the moon, which is necessary for Sarvilak's introduction, shows that there is an interval of about fifteen days between the events of the last Act and those of this; see Introd. Time-Analysis. **पादौ धावितुं**—The custom of washing the feet on coming home still obtains among the Hindus. "It was equally the practice of the Greeks; thus *Philocleon* in the *Wasps*:

"Next my girl, sprightly nymph, brings her napkin and lymph,
Feet and ankles are quick in ablution."

**अलं सुप्तजनं** &c.—This shows Charudatta's tenderness of feeling towards his servants, and also brings out the nobility of his mind. *Cf* for the use of अलं with the Inf अलमात्मस्तवं कर्तुं Pancharatra II, and अलमात्मानं खेदयितुं Veni. II. p. 43.

P. 108. **यथा डुण्डुभः**—Vidu humourously compares himself to a *dundubha* for which nobody cares; so he being a Brahmana without the qualifications of one, deserves not such regard from anyone. निद्राचौरं—It did not allow him to sleep comfortably, as he had to guard it carefully during the night. नापहरति—This is meant to serve as a precursor of Sarvilaka's entrance on the stage. अभ्यन्तरचतुःशालं—*i.e.* where Charu.'s wife kept her ornaments. Charu , who had great regard for his wife, would not like the idea of having the ornaments worn by a public woman kept in a spot where his own wife placed hers, and hence he says अलं &c.

ललाटदेशात्—The first impulse to sleep is felt in the forehead; old age also is metaphorically said to come over a man from the forehead, as its first sign, the greyness of hair is first observed round the forehead. *Cf.* the well known sl कृतान्तस्य दूती जरा कर्णमूले समागत्य वक्तीति लोकाः शृणुध्वम् । &c. The sl. occurs in the Charu. with the readings अदृश्यमाना and मनुष्यवीर्यम्.

P. 110 परिणाहः—'bulk'; implies hugeness of body. शिक्षा—training in the art of thieving. कर्ममार्ग—an opening or breach in the wall; a technicality of thieves. निर्मुच्यमानः—being left by the slough or outer skin; *i. e.* casting off his slough जीर्णतनुं—*v l.* In this case निर्मुच्यमानः must be taken in an active sense, as the pres. part of the root मुच् A'., being included in the list of roots of the 4th class. This sl. is the same as Charu III. 5.

नृपतिपुरुष &c.—In this sl the night allowing him to do his work under cover of dense darkness is compared to a mother. The comparison may not be stretched beyond this. If necessary, however, the epithets may be made applicable to both. नृपतिपुरुष—(1) the city-guards; (2) king's officers प्रचार—(1) movements, treadings; (2) course of conduct. परगृह॰—For comp. see com दूषण—(1) despoiling of; committing a theft in; (2) परगृहदूषण bringing great disgrace to the family घनतिमिर॰ भावाः (1) things; (2) feelings. घनपटलतमोनिरुद्धतारा *v. l.*—घनं thick पटलं mass यस्य तादृक् तमः तेन निरुद्धास्ताराः यस्यां in which the stars are obstructed, *i. e.* hidden by the dense darkness; or घनपटलेन तमसा च by the mass of clouds and darkness But this reading does not give a good meaning as applying to the mother. The other meaning is—'whose pupil (तार) is obstructed, *i. e.* obscured, by the darkness caused by dense opacity, or obstructed by cataract and blindness.' But this has no propriety. There is some objection to the comp. एकवीर; strictly the proper form is वीरैक:, by पूर्वापरप्रथम...मध्यमवीराश्च Pan. II. 1. 58. So this should be taken as irregular: कथमेकवीर इति । पूर्वकालैकेति (by this the form should be एकवीर) बाधित्वा परत्वात् (the first Sutra being overruled by this, which is subsequent) समासे वीरैक इति स्यात् । बाहुलकाद्भविष्यति । Sid Kau. The alternative explanation suggested in the Manorama and the Tattvabodhini is एकेषु वीरयते इति. In the present case we may take the comp. as एक: असहाय: वीर:. **दूषयामि**—Injure, spoil, *i. e.* make a hole in it.

P. 112. **कामं** &c.—**कामं** 'I grant that'; this particle is used when the speaker gives his consent unwillingly, or not fully. **वर्धते**—gains ground is better accomplished. This gives the हेतु of its being called नीच. **वञ्चनापरिभव**:—insult in the form of deception; or वञ्चनया परिभव: getting the better of them by deception. **वचनीयता**—a censurable deed. **मार्गो ह्येष** *scil.* gaining one's end by foul means. **नरेन्द्र०**—सौप्तिक from सुप्त + इक (ठञ्); see com.; that which belonged to, hence happened in, sleep Sar. means—When a great warrior like Asva. slaughtered sleeping kings, it would be no heinous crime to commit a theft. When almost all the warriors on the side of the Kauravas were killed and Duryodhana lay mortally wounded, Asva. one night saw an owl quietly killing its enemies at night while they were in sleep. This furnished him a hint as to what was to be done, and he at night stealthily entered the camp of the Pandavas while they were absent from it, killed their sons, and also slaughtered Dhrishtadyumna and Sikhandin and then went away. See A. Dic. The sl. occurs in the Charu. with the variants विबुधा: सुप्तेषु यद्वर्तते विश्वस्तेषु हि...शौर्यं न कार्कश्यता । वचनीयताऽपि तु...मार्गश्चैष.

**दर्शनान्तरगत:**—standing within range of sight; easily visible. **कराल**:—unevenly formed, rough; or wide. P. takes दर्शनान्तरगत: in the sense of 'according to the principles of, or as found in the special science of, thieving; and कराल in that of 'not opposed to or against the direction of science.' But this is far-fetched. He merely means—'where the breach will not easily attract the attention of policemen,' while he is in the house. **लोष्टककृशं**—Properly कृशलोष्टकं; so this must be taken as a comp of the आहिताग्नि class **स्त्रीजन० न भवेत्**—The Sastra advises thieves to avoid the sight of women; for, women being light in their sleep might at once raise an alarm on beholding a thief, and no violent hands can be laid on them. The sl. occurs in the Charu. with the readings--छेदादशब्दो भवेत् भित्तीनां क्व नु दर्शिनान्तरसुखः, चलेष्टककृशं, कुत्र स्त्री० स्वन्तश्च यत्नो भवेत् ॥.

नित्यादित्य &c.--Arghyas were offered to the sun every day at his rise, and water thrown on the ground near the wall, which was thus weakened by being constantly moistened. मूषिकोत्कर—rubbish thrown up by the mice; उत्कीर्यते इति उत्करः fr. कृ and aff. अ (अप्). स्कन्दपुत्राणां—In such cases पुत्र has the sense of 'a pupil or follower of;' here 'thieves,' the devotees of Skanda. *Cf.* भरतपुत्र an actor. Strangely enough Skanda, the elder son of Siva, is regarded like his mother Chandika, as the patron-deity of thieves, resembling in this respect the Grecian Mercury, and St. Nicholas of England. सिद्धिल०--*viz.* the discovery of a suitable ground for the breach. कनकशक्तिः—The wielder of the golden spear (Sakti is a kind of weapon), Karttikeya. See, however, next page.

P. 114. पद्मव्याकोशं &c.--The first two lines mention the names, which are self-explanatory, of the seven kinds of breaches to be made in a brick wall. पद्मव्या०--*i. e.* having the shape of a full-blown lotus. बालचन्द्र--crescent shaped. वापी--round like a wall. विस्तीर्णं—oblong in shape. स्वस्तिकं--of the shape of a *Svastika* ( a kind of auspicious diagram ) *i. e.* with a large gap in the centre with five triangles all round. शिल्प--architectural skill. In the Charu. the names are differently given, *viz.* सिंहाक्रान्तं पूर्णचन्द्रं झषास्यं चन्द्रार्धं वा व्याघ्रवक्त्रं त्रिकोणम् । संधिच्छेदः पीठिका वा गजास्यमस्मत्पक्ष्या विस्मितास्ते कथं स्युः ॥

विषमासु कल्प०--Hard structures; buildings so constructed as to keep off thieves or to baffle their attempts at house-breaking. कल्पनासु does not mean 'creations of breach.' दोषांश्च मे वदति—People have pointed out my faults. It seems from this that in his previous thefts Sar. had tried the other kinds of breaches and was found fault with. He, therefore, thinks of the *Kumbha* kind now This Sl occurs in the Charu. with the readings--अद्यास्य भित्तिषु ... च्छेदात्समासु सकृदर्पितकाकलीषु । काल्यं विषादविमुखः प्रतिवेशवर्गो...वदतु कर्मसु. कुमारकार्त्तिकेयाय--Karttikeya in his military character resembles the Grecian Mars. Although the son of Siva, he is variously called as Karttikeya, Sarajanman, Agnibhu, &c. For the story of his birth see A. Dic. He led the divine army against the powerful demon Taraka whom he slew, and so is named सेनानी. He is called Kumara because of his vow ever to

5

remain a celibate. He is worshipped by the people for the recovery of stolen property. And it is for this reason perhaps that thieves paid their homage to him, though he slowly lost his character as the patron of thieves afterwards. In the Charu. Sajjalaka says-नमः खरपटाय । नमो रात्रिगोचरेभ्यो देवेभ्यः.

**नमः कनकशक्तये** &c.--Some think that Kanak., Bhaskaranandin and Yogacharya are three writers on, and the teachers of, the art of thieving. It seems, however, from the epithets कनक०, ब्रह्मण्य० and देवव्र०, that Karttikeya himself is meant again, a double salutation being due to him on account of his being the परमगुरु ब्रह्मणि साधुः ब्रह्मण्यः favourable to the Brahmanas or the Vedic law; स चासौ देवश्च. **देवव्रत**--देवानां व्रतं यस्मिन् fit to be worshipped even by the gods; or it may mean 'whose law is divine (Vedic).' **योगाचार्य**—The reputed author of a treatise on the black art. The Das.-Ch attributes the authorship of the standard work on house-breaking to Karnisuta; see p. 76. **योगरोचना**--a magic ointment. योगेन साधिता रोचना योगरोचना; योग in such cases means 'having magic virtue;' *cf.* योगचूर्ण, योगवर्ति &c. **समालब्ध**--annointed or besmeared with. **प्रमाणसूत्रं**--प्रमाणार्थं सूत्रं a measuring tape or thread. For the implements of a thief *cf.* **बद्धतीक्ष्णकौक्षेयकः फणिमुख** (a hoodshaped instrument for diggging) काकलीसंदंशकपुरुषशीर्षकयोगचूर्णयोगवर्तिकामानसूत्रकर्कटकरज्जुदीपभाजनभ्रमरकरण्डकप्रभृत्यनेकोपकरणकयुक्तः &c:; Das.-Ch. II. p. 77.

**संप्रयोगान्**—the fastenings of; the sacred thread serves as a cord for loosening bracelets &c **उद्घाटकः**--The opener of, *i.e.* by helping in the operation. **यन्त्रदृढे**— held fast by a bolt or latch &c. **परिवेष्टन**--a ligature, a tourniquet.

P. 116. **स्वस्थः**--स्वस्मिन् ( one's original state ) तिष्ठतीति; restored to health. **शिखा प्रदीपस्य** &c --Here we have a fine simile. As soon as he made a small opening in the wall, the reddish yellow light of the lamp burning inside streamed through it and lay on the ground surrounded by darkness, and looked like a streak of gold on a black touch stone. **प्रतिपुरुष**--A dummy or effigy of a man ( probably the head only, see the quotation from the Das.-Ch. above ) made of wood, straw or some such material, to be first inserted in the hole for ascertaining if any of the inmates of the house were awake. Such a precaution was necessary for a thief; for in case some one was awake in the house the dummy would be caught and the thief would escape.

**प्रतीक्ष्य**--Having waited; that is 'gently;' or, पृष्ठेन प्रतीक्ष्य may mean 'looking behind, to see if any body was coming.' **लक्ष्यसुप्त**–pretending to sleep, feigning sleep, as opposed to परमार्थसुप्त. **त्रासयित्वा**--Disturbing or frightening them, by raising a sword before them, or holding the lamp before their eyes, and so on.

शङ्कित:--शङ्का अस्य संजाता असौ, *i.e.* betraying fear. **सुविशद:**—quite distinct, showing that the respiration is free. **तुल्यान्तरं**—(the inhalations and exhalations) happening at equal intervals; regular (being natural). **स्वप्नान्तरं वर्तते** *v.l.*–the subj. is नि:श्वास:; goes on in sleep (looks like that of a man in deep sleep). **विकला**—partially open (विगता कला यस्या:). **स्रस्त** &c.—See com. स्रस्त—relaxed. शिथिल—lying loosely This sl. is found in the Charu. with the readings---विषमस्तुल्यान्तरं जायते गात्रं संधिषु दीर्घतामुपगतं... दृष्टिर्गा०..चपलं पक्ष्मान्तरं जायते दीपं चैव...दभिमुख: स्याल्लक्ष्यसुप्तो यदि ॥

दर्दुर—a kind of flute. **वंशा:**—Bamboo-pipes; windinstruments. **पुस्तका**:—images or dolls made of wood, cloths &c. useful for being exhibited; मृदा वा दारुणा वाऽथ वस्त्रेणैवाथ चर्मणा । लोहरत्नै: कृतं वाऽपि पुस्तमित्यभिधीयते ॥ *Cf* पुस्तकमय्यपि इन्द्रजालमाचरति Kad. p. 174. The *mas.* gender is irregulas. **भवनप्रत्ययात्**—Through belief, *i. e.* expectation created by the grand appearance of the building.

P. 118. **तन्ममापि नाम शर्विलकस्य** &c.—This passage is misunderstood by Dr. Ryder. The meaning is–'Can any treasure be hidden to me, Sarvilaka (such an adept in the art of thieving)? That is, 'I can find out any hidden treasure by my art' Nearly the same expression occurs at p. 120 *Cf.* for a similar construction–आ: ममापि नाम दुर्योधनस्य शङ्कास्थानं पाण्डवा: Veni. II. p. 50; or ममापि नामाश्वत्थाम्न: अनिमित्तानि समरगमनविघ्नमुत्पादयन्ति । *Ibid.* III. p. 59. **न स्फारीभवति**—does not expand or multiply; a *chvi*-formation. According to the treatise on house-breaking, enchanted seeds, when scattered on the ground, expand or multiply where there is a treasure buried underneath.

**उत्स्वप्नायते**—Talks in sleep; a Denom. Atm. fr. उत्स्वप्न; उद्गत: प्रलपितादिना प्रकटीभूत: स्वप्न: यस्य स उत्स्वप्न: स इवाचरति । अन्ये तु सान्द्रनिद्रित एव जनो यत्र जल्पत्याक्रोशति हसति रोदिति विपरिवर्तते उत्तिष्ठति च स उच्यते उत्स्वप्न: इति । स्वप्नविशेष इत्यर्थ: । अत एव उत्कृष्ट: स्वप्न उत्स्वप्न इत्यवयवार्थोऽपि संगच्छते इत्याहु: । Srinivasacharya.

**भो वयस्य** &c.--The thought of theft was uppermost in the mind of Vidu. when he went to bed, and so he thus raves in his sleep. **लघुत्वात्**—Being weak-minded, through timidity. **जर्जरस्नान०**—A tattered bathing-garment. This belonged to the Vidu., and so he asks for it when Vas. comes to see Char. **गोब्राह्मणकाम्यया**—काम्या desire. Here the word must not be formed by affixing काम्यच् to ब्राह्मण (like पुत्रकाम्या; see Ragh. I. 35), as that will mean 'desire for a Brahmana', but by deriving the word काम्या separately from कम् and aff. य. The desire of a Brahmana and a cow must not be disregarded, both being objects of veneration. One disappointing them is guilty of great sin. See com. In the Char. Vid. says—मम ब्रह्मत्वेन शापितोऽसि यदि न गृह्णासि। Hence Sar. says अनतिक्रमणीया भ० etc. **अथवा**—'or rather, I shall not take it;' so this has the force of 'but' here **अस्ति**—is used here as an introductory particle. **आग्नेयः**—अग्नेः अयं that deals with (*i. e.*extinguishes) fire.

P. 76. **यात्वैव**—The reading यात्येव will require च after विचरति. The other reading has no propriety. **भद्रपीठ**—name of the insect. **ब्राह्मणकुले कृतमन्धकारं**—That is—I have tarnished the fair name of my family by this foul deed. न धिक्कृतमन्ध०—*v.l.* I did not despise this darkness, *viz.* the foul deed. **अप्रतिग्राहकस्य**—A Brahmana who does not accept a gift is considered as honourable; *cf.* प्रतिग्रहसमर्थोऽपि नादत्ते यः प्रतिग्रहम् । ये लोका दानशीलानां स तानाप्नोति पुष्कलान् ॥ Yaj. S. I. 213. प्रतिग्रह brings on loss of Brahamanic power; *cf.* प्रतिग्रहेण ह्यस्याशु ब्राह्मं तेजः प्रशाम्यति । Manus. IV. 186. **प्रणयं करोमि**—I will gratify his request; for this meaning of प्रणय, *cf.* नार्हसि त्वं संबधिनो मे प्रणयं विहन्तुम् । Ragh. II. 58; *supra*, I. 45; and *infra*, after VII. 6 **अग्रहस्तः**—अग्रश्चासौ हस्तश्च । Karm comp.; in a Karm. there must be सामानाधिकरण्य, as in the case of नीलोत्पल, both being identical. But हस्त and अग्र are not identical; however, they may be so regarded through their relation of अवयव (a part) and अवयवी (the whole of which it is a part); *cf.* Vamana हस्ताग्राग्रहस्तादयो गुणगुणिनोर्भेदाभेदात् । (तत्र भेदात् हस्ताग्रादयः । अभेदादग्रहस्तादयः); Ala. Sut. V. 2. 20.

P. 120. **महाब्राह्मण**—said in joke; see *supra*, p. 48. **अनिर्वेदित** &c.—The commentators take this in the sense of 'undecided'; नितरां वेदितं निर्वेदितं न निर्वे० अनिर्वे०; poverty in which one's valour remains undecided, as to the doing of a thing good or bad. But the usual sense of निर्वेद is 'disgust for, objection'; so it seems better to take अनिर्वेदित in the sense of 'in which prowess does not feel disgust at doing even a censurable thing;' poverty forces a man to exert his strength even in doing a reprehensible act;'

this explains why he says धिगस्तु &c.; the second half also is in better accord with this explanation. अनिर्वेदित० *v. l.*—which does not allow one to display one's power. It is difficult to see how some commentators derive the meaning अगणित from this. This sl. occurs in the Charu. with the readings अनिर्वेदं च यौवनम् । यदिदं दारुणं.

**ममापि नाम**—That is, are they of any account to me, does Sar. care for these ? *Cf. supra* p. 118, l. 2.

**क्रमणे**—In jumping over; or, in climbing. **ग्रहालु०**—see com.; in seizing and tearing to pieces. **सुप्तासुप्त०**—*i.e.* in seeing whether a man is fast asleep or only lightly sleeping.

**माया**—magic; or, the power by which one creates fantoms or illusory forms; or this may mean 'the yaugic or willpower by which one can create things;' *cf.* for this sense माया-विकल्परचितैरपि ये तदीयैः &c. Ragh. XIII. 75. **रूपशरीर** &c.—changing the features, distorting the body, changing the dress, &c. in such a way as not to be recognizable by others. डुडुभः (or—मः)–Perhaps this is the same as डुण्डुभ that has occurred before; see p. 108. It is a very tenacious reptile and remains fast-stuck to something when an attempt is made to drive it away. Here various senses are attributed to it, *e. g.* झटिति छिद्रान्तरप्रवेशपटुर्गृहगोधिका (a lizard) स्वात्मरक्षासमर्थः सरटः ( a chameleon, सरडा or घोरपड in Marathi ); अश्वतरः (a mule) &c. But these senses are conjectural. The Sl. occurs in the Charu with the readings प्लवने वृकोऽपसरणे श्येनो गृहालोकने निद्रा सुप्त० संसर्पणे...। माया वर्णशरीरभेदकरणे...संकटे च तिमिरं वायुः.

**भवनावलोकने**—in kenning or inspecting the ground to find a place for hiding in.

P. 122. **चौरं कर्तयित्वा**—Vidu., not knowing that Rad. was really serious, speaks in a jesting vein, as is usual with him.

**हताश**—हताः आशाः यस्य (one whose hopes are frustrated (on account of their wickedness); this has become slang for 'you cursed or wretched fellow.' **अहो दर्शनीयः** &c.—Mark the nobility of Charu.'s mind. Instead of getting agitated he praises the art of the robber. **शिरसि तनुः**—Because the breach was of the form of a *Kumbha*. **असदृशजन०**—संप्रयोग action, operation. Charu. thinks that the noble edifice was, as it were, afraid of the insult it would receive by being touched and worked upon by an improper man.

वेदितवान्—Properly this should be विदितवान्; so this must be taken as the Act p p. of विद् cau. in the primitive sense (स्वार्थिकणिचि निष्ठायां रूपम्). Charu. means—Since the people inside the house were in sound sleep, and nobody woke up while he was going on with his work, he ought to have known that there was nothing in the house and gone away; since he proceeded with his operation, he must have been a stranger.

संधिच्छेदन &c.—He must have long toiled at the breach and gone away disappointed. सुहृद्भ्य: &c.—This brings out the extreme magnanimity of Charu; some may perhaps call it a mistaken notion of dignity. But it is not so. Charu. is not to be judged by the ordinary criteria of judgment. The poet wants to paint his character as that of a man of exceptional generosity that feels for others; and he has already told us that his hero lived for others. *Cf. supra*, I. 48; and किं बहुना.. दक्षिणतया परकीयमिवात्मानमवगच्छति । p. 88.

P. 124. तुलयिष्यति—Will regard me as equal to that, *viz.* the act of appropriating the deposit, have a low opinion of me; see *supra*, note on तुलयसि p. 20. तूलयि०—*v. l* will think lightly of me (तूलमिव लघुं करिष्यति). शङ्कनीया—*Cf. supra*, पापं कर्म च यत् &c. I. 36. निष्प्रतापा—निर्गत: प्रतापो यस्यां in which one's power or greatness is lost sight of; and hence शङ्कनीया. This Sl. occurs in Charu. with the reading शङ्कनीया हि दोषेषु निष्प्रभावा.

प्रणय: (अर्थेषु)—a desire to possess. नृशंसेन—The word is appropriately used here; 'one who wants to do injury to men.' नॄन् शंसति इति; fr. शंसु हिंसायां; कर्मण्यण्.

P. 126. अपलप्—To talk away or hide by talking; hence, to deny the knowledge of. अहमिदानीं &c –is a question. प्रतिक्रिया—the repayment of; the equivalent value in money of. आर्यघूतायै &c.—This speech must be स्वगतं.

वरमिदानीं स &c. Mark how tender-hearted Dhuta is. She has the same apprehension as her husband that people might take a wrong view of the incident. She would rather have her husband suffer bodily than in character. In the *Charudatta* we do not find this noble sentiment expressed. पुष्करपत्र &c.—The water lying on a lotus-leaf is taken as a type of unsteadiness; *cf.* नलिनीदलगतजलमतितरलं Mohamudgara. दरिद्र &c.—Fate takes a sort of cruel pleasure in more readily depriving poor men of their money. इयं च मे एका &c. —In the Charu. Dhuta first touches her ears, hoping to find some ornament there; but not finding any she says—किमिदानीं करिष्यामि । भवतु । दृष्टम् । मम ज्ञातिकुलाल्लब्धा शतसहस्रमूल्या मुक्तावली । तामप्यार्यपुत्रः शौण्डीरतया प्रतीच्छति । [ Perhaps a न is wanting here. ] अतिशौण्डीरतया—On acconnt of his very great nobility or magnanimity; loftiness of spirit. *Cf* for this sense शौण्डीर्यं धृतिविनयं दयां स्वपक्षे &c. Panchar. II. 54. The word शौण्डीर is of rare occurrence in later plays, but occurs in the plays of Bhasa, and in ancient works like the Ramayana.

P. 128. पुरस्तान्मुखः—With the face turned to the east; for a religious gift (दान) is to be received with the face turned to the east. पौरस्त्या० *v. l.*—पुरो भवा पौरस्त्या दिक् the east; दक्षिणापश्चात्पुरसस्त्यक्; त्यक् (त्य) is added to दक्षिणा, पश्चात् and पुरस् in this sense.

रत्नषष्ठी—So called because a jewel is to be presented to a Brahmana on that day यथाविभवा०—यथाविभवस्यानुसारः—following, *i.e.* according to, one's own means. प्रतिग्राहयितव्यः—प्रतिग्रहं कारयितव्यः should be made to accept a gift. In the Char. Dhuta says—सर्वसारविभवेन ब्राह्मणेन स्वस्ति वाचयितव्यमित्येषोऽस्यागमः। तस्य कृते—may mean—(1) तस्य व्रतस्य कृते for the completion of that vow; or (2) तस्य ब्राह्मणस्य कृते for the sake of, on behalf of, that Brahmana meaning thereby Charudatta. This is the sense intended here. There are certain gifts which may be given by the wife to her husband ( as to a Brahmana ); and a religious gift cannot be refused. Dhuta uses this device, as Charudatta would not have taken that jewel-necklace from her to be given to Vasant. in exchange for her ornaments. His sense of honour would not have allowed him to do it. But when the necklace became his property he could use it in any way he liked. She could not have given it to Maitreya; for in that case Charudatta would not have accepted it from him also; for that would have been charity. So the plan adoped by Dhuta was the only way out of the difficulty.

मा खलु मां लज्जितां &c.—Which would happen if Charu. would refuse to accept the gift. She therefore requests Maitreya, so to manage it that Charu. would accept the gift.

वैक्लव्यात्—Through mental weakness. अकार्यं—Charu. fears that Vidu. might put an end to his existence rather than behold his friend disgraced. Hence in agitation he calls out to him.

सदृशदार०—In the Charu. we have सदृशकुलदार०. ब्राह्मणी—Charu. does not say धूता, as it is against Hindu etiquette to utter the name of one's wife. **अस्मि दरिद्रः**—In the Char. we have हतोऽस्मि.

**अर्थतः पुरुषो नारी**—For it is the man who gives riches to his wife or relieves her wants; but when a woman does that the relation is reversed. The sl. occurs in the Charu. with the first line read as मयि द्रव्यक्षयक्षीणे.

**विभवानुगता**—Following me in the vicissitudes of fortune. *i. e.* loving me equally in prosperous or adverse circumstances. Or this may mean 'rich' (विभवेनानुगता). **यद्**—which three.

P. 130. महतः **प्रत्ययस्य**--Great because she trusted me although poor. The sl. occurs in the Charu. with the readings यं समालक्ष्य ...कृतस्तया ।..प्रत्ययस्य प्रदीयताम् ॥. This is repeated in Act V.; ( sl. 7 ). **०शरीरस्पृष्टिकया**--Touching the body gives greater solemnity to an oath and makes it inviolable So in the Veni. गच्छ जयंधर अस्मच्छरीरस्पृष्टिकया शापितेन भवता &c. Act VI 153.

**परिवादबहल०**—परिगतो वादः परिवादः or परी०; what is talked all round or over again; hence a slanderous talk, an ill report; here accusation, blame. परिवाद एव बहलः दोष; on account of the serious fault of its giving rise to an accusation. Or परिवादस्य बहलः many-sided दोषः; on account of the many evils of idle gossip (which I wish to avoid). **रक्षां**—its preservation (from the public gaze), *i. e.* its being made or filled up; J. V. also (in his new ed.) says रक्षां रक्षणं स्वस्वरूपेणावस्थापनम् । संधिमपूरितं रक्षितुं न शक्नोमीत्यर्थः. Here रक्ष् has the sense of 'to keep away or conceal from;' as in दर्शनपथाद्रक्ष्यते Rat. I; or *infra,* सखीजनादुपहसनीयतां रक्षामि p. 134. रक्षा not being understood in this sense has puzzled some interpreters and led them to propose strange readings and far fetched interpretations. Thus some propose to read नयस्य as one word; in this case we should read रक्षान् for रक्षां; while others propose नृपस्य रक्षान्. In both cases the meaning is—I wish to avoid the policemen, who else would be busy with it and make the matter public. This will be clear from the following extracts from Dr. Ryder's long note on this—" The words न यस्य रक्षां are difficult of interpretation. This difficulty doubtless explains the presence of the variant नृपस्य रक्षान्, which Stenzler adopts...It is easy to see how न यस्य रक्षां might be altered by a puzzled reader into नृपस्य रक्षान्......The commentators give little help P and L. D. are silent. J. V [3rd ed.] has यस्य संधेः रक्षां न परिहरामि न त्यजामि । सततमेव संधिं रक्षामीत्यर्थः. This reads almost like nonsense, for it makes the second half of the verse contradict the first half; the last thing which Char. desires is the preservation of the breach. The Calcutta com. [ of Ramamaya ] is hardly more successful; यस्य संधेः रक्षां रक्षणं स्वरूपेणावस्थानमिति यावत् न परिहरामि नोपेक्षे । संधिं रक्षितुं न शक्नोमीत्यर्थः. Here the explanation of रक्षा as "the preservation (of the breach) in its present form" is ingenious enough; but the com. is forced to give to न परिहरामि a meaning exactly the reverse of that which the phrase should have. Surely न (संधेः) रक्षां परिहरामि must needs mean: "I do not avoid the preservation (of the breach) in its present form," which is precisely the opposite of what the speaker wishes to say......Obviously, the trouble lies in the न. The clause becomes plain enough if we read नयस्य...The verse may then be translated : "..I avoid the preservation of justice..".. He means to say : "Scandal is such a dreadful evil that I am justified in departing from the course of conduct which strict justice demands."

**अकृपणशौण्डीर्यं**—Strictly, the meaning is : अकृपणं not a little शौण्डीर्यं pride or dignity यस्मिन्कर्मणि; see com.; 'in a very noble way, with great dignity;' while the speaker's intention seems to be 'in a noble and yet becoming way;' but then we should expect अकृपणशौण्डीरं or अकृपणं सशौण्डीर्यम्. **भो दरिद्रः किं** &c —may mean—(1) 'what noble thing (किं) can a poor man say?'; or (2) 'can a poor man speak nobly?' **कृतशौचः**—having purified the body by cleansing the mouth, bathing &c.

# ACT IV

The fourth Act opens with a scene between Vasantasena and her maid Madanika, meant to show the further development of the former's love for Charudatta. The next scene consists of the meeting of Sarvilaka and Madanika. This has very little to do with the general *denouement* of the plot, but serves the purpose of pointing out the first stage in the development of the under-plot, *viz.* Sarvilaka's determination to set free his friend Aryaka, who was put into prison by king Palaka. The Act closes with the scene between Vasanta. and Maitreya sent to her by Charu. to hand over to her the necklace of jewels in exchange for the casket of ornaments stolen away. Vasant. accepts the necklace and makes up her mind to pay Charu. a visit that evening.

P. 132. चित्रफलक०—Vasanta. is introduced as looking intently at a picture-board on which she had drawn a likeness of her lover to beguile her longing. For the device used here see com. वेशवासदाक्षिण्येन—Vasant. was not perfectly sure that the picture bore exact resemblance to the original, and thought that Mada.'s answer that it was quite faithful to the original was merely meant to please her, and hence the question. य एव—whoever; *i.e.* every one without exception. नानापुरुष &c —Because courtesans have to please people of different sorts, whether good or bad, and hence to be falsely courteous.

तस्य कारणं—तस्य refers to the अभिरमण of the eyes and heart of Vasantasena. She means-' When my lady's heart and eyes take such delight in the picture, why should the reason of it be asked ?—it must be the exact faithfulness of the picture to the original.'

P. 134. सखीजनादुप०—For in case the picture failed to represent the exact beauty of her lover, her friends, who would judge of his beauty from the picture, might ridicule her for loving a person even externally unworthy of her. सखीजनचित्तानुवर्ती—Acting in accordance with the liking of a friend. She means-' You need not have any misgivings as to what your friends would say about your love to Charu.; women are always ready to approve of the choice of their friend and to sympathize with her. So you need not be anxious on that score.' प्रवहणं—

Although given in Amara. as a synonym of कर्णीरथ (a kind of vehicle like a palanquin or *mena* borne by men on the shoulders; कर्णीरथः प्रवहणं डयनं च समं त्रयम्। त्रीणि पुरुषस्कन्धवाह्यस्य यानविशेषस्य Bhanuji Dikshita), it is used here in the sense of 'a sort of veiled chariot drawn by bullocks.' ०साहस्रिकः—सुवर्णानां दशसहस्रं सुवर्णदशसहस्रं तेन मूल्येन लभ्यः or क्रीतः ०साहस्रिकः; by adding ठञ् (इक) by तेन परिजय्यलभ्यकार्यसुकरम् or तेन क्रीतम् Pan. V. 1 93, 37. The वृद्धि of the अ of सहस्र is irregular (दाशसाहस्रिकं would have done); it may be treated as a Prakrit irregularity. संदेशेन—Being charged with a message, which I had to deliver. It was not my fault that I said so. The Instr. may be हेतौ (object or purpose for which a thing is done).

दत्त्वा निशाया &c.—Having committed a theft I laid the blame at the door of the night; *i.e.* people will say that if such crimes are committed it is the fault of the night; *cf. supra* बहुदोषा हि शर्वरी I. 58. रक्षान्—The city-guards or policemen. The reading रक्ष्यान् is bad, as it means 'the people to be protected.' जित्वा—*i.e.* having eluded their watch. मन्दरश्मिः—(1) with my activities slackened; (2) with rays dimmed or paled. The Sl. occurs in the Charu. with the readings—कृत्वा निशायां...निद्रां च हित्वा तिमिरं भयं च।...मन्दवीर्यः (this is better) शनैर्दिवा चंन्द्र इवास्मि मन्दः (भीतः)॥.

P. 136. त्वरितगतिं—*v.l.* त्वरितगतिः qualifies यः कश्चित् The reading in the text is better, as it gives a contrast with स्थितं in the next line; if I walk with a quick step and somebody eyes me attentively, or when I step &c संभ्रान्तं—is better taken with स्थितं. तुलयति—regards suspiciously. दूषितो०—*i e.* my conscience being guilty. स्वैर्दोषैः &c.—Wilson compares—'Thus conscience does make cowards of us all.' *Hamlet*, III. The Sl occurs in the Charu.; but not after the above Sl.; Sarvi. ( Sajjalaka ) repeats it when he goes to deliver the stolen ornaments to Vasant.; the readings there are—चकितगतिर्नि०, संभ्रान्तो...स्थितो वा। सर्वांस्तांस्तुलयति दोषतो मनो मे. नारीनाथं—When a woman was the head; *i. e.* which had no male to look after its affairs. This may have been out of pity; or out of the fear that a woman might raise an alarm on seeing a robber and was not to be killed ; see *supra.*, note on कस्मिन्स्त्री-जनदर्शनं न च भवेत् &c. III. 12. Sarvilaka shows that he used discrimination even in breaking into a house. गृहदारुवत्—*Cf.* स्तम्भीभूत्वा तिष्ठामि p. 120. दिवसीकृता—अदिवसः दिवसः संपद्यमाना कृता;

अभूततद्भावे च्विः. 'I was busy doing something or another during the whole night, and so turned it into a day as it were.'

**इमं तावच्चित्रफलकं** &c —This is a device used by the poet to give Madanika an opportunity to see Sarvilaka. **मदनमपि** &c.—**विशेषयन्ती** is generally taken to mean 'surpassing, excelling;' and it has this sense, no doubt; *cf.* रक्ताशोकरुचा विशेषितगुणो बिम्बाधरालक्तकः Malav. III. 5. But it is strange that the poet should make her surpass Madana in beauty; **रति** would have been very proper So it will be better to take **विशेषयन्ती** in the sense of 'adding charm to, setting off'; see com.; 'so beautiful as to add grace to Madana himself' **येयं**—goes with **करोति. चन्दन०**—चन्दनेन शीतलम्. Fig. of speech उत्प्रेक्षा.

P. 138. **निध्यायति**—looks intently at; for this sense *cf.* तत्र खलु... विद्याधरदारिकोदयवती नाम तेन राजर्षिणा चिरं निध्यातेति कुपितोर्वशी । Vik. IV. p180; and भर्त्राऽन्या मुहुरभिलष्यता निदध्ये । Sis. VIII. 69. 'निध्यानमवलोकनम्' इति वैजयन्ती. **अभजिष्यां--भुजिष्या** may mean here a concubine; or a servant-girl; **भुज्यते इति**; from **भुज्** and the Unadi affix इष्य by **रुचिभुजिभ्यां किष्यन्** Unadi (IV. 179). **अभुजिष्या**—one not a slave or concubine; Sar wanted to make her his wife by buying up her freedom and so to prevent her from being a prostitute.

**गवाक्षेण**--गवामक्षीव गवाक्षः a latticed window (*lit.* having holes like the eyes of a bull). **अ** is substituted for the final of **अक्षि** when it does not mean 'an eye' by **अक्ष्णोऽदर्शनात्** । Pan. V. 4. 76 It is also explained as गावो **जलानि** किरणा वा अक्षन्ति व्याप्नुवन्ति एतमनेन वा; from अक्ष् and aff. अ (घञ्) अकर्तर्यर्थे.

**उद्वेजनीया**--producing horror in the minds of others; causing disgust or abhorrence; *cf.* रमणीयाऽप्युद्वेजयति Kad. p. 25.

P. 140. **साहसे श्रीः** &c.—So in the Charu —साहसे खलु श्रीर्वसति; *cf.* for the idea उद्योगः प्रस्तुतः कस्माच्छ्रीर्न संतोषमिच्छति । Pancharatra, II. 8 **अखण्डित०**—Madanika knew that Sar.'s previous life was stainless **खण्डित**—broken up by an evil deed; **अखण्डित** uniformly pure, without a stain **न खलु**—Here **खलु** has the sense of an inquiry—as a softened question. **अत्यन्तविरुद्धं**—exceedingly opposed to morals or shocking to the mind.

**विप्रस्वं**—A Brahmana's wealth or property. As the Brahmanas in ancient times were solely devoted to the performance of holy rites, the usual gates of acquiring money were shut out to them, being left to the other classes; and what money they got was in the shape of Dakshina received from kings, or householders. And even when got in any other way, it was devoted to holy purposes. Hence a Brahmana's property came to be regarded as sacred, and was not to be stolen; and if stolen, the penalty was very great. *Cf.* ब्राह्मणस्वापहरणात्सर्वाङ्गेषु प्रजायते । वेदना दारुणा तप्तज्वरश्चैव भवेत्सदा ॥ देवब्राह्मणद्रव्यचौरः कृष्णसर्पः पवनेतरभोगरहितः । Ranavirakarita Prayaschitta-Bhaga (as quoted by Pandit Hirananda Sastri); and देवस्वं ब्राह्मणस्वं वा लोभेनोपहिनस्ति यः । स पापात्मा परे लोके गृध्रोच्छिष्टेन जीवति ॥ Ms. XI. 26. The theft of gold also is considered as a heinous sin. **बालं**—a baby (having ornaments on). **अप्रकाशः**--see com.; not to be worn publicly, *i.e.* in private; at home. Sar. gives this caution in order that it should not be recognized and the theft discovered. In the Charu. we have अप्रकाश्यः, not fit to be shown outside. **अयं च जनः**--*i.e.* Vasanta., who is a courtesan. Courtesans have to go out decorated; what is the use to them of wearing ornaments at home?

**मदनिका च मूर्छा** &c.—shows how deeply Mada. loved Vasantasena. She thought that Sar. must have laid violent hands on Charu. and got the ornament, and so she faints. The idea was as shocking to her as to Vasant. herself.

P. 142. **विषाद**—pain, dismay. **संभ्रम**—fear. **नीयमानाऽभुजि०**--Sarvilaka expected her to rejoice at the thought of her freedom from servitude; but he was surprised to see that on the contrary she fainted on hearing the name of Charu. mentioned. The sl. occurs in the Charu with the readings संभ्रमोत्फुल्ललोचना । मृगीव शरविद्धाङ्गी कम्पसे चानु०.

**मदनिके भीते** &c--In the Charu. Sajjalaka says—मदनिके एतावत्किं न पर्याप्तं द्वितीयमप्यकार्यं करिष्यामि । न खल्वत्र शस्त्रेण कश्चित्परिक्षतो व्यापादितो वा । **सेर्ष्यं**--Madanika's word प्रियं excited Sar.'s jealousy. Since she fainted even at the thought of the possibility of harm having been done to Charu., he concluded that Madanika was in love with him also.

**सद्वृत्त०**—He means-'I have done an execrable deed even at the sacrifice of the honour of my family; so intense is *my* love for you; and *you* love another man.' **मन्मथ** &c.—विपन्न dead. Although my other virtues have died in me. *i. e* I have subordinated them to the gratification of my passion, still I have retained my self respect intact **मान**—pride, sense of self-respect. Some render it by 'discernment' ( युक्तायुक्तविचार ), but this is not meant here देहं–*v. l.* for मानं–has no propriety; it is, however, supported by शरीरं in the Charu , where it is appropriate **व्यपदिशसि**—falsely represent or call. The Sl. occurs in the Charu. with the variations--संतुष्टपूर्वं॰ रक्षामि मन्मथगृहीतमिदं शरीरं.

**सर्वस्वफलिनः**--सर्वाणि स्वानि ( wealth of every kind ) एव फलानि येषां; the comparison to fruits shows that their wealth is used in maintaining not only their families, but servants &c. **अलं**—completely. **वेश्याविहग**—The comparison to birds that are not confined to one fruit-bearing tree is very happy; for the fig. of speech, see com. **प्रणयेन्धनः**—प्रणय ( the making of love) is fitly compared to fuel as it inflames passion. पूर्वश्लोके वेश्यादोष उक्तः । अत्र तु वैशिकपुरुषदोष इति विशेषः । *Cf.*—वेश्याऽसौ मदनज्वाला रूपेन्धनसमेधिता । कामिभिर्यत्र हूयन्ते यौवनानि धनानि च ॥. **श्रियो हि**—Here he speaks about women in general, of course excluding virtuous ladies of family. **भुजङ्गकन्यापरि॰**—They move away as suddenly and tortuously as female snakes. The comparison to snakes indicates the spirit of resentment with which women turn away from a man when displeased.

P. 144. **विरक्तभावा**—Not only not loving but grown cold towards. For the sentiment here expressed, *cf.* **अनातुरोत्कण्ठितयोः** प्रसिध्यता समागमेनापि रतिर्न मां प्रति । Malav. III. 15

**सुष्ठु खल्विदमुच्यते**—This shows that the following sl. is a quotation from what are known as ***Subhashitas,*** as it occurs in Bhartrihari's Vairagyasataka also, (being the 19th sl.) with the variants कार्यहेतोः, च परं for पुरुषं, नार्यः for वेश्याः and श्मशानघटिकाः. **एता हसन्ति** &c.–Now he refers specially to courtesans. **श्मशानसुमनाः**—सुमनस् 'a flower'; or better still 'jasmine flowers'; see com. The jasmine flowers, although attractive, are odious because they grow in the cemetery; so prostitutes, though attractive, should be shunned because of the faults mentioned above. Here वेश्याः, a noun in the plural, are compared with सुमनाः, a noun in the sing; and this ought to constitute a fault in the case of a simile; but it does not do so here, as it is said to give a charming sense; see com. *Cf* हसन्तं प्रहसन्त्येता रुदन्तं प्ररुदन्त्यपि । अप्रियं प्रियवाक्यैश्च गृह्णन्ति कालयोगतः ॥ Subhashita. संमोहयन्ति मदयन्ति विडम्बयन्ति निर्भर्त्सयन्ति रमयन्ति विषादयन्ति । एताः प्रविश्य सदयं हृदयं नराणां किं नाम वामनयना न समाचरन्ति ॥ Bhar. Vai. 34.

**वीची**—a wave; also वीचि: *m. f.* ; वयति ऊयते वा इति वीचि:; fr. वे + ईचि Unadi (IV. 72). ०**भ्रलेखा**—It is lit up by the light of the setting sun, which is evanescent. Here वीची and लेखा should better have been in the plural, as स्त्रिय: the object of comparison is in the pl.; however, see above, note on ०सुमना:. ०**मुहूर्तरागा**:—A pun on the word राग—( 1 ) redness; ( 2 ) love. **हृतार्था**:—हृत: अर्थ: money याभि: **निरर्थं**—निर्गत: अर्थ: यस्य तम् **अलक्तक:**—Red lac or a kind of paint prepared from the red resin-sap of certain trees, often mentioned in ancient Kavyas as being used by women for dyeing certain parts of their bodies, especially the feet and lips; see Kum. V. 34, 68; VII. 58; Ragh. VII, 7 &c. **त्यजन्ति**—*Cf.* अलक्तको यथा रक्तो निष्पीड्य पुरुषस्तथा । अबलाभिर्बलाद्रक्त: पादमूले निपात्यते ॥.

**नाम**—as is well known. **चपला**:—Fickle, *i. e.* not confined to one person. **मदप्रसेकं**—is translated as 'they pour the effusion of their bloom, or the ejecting of wine from their mouth.' The real sense is rather obscene. **शरीरेण**—For the purpose of embracing, kissing &c. (what is called बाह्यरत ), Comp. for similar ideas—जल्पन्ति सार्धमन्येन पश्यन्त्यन्यं सविभ्रमम् । हृदये चिन्तयन्त्यन्यं प्रिय: को नाम योषिताम् ॥ नयनविकारैरन्यं वचनैरन्यं विचेष्टितैरन्यम् । रमयति सुरतेनान्यं स्त्री बहुरूपा निजा कस्य ॥ Sarngadhara एकेन स्मितपाटलाधररुचो जल्पन्त्यनल्पाक्षरं वीक्षन्तेऽन्यमित: स्फुटत्कमलिनीफुल्लोल्लसल्लोचना: । दूरोदारचरित्रचित्रविभवं ध्यायन्ति चान्यं धिया केनेत्थं परमार्थतोऽर्थवदिव प्रेमास्ति वामभ्रुवाम् ॥

* **न पर्वताग्रे** &c.—L. D. calls this a strange metre; but it is not so; it is a case of उपजाति, the second line being in उपेन्द्रवज्रा and the other three in वंशस्थ; the last syllable of the first line may be taken as long for the sake of the metre, the ganas thus becoming ज त-ज-र. **अयं न भवसि**—Here you will cease to exist, *i. e.* I will just kill you. Sarv. purposely says this to mark its effect on Madanika and thereby to know the real state of her heart.

**असंबद्ध**०—Because he talked of killing Charudatta, which was most unreasonable. **असभावनीये**—For what can never be conceived or thought possible, *i. e.* her being in love with Charudatta. **एष खलु अलं**०—She wanted to tell him that her

* On the aspersions cast here on the female sex in general, Wilson remarks—"The Hindu poets very rarely disprasie women; they almost invariably represent them as amiable and affectionate. In this they might give a lesson to the bards of more lofty nations, and particulary to the Greeks, who both in tragedy and comedy pursued fair sex with implacable rancour."

mistress was in love with Charu. and so it was impossible for her to love Charudatta. Sar., however, interrupts her and asks ततः किम्. **कर्णे एवमिव**--Mad. explains to him how her mistres was deep in love with Char., and also tells why she had deposited the ornament with him.

P. 146. **सवैलक्ष्यं**--Sarv. is embarrassed to find himself baffled in his object. **छायार्थं**--छाया is the pleasure he was to derive by having procured the freedom of Madanika and his consequent marriage with her. **ग्रीष्मसंतप्तः**--*i.e.* tormented by his love for Madanika. **पत्रैः वियोजिता**--He robbed Vasanta. of her ornament, which made it difficult for him to approach her.

**निसर्गादेव पण्डिताः**—*Cf.* स्त्रीणामशिक्षितपटुत्वममानुषीषु संदृश्यते किमुत याः प्रतिबोधवत्यः। Sak V. 22.

**न चन्द्रादातपो** &c.--She means—' As one cannot expect heat from the moon, so you need not apprehend any harm from Charudatta.'

**साहसे अस्मिन्**--The commentators understand by साहस his late adventure, *viz.* the theft of the golden casket. It rather means the hazardous task of going to Charu. and returning the ornament to him, which would involve his confession of the theft, as is clear from his words तथाऽपि नीतिविरुद्धमेतत्. **कथयसि**&c --As it was neither sorrow nor fear that would deter him from going to Charu., there was no need for praising his virtues to him. **जनयति मम वेदं**--is a question **कुत्सितं कर्म**—*i e.* the theft. He says this to Madanika; he was not ashamed of the deed as it was done deliberately with a good object in view. **नेदं**—*v. l.* for **वेदं**—is simpler.

P. 148. **अन्यथाऽतिसाहसं**—In the Charu. she says अथ वा अज्जुकां च पुनर्वञ्चयित्वा पुनरेव दासभावो भवेत्. **अभुजिष्ययेव**—*i.e.* like a noble-born lady. Like a low-born servant-girl she did not ask him to go away and keep the ornament for herself secretly. **महती**--of great consequence; very proper **निशायां**--*i.e.* his ignorance as to what course he had to adopt ( due to his reason being clouded). **कामदेवगेहे**--the temple of Kama that was in Vasantasena's garden.

**आत्मसंबन्धिनं**---One connected with us through his connexion with Charu., your beloved. Here Mada. speaks, identifying herself with her mistress Vasantasena. **युज्यते**—It is proper that Mad. should thus pass off the matter.

P. 150. **विज्ञातोऽहमनया**--I am known, as regards my real object, by her; *i. e.* that I was the man who wished to purchase Madanika's freedom and make her my wife. It cannot mean 'my real character, as one who stole the ornament from Charu.'s house;' for Sarvilaka was not at all aware of having been overheard by Vasantasena. Had that been his real meaning he would have given some explanation of his conduct. In the Charu Sajjalaka says to himself--कथं विदितोऽस्म्यनया after Vasant. had said—अहं जानामि तस्य गेहे साहसं कृत्वाऽऽनीतोऽयमलंकारः। तस्य गुणाननुकम्पतामार्यः। **साधु आर्यचारु०** &c —Sar. bursts out thus, thinking that it was his connexion with Charu. that made Vasantasena bestow Madanika on himself.

**गुणाः**--virtues, personal excellences. **ईश्वरैः**—rich men. *Cf.* for this sense--क्षुद्राणामविवेकमूढमनसां यत्रेश्वराणां सदा वित्तव्याधिविकारविह्वलगिरां नामापि न श्रूयते। Bh. Vair 27 **न समः**—*i.e.* superior to **न किंचिदप्रा०**--He speaks from his own experience; for, being impressed by Charu.'s merits alone, Vasa. bestowed Mad. on him. उडुप-उडु *f. n.* a star; उडूनि पातीति उडुपः the moon. It also means 'a boat,' for which see *infra* VIII. 23 उडु is derived as अवति इति ऊः; उ *n.* by ह्रस्वो नपुंसके &c. (Pan. I. 2. 47); उ च तत् डु च उडु; ऊश्च डुश्च when fem; उं क्रोधं डयते, उना शंभुना डीयते (डी and aff डु, *i.e.* उ) इति वा. *Cf.* गुणेषु क्रियतां यत्नः किमाटोपैः प्रयोजनम्। गुणैर्गौरवमायाति न महत्याऽपि संपदा। पूर्णेन्दुर्न तथा वन्द्यो निष्कलङ्को यथा कृशः॥. **प्रवहणिकः**--प्रवहणमस्यास्तीति प्रवहण + इक (ठन्), a *matub* aff, by अत इनिठनौ; it means 'one in charge of a carriage, a driver.' **प्रविश्य सप्रवहणः**--Wilson remarks on the introduction of a car on the stage--

> "The introduction of this kind of stage-property is so constant and essential that it must have been real, and shows that the place appropriated to the representation must have been level and spacious."

**सुदृष्टां** &c.--This shows the affection Vasant. had for her servants. She asks Mada. to take a good survey of her features, so that they may be firmly impressed on her memory, and she may not forget her after separation. This kindness affects Mada. deeply and brings tears to her eyes.

P. 152. **त्वमेव वन्दनीया**-Because she was the wife of a Brahmana now and socially had a higher status than a courtesan, however rich the latter was. In the Charu. Vasa says आर्या खल्विदानीमसि संवृत्ता; and taking her by the hand she gives her to

6

Sajjalaka. आरोह प्रवहणं--In the Charu, Vasanta adorns Mada. with the ornaments on her person before she asks her to mount the car. शिरसा वन्द्यतां--Because Vasant. was her benefactress, and she was not formally married yet. यत्र--यस्याः; here त्र has the sense of the Abl · some take the Loc as हेतौ (यस्मिञ्जने हेतुभूते). वधूशब्दा०--वधूशब्द एवाव ; the veil in the form of the title of 'wife', *i. e.*, the dignity of wifehood. Some take this to mean वधूशब्दस्यावगु०, the veil or dress proper for a कुलाङ्गना. प्राप्त ०गुण्ठने *v. l.*--वधूशब्दश्च अवगुण्ठनं च । वधूनामेव हि परपुरुषानवलोकनीयत्वात् । JV.

राष्ट्रियः--fr. राष्ट्र and aff इय (घ); see com; the word seems to be used here in the sense of 'the chief magistrate of the city.' It does not refer to संस्थानक; for, as Dr. Ryder remarks, he nowhere appears as a government officer, giving sensible orders in Sanskrit. Of course in Acts IX and X. the term राष्ट्रिय refers to the king's brother-in-law सिद्धादेश०--see *supra*. p 84. घोषः--From घुष् and aff अ (घञ् भावे ; a hamlet or residence of cowherds) अप्रमत्तैः--Carefully watchful (in case Aryaka escapes). भवितव्यम्--We should expect an इति after this सम्प्रति--Now (that a friend is in peril); in troublesome times like this. विशिष्टतमः--We should rather expect ०तरः In the Charu. there is no reference to Aryaka's arrest. Sajjalaka departs after Vasa. hands over Madanika to him, saying (आत्मगतं)--भोः कदा खलु अस्याः प्रतिकर्तव्यं भविष्यति । &c.

ससंभ्रममञ्जलिं बद्ध्वा &c --Mark the humility and good sense of Madanika. She did not like the idea of her husband's leaving her thus abruptly. She could not have gone back to Vasanta-sena now, as she was a wife She, therefore, requests Sarv to do what she could have most reasonably asked him to do under the circumstances. रेभिलस्य सार्थवाहस्य--This Rebhila is the same that we have met with in the beginning of the 3rd Act. Dr Ryder observes--"This is the only indication in the play that Sarvilaka is the son of Rebhila". But this does not appear to be correct. Had Sar. been Rebhila's son he would have known Charudatta and his house, as the latter was Rebhila's friend Rebhila, it appears, was some distant relative of Sarvilaka.

अप्रमत्तेन &c --Although not yet actually married to Sar, Madanika evinces the same anxiety for his safety that a married woman does for that of her husband when about to be engaged in a perilous adventure. ज्ञातीन्--Kinsmen, either of Palaka or of Aryaka; preferably the former; these are called सहजशत्रव: by Kamandaka (as they are inwardly jealous of a king). विटान्--Vitas are men who know one art (एकविद्यो विटश्चान्य:) and who hang on rich men as parasites; these have no fixed principles of their own, and are ready to accept any proposal. Thus Samsthanaka's Vita deserts his master and goes over to the side of Aryaka; see Act VIII. लब्धवर्णान्--who have earned distinction (वर्ण distinction, reputation), *i. e.* men who are ready to welcome any new enterprise.

उत्तेजयामि--incite against, fire their spirit. यौगंधरायण:--The faithful minister of king Udayana (Vatsa); a great politiician and ever devoted to his master's cause. उदयनस्य--Udayana, also known as Vatsa or Vatsaraja, was decoyed into captivity by Chanda-Mahasena, king of Ujjayini, but was set free by his minister, Yaugandharayana, by using a clever stratagem; see Kathasar. II, 5.

Udayana was a king of the lunar race, the son of Sahasranika and the grandson of Satanika (son of Janamejaya) who transferred the capital of upper India from Hastinapura to Kausambi. According to the Vishnupurana he was the son of a second Satanika, who was 19th in succession from Janamejaya. He was so named because he was educated on the Eastern (उदय) Mountain by the sage Jamadagni. His capital was Kausambi. Mahasena, also called Chanda-Mahasena, had a daughter, named Vasavadatta. She once saw Udayana in a dream, and being enamoured of him contrived to inform him of her love. Udayana, who was decoyed to Ujjayini by Mahasena, and who was engaged to teach music to Vasavadatta, managed to elope with her to his capital, following the advice of his minister Yaugandharayana. They were afterwards married in great pomp. The whole account is given by Subandhu in his *Vasavadatta*. Udayana is the hero of the *Ratnavali*, a play by Sriharsha. His account is given in the Kathasaritsagara, in Tarangas 11 to 24.

P. 154. असाधुभि:--Wicked, acting unjustly. आहिताश०-entertaining imaginary fears. अभिपत्य--having attacked the guards. This shows that Sar was the leader of the party of the friends of Aryaka secretly plotting against Palaka, and to which reference was made by Darduraka; see p. 84. राहुमुखे--When Amrita was being served out to the gods after it was churned from the ocean, Rahu, disguised as a god, joined the rank of the gods. Nectar was poured out to him; but the fraud was detected by the Sun and the Moon who informed Vishnu of it. The latter severed the head of the demon just as he was swallowing the nectar. As he had tasted a little of the quantity of nectar, the head became immortal, and it is supposed to wreak its vengeance on the Sun and the Moon. Astronomically, Rahu is the ascending node personified as a demon. He is also considered as one of the planets, as King of Meteors and guardian of the Southwest quarter. **शशाङ्कबिम्बमिव**—The simile is bad. The only significance it has is that Sar.'s friend was under a cloud, like the Moon in the grasp of Rahu.

**चारुदत्तसकाशात्** &c.—In the Charu. Maitreya comes from Charu. just after Madanika leaves Sajjalaka, asking him to wait for her in the temple of Kama. And after his interview is over Sajjalaka is introduced to Vasantasena.

**अहो रमणीयता** &c.—Vasant. thus exclaims because she had done one good act. It was closely followed by the arrival of Vidu. from Charu.; and nothing gave her more delight than anything connected with her lover Even when Sakara is about to strangle her, saying तद्दरिद्रसार्थवाहकमनुष्यकामुकि तिष्ठ तिष्ठ, she exclaims—**भण** भण पुनरपि श्लाघनीयानि एतानि अक्षराणि। Act VIII. **बन्धुल**—a bastard. **बन्धुलेन सह**—Vasa. wants to have Maitreya brought in like some great personage, attended upon by her gay servants.

**ही ही भोः**—is a combination of particles expressing joy or surprise. It is peculiar to the Vidushaka. **तपश्चरण** &c.—Because Ravana became invincible to the gods after he had practised very severe austerities and propitiated Brahma. See Ragh. X. 43. **पुष्पक**—The celebrated aerial car of Kubera, which Ravana had wrested from him. Dr. Ryder thinks that there is a pun on पुष्पक and translates—'I travel with another sort of a blossom (पुष्पक) —a woman of the town.' **अहं पुनर्ब्राह्मणः** &c —Vidu. thinks that he is happier than Ravana, as he was being attended upon by gay people without having to practise rigid penance for it. **नरनारीजनेन**—Dr. Ryder prefers the reading नगरनारीजनेन, meaning thereby 'prostitutes.' But नर is necessary as बन्धुल was with him. He compares the large mansion of Vasant. to the spacious Pushpaka car.

P. 156. **सविस्मयम्**—Vidu. was wonderstruck to see the majestic appearance of the very entrance to Vasant.'s palatial dwelling;

and he is tempted to describe it. Dr. Ryder remarks—"The pompous language of this description of the portal makes one wonder whether it is not an intentional travesty.'' Some consider the lengthy descriptions by the Vidu. of the gate and the courts to be interpolations. But that does not seem to be a correct view. Ths poet seizes this opportunity to describe the mansion of Vasantasena. The words of the *Cheti*, viz. 'प्रेक्षतामार्योऽस्मदीयं गेहद्वारं,' are suggestive. They lead the Vidu. to describe the various rooms in detail Vasanta's house is described here as having eight spacious courts or quadrangles. Such houses, it seems, were not a rarity in ancient India. In the Kathasaritsagara, Madanamala's house is described as having seven courts (कक्षाs):— तत्र वारविलासिन्या नरेन्द्रसदनोपमम् । ययौ मदनमालेति ख्याताया वरमन्दिरम् ॥ कृताह्वानमिव प्रांशुप्राकारशिखरोच्छ्रितैः * * * क्वचिदाबद्धमातङ्गघटासंघट्टसंचरम् । क्वचिदायुधसंदर्भगम्भीराकारगुम्फितम् ॥ * * क्वचिन्निबद्धसंगीतमृदङ्गध्वनिनादितम् ॥ सप्तकक्षाविभक्तं तत्स पश्यन्सपरिच्छदः । प्रापन्मदनमालाया वासप्रासादमुन्नतम् ॥ Lambaka 7, Taranga 4, slokas 19-27. Wilson remarks—'The interior of the houses at Pompeii conveys some idea of an Indian house, which, like them is a set of chambers of one or two stories, surrounding a central unroofed square. A house of a superior description is merely denoted by the superior extent of this square, and by its comprising a set or series of them as in the text." In the Charu. however, there is no mention of these eight courts. The Vidu. discusses the whole thing in four sentences, *viz.* अहो गणिकावाटस्य सश्रीकता । नानापट्टणसमागतैरागमिकैः पुस्तकानि वाच्यन्ते । संयोज्यन्ते चाहारप्रकाराः । वीणा वाद्यन्तें । सुवर्णकारा अलंकारप्रकारानादरेण योजयन्ति ।

The epithets in the Genitive qualify वसन्तसेनाभवनद्वारस्य. ०हरितोपलेपनस्य—besmeared with cow-dung, or with some green paint. कुसुमोपहार०–the floor was ornamentally decked with strewings of flowers. गगनतला०—expresses the extreme height of the turret of the portal दूरोन्नामित—read ०न्नमित and in the Prakrit ण्णमिद (as given in the foot-note). उन्नामित is grammatically inaccurate. It may, however, be defended; see note on विनामिताः *infra*, VIII. 8. मल्लिका—a kind of jasmine; the festoon was very thick and white and waving; and so it looked like the trunk of Airavata, which is also white. भ्रमायित—p. p. p. of the denom. भ्रम doubt and aff. क्यङ् (य—भ्रमायते); some take

भ्रमागत as the *chhaya.* महारत्नोपराग०– *i. e.* the lustre of precious jewels attached to the staff of the flags. The Sanskrit rendering महारजनोप०, however, is better; it means 'bright with the dye of the safflower.' ललत् gracefully moving and so चञ्चल tremulous. ०अग्रहस्तेन—the fringes of the flags are considered as the hands by which they betoken the Vidu. to come in सौभाग्यपताका--सौभाग्यसूचका: or ०लक्षका: पताका: flags indicative of good fortune. ०मोभयपार्श्वस्य– It was held auspicious to place two pots of gold or silver or copper or crystal filled with water on either side of an entrance door. Such pots were (and are, when used on auspicious occasions) covered at their mouth with bunches of mango leaves. ०ललाम--charming or graceful with. महासुर०—The comparison is queer like many others used by the poet Some understand हिरण्यकशिपु by महासुर. वज्रनिरन्तर०—Thickly studded with diamonds. Some take वज्र to mean 'steel-nails,' but that is not possible as the panels of the door were made of gold दुर्गत०—It forbade the entrance of poor men, as they had no money to pay.

P. 158. ०सच्छाया:—having the beauty of, resembling. विनिहितचूर्णमुष्टि०—It is difficult to see what this exactly means. In translating we have followed the commentators. But the sense of 'handfuls of chunam' has no propriety. Again, विनिहित does not fit in well with this explanation. So the right meaning seems to be–'white with the ornamental fist-like studs of chunam.' Or, this should be read as part of the following attribute, ०पाण्डुरविविध० &c.; then this will give a nice meaning. चूर्णमुष्टि will now mean 'handfuls of decorative powder' (रांगोळी in Marathi). The whole will mean—'decked with stairs of gold inlaid with various kinds of gems and white with handfuls of powder' &c. It is customary even now to deck the steps of a staircase with powder–drawings. निर्ध्यायति—Better read निध्यायति 'meditates upon,' *i. e.* looks intently or steadfastly at; see *supra*, p, 138, श्रोत्रिय:—A learned Brahmana. जन्मना ब्राह्मणो ज्ञेय: संस्कारैर्द्विज उच्यते । विद्यया याति विप्रत्वं त्रिभि: श्रोत्रिय उच्यते ॥. कलम—see *supra* p 62. बुस—the husks of grain बलीवर्द:—An excellent bull; अतिशयितं बलमस्य बली; ई wealth; वर् what is desired; ईश्व वर् च ईवरौ तौ ददातीति ईवर्द:; बली चासौ ईवर्दश्च. सैरिभ:—a buffalo; सीरिणां (of plough-bearers) इभ इव सीरिभ: (a word of the शकन्ध्वादि group); सीरिभ एव सैरिभ: by adding अ (अण) स्वार्थे. अपनीतयुद्धस्य—अपनीतं युद्धमस्य removed from its duel or pugilistic encounter. केशकल्पना—The arranging or dressing of the hair of. **पाटच्चरः**—a thief; पाटयंश्चरति; a comp. of the पृषोदरादि class; or पटच्चर एव पाटच्चरः by adding अ (स्वार्थे).

**मन्दुरायां शाखामृगः**—"Monkeys are kept in stables as a sort of scare-goats apparently; hence the Persian proverb—The misfortune of the stable on the head of the monkey (*Bilai tavileh ber seri maimun*)". Wilson. A big monkey was kept in a house-stable to prevent any mishap to the horses, due to evil-eye influence &c. *Cf.* मन्दुरान्ते तथा धार्यो रक्तवक्त्रो महाकपिः। सर्वोपद्रवनाशाय वाजीनां च विवृद्धये ॥ Salihotra. and प्रभष्टोऽय प्लवंगः प्रविशति नृपतेर्मन्दिरं मन्दुरायाः। Ratn. II. 2. **कूरच्युत** &c.—The old commentators take कूर in the sense of 'boiled rice' and तैल in that of 'ghee'; so this seems to mean according to them 'ghee mixed with boiled rice' and then pressed out of it; this was mixed with wheat-flour to make it tasteful and digestible; and then balls or cakes were made of it and given to elephants. JV. understands by this 'oil extracted from Kura (a kind of seed).' In this case the meaning will be–'a ball of boiled rice mixed with oil extracted from *kura.*' He also notices the reading कूरात्थअ and says इति पाठान्तरे कूरास्थिज, कुलित्थज इति वा संस्कृतम्. **पिण्ड**—a roll of cakes; a mouthful.

P. 160. **पाशकपीठे**—Agambling table; L. D. रज्जुनिर्मिते पुस्तकासने वा। Srinivasa Sastri says मञ्चे; but this seems to be far-fetched; perhaps we should read पार्श्वकपीठ, a stool placed by the side of one for putting things on; these meanings are suggested because पाशकपीठ occurs again in the next line. The difficulty, however, may be removed by taking the second पाशकपीठ to mean the board or piece of cloth marked with the four straps containing the necessary squares (called पट in Marathi) for playing at *Somgatis.* **मणिमयसारिका**—play-men or pieces called *Somgatis* in Marathi, made of jewels. **स्वाधीनमणिमय०**—*v. l.* where स्वाधीन according to the old commentators means अकृत्रिम, 'not artificial, real' (gems); or it may mean 'placed in it or belonging to it.' **मदनसंधिविग्रह०**—मदनसंबन्धी संधिः विग्रहश्च तयोः चतुराः skilled in stirring up a quarrel between lovers and in reconciling angry lovers with each other. **वर्णिका**—paint. For अग्रहस्त see *snpra* p. 156.

**क्षीणपुण्या इव** &c.—This refers to the notion that individuals, who, by the force of their merit, are raised to the dignity of stars or are starified, enjoy pleasure there for a period of time proportionate to the sum of their good actions, and when it is exhausted they come down to the earth and are often seen as falling stars. *Cf* स्वल्पीभूते सुचिरतफले स्वर्गिणां गां गतानां Megh. I, 30; ते तं भुक्त्वा स्वर्गलोकं विशालं क्षीणे पुण्ये मर्त्यलोकं विशन्ति Bg. IX 21; and नाकस्य पृष्ठे ते सुकृतेऽनुभूत्वेमं लोकं हीनतरं चाविशन्ति. Mund. Up. I. 2. 10. **कांस्यतालाः**—the strikings of the cymbals of bell-metal for marking musical time. The simile indicates the rapidity with which they are struck. **प्रणयकोप**—anger due to love or coquettish anger; *i.e.* not real, but outwardly manifested towards a lover who attends to somebody else. *Cf.* मानः कोपः स तु द्वेधा प्रणयेर्ष्यासमुद्भवः । Sah-Dar. III. 198. **कररुहपरामर्शेन**—(1) by being gently touched or stroked with the nails as a sign of endearment; (2) by being struck with the nails (when going with वीणा) **सार्यते**—is played upon. *Cf.* प्रतियोजयितव्यवल्लकीसमवस्था &c. Ragh VIII. 41. **प्रगीताः**—प्रकृष्टं गीतं यासां ताः that have sung; or प्रगीतं विद्यते यासां by adding अ (मत्वर्थीय). **नर्त्यन्ते**—are made *i. e.* taught to dance. **नाट्यं** &c.—are taught dramatic representation with erotic gesticulations. Read ससिंगारअं instead of ससिंगारओ in the Prakrit.

**अपवल्गिताः**—suspended so as to be moving about. **गर्गरी**—a vessel for holding water; *cf.* Marathi घागर; fr. गॄ (गिरति जलं) and aff. गर with the fem. ई. **आहरति**--attracts one **उपचित**—grown strong by being accumulated; plentiful.

P. 162. **धूमोद्गारैः**—The effusions of smoke are looked upon as the sighs or breathings out of the kitchen. **पटच्चर**—an old or worn-out garment. **पेशि**—may mean 'a ball of flesh;' or, better still, the bag of the stomach, as the comparison to पटच्चर shows. **रूपिदारकः**—see com.; रूप an animal. **आहारविकारं**—different preparations or articles of food. **वर्धितं**—food with condiments &c; a full meal; or, rich food.

**परधननिरताः**—delighting in enjoying others' wealth *i. e.* we induce people to come here and grow rich by their money. **गुणेष्ववाच्याः**—*i. e.* our merits should not be discussed; no one should ask us what merits we possess. **ललामः**—move about or sport gaily. Some consider this sl. to be an interpolation on the ground that the pages are not expected to speak of themselves so disparagingly. But looking to the state of the society then and the position of harlots in it, it was no disparagement for bastards to speak of themselves in this fashion. *Cf.* Shakespeare:—

Bastard—Most certain of one mother, mighty king,

That is well known: and, as I think, one father :
Of that I doubt......

Bastard—Brother by the mother's side, give me your hand :
My father gave me honour, yours gave land.

[*King John*, I.I. 59-60, 63; 163, 164 'where Philip, the illegitimate son of Richard I., speaks about himself].

P. 164. **कर्मंतोरणानि**—For comp. see com.; architectural arches. **नीलरत्न०**—Properly this should be विनिक्षिप्तनीलरत्नानि (set with sapphires); but as it is it must be taken as नीलरत्नेषु विनिक्षिप्तानि. **वैदूर्य**— *lapis lazuli*; विदूरे गिरौ भवं वैदूर्यं; fr विदूर and य (ष्यञ्). **विदूर**—name of a mountian said to be in Ceylon, from which the jewel is brought; *cf.* Bhoja—अस्ति शैलो विदूराख्यः पर्यन्ते तत्र काचन। मही रत्नाकरीभूता वैदूर्यं तत्र जायते॥ See also Malli. on Kum. I. 24. **इन्द्रनील**—इन्द्र इव नीलः; a sapphire. **कर्केतर-क**—a kind of gem. also called कर्केतन. **विचारयन्ति**—discuss the quality of; examine (in consultation with each other).

**घृष्यन्ते**—are ground. **धीरं**—patiently, steadily. **कुङ्कुम॰ प्रस्तराः**—patches of wet pulverized saffron. **सार्यते**—is being sifted or refined; 'is being moistened' (according to the commentator). **गन्धयुक्तय**—The preparations or mixtures of scents. **अवधीरित** &c.—*i. e.* who are after the concubines regardless of their wives, &c. **आसवकरक**—a wine-cup. **मुक्ताः**—deserted, whose company is left by; *i. e.* who are drinking alone. **विहंगवाटी**—An aviary; dovecots. **दधिभक्त०**—goes with ब्राह्मण and शुक. **सूक्त**—(1) beautiful words; a hymn of the Veda.

P. 166. **लब्धप्रसरा**—प्रसर scope for action, influence, ascendancy; *cf.* श्रीर्लब्धप्रसरेव वेशवनिता दुःखोपचर्या भृशम्। Mud. III 5. **कुरकुरायते**—A denom. formed by adding य (क्यण) which forms A'tm. verbs; see *supra*, note on **खटखटायेते** p. 10. **मदनसारिका**—A starling or *Maina*, so called probably because she was taught words capable of exciting love in persons coming in; and therefore she began to cackle all the more at the sight of the Vidushaka. We have such a *Maina* mentioned in the *Ratnavali*. **प्रहृष्टकण्ठा**—With the throat delighted; *i. e.* singing cheerfully and lustily. **कुम्भदासी**—A procuress; fr. **कुम्भ** the paramour of a harlot and **दासी** the maid attending on; **कुम्भः स्यात्कुम्भकर्णस्य सुते वेश्यापतौ**

घटे । Visva. She also gets fruits of various sorts to eat. Some take this in the sense of 'a water–jar–carrying maid.' परपुष्टा—So called because the eggs of the cuckoo are supposed to be hatched by a female crow and hence such names as परभृत; *cf.* प्रागन्तरिक्षगमनात्स्वमपत्यजातमन्यैर्द्विजैः परभृताः खलु पोषयन्ति। S'ak. V. 22. नागदन्त—a peg (made of, or jutting forth like, an elephant's tusk). लावक—a quail. कपिञ्जल—a partridge; or a *Chataka* प्रेष्यन्ते—are sent out for being taught fighting; or it may simply mean 'sent out' (as they were taught to return to their cages). विधुवति—fans ०महल्लक—a eunuch (a word derived from the Arabic *mahal*). L. D. translates this as वृद्धश्रेष्ठाः, probably mistaking महल्लक for मतल्लिका. प्रसारणं कृतं—an extension is made, *i. e.* have spread in every quarter; a diverse view is presented. Some take प्रसारण to mean कीर्तिप्रतिष्ठापन—the birds have given her a name. The com. reads differently.

पट्टप्रावरक—a silk cloak; पट्ट a silken garment. पुनरुक्तालं० —a double set of ornaments. अङ्गभङ्ग—distortions or awkward movements of the body. आर्य एष&c.—Some read अयं after आर्यायाः. In this case आर्य एषः should be taken as a separate sentence forming a question. कियत्तपः &c.—For Maitreya first thought he was most lucky. मा तावत्—It cannot be so; *i. e.* his position is not so enviable.

सुगन्धः—fragrant, *i. e.* using perfumes; mark the ending of the comp.; it does not take the final इ as the smell is separable; otherwise सुगन्धि कमलं. चम्पकवृक्षः—*i. e.* although the *Champaka* tree is the best by itself; *cf* the sl. पुष्पेषु चम्पा नगरीषु लङ्का दासीषु रम्भा पुरुषेषु विष्णुः &c. Although this looks like a verse in the A'rya metre and has been printed here as such, it is doubtful whether the passage was intended as verse or prose. Dr. Ryder has a long note on this as follows:—

"This passage is printed by Stenzler, Godabole and J. V. as prose; only Parab (N. E.) regards it as a verse. The matter is of a sort which the Viduāhaka would be apt to put into verse; it is not narration, nor description, but a kind of humorous moralizing. If we regard the passage as verse, it falls into five padas, the scheme of which is 12, 17, 13, 14, 15. Now if we disregard the fifth pada, and apply the rule पादान्तस्थं विकल्पेन (—श्रुतबोध) or वा पादान्ते (—वृत्तरत्नाकरं), we obtain the scheme 12, 18, 12, 14, which makes a pretty fair A'rya. But what becomes of the words अणहिगमणीओ लोअस्स? It is of course possible that they were intended by S'udraka as a prose remark following the verse; but this is improbable."

[Dr. Ryder further adds that these words might have been a marginal comment by some reader afterwards incorporated into the text by some scribe, and cites the instance of the passage in Sanskrit—किं शब्दविचार: &c.—added after Chandanaka's speech in Prakrit after VI. 20. See the foot-note there.]

P. 168 **पुष्पप्रावारक**—A garment or mantle embroidered with flowers, or having flowers worked out in it. फुल्लप्रा० *v. l.*— has the same meaning. **कपर्दकडाकिनी**—कपर्द is a *cowrie* and डाकिनी a kind of female goblin or sprit; the comp. simply means here 'a worthless hag'. करट्टडाकिनी is another reading where करट्ट means 'dirty'; see com Dr. Ryder prefers this reading, perhaps not knowing that कपर्द is used in India as a term expressive of extreme valuelessness or insignificance **उदरविस्तार:**—The speech of the Vidu. here is in a vein of good humour, which forms a trait of his character **महादेवमिव** &c —When a huge idol of a deity like Siva, Vetala, &c is to be set up in the inner shrine of a temple, it is planted there first and then the door is built up, as it is intended to be narrow to avoid the rush of people inside at a time. **द्वारशोभा**—is equivalent to शोभनं द्वारं, 'the beautiful door.' **चातुर्थिक**—a quartan fever. This is dangerous. It is thus described in medical works—(ज्वर:)अस्थिमज्जगत: पुन: । कुर्याच्चातुर्थिकं घोरमन्तकं रोगसंकरम् ॥

**एतेन उपकारेण** &c.—Vidu. means to say—'If a person becomes so fat and burly by the effect of a quartan fever, I should also like to be blessed by it.' **हताश**—is used here appropriately. It means 'one whose wish is frustrated on account of his wickedness;' hence, here, 'You silly fellow.' **शूनपीन**—शून swollen; p. p. p. of श्वि; पीन, having the same meaning, is from प्यै. ०**जठर:**—*i. e.* a person having such a belly.

**सीधुसुरासव**—There are three different kinds of wine. सीधु is wine distilled from boiled sugar-cane juice. आसव is one prepared from unboiled cane-juice grapes &c.; see com. सुरा is fermented liquor made from rice &c.; शालिषष्टिकपिष्टादिकृतं मद्यं सुरा स्मृता; it is of three kinds-गौडी पैष्टी च माध्वी च विज्ञेया त्रिविधा सुरा । Manus. XI. 94. **यदि म्रियते** &c —Here Vidu carries his humour rather too far. **यानपात्राणि** &c.—Vidu. means by asking this question that such princely wealth as Vasanta. possessed could not be had unless one had ships sailing to distant countries for carrying on trade. This shows that Ujjain had an extensive sea-borne trade in those days.

P. 170. **बहुवृत्तान्त**—With its multifarious affairs and contents. **त्रिविष्टपं**—त्रीणि विष्टपानि तेषां समहार: the three worlds; *i. e.* the things in the three worlds collected together. Some take **त्रिविष्टप** in the sense of 'the celestial abode of the the gods,' which is not the meaning here, as it goes against एकस्थमिव. **परिच्छेद:**—a section or a portion cut off; *cf.* स्वर्गिणां गां गतानां शेषै: पुण्यैर्हृतमिव दिव: कान्तिमत्खण्डमेकम् । Megh. I. 30.

**अच्छरीति० रोपिता:**—Planted in such a way as to enable them to put forth flowers in a beautiful manner; *i. e.* being pruned of their superfluous branches and parasitical overgrowth. The reading अच्छरीअकुसुमा ( आश्चर्यकुसुमा: ) 'having wonderful flowers,' is not bad. **निरन्तर०**—growing close to one another; *i. e.* affording thick shade; the swings could be suspended from such trees only. **सुवर्ण०**—Names of different flowers. Some take सुवर्णयूथिका as one word, meaning 'the yellow jasmine.' **यूथिका**—a kind of a jasmine (called जुई in Marathi ) and much liked by women; *cf.* गजयूथपयूथिकाशबलकेशी । Vik. IV. 24. **शेफालिका**—(नेवाळी in Mar.) is a fragrant white flowers; *cf.* शेफालिकाकुसुमगन्धमनोहराणि। Rit III. 14. **मालती**—(चमेली in Mar.), and **मल्लिका** (जाई in Mar.), are kinds of jasmine called respectively 'jasminum grandiflorum,' and 'jasminum zambac;' these are also often referred to by poets; for मालती see Megh; II. 38, Rit II. 24; and for मल्लिका Ragh. XVI. 47. **नवमालिका**—Double jasmine. **कुरबक**—( तांबडी कोरांटी in Mar.) is red amaranth. **अतिमुक्त**—( मोगरी in Mar. ) is the spring creeper, so called because it has white flowers bigger than pearls. **लघूकरोति** &c.—Because Indra's garden has five kinds of trees (पञ्चैते देवतरव: Amara.) only, while Vasanta.'s garden has so many varieties of flowering plants. **दीर्घिका**—an oblong tank or a large well in a garden with lotus-plants in it; see Malav. II. 12:

**अशोकवृक्ष:**—Here the red Asoka (Jonesia Asoka); न शोक: अस्मादिति अशोक:—so called because it is delight-giving to the eyes and is mentioned in connexion with love-affairs or the god of love. With regard to this tree Sir William Jones says—'The vegetable world scarcely exhibits a richer sight than an Asoka tree in blossom.' **घनलोहितपङ्क०**—**चर्चा** is 'anointing or besmearing the body with an unguent;' here the fresh and therefore reddish leaves and the red flowers of the Asoka are compared to the thickened blood from the wounds, received by a brave warrior in a fight:

P. 172. संस्कृतमाश्रित्य—Prakrit-speaking characters may, at intervals, be made to speak in Sanskrit, to show their literary accomplishment, according to the precept of Bharata—कार्यतश्चोत्तमादीनां कार्यो भाषाविपर्ययः । योषित्सखीबालवेश्याकितवाप्सरसां तथा । वैदग्ध्यार्थं प्रदातव्यं संस्कृतं चान्तरान्तरा ॥ See also p. 14 com.

गुणप्रवालं—By a highly-wrought metaphor, Vasanta. compares Charudatta to a tree. गुणाः accomplishments एव प्रवालाः foliage यस्य तं. विश्रम्भमूल—विश्रम्भ people's confidence that he will ever act nobly. महनीयपुष्पं—महनीय is here used in the sense of a noun (महनीयत्वं), 'loftiness of character, magnanimity;' or महितुं योग्यं महनीयं यशः fame तदेव पुष्पं यस्य. स्वगुणैः—The natural qualities of the soul; see com. सुहृद्विहंगाः &c.—'Do his friends still cling to him affectionately, or have they gone away like birds leaving a tree when it is destitute of fruit ?' Although asking a general question, she pointedly refers to Maitreya—'Do you still continue to be faithful to him ?'

सुष्ठूप०—*i. e.* she has well marked these traits of Charudatta's character. राजवार्ताहारी—As keeper of a licensed gaming house, it was the duty of the Sabhika to keep the king informed of what happened at the house and of the profits made. See *supra*, note on Sabhika p. 72. Or this may mean 'on some errand of the king.' The variant राजापथ्यकारी is bad, as there was nothing wrong in presiding over a gambling house. The talk about gambling is an invention of the Vidu. and bears testimony to his ready wit. He had strict instructions from his master and friend not to return without making Vasanta. accept the ornament; see *supra*, p. 130. He had to account for the loss of Vasanta.'s casket some way or other. Were he to say that it was stolen, Vasanta. would not have accepted anything in exchange for it. So the only way out of the difficulty was to account for the loss in the way the Vidu. does.

आर्ये दिष्टया वर्धसे—The Cheti congratulates her mistress on Charu.'s having turned a gambler, as he was in that case expected to be more attached to her. शौण्डीर्यता—nobility of heart, magnanimity; see *supra*, p. 130.

P. 174. किं तावत् &c.—Although faithfully carrying out his friend's instructions, the Vidu. has some faint hope that Vasanta. might decline to accept the jewel necklace, and asks her a suggestive question. In the Charu. the Vidu does nothing of the kind; he simply hands over the ornament **विहस्य**--smiling (perceptibly) Technically, विहसितं is midway between स्मित (a gentle smile) and हास or प्रहास; it is defined as आकुञ्चितकपोलाक्षं सस्वनं निःस्वनं तथा । प्रस्तावोत्थं सानुरागमाहुर्विहसितं बुधाः ।। स्याद्दाच्छुरितकं हासः सोत्प्रासः स मनाक् स्मितम् । मध्यमः स्याद्विहसितं; Amara I. 7. 34, 35. Vasanta. smiled because she understood what the Vidu meant by his question **पार्श्वे स्थापयति**--She did not wear it; for she wanted to return it herself, paying a visit to Charu. apparently in connexion with that; see p 204. **कथं हीनकुसु०**--Vasanta. wonders how a costly necklace of jewels like that could still be found with Charudatta Charu. with his wealth lost is compared to a mango-tree without blossoms. **प्रसङ्गात्**—His contact with; his having anything to do with. **अभिरन्तुं गच्छावः**—In the Charu. Vasanta. speaks more modestly and says—एहि इममलकारं गृहीत्वाऽऽर्यचारुदत्त-मभिसरिष्यावः. **दुर्दिन**—Properly, a cloudy day; here, by लक्षणा, the clouds overcasting the sky **वर्षं**—From वृष् and अ (अच्); when meaning rain, it is *m.* and *neu.*; पुंनपुंसकयोर्वर्षं जम्बुद्वीपाद्यवृष्टिषु --इति रुद्रः।. These last two speeches serve to introduce the subject-matter of the next Act.

## ACT V.

The fifth Act describes the visit of Vasantasena to Charudatta as indicated at the close of the last Act, in the midst of heavy rain, thunderstorm and terrible lightning-flashes. Also in it, the consummation of Vasantasena's love for Charudatta is reached. The poet seizes this opportunity to describe the rainy season; his description, however, is for the most part conventional, is full of repetitions, and is carried to a tedious length.

P. 176. **सोत्कण्ठ** – For उत्कण्ठा see p. 66 and notes thereon. **शिखण्डिभिः**—शिखण्डः the crest or plume अस्यास्तीति शिखण्डी a peacock. **उत्कलापैः**—The peacocks raised their plumage and danced in joy, as is their wont at the approach of the rainy season, according to the poets **यियासुभिः**—यियासु is a noun in उ from the desiderative base of या to go. **अपाकृतं**—*lit* looked askance at, despised by. **उन्मनस्कैः**—उत्कण्ठितं मनः येषां तैः; anxious to go to the Manasa lake. This also is according to poetic convention; *cf*. तच्छ्रुत्वा ते श्रवणसुभगं गर्जितं मानसोत्काः संपत्स्यन्ते नभसि भवतो राजहंसाः सहायाः। Megh I. 11; also हंसा नदन्मेघभयाद् द्रवन्ति निशामुखान्यद्य न चन्द्रवन्ति। नवाम्बुमत्ताः शिखिनो वदन्ति मेघागमे कुन्दसमा नदन्ति ॥ Ghatakarpara For these and other conventions of poets, *cf* मालिन्यं व्योम्नि पापे यशसि धवलता वर्ण्यते हासकीर्त्योः। ज्योत्स्ना पेया चकोरैर्जलधरसमये मानसं यान्ति हंसाः। मेघध्वानेषु नृत्यं भवति च शिखिनां नाप्यशोके फलं स्यात्। &c. &c. Sah.-Dar. VII. 23 25

(**हंस**)—"The wild grey goose, which bird is supposed to migrate annually to the Himalaya Mountains, particularly to the Manasa lake, whence it is termed *Manasaukas*, 'the dweller of Manasa.' Mr. Moorcroft, in his adventurous visit to this like in 1812, found the birds in vast flocks along the beach and on the water, and concluded from what he saw, that they were accustomed to frequent the lake and breed in the surrounding rocks, when the swell of the rivers of Hindustan and the inundation of the plains conceal their usual food."—Wilson.

**उत्कण्ठितस्य हृदयं च**—*Cf* मेघालोके भवति सुखिनोऽप्यन्यथावृत्ति चेतः कण्ठाश्लेषप्रणयिनि जने किं पुनर्दूरसंस्थे। Megh. I. 3.

**मेघो जलार्द्र°** &c.—In this Sl. the cloud is compared to the dark-blue body of Vishnu, by means of common attributes. **जलार्द्र°**—applies equally to both; जलार्द्र goes with महिषोदर only, and is employed to make it more dark. **विद्युत्प्रभा** &c.—Vishnu wears a bright-yellow garment; it is supplied in the case of the cloud by the bright-yellowish flashes of lightning; for the diss.

of the comp see com. **संहतबलाक** &c.—Vishnu has in his hand the big conch called पाञ्चजन्य (formed, according to some, from the skeleton of the sea-demon Panchajana); the cloud also has a conch in the shape of the flock of the cranes going up to meet it; to bear out the comparison with Panchajanya, a flock is taken, as a single crane cannot resemble it For the Balakas (a species of cranes) flying up into the sky, *cf.* गर्भाधानक्षणपरिचयान्नूनमाबद्धमाला: सेविष्यन्ते नयनसुभगं खे भवन्तं बलाका: । Megh. I. 10. **खं केशव:** &c.—Thus the cloud looks like a second Vishnu as it were. There may also be a reference here to the Dwarf incarnation of Vishnu (Vamana), who, in order to punish Bali, appeared before him as Vamana, asked for land measuring three steps, and when the requst was granted, assumed a gigantic form, covered with two steps the earth and the sky, and, planting the third step on the head of Bali, pressed him down to the nether world. The story is too well-known to students to require further details here.

P. 178. **केशवगात्र०**—This is a mere repetition of the preceding sl. in a compressed form, and thus forms a rhetorical defect (पुनरुक्त). **केशवगात्र०**—when taken with **चक्रधर** this must be taken as केशवश्चासौ गात्रश्यामश्च; प्रशस्ता: केशा: सन्त्यस्य इति केशव:; there is no propriety in saying चक्रधर: केशवगात्रमिव श्याम:. This sl. is probably an interpolation.

**एता निषिक्त** &c.—An instance of high-flown fancy, a happy idea being clothed in verse. अम्बरपट and विद्युत्प्रदीप are two Utprekshas. *V. l.* **नष्टदृष्टा:**—is not good, as they are first seen and then vanish from view. **दशा:**—They are compared to the fringes of the vast cloth of the sky, as they are not universally seen, but only when lit up by the flash of lightning.

**संसक्तैरिव** &c.—The description in the previous Sl. must be taken as referring to rain in the distance. Now he looks overhead (इह), and describes the appearance of the sky chequered by clouds of various shapes **हंसै:**—*i. e.* moving in a body. **व्याविद्धै:**—tossed about, scattered without order. **प्रोच्छ्रितै:**—lofty. **आकृतिविस्तरै:**—is instrumental to अनुगतै:; आकृतिविस्तरै: अनुगता: तै: मेघै:. **पत्रच्छेद्यमिव**—Variegated with ornamental paintings or drawings. **एतत्तद्** &c.—This description is again conventional. **धृतराष्ट्रचक्रं**—The kingdom of Dhritarashtra. The reading ०वक्त्रसदृशं has no propriety. His face could not have been dark on account of the absence of sight. The sky overcast with clouds is compared to the kingdom of Dhri., the points of similarity being given in the following three lines. The sky being covered with clouds, the peacock is shrieking with delight, like Duryodhana in the kingdom of Dhri., वा has here the sense of इव; *cf.* पद्मिनीं वाऽन्यरूपां Megh. II. 23; इववत् वायथाशब्दौ । Dandin. In translating the first line we have followed L. Dikshita who takes चक्र in the sense of 'an army.' But there is no point in this; an army is not always on march; and there is no reason why Dhri.'s army alone should have been chosen. So read 'kingdom' for 'army' in the translation.

अध्वानं--(1) journey; (2) silence; see com. **अज्ञातचर्या-चर्या** (1) motion; (2) residence (in the case of the Pandavas). The story of Yudhishthira's having gambled away his kingdom is well known. According to the conditions imposed upon them by Duryodhana, the Pandavas had to lead a solitary life for twelve years in a forest and to remain incognito for one year. This year they passed in the city of Virata. The geese, too, pass secretly to unknown regions (*i. e.* of the Manasa lake).

P. 180. (**न कथाऽपि कृता**) **अन्या**–*i. e.* other than what related to Charudatta (for instance, she did not ask me anything about myself, nor asked her servants to give any sweetmeats to me). Some read कथाऽपि न कृताऽनया । अनादरेणैव अभणित्वा किमपि &c.; but this is against facts; Vasanta. did say something to Vidu. **किमपि**—goes with भणित्वा and not with एवमेव, which means 'just in this way, without saying one word of refusal, without much ceremony.' **मल्लक**—a cup. **कन्द:**—a bulbous root. **अञ्जलिं मस्तके कृत्वा**—*i. e.* with thanks, with the greatest willingness.

P. 182. **पादुका**—a shoe or sandal. **लेष्टुका**—a small stone, pebble; अल्प: लेष्टु: लेष्टुक:; क्षुद्रार्थे क:, with the fem. off. **आ. प्रत्यवाय**—may mean 'impediments', or shortcomings, or sins. **कायस्थ:**—A man of mixed origin, being the offspring of a Kshatriya father and a Sudra mother. The Kayasthas formed the writer class. 'Men of this tribe were usually employed by the Hindu princes in the collection and record of their revenue, and their character for a spirit of extortion became proverbial.' (Wilson). It was on account of this their spirit of extortion and treacherous disposition, that they came to be hated by the people. Kshemendra in his कलाविलास has a scathing satire on them, and in his भारतमञ्जरी he says–सर्वापहारचतुरा लेखचीत्कारकारिणः । कायस्थाः क्षमा करिष्यन्ति सुषिरां मूषका इव ॥. Mr. Sarma quotes the verse—कायस्थेनोदरस्थेन मातुर्मांसं न भक्षितम् । दयाहेतुर्न चैवात्र दन्ताभावो हि कारणम्* ॥ **चाट**—a rogue; a cheat; चट् (भेदे) + अच्. Some take चाट in the sense of 'a vile seeker of sensual pleasures.' **चाट** is mentioned along with the Kayasthas in the Yaj. Smrit—चाटतस्करदुर्वृत्तमहासाहसिकादिभिः । पीड्यमानाः प्रजा रक्षेत्कायस्थैश्च विशेषतः ॥ I. 336, whereon the Mitakshara says—चाटाः प्रतारकाः विश्वास्य ये धनमपहरन्ति । कायस्था लेखका गणकाश्च । तेभ्यः रक्षेत् । तेषां राजवल्लभतयाऽतिमायावित्त्वाच्च दुर्निवारत्वात् ।. **रासभ**—Because an ass is a voracious eater of corn, and is looked down upon as an inauspicious animal leading to poverty (**अपचयहेतुः** . **दुष्टाः**—L. D. takes this in the sense of **दोषाः** (remarking भावे क्तः; but then we should expect **दुष्टं** instead of **दुष्टः**) and says—न जायन्ते अपि तु जायन्ते एव ।. **न जायन्ते**—*i. e.* these do not allow a person to prosper. Some render जाअन्ति by **यान्ति** ; then the meaning is—Even wicked people do (should) not go there; what to say then about good men ?

**सवं परिवादं**—Condemnation in every way. *V. l.* **सर्वपरिवादं**—the traducing of everything. **तुरगः**—*i. e.* a wearied horse. **प्राणव्ययात्**—प्राणस्य शक्तेः व्ययात् owing to the loss of energy or mettle. **स्वभावाः**—natural dispositions ; here, desires or fancies. **खिन्नाः** &c.—*Cf* उत्थाय हृदि लीयन्ते निर्धनानां मनोरथाः । and **उत्पद्यन्ते** विलीयन्ते दरिद्राणां मनोरथाः । Subhashitas. **कामो वाम इति**—वाम perverse, obstinately bent on doing mischief. *Cf.* कामस्य वामा गतिः Git. XII Dr. Ryder remarks—'In कामो वामः the Vidu. makes use of his third homely prose proverb in this Scene. This is one of the touches which make Maitreya a living character, very different from the stock Vidushaka.'

P. 184. **अवेत**—Know, understand. Dr. Ryder rightly observes—'Stenzler and J. V. are wrong in rendering **अवेध** by **अपेत**.' अपेत makes no sense here. **अभ्रखण्ड**—a detached collection of clouds, and not 'a broken cloud (**अभ्रशकल**)' as some take it, as it cannot give continuous rain. **तिम्यति**—तिम् 4. P. to be wet.

**वंशं वादयामि** &c.—It is difficult to see the propriety of this sl., which has no connexion here. Perhaps it is intended to indi-

---

* "Parasari gives a fanciful (but humorous) derivation of the word according to its letters ; *e. g.* क is taken from काक (crow) whose excessive passion or desire is found in the Kayasthas, &c. &c."

cate one of the qualifications of a *Cheta, viz.* that he must know instrumental and vocal music. **सुशब्दं**—may be an adv. modifying वादयामि (so as to produce sweet notes.), or an adj. to वंश (sweet sounding) **वीणां सप्ततन्त्रीं**—An instrument like the modern *Sitar*, said to have been invented by Narada. **गर्दभस्या०**—said for fun. **तुम्बुरु**—A Gandharva with a horse's head. Narada, son of Brahma, and Tumburu, are described as the best of the heavenly musicians, the former excelling in playing on the lute, the latter in music.

**प्रविष्टकेन**—प्रविष्टं (भावे क्तः—त added in the sense of a noun) entrance; प्रविष्टमेव प्रविष्टकं तेन; used in the sing. only, as a stage direction; 'gesticulating entrance.' **प्राकार**—a fence or enclosure. **कपित्थ**—the wood-apple (Feronia Elephantum; कवठ in Mar ) It is an inferior fruit, sour in taste. *Cf.* VI. 21, where it seems to have been used in the sense of the Marathi कंवडळ which, although attractive from outside, is worthless when broken.

**प्रासादवेदिका**—a raised seat or terrace of the pleasure-house.

P. 186. **तिष्ठतु दयितास०**:—Charu., who knows now what longing is, feels sympathy for the pigeon in the enjoyment of the company of his mate. We have a similar scene in Ratn. after II. 6 where the Vidu. wants to knock off a *Sarika* like a Kapittha fruit with his cudgel, whereupon the king says—मूर्ख किमप्येषा रमणीयं व्याहरति। तत्किमेनां त्रासयसि। **दुर्दिनेऽन्धकारे**—in darkness on such a cloudy day. Dr. Ryder would have a च after अन्धकारे, which will, however, spoil the sense. It is the darkness of a cloudy day which is more intense that is meant here, and not the two, a दुर्दिन and darkness. **रङ्कः**—a beggar (who sighs after being fatigued by wandering here and there for alms). **श्वासायसे**—is a demom from श्वास, meaning 'to breathe heavily.'

**इन्द्रमहकामुकः**—इन्द्रमहे कामुकः eager to get oblations; काकः इत्यर्थः. Some take ०कामुकः in the sense of 'a dog,' which is not appropriate, as is shown by the verb काकायसे.

Indramaha was a festival held in honour of Indra in ancient India. It was also called Indradhvajotthapana, or the raising of Indra's flag. It was celebrated for five days from the eighth of the bright half of Bhadrapada to the 12th, for getting timely rain and general prosperity. Its chief feature was the erection of a post with a flag attached to it; for this purpose a tall tree was felled in a forest for making a pole and was solemnly brought to the city. It was again removed to the forest on the last day. See *infra* चतुरस्र ध्वजाकार

राजद्वारे प्रतिष्ठितम् । आहुः शक्रध्वजं नाम पौरलोकसुखावहम् ॥ Bhavishyottara-Purana. For its full description, see our Sanskrit note on Ragh. IV. 3, and Brihatsam. Ch. 43. A crow is supposed to be the son of Indra; for Jayanta, Indra's son, according to one account, came in that form to test the power of Rama as Vishnu. See Ragh. XII. 22. A crow is given a share in a sacrifice; and hence is called बलिभुक्. The Mahabharata relates—A king named Vasu Uparichara, who ruled over Chedi, laid down his arms and lived in a hermitage, practising penance. Indra and the other gods came to him there and induced him to cease from ascetic practices. Indra gave him an aerial car, a triumphant garland of lotuses (ददामि ते वैजयन्तीं मालामम्लानपङ्कजां &c.) and a bamboo pole. This last he planted into the ground for the purpose of worshipping Indra. From that time all kings erect a staff with a flag in honour of Indra. See Adip. Ch. 63, slokas 1—21).

अहं ते मस्तके &c.— *i. e.* I defy you; I shall easily solve your riddle जानीहि तावत् तेन हि—If so, then first guess, man, this.

P. 188 रथ्या—रथानां समूहः a collection of *rathas* or fighting cars; or cars bringing corn to the city. It does not and cannot mean 'a street' here; in that case the word सुसमृद्ध loses its force. The Vidu.'s answers are near, though not exactly to, the point; *cf.* above ग्रीष्मः. सेनावसन्त—Vidu. purposely puts the words in wrong order, that there should be room for some quibbling further on. परिवर्त्य—Cheta means—'transposing the words सेना and 'वसन्त.' Maitreya, quibbling on the word, understands by it देहं परिवर्त्य, and repeats the same thing again, bodily turning round. There is similarly a pun on the word पदे again, पदे meaning the words of the compound सेनावसन्त, and feet. Wilson remarks—" The very term might be suspected of etymological affinity to the English 'Pun', being Pahna, the Prakrit form of Prasna, a question." धनिकः—A creditor. The Vidu. humorously calls Vasantasena thus, meaning thereby that she has come to claim more money for her *Suvarnabhanda*. यदि कुले नास्ति—The Vidu. makes a pun upon the word कुल, which means 'a family', as well as 'a house'.

P 190 अभिसारिका—A woman who, under the influence of passion, makes her lover come to her (-this happens rarely-) or herself goes to meet him. अभिसारयते कान्तं या मन्मथवशंवदा । स्वयं वाऽभिसरत्येषा धीरैरुक्ताऽभिसारिका । Sah.-D. III. 76. When a courtesan is an *abhisarika*, she must go in a splendid dress, with a smiling countenance and with jingling ornaments; see Sah.-D. III. 78, quoted in the com.

**अपद्मा श्रीरेषा** &c.—This is a general description of Vasant. and has no reference to her present visit to Charudatta's house. अपद्मा—' But without the lotus that forms her seat.' **ललितं**—graceful; *cf.* उर्वशी सुकुमारं प्रहरणं महेन्द्रस्य । Vik. I. p. 10; इदमिह मदनस्य जैत्रमस्त्रं Mal.-Madh. II 6. कुलस्त्रीणां शोकः—For her exquisite beauty was sure to attract their husbands away, and make them cease to love them. कुसुमं—She is compared to a flower, because young men were captivated and drawn to her as bees are by the honey and fragrance of a flower. **सलीलं गच्छन्ती** &c.—Construe रतिसमयलज्जाप्रणयिनी (feeling bashful even as regards the time of sexual sports, *i. e.* not seeking them, out of bashfulness) रतिक्षेत्रे रङ्गे सलीलं गच्छन्ती (walking gracefully along the stage in the form of the field of love, *i e* exciting passion by her maddening youthful charms) प्रियपथिकसार्थैरनुगता च (she is followed by crowds of loving persons, *i e.* gallants going after her); and hence कुलस्त्रीणां शोकः &c. The idea is the same as in यदालोकस्थाने भवति पुरमुन्मादतरलैः कटाक्षैर्नारीणां कुवलयितवातायनमिव । Mal.-Madh. II. 11, though in this case it is a male that excites passion. The passage is misunderstood by commentators and annotators. If we take गच्छन्ती in connexion with her present visit to Charudatta, the fourth line remains unconnected. Again, सलीलगमन was not possible amid heavy rain and thunderstorm. रतिसमय० also cannot be properly explained. She was going with the avowed purpose of enjoying the company of Charudatta; there was no लज्जा about it. *Cf.* her speech चारुदत्तमभिरन्तुं गच्छाव: and sl.33, p. 174.

**०बिम्बाः**—Disc-like round forms; *cf.* दरीगृहद्वारविलम्बिबिम्बाः Kum. I. 14. **वियुक्तवनिता०**—The dark clouds are compared to the sorrow stricken and therefore dark hearts of women separated from their husbands. The hearts are dark because they are void of joy, which is poetically considered white. मणिमयैः इव—The plumages of the peacocks, on account of their eyes of bright and various colours, resembled fans set with jewels. **ख वीज्यते**—Although the eyes on the tails of the peacocks were not actually seen in the darkness, he says so on seeing the peacocks flapping their wings.

**बर्हिणः**—a peacock; from बर्ह (a peacock's tail or feathers; see Sis. VIII. 11) अस्यास्तीति; and इन (इनिन्) which is added to फल and बर्ह; so फलिनः having fruit; बर्ह also takes इन्, when we have **बर्ही. नीपः प्रदीपायते**—The Nipa, also known as Kadamba, has bright buds and blossoms at the roaring thunder, when sprinkled with fresh rain-water. *Cf.* सीमन्ते च त्वदुपगमजं यत्र नीपं वधूनां Megh. II. 2; also I. 25; मरुन्नवाम्भःप्रविधूतसिक्ता कदम्बयष्टिः स्फुटकोरकेव Uttar. III. 42. Some take समदनः with नीपः, 'with the Madana tree.' **संन्यासः कुल०**—यथा संन्यासः क्रियते, as Samnyasa is readily embraced by people of an ignominious character and brought into disrepute by them, so the moon is obscured by the clouds and brought into disrepute for not giving light. People who lead a dissolute life readily become Samnyasins, as a means of covering their vile deeds; and, not being able to follow the rules of the life of a recluse, they generally bring a stigma on it. **नीचकुलो०**—Here by नीच is meant a family of females leading a debauched life; or a harlot; such a woman does not remain faithful to one man. **संतिष्ठते--स्था**, with सम् अव, प्र, and sometimes वि, is Atm. by समवप्रविभ्यः स्थः Pan. I. 3. 22; for the simile *cf. supra* I. 35.

P. 192. **मूढे** &c.—Vasant. calls the night her rival-wife, addressing her as **मूढे** &c. **निरन्तरपयोधरया**—With the night–'having clouds close together;' with the rival wife—' with breasts leaving no space between,' *i. e.* so plump as to touch each other (**इति विनिवारयन्ती**)—stands for the sentence formed by the first two lines. It is not a happy idea to make the night Charudatta's beloved and Vasant.'s rival. There is nothing to support such a supposition except the quibbling on **निरन्तरपयोधरया.**

**स्त्रीस्वभावदुर्विदग्धया**—दुर्विदग्धा badly wise, not giving up her point; hence, obstinate (as is the nature of women). These words should rather have been put in the mouth of Vita, as Vasant. herself is a **स्त्री. मुञ्चन्त्वशनि**--hold up the thunderbolt, *i. e.* lightning.

**पवनचपलवेगः** &c.--The epithets have a double application as they go with **मेघ** and **नृप**; for these see Com. and translation. **करसमूहं**--(2) the amount of collected taxes. The moon shining with mild light is compared to a feeble enemy who is easily overpowered. *Cf.* सशीकराम्भोधरमत्तकुञ्जरस्तडित्पताकोऽशनिशब्दमर्दलः । समागतो राजवदुद्धतद्युतिर्घनागमः कामिजनप्रियः प्रिये ॥ Rit. II. 1. **एतैरेव** &c.—The idea is– When the roaring clouds have already sufficiently wounded the hearts of women separated from their husbands, and made them long for their husbands, it is a pity that the malicious stork should make their case worse by actually uttering the words ' the rainy season--the rainy season. ' The cry of the *Baka* resembles in sound the word Pravrit. *Cf.* मेघालोके भवति &c. quoted on p 95 of our notes. आध्मात०--L.-D. says (see Com ) आध्माता: शब्दायमाना: &c ; but this is not a good way, as the word गर्जद्भि: already occurs further on. शबल—variegated. सशल्यं—*Salya* is an arrow-head which causes pain where it is lodged; here the yearning caused by the appearance of the clouds is the शल्य, as it causes pain in their hearts. प्रोषितभर्तृ०—प्रोषिता: (gone on a journey) भर्तार: यासां ता:; the final क which must be added to such words (see sl. 20 below) at the end of a Bah. is not added, as the rule is not absolutely binding; see Com.; तासां वध्यपटह: । वध्यसंबन्धी पटह: वध्यपटह:, a drum beaten to announce the slaughter of a victim. The cry of the stork is just like the sound of the death-drum announcing the near approach of death. प्रावृट्—this would resemble the cry of the crane in sound. क्षारं क्षते &c.--This expression has become proverbial, and means ' to add misery to misfortune, ' to make a case worse; *cf* क्षते क्षारमिवासह्यं जातं तस्यैव दर्शनम् Uttar. IV. 7. The hearts of the women were already wounded (सशल्यं); the cry of the crane, which constantly reminded them of the rainy reason, made their case worse and thus acted like salt cast on a wound. *Cf.* दग्धा पूर्वमहं वसन्तसमये चूताङ्कुरै: कोकिलै: पाप प्रावृषि गर्जितै: किमपरं कर्तव्यमन्यत्त्वया । दीना कान्तवियोगदु:खविधुरा क्षामा तनुर्वर्तते क्षारं प्रक्षिपसि क्षते जलधर प्राणावशेषस्थिते: ।। For the rainy season being extremely unbearable to women, *cf.* शिखिनि कूजति गर्जति तोयदे स्फुटति जातिलताकुसुमाकरे । अहह पान्थ न जीवति ते प्रिया नभसि मासि न यासि गृहं यदि ।।.

P. 194. उष्णीषं--उष्णमीषते हिनस्ति (destroys) removes इति; fr. ईष्+अ (क:); a head-dress, or turban. आपीत—completely or entirely drunk up, *i. e.* obscured. सीदन्ति--(1) sink down; (2) crouch low; or experience pain. वनिता--a beautiful woman with passion; वनिता जनितात्यर्थानुरागायां च योषिति । Amara. कक्षा—(1) the middle part; (2) arm-pits. रूप्यरज्ज्वा—The white streams of water are looked upon as silver chains. आध्मातै:--thundering, roaring (com); or, better, inflated or swollen (by being driven together). गन्धोद्दामा--(1) sending forth a powerful smell; (2) insolent with pride; see com. नवहरित०—explains the comparison to मणिमय शरs. The glossy green shoots of grass look like arrows of gems (emeralds or sapphires) pierced (fixed) into the earth. There is a confusion of ideas in this sl. The clouds are compared to the seas and yet they are described as shooting arrows. विद्युत्पक्षैः has no propriety. It is simply brought in to explain the चलत्व of the clouds. The comparison of lightning to wings is not happy. धारापातैः should better have been omitted; then we could have got a fine Utpreksha.

P. 196. पटुतरं--Very cleverly or loudly. आक्रन्दितः Hailed, greeted; *cf.* शुक्लापाङ्गैः सजलनयनैः स्वागतीकृत्य केकाः प्रत्युद्यातः Megh. I. 23; मयूरकेकाभिरिवाभ्रवृन्दम् Ragh. VII. 69.

बलाकया--by a row of cranes. सोत्कण्ठं--longingly. *Cf.* गर्भाधानक्षणपरिचयान्नूनमाबद्धमालाः सेविष्यन्ते नयनसुभगं खे भवन्तं बलाकाः। Megh. I. 10. अञ्जनमेचका :--मेचक dark blue; better dissolve अञ्जनेन मेचकाः; अञ्जनवन्मेचकाः will make the quarters deep dark like collyrium, which they were not.

निष्पन्दीकृत &c.--In this sl. the world is fancied as sleeping in the house formed of rain-showers under the canopy of clouds, with its eyes in the form of the beds of lotuses closed and its face in the shape of the circle of quarters muffled, with all distinction of night and day lost. पद्मषण्ड--a bed of lotuses. क्षपा—क्षपयति चेष्टां (the actions or movements of creatures) इति क्षपा; fr. क्षै 1st Conj. P., to cause to cease, to dispel, and aff. अ (अच्). निश्चेष्टं Its movements stopped owing to heavy rain. पयोधारागृहा०--The enveloping showers are compared to the walls forming a house; but the idea is very strange. स्फीताम्भोधर०--For the comp. see Com.; छत्रापिधानं--the multitudinous clouds gathered in the wide expanse of the sky are the umbrellas forming the canopy of the धारागृह. Some take स्फीताम्भोधरधाम separately, स्फीतं अम्भोधरा एव धाम यस्य; but it not a good way, as it is tantalogous with धारागृहा०. The idea expressed in this sl. is not properly worked out. The world, although निश्चेष्ट in the rain, does not lose consciousness as in sleep. The torrents of water falling all round cannot be fitly compared to the walls forming a house. The last line is laboured, and the idea is faulty in that the canopy is not *above* but *in* the house.

उपकृतं &c.—*Cf.* असत्पुरुषसेवेव दृष्टिर्विफलतां गता *supra* I. 34. वियुक्ताः कान्तेन &c.—Because women, when separated from their husbands, do not attend to their toilet; *cf.* Manu. प्रोषिते मलिना कृशा. In sl. 13 (*supra*) the hearts of women in separation are said to be dark; here their external appearance is referred to. त्रिदश० — *i. e.* the thunderbolt. त्रिदशाः—the gods; त्रिदश 30 standing for 33. Or तिस्रः जन्मसत्ताविनाशाख्याः दशाः येषां; or तृतीया यौवनाख्या दशा येषां ते.

प्रथमश्रीरिव—A man who obtains a large fortune for the first time, *i. e.* being poor suddenly becomes rich; an upstart. करोति रूपाणि &c.—'puts on various appearances;' this is explained in the first half. उन्नमति—(1) rises up; (2) walks with a standing gait, displays haughtiness. नमति—(1) sinks low; hangs down; (2) stoops to low things; or acts humbly. वर्षति—showers (1) water, (2) gifts or money indiscriminately. गर्जति—(1) thunders; (2) talks of himself boastfully; speaks proudly. तिमिरौघं—(1) a number of black *i. e.* evil deeds; stores up sin.

संविहसतीव—Because the cranes are of a white colour, and smiles are supposed by poetic convention to be white. माहेन्द्रेण धनुषा—*i. e.* the rain-bow. विवल्गति—displays activity; leaps forth with energy (for fighting as it were). वल्ग् with अप occurs in I. 19. How the cranes can be seen in the nocturnal darkess, or how we can have a rain-bow (which is due to the solar rays) at night, are questions with which poets are not concerned, for the descriptions of poets are not fettered by the laws of nature, as observed by Mammata—नियतिकृतनियमरहितां ...... नवरसरुचिरां निर्मितिमादधती भारती कवेः. आघूर्णति—Reels or whirls about. अनिलैः—tempestuous winds. अहिभिः—The black clouds sailing in the sky are compared to black serpents gliding on. धूपायति—Becomes possessed of the smoke of incense etc.; for this sense of धूप *cf.* धूपोष्मणा त्याजितमार्द्रभावं &c. Kum. VII. 14. We should rather have read धूमायति 'looks covered or filled with smoke;' for what is intended here is to express the resemblance of clouds to smoke; *cf.* धूमज्योतिः—सलिलमरुतां संनिपातः क्व मेघः Megh. I. 5 The verb is formed from धूम by adding य (क्यष्) which is added to the words of the लोहितादि group, the verbs so formed being optionally Parasmaipadi; and धूम forms one of the words of the लोहितादि group which is an आकृतिगण. *Cf.* धूमायिता दश दिशो दलितारविन्दाः Bv. I. 104.

निर्लज्जस्त्वं—For you frighten me and at the same time touch or seize me with your hands.

P. 198. पूर्वरतिप्रसक्ता—पूर्वा रतिः तस्यां प्रसक्ता deeply attached to you by love first made. प्रियकाङ्क्षितायाः—It would be natural to take the comp. as प्रियेण काङ्क्षितायाः, but this is against the fact; so we have to take it as प्रियः काङ्क्षितो यस्याः

**यद्वदहल्याहेतोः**—The allusion here is to Ahalya's seduction by Indra. Ahalya, the daughter of Brahma, was the wife of the sage Gotama. Indra once saw her and became enamoured of her. On one occasion, as Gotama went out early in the morning for bathing and performing the proper religious duties, Indra deceived her by the device of assuming her husband's shape and ravished her. For other particulars see our note on दीर्घतपसः परिग्रहः &c. Ragh. XI. 33. This absurd story of the Puranas had its origin in the allegorical description of Indra ( the sun ) giving chase to Ahalya the night (अहः लीयतेऽस्यां), and carrying away the shades of the night; the story is found in the Taittiriya Samhita of the Yajurveda and the Satapatha-Brahmana (*Cf.* इन्द्रागच्छेति गौरावस्कन्दिन्नहल्यायै जारेति० शतपथब्रा० का०३ अ० ३). Gotama is the moon. The Ramayana, speaking of Ahalya as the first-born daughter of Brahma, evidently refers to the night or the primeval darkness that prevailed before the creation of the world. This myth is also explained in another way. Indra is the god of rain, and Ahalya is unploughed land (अ not and हल the plough and aff. यत्); so this connexion of Indra with Ahalya is nothing more than the conversion of cultivable unploughed land into a fertile one by means of rain.

**मृषा वजसि** &c.—When Indra approached Ahalya in the form of her husband, she was surprised to find him come back so soon; but he dispelled her doubts by saying—'I am Gotama, come back so soon to meet you, being unable to overcome the influence of passion'. **तद्वन्ममापि दुःखं**—She means—'As you suffered pain on account of your longing for Ahalya, so do I.'

**निरपेक्ष**—'O you regardless of the torment of others!'. **निरवेक्ष्य** *v.l.*—is connected with दुःखं; ममापि दुःखं निरवेक्ष्य (having realized, taking into consideration) निवार्यतां &c.

**अयि विद्युत्** &c.—She means—As a female you ought to know how anxious women are to meet their lovers, and therefore you ought to sympathize with me and not put obstacles in my way. Mr. Sarma quotes–सोत्साहा नववारिभारगुरवो मुञ्चन्तु नादं घना वाता वान्तु कदम्बरेणुशबला नृत्यन्तु सर्पद्विषः। मग्नां कान्तवियोगदुःखजलधौ मां वीक्ष्य दीनाननां विद्युत्कि स्फुरसि त्वमप्यकरुणे स्त्रीत्वेऽपि तुल्ये सति ॥ Subhashita.

**ऐरावतः**—इरा उदकानि सन्त्यस्मिन्निति इरावान् the sea; इरावति भवः ऐरावतः by affixing अण्. **आखण्डलः**—Indra; आखण्डयति पर्वतान् इति; by the Unadi aff. कलच् (अल). **स्नेहः प्रलापयति**—*Cf.* तथाऽपि भवद्गुणसंतोषो मामेवं मुखरीकृतवान् । Kad. p. 180.

**कोपेन विना**—For feigned anger gives zest to pleasure; *cf.* न विना विप्रलम्भेन संभोगः पुष्टिमश्नुते । Sah.-Dar. **कदम्बनीप**—Since here the two are differently mentioned, नीप must be taken in the sense of the *Bandhuka* tree. नूपुरयोः लग्नः कर्दमस्तस्य धरौ.

P. 200. **एषा छत्रधारिका** &c.—This is a very clever way of suggesting that the Vita might now retire with the umbrella-bearer, as their services were no longer wanted.

**साटोपकूट**&c.—It is strange that the poet should make Vasanta.'s own Vita speak of the profession of a courtesan in such terms as he has done here. This shows that the profession was not held in high esteem even in those times. The poet has succinctly given us here his own idea of a courtesan's life already amplified by him in the fourth Act. **आटोप**—display of pride, arrogance. **कूट**—a secret plan to deceive or entrap one. **कपट**—fraud. See com. **शाठ्यात्मकस्य**—The very soul of which is roguery, *i.e.* which is based on it. **रतिकेलि०**—see com; a bad comp. **वेश्यापणस्य**—वेश्यारूपः आपणः (the market-place) तस्य; the profession of a harlot is compared here to a market-place **सुरतोत्सव०**—Where the commodities stored up (संगृह्यन्ते इति संग्रहाः) for sale are the festivities of sexual enjoyment. **दाक्षिण्यपण्य** &c.—दाक्षिण्यमेव पण्यं price तेन यः सुखस्य निष्क्रयः the sale of happpiness तस्य सिद्धिः success in. The idea is that Vasant. should sell the happiness she has in her possession (*cf.* सुरतोत्सवसंग्रहस्य *i.e.* at her disposal) for दाक्षिण्य (generosity or politeness), which only Charudatta can give her in exchange for her love;—thus, thinks the Vita, can a courtesan's love, which has hitherto been sold for money only, appear in its noblest aspect. The line may also be explained as पण्यरूपं सुखं पण्यसुखं; दाक्षिण्येन यत्पण्यसुखं तस्य निष्क्रयः purchase or price तस्य सिद्धिः *i.e.* show courtesy (be very polite) to Charudatta and obtain from him happiness as its price. The line is also explained as दाक्षिण्यं परचित्तानुरञ्जनमेव यत्पण्यं विक्रेयवस्तु तस्य सुखेन अनायासेन निष्क्रयसिद्धिः मूल्यप्राप्तिः अस्तु. Dr Ryder, who prefers the reading ०मुखनिष्क्रयसिद्धिः of the Nir. Ed. says—"The genitives modify ०मुख० as if we had दाक्षिण्यपण्यस्य मुखस्य &c.," and translates—"May you have success in the sale of your face, the birth-place of fraud &c. consisting of perfidy, in which love-sports have made their home; the courtesan's stock-in-trade, the compendium of amorous festivals; the price of which is courtesy But we do not see the propriety of making Vasant. sell her face."

**निष्क्रान्तो विटः**—It seems that Vita departs alone, although Vasant. had desired him to return with her maid. It is this maid who figures in the next Scene as the *Cheti*. **कुत्र युष्माकं द्यूतकरः**—Vasant. jokingly calls Charudatta a gamester, referring to his explanation given through the Vidu. of how the ornaments deposited with him were lost. द्यूतकर इति भणन्त्या &c.—The Vidu., unable to appreciate the spirit of the joke, ironically says this. He is surpised to find Vasant. addressing Charudatta as though he were a habitual gamester. Some think that the Vidu. really takes it as a compliment to his friend, since Vasant. shows thereby that she did not suspect him of having appropriated the casket of ornaments, and that she believed that it was really lost in gambling; but the word आश्चर्यं goes against this view. **का युष्माकं शुष्क—वृक्ष०**—Vasant., not knowing what to make of the expression शुष्कवृक्ष०—whether it was शुष्काणां वृक्षाणां वाटिका or शुष्का वृक्ष० asks the Vidu. to know what he meant by it. **यत्र न खाद्यते** &c.—This reply of the Vidu. is quite in keeping with his spirit of gormandism, and it makes Vasant smile on hearing it. He means—'It is a place where no banquets are given now.'

P. 202. **अपि पारयिष्यामि**—*i. e.*, to address him as a द्यूतकर, although it be in joke. Vasant. feels diffident as to her being able to address Char. in that way when actually in his presence. **अवसर एव** &c.—The Cheti cheers her up by saying that the occasion itself will give her courage to say it. Mr. Paranjpe puts this in contrast with Sita's words in the Uttar.—'भवतु कोपिष्यामि यदि तं प्रेक्षमाणाऽऽत्मनः प्रभविष्यामि' (Act I.) with the remark—'What a difference between Vasant. and Sita!' But the comparison is out of place, as the two occasions and situations are quite different. Besides, the one is a courtesan, the other a high-born married woman. **पुष्पैस्ताडयन्ती**—Vasant. soon overcomes her momentary nervousness, and knowing how to please her lover with the true genius of a courtesan strikes him with flowers. **प्रदोषः**—which usually means 'the first watch of the night' (see Kum. V. 44) is used here in the sense of 'the first half of the night.' त्वया समेतस्य &c.—*Cf.* पादास्त एव शशिनः सुखयन्ति गात्रं &c. Vik. III. 20.

कदम्बेन—The Kadamba flower used as an earornament. यौवराज्यस्थ:—A prince who is being installed as heirapparent. The simile is bad; there is no point of similarity between the two, except in so much as both are अभिषिक्त. The 'kingdom' meant here is the occupation of the lover's heart through the power of love. प्रधानवाससी--fine garments (as would suit her dignity).

P. 204. अहमेवार्यां &c.--shows that the Cheti had with her a pair of dry garments brought for the very purpose, as those of Vasant. were then expected to get wet. शुश्रूषयिष्यामि—The Causal in the primitive sense, used for शुश्रूषिष्ये. अपवारितकेन–same ss अपवार्य. This stage-direction is used when a character turns to another and communicates a secret. तद्भवेदपवारितम् । रहस्यं तु यदन्यस्य परावृत्य प्रकाश्यते । Sah.-Dar. ऋजुक:--Simple-minded, since he asks such a question. Had he known the power of love he would not have asked it. जनान्तिकं--see p. 40 and notes thereon. भणितं मया &c.--see *supra* p. 190. We should expect an इति after आगता.

मन्त्रितमेव--For these were the words addressed to Vasant. when accounting for the loss of the casket of ornaments. निध्यायति--looks intently at, eyes carefully. वञ्चितोऽसि--since you have not recognized it.

P. 206. किं तु सत्यं &c --किं तु इदं सत्यं यद्वा विडम्बना—'Is this the truth, *i e.* is this the same ornament, or is it a great story and they are going to joke with us ?' प्रियं नः प्रियं--Charu. is glad to see that Vasant. got back her ornament; for, although he had given her the *Ratnamala*, it was after all a settlement of the matter.

विदू०—एवमिव—'I mean to ask you something like this, *viz.* was the thief set on by you wishing to play a good joke upon us and to test our veracity ?' Hence he asks the question in a whisper. Had he wanted simply to ask how Vasant. came by it, he would have done that openly. चेटी—(वि० कर्णे ।) एवमिव—*i. e.* 'Not that; it was thus'—(she relates the Madanika episode). बाह्या:—*i.e.* am I to be excluded from the secret; is it not meant for my ear ? अनङ्गुलीयकं &c.—This shows that Charu. has only recently been reduced to poverty; it has not yet been an established fact with him and so his hand passes to his ring which he believed to be there. अत एव—For this magnanimity of yours; you show that you are the same in affluence as well as in indigence; for संपत्तौ च विपत्तौ च महतामेकरूपता. Vasant. has often given expression to this her sentence.

P. 208. आवित एव—goes with विफलीभवन्ति; he is not able to do anything in the least to show them. शून्यैः गृहैः—As there is nothing to be found in a vacant house, so nothing is to be got from a poor man. तरुभिश्च &c.—which cannot yield fruit. The similes are not very happy.

दृष्टपूर्वं &c.—An awkward comp., as Sudraka's often are; see com. विस्मृतं must be taken as विस्मृतं विस्मरणमस्त्येषां by affixing अ (अच्), which is added to the words of the अर्शआदि group. The word is to be explained like पीता गावः, विभक्ता भ्रातरः &c.; see Malli. on विदितः Kir. I 1. Charu. means to say that he forgot his poverty in his ecstasy of joy on meeting with Vasantasena. पूर्वजन is to be understood in the sense of प्रेयोजन, as meeting with an ordinary person would not make a man forget himself so far as not to remember his proper position. समर्प्यतां मम स्नानशाटिका—He refers to the bath-clout, in which the ornaments were wrapped when they were stolen, mentioned at p. 118. The Vidu. says this to divert Charu.'s attention to Vasant. again.

रत्नावल्या तुलयितुं—*Lit.* to balance me against; to know my worth by offering me this necklace, *i. e.* to suppose me to be so very greedy of money as to require a recompense from you. The poet seems to be very fond of this verb which he uses frequently in this play.

कः श्रद्धास्यति &c.—has occurred before; see III. 24. अतिमात्रं &c.—For he had asked a similar question before and was criticized; so she now knew that he was doing it purposely. अपसारयन्निव—The Vidu. drops this as a hint to Charu. that he should enter the house and retire to enjoy Vasant.'s company पङ्कान्तराणीव—&c.—The simile is based on false analogy. The shoots of the lotus-stalks break through the mire, while the streams of water fall from, and do not pass through, the clouds. चन्द्रव्यसनात्—The sky is fancied as being sorry and shedding tears on account of the moon being obscured by the clouds.

P. 210. अर्जुनशरप्रतिकर्कशाभिः—This is a Sakarian simile. For there is no propriety in comparing the showers to the shafts of Arjuna which flew with such an impact as to clear the ground before him for one *Krosa*. **बलदेवपट०**—Balarama is desc1lbed as wearing blue garments, and hence is called **नीलाम्बर.** *Cf.* संकर्षण-पटनीलच्छाययोपहसत इव &c. Kad. p. 62; and वहसि वपुषि विशदे वसनं जलदाभं Gitagovinda I.

**पिष्टतमाल०**—An unguent of ground *tamala* leaves. आलिप्तं and उपवीजितं indicate the feverish condition of the sky which is fancied as the lover of lightning **अम्भोदसम गम०**—There is a confusion of ideas here; lightning, fancied as a Nayika, is described as longing for a union with अम्भोद and (in the next line) is made to embrace the Sky. The poet should have at least selected a word of the masc. gender. **रक्ता**—(1) red; (2) in love, attached to. **समालिङ्गति**—by this Charu. suggests that Vasant. also should embrace him similarly.

**रोमाञ्चित**—रोमाञ्चाः संजाता अस्य तत्. **जातरागं**—with passion produced. **कदम्ब०**—The body thrilling with joy at the touch &c. of a beloved is often compared to the Kadamba tree suddenly putting forth buds at roaring of clouds. *Cf.* त्वत्संपर्कात्पुलकितमिव प्रौढपुष्पैः कदम्बैः Megh. I. 25; प्रथमप्रियावचनसंश्रवस्फुरत्पुलकेन संप्रति मया विडम्ब्यते &c. Mal. Madh. III. 7; for a similar effect on the female, *cf.* सस्वेदरोमाञ्चितकम्पिताङ्गी जाता प्रियस्पर्शसुखेन बाला। मरुन्नवाम्भः—प्रविधूतसिक्ता कदम्बयष्टिः स्फुटकोरकेव ॥ Uttar. III. 42.

**अस्मद्विध०**—मम इव विधा यस्य, *i. e.* a poor man like myself. *Cf.* the Subhashita–रटतु जलधरः पतन्तु धाराः स्फुरतु तडिन्मरुतोऽपि वान्तु शीताः। इयमुरसि महौषधीव कान्ता सकलभयप्रतिघातिनी स्थिता मे ॥.

**कामिनीनां**—भूयान् कामो यासां ताः कामिन्यः women stirred up with great passion. **इन्** here shows excess. **गात्रेषु**—अनङ्गतप्तेषु (implied) **परिष्वजन्ति**—*v. l.* The Par. may be defended on the general principle अनुदात्तेत्त्वप्रयुक्तस्यात्मनेपदस्यानित्यत्वात्.

P. 212. **स्तम्भेषु**—goes with धार्यते. **प्रचलित** &c.—प्रचरितः moved from its joints, dislocated वेदिसंचयस्य of the construction of the pedestal **अन्तः** extremities or edges यस्य; loosened from its borders **स्फुटित** &c—स्फुटित cracked; **०लेपात्**—*i. e.* सुधाद्रवानुलेपस्य स्फुटितत्वात् He means—The ceiling might come down at any time owing to the cracked condition of the masonry of the upper floor, and the walls being drenched with water might give way; so it is dangerous to sit here in such rain.

अये इन्द्रधनुः &c.—See our remark on माहेन्द्रेण धनुषा sl. 27, *supra*. महेन्द्र०—A man when yawning often raises his arm, and so the rain-bow is aptly considered as the arm of the sky. विवृद्धहनुना—The chin also is extended in the act of yawning. तालानुसारेण—As a lute is struck so as to produce high-pitched or low-pitched or gentle musical notes, or according to the variations in the voice of the singer, and to the marking of musical intervals.

---

## ACT VI.

The present Act is important in more ways than one. In the first place it contains the incident which gtves its name to the play, *viz.* the filling up of the clay-cart of Rohasena with her ornaments by Vasantasena. For it is these ornaments which, falling down from Maītreya's arm-pit, convince the judges later on of Charudatta's crime, serving as direct proof of Vasantasena's murder by him. In it also are mentioned the two events which are necessary for the further development of the plot, *viz.* Vasanta.'s sitting by a curious accident in Sakara's car and Aryaka's escape from prison and his sitting by chance in the car meant for conveying Vasantasena to the Pushpakarandaka garden, where Charudatta had already gone to enjoy her company. Charudatta thus finds there Aryaka instead of Vasant., and the two come to be friends. It will thus be seen that the action of the play, which was tardily progressing so long, now begins to move with great rapidity and the curiosity of the beholder to know the final catastrophe is ever kept on the stretch.

P. 214. **युष्माकं द्यूतकरः**—Vasanta. still addresses Charudatta as द्यूतकर although the facts were cleared up, because that is the name most dear to her on account of the ideas associated with it. **पुष्पकरण्डकं**—*Lit.* 'the basket of flowers;' abounding in flower-plants. **योजय रात्रौ**—*i. e.* while it was still night; meaning. 'before day-break.' **कुत्र गया गन्तव्यं**—She asks this question because she fears that Charu. might have asked Vardha. to take her back to her own house. **निध्यातः**—seen closely. **किं प्रविष्टा** &c—*i. e.* admitted as an inmate of the house.

**अपि संतप्यते०**—For she fears that the servants may not like their master's action in admitting a courtesan in the house.

P. 216. **मया प्रथमं संत०**—*i. e.* I shall be the first to feel the pangs of separation. **गुणनिर्जिता**—*i. e.* न धननिर्जिता, and so my love is pure and sincere. **आर्यपुत्र एव ममाभरण०**—How noble is the sentiment expressed here! Her husband is her all-in-all. Dhuta is shown here to be no ordinary wife, who is tempted by jewels; she is the worthy spouse of Charudatta who set no value on earthly riches

Read (स्वगतं) before तद्यावद्विनोदयाम्येनं, which is necessary before it and which is found in some editions.

P. 218. **प्रतिवेशि०**—प्रतिवेशः अस्यास्तीति प्रतिवेशी a neighbour; also प्रातिवेशिकः, by अत इनिठनौ. **भगवन् कृतान्त** &c.—this has occurred before; see p. 126, ll. 18–19. Cf. *infra*, X. 60. **एषेदानीं**—Now that she has dropped her ornaments (अनलंकृता यथा तव माता)

P. 220. **अपेहि**—अवेहि *v. l.* 'know' (that I won't take). **जात**--*Lit.* 'one who is as good as born;' a term of affection to be used by an elderly person when addressing a younger person *Cf.* गान्धारी (addressing दुर्योधन)--जात अलं परिदेवितेन Veni V. अपवारितं--covered (as Vasant. was to be carried in it). अवघाटितं *v. l.*--'open', which is against the fact. **यानास्तरणं**--The carriage cushions. **नासिकारज्जुकटुकौ**--resenting the insertion of--not bearing--nose-string. He means--If left alone they would get unruly and carry away the car.

P. 222. **कथमेषोऽपरः** &c.--This is Aryaka, who has just escaped from the prison; the reference to him here is meant to prepare the audience for his entrance. **शूरः**--The brave servant of; a great man who should not be asked to do such deeds.

**किं न्विदं स्फुरति** &c.--The throbbing of the right eye, or of any part on the right side of a woman, is looked upon as an evil omen, and is supposed to indicate some future evil; while the opposite is the case with regard to males (see *infra*, IX. 10); *cf.* पुंसां सदा दक्षिणदेहभागे स्त्रीणां तु वामावयवे प्रजातः। स्पन्दः फलान्ति प्रदिशत्यवश्यं निहन्त्यनुक्ताङ्गविपर्ययेण ॥ Vasantarajiya. **अथ वा चारुदत्तस्यैव दर्शनं** &c.—The sight of a pious man, the mention of favourite deities, the worship of the Brahmanas &c. are supposed to remove the effect of evil omens. Here, however, by an irony of fate, this wish of Vasanta. is not fulfilled. She does not see Charu. as expected by her.

P. 224. **भारवत्प्रवहणं** &c.—Sthavaraka felt that the carriage was heavy; but, as it was covered and he did not expect any one to get in, he did not care to examine the inside, but satisfied himself as mentioned in the text and went on.

**दौवारिकाः**—द्वारे नियुक्ताः from द्वार and इक (ठक्) by तत्र नियुक्तः Pan. IV. 4. 69; gate-keepers, sentinels posted at the door to keep watch. **गुल्मस्थानेषु**—At the police-stations, or stations generally at the four gates of a city, with small bands of armed men to keep guard and give signal of danger, and also to look after the protection of the city and to maintain order in it by patrolling the streets at night and so on. Manu lays down that for the maintenance of order there should be a *gulma* for each group of two, three or five villages according to their size, and a larger one for a hundred villages; *cf.* द्वयोस्त्रयाणां पञ्चानां मध्ये गुल्ममधिष्ठितम् । तथा ग्रामशतानां च कुर्याद्राष्ट्रस्य संग्रहम् ॥ Manu. VII. 114. गुप्ति—The prison; here the walls of the room in which he was confined.

**नरपतिबन्धना०**—For the comp. see com.; here व्यापत्ति must be taken to mean death or destruction, as is clear from the word विशसने in the prose passage following this sl.; for this sense *cf.* अव्यापन्नः कुशलमबले पृच्छति त्वां वियुक्तः &c. Megh. II 41; पितृव्यापत्तिशोकयोः Ragh. XII. 56. It refers here to death under the guise of imprisonment by the king. He was sure that he was confined solely for the purpose of being slowly put to death. Some translate the passage as—'the great ocean of misery and woe called the king's prison;' or 'the ocean of woe resulting from misery under the guise of' &c. But this does not seem to be intended. Dr. Ryder remarks—"The slight awkwardness observable when Sudraka attempts to form long compounds as in this verse (twice) and in V. 24, serves at least to help our appreciation of Bhavabhuti's exquisite skill in handling them." **निगडैकपाश**—one fastening chain.

**विशसने**—must be taken in the sense of 'that which kills,' (वि + शस् + अन being added कर्तरि), being in apposition with कोष्टागारे. It cannot be taken as the loc. of purpose. For it is not a case exactly governed by the Varttika निमित्तात्कर्मयोगे, as there is no *karmayoga* here, as in the case of चर्मणि द्वीपिनं हन्ति &c. **प्रियसुहृच्छविलकप्रसादेन**—see *supra*, IV. 27.

**वन्यनाग इव**—the simile indicates the unmerited severity of the punishment and want of judgment on the part of the king. **दैवी च सिद्धिः**—The accomplishment of an object brought on by fate; what fate means to accomplish. **सिद्धि** does not mean here 'superhuman power.' The idea is the same as that in को नाम पाकाभिमुखस्य जन्तोर्द्वाराणि दैवस्य पिधातुमीष्टे Uttar. VII. 4, though somewhat differently expressed.

P. 226. **अदत्तदण्डः**—With the fastening rod not drawn out; *i. e.* open. **अनायतार्गलं** *v. l.*—अनायता not very long *i. e.* partly broken अर्गला the festening bolt or rod यस्य; qualifies गृहं. **मम तुल्यभाग्यः**—shows that his house also was demolished by the king's order when he was taken prisoner.

अत्र तावत्प्रविश्य—Because the owner being similarly circumstanced would take pity on him and would not hand him over to the police in case he was discovered.

गोष्ठी—a company, a pleasure-party. विषमशीलैः— Perverse-tempered; *i. e.* who would not sympathize with a sufferer. विविक्तत्वात्—On account of its being unattended by men, solitary.

बहिर्यानं—बहिर्यानं गमनं अस्य that has to go out, *i. e.* going outside the city. कथं नूपुरशब्दः—It is strange that the driver should have mistaken the clank of the chain for the jingle of anklets, even supposing Aryaka to have walked very cautiously to the carriage. The poet himself sees the impropriety of this, since he adds further on the epithet पादोत्फालचालितानां by way of explanation. Again, it is difficult to understand how he should have asked Vasant. to mount the car without assistance, when she required assistance even in getting down; see *infra,* p. 246 ll. 13, 14;—or without raising the yoke to allow her to do that, when even a male like Chandanaka required it in order to get in; see p. 234 (अरे उन्नमय धुरं);—or without removing the screen, as the carriage was covered.

पादोत्फाल०—Set in motion or shaken by the raising up of the feet when mounting the car. विश्रब्धाः—in full confidence, calmly, as if nothing has happened. भित्त्वा—(1) piercing with alaram (in the case of the king).

P. 228. प्रतोली—The central or main road ( ग्राममध्यमार्गः ) प्राकारखण्डः—Part of a broken rampart. विश्वस्ताः—Full of trust, *i. e.* without fear; or it may be taken as a voc.; 'my trusty men.' गोत्रान्तरं—To another dynasty; *cf.* उच्छिन्नाश्रयकातरेव कुलटा गोत्रान्तरं श्रीर्गता Mud. VI. 5. लघु कुरुत—take quick action, look sharp.

तं तं—*scil.* देशं region; यत्र यत्र शङ्का जायते तं तं देशं. is the construction; it may also be rendered as तत्तत्स्थानं. Some give योजयत as the Chhaya of जोहह, in which case the meaning is तं तं पुरुषं योजयत अन्वेष्टुं. *Cf.* with this Veni. VI. 2.

Having given the above directions to his followers, Chan. turns to Viraka and says—किं किं दर्शयसि—'What, what is it that you are bringing to my notice? You say with confidence (that Aryaka has escaped). What fated man is he who having broken off the fetters is taking away &c.' Chand. says this, as he was sure that Aryaka could not have escaped from the prison without the help of an accomplice.

**कस्याष्टमो** &c.—He means—'Who is he whose death has approached ?' The positions of the planets from one's natal zodiacal sign mentioned indicate dire calamity and death. Thus, the sun in the 8 th zodiacal sign from one's natal sign indicates death; the moon in the fourth, a stomach-disease (कुक्षिरोग:); Venus in the sixth, mental depravity; Mars in the fifth, destruction or loss; Jupiter in the sixth, sorrow and trouble from the enemy; and Saturn in the ninth, loss of wealth, indigence. See com. Prithvidhara quotes from Varahamihira's Brihatsamhita Adh. 104, slokas 6, 8, 36, 14, 25, 28, 44. In these quotations the last line contains the name of the metre of sl. The correted text of Pri.'s com. is as under—

रुक्त्रासौ **चाष्टमस्थे** भवति सुवदना न स्वाऽपि वनिता। इत्यष्टमरविफलम्। चतुर्थेऽविश्वास: शिखरिणि भुजङ्गेन सदृश:। इति चतुर्थचन्द्रफलम्। षष्ठो भृगु: परिभवरोगतापद:। इति षष्ठभार्गवफलम्। रिपुगदकोपभयानि पञ्चमे तनयकृताश्च शुचो महीसुते। द्युतिरपि नास्य चिरं भवेत्स्थिरा शिरसि कपेरिव मालती कृता॥ इति पञ्चममङ्गलफलम्। न सखीवदनं तिलकोज्ज्वलं न च वनं शिखिकोकिलनादितम्। हरिणप्लुतशावविचित्रितं रिपुगते मनस: सुखदं गुरौ॥ इति षष्ठजीवफलम्। गच्छत्यध्वानं सप्तमे चाष्टमे च हीन: स्त्रीपुत्रै: सूर्यजे दीनचेष्ट:। तद्वद्धर्मस्थे वैरहृद्रोगबन्धैर्धर्मोऽप्युच्छिद्येद्वैश्वदेवी क्रियाद्य:॥ इति नवमशनैश्चरफलम्॥. In these quotations रिपु means the 6th and धर्म the 9th position. The position referred to here are from the *chara* point of view, *i. e.* to be measured from the zodiacal sign in which the moon is at the time of the birth of a person. **जीवति चन्द०**—He means—While Chan lived, the offender cannot live. We shall soon find that this resolve of his is only lukewarm, and yields to the higher sentiment of sympathy for the deserving sufferer. The gist of Chand.'s speech is that the terror of his name ought to deter any one from effecting Aryaka's release, and that he would rather disbelieve the story of his escape.

P. 230. **चन्दनक शपे** &c—Viraka, finding that Chand. is loath to believe him, solemnly declares that what he said was the fact. **खुटित:—पलायित:** (has escaped), acc. to L. D.; **छिन्नबन्ध:** ( has broken his bonds and run away ), according to others. **अपवारितं**—Veiled, covered. Pri. reads उद्घाटितं, which means manifest to view, ' *i. e.* in broad daylight.

**आर्यचारुदत्तस्य**—*i. e.* having absolute confidence in the loyalty of Charudatta ( who would not do anything against the king ).

P. 232. **कः आर्यचारुदत्तः**—Viraka means–Of what significance is Char. or Vasant. ? ' *i. e.* that is no consideration with us when we have to do an imperative duty. **यद्यार्यचारुदत्तं** &c.—This shows what profound regard Chan. had for the two.

**गुणारविन्दं**—Who is attractive by his virtues as a lotus is by its fragrance and beauty. **शीलमृगाङ्कं**—शीले शीलेन वा **मृगाङ्क इव आह्लादकरस्तं** as gladdening as the moon by his disposition; or, as in the Com., ' from whom shines शील ( virtuous conduct ) like moon-light from the moon '. **आपन्नदुःखमोक्षं**--wherein the misery of the people in distress finds its end, *i. e.* who puts an end to &c. **तिलकभूतौ**-- **तिलकौ भूतो** a comp **सुप्सुपा. प्राप्ते च राजकार्ये** &c.-- This shows Viraka's high sense of duty and his unflinching loyalty to his master.

**पूर्ववैरी, पूर्वबन्धुः**--The one is my enemy, the other a friend, in a former life. **विवाहे च** &c.—एककार्यनियोगे in this case means दहनकर्मणि. Both the fires discharge the same duty, *viz.* that of consuming what is thrown in them; but the one is auspicious, as it leads to the union of the husband and wife, and contributes to happiness; and the other is dismal and causes pain and sorrow ( ०दहनकर्मनियुक्तयोरपि एकः शुभोऽन्यस्त्वशुभः ).

**तन्त्रिलः**--' taking care of the king's affairs' (and not negligent like myself) this is meant as a taunt to him. **सेनापतिः**--Viraka was the chief of the police-force (नगररक्षाधिकृतः Act IX.) and also the chief magistrate of the city ( प्रधानदण्डधारकः &c. p. 242 ). Chand., it seems, was a military officer, and perhaps had a higher authority than Viraka. **त्वमपि राज्ञः** &c.—Viraka says this to please Chandanaka.

**भीमस्यानुकरिष्यामि**—Bhima required no other weapons than his arms when fighting. This is in imitation of Bhasa—सहजौ मे प्रहरणं भुजौ पीनांसकोमलौ । तावाश्रित्य प्रयुध्येयं दुर्बलैर्गृह्यते धनुः ।। बाहूरक्षौहिणी यस्य निर्व्याजो यस्य विक्रमः। Pancharatra II. 55, 56. **व्यायच्छतः**—struggling, contending with arms.

**यः खलु शरणागतं त्यजति**—*Cf.* the words of Rama who quotes the sage Kandu in support of his statement when he extended protection to Bibhishana:—बद्धाञ्जलिपुटं दीनं याचन्तं शरणागतम् । न

हन्यादानृशंस्यार्थमपि शत्रुं परंतप ॥ आर्तो वा यदि वा दृप्तः परेषां शरणं गतः। अरिः प्राणान्परित्यज्य रक्षितव्यः कृतात्मना ॥ स चेद्भयाद्वा मोहाद्वा कामाद्वाऽपि न रक्षति। स्वया शक्त्या यथान्यायं तत्पापं लोकगर्हितम् ॥ विनष्टः पश्यतस्तस्य रक्षिणः शरणं गतः। आदाय सुकृतं तस्य सर्वं गच्छेदरक्षितः ॥ एवं दोषो महानत्र प्रपन्नानामरक्षणे। अस्वर्ग्यं चायशस्यं च बलवीर्यविनाशनम् ॥ Yuddha-K. Ch. 18, Sls. 27-31.

**पत्ररथः**—A bird; पत्रं the wing रथ इव यस्य. **शाकुनिकः**—A fowler, a bird catcher; शकुनान् हन्ति इति; fr. शकुन and इक (ठक्). **एषोऽनपराध**: &c.—On seeing Aryaka in the carriage and having given him the word of safety, Chan. finds himself in a fix. He remembers his duty to the king. Aryaka, however, was innocent; he was the friend of Sarvilaka to whom he owed a debt of gratitude for having saved his life (which is, however, not referred to in the play); the carriage belonged to Charudatta who would be involved in the matter for no fault of his. All these considerations weigh heavily with him, and he determines to carry out his promise to Aryaka.

**भीताभयप्रदानं** &c.—*Cf.* न गोप्रदानं न महीप्रदानं न चान्नदानं न तथाऽऽत्मदानम्। यथा वदन्तीह महाप्रदानं सर्वप्रदानेष्वभयप्रदानम् ॥ सर्वकालसमृद्धस्य अश्वमेधस्य यत्फलम्। तत्फलं लभ्यते त्रस्ते रक्षिते शरणागते ॥ Hit. IV. 62, 63.*

**दृष्ट आर्य** :—Chand. got down so quickly that he had scarcely time to collect his thoughts; and in his hurry and confusion he was about to say आर्यकः; but he suddenly checks himself and says आर्यः.

P. 236. **घर्घर**—*Lit.* gurgling, faltering. **त्वमपि**—Even a sturdy and brave man like you.

**खशखत्ति** &c.—**म्लेच्छजातीनां**; here 'mlechchha' means a non-Aryan, a barbarian. Some of the tribes mentioned here, which must have been well-known in the days of the poet, cannot be identified now, as observed by Wilson; but they were mostly natives of South India **खश**—The Khasas are mentioned in Mud. V. 11; but they were a northern tribe and cannot be intended here. विड probably stands for विराट or Berar; द्राविड is आन्ध्र or Tailangana; चोल is the modern Tanjore; it is men-

* The importance attached to the duty of affording protection to those who solicit it is repeatedly urged in the Hindu writings. This feeling seems to have pervaded the heroic times both of Greece and Rome, and to have secured Adrastus an asylum at court of Croesus and Coriolanus a refuge in the halls of Aufidius. (Wilson).

tioned in the Vikramankadevacharita; see III. 66, &c. The mlechchhas did not, it seems, much observe the distinction of gender. *Cf.* the precept दुष्टाञ्शब्दान्मा प्रयुंक्ष्महि म्लेच्छाश्च मा भूमेत्यध्येयं व्याकरणम् ।

**कर्णाटकलह**—seems to mean, from the context, a quarrel purposely stirred up. It seems that the people of Karnataka were notorious, in the days of the poet, for their spirit of quarrelling and using grossly abusive language. **कस्त्वं**—'who are you to question my testimony?' **पूज्यमान:** &c.—As you are respected by the people, being the king's favourite, you do not remember your low caste. **को भणतु**—Who will declare it? It is so execrable.

P. 238. **शीलविभवेन**—owing to the nobility of my disposition; I am too noble-minded to utter it. **कपित्थेन भग्नेन**—'What is the use of breaking a *kapittha* fruit? Only its worthless and ugly inside would become known.' From this it seems that *kapittha* is here used in the sense of the Marathi कंवडळ, which has a gaudy exterior but is worthless when broken. **संज्ञां** ददाति—he indicates by gesticulating several acts of a barber that he is a barber. These are explained in sl. 22.

**कूर्चग्रन्थि**—The beard-root, *i. e.* the whole beard taken together. संस्थापन:—*Lit.* one who gives it a proper shape; hence, trims it. संज्ञां ददाति—*i. e.* to indicate that he belongs to the family of a shoe-maker, or leather-tanner.

जातिस्तव विशुद्धा—said ironically. **भेरी**—A large kettle-drum; बिभेत्यस्या रवात् इति भेरी. पटह–A drum with a less frightful sound; *cf.* पटुपटहध्वनिभिर्विनीतनिद्र: Ragh. IX. 71. **अहं चर्मकार:**—In Shakespeare's *Henry VIII.* the lords call Wolsey 'a butcher's cur.'

P. 240. **चतुरङ्गं** &c.—चतुर्णामङ्गानां समाहार: चतुरङ्गं *viz.* the two hands and the two feet, with which he had struck him. **कल्पयामि**—L. D. gives कर्तयामि as the Chhaya; in either case the meaning is 'cause to be cut' ( राजभटैरिति शेष: L. D. ); hence, 'I shall have you quartered.' Srinivasa Sastri takes **चतुरङ्गं** in the sense of पुष्टमङ्गं ( your fat and burly body ), remarking **बभूव** तस्याश्चतुरस्रशोभि, सर्वं॰ चतुरस्रं, इत्यादिषु पूर्णे चतुरस्रपदप्रयोगादिहायमर्थ:. But is this far-fetched and quite beside the mark. **शुनकसदृशेन**—merely barking like a dog; nothing serious can come out of your threats. **आर्ये वसन्तसेने**—He addresses Aryaka as Vasant. in order to lull all suspicion on the part of the driver and the bystanders.

स्पन्दते दक्षिणो भुजः--The throbbing of the right arm in the case of males augurs good fortune. *Cf.* अङ्गदक्षिणभागे तु शस्तं प्रस्फुरणं भवेत् । अप्रशस्तं तथा वामे पृष्ठस्य हृदयस्य च ॥ Matsya-purana. See *supra* p. 222, and comp. अभिमतफलशंसी चारु पुस्फोर बाहुः । Bhatti. I. 27. विज्ञप्ता--(1) Requested by me; (2) To whom I have made known myself. प्रत्ययिता--(1) In whom confidence is produced about safety by me; (2) If you realize the prophecy; प्रत्ययः संजातोऽस्याः. न...लुब्धः--I do not say so through greed of a reward in case the prophecy is fulfilled. ब्रूमः-The pl. is by अस्मदो द्वयोश्च Pan. I. 2. 59. अस्मद् may be optionally used in the pl. even when the speaker happens to be one individual.

चन्द्रशीलाढ्यः--चन्द्रवच्छीलं तेन आढ्यः richly endowed with. चन्दनं भोः स्मरिष्यामि--This speech is जनान्तिकं ( not to be heard by the driver ) अभयं &c.--Construe यथा देवी शुम्भनिशुम्भौ हत्वा देवेभ्योऽभयमददात्तथा हरः इ० तव शत्रुपक्षं हत्वा &c.

Sumbha and Nisumbha were two demons, brothers, who practised penance for thousands of years and propitiated Siva who conferred upon them a boon that in riches and strength they should excel the gods. In their exultation they warred against the gods and oppressed the world. The gods, at the advice of Brahma, Vishnu and Siva, applied to Durga, who fought with them, defeated their forces, slew their commanders Chanda and Munda, and finally killed them. This story is given in the 5th and the following Sections of the Chandipatha, of the Markandeya-purana.

P. 242. अरे निष्क्रामतः &c.—( Read निष्क्रामतः for निष्क्रमतः ); अरे shows surprise. निष्क्रामतः qualifies आर्यकस्य ( to be supplied from the context ). L. D. also says the same Chand. looks at the curtain and beholds Sarvilaka following the car at close quarters. Sarvilaka, it seems, was brought there by chance. He did not know that Aryaka was in the car. Had he known it, he would have asked his friend to get down at some suitable place on going out of the city. But we find no trace of him in the next Act. The poet has achieved a double object by thus suddenly introducing him here. He gives Chandanaka to understand that Sarvilaka had his hand in the release of Aryaka. But he keeps him off from Charudatta; for, his introduction to him at this stage would not have served any dramatic purpose. It would have marred the effect which is produced by his introduction to Charu in the tenth Act as the chief organizer of the whole plan. **भवतु**—Well, let him go; it is a desirable thing. **प्रधानदण्ड०**—*cf. supra,* प्रधानसभिको माथुरो मया विरोधितः &c. p. 84. **अहमपि**—I also (like Sarvilaka).

## ACT VII.

This is the shortest Act in the play containing only one incident; but it is an important one; it is the accidental friendship between Charudatta and Aryaka.

P. 244. **वणिज इव** &c.—Similarly Kalidasa compares mountains to merchants in Vik. IV. 4 (धारासारोपनयनपरा नैगमाः सानुमन्तः). **शुल्कं**—the tax or toll due to the king; घट्टादिदेयं शुल्कोऽस्त्री। Amara. The bees gathering honey are here compared to men collecting taxes, but it is not a happy simile; toll is not collected from every article for sale. **अक्षः**—The axle. **परिवर्तनं**—change (of the axle, *i. e.* putting in another). **छिन्नोऽथ वा**—This cannot cause any perceptible delay. **वर्त्मान्तो०**—कर्मान्तो० *v. l.* left on the road at the close of the work (repair of the road &c.), is preferable to वर्त्मान्तो०, where अन्त has to be taken in the sense of मध्ये 'in the middle,' which is rather forced. **स्वैरं**—easily, as he lists. **गुप्तार्यक०**—गुप्तः आर्यकः यस्मिंस्तत्प्रवहणम्.

**सावशेषापसारः**—whose escape is incomplete, yet to be fully effected. **साधोस्तु याने**—The fact that the carriage belonged to a good man, who would never betray him, is, however, assuring to him. **परभृत इव** &c.—The simile refers to the habit of the cuckoos to get their eggs hatched by crows. *Cf.* Sak. स्वमपत्यजातमन्यैर्द्विजैः परभृताः खलु पोषयन्ति। V. 22.

Dr. Ryder quotes the following (which will be interesting to the student) from D. D. Cunningham, *Indian Friends and Acquaintances* (New York 1904) pp. 64-65—"The order of events is this—When everything is ready and a desirable nest has been chosen, the cock-koil, conspicuous in his shining black plumage and crimson eyes, seats himself on a prominent perch, whilst the hen, in modest speckled grey garb, lurks hidden among dense masses of neighbouring foliage. He then lifts up his voice and shouts aloud, his voice......very soon attracting the attention of the owners of the nest, who rush out to the attack and chase him away. Now comes the chance for his wife, who forthwith nips in to deposit her egg."

P. 246. **अस्मात्**—The reading व्यसनार्णवोत्थितं is more forcible, no doubt, than the one in the text; but then grammatical structure becomes rather loose, as अस्मात् must be taken with the prior member of the Comp. अस्मात् may also be taken separately in the sense of 'from my doing so;' but it is not a good way. **ईदृशीं दशां**—*i. e.* wearing fetters. **धृतं**—supported; or, saved. *Cf. infra*, Sl. 7.

किं निगडेन बद्धो &c.—The Vidu.'s witticisms are often so meant as to foreshadow some event of that sort. *Cf.* with this किमत्रोज्जयिन्यां चौरोऽपि नास्ति p. 108. वसन्तसेनः—The Vidu., on seeing Aryaka in the carriage, humorously describes him thus. JV. explains—वसन्तः the spring सेना यस्य सः कामदेवः. करिकरसम०—That is, having long and very stout hands. *Cf.* करिवरकरबाहुः Bhasa's Madhyamavyayoga I. 6. These physical marks indicate royalty. पृथुतरसमवक्षाः—is the same as Kalidasa's कपाटवक्षाः (Ragh III. 34). ताम्र०—ताम्रत्व indicates martial spirit. असमानं—A thing unworthy of him. गोपालप्रकृतिः—गोपालः प्रकृतिर्यस्य born of a cowherd; *i. e.*, a cowherd by birth

P. 246. स्नेहमयानि &c —He means–You have bound me (to you) by chains of love which are harder than those of steel. संगच्छस्व निग०—Maitreya says this to Charudatta. 'Accept these fetters of love, which bind him and you;' *i. e.*, accept his friendship एषोऽपि मुक्तः—Or एष विमुक्तः, he is entirely set free. Some take संग० to mean 'come in contact with;' 'put these fetters on your feet;' but the very conception of this idea is horrible. Maitreya, although sometimes apparently uncharitable in his remarks, is not so silly as to say this at such a time and in the very presense of Aryaka, the future, king. His love for Charu. would never allow him to think of fetters on Charudatta's feet. Again, to have this meaning, we expect निगडानि to be in the Instrumental. Or, the Vid. may be saying this to the Cheta Take up those chains (for being thrown away)'. Dr. Ryder also says—There seems no reason why Mait. should say 'Be united with the fetters.'

'It is just possible,' he adds, that 'there is a smutty pun in संगच्छस्व, that Mait. means to hint that Charu., not being able to be united with Vasant., must be content with what has actually come in the cart, namely the fetters.' We have quoted this as a fine specimen of the exercise of critical wit. The Doctor himself observes: 'But this does not explain the case of णिअडाइं.'

धिक् शान्त—Charudatta does not like the idea of leaving Aryaka so abruptly. स्वयंग्राहप्रणयेन—स्वयं ग्राहः the acceptance of the car for driving in; तत्र प्रणयः courtesy or favour. *Cf.* कण्ठे स्वयंग्राहनिषक्तबाहुम् । Kum. III. 7. Some grammarians object to the form ग्राह; it should be ग्रह. Others hold that it is allowable. For the full discussion of this point see our note on the sl. from Kum. अलघुसंचारा—He means—On account of the feet being heavily fettered for a long time he would not be able to walk quickly (with natural ease); and this will rouse suspicion. लघुसंचारा—v. l. Will make little progress. संवारा—V. l. The concealment of your being fettered will not be easy, as you will have to trudge on. प्रवहणं विश्वासम्०—For, nobody would think that a state criminal can be driving in a carriage. क्षेमेण व्रज &c.—The dialogue here is in the Sardulavikridita metre, broken up as necessary. This practice is not rare in Sanskrit; *cf.* Uttar. 1. 33; Mal. Madh. III. 18, X. 8; and such subhashitas as कस्त्वं भोः कथयामि दैवहतकं मां विद्धि शाखोटकं &c.,—or कस्त्वं भद्र खलेश्वरोऽहमिह किं घोरे वने स्थीयते &c. Sometimes the speaker is the same, but his speech is interrupted by prose passages spoken by others; Mud. VI. 16, and Ratn. IV 19 will serve as in tances. स्वात्मा़ऽपि &c.—may be a question—'Can anyone' &c.; or we may supply (and this is better) त्वां विस्मरिष्यामि चेत् I shall forget myself as well. The meaning is, 'you are my very soul.'

P. 250. यद्युद्यते पालके &c.—With the readings in the foot-note and the omission of न, the meaning is–When Palaka is bestirring himself with effort, there is great guarding, *i. e.* every nook and corner is vigilantly guarded (by the officers). व्यलीकं—a very serious or heinous crime. This is a word of constant occurrence; see Sak VII. 24, Ratn. III 15 &c. चारदृष्टचा—see Kam. Nit. XIII. 29. *Cf.* गावः पश्यन्ति गन्धेन वेदैः पश्यन्ति च द्विजाः। चारैः पश्यन्ति राजानश्चक्षुर्भ्यामितरे जनाः ॥ And Ramayana—यस्मात्पश्यन्ति दूरस्थाः सर्वानर्थान्नराधिपाः। चारेण तस्मादुच्यन्ते राजानश्चारचक्षुषः ॥ See also Kir. I. 4.

अनाभ्युदयिकं—see Com.; not leading to prosperity, inauspicious. श्रमणक०—The sight of Sramanaka was considered inauspicious, probably because of his shaven and uncovered face. The Sramanaka is the same as the Samvahaka of Act II.

# ACT VIII

ACT VIII. is a continuation of the second part of the preceding Act; the scene is the same, *viz.* the garden *Pushpakarandaka*; and it is introduced by the entrance of the Sramanaka mentioned at the end of the last Act. Its principal events are the strangling of Vasantasena by Sakara followed by her apparent death, and the ascetic's noticing her revive and taking her to his abode. The narrative proceeds smoothly, being interrupted out of dramatic necessity only in two places, once at p. 264, and again at p. 290.

P. 252. **चीवरं**—a garment worn by ascetics (मुनिवासः। शाक्यभिक्षुप्रावरणमिति सुभूतिः।). **संयच्छत निजोदरं**—Restrain the cravings of your stomach; do not be solely devoted to the feeding of the body. **नित्यं जागृत** &c.—Keep awake by sounding the drum of contemplation; thinking of God, always remember that the happiness the world gives is not permanent This is the Vedic precept also. *Cf.* उत्तिष्ठत जाग्रत प्राप्य वरान्निबोधत। Kathopanishad III. 14; and या निशा सर्वभूतानां तस्यां जागर्ति संयमी। Bg. II. 69. **विषमाः**—Difficult to be caught *i. e.* controlled. **अनित्यतया**—अनित्यमिति शरीरादिकं सर्वमिति शेषः; looking upon all mundane things as not permanent. **धर्माणां शरणमस्मि**—I have become the abode of religious duties only, *i. e.* am solely devoted to their performance.

**पञ्चजनाः**—The five persons, *i. e.* the five senses, which lead away a man. The comp. with a numeral is allowed when the whole is a संज्ञा (a name or a technical term of science); *e. g.* सप्तर्षयः, पञ्चजनाः &c. *Cf.* यस्मिन्पञ्च पञ्चजना आकाशश्च प्रतिष्ठितः। Bri. Up. IV. 4. 17. **स्त्रियं**—the woman, *i. e.* अविद्या wrong knowledge, Nescience. For the effects of अविद्या see Mund. Up. 1. 2. 8–10. The doing away with Avidya, the purification of the mind, and the destruction of Ahamkara, are necessary for the attainment of Moksha even according to the Vedanta theory.

**ग्रामः**—The village, *i. e.* the body with the जीवात्मा in it. **रक्षितः**—prevented from going astray. **अबलः चण्डालः**—The fiend Egoism, अबलः कृतः being rendered helpless (अविद्यातत्कार्यसहायरहितः कृतः). **स्वर्गं गाहते**—attains *summum bonum.* The word स्वर्ग is used here in the sense of 'permanent happiness' (and not that obtained in Indra's *svarga*); *cf.* यन्न दुःखेन संभिन्नं न च ग्रस्तमनन्तरम्। अभिलाषोपनीतं यत्तत्सुखं स्वःपदास्पदम्॥ Pri. reads **अबलः क्व चा०.** where

क्व ( where, by whom ) does not fit in with the context. A the best it may be taken as चण्डाल: अबल: निर्बल: सन् क्व मारितः, अबल: कृतश्चेत् स्वयमेव नश्येत् इत्यर्थः ।. The metre is faulty; some long syllables must be read as short and *vice versa*; see Com. This enigmatical way of presenting some of the truths of Vedantism has been popular with writers from the Vedic period down to the time of Marathi writers like ज्ञानेश्वर, एकनाथ and others. **शिरो मुण्डितं**—Like the Buddhas, the Brahmana-bhikshu also must have his head and chin shaved; *cf.* क्लृप्तकेशनखश्मश्रुः पात्री दण्डी कुसुम्भवान् विचरेन्नियतो नित्यं सर्वभूतान्यपीडयन् ॥ Manu. VI. 52.

**किमर्थं मुण्डितं**—He means—Unless there is *Chitta-suddhi* outward shaving is useless; it becomes a mockery. **गृहीतकषायो०**—*i. e.*, immersed in a liquid of a dull red colour ( made from a paste of an ochreous clay ).

P. 254. **गामिवापवाहयति**—Mr. Apte in his Dic. gives to अपवह् *Caus.* the sense of 'to cause to carry the yoke,' and cites this passage in illustration; so he evidently bases his meaning on this passage alone. But it seems to be conjectural. The idea of making one bullock carry a yoke is very strange. So the real meaning seems to be 'turns him away' by seizing him by the nose like a bull after having passed a rope through the septum of his nose ( भृत्येन गामिव नासिकां विद्ध्वा भिक्षुमपवाहयति ) **आपानक०**—आ संभूय पिबन्त्यत्र इति आपानं; from पा and aff. अन (ल्युट्) अधिकरणे; आपानमेव आपानकं a drinking party (कन् स्वार्थे); for this sense *cf.* सर्व एव सिद्धविद्याधरलोकः कुसुमाकरोद्याने आपानकसुखमनुभवति &c. Nag III. p. 50; ताम्बूलीनां दलैस्तत्र रचितापानभूमयः । Ragh. IV. 42. **रक्तमूलकं**—It was a practice of drinkers, it seems, to eat a red radish as a relish to induce thirst and to give zest to liquor.

**निर्वेदधृतकाषायं**—काषाये धृ means 'to turn a recluse.' He has become a Bhikshu, being tired of the world, and so deserves pity and not molestation.

**अशरणशरण०**—अशरणानां शरणाः the refuge of; प्रमोदाः भूताः प्रमोदभूताः । सह सुपेति समासः । अशरणशरणाश्च ते प्रमोदभूताश्च तैः or ०शरणानां प्रमोदार्थं भूतैः उत्पन्नैः. **क्रियमाणचारुकर्म**—This should better have been compounded as **०प्रमोदभूततरुक्रियमाण०**; but the connexion can be easily understood, and so it is left out (सापेक्षत्वान्नित्यसमासः); क्रियमाणं चारु कर्म (such as supplying shade, providing fruit and flowers &c.) यस्मिन्. **अगुप्त**—A pun on the word **गुप्त**—

(1) not protected from, open or accessible to all; (2) not guarded, unrestrained, licentious. The word शुभात्मनां instead of दुरात्मनां would have made the simile very appropriate; but the poet intends a secret fling at Sakara ( तव हृदयमिव ) and so uses the word दुरात्मनां, to the detriment of the beauty of the simile **अनिर्जितोपभोग्यं**--(1) अनिर्जितं च तदुपभोग्यं च to be enjoyed and to be considered as not conquered; *i. e.* giving full freedom to the people in the pursuit of their pleasures, so that they should not feel that they are conquered. A king who has to gain the affection and loyalty of his new subjects has to do this. (2) To be enjoyed without restraint; अनिर्जितमनिर्बन्धं यथा तथोपभोग्यम् ।. उपासक:--' A worshipper of Buddha;' a formal way of addressing a stranger, whether a follower of Buddha or not. Also, one who ministers to the comfort of others, such as a sudra, a barber &c., in which sense Sakara purposely understands it. This shows that the Sakara is not altogether a fool.

**शलावके** ( **चार्वाक:** )--L. D. चारु: मनोहर: लोकसंमतत्वात् वाको वाक्यं यस्य. Name of a sophistical philosopher ( said to have been a pupil of Brihaspati), who was an atheist out and out and advocated materialistic doctrines, denying God or heaven alike. Sakara again puns or blunders on the words धन्य and पुण्य. By धन्य he understands 'a materialist, an infidel; धनमर्हतीति धन्य: one who thinks of money (अर्थ) only, *i.e.* the pleasures it brings one, and does not care for धर्म; or धनं लब्धा, यत् being added by धनगणं लब्धा Pan. IV. 4. 84. Some render शलावके by शरावक: in Sanskrit, taking it to mean 'an earthen pot' (for keeping corn), the prakrit धण्णे being rendered by धान्य. Next Sakara understands पुण्य in the sense of a कोष्ठक which L. D. takes to mean 'a brick-trough for watering cattle' ( which gives पुण्य to one constructing it—यत्र पशव: पानीयं पिबन्ति तत् कोष्ठकं हि पुण्यं प्राण्यनुग्रहात्). Or कोष्ठक may mean 'a granary' पुण्णे Prak. being rendered by पूर्ण. Next Sak. perversely asks 'Am I a potter ?' A potter obliges poor people by making cheap pots for them. पुणति (fr. पुण् 6 P. to do a good thing ) इति पुण: ( इगुपधत्वात्क:) ; पुणे साधु: पुण्य:; तत्र साधुरिति यत्. **कुलित्थयूष**—यूष: षं is a technical term in medicine; it means the liquid turned somewhat viscous, obtained by boiling in water some corn (generally मुद्ग) Marathi मूग, here *Kulittha,* Marathi कुळीथ).

शबलानि *v. l.*—of a varied colour. " This reading of Stenzler and J. V. seems preferable and has considerable authority. " Dr. Ryder. ०प्रहारिकं—एकः प्रहारः जीवितापहारित्वेनास्त्यस्य by adding इक (ठन्); one to be killed with one stroke; *i.e.* 'I'll ' dispatch you with one blow.'

तथैव—Just as it was when he got shaved and entered upon an ascetic's course of life. केशविरहात् is significant. Although there is no hair, his brow is not darkened being sunburnt; hence his conversion must be very recent. चीवरकृतः—Because the Bhikshus wear one garment in their peculiar manner, one end of which they pass lightly across the shoulder which by its friction causes a scar there. नाभ्यस्ता &c.—His manner of wearing the brown garment which is harsh to touch shows that he has not yet been inured to it. कषायरक्तं वस्त्रं कषायवस्त्रं; a comp. of the Sakaparthivadi class; otherwise we should expect काषाय०. By रचना Pri. understands the proper dyeing of the garment also; see com. दूरं निगूढान्तरः—(the other hem of the garment) which has covered the body to a great distance below (*i. e.* more than enough-which shows that he is not yet properly used to it). पटोच्छ्रयात्—on account of the bagging of the body of the garment. " And he has not learned the (proper) arrangement of the yellow robe; and the hem of the garment, by which the middle part is quite concealed, loose because of the bagging of the cloth, does not fit on his shoulder." Dr. Ryder.

P. 258. विपर्यस्त०—विपर्यस्ताः perverse मनसश्चेष्टाः the operations of the mind येषां or विपर्यस्ताः मनः चेष्टाः actions च येषां. वर्ष्मन् the body; वर्ष्म देहप्रमाणयोः Amara.; for the other sense see Ragh. IV. 76.

कठोरनिष्पन्द०—कठोराः full grown निष्पन्दाः steady, *i.e.* close-sticking लताः &c.; see Com; or, 'in a mercilessly hard and steady embrace'. निवृतिं यान्ति—Feel entirely happy; *cf.* सदृशमिष्टसमागमनिर्वृतिं वनितयाऽनितया रजनीवधः । Ragh. IX 38.

P. 260. पनसफलानीव--We can expect such a simile from Sakara only सूरः—The sun; सुवति प्रेरयति कर्मणि लोकान् (impels men to action) इति सूरः; fr. सू 6 P. and र (Unadi क्रन्). कुपितवानर०--Here a red-faced monkey is to be taken. समान इव पश्यति सदृक्षः. Another simile worthy of Sakara's wit. हतपुत्रशतेव--This is one of the rare instances in which Sakara's knowledge of history is correct.

गान्धारी—गन्धाराणां जनपदानां राजा गान्धार: तस्य अपत्यं स्त्री गान्धारी. She was the daughter of Subala, king of the Gandhara country, and wife of Dhritarashtra. As her husband was blind and lost to the comforts of sight, she, like a true Pativrata, wore a screen over her eyes to reduce herself to his condition. गोकुलं--A herd of cows. सजातीयै: कुलं Amara. *Cf.* पत्रच्छायासु हंसा मुकुलितनयना दीर्घिकापद्मिनीनां &c. Malav. II. 12.

P. 262. भाव, भात्र, शकुनि खग &c. नर पुरुष &c., and गृह शरण, are instances of Sakara's tautology. गृहशरण may, however, be taken as गृहं शरणं sole refuge येषां ते गृहशरणा: तथा निषण्णा:; मम शिरसि निलीन: is व्याहतं, मध्याह्नसूर्यकिरणानां सवत्र प्रसृतत्वात् छायानिषण्णत्वाद्वा निर्वहन्ति—pass the heat (*i.e.* noontime). जीरक—Cumin-seed. भद्रमुस्ता--Orris-root. वचा—a kind of aromatic root (उग्रगन्धा). गन्धयुक्ति:—A pounding together of fragrant substances. Although the things mentioned here have a strong smell, they are not all pleasant ones and they have nothing to do with the improvement of voice. Sakara is evidently punning on the word गन्ध in गन्धर्व.

व्याघारितं--Amply sprinkled over with ghee, and fried. पारभृतीय--From परभृत a cuckoo.

P. 264. विसंष्ठुलं--'out of joint;' 'changed upside down

घुरघुरायमाणं—Croaking, rattling; Pres. p. A'. of the Denom. fr. घुरघुर; घुरघुरो भवति घुरघुरायति-ते। लोहितादिडाज्भ्य: इति क्यष् (य) See note on खटखटायेते p. 10.

P. 266. अहमात्मीयो न भवि०--I shall lose myself, I shall die, it will be no loss to anybody else ( *cf* Marathi मी आपला ). अभ्यन्तरक:—Admitted to one's secrets; a confidant

P. 268. मृतोऽसि--Sak. says this humorously instead of saying मृतोऽस्मि. Sakara, who is far more cunning and shrewd than he appears to be, must have known at a glance that the woman was Vasantasena; but he says so purposely, probably to see what Vita might do See Sak.'s speech on p 271 (यदि राक्षसी &c . मुषितौ &c.—is विपरीतोक्ति: (see com ) as is Sak.'s characteristic. ०च्छिन्नदृष्टे:—with your eyes obscured, *i e.* dazzled by the glare of the mid-day sun. You might have mistaken the robed figure of Sthav., which was before your eyes, for that of a woman. **सकञ्चुकां**—is necessary for the figure being mistaken for that of a woman.

**अवनतशिरस:**—For a gentleman must not look up and gaze at a stranger woman's face. This brings out Vita's sense of modesty and decorum. He wants to be reckoned asa gentleman in an assembly ( सदसि गौरवप्रियस्य ). **पथि वृषभा इव**—This is the habit of bullocks. For the idea *cf.* एता रावणजीमूताद्बाष्पधारा विनिःसृताः । विभान्ति राममासाद्य वारिधारा वृषं यथा ॥ Bhasa's Abhisheka, VI. 10; and आसारवर्षमिव गोवृषभः सलीलः । Madhyamavya. 40
**संशयितास्मि**—I am placed in jeopardy. **को दोष:**—'What harm, what danger is there in this ?' Vita says this as he found his master accusing Cheta of cowardice.

P. 70. **कथं शृगाला:** &c.—Sakara says this in his usual humorous way to frighten Vita. These are bad omens.

**०प्रतीकाशं**—Words like नीकाश, प्रतीकाश express सादृश्य or resemblance when used at the end of compounds. **पुलिना०**—implies a spotless way of living. Here Char. and Sakara are indirectly described, and so the fig. of speech is अप्रस्तुतप्रशंसा.

**वसन्तसेने**—This is of course said in a suppressed voice. **जननीवशात्**—Yielding to the persuasion of your mother. Ignorant of the true fact, Vita naturally makes a supposition. For he knows how his master had sent a carriage with a costly present previously to Vasan.'s mother, asking her to send her daughter to his mansion. See. p. 134.

**अशौण्डीर्यस्वभावेन** &c.—Vita wanted to complete his sentence by adding आगतासि &c. But on finding her nod a 'no' for what he said, he says—'If you did not come at the bidding of your mother (यदि न जननीवशात् तर्हि) then it must be I think (इति मन्यते) on account of the natural propensity of a courtesan that disregards self-respect or pride and leads her to serve a great man.' It cannot properly be taken to mean 'Sakara is thus honoured by you', as some take it; not knowing the real fact he makes this guess, and that she should not feel abashed he adds ननूक्तं &c. समभुपचर भद्रे &c.—See I. 31.

**यदि राक्षसी** &c.—Sakara is too shrewd to be deceivd by Vita. **किमनेन निरू०**—What is the use of scrutinizing the matter ? Why go deep into it ? **उद्यानपरंपरया**—so as to avoid the sun.

**धुर्याणां**—He uses the pl., as he is speaking in general; 'thus the bullocks get rest.' धुरं वहतीति धुर्यः; धुरं takes in this sense the affixes य (यत्) and ढक् (एय); so धौरेय also. **तिष्ठ तिष्ठ, न हि न हि**—This shows the extreme fickleness of Sakara's mind.

P. 272. **दुष्करं विषं** &c,—*i.e.* it is difficult to turn a villain into a good man. Pandit Hiranand quotes—न विषममृतीकर्तुं शक्यं प्रयत्नशतैरपि त्यजति कटुतां न स्वां निम्बः स्थितोऽपि पयोह्रदे गुणपरिचितामार्यां वाणीं न जल्पति दुर्जनश्चिरमपि बलाध्माते लोहे कुतः कनकाकृतिः ॥ दुर्जनः सुजनीकर्तुं यत्नेनापि न शक्यते । संस्कारेणापि लशुनं कः सुगन्धीकरिष्यति ॥

**वासुदेवकं**—Sakara is very fond of the affix क. The order should rather be मनुष्यं प्रवरपुरुषं वा०. He calls himself Vasudeva probably looking to the amorous side of that god's life. See p. 36.

**दशनखे**—दशानां नखानां समूहः दशनखं तत्र. 'I fold my hands and place them at your feet'. See com If taken as voc. sing., it has no propriety, even supposing that Sak. is the speaker. **यत्तव मयाऽपकृतं**—He refers to his threats in I. 29, 30. **मदनातुरेण**—आतुर affected or afflicted by; *fr.* तुर् 3 cl. (तुतोर्ति इति) and क (अ) **तत्क्षामिताऽसि**—For a similar idea *cf.* यच्चावहासार्थमसत्कृतोऽसि विहारशय्यासनभोजनेषु । एकोऽथ वाऽप्यच्युत तत्समक्षं तत्क्षामये त्वामहमप्रमेयम् ॥ Bg. XI. 42.

**अम्बिकामातृकाभिः**—The tautology is Sakarian. **वने शृगालेन**—indicates the extreme gravity of the offence. The simile is faulty in that Vasant. is compared to a शृगाल which is *masc.*; it should have been शृगाल्या.

P. 274. **चाटुशतताडन** &c.—He means—Had you accepted me my hands were eager to pat you with a hundred words of blandishment. But now with the same I must pull you down from my car. By this he indirectly hints that she should still accept him. **कर्षामि ते**—One ते is superfluous. We cannot connect the first ते with हस्ताभ्यां; for, if he is to pull by seizing her hands, then केशेषु becomes superfluous; again, the epithet चाटुशत० loses its propriety. If we connect one ते with वरतनुं and the other with केशेषु, then the constr. becomes awkward, and there is दूरान्वय also. **वालिदयितां**—This was Tara. **यथा जटायुः**—Jatayu had nothing to do with Vali's wife. So this is an instance of Sakara's speech being हतोपम.

P. 276. न लता: &c.—*Cf. supra,* न पुष्पमोषमर्हत्युद्यानलता p. 34.

सूत्रशतैः &c.—This seems to mean—'interwoven with ornamental figures with various kinds of threads.' मंश–मश्शं *v. l.* मत्स्यं fish. चुहू &c.—are the various sounds produced at the time of sucking the marrow from the bones, chewing &c.

अकार्यं—A sinful or condemned deed. अप्रशस्तं कार्यमकार्यं; the sense of the neg. particle here is अप्राशस्त्य. अकार्यस्य गन्धोऽपि &c.—Sakara purposely misunderstands the word अकार्य and takes it to mean 'something that cannot be done,' and says 'It is no अकार्य at all;' and to make it clear he adds 'राक्षसी नास्ति'. गन्धोऽपि *lit.* means 'not even the smell of,' not to speak of the original. Hence गन्ध sometimes means 'a little' or 'a particle of;' *Cf.* घृतगन्धि भोजनं (गन्धशब्दोऽल्पपर्यायः। Kasika on अल्पाख्यायाम् Pan. V. 4. 136) and Yogasu. I. 48, न तत्र विपर्यासगन्धोऽप्यस्ति। अवेशसदृशप्रणयोपचारां—For the Comp. see Com.; he means—who is not like an ordinary courtesan; whose love is pure like that of a woman of family free from all desire of pelf उडुपेन—a boat; see *supra* p. 150 and our note thereon; so called probably because formed after the crescent-moon in shape. उडुपं दास्यामि—Sakara treats the matter jestingly and says 'I shall give you a boat.'

P. 278. पश्यन्ति—द्यौर्भूमिरापो हृदयं चन्द्रार्काग्नियमानिलाः। रात्रिः संध्ये च धर्मश्च वृत्तज्ञाः सर्वदेहिनाम्॥ Manu. VIII 86, and the well known Sl. आदित्यचन्द्रावनिलोऽनलश्च &c. साक्षिभूता—साक्षिणी भूता, the eye witness of. The affix इन् is added to साक्षात् in the sense of 'an eye-witness of', and the word so formed is a संज्ञा (*i. e.* limited to the third party witnessing a transaction between two persons who also see it) by साक्षाद्द्रष्टरि संज्ञायाम् Pan V. 2. 91. This is to be taken with each of the other nouns, with the necessary change of number and gender.

पटान्ताप०—brings out the childish folly of Sakara. He thinks that an act done under the covering of a piece of cloth would not be observed by the usual witnesses mentioned above. अपध्वस्तः—one deserving destruction on account of his wickedness, and therefore to be discarded; hence, one lost to all sense of right and virtue.

वृद्धश्रृगालः—some translate कोले by कोलः which means 'a hog'. महत्तरक—महत्तर एव महत्तरकः. मयाऽनार्येण आनीता—He means—In the first place I am guilty of having brought her here inconsiderately. It was my duty to see who got in.

P. 280. प्रभवति भट्टकः शरीरस्य—*Cf.* Shakespeare—

> " My life thou shalt command, but not my shame :
> The one my duty owes; but my fair name,
> Despite of death that lives upon my grave,
> To dark dishonour's use thou shalt not have."

—*King Richard II.*, I. 1. 166-169.

येन—कर्मणा प्रारब्धेन. Fate (the sum of the actions in a previous life which are ready to give their fruits and which shape the present life). भागधेयदोषैः—implies the multiple nature of his sin. अधिकं न क्रेष्यामि—I do not wish to add to my past sins. तेन—For this reason.

परिभूतदशः—परिभूता despised by all दशा यस्य; or rather परिभूतं तिरस्कारोऽस्या अस्तीति परिभूता an abode of contempt; like पीता गावः; now see com. प्रेष्यः—one fit to be sent on an errand; a servant. तस्मादमी &c.—अमी *i. e.* men like Sakara. The connexion between the first half and the second half is this—Even men in an abject state like Sthavaraka's hate sin and desire the fruit of meritorious deeds; while men like Sakara, who ought to know better, multiply sin, and so deserve instantaneous destruction.

P. 282. रन्ध्रानुसारी &c.—What Vita means is this—Since Sthavaraka has nobler and pious thoughts, he must be having a large fund of religious merit in store; but fate is रन्ध्रानुसारी and so notices the small portion of Sthavaraka's sins and punishes him with slavery. Again, since Sakara has wicked thoughts, the fund of his religious merit must be very small compared to his store of sins; but fate is विषम in dispensing fruits, and it rewards Sakara for the small store of his religious merit and makes him the master and Sthavaraka his slave.

सर्वकालं &c.—This must be a स्वगत speech. शिरश्चालनसंज्ञा —This must have been when Vita seized him by the neck. He has given me a hint by shaking his ( or shaking off my ) head that he won t allow me to do it; शिरश्चालनेन शिरश्चालनरूपा वा संज्ञा. So I must send him away. This is the remedy he speaks of. Samjna could not have been given to Vasantasena with the head; it would have been a नेत्रसंज्ञा.

**मल्लकप्रमाणैः**:—मल्लक according to the old Com. means a small vessel or cup formed of leaves (द्रोण in Marathi); or it may mean 'a wine-cup' Some take it in the sense of 'a jasmine flower.' The comparison occurs again in Act IX. This word, with its variants गल्लक, गल्लकं, has occrred before. Sakara in his usual absurd way calls his family बृहत्तर and compares it to a *mallaka*, which is very small, instead of to something very great; समुद्रप्रमाणैरिति वक्तव्ये मल्लकः पत्रपुटस्तेन कुलस्य महत्त्वं मौर्ख्यादुपमिनोति शकारः (L. D.) Some propose to take *mallaka* in the sense of 'a wrestler whose dimensions are very huge;' but this is far-fetched and in bad taste. Had Sakara to refer to a wrestler he would rather have referred to a पर्वत. Sl. 29 occurs again at IX. 7 with the reading नितरां for सुतरां.

P. 284. **विविक्तविश्रम्भरसः**:—See com; love has its flavour *i.e.* is properly enjoyed in the confidence of privacy (when the lovers are left to themselves).

**न्यासेन**—The cunning Sakara apparently accepts the charge, saying णाशेण which stands as well for नाशेन (for killing, that I should kill her), which he really means.

**अथ वा कपटकापटिकः** &c.—Shows that Sakara is really very shrewd. As कापटिक already means 'one acting fraudulently or cunningly' (see com.), so the addition of कपट is intended to intensify the meaning; 'the clever rogue.' Here it cannot be taken as अपार्थं वचः हुलुभुलि—is a dialectic word for the Sanskrit कपटं (*Cf.* Marathi भूल). **बाले बाले**—वासु वासु is also the छाया. **कामी**—भूयान्कामः अस्यास्तीति one whose passion is stored up or excessive; *Cf.* अहो कामी स्वतां पश्यति । Sak. II. 2; कयाऽसि कामिन् Kum. III. 8.

**कष्टमयाः**:—क्लेशप्रचुराः. Sakara, finding his suit not granted, says this—'(Since you do not accept me as your slave then indeed), men are full of hardships, have to live a life full of misery.' Some read किं ते वयं काष्ठमया मनुष्याः—'Are then we, thus despised (ते), made of wood, merely wooden images, having no feelings, *i.e.* who cannot feel the sting of rejection.' But it is difficult to render शे by ते in Sanskrit; and as remarked by Dr. Ryder, this seems to be an unnatural rendering in itself, and has no support in the context.

P. 286. **अवनतमुखी**—She hangs down her face (does not look at him), to indicate her extreme dislike to him **खलचरित निकृष्ट**—J. V suggests अथ वा हे खल चरितनिकृष्ट (चरितेन स्वभावेन पापकर्मणा निकृष्ट base); but the parallelism with सुचरिचरितं shows that the first way is better. **जातदोषः**—May mean—(1) who have given me offence or affronted me; or (2) are sinfully or wickedly disposed. J. V. says अथ वा जाते जनने दोषः अपवादः यस्य सः जारज इत्यर्थः But this is far-fetched. **परिलोभसे**—We should expect परिलोभयसे or ०यसि, but, as the metre would not allow it, the author uses परिलोभसे, taking लुभ् as a root of the first conjugation, in which class, which is an आकृति गण, लुभ् may be included.

**सुचरितचरितं विशुद्ध०**—Also refers to Charudatta by implication. **सुचरितं०**—(1) of good actions, in that it gives delight, fragrance and honey; (2) of noble or virtuous life. **विशुद्ध०**—(1) bright or beautiful in form; (2) pure, sinless or bright in body. **मधुपाः**—which are मकरन्दमार्मिका.; hence, those who know how to apppreciate pure and steady love This is made clear in the following sloka (यत्नेन &c.). J. V. remarks—गुणिषु गुणज्ञो रमते नागुणिषु हि तस्य परितोषः। अलिरेति वनात्कमलं न हि भेकस्त्वेकवासोऽपि ॥ इति न्यायात्.

**पलाशः कृतः किंशुकोऽपि** &c.—The Palasa tree is also called Kimsuka; so both are the same. The Palasa has bright red flowers which have no smell; so by comparing Sak. to the Palasa tree Vasant. meant to imply that he had wealth but no merits. But Palasa also means a raw-flesh-eater, a demon. So Sakara thought that she purposely used the word Palasa in order to indirectly call him a demon; and herein lay the abuse.

**मोटयामि**—मुट् 10 cl. to pound with blows, hence to strangle; (*cf.* Marathi मुटकणें). **सार्थवाहमनुष्यकामुकिनि**—Put in contrast with himself who is वरपुरुषवासुदेवकः.

**किं स शक्रः** &c.—We have again Sakara's absurdities. **शक्र** and **महेन्द्र** are the same; so this is पुनरुक्त. वालिपुत्र is Angada and not Mahendra; so this is आगमविरुद्ध (against history); similarly in other cases. **रम्भापुत्र**;—A son of Rambha is not known. Moreover, कालनेमि is not the son of Rambha; Kalanemi was an *asura*, son of Virochana and the grandson of Hiranyakasipu; he was slain by Vishnu. He was, however, born again as Kamsa. *Cf.* आत्मानमिह संजातं जानन्प्राग्विष्णुना हतम् । महासुरं कालनेमिं यदुभिः सत्यरुध्यत ।। Bhag. P. X. Purvardha Adh. I. 68. Kalanemi is also mentioned in the Rama. as an uncle of Ravana who was deputed by him to cause delay to and to kill Hanumat when he went to the mountain Gandhamadana to bring medicinal herbs. Hanumat, however, came to know him, and seizing him by the feet hurled him whirling through air to Lanka where he fell before Ravana's throne and died. *Cf.* कालनेमिं दुराधर्षं रक्षः परमदुर्जयम् । चतुरास्यं चतुर्हस्तमष्टनेत्रं भयावहम् ।। Ramayana.

**सुबन्धुः** may be a person named in the *Brihatkatha*; Subandhu, the poet and author of the *Vasavadatta,* cannot be meant here, as he is of a later date. **द्रोणपुत्रः**—is Asvatthama, one of the celebrated heroes of the Mahabharata. **चाणक्यः**—A well-known statesman and writer on civil policy and the minister of Chandragupta, also called **कौटिल्य** and विष्णुगुप्त in the *Mudrarakshasa*. **धुन्धुमारः**—A king of Ayodhya, of the solar race, properly named Kuvalayasva. He was called Dhundhumara from his having slain Dhundhu, a demon who annoyed the sage Uttanka. **त्रिशङ्कुः**—A celebrated king of the solar race, father of Harischandra. He loved his human body so much that he wanted to go in it to heaven. With that view he asked his family-priest Vasishtha to perform a sacrifice for him. He having refused he applied to Visvamitra, who underlook to perform the necessary sacrifice and invited all the gods to partake of it; they refused to do so whereupon Visvamitra raised him to heaven by his superhuman power. The king rose higher and higher till his head reached the vault of heaven; whereupon Indra hurled him down He fell head downwards, when Visvamitra arrested his downward motion by saying 'Stay Trisanku, stay;' and the poor monarch remained suspended in space as a constellation in the southern hemisphere.

P. 288. **भारते युगे**—The age characterized by the story of the Bharatas (the Bharata war). This is absurd; for Sita lived in the early part of the Dvapara age. Some think that this should have been भारते वर्षे; but there is no propriety in saying 'in the Bharata land.'

**असंपूर्णमनोरथः**—For she had come there to enjoy Charudutta's company, and this her desire remained unfulfilled.

**अथ वा वसन्तसेनोर्ध्वं** &c.—Although there was nobody to hear her cry, Vasanta. thought that she, so modest, so graceful in her behaviour, should be ashamed of herself, if she were to cry aloud, fearing death; with this determination she allows herself to be strangled without a groan.

**एतां दोषकरण्डिकां** &c.—Such is the picture of the virtuous Vasant. which Sakara's wicked mind presents to him The accusatives must be explained by supplying हत्वा or हतवान् (अहं). **रक्तां तस्य** &c—The second and the fourth lines are somewhat ambiguous. The best way of taking the 2nd line seems to be—(तस्मिन्) रक्तां (अत्र) आगतस्य किल तस्य रमणे (loc. for the dat.) आगतां (किं तु) कालागतां; who, in love with him, came here, as I near (किल), to sport with him, who (Ch.) had come here, but who (V.) (really) came here to meet her doom. Some separate किलागतस्य as किल+अगतस्य (see com.), 'who is in adverse circumstances;' but the context requires आगतस्य. From Sthavaraka's speech at p. 274. Sakara guesses that Char. had been waiting in the garden for Vasant. for whom a carriage was kept at his door; but that she got into the wrong carriage, and came there when he had left after uselessly waiting for her. **निःश्वासाऽपि** &c.—**अम्बा** is a term of pity like तात (and not of endearment); 'the poor woman.' As the Chhaya stands, the meaning is—How should I describe my prowess here ? The miserable woman, deprived of her breath (मया निःश्वासा कृता) dies so as never to rise again. Here अपि is redundant and is a Sakarian peculiarity. He means—I did not use violence; I merely stopped her breath and she died. निःश्वासेऽपि is another reading in the Chhaya (and from the Prakrit form of the word this seems to be better). In this case the meaning will be—'Why should I boast of the prowers of my arms ? She dies even at my breathing.' But this does not appear to be intended In the first place it is too much even for Sakara to say that Vasant. should die even at his breath. Secondly, it cannot be well taken with Sita; we can somehow take निःश्वासा with Sita (यथा भारते सीता निःश्वासा सती अम्रियत). Thirdly, सुमृता cannot be properly understood. And fourthly, this meaning does not fit in well with the following Sloka wherein Sakara boasts of the valour of his *arms* So the reading in the text is preferable. **अम्बा**—The Prakrit form अम्ब cannot be properly rendered as अम्बा. One MS. reads अम्बशुमले (अम्बस्मरा) 'fit to be remembered like a mother' which may be taken with सीता; but this has no propriety. **सीता यथा भारते**—Sita has nothing to do with the Mahabharata. Again, Sita did not die of violence. So this is आगमविरुद्ध and हतोपम.

P. 290. **शून्ये पुष्पकरण्डके**—The constr. is शून्ये पुष्पकरण्डके इति उत्त्रासिता सती मया सहसा पाशेन मारिता, who was frightened as the garden was lonely (and so no help could be expected). इति is ungrammatical after the loc. ०करण्डके; we should expect शून्यं पुष्पकरण्डकमिति. **सेवावञ्चित:** &c.—This line is somewhat hard. Dr. Ryder says—The third line is desperate, so desperate that Regnaud does not attempt to translate it......We may tentatively translate 'My brother was disappointed of his honour, and my father, and my mother (who in this respect is) like that Draupadi'......But the line seems nearly hopeless". We do not think it is so hopeless. सेवा means 'an agreeable service that brings pleasure to one'; *cf.* for this sense सेवितं नाम आवुत्तेन Sak. VI. p. 202 ; a son's exploit brings pleasure to his parents and to his brother, and so in a sense it is an act of service done towards them. So this means—'My brother was deceived in that he did not see this agreeable act of his brother, *viz.* this his exploit, his act of bravery (शूरत्वं);' see com. जे (Prakrit) may stand for य: or या. The *Chhaya* स वा वञ्चित: removes the difficulty. स वा वञ्चितभ्रातृक: मम पिता *v.l.*, which means 'my father who deceived his brother (वञ्चित: भ्राता येन)' is to be rejected as being against the context; Sakara is not likely to speak disparagingly of his father.

**अनेन पतता स्त्री व्या०**—This is the dead woman whom Viraka sees in the trial scene; Act IX. **पातिता:**—we have been degraded or made sinners. For not only he who commits sin is a sinner but also one who sees it being committed.

P. 292. **अत्याकुलं**—may be an adv.; 'in a very confused manner'; or a substantive, 'what is very contradictory or distressing'. **न शुद्ध्यति**—does not become bright or clear, *i. e.*, free from misgivings. **शीर्षं**—ought to be शीर्षेण; so this is a Sakarism.

**उदकवाहिनी**—A river. **विगलिता**—flowed out; dried up. **अलंकृतभूषणे**—*cf.* आभरणस्याभरणं Vik. II. 3. **क्रीडारसो०**—resplendent or graceful with the pleasure you took in amorous sports; or क्रीडारसस्य उद्भासिनि—you who added splendour to amorous sports, made them more charming. **सौजन्यनदि**—The repetition of the same comparison in the same verse mars poetic charm. **विपणि:** and **पण्याकर:**—are used here in the secondary sense of 'a store house of' (and not a market-place where love is sold, as it goes against the general drift of the sloka), where these exist in their fullness. *Cf.* with this--सौन्दर्यस्य तरङ्गिणी तरुणिमोत्कर्षस्य हर्षोद्गम: कान्ते: कार्मणकर्म नर्मरहसामुल्लासनावासभू: । विद्या वक्रगिरां विधेरनवधिप्रावीण्यसाक्षात्क्रिया बाणा: पञ्च शिलीमुखस्य ललनाचूडामणि: सा प्रिया ॥. The Sl. depicts karuna rasa.

P. 294. **कार्षापणं**-कर्षस्यायं कार्ष: कार्षस्य कार्षेण वा आपण: कार्षापण:; a coin of different values. According to Manusmriti (कार्षापणस्तु विज्ञेयस्ताम्रिक: कार्षिक: पण: VIII. 136) it was a copper coin; according to Amara, it was of silver. Probably it was of both. According to Pri. it was worth a rupee **सवोडिकं**--According to Pri **वोडी** is a coin worth 20 cowries current in the Gauda country. This is variously read as-(1) सवेष्टिकं with a turban; (or, loin-cloth); (2) सवेषिकं with a dress or clothes; (3) सपोषणं with nourishing or nutricious things. Dr. Ryder prefers the reading सकोटिकं (with a *Koti* or ten millions). **एष दोषस्थानं** &c.—'Let this my exploit which is criminal (*lit.* the cause of censure) be common with other men'—a roundabout way of saying 'Let the author of the crime remain unknown; do not give out his name.' **एष दु:शब्दानां फलक्रम: मे** &c.--*v. l.* 'let this continued reward of abusive words (charge of murder) be common to all men,' which virtually means the same thing; but the first reading is better.

**अप्रीति:**--Absence of joy, sorrow, repentance; 'feel sorry for what you have done.' **प्रीति**--friendship with you. **परिभव०**—causing disgrace, humiliating. **अनार्य**—dishonourable, ignoble. **निर्गुणं**--(1) void of virtues, wicked; (2) without string.

P, 296. **नगरस्त्रीशङ्किता०**--For comp. see com.; 'beheld with half-closed eyes with fear by the towns-women;' *i.e.* they will hesitate to look at you lest they might be similarly treated by you. **अन्यस्यां जातौ**--जाति is used here in the sense of birth; 'in your next life.'

**व्यवहारं देहि**--व्यवहार is a law suit, judicial proceedings; see com. on the word, at p. 306; he means—'I shall lodge a complaint against you before the king and you will have to answer for your crime.' **यावत्यां वेलायां** &c.--These ornaments are your property; but as you cannot wear them, I shall take them from you for wearing; and they will be mine so long only as I wear them. अण्णं is also translated as अन्यां (वेलां). Some read मया तावद्दत्तं as part of the next sentence ending with वेलां and मम अण्णं तव as मम आज्ञा तव, and explain यावतीं वेलां यावत्कालपर्यन्तमात्मनामलंकरोमि तावतीं वेलां त्वमात्मानमलंकुरु इति शेषः But this is not a good way. What ground is there for supplying त्वमात्मानमलंकुरु? It is merely gratuitous; also, no purpose is served by saying 'Put on the ornaments just in the space of time required by me to do so.' Again, अण्णं the Acc. has to be taken in the sense of the Nom. **प्रासादबालाग्रप्रतोलिका**--प्रासादबालाग्र has occurred before; see p. 56. प्रतोलिका properly means 'a street'; but here it has the secondary meaning of 'the corridor or aisle of the turret;' for it will be seen from Sakara's speech on the next page that Sthavaraka was confined there after Sakar went to his palace, and from the side of which he leaps down afterwards; see Act X.

P. 298. **आत्मपरित्राणे**—Loc. for the Dat. **मन्त्रः**—The secret *viz.* his having murdered Vasantasena. **नामाङ्कितः**—Marked with my name Pri. says वसन्तसेनाया इति (see com.), but that is not meant; for it was not Sakara's object to keep secret the name of Vasantsena. **आर्यपुरुषः**—A respectable man (whose testimony will be trustworthy). **वाताली**—a gust of wind or gale. **विशुद्धायां**—is emphatic. It appears that the slaughter of an animal was not allowed in the midst of a city inhabited by righteous people. **अविद मादिके**—expresses surprise mingled with fear.

**नासां छित्त्वा**—*i. e.* having pierced the middle part of his nose. It does not appear from the play when this was done. **वाहितः**—वाधितः *v. l.*

P. 300. **त्वरितत्वरितः**—making great haste. लङ्कानगर्यां गगने should be ०नगरीं गगनेन. **हनूम० इव महेन्द्रः**— Like (the monkey) Mahendra jumping upon the peak of Hanumat. This is a Sakarian absurdity. He should have properly said–As Hanumat going to Lanka through space leaped over the earth, the nether world and the peak of the mountain Mahendra. **महेन्द्रः**—One of the seven Kula-Parvatas or chief mountains, each lying in each division of the continent; *viz.* महेन्द्रो मलयः सह्यः शक्तिमानृक्षपर्वतः। विन्ध्यश्च पारियात्रश्च सप्तैते कुलपर्वताः ॥. It is identified with Mahendramala which divides Ganjam from the valley of the Mahanadi and which probably included the whole of the eastern Ghats between the Mahanadi and the Godavari.

**स्तिमितानि**—Read तिमितानि ( wetted ). **विस्तीर्णपत्राणि**—with the feathers (forming the wing) spread out. **पत्राणि इव** like wings. As Vasantasena came back to consciousness, she moved inside the heap of leaves, so that the leaves on both the sides moved up like the wings of a bird when extended. L. D. translates पत्ता by **पत्रा:** which he takes in the sense of birds.' But **पत्र** by itself rarely occurs in the sense of a bird. To make पत्र have that sense we must add the possessive aff. **अ (अच्)** which is added to the group अर्शआदि (Pan. V. 2. 127); पत्राणि एषां विद्यन्ते इति पत्रा:. Pri seems to have read एतानि विस्तीर्णप्राप्तानि (विस्तीर्णं विस्तारम्। भावे क्तः। प्राप्तानि extended) पत्राणि इव स्फुरन्ति. Dr. Ryder takes **पत्र** to mean 'a leaf' all through. **हस्तं दर्शयति**—दर्शयति does not mean 'shows', but 'puts out.'

P. 302. **न पुनर्यथाऽऽर्यो भणति**—'But not in the way as your reverence says it, *i. e.* as having conferred any benefaction on you.' This brings out the nobility of her mind. **लतामवलम्ब्य**—For, as a holy man the Bhikshu could not touch her so as to lend her the support of his hand. **एषा तरुणी** &c—Here is a young woman; here a Bhikshu, walking by her side without touching her; thus (इति) my pursuit of piety is pure (above reproach).

P. 304. **हस्तसंयत:** &c.—See com. **राजकुलं**—A king's court or relatives. These have no power over such a man, as no guilt can be proved against him. In Mr. Godbole's Ed this verse is printed as prose. The metre is an irregular Arya—the syllabic instants being 15, 17, 12 and 18 in the four padas respectively.

# ACT IX.

The chief subject of this Act is the precipitate order of King Palaka to impale Charudatta, on the judge's submitting of his finding to him—an order which serves to add to the unpopularity of the king. The judge had a good opinion of Charudatta, who was thought to be above such a crime. But circumstances creep up in such a way as to lend support to Sakara's statement and to raise doubts about Charudatta's character. Charudatta at first pleads not guilty, but finding Vasantasena gone and life without interest on that account, confesses the crime. And the dropping of gold ornaments from Maitreya's arm-pit in his struggle with Sakara settles the point.

P. 306 **शोधनकः**—The court-attendant who had also to clean the seats and keep the court-house in order (as the root शुध् shows). **अधिकरणभोजकैः**—अधिकरण is the place where disputes are decided; a court of justice; **तस्य भोजकाः**—the masters, persons in charge; the judge, and the other functionaries, such as the श्रेष्ठिन्, the Kayastha, &c. When merely the judge is meant the word अधिकरणिक is used; see com. **व्यवहारः**—The decision of a case after hearing the arguments of both the parties; judicial procedure; see com ; and *cf.* Katyayana—वि नानार्थेऽत्र संदेहे हरणं हार उच्यते। नानासंदेहहरणाद् व्यवहार इति स्मृतः ॥. **मण्डपं**—The court. **विविक्तः**—clean. **अधिकरणिकानां**—The judge and his assistants. The pl does not seem to be used out of respect; for Sakara also uses the pl further on.

**सलिलजलैः**—The repetitions in the sl. are a characteristic of Sakara's speech, as often remarked. **सुविहितैः**—Well decorated. The Gandharvas are well known for their singing and scarcely for the beauty of their limbs or dress. गन्धर्वेहिं गन्धर्वैः) *v. l.*–Pri. says **प्रथमार्थे तृतीया** Dr. Ryder trenslates this as with Gandharvic, well turned limbs'; and remarks—'The fact that the Gandharvas are male creatures, and the persons mentioned in the third line female need not trouble us, as the blunder may be attributed to Samsthanaka's ignorance.'

P. 308. **क्षणेन ग्रन्थिः** &c.—It seems that Sakara, fresh from a bath, directly walked to the court, witb his turban not put on now tying up his hair, now turning them and so on, as his whims guided him **जूटकः**—is the peculiar knot of hair worn by ascetics. मुक्ताः—set free and allowed to hang loose. The repetitions will be easily noticed.

विषग्रन्थि—By this he refers to his dreadful crime. Some render विशगण्ठि by बिसग्रन्थि (a knot of the lotus-stalk) in the case of कीट. महदन्तरं—A broad passage; *i. e.* I have hit upon a fine remedy, *viz.* to fasten the guilt on somebody. दुर्वाचत्वरे—A quadrangular spot covered with the Durva grass.

श्रेष्ठिकायस्थादिपरि०—श्रेष्ठिन् was the recognized chief of merchants. His presence was necessary for testing ornaments, counting money, &c. and for dealing with questions referring to mercantile law. For Kayastha, see *supra* p. 182. His duty in the court was to take down evidence, make notes for the judge at his dictation, &c. In fact the Kayasthas discharged the duties of notaries and attorneys. "From the way in which they interfere," remarks Wilson, "they seem to sit as joint assessors or commissioners with the judges." The judge could be either a Brahamana, or a Kshatriya or a Vaisya; but the assessors were to be Brahmanas alone. Later on, however, merchants were called in as appears from the Mitakshara. *Cf.* लोकरञ्जनार्थं कतिपयैर्वणिग्भिरधिष्ठितं सदः कर्तव्यम् See also Katyayana quoted in the com. The judge submitted his finding on the issues of a case to the king who as the dispenser of justice passed the final order; *cf.* निर्णये वयं प्रमाणं शेषे तु राजा later on.

व्यवहारपराधीनतया—व्यवहार judicial administration; technically it means the finding out of the true facts, leading to final decision, from the statements of the parties, the evidence got by counsels, by questionings, cross examination of the witnesses, consideration of the doubts expressed, &c. ०पराधीनतया—as this depends on others, *viz.* the conflicting parties, their witnesses, &c. The same is made clear in the next Sl.; *cf.* व्यवहारनीतयः Sl. 25 *infra*.

P. 310. छन्नं—Buried in doubt, not clear, truth being presented as untruth, and *vice versa.* पक्ष—Party of the plaintiff; अपरपक्ष of the defendant. अपवादः—blame or ensure, when a case is decided wrongly though on the strength of the evidence before the court.

**सन्त:**—good men, this seems to mean counsels engaged by the parties who, although good, *i. e.* upright. share the faults of their clients, as they have to depend upon their statements.

**शास्त्र**—The legal lore. **कपटानुसार**—following up, tracing out, fraud or deceit. **तुल्यो मित्र०**—*i. e.* a judge must be impartial; no consideration like—'This is my friend; this is my enemy'—ought to weigh with him. **स्वका:**—one's relatives. *Cf.* श्रुताध्ययनसंपन्ना धर्मज्ञाः सत्यवादिनः। राज्ञा सभासदः कार्या रिपौ मित्रे च ये समा:॥ Yaj.-Sm. II. 2.

**चरितं**---The action, the course of arguments (put forth by the parties); or the true facts. **दृष्ट्वा**--after carefully investigating or finding out. **धर्म्य:**--not departing or swerving from justice or virtue, righteous **धर्म्योऽतिलोभान्वित:** *v. l.*-Execedingly *i. e.* assiduously) fond of doing justice or just acts; **धर्म्यं धर्मादनपेते कर्मणि**; this is not a good reading, as अतिलोभा० has no special propriety. **द्राभवि**—This has puzzled the commentators; one takes this as भावे द्राः भावे पराभिप्रायविषये द्राः द्राभूतः। द्वारवत्प्रवेशयोग्यः। पराशयग्राहीत्यर्थः।. But this is forced and far-fetched; some interpret it as द्राभवि when there is a door or opening, *i. e.* scope for it (as in the com.), but take it with परतत्त्व &c.—firmly setting his heart on discovering, *i. e.* firmly resolved to find out, the absolute or final truth, (when there is a remedy or means for it). But this has no propriety; for wherein then will lie the skill or legal acumen of the judge, if he finds out the truth when there is the means for finding it out? So it seems it is better to take this with न लोभान्वितः; द्राभवि (when there is scope for it, some one offers bribe) न लोभान्वितः. *Cf.* विकारहेतौ सति विक्रियन्ते येषां न चेतांसि त एव धीराः। Kum. I. 59 Or, we should supply स्थित: सन् परतत्त्व etc. Dr. Ryder notices the reading द्राभ्यां वै and says—'(it) is much easier; (his heart devoted to others' interests) in behalf of both parties (plaintiff and defendant). But it is difficult to see how to get this meaning out of the reading. **परतत्त्व**—The highest or absolute truth; see com. **राज्ञश्च कोपा०**—For, sometimes a judge has to incur the king's anger by deciding a case against the king's wish or understanding.

**चन्द्रालोके** &c.—By this they compliment the judge on being complacent and habitually disposed to please all. **कार्यार्थी**—कार्य is a suit to be decided; कार्येण अर्थी; one wishing to lodge a plaint or suit; a litigant.

P. 312. व्यवहारे—seems here to be used in the sense of 'the court'; or it may mean 'litigation'. व्याकुलेन—Causing disturbance, hard and perplexing, as involving the ruin or death of some great man (as Sakara was the complainant). भवितव्यं—is bound, sure, to be. The interpretation 'to-day we shall have a very busy day' is not supported by the context. भगिनीपति—is redundant after आवुत्तं भगिनीं मातरं च—is meant to convince Sodhanaka that he would do it by trying to bring every influence to bear on Palaka. The Sakara's threat and the judge's consequent admission of the suit are intended to show the readiness of King Palaka to yield to back-door influence and to take action under it without further inquiry.

P. 314. भीतभीता:—Much frightened. यद्यदहं—The shrewd Sakara concludes from the judge's yielding to his threat that he would force the court to accept as truth whatever he would say.

युष्माकमपि—He means—It is in my power to make you happy or unhappy—implying thereby that the judge and his assistants must not go against his wishes. स्थिरसंस्कारता—Oh, the permanence—unchangeableness—of the impressions—mental culture—of one who is a complainant. Said with reference to Sakara's words युष्माकमपि सुखं &c. which was an echo of the threat held out to the judge. Sakara should not have spoken such words in the open court at least. The judge means that the fellow would not give up his fooleries under any circumstances; and this is proved by the next speech of Sakara.

भवान् कार्यार्थी—The question is according to the prescribed procedure for the conduct of a case in a court of law. *Cf.* काले कार्यार्थिनं पृच्छेत्प्रणतं पुरतः स्थितम् । किं कार्यं का च ते पीडा--इति । Vyavahara-Mayukha. मल्लकप्रमाणस्य—See *supra* p. 282 and our note thereon.

राजश्वशुर:—Sakara wants to impress on the judge the fact of his being connected with the king, in order to secure a favourable judgement from him. किं कुलेनोपदिष्टेन—this sl. has occurred before (VIII. 29). *Cf.* what Vidura says to Duryodhana—न कुलं वृत्तहीनानां प्रमाणमिति मे मतिः । अन्तेष्वपि हि जातानां वृत्तमेव विशिष्यते ॥ Mahabharata.

P. 316. न पश्यामि वा—is a Sakarism. काञ्चनशत०—काञ्चनस्य शतं भूषणानि यस्यास्ताम्. प्रविश्य--better read प्रवेश्य (which is followed in the translation). बाहुपाश०--बाहुरेव पाशः तस्य बलात्कारेण.

**न मयेति** &c.—**व्यवहारपदं** a legal point. For the words **न मया** which Sakara uttered in his eagerness to deny his hand in the matter, and the manner in which he bit his lips afterwards, created a suspicion about his being the murderer in the mind of the judge, and he asked the scribe to write down those words as likely to serve as a clue to the unravelling of the mystery A judge ought to attach great importance to the words falling from the lips of a party unconsciously. *Cf.* स्वभावेनैव यद्ब्रूयुस्तद्ग्राह्यं व्यावहारिकम् । अतो यदन्यद्विब्रूयुर्धर्मार्थं तदपार्थकम् ।। Manu. VIII. 78.

**उत्त्वरायमाणेन**—(1) rising up quickly; (2) making haste. Some read त्वरां कुर्वाणेन as the Chhaya. **पायसपिण्डारकः**—पायस is a dainty preparation of rice boiled in milk with sugar; or it may simply mean पयसः अयं पायसः 'of milk;' पिण्डं पिण्डाकारं ऋच्छतीति पिण्डारः (fr पिण्ड + ऋ to go + affix अ), पिण्डार एव पिण्डारकः, the swelling up in the form of a ball of milk or Payasa. (**पयसः** त्वरयोद्गमनं यथा स्वनाशाय भवति तथा ). J. V. takes this in the sense of greedy or eager for' (पायसपिण्डलोभिना) and sees a reference in **पायस** to Charudatta's destruction ( like a man greedily swallowing hot **पायसान्न** and getting his tongue burnt ). But in this case we don't get he meaning directly; we have to suppose the milk porridge to be very hot. Some take पिण्डारक in the sense of 'a beggar' (पिण्डारो भिक्षुके द्रुमे), *lit.* one who goes out for food. "A mendicant feasting on a preparation of milk. The story of a beggar who in his voracity swallowed hot milk-dish and killed himself, must have been current in Sudraka s time, and Sakara refers to it in the manner of Sam Weller." Paranjpe.

**ननु भणामि मयेव दृष्टा**—Sakara explains away the matter saying 'I did not want to say **ण मए**; you did not hear me properly. I was going to say—णं मए एव्व दिट्ठा.' **कथं त्वया ज्ञातं** &c.—From this speech of the judge it appears that he did not find fault with Sakara for wiping off what was written. For according to law the judge is not to regard a statement made by a party spontaneously as final, but should have it written down tentatively to be corrected or modified afterwards according to subsequent evidence; *cf* पूर्वपक्षं स्वभावोक्तं प्राड्विवाकोऽभिलेखयेत् । पाण्डुलेखेन (with a piece of chalk) फलके (on a board) ततः पत्रे विशोधितम् । शोधयेत्पूर्ववादं तु यावन्नोत्तरदर्शनम् ।। Vya.—May **शूनशूना**—Very much swollen; शून P. p. p. of श्वि. **मोघ**—रिक्त (empty, destitute of). **ग्रीवालिका—**

neck; see com,; a Sakarian peculiarity, as the word **आलि** is added to **ग्रीवा** without authority or sense.

P. 318. **अवलम्बते**—depends for proof **अर्थानुसारेण**—By following up the facts, what transpires in the course of the conduct of a case. ०**निष्पाद्यः**—*i. e.* the judge has to bring his legal acumen to bear on the facts supplied and to sift the truth from them and to give his decision.

**कुट्टिनि**—Better read कुट्टनि. Mark Sakara's levity of mind and wickedness. He hates Vasantasena's mother for no fault of hers.

P. 320. **चारुदत्तो मित्रमिति**—This is a reply to Sakara. That Charudatta is Vasantasena's friend proves nothing against him. **प्रथम पादः**—According to writers on law litigation has four Padas—चतुष्पाद् व्यवहारोऽयं विवादेषूपदर्शितः । Yaj, Vyavaharadhaya Sl. 8. तत्र प्रत्यर्थिनोऽग्रतो लेख्यमिति भाषापादः प्रथमः। यथोक्तं—परस्परं मनुष्याणां स्वार्थविप्रतिपत्तिषु। वाक्यन्यायाद्व्यवस्थानं व्यवहार उदाहृतः। भाषोत्तरक्रियासाध्यसिद्धिभिः क्रमवृत्तिभिः। आक्षिप्तचतुरंशस्तु चतुष्पादभिधीयते ।। Mitakshara on the above.

**स्वैरं**—gently (and not in the tone of authority as in the case of a culprit). Mark the *samdhi*-स्व + ईरः (ईर् to go and अच्). **अवस्थामभिशङ्कते**—*Lit.* the summons suspects my (miserable) state (poverty); *i. e.* since the king has called me, it shows, that he has entertained a suspicion about me on account of my poverty.

P. 322. **ज्ञातः**—*i. e.* from the reports of his officers. **अभियुक्त इव**—As if charged with some crime, under arrest. Charu. had offended the king in no way; so the only crime he could think of, as being the probable cause of his being summoned now, was the help he gave to Aryaka in making good his escape.

**वाशति**—वाश् 4 conj. is Atm ; *cf.* (शिवाः) प्रतिभयं ववाशिरे Ragh. XI. 61; क्रूरा ध्वाङ्क्षा ववाशिरे Bhatti. XIV 76. So the para. here is anomalous Some defend it on the principle अनुदात्तत्वलक्षणमात्मनेपदमनित्यम्. Or this may be explained as वाशं करोति वाशति. **अमात्य**—here the judge, as a minister of justice. **अनिमित्तानि**—For these ominous signs see com.

**शुष्कवृक्ष**०—*Cf.* किं नु खलु एष वायस...आदित्याभिमुखं विस्वरं विलपति । Bhasa's Panch. II. A crow, sitting on a withered tree, facing the sun and uttering harsh cries, forebodes dire calamity. See com. **घोरमसंशयम्**—Some take घोरं as qualifying चक्षुः. It is, however, better to take it separately असंशयं घोरं वर्तते (see trans.); for, if taken with the preceding sentence, असंशयं has no propriety.

जिह्मित—rendered crooked, coiled. भुजगपतिः—The sight of a serpent confronting a person is ominous. It is strange that a snake should be found in a street of such a crowded city as Ujjayini, and that too during day time. But the poet brings in one in his anxiety to bring together all ominous sights.

P. 324. नयनं—the left eye; see *supra* p. 250. And शार्ङ्गधरपद्धति—वामस्याधःस्फुरणमसकृत्सङ्गरे भेदहेतुस्तस्यैवोर्ध्वं हरति नितरां मानसं दुःखजालम्। नेत्रोपान्ते हरति च धनं नेत्रकोणे च बन्धुं सव्ये चैतत्फलमविकलं व्यत्ययं चापसव्ये ॥. See also our note on किं न्विदं स्फुरति p. 222. शकुनिरपरः—may be a crow or a vulture. The science of augury is called शाकुनं after शकुनि.

चिन्तासक्त &c.—In this sl. the court is compared to the ocean on account of the vast conclave of men gathered there and the presenee of animals like horses and elephants, serving as the instruments of destruction. This shows that several judges sat in different compartments of the same building. आसक्त devoted to; निमग्न plunged in; the whole means 'deeply engulfed or buried in thought.' मन्त्रिन्—A counsel. दूताः—envoys or the wrangling advocates चार—spies or informers; they are compared to sharks because they furnish secret information to the court and lead to men's ruin. हिंस्राः—the sea-monsters. वाशक—pettifoggers, or law-agents, who incite people to enter into litigation with one another. These are compared to the herons that hover about to catch their prey. कंकस्तु लोहपृष्ठः स्यात्संदंशवदनः खरः। रणालंकरणः क्रूरः स च स्यादामिषप्रियः ॥ Rajanighanta. नानावासक—*v. l.*—those who put on various dresses (वस् to dress), *i. e.* disguises; spies, detectives.

नीतिक्षुण्णतटं—With its bounds broken by policy (like the shore of the sea broken by rivers); or नीतिः (subtle argumentation) एव क्षुण्णं तटं यस्य; hence difficult or dangerous to approach J–V. comments नीत्याः......कदाचिदसत्यमपि सत्यवत्सत्यमप्यसत्यवत् क्रियते नीतिविद्भिरिति विचारशैल्याः दुर्गमत्वात्सुखेनावबोधाभावाच्च क्षुण्णतटसाम्यमवगन्तव्यम्। एतेन यथा हि बन्धुरतटभूमिषु अध्वगस्य पादस्खलनं नियतमव्यभिचारि तथैव कुटिलायां दुरवग्रहायां च राजनीतौ विचक्षणस्यापि स्खलनं स्वतः संभवीति प्रतीयते।. हिंस्रैः—उपलक्षितं marked by its cruel deeds; or, on account the things dangerous to life, *viz.* water &c. mentioned above. दैवतः—abl. in तस् of दैव; coming from fate; or, दैवतः may mean 'god' or the gods, for he says above सर्वथा देवताः स्वस्ति करिष्यन्ति।

According to Amara. दैवत may be also *mas*. (दैवतानि पुंसि वा). Mammata criticizes the use of such words, though given as *mas*., as open to the fault अप्रयुक्तत्वं, they being not so used by poets (अप्रयुक्तत्वं तथाम्नातमपि कविभिरनादृतम्). J. V. quotes the following sl. to show that दैवतः *mas* is used by poets—यथाऽयं दारुणाचारः सर्वदैव विभाव्यते। तथा मन्ये दैवतोऽस्य पिशाचो राक्षसोऽथ वा॥.

घोणोन्नत—should properly be उन्नतघोणं; so this must be taken as a case of the आहिताग्न्यादि class; आहिताग्निः, अग्न्याहितः. अकारण०—It is better to take the comp. as in the com.; "it ought not to be the abode of crimes attributed to it wilfully." If we say 'causeless', crimes then it will follow that it can be the पात्र of सकारणदूषणs; while the author means that such persons can never be guilty of sinful acts.

न ह्याकृतिः &c.—*cf*. Das.-Ch. सेयमाकृतिर्न व्यभिचरति शीलम्; also यत्राकृतिस्तत्र गुणा वसन्ति; आकृतिमनुगृह्णन्ति गुणाः (Viddh.-Bhanj.); and for the same thought differently expressed—यदुच्यते पार्वति पापवृत्तये न रूपमित्यव्यभिचारि तद्वचः। Kum. V. 36.

P. 326. नियुक्ताः—has a technical meaning. It means 'assessors' who are non-Brahmanas; here the श्रेष्ठी and the Kayastha. ब्राह्मणोऽनियुक्तः। सभ्यास्तु नियुक्ताः। Vya.-M. II. प्रसक्तिः—Connexion, friendship.

P. 328. भट्टकः—Some take this as referring to Charudatta and the whole sl. as one sentence. लज्जया भीरुतया वा भट्टकः (the master, *i. e.*, Charudatta—so called ironically) तन्न गूहति किं अपि तु गूहत्येव—Will not master (*i. e.* Charu.) hide it now? he *will*. J. V. suggests an alternative meaning—तस्मात् भवान् न भट्टकः पण्डितः। स्वदोषनिगूहनादतिनीच एव।. Pri. reads नष्टकः (is he one not doomed? He is).

सविघ्नः—Full of danger (on account of the gravity of the crime); or supply भवेत् after सविघ्नः; the conduct of the case will be obstructed *i. e.* delayed (if you won't reply promptly). अलं धैर्यं—We should expect धैर्येण; as it is, construe धैर्यमलमस्तु सत्यकथनायेति शेषः; have firmness of mind sufficient to enable you to tell the truth. छलं—equivocation, verbal quibbling कपटकापटिकः—कपटेन जयति कापटिकः; (कपट+ठक्—इक); कपटयुक्तः कापटिकः कपटकापटिकः; the tautology is Sakarian.

P. 330. अभ्युक्षितोऽसि &c.—It is difficult to see what the poet's idea was when he wrote the first two lines of this Sloka;

and no satisfactory explanation of these can be given. Dr. Ryder also says—this verse is desperately hard. बलाहक is a cloud; वारीणां वाहकः बलाहकः a comp. of the पृषोदरादि class (irregular). According to J. V. (5th ed.) the meaning is—You are not wet with rain-water and yet your forehead is drenched in perspiration (like that of one conscious of having told a lie). This may have been intended. But, why चाषाग्रपक्षसदृशं ? And what is the propriety of भृशं ? Other commentators give no help. Some say—चाषाग्रपक्षा हि वारिसंपर्केण मलिना भवन्ति त्वन्मुखं तु तत्संपर्काभावेऽपि निष्प्रभं &c 'The wings of the blue jay turn dark when sprinkled over with water; your face is darkened though not thus sprinkled.' But चाषाग्रपक्षमिव cannot be legitimately taken with त्वन्मुखं; and J. V. has given up this interpretation in his new ed. (1917). हेमन्तपद्ममिव—Because the lotuses in winter being blighted by frost lose their freshness and bloom. *Cf.* जातां मन्ये शिशिरमथितां पद्मिनीं वाऽन्यरूपां; Megh. II. 23; and मृणालिनी हैममिवोपरागम् । Ragh. XVI. 7. Sakara got perspiration on his forehead and changed colour as Charu. fixed his gaze on him. Hence he says—your statement is false *Cf.* ललाटं स्विद्यते चास्य मुखं वैवर्ण्यमेति च । अभियोगे च साक्ष्ये वा दुष्टः स परिकीर्तितः । Yaj. II. 13, 5.

तारणं— The swimming of. दूषणं—attributing of crime to. *Cf.* दोर्भ्यां तितीर्षति तरङ्गवतीभुजङ्गमादातुमिच्छति करे हरिणाङ्कबिम्बम् । मेरुं लिलङ्घयिषति ध्रुवमेष देव यस्ते गुणान्गदितुमुद्यममातनोति ॥.

P. 332. प्राकृतः—A low-born fellow. प्रकृष्टं अकृतं अकार्यं (wicked or sinful deeds) यस्य. न च ते जिह्वा &c.—Your action in impeaching Char. is as heinous as that of an outcast expounding the Vedas, the penalty for which is the falling off of the tongue. चलयसि—by bringing accusation against him. न च देहं हरति भूः—The earth ought to open up and swallow you down. She does not do it; this is wonderful. *Cf.* उपकारिणि विश्रब्धे शुद्धमतौ यः समाचरति पापम् । तं जनमसत्यसंधं भगवति वसुधे कथं वहसि ॥ Hit.

उदकोच्छ्रय—Its swelling mass of water. ०मात्रशेषं *i. e.* having deprived it of all its wealth, pearls, &c. अवीर—a low-minded person; Charu being a दानवीर will never stoop to such a mean thing अवैरिजुष्टं— *V. l.* 'not committed (even) by one's foes'. This is not a good reading. हा जाते &c.—Vasantasena's mother, believing that her daughter was killed either by Sakara himself or by some one else, mourns her loss.

परिभव—gross insult ar wrong; स एव विमानना disrespecting; or better still परिभवेन विमानना (its result, *i. e.* shame or chagrin caused by it, humiliation).

P. 334. चन्दनमहत्तरकेण–' By the great Chandanaka'; this is said ironically, meaning thereby —' unduly proud of his post and insolent.'

निर्मल० शशी—*i. e.* Charu. of spotless fame. राहुणा—*i. e.* by Sakara seeking to inculpate him. कूलावपातेन—By the subsidence of, tumbling down into (the stream). *Cf.* कूलंकषेव सिन्धु: प्रसन्नमम्भस्तटतरुं च। Sak. V. 21; गङ्गा रोधः पतनकलुषा Vik. I. 7.

वैषम्यं &c.—' The adverseness of worldly transactions or incidents. ' It is better to take लोकव्यवहार in this sense than in that of administration of law;' for in that case he would have said simply व्यवहारस्य. The judge was sure that Charudatta was innocent, but outward incidents had so combined as to prove him guilty. See below, note on व्यवहारनीतयः.

इदं—may refer to चारुदत्तवृत्तं or कार्यं ( this case ). संकटं—dangerous, intricate; संकटति (that which covers from all sides); fr. कट + अ ( अच् ); or सं dangerous and aff. कट ( कटच् ); संबाधार्थात्संशब्दात्स्वार्थे कटच्. अहो—expresses surprise and sorrow. सुसन्नाः—Well-connected. ०नीतयः—The legal points or proofs (which almost showed that Charu. was guilty ). For in the first instance Vasantasena's mother admitted that her daughter had gone to Charudatta's house Secondly, there was Viraka's statement that Vasantasena was being taken to the P. garden in Charudatta's carriage that was covered. Thirdly, the remains of the dead body of a woman actually found there proved Sakara's assertion to that effect. This made the judge dubious about his own conviction that Charudatta was innocent, and he was at a loss to know how to set aside the evidence as worthless and declare Charu. not guilty. Hence his remark मतिस्तु &c.

एवं मनुष्यस्य &c —The Upama here is vitiated by the fault अनुचितत्व, as the bees delightfully alighting on full-blown flowers are compared to misfortunes. छिद्रेष्वनर्था &c.—is also the fourth line of the well-known Subhashita क्षते प्रहारा निपतन्त्यभीक्ष्णं धनक्षये दीप्यति जाठराग्निः। आपत्सु वैराणि समुल्लसन्ति छिद्रेष्व० ॥; and also of the Sl in Hitop. एकस्य दुःखस्य &c. I. 205

P. 336. कि--this should be taken with the last line; किं तद्ग्राह्यं भवति, न तद्विचारणीयं किम्; or, न may be a reply to the first question; किं तद्ग्राह्यं भवति । न ( not at all ); तद्विचारणीयमेव. अवचय--By the rule हस्तादाने चेरस्तेये Pan. III. 3. 40, the root चि takes घञ् ( अ causing वृद्धि ) when the sense is " taking something with the hand, except in the case of stealing." So we should have अवचाय. But we find the form अवचय in use; how to defend it ? The वृत्तिकार says हस्तादानग्रहणे प्रत्यासत्तिरादेयस्य लक्ष्यते, *i. e.* the Sutra implies 'nearness' of the thing to be plucked. When such is not the case, the root takes अच् and we get अवचय. Here also the flowers were out of the reach of the hand, as Char. speaks of 'bending down the creepers;' and so अवचय is right. ह्री अनेन—By this *i. e.* Charu.'s being unseated, which showed that his guilt was taken as proved.

हा ब्राह्मणि—He refers to his wife Dhuta मिथ्यैव नन्दसि &c.—The line is rather obscure, owing to the difficulty of the meaning to be assigned to परव्यसनेन. It is variously interpreted as, 'although beset by terrible misfortune', (परेण श्रेष्ठेन व्यसनेनोपलक्षितः ); with mere childish amusements or sports' ( परेण केवलेन व्यसनेन बाल्यसुलभेन क्रीडनेन J. V. ); but this seems to be unusual. It is better to take परव्यसनेन as 'misfortune being far removed from you' (परं दूरं यद् व्यसनं तेन); you not knowing what misfortune is. Another way is परं व्यसनं यस्मात्तेन मया; 'you always take delight in my company thinking me to be beyond the reach of misfortune; but you do not know what has befallen me to day.' *Cf. supra* एतेनार्यचारुदत्त आत्मानं विनोदयति । P 218.

P. 338. अस्या आभरणं—Read अस्य आभरणं. The masc. form इमस्स cannot refer to Vasantasena, as observed by Dr. Ryder, who translates—" It was right for her to give him the jewels (to stop his crying), but not ( for me ) to receive them. "

रतिर्वा—Or rather, Rati of this world. रति may also mean 'the sentiment or flavour of love' अविशेषेण—Without distinction, the very embodiment of We may also separate as विशेषेण '(who can be) particularly, or eminently, called' &c शेषं &c --He could not say 'बाहुपाशेन घातिता;' he loved Vasanta. so tenderly.

P. 340. तपस्वी--He pities him for being so wicked as to be the tool of the god of death. He means--It is the god of death who wants to kill me; this fellow is निमित्तमात्रं. उह्यमानमपि--See IX. 32. दोषात्--owing to my labouring under the disadvantage of poverty.

विहार:--See p. 302. आराम--a delightful garden; आरमन्ति जना अत्र; रम् with आ and अ( घञ् ).

अनीश:—Not rich; poor. उच्छृङ्खल—*Lit.* one who has broken through all social and moral bonds; a perfect libertine. ०भण्ड—a reviler or utterer of abusive language, a rogue. This may also be taken saparately. Some read ०भाण्ड; कृता: जनस्य दोषास्तेषां भाण्ड the vessel of crimes you ( falsely ) impute to others. One Com has taken कृत in the sense of हिंसित, taking हिंसित as a noun, and the comp. कृतजन as one of the शाकपार्थिवादि class—हिंसाप्रधाना जना: ( murderous people ) तेषां दोषा: तेषां भाण्ड; but this is useless labour, and the meaning attributed to कृत is obscure.

काकपद &c.—See *supra* p. 54.

P 342. The ornaments were actually found with Maitreya. This was to all appearances the last and the most convincing proof of Charudatta's guilt. So the officers hang down their faces, as they had openly declared their opinion that Charu. would never be guilty of a crime of that kind. विस्तर:—a collection or number of. Mark the Samdhi; we have विष्टर: when the meaning is 'a seat or a tree'; वृक्षासनयोर्विष्टर: Pan. VIII. 3. 93.

भूतार्थ:—The fact, *viz.* that the ornaments were given by Vasantasena herself to his son for making a golden toy-cart with, but that they were given in his ( Maitreya's ) charge to be returned to her as he ( Charu. ) did not like to keep them. नृपतेश्चक्षु:—Here the judge. He is दुर्बल because his ken is limited by the facts proved before him and cannot penetrate beyond them and see the real thing. दैन्यं—Miserableness, helplessness. For it will be taken to be a lie invented to explain away the matter somehow, as Vasanta. was not alive to bear testimony to it It will spoil the judge's opinion and lead to an inglorious death. What Charu. says here is not true. The judge had openly expressed his belief in his innocence and his attitude towards him is sympathetic throughout this scene. So had Charu. told the truth, with Maitreya to corroborate it, the judge would have readily believed it. He again misses an opportunity when the assessors ask him the suggestive question कथमेतानि &c. ( see page 344 ) and he evades the answer by simply saying एवं गतानि । आं इदम्. This shows that the poet does not want him to do it. He wanted to have Char.'s crime proved somehow and has done it at the expense of his hero. This is a flaw in the construction of the plot. The poet should better have dropped these two speeches.

अङ्गारक०—In this sl. Charu. is compared to Jupiter, a planet of the Brahmana class, Sakara to Mars, a malignant planet and opposed to him, and Vidu. to a comet suddenly appearing by his side to help the destructive influence of Mars. The comp. अङ्गारकवि०, if dissolved as अङ्गारकः विरुद्धः यस्य, must be taken as one of the आहिताग्न्यादि class. Brihaspati is represented as in the lowest position and therefore not powerful enough to resist the adverse action of Mars on him. Here Mars is represented as the enemy of Jupiter. This is according to the opinion of the ancient astrologers. Modern astrologers, headed by Varahamihira, do not regard Mars as an enemy of Jupiter. *Cf.* जीवेन्दूष्णकराः कुजस्य सुहृदः; Brihajjataka II 16; and जीवो जीवबुधौ सितेन्दुतनयौ व्यर्का विभौमाः क्रमात् । वीन्द्वर्का विकुजेन्दवश्च सुहृदः केषांचिदेवं मतम् ।। *Ibid.* II. 15. This is one of the proofs of the antiquity of the play. अक्षिभ्यां &c.—Your eyes have convinced you that these are the same ornaments; but you do not say it in words.

P. 344. ननु भणामि &c.—The sentence ends at the second न खलु, जानामि being understood. अनभिज्ञातः—It is not recognized by me. The छाया should rather have been अनभिज्ञातं to suit the context, as in the case of सो ज्जेव एसो ण वेत्ति p. 342. घटितः—should also be read as घटितं. She means—These may be the imitations of the ornaments of my daughter made by the same workman.

The judge endorses the same view by saying वस्त्वन्तराणि &c. भूषणगुणस्य— is equivalent to गुणवतो भूषणस्य excellent ornaments. कृतहस्तता--dexterity of hand got by practice. आर्यचारुदत्तीयानि-- This is addressed to the mother. एवं गतानि &c.--Here Charu. shows his weak-mindedness. सत्यमिति द्वे अक्षरे—सत्य, these are two syllables only; but how potent are they ! ( As shown above ). अलीकेन--by अलीक, which is trisyllabic. Or, सत्यमिति द्वे

only the two syllables स and त्य are अक्षरे everlasting; so hide not these by अलीक, falsehood, which is not everlasting.

आभरणानि &c.—Charu. gets a little irritated and says this. 'I do not know much about the ornaments about which so much fuss is made; I only know that' etc अस्मद्गृहात्—and not from the Pushpa. garden.

P. 346. कर्कशा: कशा:—*i. e.* strokes of the whip. mercilessly inflicted (for getting a confession from you). सहास्माकं मनो०—See trans. The judge still hopes that Charu. would tell the truth and establish his innocence and thus enable him to let him off. स्त्रीरत्नं —Better read स्त्री रत्नं separately for Sakara says व्यापादिता, which agrees with स्त्री. शारीरो दण्ड:—Capital punishment, death by being impaled.

प्रसीदन्तु &c —Mark the nobility of the old lady's mind. Fully convinced inwardly of the innocence of Charu., she wishes that he at least should be saved, if her daughter was gone. अहमर्थिनी—She means—'It is my daughter who is killed; I am therefore the proper person to lodge a complaint. I do not wish to do it. Why should you then order his death?' Poor woman! She did not know that according to criminal law the plaint lay between the king on one side and the culprit on the other; it did not matter who gave the information. आत्मन: सदृशं—Worthy of my great power.

P. 348. निर्णये &c.—*Cf.* वधाध्यक्षो नृप: शास्ता सभ्या: कार्यपरीक्षका:। Vya—May.; see *supra*, notes to p. 310. मनुरब्रवीत्—See com. The Brahmanas were exempted from capital punishment by Manu, not out of partiality, but because at his time they were men given to holy pursuits and committed atrocious crimes very rarely; and if one was guilty of such a crime, ignominious banishment was more torturing than death to one who was held in reverence by the people. *Cf.* what the Mahabharata says:—वपनं द्रविणादानं स्थानान्निर्वपणं तथा। एषो हि ब्रह्मबन्धूनां वधो नान्योऽस्ति दैहिक.॥ Adi. 7. 57. अक्षतं:—unimpaired, intact. शूले भञ्जक्त—Break up his body on a stake, *i. e.* impale him.

निकार—extreme humiliation, insult (here, mutilation of the body); *cf.* सुदु:सहं प्राप्य निकारमीदृशम् Kir. I. 43. अविमृश्यकारी—For he ordered his death without considering his previous unimpeachable character. A king ought to decide a case impartially—धर्मशास्त्रं पुरस्कृत्य प्राड्विवाकमते स्थित:। समाहितमति: पश्येद् व्यवहारान-

नुक्रमात् ॥ Naradasmriti. श्वेतकाकीयैः—who make false statements; from श्वेतकाक (which does not exist) and ईय; see com. Some explain it as 'resembling a dog (श्वा), a deer (एत) and a crow'; *i. e.* servile, timid and cuuning. See Nilakanta on उपायैः श्वेतकाकीयैः प्रियकामा यशस्विनी। Mah.-Bha. Adi. 47. 11. शासनदूषकैः—Who bring a stigma on the king's administration (his wish being to do absolute justice). This is the व्यवहारदुष्टता referred to in I. 7. It will be seen that this attack on the judge is quite groundless. Perhaps he refers by श्वेतकाकीयैः to Sakara, who, he thinks, might have gone to the king and advised him to pass capital punishment on him; see sl. 43 below (अथ रिपुवचनाद्वा).

**अम्बां**—His mother. **अपश्चिमं**—नास्ति पश्चिमं (posterior) यस्य तद्यथा in a manner in which there is none posterior to it; for the last time. पश्चिमं *v. l.* means the same thing; but अपश्चिम constantly occurs in plays; *cf.* अयमपश्चिमस्ते रामस्य शिरसा पादपङ्कजस्पर्शः। Uttar. I.; अयमत्र ते जन्मन्यपश्चिमः पश्चिमावस्थाप्रार्थितो मकरन्दबाहुपरिष्वङ्गः। Mal.-Madh. IX; तात अम्ब मेऽपश्चिमः प्रणामः। Nag V. **मूले छिन्ने**—मूल is the father Char. **देहप्रतिकृतिः**—The bodily representative. See com.

P. 350. **बटुः**—often used as a depreciatory term or to show contempt; *cf.* चाणक्यबटुः Mud.; निवार्यतामालि किमप्ययं बटुः &c., Kum. V. 83.

**विषसलिल** &c.—These are the different ordeals for proving one's innocence. *Cf.* तुलाग्न्यापो विषं कोशो दिव्यानीह विशुद्धये। महाभियोगेष्वेतानि शीर्षकस्थेऽपि योक्तरि ॥ Yaj.-S. II. 95. **०प्रार्थिते**—sought (*i. e.* proper) to be decided by **विचारे**—my case; *lit.* the consideration of my crime. **वीक्ष्य**—having looked into (*i. e.* proved) my crime. Four of the five modes of te ting one's innocence by an ordeal mentioned by Yajnavalkya are given here; *viz.* (1) making a man taste poison without being affected or harmed by it; or (2) keeping him under water while another swift-going man ran the distance covered by an arrow discharged and brought it back; or (3) by placing him in a scale-pan with equal weights put in the other, and then seeing that his pan rises up if innocent; or (4) by observing that he remains unburnt in fire for a certain space of time, after the performance of some preliminary rites. These are thus given by Yaj.—त्वं विष ब्रह्मणः पुत्र सत्यधर्मे व्यवस्थित। त्रायस्वास्माद्भीतिपाशात्सत्येन भव मेऽमृतम् ॥ एवमुक्त्वा विषं शार्ङ्गं भक्षयेद्धिमशैलजम्। यस्य वेगैर्विना जीर्येत्तस्य शुद्धिं विनिर्दिशेत् ॥ (110, 111). सत्येन

माऽभिरक्ष त्वं वरुणेत्यभिशाप्य कम् । नाभिदघ्नोदकस्थस्य गृहीत्वोरू जलं विशेत् ॥ समकालमिषुं मुक्तमानीयाद्यो जवी नरः । गते तस्मिन्निमग्नाङ्गं पश्येच्चेच्छुद्धिमाप्नुयात् ॥ (108, 109). तुलाधारणविद्वद्भिरभियुक्तस्तुलाश्रितः । प्रतिमानसमीभूतो रेखां कृत्वाऽवतारितः ॥ त्वं तुले सत्यधामाऽसि पुरा देवैर्विनिर्मिता । तत्सत्यं वद कल्याणि संशयान्मां विमोचय ॥ यद्यस्मि पापकृन्मातस्ततो मां त्वमधो नय । शुद्धश्चेद्गमयोर्ध्वं मां तुलामित्यभिमन्त्रयेत् ॥ (100, 101, 102). करौ विमृदितव्रीहेर्लक्षयित्वा ततो न्यसेत् । सप्ताश्वत्थस्य पत्राणि तावत्सूत्रेण वेष्टयेत् ॥ त्वमग्ने सर्वभूतानामन्तश्चरसि पावक । साक्षिवत्पुण्यपापेभ्यो ब्रूहि सत्यं करे मम ॥ तस्येत्युक्तवतो लोहं पञ्चाशत्पलिकं समम् । अग्निवर्णं न्यसेत्पिण्डं हस्तयोरुभयोरपि ॥ &c. ( 103, 104, 105 ).

**दातव्यं**—should have been given (had I been found guilty). **ब्राह्मणं**—may be derived as—(1) ब्रह्मण: अपत्यं; by adding अ (तस्यापत्यमिति अण्); or (2) ब्रह्म वेदमधीते । तदधीते तद्वेद इति अण्; or (3) ब्रह्म जानाति इति; by adding अण् by शेष । Pan. IV. 2, 92. **पतसि नरकमध्ये**—For अदण्ड्यान्दण्डयन्राजा दण्ड्यांश्चैवाप्यदण्डयन् । अयशो महदाप्नोति नरकं चैव गच्छति ॥ Manu. VIII. 128. It is difficult to understand this chafing and wrath of Charu., when the evidence went aganist him and was supported by his own admission finally.

# ACT X

This, the last act of the play, contains its twofold catastrophe, *viz.* (1) that of the principal part, the acquisition of Vasantasena, raised to the dignity of a wife by royal order, and (2) that of the underplot, *viz* the acquisition of the kingdom of Palaka by Aryaka. Charu. is conducted through the streets of Ujjayini to the place of execution. In the meantime Vasantasena who was revived by the Bhikshu who accidentally saw her, arrives on the scene of execution, escorted by him, just at the time when the executioners are about to kill Charudatta. Her appearance fills the Chandalas with joy, who release Charudatta and wish to kill Sakara instead. Sarvilaka comes to the place just then and relates to Charudatta how Palaka was killed and Aryaka set on the throne. He also further tells him that the kingdom of Kusavati was conferred on him (Char.) by the new king and also that Vasantasena was raised to the dignity of a wife.

P. 352. तर्त्कि &c —This seems to be addressed to Charudatta तर्त्कि—What then ? What help is there ? You must follow us. न कलय कारणं—Do not think of the reason The King's command is absolute. The Chandalas then offer some consolation to Char, telling him that they would execute their duty with such skill as to make him feel the pain of death as little as possible. नववध &c. See com.–(1) in effecting the slaughter and fettering (of a person) newly condemned; or (2) in managing to bind a man for the first time for being put to death; or better still; (3) in leading (to the place of execution) the man bound for being &c. (नव: वधार्थं बन्ध: यस्य तस्य नयने).*

करवीर—(Mar. कण्हेर) Oleander. 'Sweet-scented Oleander or rose-bay' (Wilson). वध्यपुरुषा०—वध्यौ appointed to kill; executioners; वध्यो च तौ पुरुषौ च; Karma. comp.; or see com. मन्द०—मन्द: little (being consumed).

पितृवनं—a cemetery. विरसं—discordantly, harshly. रक्तगन्धा०—anointed with red sandal; (2) with बलि—besmeared with drops (गन्ध) of blood; or the smell of blood. बलि—not

* "The difficulties of this verse are diminished if we can regard Karana as the representative of the Sanskrit Karana 'pain'. We may then translate—'What then? Do not consider the pain; being adepts in the new-fangled managing of executions and fetterings, we are skilful in cutting off heads and impaling in short order'." Dr. Ryder.

the usual काकबलि daily offered after the Vaisvadeva, but a special offering to some deity or a ghost &c., of cooked rice covered with flowers, blood &c. तर्कयन्ति—eagerly expect. *Cf.* तस्याः पातुं.....तर्कयेस्तिर्यगम्भः Megh. I. 53.

"The paraphernalia and circumstances of a public execution according to Hindu fashions are interestingly described here; the scantiness of the official attendance shows that the people were as easily managed then as at any subsequent period. The character of the executioner corresponds precisely with that of the Roman carnifex, and in like manner the place of execution is the public cemetery, or place of burning the dead. The criminal is dressed as a victim with very classical decorations." Wilson

P. 354. कालपरशु०—The comp. may also be taken as—कालरूपः deadly परशुधाराः ( the strokes of the edge of ) ताभिः सज्जनपुरुषद्रुमं—The tree in the form of a man (yielding shade to) good men–to avoid the repetition of ideas. सज्जन may be taken in the sense of 'good' ( see trans. ); सज्जनः पुरुषः एव द्रुमः तम् *cf. supra,* IV. 32. व्यापाराः—Actions, modes of operation. ०हस्तकैः—impressions of the extended palm. पिष्टचूर्ण—(1) rice-flour; or पिष्टं and चूर्णं sesamum powder; see also com. पशूकृतः—turned into a beast that is to be victimized. तारतम्य—तरतमस्य भावः; discretion, proper judgement. एतद्—this ( calamity or misfortune ). इन्द्रः—*i. e.* the high pole set up in the Indra festival ( see note on इन्द्रमह p. 186 ); it was to be secretly removed. See Kalikapurana quoted in the com. Some understand by इन्द्र a king, being deposed and banished.

हण्ड—and हण्डे are vocative particles used in addressing persons of the lowest class. आहीन्त and गोह are the names of the two Chandalas. किं रोदिति &c—As the women of the city, looking out of the windows of houses lining the street through which Charu. was being conducted, were shedding a profusion of tears, the executioner mistook it for torrents of rain-water, and asks the question पतति वज्रं—The fall of the thunderbolt; a thunder-clap is the sign of rain.

P. 356. प्रणालीभिः—प्रणाली (*cf.* Marathi पन्हळ) is a conduit for carrying away rain-water from the tiles; an aqueduct.

सलोप्त्रः—with the stolen things or property; fr. लुप् 6 cl. P. A. to steal, and त्र (ष्ट्रन्); also written as लोत्र ( fr. लू ): *cf.* लोप्त्रेण गृहीतस्य कुम्भीलकस्यास्ति वा प्रतिवचनम्। Vik. II. p. 59.

P. 358. मखशत०—Performed from time to time by his ancestors and by himself before he was reduced to poverty. सदसि—in the sacrificial assembly. निबिडचैत्य—निबिड crowded with sacrificial priests and Brahmanas. चैत्यं —A sacrificial shed or place of worship. चीयते असौ चित्य: the sacred fire got by rubbing; चित्या the generation of fire; तस्य तस्या वा इदं ( स्थानं ), by adding अ ( अण् ), तद् —*scil.* गोत्रं his race ( because the Chandalas named his father and grandfather ). असदृश० घुष्यते— He was sorry as the sacred name of his family was defiled by being uttered by the Chandalas. Some take तदसदृश० as one word in the sense of 'a completely different type from that of the Brahmanas'; but तद् cannot syntactically refer to ब्रह्म in निबिड &c. If so taken it may refer to कुलं; but in this case recourse must be had to Lakshana, कुल meaning कुलपुरुष. This sl. with the readings यद् for मे and निधन for मरण, and the speech read as एष सागरदत्तस्य सुत आर्यविनयदत्तस्य नप्ता...गणिका वसन्तसेना सुवर्णलोभेन मारितेति, is quoted in the D-Rup. under I. 46 as an instance of प्रसङ्ग, one of the angas of अवमर्शसंधि; it is also quoted in the Sah.-Dar. under VI. 104 The principal fig. of speech in this sl. is उदात्त; see K.-P. X. 29.

सुरुचिर०—The comp. is a नित्यसमास. सुरुचिर is added, as an ordinary coral may be of a very faint colour; or सुरुचिर may be taken with अधरोष्ठ. संनिभाधरोष्ठि—see com.; or we may dissolve अधर: ( the lower lip ) ओष्ठ: ( the upper lip ) च अधरोष्ठं ०संनिभमधरोष्ठं यस्या:; some take अधरोष्ठ as a comp. of the शाकपार्थिवादि class (अधरसहित: ओष्ठ: अधरोष्ठ:). The figures of speech in this sl. are two Upamas, Vishama (since the two contradictory things अमृतपान and विषपान are mentioned) and also रसवदलंकार, as the शृङ्गार implied herein subserves the Karuna. See Sah.-Dar. X. 95, 96.

गुणरत्ननिधि:—see com.; रत्ननिधि may also mean 'the ocean'. असुवर्ण—The reading असुवर्णमण्डनकं, which is explained as नास्ति सुवर्णमण्डनं यस्मिंस्तद्यथा तथा ( without any gold ornaments ), violates the metre, as we get 11 instead of 12 Matras in the *pada*. सर्व: खलु &c.—Mark how the Chandalas express noble sentiments throughout this scene. चिन्तायुक्त:—Uneasy or distressed with anxiety; *i. e.* they express anxiety on account of.

वस्त्रान्त०—वस्त्रान्तररुद्ध *v. l.* वस्त्रान्तरे inside the garment रुद्धं &c. Herein Charu. endorses the sentiment expressed in the last verse. परोऽपि बन्धु: &c.—*Cf.* the Subhashita इह लोके हि धनिनां परोऽपि

स्वजनायते । स्वजनोऽपि दरिद्राणां तत्क्षणाद्दुर्जनायते ॥; and for the idea more poetically expressed रिक्तः सर्वो भवति हि लघुः पूर्णता गौरवाय । Megh. I. 20. **स्वजातिमहत्तर**—Charu. so addresses one of the Chandalas on account of the noble sentiments expressed by them in their speeches. **किमस्माकं हस्तात्** &c — For it is sinful for a Brahmana to receive Dakshina or any charity from a low-caste person.

P. 360. **तत्परलोकार्थं** &c.—*Cf.* पुन्नाम्नो नरकाद्यस्मात्त्रायते पितरं सुतः । तस्मात्पुत्र इति प्रोक्तः स्वयमेव स्वयंभुवा ॥ Manu. IX. 138.

**आवुक**—in Prakrit stands for पितः; *cf.* अथावुकः जनकः Amara. **चिरं**—long ( until my son reaches manhood ). **इदं निवापोदकभोजनं**—निवाप ( fr. वप् with नि and aff घञ *i. e.* अ added कर्मणि or भावे; न्युप्यते निवपनं वा ) is the offering, generally libation of water, to the Pitris or manes. He means—Rohasena being a boy, the water he will offer by his tiny hands would not be sufficient to allay his ( Char.'s ) thirst. It is a Hindu belief that the departed forefathers subsist on the food and water offered to them. by their descendants. For the rite see Manu. III. 203, 215, 223. *Cf.* the lamentation of Dushyanta at Sak. VI. 25.

**यज्ञोपवीतं**—यज्ञार्थमुपवीतं यज्ञोपवीतं; उपवीत is the sacred thread ( see Ragh. XI. 64 ) in its proper position ( also called **सव्य** ) *viz.* it being placed on the left shoulder and worn crosswise, passing under the right arm; this is the position when rites are performed with reference to the gods; the other positions are प्राचीनावीत—also called अपसव्य—( when the sacred thread is placed on the right shoulder ) and निवीत (when it is placed round the neck and hangs down both ways). निवीतं मनुष्याणां प्राचीनावीतं पितॄणामुपवीतं देवानाम्। Jaiminiyanyayamalavistara. See Amara. II. 7, 49, 50.

**अमौक्तिकं**—मौक्तिकादन्यत् सौवर्णादन्यत् असौवर्णं; here the sense of the negative particle is तदन्यत्व; or नास्ति मौक्तिकं यस्मिन् &c. **ब्राह्मणानां**—The sacred thread, although commonly worn by the three upper classes, came to be the chief badge of the Brahmana class, like the bow of the Kshatriyas. **देवतानां** &c.—For the necessary position of the sacred thread when making offerings to gods or the Pitris, see note above.

P. 362. **निरुपपदेन**—उपपद a word or epithet of respect prefixed to a name as आर्य, श्री &c.; *cf.* **कथं** निरुपपदमेव चाणक्यमिति

नार्यंचाणक्यमिति । Mud. III **अहतमार्गा**—(1) with its course unimpeded, wilfully; (2) with her motion unobstructed. **उद्दामा**—उद्गता दाम्नः, broken off from restraint. **किशोरी**—a young mare. **प्रत्येषितुं**—To override, to tax; here पुरुषं must be supplied as the object. Some read प्रतीष्टं as the छाया of पडिच्छिदुं, which means (1) the desired end, (2) the desired place; or it may be an adv., 'as it (fate), or she (mare), likes.'

**व्यपदेशाः**—व्यपदिश्यतेऽनेन that by which a person is known or distinguished; titles, distinctive appellations, &c. **शुष्काः**—are dried up, *i.e.* gone, have become extinct; and yet should not the head &c.; or this may be taken as a question—Are all his titles gone, or empty, *i.e.* vain, (because a murder is imputed to him)? 'Should not the head' &c. The reading पणमिअ मत्थके is better. With this reading the meaning will be व्यपदेशाः शुष्काः (titles or appellations are vain); अस्य किं प्रणम्य मस्तके न कर्तव्यं what of him should not be borne on the head with a bow; *i.e.* what circumstance in connexion with him is here which does not deserve high honour? Pri. reads शुष्का अपि प्रदेशाः विनमितमस्तकेन &c paraphrasing प्रदेशाः by अङ्गानि. 'His limbs even are parched; what has he to do with bent head; *i.e.* he should not bend his head; although he has killed a woman and hung down his head, no one can blame him.' But this explanation is very unsatisfactory.

**जनपदस्य**—जनः पद्यन्ते move अत्र इति जनपदो देशः a country, *i.e.* its people; or जनपद the people; भवेज्जनपदो जानपदोऽपि जनदेशयोः । Medini. The comparison to the eclipsed moon shows that Charu. also would soon be freed from the imputation and his character cleared up **अंसेन**—Across the shoulders, *i.e.* round the neck. **करवीर**०—It was customary to cast a red garland round the neck of the person to be executed and to make him carry the stake also. *Cf.* Mud. II. 21. VII 4; and ततः प्रावेशति......वध्यवेषधारी शूलं स्कन्धेनादाय...चन्दनदासः । *Ibid.* VII.

**आघातं**—The place of execution; आहन्यते अत्र; हन् and aff. अ (घञ् अधिकरणे). **अनुप्रयामि**—walk on and on towards. *Cf.* आसन्नतरतामेति मृत्युर्जन्तोर्दिने दिने । आघातं नीयमानस्य वध्यस्येव पदे पदे ॥ Hit. IV. 72. **शामित्रं**—शमितुः इदं शामित्रं (by adding अ (अण्) in the sense of तस्येदं); the place of the शमिता or the carver and immolator, *i.e.* the place where the sacrificial animal is killed

**आलब्धुं**--To be killed; लभ् with आ ( Atm. ) means 'to kill' and immolate an animal at a sacrifice; *cf.* प्रातेर्वै पशूनालभन्ते । Sat. Brah. As the root is transitive, the infinitive here has a passive force; but as this is grammatically inaccurate, the reading आलब्ध इव is preferable; here, however, आलब्ध must be taken in the sense of consecrated (अभिमन्त्रित:) for a sacrifice, and not in that of killed, as it would go against the simile.

**चाण्डालौ**--He means—We are not Chandalas by our actions (कर्मणा); we have not got the sinfulness and cruelty &c. that characterize the Chandala class. This is made clear in the second half. **येऽभिभवन्ति** &c.—By this they indirectly refer to Sakara and Palaka.

P. 364. **सात्त्रं**— adv.; or adj. qualifying पुत्र. इदं तत् &c.—*Cf.* प्रसव: खलु प्रकर्षपर्यन्त: स्नेहस्य । अन्त:करणतत्त्वस्य दाम्पत्यो: स्नेहसश्रयात् । आनन्दग्रन्थिरेकोऽयमपत्यमिति बध्यते ॥ Uttar. III. 17. **अचान्दनं** &c.—चन्दनस्येदं चान्दनं; उशीरस्येदमौशीरं तन्न भवतीति अनौशीरं not made of Usira (the fragrant root of the herb *Andropogon Muricatus*, called वाळा in Marathi); *cf.* नन्दयति चन्द्रचन्दननिष्यन्द-जडस्तव स्पर्श: । Uttar. VI. 13. This is an instance of वत्सल रस; see Sah.-Dar. III. 251.

**काञ्चनकलश०**—He is compared to a pot of gold (and not of earth), to show that he will bear the strain and remain unharmed. डुब्बन्तं (मज्जन्तं)—*Cf.* Marathi डुबणें.

P. 366. **व्यसनकृतां**—व्यसन may mean poverty, adversity, or the calamity, *viz.* his being charged with the crime of murder. ०कृशां *v.l.*—reduced, *i.e.* wretched, disgraceful, owing to व्यसन. **मया**—The reading त्वया is not good, as the proclamation was अनेन चारुदत्तेन मारिता.

**वासपादप:**—*Cf. supra* सुजनशकुनाधिवासं sl 4, p. 354. **दण्डनिगड:**—The chains fastened crosswise to restrict his motion. It does not mean 'stocks', as the *cheta* was not put into stocks. **शृणाथ इति पूर्वोक्तं**—*i.e.* as far as न पुनरेतेनार्येण.

**द्रोणमेघ:**—A particular class of clouds discharging rain plentifully and producing luxuriant crops; see com. For the idea *cf.* अभिवृष्य मरुत्सस्यं कृष्णमेघस्तिरोदधे । Ragh. X. 48. This occurs again in sl. 39 below.

P. 368. **सूपेन**—सुवति रसमिति सूप:. **शालीयकूरेण**—कूर *m. n.* boiled rice, food; *cf. supra* इतश्च कूरच्युततैलमिश्रं &c. IV. p. 158.

खङ्खण—A sharp ringing sound. शत्रुविनाशो नाम &c.—This and the following sentence are an instance of Sakara's spiteful nature and levity of mind. Death he can lightly treat of. His typical humour is also seen further on in that he says—यस्यां वेलाया-मस्मादृशो प्रवरमानुषः &c.; see page 370. विणाशे नाम—विणाशेण *v.l.* वावादअन्तं—is to be properly rendered by व्यापादयन्तं which means 'killing', but is used for व्यापाद्यमानं, being a Sakarian peculiarity; or we should read वावादिज्जन्तं as some do.

P. 370. अविनय—Immodesty, haughtiness, arrogance. दुष्टबलीवर्दः—*scil.* Sakara. This shows how unpopular Sakara was, being held in contempt even by Chandalas. द्वारं पिधत्त—otherwise he will enter in and bring some disaster on you. प्रणयिजनकल्पपादप—see *supra* p. 52 (notes p. 32). रत्नकुम्भसदृशः—*i.e.* a superbly rich and a worthy person.

P. 372. अपवारितकेन--see *supra* p. 58. एतत्तत्सुवर्णकं &c.—Mark the ready-wittedness of Sakara which enables him to turn an incident to his advantage. शोभनं भणति--The Chandalas, although noble-minded, not having the penetrating eye of a judge, are easily led to believe in the story of Sakara by the scars on Cheta's back.

P. 235. एतावान्मे विभवः--*Cf.* विदू०--एतावान्मे मतिविभवो भवन्तं सेवितुम्। Malav. II. p. 58 निष्कारणो०--Karm. comp; ०पगतश्चासौ बान्धवश्च. This may be separated as ०पगत बान्धव; but it will spoil the sense. धर्मशील—As shown by his pious desire to save the life of an innocent man, even at the risk of losing his master's favour. न संवदति—is not in agreement with it, does not favour it.

P. 374. आश्रमं--To a hermitage; *i.e.* leave the town and retire to a forest. त्वमप्येवं--For his fear was roused by Sakara's asking the Chandalas to kill his son together with him. *Cf.* the similar advice of Chandanadasa to his son in the Mudra.—पुत्र चाणक्यविरहिते देशे वस्तव्यम्। Act VII. p. 346

न युज्यते प्राणपरित्यागः—For if one commits suicide the penalty is—असूर्या नाम ते लोका अन्धेन तमसावृताः। तांस्ते प्रेत्याभिगच्छन्ति ये के चात्महनो जनाः॥. Isavasyopanishad 3.

P. 376. शङ्खल--The stick used for beating the drum. पालिका—Turn; *cf.* Marathi पाळी. अरे तव--This shows that even the Chandalas considered it a horrible sin to kill Charu., and so each wanted the other to do it. बहुविधं लेखकं कृत्वा—Drawing lines or making marks in various ways. It is difficult to know what their mode of decision exactly was. It was not certainly casting lots, as is shown by this stage direction. So probably it was as Mr. Sharma has it:—They drew lines without counting them. Then marked every third line. If after the last mark there remained one line, it was the turn of the first headsman; if two, of the second. If nothing remained, then they had to draw lines again. लेख ( or लेखक ) may mean a scratch or a line.

P. 378. वृद्धिमहोत्सवेन—On the festive occasion of the blissful or joyous event; or वृद्धि may mean 'the extension of the race.' राजपरिवर्तः—Mark the poet's skill in gently introducing the revolution to be shortly announced किं किं राजपरिवर्तः &c.—Sakara is alarmed at the very mention of a change of kings; for where would he be if his brother in law, Palaka, would lose his throne? वध्यपालिकायाः—L. D. says-लेखं कियत्यः पालिकास्तव मम च कियत्य आसन्नावाभ्यामुपभुक्ता वा काः का इत्येवं गणनरूपं लिखितदर्शनरूपं च व्यवहारमित्यर्थः। This was a device to delay the execution of Charudatta.

धर्मः—Religious merit. प्रबलपुरुष—He refers by this to the Judge, king Palaka and Sakara. स्वस्वभावेन—Her own natural disposition, *i.e.* magnanimity.

प्रतिवृत्तं—Turned or hanging down परिवृत्तं *v.l.*—turned upside down, (being pierced through) दीर्घ—With outstretched bodies ( to reach the dead body ). वेश इव—like the dress *i.e.* form of grim laugh ( अट्ट–विकट ).

P. 380. उत्तिष्ठत्प०—उत्तिष्ठतः पश्चात्पततः. वसनपातिका—The falling down of a garment which is taken up again. शवस्य—of the dead body which rises up again in a new form. This is a reflex of the sentiment expressed in वासांसि जीर्णानि यथा विहाय &c. Bg. II. 22. *Cf.* मृतः को वा न जायते; Hit.

अस्थानपरिश्रांतां—exhausted ( fainted ) in an improper, *i. e.* out-of-the-way place; or अस्थाने may mean in a place out of her house (स्नानादन्यत्र अस्थाने). विषमभरक्रान्ता—Weighed under an uneven load. This simile has occurred before; see p. 98.

P. 382. उत्तानः—lying supine or flat (on the back). समं—evenly, in a straight line. एकप्रहारेण &c.—This was against the king's order which was to impale Charudatta; the Chandalas were doing it on their own responsibility, as the lesser of the two evils. Death on the stake would have been more agonizing. **सह्यवासिनी**—The goddess Durga in her fierce form known as Chandika, the patron-deity of the Chandalas, Bhils, and such other fierce tribes. She was also called after the mountain on which her temple was located; *e. g.* सह्यवासिनी, विन्ध्यवासिनी, &c. Here she is called **सह्य०** which shows that the Chandalas came from the mountain Sahya.

P. 384. **यथाज्ञप्तं**—The second Chandala thinks that the sword fell down because they tried to go against the king's order. **त्वरितमेषा**—Pri. seems to omit एषा. **चिकुर**—The hair of the head (चि इति अव्यक्तं कुरति sounds). **उरसि पतति**—For Charu. was lying supine on the ground. **जीवति चारु०**—is a question. **यज्ञवाटगतस्य**—वाट *m. n.* an enclosure, a piece of enclosed ground; *cf.* similar words such as वेशवाट, श्मशानवाट &c. The Chandalas being connected with the court knew that the king was engaged in a sacrifice.

P. 386. Sl. 39.—*Cf. supra* sl. 26 **भ्रान्तं मनः** &c.—Construe **वा अथ** वा मम भ्रान्तं (under delusion) मनः एनां पश्यति । अथ वा वसन्तसेना न मृता सा एव इयम् ।. **जीवातुकाम्यया**—With the desire to restore me to life; from जीवातु and aff. काम्या; *cf.* गोकाम्या *supra* p. 118. जीवातु means 'revival' (जीवित), or the elixir of life (जीवनौषधि); जीवातुरस्त्रियां भक्ते जीविते जीवनौषधौ । Medini *Cf.* रे हस्त दक्षिण मृतस्य शिशोर्द्विजस्य जीवातवे विसृज शूद्रमुनौ कृपाणम् । Uttar. II. 10; जीव्यते अनेन इति जीवातुः fr. जीव् and the Unadi aff. आतु; see Unadi I. 79 **रूपानुरूपेण**—रूपस्यानुरूपेण सादृश्येन लक्षितेत्यर्थः. **अन्या**—Some other, *i. e* some nymph of heaven who can assume the desired form. **निमीलिताक्ष एव**—Such is the effect, described by poets, of the thrilling joy experienced by a lover at the touch of his love after separation; *cf.* **रामः**—(आनन्दनिमीलिताक्षः एव ।) सखि वासन्ति दिष्ट्या वर्धसे । Uttar. III. p 88; **राजा**—(निमीलिताक्ष एव । स्पर्शं रूपयित्वा । अये उर्वशीगात्रसंपर्कात् &c. Vik. IV. p. 212.

**विद्या इव**—*i. e.* like the Samjivani (life-reviving) Vidya or spell, (which was first known and practised by Sukra, the preceptor of the *Daityas.*) For the संजीवनौषधिस, see Agni Purana, Adh. 284.

P. 388 **देहं**—is neu. here; see com. **अहो प्रभावः** &c.—*Cf.* as a parallel what Pururavas says in Vik.—अहो विरुद्धार्थसंपादयितेप्सितलाभो नाम । पादास्त एव शशिनः सुखयन्ति गात्रं बाणास्त एव मदनस्य ममानुकूलाः &c., III. 20.

वरवस्त्रं—It is better to take this in the sense of 'the bride-groom's garment.' From this it seems that it was customary to give red garments to bride-grooms to wear. We read in the Nagananda, 4th Act, of red marriage–garments being given to Jimutavahana which he uses as the insignia of death.

अतिदक्षिणतया—Vasa. thinks that in his extreme kindness of heart or generosity Char. must have sacrificed himself for some one else, and must not have told the fact that he was quite innocent in the matter.

प्रभविष्णुता—Powerful, as he had high influence with the king. मनाक्—a little; almost. Char. thinks lightly of the great calamity that had threatened his life.

P. 390. वृषभकेतुः—The bull-emblemed god, Siva. दक्षयज्ञस्य हन्ता—The destroyer of the sacrifice of Daksha, his-father-in-law. He first glorifies Siva, and afterwards his friend Aryaka, who also had destroyed the sacrifice of Palaka, killing him, as Daksha was killed by Siva.

Daksha was one of the ten sons of Brahman, being born from his right thumb, and the chief of the ten Prajapatis or patriarchs of mankind. One of his many daughters was Sati, who was espoused by Siva. Once Daksha performed a great sacrifice, to which all the gods and sages were invited, but neither his daughter Sati nor her husband Siva. Sati, however, decided to attend the sacrifice herself; but when she went there she was greatly insulted, whereupon she threw herself into the fire and perished ( see also Kum. I. 21, and our note *ad loc.* ) When Siva heard this he was exceedingly wroth, and, according to one account, himself went to the sacrifice, completely destroyed it, and pursued Daksha who ran away in the from of a deer, and at last decapitated him. According to another account, Siva tore off a hair form his *Jata* and dashed it on the ground; whence there arose the mighty Virabhadra, who was ordered by the god to go and demolish Daksha's sacrifice. Thereupon he, accompanied by several *ganas*, went to the sacrifice, completely routed it, putting to flight all the gods and the sages, and according to one account beheaded Daksha himself.

भेत्ता षण्मुखः--षण्मुख is a name of Karttikeya, the Indian Mars ( god of war ). He is said to have pierced the mountain Krauncha, whence he is called *Krauncha-darana.* Krauncha is also the name of a demou ( who had lurked in the mountain Krauncha ) slain by Karttikeya. Here he fitly refers to Karttikeya as the great leader of the divine forces against the demons. तदनु--shows that next in rank stands Aryaka as a great hero.

**शेषभूतां**—like the **शेष** or **शेषा**, the garland of flowers cast off from an idol which is held sacred and received with veneration. This shows implicit obedience with reverence. *Cf.* तथेति शेषामिव भर्तुराज्ञामादाय मूर्ध्ना मदनः प्रतस्थे । Kum. III. 22; गुणानुरागेण शिरोभि ह्यते नराधिपैर्माल्यमिवास्य शासनम् । Kir. I. 21; and इमं देवशेषापदेशेन ( *v. l.* ) तस्य हस्तं प्रापयिष्यामि । Sak. III. p. 73.

**०मन्त्रहीनं**—*Cf.* दौर्मन्त्र्यान्नृपतिर्विनश्यति Bh. Nit. 42. **प्रकर्षात्**—may be taken as used adverbially; 'greatly, in a high degree'; or as the Abl. of **प्रकर्ष** excellence, greatness of power. **राज्यं**—should have been omitted; as it is, we may construe—बलारेः राज्यमिव वसुधाधिराज्यं शत्रुराज्यं प्राप्तम्. **बलारि**—The enemy, *i. e.* killer, of Bala, brother of Vritra. In several passages of the Rigveda Bala appears as *Vala*, being the name of the cloud fancied as the demon of darkness; also called **वृत्र**—fr. वृ to cover; see our note on that world at Ragh. III. 62. Vala *lit.* means the coverer of the heavenly cows – the pent-up rain-water. Indra destroys the demon with his thunderbolt and sets free the cows. *Cf.* **इन्द्रो यद्वज्री धृष्यमाणो** अन्धसाऽभिनद्वलस्य परिधीन् Rv. I 52. 5; यो गा उदाजदपधा वलस्य II. 2 3; see also X. 67. 8

**जाल्मा**—'You thoughtless men' ( जाल्मोऽसमीक्ष्यकारी स्यात् Amara. ), as they were thronging there for nothing.

**गुणधृतया**—( 1 ) held *i. e.* drawn by his merits; ( 2 ) held by a rope. A boat also when nearing the shore is drawn to it by means of a rope. **ज्योत्स्ना०**—जोत्स्ना in the case of Char. is Vasantasena. **उपरागः**—An eclipse; उपरज्यते इति fr. रज् with the aff. अ ( घञ् ). **आर्जवं**—ऋजोर्भावः straightforwardness, an open confession of one's crime.

P. 392. **महापापः**—Theft was held a great sin; *cf.* ब्रह्महत्या सुरापानं स्तेयं गुर्वङ्गनागमः । महान्ति पातकान्याहुः संसर्गश्चापि तैः सह ॥ Manu. XI. 54. **आर्यवृत्तेन**–This is put in to justify his action ( आर्यवृत्तः अकार्यं न करिष्यति ); he did it in the interest of the people ( as Palaka was a bad king ). **यथाऽऽह तत्रभवान्**—Read rather **अत्रभवान्**.

**उज्जयिन्यां**—goes with प्रतिष्ठितमात्रेण. **वेणातटे**—Vena, a tributary of the Narmada on the bank of which Kusavati was situated. **कुशावत्याः**—Kusavati, also called **कुशस्थली**, the city founded by Kusa, Rama's son (see Ragh. XV. 97) was the capital of Dakshina Kosala, situated in the defiles of the Vindhya mountain. It must have been to the north of the Narmada, but south of the Vindhya, and is probably the same as Ramnagar in Bundelkhand. **उपयुज्यतां**—It should be enjoyed by you, *i. e.* it is at your service.

**०बाहुबद्धः**—should be **०बद्धबाहुः**; Sudraka is very fond of such compounds.

P. 394. **उद्दाम इव गर्दभः**--Sakara's humour does not leave him even in distress.

**राष्ट्रियबन्धः**--may mean ( 1 ) राष्ट्रियस्य मम बन्धः; the being bound, the seizure, of me, the king's brother-in-law; *i. e.* people are ready from all sides to seize me. Some take **बन्ध** in the sense of enemies ( बध्यते अनेनेति बन्धः विपक्षः ), my enemies have surrounded me from all sides;--or ( 2 ) the king's men have surrounded me &c. **व्यापादयाव**--We have used the dual as this is said by the two Chandalas who had gone in search of Sakara; see p. 386; many editions, however, give the plural **व्यापादयाम** in the *chhaya*; in that case it refers to the people.

P. 396. **शरणमुपेत्य पादयोः पतितः** &c. —*Cf.* बद्धाञ्जलिपुटं दीनं याचन्तं शरणागतम् । न हन्यादानृशंस्यार्थमपि शत्रुं परंतप ॥ Rama. Yudh.-K. 18; and अवध्या ब्राह्मणा गावो ज्ञातयः शिशवः स्त्रियः । येषां चान्नानि भुञ्जीत ये च स्युः शरणागताः ॥ Maha. Udyog. 36, 66. The metre of stanza 55 is defective, the second pada being short by two matras; some propose, therefore, to read either यःशरणमुपेत्य or शरणं समुपेत्य to remedy the deficiency. It is also suggested that the last pada should be read as कर्तव्यस्तूपकारहतः, to avoid the absence of *Samdhi* between the third and the fourth padas as they are. These conjectures, however, are not supported by any MS. authority.

**नेपथ्ये कलकलः**--The passage from here to Charudatta's speech युष्मत्प्रसादेन on p. 402, is an interpolation by one Nila Kantha (see com ) who says that as the author had not brought all his characters together at the close, for fear of the representation of the play lasting till sunrise, he supplied the omission. See the verse quoted in the com. See also remarks on this scene in the Introduction.

P. 398. **महीतल** &c.—*i. e.* you deserve a place in heaven. **पतिव्रते**—is significant; you are a *Pativrata*, who should die only when I am dead; *cf.* Harita–आर्ताऽऽर्ते मुदिते हृष्टा प्रोषिते मलिना कृशा । मृते म्रियेत या पत्यौ सा स्त्री ज्ञेया पतिव्रता ॥ **त्वरया सर्पणं**--supply **आवश्यकं**; for each moment was important. **भिन्नत्वेन**—*i. e.* without the dead body of the husband; *cf.* J. V.-तथा च उशनसोक्ता शुद्धितत्त्व-धृता स्मृतिः—'पृथक् चितिं समारुह्य न विप्रा गन्तुमर्हति। अन्यासामेव नारीणां स्त्रीधर्मोऽयं परः स्मृतः'॥ इति।.

P. 400 **यथोपदेशिनी**--Acting according to the instruction I have received from your action; *i. e.* I will follow your example and throw myself into the fire. **तिलोदकपानाय**—Water mixed with sesamum ought to be offered to the dead every day; at least on all the days sacred to the manes. **पर्यवस्थापयाति**--पर्यवस्थापय् seems to be used here in the sense of 'to look after the welfare of.'

P. 402. **प्रेयसि**--Voc. sing. of प्रेयसी; the second प्रेयसि is loc. sing. of प्रेयस्, the much-loved one, the husband. **व्यवसायः**—a determined purpose, resolve; *cf.* मन्दीचकार मरणव्यवसायबुद्धिं। Kum. IV. 45; अहमेकरसस्तथाऽपि ते व्यवसायः प्रतिपत्तिनिष्ठुरः। Ragh. VIII. 65. **अम्भोजिनी**--is here used in the sense of पद्मिनी, the day-lotus. *Cf.* ( when the sun set ) पद्मिनी किमु करोति वराकी मीलिताम्बुरुहनेत्रपुटाऽभूत्। **अचेतना**—not acting consciously, only following the law of nature. *Cf.* अत एव ता मधुकर्य उच्यन्ते; *supra* p. 70. **संविधानकं**—The happy turn of events. He also praises the arrangement of the incidents of the plot; we have the same expression in Uttar. III. p. 97. **परितुष्टो राजा**—The king as the supreme head of the वर्णs and the आश्रमs. **अवगुण्ठ्य**--As was necessary for a woman of family.

P. 404. **जीवापिताऽस्मि**--Some read जीविताऽस्मि as the *chhaya.* for जीवाविदम्हि, which is easier. जीवापिता is explained by J. V. as जीवमापिता.

**दण्डपालकः**—A magistrate. **चारित्रं**—चरित्रमेव चारित्रं; स्वार्थे ष्यञ्. **प्रोत्खात**--Completely destroyed. **अचला**—The earth ( अचलाः mountains सन्त्यस्यां ). **प्रियसुहृदि** &c.--For the constr. see com. We do not find the meeting of Dhuta and her son with Char. mentioned in this sl.; this shows that the preceding scene relating that is an interpolation.

P. 406. **तुच्छयति**--Makes light or poor, empties; a denom. from तुच्छ. **आकुलान्**—(1) In a disturbed state; not fully happy; (2) hanging loose and half-filled. **प्रतिपक्ष॰**—For comp see com; प्रतिपक्ष opposites, such as the state of being emptied or filled up ( poverty and affluence ), &c. **लोकस्थिति**--The course or conduct of the world, or worldly existence; *cf.* the sl. from the Sak. quoted in the com. **कूपघटिकान्याय**--The maxim of the action of the water-wheel and the buckets; *viz.* as the wheel turns, some of the buckets filled with water go up, some are emptied of their contents, while there are some that move up half-filled. being loosened. It is thus used to denote the various vicissitudes of worldly existence. It is also called घटीयन्त्रन्याय. *Cf.* आपद्गतं हससि किं द्रविणान्ध मूढ लक्ष्मीः स्थिरा न भवतीति किमत्र चित्रम् । किं त्वं न पश्यसि घटीर्जलयन्त्रचक्रे रिक्ता भवन्ति भरिता भरिताश्च रिक्ताः ॥ *Prabandhachintamani*, as quoted by Col. Jacob in his *Laukika-nyayanjali*, Part II **घटिकाः**—क्षुद्रः घटः घटकः ह्रस्वे इति कन्; and the fem. aff. आ.

**भरतवाक्य**—The last stanza of a play is so called, because it is chanted by the actor, divested of his dramatic character, the play having already ended; see com.; it generally contains an expression of good wishes for general prosperity, &c. It may have been also so called after Bharata, the father of the Indian drama, to perpetuate his memory.

**क्षीरिण्यः**--प्रभूतं क्षीरमासां विद्यते इति; इन् shows excess. **सर्व-संपन्न०**--The comp. should rather have been संपन्नसर्वसस्या. As it is, it must be taken as सर्वाणि च तानि संपन्नानि च सस्यानि यस्यां ( खञ्जकुब्जादिवत्समासः ). **सन्तः**--Good men; or learned men, as they are generally poor; *cf.* for this sense **तं सन्तः** श्रोतुमर्हन्ति सदसद्व्यक्तिहेतवः । Ragh. I. 10. **श्रीमन्तः**--The presence of the word श्री in the concluding stanza is auspicious. For, as Patanjali says, मङ्गलादीनि मङ्गलमध्यानि मङ्गलान्तानि च शास्त्राणि प्रथन्ते.

**०रिपवः**—रिपु fr. रप् 1 P. to speak out distinctly ( रपति दोषं ) and the. Unadi aff. उ ( कुः ), र being changed to रि, by Unadi. 1, 26. **धर्मनिष्ठाः**--Firmly devoted to their duty, which is pre-eminently the protection of the subjects; *cf.* क्षत्रियस्य परो धर्मः प्रजानामेव पालनम् । Manu. VII. 144 or धर्मनिष्ठाः सन्तः पृथ्वीं पान्तु govern the earth being unflinchingly dutiful or just. Some construe the last two lines as--जन्मभाजः सततमभिमताः परस्परसंमताः सन्तः मोदन्तां, ब्राह्मणाः सन्तः सन्तु, श्रीमन्तः प्रशमितरिपवः धर्मनिष्ठाः च भूपाः &c. **संहारो नाम**--संहारः that in which all the incidents are brought to one focus, their legitimate end, the catastrophe.

# APPENDICES

## I.

### The Metres Used in the Play, Their Definitions and Schemes.

1. Sanskrit Verse is regulated by quantity, and not by accent as in English A पद्य or stanza consists of four पादs or quarters. A *Pada* is regulated by the number of syllables (अक्षरs) or syllabic instants (मात्राs). When the *padas* are all in one metre, it is called a सम वृत्त, to which type most of the metres conform; those are अर्धसम वृत्तs wherein the first *pada* corresponds with the third and the second with the fourth, called respectively the 'odd' and the 'even' *padas*. A third class is विषम वृत्तs, which are very rare.

2. The vowels अ, इ, उ, ऋ and ऌ are short, and the rest long. The quantity of a syllable is determined by its vowel. A syllable with a short vowel is called लघु ( light ), and one wlth a long vowel is called गुरु (heavy).

3. But a लघु syllable becomes गुरु if it is followed by an *Anusvara* or a *Visarga*, or a conjunct consonant, or when it occurs at the end of a *pada*[1].

4. Three successive syllables form a गण (foot); marking a short syllable as ⏑ and a long one as—, the different गणs, which are eight in number, may be exhibited as follows[2]:—

य ⏑ – – ; र – ⏑ – ; त – – ⏑ ; भ – ⏑ ⏑ ; ज ⏑ – ⏑ ; स ⏑ ⏑ – ; म – – – ; and न ⏑ ⏑ ⏑. A short syllable is often indicated in the Definition by the letter ल and a long one by ग.

5. The *Mrichchhakatika* contains in all 21 varieties of Sanskrit metres, which we give below in alphabetical order. The metres are also named, in most, cases, in the com. in this edition.

---

1 सानुस्वारश्च दीर्घश्च विसर्गी च गुरुर्भवेत् ।
वर्णः संयोगपूर्वश्च तथा पादान्तगोऽपि वा ॥

2 आदिमध्यावसानेषु यरता यान्ति लाघवम् ।
भजसा गौरवं यान्ति मनौ तु गुरुलाघवम् ॥

The Prakrit metres are not given here, as they are not needed by the University students, and also because of the p evalent uncertaityn of readings in Prakrit. The curious reader may consult *Prakrita-Pingala* or similar works.

**अनुष्टुभ्**—(Also called श्लोक). Def श्लोके षष्ठं गुरु ज्ञेयं सर्वत्र लघु पञ्चमम्। द्विचतुष्पादयोर्ह्रस्वं सप्तमं दीर्घमन्ययोः ॥. There are many variations of this metre, but the one defined is the commonest. Each *pada* of it consists of eight syllables of which the sixth is long and the fifth short and the seventh in the 2nd and 4th *padas* is short and the 1st and 3rd *padas* long. The rest of the syllables may be either short or long. This is the shortest metre in general use, and is easily recognizable.

*Examples*—

I. 2, 16, 34, &c.

**आर्या**—Def यस्याः प्रथमे पादे द्वादश मात्रास्तथा तृतीयेऽपि। अष्टादश द्वितीये चतुर्थके पञ्चदश साऽऽर्या ॥. This belongs to the class of metres regulated by the number of मात्राs or syllabic instants. The four *padas* contain respectively 12, 18, 12 and 15 *matras*. Like an *Anushtubh*, an *Arya* too, is easily recognizable. Ex — 1. 8, 11, 33, &c.

**इन्द्रवंशा**—Def. [जतौ तु वंशस्थमुदीरितं जरौ] तच्चेन्द्रवंशा प्रथमाक्षरे गुरौ।. This is the same as वंशस्थ (see below) with the first syllable long. This does not occur independently in this play, but is employed in I. 46 and III. 7, which are thus उपजातिs (see below).

**इन्द्रवज्रा**—Def. स्यादिन्द्रवज्रा यदि तौ जगौ गः।. 11 Syllables. Scheme—त, त, ज, ग, ग. Ex.—IV. 16; V. 49; X. 11, 21, 48, 58.

**उपजाति**—Def. [स्यादिन्द्रवज्रा यदि तौ जगौ गः। उपेन्द्रवज्रा जतजास्ततो गौ ॥] अनन्तरोदीरितलक्ष्मभाजौ पादौ यदीयावुपजातयस्ताः ॥ [इत्थं किलान्यास्वपि मिश्रितासु वदन्ति जातिष्विदमेव नाम ॥]. An *Upajati* is a mixture of one or more *padas* of इन्द्रवज्रा (see above) with one or more of उपेन्द्रवज्रा (see below), so as to form one stanza. A mixture of other metres also in this manner is called an *Upajati*. Thus in I 46 we find one *pada* of इन्द्रवंशा and three of वंशस्थ; and in III. 7 two *padas* are in उपेन्द्रवज्रा, one in इन्द्रवज्रा, and one in इन्द्रवंशा. Both of these are *Upajatis* The student is recommended to scan the metre of each *pada* and find out its name for himself in each case. The other examples of *Upajati* are--I. 38; III. 6; IV. 1, 12, 15, 32; V. 21, 29. 40, 44, 47, 52. VIII. 27, 30; IX. 10, 26; X. 6, 16, 40, 43.

**उपेन्द्रवज्रा**--Def. उपेन्द्रवज्रा जतजास्ततो गौ ।. 11 Syllables, Scheme— ज, त, ज, ग, ग. Ex.--I. 6; IV. 23; VI. 3.

[ **औपच्छन्दसिक**—See Malabharini below ].

**गीति**—Def. आर्यापूर्वार्धसमं द्वितीयमपि यत्र भवति हंसगते । छन्दोविदस्तदानीं गीतिंताममृतवाणि भाषन्ते ॥. This is just like an *Arya* except that the last *pada* contains 18 *matras* instead of 15, so that both the halves of the stanza are similar. *Ex.*-- V. 34.

**पुष्पिताग्रा**--Def. अयुजि नयुगरेफतो यकारो युजि च नजौ जरगाश्च पुष्पिताग्रा ॥. Odd *padas*-12 Syllables. Sch. -- न, न, र, य. Even *padas*-13 Syllables. Sch.--न, ज, ज, र, ग. This is an अर्धसम वृत्त. *Ex.*--I. 24, 56; II. 7; III. 10, 21, 22; IV. 4, 27, 28; VIII. 4, 8, 15, 32; X. 13.

**प्रमिताक्षरा** --Def. प्रमिताक्षरा सजससैः कथिता ।. 12 Syllables. Scheme - स, ज, स, स. *Ex.* X. 56.

**प्रहर्षिणी**--Def. म्नाशाभिर्मनजरगाः प्रहर्षिणीयम् । 13 Syllables. Scheme - म, न, ज, र, ग. The pause occurs after the third syllable. *Ex.*--IV. 2; V. 50; VI. 1; VII. 8; VIII. 41; IX. 27; X. 25, 33, 47, 49.

**मालभारिणी**--( Also called औपच्छन्दसिक, of which it forms a special variety ) Def. विषमे ससजा गुरू समे चेत्सभरा येन तु मालभारिणीयम् ॥. Odd *pada*-11 Syllables. Sch.-स, स, ज, ग, ग. Even *pada*-12 Syllables. Sch.—स, भ, र, य. This is an अर्धसम वृत्त. *Ex*.—I. 3, 5.

**मालिनी**--Def. ननमयययुतेयं मालिनी भोगिलोकैः । 15 Syllables. Sch.— न, न, म, य, य. The pause occurs after the eighth syllable. *Ex.*—I. 31 57; IV. 20; V. 17; VII. 3, 5; VIII. 42; IX. 12, 43; X. 3, 12, 34, 46.

**वंशस्थ**--Def. जतौ तु वंशस्थमुदीरितं जरौ ।. 12 Syllables. Sch.—ज, त, ज, र. *Ex.*—I. 7, 10, 53; II. 10; III. 8, 17; V. 37; VII. 4; VIII. 7; IX 25. This is also called वंशस्थविल.

**बसन्ततिलका**—Def. उक्ता वसन्ततिलका तभजा जगौ गः ।. 14 Syllables Sch.—त, भ, ज, ज, ग, ग. *Ex.*—I. 9, 12, 13, 17, 20, 22, 27, 35, 49; III. 3, 4, 9, 14, 16; IV 9, 14, 26; V. 1, 2, 4, 8, 13, 15, 33, 36, 42, 45; VI. 2; VIII. 23, 24, 26; IX. 9, 16, 19, 22, 28, 29, 34; X. 31, 44.

**विद्युन्माला**—Def. मो मो गो गो विद्युन्माला ।. 8 Syllables. Scheme—म, म, ग, ग. *Ex.*—II. 8.

**वैश्वदेवी**—Def. बाणाश्वैश्छिन्ना वैश्वदेवी ममौ यौ ।. 12 Syllables. Scheme—म, म, य, य. The pause occurs after the fifth syllable. *Ex*—III. 13.

**शार्दूलविक्रीडित**—Def. सूर्याश्वैर्यदि मः सजौ सततगाः शार्दूलविक्रीडितम् ।. 19 Syllables. Sch.—म, स, ज, स, त, त, ग. The pause occurs after the twelfth syllable. *Ex.*—I. 14, 32, 36, 37; II. 12; III. 5, 11, 12, 18, 20, 23; IV. 6; V. 5, 6, 14, 18, 20, 23, 24, 27, 35, 46; VII. 2, 7; VIII. 5, 11, 38; IX. 3, 4, 5, 14; X. 60.

**शिखरिणी**— Def. रसै रुद्रैश्छिन्ना यमनसभला गः शिखरिणी ।. 17 Syllables. Sch.—य, म, न, स, भ, ल, ग. The pause occurs after the sixth syllable. *Ex.*—I. 15; V. 12, 22, 25; VI. 4.

**सुमधुरा**—Def. म्रौ भ्नौ मो नो गुरुश्चेद् हयऋतुरसैरुक्ता सुमधुरा ।. 19 Syllables. Scheme—म, र, भ, न म, न, ग. The pauses occur after the seventh and the thirteenth syllables *Ex.*—IX. 21.

**स्रग्धरा**—Def. म्रभ्नैर्यानां त्रयेण त्रिमुनियतियुता स्रग्धरा कीर्तितेयम् ।. 21 Syllables. Scheme—म, र, भ, न, य, य, य. The pauses occur after the seventh and the fourteenth syllables. This is the longest metre in common use. *Ex.*—I. 1, 4, 48; X. 59, 61.

**हरिणी**—Def. नसमरसला गः षड्वेदैर्हयैर्हरिणी मता ।. 17 Syllables. Scheme—न स, म, र, स, ल, ग. The pauses occur after the sixth and the tenth syllables. *Ex.*—IV. 3; IX. 13.